READER IN COMPARATIVE RELIGION

An Anthropological Approach

FOURTH EDITION

WILLIAM A. LESSA
Professor Emeritus
University of California, Los Angeles

EVON Z. VOGT
Harvard University

With the assistance of
John M. Watanabe
Harvard University

HarperCollins*Publishers*

Sponsoring Editor: Richard Heffron
Project Editor: Holly Detgen
Production Manager: Stefania J. Taflinska
Compositor: TriStar Graphics
Printer and Binder: Hamilton Printing Co.
Art Studio: Vantage Art Inc.

READER IN COMPARATIVE RELIGION:
An Anthropological Approach,
Fourth Edition

Library of Congress Cataloging in Publication Data

Lessa, William Armand, ed.
Reader in comparative religion.

Bibliography: p.
Includes indexes.
1. Religions—Addresses, essays, lectures.
I. Vogt, Evon Zartman, Date — joint ed.
II. Title.
BL80.2.L44 1979 200′.8 78-13409
ISBN 0-06-043991-2

CONTENTS

FOREWORD

Three things appear to distinguish man from all other living creatures: the systematic making of tools, the use of abstract language, and religion. Some observers think they have detected among certain birds, mammals, and even other organisms the analogues of ritual. But no one has seriously suggested the presence of myth or theology. For these, another of the three distinctively human phenomena—abstract language—is surely a precondition.

Until the emergence of Communist societies we know of no human groups without religion. Even the Communists, as has often been said, have their "secular religion." While they repudiate the supernatural, they give allegiance in feeling as well as in thought to a body of doctrine that purports to provide life with a fairly immediate meaning. Nor is communism without its ritual and ceremonial side.

The universality of religion (in the broadest sense) suggests that it corresponds to some deep and probably inescapable human needs. All of these are repeatedly discussed in this book. There is the need for a moral order. Human life is necessarily a moral life precisely because it is a social life, and in the case of the human animal the minimum requirements for predictability of social behavior that will ensure some stability and continuity are not taken care of automatically by biologically inherited instincts, as is the case with the bees and the ants. Hence there must be generally accepted standards of conduct, and these values are more compelling if they are invested with divine authority and continually symbolized in rites that appeal to the senses. But no religion is solely a system of ethics. All religions also represent a response to the wonder and the terror of the ineluctable process of nature. They supply some answer to the profound uncertainties of experience, most especially to the homogeneity of death—even though some religions make a pure acknowledgment of death and erectly, carelessly, undauntedly admit nothingness.

The needs met by religion are not, however, by any means limited to those of constituting or bolstering a social order or of providing cognitive "explanations." Man is a symbolic as well as a tool-making creature. Cassirer understandably considers myth as an autonomous form of symbolism comparable to language, art, and science. In many and varied respects religion is an expressive activity: an outlet in drama, poetry, dance, and the plastic and graphic arts for the diverse temperaments of individuals, for particular subgroups, for the total community or society. My teacher, R. R. Marett, used to say "primitive religion is danced, not believed."

He did not intend, of course, that this aphorism should be taken literally. And one of the strong points of this book is that Professors Lessa and Vogt have resolutely emphasized the continuity of all religious phenomena. Yet there is one matter on which the equivocal word "primitive" gives us a useful reminder. In so-called primitive societies religion encompasses philosophy, theater, "science," ethics, diversion, and other behavior spheres which recent Western civilization has tended to segregate. The student must be aware of this fact, though the adjective "comparative" in the title of this book is altogether factual.

Indeed this reader is more genuinely comparative than any volume I know. Careful study of it should free any student from a narrow and culture-bound conception of religion. And it will become quite apparent that at least the symbolic forms of all religions derive from the particular nature and specific experience of the peoples that created these forms. As Xenophanes (560–475 B.C.) wrote:

Yes, and if oxen and horses or lions had hands, and could paint with their hands, and produce works of art as men do, horses would paint the forms of their gods like horses, and oxen like oxen, and make their bodies in the image of their several kinds. . . . The Ethiopians make their gods black and snub-nosed: the Thracians say theirs have blue eyes and red hair.

All religious systems—in practice if not in theory—have had to make some concessions to the frailties of human nature.

Because religious beliefs and practices, learned so early in contexts intimately associated with the most intense human experiences, are the targets of strong positive and negative feelings on the part of both participants and observers and because religion embraces such a wide and such a complex area of human life, the scientific study of religion is peculiarly difficult. The most honest and best course is the one which the editors have followed with great sensitivity and skill: achieve a decent balance between data and interpretation; present opposing points of view fairly and in historical depth; be as wide-ranging and comprehensive as space will allow. Nevertheless, thanks to the introductions to each chapter and the paragraphs linking the selections, the editors have succeeded in making judicious contributions to the establishment of regularities, to general theory. At the same time, the rich bibliographic aids make it easy for teacher and student to check and control the inductive generalizations which Professors Lessa and Vogt set forth on all the major topical areas of religion.

This, surely, is no parochial book. There are passages from the sacred texts of many religions. These passages and the descriptive accounts swing through the centuries and all the continents. The authors represent many nationalities and professions. We have bishops and anthropologists, literary critics and sociologists, psychiatrists and clergymen, administrators and psychologists. And the full gamut of the religious experience merges in the materials: rationality and passion; the supplication of bliss and of dread; a lurking, snakelike fear; the carrion gobbling of the garbage of sensations; mistrust and lurking insolence, insolence against a higher creation; the drift of spent souls; the striving for a center to life; the wheeling upon a dark void; the unquenched desire to worship.

CLYDE KLUCKHOHN

PREFACE

The basic purpose of this book of readings is to provide the student with a guide to the literature concerning what anthropologists have found out about religion in the last 100 years. In a few cases we have included selections from the pens of sociologists, historians, and others, and particularly from scholars in these related fields whose works have especially influenced anthropological thinking or who have dealt with data from primitive cultures.

The book grew out of a need felt by the two editors as they attempted to teach courses in comparative and primitive religion at the University of California at Los Angeles and at Harvard University and discovered that many of the best materials were published in obscure journals or were inaccessible to large numbers of our students.

There are a number of interesting introductory texts on primitive religion, including Annemarie De Waal Malefijt's *Religion and Culture: An Introduction to Anthropology of Religion*, Evans-Pritchard's *Theories of Primitive Religion*, Fadwa El Guindi's *Religion in Culture*, William J. Goode's *Religion Among the Primitives*, W. W. Howells' *The Heathens*, Robert H. Lowie's *Primitive Religion*, Edward Norbeck's *Religion in Primitive Society*, Paul Radin's *Primitive Religion*, Anthony F. C. Wallace's *Religion: An Anthropological View*, J. Milton Yinger's two books *Religion, Society, and the Individual* and *The Scientific Study of Religion*. But after students have read one of these texts in the opening weeks of a school term, there is then little for them to do except turn to the long, specialized monographs, or some of the smaller monographs such as "Case Studies in Cultural Anthropology," edited by George and Louise Spindler. It is hoped that this collection of readings will fill the gap between the introductory texts and the monographs and will give the student a significant overview of the anthropological literature. Additional useful collections of readings may be found in the recent books edited by John Middleton, including *Myth and Cosmos* (1967), *Gods and Rituals* (1967), and *Magic, Witchcraft, and Curing* (1967) and a volume edited by Charles Leslie, *Anthropology of Folk Religion* (1960). The teaching procedure that we recommend is, first, an introductory text; second, this volume; and third, exposure of the students to one or more of the monographs. We have included a selected list of the longer, specialized monographs on religion that we have found useful.

The fourth edition of this volume has been made possible by the reception given the first, second, and third, and so we must reaffirm the help given us in the past before we can go on to express our new indebtedness.

When the editors first contemplated the compilation of a book of readings that would be useful to them and possibly to others in teaching comparative and primitive religion they received much encouragement and many significant suggestions from their friends and associates, particularly the late Clyde Kluckhohn, Robert N. Bellah, Clifford Geertz, and Melford E. Spiro, whose advice was gratefully absorbed in molding the form and content of the *Reader*. The junior editor, while at the Center for Advanced Study in the Behavioral Sciences during 1956 and 1957, received further reinforcement through stimulating discussions with the late E. E. Evans-Pritchard, Morris E. Opler, and John M. Roberts. When it came time to put words on paper, Robert B. Edgerton and Roger C. Owen skillfully assisted in preparing some of the introductions to the selections and generally served as intellectual sounding boards, while Barbara Metzger wrote most of the original notes for the monographs on non-Western religious systems.

The second edition turned once more to some of its old supporters and at the same time added new names to its roster of collaborating colleagues, these being John W. M. Whiting, Michael G. Smith, and Philip L. Newman. We were also indebted to Jack Stauder for comments on the second edition.

The student assistants at the University of California, Los Angeles, who helped prepare the manuscript of the second edition for presentation to the publisher should also be given the recognition that belongs to them. Building on the foundation laid by Carol Romer Jones, who almost single-handedly worked on the first edition, Claudia Stevens, Carol Swartout, and Judy Wiseman collaborated on the second, which, strange to say, made more demands on time, patience, and ingenuity than one would have imagined necessary.

The work for the third edition was almost all done at Harvard University where the junior editor had the expert and devoted assistance of Kirk M. Endicott, Gary H. Gossen, Priscilla Rachun Linn, Michelle Zimbalist Rosaldo, and Renato I. Rosaldo, Jr., who collaborated with him from the beginning in selecting new materials, abridging the selections, and drafting the introductions for chapters and articles. Without their competent help, the third edition would never have appeared in print on schedule. Throughout the process of planning the third edition, we also profited from the research assistance of Catherine C. Vogt and from the bibliographic suggestions and advice of James J. Fox. The technical task of typing and assembling the manuscript for the third edition was efficiently accomplished by Dolores Vidal.

The work for the fourth edition was again almost all accomplished at Harvard University where the junior editor had the magnificent assistance of John M. Watanabe, who helped select new materials and draft introductions to chapters and articles, and Sarah L. Nordgren who typed, assembled, and proofread the manuscript. We are deeply indebted to these talented assistants who worked together so productively to meet our deadlines.

Finally, we must express our gratitude to the publishers, editors, and authors whose selections appear in this latest edition. Indeed, in several instances they offered to substitute, add, or revise selections. A number of them suggested that they were flattered to be included, although of course we look at this the other way around. There would have been no *Reader* without their contributions.

William A. Lessa
Evon Z. Vogt

GENERAL INTRODUCTION

I

Although the problem of the nature of religion has for centuries absorbed the imagination and energies of scholars in different cultures, the detached comparative approach to the matter is a relatively recent experience in history. Indeed, the first sustained and systematic efforts to understand and interpret the phenomenon stem from the works of nineteenth- and early twentieth-century British scholars, especially Sir Edward B. Tylor, William Robertson Smith, Andrew Lang, Sir James Frazer, and R. R. Marett. Many of these men were merely amateur or quasi-professional anthropologists, but they were endowed with inquiring minds and fine intellects.

These writers were for the most part influenced by the Darwinian concept of biological evolution and were interested in describing what they conceived to be the stages in cultural evolution. They turned to the study of "primitive" peoples living in the far corners of the world because they believed that these cultures represented what amounted to an earlier evolutionary stage in our own cultural development. They were motivated by a basic question: What are the origins of religion in mankind's development? By careful study of the accounts of missionaries and travelers among primitive peoples—they did no field work themselves—they attempted to reconstruct what the earlier stages of religion were like and to answer such questions as: How did man first create myths and develop ritual? Was animism the first form of religion, or was there a preanimistic religion? Did an age of magic precede an age of religion? Was totemism or ancestor worship the most ancient form of religion?

A special problem related to this question of origins involved the inquiry into whether or not the most "primitive" peoples, such as the Ona and the Yahgan of Tierra del Fuego, the Eskimo, or the Ainu of Japan, worshipped a "primitive high god" or "Supreme Being." The implication was that perhaps mankind developed polytheistic religions only later in history, and did not return to monotheism until the development of the great religions in the Near East. Father Wilhelm Schmidt was one of the principal investigators of this problem.

Several other theoretical approaches to the question of origins were taken. One trend of thought, exemplified by the writings of Tylor and Frazer, took a rationalistic or intellectualistic approach. For Tylor, religious beliefs were derived from the concept of a soul separable from the body which arose from man's need to explain sleep, dreams, hallucinations, death, and the like. This doctrine of the soul was then expanded to the worship of ancestors, spirits, deities, and finally to the monotheistic God. On the other hand, Frazer placed greater emphasis on death, the fear of death, and fear of the dead in accounting for the origin of the soul concept. Both theorists based their conjectures on the assumption that a rational need to explain physiological phenomena underlay religious beliefs and beliefs in the supernatural.

A second theoretical approach is found in the works of the so-called French sociological school, and particularly in the work of Émile Durkheim. Some of Durkheim's ideas are foreshadowed in Fustel de Coulanges' *The Ancient City* (1877), an elucidation of the dynamic role religion played in ancient Greek and Roman society and the extent to which religion permeated Greco-Roman social and political organization, especially in the family, marriage, property, morals, law, political authority, social class, and citizenship. For Durkheim and his students, religion originates in the moral order of society itself. The affective power of religious symbols and beliefs stems from the sense of interdependence and obligation every individual experiences as a social being, in possessing learned culture rather than innate instincts. Evolutionary thinking still influences Durkheim's treatment of religion as an integral part of society. In *The Elementary Forms of the Religious Life* (1915), he selects Australian totemism to illustrate his theory because for him it is the most primitive—and therefore the most pristine—form of religion. The works of this school are of crucial importance because they form a kind of historical bridge between the earlier interests in evolutionary origins and the later interests in the functions of religion, whatever its origin. The French school has exerted considerable influence outside its own national boundaries, thanks mostly to the prestige and expertise of two English social anthropologists, A. R. Radcliffe-Brown and E. E. Evans-Pritchard.

As the search for laws of social evolution lost currency in social anthropology, the preoccupation with the origins of religion was supplanted by other theoretical concerns. One such theoretical development is found in the work of the German sociologist Max Weber, especially in his explorations of the relationships between religious and economic institutions and his clear recognition of the fundamental importance of the problem of meaning. This problem has two aspects: one is the difficulty of answers to the question of why unpredictable, unfortunate events occur in human life. Interest in this question continues and is dealt with very perceptively in a selection from Evans-Pritchard, who shows with incisive clarity how witchcraft explains unfortunate events in Azande life. The second aspect has to do with the relationships between major institutional forms in a society. That is, the economic system must have some meaning in terms of the religious system and vice versa. Although we have not included a selection from Weber, his influence is evident in the writings of Talcott Parsons, and the questions we raise are clearly dealt with in the selection entitled "Religious Perspectives in Sociology and Social Psychology."

Another major theoretical approach to the comparative study of religion comes from Sigmund Freud. His psychoanalytic insights have exerted a crucial influence on ideas about the nature of religion. Especially important are his views on the relationship of religious thought and emotions to unconscious motivation and the treatment of religion as a projective system. This approach views religion as essentially a collective attempt to resolve the guilt and anxiety stemming from conflicts inherent in the individual personality. This is clearly evident in Freud's theory of the origin of the incest taboo outlined in *Totem and Taboo*. Other writers have carried on the tradition, especially Géza Róheim and Bruno Bettelheim.

Meanwhile, influenced in part by the French sociological school and by their own firsthand field researches with primitive peoples, two major figures emerged who were to have a lasting impact on the anthropological treatment of religion: Malinowski and Radcliffe-Brown. In their functional approach to religion the question of origins in the older classical sense has shifted to a different question: What is the function of religion, whatever its origin, in any society, and in particular societies? In other words, what does religion do for people and for social groups? There are great similarities but also important differences in the theoretical approaches of these two scholars; Homans attempts to resolve the differences.

As theoretical concerns with social structure, kinship, politics, and language assumed preeminence in anthropology, the study of religion became sporadic. Interest and research in the field, however, have quickened during the last two decades both in the United States and in Europe, as well as in Australia. A number of works by the American anthropologists A. Irving Hollowell, Morris Opler, and Clyde Kluckhohn favored a synthesis of the functional and psychoanalytical approaches to religion. Other American and some British anthropologists began studying religions that emerged in acculturation situations, such as the Ghost Dance, Peyote Cult, and Cargo Cults, and produced a number of remarkable publications like Anthony Wallace's "Revitalization Movements" (1956), which is reprinted in Chapter Nine. Other American scholars began applying anthropological concepts to the study of the religions of the high cultures of the Far East, India, and Southeast Asia, and to the analysis of certain aspects of ritual in our own culture.

More recent work on the anthropology of religion has shifted from a strict preoccupation with social function to a concern with the meaning of religious symbols and beliefs. In his book, *Theories of Primitive Religions* (1965), Evans-Pritchard indicates the inadequacies of purely sociological or psychological explanations of religion and stresses the importance of belief, meaning, and translation in the study of religion. A growing awareness of the need for such a "sociology of ideas" and an understanding of the manner in which these ideas are communicated have produced a number of excellent monographs on ritual, religion, and symbolism which we cite in various chapters in the *Reader*. An article by Victor Turner, "Symbolic Studies" (1975), provides a succinct overview of current directions in the field. Other books by Turner, including *The Forest of Symbols* (1967), *The Drums of Affliction* (1968), *The Ritual Process* (1969), and *Dramas, Fields, and Metaphors* (1974), have proven invaluable contributions to the field.

Of special note are several collections of articles: *Anthropological Approaches to the Study of Religion* (1966) edited by Michael Banton, *The Structural Study of Myth and Totemism* (1967) edited by E. R. Leach, *The Interpretation of Ritual* (1972) edited by J. S. La Fontaine, *Modes of Thought* (1973) edited by Robin Horton and Ruth Finnegan, and *The Interpretation of Symbolism* (1975) edited by Roy Willis. The series of volumes on symbol, myth, and ritual edited by Victor Turner also deserves mention, especially *Australian Religions* (1973) by M. Eliade, *Symbols: Public and Private* (1973) by Raymond Firth, *Walbiri Iconography* (1973) by Nancy Munn, *The Peyote Hunt* (1974) by Barbara Myerhoff, and *The Transformation of the Hummingbird* (1977) by Eva Hunt. Also in this tradition of symbolic analysis are Gary Gossen's *Chamulas in the World of the Sun: Time and Space in a Maya Oral Tradition* (1974) and Evon Vogt's *Tortillas for the Gods: A Symbolic Analysis of Zinacanteco Ritual* (1976). Two books by Mary Douglas, *Natural Symbols* (1970) and *Implicit Meanings* (1975), and a volume edited by Rodney Needham entitled *Right and Left* (1973) represent in-depth investigations into the role of symbols in social life. A recent summary of the general structuralist approach to the study of cultural symbols can be found in E. R. Leach's *Culture and Communication* (1976).

The anthropology of religion has also been stimulated by the work of the French anthropologist, Claude Lévi-Strauss whose publications on myth and aspects of ritual offer novel and provocative insights. Three of his articles, "The Effectiveness of Symbols" (1949), "The Structural Study of Myth" (1955; revised 1963), and "The Bear and the Barber" (1963), have been included in the *Reader*. But the student should read his other publications containing materials on religion, especially *Totemism* (1963), *Structural Anthropology* (1963), *The Savage Mind* (1966), *The Raw and the Cooked* (1969), *From Honey to Ashes* (1973), *Structural Anthropology II* (1976), *Mythologiques: L'Origine des Maniéres de Table* (1969), and *Mythologiques: L'Homme Nu* (1971), as well as the Festschrift in his honor entitled *Échanges et Communication* (1970) edited by Jean Pouillon and Pierre Maranda. A good introduction to Lévi-Strauss's work is *Claude Lévi-Strauss* (1970) by E. R. Leach; an evaluation and critique of Lévi-Strauss's structuralism can be found in a collection of essays entitled *The Unconscious in Culture* (1974) edited by Ino Rossi.

This growing field of symbolic analysis encompasses a wide range of approaches, varying from the interpretation of the role of cultural symbols in social life epitomized by Victor Turner and Clifford Geertz to the analysis of the self-contained logic of symbol systems developed by Claude Lévi-Strauss. Many other anthropologists have turned to fields such as philosophy, psychology, literary criticism, aesthetics, linguistics, information theory, and semiotics (the science of signs) for insights into the analysis of symbols and their uses. We have attempted to include both a representative sample of these various approaches in this new edition of the *Reader* as well as examples of more traditional analyses of religious systems.

The anthropological study of religion has moved from concern with the origins of religion to the elucidation of the sociological and psychological functions that religion fulfills to an inquiry into the way in which religious beliefs and thought are structured and expressed. But progress in theoretical treatment and methodological sophistication still lags behind the study of other aspects of culture (e.g. social structure, kinship, language), and we hope that this volume will stimulate younger generations of students to continue this inquiry into the nature and functions of religion.

II

At this point it may be appropriate to explain to some readers our seeming brashness in appropriating to our own use the term "comparative religion," in view of the fact that it has had different connotations for older students of religion as well as for modern theologians. Actually, the editors are not giving a special meaning to the term. It reflects a whole point of view in anthropology, and accordingly there occurs in the anthropological literature a series of related expressions, such as "comparative law," "comparative art," "comparative folklore," and "comparative institutions." The philosophy behind these terms will shortly be explained, but for the moment it will be well to examine the older and more traditional meaning of comparative religion.

Earlier studies of religion purported to be comparative—and indeed they often were—but these early studies used comparison as a sort of apologetic for the dominant Judaic-Christian religions.[1] During the latter stages of the nineteenth century several factors were combining to emancipate the comparative study of religion from this earlier goal of providing data for the validation of the origins and authority of Judaism or Christianity. One such factor was the accreting store of knowledge about primitive religions that was being collected by travelers, soldiers, missionaries, and administrators. Another was the Darwinian theory of biological evolution, which led to studies of other forms of evolution—among them that of religion. Several scholarly disciplines began to contribute stimuli to objective comparative studies; sociology, anthropology, philology, mythology, folk psychology, and history all began to eschew apologetics for science.

The new comparative religion as represented by the anthropological approach makes no effort to evaluate, and it encompasses all the religions of the world, past and present, about which there is any information. By going beyond the complex cults of the great contemporary civilizations it is possible to gain not only a wider range of variation but also a greater degree of detachment. For example, those who are close to Christianity cannot always divorce themselves from the cultural and emotional associations that they entertain toward it. And they are apt to have preconceived notions regarding religions, such as Judaism and Islam, which have had intimate historical relationships with it. It is much more possible to retain an objective point of view when treating of the beliefs of the Koryak, Betsimisarka, Kankanay, Witoto, or Ewe. In addition, the religions of the simpler societies have the advantage of being divested of the complex trappings characteristic of the faiths of civilized groups. They are more internally consistent, possessed of fewer alternatives of dogma, less complicated by sophisticated metaphysics, and freer of hierarchical superstructure. In short, they permit one to get down to the core—the fundamentals—of religion and its place in human life.

But what is the comparative method? Unfortunately, since it has meant many things to different people, the answer is not simple. Essentially, it is a method that attempts to achieve generalization through comparison of similar kinds of phenomena. It seeks to extract common denominators from a mass of variants. But the methods for which comparison has been utilized and the goals toward which these methods have been directed have not always been the same. The most comprehensive and fruitful effort to bring order out of the chaotic state into which the meaning of the expression has fallen is one made by Oscar Lewis in an article entitled "Comparisons in Cultural Anthropology" (1955). We shall take the liberty of reviewing some of his analysis.

According to Professor Lewis, there are two broad types of comparative studies in anthropology. The first examines societies that are historically related. Their common culture provides controls against which variables may be tested. This type, which has been given little recognition as an aspect of the comparative method, may involve comparisons within a single culture or community, with a single culture area, or within a single nation. There are many advantages to comparative studies of this more limited kind. The data are more intensively studied, usually along comparable lines, so there is greater assurance of comparability. The culture is seen as a whole and not in fractions, so that all aspects of the culture appear in context. Moreover, a large number of variables can be studied functionally. The objectives are usually modest and the research

[1] In recent years theologians and others working in this more traditional and restricted field have veered away from the term "comparative religion" and substituted "history of religions" and "phenomenology of religions"—terms growing out of the general body of knowledge originally known as *Allgemeine Religionswissenschaft* (see Joseph M. Kitagawa, "The Nature and Program of the History of Religions Field," *Divinity School News*, November, 1957, pp. 13–25).

designs closer to those made in truly experimental studies. It is here that we find the greater proportion of recent studies based on comparative field research. The greatest drawback to the limited approach is that it has narrow vistas.

The second broad type of comparative study compares historically unrelated societies, taking a broader and more ambitious approach, often of a holistic character. It may make comparisons within a continent, between continents or nations, or on a random or global scale. The purpose is to utilize similarities in form, structure, and process as a basis for deriving typologies or establishing causal relationships among various aspects of culture. It might be observed parenthetically that in this case we are dealing with headier wine. This kind of comparison looks for universals, worldwide typologies, or evolutionary sequences. Here is where the work of men such as Tylor, Freud, Durkheim, and Radcliffe-Brown fits in. The weakness of this overall approach is that it does not have many of the controls possible in the more limited studies described in the previous paragraph. Moreover, when statistics are used they often artificially quantify the culture elements and control only a few of the variables. Recently there have been more sophisticated comparative studies along these lines in the "cross-cultural" works of Murdock, Whiting, and others who have used the Human Relations Area Files as a basis for careful samples of the world's societies and have successfully arrived at generalizations with high validity, as for example in Murdock's *Social Structure* (1949). Whiting's helpful paper "The Cross-Cultural Method" (1954) provides an excellent description of the general approach.

Evans-Pritchard ("Religion," 1956) has in effect advocated a combination of these two approaches if we are to retain the objectivity necessary to reach general and significant conclusions regarding the nature of primitive religions as a whole. He says that we must, for example, first investigate the religion of one Melanesian people, then compare the religion of that group with several other Melanesian societies that are nearest to it in their culture. After that would come a comparative study of all Melanesian groups, and only then could one say something about Melanesian religion in general. This laborious kind of research is the only hope for eventually achieving broader conclusions about religion. This newer stress on careful comparisons on a smaller scale has also been emphasized by others, especially Eggan, who writes, "My own preference is for the utilization of the comparative method on a smaller scale and with as much control over the frame of comparison as it is possible to secure" ("Social Anthropology and the Method of Controlled Comparison," 1954). Eggan's masterful discussion of controlled comparisons shows that he is aware that there is much work ahead, and that no one approach is sufficient—the anthropological concepts of structure and function can and should be combined with the ethnological concepts of process and history.

More than mere painstaking labor is needed for valid comparisons. We must be sure that a comparative analysis is based on comparable data. Franz Boas' old warnings on this score are still valid and have been eloquently renewed by Clyde Kluckhohn in a paper entitled "Universal Categories of Culture" (1953). As one of his examples he makes specific mention of the field of religion, which he says is a recurring pattern but not a uniform phenomenon, as evidenced by the lack of a clear-cut distinction between magic and religion. These concepts, he says, have heuristic usefulness in given situations but are not sufficiently distinct to serve as units from which larger concepts can be built up.

As for the aims which anthropologists have in their comparisons, Lewis (1955) says that there are several: to establish general laws or regularities; to document the range of variation in the phenomena studied; to document the distribution of traits or aspects of culture; to reconstruct culture history; to test hypotheses derived from non-Western societies. This is a broad range, and it should be noted that it covers all the approaches in cultural anthropology, whether functional, diffusionist, *kulturkreis*, or evolutionary. The difference lies both in the ways in which they are used and in the objectives toward which they are directed.

The present volume is not concerned with documenting distributions or reconstructing history. Rather, as a work of science, it is concerned with comparison only insofar as it helps to establish regularities in religious phenomena. Of course, this would presuppose the testing of hypotheses in different cultural contexts. Some of the articles in the pages that follow do not explicitly state their aims, but these can be interpreted with reasonable accuracy. Many of the articles seem to be essentially descriptive or historical, but our purpose has been to use them as contributions to general theory and not as particular and discrete facts.

We can conclude by warning that anthropology cannot claim comparison as its brain child. Aside from the impressionistic comparisons of the layman, there are the systematic and controlled ones of all scientific disciplines, which use correlation and covariation in their study of similarities and differences. If we may at this point venture an opinion, it would be to the effect that anthropology can at least take pride in the fact that of all the social sciences it has most expanded the possibilities of comparison by adding to the general pool the thousands of case histories made available by its study of tribal societies.

ONE
THE ORIGIN AND DEVELOPMENT OF RELIGION

Introduction

The origins of religion can only be speculated upon; they can never be discovered. Theories with enormous "documentation" and nimble imagination may temporarily delude the impressionable reader into believing that answers have been found, but sober reflection will always show the futility of accepting any one of them as constituting more than a scholarly guess. Should we on this account turn away from such speculations? Not at all. The better and more responsible of these hypotheses have pointed the way to rewarding lines of investigation. Not only have they caused an immense amount of field data to be collected and studied, but they have been ultimately responsible for analytic contributions of lasting value. Even scholars who have consciously renounced historical interests in religion owe a great debt to others who have had such interests and helped found a science of religion.

One might ask what gave these early students the courage to proceed with reconstructions in the face of our inability to recover the past from actual documentary evidence. What did they substitute for fact? The answer is, schemes, analogies, and assumptions, all overlaid with rich imagination. One method of approach was through the so-called comparative method. "Evidences" from tribes all over the world were taken out of context and arranged in a sequential scheme. But this was done only according to a preconceived plan and was justified on the grounds that it arranged the data in such a way that they conformed to the scheme and therefore proved its validity. Another method was through the use of so-called survivals—"processes, customs, opinions, and so forth, which have been carried on by force of habit into a new state of society different from that in which they had their original home, and thus they remain proofs and examples of an older condition of culture out of which a newer had been evolved" (Tylor, 1873). In brief, existing survivals throw light on the history of the past. But in the absence of written records there is no way of knowing that a custom is actually a vestigial remnant of a formerly widespread condition. Again, reliance was firmly placed on the principle of the psychic unity of mankind—human nature is basically uniform, therefore similar results have come independently from the same causes. The implication of such panhumanism is that processes and reactions which we can study and understand today can be used to reconstruct the past because man's mind always reacts in the same way to similar external stimuli. Although anthropologists admit the great force of such psychic unity, they feel that the evolutionists did not take sufficient cognizance of the even greater effects of diffusion in producing cultural similarity. Thus specific religious phenomena with which we are acquainted through firsthand experience may not be used to project back into the past, because religious traits may be borrowed instead of developed independently. Such borrowing can disturb any picture of uniform development. Some evolutionists, notably Herbert Spencer, were guided by the principle of progress—society keeps advancing from a less desirable state to a better and better one. The way in which this principle operates is to regard the civilization of western Europe as the acme of man's achievements and to assume that the situation in the childhood of mankind must for each human institution have been exactly the opposite, with intermediate stages grading off from the one to the other. Thus if monotheism prevails today in western Europe, the belief in many spirits must have been a very early condition, polytheism being a less enlightened stage than belief in one God. Since progress is a matter of opinion and merely begs the question as to what is a desirable kind of change, such a theoretical plan rests on a tenuous base; it cannot tell us what the situation was like in primeval times. Moreover, the principle of progress as used by Spencer demands that it be regarded as an irresistible trend, an assumption that finds many objections. To reconstruct the past the surest evidences must come from archaeology; valuable leads have indeed been suggested by the study of old cultural remains. The burials of Neanderthal man and Cro-Magnon man have strong implications for the theory that they indicate an ancient belief in the soul and the afterworld. But since archaeological interpretations must so often rely on analogies with contemporary primitives they are not always conclusive. There is justifiable reason for being cautious in using archaeological data to say that the art of the Upper Paleolithic is magico-religious in nature.

The articles selected for this chapter consist of both theories of origins and critiques of such theories. It will be noticed that for the most part they do not bear a recent date, a reflection of the fact that the problem of origins is not a pressing current issue. But one should not minimize the value of these ideas, for they command serious attention as exploratory efforts and have had far-reaching and often fruitful effects. The first article is by Tylor, and represents the earliest of the major anthropological hypotheses of origins; it views religion as being rooted in the idea of the soul, and argues that out of this rational creation by primeval man came the subsequent belief that a plurality of spirits is associated with various spheres of nature, human activities, and so on. Tylor's basic position was challenged by Father Wilhelm Schmidt of the *Kulturkreis* school of anthropological thought that developed especially in Vienna. Schmidt (1931) maintained that in the beginning man had belief in one Spirit and that the multiplicity of gods we see in some contemporary societies is a degeneration from the earliest position. Another approach to the problem of origins was offered by W. Robertson Smith (1889; reprinted in paperback, 1956), who wrote especially on the origin of sacrifice. He was influential in shaping the ideas of many subsequent writers, among them Freud, whose views in *Totem and Taboo* (paperback edition, 1952) are here represented only indirectly through two articles by Kroeber, who was at variance with the psychoanalytic interpretation of the origin not only of sacrifice but of religion in general. Durkheim's provocative theory of the origin of religion, which has had a strong and lasting influence in contemporary thinking, is presented in the form of selections from *The Elementary Forms of the Religious Life*.

One important historical theory is not represented in the selections and deserves special notice. It is the naturism explanation originally offered in 1856 by F. Max Müller and subsequently expanded by him and other students of Sanskrit. The discovery of the ancient Vedas of the Hindus influenced Müller's ideas. The impulse to religious thought and language, he maintained, arises in the first instance from sensuous experience—from the influence of external nature on man. Nature contains surprise, terror, marvels, miracles. This vast domain of the unknown and infinite, rather than the known and finite, is what provided the sensation from which religions are derived. Fire, for example, could create such an impression on the mind of man. So could the sun and rivers and the wind, to name but a few phenomena. Religions only came into being, however, when the forces of nature were transformed by man from abstract forces to personal agents, that is, spirits. This came about through a "disease of language." Language influences the way in which people classify newly learned things. Natural phenomena came to be compared to human acts, and expressions originally used for human acts came to be applied to natural objects. A thunderbolt was called Something that tears up the soil or spreads fire, the wind Something that sighs or whistles, a river Something that flows, and so on. After this had been done, spirits had to be invented to account for the acts attributed to them by their names, and so arose pantheons of gods. The myth-making process then took hold and carried matters still further by endowing each god with a biography. Thus religion is really a fabric of errors. The supernatural world was composed of beings created out of nothing. In this developmental scheme Müller did not ignore Tylor's later theory of the origin of the soul, but he felt that it was a secondary idea. His chief error was in explaining primitive personalism about nature as if it were some sort of cognitive mistake—a disease of language—as if the primitive first saw the world in coldly objective and scientific terms and then through cognitive error lost this view. But the primitive never had such a world view, which was itself the product of cultural development. Müller's other error was in supposing that he could take ancient historic records from India and attribute religious developments there to the whole world. Writing is, after all, a recent phenomenon and does not even approach the antiquity ascribed to religion.

Edward B. Tylor
ANIMISM

More than any other anthropologist, Sir Edward B. Tylor stressed the importance of the soul both in defining religion and in understanding the evolutionary stages through which religious phenomena have passed. To him, the belief in spirit beings—animism—constitutes the minimum definition of religion.

The present passage from Tylor's extensive account of animism does not clearly reveal his evolutionary position, but it is apparent that he is concerned with origin and development. First he delves into the question of how men came to create the concept of the soul, and finds the answer in men's efforts to interpret dreams, hallucinations, and other aberrant psychic phenomena which puzzle them. Tylor adduces what he considers to be evidences from primitive peoples that the idea of the soul is not only universal but is also consistent with his dream theory. Along the way he accounts for the origin of human sacrifice by asserting that it is a way of freeing the soul from the body and putting it into the service of the dead. It is only a reasonable step that early man should next extend the idea of the soul to animals, and then to plants, for they too live and die, enjoy health and suffer disease. This accounts for animal sacrifice, which is designed to aid the dead in the afterlife; however, there does not exist a counterpart among plants, for they are not sacrificed for the purpose of enlisting their souls for the service of the dead. Continuing to reason by analogy, says Tylor, early man extended the theory of the soul to stones, weapons, food, ornaments, and other objects which we who are civilized would endow with neither a soul nor life.

The portions of Tylor's theory of animism which have not been included in the accompanying article are lengthy, constituting six chapters of his *Primitive Culture*. They deal with such matters as transmigration and the future life; the expanding of the original theory of souls into a wider doctrine of spirits, that is, an animistic theory of

Reprinted in abridged form from Edward B. Tylor, *Primitive Culture* (2 vols.; 2d ed.; London: John Murray, 1873), Chap. 11.

nature; the development of the view that spirits are personal causes of phenomena of the world; the origin of guardian spirits and nature spirits; the origin of polytheism; and, finally, the development of the idea of monotheism as the completion of the polytheistic system and the outcome of the animistic philosophy. All these are fitted into an unsystematic unilinear scheme of development, in which certain inevitable stages are passed through.

The first aspect of Tylor's theory, which is contained in the article that follows, has been attacked with far less severity than the evolutionary aspect, and even today it continues to impress scholars with its plausibility. The usual criticism is that it is an intellectualistic explanation, and that a rational need to explain the physiological phenomena of such unusual psychic states as dreams not only does not concern the primitive but fails to produce the emotional quality necessary for religion. It is for this reason that some theorists have substituted the criterion of supernaturalism for that of animism as a minimum requirement for religion. Another criticism is that primitive man could not have developed the concept of the soul through dreams because it would have been too easy for him to be contradicted when trying to check with his tribal mates on his hallucinatory experiences. Nevertheless, Tylor's theory has its admirers. Lowie remarks that it not only has a "high degree of probability" but to his knowledge has no serious competitor among rival theories. Even Marett, who put forth the theory that animatism preceded animism, expressed appreciation of Tylor's hypothesis and asserted that he himself was "no irreconcilable foe who has a rival theory to put forward concerning the origin of religion."

Greater vulnerability attaches to the second aspect of Tylor's theory, for when he attempts to show that out of the concept of the soul there evolved the concept of animism, then polydaemonism, then polytheism, and finally monotheism, he falls into most of the fallacies of the evolutionists of his time. In treating primitive man as primeval he had to assume that over a period of hundreds of thousands of years some of the simpler peoples of the world had retained religious beliefs unchanged. One could argue that religion shows a remarkable tenacity and indeed undergoes less alteration than other aspects of culture; but in this case it is asking too much. And, one could argue, too, as did the irrepressible Andrew Lang, that among the simplest peoples of the world there frequently appears a high god; therefore, while the idea of the soul as outlined by Tylor might itself be valid, it need not be supposed that it evolved into the concept of the high god. Other deficiencies in Tylor's chronological scheme could be mentioned, but they are mostly reducible to the use he made of survivals and the faulty comparative method of contemporary evolutionists.

Notwithstanding these limitations, there can be no doubt that Tylor made a challenging attempt to describe the origin of the soul and the general history of religion, and it stimulated subsequent and more sophisticated efforts.

The first requisite in a systematic study of the religions of the lower races is to lay down a rudimentary definition of religion. By requiring in this definition the belief in a supreme deity or of a judgment after death, the adoration of idols or the practice of sacrifice, or other partially diffused doctrines of rites, no doubt many tribes may be excluded from the category of religious. But such narrow definition has the fault of identifying religion rather with particular developments than with the deeper motive which underlies them. It seems best to fall back at once on this essential source, and simply to claim, as a minimum definition of religion, the belief in Spiritual Beings. So far as I can judge from the immense mass of accessible evidence, we have to admit that the belief in spiritual beings appears among all low races with whom we have attained to thoroughly intimate acquaintance; whereas the assertion of absence of such belief must apply either to ancient tribes, or to more or less imperfectly described modern ones.

I purpose here, under the name of Animism, to investigate the deep-lying doctrine of Spiritual Beings, which embodies the very essence of Spiritualistic as opposed to Materialistic philosophy. Animism is not a new technical term, though now seldom used. From its special relation to the doctrine of the soul, it will be seen to have a peculiar appropriateness to the view here taken of the mode in which theological ideas have been developed among mankind. The word "Spiritualism," though it may be, and sometimes is, used in a general sense, has this obvious defect to us, that it has become the designation of a particular modern sect, who indeed hold extreme spiritualistic views, but cannot be taken as typical representatives of these views in the world at large. The sense of Spiritualism in its wider acceptation, the general belief in spiritual beings, is here given to Animism.

Animism characterizes tribes very low in the scale of humanity, and thence ascends, deeply modified in its transmission, but from first to last preserving an unbroken continuity, into the midst of high modern culture. Doctrines adverse to it, so largely held by individuals or schools, are usually due not to early lowness of civilization, but to later changes in the intellectual course, to divergence from, or rejection of, ancestral faiths; and such newer developments do not affect the present inquiry as to the fundamental religious condition of mankind. Animism is, in fact, the groundwork of the Philosophy of Religion, from that of savages up to that of civilized men. And although it may at first sight seem to afford but a bare and meager definition of a minimum of religion, it will be found practically sufficient; for where the root is, the branches will generally be produced. It is habitually found that the theory of Animism divides into two great dogmas, forming parts of one consistent doctrine; first concerning souls of individual creatures, capable of continued existence after the death or destruction of the body; second, concerning other spirits, upward to the rank of powerful deities. Spiritual beings are held to affect or control the events of the material world, and man's life here and hereafter; and it being considered that they hold intercourse with men, and receive pleasure or displeasure from human actions, the belief in their existence leads naturally, and it might almost be said inevitably, sooner or later to active reverence and propitiation. Thus Animism, in its full development, includes the belief in souls and in a future state, in controlling deities and subordinate spirits, these doctrines practically resulting in some kind of active worship. One great element of religion, that moral element which among the higher nations forms its most vital part, is indeed little represented in the religion of the lower races. It is not that these races have no moral sense or no moral standard, for both are strongly marked among them, if not in formal precept, at least in that traditional consensus of society which we call public opinion, according to which certain actions are held to be good or bad, right or wrong. It is that the conjunction of ethics and Animistic philosophy, so intimate and powerful in the higher culture, seems scarcely yet to have begun in the lower. I propose here hardly to touch upon the purely moral aspects of religion, but rather to study the animism of the world so far as it constitutes, as unquestionably it does constitute, an ancient and world-wide philosophy, of which belief is the theory and worship is the practice. Endeavoring to shape the materials for an inquiry hitherto strangely undervalued and neglected, it will now be my task to bring as clearly as may be into view the fundamental animism of the lower races, and in some slight and broken outline to trace its course into higher regions of civilization. Here let me state once and for all two principal conditions under which the present research is carried on. First, as to the religious doctrines and practices examined, these are treated as belonging to theological systems devised by human reason, without supernatural aid or revelation; in other words, as being developments of Natural Religion. Second, as to the connection between similar ideas and rites in the religions of the savage and the civilized world. While dwelling at some length on doctrines and ceremonies of the lower races, and sometimes particularizing for special reasons the related doctrines and ceremonies of the higher nations, it has not seemed my proper task to work out in detail the problems thus suggested among the philosophies and creeds of Christendom. Such applications, extending farthest from the direct scope of a work on primitive culture, are briefly stated in general terms, or touched in slight allusion, or taken for granted without remark. Educated readers possess the information required to work out their general bearing on theology, while more technical discussion is left to philosophers and theologians specially occupied with such arguments.

The first branch of the subject to be considered is the doctrine of human and other souls, an examination of which will occupy the rest of the present theory of its development. It seems as though thinking men, as yet at a low level of culture, were deeply impressed by two groups of biological problems. In the first place, what is it that makes the difference between a living body and a dead one; what causes waking, sleep, trance, disease, death? In the second place, what are those human shapes which appear in dreams and visions? Looking at these two groups of phenomena, the ancient savage philosophers probably made their first step by the obvious inference that every man has two things belonging to him, namely, a life and a phantom. These two are evidently in close connection with the body, the life as enabling it to feel and think and act, the phantom as being its image or second self; both, also, are perceived to be things separable from the body, the life as able to go away and leave it insensible or dead, the phantom as appearing to people at a distance from it. The second step would seem also easy for savages to make, seeing how extremely difficult civilized men have found it to unmake. It is merely to combine the life and the phantom. As both belong to the body, why should they not also belong to one another, and be manifestations of one and the same soul? Let them then be considered as united, and the result is that well-known conception which may be described as an apparitional soul, a ghost-soul. This, at any rate, corresponds with the actual conception of the personal soul or spirit among the lower races, which may be defined as follows: It is a thin unsubstantial human image, in its nature a sort of vapor, film, or shadow; the cause of life and thought in the individual it animates; independently possessing the personal consciousness and volition of its corporeal owner, past or present; capable of leaving the body far behind, to flash swiftly from place to place; mostly impalpable and invisible, yet also manifesting physical power, and especially appearing to men waking or asleep as a phantasm separate from the body of which it bears the likeness; continuing to exist and appear to men after the death of that body; able to enter into, possess, and act in the bodies of other men, of animals, and even of things. Though this definition is by no means of universal application, it has sufficient generality to be taken as a standard, modified by more or less divergence among any particular people. Far from these worldwide opinions being arbitrary or conventional products, it is seldom even justifiable to consider their uniformity among distant races as proving communication of any sort. They are doctrines answering in the most forcible way to the plain evidence of men's senses, as interpreted by a fairly consistent and rational primitive philosophy. So well, indeed, does primitive animism account for the facts of nature, that it has held its place into the higher levels of education. Though classic and medieval philosophy modified it much, and modern philosophy has handled it yet more unsparingly, it has so far retained the traces of its original character, that heirlooms of primitive ages may be claimed in the existing psychology of the civilized world. Out of the vast mass of evidence, collected among the most various and distant races of mankind, typical details may now be selected to display the earlier theory of the soul, the relations of the parts of this theory, and the manner in which these parts have been abandoned, modified, or kept up, along the course of culture.

To understand the popular conceptions of the human soul or spirit, it is instructive to notice the words which have been found suitable to express it. The ghost or phantasm seen by the dreamer or the visionary is an unsubstantial form, like a shadow, and thus the familiar term of the *shade* comes in to express the soul. Thus the Tasmanian word for the shadow is also that for the spirit; the Algonquin Indians describe a man's soul as *otahchuk*, "his shadow," the Quiché language uses *natub* for "shadow, soul"; the Arawac *ueja* means "shadow, soul, image"; the Abipones made the one word *loâkal* serve for "shadow, soul, echo, image." The Zulus not only use the word *tunzi* for "shadow, spirit, ghost," but they consider that at death the shadow of a man will in some way depart from the corpse, to become an ancestral spirit. The Basutos not only call the spirit remaining after death the *seriti* or "shadow," but they think that if a man walks on the river bank a crocodile may seize his shadow in the water, and draw him in; while in Old Calabar there is found the same identification of the spirit with the *ukpon* or "shadow," for a man to lose which is fatal. There are thus found among the lower races not only the types of those familiar classic terms, the *skia* and *umbra*, but also what seems the fundamental thought of the stories of shadowless men still current in the folklore of Europe, and familiar to modern readers in Chamisso's tale of Peter Schlemihl. Thus the dead in Purgatory knew that Dante was alive when they saw that, unlike theirs, his fingers cast a shadow on the ground. Other attributes are taken into the notion of soul or spirit, with especial regard to its being the cause of life. Thus the Caribs, connecting the pulses with spiritual beings, and especially considering that in the heart dwells man's chief soul, destined to a future heavenly life, could reasonably use the one word *iouanni* for "soul, life, heart." The Tongans supposed the soul to exist throughout the whole extension of the body, but particularly in the heart. On one occasion, the natives were declaring to a European that a man buried months ago was nevertheless still alive. "And one, endeavoring to make me understand what he meant, took hold of my hand, and squeezing it, said, 'This will die, but the life that is within you will never die'; with his other hand pointing to my heart." So the Basutos say of a dead man that his heart is gone, and of one recovering from sickness that his heart is coming back. This corresponds to the familiar Old World view of the heart as the prime mover in life, thought, and passion. The connection of soul and blood, familiar to the Karens and Papuas, appears prominently in Jewish and Arabic philosophy.

The act of breathing, so characteristic of the high animals during life, and coinciding so closely with life in its departure, has been repeatedly and naturally identified with the life or soul itself. It is thus that West Australians used one word *waug* for "breath, spirit, soul"; that in the Netela language of California, *piuts* means "life, breath, soul"; that certain Greenlanders reckoned two souls to man, namely, his shadow and his breath; that the Malays say the soul of the dying man escapes through his nostrils, and in Java use the same word *nawa* for "breath, life, soul." The conception of the soul as breath may be followed up through Semitic and Aryan etymology, and thus into the main streams of the philosophy of the world. Hebrew shows *nephesh*, "breath" passing into all the meanings of "life, soul, mind, animal," while *ruach* and *neshamah* make the like transition from "breath" to "spirit"; and to these the Arabic *nefs* and *ruh* correspond. The same is the history of Sanskrit *atman* and *prana*, of Greek *psyche* and *pneuma*, of Latin *animus*, *anima*, *spiritus*. German *geist* and English *ghost*, too, may possibly have the same original sense of breath. And if any should think such expressions due to mere metaphor, they may judge the strength of the implied connection between breath and spirit by cases of most unequivocal significance. Among the Seminoles of Florida, when a woman died in childbirth, the infant was held over her face to receive her parting spirit, and thus acquire strength and knowledge for its future use. These Indians could have well understood why at the deathbed of an ancient Roman, the nearest kinsman leant over to inhale the last breath of the departing (*ex excipies hanc animam ore pio*) [you will receive this spirit from a devout mouth]. Their state of mind is kept up to this day among Tyrolese peasants, who can still fancy a good man's soul to issue from his mouth at death like a little white cloud.

Among rude races, the original conception of the human soul seems to have been that of ethereality, or vaporous materiality, which has held so large a place in human thought ever since. In fact, the later metaphysical notion of immateriality could scarcely have conveyed any meaning to a savage. It is moreover to be noticed that, as to the whole nature and action of apparitional souls, the lower philosophy escapes various difficulties which down to modern times have perplexed metaphysicians and theologians of the civilized world. Considering the thin ethereal body of the soul to be itself sufficient and suitable for visibility, movement, and speech, the primitive animists had no need of additional hypotheses to account for these manifestations, theological theories such as we may find detailed by Calmet, as that immaterial souls have their own vaporous bodies provided for them by supernatural means to enable them to appear as specters, or that they possess the power of condensing the circumambient air into phantomlike bodies to invest themselves in, or of forming from it vocal instruments. It appears to have been within systematic schools of civilized philosophy that the transcendental definitions of the immaterial soul were obtained, by abstraction from the primitive conception of the ethereal-material soul, so as to reduce it from a physical to a metaphysical entity.

Departing from the body at the time of death, the soul or spirit is considered set free to linger near the tomb, to wander on earth or flit in the air, or to travel to the proper region of spirits—the world beyond the grave. The principal conceptions of the lower psychology as to a Future Life will be considered in the following chapters, but for the present purpose of investigating the theory of souls in general, it will be well to enter here upon one department of the subject. Men do not stop short at the persuasion that death releases the soul to a free and active existence, but they quite logically proceed to assist nature, by slaying men in order to liberate their souls for ghostly uses. Thus there arises one of the most widespread, distinct, and intelligible rites of animistic religion—that of funeral human sacrifice for the service of the dead. When a man of rank dies and his soul departs to its own place, wherever and whatever that place may be, it is a rational inference of early philosophy that the souls of attendants, slaves, and wives, put to death at his funeral, will make the same journey and continue their service in the next life, and the argument is frequently stretched further, to include the souls of new victims sacrificed in order that they may enter upon the same ghostly servitude. It will appear from the ethnography of this rite that it is not strongly marked in the very lowest levels of culture, but that, arising in the higher savagery, it develops itself in the barbaric stage, and thenceforth continues or dwindles in survival.

Of the murderous practices to which this opinion leads, remarkably distinct accounts may be cited from among tribes of the Indian Archipelago. The following account is given of the funerals of great men among the savage Kayans of Borneo: "Slaves are killed in order that they may follow the deceased and attend upon him. Before they are killed the relations who surround them enjoin them to take great care of their master when they join him, to watch and shampoo him when he is indisposed, to be always near him, and to obey all his behests. The female relatives of the deceased then take a spear and slightly wound the victims, after which the males spear them to death." Again, the opinion of the Idaan is "that all whom they kill in this world shall attend them as slaves after death. This notion of further interest in the destruction of the human species is a great impediment to an intercourse with them, as murder goes further than present advantage or resentment. From the same principle they will purchase a slave, guilty of any capital crime, at fourfold his value, that they may be his executioners." With the same idea is connected the ferocious custom of "head-hunting," so prevalent among the Dayaks before Rajah Brooke's time. They considered that the owner of every human head they could procure would serve them in the next world, where, indeed, a man's rank would be according to his number of heads in this. They would continue the mourning for a dead man till a head was brought in, to provide him with a slave to accompany him to the "habitation of souls"; a father who lost his child would go out and kill the first man he met, as a funeral ceremony; a young man might not marry till he had procured a head, and some tribes would bury with a dead man the first head he had taken, together with spears, cloth, rice, and betel. Waylaying and murdering men for their heads became, in fact, the Dayaks' national sport, and they remarked "the white men read books, we hunt heads instead." Of such rites in the Pacific islands, the most hideously purposeful accounts reach us from the Fiji group. Till lately, a main part of the ceremony of a great man's funeral was the strangling of wives, friends, and slaves, for the distinct purpose of attending him into the world of spirits. Ordinarily the first victim was the wife of the deceased, and more than one if he had several, and their corpses, oiled as for a feast, clothed with new fringed girdles, with heads dressed and ornamented, and vermilion and turmeric powder spread on their faces and bosoms, were laid by the side of the dead warrior. Associates and inferior attendants were likewise slain, and these bodies were spoken of as "grass for bedding the grave." When Ra Mbithi, the pride of Somosomo, was lost at sea, seventeen of his wives were killed; and after the news of the massacre of the Namena people, in 1839, eighty women were strangled to accompany the spirits of their murdered husbands.

In now passing from the consideration of the souls of men to that of the souls of the lower animals, we have first to inform ourselves as to the savage man's idea, which is very different from the civilized man's, of the nature of these lower animals. A remarkable group of observances customary among rude tribes will bring this distinction sharply into view. Savages talk quite seriously to beasts alive or dead as they would to men alive or dead, offer them homage, ask pardon when it is their painful duty to hunt and kill them. A North American Indian will reason with a horse as if rational. Some will spare the rattlesnake, fearing the vengeance of its spirit if slain; others will salute the creature reverently, bid it welcome as a friend from the land of spirits, sprinkle a pinch of tobacco on its head for an offering, catch it by the tail and dispatch it with extreme dexterity, and carry off its skin as a trophy. If an Indian is attacked and torn by a bear, it is that the beast fell upon him intentionally in anger, perhaps to revenge the hurt done to another bear. When a bear is killed, they will beg pardon of him, or even make him condone the offense by smoking the peace-pipe with his murderers, who put the pipe in his mouth and blow down it, begging his spirit not to take revenge. So in Africa, the Kafirs will hunt the elephant, begging him not to tread on them and kill them, and when he is dead they will assure him that they did not kill him on purpose, and they will bury his trunk, for the elephant is a mighty chief, and his trunk is his hand that he may hurt withal. The Congo people will even avenge such a murder by a pretended attack on the hunters who did the deed. Such customs are common among the lower Asiatic tribes. The Stiens of Kambodia ask pardon of the beast they have killed; the Ainos of Yesso kill the bear, offer obeisance and salutation to him, and cut up his carcase. The Koriaks, if they have slain a bear or wolf, will flay him, dress one of their people in the skin, and dance round him, chanting excuses that they did not do it, and especially laying the blame on a Russian. But if it is a fox, they take his skin, wrap his dead body in hay, and sneering tell him to go to his own people and say what famous hospitality he has had, and how they gave him a new coat instead of his old one. The Samoyeds excuse themselves to the slain bear, telling him that it was the Russian who did it, and that a Russian knife will cut him up. The Goldi will set up the slain bear, call him "my lord" and do ironical homage to him, or taking him alive will fatten him in a cage, call him "son" and "brother," and kill and eat him as a sacrifice at a solemn festival. In Borneo, the Dayaks, when they have caught an alligator with a baited hook and rope, address him with respect and soothing till they have his legs fast, and then mocking call him "rajah" and "grandfather." Thus when the savage gets over his fears, he still keeps up in ironical merriment the reverence which had its origin in trembling sincerity. Even now the Norse hunter will say with horror of a bear that will attack man, that he can be "no Christian bear."

The sense of an absolute psychical distinction between man and beast, so prevalent in the civilized world, is hardly to be found among the lower races. Men to whom the cries of beasts and birds seem like human language, and their actions guided as it were by human thought, logically enough allow the existence of souls to beasts, birds, and reptiles, as to men. The lower psychology cannot but recognize in beasts the very characteristic which it attributes to the human soul, namely, the phenomena of life and death, will and judgment, and the phantom seen in vision or in dream. As for believers, savage or civilized, in the great doctrine of metempsychosis, these not only consider that an animal may have a soul, but that this soul may have inhabited a human being, and thus the creature may be in fact their own ancestor or once familiar friend. A line of facts, arranged as waymarks along the course of civilization, will serve to indicate the history of opinion from savagery onward, as to the souls of animals during life and after death. North American Indians held every animal to have its spirit, and these spirits their future life; the soul of the Canadian dog went to serve his master in the other world; among the Sioux, the prerogative of having four souls was not confined to man, but belonged also to the bear, the most human of animals. The Greenlanders considered that a sick human soul might be replaced by the sorcerer with a fresh healthy soul of a hare, reindeer, or a young child. Maori taletellers have heard of the road by which the spirits of dogs descend to Reinga, the Hades of the departed; the Hovas of Madagascar know that the ghosts of beasts and men, dwelling in a great mountain in the south called Ambondrombe, come out occasionally to walk among the tombs or execution-places of criminals. The Kamchadals held that every creature, even the smallest fry, would live again in the underworld. The Kukis of Assam think that the ghost of every animal a Kuki kills in the chase or for the feast will belong to him in the next life, even as the enemy he slays in the field will then become his slave. The Karens apply the doctrine of the spirit or personal life-phantom, which is apt to wander from the body and thus suffer injury, equally to men and to animals. The Zulus say the cattle they kill come to life again, and become the property of the dwellers in the world beneath. The Siamese butcher, when in defiance of the very principles of his Buddhism he slaughters an ox, before he kills the creature has at least the grace to beseech its spirit to seek a happier abode. In connection with such transmigration, Pythagorean and Platonic philosophy gives to the lower animals undying souls, while other classic opinion may recognize in beasts only an inferior order of soul, only the "anima" but not the human "animus" besides. Thus Juvenal:

Principio indulsit communis conditor illis / Tantum animas; nobis animum quoque. . . . [In the beginning to them the universal creator granted only a lower type of soul, but to us also an intellective soul.]

Through the middle ages, controversy as to the psychology of brutes has lasted on into our own times, ranging between two extremes; on the one the theory of Descartes which reduced animals to mere machines, on the other what Mr. Alger defines as "the faith that animals have immaterial and deathless souls." Among modern speculations may be instanced that of Wesley, who thought that in the next life animals will be raised even above their bodily and mental state at the creation, "the horridness of their appearance will be exchanged for their primeval beauty," and it even may be that they will be made what men are now, creatures capable of religion. Adam Clarke's argument for the future life of animals rests on abstract justice: whereas they did not sin, but yet are involved in the sufferings of sinful man, and cannot have in the present state the happiness designed for them, it is reasonable that they must have it in another. Although, however, the primitive belief in the souls of animals still survives to some extent in serious philosophy, it is obvious that the tendency of educated opinion on the question whether brutes have soul, as distinguished from life and mind, has for ages been in a negative and skeptical direction.

Animals being thus considered in the primitive psychology to have souls like human beings, it follows as the simplest matter of course that tribes who kill wives and slaves, to dispatch their souls on errands of duty with their departed lords, may also kill animals in order that their spirits may do such service as is proper to them. The Pawnee warrior's horse is slain on his grave to be ready for him to mount again, and the Comanche's best horses are buried with his favorite weapons and his pipe, all alike to be used in the distant happy hunting-grounds. In South America not only do such rites occur, but they reach a practically disastrous extreme. Patagonian tribes, says D'Orbigny, believe in another life, where they are to enjoy perfect happiness, therefore they bury with the deceased his arms and ornaments, and even kill on his tomb all the animals which belonged to him, that he may find them in the abode of bliss; and this opposes an insurmountable barrier to all civilization, by preventing them from accumulating property and fixing their habitations. Not only do Pope's now hackneyed lines express a real motive with which the Indian's dog is buried with him, but in the North American continent the spirit of the dog has another remarkable office to perform. Certain Eskimos, as Cranz relates, would lay a dog's head in a child's grave, that the soul of the dog, who ever finds his home, may guide the helpless infant to the land of souls. In accordance with this, Captain Scoresby in Jameson's Land found a dog's skull in a small grave, probably a child's. Again, in the distant region of the Aztecs, one of the principal ceremonies was to slaughter a techichi, or native dog; it was burnt or buried with the corpse, with a cotton thread fastened to its neck, and its office was to convey the deceased across the deep waters of Chiuhnahaupan, on the way to the Land of the Dead. The dead Buraet's favorite horse, led saddled to the grave, killed, and flung in, may serve for a Tartar example. In Tonquin, even wild animals have been customarily drowned at funeral ceremonies of princes, to be at the service of the departed in the next world. Among Semitic tribes, an instance of the custom may be found in the Arab sacrifice of a camel on the grave, for the dead man's spirit to ride upon. Among the nations of the Aryan race in Europe, the prevalence of such rites is deep, wide, and full of purpose. Thus warriors were provided in death with horses and housings, with hounds and falcons. Customs thus described in chronicle and legend are vouched for in our own time by the opening of old barbaric burial places. How clear a relic of savage meaning lies here may be judged from a Livonian account as late as the fourteenth century, which relates how men and women, slaves, sheep, and oxen, with other things, were burnt with the dead, who, it was believed, would reach some region of the living, and find there, with the multitude of cattle and slaves, a country of life and happiness. As usual, these rites may be traced onward in survival. The Mongols, who formerly slaughtered camels and horses at their owner's burial, have been induced to replace the actual sacrifice by a gift of the cattle to the Lamas. The Hindus offer a black cow to the Brahmans, in order to secure their passage across the Vaitarani, the river of death, and will often die grasping the cow's tail as if to swim across in herdsman's fashion, holding on to the cow. It is mentioned as a belief in Northern Europe that he who has given a cow to the poor will find a cow to take him over the bridge of the dead, and a custom of leading a cow in the funeral procession is said to have been kept up to modern times. All these rites probably belong together as connected with ancient funeral sacrifice, and the survival of the custom of sacrificing the warrior's horse at his tomb is yet more striking. Saint-Foix long ago put the French evidence very forcibly. Mentioning the horse led at the funeral of Charles VI, with the four valets-de-pied in black, and bareheaded, holding the corners of its caparison, he recalls the horses and servants killed and buried with pre-Christian kings.

Plants, partaking with animals the phenomena of life and death, health and sickness, not unnaturally have some kind of soul ascribed to them. In fact, the notion of a vegetable soul, common to plants and to the higher organisms possessing an animal soul in addition, was familiar to medieval philosophy, and is not yet forgotten by naturalists. But in the lower ranges of culture, at least within one wide district of the world, the souls of plants are much more fully identified with the souls of animals. The Society Islanders seem to have attributed "varua," i.e., surviving soul or spirit, not to men only but to animals and plants. The Dayaks of Borneo not only consider men and animals to have a spirit of living principle, whose departure from the body causes sickness and eventually death, but they also give to the rice its "samangat padi," or "spirit of the paddy," and they hold feasts to retain this soul securely, lest the crops should decay. The Karens say that plants as well as men and animals have their "la" ("kelah"), and the spirit of sickly rice is here also called back like the human spirit considered to have left the body. There is reason to think that the doctrine of the spirits of plants lay deep in the intellectual history of South-East Asia, but was in great measure superseded under Buddhist influence. The Buddhist books show that in the early days of their religion it was a matter of controversy whether trees had souls, and therefore whether they might lawfully be injured. Orthodox Buddhism decided against the tree-souls, and consequently against the scruple to harm them, declaring trees to have no mind nor sentient principle, though admitting that certain dewas or spirits do reside in the body of trees, and speak from within them. Buddhists also relate that a heterodox sect kept up the early doctrine of the actual animate life of trees, in connection with which may be remembered Marco Polo's somewhat doubtful statement as to certain austere Indians objecting to green herbs for such a reason, and some other passages from later writers. Generally speaking, the subject of the spirits of plants is an obscure one, whether from the lower races not having definite opinions, or from our not finding it easy to trace them. The evidence from funeral sacrifices, so valuable as to most departments of early psychology, fails us here, from plants not being thought suitable to send for the service of the dead. Yet, as we shall see more fully elsewhere, there are two topics which bear closely on the matter. On the one hand, the doctrine of transmigration widely and clearly recognizes the idea of trees or smaller plants being animated by human souls; on the other the belief in tree-spirits and the practice of tree-worship involve notions more or less closely coinciding with that of tree-souls, as when the classic hamadryad dies with her tree, or when the Talein of South-East Asia, considering every tree to have a demon or spirit, offers prayers before he cuts one down.

Thus far the details of the lower animistic philosophy are not very unfamiliar to modern students. The primitive view of the souls of men and beasts as asserted or acted on in the lower and middle levels of culture, so far belongs to current civilized thought, that those who hold the doctrine to be false, and the practices based upon it futile, can nevertheless understand and sympathize with the lower nations to whom they are matters of the most sober and serious conviction. Nor is even the notion of a separable spirit or soul as the cause of life in plants too incongruous with ordinary ideas to be readily appreciable. But the theory of souls in the lower culture stretches beyond this limit, to take in a conception much stranger to modern thought. Certain high savage races distinctly hold, and a large proportion of other savage and barbarian races make a more or less close approach to, a theory of separable and surviving souls or spirits belonging to sticks and stones, weapons, boats, food, clothes, ornaments, and other objects which to us are not merely soulless but lifeless.

Yet, strange as such a notion may seem to us at first sight, if we place ourselves by an effort in the intellectual position of an uncultured tribe, and examine the theory of object souls from their point of view, we shall hardly pronounce it irrational. In discussing the origin of myth, some account has been already given of the primitive stage of thought in which personality and life are ascribed not to men and beasts only, but to things. It has been shown how what we call inanimate objects—rivers, stones, trees, weapons, and so forth—are treated as living intelligent beings, talked to, propitiated, punished for the harm they do. Hume, whose *Natural History of Religion* is perhaps more than any other work the source of modern opinions as to the development of religion, comments on the influence of this personifying stage of thought. "There is a universal tendency among mankind to conceive all beings like themselves, and to transfer to every object those qualities with which they are familiarly acquainted, and of which they are intimately conscious. . . . The *unknown causes*, which continually employ their thought, appearing always in the same aspect, are all apprehended to be of the same kind or species. Nor is it long before we ascribe to them thought and reason, and passion, and sometimes even the limbs and figures of men, in order to bring them nearer to a resemblance with ourselves." Auguste Comte has ventured to bring such a state of thought under terms of strict definition in his conception of the primary mental condition of mankind—a state of "pure fetishism, constantly characterized by the free and direct exercise of our primitive tendency to conceive all external bodies soever, natural or artificial, as animated by a life essentially analogous to our own, with mere differences of intensity." Our comprehension of the lower stages of mental culture depends much on the thoroughness with which we can appreciate this primitive, childlike conception, and in this our best guide may be the memory of our own childish days. He who recollects when there was still personality to him in posts and sticks, chairs and toys, may well understand how the infant philosophy of mankind could extend the notion of vitality to what modern science only recognizes as lifeless things; thus one main part of the lower animistic doctrine as to souls of objects is accounted for. The doctrine requires for its full conception of a soul not only life, but also a phantom or apparitional spirit; this development, however, follows without difficulty, for the evidence of dreams and visions applies to the spirits of objects in much the same manner as to human ghosts. Everyone who has seen visions while light-headed in fever, everyone who has ever dreamt a dream, has seen the phantoms of objects as well as of persons. How then can we charge the savage with farfetched absurdity for taking into his philosophy and religion an opinion which rests on the very evidence of his senses? The notion is implicitly recognized in his accounts of ghosts, which do not come naked, but clothed, and even armed; of course there must be spirits of garments and weapons, seeing that the spirits of men come bearing them. It will indeed place savage philosophy in no unfavorable light, if we compare this extreme animistic development of it with the popular opinion still surviving in civilized countries, as to ghosts and the nature of the human soul as connected with them. When the ghost of Hamlet's father appeared armed cap-a-pie,

Such was the very armour he had on,
When he the ambitious Norway combated.

And thus it is a habitual feature of the ghost stories of the civilized, as of the savage world, that the ghost comes dressed, and even dressed in well-known clothing worn in life. Hearing as well as sight testifies to the phantoms of objects: the clanking of ghostly chains and the rustling of ghostly dresses are described in the literature of apparitions. Now by the savage theory, according to which the ghost and his clothes are alike imaginary and subjective, the facts of apparitions are rationally met. But the modern vulgar who ignore or repudiate the notion of ghosts of things, while retaining the notion of ghosts of persons, have fallen into a hybrid state of opinion which has neither the logic of the savage nor of the civilized philosopher.

It remains to sum up in a few words the doctrine of souls, in the various phases it has assumed from first to last among mankind. In the attempt to trace its main course through the successive grades of man's intellectual history, the evidence seems to accord best with a theory of its development, somewhat to the following effect. At the lowest levels of culture of which we have clear knowledge, the notion of a ghost-soul animating man while in the body, is found deeply ingrained. There is no reason to think that this belief was learnt by savage tribes from contact with higher races, nor that it is a relic of higher culture from which the savage tribes have degenerated: for what is here treated as the primitive animistic doctrine is thoroughly at home among savages, who appear to hold it on the very evidence of their senses, interpreted on the biological principle which seems to them most reasonable. We may now and then hear the savage doctrines and practices concerning souls claimed as relics of a high religious culture pervading the primeval race of man. They are said to be traces of remote ancestral religion, kept up in scanty and perverted memory by tribes degraded from a nobler state. It is easy to see that such an explanation of some few facts, sundered from their connection with the general array, may seem plausible to certain minds. But a large view of the subject can hardly leave such argument in possession. The animism of savages stands for and by itself; it explains its own origin. The animism of civilized men, while more appropriate to advanced knowledge, is in great measure only explicable as a developed product of the older and ruder system. It is the doctrines and rites of the lower races which are, according to their philosophy, results of point-blank natural evidence and acts of straightforward practical purpose. It is the doctrines and rites of the higher races which show survival of the old in the midst of the new, modification of the old to bring it into conformity with the new, abandonment of the old because it is no longer compatible with the new. Let us see at a glance in what general relation the doctrine of souls among savage tribes stands to the doctrine of souls among barbaric and cultured nations. Among races within the limits of savagery, the general doctrine of souls is found worked out with remarkable breadth and consistency. The souls of animals are recognized by a natural extension from the theory of human souls; the souls of trees and plants follow in some vague partial way; and the souls of inanimate objects expand the general category to its extremest boundary. Thenceforth, as we explore human thought onward from savage into barbarian and civilized life, we find a state of theory more conformed to positive science, but in itself less complete and consistent. Far on into civilization, men still act as though in some half-meant way they believed in souls or ghosts of objects, while nevertheless their knowledge of physical science is beyond so crude a philosophy. As to the doctrine of souls of plants, fragmentary evidence of the history of its breaking down in Asia has reached us. In our own day and country, the notion of souls of beasts is to be seen dying out. Animism, indeed, seems to be drawing in its outposts, and concentrating itself on its first and main position, the doctrine of the human soul. This doctrine has undergone extreme modification in the course of culture. It has outlived the almost total loss of one great argument attached to it—the objective reality of apparitional souls or ghosts seen in dreams and visions. The soul has given up its ethereal substance, and become an immaterial entity, "the shadow of a shade." Its theory is becoming separated from the investigations of biology and mental science, which now discuss the phenomena of life and thought, the sense and the intellect, the emotions and the will, on a groundwork of pure experience. There has arisen an intellectual product whose very existence is of the deepest significance, a "psychology" which has no longer anything to do with "soul." The soul's place in modern thought is in the metaphysics of religion, and its especial office there is that of furnishing an intellectual side to the religious doctrine of the future life. Such are the alterations which have differenced the fundamental animistic belief in its course through successive periods of the world's culture. Yet it is evidence that, notwithstanding all this profound change, the conception of the human soul is, as to its most essential nature, continuous from the philosophy of the savage thinker to that of the modern professor of theology. Its definition has remained from the first that of an animating, separable, surviving entity, the vehicle of individual personal existence. The theory of the soul is one principal part of a system of religious philosophy, which unites, in an unbroken line of mental connection, the savage fetish-worshiper and the civilized Christian. The divisions which have separated the great religions of the world into intolerant and hostile sects are for the most part superficial in comparison with the deepest of all religious schisms, that which divides Animism from Materialism.

Alfred L. Kroeber

TOTEM AND TABOO: AN ETHNOLOGIC PSYCHOANALYSIS

In lieu of an abridgment of Freud's *Totem and Taboo* a critique has been offered instead, because while Freud's theory of the origin of sacrifice is well known and his book is available in reprinted forms, not too much is known of the anthropological reservations which have been made regarding it. Kroeber was admirably qualified to comment on the work, not only because of his regnant position in historical anthropology but also because of his experience as a practicing psychoanalyst from 1920 to 1923.

Freud's theory may be sharply different from that of others, but it was not derived out of thin air or psychoanalysis alone. He drew upon ideas from Bachofen, Atkinson, and Robertson Smith, to mention but a few.

Reprinted from *American Anthropologist*, XXII (1920), 48–55, by permission of the American Anthropological Association.

His "evidences" came from myth, totemic practices, and psychoanalysis, none of them documentary sources of the kind that historians or even anthropologists use to reconstruct the past. As a work of history, which it purports to be, Freud's reconstruction of the primal horde and the events which led to the slaying of the father and the instituting of commemorative sacrificial rites is the work of a fertile imagination. Prehistory is usually a reconstruction of a very tentative sort and all we can do is judge its plausibility. In this case the plausibility is low indeed.

Totem and Taboo, then, really falls back on whatever support it can derive from psychoanalytic theory. It is based on the assumption that the Oedipus complex is innate and universal. It is normal for the child to wish to have a sexual relationship with the mother and unwittingly will the death of its rival, the father, and this is often achieved vicariously through fantasy. In the primal horde, sexual gratification with their mothers was never consummated after the father had been slain by his sons; in fact, the sons set up specific taboos against sexual relations with their mothers, thus denying themselves the rewards of victory over the old man. The ritual slaughtering of an animal was instituted in order to commemorate the original parricide, says Freud, and in support of his view he points out that in the child's unconscious he frequently identifies his father with some animal. After the primal father had been killed, his sons felt some remorse for their action because they had felt some degree of admiration for his strength and protection. This ambivalent attitude is seen in the sacrificial ritual, which expresses not only the death-wish but rapprochement as well. The symbolism of the totem feast, then, is that it not only reenacts the original act of parricide, but establishes communion and reconciliation with the father through the father-substitute. Freud went so far as to say that all culture originated from the first sacrificial ritual.

Neo-Freudians discount the hereditary implications of the events in the primal horde. They feel that the Oedipus complex arises anew each time out of a familial configuration. Some even doubt that it is universal. The British psychoanalyst Money-Kyrle (*The Meaning of Sacrifice*, 1930) has modified Freud's position and attempted to make it more palatable by denying the implications of a racial mind and the inheritance of acquired memory; instead, he says, sacrifice should be viewed as the symbolic expression of an unconscious desire for parricide that each individual has acquired for himself. Malinowski, the ethnologist (*Sex and Repression in Savage Society*, 1927), long ago showed that the complex was modifiable in terms of social structure. More recently Lessa ("Oedipus-Type Tales in Oceania," 1956) has indicated that Oedipus stories not only reflect such modifications, but apparently are not universal, being present only in a contiguous band extending eastward from Europe to the south-west Pacific. As Kroeber and many others have insisted, Freud was brilliant in his insights into psychological motivation, but his attempt to explain sacrifice as the result of an historic incident does not bear up under scrutiny. In all fairness, it should be pointed out that at least some have interpreted the "historical" description in *Totem and Taboo* as a brilliant image not to be taken literally as an historical event.

The recent translation into English of Freud's interpretation of a number of ethnic phenomena[1] offers an occasion to review the startling series of essays which first appeared in *Imago* a number of years ago. There is the more reason for this because, little as this particular work of Freud has been noticed by anthropologists, the vogue of the psychoanalytic movement founded by him is now so strong that the book is certain to make an impression in many intelligent circles.

Freud's principal thesis emerges formally

[1] Sigmund Freud, *Totem and Taboo: Resemblances Between the Psychic Life of Savages and Neurotics*. Authorized English Translation, with Introduction, by A. A. Brill (New York: Moffat Yard & Co., 1918).

only toward the end of his book, but evidently has controlled his reasoning from the beginning, although perhaps unconsciously. This thesis is "that the beginnings of religion, ethics, society, and art meet in the Oedipus complex." He commences with the inference of Darwin, developed farther by Atkinson, that at a very early period man lived in small communities consisting of an adult male and a number of females and immature individuals, the males among the latter being driven off by the head of the group as they became old enough to evoke his jealousy. To this Freud adds the Robertson Smith theory that sacrifice at the altar is the essential element in every ancient cult, and that such sacrifice goes back to a killing and eating by the clan of its totem animal, which was regarded as of kin with the clan and its god, and whose killing at ordinary times was therefore strictly forbidden. The Oedipus complex directed upon these two hypotheses welds them into a mechanism with which it is possible to explain most of the essentials of human civilization, as follows. The expelled sons of the primal horde finally banded together and slew their father, ate him, and appropriated the females. In this they satisfied the same hate impulse that is a normal infantile trait and the basis of most neuroses, but which often leads to unconscious "displacement" of feelings, especially upon animals. At this point, however, the ambivalence of emotions proved decisive. The tender feelings which had always persisted by the side of the brothers' hate for their father, gained the upper hand as soon as this hate was satisfied, and took the form of remorse and sense of guilt. "What the father's presence had formerly prevented they themselves now prohibited in the psychic situation of 'subsequent obedience' which we know so well from psychoanalysis. They undid their deed by declaring that the killing of the father substitute, the totem, was not allowed, and renounced the fruits of their deed by denying themselves the liberated women. Thus they created the two fundamental taboos of totemism." These are "the oldest and most important taboos" of mankind: "namely not to kill the totem animal and to avoid sexual intercourse with totem companions of the other sex," alongside which many if not all other taboos are "secondary, displaced and distorted." The renunciation of the women or incest prohibition had also this practical foundation: that any attempt to divide the spoils, when each member of the band really wished to emulate the father and possess all the women, would have disrupted the organization which had made the brothers strong. The totem sacrifice and feast reflected the killing and eating of the father, assuaged "the burning sense of guilt," and brought about "a kind of reconciliation" or agreement by which the father-totem granted all wishes of his sons in return for their pledge to honor his life. "All later religions prove to be . . . reactions aiming at the same great event with which culture began and which ever since has not let mankind come to rest."

This mere extrication and presentation of the framework of the Freudian hypothesis on the origin of socio-religious civilization is probably sufficient to prevent its acceptance; but a formal examination is only just.

First, the Darwin-Atkinson supposition is of course only hypothetical. It is a mere guess that the earliest organization of man resembled that of the gorilla rather than that of trooping monkeys.

Second, Robertson Smith's allegation that blood sacrifice is central in ancient cult holds chiefly or only for the Mediterranoid cultures of a certain period—say the last two thousand years B.C.—and cultures then or subsequently influenced by them. It does not apply to regions outside the sphere of affection by these cultures.

Third, it is at best problematical whether blood sacrifice goes back to a totemic observance. It is not established that totemism is an original possession of Semitic culture.

Fourth, coming to the Freudian theory proper, it is only conjecture that the sons would kill, let alone devour, the father.

Fifth, the fact that a child sometimes displaces its father-hatred upon an animal—we are not told in what percentage of cases—is no proof that the sons did so.

Sixth, if they "displaced," would they retain enough of the original hate impulse to slay the father; and if so, would the slaying not resolve and evaporate the displacements? Psychoanalysts may affirm both questions; others will require more examination before they accept the affirmation.

Seventh, granting the sons' remorse and resolve no longer to kill the father-displacement-totem, it seems exceedingly dubious whether this resolve could be powerful and enduring enough to suppress permanently the gratification of the sexual impulses which was now possible. Again there may be psychoanalytic evidence sufficient to allay the doubt; but it will take a deal of evidence to convince "unanalytic" psychologists, ethnologists, and laymen.

Eighth, if the band of brothers allowed

strangers—perhaps expelled by their jealous fathers—to have access to the women whom they had renounced, and matrilinear or matriarchal institutions thus came into existence, what would be left for the brothers (unless they were able to be content with life-long celibacy or homosexuality), other than individual attachments to other clans; which would mean the disintegration of the very solidarity that they are pictured as so anxious to preserve, even by denying their physiological instincts?

Ninth, it is far from established that exogamy and totem abstinence are the two fundamental prohibitions of totemism. Freud refers to Goldenweiser's study of the subject, which is certainly both analytical and conducted from a psychological point of view even though not psychoanalytical; but he fails to either accept or refute this author's carefully substantiated finding that these two features cannot be designated as primary in the totemic complex.

Tenth, that these two totemic taboos are the oldest of all taboos is pure assertion. If all other taboos are derived from them by displacement or distortion, some presentation of the nature and operation and sequence of these displacements is in order. An astronomer who casually said that he believed Sirius to be the center of the stellar universe and then proceeded to weave this opinion into the fabric of a still broader hypothesis, would get little hearing from other astronomers.

A final criticism—that the persistence into modern society and religion of this first "great event with which culture began" is an unexplained process—will not be pressed here, because Freud has anticipated it with a *tu quoque:* social psychologists assume a "continuity in the psychic life of succeeding generations" without in general concerning themselves much with the manner in which this continuity is established.

No doubt still other challenges of fact or interpretation will occur to every careful reader of the book. The above enumeration has been compiled only far enough to prove the essential method of the work; which is to evade the painful process of arriving at a large certainty by the positive determination of smaller certainties and their unwavering addition irrespective of whether each augments or diminishes the sum total of conclusion arrived at. For this method the author substitutes a plan for multiplying into one another, as it were, fractional certainties—that is, more or less remote possibilities—without recognition that the multiplicity of factors must successively decrease the probability of their product. It is the old expedient of pyramiding hypotheses; which if theories had to be paid for like stocks or gaming cards, would be less frequently indulged in. Lest this criticism be construed as unnecessarily harsh upon a gallant and stimulating adventurer into ethnology, let it be added that it applies with equal stricture upon the majority of ethnologists from whom Freud has drawn an account of the renown or interest of their books: Reinach, Wundt, Spencer and Gillen, Lang, Robertson Smith, Durkheim and his school, Keane, Spencer, Avebury; and his special *vade mecum* Frazer.

There is another criticism that can be leveled against the plan of Freud's book: that of insidiousness, though evidently only as the result of the gradual growth of his thesis during its writing. The first chapter or essay, on the Savage's Dread of Incest, merely makes a case for the applicability of psychoanalysis to certain special social phenomena such as the mother-in-law taboo. In the second, the psychoanalytic doctrine of the ambivalence of emotions is very neatly and it seems justly brought to bear on the dual nature of taboo as at once holy and defiling. Concurrently a foundation is laid, though not revealed, for the push to the ultimate thesis. The third chapter on Animism, Magic, and the Omnipotence of Thought refrains from directly advancing the argument, but strengthens its future hold on the reader by emphasizing the parallelism between the thought systems of savages and neurotics. The last chapter is not, in the main, a discussion of the Infantile Recurrence of Totemism, as it is designated, but an analysis of current ethnological theories as to the origin of totemism in society and the presentation of the theory of the author. This hypothesis, toward which everything has been tending, does not however begin to be divulged until page 233; after which, except for tentative claims to a wide extensibility of the principle arrived at and some distinctly fair admissions of weakness, the book promptly closes without any re-examination or testing of its proposition. The explanation of taboo on pages 52–58 is an essential part of the theory developed on pages 233 seq., without any indication being given that it is so. Then, when the parallelism of savage and neurotic thought has been driven home by material largely irrelevant to the final and quite specific thesis, this is suddenly sprung. Freud cannot be charged with more than a propagandist's zeal and perhaps haste of composition; but the consequence is that this book is keen without orderliness, intricately rather than closely reasoned, and endowed with an unsubstantiated convincingness. The critical reader will ascertain these qualities; but the book will fall into the hands of many who are lacking either in care or independence of judgment and who, under the influence of a great name and in the presence of a bewilderingly fertile imagination, will be carried into an illusory belief. Again there is palliation—but nothing more—in the fact that the literature of theoretical anthropology consists largely of bad precedent.

But, with all the essential failure of its finally avowed purpose, the book is an important and valuable contribution. However much cultural anthropology may come to lean more on the historical instead of the psychological method, it can never ultimately free itself, nor should it wish to, from the psychology that underlies it. To this psychology the psychoanalytic movement initiated by Freud has made an indubitably significant contribution, which every ethnologist must sooner or later take into consideration. For instance, the correspondences between taboo customs and "compulsion neuroses" as developed on pages 43–48 are unquestionable, as are also the parallelism between the two aspects of taboo and the ambivalence of emotions under an accepted prohibition. Again the strange combination of mourning for the dead with the fear of them and taboos against them is certainly illumined if not explained by this theory of ambivalence.

It is even possible to extend Freud's point of view. Where the taboo on the name of the dead is in force we find not only the fear that utterance will recall the soul to the hurt of the living, but also actual shock at the utterance as a slight or manifestation of hostility to the dead. It is a fair question whether this shock may not be construed as a reaction from the unconscious hate carried toward the dead during their life, as if speaking of them were an admission of satisfaction at their going. The shock is certainly greatest where affection was deepest; persons who were indifferent were mentioned without emotional reluctance if circumstances permit, whereas enemies, that is individuals toward whom hate was avowed instead of repressed, may have the utterance of their names gloated over.

Of very broad interest is the problem raised by Freud's conjecture that the psychic impulses of primitive people possessed more ambivalence than our own except in the case of neurotics: that their mental life, like that of neurotics, is more sexualized and contains fewer social components than ours. Neurosis would therefore usually represent an atavistic constitution. Whatever its complete significance, there exists no doubt a remarkable similarity between the phenomena of magic, taboo, animism, and primitive religion in general, and neurotic manifestations. In both a creation that has only psychic validity is given greater or less preference over reality. As Freud says, the two are of course not the same, and the ultimate difference lies in the fact that neuroses are asocial creations due to a flight from dissatisfying reality. This is certainly not to be denied on any ethnological grounds; yet the implication that savages are essentially more neurotic than civilized man may well be challenged, although it cannot be dismissed offhand.

The experience of firsthand observers will probably be unanimous that primitive communities, like peasant populations, contain very few individuals that can be put into a class with the numerous neurotics of our civilization. The reason seems to be that primitive societies have institutionalized such impulses as with us lead to neuroses. The individual of neurotic tendency finds an approved and therefore harmless outlet in taboo, magic, myth, and the like, whereas the non-neurotic, who at heart remains attached to reality, accepts these activities as forms which do not seriously disturb him. In accord with this interpretation is the fact that neurotics appear to become numerous and characteristic in populations among whom religion has become decadent and "enlightenment" active, as in the Hellenistic, Roman Imperial, and recent eras; whereas in the Middle Ages, when "superstition" and taboo were firmly established, there were social aberrations indeed, like the flagellants and children's crusade, but few neurotics. Much the same with homosexuality, which the North American and Siberian natives have socialized. Its acceptance as an institution may be a departure from normality, but has certainly saved countless individuals from the heavy strain which definite homosexualists undergo in our civilization. It would be unfitting to go into these matters further here: they are mentioned as an illustration of the importance of the problems which Freud raises. However precipitate his entry into anthropology and however flimsy some of his syntheses, he brings to bear keen insight, a fecund imagination, and above all a point of view which henceforth can never be ignored without stultification.

While the book thus is one that no ethnologist can afford to neglect, one remark may be extended to psychologists of the unconscious who propose to follow in Freud's footsteps: there really is a great deal of ethnology not at all represented by the authors whom Freud discusses. To students of this side of the science the line of work initiated by Tylor and developed and most notably represented among the living by Frazer, is not so much ethnology as an attempt to psychologize with ethnological data. The cause of Freud's leaning so heavily on Frazer is clear. The latter knows nothing of psychoanalysis and with all acumen his efforts are prevailingly a dilettantish playing; but in the last analysis they are psychology, and as history only a pleasing fabrication. If psychoanalysts wish to establish serious contacts with historical ethnology, they must first learn to know that such an ethnology exists. It is easy enough to say, as Freud does, that the nature of totemism and exogamy could be most readily grasped if we could get into closer touch with their origins, but that as we cannot we must depend on hypotheses. Such a remark rings a bit naïve to students who have long since made up their minds that ethnology, like every other branch of science, is work and not a game in which lucky guesses score; and who therefore hold that since we know nothing directly about the origin of totemism or other social phenomena but have information on these phenomena as they exist at present, our business is first to understand as thoroughly as possible the nature of these existing phenomena; in the hope that such understanding may gradually lead to a partial reconstruction of origins—without undue guessing.

Alfred L. Kroeber

TOTEM AND TABOO IN RETROSPECT

Almost two decades after writing the foregoing critique, Kroeber, in an issue of the *American Journal of Sociology* that was devoted to Freud in appreciation rather than in criticism of his contributions, again criticizes Freud's historical fantasies. He was writing at a time when anthropology was reaching the apex of psychoanalytic interest. In 1948 (*Anthropology*) he maintained perhaps an even stronger position, saying "the psychoanalytic explanation of culture is intuitive, dogmatic, and wholly unhistorical." In even more recent years he reiterated his disillusionment with the possibility of using psychoanalysis for historical reconstruction and was especially caustic concerning Freud's failure to advance beyond outmoded materials and approaches: "Freud preferred to forage in Frazer rather than to read the intellectually sophisticated works of his own age-mate Boas" (*The Nature of Culture*, 1952).

Reprinted from the *American Journal of Sociology*, XLV (1939), 446–451, by permission of The University of Chicago Press.

Nearly twenty years ago I wrote an analysis of *Totem and Taboo*—that brain child of Freud which was to be the precursor of a long series of psychoanalytic books and articles explaining this or that aspect of culture, or the whole of it.[1] It seems an appropriate time to return to the subject.

I see no reason to waver over my critical analysis of Freud's book. There is no indication that the consensus of anthropologists during these twenty years has moved even an inch nearer acceptance of Freud's central thesis. But I found myself somewhat conscience-stricken when, perhaps a decade later, I listened to a student in Sapir's seminar in Chicago making his report on *Totem and Taboo*, who, like myself, first spread out its gossamer texture and then laboriously tore it to shreds. It is a procedure too suggestive of breaking a butterfly on the wheel. An iridescent fantasy deserves a more delicate touch even in the act of demonstration of its unreality.

Freud himself has said of my review that it characterized his book as a *Just So* story. It is

[1] "Totem and Taboo: An Ethnologic Psychoanalysis," *American Anthropologist* XXII (1920), 48–55.

a felicitous phrase, coming from himself. Many a tale by Kipling or Andersen contains a profound psychological truth. One does not need therefore to cite and try it in the stern court of evidential confrontation.

However, the fault is not wholly mine. Freud does speak of the "great event with which culture began." And therewith he enters history. Events are historical and beginnings are historical, and human culture is appreciable historically. It is difficult to say how far he realized his vacillation between historic truth and abstract truth expressed through intuitive imagination. A historic finding calls for some specification of place and time and order; instead of which, he offers a finding of unique cardinality, such as history feels it cannot deal with.

Freud is reported subsequently to have said that his "event" is to be construed as "typical." Herewith we begin to approach a basis of possible agreement. A typical event, historically speaking, is a recurrent one. This can hardly be admitted for the father-slaying, eating, and guilt sense. At any rate, there is no profit in discussing the recurrence of an event which we do not even know to have occurred once. But there is no need sticking fast on the word "event" because Freud used it. His argument is evidently ambiguous as between historical thinking and psychological thinking. If we omit the fatal concept of event, of an act as it happens in history, we have left over the concept of the psychologically potential. Psychological insight may legitimately hope to attain to the realization and definition of such a potentiality; and to this, Freud should have confined himself. We may accordingly properly disregard any seeming claim, or half-claim, to historic authenticity of the suggested actual happening, as being beside the real point, and consider whether Freud's theory contains any possibility of being a generic, timeless explanation of the psychology that underlies certain recurrent historic phenomena or institutions like totemism and taboo.

Here we obviously are on better ground. It becomes better yet if we disregard certain gratuitous and really irrelevant assumptions, such as that the self-imposed taboo following the father-slaying is the original of all taboos, these deriving from it as secondary displacements or distortions. Stripped down in this way, Freud's thesis would reduce to the proposition that certain psychic processes tend always to be operative and to find expression in wide-spread human institutions. Among these processes would be the incest drive and incest repression, filial ambivalence, and the like; in short, if one likes, the kernel of the Oedipus situation. After all, if ten modern anthropologists were asked to designate one universal human institution, nine would be likely to name the incest prohibition; some have expressly named it as the only universal one. Anything so constant as this, at least as regards its nucleus, in the notoriously fluctuating universe of culture, can hardly be the result of a "mere" historical accident devoid of psychological significance. If there is accordingly an underlying factor which keeps reproducing the phenomenon in an unstable world, this factor must be something in the human constitution—in other words, a psychic factor. Therewith the door is open not for an acceptance *in toto* of Freud's explanation but at any rate for its serious consideration as a scientific hypothesis. Moreover, it is an explanation certainly marked by deeper insight and supportable by more parallel evidence from personal psychology than the older views, such as that familiarity breeds sexual indifference, or recourse to a supposed "instinct" which is merely a verbal restatement of the observed behavior.

Totemism, which is a much rarer phenomenon than incest taboo, might then well be the joint product of the incest-drive-and-repression process and of some other less compelling factor. Nonsexual taboo, on the other hand, which rears itself in so many protean forms over the whole field of culture, might be due to a set of still different but analogous psychic factors. Anthropologists and sociologists have certainly long been groping for something underlying which would help them explain both the repetitions and the variations in culture, provided the explanation were evidential, extensible by further analysis, and neither too simplistic nor too one-sided. Put in some such form as this, Freud's hypothesis might long before this have proved fertile in the realm of cultural understanding instead of being mainly rejected or ignored as a brilliant fantasy.

What has stood in the way of such a fruitful restatement or transposition? There seem to be at least three factors: one due to Freud himself, another jointly to himself and his followers, the third mainly to the Freudians.

The first of these is Freud's already mentioned ambiguity which leads him to state a timeless psychological explanation as if it were also a historical one. This tendency is evident elsewhere in his thinking. It appears to be the counterpart of an extraordinarily explorative imagination, constantly impelled to penetrate into new intellectual terrain. One consequence is a curious analogy to what he himself has discovered in regard to the manifest and the latent in dreams. The manifest is there, but it is ambiguous; a deeper meaning lies below; from the point of view of this latent lower content, the manifest is accidental and inconsequential. Much like this, it seems to me, is the historical dress which Freud gives his psychological insight. He does not repudiate it; he does not stand by it as integral. It is really irrelevant; but his insight having manifested itself in the dress, he cannot divest himself of this "manifest" form. His view is overdetermined like a dream.

A second factor is the curious indifference which Freud has always shown as to whether his conclusions do or do not integrate with the totality of science. This led him at one time to accept the inheritance of acquired traits as if it did not clash with standard scientific attitude. Here again we have the complete explorer who forgets in his quest, or represses, knowledge of what he started from or left behind. In Freud himself one is inclined not to quarrel too hard with this tendency; without it, he might have opened fewer and shorter vistas. Of his disciples, however, who have so largely merely followed, more liaison might be expected. I recall Rank, while still a Freudian, after expounding his views to a critically sympathetic audience, being pressed to reconcile certain of them to the findings of science at large and, after an hour, conceding that psychoanalysts held that there might be more than one truth, each on its own level and independent of the other. And he made the admission without appearing to realize its import.

A third element in the situation is the all-or-none attitude of most avowed psychoanalysts. They insist on operating within a closed system. At any rate, if not wholly closed, it grows only from within; it is not open to influence from without. A classical example is Ernest Jones's resistance to Malinowski's finding that among the matrilineal Melanesians the effects directed toward the father in our civilization are largely displaced upon the mother's brother, the relation of father and children being rather one of simple and relatively univalent affection. Therewith Malinowski had really vindicated the mechanism of the Oedipus relation. He showed that the mechanism remained operative even in a changed family situation; a minor modification of it, in its direction, conforming to the change in given condition. Jones, however, could not see this, and resisted tooth and nail. Because Freud in the culture of Vienna had determined that ambivalence was directed toward the father, ambivalence had to remain directed to him universally, even where primary authority resided in an uncle.

The same tendency appears in Roheim, whose "Psycho-analysis of Primitive Cultural Types" contains a mass of psychological observations most valuable to cultural anthropologists, but so organized as to be unusable by them. None have used it, so far as I know. This is not due to lack of interest on the part of anthropologists in psychological behavior within cultures, for in recent years a whole series of them have begun avowedly to deal with such behavior. Nor is it due to any deficiency of quality in Roheim's data: these are rich, vivid, novel, and valuable. But the data are so presented as to possess organization only from the point of view of orthodox psychoanalytic theory. With reference to the culture in which they occur, or to the consecutive life histories of personalities, they are inchoate. The closing sentence of the monograph—following immediately on some illuminative material—is typical: "We see then, that the sexual practices of a people are indeed prototypical and that from their posture in coitus their whole psychic attitude may be inferred." Can a conclusion be imagined which would appear more arbitrarily dogmatic than this to any psychologist, psychiatrist, anthropologist, or sociologist?

The fundamental concepts which Freud formulated—repression, regression and infantile persistences, dream symbolism and overdetermination, guilt sense, the effects toward members of the family—have gradually seeped into general science and become an integral and important part of it. If one assumes that our science forms some kind of larger unit because its basic orientation and method are uniform, these concepts constitute the permanent contribution of Freud and psychoanalysis to general science; and the contribution is large. Beyond, there is a further set of concepts which in the main have not found their way into science: the censor, the superego, the castration complex, the explanation of specific cultural phenomena. To these concepts the several relevant branches of science—sociology, anthropology, psychology, and medicine alike—remain impervious about as consistently as when the concepts were first developed. It may therefore be inferred that science is likely to remain negative to them. To the psychoanalysts, on the contrary, the two classes of concepts remain on the same level, of much the same value, and inseparably interwoven into one system. In this quality of nondifferentiation between what the scientific world accepts as reality and rejects as fantasy, between what is essential and what is incidental, the orthodox psychoanalytic movement reveals itself as partaking of the nature of a religion—a system of mysticism; even, it might be said, it shows certain of the qualities of a delusional system. It has appropriated to itself such of the data of science—the cumulative representative of reality—as were digestible to it and has ignored the larger remainder. It has sought little integration with the totality of science, and only on its own terms. By contrast, science, while also of course a system, has shown itself a relatively open one: it has accepted and already largely absorbed a considerable part of the concepts of psychoanalysis. It is indicative of the largeness of Freud's mind that, although the sole founder of the movement and the originator of most of its ideas, his very ambiguities in the more doubtful areas carry a stamp of tolerance. He may persist in certain interpretations; he does not insist on them; they remain more or less fruitful suggestions. Of this class is his theory of the primary determination of culture. As a construct, neither science nor history can use it; but it would seem that they can both accept and utilize some of the process concepts that are involved in the construct.

I trust that this reformulation may be construed not only as an *amende honorable* but as a tribute to one of the great minds of our day.

NOTE: Since the above was written and submitted, Freud has published *Moses and Monotheism.* The thesis of *Totem and Taboo* is reaffirmed: "I still hold to this construction." One concession in the direction of my argument is made: the father-killing was not a unique event but "extended in reality over thousands of years." Of his stimulator, Robertson Smith, Freud says superbly: "with his opponents I will never agree." We, on our part, if I may speak for ethnologists, though remaining unconverted, have met Freud, recognize the encounter as memorable, and herewith resalute him.

Émile Durkheim
THE ELEMENTARY FORMS OF THE RELIGIOUS LIFE

Few books on the science of religion stand out as powerfully as Émile Durkheim's *The Elementary Forms of the Religious Life*, published originally in 1912 in France under the title *Les Formes élémentaires de la vie religieuse: Le Système totémique en Australie*. The author had already foreshadowed his views on religion in his *Le Suicide* (1897) and an article in the *Année Sociologique* (1899), and had even published some of the first portions of his forthcoming book. What Durkheim had to say has had a deep impact on subsequent theoreticians, particularly Radcliffe-Brown, Evans-Pritchard, and Warner. Durkheim's realization that religion plays a vital part in social life was impressed upon him by the writings of Robertson Smith and those British anthropologists who had been concerned with the subject of religion. While Durkheim was in Paris in 1885 for the purpose of rounding out his training, Lucien Herr, the librarian of the École Normale, guided him toward Frazer's articles on totemism, and from then on he made it his concern to study primitive religion so that he could understand the role of religion in general.

Durkheim became convinced that in order to understand this role one must examine religion in its simplest and original form, totemism; therefore he used materials from Australia to make his analysis. Totemism, he maintained, embodies all the essential aspects of religion: the division of things into sacred and profane; the notion of the soul, spirits, mythical personalities, and divinity; a negative cult with ascetic practices; rites of oblation and communion; imitative rites; commemorative rites; and expiatory rites. The sacred attitude necessary for religion is to be seen in the totem, which derives its sacredness from the fact that it is essentially the symbol of society. The totem represents the clan, which to the aborigine is virtually society itself. Primitive man, especially as a consequence of the social environment that results when he meets in large ceremonial gatherings, realizes, however unconsciously, that as a member of society he can survive but that as a lone individual he cannot. He comes to view society as something sacred because he is utterly dependent on it as a source of strength and culture. But it is easier for him to visualize and direct his feeling of awe and respect toward a symbol than toward so complex a thing as a clan. The totem becomes the object of the sacred attitude. It is virtually God. Society, in effect, deifies itself. Durkheim equates Society with God. Not only are the members of society sacred, but so are all things which stand for society: the totemic plants and animals and the images of such totems. They become the object of a cult because they possess mana. As Lowie (*Primitive Religion*, 1948) has so aptly put it, "In this interpretation of totemism there is something like an anticipation of the Freudian interpretation of dreams. Things are not what they seem on the surface but have a hidden meaning."

His preoccupation with origins was merely incidental to Durkheim's main goal, which was to study the role of religion. In effect, Durkheim saw religion as a vast symbolic system which made social life possible by expressing and maintaining the sentiments or values of the society. He especially analyzed the role of ceremonial and ritualistic institutions, and concluded that they are disciplinary, integrating, vitalizing, and euphoric forces. His method was what only in later years came to be labeled "functional." It stemmed from such predecessors as Fustel de Coulanges (who was one of his professors at the École Normale and whose *La Cité antique* [1864] linked religion with political organization and other institutions in a complex of interdependent relations) and Robertson Smith.

Religious phenomena are naturally arranged into two fundamental categories: beliefs and rites. The first are states of opinion, and consist in representations; the second are determined modes of action. Between these two classes of facts there is all the difference which separates thought from action.

The rites can be defined and distinguished from other human practices, moral practices, for example, only by the special nature of their object. A moral rule prescribes certain manners of acting to us, just as a rite does, but which are addressed to a different class of objects. So it is the object of the rite which must be characterized, if we are to characterize the rite itself. Now it is in the beliefs that the special nature of this object is expressed. It is possible to define the rite only after we have defined the belief.

All known religious beliefs, whether simple or complex, present one common characteristic: they presuppose a classification of all the things, real and ideal, of which men think, into two classes or opposed groups, generally designated by two distinct terms which are translated well enough by the words *profane* and *sacred* (*profane*, *sacré*). This division of the world into two domains, the one containing all that is sacred, the other all that is profane, is the distinctive trait of religious thought; the beliefs, myths, dogmas, and legends are either representations or systems of representations which express the nature of sacred things, the virtues and powers which are attributed to them, or their relations with each other and with profane things. But by sacred things one must not understand simply those personal beings which are called gods or spirits; a rock, a tree, a spring, a pebble, a piece of wood, a house, in a word, anything can be sacred. A rite can have this character; in fact, the rite does not exist which does not have it to a certain degree. There are words, expressions, and formulae which can be pronounced only by the mouths of consecrated persons; there are gestures and movements which everybody cannot perform. If the Vedic sacrifice has had such an efficacy that, according to mythology, it was the creator of the gods, and not merely a means of winning their favor, it is because it possessed a virtue comparable to that of the most sacred beings. The circle of sacred objects cannot be determined, then, once for all. Its extent varies infinitely, according to the different religions. That is how Buddhism is a religion: in default of gods, it admits the existence of sacred things, namely, the four noble truths and the practices derived from them.

. . .

. . . The real characteristic of religious phenomena is that they always suppose a bipartite division of the whole universe, known and knowable, into two classes which embrace all that exists, but which radically exclude each other. Sacred things are those which the interdictions protect and isolate; profane things, those to which these interdictions are applied and which must remain at a distance from the first. Religious beliefs are the representations which express the nature of sacred things and the relations which they sustain, either with each other or with profane things. Finally, rites are the rules of conduct which prescribe how a man should comport himself in the presence of these sacred objects.

. . .

The really religious beliefs are always common to a determined group, which makes profession of adhering to them and of practicing the rites connected with them. They are not merely received individually by all the members of this group; they are something belonging to the group, and they make its unity. The individuals which compose it feel themselves united to each other by the simple fact that they have a common faith. A society whose members are united by the fact that they think in the same way in regard to the sacred world and its relations with the profane world, and by the fact that they translate these common ideas into common practices, is what is called a "Church." In all history, we do not find a single religion without a Church. Sometimes the Church is strictly national, sometimes it passes the frontiers; sometimes it embraces an entire people (Rome, Athens, the Hebrews), sometimes it embraces only a part of them (the Christian societies since the advent of Protestantism); sometimes it is directed by a corps of priests, sometimes it is almost completely devoid of any official directing body. But wherever we observe the religious life, we find that it has a definite group as its foundation. Even the so-called "private" cults, such as the domestic cult or the cult of a corporation, satisfy this condition; for they are always celebrated by a group, the family, or the corporation. Moreover, even these particular religions are ordinarily only special forms of a more general religion which embraces all; these restricted Churches are in reality only chapels of a vaster Church which, by reason of this very extent, merits this name still more.

It is quite another matter with magic. To be sure, the belief in magic is always more or less general; it is very frequently diffused in large masses of the population, and there are even peoples where it has as many adherents as the real religion. But it does not result in binding together those who adhere to it, nor in uniting them into a group leading a common life. *There is no Church of magic.* Between the magician and the individuals who consult him, as between these individuals themselves, there are no lasting bonds which make them members of the same moral community, comparable to that formed by the believers in the same god or the observers of the same cult. The magician has a clientele and not a Church, and it is very possible that his clients have no other relations between each other, or even do not know each other; even the relations which they have with him are generally accidental and transient; they are just like those of a sick man with his physician. The official and public character with which he is sometimes invested changes nothing in this situation; the fact that he works openly does not unite him more regularly or more durably to those who have recourse to his services.

. . .

Thus we arrive at the following definition: *A religion is a unified system of beliefs and practices relative to sacred things, that is to say, things set apart and forbidden—beliefs and practices which unite into one single moral community called a Church, all those who adhere to them.* The second element which thus finds a place in our definition is no less essential than the first; for by showing that the idea of religion is inseparable from that of the Church, it makes it clear that religion should be an eminently collective thing.

. . .

LEADING CONCEPTIONS OF THE ELEMENTARY RELIGION

Even the crudest religions with which history and ethnology make us acquainted are already of a complexity which corresponds badly with the idea sometimes held of primitive mentality. One finds there not only a confused system of beliefs and rites, but also such a plurality of different principles, and such a richness of essential notions, that it seems impossible to see in them anything but the late product of a rather long evolution. Hence it has been concluded that to discover the truly original form of religious life, it is necessary to descend by analysis beyond these observable religions, to resolve them into their common and fundamental elements, and then to seek among these latter some one from which the others were derived.

To the problem thus stated, two contrary solutions have been given.

There is no religious system, ancient or recent, where one does not meet, under different forms, two religions, as it were, side by side, which, though being united closely and mutually penetrating each other, do not cease, nevertheless, to be distinct. The one addresses itself to the phenomena of nature, either the great cosmic forces, such as winds, rivers, stars, or the sky, etc., or else the objects of various sorts which cover the surface of the earth, such as plants, animals, rocks, etc.; for this reason it has been given the name of *naturism.* The other has spiritual beings as its object, spirits, souls, geniuses, demons, divinities properly so-called, animated and conscious agents like man, but distinguished from him, nevertheless, by the nature of their powers and especially by the peculiar characteristic that they do not affect the senses in the same way: ordinarily they are not visible to human eyes. This religion of spirits is called *animism.* Now, to explain the universal coexistence of these two sorts of cults, two contradictory theories have been proposed. For some, animism is the primitive religion, of which naturism is only a secondary and derived form. For the others, on the contrary, it is the nature cult which was the point of departure for religious evolution; the cult of spirits is only a peculiar case of that.

These two theories are, up to the present, the only ones by which the attempt has been made to explain rationally the origins of religious thought.

. . .

Finally, the animistic theory implies a consequence which is perhaps its best refutation.

If it were true, it would be necessary to admit that religious beliefs are so many hallucinatory representations, without any objective foundation whatsoever. It is supposed that they are all derived from the idea of the soul because one sees only a magnified soul in the spirits and gods. But according to Tylor and his disciples, the idea of the soul is itself constructed entirely out of the vague and inconsistent images which occupy our attention during sleep: for the soul is the double, and the double is merely a man as he appears to himself while he sleeps. From this point of view, then, sacred beings are only the imaginary conceptions which men have produced during a sort of delirium which regularly overtakes them every day, though it is quite impossible to see what useful ends these conceptions serve, nor what they answer to in reality. If a man prays, if he makes sacrifices and offerings, if he submits to the multiple privations which the ritual prescribes, it is because a sort of constitutional eccentricity has made him take his dreams for perceptions, death for a prolonged sleep, and dead bodies for living and thinking beings. Thus not only is it true, as many have held, that the forms under which religious powers have been represented to the mind do not express them exactly, and that the symbols with the aid of which they have been thought of partially hide their real nature, but more than that, behind these images and figures there exists nothing but the nightmares of private minds. In fine, religion is nothing but a dream, systematized and lived, but without any foundation in reality. Thence it comes about that the theorists of animism, when looking for the origins of religious thought, content themselves with a small outlay of energy. When they think that they have explained how men have been induced to imagine beings of a strange, vaporous form, such as those they see in their dreams, they think the problem is resolved.

In reality, it is not even approached. It is inadmissible that systems of ideas like religions, which have held so considerable a place in history, and from which, in all times, men have come to receive the energy which they must have to live, should be made up of a tissue of illusions. Today we are beginning to realize that law, morals, and even scientific thought itself were born of religion, were for a long time confounded with it, and have remained penetrated with its spirit. How could a vain fantasy have been able to fashion the human consciousness so strongly and so durably? Surely it ought to be a principle of the science of religions that religion expresses nothing which does not exist in nature; for there are sciences only of natural phenomena.

. . .

The spirit of the naturistic school is quite different.

. . .

They talk about the marvel which men should feel as they discover the world. But really, that which characterizes the life of nature is a regularity which approaches monotony. Every morning the sun mounts in the horizon, every evening it sets; every month the moon goes through the same cycle; the river flows in an uninterrupted manner in its bed; the same seasons periodically bring back the same sensations. To be sure, here and there an unexpected event sometimes happens: the sun is eclipsed, the moon is hidden behind clouds, the river overflows. But these momentary variations could only give birth to equally momentary impressions, the remembrance of which is gone after a little while; they could not serve as a basis for these stable and permanent systems of ideas and practices which constitute religions. Normally, the course of nature is uniform, and uniformity could never produce strong emotions. Representing the savage as filled with admiration before these marvels transports much more recent sentiments to the beginnings of history. He is much too accustomed to it to be greatly surprised by it. It requires culture and reflection to shake off this yoke of habit and to discover how marvellous this regularity itself is. Besides, as we have already remarked, admiring an object is not enough to make it appear sacred to us, that is to say, to mark it with those characteristics which make all direct contact with it appear a sacrilege and a profanation. We misunderstand what the religious sentiment really is, if we confound it with every impression of admiration and surprise.

But, they say, even if it is not admiration, there is a certain impression which men cannot help feeling in the presence of nature. He cannot come in contact with it, without realizing that it is greater than he. It overwhelms him by its immensity. This sensation of an infinite space which surrounds him, of an infinite time which has preceded and will follow the present moment, and of forces infinitely superior to those of which he is master, cannot fail, as it seems, to awaken within him the idea that outside of him there exists an infinite power upon which he depends. And this idea enters as an essential element into our conception of the divine.

But let us bear in mind what the question is. We are trying to find out how men came to think that there are in reality two categories of things, radically heterogeneous and incomparable to each other. Now how could the spectacle of nature give rise to the idea of this duality? Nature is always and everywhere of the same sort. It matters little that it extends to infinity: beyond the extreme limit to which my eyes can reach, it is not different from what it is here. The space which I imagine beyond the horizon is still space, identical with that which I see. The time which flows without end is made up of moments identical with those which I have passed through. Extension, like duration, repeats itself indefinitely; if the portions which I touch have of themselves no sacred character, where did the others get theirs? The fact that I do not see them directly, is not enough to transform them. A world of profane things may well be unlimited; but it remains a profane world. Do they say that the physical forces with which we come in contact exceed our own? Sacred forces are not to be distinguished from profane ones simply by their great intensity, they are different; they have special qualities which the others do not have. Quite on the contrary, all the forces manifested in the universe are of the same nature, those that are within us just as those that are outside of us. And especially, there is no reason which could have allowed giving a sort of pre-eminent dignity to some in relation to others. Then if religion really was born because of the need of assigning causes to physical phenomena, the forces thus imagined would have been no more sacred than those conceived by the scientist today to account for the same facts. This is as much as to say that there would have been no sacred beings and therefore no religion.

. . .

TOTEMISM AS AN ELEMENTARY RELIGION

Since neither man nor nature have of themselves a sacred character, they must get it from another source. Aside from the human individual and the physical world, there should be some other reality, in relation to which this variety of delirium which all religion is in a sense, has a significance and an objective value. In other words, beyond those which we have called animistic and naturistic, there should be another sort of cult, more fundamental and more primitive, of which the first are only derived forms or particular aspects.

In fact, this cult does exist: it is the one to which ethnologists have given the name of *totemism*.

. . .

With one reservation which will be indicated below, we propose to limit our research to Australian societies. They are perfectly homogeneous, for though it is possible to distinguish varieties among them, they all belong to one common type. This homogeneity is even so great that the forms of social organization are not only the same, but that they are even designated by identical or equivalent names in a multitude of tribes, sometimes very distant from each other. Also, Australian totemism is the variety for which our documents are the most complete. Finally, that which we propose to study in this work is the most primitive and simple religion which it is possible to find. It is therefore natural that to discover it, we address ourselves to societies as slightly evolved as possible, for it is evidently there that we have the greatest chance of finding it and studying it well. Now there are no societies which present this characteristic to a higher degree than the Australian ones. Not only is their civilization most rudimentary—the house and even the hut are still unknown—but also their organization is the most primitive and simple which is actually known; it is that which we have elsewhere called *organization on basis of clans.*

. . .

Among the beliefs upon which totemism rests, the most important are naturally those concerning the totem; it is with these that we must begin.

At the basis of nearly all the Australian tribes we find a group which holds a preponderating place in the collective life: this is the clan. Two essential traits characterize it.

In the first place, the individuals who compose it consider themselves united by a bond of kinship, but one which is of a very special nature. This relationship does not come from the fact that they have definite blood connections with one another; they are relatives from the mere fact that they have the same name. They are not fathers and mothers, sons or daughters, uncles or nephews of one another in the sense which we now give these words; yet they think of themselves as forming a single family, which is large or small according to the dimensions of the clan, merely because they are collectively designated by the same word. When we say that they regard themselves as a single family, we do so because they recognize duties toward each other which are identical with those which have always been incumbent upon kindred: such duties as aid, vengeance, mourning, the obligations not to marry among themselves, etc.

. . .

The species of things which serves to designate the clan collectively is called its *totem.* The totem of the clan is also that of each of its members.

Each clan has its totem, which belongs to it alone; two different clans of the same tribe cannot have the same. In fact, one is a member of a clan merely because he has a certain name. All who bear this name are members of it for that very reason; in whatever manner they may be spread over the tribal territory, they all have the same relations of kinship with one another. Consequently, two groups having the same totem can only be two sections of the same clan. Undoubtedly, it frequently happens that all of a clan does not reside in the same locality, but has representatives in several different places. However, this lack of a geographical basis does not cause its unity to be the less keenly felt.

. . .

In a very large proportion of the cases, the objects which serve as totems belong either to the animal or the vegetable kingdom, but especially to the former. Inanimate things are much more rarely employed. Out of more than 500 totemic names collected by Howitt among the tribes of southeastern Australia, there are scarcely forty which are not the names of plants or animals; these are the clouds, rain, hail, frost, the moon, the sun, the wind, the autumn, the summer, the winter, certain stars, thunder, fire, smoke, water, or the sea. It is noticeable how small a place is given to celestial bodies and, more generally, to the great cosmic phenomena, which were destined to so great a fortune in later religious development.

. . .

But the totem is not merely a name; it is an emblem, a veritable coat-of-arms whose analogies with the arms of heraldry have often been remarked. In speaking of the Australians, Grey says, "each family adopt an animal or vegetable as their crest and sign," and what Grey calls a family is incontestably a clan. Also Fison and Howitt say, "the Australian divisions show that the totem is, in the first place, the badge of a group."

. . .

These totemic decorations enable us to see

that the totem is not merely a name and an emblem. It is in the course of the religious ceremonies that they are employed; they are a part of the liturgy; so while the totem is a collective label, it also has a religious character. In fact, it is in connection with it, that things are classified as sacred or profane. It is the very type of sacred thing.

The tribes of Central Australia, especially the Arunta, the Loritja, the Kaitish, the Unmatjera, and the Ilpirra, make constant use of certain instruments in their rites which are called the *churinga* by the Arunta according to Spencer and Gillen, or the *tjurunga*, according to Strehlow. They are pieces of wood or bits of polished stone, of a great variety of forms, but generally oval or oblong. Each totemic group has a more or less important collection of these. *Upon each of these is engraved a design representing the totem of this same group.* A certain number of the churinga have a hole at one end, through which goes a thread made of human hair or that of an opossum. Those which are made of wood and are pierced in this way serve for exactly the same purposes as those instruments of the cult to which English ethnographers have given the name of "bull-roarers." By means of the thread by which they are suspended, they are whirled rapidly in the air in such a way as to produce a sort of humming identical with that made by the toys of this name still used by our children; this deafening noise has a ritual significance and accompanies all ceremonies of any importance. These sorts of churinga are real bull-roarers. But there are others which are not made of wood and are not pierced; consequently they cannot be employed in this way. Nevertheless, they inspire the same religious sentiments.

In fact, every churinga, for whatever purpose it may be employed, is counted among the eminently sacred things; there are none which surpass it in religious dignity. This is indicated even by the word which is used to designate them. It is not only a substantive but also an adjective meaning sacred. Also, among the several names which each Arunta has, there is one so sacred that it must not be revealed to a stranger; it is pronounced but rarely, and then in a low voice and a sort of mysterious murmur.

. . .

Now in themselves, the churinga are objects of wood and stone like all others; they are distinguished from profane things of the same sort by only one particularity; this is that the totemic mark is drawn or engraved upon them. So it is this mark and this alone which gives them their sacred character.

. . .

But totemic images are not the only sacred things. There are real things which are also the object of rites, because of the relations which they have with the totem: before all others, are the beings of the totemic species and the members of the clan.

. . .

Every member of the clan is invested with a sacred character which is not materially inferior to that which we just observed in the animal. This personal sacredness is due to the fact that the man believes that while he is a man in the usual sense of the word, he is also an animal or plant of the totemic species.

In fact, he bears its name; this identity of name is therefore supposed to imply an identity of nature. The first is not merely considered as an outward sign of the second; it supposes it logically. This is because the name, for a primitive, is not merely a word or a combination of sounds; it is a part of the being, and even something essential to it. A member of the Kangaroo clan calls himself a kangaroo; he is therefore, in one sense, an animal of this species.

. . .

We have seen that totemism places the figured representations of the totem in the first rank of the things it considers sacred; next come the animals or vegetables whose name the clan bears, and finally the members of the clan. Since all these things are sacred in the same way, though to different degrees, their religious character can be due to none of the special attributes distinguishing them from each other. If a certain species of animal or vegetable is the object of a reverential fear, this is not because of its special properties, for the human members of the clan enjoy the same privilege, though to a slightly inferior degree, while the mere image of this same plant or animal inspires an even more pronounced respect. The similar sentiments inspired by these different sorts of things in the mind of the believer, which give them their sacred character, can evidently come only from some common principle partaken of alike by the totemic emblems, the men of the clan and the individuals of the species serving as totem. In reality, it is to this common principle that the cult is addressed. In other words, totemism is the religion, not of such and such animals or men or images, but of an anonymous and impersonal force, found in each of these beings but not to be confounded with any of them. No one possesses it entirely and all participate in it. It is so completely independent of the particular subjects in whom it incarnates itself, that it precedes them and survives them. Individuals die, generations pass and are replaced by others; but this force always remains actual, living, and the same. It animates the generations of today as it animated those of yesterday and as it will animate those of tomorrow.

. . .

Thus the totem is before all a symbol, a material expression of something else. But of what?

From the analysis to which we have been giving our attention, it is evident that it expresses and symbolizes two different sorts of things. In the first place, it is the outward and visible form of what we have called the totemic principle or god. But it is also the symbol of the determined society called the clan. It is its flag; it is the sign by which each clan distinguishes itself from the others, the visible mark of its personality, a mark borne by everything which is a part of the clan under any title whatsoever, men, beasts, or things. So if it is at once the symbol of the god and of the society, is that not because the god and the society are only one? How could the emblem of the group have been able to become the figure of this quasidivinity, if the group and the divinity were two distinct realities? The god of the clan, the totemic principle, can therefore be nothing else than the clan itself, personified and represented to the imagination under the visible form of the animal or vegetable which serves as totem.

But how has this apotheosis been possible, and how did it happen to take place in this fashion?

In a general way, it is unquestionable that a society has all that is necessary to arouse the sensation of the divine in minds, merely by the power that it has over them; for to its members it is what a god is to his worshipers. In fact, a god is, first of all, a being whom men think of as superior to themselves, and upon whom they feel that they depend. Whether it be a conscious personality, such as Zeus or Jahveh, or merely abstract forces such as those in play in totemism, the worshiper, in the one case as in the other, believes himself held to certain manners of acting which are imposed upon him by the nature of the sacred principle with which he feels that he is in communion. Now society also gives us the sensation of a perpetual dependence. Since it has a nature which is peculiar to itself and different from our individual nature, it pursues ends which are likewise special to it; but, as it cannot attain them except through our intermediacy, it imperiously demands our aid. It requires that, forgetful of our own interests, we make ourselves its servitors, and it submits us to every sort of inconvenience, privation, and sacrifice, without which social life would be impossible. It is because of this that at every instant we are obliged to submit ourselves to rules of conduct and of thought which we have neither made nor desired, and which are sometimes even contrary to our most fundamental inclinations and instincts.

Since religious force is nothing other than the collective and the anonymous force of the clan, and since this can be represented in the mind only in the form of the totem, the totemic emblem is like the visible body of the god. Therefore, it is from it that those kindly or dreadful actions seem to emanate, which the cult seeks to provoke and prevent; consequently, it is to it that the cult is addressed. This is the explanation of why it holds the first place in the series of sacred things.

But the clan, like every other sort of society, can live only in and through the individual consciousnesses that compose it. So if religious force, in so far as it is conceived as incorporated in the totemic emblem, appears to be outside of the individuals and to be endowed with a sort of transcendence over them, it, like the clan of which it is the symbol, can be realized only in and through them; in this sense, it is immanent in them and they necessarily represent it as such. They feel it present and active within them, for it is this which raises them to a superior life. This is why men have believed that they contain within them a principle comparable to the one residing in the totem, and consequently, why they have attributed a sacred character to themselves, but one less marked than that of the emblem. It is because the emblem is the pre-eminent source of the religious life; the man participates in it only indirectly, as he is well aware; he takes into account the fact that the force that transports him into the world of sacred things is not inherent in him, but comes to him from the outside.

But for still another reason, the animals or vegetables of the totemic species should have the same character, and even to a higher degree. If the totemic principal is nothing else than the clan, it is the clan thought of under the material form of the totemic emblem; now this form is also that of the concrete beings whose name the clan bears. Owing to this resemblance, they could not fail to evoke sentiments analogous to those aroused by the emblem itself. Since the latter is the object of a religious respect, they too should inspire respect of the same sort and appear to be sacred. Having external forms so nearly identical, it would be impossible for the native not to attribute to them forces of the same nature. It is therefore forbidden to kill or eat the totemic animal, since its flesh is believed to have the positive virtues resulting from the rites; it is because it resembles the emblem of the clan, that is to say, it is in its own image. And since the animal naturally resembles the emblem more than the man does, it is placed on a superior rank in the hierarchy of sacred things. Between these two beings there is undoubtedly a close relationship, for they both partake of the same essence: both incarnate something of the totemic principle. However, since the principle itself is conceived under an animal form, the animal seems to incarnate it more fully than the man. Therefore, if men consider it and treat it as a brother, it is at least as an elder brother.

But even if the totemic principle has its preferred seat in a determined species of animal or vegetable, it cannot remain localized there. A sacred character is to a high degree contagious; it therefore spreads out from the totemic being to everything that is closely or remotely connected with it. The religious sentiments inspired by the animal are communicated to the substances upon which it is nourished and which serve to make or remake its flesh and blood, to the things that resemble it, and to the different beings with which it has constant relations. Thus, little by little, subtotems are attached to the totems and form the cosmological systems expressed by the primitive classifications. At last, the whole world is divided up among the totemic principles of each tribe.

We are now able to explain the origin of the ambiguity of religious forces as they appear in history, and how they are physical as well as human, moral as well as material. They are moral powers because they are made up entirely of the impressions this moral being, the group, arouses in those other moral beings, its individual members; they do not translate the manner in which physical things affect our senses, but the way in which the collective consciousness acts upon individual consciousnesses. Their authority is only one form of the moral ascendancy of society over its members. But, on the other hand, since they are conceived of under material forms, they could not fail to be regarded as closely related to material things. Therefore they dominate the two worlds. Their residence is in men, but at the same time they are the vital principles of things. They animate minds and discipline them, but it is also they who make plants grow and animals reproduce. It is this double nature which has enabled religion to be like the womb from which come all the leading germs of human civilization. Since it has been made to embrace all of reality, the physical world as well as the moral one, the forces that move bodies as well as those that move minds have been conceived in a religious form. That is how the most diverse methods and practices, both those that make possible the continuation of the moral life (laws, morals, beaux-arts) and those serving the material life (the natural, technical, and practical sciences), are either directly or indirectly derived from religion.

TWO
THE FUNCTION OF RELIGION IN HUMAN SOCIETY

Introduction

While the earlier scholars, especially the writers on comparative religion in the nineteenth century, were concerned with the basic question of how various forms of religion originated in human history, the emphasis shifted in the twentieth century to the basic question of what functions religion has in human society. This shift of interest is well expressed by Radcliffe-Brown when he contrasts his own position with that of Sir James Frazer. He writes that

> *Sir James accounted for the taboos of savage tribes as the application in practice of beliefs arrived at by erroneous processes of reasoning, and he seems to have thought of the effect of these beliefs in creating or maintaining a stable orderly society as being accidental. My own view is that the negative and positive rites of savages exist and persist because they are part of the mechanism by which an orderly society maintains itself in existence, serving as they do to establish certain fundamental social values. . . . I would suggest that what Sir James Frazer seems to regard as the accidental results of magical and religious beliefs really constitute their essential function and the ultimate reason for their existence (Taboo).*

In other words, scholars began to be less concerned with the question of how religious beliefs and practices arose out of human experience, and more concerned with the study of what these beliefs and practices *do* for individuals and societies, whatever their origins. When the question was posed in this fashion, there began to be less disposition to study historical origins and stages of development, and less tendency to become embroiled in theological arguments. Instead, the student of comparative religion could start with the fundamental hypothesis that given the biological and social nature of man on this planet, some kind of religious system is a cultural universal; no human society can get along without a religion any more than it can survive without an economic system. The actual cultural content found in the religions of different societies may vary enormously, but underlying this diversity there may be impressive similarities in basic functions, involving the culturally prescribed solutions of human social and psychological problems and the ways of expressing and reaffirming the central values of a society. Viewed in this light, religion appears to be an essential ingredient of society.

To start with this position and to pose these

questions, then, is a call for cross-cultural research and theoretical thinking that will lead both to a clear specification of those aspects of the human situation that require religious patterns and to a precise delineation of the functions religion does perform. We want to know what social and psychological problems are solved by religious beliefs and practices and how. We want to know to what extent and how a religious system helps to express, codify, and reaffirm the central values of a society in such a way as to maintain the social fabric of that society.

The following selections are from writers who have established landmarks in the development of functional thinking about the nature of religion and associated beliefs and practices. The works of Malinowski and Radcliffe-Brown are clearly classics in this development of functionalism, and their publications have sparked a stimulating controversy over the concept of function as well as a disagreement over the relationships of anxiety to ritual. Malinowski's use of the concept of function revolved around the question: What human needs (individual and social) are fulfilled by cultural patterns? Radcliffe-Brown's use of the concept was based upon his "organismic analogy"; that is, just as an organ of the body has a function in preserving the successful maintenance of the body as a whole, so does a social custom or usage have a function in preserving the maintenance of a society as a whole. This conceptual difference led to the disagreements between Malinowski and Radcliffe-Brown over the relationship of anxiety to ritual—a disagreement which Homans attempts to resolve in his paper.

Drawing upon these theories of the functions of religion, as well as upon the earlier work of Émile Durkheim, Max Weber, Vilfredo Pareto, and others, the selection from Talcott Parsons represents a recent synthesis of our theoretical knowledge concerning the role and functions of religion in human society. The selection by Clyde Kluckhohn, "Myths and Rituals: A General Theory," makes a two-fold contribution to the functional analysis of religion. First, he demonstrates the functional interrelation between myth and ritual, showing that one is not necessarily prior to the other. Second, the role of religion as an adaptive and adjustive response to physical and psychological threats to the individual is examined.

While functional explanations of religion are intuitively powerful, a strict sociological or psychological reductionism cannot explain why it is that religion, rather than some other aspect of culture, comes to fulfill these functions. Clifford Geertz, in the final essay of this chapter, takes up this question by examining the nature and efficacy of religious symbols. He attempts to show not only what religion *does,* but also why religious symbols are especially well suited to fulfill these functions and precisely how they establish cultural order and meaning in the world.

Bronislaw Malinowski

THE ROLE OF MAGIC AND RELIGION

Few writers in modern times have written as lucidly and with as much firsthand field experience on the subject of magic and religion as has Bronislaw Malinowski. His classic paper on the subject is "Magic, Science, and Religion," which was first published in James Needham (ed.), *Science, Religion and Reality,* in 1925. But since this famous paper was reprinted by the Free Press in a book by the same name in 1948, and then in 1954 became available in a Doubleday Anchor Book edition, we are presenting a briefer statement of most of the same theoretical ground drawn from his article, "Culture," which appeared in the *Encyclopedia of the Social Sciences.* For a more detailed version

Excerpted from "Culture" by Bronislaw Malinowski. Reprinted with permission of the publisher from *Encyclopedia of the Social Sciences,* Seligman and Johnson, editors. Volume IV, 634–642.

of the argument, the reader may turn to the readily available Anchor Book entitled *Magic, Science, and Religion.*

To understand Malinowski's thesis that every society, even the most primitive, has perfectly sound empirical knowledge to carry out many of its practical activities, that "magic is to be expected and generally to be found whenever man comes to an unbridgeable gap, a hiatus in his knowledge or in his powers of practical control, and yet has to continue in his pursuit," and that "religion is not born out of speculation or reflection, still less out of illusion or misapprehension, but rather out of the real tragedies of human life, out of the conflict between human plans and realities," one has to understand some of the thinking that was current about primitive religion at the time he wrote. Tylor had made primitive man into a kind of rational philosopher who tried to find answers to such problems as the difference between the living and the dead, and had developed the belief in animistic spirits which he regarded as the basis for primitive religion; Frazer had been concerned with showing that magic was a kind of "false science" and that an age of magic preceded an age of religion; Lévy-Bruhl had been engaging in brilliant speculations concerning the prelogical and mystical character of primitive thought. Into this cluster of ideas Malinowski brought some new insights—insights that were based for the first time on extensive, firsthand field experience. He was able to invite his readers "to step outside the closed study of the theorist into the open air of the Anthropological field," in this case the Trobriand Islands.

In addition to clarifying the relationships among magic, science, and religion, Malinowski clearly showed that the myths of primitive peoples also have important functions in social life. Thus he writes in the following article that "the function of myth is to strengthen tradition and to endow it with a greater value and prestige by tracing it back to a higher, better, more supernatural and more effective reality of initial events." For a more detailed version of his thesis on myths, and his classification of the oral literature into myths, legends, and folk tales, the reader may turn to his book *Myth in Primitive Psychology* (1926), which is also reprinted in the Anchor Book edition of *Magic, Science, and Religion.*

In spite of the various theories about a specific non-empirical and prelogical character of primitive mentality there can be no doubt that as soon as man developed the mastery of environment by the use of implements, and as soon as language came into being, there must also have existed primitive knowledge of an essentially scientific character. No culture could survive if its arts and crafts, its weapons and economic pursuits were based on mystical, non-empirical conceptions and doctrines. When human culture is approached from the pragmatic, technological side, it is found that primitive man is capable of exact observation, of sound generalizations and of logical reasoning in all those matters which affect his normal activities and are at the basis of his production. Knowledge is then an absolute derived necessity of culture. It is more, however, than a means to an end, and it was not classed therefore with the instrumental imperatives. Its place in culture, its function, is slightly different from that of production, of law, or of education. Systems of knowledge serve to connect various types of behavior; they carry over the results of past experiences into future enterprise and they bring together elements of human experience and allow man to co-ordinate and integrate his activities. Knowledge is a mental attitude, a diathesis of the nervous system, which allows man to carry on the work which culture makes him do. Its function is to organize and integrate the indispensable activities of culture.

The material embodiment of knowledge consists in the body of arts and crafts, of technical processes and rules of craftsmanship. More specifically, in most primitive cultures and certainly in higher ones there are special implements of knowledge—diagrams, topographical models, measures, aids to orientation or to counting.

The connection between native thought and language opens important problems of function. Linguistic abstraction, categories of space, time and relationship, and logical means of expressing the concatenation of ideas are extremely important matters, and the study of how thought works through language in any culture is still a virgin field of cultural linguistics. How primitive language works, where it is embodied, how it is related to social organization, to primitive religion and magic, are important problems of functional anthropology.

By the very forethought and foresight which it gives, the integrative function of knowledge creates new needs, that is, imposes new imperatives. Knowledge gives man the possibility of planning ahead, of embracing vast spaces of time and distance; it allows a wide range to his hopes and desires. But however much knowledge and science help man in allowing him to obtain what he wants, they are unable completely to control change, to eliminate accidents, to foresee the unexpected turn of natural events, or to make human handiwork reliable and adequate to all practical requirements. In this field, much more practical, definite, and circumscribed than that of religion, there develops a special type of ritual activities which anthropology labels collectively as magic.

The most hazardous of all human enterprises known to primitive man is sailing. In the preparation of his sailing craft and the laying out of his plans the savage turns to his science. The painstaking work as well as the intelligently organized labor in construction and in navigation bears witness to the savage's trust in science and submission to it. But adverse wind or no wind at all, rough weather, currents and reefs are always liable to upset his best plans and most careful preparations. He must admit that neither his knowledge nor his most painstaking efforts are a guaranty of success. Something unaccountable usually enters and baffles his anticipations. But although unaccountable it yet appears to have a deep meaning, to act or behave with a purpose. The sequence, the significant concatenation of events, seems to contain some inner logical consistency. Man feels that he can do something to wrestle with that mysterious element or force, to help and abet his luck. There are therefore always systems of superstition, of more or less developed ritual, associated with sailing, and in primitive communities the magic of sailing craft is highly developed. Those who are well acquainted with some good magic have, in virtue of that, courage and confidence. When the canoes are used for fishing, the accidents and the good or bad luck may refer not only to transport but also to the appearance of fish and to the conditions under which they are caught. In trading, whether overseas or with near neighbors, chance may favor or thwart the ends and desires of man. As a result both fishing and trading magic are very well developed.

Likewise in war, man, however primitive, knows that well-made weapons of attack and defense, strategy, the force of numbers, and the strength of the individuals ensure victory. Yet with all this the unforeseen and accidental help even the weaker to victory when the fray happens under the cover of night, when ambushes are possible, when the conditions of the encounter obviously favor one side at the expense of the other. Magic is used as something which over and above man's equipment and his force helps him to master accident and to ensnare luck. In love also a mysterious, unaccountable quality of success or else a predestination to failure seems to be accompanied by some force independent of ostensible attraction and of the best laid plans and arrangements. Magic enters to insure something which counts over and above the visible and accountable qualifications.

Primitive man depends on his economic pursuits for his welfare in a manner which makes him realize bad luck very painfully and directly. Among people who rely on their fields or gardens what might be called agricultural knowledge is invariably well developed. The natives know the properties of the soil, the need of a thorough clearing from bush and weed, fertilizing with ashes and appropriate planting. But however well chosen the site and well worked the gardens, mishaps occur. Drought or deluge coming at most inappropriate seasons destroys the crop altogether, or some blights, insects, or wild animals diminish them. Or some other year, when man is conscious that he deserves but a poor crop, everything runs so smoothly and prosperously that an unexpectedly good return rewards the undeserving gardener. The dreaded elements of rain and sunshine, pests and fertility seem to be controlled by a force which is beyond ordinary human experience and knowledge, and man repairs once more to magic.

In all these examples the same factors are involved. Experience and logic teach man that within definite limits knowledge is supreme; but beyond them nothing can be done by rationally founded practical exertions. Yet he rebels against inaction because although he realizes his impotence he is yet driven to action by intense desire and strong emotions. Nor is inaction at all possible.

Once he has embarked on a distant voyage or finds himself in the middle of a fray or halfway through the cycle of garden growing, the native tries to make his frail canoe more seaworthy by charms or to drive away locusts and wild animals by ritual or to vanquish his enemies by dancing.

Magic changes its forms; it shifts its ground; but it exists everywhere. In modern societies magic is associated with the third cigarette lit by the same match, with spilled salt and the need of throwing it over the left shoulder, with broken mirrors, with passing under a ladder, with the new moon seen through glass or on the left hand, with the number thirteen or with Friday. These are minor superstitions which seem merely to vegetate among the intelligentsia of the western world. But these superstitions and much more developed systems also persist tenaciously and are given serious consideration among modern urban populations. Black magic is practiced in the slums of London by the classical method of destroying the picture of the enemy. At marriage ceremonies good luck for the married couple is obtained by the strictest observance of several magical methods such as the throwing of the slipper and the spilling of rice. Among the peasants of central and eastern Europe elaborate magic still flourishes and children are treated by witches and warlocks. People are thought to have the power to prevent cows from giving milk, to induce cattle to multiply unduly, to produce rain and sunshine and to make people love or hate each other. The saints of the Roman Catholic Church become in popular practice passive accomplices of magic. They are beaten, cajoled and carried about. They can give rain by being placed in the field, stop flows of lava by confronting them and stop the progress of a disease, of a blight or of a plague of insects. The crude practical use made of certain religious rituals or objects makes their function magical. For magic is distinguished from religion in that the latter creates values and attains ends directly, whereas magic consists of acts which have a practical utilitarian value and are effective only as a means to an end. Thus a strictly utilitarian subject matter or issue of an act and its direct, instrumental function make it magic, and most modern established religions harbor within their ritual and even their ethics a good deal which really belongs to magic. But modern magic survives not only in the forms of minor superstitions or within the body of religious systems. Wherever there is danger, uncertainty, great incidence of chance and accident, even in entirely modern forms of enterprise, magic crops up. The gambler at Monte Carlo, on the turf, or in a continental state lottery develops systems. Motoring and modern sailing demand mascots and develop superstitions. Around every sensational sea tragedy there has formed a myth showing some mysterious magical indications or giving magical reasons for the catastrophe. Aviation is developing its superstitions and magic. Many pilots refuse to take up a passenger who is wearing anything green, to start a journey on a Friday, or to light three cigarettes with a match when in the air, and their sensitiveness to superstition seems to increase with altitude. In all large cities of Europe and America magic can be purchased from palmists, clairvoyants, and other soothsayers, who forecast the future, give practical advice as to lucky conduct, and retail ritual apparatus such as amulets, mascots, and talismans. The richest domain of magic, however, is, in civilization as in savagery, that of health. Here again the old venerable religions lend themselves readily to magic. Roman Catholicism opens its sacred shrines and places of worship to the ailing pilgrim, and faith healing flourishes also in other churches. The main function of Christian Science is the thinking away of illness and decay; its metaphysics are very strongly pragmatic and utilitarian and its ritual is essentially a means to the end of health and happiness. The unlimited range of universal remedies and blessings, osteopathy and chiropractic, dietetics and curing by sun, cold water, grape or lemon juice, raw food, starvation, alcohol or its prohibition—one and all shade invariably into magic. Intellectuals still submit to Coué and Freud, to Jaeger and Kneipp, to sun worship, either direct or through the mercury-vapor lamp—not to mention the bedside manner of the highly paid specialist. It is very difficult to discover where common sense ends and where magic begins.

The savage is not more rational than modern man nor is he more superstitious. He is more limited, less liable to free imaginings and to the confidence trick of new inventions. His magic is traditional and he has his stronghold of knowledge, his empirical and rational tradition of science. Since the superstitious or prelogical character of primitive man has been so much emphasized, it is necessary to draw clearly the dividing line between primitive science and magic. There are domains on which magic never encroaches. The making of fire, basketry, the actual production of stone implements, the making of strings or mats, cooking and all minor domestic activities although extremely important are never associated with magic. Some of them become the center of religious practices and of mythology, as, for example, fire or cooking or stone implements; but magic is never connected with their production. The reason is that ordinary skill guided by sound knowledge is sufficient to set man on the right path and to give him certainty of correct and complete control of these activities.

In some pursuits magic is used under certain conditions and is absent under others. In a maritime community depending on the products of the sea there is never magic connected with the collecting of shellfish or with fishing by poison, weirs, and fish traps, so long as these are completely reliable. On the other hand, any dangerous, hazardous, and uncertain type of fishing is surrounded by ritual. In hunting, the simple and reliable ways of trapping or killing are controlled by knowledge and skill alone; but let there be any danger or any uncertainty connected with an important supply of game and magic immediately appears. Coastal sailing as long as it is perfectly safe and easy commands no magic. Overseas expeditions are invariably bound up with ceremonies and ritual. Man resorts to magic only where chance and circumstances are not fully controlled by knowledge.

This is best seen in what might be called systems of magic. Magic may be but loosely and capriciously connected with its practical setting. One hunter may use certain formulae and rites, and another ignore them; or the same man may apply his conjurings on one occasion and not on another. But there are forms of enterprise in which magic must be used. In a big tribal adventure, such as war, or a hazardous sailing expedition or seasonal travel or an undertaking such as a big hunt or a perilous fishing expedition or the normal round of gardening, which as a rule is vital to the whole community, magic is often obligatory. It runs in a fixed sequence concatenated with the practical events, and the two orders, magical and practical, depend on one another and form a system. Such systems of magic appear at first sight an inextricable mixture of efficient work and superstitious practices and so seem to provide an unanswerable argument in favor of the theories that magic and science are under primitive conditions so fused as not to be separable. Fuller analysis, however, shows that magic and practical work are entirely independent and never fuse.

But magic is never used to replace work. In gardening the digging or the clearing of the ground or the strength of the fences or quality of the supports is never scamped because stronger magic has been used over them. The native knows well that mechanical construction must be produced by human labor according to strict rules of craft. He knows that all the processes which have been in the soil can be controlled by human effort to a certain extent but not beyond, and it is only this beyond which he tries to influence by magic. For his experience and his reason tell him that in certain matters his efforts and his intelligence are of no avail whatever. On the other hand, magic has been known to help; so at least his tradition tells him.

In the magic of war and of love, of trading expeditions and of fishing, of sailing and of canoe making, the rules of experience and logic are likewise strictly adhered to as regards technique, and knowledge and technique receive due credit in all the good results which can be attributed to them. It is only the unaccountable results, which an outside observer would attribute to luck, to the knack of doing things successfully, to chance or to fortune, that the savage attempts to control by magic.

Magic therefore, far from being primitive science, is the outgrowth of clear recognition that science has its limits and that a human mind and human skill are at times impotent. For all its appearances of megalomania, for all that it seems to be the declaration of the "omnipotence of thought," as it has recently been defined by Freud, magic has greater affinity with an emotional outburst, with daydreaming, with strong, unrealizable desire.

To affirm with Frazer that magic is a pseudo-science would be to recognize that magic is not really primitive science. It would imply that magic has an affinity with science or at least that it is the raw material out of which science develops—implications which are untenable. The ritual of magic shows certain striking characteristics which have made it quite plausible for most writers from Grimm and Tylor to Freud and Lévy-Bruhl to affirm that magic takes the place of primitive science.

Magic unquestionably is dominated by the sympathetic principle: like produces like; the whole is affected if the sorcerer acts on a part of it; occult influences can be imparted by contagion. If one concentrates on the form of the ritual only, he can legitimately conclude with Frazer that the analogy between the magical and the scientific conceptions of the world is close and that the various cases of sympathetic magic are mistaken applications of one or the other of two great fundamental laws of thought, namely, the association of ideas by similarity and the association of ideas by contiguity in space or time.

But a study of the function of science and the function of magic casts a doubt on the sufficiency of these conclusions. Sympathy is not the basis of pragmatic science, even under the most primitive conditions. The savage knows scientifically that a small pointed stick of hard wood rubbed or drilled against a piece of soft, brittle wood, provided they are both dry, gives fire. He also knows that strong energetic, increasingly swift motion has to be employed, that tinder must be produced in the action, the wind kept off, and the spark fanned immediately into a glow and this into a flame. There is no sympathy, no similarity, no taking the part instead of the legitimate whole, no contagion. The only association or connection is the empirical, correctly observed and correctly framed concatenation of natural events. The savage knows that a strong bow well handled releases a swift arrow, that a broad beam makes for stability and a light, well-shaped hull for swiftness in his canoe. There is here no association of ideas by similarity or contagion or *pars pro toto*. The native puts a yam or a banana sprout into an appropriate piece of ground. He waters or irrigates it unless it be well drenched by rain. He weeds the ground around it, and he knows quite well that barring unexpected calamities the plant will grow. Again there is no principle akin to that of sympathy contained in this activity. He creates conditions which are perfectly scientific and rational and lets nature do its work. Therefore in so far as magic consists in the enactment of sympathy, in so far as it is governed by an association of ideas, it radically differs from science; and on analysis the similarity of form between magic and science is revealed as merely apparent, not real.

The sympathetic rite although a very prominent element in magic functions always in the context of other elements. Its main purpose always consists in the generation and transference of magical force and accordingly it is performed in the atmosphere of the supernatural. As Hubert and Mauss have shown, acts of magic are always set apart, regarded as different, conceived and carried out under distinct conditions. The time when magic is performed is often determined by tradition rather than by the sympathetic principle, and the place where it is performed is only partly determined by sympathy or contagion and more by supernatural and mythological associations. Many of the substances used in magic are largely sympathetic but they are often used primarily for the physiological and emotional reaction which they elicit in man. The dramatic emotional elements in ritual enactment incorporate, in magic, factors which go far beyond sympathy or any scientific or pseudo-scientific principle. Mythology and tradition are everywhere embedded, especially in the performance of the magical spell, which must be repeated with absolute faithfulness to the traditional original and during which mythological events are recounted in which the power of the prototype is invoked. The supernatural character of magic is also expressed in the abnormal character of the magician and by the temporary taboos which surround its execution.

In brief, there exists a sympathetic principle: the ritual of magic contains usually some reference to the results to be achieved; it foreshadows them, anticipates the desired events. The magician is haunted by imagery, by symbolism, by associations of the result to follow. But he is quite as definitely haunted by the emotional obsession of the situation which has forced him to resort to magic. These facts do not fit into the simple scheme of sympathy conceived as misapplication of crude observations and half-logical deductions. The various apparently disjointed elements of magical ritual—the dramatic features, the emotional side, the mythological allusions, and the anticipation of the end—make it impossible to consider magic a sober scientific practice based on an empirical theory. Nor can magic be guided by experience and at the same time be constantly harking back to myth.

The fixed time, the determined spot, the preliminary isolating conditions of magic, the taboos to be observed by the performer, as well as his physiological and sociological nature, place the magical act in an atmosphere of the supernatural. Within this context of the supernatural the rite consists, functionally speaking, in the production of a specific virtue or force and of the launching, directing, or impelling of this force to the desired object. The production of magical force takes place by spell, manual and bodily gesticulation, and the proper condition of the officiating magician. All these elements exhibit a tendency to a formal assimilation toward the desired end or toward the ordinary means of producing this end. This formal resemblance is probably best defined in the statement that the whole ritual is dominated by the emotions of hate, fear, anger, or erotic passion, or by the desire to obtain a definite practical end.

The magical force or virtue is not conceived as a natural force. Hence the theories propounded by Preuss, Marett, and Hubert and Mauss, which would make the Melanesian mana or the similar North American concepts the clue to the understanding of all magic, are not satisfactory. The mana concept embraces personal power, natural force, excellence and efficiency alongside the specific virtue of magic. It is a force regarded as absolutely *sui generis*, different either from natural forces or from the normal faculties of man.

The force of magic can be produced only and exclusively within traditionally prescribed rites. It can be received and learned only by due initiation into the craft and by the taking over of the rigidly defined system of conditions, acts, and observances. Even when magic is discovered or invented it is invariably conceived as true revelation from the supernatural. Magic is an intrinsic, specific quality of a situation and of an object or phenomenon within the situation, consisting in the object being amenable to human control by means which are specifically and uniquely connected with the object and which can be handled only by appropriate people. Magic therefore is always conceived as something which does not reside in nature, that is, outside man, but in the relation between man and nature. Only those objects and forces in nature which are very important to man, on which he depends and which he cannot yet normally control elicit magic.

A functional explanation of magic may be stated in terms of individual psychology and of the cultural and social value of magic. Magic is to be expected and generally to be found whenever man comes to an unbridgeable gap, a hiatus in his knowledge or in his powers of practical control, and yet has to continue in his pursuit. Forsaken by his knowledge, baffled by the results of his experience, unable to apply any effective technical skill, he realizes his impotence. Yet his desire grips him only the more strongly. His fears and hopes, his general anxiety, produce a state of unstable equilibrium in his organism, by which he is driven to some sort of vicarious activity. In the natural human reaction to frustrated hate and impotent anger is found the *materia prima* of black magic. Unrequited love provokes spontaneous acts of prototype magic. Fear moves every human being to aimless but compulsory acts; in the presence of an ordeal one always has recourse to obsessive daydreaming.

The natural flow of ideas under the influence of emotions and desires thwarted in their full practical satisfaction leads one inevitably to the anticipation of the positive results. But the experience upon which this anticipatory or sympathetic attitude rests is not the ordinary experience of science. It is much more akin to daydreaming, to what the psychoanalysts call wish fulfillment. When the emotional state reaches the breaking point at which man loses control over himself, the words which he utters, the gestures to which he gives way, and the physiological processes within his organism which accompany all this allow the pent-up tension to flow over. Over all such outbursts of emotion, over such acts of prototype magic, there presides the obsessive image of the desired end. The substitute action in which the physiological crisis finds its expression has a subjective value: the desired end seems nearer satisfaction.

Standardized, traditional magic is nothing else but an institution which fixes, organizes and imposes upon the members of a society the positive solution in those inevitable conflicts which arise out of human impotence in dealing with all hazardous issues by mere knowledge and technical ability. The spontaneous, natural reaction of man to such situations supplies the raw material of magic. This raw material implies the sympathetic principle in that man has to dwell both on the desired end and on the best means of obtaining it. The expression of emotions in verbal utterances, in gestures, in an almost mystical belief that such words and gestures have a power, crops up naturally as a normal, physiological reaction. The elements which do not exist in the *materia prima* of magic but are to be found in the developed systems are the traditional, mythological elements. Human culture everywhere integrates a raw material of human interests and pursuits into standardized, traditional customs. In all human tradition a definite choice is made from within a variety of possibilities. In magic also the raw material supplies a number of possible ways of behavior. Tradition chooses from among them, fixes a special type and endues it with a hallmark of social value.

Tradition also reinforces the belief in magical efficacy by the context of special experience. Magic is so deeply believed in because its pragmatic truth is vouched for by its psychological or even physiological efficacy, since in its form and in its ideology and structure magic corresponds to the natural processes of the human organism. The conviction which is implied in these processes extends obviously to standardized magic. This conviction is useful because it raises the efficiency of the person who submits to it. Magic possesses therefore a functional truth or a pragmatic truth, since it arises always under conditions where the human organism is disintegrated. Magic corresponds to a real physiological need.

The seal of social approval given to the standardized reactions, selected traditionally out of the raw material of magic, gives it an additional backing. The general conviction that this and only this rite, spell or personal preparation enables the magician to control chance makes every individual believe in it through the ordinary mechanism of molding or conditioning. The public enactment of certain ceremonies, on the one hand, and the secrecy and esoteric atmosphere in which others are shrouded add again to their credibility. The fact also that magic usually is associated with intelligence and strong personality raises its credit in the eyes of any community. Thus a conviction that man can control by a special, traditional, standardized handling the forces of nature and human beings is not merely subjectively true through its physiological foundations, not merely pragmatically true in that it contributes to the reintegration of the individual, but it carries an additional evidence due to its sociological function.

Magic serves not only as an integrative force to the individual but also as an organizing force to society. The fact that the magician by the nature of his secret and esoteric lore has also the control of the associated practical activities causes him usually to be a person of the greatest importance in the community. The discovery of this was one of the great contributions of Frazer to anthropology. Magic, however, is of social importance not only because it gives power and thus raises a man to a high position. It is a real organizing force. In Australia the constitution of the tribe, of the clan, of the local group, is based on a system of totemic ideas. The main ceremonial expression of this system consists in the rites of magical multiplication of plants and animals and in the ceremonies of initiation into manhood. Both of these rites underlie the tribal framework and they are both the expression of a magical order of ideas based on totemic mythology. The leaders who arrange the tribal meetings, who conduct them, who direct the initiation and are the protagonists in dramatic representations of myth and in the public magical ceremonies, play this part because of their traditional magical filiation. The totemic magic of these tribes is their main organizing system.

To a large extent this is also true of the Papuan tribes of New Guinea, of the Melanesians and of the people of the Indonesian archipelagoes, where magical rites and ideas definitely supply the organizing principle in practical activities. The secret societies of the Bismarck Archipelago and West Africa, the rain makers of the Sudan, the medicine men of the North American Indians—all combine magical power with political and economic influence. Sufficient details to assess the extent and the mechanism by which magic enters and controls secular and ordinary life are often lacking. But among the Masai or Nandi in East Africa the evidence reveals that the military organization of the tribe is associated with war magic and that the guidance in political affairs and general tribal concerns depends on rain magic. In New Guinea garden magic, overseas trading expeditions, fishing and hunting on a big scale show that the ceremonial significance of magic supplies the moral and legal framework by which all practical activities are held together.

Sorcery in its major forms is usually specialized and institutionalized; that is, either the sorcerer is a professional whose services can be bought or commanded or sorcery is vested in a secret society or special organization. In all cases sorcery is either in the same hands as political power, prestige and wealth or else it can be purchased or demanded by those who can afford to do so. Sorcery thus is invariably a conservative force used at times for intimidation but usually for the enforcement of customary law or of the wishes of those in power. It is always a safeguard for the vested interests, for the organized, established privileges. The sorcerer who has behind him the chief or a powerful secret society can make his art felt more poignantly than if he were working against them or on his own.

The individual and sociological function of magic is thus made more efficient by the very mechanisms through which it works. In this and in the subjective aspect of the calculus of probability, which makes success overshadow failure, while failure again can be explained by countermagic, it is clear that the belief is not so ill founded nor due to such extravagant superstitiousness of the primitive mind as might at first appear. A strong belief in magic finds its public expression in the running mythology of magical miracles which is always found in company with all important types of magic. The competitive boasting of one community against another, the fame of outstanding magical success, the conviction that extraordinary good luck has probably been due to magic, create an ever nascent tradition which always surrounds famous magicians or famous systems of magic with a halo of supernatural reputation. This running tradition usually culminates retrospectively in a primeval myth, which gives the charter and credentials to the whole magical system. Myth of magic is definitely a warrant of its truth, a pedigree of its filiation, a charter of its claims to validity.

This is true not only of magical mythology. Myth in general is not an idle speculation about the origins of things or institutions. Nor is it the outcome of the contemplation of nature and rhapsodical interpretation of its laws. The function of myth is neither explanatory nor symbolic. It is the statement of an extraordinary event, the occurrence of which once for all had established the social order of a tribe or some of its economic pursuits, its arts and crafts or its religious or magical beliefs and ceremonies. Myth is not simply a piece of attractive fiction which is kept alive by the literary interest in the story. It is a statement of primeval reality which lives in the institutions and pursuits of a community. It justifies by precedent the existing order and it supplies a retrospective pattern of moral values, of sociological discriminations and burdens and of magical belief. In this consists its main cultural function. For all its similarity of form myth is neither a mere tale or prototype of literature or of science nor a branch of art or history nor an explanatory pseudo-theory. It fulfills a function *sui generis* closely connected with the nature of tradition and belief, with the continuity of culture, with the relation between age and youth and with the human attitude toward the past. The function of myth is to strengthen tradition and to endow it with a greater value and prestige by tracing it back to a higher, better, more supernatural and more effective reality of initial events.

The place of religion must be considered in the scheme of culture as a complex satisfaction of highly derived needs. The various theories of religion ascribe it to either a religious "instinct" or a specific religious sense (McDougall, Hauer) or else explain it as a primitive theory of animism (Tylor) or preanimism (Marett) or ascribe it to the emotions of fear (Wundt) or to aesthetic raptures and lapses of speech (Max Müller) or the self-revelation of society (Durkheim). These theories make religion something superimposed on the whole structure of human culture, satisfying some needs perhaps, but needs which are entirely autonomous and have nothing to do with the hard-worked reality of human existence. Religion, however, can be shown to be intrinsically although indirectly connected with man's fundamental, that is, biological, needs. Like magic it comes from the curse of forethought and imagination, which fall on man once he rises above brute animal nature. Here there enter even wider issues of personal and social integration than those arising out of the practical necessity of hazardous action and dangerous enterprise. A whole range of anxieties, forebodings and problems concerning human destinies and man's place in the universe opens up once man begins to act in common not only with his fellow citizens but also with the past and future generations. Religion is not born out of speculation or reflection, still less out of illusion or misapprehension, but rather out of the real tragedies of human life, out of the conflict between human plans and realities.

Culture entails deep changes in man's personality; among other things it makes man surrender some of his self-love and self-seeking. For human relations do not rest merely or even mainly on constraint coming from without. Men can only work with and for one another by the moral forces which grow out of personal attachments and loyalties. These are primarily formed in the processes of parenthood and kinship but become inevitably widened and enriched. The love of parents for children and of children for their parents, that between husband and wife and between brothers and sisters, serve as prototypes and also as a nucleus for the loyalties of clanship, of neighborly feeling, and of tribal citizenship. Co-operation and mutual assistance are based, in savage and civilized societies, on permanent sentiments.

The existence of strong personal attachments and the fact of death, which of all human events is the most upsetting and disorganizing to man's calculations, are perhaps the main sources of religious belief. The affirmation that death is not real, that man has a soul and that this is immortal, arises out of a deep need to deny personal destruction, a need which is not a psychological instinct but is determined by culture, by co-operation and by the growth of human sentiments. To the individual who faces death the belief in immortality and the ritual of extreme unction, or last comforts (which in one form or another is almost universal), confirm his hope that there is a hereafter, that it is perhaps not worse than the present life and may be better. Thus the ritual before death confirms the emotional outlook which a dying man has come to need in his supreme conflict. After death the bereaved are thrown into a chaos of emotion, which might become dangerous to each of them individually and to the community as a whole were it not for the ritual of mortuary duties. The religious rites of wake and burial—all the assistance given to the departed soul—are acts expressing the dogma of continuity after death and of communion between dead and living. Any survivor who has gone through a number of mortuary ceremonials for others becomes prepared for his own death. The belief in immortality, which he has lived through ritually and practiced in the case of his mother or father, of his brothers and friends, makes him cherish more firmly the belief in his own future life. The belief in human immortality therefore, which is the foundation of ancestor worship, of domestic cults, or mortuary ritual and of animism, grows out of the constitution of human society.

Most of the other forms of religion when analyzed in their functional character correspond to deep although derived needs of the individual and of the community. Totemism, for example, when related to its wider setting affirms the existence of an intimate kinship between man and his surrounding world. The ritual side of totemism and nature worship consists to a large extent in rites of multiplication or of propitiation of animals or in rites of enhancing the fertility of vegetable nature which also establish links between man and his environment. Primitive religion is largely concerned with the sacralization of the crises of human life. Conception, birth, puberty, marriage, as well as the supreme crisis death, all give rise to sacramental acts. The fact of conception is surrounded by such beliefs as that in reincarnation, spirit entry and magical impregnation. At birth a wealth of animistic ideas concerning the formation of the human soul, the value of the individual to his community, the development of his moral powers, the possibility of forecasting his fate, become associated with and expressed in birth ritual. Initiation ceremonies, prevalent in puberty, have a developed mythological and dogmatic context. Guardian spirits, tutelary divinities, culture heroes, or a tribal All-Father are associated with initiation ceremonies. The contractual sacraments, such as marriage, entry into an age grade, or acceptance into a magical or religious fraternity, entail primarily ethical views but very often are also the expression of myths and dogmas.

Every important crisis of human life implies a strong emotional upheaval, mental conflict and possible disintegration. The hopes of a favorable issue have to struggle with anxieties and forebodings. Religious belief consists in the traditional standardization of the positive side in the mental conflict and therefore satisfies a definite individual need arising out of the psychological concomitants of social organization. On the other hand, religious belief and ritual, by making the critical acts and the social contracts of human life public, traditionally standardized, and subject to supernatural sanctions, strengthen the bonds of human cohesion.

Religion in its ethics sanctifies human life and conduct and becomes perhaps the most powerful force of social control. In its dogmatics it supplies man with strong cohesive forces. It grows out of every culture, because knowledge which gives foresight fails to overcome fate; because lifelong bonds of cooperation and mutual interest create sentiments, and sentiments rebel against death and dissolution. The cultural call for religion is highly derived and indirect but is finally rooted in the way in which the primary needs of man are satisfied in culture.

A. R. Radcliffe-Brown

TABOO

Another anthropological scholar whose writings on the function of religion in primitive society have been of major significance is Radcliffe-Brown. His three most important works on this subject are portions of his book, *The Andaman Islanders* (1922), his Frazer Lecture,

Reprinted from A. R. Radcliffe-Brown, *Taboo* ("The Frazer Lecture," 1939). Cambridge University Press, 1939. Reprinted by permission of the publisher.

Taboo (which is herewith reprinted), and a later paper, "Religion and Society" (1945).

Radcliffe-Brown's central thesis, that religious and magical rituals exist and persist because they are part of the mechanism by which society maintains itself in existence by establishing certain fundamental social values, should be understood in the wider context of his contributions toward the concepts and methods needed to pursue a systematic comparative study of societies, and especially of his thinking about the concept of "function." His series of papers reprinted in *Structure and Function in Primitive Society* (1952) are particularly useful.

In this paper on taboo Radcliffe-Brown begins by discussing the nature of one of the classic ideas in the primitive religions of Polynesia, but goes on to expound his thoughts on ritual and ritual values and their relationship to the essential constitution of a society. He reaches the conclusion that "the primary basis of ritual is the attribution of ritual value to objects and occasions which are either themselves objects of important common interests linking together the persons of a community or are symbolically representative of such objects." He then argues that men are more likely to experience concern and anxiety when a customary ritual is not performed than they are to turn to ritual procedures when they feel anxious.

The purpose of this lecture, which you have done me the honor of inviting me to deliver, is to commemorate the work of Sir James Frazer, as an example of lifelong, single-minded devotion to scientific investigation and as having contributed, in as large a measure as that of any man, to laying the foundations of the science of social anthropology. It therefore seems to me appropriate to select as the subject of my discourse one which Sir James was the first to investigate systematically half a century ago, when he wrote the article on "Taboo" for the ninth edition of the *Encyclopaedia Britannica*, and to the elucidation of which he has made many successive contributions in his writings since that time.

The English word "taboo" is derived from the Polynesian word "tabu" (with the accent on the first syllable). In the languages of Polynesia the word means simply "to forbid," "forbidden," and can be applied to any sort of prohibition. A rule of etiquette, an order issued by a chief, an injunction to children not to meddle with the possessions of their elders, may all be expressed by the use of the word "tabu."

The early voyagers in Polynesia adopted the word to refer to prohibitions of a special kind, which may be illustrated by an example. Certain things such as a newly born infant, a corpse or the person of a chief are said to be tabu. This means that one should, as far as possible, avoid touching them. A man who does touch one of these tabu objects immediately becomes tabu himself. This means two things. In the first place, a man who is tabu in this sense must observe a number of special restrictions on his behavior; for example, he may not use his hands to feed himself. He is regarded as being in a state of danger, and this is generally stated by saying that if he fails to observe the customary precautions he will be ill and perhaps die. In the second place he is also dangerous to other persons—he is tabu in the same sense as the thing he has touched. If he should come in contact with utensils in which, or the fire at which, food is cooked, the dangerous influence would be communicated to the food and so injure anyone who partook of it. A person who is tabu in this way, as by touching a corpse, can be restored to his normal condition by rites of purification or desacralization. He is then said to be *noa* again, this term being the contrary of tabu.

Sir James Frazer has told us that when he took up the study of taboo in 1886 the current view of anthropologists at the time was that the institution in question was confined to the brown and black races of the Pacific, but that as a result of his investigations he came to the conclusion that the Polynesian body of practices and beliefs "is only one of a number of similar systems of superstition which among many, perhaps all the races of men have contributed in large measure, under many different names and with many variations of detail, to build up the complex fabric of society in all the various sides or elements of it which we describe as religious, social, political, moral, and economic."

The use of the word taboo in anthropology

for customs all over the world which resemble in essentials the example given from Polynesia seems to me undesirable and inconvenient. There is the fact already mentioned that in the Polynesian language the word tabu has a much wider meaning, equivalent to our own word "forbidden." This has produced a good deal of confusion in the literature relating to Polynesia owing to the ambiguity resulting from two different uses of the same word. You will have noticed that I have used the word "taboo" (with the English spelling and pronunciation) in the meaning that it has for anthropologists, and "tabu" (with the Polynesian spelling and pronunciation) in special reference to Polynesia and in the Polynesian sense. But this is not entirely satisfactory.

I propose to refer to the customs we are considering as "ritual avoidances" or "ritual prohibitions" and to define them by reference to two fundamental concepts for which I have been in the habit of using the terms "ritual status" and "ritual value." I am not suggesting that these are the best terms to be found; they are merely the best that I have been able to find up to the present. In such a science as ours words are the instruments of analysis and we should always be prepared to discard inferior tools for superior when opportunity arises.

A ritual prohibition is a rule of behavior which is associated with a belief that an infraction will result in an undesirable change in the ritual status of the person who fails to keep to the rule. This change of ritual status is conceived in many different ways in different societies, but everywhere there is the idea that it involves the likelihood of some minor or major misfortune which will befall the person concerned.

We have already considered one example. The Polynesian who touches a corpse has, according to Polynesian belief, undergone what I am calling an undesirable change of ritual status. The misfortune of which he is considered to be in danger is illness, and he therefore takes precautions and goes through a ritual in order that he may escape the danger and be restored to his former ritual status.

Let us consider two examples of different kinds from contemporary England. There are some people who think that one should avoid spilling salt. The person who spills salt will have bad luck. But he can avoid this by throwing a pinch of the spilled salt over his shoulder. Putting this in my terminology, it can be said that spilling salt produces an undesirable change in the ritual status of the person who does so, and that he is restored to his normal or previous ritual status by the positive rite of throwing salt over his shoulder.

A member of the Roman Catholic Church, unless granted a dispensation, is required by his religion to abstain from eating meat on Fridays and during Lent. If he fails to observe the rule he sins, and must proceed, as in any other sin, to confess and obtain absolution. Different as this is in important ways from the rule about spilling salt, it can and must for scientific purposes be regarded as belonging to the same general class. Eating meat on Friday produces in the person who does so an undesirable change of ritual status which requires to be remedied by fixed appropriate means.

We may add to these examples two others from other societies. If you turn to the fifth chapter of Leviticus you will find that amongst the Hebrews if a "soul" touch the carcase of an unclean beast or of unclean cattle, or of unclean creeping things, even if he is unaware that he does so, then he is unclean and guilty and has sinned. When he becomes aware of his sin he must confess that he has sinned and must take a trespass offering—a female from the flock, a lamb, or a kid of the goats—which the priest shall sacrifice to make an atonement for the sin so that it shall be forgiven him. Here the change in ritual status through touching an unclean carcase is described by the terms "sin," "unclean," and "guilty."

In the Kikuyu tribe of East Africa the word *thahu* denotes the undesirable ritual status that results from failure to observe rules of ritual avoidance. It is believed that a person who is *thahu* will be ill and will probably die unless he removes the *thahu* by the appropriate ritual remedies, which in all serious cases require the services of a priest or medicine man. Actions which produce this condition are touching or carrying a corpse, stepping over a corpse, eating food from a cracked pot, coming in contact with a woman's menstrual discharge, and many others. Just as amongst the Hebrews a soul may unwittingly be guilty of sin by touching in ignorance the carcase of an unclean animal, so amongst the Kikuyu a man may become *thahu* without any voluntary act on his part. If an elder or a woman when coming out of the hut slips and falls down on the ground, he or she is *thahu* and lies there until some of the elders of the neighborhood come and sacrifice a sheep. If the side-pole of a bedstead breaks, the person lying on it is *thahu* and must be purified. If the droppings of a kite or crow fall on a person he is *thahu*, and if a hyena defecates in a village, or a jackal barks therein, the village and its inhabitants are *thahu*.

I have purposely chosen from our own society two examples of ritual avoidances which are of very different kinds. The rule against eating meat on Friday or in Lent is a rule of religion, as is the rule, where it is recognized, against playing golf or tennis on Sunday. The rule against spilling salt, I suppose it will be agreed, is nonreligious. Our language permits us to make this distinction very clearly, for infractions of the rules of religion are sins, while the nonreligious avoidances are concerned with good and bad luck. Since this distinction is so obvious to us it might be thought that we should find it in other societies. My own experience is that in some of the societies with which I am acquainted this distinction between sinful acts and acts that bring bad luck cannot be made. Several anthropologists, however, have attempted to classify rites into two classes, religious rites and magical rites.

For Émile Durkheim the essential distinction is that religious rites are obligatory within a religious society or church, while magical rites are optional. A person who fails in religious observances is guilty of wrongdoing, whereas one who does not observe the precautions of magic or those relating to luck is simply acting foolishly. This distinction is of considerable theoretical importance. It is difficult to apply in the study of the rites of simple societies.

Sir James Frazer defines religion as "a propitiation or conciliation of superhuman powers which are believed to control nature and man," and regards magic as the erroneous application of the notion of causality. If we apply this to ritual prohibitions we may regard as belonging to religion those rules the infraction of which produces a change of ritual status in the individual by offending the superhuman powers, whereas the infraction of a rule of magic would be regarded as resulting immediately in a change of ritual status, or in the misfortune that follows, by a process of hidden causation. Spilling salt, by Sir James Frazer's definition, is a question of magic, while eating meat on Friday is a question of religion.

An attempt to apply this distinction systematically meets with certain difficulties. Thus with regard to the Maori, Sir James Frazer states that "the ultimate sanction of the taboo, in other words, that which engaged the people to observe its commandments, was a firm persuasion that any breach of those commandments would surely and speedily be punished by an *atua* or ghost, who would afflict the sinner with a painful malady till he died." This would seem to make the Polynesian taboo a matter of religion, not of magic. But my own observation of the Polynesians suggests to me that in general the native conceives of the change in his ritual status as taking place as the immediate result of such an act as touching a corpse, and that it is only when he proceeds to rationalize the whole system of taboos that he thinks of the gods and spirits—the *atua*—as being concerned. Incidentally, it should not be assumed that the Polynesian word *atua* or *otua* always refers to a personal spiritual being.

Of the various ways of distinguishing magic and religion I will mention only one more. For Professor Malinowski a rite is magical when "it has a definite practical purpose which is known to all who practice it and can be easily elicited from any native informant," while a rite is religious if it is simply expressive and has no purpose, being not a means to an end but an end in itself. A difficulty in applying this criterion is due to uncertainty as to what is meant by "definite practical purpose." To avoid the bad luck which results from spilling salt is, I suppose, a practical purpose though not very definite. The desire to please God in all our actions and thus escape some period of Purgatory is perhaps definite enough, but Professor Malinowski may regard it as not practical. What shall we say of the desire of the Polynesian to avoid sickness and possible death which he gives as his reason for not touching chiefs, corpses, and newly born babies?

Seeing that there is this absence of agreement as to the definitions of magic and religion and the nature of the distinction between them, and seeing that in many instances whether we call a particular rite magical or religious depends on which of the various proposed definitions we accept, the only sound procedure, at any rate in the present state of anthropological knowledge, is to avoid as far as possible the use of the terms in question until there is some general agreement about them. Certainly the distinctions made by Durkheim and Frazer and Malinowski may be theoretically significant, even though they are difficult to apply universally. Certainly, also, there is need for a systematic classification of rites, but a satisfactory classification will be fairly complex and a simple dichotomy between magic and religion does not carry us very far toward it.

Another distinction which we make in our own society within the field of ritual avoidances is between the holy and the unclean. Certain things must be treated with respect because they are holy, others because they are unclean. But, as Robertson Smith and Sir James Frazer have shown, there are many societies in which this distinction is entirely unrecognized. The Polynesian, for example, does not think of a chief or a temple as holy and a corpse as unclean. He thinks of them all as things dangerous. An example from Hawai'i will illustrate this fundamental identity of holiness and uncleanness. There, in former times, if a commoner committed incest with his sister he became *kapu* (the Hawai'ian form of tabu). His presence was dangerous in the extreme for the whole community, and since he could not be purified he was put to death. But if a chief of high rank, who by reason of his rank was, of course, sacred (*kapu*), married his sister he became still more so. An extreme sanctity or untouchability attached to a chief born of a brother and sister who were themselves the children of a brother and sister. The sanctity of such a chief and the uncleanness of the person put to death for incest have the same source and are the same thing. They are both denoted by saying that the person is *kapu*. In studying the simpler societies it is essential that we should carefully avoid thinking of their behavior and ideas in terms of our own ideas of holiness and uncleanness. Since most people find this difficult it is desirable to have terms which we can use that do not convey this connotation. Durkheim and others have used the word "sacred" as an inclusive term for the holy and the unclean together. This is easier to do in French than in English, and has some justification in the fact that the Latin *sacer* did apply to holy things such as the gods and also to accursed things such as persons guilty of certain crimes. But there is certainly a tendency in English to identify sacred with holy. I think that it will greatly aid clear thinking if we adopt some wide inclusive term which does not have any undesirable connotation. I venture to propose the term "ritual value."

Anything—a person, a material thing, a place, a word or name, an occasion or event, a day of the week or a period of the year—which is the object of a ritual avoidance or taboo can be said to have ritual value. Thus in Polynesia chiefs, corpses, and newly born babies have ritual value. For some people in England salt has ritual value. For Christians, all Sundays and Good Friday have ritual value, and for Jews all Saturdays and the Day of Atonement. The ritual value is exhibited in the behavior adopted towards the object or occasion in question. Ritual values are exhibited not only in negative ritual but also in positive ritual, being possessed by the objects towards which positive rites are directed and also by objects, words, or places used in the rites. A large class of positive rites, those of consecration or sacralization, have for their purpose to endow objects with ritual value. It may be noted that in general anything that has value in positive ritual is also the object of some sort of ritual avoidance or at the very least of ritual respect.

The word "value," as I am using it, always refers to a relation between a subject and an object. The relation can be stated in two ways by saying either that the object has a value for the subject, or that the subject has an interest in the object. We can use the terms in this way to refer to any act of behavior towards an object. The relation is exhibited in and defined by the behavior. The words "interest" and "value" provide a convenient shorthand by which we can describe the reality, which consists of acts of behavior and the actual relations between subjects and objects which those acts of behavior reveal. If Jack loves Jill, then Jill has the value of a loved object for Jack, and Jack has a recognizable interest in Jill. When I am hungry I have an interest in food, and a good meal has an immediate value for me that it does not have at other times. My toothache has a value to me as something that I am interested in getting rid of as quickly as possible.

A social system can be conceived and studied as a system of values. A society consists of a number of individuals bound together in a network of social relations. A social relation exists between two or more persons when there is some harmonization of their individual interests, by some convergence of interest and by limitation or adjustment of divergent interests. An interest is always the interest of an individual. Two individuals may have similar interests. Similar interests do not in themselves consititute a social relation; two dogs may have a similar interest in the same bone and the result may be a dogfight. But a society cannot exist except on the basis of a certain measure of similarity in the interests of its members. Putting this in terms of value, the first necessary condition of the existence of a society is that the individual members shall agree in some measure in the values that they recognize.

Any particular society is characterized by a certain set of values—moral, aesthetic, economic, etc. In a simple society there is a fair amount of agreement amongst the members in their evaluations, though of course the agreement is never absolute. In a complex modern society we find much more disagreement if we consider the society as a whole, but we may find a closer measure of agreement amongst the members of a group or class within the society.

While some measure of agreement about values, some similarity of interests, is a prerequisite of a social system, social relations involve more than this. They require the existence of common interests and of social values. When two or more persons have a common interest in the same object and are aware of their community of interest a social relation is established. They form, whether for a moment or for a long period, an association, and the object may be said to have a social value. For a man and his wife the birth of a child, the child itself and its well being and happiness or its death, are objects of a common interest which binds them together and they thus have, for the association formed by the two persons, social value. By this definition an object can only have a social value for an association of persons. In the simplest possible instance we have a triadic relation; Subject 1 and Subject 2 are both interested in the same way in the Object and each of the Subjects has an interest in the other, or at any rate in certain items of the behavior of the other, namely those directed toward the object. To avoid cumbersome circumlocutions it is convenient to speak of the object as having a social value for any one subject involved in such a relation, but it must be remembered that this is a loose way of speaking.

It is perhaps necessary for the avoidance of misunderstanding to add that a social system also requires that persons should be objects of interest to other persons. In relations of friendship or love each of two persons has a value for the other. In certain kinds of groups each member is an object of interest for all the others, and each member therefore has a social value for the groups as a whole. Further, since there are negative values as well as positive, persons may be united or associated by their antagonism to other persons. For the members of an anti-Comintern pact the Comintern has a specific social value.

Amongst the members of a society we find a certain measure of agreement as to the ritual value they attribute to objects of different kinds. We also find that most of these ritual values are social values as defined above. Thus for a local totemic clan in Australia the totem-centers, the natural species associated with them, i.e., the totems, and the myths and rites that relate thereto, have a specific social value for the clan; the common interest in them binds the individuals together into a firm and lasting association.

Ritual values exist in every known society, and show an immense diversity as we pass from one society to another. The problem of a natural science of society (and it is as such that I regard social anthropology) is to discover the deeper, not immediately perceptible, uniformities beneath the superficial differences. This is, of course, a highly complex problem which will require the studies begun by Sir James Frazer and others to be continued by many investigators over many years. The ultimate aim should be, I think, to find some relatively adequate answer to the question, *What is the relation of ritual and ritual values to the essential constitution of human society?* I have chosen a particular approach to this study which I believe to be promising—to investigate in a few societies studied as thoroughly as possible the relations of ritual values to other values including moral and aesthetic values. In the present lecture, however, it is only one small part of this study in which I seek to interest you—the question of a relation between ritual values and social values.

One way of approaching the study of ritual is by the consideration of the purposes or reasons for the rites. If one examines the literature of anthropology one finds this approach very frequently adopted. It is by far the least profitable, though the one that appeals most to common sense. Sometimes the purpose of a rite is obvious, or a reason may be volunteered by those who practice it. Sometimes the anthropologist has to ask the reason, and in such circumstances it may happen that different reasons are given by different informants. What is fundamentally the same rite in two different societies may have different purposes or reasons in the one and in the other. The reasons given by the members of a community for any custom they observe are important data for the anthropologist. But it is to fall into grievous error to suppose that they give a valid explanation of the custom. What is entirely inexcusable is for the anthropologist, when he cannot get from the people themselves a reason for their behavior which seems to him satisfactory, to attribute to them some purpose or reason on the basis of his own preconceptions about human motives. I could adduce many instances of this from the literature of ethnography, but I prefer to illustrate what I mean by an anecdote.

A Queenslander met a Chinese who was taking a bowl of cooked rice to place on his brother's grave. The Australian in jocular tones asked if he supposed that his brother would come and eat the rice. The reply was "No! We offer rice to people as an expression of friendship and affection. But since you speak as you do I suppose that you in this country place flowers on the graves of your dead in the belief that they will enjoy looking at them and smelling their sweet perfume."

So far as ritual avoidances are concerned the reasons for them may vary from a very vague idea that some sort of misfortune or ill-luck, not defined as to its kind, is likely to befall anyone who fails to observe the taboo, to a belief that nonobservance will produce some quite specific and undesirable result. Thus an Australian aborigine told me that if he spoke to any woman who stood in the relation of mother-in-law to him his hair would turn gray.

The very common tendency to look for the explanation of ritual actions in their purpose is the result of a false assimilation of them to what may be called technical acts. In any technical activity an adequate statement of the purpose of any particular act or series of acts constitutes by itself a sufficient explanation. But ritual acts differ from technical acts in having in all instances some expressive or symbolic element in them.

A second approach to the study of ritual is therefore by a consideration not of their purpose or reason, but of their meaning. I am here using the words "symbol" and "meaning" as coincident. Whatever has a meaning is a symbol and the meaning is whatever is expressed by the symbol.

But how are we to discover meanings? They do not lie on the surface. There is a sense in which people always know the meaning of their own symbols, but they do so intuitively and can rarely express their understanding in words. Shall we therefore be reduced to guessing at meanings as some anthropologists have guessed at reasons and purposes? I think not. For as long as we admit guesswork of any kind social anthropology cannot be a science. There are, I believe, methods of determining, with some fair degree of probability, the meanings of rites and other symbols.

There is still a third approach to the study of rites. We can consider the effects of the rite—not the effects that it is supposed to produce by the people who practice it but the effects that it does actually produce. A rite has immediate or direct effects on the persons who are in any way directly concerned in it, which we may call, for lack of a better term, the psychological effects. But there are also secondary effects upon the social structure, i.e., the network of social relations binding individuals together in an ordered life. These we may call the "social effects." By considering the psychological effects of a rite we may succeed in defining its psychological function; by considering the social effects we may discover its social function. Clearly it is impossible to discover the social function of a rite without taking into account its usual or average psychological effects. But it is possible to discuss the psychological effects while more or less completely ignoring the more remote sociological effects, and this is often done in what is called "functional anthropology."

Let us suppose that we wish to investigate in Australian tribes the totemic rites of a kind widely distributed over a large part of the continent. The ostensible purpose of these rites, as stated by the natives themselves, is to renew or maintain some part of nature, such as a species of animal or plant, or rain, or hot or cold weather. With reference to this purpose we have to say that from our point of view the natives are mistaken, that the rites do not actually do what they are believed to do. The rainmaking ceremony does not, we think, actually bring rain. In so far as the rites are performed for a purpose they are futile, based on erroneous belief. I do not believe that there is any scientific value in attempts to conjecture processes of reasoning which might be supposed to have led to these errors.

The rites are easily perceived to be symbolic, and we may therefore investigate their meaning. To do this we have to examine a considerable number of them and we then discover that there is a certain body of ritual idiom extending from the west coast of the continent to the east coast with some local variations. Since each rite has a myth associated with it we have similarly to investigate the meanings of the myths. As a result we find that the meaning of any single rite becomes clear in the light of a cosmology, a body of ideas and beliefs about nature and human society, which, so far as its most general features are concerned, is current in all Australian tribes.

The immediate psychological effects of the rites can be to some extent observed by watching and talking to the performers. The ostensible purpose of the rite is certainly present in their minds, but so also is that complex set of cosmological beliefs by reference to which the rite has a meaning. Certainly a person performing the rite, even if, as sometimes happens, he performs it alone, derives therefrom a definite feeling of satisfaction, but it would be entirely false to imagine that this is simply because he believes that he has helped to provide a more abundant supply of food for himself and his fellow tribesmen. His satisfaction is in having performed a ritual duty, we might say a religious duty. Putting in my own words what I judge, from my own observations, to express what the native feels, I would say that in the performance of the rite he has made that small contribution, which it is both his privilege and his duty to do, to the maintenance of that order of the universe of which man and nature are interdependent parts. The satisfaction which he thus receives gives the rite a special value for him. In some instances with which I am acquainted of the last survivor of a totemic group who still continues to perform the totemic rites by himself, it is this satisfaction that constitutes apparently the sole motive for his action.

To discover the social function of the totemic rites we have to consider the whole body of cosmological ideas of which each rite is a partial expression. I believe that it is possible to show that the social structure of an Australian tribe is connected in a very special way with these cosmological ideas and that the maintenance of its continuity depends on keeping them alive, by their regular expression in myth and rite.

Thus any satisfactory study of the totemic rites of Australia must be based not simply on the consideration of their ostensible purpose and their psychological function, or on an analysis of the motives of the individuals who perform the rites, but on the discovery of their meaning and of their social function.

It may be that some rites have no social function. This may be the case with such taboos as that against spilling salt in our own society. Nevertheless, the method of investigating rites and ritual values that I have found most profitable during work extending over more than thirty years is to study rites as symbolic expressions and to seek to discover their social functions. This method is not new except in so far as it is applied to the comparative study of many societies of diverse types. It was applied by Chinese thinkers to their own ritual more than twenty centuries ago.

In China, in the fifth and sixth centuries B.C., Confucius and his followers insisted on the great importance of the proper performance of ritual, such as funeral and mourning rites and sacrifices. After Confucius there came the reformer Mo Ti who taught a combination of altruism—love for all men—and utilitarianism. He held that funeral and mourning rites were useless and interfered with useful activities and should therefore be abolished or reduced to a minimum. In the third and second centuries B.C. the Confucians, Hsün Tze and the compilers of the *Li Chi* (Book of Rites), replied to Mo Ti to the effect that though these rites might have no utilitarian purpose they none the less had a very important social function. Briefly the theory is that the rites are the orderly (the *Li Chi* says the beautified) expression of feelings appropriate to a social situation. They thus serve to regulate and refine human emotions. We may say that partaking in the performance of rites serves to cultivate in the individual sentiments on whose existence the social order itself depends.

Let us consider the meaning and social function of an extremely simple example of ritual. In the Andaman Islands when a woman is expecting a baby a name is given to it while it is still in the womb. From that time until some weeks after the baby is born nobody is allowed to use the personal name of either the father or the mother; they can be referred to by teknonymy, i.e., in terms of their relation to the child. During this period both the parents are required to abstain from eating certain foods which they may freely eat at other times.

I did not obtain from the Andamanese any statement of the purpose or reason for this avoidance of names. Assuming that the act is symbolic, what method, other than that of guessing, is there of arriving at the meaning? I suggest that we may start with a general working hypothesis that when, in a single society, the same symbol is used in different contexts or on different kinds of occasions there is some common element of meaning, and that by comparing together the various uses of the symbol we may be able to discover what the common element is. This is precisely the method that we adopt in studying an unrecorded spoken language in order to discover the meanings of words and morphemes.

In the Andamans the name of a dead person is avoided from the occurrence of the death to the conclusion of mourning; the name of a person mourning for a dead relative is not used; there is avoidance of the name of a youth or girl who is passing through the ceremonies that take place at adolescence; a bride or bridegroom is not spoken of or to by his or her own name for a short time after the marriage. For the Andamanese the personal name is a symbol of the social personality, i.e., of the position that an individual occupies in the social structure and the social life. The avoidance of a personal name is a symbolic recognition of the fact that at the time the person is not occupying a normal position in the social life. It may be added that a person whose name is thus temporarily out of use is regarded as having for the time an abnormal ritual status.

Turning now to the rule as to avoiding certain foods, if the Andaman Islanders are asked what would happen if the father or mother broke this taboo the usual answer is that he or she would be ill, though one or two of my informants thought it might perhaps also affect the child. This is simply one instance of a standard formula which applies to a number of ritual prohibitions. Thus a person in mourning for a relative may not eat pork and turtle, the most important flesh foods, and the reason given is that if they did they would be ill.

To discover the meaning of the avoidance of foods by the parents we can apply the same method as in reference to the avoidance of their names. There are similar rules for mourners, for women during menstruation, and for youths and girls during the period of adolescence. But for a full demonstration we have to consider the place of foods in Andamanese ritual as a whole, and for an examination of this I must refer to what I have already written on the subject.

I should like to draw your attention to another point in the method by which it is possible to test our hypotheses as to the meanings of rites. We take the different occasions on which two rites are associated together, for example the association of the avoidance of a person's name with the avoidance by that person of certain foods, which we find in the instance of mourners on the one hand and the expectant mother and father on the other. We must assume that for the Andamanese there is some important similarity between these two kinds of occasions—birth and death—by virtue of which they have similar ritual values. We cannot rest content with any interpretation of the taboos at childbirth unless there is a parallel interpretation of those relating to mourners. In the terms I am using here we can say that in the Andamans the relatives of a recently dead person, and the father and mother of a child that is about to be, or has recently been born, are in an abnormal ritual status. This is recognized or indicated by the avoidance of their names. They are regarded as likely to suffer some misfortune, some bad luck, if you will, unless they observe certain prescribed ritual precautions of which the avoidance of certain foods is one. In the Andaman Islands the danger in such instances is thought of as the danger of illness. This is the case also with the Polynesian belief about the ritual status of anyone who has touched a corpse or a newly born baby. It is to be noted that for the Polynesians as well as for the Andamanese the occasion of a birth has a similar ritual value to that of a death.

The interpretation of the taboos at childbirth at which we arrive by studying it in relation to the whole system of ritual values of the Andamanese is too complex to be stated here in full. Clearly, however, they express, in accordance with Andamanese ritual idiom, a common concern in the event. The parents show their concern by avoiding certain foods; their friends show theirs by avoiding the parents' personal names. By virtue of these taboos the occasion acquires a certain social value, as that term has been defined above.

There is one theory that might seem to be applicable to our example. It is based on a hypothesis as to the psychological function of a class of rites. The theory is that in certain circumstances the individual human being is anxious about the outcome of some event or activity because it depends to some extent on conditions that he cannot control by any technical means. He therefore observes some rite which, since he believes that it will ensure good luck, serves to reassure him. Thus an aeronaut takes with him in a plane a mascot which he believes will protect him from accident and thus carries out his flight with confidence.

The theory has a respectable antiquity. It was perhaps implied in the *Primus in orbe deos fecit timor* [the first fear made gods on the earth] of Petronius and Statius. It has taken various forms from Hume's explanation of religion to Malinowski's explanation of Trobriand magic. It can be made so plausible by a suitable selection of illustrations that it is necessary to examine it with particular care and treat it with reasonable skepticism. For there is always the danger that we may be taken in by the plausibility of a theory that ultimately proves to be unsound.

I think that for certain rites it would be easy to maintain with equal plausibility an exactly contrary theory, namely, that if it were not for the existence of the rite and the beliefs associated with it the individual would feel no anxiety, and that the psychological effect of the rite is to create in him a sense of insecurity or danger. It seems very unlikely that an Andaman Islander would think that it is dangerous to eat dugong or pork or turtle meat if it were not for the existence of a specific body of ritual the ostensible purpose of which is to protect him from those dangers. Many hundreds of similar instances could be mentioned from all over the world.

Thus, while one anthropological theory is that magic and religion give men confidence, comfort, and a sense of security, it could equally well be argued that they give men fears and anxieties from which they would otherwise be free—the fear of black magic or of spirits, fear of God, of the Devil, of Hell.

Actually in our fears or anxieties as well as in our hopes we are conditioned (as the phrase goes) by the community in which we live. And it is largely by the sharing of hopes and fears, by what I have called common concern in events or eventualities, that human beings are linked together in temporary or permanent associations.

To return to the Andamanese taboos at childbirth, there are difficulties in supposing that they are means by which parents reassure themselves against the accidents that may interfere with a successful delivery. If the prospective father fails to observe the food taboo it is he who will be sick, according to the general Andamanese opinion. Moreover, he must continue to observe the taboos after the child is safely delivered. Further, how are we to provide a parallel explanation of the similar taboos observed by a person mourning for a dead relative?

The taboos associated with pregnancy and parturition are often explained in terms of the hypothesis I have mentioned. A father, naturally anxious at the outcome of an event over which he does not have a technical control and which is subject to hazard, reassures himself by observing some taboo or carrying out some magical action. He may avoid certain foods. He may avoid making nets or tying knots, or he may go round the house untying all knots and opening any locked or closed boxes or containers.

I wish to arouse in your minds, if it is not already there, a suspicion that both the general theory and this special application of it do not give the whole truth and indeed may not be true at all. Skepticism of plausible but unproved hypotheses is essential in every science. There is at least good ground for suspicion in the fact that the theory has so far been considered in reference to facts that seem to fit it, and no systematic attempt has been made, so far as I am aware, to look for facts that do not fit. That there are many such I am satisfied from my own studies.

The alternative hypothesis which I am presenting for consideration is as follows. In a given community it is appropriate that an expectant father should feel concern or at least should make an appearance of doing so. Some suitable symbolic expression of his concern is found in terms of the general ritual or symbolic idiom of the society, and it is felt generally that a man in that situation ought to carry out the symbolic or ritual actions or abstentions. For every rule that *ought* to be observed there must be some sort of sanction or reason. For acts that patently affect other persons the moral and legal sanctions provide a generally sufficient controlling force upon the individual. For ritual obligations conformity and rationalization are provided by the ritual sanctions. The simplest form of ritual sanction is an accepted belief that if rules of ritual are not observed some undefined misfortune is likely to occur. In many societies the expected danger is somewhat more definitely conceived as a danger of sickness or, in extreme cases, death. In the more specialized forms of ritual sanction the good results to be hoped for or the bad results to be feared are more specifically defined in reference to the occasion or meaning of the ritual.

The theory is not concerned with the historical origin of ritual, nor is it another attempt to explain ritual in terms of human psychology; it is a hypothesis as to the relation of ritual and ritual values to the essential constitution of human society, i.e., to those invariant general characters which belong to all human societies, past, present, and future. It rests on the recognition of the fact that while in animal societies social coaptation depends on instinct, in human societies it depends upon the efficacy of symbols of many different kinds. The theory I am advancing must therefore, for a just estimation of its value, be considered in its place in a general theory of symbols and their social efficacy.

By this theory the Andamanese taboos relating to childbirth are the obligatory recognition in a standardized symbolic form of the significance and importance of the event to the parents and to the community at large.

They thus serve to fix the social value of occasions of this kind. Similarly I have argued in another place that the Andamanese taboos relating the animals and plants used for food are means of affixing a definite social value to food, based on its social importance. The social importance of food is not that it satisfies hunger, but that in such a community as an Andamanese camp or village an enormously large proportion of the activities are concerned with the getting and consuming of food, and that in these activities, with their daily instances of collaboration and mutual aid, there continuously occur those interrelations of interests which bind the individual men, women, and children into a society.

I believe that this theory can be generalized and with suitable modifications will be found to apply to a vast number of the taboos of different societies. My theory would go further for I would hold, as a reasonable working hypothesis, that we have here the primary basis of all ritual and therefore of religion and magic, however those may be distinguished. The primary basis of ritual, so the formulation would run, is the attribution of ritual value to objects and occasions which are either themselves objects of important common interests linking together the persons of a community or are symbolically representative of such objects. To illustrate what is meant by the last part of this statement two illustrations may be offered. In the Andamans ritual value is attributed to the cicada, not because it has any social importance itself but because it symbolically represents the seasons of the year which do have importance. In some tribes of Eastern Australia the god Baiame is the personification, i.e., the symbolical representative, of the moral law of the tribe, and the rainbow-serpent (the Australian equivalent of the Chinese dragon) is a symbol representing growth and fertility in nature. Baiame and the rainbow-serpent in their turn are represented by the figures of earth which are made on the sacred ceremonial ground of the initiation ceremonies and at which rites are performed. The reverence that the Australian shows to the image of Baiame or towards his name is the symbolic method of fixing the social value of the moral law, particularly the laws relating to marriage.

In conclusion let me return once more to the work of the anthropologist whom we are here to honor. Sir James Frazer, in his *Psyche's Task* and in his other works, set himself to show how, in his own words, taboos have contributed to build up the complex fabric of society. He thus initiated that functional study of ritual to which I have in this lecture and elsewhere attempted to make some contribution. But there has been a shift of emphasis. Sir James accounted for the taboos of savage tribes as the application in practice of beliefs arrived at by erroneous processes of reasoning, and he seems to have thought of the effects of these beliefs in creating or maintaining a stable orderly society as being accidental. My own view is that the negative and positive rites of savages exist and persist because they are part of the mechanism by which an orderly society maintains itself in existence, serving as they do to establish certain fundamental social values. The beliefs by which the rites themselves are justified and given some sort of consistency are the rationalizations of symbolic actions and of the sentiments associated with them. I would suggest that what Sir James Frazer seems to regard as the accidental results of magical and religious beliefs really constitute their essential function and the ultimate reason for their existence.

NOTE: The theory of ritual outlined in this lecture was first worked out in 1908 in a thesis on the Andaman Islanders. It was written out again in a revised and extended form in 1913 and appeared in print in 1922. Unfortunately the exposition contained in *The Andaman Islanders* is evidently not clear, since some of my critics have failed to understand what the theory is. For example, it has been assumed that by "social value" I mean "utility."

The best treatment of the subject of value with which I am acquainted is Ralph Barton Perry's *General Theory of Value*, 1926. For the Chinese theory of ritual the most easily accessible account is in Chapter XIV of Fung Yu-lan's *History of Chinese Philosophy*, 1937. The third chapter, on the uses of symbolism, of Whitehead's *Symbolism: Its Meaning and Effect*, is an admirable brief introduction to the sociological theory of symbolism.

One very important point that could not be dealt with in the lecture is that indicated by Whitehead in the following sentence: "No account of the uses of symbolism is complete without the recognition that the symbolic elements in life have a tendency to run wild, like the vegetation in a tropical forest."

George C. Homans

ANXIETY AND RITUAL: THE THEORIES OF MALINOWSKI AND RADCLIFFE-BROWN

With the publication of Malinowski's various books and papers on the function of ritual in allaying anxiety and inspiring confidence in men faced with an unbridgeable gap in their empirical knowledge, and of Radcliffe-Brown's lecture *Taboo*, which presents the thesis that anxiety is frequently experienced when a customary ritual is *not* performed, students of religion and magic were confronted by a theoretical dilemma of how to resolve these two essentially opposing theories.

In this brief but penetrating paper Homans suggests a resolution by introducing the concepts of "primary" and "secondary" anxieties and rituals and by clarifying the relationship between the individual and societal level of analysis. His use of the term "rationalization" for the native's justification of his ritual may be misleading to some readers. This is rationalization not from the native's point of view—he *believes* in his rituals and thinks they are efficacious—but from the outside observer's point of view.

Reprinted from *American Anthropologist*, XLIII (1941), 164–172, by permission of the author and the American Anthropological Association.

In his Frazer Lecture for the year 1939, recently published as a pamphlet under the title *Taboo*, Professor A. R. Radcliffe-Brown restates certain of his views on magic and religion.[1] At the same time, he makes certain criticisms of Professor Malinowski's theories on the subject. The appearance of *Taboo*, therefore, offers the anthropologist an occasion for examining the present status of the theory of ritual by means of a study of a controversy between what are perhaps its two most important experts. Incidentally, the reader will find illustrated a type of behavior common in disputes in the world of science.

Malinowski's theory of magic is well known and has been widely accepted.[2] He holds that any primitive people has a body of empirical knowledge, comparable to modern scientific knowledge, as to the behavior of nature and the means of controlling it to meet man's needs. This knowledge the primitives apply in a thoroughly practical manner to get the results they desire—a crop of tubers, a catch of fish, and so forth. But their techniques are seldom so powerful that the accomplishment of these results is a matter of certainty. When the tiller of the soil has done the best he can to see that his fields are properly planted and tended, a drought or a blight may overwhelm him. Under these circumstances the primitives feel a sentiment which we call "anxiety"[3] and they perform magical rites which they say will ensure good luck. These rites give them the confidence which allows them to attack their practical work with energy and determination.

Malinowski clinches his argument with an observation made in the course of his field work:

> *An interesting and crucial test is provided by fishing in the Trobriand Islands and its magic. While in the villages on the inner Lagoon fishing is done in an easy and absolutely reliable manner by the method of poisoning, yielding abundant results without danger and uncertainty, there are on the shores of the open sea dangerous modes of fishing and also certain types in which the yield varies greatly according to whether shoals of fish appear beforehand or not. It is most significant that in the Lagoon fishing, where man can rely completely upon his knowledge and skill, magic does not exist, while in the open-sea fishing, full of*

[1] Elsewhere most prominently stated in *The Andaman Islanders* (new ed., 1933).

[2] See "Magic, Science, and Religion," in J. Needham (ed.), *Science, Religion and Reality; Coral Gardens and Their Magic;* and *Foundations of Faith and Morals* ("Riddell Memorial Lectures").

[3] The word "anxiety" is used here in its ordinary commonsense meaning. This use is not to be confused with the psychoanalytic one, though of course the two are related.

danger and uncertainty, there is extensive magical ritual to secure safety and good results.[4]

On this understanding of magic, Malinowski bases a distinction between magical and religious ritual. A magical rite, he says,

has a definite practical purpose which is known to all who practice it and can be easily elicited from any native informant.

This is not true of a religious rite.

While in the magical act the underlying idea and aim is always clear, straightforward, and definite, in the religious ceremony there is no purpose directed towards a subsequent event. It is only possible for the sociologist to establish the function, the sociological raison d'être *of the act. The native can always state the end of the magical rite, but he will say of a religious ceremony that it is done because such is the usage, or he will narrate an explanatory myth.*[5]

This argument is the first with which Professor Radcliffe-Brown takes issue, and his criticism seems to the writer justified. He points out that the difficulty in applying this distinction between magic and religion lies in uncertainty as to what is meant by "definite, practical purpose." What is, in fact, the definite, practical purpose of a magical rite? To an anthropologist from western civilization, a magical rite and a religious rite are equally devoid of definite, practical results, in the usual sense of the phrase. The distinction between them must be based on other grounds. A scrutiny of the methods we actually use to determine the purpose of a magical rite reveals that what we take to be the purpose of the rite is the purpose as stated by a native informant. The native performs one rite and says that it has a definite, practical purpose. He performs another rite and says that it is performed as a matter of custom. If we call the first rite magic and the second religion, we are basing our distinction on a difference between the verbal statements a native makes about the rites. For some purposes the distinction may be a useful one, but one of the truisms of the social sciences is that we shall do well to look at the statements men make about what they do with extreme care before we take the statements at their face value. Or, to use Radcliffe-Brown's own words:

The reasons given by the members of a community for the customs they observe are important data for the anthropologist. But it is to fall into grievous error to suppose that they give a valid explanation of the custom.[6]

[4] *Science, Religion and Reality*, p. 32.
[5] *Ibid.*, p. 38.
[6] *Taboo*, p. 25.

Without doubt there are many factors involved in the performance of magic, but the least number which must be taken into consideration are apparently the following. A sentiment which we call anxiety arises when men feel certain desires and do not possess the techniques which make them sure of satisfying the desires. This sentiment of anxiety then manifests itself in ritual behavior. We may recall to mind here Pareto's third class of residues—the need of expressing sentiments by external acts. The situation is familiar in American folklore: a man and his wife are held up in a taxi in New York traffic and in danger of missing their liner to Europe. There is nothing that either one of them can do that would be of any use, but the wife screams to her husband: "But do something, can't you?" Furthermore, the action taken under such circumstances, however useless it may be, does do something to relieve the anxiety. In the usual phrase, it "works it off."

A better statement, from the point of view of psychology, is the following:

From clinical, physiological, and psychological data, it has been shown that throwing into conflict powerful excitations toward and against motor reaction regularly results in disorganization of behavior, subjective distress, and persistent drive toward relief. This syndrome has been called variously "affect," "tension," "anxiety," and "neurosis." . . . The drive toward relief tends to set into operation implicit or explicit forms of behavior, the principal characteristic of which is their abbreviated or condensed or symbolic character and their relative indifference and impermeability (because of the necessity of attaining relief as quickly as possible) to the ordinary checks, delays, and inhibitions imposed by objective reality; thus they are objectively non-adaptive, but are subjectively adaptive to the extent that the relief aimed at is actually effected.[7]

In magic in a primitive society there is a further factor which must be taken into consideration. The primitives feel anxiety and perform ritual actions which have some effect in relieving the anxiety, but they also produce a statement. They say that magical action does in fact produce a "definite, practical result." This statement is to be taken simply as a rationalization, similar in character to other rationalizations. If the rationalization is to be used as a means of distinguishing magic from religion, it should at least be recognized for what it is.

The writer doubts whether the distinction between magic and religion, as formulated

[7] R. R. Willoughby, "Magic and Cognate Phenomena: An Hypothesis," in C. Murchison (ed.), *Handbook of Social Psychology*, p. 471.

by Malinowski, is a useful one. In an effort to get away from the rationalizations, magic might be defined as the ritual which is closely associated with practical activities: hunting, fishing, husbandry. Then religion would be the ritual which is not associated with practical activities, in the sense that, for instance, the Mass of the Catholic Church is not so associated. But could a distinction be made in many societies between magic and religion as so defined? Anthropologists will be aware that in many primitive societies native informants say of the most fundamental and sacred rituals, i.e., those ordinarily called religious, that if they are not performed the food supply will fail. Are these rituals closely associated with practical activities? The food supply is certainly a practical concern. Once more we are involved in the native rationalizations. In a sense these rituals are both magical and religious.

Nevertheless, Malinowski's general theory of magic seems sound, and it may be well to cite one of his statements as a summary:

We have seen that all the instincts and emotions, all practical activities, lead man into impasses where gaps in his knowledge and the limitations of his early power of observation and reason betray him at a crucial moment. The human organism reacts to this in spontaneous outbursts, in which rudimentary modes of behavior and rudimentary beliefs in their efficiency are engendered. Magic fixes upon these beliefs and rudimentary rites and standardizes them into permanent traditional forms.[8]

One word of explanation is needed here. The present paper is concerned with ritual so far as it arises out of the sentiment we call anxiety. But there is no implication that other sentiments besides anxiety do not give rise to ritual behavior.

There are other and more important criticisms which Radcliffe-Brown makes of Malinowski's theory of ritual. He wisely bases them upon a consideration of an actual case, the ritual of birth in the Andaman Islands. In order to follow his discussion, his material should first be cited:

In the Andaman Islands when a woman is expecting a baby a name is given to it while it is still in the womb. From that time until some weeks after the baby is born nobody is allowed to use the personal name of either the father or the mother; they can be referred to only by teknonymy, i.e., in terms of their relation to the child. During this period both the parents are required to abstain from eating certain foods which they may freely eat at other times.[9]

To be sure, this is an example of negative ritual—avoidance of behavior which under other circumstances might be proper— rather than of positive ritual, but the same problems arise in either case.

Radcliffe-Brown admits that Malinowski's theory might seem to be applicable as an interpretation of this body of ritual. For a woman, childbirth is always a dangerous process, in which tragedy may suddenly appear for inexplicable reasons. It is dangerous today; it was supremely dangerous under primitive conditions. Under these circumstances, the woman may feel great anxiety, and the husband is naturally interested in the fate of his wife. But the husband and the wife perform certain rites and say that they are efficacious in warding off the dangers of childbirth. Therefore their fears are, to a certain extent, lulled.

Without explicitly rejecting Malinowski's interpretation, Radcliffe-Brown offers an alternative. He writes:

The alternative hypothesis which I am presenting for consideration is as follows. In a given community it is appropriate that an expectant father should feel concern or at least make an appearance of doing so. Some suitable symbolic expression of his concern is found in terms of the general ritual or symbolic idiom of the society, and it is felt generally that a man in that situation ought to carry out the symbolic or ritual actions or abstentions.[10]

Radcliffe-Brown presents this interpretation as an alternative to Malinowski's. The point to be made here is that the question is not one of either/or. The hypothesis is not an alternative but a supplement: both hypotheses must be taken into consideration.

In fact the problem which is raised is the ancient one of the individual and his society. Malinowski is looking at the individual, Radcliffe-Brown at society. Malinowski is saying that the individual tends to feel anxiety on certain occasions; Radcliffe-Brown is saying that society expects the individual to feel anxiety on certain occasions. But there is every reason to believe that both statements are true. They are not mutually exclusive. Indeed the writer has difficulty in believing that it should have ever come about that "in a given community it is appropriate that an expectant father should feel concern" if individual fathers had not in fact showed such concern. Of course, once the tradition had been established, variations in two directions would naturally be produced. There would be, on the one hand, fathers who felt no

[8] *Science, Religion and Reality*, p. 82.
[9] *Taboo*, p. 33.
[10] *Ibid.*, p. 41.

concern but thought that the expedient thing to do was to put on a show of concern, and on the other hand, fathers who felt concern but did not express it in the manner appropriate in the given society. But on the whole these persons would be few. The average citizen would feel concern at the birth of his child but also would express his concern in the traditional manner. The custom of the society would provide the appropriate channel of his sentiments. In short, a theory adequate to the facts would combine the hypotheses of Malinowski and Radcliffe-Brown.

A statement made by Malinowski in another connection is appropriately quoted here:

The tendency represented largely by the sociological school of Durkheim, and clearly expressed in Professor Radcliffe-Brown's approach to primitive law and other phenomena, the tendency to ignore completely the individual and to eliminate the biological element from the functional analysis of culture, must in my opinion be overcome. It is really the only point of theoretical dissension between Professor Radcliffe-Brown and myself, and the only respect in which the Durkheimian conception of primitive society has to be supplemented in order to be really serviceable in field work, in theoretical studies, and in the practical application of sociology.[11]

Radcliffe-Brown makes a second and more important objection in applying Malinowski's theory to the ritual of childbirth in the Andamans. While a woman is expecting a child, and for some weeks after the birth of the child, both parents are required to abstain from eating certain foods which they may properly eat under ordinary circumstances, these foods apparently being dugong, pork, and turtle meat. Furthermore,

If the Andaman Islanders are asked what would happen if the father or mother broke this taboo, the usual answer is that he or she would be ill, though one or two of my informants thought it might perhaps also affect the child. This is simply one instance of a standard formula which applies to a number of ritual prohibitions.[12]

On the basis of this observation, Radcliffe-Brown goes on to make the following attack on Malinowski's anxiety theory:

I think that for certain rites it would be easy to maintain with equal plausibility an exactly contrary theory, namely, that if it were not for the existence of the rite and the beliefs associated with it the individual would feel no anxiety, and that the psychological effect of the rite is to create in him a sense of insecurity or danger. It seems very unlikely that an Andaman Islander would think that it is dangerous to eat dugong or pork or turtle meat if it were not for the existence of a specific body of ritual the ostensible purpose of which is to protect him from those dangers. Many hundreds of similar instances could be mentioned from all over the world.[13]

This attack on Malinowski's theory appears at first glance to be devastating. But let us examine it a little more closely. Put in simpler language, what Radcliffe-Brown is saying is that the Andaman mother and father do not apparently feel anxiety at the fact of approaching childbirth. They feel anxiety only when the ritual of childbirth is not properly performed. There is no doubt that similar observations could be made of backward peoples all over the world. It is true that their techniques do not allow them to control completely the natural forces on which their lives depend. Nevertheless when they have done their practical work as well as they know how and have performed the proper rituals, they display little overt anxiety. If anxiety is present, it remains latent. They are, as we say, fatalists. What Thomas and Znaniecki have observed of the Polish peasant seems to be true of most primitive peoples. They write:

The fact is that when the peasant has been working steadily, and has fulfilled the religious and magical ceremonies which tradition requires, he "leaves the rest to God," and waits for the ultimate results to come; the question of more or less skill and efficiency of work has very little importance.[14]

When the primitive or the peasant has done his practical work as well as he knows how, and has "fulfilled the religious and magical ceremonies which tradition requires," he displays little overt anxiety. But he does feel anxiety if the ceremonies have not been properly performed. In fact he generalizes beyond this point and feels that unless all the moralities of his society are observed, nature will not yield her fruits. Incest or murder in the camp will lead to a failure of the crops just as surely as will a breach of ritual. In the shape of famine, pestilence, or war, God will visit their sins upon the people. Accordingly when, in a village of medieval Europe, the peasants, led by the parish priest, went in procession about the boundaries of the village in the Rogation Days in order to bless the growing crops, they offered up prayers at the same time for the forgiveness of sins. This associ-

[11] I. Hogbin, *Law and Order in Polynesia,* xxxviii. The introduction is by Malinowski.

[12] *Taboo,* p. 35.

[13] *Ibid.,* p. 39.

[14] W. I. Thomas and F. Znaniecki, *The Polish Peasant in Europe and America,* I, 174.

ation of ideas is characteristic: nature and morality are mutually dependent.

As a matter of fact, the above observations are implicit in Malinowski's theory, and he was undoubtedly aware of them. He points to the initial anxiety situation, but he also states that ritual dispels the anxiety, at least in part, and gives men confidence. He implies, then, that anxiety remains latent so long as ritual is properly performed. Radcliffe-Brown's criticism does not demolish Malinowski's theory but takes the necessary further step. Once again, it is not an alternative but a supplement. Using the ritual of childbirth in the Andamans as an example, he asks what happens, or rather what would happen, if the ritual is not performed. And he shows that this occasion is the one in which the natives feel anxiety. The anxiety has, so to speak, been displaced from the original situation. But even granted that it has been displaced, Malinowski's general theory is confirmed by the existence of a secondary ritual which has the function of dispelling the secondary anxiety which arises from a breach of ritual and tradition. We call this the ritual of purification, of expiation.

In his description of the Australian Murngin, W. L. Warner sums up admirably what the writer has been trying to say. He writes:

> *The Murngin in their logic of controlling nature assume that there is a direct connection between social units and different aspects of nature, and that the control of nature lies in the proper control and treatment of social organization. Properly to control the social organization, the rituals must also be held which rid society of its uncleanliness. The society is disciplined by threat of what will happen to nature, the provider, if the members of the group misbehave.*[15]

In summary, it appears from the discussion of the theories of Malinowski and Radcliffe-Brown that at least seven elements must be taken into consideration in any study of the rituals we are accustomed to call magic. Of course, there are other elements which are not considered here. The seven are the following:

1. *Primary anxiety*. Whenever a man desires the accomplishment of certain results and does not possess the techniques which will make him certain to secure these results, he feels a sentiment which we call anxiety.

2. *Primary ritual*. Under these circumstances, he tends to perform actions which have no practical result and which we call ritual. But he is not simply an individual. He is a member of a society with definite traditions, and among other things society determines the form of the ritual and expects him to perform the ritual on the appropriate occasions. There is, however, evidence from our own society that when ritual tradition is weak, men will invent ritual when they feel anxiety.

3. *Secondary anxiety*. When a man has followed the technical procedures at his command and performed the traditional rituals, his primary anxiety remains latent. We say that the rites give him confidence. Under these circumstances, he will feel anxiety only when the rites themselves are not properly performed. In fact this attitude becomes generalized, and anxiety is felt whenever any one of the traditions of society is not observed. This anxiety may be called secondary or displaced anxiety.

4. *Secondary ritual*. This is the ritual of purification and expiation which has the function of dispelling secondary anxiety. Its form and performance, like those of primary ritual, may or may not be socially determined.

5. *Rationalization*. This element includes the statements which are associated with ritual. They may be very simple: such statements as that the performance of a certain magic does ensure the catching of fish, or that if an Andaman mother and father do not observe the food taboos they will be sick. The statements may be very elaborate. Such are the statements which accompany the fundamental rituals of any society: the equivalents of the Mass of the Catholic Church.

6. *Symbolization*. Since the form of ritual action is not determined by the nature of a practical result to be accomplished, it can be determined by other factors. We say that it is symbolic, and each society has its own vocabulary of symbols. Some of the symbolism is relatively simple: for example, the symbolism of sympathies and antipathies. Some is complicated. In particular, certain of the rituals of a society, and those the most important, make symbolic reference to the fundamental myths of the society. The ceremonies of the Murngin make reference to the fundamental myths of that society just as surely as the Mass makes reference to Christ's sacrifice on Calvary.

7. *Function*. Ritual actions do not produce a practical result on the external world—that is one reason why we call them ritual. But to make this statement is not to say that ritual has no function. Its function is not related to the world external to the society but to the internal constitution of the society. It gives

[15] W. L. Warner, *A Black Civilization*, p. 410.

the members of the society confidence; it dispels their anxieties; it disciplines the social organization. But the functions of ritual have been discussed elsewhere, and in any case they raise questions which are beyond the scope of the present paper.

Finally, a study of the theories of Malinowski and Radcliffe-Brown illustrates a common feature of scientific controversies: two distinguished persons talking past one another rather than trying to find a common ground for discussion, presenting their theories as alternatives when in fact they are complements. Such a study suggests also that the theory necessary for an adequate description of any phenomenon is often more complicated than the theories of the phenomenon which exist at any given time.

Talcott Parsons

RELIGIOUS PERSPECTIVES IN SOCIOLOGY AND SOCIAL PSYCHOLOGY

Among the works of recent American sociologists, those of Talcott Parsons have been of the most general significance in defining the role and function of religion in human society. Parsons' classic paper on this subject is "The Theoretical Development of the Sociology of Religion," in which he synthesizes the theories of Durkheim, Pareto, Weber, and Malinowski. Since this earlier paper is readily available in his *Essays in Sociological Theory* (1949), a briefer and less available essay has been selected for inclusion in this volume.

In addition to setting forth a definition of religion as a universal feature of human society, Parsons (following leads suggested by Malinowski) also provides a cogent discussion of the two main types of frustration in the human situation that provide focal points for the development of religious patterns. One of these types is due to the fact that men are "hit" by events which they cannot either foresee and prepare for or control, such as the occurrence of premature death. The second type is present where there is a strong emotional investment in the success of human endeavor, where energy and skill count for much, but where unknown or uncontrollable factors often intervene to upset the balance between effort and success, such as in the exposure of agriculture to uncontrollable weather.

These frustrations of established expectations pose "problems of meaning," in the sense that Max Weber wrote much about; that is, we can explain how an automobile accident caused a premature death, but we cannot explain why it had to happen to a particular person at a particular time; we can explain how it is that "the wicked flourish like a green bay tree," but not why it has to come out this way in societies. Hence the significance of religion in human life is that it is made up of those aspects of the life situation to which men cannot remain indifferent, which they cannot in the long run evade, but which they cannot control or adjust to through the ordinary techniques and attitudes of practical utilitarian life.

Adapted from Talcott Parsons, "Sociology and Social Psychology," in Hoxie N. Fairchild (ed.), *Religious Perspectives in College Teaching* (New York: Ronald Press, 1952), pp. 286–305.

The present essay is written from the point of view of the social scientist, not that of the representative of any religious denomination.

Sociology we will define as the science interested in the institutional structure of social systems, and the motivational processes in human beings which are involved in the maintenance and change of institutions. Social psychology is an interstitial science between psychology and sociology, much like biochemistry in the natural sciences. It is concerned with the study of motivational processes of behavior and the structure of personalities, in the context of their relevance to social systems and their problems, notably their institutional structure.

A religion we will define as a set of beliefs, practices and institutions which men have evolved in various societies, so far as they can be understood, as responses to those aspects of their life and situation which are believed not in the empirical-instrumental sense to be rationally understandable and/or controllable, and to which they attach a significance which includes some kind of reference to the relevant actions and events to man's conception of the existence of a "supernatural" order which is conceived and felt to have a fundamental bearing on man's position in the universe and the values which give meaning to his fate as an individual and his relations to his fellows.

Defined in this way, a religion or religious system will include at a minimum: (1) a more or less integrated set of beliefs concerning entities which are "supernatural," sacred, or, as Durkheim said, "set apart" from the ordinary objects and events of utilitarian or instrumental significance of human affairs and interests on his relation to which the meaning of man's life is fundamentally dependent; (2) a system of symbols, objects, acts, persons, empirical and non-empirical, which have the quality of sacredness and in relation to which men express the emotional states relevant to the religious sphere, in short, a system of expressive symbols; (3) a set of more or less definitely prescribed activities which are interpreted as important and often obligatory in the light of the beliefs involved, but which from the point of view of the instrumental interests of daily life are "useless" in that they do not "accomplish anything." These activities will usually be prescribed for different types of occasions, forbidden on others and may be differentiated for different statuses in the social group; (4) to some degree a sense that "we" who share common beliefs of this character, and participate in what is felt to be an integrated system of such activities, constitute a "collectivity"—a group which by virtue of that fact is bound together in what Durkheim called a "moral community"; finally, (5) a sense that man's relation to the supernatural world is in some way intimately connected with his moral values, with the nature of the goals he is called upon to live for and the rules of conduct he is expected to comply with. The sharing of these common moral values as well as more specifically "religious" beliefs and practices will be constitutive of the moral community spoken of above.

In addition to these five minimum features of what the sociologist would call a religion or religious system, certain others may be expected to appear in different types of religious systems. These are all aspects of the differentiation and corresponding modes of organization of the social relationship systems which religious beliefs and practices involve. The most important aspect of differentiation is the differentiation of the roles of individuals and of classes of them relative to those of others participating in the same religious system. There are in turn two main aspects of this differentiation. The first is the differentiation of types of individuals and groups relative to their relations to the sacred and supernatural sphere independent of functions on behalf of the religious collectivity, while the second is differentiation of roles with such specialized functions. In the first direction we find such types as the individual ascetic or monastic order. In the second falls the minister or priest who functions on behalf of his congregation. The prophet can be regarded in both contexts, as having established a *new* relation to the supernatural and as the leader of a *movement* to implement its implications in the life of society.

Closely related to the differentiation of roles is the development of the character of the religious collectivity itself. There are several important aspects of this but two may be singled out for mention here. One is the mode of integration—or lack of it—of the religious collectivity itself with the rest of the group structure of the society. Thus it may be an aspect of a single overall collective organization as in the case of the most nonliterate societies, or there may be a distinctive religious grouping as with the Christian church or denominational organization. The other aspect is that of the internal organization of the religious collectivity above all the ways and extent of the development of formal organization of explicit canons formally interpreted and enforced, and the like.

The analysis of the conditions determining the specific type of belief or symbol system, of activities or moral roles, of differentiation of roles, of modes of collectivity organization, constitutes one main aspect of the sociology of religion in a more detailed sense. The other main aspect concerns the ways in which differences of religious systems in these respects are interdependent with other aspects of the social systems of which they are a part. Unfortunately limitations of space preclude entering into the fascinating analysis of these problems here. The reader should, however, keep in mind that solid grounding of many of the empirical generalizations stated in later sections of this essay would require carrying through the relevant analysis on this level in full detail. It is only space limitation which makes this impossible.

MOTIVATION OF RELIGIOUS BELIEF AND BEHAVIOR

With the above sketch of some of the principal components of religious systems on the social level in mind we may now turn to some aspects of the "social psychology" of religion, of the characteristic of man as an "actor" in a situation, and of that situation, which helps us to understand his need for and relations to religious institutions. We will develop this theme in two sections; in the present one we will attempt to sketch some of the main sources of the motivation to religious belief and behavior, and in that following to indicate some of the complicated interrelations between religious and secular motivations on this level.

Man is distinguished from the other animals, from the point of view of the social scientist, above all by the fact that he is a creator and bearer of culture. He creates and lives by systems of symbols and of artifacts; he not only modifies his environment but his orientation to it is generalized in terms of systems of symbolic meaning; he communicates with his fellow men through language and other symbols; he perpetuates and develops his knowledge, and he expresses his feelings, not directly and crudely, but in elaborately symbolic form.

A "culture" is not and cannot be just a discrete collection of disconnected artifacts and symbols, but to a greater or lesser degree must constitute a *system*. It must, that is, have coherence as a set of orientations which tie together the many particular aspects of men's experience and needs. Above all it has three types of functions. In the cognitive aspects, as a system of beliefs, it attempts to answer man's questions about himself and the world he lives in, and we all know that we cannot consciously hold contradictory beliefs without strain. Second, it provides "forms" or expressive symbols for expressing and communicating his feelings, forms which conform to standards of "taste." Finally, and from the sociological point of view perhaps most important, it provides standards for evaluation, above all the moral standards which regulate man's conduct, particularly in his relation with his fellows. It can be proved quite definitely that once the step from regulation by "instinct" to the plastic dependence on learned patterns of behavior has been taken by man as organism, a society of men cannot subsist without what sociologists call the institutionalization of a relatively consistent system of patterns of culture, above all of moral values.

The role of culture in human life implies that men must be concerned, in a sense somewhat different from the animals, with the *meaning* of their experience, that is, not merely with whether a given experience gratifies a wish or fills a need or contrariwise involves pain or deprivation, but also with the *fit* between the *expectations* of experience which have been defined for him in his culture, and the actuality which he himself experiences.

There is in every system of human action, in every society, a smooth, "normal" pattern of everyday functioning, of ways in which people go "about their business" without particular strain, where the means available to them are adequate to attain the goals they have been taught to strive for, and where the all-important other people fulfill their expectations. But if all human life were like that, religion would certainly not have the significance that it does. We would be much more likely to think of the "problems" of life as mainly of a practical "utilitarian" kind, to be solved by good "horse sense."

There are certain fundamental respects in which this is an inadequate picture of the human life situation. In whatever kind of society *some* human expectations, in the fulfillment of which people have acquired a deep emotional investment, are doomed to frustration. These frustrations are of two main types. One of them consists in the fact that men are "hit" by events which they either cannot foresee and prepare for, or control, or both; to which, however, they must make major adjustments, sometimes practical but always emotional. The type case of this kind of frustration is the occurrence of premature death. Certainly the fact that though we all know we have to die almost no man knows when he will die is one of the cardinal facts of the human situation. But not only for the person facing death himself, if he has time to think about it, but quite clearly for the survivors, there is a major problem of adjustment, for the simple reason that the human individual as an object of emotional attachment is of such fundamental importance. Even the loss of a "beloved enemy" can, we know, be very upsetting. Though religious orientations to death, which are universal and fundamental to religion, contain many shadings of belief about the "life after death," the fundamental feature of this orientation is not "wishful thinking." As one historian of religion has put it, "No major religion has ever claimed to be able to 'beat death.'" The dead are dead, and cannot be brought back to life; but the living must still adjust themselves to that fact. From the point of view of the social scientist, what they believe and do in this situation has significance as a set of "mechanisms" which in some ways facilitate this adjustment. From the secular social point of view to hold funeral ceremonies does not "accomplish anything," the functions of such ceremonies are "latent," but they may none the less be highly important.

In general it is extremely conspicuous that ceremonialism not only concerns the directly bereaved, but directly symbolizes the belongingness of the deceased and of the bereaved in larger social groupings. On the one hand these larger groups which are not so directly affected give their "support" to the bereaved, but on the other they set a "tone" for the occasion which in general says, "the traditional values of the society must be upheld." Death must be only a temporary interruption, the important thing on one level is to "get over it" and to go on living. Though it is by no means obvious, there are many features of funeral ceremonies which are closely similar to those of psychotherapy.

There are other types of uncontrollable events besides death which have what in certain respects is a similar bearing on human interests, natural catastrophes being one of them. Furthermore it should be noted that not only frustration in the usual sense, but unexpected and therefore "unearned" good fortune may also have an upsetting effect and require processes of adjustment. Perhaps our own Thanksgiving fits in that category. The Pilgrim Fathers may well have felt that they were extremely "lucky," or as they said, favored by God, to have survived their first terrible year in the wilderness at all.

A second type of frustrating experience is connected with what has come to be called in a special sense "uncertainty." By this is meant the very common type of situation where there is a strong emotional investment in the success of certain human endeavors, where energy and skill undoubtedly count for much, but where unknown and/or uncontrollable factors may and often do intervene to upset any "reasonable" balance between action and success. The exposure of agriculture the world over, with few exceptions, to the vagaries of uncontrollable and unpredictable weather, is one of the most important examples. No matter how industrious and capable a farmer may be, his crops may be ruined by drought or flood. The field of health is another classic example, and there are a variety of others. The unpredictable character of human conduct in many fields, from love to war, is also prominent.

In all these situations rational techniques must of course loom large; no farmer ever grew good crops by magic alone. But these are the classic situations in which what anthropologists call "magic" flourishes. Whatever the distinction made, magic is always continuous with religion, it always involves some relation to the strains occasioned by uncertainty, and to human emotional adjustment to such situations. Magical beliefs and practices constitute, from the point of view of social psychology, mechanisms of adjustment to these situations of strain. They give an opportunity to "act out" some of the psychological products of that strain, thus to "place the blame" for the frustration—most conspicuous in the cases of belief in witchcraft. They give people the sense of "doing something about it" in areas where their rational techniques are powerless or untrustworthy. Above all they act as a tonic to self-confidence; they are a protection against allowing the risk of failure to lead to a fatalistic discouragement, the attitude that since success cannot be assured, it is no use trying at all. At the same time, magic may act as a stereotyping agency in situations where empirical knowledge and technique are applicable, and thus block technological advance—this in spite of the fact which Malinowski makes so clear, that magic cannot take the place of rational technique. The Trobriand Islander does not believe that he can make up for failing to cultivate his garden properly by more or better magic; it is a supplement, not a substitute.

The frustrations of established expectations of which we have been speaking pose "problems of meaning" in a double sense. On the one hand, man, being a culture-bearing animal, does not merely "take it" when things go as he does not expect. He has to give these things a meaning, in the first instance emotionally, so that his adjustments to such experiences can become integrated in the *system* of experience, which means among other things that his reactions are coordinated and organized with those of his fellows; he can communicate his feelings and receive adequate responses to his expressions of them.

But beyond this, as we have noted at the beginning of this section, the culture in which a social group lives constitutes a more or less integrated system. As such it must have a certain level of consistency; it must "cover" the principal ranges of men's experience in such a way that all of them to some degree "make sense," together as a whole.

Besides the direct problem of emotional adjustment to the frustration of particular experiences, the "generalization" which is involved in the integration of a cultural system brings up two further particularly crucial "problem" areas. The culture links the experience and expectations of any particular individual or subgroup with those of others in a society. There is not only the question of why must this happen *to me*, or to those close to me, but why must it happen at all to anyone? Above all, since men universally seek gratification of their wishes and needs there is the generalized problem of suffering, of why men must endure deprivation and pain and so unequally and haphazardly, or, indeed, at all, and, since all societies must live by moral standards, there is equally the problem of "evil," of why men violate the moral standards of their society and why the "economy" of rewards and punishments fails, as it *always* does to some extent, to balance out. Good fortune and suffering must always, to cultural man, be endowed with meaning. They cannot, except in limiting cases, be accepted as something that "just happens." Similarly it is impossible to live by moral standards and yet be wholly indifferent either to the extent of conformity with them or to the fate of conformists and violators respectively. It is necessarily disconcerting that to some degree "the good die young while the wicked flourish as the green bay tree."

The sociologist is in a position to state that some significant degree of discrepancy between expectations in both these respects and the actual state of affairs in a society is inevitable, though it varies greatly in degree and in incidence. Both expectations of gratification and moral standards vary from society to society, but this fundamental fact of discrepancy seems to be a constant, grounded in the nature of human personality, society, and culture and their relations to each other.

This complex of circumstances constitutes from a certain sociological point of view the primary focus of the differential significance of religion in human life. It is made up of aspects of the life situation to which men, being what they are, cannot remain emotionally indifferent, and which at the same time in the long run they cannot evade. But adequate adjustment on either the emotional or the cognitive level to these situations cannot be worked out through the "ordinary" techniques and attitudes of practical utilitarian life. The content and incidence of the problems vary, but their presence is a constant. Almost another way of putting the essential point is to say that tragedy is of the essence of the human situation.

Clyde Kluckhohn

MYTHS AND RITUALS: A GENERAL THEORY

The question of the functional relationship of myths to rituals is one that has concerned students of comparative religion for over a century. Are rituals developed as enactments of myths? Or are myths developed to justify rituals? This latter point of view is vigorously held to by such scholars as Lord Raglan (*The Hero*, 1936) and Stanley Edgar Hyman ("The Ritual View of Myth and the Mythic," 1955) but opposed by Bascom ("The Myth-Ritual Theory," 1957) and others.

In this illuminating paper Kluckhohn discusses the theoretical issues involved, and then shows that there is no necessary primacy of myth over ritual, or vice versa. In some cases, myths were composed to justify

Reprinted with minor abridgments by permission of the President and Fellows of Harvard College from Clyde Kluckhohn, "Myths and Rituals: A General Theory," *Harvard Theological Review*, XXXV (January, 1942), 45–79. The author kindly undertook some minor reworking of the text and deleted most of the footnotes.

rituals. But, in general, there is a tendency for the two to be intricately interrelated and to have important functional connections with the social and psychological life of a particular people. Kluckhohn then tests these generalities by a review of the Navaho Indian case in which he shows in detail the interconnections between myth and ritual and the functions of both in Navaho society.

The identification of a "type anxiety" (that of concern for health) and the function of the ceremonial system (which in Navaho society is almost entirely composed of curing ceremonies) in dealing with this anxiety at both the societal and individual level brings the discussion into sharp focus and shows clearly how myths and rituals can be systematically studied as cultural products.

I

Nineteenth-century students strongly tended to study mythology apart from associated rituals (and indeed apart from the life of the people generally). Myths were held to be symbolic descriptions of phenomena of nature. One prominent school, in fact, tried to find an astral basis for all mythic tales. Others, among whom Andrew Lang was prominent, saw in the myth a kind of primitive scientific theory. Mythology answered the insistent human HOW? and WHY? How and why was the world made? How and why were living creatures brought into being? Why, if there was life, must there be death? To early psychoanalysts such as Abraham and Rank myths were "group fantasies," wish fulfillments for a society strictly analogous to the dream and daydream of individuals. Mythology for these psychoanalysts was also a symbolic structure par excellence, but the symbolism which required interpretation was primarily a sex symbolism which was postulated as universal and all-pervasive. Reik recognized a connection between rite and myth, and he, with Freud, verbally agreed to Robertson Smith's proposition that mythology was mainly a description of ritual. To the psychoanalysts, however, mythology was essentially (so far as what they did with it is concerned) societal phantasy material which reflected impulse repression. (Many psychoanalysts today consider myths simply "a form of collective daydreaming." I have heard a prominent psychoanalyst say "Creation myths are for culture what early memories (true or fictitious) are to the individual.") There was no attempt to discover the practical function of mythology in the daily behaviors of the members of a society nor to demonstrate specific interactions of mythology and ceremonials. The interest was in supposedly panhuman symbolic meanings, not in the relation of a given myth or part of a myth to particular cultural forms or specific social situations.

To some extent the answer to the whole question of the relationship between myth and ceremony depends, of course, upon how wide or how restricted a sense one gives to "mythology." In ordinary usage the Oedipus tale is a "myth," but only some Freudians believe that this is merely the description of a ritual! The famous stories of the Republic are certainly called "μῦθος," and while a few scholars believe that Plato in *some* cases had reference to the Orphic and/or Eleusinian mysteries there is certainly not a shred of evidence that all of Plato's immortal "myths" are "descriptions of rituals." To be sure, one may justifiably narrow the problem by saying that in a technical sense these are "legends," and by insisting that "myths" be rigorously distinguished from "legends," "fairy tales," and "folk tales." If, however, one agrees that "myth" has Durkheim's connotation of the "sacred" as opposed to the "profane" the line is still sometimes hard to draw in concrete cases. What of "creation myths"? In some cases (as at Zuni) these are indeed recited during ritual performances (with variations for various ceremonies). In other cases, even though they may be recited in a "ritual" attitude, they do not enter into any ceremonial. Nevertheless, they definitely retain the flavor of "the sacred." Moreover, there are (as again at Zuni) exoteric and esoteric forms of the same myth. Among the Navaho many of the older men who are not ceremonial practitioners know that part of a myth which tells of the exploits of the hero or heroes but not the portion which prescribes the ritual details of the chant. Granting that there are sometimes both secular and sacred versions of the same tale and that other difficulties obtrude themselves in particular cases, it still seems possible to use the connotation of the sacred as that which differentiates "myth" from the rest of folklore.

But defining "myth" strictly as "sacred tale" does not carry with it by implication a warrant for considering mythology purely as a description of correlative rituals. Generally speaking, we do seem to find rich ritualism and a rich mythology together. But there are cases (like the Toda) where an extensive ceremonialism does not appear to have its equally extensive mythological counterpart and instances (like classical Greece) where a ramified mythology appears to have existed more or less independent of a comparatively meager rite system. For example, in spite of the many myths relating to Ares the rituals connected with Ares seem to have been few in number and highly localized in time and space. The early Romans, on the other hand, seemed to get along very well without mythology. The poverty of the ritual which accompanies the extremely complex mythology of the Mohave is well known. Kroeber indeed says, "Public ceremonies or rituals as they occur among almost all native Americans cannot be said to be practiced by the Mohave." The Bushmen likewise had many myths and very little ritual. On the other hand, one can point to examples like the Central Eskimo, where every detail of the Sedna myth has its ritual analogue in confessional, other rites, or hunting taboos, or, for contrast, to the American Indian tribes (especially some Californian ones) where the creation myth is never enacted in ceremonial form. In different sectors of one culture, the Papago, all of these possibilities are represented. Some myths are never ceremonially enacted. Some ceremonies emphasize content foreign to the myth. Other ceremonies consisting only of songs have some vague place in the mythological world; between these and the myths "there is a certain tenuous connection which may be a rationalization made for the sake of unity."

The anthropology of the past generation has tended to recoil sharply from any sort of generalized interpretation. Obsessed with the complexity of the historical experience of all peoples, anthropologists have (perhaps overmuch) eschewed the inference of regularities of psychological reaction which would transcend the facts of diffusion and of contacts of groups. Emphasis has been laid upon the distribution of myths and upon the mythological patterning which prevailed in different cultures and culture areas. Study of these distributions has led to a generalization of another order which is the converse of the hypothesis of most nineteenth-century classical scholars that a ritual was an enactment of a myth. In the words of Boas: "The uniformity of many such rituals over large areas and the diversity of mythological explanations show clearly that the ritual itself is the stimulus for the origin of the myth. . . . The ritual existed, and the tale originated from the desire to account for it."

While this suggestion of the primacy of ritual over the myth is probably a valid statistical induction and a proper statement of the modal tendency of our evidence, it is, it seems to me, as objectionably a simple unitary explanation (if pressed too far) as the generally rejected nineteenth-century views. Thus we find Hocart recently asking: "If there are myths that give rise to ritual where do these myths come from?" A number of instances will shortly be presented in which the evidence is unequivocal that myths did give rise to ritual. May I only remark here that—if we view the matter objectively—the Christian Mass, as interpreted by Christians, is a clear illustration of a ritual based upon a sacred story. Surely, in any case, Hocart's question can be answered very simply: from a dream or a waking fantasy or a personal habit system of some individual in the society. The basic psychological mechanisms involved would seem not dissimilar to those whereby individuals in our own (and other) cultures construct private rituals or carry out private divination—e.g., counting and guessing before the clock strikes, trying to get to a given point (a traffic light, for instance) before something else happens. As DuBois has suggested, "the explanation may be that personal rituals have been taken over and socialized by the group." These "personal rituals" could have their genesis in idiosyncratic habit formations (similar to those of obsessional neurotics in our culture) or in dreams or reveries. Mrs. Seligman has convincingly suggested that spontaneous personal dissociation is a frequent mechanism for rite innovations. The literature is replete with instances of persons "dreaming" that supernaturals summoned them, conducted them on travels or adventures, and finally admonished them thereafter to carry out certain rites (often symbolically repetitive of the adventures).

Moreover, there are a number of well-documented actual cases where historical persons, in the memory of other historical persons, actually instituted new rituals. The ritual innovations of the American Indian Ghost Dance cult and other nativistic cults of the New World provide striking illustration. In these cases the dreams or fantasies—told by the innovators before the ceremonial was ever actualized in deeds—became an important part of traditionally accepted rite-myths. Lincoln has presented plausible evidence that dreams are the source of "new" rituals. Morgan, on the basis of Navaho material, says:

. . . delusions and dreams . . . are so vivid and carry such conviction that any attempt to reason

about them afterwards on the basis of conscious sense impressions is unavailing. Such experiences deeply condition the individual, sometimes so deeply that if the experience is at variance with a tribal or neighborhood beliefs, the individual will retain his own variation. There can be no doubt that this is a very significant means of modifying a culture.

Van Gennep asserts that persons went to dream in the sanctuary at Epidaurus as a source for new rites in the cult of Asclepius. To obtain ceremony through dream is, of course, itself a pattern, a proper traditional way of obtaining a ceremony or power. I do not know of any cases of a society where dreaming is generally in disrepute, as at Zuni, and where ceremony has yet demonstrably originated through dream. But where dreaming is accepted as revelation it must not be assumed that the content (or even, entirely, the structure) of a new myth and its derived ceremony will be altogether determined by pre-existent cultural forms. As Lowie has remarked, "That they themselves (dreams) in part reflect the regnant folklore offers no ultimate explanation." Anthropologists must be wary of what Korzybski calls "self-reflexive systems"—here, specifically, the covert premise that "culture alone determines culture."

The structure of new cultural forms (whether myths or rituals) will undoubtedly be conditioned by the pre-existent cultural matrix. But the rise of new cultural forms will almost always be determined by factors external to that culture: pressure from other societies, biological events such as epidemics, or changes in the physical environment. Barber has recently shown how the Ghost Dance and the Peyote Cult represent alternative responses of various American Indian tribes to the deprivation resultant upon the encroachment of whites. The Ghost Dance was an adaptive response under the earlier external conditions, but under later conditions the Peyote Cult was the more adaptive response, and the Ghost Dance suffered what the stimulus-response psychologists would call "extinction through non-reward." At any rate, the Ghost Dance became extinct in some tribes; in others it has perhaps suffered only partial extinction.

There are always individuals in every society who have their private rituals; there are always individuals who dream and who have compensatory fantasies. In the normal course of things these are simply deviant behaviors which are ridiculed or ignored by most members of the society. Perhaps indeed one should not speak of them as "deviant"—they are "deviant" only as carried to extremes by a relatively small number of individuals, for everyone probably has some private rituals and compensatory fantasies. When, however, changed conditions happen to make a particular type of obsessive behavior or a special sort of fantasy generally congenial, the private ritual is then socialized by the group, the fantasy of the individual becomes the myth of his society. Indeed there is evidence that when pressures are peculiarly strong and peculiarly general, a considerable number of different individuals may almost simultaneously develop substantially identical fantasies which then become widely current.

Whether belief (myth) or behavior (ritual) changes first will depend, again, both upon cultural tradition and upon external circumstances. Taking a very broad view of the matter, it does seem that behavioral patterns more frequently alter first. In a rapidly changing culture such as our own many ideal patterns are as much as a generation behind the corresponding behavioral patterns. There is evidence that certain ideal patterns (for example, those defining the status of women) are slowly being altered to harmonize with, to act as rationalizations for, the behavioral actualities. On the other hand, the case of Nazi Germany is an excellent illustration of the ideal patterns ("the myth") being provided from above almost whole cloth and of the state, through various organizations, exerting all its force to make the behavioral patterns conform to the standards of conduct laid down in the Nazi mythology.

Some cultures and subcultures are relatively indifferent to belief, others to behavior. The dominant practice of the Christian Church, throughout long periods of its history, was to give an emphasis to belief which is most unusual as seen from a cross-cultural perspective. In general, the crucial test as to whether or not one was a Christian was the willingness to avow belief in certain dogmas. The term "believer" was almost synonymous with "Christian." It is very possibly because of this cultural screen that until this century most European scholars selected the myth as primary.

II

To a considerable degree, the whole question of the primacy of ceremonial or mythology is as meaningless as all questions of "the hen or the egg" form. What is really important, as Malinowski has so brilliantly shown, is the intricate interdependence of myth (which is one form of ideology) with ritual and many other forms of behavior. He examines myths not as curiosa taken out of their total context but as living, vitally important elements in the day-to-day lives of his Trobrianders, interwoven with every other abstracted type of activity. From this point of view one sees the fallacy of all unilateral explanations. One also sees the aspect of truth in all (or nearly all) of them. There are features which seem to be explanatory of natural phenomena. There are features which reveal the peculiar forms of wish fulfillments characteristic of the culture in question (including the expression of the culturally disallowed but unconsciously wanted). There *are* myths which are intimately related to rituals, which may be descriptive of them, but there are myths which stand apart. If these others are descriptive of rituals at all, they are, as Durkheim (followed by Radcliffe-Brown and others) suggested, descriptions of rituals of the social organization. That is, they are symbolic representations of the dominant configurations of the particular culture. Myths, then, may express not only the latent content of rituals but of other culturally organized behaviors. Malinowski is surely in error when he writes "... myth ... is not symbolic. ..." Durkheim and Mauss have pointed out how various nonliterate groups (notably the Zuni and certain tribes of southeastern Australia) embrace nature within the schema of their social organization through myths which classify natural phenomena precisely according to the principles that prevail in the social organization.

Boas, with his usual caution, is skeptical of all attempts to find a systematic interpretation of mythology. But, while we can agree with him when he writes "... mythological narratives and mythological concepts should not be equalized; for social, psychological, and historical conditions affect both in different ways," the need for scrupulous inquiry into historical and other determinants must not be perverted to justify a repudiation of all attempts to deal with the symbolic processes of the all-important covert culture. At all events, the factual record is perfectly straightforward in one respect: neither myth nor ritual can be postulated as "primary."

This is the important point in our discussion at this juncture, and it is unfortunate that Hooke and his associates in their otherwise very illuminating contributions to the study of the relations between myth and ritual in the Near East have emphasized only one aspect of the system of interdependences which Malinowski and Radcliffe-Brown have shown to exist. When Hooke points out that myths are constantly used to justify rituals this observation is quite congruent with the observed facts in many cultures. Indeed all of these data may be used toward a still wider induction: man, as a symbol-using animal, appears to feel the need not only to act but almost equally to give verbal or other symbolic "reasons" for his acts. Hooke rightly speaks of "the vital significance of the myth as something that works," but when he continues "and that dies apart from its ritual" he seems to imply that myths cannot exist apart from rituals and this, as has been shown, is contrary to documented cases. No, the central theorem has been expressed much more adequately by Radcliffe-Brown: "In the case of both ritual and myth the sentiments expressed are those that are essential to the existence of the society." This theorem can be regarded as having been well established in a general way, but we still lack detailed observations on change in myths as correlated with changes in ritual and changes in a culture generally. Navaho material gives certain hints that when a culture as a whole changes rapidly its myths are also substantially and quickly altered.

In sum, the facts do not permit any universal generalizations as to ritual being the "cause" of myth or vice versa. Their relationship is rather that of intricate mutual interdependence, differently structured in different cultures and probably at different times in the same culture. As Benedict has pointed out, there is great variation in the extent to which mythology conditions the religious complex—"the small role of myth in Africa and its much greater importance in religion in parts of North America." Both myth and ritual satisfy the needs of a society and the relative place of one or the other will depend upon the particular needs (conscious and unconscious) of the individuals in a particular society at a particular time. This principle covers the observed data, which show that rituals are borrowed without their myths, and myths without any accompanying ritual. A ritual may be reinforced by a myth (or vice versa) in the donor culture, but satisfy the carriers of the recipient culture simply as a form of activity (or be rationalized by a quite different myth which better meets their emotional needs). In short, the only uniformity which can be posited is that there is a strong tendency for some sort of interrelationship between myth and ceremony and that this is dependent upon what appears, so far as present information goes, to be an invariant function of both myth and ritual: the gratification (most often in the negative form of anxiety reduction) of a large proportion of the individuals in a society.

If Malinowski and Radcliffe-Brown (and their followers) turned the searchlight of their interpretations as illuminatingly upon specific human animals and their impulses as upon cultural and social abstractions, it might be possible to take their work as providing a fairly complete and adequate general theory of myth and ritual. With Malinowski's notion of myth as "an active force" which is intimately related to almost every other aspect of a culture we can only agree. When he writes: "Myth is a constant by-product of living faith which is in need of miracles; of sociological status, which demands precedent; of moral rule which requires sanction," we can only applaud. To the French sociologists, to Radcliffe-Brown, and to Warner we are indebted for the clear formulation of the symbolic principle. Those realms of behavior and of experience which man finds beyond rational and technological control he feels are capable of manipulation through symbols. Both myth and ritual are symbolical procedures and are most closely tied together by this, as well as by other, facts. The myth is a system of word symbols, whereas ritual is a system of object and act symbols. Both are symbolic processes for dealing with the same type of situation in the same affective mode.

But the French sociologists, Radcliffe-Brown, and—to a lesser extent—Malinowski are so interested in formulating the relations between conceptual elements that they tend to lose sight of the concrete human organisms. The "functionalists" do usually start with a description of some particular ritualistic behaviors. Not only, however, do the historical origins of this particular behavioral complex fail to interest them. Equally, the motivations and rewards which persons feel are lost sight of in the preoccupation with the contributions which the rituals make to the social system. Thus a sense of the specific detail is lost and we are soon talking about myth in general and ritual in general. From the "functionalist" point of view specific details are about as arbitrary as the phonemes of a language are with respect to "the content" of what is communicated by speech. Hence, as Dollard says, "What one sees from the cultural angle is a drama of life much like a puppet show in which 'culture' is pulling the strings from behind the scenes." The realization that we are really dealing with "animals struggling in real dilemmas" is lacking.

From this angle, some recent psychoanalytic interpretations of myth and ritual seem preferable. We may regard as unconvincing Roheim's attempts to treat myths as historical documents which link human phylogenetic and ontogenetic development, as we may justly feel that many psychoanalytic discussions of the latent content of mythology are extravagant and undisciplined. Casey's summary of the psychoanalytic view of religion, ". . . ritual is a sublimated compulsion; dogma and myth are sublimated obsessions," may well strike us as an oversimplified, overneat generalization, but at least our attention is drawn to the connection between cultural forms and impulse-motivated organisms. And Kardiner's relatively sober and controlled treatment does "point at individuals, at bodies, and at a rich and turbulent biological life"—even though that life is admittedly conditioned by social heredity: social organization, culturally defined symbolic systems, and the like.

In a later section of this paper, we shall return to the problem of how myths and rituals reinforce the behavior of individuals. But first let us test the generalities which have been propounded thus far by concrete data from single culture, the Navaho.

III

The Navaho certainly have sacred tales which, as yet at all events, are not used to justify associated rituals. A striking case, and one where the tale has a clear function as expressing a sentiment "essential to the existence of the society," is known from different parts of the Navaho country. The tales differ in detail but all have these structural elements in common: one of "the Holy People" visits one or more Navahos to warn them of an impending catastrophe (a flood or the like) which will destroy the whites—but believing Navahos will be saved if they retire to the top of a mountain or some other sanctuary. It is surely not without meaning that these tales became current at about the time that the Navahos were first feeling intensive and sustained pressure (they were not just prisoners of war as in the Fort Sumner epoch) from the agents of our culture. Father Berard Haile has recently published evidence that Navaho ceremonials may originate in dreams or visions rather than being invariably *post hoc* justifications for existent ritual practices. A practitioner called "son of the late Black Goat" instituted a new ceremonial "which he had learned in a dream while sleeping in a cave." Various informants assured Father Berard that chantway legends originated in the "visions" of individuals. We have, then, Navaho data for (*a*) the existence of myths without associated rituals, and (*b*) the origin of both legends and rituals in dreams or visions.

It is true that all ceremonial practice among the Navaho is, in cultural theory, justified by an accompanying myth. One may say with Dr. Parsons on the Pueblos: "Whatever the original relationship between myth and ceremony, once made, the myth supports the ceremony or ceremonial office and may suggest ritual increments." One must in the same breath, however, call attention to the fact that myth also supports accepted ways of secular behavior. As Dr. Hill has pointed out, "Women are required to sit with their legs under them and to one side, men with their legs crossed in front of them, because it is said that in the beginning Changing Woman and the Monster Slayer sat in these positions." Let this one example suffice for the many which could easily be given. The general point is that in both sacred and secular spheres myths give some fixity to the ideal patterns of cultures where this is not attained by the printed word. The existence of rituals has a similar effect. Although I cannot agree with Wissler that "the primary function" of rituals is "to perpetuate exact knowledge and to secure precision in their application," there can be no doubt that both myths and rituals are important agencies in the transmission of a culture and that they act as brakes upon the speed of culture change.

Returning to the connections between myth and rite among the Navaho, one cannot do better than begin by quoting some sentences from Washington Matthews: "In some cases a Navajo rite has only one myth pertaining to it. In other cases it has many myths. The relation of the myth to the ceremony is variable. Sometimes it explains nearly everything in the ceremony and gives an account of all the important acts from beginning to end, in the order in which they occur; at other times it describes the work in a less systematic manner. . . . Some of the myths seem to tell only of the way in which rites, already established with other tribes, were introduced among the Navajos. . . . The rite-myth never explains all of the symbolism of the rite, although it may account for all the important acts. A primitive and underlying symbolism which probably existed previous to the establishment of the rite, remains unexplained by the myth, as though its existence were taken as a matter of course, and required no explanation."

To these observations one may add the fact that knowledge of the myth is in no way prerequisite to the carrying out of a chant. Knowledge does give the singer or curer prestige and ability to expect higher fees, and disparaging remarks are often heard to the effect "Oh, he doesn't know the story," or "He doesn't know the story very well yet." And yet treatment by a practitioner ignorant of the myth is regarded as efficacious. Navahos are often a little cynical about the variation in the myths. If someone observes that one singer did not carry out a procedure exactly as did another (of perhaps greater repute) it will often be said "Well, he says *his* story is different." Different forms of a rite-myth tend to prevail in different areas of the Navaho country and in different localities. Here the significance of the "personality" of various singers may sometimes be detected in the rise of variations. The transvestite "Left-handed" who died a few years ago enjoyed a tremendous reputation as a singer. There is some evidence that he restructuralized a number of myths as he told them to his apprentices in a way which tended to make the hermaphrodite *be ˀgočidí* a kind of supreme Navaho deity—a position which he perhaps never held in the general tradition up to that point. I have heard other Navaho singers say that sand paintings and other ceremonial acts and procedures were slightly revised to accord with this tenet. If this be true, we have here another clear instance of myth-before-ritual.

Instances of the reverse sort are also well documented. From a number of informants accounts have been independently obtained of the creation (less than a hundred years ago) of a new rite: Enemy Monster Blessing Way. All the information agreed that the ritual procedures had been devised by one man who collated parts of two previously existent ceremonials and added a few bits from his own fancy. And three informants independently volunteered the observation "He didn't have any story. But after a while he and his son and another fellow made one up." This is corroborated by the fact that none of Father Berard's numerous versions of the Blessing Way myth mentions an Enemy Monster form.

Besides these notes on the relations between myth and rite I should like to record my impression of another function of myth—one which ranges from simple entertainment to "intellectual edification." Myth among the Navaho not only acts as a justification, a rationale for ritual behavior and as a moral reinforcement for other customary behaviors. It also plays a role not dissimilar to that of literature (especially sacred literature) in many literate cultures. Navahos have a keen expectation of the long recitals of myths (or portions of them) around the fire on winter nights.[1] Myths have all the charm of the familiar. Their very familiarity increases their efficacy, for, in a certain broad and loose sense, the function of both myths and rituals is "the discharge of the emotion of individuals in socially accepted channels." And Hocart acutely observes: "Emotion is assisted by the repetition of words that have acquired a strong emotional coloring, and this coloring again is intensified by repetition." Myths are expective, repetitive dramatizations—their role is similar to that of books in cultures which have few books. They have the (to us) scarcely understandable meaningfulness which the tragedies had for the Greek populace. As Matthew Arnold said of these, "their significance appeared inexhaustible."

IV

The inadequacy of any simplistic statement of the relationship between myth and ritual has been established. It has likewise been maintained that the most adequate generalization will not be cast in terms of the primacy of one or the other of these cultural forms but rather in terms of the general tendency for the two to be interdependent. This generalization has been arrived at through induction from abstractions at the cultural level. That is, as we have sampled the evidence from various cultures we have found cases where myths have justified rituals and have appeared to be "after the fact" of ritual; we have also seen cases where new myths have given rise to new rituals. In other words, the primary conclusion which may be drawn from the data is that myths and rituals tend to be very intimately associated and to influence each other. What is the explanation of the observed connection?

The explanation is to be found in the circumstance that myth and ritual satisfy a group of identical or closely related needs of individuals. Thus far we have alluded only occasionally and often obliquely to myths and rituals as cultural forms defining individual behaviors which are adaptive or adjustive responses. We have seen how myths and rituals are adaptive from the point of view of the society in that they promote social solidarity, enhance the integration of the society by providing a formalized statement of its ultimate value-attitudes, and afford a means for the transmission of much of the culture with little loss of content—thus protecting cultural continuity and stabilizing the society. But how are myth and ritual rewarding enough in the daily lives of individuals so that individuals are instigated to preserve them, so that myth and ritual continue to prevail at the expense of more rational responses?

A systematic examination of this question, mainly again in terms of Navaho material, will help us to understand the prevailing interdependence of myth and ritual which has been documented. This sketch of a general theory of myth and ritual as providing a cultural storehouse of adjustive responses for individuals is to be regarded as tentative from the writer's point of view. I do not claim that the theory is proven—even in the context of Navaho culture. I do suggest that it provides a series of working hypotheses which can be tested by specifically pointed field procedures.

We can profitably begin by referring to the function of myth as fulfilling the expectancy of the familiar. Both myth and ritual here provide cultural solutions to problems which all human beings face. Burke has remarked, "Human beings build their cultures, nervously loquacious, upon the edge of an abyss." In the face of want and death and destruction all humans have a fundamental insecurity. To some extent, all culture is a gigantic effort to mask this, to give the future the simulacrum of safety by making activity repetitive, expective—"to make the future predictable by making it conform to the past." From one angle our own scientific mythology is clearly related to that motivation, as is the obsessive, the compulsive tendency which lurks in all organized thought.

When questioned as to why a particular ceremonial activity is carried out in a particular way, Navaho singers will most often say "because the *diyin diné*—the Holy People—did it that way in the first place." The *ultima ratio* of nonliterates strongly tends to be "that is what our fathers said it was." An Eskimo said to Rasmussen: "We Eskimos do not concern ourselves with solving all riddles. We repeat the old stories in the way they were told to us and with the words we ourselves remember." The Eskimo saying "we keep the old rules in order that we may live untroubled" is well known.

. . .

[1] Why may the myths be recited only in winter? In Navaho feeling today this prohibition is linked in a wider configuration of forbidden activities. There is also, as usual, an historical and distributional problem, for this same prohibition is apparently widely distributed in North America. For example, it is found among the Berens River Salteaux and among the Iroquois. But I wonder if in a certain "deeper" sense this prohibition is not founded upon the circumstance that only winter affords the leisure for telling myths, that telling them in summer would be unfitting because it would interfere with work activities?

Goldstein, a neurologist, recognizes a neurological basis for the persistence of such habit systems: "The organism tends to function in the accustomed manner, as long as an at least moderately effective performance can be achieved in this way."

Nevertheless, certain objections to the position as thus far developed must be anticipated and met. It must be allowed at once that the proposition "man dreads both spontaneity and change" must be qualified. More precisely put, we may say "most men, most of the time, dread both spontaneity and change in most of their activities." This formulation allows for the observed fact that most of us *occasionally* get irked with the routines of our lives or that there are certain sectors of our behavior where we fairly consistently show spontaneity. But a careful examination of the totality of behavior of any individual who is not confined in an institution or who has not withdrawn almost completely from participation in the society will show that the larger proportion of the behavior of even the greatest iconoclasts is habitual. This must be so, for by very definition a socialized organism is an organism which behaves mainly in a predictable manner. . . .

Existence in an organized society would be unthinkable unless most people, most of the time, behaved in an expectable manner. Rituals constitute "tender spots" for all human beings, people can count upon the repetitive nature of the phenomena. For example, in Zuni society (where rituals are highly calendrical) a man whose wife has left him or whose crops have been ruined by a torrential downpour can yet look forward to the Shalako ceremonial as something which is fixed and immutable. Similarly, the personal sorrow of the devout Christian is in some measure mitigated by anticipation of the great feasts of Christmas and Easter. Perhaps the even turn of the week with its Sunday services and mid-week prayer meetings gave a dependable regularity which the Christian clung to even more in disaster and sorrow. For some individuals daily prayer and the confessional gave the needed sense of security. Myths, likewise, give men "something to hold to." The Christian can better face the seemingly capricious reverses of his plans when he hears the joyous words "lift up your hearts." Rituals and myths supply, then, fixed points in a world of bewildering change and disappointment.

If almost all behavior has something of the habitual about it, how is it that myths and rituals tend to represent the maximum of fixity? Because they deal with those sectors of experience which do not seem amenable to rational control and hence where human beings can least tolerate insecurity. That very insistence upon the minutiae of ritual performance, upon preserving the myth to the very letter, which is characteristic of religious behavior must be regarded as a "reaction formation" (in the Freudian sense) which compensates for the actual intransigence of those events which religion tries to control.

To anticipate another objection: do these "sanctified habit systems" show such extraordinary persistence simply because they are repeated so often and so scrupulously? Do myths and rituals constitute repetitive behavior par excellence not merely as reaction formations but because the habits are practiced so insistently? Perhaps myths and rituals perdure in accord with Allport's "principle of functional autonomy"—as interpreted by some writers? No, performances must be rewarded in the day-to-day lives of participating individuals. Sheer repetition in and of itself has never assured the persistence of any habit. If this were not so, no myths and rituals would ever have become extinct except when a whole society died out. It is necessary for us to recognize the somewhat special conditions of drive and of reward which apply to myths and rituals.

It is easy to understand why organisms eat. It is easy to understand why a defenseless man will run to escape a charging tiger. The physiological bases of the activities represented by myths and rituals are less obvious. A recent statement by a stimulus-response psychologist gives us the clue: "The position here taken is that human beings (and also other living organisms to varying degrees) can be motivated either by organic pressures (needs) that are currently felt or by the mere anticipation of such pressures, and that those habits tend to be acquired and perpetuated (reinforced) which effect a reduction in either of these two types of motivation." That is, myths and rituals are reinforced because they reduce the anticipation of disaster. No living person has died—but he has seen others die. The terrible things which we have seen happen to others may not yet have plagued us, but our experience teaches us that these are at least potential threats to our own health or happiness.

If a Navaho gets a bad case of snow blindness and recovers after being sung over, his disposition to go to a singer in the event of a recurrence will be strongly reinforced. And, by the principle of generalization, he is likely to go even if the ailment is quite different.

Likewise, the reinforcement will be reciprocal—the singer's confidence in his powers will also be reinforced. Finally there will be some reinforcement for spectators and for all who hear of the recovery. That the ritual treatment rather than more rational preventatives or cures tends to be followed on future occasions can be understood in terms of the principle of the gradient of reinforcement. Delayed rewards are less effective than immediate rewards. In terms of the conceptual picture of experience with which the surrogates of his culture have furnished him, the patient *expects* to be relieved. Therefore, the very onset of the chant produces some lessening of emotional tension—in technical terms, some reduction of anxiety. If the Navaho is treated by a white physician, the "cure" is more gradual and is dependent upon the purely physicochemical effects of the treatment. If the native wears snow goggles or practices some other form of prevention recommended by a white, the connection between the behavior and the reward (no soreness of the eyes) is so diffuse and so separated in time that reinforcement is relatively weak. Even in those cases where no improvement (other than "psychological") is effected, the realization or at any rate the final acceptance that no help was obtained comes so much later than the immediate sense of benefit that the extinction effects are relatively slight.

Navaho myths and rituals provide a cultural storehouse of adjustive[2] responses for individuals. Nor are these limited to the more obvious functions of providing individuals with the possibility of enhancing personal prestige through display of memory, histrionic ability, etc. Of the ten "mechanisms of defense" which Anna Freud suggests that the ego has available, their myths and rituals afford the Navaho with institutionalized means of employing at least four. Reaction formation has already been discussed. Myths supply abundant materials for introjection and likewise (in the form of witchcraft myths) suggest an easy and culturally acceptable method of projection of hostile impulses. Finally, rituals provide ways of sublimation of aggression and other socially disapproved tendencies, in part, simply through giving people something to *do*.

All of these "mechanisms of ego defense" will come into context only if we answer the question, "adjustive with respect to what?" The existence of motivation, of "anxiety," in Navaho individuals must be accounted for by a number of different factors. In the first place—as in every society—there are those components of "anxiety," those "threats" which may be understood in terms of the "reality principle" of psychoanalysis: life *is* hard—an unseasonable temperature, a vagary of the rainfall does bring hunger or actual starvation; people *are* organically ill. In the second place, there are various forms of "neurotic" anxiety. In our own society it is probably sexual, although this may be true only of those segments of our society who are able to purchase economic and physical security. In most Plains Indians sexual anxiety, so far as we can tell from the available documents, was insignificant. There the basic anxiety was for life itself and for a certain quality of that life (which I cannot attempt to characterize in a few words).

Among the Navaho the "type anxiety" is certainly that for health. Almost all Navaho ceremonials (essentially every ceremonial still carried out today) are curing ceremonials. And this apparently has a realistic basis. A prominent officer of the Indian Medical Service stated that it was his impression that morbidity among the Navaho is about three times that found in average white communities. In a period of four months' field work among the Navaho, Drs. A. and D. Leighton found in their running field notes a total of 707 Navaho references to "threats" which they classified under six headings. Of these, sixty percent referred to bodily welfare, and are broken down by the Leightons as follows:

> *Disease is responsible for sixty-seven percent, accidents for seventeen percent, and the rest are attributed to wars and fights. Of the diseases described, eighty-one percent were evidently organic, like smallpox, broken legs, colds, and sore throats; sixteen percent left us in doubt as to whether they were organic or functional; and three percent were apparently functional, with symptoms suggesting depression, hysteria, etc. Of all the diseases, forty percent were incapacitating, forty-three percent were not, and seventeen percent were not sufficiently specified in our notes to judge. From these figures it can easily be seen that lack of health is a very important concern of these Navahos, and that almost half of the instances of disease that they mentioned interfered with life activities* ("Some Types of Uneasiness," p. 203).

[2] It is not possible to say "adaptive" here because there are not infrequent occasions on which ceremonial treatment aggravates the condition or actually brings about death (which would probably not have supervened under a more rational treatment or even if the patient had simply been allowed to rest). From the point of view of the society, however, the rituals are with little doubt adaptive. Careful samples in two areas and more impressionistic data from the Navaho country generally indicate that the frequency of ceremonials has very materially increased concomitantly with the increase of white pressure in recent years. It is tempting to regard this as an adaptive response similar to that of the Ghost Dance and Peyote Cult on the part of other American Indian tribes.

While I am inclined to believe that the character of this sample was somewhat influenced by the fact that the Leightons were white physicians—to whom organic illnesses, primarily, would be reported—there is no doubt that these data confirm the reality of the health "threat." In terms of clothing and shelter which are inadequate (from our point of view at least), of hygiene and diet which similarly fail to conform to our health standards, it is not altogether surprising that the Navaho need to be preoccupied with their health. It is unequivocally true in my experience that a greater proportion of my Navaho friends are found ill when I call upon them than of my white friends.

The Navaho and Pueblo Indians live in essentially the same physical environment. Pueblo rituals are concerned predominantly with rain and with fertility. This contrast to the Navaho preoccupation with disease cannot (in the absence of fuller supporting facts) be laid to a lesser frequency of illness among the Pueblos, for it seems well documented that the Pueblos, living in congested towns, have been far more ravaged by endemic diseases than the Navaho. The explanation is probably to be sought in terms of the differing historical experience of the two peoples and in terms of the contrasting economic and social organizations. If one is living in relative isolation and if one is largely dependent (as were the Navaho at no terribly distant date) upon one's ability to move about hunting and collecting, ill-health presents a danger much more crucial than to the Indian who lives in a town which has a reserve supply of corn and a more specialized social organization.

That Navaho myths and rituals are focused upon health and upon curing has, then, a firm basis in the reality of the external world. But there is also a great deal of uneasiness arising from interpersonal relationships, and this undoubtedly influences the way the Navaho react to their illnesses. Then, too, one type of anxiousness always tends to modify others. Indeed, in view of what the psychoanalysts have taught us about "accidents" and of what we are learning from psychosomatic medicine about the psychogenic origin of many "organic" diseases we cannot regard the sources of disease among the Navaho as a closed question. Some disorders (especially perhaps those associated with acute anxieties) may be examples of what Caner has called "superstitious self-protection."

Where people live under constant threat from the physical environment, where small groups are geographically isolated and "emotional inbreeding" within the extended family group is at a maximum, interpersonal tensions and hostilities are inevitably intense. The prevalence of ill-health which throws additional burdens on the well and strong is in itself an additional socially disruptive force. But if the overt expression of aggressive impulses proceeds very far the whole system of "economic" co-operation breaks down and then sheer physical survival is more than precarious. Here myths and rituals constitute a series of highly adaptive responses from the point of view of the society. Recital of or reference to the myths reaffirms the solidarity of the Navaho sentiment system. In the words of a Navaho informant: "Knowing a good story will protect your home and children and property. A myth is just like a big stone foundation—it lasts a long time." Performance of rituals likewise heightens awareness of the common system of sentiments. The ceremonials also bring individuals together in a situation where quarreling is forbidden. Preparation for and carrying out of a chant demands intricately ramified co-operation, economic and otherwise, and doubtless thus reinforces the sense of mutual dependency.

Myths and rituals equally facilitate the adjustment of the individual to his society. Primarily, perhaps, they provide a means of sublimation of his antisocial tendencies. It is surely not without meaning that essentially all known chant myths take the family and some trouble within it as a point of departure. While as a total explanation the following would be oversimple, it seems fair to say that the gist of this may be interpreted as follows: the chant myth supplies a catharsis for the traumata incident upon the socialization of the Navaho child. That brother and sister are the principal *dramatis personae* fits neatly with the central conflicts of the Navaho socialization process. This is a subject which I hope to treat in detail in a later paper.

Overt quarrels between family members are by no means infrequent, and, especially when drinking has been going on, physical blows are often exchanged. Abundant data indicate that Navahos have a sense of shame which is fairly persistent and that this is closely connected with the socially disapproved hostile impulses which they have experienced toward relatives. It is also clear that their mistrust of others (including those in their own extended family group) is in part based upon a fear of retaliation (and this fear of retaliation is soundly based upon experience in actual life as well, as, possibly, upon "unconscious guilt"). Certain passages in the myths indicate that the Navaho have a somewhat conscious realization that the ceremonials act as a cure, not only for physical illness, but also for antisocial tendencies. The following extract from the myth of the Mountain Top Way Chant will serve as an example: "The ceremony cured Dsiliyi Neyani of all his strange feelings and notions. The lodge of his people no longer smelled unpleasant to him."

Thus "the working gods" of the Navaho are their sanctified repetitive ways of behavior. If these are offended by violation of the culture's system of scruples, the ceremonials exist as institutionalized means of restoring the individual to full rapport with the universe: nature and his own society. Indeed "restore" is the best English translation of the Navaho word which the Navaho constantly use to express what the ceremonial does for the "patient." The associated myths reinforce the patient's belief that the ceremonial will both truly cure him of his illness and also "change" him so that he will be a better man in his relations with his family and his neighbors. An English-speaking Navaho who had just returned from jail where he had been put for beating his wife and molesting his stepdaughter said to me: "I am sure going to behave from now on. I am going to be changed—just like somebody who has been sung over."

Since a certain minimum of social efficiency is by derivation a biological necessity for the Navaho, not all of the hostility and uneasiness engendered by the rigors of the physical environment, geographical isolation, and the burdens imposed by illness is expressed or even gets into consciousness. There is a great deal of repression and this leads, on the one hand, to projection phenomena (especially in the form of fantasies that others are practicing witchcraft against one) and, on the other hand, the strong feelings of shame at the conscious level are matched by powerful feelings of guilt at the unconscious level. Because a person feels guilty by reason of his unconscious hostilities towards members of his family (and friends and neighbors generally), some individuals develop chronic anxieties. Such persons feel continually uncomfortable. They say they "feel sick all over" without specifying organic ailments other than very vaguely. They feel so "ill" that they must have ceremonials to cure them. The diagnostician and other practitioners, taking myths as their authority, will refer the cause of the illness to the patient's having seen animals struck by lightning, to a past failure to observe ritual requirements, or to some similar violation of a cultural scruple. But isn't this perhaps basically a substitution of symbols acceptable to consciousness, a displacement of guilt feelings?

It is my observation that Navahos other than those who exhibit chronic or acute anxieties tend characteristically to show a high level of anxiety. It would be a mistake, however, to attribute all of this anxiety to intrafamilial tensions, although it is my impression that this is the outstanding pressure. Secondary drives resultant upon culture change and upon white pressure are also of undoubted importance. And it is likewise true, as Mr. Homans has pointed out, that the existence of these ritual injunctions and prohibitions (and of the concomitant myths and other beliefs) gives rise to still another variety of anxiety. In other words, the conceptual picture of the world which Navaho culture sets forth makes for a high threshold of anxiety in that it defines all manner of situations as fraught with peril, and individuals are instigated to anticipate danger on every hand.

But the culture, of course, prescribes not only the supernatural dangers but also the supernatural means of meeting these dangers or of alleviating their effects. Myths and rituals jointly provide systematic protection against supernatural dangers, the threats of ill-health and of the physical environment, antisocial tensions, and the pressures of a more powerful society. In the absence of a codified law and of an authoritarian "chief" or other father substitute, it is only through the myth-ritual system that Navahos can make a socially supported, unified response to all of these disintegrating threats. The all-pervasive configurations of words symbols (myths) and of act symbols (rituals) preserve the cohesion of the society and sustain the individual, protecting him from intolerable conflict. As Hoagland has remarked:

> *Religion appears to me to be a culmination of this basic tendency of organisms to react in a configurational way to situations. We must resolve conflicts and disturbing puzzles by closing some sort of a configuration, and the religious urge appears to be a primitive tendency, possessing biological survival value, to unify our environment so that we can cope with it.*

V

The Navaho are only one case. The specific adaptive and adjustive responses performed by myth and ritual will be differently phrased in different societies according to the historical experience of these societies (including the specific opportunities they have had for borrowing from other cultures), in accord with prevalent configurations of other aspects of the culture, and with reference to pressures exerted by other societies and by the physical and biological environment. But the general nature of the adaptive and adjustive responses performed by myth and ritual appears very much the same in all human groups. Hence, although the relative importance of myth and of ritual does vary greatly, the two tend universally to be associated.

For myth and ritual have a common psychological basis. Ritual is an obsessive repetitive activity—often a symbolic dramatization of the fundamental "needs" of the society, whether "economic," "biological," "social," or "sexual." Mythology is the rationalization of these same needs, whether they are all expressed in overt ceremonial or not. Someone has said "every culture has a type conflict and a type solution." Ceremonials tend to portray a symbolic resolvement of the conflicts which external environment, historical experience, and selective distribution of personality types have caused to be characteristic in the society. Because different conflict situations characterize different societies, the "needs" which are typical in one society may be the "needs" of only deviant individuals in another society. And the institutionalized gratifications (of which rituals and myths are prominent examples) of culturally recognized needs vary greatly from society to society. "Culturally recognized needs" is, of course, an analytical abstraction. Concretely, "needs" arise and exist only in specific individuals. This we must never forget, but it is equally important that myths and rituals, though surviving as functioning aspects of a coherent culture only so long as they meet the "needs" of a number of concrete individuals, are, in one sense, "supra-individual." They are usually composite creations; they normally embody the accretions of many generations, the modifications (through borrowing from other cultures or by intra-cultural changes) which the varying needs of the group as a whole and of innovating individuals in the group have imposed. In short, both myths and rituals are cultural products, part of the social heredity of a society.

Clifford Geertz

RELIGION AS A CULTURAL SYSTEM

While affirming the functional importance of religion in human society, Clifford Geertz, in this splendidly written exposition on religion, goes beyond reductionist functional interpretations to elucidate the power of religious symbols as culturally conceived conceptualizations of the world and man's place in it. His fundamental assumption is that any religion, like the wider cultural system of which it is a part, affirms notions of what reality is all about, what it "means," and how one is to act within it. But chaos—the lack of interpretability—assails purely commonsense notions of the really real at the limits of man's analytical, emotional, and moral capacities. Religion denies that these problems of incomprehensibility, suffering, and evil are fundamental characteristics of the world through the culturally constituted concepts embodied in sacred symbols.

For Geertz, a symbol means any object, act, event, quality, or relation that serves as a vehicle for a conception, the conception being the symbol's meaning. Cultural patterns are of course symbolic systems, religious symbols being those that induce and define dispositions in man. Geertz's aim is to demonstrate that sacred symbols deal with

Reprinted in greatly abridged form from Michael Banton (ed.), *Anthropological Approaches to the Study of Religion* ("Association of Social Anthropologists Monographs," No. 3 [London: Tavistock Publications, 1965]), by permission of the Association of Social Anthropologists, the publisher, and the author. This monograph is distributed in the United States by Barnes & Noble Books, New York.

bafflement, pain, and moral paradox by synthesizing a people's ethos and their world view. The ethos of the group is rendered intellectually more reasonable by religious belief and practice. If man's denial of chaos comes to be believed in it is because of the special perspective of religion, which goes outside the realities of daily life to wider realities that complete them in a context of faith. Ritual is a powerful means for providing the conviction that religious concepts are truthful and that religious directives are sound, and the latter effective because they induce moods and motivations. They help make the group's ethos intellectually reasonable.

This article, which must be read in its unabridged form for substantiation of many of the author's premises, is at once both an interpretation of the role of symbolism and an appreciation of the importance of religion in transcending the chaos that threatens man.

The general analytical approach taken here is elaborated in other essays by Geertz collected in his book, *The Interpretation of Cultures* (1973).

Any attempt to speak without speaking any particular language is not more hopeless than the attempt to have a religion that shall be no religion in particular. . . . Thus every living and healthy religion has a marked idiosyncrasy; its power consists in its special and surprising message and in the bias which that revelation gives to life. The vistas it opens and the mysteries it propounds are another world to live in; and another world to live in—whether we expect ever to pass wholly over into it or not—is what we mean by having a religion.

—Santayana: *Reason in Religion* (1906)

As we are to deal with meaning, let us begin with a paradigm: *viz.*, that sacred symbols function to synthesize a people's ethos—the tone, character and quality of their life, its moral and aesthetic style and mood—and their world-view—the picture they have of the way things in sheer actuality are, their most comprehensive ideas of order. In religious belief and practice a group's ethos is rendered intellectually reasonable by being shown to represent a way of life ideally adapted to the actual state of affairs the world-view describes, while the world-view is rendered emotionally convincing by being presented as an image of an actual state of affairs peculiarly well-arranged to accommodate such a way of life. This confrontation and mutual confirmation has two fundamental effects. On the one hand, it objectivises moral and aesthetic preferences by depicting them as the imposed conditions of life implicit in a world with a particular structure, as mere common sense given the unalterable shape of reality. On the other, it supports these received beliefs about the world's body by invoking deeply felt moral and aesthetic sentiments as experiential evidence for their truth. Religious symbols formulate a basic congruence between a particular style of life and a specific (if, most often, implicit) metaphysic, and in so doing sustain each with the borrowed authority of the other.

Phrasing aside, this much may perhaps be granted. The notion that religion tunes human actions to an envisaged cosmic order and projects images of cosmic order onto the plane of human experience is hardly novel. But it is hardly investigated either, so that we have very little idea of how, in empirical terms, this particular miracle is accomplished. We just know that it is done, annually, weekly, daily, for some people almost hourly; and we have an enormous ethnographic literature to demonstrate it. But the theoretical framework which would enable us to provide an analytic account of it, an account of the sort we can provide for lineage segmentation, political succession, labor exchange or the socialization of the child, does not exist.

Let us, therefore, reduce our paradigm to a definition, for although it is notorious that definitions establish nothing in themselves they do, if they are carefully enough constructed, provide a useful orientation, or reorientation, of thought, such that an extended unpacking of them can be an effective way of developing and controlling a novel line of inquiry. They have the useful virtue of explicitness: they commit themselves in a way discursive prose, which, in this field especially, is always liable to substitute rhetoric for argument, does not. Without ado, then, a *religion* is: (1) a system of symbols which acts to (2) establish powerful, pervasive and long-lasting moods and motivations in men by (3) formulating conceptions of a general order of existence and (4) clothing these conceptions with such an aura of factuality that (5) the moods and motivations seem uniquely realistic.

1. . . . A SYSTEM OF SYMBOLS WHICH ACTS TO . . .

Such a tremendous weight is being put on the term "symbol" here that our first move must be to decide with some precision what we are going to mean by it. This is no easy task, for, rather like "culture," "symbol" has been used to refer to a great variety of things, often a number of them at the same time. In some hands it is used for anything which signifies something else to someone: dark clouds are the symbolic precursors of an oncoming rain. In others it is used only for explicitly conventional signs of one sort or another: a red flag is a symbol of danger, a white of surrender. In others, it is confined to something which expresses in an oblique and figurative manner that which cannot be stated in a direct and literal one, so that there are symbols in poetry but not in science, and symbolic logic is misnamed. In yet others, however, it is used for any object, act, event, quality or relation which serves as a vehicle for a conception—the conception is the symbol's "meaning"—and that is the approach I shall follow here. The number "6," written, imagined, laid out as a row of stones, or even punched into the program tapes of a computer is a symbol. But so also is the Cross, talked about, visualized, shaped worriedly in air or fondly fingered at the neck, the expanse of painted canvas called "Guernica" or the bit of painted stone called a churinga, the word "reality," or even the morpheme "-ing." They are all symbols, or at least symbolic elements, because they are tangible formulations or notions, abstractions from experience fixed in perceptible forms, concrete embodiments of ideas, attitudes, judgments, longings or beliefs. To undertake the study of cultural activity—activity in which symbolism forms the positive content—is thus not to abandon social analysis for a Platonic cave of shadows, to enter into a mentalistic world of introspective psychology or, worse, speculative philosophy and wander there forever in a haze of "Cognitions," "Affections," "Conations" and other elusive entities. Cultural acts, the construction, apprehension and utilization of symbolic forms, are social events like any other; they are as public as marriage and as observable as agriculture.

They are not, however, exactly the same thing; or, more precisely, the symbolic dimension of social events is, like the psychological, itself theoretically abstractable from those events as empirical totalities. There is still, to paraphrase a remark of Kenneth Burke's, a difference between building a house and drawing up a plan for building a house, and reading a poem about having children by marriage is not quite the same thing as having children by marriage. Even though the building of the house may proceed under the guidance of the plan or—a less likely occurrence–the having of children may be motivated by a reading of the poem, there is something to be said for not confusing our traffic with symbols with our traffic with objects or human beings, for these latter are not in themselves symbols, however often they may function as such. No matter how deeply interfused the cultural, the social and the psychological may be in the everyday life of houses, farms, poems and marriages, it is useful to distinguish them in analysis, and, so doing, to isolate the generic traits of each against the normalized backgrounds of the other two.

So far as culture patterns, i.e., systems or complexes of symbols, are concerned, the generic trait which is of first importance for us here is that they are extrinsic sources of information. By "extrinsic," I mean only that—unlike genes, for example—they lie outside the boundaries of the individual organism as such in that intersubjective world of common understandings into which all human individuals are born, pursue their separate careers, and leave persisting behind them after they die. By "sources of information," I mean only that—like genes—they provide a blueprint or template in terms of which processes external to themselves can be given a definite form. As the order of bases in a strand of DNA forms a coded program, a set of instructions or a recipe, for the synthesization of the structurally complex proteins which shape organic functioning, so culture patterns provide such programs for the institution of the social and psychological processes which shape public behavior. Though the sort of information and the mode of its transmission are vastly different in the two cases, this comparison of gene and symbol is more than a strained analogy of the familiar "social heredity" sort. It is actually a substantial relationship, for it is precisely the fact that genetically programmed processes are so highly generalized in men, as compared with lower animals, that culturally programmed ones are so important, only because human behavior is so loosely determined by intrinsic sources of information that extrinsic sources are so vital. To build a dam a beaver needs only an appropriate site and the proper materials—

his mode of procedure is shaped by his physiology. But man, whose genes are silent on the building trades, needs also a conception of what it is to build a dam, a conception he can get only from some symbolic source—a blueprint, a textbook or a string of speech by someone who already knows how dams are built, or, of course, from manipulating graphic or linguistic elements in such a way as to attain for himself a conception of what dams are and how they are built.

This point is sometimes put in the form of an argument that cultural patterns are "models," that they are sets of symbols whose relations to one another "model" relations among entities, processes or what-have-you in physical, organic, social or psychological systems by "paralleling," "imitating" or "simulating" them. The term "model" has, however, two senses—an "of" sense and a "for" sense—and though these are but aspects of the same basic concept they are very much worth distinguishing for analytic purposes. In the first, what is stressed is the manipulation of symbol structures so as to bring them, more or less closely, into parallel with the preestablished non-symbolic system, as when we grasp how dams work by developing a theory of hydraulics or constructing a flow chart. The theory or chart models physical relationships in such a way—i.e., by expressing their structure in synoptic form—as to render them apprehensible: it is a model *of* "reality." In the second, what is stressed is the manipulation of the non-symbolic systems in terms of the relationships expressed in the symbolic, as when we construct a dam according to the specifications implied in an hydraulic theory or the conclusions drawn from a flow chart. Here, the theory is a model under whose guidance physical relationships are organized: it is a model *for* "reality." For psychological and social systems, and for cultural models that we would not ordinarily refer to as "theories," but rather as "doctrines," "melodies" or "rites," the case is in no way different. Unlike genes, and other non-symbolic information sources, which are only models *for*, not models *of*, culture patterns have an intrinsic double aspect: they give meaning, i.e., objective conceptual form, to social and psychological reality both by shaping themselves to it and by shaping it to themselves.

It is, in fact, this double aspect which sets true symbols off from other sorts of significative forms. Models *for* are found, as the gene example suggests, through the whole order of nature, for wherever there is a communication of pattern such programs are, in simple logic, required. Among animals, imprint learning is perhaps the most striking example, because what such learning involves is the automatic presentation of an appropriate sequence of behavior by a model animal in the presence of a learning animal which serves, equally automatically, to call out and stabilize a certain set of responses genetically built into the learning animal. The communicative dance of two bees, one of which has found nectar and the other of which seeks it, is another, somewhat different, more complexly coded, example. Craik has even suggested that the thin trickle of water which first finds its way down from a mountain spring to the sea and smoothes a little channel for the greater volume of water which follows after it plays a sort of model *for* function. But models *of*—linguistic, graphic, mechanical, natural, etc., processes which function not to provide sources of information in terms of which other processes can be patterned, but to represent those patterned processes as such, to express their structure in an alternative medium—are much rarer and may perhaps be confined, among living animals, to man. The perception of the structural congruence between one set of processes, activities, relations, entities, etc., and another set for which it acts as a program, so that the program can be taken as a representation, or conception—a symbol—of the programmed, is the essence of human thought. The inter-transposability of models *for* and models *of*, of which symbolic formulation makes possible, is the distinctive characteristic of our mentality.

2. . . . TO ESTABLISH POWERFUL, PERVASIVE AND LONG-LASTING MOODS AND MOTIVATIONS IN MEN BY . . .

So far as religious symbols and symbol systems are concerned this inter-transposability is clear. The endurance, courage, independence, perseverance and passionate willfulness with which the Plains Indian practices the vision quest are the same flamboyant virtues by which he attempts to live: while achieving a sense of revelation he stabilizes a sense of direction. The consciousness of defaulted obligation, secreted guilt and, when a confession is obtained, public shame in which [a] Manus' seance rehearses him are the same sentiments that underlie the sort of duty ethic by which his property-conscious society is maintained: the gaining of an absolution involves the forging of a conscience. And the same self-discipline which rewards a Javanese mystic staring fixedly into the flame of a lamp with what he takes to be an intimation of divinity drills him in that rigorous control of emotional expression which is necessary to a man who would follow a quietistic style of life. Whether one sees the conception of a personal guardian spirit, a family tutelary or an immanent God as synoptic formulations of the character of reality or as templates for producing reality with such a character seems largely arbitrary, a matter of which aspect, the model *of* or model *for*, one wants for the moment to bring into focus. The concrete symbols involved—one or another mythological figure materializing in the wilderness, the skull of the deceased household head hanging censoriously in the rafters, or a disembodied "voice in the stillness" soundlessly chanting enigmatic classical poetry—point in either direction. They both express the world's climate and shape it.

They shape it by inducing in the worshipper a certain distinctive set of dispositions which lend a chronic character to the flow of his activity and the quality of his experience. A disposition describes not an activity or an occurrence but a probability of an activity being performed or an occurrence occurring under certain circumstances: "When a cow is said to be a ruminant, or a man is said to be a cigarette smoker, it is not being said that the cow is ruminating now or that the man is smoking a cigarette now. To be a ruminant is to tend to ruminate from time to time, and to be a cigarette-smoker is to be in the habit of smoking cigarettes." Similarly, to be pious is not to be performing something we would call an act of piety, but to be liable to perform such acts. So, too, with the Plains Indian's bravura, the Manus' compunctiousness or the Javanese's quietism which, in their contexts, form the substance of piety. The virtue of this sort of view of what are usually called "mental traits" or, if the Cartesianism is unavowed, "psychological forces" (both unobjectionable enough terms in themselves) is that it gets them out of any dim and inaccessible realm of private sensation into that same well-lit world of observables in which reside the brittleness of glass, the inflammability of paper and, to return to the metaphor, the dampness of England.

So far as religious activities are concerned (and learning a myth by heart is as much a religious activity as detaching one's finger at the knuckle), two somewhat different sorts of disposition are induced by them: moods and motivations.

The major difference between moods and motivations is that where the latter are, so to speak, vectorial qualities, the former are merely scalar. Motives have a directional cast, they describe a certain overall course, gravitate toward certain, usually temporary, consummations. But moods vary only as to intensity: they go nowhere. They spring from certain circumstances but they are responsive to no ends. Like fogs, they just settle and lift; like scents, suffuse and evaporate. When present they are totalistic: if one is sad everything and everybody seems dreary; if one is gay, everything and everybody seems splendid. Thus, though a man can be vain, brave, willful and independent at the same time, he can't very well be playful and listless, or exultant and melancholy at the same time. Further, where motives persist for more or less extended periods of time, moods merely recur with greater or lesser frequency, coming and going for what are often quite unfathomable reasons. But perhaps the most important difference, so far as we are concerned, between moods and motivations is that motivations are "made meaningful" with reference to the ends toward which they are conceived to conduce, while moods are "made meaningful" with reference to the conditions from which they are conceived to spring. We interpret motives in terms of their consummations, but we interpret moods in terms of their sources. We say that a person is industrious because he wishes to succeed, we say that a person is worried because he is conscious of the hanging threat of nuclear holocaust. And this is no less the case when the interpretations invoked are ultimate. Charity becomes Christian charity when it is enclosed in a conception of God's purposes; optimism is Christian optimism when it is grounded in a particular conception of God's nature. The assiduity of the Navaho finds its rationale in a belief that, as "reality" operates mechanically, it is coercible; their chronic fearfulness finds its rationale in a conviction that, however "reality" operates, it is both enormously powerful and terribly dangerous.

3. . . . BY FORMULATING CONCEPTIONS OF A GENERAL ORDER OF EXISTENCE AND . . .

That the symbols or symbol systems which induce and define dispositions we set off as religious and those which place those dispositions in a cosmic framework are the same symbols ought to occasion no surprise. For what else do we mean by saying that a particular mood of awe is religious and not secular except that it springs from entertaining a conception of all-pervading vitality like mana and not from a visit to the Grand Canyon? Or that a particular case of asceticism is an example of a religious motivation except that it is directed toward the achievement of an unconditioned end like nirvana and not a conditioned one like weight-reduction? If sacred symbols did not, at one and the same time, induce dispositions in human beings and formulate, however obliquely, inarticulately or unsystematically, general ideas of order, then the empirical differentia of religious activity or religious experience would not exist. A man can indeed be said to be "religious" about golf, but not merely if he pursues it with passion and plays it on Sundays: he must also see it as symbolic of some transcendent truths. And the pubescent boy gazing soulfully into the eyes of the pubescent girl in a William Steig cartoon and murmuring, "there is something about you, Ethel, which gives me a sort of religious feeling," is, like most adolescents, confused. What any particular religion affirms about the fundamental nature of reality may be obscure, shallow or, all too often, perverse, but it must, if it is not to consist of the mere collection of received practices and conventional sentiments we usually refer to as moralism, affirm something. If one were to essay a minimal definition of religion today it would perhaps not be Tylor's famous "belief in spiritual beings," to which Goody, wearied of theoretical subtleties, has lately urged us to return, but rather what Salvador de Madariaga has called "the relatively modest dogma that God is not mad."

Usually, of course, religions affirm very much more than this: we believe, as James remarked, all that we can and would believe everything if we only could. The thing we seem least able to tolerate is a threat to our powers of conception, a suggestion that our ability to create, grasp and use symbols may fail us, for were this to happen we would be more helpless, as I have already pointed out, than the beavers. The extreme generality, diffuseness and variability of man's innate (i.e., genetically programmed) response capacities means that without the assistance of cultural patterns he would be functionally incomplete, not merely a talented ape who had, like some under-privileged child, unfortunately been prevented from realizing his full potentialities, but a kind of formless monster with neither sense of direction nor power of self-control, a chaos of spasmodic impulses and vague emotions. Man depends upon symbols and symbol systems with a dependence so great as to be decisive for his creatural viability and, as a result, his sensitivity to even the remotest indication that they may prove unable to cope with one or another aspect of experience raises within him the gravest sort of anxiety.

There are at least three points where chaos—a tumult of events which lack not just interpretations but *interpretability*—threatens to break in upon man: at the limits of his analytic capacities, at the limits of his powers of endurance, and at the limits of his moral insight. Bafflement, suffering and a sense of intractable ethical paradox are all, if they become intense enough or are sustained long enough, radical challenges to the proposition that life is comprehensible and that we can, by taking thought, orient ourselves effectively within it—challenges with which any religion, however "primitive," which hopes to persist must attempt somehow to cope.

Of the three issues, it is the first which has been least investigated by modern social anthropologists (though Evans-Pritchard's classic discussion of why granaries fall on some Azande and not on others, is a notable exception). Even to consider people's religious beliefs as attempts to bring anomalous events or experiences—death, dreams, mental fugues, volcanic eruptions or marital infidelity—within the circle of the at least potentially explicable seems to smack of Tyloreanism or worse. But it does appear to be a fact that at least some men—in all probability, most men—are unable to leave unclarified problems of analysis merely unclarified, just to look at the stranger features of the world's landscape in dumb astonishment or bland apathy without trying to develop, however fantastic, inconsistent or simple-minded, some notions as to how such features might be reconciled with the more ordinary deliverances of experience. Any chronic failure of one's explanatory apparatus, the complex of received culture patterns (common sense, science, philosophical speculation, myth) one has for mapping the empirical world, to explain things which cry out for explanation, tends to lead to a deep disquiet—a tendency rather more widespread and a disquiet rather deeper than we have sometimes supposed since the pseudoscience view of religious belief was, quite rightfully, deposed. After all, even that high priest of heroic atheism, Lord Russell, once remarked that although the problem of the existence of God has never bothered him, the ambiguity of certain mathematical axioms had threatened to unhinge his mind. And Einstein's profound dissatisfaction with quantum mechanics was based on a—surely religious—inability to believe that, as he put it, God plays dice with the universe.

But this quest for lucidity and the rush of metaphysical anxiety that occurs when empirical phenomena threaten to remain intransigently opaque is found on much humbler intellectual levels. Certainly, I was struck in my own work, much more than I had at all expected to be by the degree to which my more animistically inclined informants behaved like true Tyloreans. They seemed to be constantly using their beliefs to "explain" phenomena: or, more accurately, to convince themselves that the phenomena were explainable within the accepted scheme of things, for they commonly had only a minimal attachment to the particular soul possession, emotional disequilibrium, taboo infringement or bewitchment hypothesis they advanced and were all too ready to abandon it for some other, in the same genre, which struck them as more plausible given the facts of the case. What they were *not* ready to do was abandon it for no other hypothesis at all; to leave events to themselves.

The second experiential challenge in whose face the meaningfulness of a particular pattern of life threatens to dissolve into a chaos of thingless names and nameless things—the problem of suffering—has been rather more investigated, or at least described, mainly because of the great amount of attention given in works on tribal religion to what are perhaps its two main loci: illness and mourning. Yet for all the fascinated interest in the emotional aura which surrounds these extreme situations, there has been, with a few exceptions such as Lienhardt's recent discussion of Dinka divining, little conceptual advance over the sort of crude confidence type theory set forth by Malinowski: *viz.*, that religion helps one to endure "situations of emotional stress" by "open [ing] up escapes from such situations and such impasses as offer no empirical way out except by ritual and belief into the domain of the supernatural." The inadequacy of this "theology of optimism," as Nadel rather drily called it, is, of course, radical. Over its career religion has probably disturbed men as much as it has cheered them; forced them into a head-on, unblinking confrontation of the fact that they are born to trouble as often as it has enabled them to avoid such a confrontation by projecting them into a sort of infantile fairy-tale world where—Malinowski again—"hope cannot fail nor desire deceive." With the possible exception of Christian Science, there are few if any religious traditions, "great" or "little," in which the proposition that life hurts is not strenuously affirmed and in some it is virtually glorified.

As a religious problem, the problem of suffering is, paradoxically, not how to avoid suffering but how to suffer, how to make of physical pain, personal loss, worldly defeat or the helpless contemplation of others' agony something bearable, supportable—something, as we say, sufferable.

The problem of suffering passes easily into the problem of evil, for if suffering is severe enough it usually, though not always, seems morally undeserved as well, at least to the sufferer. But they are not, however, exactly the same thing—a fact I think Weber, too influenced by the biases of a monotheistic tradition in which, as the various aspects of human experience must be conceived to proceed from a single, voluntaristic source, man's pain reflects directly on God's goodness, did not fully recognize in his generalization of the dilemmas of Christian theodicy Eastward. For where the problem of suffering is concerned with threats to our ability to put our "undisciplined squads of emotion" into some sort of soldierly order, the problem of evil is concerned with threats to our ability to make sound moral judgments. What is involved in the problem of evil is not the adequacy of our symbolic resources to govern our affective life, but the adequacy of those resources to provide a workable set of ethical criteria, normative guides to govern our action. The vexation here is the gap between things as they are and as they ought to be if our conceptions of right and wrong make sense, the gap between what we deem various individuals deserve and what we see that they get—a phenomenon summed up in that profound quatrain:

The rain falls on the just
And on the unjust fella;
But mainly upon the just,
Because the unjust has the just's umbrella.

Or if this seems too flippant an expression of an issue that, in somewhat different form, animates the Book of Job and the Baghavad Gita, the following classical Javanese poem, known, sung, and repeatedly quoted in Java by virtually everyone over the age of six, puts the point—the discrepancy between moral prescriptions and material rewards, the seeming inconsistency of "is" and "ought"—rather more elegantly:

We have lived to see a time without order
In which everyone is confused in his mind.
One cannot bear to join in the madness,
But if he does not do so
He will not share in the spoils,
And will starve as a result.
Yes, God; wrong is wrong:
Happy are those who forget,
Happier yet those who remember and have deep insight.

The problem of evil, or perhaps one should say the problem *about* evil, is in essence the same sort of problem of or about bafflement and the problem of or about suffering. The strange opacity of certain empirical events, the dumb senselessness of intense or inexorable pain, and the enigmatic unaccountability of gross iniquity all raise the uncomfortable suspicion that perhaps the world, and hence man's life in the world, has no genuine order at all—no empirical regularity, no emotional form, no moral coherence. And the religious response to this suspicion is in each case the same: the formulation, by means of symbols, of an image of such a genuine order of the world which will account for, and even celebrate, the perceived ambiguities, puzzles and paradoxes in human experience. The effort is not to deny the undeniable—that there are unexplained events, that life hurts or that rain falls upon the just—but to deny that there are inexplicable events, that life is unendurable and that justice is a mirage. The principles which constitute the moral order may indeed often elude men in the same way as fully satisfactory explanations of anomalous events or effective forms for the expression of feeling often elude them. What is important, to a religious man at least, is that this elusiveness be accounted for, that it be not the result of the fact that there are no such principles, explanations or forms, that life is absurd and the attempt to make moral, intellectual or emotional sense out of experience is bootless.

The Problem of Meaning in each of its intergrading aspects (how these aspects in fact intergrade in each particular case, what sort of interplay there is between the sense of analytic, emotional and moral impotence, seems to me one of the outstanding, and except for Weber untouched, problems for comparative research in this whole field) is a matter of affirming, or at least recognizing, the inescapability of ignorance, pain and injustice on the human plane while simultaneously denying that these irrationalities are characteristic of the world as a whole. And it is in terms of religious symbolism, a symbolism relating man's sphere of existence to a wider sphere within which it is conceived to rest, that both the affirmation and the denial are made.

4. . . . AND CLOTHING THOSE CONCEPTIONS WITH SUCH AN AURA OF FACTUALITY THAT . . .

There arises here, however, a profounder question: how is it that this denial comes to be believed? how is it that the religious man moves from a troubled perception of experienced disorder to a more or less settled conviction of fundamental order? just what does "belief" mean in a religious context? Of all the problems surrounding attempts to conduct anthropological analysis of religion this is the one that has perhaps been most troublesome and therefore the most often avoided, usually by relegating it to psychology, that raffish outcast discipline to which social anthropologists are forever consigning phenomena they are unable to deal with within the framework of a denatured Durkheimianism. But the problem will not go away, it is not "merely" psychological (nothing social is), and no anthropological theory of religion which fails to attack it is worthy of the name. We have been trying to stage Hamlet without the Prince quite long enough.

It seems to me that it is best to begin any approach to this issue with frank recognition that religious belief involves not a Baconian induction from everyday experience—for then we should all be agnostics—but rather a prior acceptance of authority which transforms that experience. The existence of bafflement, pain and moral paradox—of The Problem of Meaning—is one of the things that drive men toward belief in gods, devils, spirits, totemic principles or the spritual efficacy of cannibalism (an enfolding sense of beauty or a dazzling perception of power are others), but it is not the basis upon which those beliefs rest, but rather their most important field of application.

In tribal religions authority lies in the persuasive power of traditional imagery; in mystical ones in the apodictic force of supersensible experience; in charismatic ones in the hypnotic attraction of an extraordinary personality. But the priority of the acceptance of an authoritative criterion in religious matters over the revelation which is conceived to flow from that acceptance is not less complete than in scriptural or hieratic ones. The basic axiom underlying what we may perhaps call "the religious perspective" is everywhere the same: he who would know must first believe.

But to speak of "the religious perspective" is, by implication, to speak of one perspective among others. A perspective is a mode of seeing, in that extended sense of "see" in which it means "discern," "apprehend," "understand" or "grasp." It is a particular way of looking at life, a particular manner of construing the world, as when we speak of an historical perspective, a scientific perspective, an aesthetic perspective, a common-sense perspective, or even the bizarre perspective embodied in dreams and in hallucinations. The question then comes down to, first, what is "the religious perspective" generically considered, as differentiated from other perspectives; and second, how do men come to adopt it.

If we place the religious perspective against the background of three of the other major perspectives in terms of which men construe the world—the common-sensical, the scientific and the aesthetic—its special character emerges more sharply. What distinguishes common-sense as a mode of "seeing" is, as Schutz (1962) has pointed out, a simple acceptance of the world, its objects and its processes as being just what they seem to be—what is sometimes called naive realism—and the pragmatic motive, the wish to act upon that world so as to bend it to one's practical purposes, to master it, or so far as that proves impossible, to adjust to it. The world of everyday life, itself, of course, a cultural product, for it is framed in terms of the symbolic conceptions of "stubborn fact" handed down from generation to generation, is the established scene and given object of our actions. Like Mt. Everest it is just there and the thing to do with it, if one feels the need to do anything with it at all, is to climb it. In the scientific perspective it is precisely this givenness which disappears (Schutz, 1962). Deliberate doubt and systematic inquiry, the suspension of the pragmatic motive in favor of disinterested observation, the attempt to analyze the world in terms of formal concepts whose relationship to the informal conceptions of common-sense become increasingly problematic—these are the hallmarks of the attempt to grasp the world scientifically. And as for the aesthetic perspective, which under the rubric of "the aesthetic attitude" has been perhaps most exquisitely examined, it involves a different sort of suspension of naive realism and practical interest, in that instead of questioning the credentials of everyday experience that experience is merely ignored in favor of an eager dwelling upon appearances, an engrossment in surfaces, an absorption in things, as we say, "in themselves": "The function of artistic illusion is not 'make-believe' . . . but the very opposite, disengagement from belief—the contemplation of sensory qualities without their usual meanings of 'here's that chair,' 'That's my telephone' . . . etc. The knowledge that what is before us has no practical significance in the world is what enables us to give attention to its appearance as such" (Langer, 1953, p. 49). And like the common-sensical and the scientific (or the historical, the philosophical and the autistic), this perspective, this "way of seeing" is not the product of some mysterious Cartesian chemistry, but is induced, mediated, and in fact created by means of symbols. It is the artist's skill which can produce those curious quasi-objects—poems, dramas, sculptures, symphonies—which, dissociating themselves from the solid world of common-sense, take on the special sort of eloquence only sheer appearances can achieve.

The religious perspective differs from the common-sensical in that, as already pointed out, it moves beyond the realities of everyday life to wider ones which correct and complete them, and its defining concern is not action upon those wider realities but acceptance of them, faith in them. It differs from the scientific perspective in that it questions the realities of everyday life not out of an institutionalized scepticism which dissolves the world's givenness into a swirl of probabilistic hypotheses, but in terms of what it takes to be wider, non-hypothetical truths. Rather than detachment, its watchword is commitment; rather than analysis, encounter. And it differs from art in that instead of effecting a disengagement from the whole question of factuality, deliberately manufacturing an air of semblance and illusion, it deepens the concern with fact and seeks to create an aura of utter actuality. It is this sense of the "really real" upon which the religious perspective rests and which the symbolic activities of religion as a cultural system are devoted to producing, intensifying, and, so far as possible, rendering inviolable by the discordant revelations of secular experience. It is, again, the imbuing of a certain specific complex of symbols—of the metaphysic they formulate and the style of life they recommend—with a persuasive authority which, from an analytic point of view is the essence of religious action.

Which brings us, at length, to ritual. For it is in ritual—i.e., consecrated behavior—that this conviction that religious conceptions are veridical and that religious directives are sound is somehow generated. It is in some sort of ceremonial form—even if that form be hardly more than the recitation of a myth, the consultation of an oracle, or the decoration of a grave—that the moods and motivations which sacred symbols induce in men and the general conceptions of the order of existence which they formulate for men meet and reinforce one another. In a ritual, the world as lived and the world as imagined, fused under the agency of a single set of symbolic forms, turn out to be the same world, producing thus that idiosyncratic transformation in one's sense of reality to which Santayana refers in my epigraph. Whatever role divine intervention may or may not play in the creation of faith—and it is not the business of the scientist to pronounce upon such matters one way or the other—it is, primarily at least, out of the context of concrete acts of religious observance that religious conviction emerges on the human plane.

However, though any religious ritual, no matter how apparently automatic or conventional (if it is truly automatic or merely conventional it is not religious), involves this symbolic fusion of ethos and world-view, it is mainly certain more elaborate and usually more public ones, ones in which a broad range of moods and motivations on the one hand and of metaphysical conceptions on the other are caught up, which shape the spiritual consciousness of a people. Employing a useful term introduced by Singer (1955) we may call these full-blown ceremonies "cultural performances" and note that they represent not only the point at which the dispositional and conceptual aspects of religious life converge for the believer, but also the point at which the interaction between them can be most readily examined by the detached observer.

Of course, all cultural performances are not religious performances, and the line between those that are, and artistic, or even political ones is often not so easy to draw in practice, for, like social forms, symbolic forms can serve multiple purposes. But the point is that, paraphrasing slightly, Indians—"and perhaps all peoples"—seem to think of their religion "as encapsulated in these discrete performances which they [can] exhibit to visitors and to themselves" (Singer, 1955). The mode of exhibition is however radically different for the two sorts of witnesses, a fact seemingly overlooked by those who would argue that "religion is a form of human art." Where for "visitors" religious performances can, in the nature of the case, only be presentations of a particular religious perspective, and thus aesthetically appreciated or scientifically dissected, for participants they are in addition enactments, materializations, realizations of it—not only models *of* what they believe, but also models *for* the believing of it. In these plastic dramas men attain their faith as they portray it.

5. . . . THAT THE MOODS AND MOTIVATIONS SEEM UNIQUELY REALISTIC.

But no one, not even a saint, lives in the world religious symbols formulate all of the time, and the majority of men live in it only at moments. The everyday world of common-sense objects and practical acts is, as Schutz says, the paramount reality in human experience—paramount in the sense that it is the world in which we are most solidly rooted, whose inherent actuality we can hardly question (however much we may question certain portions of it), and from whose pressures and requirements we can least escape. A man, even large groups of men, may be aesthetically insensitive, religiously unconcerned and unequipped to pursue formal scientific analysis, but he cannot be completely lacking in common-sense and survive. The dispositions which religious rituals induce thus have their most important impact—from a human point of view—outside the boundaries of the ritual itself as they reflect back to color the individual's conception of the established world of bare fact. The peculiar tone that marks the Plains vision quest, the Manus confession or the Javanese mystical exercise pervades areas of the life of these peoples far beyond the immediately religious, impressing upon them a distinctive style in the sense both of a dominant mood and a characteristic movement. Religion is sociologically interesting not because, as vulgar positivism would have it, it describes the social order (which, insofar as it does, it does not only very obliquely but very incompletely), but because, like environment, political power, wealth, jural obligation, personal affection, and a sense of beauty, it shapes it.

The movement back and forth between the religious perspective and the common-sense perspective is actually one of the more obvious empirical occurrences on the social scene, though, again, one of the most neglected by social anthropologists, virtually all of whom have seen it happen countless times. Religious belief has usually been presented as an homogeneous characteristic of an individual, like his place of residence, his occupational role, his kinship position, and so on. But religious belief in the midst of ritual, where it engulfs the total person, transporting him, so far as he is concerned, into another mode of existence, and religious belief as the pale, remembered reflection of that experience in the midst of everyday life are not precisely the same thing, and the failure to realize this has led to some confusion, most especially in connection with the so-called "primitive mentality" problem. Much of the difficulty between Lévy-Bruhl and Malinowski on the nature of "native thought," for example, arises from a lack of full recognition of this distinction; for where the French philosopher was concerned with the view of reality savages adopted when taking a specifically religious perspective, the Polish-English ethnographer was concerned with that which they adopted when taking a strictly common-sense one. Both perhaps vaguely sensed that they were not talking about exactly the same thing, but where they went astray was in failing to give a specific accounting of the way in which these two forms of "thought"—or as I would rather say, these two modes of symbolic formulation—interacted, so that where Lévy-Bruhl's savages tended to live, despite his postludial disclaimers, in a world composed entirely of mystical encounters, Malinowski's tended to live, despite his stress on the functional importance of a religion, in a world composed entirely of practical actions. They became reductionists (an idealist is as much of a reductionist as a materialist) in spite of themselves because they failed to see man as moving more or less easily, and very frequently, between radically contrasting ways of looking at the world, ways which are not continuous with one another but separated by cultural gaps across which Kierkegaardian leaps must be made in both directions.

For an anthropologist, the importance of religion lies in its capacity to serve, for an individual or for a group, as a source of general, yet distinctive conceptions of the world, the self and the relations between them on the one hand—its model *of* aspect—and of rooted, no less distinctive "mental" dispositions—its model *for* aspect—on the other. From these cultural functions flow, in turn, its social and psychological ones.

Religious concepts spread beyond their specifically metaphysical contexts to provide a framework of general ideas in terms of which a wide range of experience—intellectual, emotional, moral—can be given meaningful form. The Christian sees the Nazi movement against the background of The Fall which, though it does not, in a casual sense, explain it, places it in a moral, a cognitive, even an effective sense. A Zande sees the collapse of a granary upon a friend or relative against the background of a concrete and rather special notion of witchcraft and thus avoids the philosophical dilemmas as well as the psychological stress of indeterminism. A Javanese finds in the borrowed and reworked concept of *rasa* ("sense-taste-feeling-meaning") a means by which to "see" choreographic, gustatory, emotional and political phenomena in a new light. A synopsis of cosmic order, a set of religious beliefs is also a gloss upon the mundane world of social relationships and psychological events. It renders them graspable.

But more than gloss, such beliefs are also a template. They do not merely interpret social and psychological processes in cosmic terms—in which case they would be philosophical, not religious—but they shape them. In the doctrine of original sin is embedded also a recommended attitude toward life, a recurring mood and a persisting set of motivations. The Zande learns from witchcraft conceptions not just to understand apparent "accidents" as not accidents at all, but to react to these spurious accidents with hatred for the agent who caused them and to proceed against him with appropriate resolution. Rasa, in addition to being a concept of truth, beauty and goodness, is also a preferred mode of experiencing, a kind of affectless detachment, a variety of bland aloofness, an unshakeable calm. The moods and motivations a religious orientation produces cast a derivative, lunar light over the solid features of a people's secular life.

The tracing of the social and psychological role of religion is thus not so much a matter of finding correlations between specific ritual acts and specific secular social ties—though these correlations do, of course, exist and are very worth continued investigation, especially if we can contrive something novel to say about them. More, it is a matter of understanding how it is that men's notions, however implicit, of the "really real" and the dispositions these notions induce in them, color their sense of the reasonable, the practical, the humane and the moral. How far it does so (for in many societies religion's effects seem quite circumscribed, in others completely pervasive); how deeply it does so (for some men, and groups of men, seem to wear their religion lightly so far as the secular world goes, while others seem to apply their faith to each occasion, no matter how trivial); and how effectively it does so (for the width of the gap between what religion recommends and what people actually do is most variable cross-culturally)—all these are crucial issues in the comparative sociology and psychology of religion. Even the degree to which religious systems themselves are developed seems to vary extremely widely, and not merely on a simple evolutionary basis. In one society, the level of elaboration of symbolic formulations of ultimate actuality may reach extraordinary degrees of complexity and systematic articulation; in another, no less developed socially, such formulations may remain primitive in the true sense, hardly more than congeries of fragmentary by-beliefs and isolated images, of sacred reflexes and spiritual pictographs. One need only think of the Australians and the Bushmen, the Toradja and the Alorese, the Hopi and the Apache, the Hindus and the Romans, or even the Italians and the Poles, to see that degree of religious articulateness is not a constant even as between societies of similar complexity.

The anthropological study of religion is therefore a two stage operation: first, an analysis of the system of meanings embodied in the symbols which make up the religion proper, and, second, the relating of these systems to social structural and psychological processes. My dissatisfaction with so much of contemporary social anthropological work in religion is not that it concerns itself with the second stage, but that it neglects the first, and in so doing takes for granted what most needs to be elucidated. To discuss the role of ancestor worship in regulating political succession, of sacrificial feasts in defining kinship obligations, of spirit worship in scheduling agricultural practices, of divination in reinforcing social control or of initiation rites in propelling personality maturation are in no sense unimportant endeavors, and I am not recommending they be abandoned for the kind of jejune cabalism into which symbolic analysis of exotic faiths can so easily fall. But to attempt them with but the most general, common-sense view of what ancestor worship, animal sacrifice, spirit worship, divination or initiation rites are as religious patterns seems to me not particularly promising. Only when we have a theoretical analysis of symbolic action comparable in sophistication to that we now have for social and psychological action, will we be able to cope effectively with those aspects of social and psychological life in which religion (or art, or science, or ideology) plays a determinant role.

THREE
THE INTERPRETATION OF SYMBOLISM

Introduction

Man is a cultural being, which in essence means that he is a symbol-using animal. Indeed, his capacity to symbolize is often proposed as a criterion placing him apart from the beasts. Language may be the most important kind of symbolization, but it is not the only one. It has been said that religion may be viewed as a vast symbolic system, as indeed it may, and it is to this possibility that the present chapter addresses itself.

Symbols take many forms and have many functions, from the numbers that stand for quantities of goods in the keeping of accounts to the actions in dreams that serve to disguise the repressed wishes of the individual subconscious. In practice, the anthropology of religion normally concerns itself with symbols of nonempirical cultural knowledge, notably cosmologies, and the symbols used in ritual (see Chapter Five), two classes which, of course, overlap considerably. Anthropologists do not restrict their inquiry into ritual symbols to the ritual context, however, for it is precisely the extension of these symbols and the concepts and principles they represent into the most mundane activities that creates the remarkable consistency of many non-Western cultures.

Like metaphors, symbols typify or represent or recall something by possession of analogous qualities or by association in fact or thought. But there is no universal meaning that any single motif may be said to symbolize, the Jungian notion of archetypes notwithstanding. Symbols and what they signify are above all culturally constructed and culturally bound. One culture's symbolic analogy is another culture's puzzle. Unlike symbols in science and mathematics, which are intended to be unambiguous, religious symbols may simultaneously encompass many referents, even some that are not strictly compatible. This is the quality called "multivocality" by Victor Turner, who has demonstrated it vividly with the ritual symbols of the Ndembu. Multivocality charges even the simplest ceremonies with multiple levels of meaning, with referents from cosmology to social relations.

It would be a mistake to assume, however, that religious symbols are purely referential, that is, that they are merely highly condensed metaphorical expressions or propositions about the objective world. Religious symbols are above all sacred symbols, and as such, they embody to the faithful the unquestionable truth of unverifiable statements about the cosmos and man's place in it. It is this characteristic of self-confirming assertions about reality that gives religious symbols both intellectual and emotional significance to the people who hold them. The power of religious symbols lies neither in the objectively or empirically establishable truth or falsity of sacred propositions nor in the concrete qualities of the objects used to convey them. Rather, their conceived efficacy, their "truth," stems precisely from the *nondiscursive* "moods and motivations," to use Clifford Geertz's phrase, which they elicit from the faithful. Sacred propositions are not postulates to be proven but assertions to be taken for granted.

The ability of religious symbols also to evoke powerful emotions seems to derive both from the historical experiences and social conditions of individuals and societies as well as from universal features of human psychology. Few symbols of any complexity can be said to be universal in significance or meaning, but there does seem to be a dimension of psychological appropriateness that restricts the theoretically infinite range of possible associations between signs and meanings. The predominance of right over left and the prominence of the colors red, white, and black around the world are examples of the skewing of probability by apparently universal principles. Whether these are explained by reference to bodily processes, as by Turner, childhood experiences, as in Freudian interpretations, or Jungian universal archetypes, some universal as well as conventional and culturally defined meanings seem almost certainly to contribute to the emotional load of religious symbols. (See Leach's "Magical Hair," 1958, for a discussion of this problem.) Not only do meanings and contexts vary in the complex analysis of symbolism, but interpretations equally may alter according to theoretical preoccupation. For example, much attention has been focused on the symbolism of subincision among the Australians. Bruno Bettelheim, in *Symbolic Wounds* (1954), has suggested that the operation is the symbolic carving of a vulva on a male penis, thus indicating that *both* sexes experience envy of the opposite's sexuality, rather than the one-sided penis envy reported for females. Years later, another theory was put forth by Philip Singer and Daniel E. DeSole, in an article entitled "The Australian Subincision Ceremony Reconsidered: Vaginal Envy or Kangaroo Bifid Penis Envy" (1967), and was followed by a communication by J. E. Cawte (1968) which endorsed the observation that the subincised penis was a symbolic representation of the naturally split kangaroo penis. The bifid penis allows for greater size and prolonged coitus, two sexual values highly prized in cultures where the fertility rite and symbol is of utmost importance. Finally, Mary Douglas mentions in *Purity and Danger* (1966) that the subincision ceremony could symbolize the carving of the two moieties of the tribe on the part of the body which helps to generate its members. This controversy illustrates the many meanings which can be read into the nature of symbolism—furthermore, all interpretations may indeed be correct, depending on one's theoretical concerns. It is necessary to agree with J. E. Cawte, who is concerned "to show that we have long passed a point at which anyone, least of all those of us interested in psychoanalysis, should expect to find a simplistic theory" (p. 963).

Despite these manifest complexities, two general approaches in current anthropological analyses of symbolism can be discerned. The first is what Victor Turner calls "processual symbology"—the study of how symbols trigger social action and the process by which symbols acquire and shed both public and private meanings. The first six articles in this chapter represent various forms that this approach can take. Ortner and Hallpike deal with general definitional and methodological problems; Myerhoff and Wolf show how symbols acquire meanings through historically and socially derived processes. Finally, Gossen illustrates the consistency with which religious symbols reflect cosmological and social conceptualizations, and Rosaldo and Atkinson seek to determine the symbolic significance of "man" and "woman" in the study of cosmologies.

The second general approach to symbolic analysis addresses the problem of symbolic classification. This investigation of native categories and their relationships derives from a theoretical position formulated by Durkheim and Mauss in their classic book, *Primitive Classification* (1963), and from the anthropological linguists Edward Sapir (1931), Benjamin Whorf (Carroll 1956), and others. The "structuralist" analyses reflected in Lévi-Strauss's work currently epitomize this approach. Structuralist studies share the conviction that symbols do not exist in isolation as merely names or labels. Symbols represent native categories; they include some things and not others, and there are rules which govern their proper understanding and use. Lest their associations appear arbitrary, the anthropologist is forced to consider symbols in relation to one another. Only in considering *systems* of classification, the relations between categories, can he begin to understand systems strange to his own.

The objective, then, is to elucidate the underlying "logic" by which systems of symbols are ordered. Lévi-Strauss attempts to derive this logic from the notion of binary oppositions borrowed from the phonological theory of "distinctive features" developed by Roman Jakobson (1956) and other linguists. According to this theory, all meaning is relational: no single sound is really "p," but we distinguish "p" from "b" by the presence or absence of a feature called "voice." Lévi-Strauss and other structuralists, by analogy, treat cultural categories as the products of binary relations. But while distinctive feature theory yields elegant accounts of phonemes, it remains, for anthropologists, more a metaphor than a technique.

The last three articles in this chapter deal with this problem of symbolic classification. The selection by Lévi-Strauss analyzes the structural "logic" of the relationship between totemic groups and castes. Douglas suggests in her article that the concept of mystical pollution is essentially a problem of order: that which is anomalous or out of place is abhorred and must be avoided. In a critical application of structuralist method, Leach, in his essay on "animal avoidance," points out that Lévi-Strauss's binary model is overhasty in abolishing analogic and qualitative modes of thought.

Finally, mention must be made of two recent developments in the study of symbolism which have not been included in the *Reader*. The first is a brief but provocative book by Dan Sperber entitled *Rethinking Symbolism* (1975). There Sperber develops the proposition that "symbolism" is not really about semiologically derived meanings at all but has to do with aspects of cognition inherent in the human mind. The second is an essay by C. R. Hallpike (1976), "Is There a Primitive Mentality?" which explores the implications of Jean Piaget's developmental psychology for the cross-cultural study of collective symbolic forms. Both of these pieces reflect some of the stimulating new work being done in the field.

Symbolic analysis represents a crucial shift from the fixed and "objective" perspective of more traditional anthropology to a more dialectical perspective which addresses itself as much to the anthropologist-observer's subjectivity and cultural concepts as it does to the observed society and culture. Students interested in pursuing the myriad complexities involved in studying symbolism in general might consult, among others, Ogden and Richards' *The Meaning of Meaning* (1927) or Whitehead's *Symbolism* (1927). For a more anthropologically oriented discussion of the problem, see James Fernandez's paper, "The Mission of Metaphor in Expressive Culture" (1974), and a book edited by Mary Douglas entitled *Rules and Meanings: The Anthropology of Everyday Knowledge* (1973).

Sherry B. Ortner

ON KEY SYMBOLS

The first step in any analysis is deciding exactly what constitutes a symbol. Many anthropologists note that an adequate understanding of another culture frequently hinges on comprehending the meaning of a few distinctive words or concepts. By what criteria are these crucial cultural symbols to be recognized? In this brief but cogent article, Sherry Ortner outlines a typology for analyzing such "key" cultural symbols. The explication of dominant cultural patterns or themes has long been a major concern in anthropology and Ortner shows how the symbols which embody such patterns or themes may be categorized according to their primary uses in thought and action. By distinguishing between "summarizing" and "elaborating" symbols, the different ways in which symbols both affect emotions and communicate information are highlighted. She elaborates on Clifford Geertz's distinction between symbols as models *of* models and models *for* in her discussion of how symbols provide *orientations* for conceptualization—root metaphors—

Reprinted in slightly abridged form from *American Anthropologist*, 75 (1973), 1338–1346, by permission of the author and the American Anthropological Association.

as well as *strategies* for action—key scenarios—for the members of a culture. Ortner is careful to point out, however, that her typology is a heuristic concept rather than a precise reflection of distinct—and distinguishable—kinds of symbols. It provides a framework within which the complexities of an unfamiliar system of cultural symbols initially may be sorted out. The proper understanding of any symbol lies in a holistic and in-depth study of the cultural context in which it operates rather than in any universal typology or theoretical model. For concrete applications of this general theoretical approach to symbolic analysis, see her essays, "Sherpa Purity" (1973) and "Gods' Bodies, Gods' Food: A Symbolic Analysis of Sherpa Ritual" (1975). An analysis of another key symbol in Sherpa culture may be found in Robert A. Paul's article, "The Sherpa Temple as a Model of the Psyche" (1976).

It is by no means a novel idea that each culture has certain key elements which, in an ill-defined way, are crucial to its distinctive organization. Since the publication of Benedict's *Patterns of Culture* in 1934, the notion of such key elements has persisted in American anthropology under a variety of rubrics: "themes" . . . , "focal values" . . . , "dominant values" . . . , "integrative concepts" . . . , "dominant orientations" . . . , and so forth. We can also find this idea sneaking namelessly into British social anthropological writing; the best example of this is Lienhardt's (1961) discussion of cattle in Dinka culture (and I say culture rather than society advisedly). Even Evans-Pritchard has said,

> *as every experienced field-worker knows, the most difficult task in social anthropological field work is to determine the meanings of a few key words, upon an understanding of which the success of the whole investigation depends (1962:80).*

Recently, as the focus in the study of meaning systems has shifted to the symbolic units which formulate meaning, the interest in these key elements of cultures has become specified as the interest in key symbols. Schneider (1968) calls them "core symbols" in his study of American kinship; Turner (1967) calls them "dominant symbols" in his study of Ndembu ritual; I called them "key symbols" in my study of Sherpa social relations.

The primary question of course is what do we mean by "key"? But I will postpone considering this problem until I have discussed the various usages of the notion of key symbols in the literature of symbolic analysis.

Two methodological approaches to establishing certain symbols as "core" or "key" to a cultural system have been employed. The first approach, less commonly used, involves analyzing the system (or domains thereof) for its underlying elements—cognitive distinctions, value orientations, etc.—then looking about in the culture for some figure or image which seems to formulate, in relatively pure form, the underlying orientations exposed in the analysis. The best example of this approach in the current literature is David Schneider's (1968) analysis of American kinship; Schneider first analyzes the kinship system for its basic components—nature and law—and then decides that conjugal sexual intercourse is the form which, given its meaning in the culture, expresses this opposition most succinctly and meaningfully. Schneider expresses his debt to Ruth Benedict, and this debt turns out to be quite specific, since the other major work which embodies this method is Benedict's *The Chrysanthemum and the Sword* (1967). The sword and the chrysanthemum were chosen by Benedict from the repertoire of Japanese symbols as most succinctly, or perhaps most poetically, representing the tension in the Japanese value system which she postulated. She did not arrive at this tension through an analysis of the meanings of chrysanthemums and swords in the culture; she first established the tension in Japanese culture through analysis of various symbolic systems, then chose these two items from the repertoire of Japanese symbols to sum up the opposition.

In the second, more commonly employed approach, the investigator observes something which seems to be an object of cultural interest, and analyzes it for its meanings. The observation that some symbol is a focus of cultural interest need not be very mysterious or intuitive. I offer here five reasonably reliable indicators of cultural interest, and there are probably more. Most key symbols, I venture to suggest, will be signaled by more than one of these indicators:

1. The natives tell us that X is culturally important.
2. The natives seem positively or negatively aroused about X, rather than indifferent.

3. X comes up in many different contexts. These contexts may be behavioral or systemic: X comes up in many different kinds of action situation or conversation, or X comes up in many different symbolic domains (myth, ritual, art, formal rhetoric, etc.).
4. There is greater cultural elaboration surrounding X, e.g., elaboration of vocabulary, or elaboration of details of X's nature, compared with similar phenomena in the culture.
5. There are greater cultural restrictions surrounding X, either in sheer number of rules, or severity of sanctions regarding its misuse.

As I said, there may be more indicators even than these of the key status of a symbol in a culture, but any of these should be enough to point even the most insensitive fieldworker in the right direction. I should also add that I am not assuming that there is only one key symbol to every culture; cultures are of course a product of the interplay of many basic orientations, some quite conflicting. But all of them will be expressed somewhere in the public system, because the public symbol system is ultimately the only source from which the natives themselves discover, rediscover, and transform their own culture, generation after generation.

It remains for us now to sort out the bewildering array of phenomena to which various investigators have been led to assign implicitly or explicitly the status of key cultural symbol. Anything by definition can be a symbol, i.e., a vehicle for cultural meaning, and it seems from a survey of the literature that almost anything can be key. Omitting the symbols established by the first approach cited above, which have a different epistemological status, we can cite from the anthropological literature such things as cattle among the Dinka and Nuer, the Naven ritual of the Iatmul, the Australian churinga, the slametan of the Javanese, the potlatch of the northwest coast, the forked stick of Ndembu rituals, and from my own research, the wheel-image in Tibet and food among the Sherpas. We could also add such intuitive examples as the cross of Christianity, the American flag, the motorcycle for the Hell's Angels, "work" in the Protestant ethic, and so on.

The list is a jumble—things and abstractions, nouns and verbs, single items and whole events. I should like to propose a way of subdividing and ordering the set, in terms of the ways in which the symbols operate in relation to cultural thought and action.

The first major breakdown among the various types of symbols is along a continuum whose two ends I call "summarizing" vs. "elaborating." I stress that it is a continuum, but I work with the ideal types at the two ends.

Summarizing symbols, first, are those symbols which are seen as summing up, expressing, representing for the participants in an emotionally powerful and relatively undifferentiated way, what the system means to them. This category is essentially the category of sacred symbols in the broadest sense, and includes all those items which are objects of reverence and/or catalysts of emotion—the flag, the cross, the churinga, the forked stick, the motorcycle, etc. The American flag, for example, for certain Americans, stands for something called "the American way," a conglomerate of ideas and feelings including (theoretically) democracy, free enterprise, hard work, competition, progress, national superiority, freedom, etc. And it stands for them all at once. It does not encourage reflection on the logical relations among these ideas, nor on the logical consequences of them as they are played out in social actuality, over time and history. On the contrary, the flag encourages a sort of all-or-nothing allegiance to the whole package, best summed up on a billboard I saw recently: "Our flag, love it or leave." And this is the point about summarizing symbols in general—they operate to compound and synthesize a complex system of ideas, to "summarize" them under a unitary form which, in an old-fashioned way, "stands for" the system as a whole.

Elaborating symbols, on the other hand, work in the opposite direction, providing vehicles for sorting out complex and undifferentiated feelings and ideas, making them comprehensible to oneself, communicable to others, and translatable into orderly action. Elaborating symbols are accorded central status in the culture on the basis of their capacity to order experience; they are essentially analytic. Rarely are these symbols sacred in the conventional sense of being objects of respect or foci of emotion; their key status is indicated primarily by their recurrence in cultural behavior or cultural symbolic systems.

Symbols can be seen as having elaborating power in two modes. They may have primarily conceptual elaborating power, that is, they are valued as a source of categories for conceptualizing the order of the world. Or they may have primarily action elaborating power; that is, they are valued as implying mechanisms for successful social action. These two modes reflect what I see as the two basic and of course interrelated functions of culture in general: to provide for its members "orientations," i.e., cognitive and affective categories; and "strategies," i.e., programs for orderly social action in relation to culturally defined goals.

Symbols with great conceptual elaborating power are what Stephen Pepper (1942) has called "root metaphors," and indeed in this realm the basic mechanism is the metaphor. It is felt in the culture that many aspects of experience can be likened to, and illuminated by the comparison with, the symbol itself. In Pepper's terms, the symbol provides a set of categories for conceptualizing other aspects of experience, or, if this point is stated too uni-directionally for some tastes, we may say that the root metaphor formulates the unity of cultural orientation underlying many aspects of experience, by virtue of the fact that those many aspects of experience can be likened to it.

One of the best examples of a cultural root metaphor in the anthropological literature is found in Godfrey Lienhardt's discussion of the role of cattle in Dinka thought. Cows provide for the Dinka an almost endless set of categories for conceptualizing and responding to the subtleties of experience. For example:

> *The Dinkas' very perception of colour, light, and shade in the world around them is . . . inextricably connected with their recognition of colour-configurations in their cattle. If their cattle-colour vocabulary were taken away, they would have scarcely any way of describing visual experience in terms of colour, light and darkness* (1961:13).

More important for Lienhardt's thesis is the Dinka conceptualization of the structure of their own society on analogy with the physical structure of the bull. " 'The people are put together, as a bull is put together,' said a Dinka chief on one occasion" (*Ibid.*: 23), and indeed the formally prescribed division of the meat of a sacrificed bull is a most graphic representation of the statuses, functions, and interrelationships of the major social categories of Dinka society, as the Dinka themselves represent the situation.

In fact, as Mary Douglas points out, the living organism in one form or another functions as a root metaphor in many cultures, as a source of categories for conceptualizing social phenomena (1966). In mechanized society, on the other hand, one root metaphor for the social process is the machine, and in recent times the computer represents a crucial modification upon this root metaphor. But the social is not the only aspect of experience which root-metaphor type symbols are used to illuminate; for example, much of greater Indo-Tibetan cosmology—the forms and processes of life, space, and time—is developed on analogy with the quite simple image of the wheel (Ortner 1966).

A root metaphor, then, is one type of key symbol in the elaborating mode, i.e., a symbol which operates to sort out experience, to place it in cultural categories, and to help us think about how it all hangs together. They are symbols which are "good to think," not exactly in the Lévi-Straussian sense, but in that one can conceptualize the interrelationships among phenomena by analogy to the interrelations among the parts of the root metaphor.

The other major type of elaborating symbol is valued primarily because it implies clear-cut modes of action appropriate to correct and successful living in the culture. Every culture, of course, embodies some vision of success, or the good life, but the cultural variation occurs in how success is defined, and, given that, what are considered the best ways of achieving it. "Key scenarios," as I call the type of key symbol in this category, are culturally valued in that they formulate the culture's basic means-ends relationships in actable forms.

An example of a key scenario from American culture would be the Horatio Alger myth. The scenario runs: poor boy of low status, but with total faith in the American system, works very hard and ultimately becomes rich and powerful. The myth formulates both the American conception of success—wealth and power—and suggests that there is a simple (but not easy) way of achieving them—singleminded hard work. This scenario may be contrasted with ones from other cultures which present other actions as the most effective means of achieving wealth and power, or which formulate wealth and power as appropriate goals only for certain segments of the society, or, of course, those which do not define cultural success in terms of wealth and power at all. In any case, the point is that every culture has a number of such key scenarios which both formulate appropriate goals and suggest effective action for achieving them; which formulate, in other words, key cultural strategies.

This category of key symbols may also include rituals; Singer seems to be making the point of rituals as scenarios when he writes of "cultural performances" (1958), in which both valued end states and effective means for achieving them are dramatized for all to see. Thus this category would include naven, the slametan, the potlatch, and others. The category could also include individual elements of rituals—objects, roles, action sequences—insofar as they refer to or epitomize the ritual as a whole, which is why one can have actions, objects, and whole events in the same category.

Further, scenarios as key symbols may include not only formal, usually named events, but also all those cultural sequences of action which we can observe enacted and reenacted according to unarticulated formulae in the normal course of daily life. An example of such a scenario from Sherpa culture would be the hospitality scenario, in which any individual in the role of host feeds a guest and thereby renders him voluntarily cooperative vis-à-vis oneself. The scenario formulates both the ideally valued (though infrequently attained) mode of social relations in the culture—voluntary cooperation—and, given certain cultural assumptions about the effects of food on people, the most effective way of establishing those kinds of relations. Once again then, the scenario is culturally valued—indicated in this case by the fact that it is played and replayed in the most diverse sorts of social contexts—because it suggests a clear-cut strategy for arriving at culturally defined success.

I have been discussing the category of key symbols which I called "elaborating" symbols, symbols valued for their contribution to the sorting out of experience. This class includes both root metaphors which provide categories for the ordering of conceptual experience, and key scenarios which provide strategies for organizing action experience. While for purposes of this discussion I have been led by the data to separate thought from action, I must hasten to put the pieces back together again. For my view is that ultimately both kinds of symbols have both types of referents. Root metaphors, by establishing a certain view of the world, implicitly suggest certain valid and effective ways of acting upon it; key scenarios, by prescribing certain culturally effective courses of action, embody and rest upon certain assumptions about the nature of reality. Even summarizing symbols, while primarily functioning to compound rather than sort out experience, are seen as both formulating basic orientations and implying, though much less systematically than scenarios, certain modes of action.

One question which might be raised at this point is how we are to understand the logical relationships among the types of key symbols I have distinguished. As the scheme stands now, it has the following unbalanced structure:

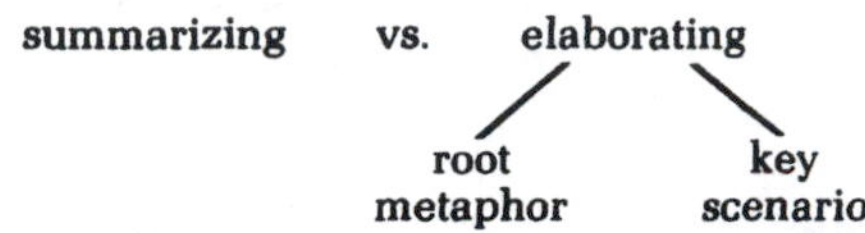

I would argue that this asymmetry follows from the content of the types: the meaning-content of summarizing or sacred symbols is by definition clustered, condensed, relatively undifferentiated, "thick," while the meaning-content of elaborating symbols is by definition relatively clear, orderly, differentiated, articulate. Thus it is possible to make distinctions among the different ordering functions of elaborating symbols, while the denseness of meaning of summarizing symbols renders them relatively resistant to subdivision and ordering by types. Nonetheless, in the interest of systematic analysis, we may raise the question of whether such subdivisions are possible, and in particular whether the thought/action distinction which subdivides elaborating symbols (into root metaphors and key scenarios) also crosscuts and subdivides summarizing symbols.

The important mode of operation of summarizing symbols, it will be recalled, is its focusing power, its drawing-together, intensifying, catalyzing impact upon the respondent. Thus we must ask whether some summarizing symbols primarily operate to catalyze thought or in any case internal states of the actor, while others primarily operate to catalyze overt action on the part of the actor. Now it does seem possible, for example, to see the cross or some other religious symbol as primarily focusing and intensifying inner attitude, with no particular implied public action, while the flag or some other political symbol is primarily geared to focusing and catalyzing overt action in the public world. Yet, intuitively at least, this distinction seems relatively weak and unconvincing compared to the easily formulated and grasped distinction between the two types of elaborating symbols: static formal images serving metaphor functions for thought (root metaphors), and dramatic, phased action sequences serving scenario functions for action (key scenarios). Of course, as I said, root metaphors may imply particular modes of, or at least a restricted set of possible modes of, action; and key scenarios presuppose certain orderly assumptions of thought. But the distinction—the former geared primarily to thought, the latter to action—remains sharp.

Summarizing symbols, on the other hand, speak primarily to attitudes, to a crystallization of commitment. And, in the mode of commitment, the thought/action distinction is not particulary relevant. There may certainly be consequences for thought and action as a result of a crystallized commitment, but commitment itself is neither thought nor action. The point perhaps illuminates the generally sacred status of summarizing symbols, for they are speaking to a more diffuse mode of orientation in the actor, a broader context of attitude within which particular modes of thinking and acting are formulated.

This is not to say that nothing analytic may be said about summarizing symbols beyond the fact that they catalyze feeling; there are a number of possible ways of subdividing the catalog of sacred symbols in the world, some no doubt more useful or illuminated than others. My point is merely that the particular factor which subdivides elaborating symbols—the thought/action distinction—does not serve very powerfully to subdivide the category of summarizing symbols, since the summarizing symbol is speaking to a different level of response, the level of attitude and commitment.

We are now in a position to return to the question of "key" or central status. Why are we justified in calling a particular symbol "key"? The indicators provided earlier for at least provisionally regarding certain symbols as key to a particular culture were all based on the assumption that keyness has public (though not necessarily conscious) manifestation in the culture itself, available to the observer in the field, or at least available when one reflects upon one's observations. But the fact of public cultural concern or focus of interest is not *why* a symbol is key; it is only a *signal* that the symbol is playing some key role in relation to other elements of the cultural system of thought. The issue of keyness, in short, has to do with the internal organization of the system of cultural meaning, as that system functions for actors leading their lives in the culture.

Broadly speaking, the two types of key symbols distinguished above, defined in terms of how they act upon or are manipulated by cultural actors, also indicate the two broad modes of "keyness" from a systemic point of view, defined in terms of the role such symbols are playing in the system; that is, a given summarizing symbol is "key" to the system insofar as the meanings which it formulates are logically or affectively prior to other meanings of the system. By "logically or affectively prior" I mean simply that many other cultural ideas and attitudes presuppose, and make sense only in the context of, those meanings formulated by the symbol. The key role of an elaborating symbol, by contrast, derives not so much from the status of its particular substantive meanings, but from its formal or organizational role in relation to the system; that is, we say such a symbol is "key" to the system insofar as it extensively and systematically formulates relationships—parallels, isomorphisms, complementarities, and so forth—between a wide range of diverse cultural elements.

This contrast between the two modes of "keyness" may be summed up in various ways, all of which oversimplify to some extent, but which nonetheless give perspective on the point. (1) "Content versus form": The keyness of a summarizing symbol derives from its particular substantive meanings (content) and their logical priority in relation to other meanings of the system. The keyness of an elaborating symbol derives from its formal properties, and their culturally postulated power to formulate widely applicable modes of organizing cultural phenomena. (2) "Quality versus quantity": The keyness of a summarizing symbol derives from the relative fundamentality (or ultimacy) of the meanings which it formulates, relative to other meanings of the system. The keyness of an elaborating symbol derives from the broadness of its scope, the extent to which it systematically draws relationships between a wide range of diverse cultural elements. (3) "Vertical versus lateral": The keyness of a summarizing symbol derives from its ability to relate lower-order meanings to higher-order assumptions, or to "ground" more surface-level meanings to their deeper bases. (The issue here is degree of generality of meaning. Whether more general meanings are termed "higher" or "deeper," "ultimate" or "fundamental," by a particular cultural analyst seems a matter of personal preference.) The keyness of an elaborating symbol by contrast derives from its ability to interconnect disparate elements at essentially the same level, by virtue of its ability to manifest (or bring into relief) their formal similarities.

All of these terminological contrasts—form/content, quantity/quality, lateral/vertical—are really perspectives upon the same basic contrast, for which we have no more general term; that is, when we say a summarizing symbol is "key" to the system, we mean that its substantive meanings have certain kinds of priority relative to other meanings of the system. When we say an elaborating symbol is key to the system, we refer to the power of its formal or organizational role in relation to the system.

But at this point we must stop short of reifying the distinctions, for, in practice, the contrast between the two broad types of key symbols and the two modes of "keyness" may break down. It seems empirically to be the case that an elaborating symbol which is accorded wide-ranging applicability in the culture—played in many contexts, or applied to many different sorts of forms—is generally not only formally apt but also substantively referential to high level values, ideas, cognitive assertions, and so forth. Indeed, insofar as such high level formulations are made, a key elaborating symbol of a culture may move into the sacred mode and operate in much the same way as does a summarizing symbol. And, on the other hand, some summarizing symbols may play important ordering functions, as when they relate the respondent not merely to a cluster of high level assumptions and values, but to a particular scenario which may be replayed in ongoing life. (One may think, for example, of the Christian cross evoking, among other things, not only a general sense of God's purpose and support, but also the particular scenario of Christ's martyrdom.)

Thus we are brought to an important point, namely, that we are distinguishing not only types of symbols, but types of symbolic functions. These functions may be performed by any given symbol—at different times, or in different contexts, or even simultaneously by different "levels" of its meaning. While there are many examples of summarizing and elaborating symbols in their relatively pure forms, the kinds of functions or operations these symbols perform may also be seen as aspects of any given symbols.

To summarize the original scheme briefly, key symbols may be discovered by virtue of a number of reliable indicators which point to cultural focus of interest. They are of two broad types—summarizing and elaborating. Summarizing symbols are primarily objects of attention and cultural respect; they synthesize or "collapse" complex experience, and relate the respondent to the grounds of the system as a whole. They include most importantly sacred symbols in the traditional sense. Elaborating symbols, on the other hand, are symbols valued for their contribution to the ordering or "sorting out" of experience. Within this are symbols valued primarily for the ordering of conceptual experience, i.e., for providing cultural "orientations," and those valued primarily for the ordering of action, i.e., for providing cultural "strategies." The former includes what Pepper calls "root metaphors," the latter includes key scenarios, or elements of scenarios which are crucial to the means-end relationship postulated in the complete scenario.

This scheme also suggests, at least by the choices of terms, the modes of symbolic analysis relevant to the different types of key symbols. The first type (summarizing symbols) suggests a range of questions pertaining to the cultural conversion of complex ideas into various kinds of relatively undifferentiated commitment—-patriotism, for example, or faith. The second type (root metaphors) suggests questions applicable to the analysis of metaphor in the broadest sense—questions of how thought proceeds and organizes itself through analogies, models, images, and so forth. And the third type (key scenarios) suggests dramatistic modes of analysis, in which one raises questions concerning the restructuring of attitudes and relationships as a result of enacting particular culturally provided sequences of stylized actions.

This article has been frankly programmatic; I am in the process of implementing some of its ideas in a monograph on Sherpa social and religious relations. Here I have simply been concerned to show that, although a method of cultural analysis via key symbols has been for the most part unarticulated, there is at least incipiently method in such analysis. It is worth our while to try to systematize this method, for it may be our most powerful entree to the distinctiveness and variability of human cultures.

C. R. Hallpike

SOCIAL HAIR

In 1958, Edmund Leach published a celebrated essay entitled "Magical Hair" in which he developed an anthropological critique of the psychoanalytic theory propounded by Dr. Charles Berg in his book, *The Unconscious Significance of Hair* (1951). The following article by C. R. Hallpike in turn takes Leach to task for favoring too psychological a theory about hair symbolism. Rather than symbolizing castration (as Berg asserts) or one kind of symbolic separation which publically moves individuals from one social status to another (as Leach asserts), Hallpike argues that the cutting of hair is a symbol of social control; that long hair is associated with being outside of society and the cutting of hair symbolizes living under a particular disciplinary regime within society. Two issues raised by this seemingly trivial argument are of central concern to the anthropological analysis of symbolism. The first issue addresses the question of why do many of the same symbolic motifs—particularly those derived from the body and bodily processes—recur in a wide variety of cultures. Rather than attributing this fact to universal subconscious psychological processes, Hallpike takes a sociological and cognitive approach, asserting that such similarities in symbolic systems derive from common concerns and experiences shared by all human beings. A similar position is taken by Mary Douglas in her book, *Natural Symbols* (1970), in which she explores and elaborates this relationship between social organization and body symbolism.

The second issue raises the problem of the relationship between public and private symbolism; between symbols which primarily communicate information "about the world" and symbols which alter individual emotional states. This distinction, however, is a hard one to maintain because many symbols both *say* something about the individual, society, and the world as well as *do* something for the individual emotionally. But the question remains, where does this affective power of symbols come from? Again, Hallpike takes an avowedly empiricist position and asserts that the purely emotional element is irrelevant to an anthropological analysis of symbolic systems. The anthropologist's task is to elucidate the structure of the symbolic system and its relationship to the people's cosmology, social organization, and values, rather than search for its sources in the subconscious personality structure of the people. The symbolism is "there" as a shared, public fact, thus it can be analyzed as such, regardless of its source or objective truth value.

Reprinted in slightly revised form from *Man*, n.s., 4 (1969), 256–264, by permission of the author and the Royal Anthropological Institute of Great Britain and Ireland.

A central problem in the interpretation of ritual is the fact that while the participants in each society may be unable to give an explicit explanation of the meaning of the symbols involved, there is a large body of symbols and symbolic acts which is common to a wide variety of cultures, and while any particular symbol may have a multiplicity of meanings from society to society, we find that these meanings constantly recur. For example, as Turner (1966) has pointed out, black, white and red are the colours most often used in ritual, where black is very often symbolic of dirt or rainclouds, white of milk or semen, and red of blood. Given, then, that there is a number of symbols, with a common signification in different cultures, we must try to explain the basis of this similarity.

Two different hypotheses suggest themselves. The first is that the meanings ascribed to symbols are related to the workings of the subconscious, which are assumed to be similar in members of every culture and, more specifically, to the mechanisms of the repression and sublimation of the sexual impulses. The second is that, given the common concern of all societies with survival, the nature of the physical environment, procreation, the social role of the sexes, youth and age, order and disorder, and similar basic concepts, there are certain symbols and symbolic acts which are inherently appropriate in expressing these concepts, and that this is why these symbols are so commonly found and often have the same meaning in different cultures. All that I mean by "inherently appropriate" is that since blood and fire, for example, are red and not green, we would expect to find that cultures which ascribe symbolic values to colours would choose red as a symbol of blood or warfare, and not green. This does not mean that only one symbol is very appropriate to express any particular concept. For example, one culture may choose red as a symbol of death through its association with bloodshed; another might choose white through its association with bone; and a third might choose black through its association with night, and the setting of the sun. The point I am making is that we elucidate the meaning of symbolism by examining the way in which people conceptualize the associations of entities in the real world. Thus the first hypothesis mentioned above regards symbols as "about" the subconscious, while the second hypothesis regards them as "about" the world and man's place in it.

The object of this article is a re-analysis of Dr. Leach's celebrated and stimulating essay "Magical Hair" (Leach, 1958) in which he advances a theory of the symbolic meaning of hair which is of the first type.

Leach examines the relationship between the significance of symbolism in the individual subconscious, as seen by a psycho-analyst, Dr. Charles Berg, and the significance of symbolism in social ritual, as interpreted by ethnographers. The particular piece of symbolism which he uses as a basis for discussion is Berg's hypothesis that there is a basic symbolic equivalence between head hair and the male genitals in the subconscious, such that hair-cutting equals castration. His problem is to explain how the conclusions of psycho-analysis about the symbolic meaning of hair in individual fantasies, as a matter of fact, though without much logical or empirical justification, turn out to be closely in accord with what ethnographers have to say about the significance of hair in ritual. His conclusion is that the psychologists and the ethnographers are discussing quite different types of phenomena (the subconscious and the social), but that the psychologists can contribute to our understanding of ritual because much of its content is designed to express, and therefore to control, our potentially dangerous emotions. Phallic symbolism occurs often in ritual because "ritual makes explicit these powerful and dangerous thoughts. . . . Phallicism in ritual is thus a form of cathartic prophylaxis; it is not an expression of the repressed unconscious of the collective individual, it is a social process which serves to prevent the individual from developing sexual repressions at all" (1958: 161). This may or may not be so; the problem with such theories is to bring them into some sort of relationship with the facts, so that they can be shown empirically to be true or false. The whole relationship between private and social symbolism is too complex to be considered here; on this occasion my immediate concern is to consider a particular symbolic theme, in the light of Leach's psychological theory, and to try to determine whether it is really true that head hair can be shown to be associated with sexuality in a wide range of societies and, more explicitly, if it is true that:

head = phallus
hair = semen
hair cutting = castration

and that:

long hair = unrestrained sexuality
short hair = restricted sexuality
close shaven hair = celibacy.

Let us first of all consider the special characteristics of hair.

1. Like the nails it grows constantly.
2. It can be cut painlessly, again like the nails.
3. It grows in great quantity, such that individual hairs are almost numberless.
4. Head hair is apparent on infants of both sexes at birth.
5. Genital/anal hair appears at puberty in both sexes.
6. In some races, males develop facial hair after puberty, and also body hair.
7. Hair on different parts of the body is of different texture, e.g. eyelashes, pubic hair, head hair.
8. In old age hair often turns white and/or falls out.
9. Hair is a prominent feature of animals, especially monkeys, man's analogue in the animal kingdom.

Now the human body is the focus of much ritual; and it is not surprising that a physical feature with such manipulative potential as hair should be used so frequently in ritual. Moreover, in view of its manifold characteristics, which I have just set out, it would be surprising if all its ritual and symbolic manifestations could be reduced to a single origin.

One of the most frequent ritual uses of hair is in association with mourning. On this point Leach says: "That hair rituals may have sexual associations has been apparent to anthropologists from the beginning, but mostly they have not regarded this as a matter of crucial significance. Tylor, for example, classed ritual haircutting as one 'of an extensive series of practices, due to various and often obscure motives, which come under the general heading of ceremonial mutilations.' Of other such practices he mentions blood-letting and the cutting-off of finger joints. He avoids reference to circumcision, but the latter rite is clearly a 'ceremonial mutilation' (Tylor, 1873: 2, 403)" (1958: 150). While conceding that ritual does not reflect the psychological condition of the individual performing it, but rather that "the structure of the social situation requires the actor to make formal symbolic statements of a particular kind" (1958: 153), he still finds Berg's hypothesis in relation to shaving the head at mourning—that loss of the loved one equals castration equals loss of hair—to be meaningful as explaining the genesis of the symbolism in the first place. Now exactly *why* people should react to grief by shaving off their hair and mutilating themselves is undoubtedly amenable to psychological explanation, but there is no *prima facie* reason to link it with castration. Certainly circumcision has no such meaning, but quite the reverse in most primitive societies.

One of the greatest weaknesses in Berg's hypothesis that shaving head hair equals castration is that women shave their heads in mourning as well as men. But what on earth does it mean to talk of "female castration"? The notion is sufficiently bizarre to require some elucidation for readers who are not psychologists. Moreover, references to shaving the head at mourning very frequently describe other mutilations such as gashing the face and body. For example, Frazer lists (1923: 377–83) besides the Jews of the Old Testament, sixty-eight societies in which some form of self-mutilation is performed at mourning, and in almost every case we find that the cutting off of the hair is accompanied by bodily laceration. In the absence of any indication to the contrary, why should we therefore assume that the cutting off of the hair is not simply a particular type of self-mutilation?

We frequently find in ethnographical literature that hair has close associations with the soul. For example, to refer to Frazer again: "The Siamese think that a spirit called *khuan* or *kwun* dwells in the human head, of which it is the guardian spirit. The spirit must be carefully protected from injury of every kind; hence the act of shaving or cutting the hair is accompanied with many ceremonies" (1922: 230); and he cites many other instances to show the sacred character of the head and consequently the peculiar nature of head hair. Since the head is the seat of reason and the sensory organs, among other things, this is surely good reason for recognising that it is a most appropriate seat of the soul, in primitive eyes. Leach concludes however that "The 'soul stuff' of such writers as Hutton and Wilken is not perhaps very different from the 'libido' of the psycho-analysts" (1958: 150). Not perhaps *very* different, but sufficiently different to require considerable demonstration of similarity, which we are not given.

Magic is another familiar ritual use of hair, which is treated, along with nail parings and bodily secretions, as symbolically equal to the person from whose body they came. Of this Leach says:

> *The psycho-analyst, being concerned with the inner feelings of the individual, categorizes all actions which cut away part of the individual's body as symbolic equivalents of "castration." He then argues that these ritual acts have emotional force for the individual because they are in fact felt to be a repression of libidinous energy. In contrast, the social anthropologist is concerned with the publicly acknowledged status of social persons, and he notes that the ritual acts in which part of the individual's body is cut off are prominent in rites de passage. . . . He might well label all such rites "circumcision." The social anthropologist's explanation of why rites of "circumcision," so defined, should be emotionally charged comes from Durkheim. The ritual situation converts the symbol into a "collective representation" of God and Society. . . . These two arguments, the psycho-analytic and the Durkheimian, appear to be sharply contrasted, yet they are not contradictory. We can accept them both simultaneously together with a third argument, borrowed from Frazer, to the effect that magical power typically resides in objects which are detached from individuals in ritual situations—e.g. the blood, hair, nail parings, etc. of persons involved in rites de passage. We cannot simply merge these three arguments, but if we recognize that they all refer to "the same thing," then we are led to conclude that magical potency, regarded as a social category, is something which inheres in "circumcision" symbols, but that such symbolization is effective because for each individual the ritual situation is felt to signify "castration"* (1958: 162).

Originally, it will be remembered, Leach was concerned to show that Berg's equation of head hair equals genitals was relevant in explaining certain ethnographical facts, but now we have gone far beyond this and are being asked to believe that *everything* cut or removed from the body has a sexual significance—specifically, castration. But if blood and body dirt as used in magic and ritual symbolise castration, does the use of personal names, garments, foot-prints and shadows, which are very prominent in magic, also symbolise castration? In fact, of course, there is a much simpler explanation of why hair, nails and blood, etc. are used in magic on a *pars pro toto* basis to symbolise the person from whom they were taken. In the first place, hair and nails grow constantly and this is surely a very good reason why they should be believed to be specially endowed with vitality; blood and semen, for different reasons, are also believed to be sources of vitality in primitive thought. But these considerations cannot apply to body dirt or nasal mucus, and still less to foot-prints, shadows, names and garments. In primitive thought we frequently find that the person is thought of as having extensions, of which personal names, personal belongings, shadows and foot-prints are examples. It seems likely, therefore, that there are two reasons why hair is chosen as a symbol of the whole person in magic. It is endowed *par excellence* with vitality (and may have associations with the soul if it has come from the head) and it also falls into the wider category of extensions of the person.

So far in this article I have tried to demonstrate something of the multiplicity of hair in its ritual aspects. For example, it can be thought of as associated with the soul, through the head, as having inherent vitality because it grows; it may figure in the general category of bodily mutilations; and its physical characteristics make it very appropriate, like dress, for expressing changes or differences in ritual or social status. There is thus no reason why a theory of hair in ritual should be obliged to reduce all the manifestations of hair to a single origin—symbolic castration. It is only when we realise that the ritual uses of hair are of widely differing types that we can attempt to explain any of them. But Leach's theory not only tries to provide a single explanation, but founders on three stubbornly empirical facts.

The first is one to which I have already referred. This is that women's hair, as well as men's, is frequently the focus of ritual attention. The second is that if head hair equals male genitals, why is it that comparatively little regard is paid to beards in ritual contexts? As I remarked earlier, head hair is common to both sexes and is present at birth, while the facial hair only develops in the male at puberty. Moreover, in texture the latter has more resemblance to pubic hair than to head hair. If there were any plausibility in the theory that head hair equals male genitals, and that cutting hair equals castration, one would expect beards to be more prominent than head hair in ritual; so it is surely strange that in fact beards have a comparatively minor role, even allowing for the fact that in some races males do not develop much facial hair. The third and most serious defect is one to which I have not so far alluded. This is the fact that ascetics commonly have long hair. Now of course, according to the equations: long hair equals unrestrained sexuality; short hair equals restricted sexuality; close shaven hair equals celibacy; this is all wrong. Leach of course is aware of the problem; but his solution, in so far as he advances one, is far from adequate.

He quotes Iyer as follows: "The *sannyasin's* freedom from social obligation and his final renunciation of the sex life is symbolised by change of dress but above all by change of hair style. According to the mode of asceticism he intends to pursue a *sannyasin* either shaves off his tuft of hair [the isolated tuft of hair is an essential social identification mark of the male Brahmin] or else neglects it altogether, allowing it to grow matted and lousy" (Leach, 1958: 156). Berg explains the long hair as follows: "Fakirs simply ignore altogether the very existence of their hair (cf. the ascetic tendency to ignore the existence of the genital organs). It grows into a matted lice-inhabited mass and may be as much a source of unremitting torment as the neglected penis itself. Apparently it is not permitted to exist as far as consciousness is concerned" (Leach, 1958: 156). Leach points out that far from the *sannyasin's* behaviour being compulsive, it is socially prescribed, "The correct hair behaviour . . . of Indian ascetics was all laid down in the *Naradaparivrajaka Upanishad* over 2,000 years ago" (1958: 156). But he agrees with Berg that "For the Brahmin the tonsured tuft 'means' sexual restraint, the shaven head 'means' celibacy and the matted head 'means' total detachment from the sexual passions" (1958: 156). But this explanation is of course quite opposed to the theory that long hair equals unrestrained sexuality.

There is a striking passage in Gibbon's *Decline and Fall of the Roman Empire* relating to long hair and asceticism.

> *The monks were divided into two classes; the Coenobites, who lived under a common and regular discipline; and the Anachorets, who indulged their unsocial, independent fanaticism. The most devout, or the most ambitious of the spiritual brethren, renounced the convent, as they had renounced the world. . . . All superfluous incumbrance of dress they contemptuously cast away; and some savage saints of both sexes have been admired, whose naked bodies were only covered by their long hair. They aspired to reduce themselves to the rude and miserable state in which the human brute is scarcely distinguished above his kindred animals; and the numerous sect of Anachorets derived their name from their humble practice of grazing in the fields with the*

common herd. They often usurped the den of some wild beast whom they affected to resemble;... The most perfect Hermits are supposed to have passed many days without food, many nights without sleep, and many years without speaking.... (1960: 516).

This illustrates very well the hypothesis I wish to advance in this article: that long hair is associated with being outside society and that the cutting of hair symbolises re-entering society, or living under a particular disciplinary regime within society. Of course, one may be outside society partially or wholly and I am not suggesting that long hair is appropriate only to hermits and outcasts. By being "outside society" I do not mean therefore the total exclusion of ascetics and similar categories, but rather an attitude or condition of rejection of which the asceticism of the anchorite or *sannyasin* is the ultimate expression, or, again, the possession of certain traits such as spiritual power by reason of which the possessor is not fully amenable to social control. To be more precise, I would formulate the theory as "cutting the hair equals social control." Dressing the hair may also be ceremonially equivalent to cutting it.

The tonsure of the monk is a familiar aspect of Christian religious life, to which Leach refers briefly (1958: 154) and which at first sight seems to support the theory that shaven head equals celibacy. But the monk takes three vows, of which chastity is only one; the others are poverty and *obedience.* The monk in fact is under discipline, ideally of a most rigorously social type. The anchorite, as Gibbon's quotation makes very clear, is under no social discipline whatsoever and indeed represents rejection of social control in its most extreme degree; yet he, like the monk, abstains from the lusts of the flesh. The monk, of course, is not the only person under the discipline of institutional life who has his hair cut short. The soldier and the convict are other well known examples, but nobody would suppose that soldiers are ideally intended to refrain from having sexual relations, even if convicts, by reason of their circumstances, are in practice deprived of sex. Thus the cropped head or tonsure in all three cases of monk, soldier and convict signifies that they are under discipline.

By contrast to these groups, we may consider three categories of person who are, in Western society, generally credited with long hair—intellectuals, juvenile rebels against society and women. It is not difficult to see that in various ways they are, or are thought to be, in some respects less subject to social control than the average man. The intellectual is someone who is, by reason of his interests, remote from the concerns of everyday life, or even positively hostile to and critical of society; and enough has been written about "hippies" to make any explanation of their long hair somewhat superfluous. But the case of women perhaps needs a little more elucidation. In the first place, they are traditionally concerned with domestic affairs and not with the running of society as a whole, and secondly, they have always been considered to be more governed by their emotions, more whimsical and less predictable than men. (Whether truly or falsely is beside the point—it is still a widely held social stereotype.) It is of course true that in past centuries men have worn long hair, but in such periods women's hair has been even longer; at the end of the eighteenth century it was not considered unmanly for men to weep publicly, but there is no indication that they outdid women in this respect.

Long hair is therefore, I suggest, a symbol of being in some way outside society, of having less to do with it, or of being less amenable to social control than the average citizen. But the means by which one attains this condition are of course various. Anchorites, witches, intellectuals, hippies and women all have long hair, but there is no single quality which they have in common besides the negative one of being partially or wholly outside society. There is however one characteristic which is often associated with being outside society, for whatever reason: this is animality.

Gibbon's irony delights in emphasising how men in their search for holiness come to resemble the beasts, and while I am not suggesting that the relationship between spiritual power and beastliness is more than outward and analogical, it is nevertheless a striking resemblance. There is considerable evidence in fact for an association of "outside society equals hairiness equals animality." The animal familiars of witches and the wild beasts over which the Egyptian saints had such power, come to mind in this connexion. Most primitive societies give animals an important place in their cosmologies and they often symbolise the chaos of untamed nature before the process of socialisation. The culture hero Dribidu of the Lugbara as described by Middleton (1960) is a good example of this association. "They [the two culture-heroes] were not human as men are now; Dribidu means 'the hairy one' since he was covered with long hair over most of his body. He is also known as 'Banyale' ('eater of men'), since he ate his children until he was discovered and driven out of his earlier home on the east bank of the Nile. . . ." (1960: 231) ". . .In our own terms the significant differences between the two periods before and after the heroes is that in the latter the personages were ordinary human beings, who behaved as people behave now, and were members of clans, whereas in the former they behaved in a contrary manner and lived in isolation, in a world in which there were no clans" (1960: 233).

The Bible provides considerable support for my hypothesis, but little for Leach's. Esau, the hunter of wild beasts, was a hairy man, while his brother Jacob, a herdsman dwelling in tents, was a smooth man. Esau also sold his birthright for food (Genesis XXV, 23–27). In Leviticus it is prescribed that a sufferer from leprosy and therefore an outcast, when cured and thereby ready to be reincorporated in society, shall shave off all his hair (Leviticus XIV, 8,9). The Nazarites, who separated themselves unto the Lord, were never allowed to cut their hair until the end of their separation, when the hair was formally shaved off at the tabernacle (Numbers VI, 1–18). In Deuteronomy (XXI, 10–14) it is prescribed that female captives taken in war if made wives shall pare their nails and shave their heads.

In the Book of Judges we are told that Samson's strength resided in his hair, and when he is shorn he is as weak as any other man (Judges XVI, 17–19). 2 Samuel XIV, 26 records that Absalom only cut his hair at yearly intervals, and that at each polling of his head his hair weighed 200 shekels (estimated as 3 5/7 lbs. avoirdupois, by Hastings 1902:904). He was not remarkable for his fertility, and begot only a daughter and three sons, who pre-deceased him (2 Samuel XIV, 27; 2 Samuel XVIII, 18). His principal claim on our attention is, of course, that he attempted to overthrow his sovereign, and his father, King David.

The description of how King Nebuchadnezzar was overthrown and made an outcast is another very clear example of the association of hairiness and the separation from society in the state of nature: ". . . and he was driven from men, and did eat grass as oxen, and his body was wet with the dew of heaven, till his hairs were grown like eagles' feathers, and his nails like birds' claws" (Daniel IV, 33). It may be significant that two major prophets, Elijah and John the Baptist, are associated with hairiness and animal clothing. In a discussion of St. Paul's injunction to women to cover their heads in church, W. F. Howard says: "It may be a sign of the husband's authority. So Stack & Billerbeck show from Rabbinical sources that the bride walked in the wedding procession with uncovered head as a token of her free maidenhood. Then, as a sign that her husband's authority was upon her, Jewish usage required that the married woman should always appear with her head covered" (Howard, 1929: I Cor. II, 3). I should emphasise that I have not been partial in my selection of these Biblical examples in order to prove a point. On the contrary, the examples are a complete list of every significant mention of hair, except those passages dealing with the cutting-off of hair in mourning, an aspect of hair already discussed.

The Bible therefore provides the following associations between long hair, or cutting the hair, and social attributes:

hairiness = hunter (Esau)
hairiness = wild beasts (Nebuchadnezzar)
hairiness = physical strength (Samson)
hairiness = asceticism, spiritual power (Elijah, John the Baptist)
growing long hair = separation from society to God (Nazarites)
shaving hair = rejoining society (Nazarites, when lepers are cured)
covering hair = discipline (women's acceptance of husbands' authority).

The only marginal case among these is that of Samson, in that taken by itself it could be cited as evidence of the association of head hair and sexuality. But it fits equally well with my hypothesis.

Stith-Thompson's *Motif-index of folk literature* (1955–1958) also provides considerable support for my hypothesis, and little for Leach's. There are twenty instances of hairiness being associated with supernatural or half-human beings, such as fairies, dwarfs, giants, water and wood spirits, devils and mermaids; seven associations with animal-human relationships; three associations with witches; three associations with vegetable-human relations; seven associations with the soul or vitality; and six with asceticism. (I have consulted only the references to "hair" and "hairy.") There were no clear references to head hair in association with sexuality, though Leach might disagree with me.

One could go on producing confirmatory data, but it seems to me that the evidence cited so far is ample confirmation that there is no frequent association of head hair and the male genitals. The chief deficiency of Leach's hypothesis however is not that it applies to a much narrower range of facts than he leads us to suppose, but that on its own ground, where social status is overtly associated with hair and with sex, it fails to provide any explanation of why long hair is associated with ascetics and with men like

Samson, and why short hair is associated with monks and soldiers.

My primary objection to Leach's theory therefore is simply that it takes account of very few of the facts. But there is a more fundamental weakness in his theory, which it shares with all such psychological theories. When an anthropologist is trying to understand the rituals of an alien culture he does not concern himself with what the symbols stand for in the subconscious of each participant; indeed, he has no means of knowing this. His mode of analysis will be two-fold. He will ask the natives what each symbol means (without necessarily eliciting a satisfactory answer) and make a list of the occurrences of each symbol in its ritual context. When he has collected sufficient data of this type he will try to discern the structure of the symbolism and its relation to the people's cosmology, social organisation and values. A good example of this procedure is Turner's paper on symbols of *passage* in Ndembu circumcision ritual (Turner 1962). Of course, the success of the interpretation will depend on the quality of the anthropologist's intelligence, imagination and training; the facts cannot interpret themselves. But the point I am making is that once the anthropologist has discerned the structure of the symbolism in the culture he is investigating, his work is complete. The structure is *there* in the symbolism, just as the structure is *there* in a language analysed by the linguist.

The advantage of treating symbolism as "about" the world, rather than "about" the subconscious is that the relations between symbols and the world are empirically verifiable, and it is accordingly possible to evaluate different explanations of a particular piece of symbolism in terms of how well they fit the facts. Thus the advantage of my theory that cutting hair equals social control is that it can be applied fairly rigorously to the logic of social situations in which hair is symbolically significant. In other words, we do not have to ask ourselves: "What is going on in the minds of people who cut off their hair after being cured of leprosy?" (quite possibly nothing at all is going on in their minds beyond the acceptance of a social rule); we simply consider the structural form of the evidence. With psychological theories such as Leach's, however, we cannot relate a people's symbolism to the facts of their natural environment and their society, but only to one of an indefinite number of theories about the subconscious.

Barbara G. Myerhoff

THE DEER-MAIZE-PEYOTE SYMBOL COMPLEX AMONG THE HUICHOL INDIANS OF MEXICO

This stimulating article by Barbara Myerhoff offers an interpretation of the heretofore puzzling relationship among deer, maize, and peyote in Huichol symbolism. She suggests that the deer symbolizes an earlier hunting stage in Huichol culture while maize symbolism concerns their present, still imperfectly developed, agricultural system. Peyote symbolically resolves this hunting-versus-agricultural opposition as the Indians return to the original Huichol homeland and way of life during the annual Peyote Hunt, a symbolic re-creation of "original times" before the present separation occurred between man and the gods, plants and animals, life and death, the natural and the supernatural, and men and women. On the peyote pilgrimage, men become gods, and when the first peyote is "slain" and eaten, the social distinctions of age, sex, ritual status, and family affiliations are eliminated in an all-encompassing unit. In her recently published book entitled *Peyote Hunt: The Sacred Journey of the Huichol Indians* (1974), Myerhoff provides more ethnographic details, including the manner in which everything is symbolically reversed as the pilgrims approach the sacred land; the known world is backward and upside down; old men become small children; that which is sad and ugly is spoken of as beautiful and

Reprinted in abridged form from *Anthropological Quarterly*, 43 (1970), 64–68, by permission of the author and the publishers.

gay; one thanks another person by saying "you are welcome"; one greets another by turning his back on him and bidding him goodbye; the sun is the moon, and the moon is the sun. Through this mystical journey embodied in the Peyote Hunt, both the past and present values of Huichol culture are expressed and affirmed.

The problem taken up by this paper is the analysis and interpretation of the Deer-Maize-Peyote symbol complex, its nature and function, among the Huichol Indians of northcentral Mexico.

At present, the majority of the 10,000 Huichols live in the more inaccessible regions of the Sierra Madre Occidental in five communities in the states of Jalisco, Nayarit, Zacatecas, and Durango. The Huichols have remained relatively unacculturated and unstudied. They seem to have escaped extensive influence by Aztecs, Spaniards, and missionaries and have retained their indigenous way of life to a remarkable degree. Their religion and ideology are quite intact, and the imposition of Mexican national political and economic institutions has been nominal.

The Huichols live on dispersed *ranchos* which consist of several households and the adjoining fields of related nuclear families. No corporate kinship groups exist, and, in fact, the only significant social groups are family, household, rancho, and community. There is no provision for systematic interaction between the five communities, nor is there any stable indigenous centralized authority. The only unity which exists among the communities is shared culture and language (the latter is a language within the Uto-Aztecan family and related to Nahuatl). Apart from the political organization imposed by the Mexican state (which operates rather superficially and infrequently), the only specialists are shaman-priests who are part-time agriculturalists as well. Each rancho sends an elder to an informal council of elders which meets irregularly to discuss matters of mutual concern, but the council lacks any authority to enforce its decisions. The integrity of Huichol society and culture is due in part to the nature and role of religion in their lives; one of the more important components of this religious system is the Deer-Maize-Peyote complex. These symbols are central not only to religion but to art, mythology, and worldview as well. Together they provide a source of personal and social integration and a bulwark against acculturation.

In this interpretation, two aspects of the Deer-Maize-Peyote complex are examined: first, consideration is given to the achievement of a fusion between each of the three individual constituents such that they become a single symbol complex; and second, the function of this fusion is seen as the transcendence or unification of a series of contradictions—societal, historical, and ideological—in Huichol life.

The achievement of this unification is manifest most dramatically in the major Huichol religious ceremony, the annual Peyote Hunt, which represents an historical and mythical return to the original Huichol homeland and way of life. The Hunt is a symbolic re-creation of "original times" before the present separation occurred between man, the gods, plants and animals; between life and death; between natural and supernatural; between the sexes. On the Peyote Hunt, the people who return to their homeland become the gods, and at the climactic moment of the ceremony, they slay and eat the peyote, which is equated with the deer and with maize. At this time, all important social distinctions are overcome. Differences due to age, sex, ritual status, regional origins, and family affiliations are eliminated. A state of unity and continuity is reached between humanity, nature, society, and the supernatural. This unity is seen by the Huichols—and by this observer—as the most important function of the Deer-Maize-Peyote symbol complex, and indeed is the goal of their religious life, value system, and worldview.

In order to understand the nature and origins of some of the contradictions which are found in present-day Huichol life and overcome by the symbol complex, it is necessary to attempt a reconstruction of their pre-Conquest and early post-Conquest history. Huichol myth and tradition, archeological and ethnobotanical evidence, and some recorded historical material converge to form a coherent and plausible interpretation. It seems most likely that the Huichols . . . were among that group known to the Aztecs as Chichimeca, the northern barbarians who lived as nomadic hunters and collectors in the high deserts to the northeast of their present abode in the Sierra. They retreated before the Spaniards into the mountains, but annually in small parties of pilgrims seeking peyote, they return to *Wirikuta*, their sacred land in San Luis Potosí. In their own tradition, they are retracing the path of the Ancient Ones who were driven out of that sacred land of their origins, and the Peyote Hunt consists of a return of the Ancient Ones and deities to their homeland and to First Times—a kind of lost paradise—when they lived as hunters and gatherers. Their transition from hunting to cultivating and from desert to mountain locale is incomplete, and it will be seen that this transitional status provides some of the striking contradictions which are resolved through the identification of the deer with the peyote and both of these with maize.

Two types of evidence which support this "incomplete transition" hypothesis may be mentioned: social-organizational and religious (see Furst and Myerhoff, "Myth as History," for corroborating archeological and ethnobotanical evidence). Many features of social organization more commonly found associated with nomadic hunters than with sedentary cultivators are evident among the present-day Huichols. Some of these are: a lack of political centralization; dispersion of households; absence of any provision for corporate action above the household level; religious autonomy of rancho elders who function as family shamans; absence of unilineal kinship groups; absence of pantribal sodalities; and so forth.

Features in the religious life of the Huichols which also support the "incomplete transition" hypothesis include a well-developed shamanic complex; the close identification of the hunter with the deer who is regarded as a sacred animal and as man's brother; a Master of the Species who sends the deer to man; the concept that success in hunting is determined by supernatural forces rather than hunting skill; the ability of the shaman to transform himself into the deer; the notion that the deer is never killed but is continually renewed and resurrected from his bones, and so forth. All of these features are evident despite the fact that at present the deer is rare in the Sierra and has no economic significance to the Huichol. There seems little reason to doubt that, although the Huichols have taken up agriculture with some success, their religious life still revolves around the deer and in many essential ways resembles a classical Hunting Ideology.

The incomplete transition of the Huichols thus occurs on several levels: geographical (from desert to mountains), ecological and economic (from nomadic hunters to sedentary agriculturalists), and religious and ideological (from deer to maize as major sacred symbol). The paradoxes which arise from transitional status of the Huichols are dealt with by the Deer-Maize-Peyote complex, which is central to the operation of Huichol culture *in toto*. This is stated most explicitly by the Huichols themselves, who say, "Now I will tell you of the maize and the peyote and the deer. These things are one. They are a unity. They are our life. They are ourselves." The association of these three symbols has puzzled previous ethnographers who worked among the Huichol. Lumholtz (1902) referred to the symbol complex as a Holy Trinity and spoke of it as a cult but did not attempt further analysis. Zingg (1938) stated that the relationship between deer, maize, and peyote was mystical and illogical. The deer, maize, and peyote are in a sense a "Holy Trinity," but this designation adds little to our understanding. Calling them a "cult" is unfortunate because the symbol complex should be distinguished from the North American peyote cult with which it has nothing in common. And as for considering their association illogical, our analysis has revealed that this relationship could not possibly be more logical, once the premises and purposes underlying the association of deer, maize, and peyote have been examined. The question, therefore, must be rephrased: What is the logical relationship among them, and then, what purpose is served by the identification of these three symbols as one?

. . .

On the belief level, the relationship between deer, maize, and peyote is quite explicit and succinctly stated by the Huichols when they say: "They are one, they are unity, they are ourselves." The simplicity of this statement can be misleading. It may be regarded as the key conceptualization in their worldview. Furthermore, it must be understood literally, not symbolically, as is demonstrated by an analysis of ceremonial and mundane behaviors toward deer, maize, and peyote. On the operational level, examination of the Huichol ceremonial cycle reveals that these symbols interlock so that the entire ceremonial life of the Huichol revolves around obtaining and using each of them in a particular sequence. The maize cannot grow without first being ceremonially anointed with deer blood. The deer cannot be sacrificed and his blood thereby obtained without consuming peyote obtained from Wirikuta during the Peyote Hunt. The ceremonies which bring the rains to the maize cannot be held without peyote from the Sacred Land. The peyote cannot be hunted until the maize has been cleansed and sanctified with deer blood, and until the children have been told the stories of the First Peyote Hunt. Thus every major ceremony is dependent ultimately on the presence of all three symbolic items, and their sequential procurement makes the entire religious calendar a closed circle.

Using data provided by beliefs and behaviors, it is possible to identify the specific referents of the deer, maize, and peyote. . . . Taking each of the components of the symbol complex separately, we arrive at the following interpretation:

Let us begin with the deer. Some of the evidence of the Huichols' recent transition to agriculture from hunting has been mentioned. If there were other large and important animals which were also hunted and which provided a major source of food, we have heard or seen nothing of them. In any event, the deer and no other animal presently stands for the lost hunting life. The life of hunters is utterly different from that of cultivators. In the past Huichols were quasi-nomadic, in all probability living in small bands, moving freely from place to place, inaccessible to the influences and challenges of other more advanced peoples, and the indignities and dangers of foreign conquerors. Insulated from the caprice of weather and seasonal changes, dependent primarily on their own efforts and the behavior of the animals, they lived in a relatively simple and direct relationship which characterizes that bond between hunter and hunted animal, a relationship in which man is more a partner than he is as the caretaker or servant of his crops. In short the Huichol hunter led a life of comparative freedom and independence.

And in citing the lost attractions of the Huichol past, it would be naive to omit the factor of excitement, the sense of potence and triumph typically experienced by hunters. Thomas (1959) has stated this simply and beautifully in her description of the Bushman hunters for whose existence foraged food is most important, but in giving joy and passion there is nothing to rival the hunt. It may be supposed, then, that the Huichol hunter led a difficult life but a life of autonomy, excitement and glory. And how does this compare with his present state? The Huichol is in bondage, at the mercy of forces nearly entirely beyond his influence. The elements themselves are quixotic, and the maize is a demanding mistress who, despite the Huichol's greatest efforts and ceaseless diligence, may or may not reward him sufficiently to allow him to avert starvation throughout the year. Then, there are the outsiders, the Mexicans who are unpredictable as the weather, often ruthless, and always reminding the Huichols of their impotence and secondary place in the scheme of things. And finally, the Huichols now are sedentary. To remain living in one place tending the fields is an onerous burden which they must continually abjure one another to endure. No Huichol, however, needs to be urged to run down the deer.

In reconstructing the Huichol past as hunters and the quality of this life, it must be noted too that this was a time dominated by men, for hunting among them was and is today the exclusive prerogative of men. Women aid and admire but do not actively participate. In agriculture, of course, female efforts are indispensable, and Huichol women are duly rewarded by being permitted an extensive participation in prestigious ritual and ideological, as well as utilitarian activities. Despite the religious and economic importance of women in everyday Huichol life, they are excluded from all that which pertains to the deer and the deer hunt, and it is only this activity from which they are barred entirely.

The deer is clearly associated with a period in the history of Huichols which was marked by masculine dominance and ascendance and an arrangement which is no longer characteristic of relationships between the sexes, which are at present almost completely equalitarian. That the former condition of masculine dominance should arouse nostalgia, particularly among Huichol males, is not surprising.

Thus the deer is the symbol of original Huichol life as hunters, of the Huichol past, idealized no doubt, and made luminous by nostalgia, but nevertheless operating with the force of reality, of those "Ancient Times" of freedom, autonomy, potence, masculine domination, and dignity. It is this past, part fantasy, part reality, which the deer represents, preserves, and carries into the present as one constituent of the Deer-Maize-Peyote complex which is so pivotal in Huichol culture.

Maize and its role in Huichol life contrasts sharply with that of the deer. Obviously it is the basic food, the plant which provides the subsistence of the present as deer was the animal source of life in the past. And while maize itself is praised as beautiful the toil and regularity required to till the soil is not. The life of the cultivator is not lauded and eulogized by the Huichols as is the running of the deer. Maize is considered delicate, touchy, unpredictable, quick to take offense and leave. It is likened to children, requiring extreme care and tending, day in day out, and even then unreliable in its rewards. And maize, one must not forget, was procured from "foreigners"—the non-Huichols who are viewed with no trust or liking. Zingg (1938) and Lumholtz (1900) both sensed a less than complete incorporation of maize into Huichol life and saw a corresponding lesser intensity in the treatment of maize during the ceremonies which involved all three symbolic components of the Deer-Maize-Peyote complex.

Maize is thus the mundane present, undeniably of great importance, but ultimately a utilitarian concern, requiring the efforts of men, women, and children in ceaseless, dull, taxing, regular effort. It belongs, of course, in a central symbol complex such as this one, for it is the present reality, but it is also the antithesis of the idealized hunting past, symbolized among the Huichol by the deer.

Of all three symbols, peyote is the most interesting. Its inclusion in the complex may be read as indicative of the peculiar *Geist* or genius of the Huichols—that turn-of-mind which makes them distinct and sets them apart from others around them. In behaviors and beliefs it can be seen repeatedly that peyote is construed as providing an essentially private experience. One should not tell of one's peyote-induced visions. Each person has his or her own, and each is different (with the exception of the conventional visions of the deities experienced by the shaman under the influence of peyote). It is something precious and beautiful. It serves no useful purpose. It does not contribute to social solidarity, and no effort is made to ritualize and exploit the camaraderie, which often accompanies shared escape from reality. Nor is it used to strengthen bonds between people. It is not given to one group as a reward and mark of special status, as was done with narcotics and intoxicating beverages used by the Aztecs. Peyote occupies a non-utilitarian place on all levels of Huichol life. Even the visions obtained by it are not used for religious illumination, didactic purposes, or intensification of experiences. They are gratuitous. And because peyote produces experiences which are only uniform in being consistently pleasant, it brings to each one who takes it something unpredictable, irregular, spontaneous, and unstructured, though still within safeguards and limits. It permits an experience which is not completely routinized, neither is it dangerous or likely to lead to individual or societal disruption. Peyote constitutes that part of human life which is private, beautiful, and unique. As such, it constitutes that part of religion which has nothing to do with shared sentiments, morals, ethics, or dogma. It is within the religious experience but separate from it, and in some philosophical systems such experiences are considered the most elevated and most intensely spiritual available to mankind. As such it is the opposite of those parts of religion which are ritualized, mechanical, and impersonal.

Peyote, then, is the Huichol provision for an unknowable and personal experience. It is intriguing that such provisions should have been devised by a people intensely concerned with order, regularity, predictability, and propriety. Through the use of peyote, spontaneity and privacy have been retained within a fixed framework of opposing values. Such an arrangement makes so much sense psychologically that one may see in it a major source of the flexibility and durability which marks Huichol life and religion. Peyote is neither mundane, like maize, nor exotic and exciting, like deer. It is that solitary, ahistorical, asocial, asexual, arational domain without which man is not complete, without which life is a lesser affair.

There is a completeness represented by this combination of deer, maize, and peyote. When the Huichol juxtapose them and consider each to be an aspect of the other, they are stating that there is a wholeness to being human, that one cannot live without a sense of the past, working for a living, or finding moments of solitary beauty. Surely this is an accurate statement of human life when it is healthy and whole. All are essential and all are part of being human. Simply, the three symbols represent a unity, as the Huichols say. The animal represents the past—hunting, masculinity, independence, adventure, and freedom; the plant is the labor of the present—food, regularity, domesticity, sharing between the sexes, routine, and persistent diligence; the cactus which grows far away is plant and animal at once—non-utilitarian, free of time, sex, and specifiable meaning, existing for its own unscrutinized, quiet gift of beauty and privacy. Truly such a vision is, as the Huichol often state it, "beautiful because it is right."

The function of the achievement of a unification between deer, maize, and peyote may be considered in the light of some of the writings on symbolism, myth, and ritual by Lévi-Strauss which can be seen to coincide closely with many of Victor Turner's (1967, 1968) views. Both of them treat the problem of how symbols can operate to overcome oppositions, or as Geertz (1966) would put it, to embrace paradox and celebrate ambiguities. It is the special purpose of symbols, in my opinion, to encompass incompatible, irresolvable sets of referents; and, the special task of symbols is the prevention of the clear, undisguised recognition of the unsatisfactory arrangements which actually exist in the lives of men. Like Gluckman's (1964, 1965) rituals of rebellion, symbols avoid real change by avoiding the accumulation of dissatisfactions with things as they really are.

Symbols are embedded in ritual, that is, in behavioral contexts in which their opposed referents cannot break through into consciousness because of the rigidity, precision, and mechanical nature of ritual itself. Rituals, by inhibiting spontaneity and idiosyncratic responses, assure that the symbols being employed are not contemplated with full consciousness and close scrutiny. Thus rituals allow symbols to exert their unifying influence while remaining uncomprehended and unchallenged. In this view, both ritual and myth contrive to mask contradictions, to fuse the oppositions among the symbols being employed through contact, and ultimately achieve an interchange of their qualities that phenomenologically blurs the contradictions between them.

The Deer-Maize-Peyote complex, seen in this light, functions to achieve a series of unifications by presenting, then embracing, many of the contradictions, oppositions, and paradoxes of Huichol life. These contradictions occur and are transcended on several levels: (a) On the societal level—Social barriers are transcended by means of the symbol complex when, during the Peyote Hunt, the shaman-priest and the pilgrims he has led back to the Sacred Land become a single entity. Distinctions between leader and led, between priest and congregation are set aside. Men, women, children, and adults participate equally and completely in receiving the sacramental First Peyote which is also the Deer and the Maize. Ritual status—determined by the number of pilgrimages made, religious knowledge attained, or the standing of the deity embodied during the pilgrimage—is irrelevant at the climactic moment when the sacred cactus (which is also the deer and the maize) is revered and eaten. (b) On a historical and ecological level—a past life as free, autonomous, desert-dwelling, nomadic hunters, living in a society dominated by men is opposed to and reconciled with the present mountain-dwelling, sedentary life, based on agriculture, requiring an equalitarian division of labor which includes and gives considerable status to the work of women. It is a life which at present requires ceaseless, monotonous attention to the crops, the seasons, and accommodating to the humiliations of dependence and subjection to an ill-understood outside society of foreigners. (c) On a biological-natural level—when the peyote is eaten in the Sacred Land of Wirikuta, distinctions are overcome between plant and animal, between man and animals, and between the natural world, the human world, and the supernatural world. Finally (d), on a psychological level—the greatest unification achieved by the symbol complex occurs when the Huichol pilgrims return to Wirikuta as the Ancient Ones regaining their original homeland to hunt the sacred peyote. Wirikuta, there is reason to believe, is the land of their origins, historically as well as mythically, thus by returning there the Huichols unify their historical past with their idealized past. As deities in the Sacred Land they retrieve their lost paradise, the timeless, placeless condition when humans and animals were brothers, before they became separated from the deities, before distinctions were made between life and death. Hence the pilgrimage to Wirikuta enables the Huichols to overcome the contradictions between the mortal and blessed condition, between the purity and complete accord which characterized the life of the Ancient Ones and the present imperfect state of humanity with its biological needs, discord, selfishness, pain and death. A union is achieved at this climactic moment between the spiritual and the mundane, and between the private, unique, and virtually uncommunicable experience of a peyote-induced vision as opposed to the daily, shared, public life of hard work and predictability.

In addition to achieving the resolution of many paradoxes, the Deer-Maize-Peyote complex can be seen to function along the lines emphasized by Geertz (1966) in his discussion of the nature and purpose of religion, namely, the elimination of that most unacceptable of all aspects of human life—the unexpected, inexplicable, and the uncanny. In other words, this symbol complex takes up the problem of moral incoherence. By making it possible to retain the past as part of the present, the need is eliminated for dealing with the question of why the world changed, why the beauty and freedom of former times has passed away, why humans lost touch with nature, and why it is no longer possible to pursue "the perfect life—to offer to the Ancient Ones and chase the deer."

These losses require a moral explanation, an answer which re-aligns the "ought" and the "is." A religion may provide such justification by postulating some sin or fault because of which humans forfeited a privileged past, thus granting assurance that life is as it should be—whether good or bad—and as such is understandable. Or a religion may provide a concept of an after-life for the inequities and sufferings of a present transient and inconsequential reality. A third alternative moral explanation is that seen in Huichol religion—denying the gratuitous and cruel state of the present by refusing to relinquish the past. Their most precious religious heritage—their past—is idealized and recovered. Even if only for a little while, by means of the Peyote Hunt, paradise may be regained. Through the Deer-Maize-Peyote complex, the deer and a life dedicated to hunting the deer is still a fact of present-day reality rather than a fading shabby memory, chewed over by old men at the end of the day. Change itself is denied; there is no history, only the timeless present.

The Huichols are aware that others have more than they materially, that they are destitute while outsiders prosper. This is yet another moral paradox which is managed by the religion. In spite of great privation, they do not see themselves as victims of the operation of blind chance, fate, or the inexorable forces of history. Consistently, the Huichols deny that their life is poor. Materially, they experience difficulty, yes, but as they are so fond of saying, "Our symbols make us rich." And the shaman-priest who probably suffers more than any individual in the society, is the richest man of all. Their wealth is aesthetic and spiritual. They envy no one, at least that is their ideal. They have in abundance life's greatest treasure—an utter sense of conviction of the meaningfulness of their life. With rare confidence the Huichols move through the world, acknowledging no one as better or master, and this though it is hard to imagine a people with less actual control over their fate or more at the mercy of forces beyond their power and comprehension. Yet they pity those who live a life different from their own. Such an attitude could be called complacent, or perhaps it is integrity. At any rate, it assures them that their present life is ideal, just as their past life was perfect. And the greatest part of this certainty may be attributed to the Deer-Maize-Peyote symbol. The deer as the past life of perfection, the maize as the mundane, human dimension, and the peyote as the spiritual, private, and free part of life merge. The mundane is elevated and refined by its association with the divine, and the gods themselves become accessible, knowable, and even mundane: thus sensual experiences are refined while spiritual experiences are made tangible by their contact with each other, and the dichotomy between them disappears. All this occurs in the land of Wirikuta when paradise and innocence are regained, and it is there that the Huichols find their destiny once more.

Geertz (1966) says that religious symbols embody attitudes, longings, and beliefs. The Huichols' symbols embody an image of a morally closed world in which nothing is neutral or gratuitous. Even the ambiguities and puzzles of that life are given significance, put in their place, put in order. The human condition becomes lucid and more than merely bearable and desirable. On the Peyote Hunt the major symbols make the imaginary life the real life, and provide that fusion of the "lived-in" with the "thought-of" order which Geertz (1966) describes as one of the major tasks of religion. Wirikuta is no imaginary place. The Huichols need not speculate or fantasize as to what it might be like. Through their own will, dedication, and virtue they are truly there, and even those who never go, know it from the reports of pilgrims. They touch the earth, feel the hairs of the deities brush their faces, feel the warmth of the fire as it sears their past sins away, taste the waters from the sacred springs, turn the peyote over in their mouths and watch with their own eyes as the surrounding world becomes a luminous and multi-colored place of magic animals and animated plants and flowers.

Thus we may regard Deer, Maize, and Peyote as constituting for the Huichols "their symbols of general orientation in nature, earth, and society . . . providing their *Lebensanschauung* and *Weltanschauung*." As Langer (1960) has said, "Such symbols are truly man's most valuable property."

Eric Wolf

THE VIRGIN OF GUADALUPE: A MEXICAN NATIONAL SYMBOL

There hardly exists a better example of a highly evocative national symbol and a clearer illustration of the relations of microcosm to macrocosm than that of the Virgin of Guadalupe of Mexico. Like her famous Polish counterpart, the Black Madonna of Czenstochowa, she embodies abstract principles and precepts of the nation to which she belongs. The complexity and heterogeneity of Mexico are reconciled in Guadalupe in a special way that no other symbol can rival. Political overtones are blended with individual and societal aspirations, particularly for the Indian, for it was to an Indian that the Virgin revealed herself in 1531. Eric Wolf provides us with a masterful analysis of Guadalupe in this article.

Reprinted with slight abridgments from the *Journal of American Folklore*, LXXI (1958), 34–39, by permission of the author and The American Folklore Society, Inc.

Occasionally, we encounter a symbol which seems to enshrine the major hopes and aspirations of an entire society. Such a master symbol is represented by the Virgin of Guadalupe, Mexico's patron saint. During the Mexican War of Independence against Spain, her image preceded the insurgents into battle. Emiliano Zapata and his agrarian rebels fought under her emblem in the Great Revolution of 1910. Today her image adorns house fronts and interiors, churches and home altars, bull rings and gambling dens, taxis and buses, restaurants and houses of ill repute. She is celebrated in popular song and verse. Her shrine at Tepeyac, immediately north of Mexico City, is visited each year by hundreds of thousands of pilgrims, ranging from the inhabitants of far-off Indian villages to the members of socialist trade union locals. "Nothing to be seen in Canada or Europe," says F. S. C. Northrop, "equals it in the volume or the vitality of its moving quality or in the depth of its spirit of religious devotion."

In this paper, I should like to discuss this Mexican master symbol, and the ideology which surrounds it. In making use of the term "master symbol," I do not wish to imply that belief in the symbol is common to all Mexicans. We are not dealing here with an element of a putative national character, defined as a common denominator of all Mexican nationals. It is no longer legitimate to assume "that any member of the [national] group will exhibit certain regularities of behavior which are common in high degree among the other members of the society." Nations, like other complex societies, must however, "possess cultural forms or mechanisms which groups involved in the same overall web of relationships can use in their formal and informal dealings with each other." Such forms develop historically, hand in hand with other processes which lead to the formation of nations, and social groups which are caught up in these processes must become "acculturated" to their usage. Only where such forms exist, can communication and coördinated behavior be established among the constituent groups of such a society. They provide the cultural idiom of behavior and ideal representations through which different groups of the same society can pursue and manipulate their different fates within a coordinated framework. This paper, then, deals with one such cultural form, operating on the symbolic level. The study of this symbol seems particularly rewarding, since it is not restricted to one set of social ties, but refers to a very wide range of social relationships.

The image of Guadalupe and her shrine at Tepeyac are surrounded by an origin myth. According to this myth, the Virgin Mary appeared to Juan Diego, a Christianized Indian of commoner status, and addressed him in Nahuatl. The encounter took place on the Hill of Tepeyac in the year 1531, ten years after the Spanish Conquest of Tenochtitlan. The Virgin commanded Juan Diego to seek out the archbishop of Mexico and to inform him of her desire to see a church built in her honor on Tepeyac Hill. After Juan Diego was twice unsuccessful in his efforts to carry out her order, the Virgin wrought a miracle. She bade Juan Diego pick roses in a sterile spot where normally only desert plants could grow, gathered the roses into the Indian's cloak, and told him to present cloak and roses to the incredulous archbishop. When Juan Diego unfolded his cloak before the bishop, the image of the Virgin was miraculously stamped upon it. The bishop acknowledged the miracle, and ordered a shrine built where Mary had appeared to her humble servant.

The shrine, rebuilt several times in centuries to follow, is today a basilica, the third highest kind of church in Western Christendom. Above the central altar hangs Juan Diego's cloak with the miraculous image. It shows a young woman without child, her head lowered demurely in her shawl. She wears an open crown and flowing gown, and stands upon a half moon symbolizing the Immaculate Conception.

The shrine of Guadalupe was, however, not the first religious structure built on Tepeyac; nor was Guadalupe the first female supernatural associated with the hill. In pre-Hispanic times, Tepeyac had housed a temple to the earth and fertility goddess Tonantzin, Our Lady Mother, who—like Guadalupe—was associated with the moon. Temple, like basilica, was the center of large scale pilgrimages. That the veneration accorded Guadalupe drew inspiration from the earlier worship of Tonantzin is attested by several Spanish friars. F. Bernardino de Sahagún, writing fifty years after the Conquest says: "Now that the Church of Our Lady of Guadalupe has been built there, they call her Tonantzin too. . . . The term refers . . . to that ancient Tonantzin and this state of affairs should be remedied, because the proper name of the Mother of God is not Tonantzin, but Dios and Nantzin. It seems to be a satanic device to mask idolatry . . . and they come from far away to visit that Tonantzin, as much as before; a devotion which is also suspect because there are many churches of Our Lady everywhere and they do not go to them; and they come from faraway lands to this Tonantzin as of old." F. Martin de León writes in a similar vein: "On the hill where Our Lady of Guadalupe is they adored the idol of a goddess they called Tonantzin, which means Our Mother, and this is also the name they give Our Lady and they always say they are going to Tonantzin or they are celebrating Tonantzin and many of them understand this in the old way and not in the modern way. . . ." The syncretism was still alive in the seventeenth century. F. Jacinto de la Serna, in discussing the pilgrimages to Guadalupe at Tepeyac, noted: ". . . it is the purpose of the wicked to [worship] the goddess and not the Most Holy Virgin, or both together."

Increasingly popular during the sixteenth century, the Guadalupe cult gathered emotional impetus during the seventeenth. During this century appear the first known pictorial representations of Guadalupe, apart from the miraculous original; the first poems are written in her honor; and the first sermons announce the transcendental implications of her supernatural appearance in Mexico and among Mexicans. Historians have long tended to neglect the seventeeth century which seemed "a kind of Dark Age in Mexico." Yet "this quiet time was of the utmost importance in the development of Mexican Society." During this century, the institution of the hacienda comes to dominate Mexican life. During this century, also, "New Spain is ceasing to be 'new' and to be 'Spain.' " These new experiences require a new cultural idiom, and in the Guadalupe cult, the component segments of Mexican colonial society encountered cultural forms in which they could express their parallel interests and longings.

The primary purpose of this paper is not, however, to trace the history of the Guadalupe symbol. It is concerned rather with its functional aspects, its roots and reference to the major social relationships of Mexican society.

The first set of relationships which I would like to single out for consideration are the ties of kinship, and the emotions generated in the play of relationships within families. I want to suggest that some of the meanings of the Virgin symbol in general, and of the Guadalupe symbol in particular, derive from these emotions. I say "some meanings" and I use the term "derive" rather than "originate," because the form and function of the family in any given society are themselves determined by other social factors: technology, economy, residence, political power. The family is but one relay in the circuit within which symbols are generated in complex societies. Also, I used the plural "families" rather than "family," because there are demonstrably more than one kind of family in Mexico. I shall simplify the available information on Mexican family life, and discuss the material in terms of two major types of families. The first kind of family is congruent with the closed and static life of the Indian village. It may be called the Indian family. In this kind of family, the husband is ideally dominant, but in reality labor and authority are shared equally among both marriage partners. Exploitation of one sex by the other is atypical; sexual feats do not add to a person's status in the eyes of others. Physical punishment and authoritarian treatment of children are rare. The second kind of family is congruent with the much more open, mobile, manipulative life in communities which are actively geared to the life of the nation, a life in which power relationships between individuals and groups are of great moment. This kind of family may be called the Mexican family. Here, the father's authority is unquestioned on both the real and the ideal plane. Double sex standards prevail, and male sexuality is charged with a desire to exercise domination. Children are ruled with a heavy hand; physical punishment is frequent.

The Indian family pattern is consistent with the behavior towards Guadalupe noted by John Bushnell in the Matlazinca speaking community of San Juan Atzingo in the Valley of Toluca. There, the image of the Virgin is addressed in passionate terms as a source of warmth and love, and the *pulque* or century plant beer drunk on ceremonial occasions is identified with her milk. Bushnell postulates that here Guadalupe is identified with the mother as a source of early satisfactions, never again experienced after separation from the mother and emergence into social adulthood. As such, Guadalupe embodies a longing to return to the pristine state in which hunger and unsatisfactory social relations are minimized. The second family pattern is also consistent with a symbolic identification of Virgin and mother, yet this time within a context of adult male dominance and sexual assertion, discharged against submissive females and children. In this second context, the Guadalupe symbol is charged with the energy of rebellion against the father. Her image is the embodiment of hope in a victorious outcome of the struggle between generations.

This struggle leads to a further extension of the symbolism. Successful rebellion against power figures is equated with the promise of life; defeat with the promise of death. As John A. Mackay has suggested, there thus takes place a further symbolic identification of the Virgin with life; of defeat and death with the crucified Christ. In Mexican artistic tradition, as in Hispanic artistic tradition in general, Christ is never depicted as an adult man, but always either as a helpless child, or more often as a figure beaten, tortured, defeated and killed. In this symbolic equation we are touching upon some of the roots both of the passionate affirmation of faith in the Virgin, and of the fascination with death which characterizes Baroque Christianity in general, and Mexican Catholicism in particular. Guadalupe stands for life, for hope, for health; Christ on the cross, for despair, and for death.

Supernatural mother and natural mother are thus equated symbolically, as are earthly and other worldly hopes and desires. These hopes center on the provision of food and emotional warmth in the first case, in the successful waging of the Oedipal struggle in the other.

Family relations are, however, only one element in the formation of the Guadalupe symbol. Their analysis does little to explain Guadalupe as such. They merely illuminate the female and maternal attributes of the more widespread Virgin symbol. Guadalupe is important to Mexicans not only because she is a supernatural mother, but also because she embodies their major political and religious aspirations.

To the Indian groups, the symbol is more than an embodiment of life and hope; it restores to them the hopes of salvation. We must not forget that the Spanish Conquest signified not only military defeat, but the defeat also of the old gods and the decline of the old ritual. The apparition of Guadalupe to an Indian commoner thus represents on one level the return of Tonantzin. As Tannenbaum has well said, "The Church-. . . gave the Indian an opportunity not merely to save his life, but also to save his faith in his own gods." On another level, the myth of the apparition served as a symbolic testimony that the Indian, as much as the Spaniard, was capable of being saved, capable of receiving Christianity. This must be understood against the background of the bitter theological and political argument which followed the Conquest and divided churchmen, officials, and conquerors into those who held that the Indian was incapable of conversion, thus inhuman, and therefore a fit subject of political and economic exploitation; and those who held that the Indian was human, capable of conversion and that this exploitation had to be tempered by the demands of the Catholic faith and of orderly civil processes of government. The myth of Guadalupe thus validates the Indian's right to legal defense, orderly government, to citizenship; to supernatural salvation, but also to salvation from random oppression.

But if Guadalupe guaranteed a rightful

place to the Indians in the new social system of New Spain, the myth also held appeal to the large group of disinherited who arose in New Spain as illegitimate offspring of Spanish fathers and Indian mothers, or through impoverishment, acculturation or loss of status within the Indian or Spanish group. For such people, there was for a long time no proper place in the social order. Their very right to exist was questioned in their inability to command the full rights of citizenship and legal protection. Where Spaniard and Indian stood squarely within the law, they inhabited the interstices and margins of constituted society. These groups acquired influence and wealth in the seventeenth and eighteenth centuries, but were yet barred from social recognition and power by the prevailing economic, social and political order. To them, the Guadalupe myth came to represent not merely the guarantee of their assured place in heaven, but the guarantee of their place in society here and now. On the political plane, the wish for a return to a paradise of early satisfactions of food and warmth, a life without defeat, sickness or death, gives rise to a political wish for a Mexican paradise, in which the illegitimate sons would possess the country, and the irresponsible Spanish overlords, who never acknowledged the social responsibilities of their paternity, would be driven from the land.

In the writings of seventeenth century ecclesiastics, Guadalupe becomes the harbinger of this new order. In the book by Miguel Sánchez, published in 1648, the Spanish Conquest of New Spain is justified solely on the ground that it allowed the Virgin to become manifest in her chosen country, and to found in Mexico a new paradise. Just as Israel had been chosen to produce Christ, so Mexico had been chosen to produce Guadalupe. Sánchez equates her with the apocalyptic woman of the Revelation of John (XII, 1), "arrayed with the sun, and the moon under her feet, and upon her head a crown of twelve stars" who is to realize the prophecy of Deuteronomy VIII, 7–10 and lead the Mexicans into the Promised Land. Colonial Mexico thus becomes the desert of Sinai; Independent Mexico the land of milk and honey. F. Francisco de Florencia, writing in 1688, coined the slogan which made Mexico not merely another chosen nation, but the Chosen Nation: *non fecit taliter omni nationi* [he did not act in such a way for every nation], words which still adorn the portals of the basilica, and shine forth in electric lights bulbs at night. And on the eve of Mexican independence, Servando Teresa de Mier elaborates still further the Guadalupan myth by claiming that Mexico had been converted to Christianity long before the Spanish Conquest. The apostle Saint Thomas had brought the image of Guadalupe-Tonantzin to the New World as a symbol of his mission, just as Saint James had converted Spain with the image of the Virgin of the Pillar. The Spanish Conquest was therefore historically unnecessary, and should be erased from the annals of history. In this perspective, the Mexican War of Independence marks the final realization of the apocalyptic promise. The banner of Guadalupe leads the insurgents; and their cause is referred to as "her law." In this ultimate extension of the symbol, the promise of life held out by the supernatural mother has become the promise of an independent Mexico, liberated from the irrational authority of the Spanish father-oppressors and restored to the Chosen Nation whose election had been manifest in the apparition of the Virgin on Tepeyac. The land of the supernatural mother is finally possessed by her rightful heirs. The symbolic circuit is closed. Mother; food, hope, health, life; supernatural salvation and salvation from oppression; Chosen People and national independence—all find expression in a single master symbol.

The Guadalupe symbol thus links together family, politics and religion; colonial past and independent present; Indian and Mexican. It reflects the salient social relationships of Mexican life, and embodies the emotions which they generate. It provides a cultural idiom through which the tenor and emotions of these relationships can be expressed. It is, ultimately, a way of talking about Mexico: a "collective representation" of Mexican society.

Gary H. Gossen

TEMPORAL AND SPATIAL EQUIVALENTS IN CHAMULA RITUAL SYMBOLISM

In this paper, prepared especially for this volume, the author describes some of the cosmological referents for the religious symbolism of a modern Maya community. In Chamula, the Ancient Maya sun and moon deities and other supernaturals appear to have merged in a meaningful way with the Christian pantheon which the Dominican missionaries introduced after the Spanish Conquest. The paper illustrates that internal consistency and meaning in religious symbolism do not necessarily atrophy in cases of culture contact and syncretism. (See, for example, the similarity between the modern Chamulas' belief system and that of the Ancient Maya [León-Portilla, 1968, and Thompson, 1970].) Chamulas believe that the sun-Christ not only delimits the spatial boundaries of their universe, but also maintains the critical temporal cycles which regulate their agricultural activity and ritual life. Hence, most of the fundamental discriminations in Chamula ritual symbolism—right/left, up/down, counterclockwise/clockwise—emphasize the primacy of the sun and all that he represents. The paper also illustrates the usefulness of Victor Turner's concept of multivocality (multiple symbolic referents) in describing and attempting to make intelligible the complexity of belief systems which are not our own.

Printed with the author's permission.

The Jews saw that it was written
That Our Father would give heat
When he ascended to the sky.
But he did not go directly to the sky.
First he went to the underworld for two days,
And for two days the Jews were sad.
On the third day Our Father returned.
And the Jews cried,
For Our Father had begun his ascent to the sky.
On the third day, the Jews gathered together awaiting their fate.
Then they felt it!
There was a bit of heat from Our Father.
Slowly the heat on the land increased.
By ten o'clock the Jews were very ill.
By the time Our Father reached the center of the sky
The Jews had perished.

—A fragment of an account of the creation, as dictated by Salvador López Sethol, age 24, a ritual assistant to the First Alcalde of Barrio San Juan, Chamula

I. INTRODUCTION

My purpose in this paper is to discuss some fundamental discriminations which appear in Chamula ritual symbolism. I shall attempt to demonstrate that some of the implicit rules which govern Chamula ritual action and symbolism seem to derive ultimately from a time-space principle whose primary cosmological referent is the sun deity, *htotik*. It will be evident from the fragment of myth text cited above that the sun and Christ are one and the same in the syncretistic belief system of the Chamulas. Furthermore, as the text fragment indicates, the sun-Christ deity was responsible for delimiting the major temporal and spatial cycles by means of his death and subsequent ascent into the sky, thus defeating the forces of chaos, cold, and evil. The sun is therefore the initial and primary symbol of ethical, spatial, and temporal order in the Chamula universe. He represents the most distant and most sacred extreme in a continuum of social categories which begins at the ceremonial center of Chamula, the "navel of the earth," in Chamula terminology, and the center of the moral universe.

Chamula is a Tzotzil-speaking municipio of approximately 40,000 modern Maya Indians which lies at the top of the Central Chiapas Highlands of southern Mexico. All Chamulas engage to a greater or lesser extent in subsistence maize, squash, and bean agriculture. Nearly all Chamula families also keep a few sheep for wool for their own clothing and for a small surplus which is sold to Indians in nearby municipios. They supplement their income by engaging in economic specializations such as pottery or furniture manufacture or in employment as day laborers in the Ladino trade center of

San Cristóbal or on maize fields or coffee plantations in the lowlands. Chamulas live virilocally in dispersed hamlets which belong to one or more of the three barrios of the municipio. The barrios are ranked in order of ritual importance: first, Barrio San Juan, which is generally east of the ceremonial center; second, Barrio San Pedro, which is generally north of the ceremonial center; finally, Barrio San Sebastián, which lies to the west and south of the ceremonial center. The three barrios converge on the ceremonial center, which has virtually no permanent population. The center serves as the symbolic focus of nearly all public ritual and administrative activity. Rental houses there provide homes for the political and religious officials while they serve their terms in office, ranging from one to three years. Chamulas are governed by a political organization which is partly traditional (Ayuntamiento Regional, consisting of sixty-three positions, or cargos) and partly prescribed by Mexican law (Ayuntamiento Constitucional, consisting of twelve positions, including that of the chief magistrate, the Presidente). A religious organization consisting of sixty-one positions supervises ceremonial activities and cults to the saints and the sun and moon deities; it also coordinates its activities with those of the political organization. Political and religious authority at the local hamlet level lies in the hands of past cargo-holders, heads of segments of patrilineages, and shamans. (See Pozas, 1959 and 1962, and Gossen, 1970, for more ethnographic background.)

Chamula is among the most conservative and self-conscious of the Indian communities of Highland Chiapas, and has apparently been a discrete cultural entity since before the time of the Spanish conquest and Dominican missionization. At present it permits no Spanish-speaking Mexicans to live permanently or to hold property within its boundaries except for one family, that of the Mexican secretary who helps the Chamulas in their dealings with the state and national governments. The Ladino (Mexican) schoolteachers, the Ladino priest, and the Instituto Nacional Indigenista doctor are permitted to stay overnight on a semi-regular basis, but all other persons must get specific permission from municipal authorities to spend the night in the municipio. Chamula is also one of the largest and most rapidly growing communities in the highlands and the population explosion is forcing people to use whatever means they can find to acquire additional land outside the municipio boundaries. They take maximum advantage of agrarian reform laws and are relocating in large and small groups throughout the state of Chiapas. These relocated groups, however, do not generally become acculturated nor do they cease to speak Tzotzil, for they generally move in units large enough to maintain a microcosm of "normal" Chamula life. Their ties to their home municipio remain very strong and they continue to regard it as "the navel of the earth," the center of the moral universe.

II. THE CHAMULA UNIVERSE

Chamulas believe that the earth is an inclined island which is higher in the east than in the west. This belief is supported by Chamula experience in the outside world. Men go frequently to the south and west to the nearby lowlands of the Grijalva River Valley to work on rented maize fields and to the Pacific slope to work on coffee plantations. This tropical lowland area is relatively close to their cool highland home, but its elevation is spectacularly lower than that of Chamula. In other words, the drop-off to the south and west is dramatic; to the north and east there is no immediate drop-off, only a continuation of small highland valleys and basins. Significantly, Tzontevitz Mountain, the highest in the Central Chiapas Highlands and the most sacred of all mountains to Chamulas, lies both to the east of Chamula ceremonial center and within Barrio San Juan, which is the highest ranking of the three barrios. Chamulas have few economic reasons to travel extensively to the north and east beyond their own boundary. This is not the case with the lowland south and west, which are relatively well known to most Chamula men. Economic activity, travel, social organization, and topography, therefore, support and reflect the prevailing belief that the island-earth is generally high in the east and low in the west. This is suggested by the Tzotzil words which are sometimes used to designate these directions: *ta ʔak'ol* ("above" or "up") means east; *ta ʔolon* ("below" or "down") means west.[1]

Chamulas believe that the earth is laced with caves and tunnels which eventually

[1] It is important to clarify that, although the tropical lowlands actually lie mostly south and slightly west of Chamula, the whole lowland area is conceptually united by the qualities of lowness and association with the setting sun. Thus, Chamulas will frequently say that they are going west (*ta ʔolon*, "down" or "below") to the coffee plantations. This is not an error in their directional sense, but simply an expression of certain conceptual equivalences in their cosmology. Furthermore, many of the traditional travel routes which Chamulas have used to reach the lowlands in the past (and

reach the edges of the earth. These limestone caves and passages are also believed to provide channels for the drainage of the highlands. Chamulas also believe that the earthlords, who live in the mountain caves, provide all forms of precipitation, including accompanying clouds, lightning, and thunder. These beliefs are supported by the fact that the Central Chiapas Highlands are in fact a karst-type limestone area in which internal drainage is extremely important. Only earthlords, snakes (which are the familiars and alternate forms of the earthlords), and demons inhabit the internal cave networks of the earth. Hence, all are associated with dampness, darkness, and lowness.

The earth is the middle of three major horizontal layers of the Chamula universe. The sky and the underworld make up the remainder. Three layers, which informants draw as concentric domes, make up the sky. The first and smallest of these domes is the only level of the sky which is visible to most human beings. This first level, however, is only a reflection of what is happening at the upper two levels. The moon (who is conceptually equivalent to the Virgin Mary, *hmeʔtik* or "Our Mother") and minor constellations travel in the second level. The sun (who is conceptually equivalent to Christ, *htotik* or "Our Father"), Saint Jerome, the guardian of animal souls, and major (bright) constellations reside and travel in the third level. The heat and brilliance of the sun's head are so great that they penetrate the two inferior layers of the sky. Thus, it is only the reflection of the sun's face and head which we perceive on earth.

The underworld is the dwelling place of the dead and is characterized by inversions of many kinds. When it is dark on earth, it is light in the underworld, for the sun travels that part of his circular path around the earth at that time. Conversely, night in the underworld occurs during the daytime on earth. There is no proper food in the underworld. The dead eat charred food and flies in place of normal food. The dead must also refrain from sexual intercourse. With these exceptions, life in the underworld is much like life on earth. People do not suffer there. Those who have murdered or committed suicide are exceptions. These are burned by the sun as he travels his circuit there during the night on earth. The underworld is also the point from which the universe is supported. Opinions vary on the nature of this support, but most Chamulas think that (1) a single earthbearer carries the universe on his back, or that (2) four earthbearers support the universe at the intercardinal points.

The whole cosmological system is bound and held together by the circular paths of the sun and the moon, who are the principal deities in the Chamula pantheon. Each day they pass by the eastern and western edges of the earth on their trips to the sky and underworld. It is not surprising that these deities effectively represent most of the fundamental assumptions which Chamulas make about order, for they mark temporal and spatial categories which are critical for the maintenance of life as Chamulas know it. In the remainder of this paper, I shall explore some of the components of the ideal order which Chamulas represent by means of ritual symbolism.

III. SOME FUNDAMENTAL DISCRIMINATIONS

THE SUN AS THE FIRST PRINCIPLE OF ORDER

A primary and irreducible symbol of Chamula thinking and symbolism is the sun, "Our Father," *htotik*. At once in the concept of the sun, most units of lineal, cyclical, and generational time are implied, as well as the spatial limits and subdivisions of the universe, vertical and horizontal. Most of the other deities (earthlords are important exceptions) and all men are related lineally or spiritually to the sun-creator, who is the son of the moon. Day and night, the yearly agricultural and religious cycles, the seasons, the divisions of the day, most plants and animals, the stars and the constellations, all are the work of the creator, *htotik*, the lifeforce itself. Only the demons, monkeys, and Jews are logically prior to and hostile to the coming of order. These forces killed the sun and forced him to ascend into the heavens, thus providing heat, light, life, and order (see text fragment which precedes Section I). Hence, the Tzotzil words for "day" *(k'ak'al)* and "fiesta" *(k'in)*, which provide fundamental time references for Chamulas, are directly related to the words for "fire" *(k'ok')* and "hot" *(k'išin)*, respectively. It is also relevant

---

continue to use in the present) take them first to the west and then back to the south and east to reach their destinations. One of these routes takes them down the Ixtapa Valley of Zinacantan. The orientation of this valley is close to "true east/up-west/down." Furthermore, this valley appears, archaeologically and historically, to have been a principal channel for trade and other forms of contact (including the Spanish Conquest) between the lowlands and the Central Highlands (see Vogt, 1969: 1-31, and Wasserstrom, 1970: 1-22). It should also be noted that names and subjective evaluation of the directions are not exactly the same in all of the Tzotzil-speaking communities of the highlands. Compare, for example, the case of Zinacantan, which shares a long boundary with Chamula (Vogt, 1969: 298, 422, 442, 602).

that one of the several names for the sun-creator is *htotik k'ak'al* or "Our Father Heat (Day)."

The fundamental spatial divisions of the universe, the cardinal directions, are also derived from the relative positions of the sun on his east-west path across the heavens:

EAST: *lok'eb k'ak'al*, "emergent heat (or day)"
WEST: *maleb k'ak'al*, "waning heat (or day)"
NORTH: *šokon vinahel ta bae'i k'ob*, "the edge of heaven on the right hand"
SOUTH: *šokon vinahel ta e'et k'ob*, "the edge of heaven on the left hand"

The principal temporal divisions of each day are also described in terms of the relative position of the sun on his path across the heavens. For example, "in the afternoon" is generally expressed in Tzotzil as *ta mal k'a-k'al*, "in the waning heat (or day)." "In the mid-morning" is expressed as *štoy ša k'ak'al*, "the heat (day) is rising now." Temporal divisions of the year are expressed most frequently in terms of the fiesta cycle. One is able to specify almost any day in the year by referring to stages of, or day before or after, one of the more than thirty religious fiestas which are celebrated annually in Chamula. In referring to a certain day in relation to the fiesta cycle, one says, for example, "*sk'an to ʔošib k'ak'al ta k'in san huan* ("It is three days until the fiesta of San Juan"). This is usually understood as I have translated it, yet the relationship and similarity of words (*k'ok'*, "fire," and *k'ak'al*, "heat" or "day"; *k'in*, "fiesta," and *k'išin*, "hot") in the concepts noted above is such that it is possible to understand this as: "three daily cycles of heat before a major (religious) cycle of heat." These are but a few examples which suggest that the sun and his lifegiving heat determine the basic categories of temporal and spatial order.

THE SUN AND THE PRIMACY OF THE RIGHT HAND

Chamula cosmological symbolism has as its primary orientation the point of view of the sun as he emerges on the eastern horizon each day, facing his universe, north on his right hand, south on his left hand (see Figure 1, which is a Chamula's drawing of this fundamental cosmological moment). This orientation helps to explain the derivation of the descriptive terms for north ("the edge of heaven on the right hand") and south ("the edge of heaven on the left hand"). Furthermore, the adjective "right," *bae'i*, is positively evaluated in innumerable words and idioms in Tzotzil. By extension, it means "actual," "very," "true," or "the most representative," as in "Tzotzil" (*bae'i k'op*), which may be translated literally as "the true language"; or "right hand," (*bae'i k'ob*), which may also be read as the "real hand" or "true hand." North is on the right hand of the sun-creator as he traverses the sky. This orientation appears to be related to the belief that north is a direction of good omen and virtue. Chamulas often express this as *mas lek sk'an yoʔnton ta bae'i k'ob li htotike*, or "Our Father's heart prefers the right hand way." This fundamental orientation may also contribute to an understanding of Chamula ritual treatment of space. It is first of all necessary to understand that religious cargo-holders themselves have an aspect of deity in that they share with the sun and the saints (the sun's kinsmen) the responsibility and the burden of maintaining the social order. While imparting a sacred aspect to themselves through exemplary behavior and constant use of sacred symbols and objects such as strong rum liquor, incense, candles, fireworks, and cigarettes, most of which have actual or metaphoric qualities of heat, they metaphorically follow the sun's pattern of motion by moving to their own right through any ritual space which lies before them. This helps to explain the overwhelming tendency of almost all Chamula ritual motion to follow a counterclockwise pattern. This direction is the horizontal equivalent of the sun's daily vertical path across the heavens from east to west. One can derive this transformation according to Chamula premises by pretending to face the universe from the eastern horizon, as the sun does each morning, and

FIGURE 1
The Sun-Christ emerging from the Eastern horizon, original by Marian López Calixto.

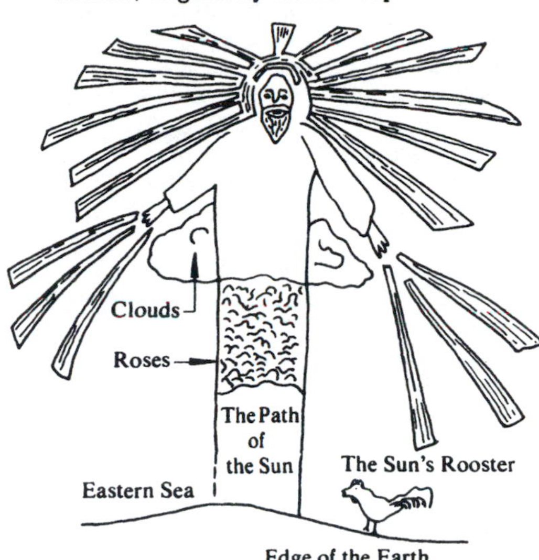

"turning" the vertical solar orbit to the right so that it lies flat on the earth. I should emphasize that no Chamula ever stated the derivation as simply as I have stated it here. However, informants consistently said that east is the sun's position at *šlok' htotik* ("the sun appears" or "dawn"); north is the horizontal equivalent to the sun's vertical position at *ʔolol k'ak'al* ("half heat," "half-day," or "noon"); west is *šbat htotik* ("the sun departs" or "sundown"); and south is the horizontal equivalent to the sun's vertical position at *ʔolol ʔak'obal* ("half-night" or "midnight"). This horizontal transformation allows cargo officials to "move as the sun moves," thereby restating symbolically both the temporal and spatial cycles for which the sun is responsible. This makes the beginning of any ritual (counterclockwise) circuit "conceptual east." North in this system becomes the horizontal equivalent of the point of "maximum heat" of the sun at noon at the zenith of his orbit; west and south also follow the solar circuit. This helps to explain why the cardinal direction north shares with the east the sign of good omen and positive orientation; west and south are generally negative in the cosmological system. I attempt to summarize some of this information in Figure 2.

The positive symbolic value of the north is also intelligible in that Chamulas are quite conscious of the fact that the apparent position of the rising sun shifts northward on the eastern horizon during the increasingly longer days between the vernal equinox and the summer solstice. This period is also associated with the first rains of the wet season (in early May) and with the beginning of the annual growing cycle for highland crops. South, on the other hand, is associated with night and the underworld in the daily cycle. South is also associated with the time of shortening days, the autumnal equinox to the winter solstice, which marks the end of the growing season and the beginning of killing frosts and death in the annual solar cycle. This helps to explain why the south is nega-

FIGURE 2
Some category relationships in Chamula cosmology, showing particularly the spatial equivalence of vertical solar and counterclockwise ritual circuits.

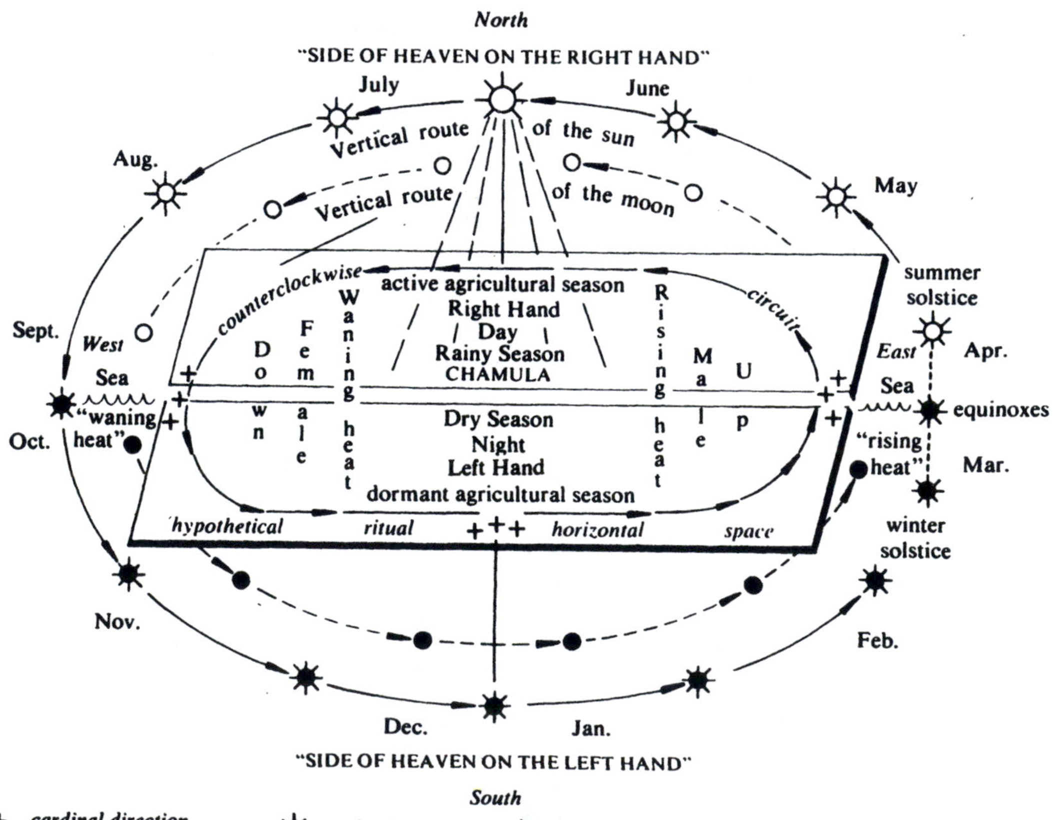

tively regarded in some respects, for it represents both night and frost, dry weather and the nonproductive agricultural season. West represents incipient death in the life cycle, twilight in the daily cycle, as well as the period between the summer solstice and the autumnal equinox. It is significant that the intercardinal direction southeast is the first point in the spatio-temporal symbolic scheme which represents an "upswing" or emergence of the sun from the negative nadir (south) of the system. This may be important in explaining why the southeast is frequently an alternate to the east as the initial position in ritual circuits and positions of ritual personnel (see Figure 2).

Ritual circuits, therefore, carry a great deal more information than they appear to at first glance. They proceed counterclockwise because that direction is the logical horizontal equivalent of the annual solar cycle and the daily solar cycle. Even though circumstances may not allow all individual circuits to begin in the actual east or southeast, the principles of the right hand and counterclockwise motion appear to serve as ritual surrogates for the eastern solar orientation and the solar cycle. Any initial ritual location can thus become "conceptual east." In this way men are better able to base their ritual orientation on the first principle of life itself, which is the sun.

THE PRIMACY OF "UP"

The primacy of the sun as giver of order implies still another symbolic discrimination: primacy of "up" over "down." Cosmologically, increasing height and goodness are associated with the rising sun; decreasing height and threat, with the setting sun. It will be recalled from the discussion above (Section II) that the eastern part of the earth is believed to be tilted upward (*ta ʔak'ol*) and the western part downward (*ta ʔolon*). Living in what they believe to be the highest place on the earth, they as a group are at a point closer to the sun when at its zenith of potency and heat (at noon) than any other Indian or Ladino community with which they are acquainted. Furthermore, Tzontevitz, the sacred mountain which lies in the highest-ranking of the three barrios, is also the home of their patron saint San Juan. In addition, as I mentioned above, Tzontevitz Mountain happens in fact to be the highest peak in the Central Highlands. Chamulas therefore enjoy an especially close relationship with the sun in a physical and metaphorical sense. This position also places the predominantly Indian Highlands in a more desirable (i.e., closer) relationship with the sun than the predominantly Ladino Lowlands. This factor is not unrelated to the Chamula view of social distance, in which the highlands are generally considered to be less dangerous and less asocial than the lowlands.

In the ritual setting, the primacy of "up" is expressed metaphorically in the positions of saints in relation to human beings. They ride and sit habitually on litters and platforms which raise them above the level of men. Cargo-holders who serve them achieve thereby elevation of goodness, virtue, and prestige. For Alféreces (religious cargo-holders who are in charge of saints' objects, particularly their banners and clothing), this ritual height is expressed by special pole and branch towers, fifteen feet high, which are constructed at their homes at the time when they leave office. A representative of the Alférez sits in the tower and thus symbolizes the new heights of the desirable which the outgoing official has achieved in his year in office. In so doing, he has helped the sun to maintain order and thus partakes of the sun's good, rising aspect.

Related to the good, rising aspect of ritual cycles is the importance of head over feet. Heads and faces of images of saints receive a great amount of attention in ritual action and symbolism, the reason being that the head is the source of their heat and power. An example of this is the cult to the sacred flagpole tips which the Pasión sponsors at the "Fiesta of Games" in February. The tips symbolize the head and halo of the sun and, by extension, the whole concept of the sun. It appears to be significant that this fiesta, which is the major annual cult to the sun deity, occurs in February, a time of drought, frost, and agricultural dormancy, but *also* the time of the beginning upswing of the solar cycle from its nadir in the symbolic system (see symbolic associations in Figure 2).

THE PRIMACY OF HEAT

The primacy of heat over cold in Chamula symbolism has been apparent in several of the above discussions. The importance of heat is ever present in Chamula life, from daily household activity to ritual settings. The daily round of Chamula domestic life centers on the hearth, which lies near the center of the dirt floor of nearly all Chamula houses. The working day usually begins and ends around the fire, men and boys sitting and eating to the right of the hearth (from the point of view of one who faces the interior from the front door), women and girls to the left of the hearth (see Figure 3). Furthermore, men in this patrifocal society always sit on tiny chairs, thus raising them above the cold, feminine ground, and wear sandals, which separate them from the ground and complement their masculine heat. Women, on the other hand, customarily sit on the ground, which is symbolically cold, and always go barefooted, which, symbolically, does not separate them, but rather gives them direct contact with the cold, feminine earth. Coldness, femininity, and lowness are logically prior to heat, masculinity, and height. This follows from the mythological account of the coming of order. The male sun was born from the womb of the female moon and was then killed by the forces of evil and darkness (the demons and the Jews). This in turn allowed him to arise into the sky as the life-giving source of order (see the myth fragment which precedes Section I).

The very words for time and space are related to heat, for the sun symbolizes the source of earthly heat as he does nearly all other aspects of cosmological order. Days, fiesta intervals, seasons, and years are all measured by increasing and decreasing cycles of heat. The opposite of order is symbolized by the cold darkness in which the demons, Jews, and monkeys lived before the forced ascension of the sun into the sky. The life cycle is also conceived as a cycle of increasing heat from a cold beginning. A baby has a dangerously cold aspect. This is reflected in the term *maš* ("monkey"), which refers to an unbaptized child. A child acquires steadily increasing heat with baptism

FIGURE 3
Space in a Chamula house.

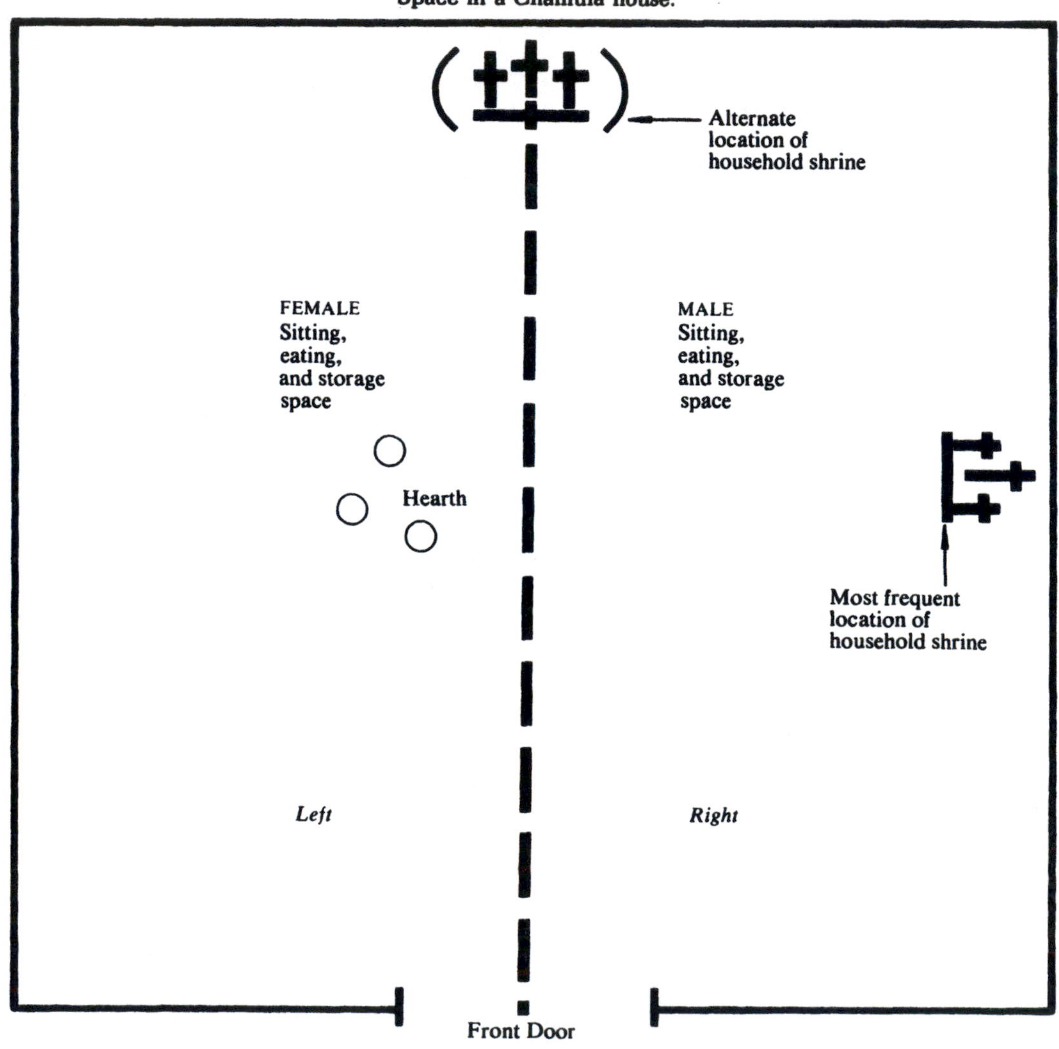

and sexual maturity. The heat of the life cycle reaches a fairly high level with social maturity, which is expressed by marriage and reproduction. The acquisition of heat may be carried further through a cargo or shamanistic career. Life and death are also elementary expressions of the hot-cold syndrome of Chamula values. Life crisis rituals and cargo initiations include symbols of both life (hot and integrative) and death (cold and disjunctive). Hot and cold are also fundamental categories in the bewildering complexity of Chamula theory of illness. In nearly all of these domains (with the exception of illness, in which a hot-cold disequilibrium is frequently a cause), increasing heat expresses the divine and order-giving will of the sun himself.

Most ritual substances also have the quality of heat, actual and metaphoric. Tobacco, rum, incense, candles, and fireworks generate or emit heat. Furthermore, the raw materials for them are believed to be of lowland, tropical origin-which is certainly true for the most part. Resin for incense, beef tallow and wax for candles, the ingredients for gunpowder, sugarcane for rum, and tobacco for cigarettes do in fact come from, or at least through, the lowlands. This tropical origin is interesting because it illustrates a paradox in Chamula thinking about the world. Although the highlands are closer than the lowlands to the sun in a vertical sense, the climate of the highlands is actually much colder than that of the lowlands. It may be that the ambiguous quality of the lowlands (physically hot yet socially distant) makes them a logical source for some sacred symbols and substances. This symbolic ambiguity may be complemented by the fact that Chamulas are economically dependent on the lowlands in many ways.

THE PRIMACY OF LIGHT

It follows from *htotik's* primordial force in Chamula symbolism that light also represents the desirable and the good. This has precedent in the cosmogonic moment when the sun ascended into the sky, creating the categories of temporal and spatial order. Light and heat were the first manifestations of the new order. Light has many other aspects—among them, heat and ability to penetrate. These are qualities which cargoholders and shamans share with the deities; all are known to have penetrating, all-seeing vision. It is also significant in a consideration of the meaning of light to note that Chamula men and boys customarily wear white wool tunics; women and girls generally wear brown and black wool skirts and blouses. The days and the seasons have greater and lesser proportions of light to darkness and generally are imbued with positive significance according to increasing proportion of light. The logical inverse of this principle is expressed in the Fiesta for the Dead (All Saints' Day, November 1, the beginning of the cold, dry season), in which a meal is prepared and served to the dead in the middle of the night and in a season of decreasing proportion of light to darkness each day. Similarly, funerals involve, among other things, nocturnal ritual sequences, the consumption of charred maize kernels (not cooked before charring) and black tortillas (made with a bluish-black variety of maize).

Another important light-dark syndrome occurs at Christmas, just after the winter solstice, when the sun begins to renew its strength. The climax ritual of the birth of Christ (which is also, of course, the birth of the sun) consists in Chamula of a midnight torchlight procession (December 24) around the church atrium. In this ritual an image of the Virgen del Rosario is carried around the atrium, preceded by the image of the Christ child. The female image is carried by widowed women who wear white shawls; the Christ child is carried by the male *sacristán* and his assistants. This is the only time in the ritual year (except for the immediately preceding *posadas*) in which a *single* female religious figure is carried around the atrium in procession. It is also the only time in the ritual year in which an equal number of male (one) and female (one) images participate in the procession. Usually there are more male images than female images in these processions. Furthermore, it is the only time in the ritual year in which the saints' procession occurs at night, precisely at midnight; the other processions occur slightly before noon or just at noon. These reversals in the Christmas ritual make cosmological sense because they occur at a time of the year when the nights are longest, when frost has already killed most plant life, and when the sun has just been ritually reborn. The forces of light will prevail as the sun grows up and the days increase in length in proportion to night. These gradually lengthening days will bring heat and a new growing season for the sun's body, which is maize, the most basic and most sacred of all Chamula foods.

THE PRIMACY OF MALENESS

The sun gave mankind maize from his body. This is reflected in a ritual term, *šohobal*, which is frequently used to refer to maize

FIGURE 4
Chamula church interior.

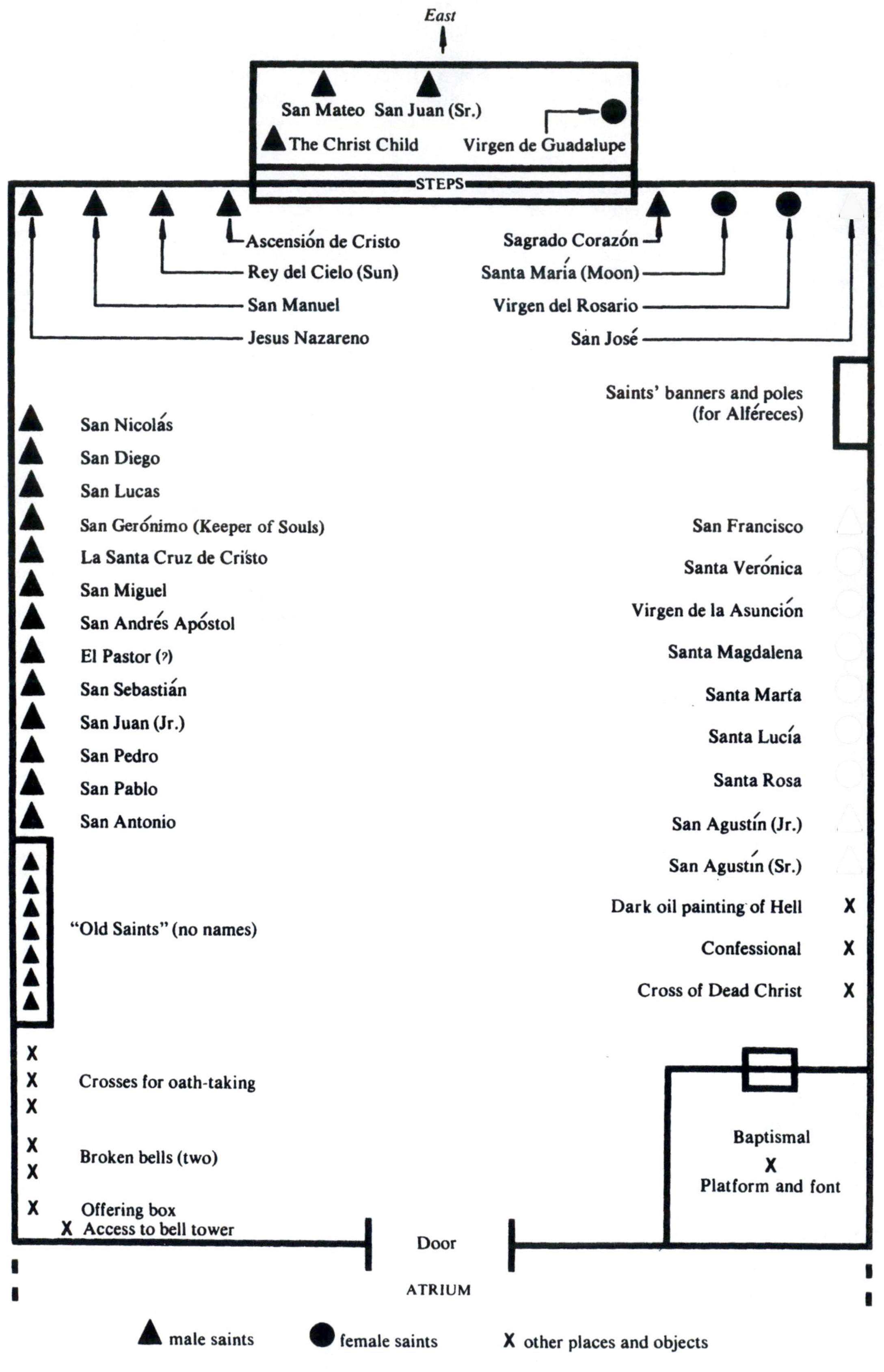

foods. It means "radiance" or "halo of the sun." According to Chamula mythology, maize (which is "hot" in the hot-cold scheme of food evaluation) came from a piece of the sun's groin (but not his penis) and included a part of his pubic hair, which is the silk of the ear of maize. The moon only gave potatoes (her breast milk) and beans (her necklace). The contrast is great, for maize is *the* staple; potatoes and beans are less important items in the diet. That relationship is analogous to that of the male principle to the female principle in this patrifocal society. Maleness receives ritual primacy; the female principle complements it. In the beginning, the moon bore the sun as her child, but very soon afterwards he asserted his authority over his mother in innumerable ways. Among other tricks, the sun blinded his mother with hot water while they were taking a sweat bath together. This explains the moon's lesser radiance and her tendency (according to Chamula belief) to follow behind the sun in the sky at a point in her circular path (second level of the sky) which is nearly always just opposite his position in his path (third level). Furthermore, the moon has the responsibility of leaving a breakfast of maize gruel for the sun each morning at the eastern horizon. In sum, she has a relationship to her son like that which prevails between the female principle and the male principle in Chamula life: one of submission within a larger sphere of economic interdependence.

The primacy of maleness is also expressed symbolically in nearly all ritual proceedings, for women have no official cargo positions. They do have some special ritual tasks, but these do not count in the cargo system. All wives of cargo-holders receive the title of their husbands, prefixed by *me?* ("mother"), suggesting a ritual relationship of male and female like that which prevails between the sun and the moon. The primacy of maleness has other expressions. In general, right, counterclockwise motion is associated with male saints; left, clockwise motion is associated with female saints. This contrast is expressed also in the distribution of sitting and working space within Chamula houses (see Figure 3). As noted above, the space to the right of the front door of a house interior (from the point of view of one looking in the front door) is male sitting and eating space. The space to the left of the front door is female sitting, eating and working space. This pattern prevails in nearly all Chamula homes which I have seen and applies only to the times of day in which both sexes are present, particularly at mealtimes. At other times during the day, women customarily work throughout the house interior. The pattern does not seem to apply to sleeping positions in the household.

In a very similar manner, the male/right–female/left rule applies to the permanent positions of all female saints and all major male saints in the Chamula church (see Figure 4). The female saints reside on the left side (south) of the church, from the point of view of the patron saint San Juan, who stands above the altar in the center of the east end of the church. While there are no female saints on the "male (north) side," there are a few unimportant male saints on the "female (south) side." I believe that it is also significant that an oil painting of Hell (a very dark one which has never been cleaned), the cross of the dead Christ, and the baptistry are all found in the "most negative," "female" part of the church, the southwestern corner. These objects are negative within the symbolic scheme. The opposite (northeastern) corner of the church is the "most positive," "most masculine" part of the church. This corner lies to the patron saint's immediate right. It is here that the major male saints and images of Christ (the sun) line the north and east walls. These ideal positions may be seen as microcosmic representations of the categories of Chamula cosmology and cosmogony. North was on the sun's right hand when he rose into the heavens in the east, just as the north is on San Juan's and Christ's right hand in the Chamula church. What more logical place could there be for the male images? When processions take place at the climax of some major fiestas in honor of male saints, the male saints march out of the church and around the atrium to the right (counterclockwise). Female saints, on the other hand, march out to the left (clockwise) around the atrium, meet at the half-way point (the west entrance to the atrium) and bow to each of the male saints in sequence. The female saints then reverse their direction of motion and line up behind the last male saint. They march around the last 180 degrees of the circuit behind the male saints, but this time in counterclockwise direction, which is associated with the male principle. The female saints thus "capitulate" symbolically to the male principle and follow the male saints as the moon follows the sun and Chamula women follow their husbands (see Figure 5). At minor fiestas in honor of male saints and at major fiestas in honor of female saints, the two sexes do not march in opposite directions. The female saints simply follow the

FIGURE 5
Pattern of male and female saints' motion in a procession.

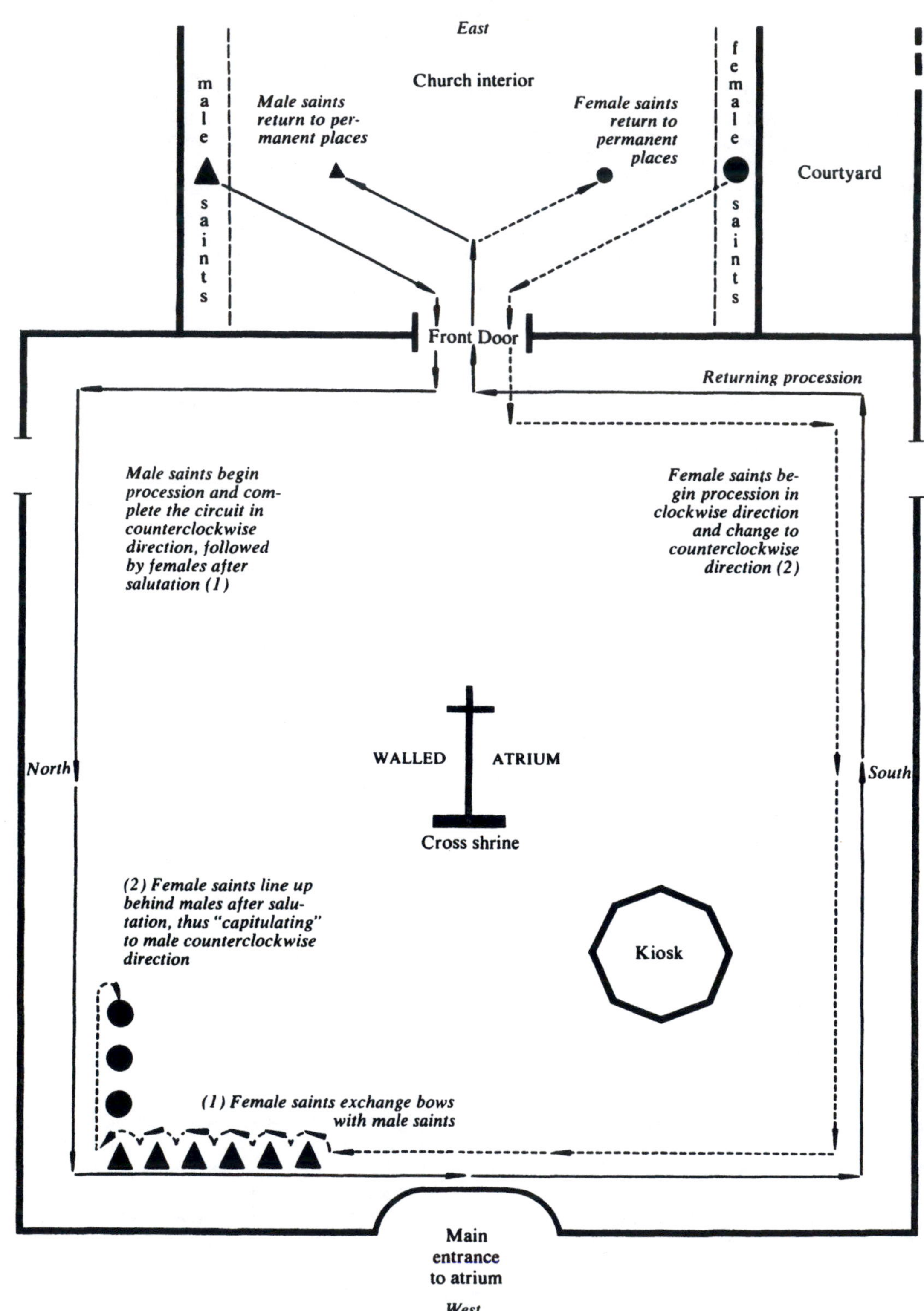

male saints all around the atrium in the male, counterclockwise direction.

Temporally, there appear to be yet other ways in which maleness asserts its primacy. The fiesta cycle, for example, does not honor a single major female saint during the half-year between the winter and summer solstices, a time which is under the influence of increasing atmospheric heat and increasing length of days in proportion to night. This is the time of the two most important fiestas in the annual cycle: Carnaval, in honor of the sun, in February; and the fiesta of San Juan, from June 21 to 24. In the latter half of the year, four major female saints are honored by fiestas (Santa Rosa and La Virgen de la Asunción, both in August; La Virgen del Rosario, in October, and La Virgen de Guadalupe in December), but these are not as important or as well attended as those which occur in the "male" half of the year.

This distribution of major female saints in the annual fiesta cycle parallels certain aspects of the female principle in each day. One-half day (from midnight to noon, a time of the sun's rising heat from the depth of the underworld to the zenith of the heavens) is believed to be the time of the sun's influence over the female principle, thus causing women to behave properly and morally during these hours. On the other hand, from noon to midnight (the time of waning heat), women are believed to be more prone to commit adultery and do evil in general, for they are under the influence of the *pukuh* (demon) at that time. This belief has mythical precedent in the fact that it was the *pukuh* (not the sun) who originally taught the first woman (not the first man) to have sexual intercourse. Hence, Chamulas believe that men, like the sun, have had to assume the major ritual responsibility for guaranteeing moral order and stability.

THE PRIMACY OF THE SENIOR PRINCIPLE

Another symbolic pattern seems to follow from the aspects of sun-primacy which have already been discussed. This is the primacy of "senior" over "junior" in the classificatory system. The sun is the senior (*bankilal*) kinsman of all of the other saints (except the Virgin and San José, who are "prior" to the sun and are sometimes difficult for Chamulas to classify). The *bankilal-ʔie'inal* (senior-junior) relationship is used in evaluating many domains, from sibling terminology in the kinship system to aspects of animal soul companions, relative rank of cargo-holders, and ranking of topographical features. It is a many-valued system in which relative age, size, distance, strength, wealth, or one of many other criteria may be applied to the ranking of a closed domain of objects or individuals. Vogt has discussed this principle at length as it exists in nearby Zinacantan (1969: 238–245). Here I should only like to point out that the "senior" primacy over "junior" has a background of time-space association which contributes to its strength as a ritual principle.

"Senior" is first of all prior to "junior" in the rather fuzzy genealogy of the deities. "Senior" aspects of domains therefore have priority over "junior" aspects of domains in ritual expressions of the social order. Spatially interpreted, this means that "senior" personnel, from their own point of view, usually stand or sit to the right of "junior" personnel. Female counterparts (usually wives) of these officials stand still further to the left, from their own point of view, or behind the male cargo officials. Whether or not they are formally placed by ritual position, individuals receive drinks and other ritual sacraments in equal portions according to the principle of more "senior" first, more "junior" last. The male principle, seniority, and higher-ranking cargo positions take precedence over the female principle, youth, and lower-ranking cargo positions. Any ritual group, then, can be ranked according to the primacy of the "senior" principle. (See Rosaldo, 1968, also reprinted in this volume, for a discussion of this ritual principle as it occurs in nearby Zinacantan.)

To confuse matters, the most "senior" official hardly ever moves in the front position of a group which is traversing a ritual circuit. In fact, he usually brings up the rear of the group. This positioning is not a paradox if one remembers that cargo-holders share certain attributes of deities, particularly of the sun himself, as they traverse ritual circuits in a counterclockwise direction. Assuming "conceptual east" as the point of orientation and beginning for a ritual circuit (discussed above), it follows that the member of the party who has greatest "heat," which is a fundamental attribute of the sun symbol of the east, should remain closest to the source of that "heat." It is a simple spatial rule of "like remains close to like." And it places the most "senior" official at the end of a procession nearly every time. While this pattern seems to prevail almost without exception in groups of male cargo-holders, it is nevertheless intriguing that females customarily follow men in daily life and in ritual processions as well. Since men in this patrifocal society outrank women for most purposes, one might assume, according to the pattern of "senior-last," that women would *precede* men. The opposite is in fact the case. It seems plausible that the female principle is both *logically prior to patrifocal order* (for the female moon gave birth to the male sun) *and subordinate (junior) to patrifocal order* for the precocious sun blinded his mother and began to give her orders shortly after his birth). I believe that this dual attribute of the female principle may be expressed in the ritual sequence which is described in Figure 5, in which female saints begin moving to their own left (clockwise)

FIGURE 6
A relationship of some expressions of the junior-senior principle to orientation of "conceptual East."

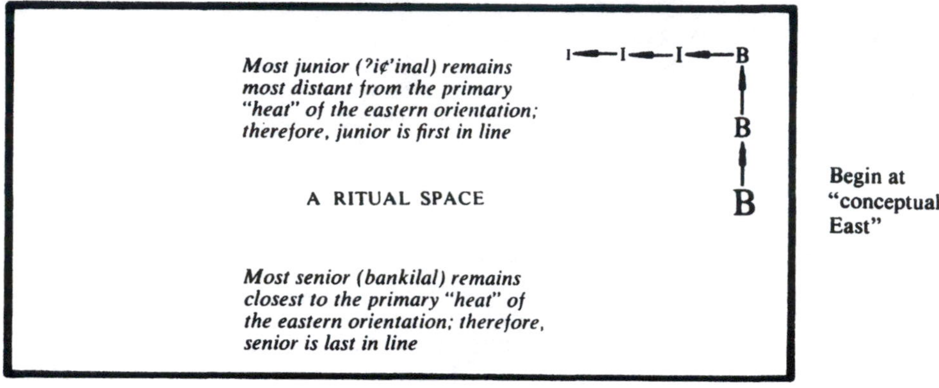

A. Junior-senior order in processions through ritual space

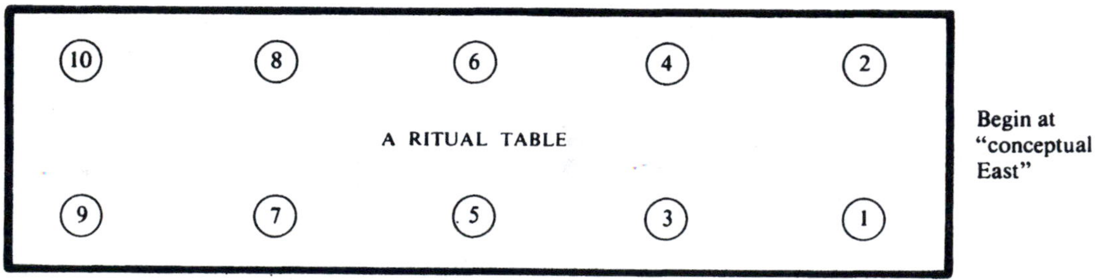

B. Junior-senior order in seating at ritual meals *(senior (bankilal) officials remain closest to "conceptual East")*

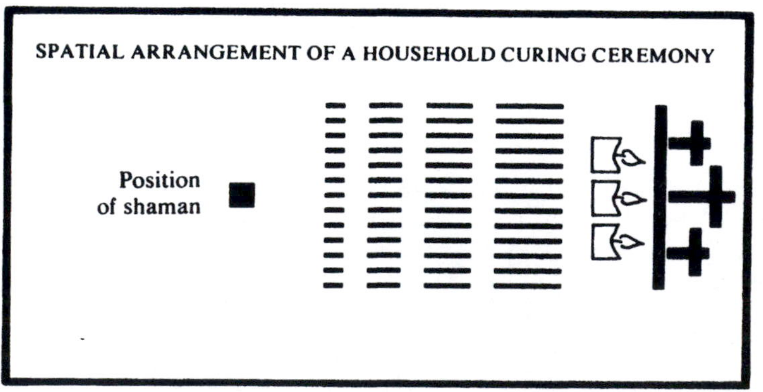

C. Junior-senior order in candle arrangement at a household curing ceremony *(largest, most expensive, and longest-burning candles remain closest to "conceptual East")*

and then line up behind the male saints, joining them to complete a counterclockwise (male) circuit.

The pattern in which most "senior" (*bankilal*) remains closest to "conceptual east" is shown in Figure 6 (Part A). Figure 6 also shows how the "senior-east" association makes intelligible such diverse spatial patterns as seating order at ritual meals (Part B) and distribution of candles at shamanistic curing rituals (Part C). In the case of the ritual table, the most senior-ranking members of the group sit closest to "conceptual east" in the cosmological microcosm and the most junior members sit closest to "conceptual west." Similarly, the cross-shrine in shamanistic rituals appears to serve as "conceptual east." The many required sizes of candles are always arranged (except in case of witchcraft rituals) so that the most "senior" candles (white, largest, longest-burning, and most expensive) are lined up closest to "conceptual east" and the most "junior" ones toward "conceptual west." I use the term "conceptual" because it is sometimes not physically possible to begin sequences or to place shrines in the position of true east. However, time-space symbolic equivalents, which appear to be assumed knowledge of most Chamulas, can make almost any situation ritually effective if the correct relationships are maintained.

IV. MICROCOSM AND REDUNDANCY

Those symbols which are most effective imply a great deal at once. The sun, the giver and maintainer of order, is such a symbol in Chamula thought. No Chamula ritual passes without innumerable references to patterns whose precedent is found in the cosmogonic moment of the sun's ascent into the heavens. All that accompanied that event is now fixed in Chamula custom and belief, for that moment provided the necessary spatial and temporal categories for an orderly social existence. The ritual task is to state what is essential about all of this in the most economical form possible. Relatively few words and actions must encapsulate what really matters; hence, the importance of sun symbolism and its multivocality, to borrow Victor Turner's useful term (1967: 50). For example, a microcosmic action such as the movement of personnel through ritual space takes its meaning from the great universe, the macrocosm of the sun. The primacy of the right hand and masculinity, the cycles of heat in the day and the year, the point of view of the eastern horizon, the counterclockwise motion—all join to recreate the past in the present and to draw in the limits of the great universe to manageable size within the sacred precincts of the Ceremonial Center. The procession of religious images around the atrium of the church at the climax of each major fiesta recreates the cosmogonic moment of the coming of the first light, the first heat, the first maize—the coming of order itself. Moreover, the procession occurs at noon, when the sun is at the zenith of the heavens, giving maximum heat. The event states not a part, but all of this at once.

Michelle Zimbalist Rosaldo and Jane Monnig Atkinson

MAN THE HUNTER AND WOMAN: METAPHORS FOR THE SEXES IN ILONGOT MAGICAL SPELLS

In this stimulating article on the metaphors for the sexes found in Ilongot magical spells, Michelle Rosaldo and Jane Atkinson combine in a highly creative manner the concepts of Victor Turner and others on "dominant" symbols and the concepts of Lévi-Strauss and others concerned with "binary oppositions." They show how the plants used in magical spells for hunting and agriculture emphasize the role of man as the hunter, the life-taker, the role of woman as the gardener, the life-giver. By opposing categories such as male/female, death/birth, forest/garden, hunter/planter, and meat/rice, these plant metaphors provide

Reprinted in abridged form from Roy Willis (ed.), *The Interpretation of Symbolism* (London: J. M. Dent & Sons Ltd.; New York: John Wiley & Sons, 1975), pp. 43–75, by permission of the authors and the publishers.

symbolic expressions of the opposition as well as the equality and complementarity of male and female domains in Ilongot life. The authors show how these symbolic distinctions are reflected in all aspects of Ilongot society, from magical spells to economic activities to procreation. They also suggest that the basic symbolic contrast between the male life-taker and the female life-giver has cross-cultural validity, and in the unabridged article they analyze comparative data from the Malay Archipelago, Indonesia, and the Philippines that support their hypothesis. They conclude that the critical difference between giving and taking life is rooted in the fact that a man's killing is always an act of will, directed toward a body other than his own; giving life through childbirth, on the other hand, is a natural function of a woman's own body. While this conclusion needs further testing with additional comparative data, the authors have clearly presented a fascinating analysis of the use of plants in magical spells as metaphors for a basic opposition in Ilongot society.

The ensemble of a people's customs always has its particular style; they form into systems. I am convinced that the number of these systems is not unlimited and that human societies, like individual human beings . . . never create absolutely: *all they can do is to choose combinations from a repertory of ideas which it should be possible to reconstitute . . .* (Lévi-Strauss 1970: 160).

For the Kayans of Borneo, as for the Aztecs of ancient Mexico, a special place in heaven was shared by women who died in childbed and men who died in war. For certain African groups, like the Ndembu, male hunting cults have counterparts in cults which guarantee female fertility and encourage childbirth. Childbirth and killing, life-giving and life-taking, constitute opposed and complementary terms which provide a framework for symbolic conceptualizations of men's and women's roles quite generally, and perhaps, universally. If, as Lévi-Strauss suggests, 'societies . . . never create absolutely' (1970: 160), if, by virtue of similarities in human experience everywhere, certain symbolic idioms are available to people around the world, then it is, perhaps, not surprising that an idiom which opposes men and women is among them. Since issues of sex-role definition appear to be inevitable both socially and psychologically, since man—in very different social systems—conceives himself as opposed and generally superior to woman, the symbolism of the sexes is a likely ground for discovering abstract and universal symbolic themes. Even the anthropologist's myth of Man the Hunter—of males, autonomous and agentic, creating the first forms of culture, cooperation, and technology—is only one culture's articulation of a very general pattern. Man the Hunter is a form of man the killer, the life-taker, opposed implicitly or explicitly to Woman the Childbearer, the giver of life through birth.

Our purpose in this paper is to show how the framework of an abstract opposition, between life-giving and life-taking, illuminates symbolic definitions of the sexes in one particular culture. By posing the problem in this way, we hope to suggest that culture-specific configurations of symbolic materials reflect a variety of constraining factors: universal themes and oppositions; symbolic materials available to historically or locally related cultures; the shaping of culture by particular social systems; and, finally, the need for human actors in specific situations to organize their experienced worlds. Although our programme, in its general outlines, resembles the one which Lévi-Strauss proposes in *Mythologiques* and elsewhere, our interest lies less in universal generalizations than in the place of general considerations in the analysis of particulars. We assume that men and women are defined everywhere in relation to one another, and that an opposition between life-givers and life-takers is often the form in which this relation is cast. Still, it is necessary to examine the realization of this opposition in any given instance, to ask how the myths, metaphors, and symbols which express it are related to their social and cultural context, and to show how these work for actors to orient, interpret, transform, or legitimize their everyday concerns.

In the interpretation of a particular culture, general assumptions of the sort we are discussing govern one's choice and, ultimately, one's ordering of data. At the same time, however, any interpretation or analysis of symbols must emerge from their actual contexts of use. The symbols and metaphors used in conventional cultural performances may be seen to exemplify or articulate themes of a general nature; through them, abstract and even universal considerations may be cast in a particular culture's mould. Yet metaphors are also produced, and experienced as meaningful, by socially situated actors. They provide an interpretation of individual needs and desires, a vehicle which orients actors towards the distinctive, intelligible, and orderly views of experience which their culture, in fact, provides.

Analysis must, then, begin with the complexities of actual cultural practice. Methodologically, we can think of two approaches from which such analysis might proceed. The first, illustrated by Turner's (1964b; 1967) discussions of "dominant symbols" or Pepper's (1942) "root metaphors," is given systematic treatment in a recent paper by Ortner (1974a). "Key" or dominant symbols are selected out of the webs of interrelated cultural expressions because they are felt to provide a focus for crucial activities, like rituals, and again, because they supply a metaphorical framework which relates a variety of cultural concerns. They may be "life" symbols (Langer, 1942) which build upon associations salient universally and address existential preoccupations important to people around the world. So, the *mudyi* or "milk tree" dominates the girl's initiation for the Ndembu, and by virtue of its associations with maternity, matriliny, women, the girl, her mother, and so on, it acquires importance as a focal expression of Ndembu feeling and thought (Turner, 1964b). In the case of our own data, such a key symbol would be headhunting, which is at once a kind of male initiation, a focus of group identity, and an image of grace, masculinity, health, and violence, all of which are (in some sense) cultural ideals. The key symbol, in other words, is laden with a variety of deeply salient meanings; its successful analysis depends on a careful explication of the ways in which its multiple metaphorical associations are realized in a wide range of activities, and the ways in which these articulate with one another in a particular focal event.

The second approach, less common in anthropological writings, begins with those cultural performances which pile image on image, in the manner of a Lévi-Straussian *bricoleur*. By combining what once was separate, by saying the "same thing" in a variety of symbolic forms, the *bricoleur* creates a context in which new meanings are realized, and the experienced world is re-ordered in terms of unique orientation or goal. In magical spells, for example, practitioners typically call on a wide range of objects (cf. Strathern and Strathern 1968; Tambiah, 1968).... Health is like a plant which glistens, like sunrise, like loose flying feathers, like a tree whose thorny trunk keeps predators from reaching its fruit. Taken together, all of those images suggest something clean, pure, and invulnerable; the various metaphors combine to establish a particular idea of health as a principle which orders and humanizes an uncontrollable natural world.

A systematic study of such essentially redundant metaphorical expressions can isolate the principles in terms of which they are selected, the particular ideas of order, the emotional orientations and cultural themes which they are intended to express. Such ideas, in turn, can be systematically related. From an analysis of actual metaphors one can begin to isolate the structural associations which underlie a multiplicity of cultural expressions. Each metaphor, taken by itself, may seem arbitrary, yet combined with others it can be shown to signify and reflect an underlying system of meanings, and to serve as a vehicle through which that system is constituted and reaffirmed.

The magical spells of the Ilongots, a group of hunters and swidden agriculturalists in Northern Luzon, Philippines, provide a rich field for the exploration of this second approach to metaphor. The spells are about things like hunting and headhunting, agriculture, accidents, and disease. They are a part of every adult Ilongot's knowledge, and, among those Ilongots who have not yet become Christians, hardly a day goes by without someone's calling on plants, birds, clouds, sweet things, or poisons, to guarantee success in the hunt or the harvest, safety and glory to the warrior, or comfort and personal good health. Our approach in this paper will, then, involve a detailed exploration of Ilongot magical metaphors. We begin by discussing spells for agriculture and hunting, which, through their relation to the life-giving/life-taking opposition, lead to a number of suggestions as to the conceptualization of men and women in the Ilongot cultural order. In a final section, comparative evidence is introduced to suggest that the Ilongot system represents one variant of what we take to be a universal or 'natural' structure of male and female associations, and we discuss the importance of postulating such universal schemata in the interpretation of any particular case.

THE ILONGOTS

There are some 2500 Ilongots living in scattered settlements in the rugged and fertile hill country just south of the Mountain Province in Northern Luzon, Philippines. Their household, community, and larger political ties are organized by relations of bilateral kinship (R. Rosaldo, 1970b). Residence on marriage tends to be uxorilocal, but when closely related men marry into a community, they provide the focus of its political identity. Relations between women and men are cooperative and relatively egalitarian; husband and wife participate equally in most family decisions, both care for young children, and both provide food for the home. Ilongot women are gardeners, producing the rice which is the staple of the family diet. Ilongot men are hunters, deft and at home in the forest, and aside from their activity in clearing the woodlands for planting, they have little to do with the production of the staple food, rice.

Power, in Ilongot society, is not the prerogative of individuals of any particular status, nor do criteria like age, esoteric wisdom, success in hunting or even in headhunting, provide grounds on which men establish fixed rankings among themselves. Young men should take heads and marry, and those who have not done so are unlikely to be influential in later community life; but the boy who has killed no one has a perfect right to resist his father's decisions; some men never take heads; some never marry; and the successful hunter and killer will be powerful only if he has the verbal precocity and human intelligence which enable him to persuade, rather than command. Formal norms dictate that everyone is his fellow's equal, and while some people have more influence than others, none has permanent authority, nor can anyone take for granted that his recommendations will be followed. This stress on individual autonomy and equality is reflected in the fact that men, women, and children all receive equal and individual portions whenever food is being distributed, and it is implicitly recognized in the artful, prolonged, and careful oratorical confrontations . . . where, again, what is desired is not the grudging compliance of subordinates, but a meeting of minds and of hearts.

Magical spells are, like oratory, a method of metaphorical persuasion. The spirits cannot be coerced, but they can be influenced, to comply with human desires. They may be frightened or threatened, coaxed or coddled, but no one can be sure they will obey. There is no single fixed form for a magical performance, no correct or certain set of expressions, images, or commands. The spells of even a single practitioner are always different. Ilongots describe their magic, like their oratory, as an attempt to find the "right words," which will win the spirits' compliance. At the same time, examination of a number of spells of any single type reveals that they are all alternative realizations of a shared and constraining sense of order, that each draws on a common repertory of possible expressions, which, in turn, reflect a small set of culturally significant themes.

The metaphors of magical spells are, for the most part, familiar to all adult members of the community. Men and women alike know that plants with red sap make a tea which cures bloody diarrhoea, that a good harvester is like a 'spinning bug' in her infinitely productive garden, that spirits are apt to be frightened when a plant known as 'toothless' is invoked in the course of a spell. They know that betel spit, which changes from green to red, suggests a change towards good fortune, and that splashing water on a patient may wash away a disease. Metaphors, in word and in gesture, are realized in a variety of forms in any particular performance. They may be associated with a particular object or action, they may be announced in a simile, or again, they may be suggested by the name or physical characteristics of a plant which is used in the spell.

Thus, when an Ilongot woman prepares for a harvest, or a man, having fed his hunt dogs, is about to set off after game, each gathers a collection of herbs which are, typically, charred with pitch or steamed over a preheated hearthstone. An object like steam is said to "quicken" the pulse of the performer, producing the feeling of excitement which foretells a successful endeavour. The hearthstone itself is a symbol of closeness and stability, of rice so thick that the harvester stays in a single spot throughout an entire day's reaping, of game which meets the hunter near to his home. The plants have names which resemble the Ilongot words for "meet," "hasten," "near," and "encounter" (cf. M. Rosaldo, 1972); they too suggest that success is available close by. Finally, the spoken spell is rich in images of plenty; it asks that the practitioner be dizzied and overwhelmed with the rice or the game he desires, that quantities—like stars in the night or leaves which fall in a windstorm—will appear before his eyes.

Hunting and agricultural spells both belong to the subset of magical performances called "preparations". . . . Agricultural spells can be performed shortly after planting, when the gardener "washes" the young shoots which are described as her "children," and again, at several points during and after the harvest (when the rice is dried, put in the granary, and first removed to eat). Similarly, hunting spells may be recited over dogs before a collective hunt; by the lone hunter who has encountered an animal's footprint, or, in the home, when preparing one's gun or one's bow. These spells differ in their typical "action metaphors"; varieties of hunting and agricultural spells may be distinguished as to whether they involve things like washing, steaming or beating the herbs, building a fence which will ward off bad spirits, tying plants around a rice stalk, or turning dirt in a footprint to signify the death of the game. On the other hand, all varieties of agricultural spells, and all spells used for hunting, tend to be relatively constant in their repertory of plants, their characteristic verbal expressions and metaphors, and these are what will concern us here.

Whether he steams his herbs on a hearthstone, or lights pitch in the footprints of game, the hunter's words are apt to be something like the following (plant names in the two following texts are asterisked*):

You, spirits who walk by the rivers, come join my steaming here!
Here I do steam magic on my hand on the hearthstone
Don't fail me, let me shoot, you spirits, my grandfathers!
They like you, hand
Hand that is steamed on the hearthstone, hand
At your finishing place, hand
May they be full hand, the wild game, hand*
They like you, hand
Make it a hoard of wild game, hand*
Make them meet you hand, the wild game, hand*
Make the eyes of the deer bulge, hand, in a clear place, hand
They like you, hand
May they be like stars to you, hand, the wild animals, hand
Don't, please, hand, go too far away, hand
Make your hunting place near, hand*
Be, hand, like the sure hand of a Negrito hunter, hand
They like you, hand. . . .

Similarly, a gardener, at the beginning or end of her harvest, when she wonders how healthy her plants are, or later, when she puts the harvested bundles in her granary for use through the rest of the year, will use much the same language and images, asking again and again that her rice supply be unending, that its "fruitfulness" remain in her field:

Here, I steam you, rice, with your fruitfulness, rice*
Rice, you have a spell performed, now, rice
Make it pile high, rice, your fruitfulness, rice*
They like you, rice
Beckon your fruitfulness,* rice*
Here is the plant called beckoning, rice*
Don't act childish, rice, don't be troublesome, rice
They like you, rice
Be like the rice of the lowlanders, rice
Make it so people everywhere speak of you, rice
They like you, rice
And may I be, please, rice, like a spinning bug in the centre of the field, rice
They like you, rice
This is the plant called hoards, rice*
Let there be hoards of you, rice*
And be full, rice*
May your fruitfulness flourish,* rice. . . .*

Such spells may be as short as the fragments recorded here, or they may go on for as much as five or ten minutes, the rhythmic tones of the practitioner rising to call on the spirits or falling to mutter a wish.

. . .

CALLING ON PLANTS

All but the simplest Ilongot spells require the use of plants and botanical metaphors (M. Rosaldo, 1971; 1972). Plants with flowing red sap are used to cure bloody diarrhoea; a grass which has thorns "pierces" shooting pains in the chest; the sweet pungent odour of a wild variety of ginger is said to bring game which "has flavour"; the sharp prongs on a rattan vine "cling" like rice in a harvester's hands. In some spells, it appears that plants are selected because they are odd or peculiar in appearance. In others, plants seem to be chosen because they grow in or near a particular spirit's home. Finally, of the 400 plants we know to be used in magic, the majority have names like "thigh," "finger," "twist," "evil," "encounter"; most of these plants have no physical characteristics which suggest that their names are appropriate, yet Ilongots say they are chosen because of their names, which make sense in the spell.

This use of plant-naming presents a number of problems for analysis. Metaphorical uses of plants have, of course, been noted elsewhere in the anthropological literature (Fox, 1972; Turner, 1964a). But why should plants have names like "twist" or "finger"? Is naming completely arbitrary? And what can be said of the significance of plants which are chosen for any particular spell? The problem has two aspects: first, what sets of names are used in what categories of magic and, second, why are these names assigned to particular kinds of plants?

To begin, an equation between plants and people is common in Ilongot metaphor (as it may be universally). Plants, especially wild species, are associated with intangible forces which give life. So, in oratory, plants are used to speak of humans; "shoots" can mean "children," and "young leaf" describes a child's growing up. In spells, on the other hand, human characteristics are used to name botanical species, which are called after body parts or feelings, emotions, or characteristic modes of action. What is more, these names are ordered. Examination of lists of all plants which can be used in any category of magic reveals that the plants used in any one kind of spell tend to have names which reflect a single semantic conception. Thus . . . plants which chase the threatening ancestors have names like "twisted," "toothless," "dizzy"—names which suggest physical defects which a troublesome spirit might avoid. Furthermore, most if not all plants used in a particular spell and having names of related semantic value appear to grow in a particular part of the physical environment. . . . In other words, all plants which can be used in a single spell may be said to signify, and participate in, two underlying systems of meaning: one having to do with the human characteristics of supernatural objects and aspirations; and the second relating to the environment in which the spirits are often found. Through the use of real plants from particular environments, aspects of the natural and spirit worlds are subordinated to human manipulation; and by naming these plants in his magic, the Ilongot connects his own sense of his body, its needs and aspirations, to external and tangible symbols from a "humanized" (and so controllable) physical world.

. . . Many of the same plants are used in two kinds of magic, making spells for agriculture and hunting unique in the Ilongot repertory. Ilongots explain this by saying that "the plants are the same because it is the same food that we eat." We would like to go further, in suggesting that these plants signify the symmetry and complementarity of female and male activities, of garden and forest, of rice and of game. Only when this is established can we begin to see why the plants come from the forest, rather than some other environment.

As we noted earlier in this essay, Ilongot women are gardeners and Ilongot men like to hunt. The products of the two—rice and game—should complement one another in the ideal diet; men and women are felt to contribute their comparable, but separate, kinds of foods. Though men may, in practice, help with hoeing and harvesting, and women occasionally hunt, this sexual division of labour extends ideally through all aspects of food production, preparation, and distribution. Aside from clearing the woodlands for planting—which pollarders describe as raping or beheading the forest—men are never obliged to assist in the cultivation or preparation of rice. We found, for example, that even though women plant between 10 and 25 varieties of rice in a single garden, their husbands did not know the variety names. And again, where men of neighbouring swidden groups may help to pound rice, or sow the seed while women dibble, Ilongots see all of these as female chores. An Ilongot woman, when she feels angry, goes to sit beneath her granary; a man runs off to the woods to think. Men hunt, butcher, and prepare meat dishes; the forest is their domain.

On another level, this opposition is mirrored in a dualistic classification of things which grow in garden and forest, and in a pair of deities, who dominate each of the two domains. The forest lord . . . is usually called . . . "from the forest," and his wife, . . . the Maiden, is also known as . . . "from the fields"; they are patrons, respectively, of hunting and agricultural pursuits. In magical and mundane contexts alike, Ilongots indicate that there is a forest world equal to, and opposing the garden, which is associated with the domestic one. . . .

Spells for hunting and agriculture can both be called . . . preparations. And spells, in both cases, can bring pain as well as success; both [the forest lord and the Maiden] are sensitive to greed, carelessness, or other abuse by their followers, and people who make themselves vulnerable by performing [spells] must, at the risk of severe illness, avoid laughing and shouting, and observe a number of taboos. In both cases, also, it is not the edge . . . which is dangerous, but the . . . "centre" of the garden or forest, where play is restricted and productive activities are the only legitimate tasks. (It is equally true in houses, that while "centres" are used for distributing and serving food, the "edges" are where people will eat, talk, and relax.) Angering either patron in its magical "centre" may bring on a sudden illness. . . .

There is, then, both a sex-linked economic opposition, and a marked symbolic parallelism, between the male and female domains. This is illustrated in Figure 1.

This parallelism, and the implied symmetrical conception of male and female activities, are signified in spells by the use of the same plants and plant verbs in both agricultural and hunting magic. The use of the same plants in both contexts corresponds to the fact that, in most situations, Ilongot men and women are seen as one another's equals, and, in terms of the production of foodstuffs, they operate in complementary spheres.

Why, then, do the plants come almost exclusively from the forest? If the sharing of plants in hunting and gardening magic suggests the symmetrical statuses and shared orientations of the sexes, why should the site of men's productive activity furnish the magical plants necessary for both men's and women's subsistence work? Certainly this imbalance hints at sexual asymmetry. But the association of the plants . . . with the forest takes on an additional interpretation in the context of Ilongot magic as a whole. To begin, with only a few exceptions, all of the 400 plants used in Ilongot spells are wild species, and these can be collected by both women and men. The forest, associated on one level with maleness, holds no sacred powers from which women are kept apart. Furthermore, Ilongot see in the forest, as in all things wild, the free and auspicious power of nature. . . . [This power] equated with nature, with sunshine, and the capacity for life in general, is sexless. It is a force which both men and women can bring to the service of life. We imagine that wild plants constitute the bulk of the Ilongot's magical repertory because of their association, not with maleness specifically, but with the all-embracing forces of a natural world which surrounds, constrains, and ultimately sustains the life enterprises of both sexes. While men surpass women in their knowledge of the forest and wild things generally, the idea of power in nature, and so, in wild botanical species, suggests that the plants [used in both agricultural and hunting rituals] have a spiritual efficacy which transcends the distinction of sex. . . .

The cultural choice of forest over garden as the source of plants suitable for both hunting and gardening magic may be compared to the linguistic observation that male, as against female, categories are 'unmarked' in most languages. The fact that forest rather than garden plants are suitable for both kinds of magic is paralleled, for example, by pronominal usage in English, which favours 'he' over 'she' when referring to a generalized third person. By analogy, the forest is opposed to the garden, but it also has an 'unmarked' status which permits it to signify both wild and domestic spheres. 'Unmarked' terms, in linguistic parlance, tend to be valued more positively than their 'marked' counterparts; perhaps here we see an expression of the asymmetry, as well as the complementarity, of Ilongot conceptions of male and female, a point to be developed in the discussion below.

SIMILES

The selection of plants and plant verbs highlights the complementarity of men and women in Ilongot cultural conceptions; the sexes are thought of as equal in emotional and spiritual orientations in so far as both are producers of food. It would be misleading, however, to assume that rice and game have equal value as foodstuffs. The asymmetry in their evaluations, suggested in our earlier observations, is reflected, perhaps, in the fact that while individual women produce rice, which is the staple of the individual family's diet, game is usually hunted by the men of the community collectively, and it is either sold for prestige goods (cloth, brass wire, and other products, which are used in the payment of brideprices and the resolution of feuds), or distributed through the community as a whole. On a cultural level, game is the most desirable part of the diet, and while Ilongots minimize expressions of sexual asymmetry, an examination of the similes used in magic suggests that hunting is equated with headhunting, that killing of animals is like killing of men, which is a focal cultural theme (cf. R. Rosaldo, 1970a).

Using the methods described earlier, we drew up a complete list of the similes used in all hunting and agricultural spells respectively. Out of a list of some 40 . . . only one,

FIGURE 1
The opposition of garden and forest.

forest	garden
forest lord	maiden
men	women
game	rice
wild boar	domestic pig
wild chicken	domestic chicken
his banana, his piper betel, etc.	cultivated banana, piper betel, etc.
magical centre	magical centre

which compares hunt dogs and rice to a sweet potato plant—which has many and closely spaced roots—is found in both kinds of spells. Beyond this, most of the similes used for hunting have violent connotations. Hunt dogs are compared to songs which celebrate the headhunter, to duelling, and to the loud call of a bird whose beak is a headhunter's ornament. They are equated with violent natural images, like whirlpools, rapids, lightning, rushing wind and water; with the crash of pollarded branches, and overgrowth that falls in the forest; with destructive, inedible animals, like roaches, bees, crocodiles, and pythons; with exchanging betel, which suggests a gift to any enemy; with fish which jump; with boiling water; with harpoon arrows; and with large-scale destructive fires. The bow is said to kill like the bows of Negritoes, who are known to use poison on their arrows. The gun claps like drums which celebrate the return of successful killers. And game is compared to flowing water, to ants, and to stars in the sky. Most of these images suggest violence, destruction, and quantity. While one might imagine equations of hunt dogs, bows, or whatever, with pacific images of closeness, a good harvest, success, the Ilongots have chosen to use similes to signify those features which hunting shares with killing. Taken together, most of these similes can be seen to be saying the same thing; and spells, by aligning these diverse images of violence, equate hunting, a mere productive activity, with a "key symbol," an idea of great cultural significance: the headhunter's taking of life.

It is more difficult to isolate a single theme which underlies the similes in spells for agriculture. Some can be interpreted in juxtaposition with complementary images for hunting. Thus, while game is like stars, rice is like clouds, and where hunt dogs are equated with destructive fires, the rice is said to be warm like the fires one lights in the hearth. Hunting similes suggest wildness, action, and quantity, while those used in agriculture indicate domesticity, passivity, and mass. This becomes clear in a number of additional examples. Rice is to 'cling' like rattan vines (and rattans have domestic uses), to be anchored like a banana, and to flourish like a few other cultivated plants; it is compared to solid rock formations, to deep pools, to sand which cannot be counted, to a plant which clings to a rock. And the harvester, too, is anchored, like a bug which burrows in the ground, or another which spins in the water. Agriculture, in these similes, is pictured as domestic, passive, and certain, none of which are virtues that are celebrated in the hunt.

Thus, where the metaphorical uses of plants suggest an equation between hunting and agriculture, the images used in similes suggest crucial differences in the emotional orientations and cultural themes associated with women and men. Hunting is violent; gardening passive. Hunting involves killing; agriculture, a kind of sympathy between the gardener and her desired object, the rice. Since headhunting is an activity which both men and women admire, the importance of hunting and, we would argue, of male activities in general, is communicated in these spells through the simile frame which transforms a complementary conception into an asymmetrical one. If hunting is like headhunting, it is also an act of will and of discipline, an activity of utmost cultural value.

ADDITIONAL EVIDENCE

By examining sets of metaphors used in spells for agriculture and hunting, we have seen that they are concerned with two opposed cultural conceptions. The use of plants and plant verbs signifies sexual complementarity and equality; male and female activities are comparable for the Ilongots because both involve the production of food. Expressions used in the simile frame point, however, to an asymmetrical conception. Hunting is equated with killing, with the most focal of cultural traditions, and so men, because they are violent, may be seen as superior to women and the functions they fulfil.

Additional, less systematic, evidence permits us to complete our description. If hunting and agriculture are conceived to be in opposition, logical considerations alone would suggest that, as hunting involves life-taking, agriculture might well be associated with the giving, or creation, of life. No such association appears in the spells we have considered; moving from those to other kinds of cultural expressions, however, we find some suggestions of their availability in the repertory of Ilongot ideas.

a. Ilongot gardeners identify their own life with the health and 'heart' of their rice crop. A woman who has begun harvesting will be reluctant, for example, to visit another's garden for fear that the 'heart' of her own rice will go to a neighbour's field. Again, after the harvest, the woman places some newly harvested stalks on her head, asking that the rice hearts live as long as she does, and that rice, like a woman, 'be big' where it is stacked.

b. Earlier in the agricultural cycle, rice plants are treated like young children. While the plants are still growing, the woman bathes them—much as a mother bathes a new baby—to make them fat. When the unripe panicles are full and almost ready to be harvested, they are described as "pregnant." And, finally, the harvester's bundle of collected herbs is combined with rice stalks, in a manner which suggests the "rice baby" of freak ears used in Malay magic (cf. Endicott, 1970), and it is "given a body" with betel spit—which, in myths, has been known to give life to skeletons and bones.

Without further evidence, these suggestions of an equation between agriculture and childbirth must, of course, remain tentative; and the fact that the association is, at best, a weak one may itself be of importance (see below). If, however, we are willing to assume that Ilongot conceptions of subsistence activities are constrained by, and represent one viariant of, a universally available pattern, we can diagram the metaphorical relations between hunting and gardening in the manner illustrated [in Figure 2].

All 'A's' in the diagram indicate some kind of positive association—between agriculture and childbirth (or life-giving), hunting and killing, and, perhaps the strongest, between gardening and the hunt. We claim that this paradigm is an adequate representation of the relationships signified in Ilongot magical metaphors, and, similarly, that it characterizes a system of deep, pervasive, and widely ramifying cultural concerns. If this is correct, we would further expect to find expressions in Ilongot cultural practice which indicate the negative relations, or incompatibilities, of all combinations marked as B. In fact, these are available.

B1. Returning headhunters, wearing ornaments which indicate their success, are not permitted to enter a rice garden; through this prohibition, killing and gardening are opposed. Shedding blood in the garden—through leech bites, cuts, or even sacrifice—is also thought to endanger the growing rice.

B2. A myth suggests the incompatibilities of headhunting and childbirth. In it, a man takes his wife's head at her granary and then brings her to life. After they have lived together for a while, he sets off hunting, and instructs her to appear again at the granary—presumably to be killed—if she has not yet given birth. On returning from his hunt, the man sees that his wife is absent from the granary and tells it to fill itself with rice if the child is a female, and to be emptied if the baby is a male. This episode occurs twice, and he has both male and female children. Had the wife failed to give birth in both instances, death rather than birth would have been the outcome, since she would have been beheaded.

B3. Evidence here (as with the positive associations between agriculture and childbirth) is weakest. Ilongots do, however, say that contact with women can damage a man's prowess in the hunt; the cure, in such a case, is the same as the ritual which is used to make a newborn baby grow. What is suggested here, though weakly, is that female fertility is dangerous; the ritual which promotes the natural development of a child is used to counteract a man's polluted state.

What does all of this tell us? Essentially, we claim to have identified a covert set of structural relationships which governs the selection of a variety of stereotyped cultural expressions, and which, in turn, is invoked every time a gardener or hunter performs an appropriate magical spell. The "strength" of the various articulations of the model depends, in turn, on the strength of these associations in Ilongot culture. The evidence from plant metaphors is most powerful because these signify the symmetry and complementarity of men and women, an idea of equality pervading most aspects of Ilongot social life. The contradictory statement, of man's violence and superiority, corresponds

FIGURE 2
Hunting and agriculture in Ilongot cultural conceptions.

	Male (Life-Taking)		*Female (Life-Giving)*	
	headhunting	hunting	agriculture	childbirth
headhunting		A. good association, similes	B1	B2
hunting			A. strong association; plants	B3
agriculture				A. weak association

to the fact that cultures universally recognize some form of sexual asymmetry; male dominance, epitomized in headhunting, is, then, indicated in the similes used in these spells. The other relations, both positive and negative, were derived on the basis of less explicit evidence. This, we suggest, reflects the fact that, while they are available or "present" in the Ilongot cultural system, they do not correspond to conceptions which Ilongots choose to stress. Ilongots place little emphasis on female sexuality or fertility; there are no rituals surrounding childbirth or sterility; menstrual taboos are absent as are any other explicit statements of woman's lesser status. Strong statements linking agriculture and fertility would, we suggest, emphasize woman's "otherness," and, implicitly, her inferiority, and would therefore be incompatible with the egalitarian ethos which governs much of Ilongot life.

MAN THE HUNTER AND WOMAN

Anthropological tradition has nurtured the myth of an early "man the hunter," the wilful creator of the first forms of culture and society. But just as man the hunter relied upon woman as food-gatherer, child-bearer, and companion, so conceptions of hunting enter a system of relationships which includes the activities of woman as well as man. Our analysis of Ilongot magical metaphors has shown, for one particular culture, that ideas about hunting and gardening are linked as terms of a fundamental opposition between life-giving and life-taking. Here, we will suggest that the structural principle underlying this set of cultural expressions is not unique to Ilongot culture, but governs cultural characterizations of the sexes around the world.

Beginning with the basic opposition of taking life and giving it, a set of logical connections can be constructed that relate the life-sustaining and life-destroying tasks of women and men. We can start with the place of hunting in this set. As a form of killing, hunting shares with warfare the act of destroying life and, like warfare, it is limited, with very few exceptions, to men. Cultural conceptions of hunting and warfare may be associated as male activities and subordinated under the rubric of life-taking, which in turn is defined in relation to cultural conceptions of its opposite, an exclusively female act, the giving of life through birth. Regardless of the degree of participation allotted to men by different cultural theories of procreation (cf. Leach, 1961: Chapter 1), women are indisputably associated with the birth and nurturance of the human infant; their bodies are the locus of earliest biological growth. If childbirth is the opposite of killing with respect to life, preparation of food may be regarded as the opposite of hunting with respect to economic productivity—that is, in its destructive aspect, hunting can be associated with warfare; in its productive aspect, with the gathering, growing, or preparing of food. The association of hunting and warfare is based upon the identity of the act of killing, as well as upon identical actors, men. The association of motherhood and the preparation of food is less direct. Metaphors may liken the preparer of food to the nursing mother, or compare the fertility of plants to the fertility of women. The ordering of relationships may be illustrated in the following way:

LIFE-GIVING	LIFE-TAKING
motherhood	warfare
cultivation, gathering, preparation of food	hunting

In the remainder of this paper, we shall discuss how this paradigm and the possibilities for associations among its elements serve as a structural framework underlying culturally diverse representations of the sexes. This paradigm isolates as well some highly general, if not universal, considerations which lend an evaluative cast to symbolic statements about the relations of women and men. This evaluative aspect of our paradigm may best be illustrated by reviewing the Ilongot example.

In the analysis above, Ilongot metaphors were seen to build upon the complementarity of men's and women's contributions to production. Diagrammed in terms of the model outlined here, the Ilongot metaphors take the form [shown in Figure 3].

Because of their emphasis upon the commonalities of men's and women's economic contributions, we suggested that Ilongot magical metaphors reflect the relatively egalitarian relations of the sexes in the Ilongot social world. At the same time, we saw that men's hunting was distinguished from and elevated above women's gardening through its symbolic affinities with headhunting. Women's gardening, by contrast, was only weakly associated with childbirth. In fact, Ilongot culture provides almost no symbolic elaboration upon the themes of birth and biological fertility. As men's complements and near equals, Ilongot women come to view their social and productive roles in an idiom which minimizes their differences from men.

The Ilongot system would appear to represent one variant of a life-giving/life-taking opposition which we assume to be quite general. It is our contention that ties between male activities (and hunting in particular) and killing provide people everywhere with a symbolic idiom which ranks and differentiates the roles of women and men. The ways in which particular cultures elaborate upon the poles of the opposition reflect variations in the social relations and cultural valuations of the sexes: emphasis on economic complementarity suggests a relatively egalitarian system; emphasis on biological fertility, absent among the Ilongots, seems to be found in cultures where the sexes are seen as different and unequal by natural right. Though we are aware that women elsewhere gain ritual and social value through cultural recognition of their reproductive functions, we imagine that emphasis on these functions derives ultimately from an assumption of deep-seated inequality. The celebration of motherhood and female sexuality implies a definition of womankind in terms of nature and biology; it traps women in their physical being, and thereby in the very general logic which declares them less capable of transcendence and of cultural achievement than men.

FIGURE 3
The form of Ilongot metaphors.

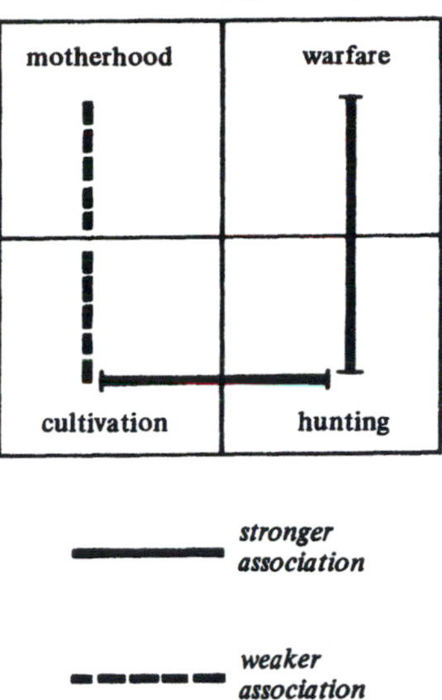

CONCLUSIONS

At the start of this paper, we posed our concern for the place of general considerations in the analysis of particulars. Assuming that certain oppositional principles constrain and organize cultural expressions universally, we sought to understand their realization in one culture's symbolic schemes. By examining the metaphors which Ilongots use in magic, we showed how a wealth of diverse images provides a redundant and affectively laden statement of the meanings which Ilongots assign to the relations of the sexes. The vivid and concrete imagery of spells speaks directly to the needs and aspirations of Ilongot cultivators and hunters. At the same time, systematic connections among metaphors give sense and order to individual experience by relating it to more abstract and generalized concerns. In interpreting the order underlying metaphors used in magic, we related them to an opposition between life-giving and life-taking, which we imagine, provides a framework for conceptualization of the sexes in diverse cultural settings. Consideration of this framework indicated, first, that magical metaphors are systematically linked to other symbolic expressions in Ilongot culture, and second, that symbolic characterizations of men and women among the Ilongots represent a locally appropriate and intelligible articulation of universal themes. The general implications of our approach were illustrated by a brief comparative analysis.

In our discussion, we have then assumed that symbolic characterizations of men and women in any culture are shaped by social and ideological factors, and that representations of one sex are dependent upon representations of the other. The particular symbolic expressions found in a culture are in no way natural or inevitable. They are choices from a number of possibilities expressed in the life-giving/life-taking paradigm and conditioned by forms of social life. Furthermore, we have assumed that the two sides of the paradigm are never equal. In all cultures, men's spheres of activity are more highly valued than women's (M. Rosaldo, 1974); and, for this reason, it seems likely that emphasis upon female biological reproduction indicates a sense of asymmetry in status between women and men. This assumption, of course, underlies our claim that the most egalitarian possibility is one which stresses economic complementarity. The Ilongots elaborate this mode of expression, although they also highlight the importance of life-taking in the hunt. Hunting, through its association with headhunting, is elevated above the productive activities of women. At the same time, the relative lack of emphasis on female reproduction minimizes a sense of women's difference from, and implicitly, their inferiority to, men.

But the question remains—in what sense is men's taking of life more valued than women's childbearing? How can we assume that in a world where men are killers, cultural emphases on the maternal role, female fertility, and female sexuality in general, necessarily imply that women are, in some sense, less than men?

The general evaluative implications of the life-giving/life-taking opposition are suggested by the fact that killing and childbearing tend to be represented asymmetrically; metaphors for men and killing, as against those for women and childbirth, associate men with cultural activities and women with natural growth. Men may work in the forest, but they do so in the name of culture, and while women are, in our examples, compared to rice and fig trees, men are portrayed as spears and arrows. Further, men, in many cultures, can assume female reproductive roles symbolically, but women are almost everywhere denied a positive role in taking life. In cultural forms as diverse as the couvade, sub-incision, "male menstruation," headhunting which grants fertility, and initiations marked by imagery of birth, men engage in what appears to be valued and auspicious androgynous existence. The converse—the assumption of life-taking roles by women—is generally regarded as unnatural and undesirable. Female killers are portrayed as sterile, virginal, and, so, incomplete as women, or as violent, childhaters, mockers of group integrity, and imagers of inauspicious times. Athena and Artemis in Greek mythology, Amazons who amputate their breasts so as better to draw their bows, the Mother Snake of Arnhem Land who swallows her own children, Ndembu women dressed as hunters to symbolize sterility, Gogo women masquerading as violent men to "turn around" bad fortune—these diverse representations of women as killers derive their impact from the antithesis of motherhood and the violence of taking life.

Motherhood is incompatible with killing, but then men conceptualized as killers can, and often do, assume positively valued symbolic roles associated with giving life. To understand the roots of the asymmetry we need to ask two questions. First, why are men and women, who play diverse and important roles in economics, politics, and religion, regarded almost everywhere as killers and childbearers? And, second, why do the experience and meanings linked to these conceptions give them an opposed and evaluative sense? The answer to the first question must lie in an account of the social fact of sexual asymmetry, the fact that men in all known social systems have been allotted roles of authority, dominance, and prestige. The opposition between life-giving and life-taking provides cultural terms in which to conceptualize and rationalize social asymmetry. Considering these structural poles in terms of their potential as "key symbols," we can see why this might be the case.

Killing, unlike childbirth, grants men wilful control over the processes of nature, and, in particular, over the natural processes of life and death. Such an association is made explicit for cultural interpretations of forms of killing as distinct as warfare in New Guinea . . . and live burial among certain African groups. . . . We would suggest, then, that the critical difference between giving and taking life is rooted in the fact that a man's killing is always an act of will, directed towards a body other than his own; giving life through childbirth, on the other hand, is a natural function of a woman's own body, and usually is something over which she has little intentional control. Men's life-taking, because of its intentionality, becomes a means of culturally transcending the biological; whereas childbearing, despite values attached to it as the means of perpetuating a social group, remains grounded in the "naturalness" of women's sexual constitution. It has been clear, since the writings of Freud, that we cannot dismiss the notion that sexuality is problematic for humans. And because women conceptualized as childbearers are less easily dissociated from their sexual functions than men are, the female side of the life-giving/life-taking model is likely to be one of cultural and psychological ambivalence.

The terms of our structural opposition are, then, by no means arbitrary. The very feelings and experiences which give universal plausibility to conceptions of the sexes as childbearers and killers also, we are suggesting, lend these conceptions an evaluative cast. In de Beauvoir's words, "it is not in giving life but in risking life that man is raised above the animal; that is why superiority has been accorded in humanity not to the sex that brings forth but to that which kills" (1952: 58).

To this we would add only one qualification: the fact that the sexes have often been epitomized as life-givers and life-takers itself requires explanation—an understanding of the roots of sexual hierarchy in the human social world.

Claude Lévi-Strauss
THE BEAR AND THE BARBER

While Lévi-Strauss ostensibly addresses himself in this article to similarities between totemic groups and castes, he is really using them to express a methodological approach wherein he tries to reduce the variables of society to certain basic means for the solution of human problems. As in his provocative book on kinship and marriage, *The Elementary Structures of Kinship* (1969), which has exerted a profound influence on current social anthropology, his goal is to demonstrate that symmetry and exchange pervade human relations. He feels in the present instance that he has found a common language to express the structural relationship between totemic groups and castes, these two systems being ways that societies have evolved for allowing their members to express affiliation with the group into which they were born. But if exchange is to be possible between groups, social diversification must be established. In societies where there is no division of labor or specialization, as among the Australians, the only possible objective model that can be used by groups to define themselves is a natural rather than cultural one, namely, the diversity of natural species. This makes it possible for exogamous groups to exchange women between themselves even though women are biologically similar. In complex societies, nature is not taken as the model for diversification; instead, cultural products and services are used, these being true social species. But women cannot be exchanged outside their castes because they are not acknowledged to be similar from one occupational group to another. Australian totemic groups and Indian castes both specialize in "controlling" something necessary to the well-being of the whole group. Both are "exopractical" in that one produces women for marriage and the other produces goods and services. Both are "endopractical" in that each is kept closely self-contained—the Australian tribes through their preferred type of matrimonial exchange, the Indian castes by virtue of their rule of endogamy.

These ideas are admittedly involved and controversial, with insufficient testing on a wide scale, but at the same time they open the way to new insights regarding the nature of symbolic classification.

Reprinted from the *Journal of the Royal Anthropological Institute*, XCIII (1963), 1-11, by permission of the author and the Royal Anthropological Institute of Great Britain and Ireland.

Human societies have evolved a number of means for allowing their members to express affiliation with the group into which they were born. Among these we shall single out two strongly contrasted ones. In one case, a given individual will make such a statement as "I am a bear," in the other case he will make such a statement as "I am a barber." One case exemplifies the so-called "totemic" groups, the other the caste system. My purpose is to examine the nature of the structural relationship—if there be one—between the two.

The words "bear" and "barber" were not chosen at random. Barbers cut and shave other people's hair, while—at least among the Chippewa Indians—people born in the Bear clan were reputed to have long, thick hair and never to grow bald. This doubly inverted relation—presence or absence of a given trait on the one hand, in respect to self or other on the other hand—plus perhaps an opposition between nature and culture (since the kind of hair one grows is a natural trait, while to remove it is a cultural custom), this threefold relation then is endowed, as I shall try to show, with an inner meaning since it symbolizes so to speak the structure of the scheme I am about to develop.

As a preliminary, I should like to caution the reader with regard to my use of the word "totemism."

Although I shall use it freely in the course of my talk, I fully endorse the general trend that has prevailed for a good many years among anthropologists to consider that there is no real institution which corresponds to the term "totemism" and that totemistic theories proceed from an arbitrary carving out of the objective facts. Nevertheless, it would be too easy simply to discard all past and present speculations concerning what is generally referred to as "totemism." If so many scholars whom we all admire have been, as it were, fascinated by the idea of "totemism," it is probably because, at a deeper level than the one they have been mistakenly considering, phenomena arbitrarily put together to make up a pseudoinstitution are endowed with some inner meaning which makes them worthy of interest. This I believe was first discovered by Radcliffe-Brown, whose position in respect to "totemism" started by being a purely negative one in his early paper, "The Sociological Theory of Totemism" (1929), but who twenty-two years later in his Huxley Memorial Lecture entitled "The Comparative Method in Social Anthropology," without reverting in the least to a conception of "totemism" as an actual institution, succeeded nevertheless in unravelling the importance of the use of animal and plant names to characterize the relationship between the segments of human society. But this process led Radcliffe-Brown to modify considerably his earlier conception of this relationship.

In 1929, he believed that primitive people attached an intrinsic importance to animals for the reason that, as food, they were supposed to arouse man's spontaneous interest; whereas, in 1951 it was his theory that both animals and plants were to be regarded as mere figures of speech—symbols as it were. Thus, while in 1929, Radcliffe-Brown believed that interest was conferred upon animals and plants because they were "eatable," in 1951 he saw clearly that the real reason for this interest lay in the fact that they are, if I may use the word, "thinkable." It is interesting to note that each one of these two successive theories is in one way more abstract and in another way more concrete than the other. The first theory is more abstract since all animals which can be consumed are merged into a vague category characterized by the one single aspect that has been abstracted: that of constituting merely animal food. From this point of view, animals that can be eaten are all regarded as similar, while men who partake of this common food are also held to be similar. Thus the link between the distinction of biological species and the segments of society is not perceived, though this first theory is also more concrete, since it only envisages the point of view of practical utility and physiological need. In its turn the second theory is more abstract, since it relies far less on the animals themselves than on the discovery that these animals or plants, or rather their properties, can be put to use as symbols to express contrasts and oppositions. Nevertheless, it is more concrete, because we are now asked in each special case to look for a definite reason which can account for the selection of a given animal and not of any other. So the choice made by one culture among the whole gamut of animals and plants which are empirically present becomes a means to express differences between men.

If Radcliffe-Brown's second theory is valid, as I believe it to be, we must admit that behind what was erroneously called "totemism" lie three very precise ideas. First, the idea of a culturally discrete set, that is, a segmentary society; second, the idea of a naturally discrete set, that is, the awareness of the empirical discontinuity of the biological species and third, the idea that there is some kind of homology between the above two systems of differences. Therefore totemic ideas appear to provide a code enabling man to express isomorphic properties between nature and culture. Obviously, there exists here some kind of similarity with linguistics, since language is also a code which, through oppositions between differences, permits us to convey meanings and since in the case of language as well as in that of "totemism," the complete series of empirical media provided in one case by vocal articulation, and in the other by the entire wealth of the biological world, cannot be called upon, but rather (and this is true in both cases) only a few elements which each language or each culture selects in order that they can be organized in strongly and unequivocally contrasting pairs. Such being the answer, we may be in a position to solve the problem raised by Boas in his paper "Mythology and Folk-tales of the North American Indians," where he says, "the essential problem regarding the ultimate origin of mythologies remains—why human tales are preferably attached to animals, celestial bodies and other personified phenomena of nature." The answer lies, so it seems, not, as the functionalist school assumes, in the utilitarian properties of biological species as mankind conceives them, but rather in their logical properties, that is, their ability to serve as symbols expressing contrasts and oppositions. This was demonstrated for a limited area by Dr. Freeman in his recent paper "Iban Augury," in which he shows how the Ibans by selecting a few species of birds out of a very large set provided by their forest environment, and by selecting for each species a very small number of significant properties, have been able to use these differential elements by opposing them and also combining them so as to convey different messages.

Having cleared up these general problems, I shall now enter into my subject proper. When going over the work of early investigators in Australia, I was struck by the fact that approximately between 1830 and 1850, these authors, although they knew that Australian sections and sub-sections were probably connected with the laws of intermarriage, nevertheless believed them to differ in rank; and to describe them, they frequently used the word "caste." This, I think, should not be neglected. In the first place, because there may have been something more "caste-like" in these divisions than what was subsequently found among interior, mostly desert, people and because it seems obvious that even from a superficial point of view there is something similar between Australian tribes and caste societies; each segment performs a special task which benefits the community as a whole and which is complementary to functions that devolve upon other segments. This appears clearly among the Australian tribes described by Spencer & Gillen in which moieties or clans are bound together by a rule of reciprocity. The Kaitish and the Unmatjera, who are northern neighbours of the Aranda, know of rules that require an individual who gathers wild seeds in a territory belonging to a totemic group named after those seeds, to obtain permission from its head before consuming them; according to these rules, each totemic group is obliged to provide others with plants or animals whose "production" it allegedly controls. Thus the totemic food prohibition appears to be in such a case merely a negative way of expressing a positive obligation towards the others. This is clearly shown in a few well documented examples presented by Spencer & Gillen. The lone hunter belonging to the Emu clan cannot touch the bird, but in company he can and must kill it so as to present it as food to hunters belonging to other clans, and conversely the hunter belonging to the Water clan is permitted to drink alone, but when in company he can drink only if the water is presented to him by members of the opposite moiety. Among the Warramunga too each totemic group is held responsible for the natural species consumed by other groups. The Warramunga and the Walpari have secondary prohibitions against consuming the maternal totem but these are lifted when food is obtained from the opposite moiety. Generally speaking, and for each totem, there is a threefold distinction between those groups who never consume it because it is their own totem, those that may consume it when obtained from the opposite moiety (in case it should be the maternal totem), and those that can consume it in all circumstances, because it is not their totem. The same is true for the sacred well which women may never approach, while uninitiated men, though they may approach them, may not drink from them, while still other groups of uninitiated men may both approach the wells and drink of the water, providing it is offered them by men belonging to the group that is allowed to drink freely.

Notwithstanding these similarities between totemic groups and castes, it is clear that the line which I have followed so far is too general to be convincing. It is well known that castes and totemic groups are widely different and opposed institutional systems, that one is linked with the highest cultures and the other with the lowest cultures with which anthropologists are acquainted. In a traditional way, totemism is linked to exogamy in its strictest forms, which in a game of free association, ninety-nine out of a hundred anthropologists would probably associate the word "caste" with the word "endogamy."

Thus the distinctive character of the extreme cases is clear, but would these appear as extreme if we could dispose of intermediary forms? In earlier writings I have tried to show that exchange in human society is a universal means of ensuring the interlocking of its constitutive parts and that this exchange can operate at different levels among which the more important are food, goods and services, and women. Two cases should be distinguished, however. Sometimes the three forms (or two of them) are called upon, so to speak, to cumulate their effects and to complement each other, either positively or negatively. In the second case, one form only is retained because it supplements the others. A good positive example of the first case is provided by those Australian groups where exchange of women and food prohibitions (which, as we have seen, can be equally well expressed as an obligatory exchange of foods), reinforce each other, and we find a negative example of the same phenomenon in some parts of Melanesia and in peasant Europe of the past, where endogamy or exogamy unwillingly practised seems to be connected with what we may call "endo-agriculture," that is, an extreme unwillingness to exchange seeds. Turning now to the second case, we may perhaps be permitted to consider the type of structure to be found in the so-called Crow-Omaha kinship systems as being in diametrical opposition to the Aranda systems in so far as, in the former, everything not forbidden is allowed, while in the latter the exact opposite is true: everything not allowed is forbidden. Now if this be granted, it is rather remarkable that in an African group such as the Nandi of Kenya, whose kinship system has been classified rightly or wrongly by Radcliffe-Brown as Omaha, there should be an extraordinary development of clan prohibitions bearing upon food and costume, and accompanied by individual marriage prohibitions based, not on clan affiliation, but on peculiar events pertaining to the individual history of each prospective groom and bride, which means that, in such a case, the structural arrangement of the alliance network—if any—would result from statistical fluctuations, exactly as happens with rules of marriage of the Crow-Omaha type. Let us consider a final example: that of the Baganda such as described by Roscoe. We are told that the Baganda had about forty clans, each possessing two totems, the first one being subject to food prohibition "so as to make it available to others in greater quantity," which is a modest counterpart of the Australian belief that, by refraining from consuming its totem, each clan acquires the power to multiply it. As in Australia too, each clan was linked to a territory which, in the case of the Baganda, was usually a sacred hill. In addition, each clan had a great many privileges, obligations, and prohibitions, as for instance, eligibility to kingship and other dignities, providing kingly wives, making and caring for regalia, providing other clans with certain kinds of food, and also special occupations. The Mushroom clan, for instance, was said to be sole maker of bark cloth and all the blacksmiths were supposed to come from the clan of the Tailless Cow. In such cases, we may well ask ourselves whether we are dealing with totemic clans, occupational castes, or with an intermediary form pertaining to both these types. Let us tackle this problem through application of our axiomatic principle.

We have seen that the so-called totemic concept amounts to a belief in an homology *not* between social groups and natural species, but between differences existing, on the one hand within the social system, and on the other within the natural system. Two systems of differences are conceived as isomorphic, although one is situated in nature, and the other in culture.

Let us now suppose that in addition to an homology of relationships, we have an homology of terms, and going one step further, that the homology of relationships shifts and becomes an homology between terms. The result will no longer be that Clan 1 can be held to differ from Clan 2 as for instance, Eagle differs from Bear, but that Clan 1 is in itself like Eagle and Clan 2 in itself like Bear. The system of differences will continue to exist, but, first, it will be conceived in reference to nature instead of to culture, and second, exogamy will inevitably break down because it implies that while women are sociologically conceived of as being different, they are naturally (though unconsciously) conceived of as similar, or else they could not be exchanged.

It so happens that this theoretical transformation may be exemplified by concrete examples. In volume 5 of the *Haddon-Rivers Expedition to Torres Straits* (p. 184) we find that at Mabuiag, for instance, "A definite physical and psychological resemblance was postulated from the human and animal members of the clan. There can be little doubt that this sentiment reacted on the clansmen and constrained them to live up to the traditional character of their respective clans." Thus the Cassowary, Crocodile, Snake, and Shark clans were reputed to love fighting, while the Shovel-nosed Skate, Ray and Sucker-Fish clans were said to be peaceable. Intermediate between the fierce and the gentle clans was the Dog clan, which was thought to be sometimes pugnacious and sometimes pacific, just like real dogs. The men of the Crocodile clan were said to be very strong and ruthless, while the men of the Cassowary clan were reputed for their long legs and their ability to run fast, like real cassowaries. Similar observations have been made in North America among Eastern Indians such as the Delaware, the Menomini, and the Chippewa. Among the latter, people of the Fish clan were reputed to be long lived, frequently to grow bald or to have thin hair, and all bald people were assumed to come from this clan. People of the Bear clan had long, thick, coarse hair that never turned white; they were said to be bellicose and quick to anger. People of the Crane clan had loud, ringing voices. Orators were always supposed to come from this clan.

From a theoretical point of view, we may now appraise the implications of these two opposite conceptions. In the first hypothesis, society on the one hand, nature on the other, will each retain its systematic integrity. Social segments will be referred to social segments; each natural species will be referred to other natural species. In the second hypothesis, instead of two "horizontal" systems situated at different levels, we shall have a plurality of "vertical" systems, considerably impoverished in fact, since instead of *two systems* each consisting of *numerous elements* we shall have *numerous systems* each consisting of *two elements*, heterogeneous (one natural, one cultural) instead of homogeneous (entirely natural or entirely cultural). Should this interpretation prove to be true, it should be possible, first to translate or recode a "totemic" system into a caste system and conversely, and also to give concrete examples of societies which have actually done so. This is what I intend to exemplify now.

Tribes of the Muskogi linguistic group in the South-Eastern United States such as, for instance, the Chickasaw and the Creek, did have clans and moieties the first of which were perhaps exogamous and the second endogamous. In any case moieties were noted for overt manifestations of exclusivism that bordered on hostility. Ritual was jealously guarded by each moiety and members of another moiety who had witnessed a ceremony, even inadvertently, were put to death (an attitude recalling that held by the Aranda in relation to their cult groups). What is even more important, moieties were said to differ by their respective ways of life and their disposition of mind; one was said to be warlike and to prefer open country, the other one to be peaceable and to live in the woods. They may also have been hierarchized, as is suggested by some of the names under which they were known, one moiety being called "their-hickory-choppings," meaning that they had substantial lodges, while the other moiety was called "their worn-out place," meaning that it consisted of inferior people living mostly under trees and in the woods. These differences were both more complex and more marked between clans, lineages, and hamlets. When informants were called upon to describe these secondary units, they used as a kind of leit-motiv, practically always the same words. "These people had ways of their own . . . they were very peculiar . . . different from all others . . . they had their own customs." These peculiarities were said to belong to different types: environment, economic activities, costume, food preferences, talents and tastes.

For instance, people of the Raccoon clan fed mostly on fish and wild fruits. Those of the Panther clan lived in mountains, avoided water, which they greatly feared, and fed on game. People of the Wild-Cat clan slept in the daytime, hunted by night since they were gifted with an especially keen sight, and were not interested in women. Those of the Bird clan woke up before daylight: "they were like real birds in that they would not bother anybody . . . the people of this clan have different sorts of minds, just as there are different species of birds . . . they had many wives . . . they did not work at all, but had an easy time going through life and went anywhere they wanted to . . . they had many offspring, as birds have."

People of the Red-Fox clan lived only in the woods, made a living by stealing from other people . . . doing whatever they liked. The "Wandering Iska" or "No-Home Iska" were a shiftless people "who did not want to own anything . . . they did not do anything for themselves . . . they were healthy looking, strong, for they did not do anything to run themselves down . . . they moved very slowly . . . they thought they were going to live forever . . . they did not care how they dressed or appeared . . . sometimes they wore dirty dresses . . . they were beggars and lazy."

The same kind of differences are emphasized between hamlets, for instance the Bending-Post-Oak-House Group lived in the wood, they were not very energetic, they loved to dance. They were prone to anxiety, had no foresight, were early risers, and made many mistakes, while people of the High-Corncrib House Group were not much esteemed by others but thought a great deal of themselves: "They were industrious, raised large crops, did not hunt much, bartered corn for venison. They were very wise, people of one mind, truthful, and they knew a great deal about the weather."

All these statements, which I have borrowed from Swanton, cannot be taken literally. They refer to a period when the traditional culture had already broken down and were obtained from old informants. They clearly belong to folk ethnology since, theoretically, it would be impossible for a human society to mimic nature to such an extent without running the risk of breaking down into several distinct groups hostile to one another. However, the testimony collected by Swanton is so rich, so concordant even when it comes from different tribes, that it must contain if not the literal truth at least the expression of a conceptual model which must have existed in the minds of the natives.

Allowing for these restrictive considerations, these statements have a threefold importance. In the first place, they describe what appears to have been a kind of caste system. In the second place, castes and their mutual relationships are being coded, so to speak, according to a natural model, after the diversity of natural species, as happens with totemic groups; and in the third place, from an historical point of view, these Muskogi tribes constituted a kind of link between the "true" totemic societies of the Plains and the only "true" caste-societies which are known to have existed in North America, such as the Natchez, Thus, I have established so far that in two parts of the world traditionally conceived as "totemistic," Australia's so-called "totemic" groups can be interpreted as occupational groups, while in America, social segments which can actually function as castes, were conceived after a "totemic" model.

Let us now shift to India, also a classical land, though of castes rather than totemic groups. Here, instead of castes being conceived after a natural model, vestiges of totemic groups tend to be conceived after a cultural model. But before exemplifying this point let me remind the reader that I am using the word "totemic" in such a way as to be able to leave entirely aside the question of whether or not there are actual vestiges of totemism in India. From my present point of view, the problem is irrelevant since, when I make loose usage of the term totemism, I never refer to a past or present institution but to a classificatory device whereby discrete elements of the external world are associated with the discrete elements of the social world. Bearing this in mind, we may be struck by the fact that whereas so-called "totemic" names in Bengal are mostly of animal or vegetable origin, further south an increasing proportion of names borrowed from manufactured objects is to be found. For instance the Devanga who are a caste of weavers in Madras, use very few plant names for their clans and almost no animal names, but rather names such as buttermilk, cattle-pen, money, dam, houses, collyrium, knife, scissors, boat, clay lamp, female cloth, clothes, ropes for hanging pots, old plough, monastery, cart, funeral pyre, tile, etc., and the Kuruba of Mysore, who have sixty-seven exogamous clans, with few plant and animal names, designate them by names such as, among others, drum, booth, cart, cup, woollen thread, bangle, gold, pick-axe, hut, gold ring, bell-metal, coloured border of a cloth, stick, blanket, measure, metal toe-ring, moustache, loom, bamboo tube, lace, ring, etc.

These manufactured objects are not only used as clan names, but they also receive attention, and serve to express obligations and prohibitions as in totemic systems. It is true that the use of manufactured objects as totemic names is well known elsewhere in the world, particularly in Northern Australia and in some parts of Africa, very good examples having been recently (1961) presented for the Dinka by Dr. Lienhardt in his book *Divinity and Experience*. However, this never happens to such an extent as in India. Thus it seems that while in America castes confusedly conceived have been contaminated by totemic classifications, in India, where products or symbols of occupational activities are clearly differentiated as such and can be put to use in order to express differences between social groups, vestiges or remnants of totemic groups have come to make use of a symbolism that is technological and occupational in origin.

This appears less surprising when one attempts to express Australian institutions (the first ones which we have envisaged) differently, and in a more direct way, in the language of the caste system. What we have done thus far was to compare Australian totemic groups one to another from the standpoint of their specialization in control of a given animal or vegetable species, while occupational castes "control" the technical activities necessary to the well-being of the whole group.

There are nevertheless two differences. In the first place, a potter caste makes pots, a laundryman caste does actual laundry work, and barbers do shave. The performances of Australian totemic groups, however, are unreal, imaginary, and even though the participants believe in their reality, we shall see later that this characteristic makes a great deal of difference. In the second place, the connexion between the sorcerer and the natural species that he claims to control is not of the same type as the link between the craftsman and his product. Only in mythical times did the animals or plants actually originate from the ancestor's body. Nowadays, kangaroos produce kangaroos and man can only help them to do so.

But the similarity is much stronger if we adopt a different point of view. An Australian section or sub-section actually produces its women for the benefit of the other sections, much as an occupational caste produces goods and services which the other castes cannot produce and must seek from this caste alone. Thus, it would be inaccurate to define totemic groups and caste systems as being simply one exogamous and another endogamous. These are not real properties existing as such, but superficial and indirect consequences of a similarity which should be recognized at a deeper level. In the first place, both castes and totemic groups are "exo-practical": castes in relation to goods and services, totemic groups in relation to marriage. In the second place, both remain to some extent "endo-practical": castes by virtue of the rule of endogamy and Australian groups as regards their preferred type of matrimonial exchange, which being mostly of the "restricted" type, keeps each tribe closely self-contained and, as it were, wrapped up in itself. It would seem that allowing for the above restrictive considerations, we have now reached a satisfactory formulation, in a common language, of the relationship between totemic groups and castes. Thus we might say that in the first case—totemic groups—women, that is, biological individuals or natural products, are begotten naturally by other biological individuals, while in the second case—castes—manufactured objects or services rendered through the medium of manufactured objects are fabricated culturally through technical agents. The principle of differentiation stems in the one case from nature and in the other from culture.

However, this kind of parallelism would be purely formal and without any concrete basis, for occupational castes are truly different from one another as regards culture, and also complementary. The same cannot be said, as regards nature, of exogamic groups which specialize, so to speak, in the production of women belonging to different "species." Occupational activities are true social species; they are objectively distinct. Women, on the other hand, even when they are born in different sections of sub-sections, belong nevertheless to one and the same natural species.

Social logic appears at this point to be caught in a dialectical trap. The assumed parallelism between natural products (actually, women) and social products is wholly imaginary. This explains why exogamous groups are so often inclined to define themselves as totemic groups, for over and above exogamy they need an objective model to express their social diversity. In societies where division of labour and occupational specialization do not exist, the only possible objective model has to be sought in the natural diversity of biological species; for there are only two objectively given models of concrete diversity: one on the level of nature, made up by the taxonomic system of natural species, the other on the level of culture, made up by the social system of trades and occupations.

The rules of exogamy establish an ambiguous system which lies somewhere in between: as regards nature, women are all alike, and only as regards culture may they be claimed to be different.

If the first point of view prevails, that is, when men borrow from nature their conceptual model of diversification, they must unconsciously abide also by a natural model of womankind. Exogamous groups make the overt claim that women are culturally different and, consequently, may be exchanged. But actually, they can only be exchanged because, at a deeper level, they are known to be similar. This provides an explanation to what I have said earlier and permits, so to speak, one to deduce exogamy from more general principles.

Conversely, when the overt conceptual model is cultural, as in the caste system, women are acknowledged to be similar only within the limits of their respective social groups and this being projected on to the natural plane, their exchange between groups consequently becomes impossible.

In other words, both the caste system and the so-called totemic systems postulate isomorphism between natural and cultural differences. The validation of this postulate involves in each case a symmetrical and inverted relationship. Castes are defined after a cultural model and must define their matrimonial exchange after a natural model. Totemic groups pattern matrimonial exchange after a cultural model, and they themselves must be defined after a natural model. Women, homogeneous as regards nature, are claimed to be heterogeneous as regards culture, and conversely, natural species, although heterogeneous as regards nature, are claimed to be homogeneous as regards culture, since from the standpoint of culture, they share common properties in so far as man is believed to possess the power to control and to multiply them.

In totemic systems, men exchange culturally the women who procreate them naturally, and they claim to procreate culturally the animal and vegetable species which they exchange naturally: in the form of foodstuffs which are interchangeable, since any biological individual is able to dispense with one and to subsist on the others. A true parallelism can therefore be said to exist between the two formulas, and it is possible to code one into the terms of the other. Indeed, this parallelism is more complex than we believed it to be at the beginning. It can be expressed in the following tortuous way: castes naturalize fallaciously a true culture while totemic groups culturalize truly a false nature. "False" in two respects: first, from a natural point of view, women belong to one and the same natural species; and second, as a natural species, men do not have the power to increase and control other natural species.

However, this symmetry can never be rigorous; soon enough it reaches its limits. During their procreative period, women are naturally equivalent; anatomical structure and physiological function are, grossly speaking, identical in all female individuals. On the other hand, foods are not so easily replaceable. Speaking of the Karuba of Mysore, Thurston quotes the Arisana gotram which bears the name of turmeric. But since it is not easy to go without turmeric it has adopted as its food-prohibition *korra* seeds which can be more easily dispensed with. And in his book already referred to, Dr. Lienhardt states something similar about clans whose divinity is the giraffe. This is an all-important food, and instead of prohibiting it, these clans content themselves with avoiding to shed its blood. The same limitation exists with occupational castes. They too have to remain to some extent endofunctional, in order to render themselves the services they give to others. Otherwise who is going to shave the barber?

By way of conclusion I should like to emphasize four points. First, totemism which has been formalized in what may be called the "language of primitiveness" can equally well be formalized in the "language of castes" which were thought to be the very opposite of primitiveness.

Secondly, in its social undertakings, mankind keeps manoeuvering within narrow limits. Social types are not isolated creations, wholly independent of each other, and each one an original entity, but rather the result of an endless play of combination and recombination, forever seeking to solve the same problems by manipulating the same fundamental elements. This game always consists in a give-and-take, and what is given or taken must always belong either to the realm of nature (natural products) or to the realm of culture (goods and services), the exchange of women being the only formula that makes it possible to overcome this duality. Thus exchange of women not only ensures a horizontal mediation between groups of men, it also ensures a mediation, which we might call vertical, between nature and culture.

Thirdly, as we have seen, the tremendous differences existing between totemic groups and caste systems, in spite of their logical inverted similarity, may be ascribed to the fact that castes are right and totemic systems are wrong, when they believe that they provide real services to their fellow groups. This should convince us that the "truth-value" is an unavoidable dimension of structural method. No common analysis of religion can be given by a believer and a nonbeliever, and from this point of view, the type of approach known as "religious phenomenology" should be dismissed.

Lastly, by analysing a specific example, I have attempted to validate a methodological approach which I have been trying to follow in France and which Dr. Leach is following in England. According to this approach societies are not made up of the flotsam and jetsam of history, but of variables; thus widely different institutions can be reduced to transformations of the same basic figure, and the whole of human history may be looked upon merely as a set of attempts to organize differently the same means, but always to answer the same questions.

Mary Douglas

THE ABOMINATIONS OF LEVITICUS

The subtle and suggestive implications of Mary Douglas's theoretical approach, first advanced in her book *Purity and Danger* (1966), have led to reconsiderations of so-called magical attitudes in all parts of the world. Douglas provides an excellent application of her ideas in her consideration of Jewish dietary laws, most specifically the taboo against eating pork. She argues that the prohibited "abominations of Leviticus" are animals which appear anomalous in the classification of natural things handed down by God in Genesis. By avoiding what in nature challenges God's order, men confirm that order. Through a dietary observance, God is made holy—separate and whole.

Reprinted in abridged form from Mary Douglas, *Purity and Danger* (London: Routledge & Kegan Paul Ltd.; New York: Frederick A. Praeger, Inc., 1966) pp. 41–58, by permission of the author and publishers.

Defilement is never an isolated event. It cannot occur except in view of a systematic ordering of ideas. Hence any piecemeal interpretation of the pollution rules of another culture is bound to fail. For the only way in which pollution ideas make sense is in reference to a total structure of thought whose keystone, boundaries, margins and internal lines are held in relation by rituals of separation.

To illustrate this I take a hoary old puzzle from biblical scholarship, the abominations of Leviticus, and particularly the dietary rules. Why should the camel, the hare and the rock badger be unclean? Why should some locusts, but not all, be unclean? Why should the frog be clean and the mouse and the hippopotamus unclean? What have chameleons, moles and crocodiles got in common that they should be listed together?

[To help follow the argument the reader is referred to Deuteronomy XIV and Leviticus XI using the text of the New Revised Standard Translation.]

. . .

All the interpretations given so far fall into one of two groups: either the rules are meaningless, arbitrary because their intent is disciplinary and not doctrinal, or they are allegories of virtues and vices. Adopting the view that religious prescriptions are largely devoid of symbolism, Maimonides said:

> *The Law that sacrifices should be brought is evidently of great use . . . but we cannot say why one offering should be a lamb whilst another is a ram, and why a fixed number of these should be brought. Those who trouble themselves to find a cause for any of these detailed rules are in my eyes devoid of sense. . . .*

. . .

Any interpretations will fail which take the Do-nots of the Old Testament in piecemeal fashion. The only sound approach is to forget hygiene, aesthetics, morals and instinctive revulsion, even to forget the Canaanites and the Zoroastrian Magi, and start with the texts. Since each of the injunctions is prefaced by the command to be holy, so they must be explained by that command. There must be contrariness between holiness and abomination which will make over-all sense of all the particular restrictions.

Holiness is the attribute of Godhead. Its root means "set apart." What else does it mean? We should start any cosmological enquiry by seeking the principles of power and danger. In the Old Testament we find blessing as the source of all good things, and the withdrawal of blessing as the source of all dangers. The blessing of God makes the land possible for men to live in.

God's work through the blessing is essentially to create order, through which men's affairs prosper. Fertility of women, livestock and fields is promised as a result of the blessing and this is to be obtained by keeping covenant with God and observing all His precepts and ceremonies (Deut. XXVIII, 1–14). Where the blessing is withdrawn and the power of the curse unleashed, there is barrenness, pestilence, confusion. For Moses said:

> *But if you will not obey the voice of the Lord your God or be careful to do all his commandments and his statutes which I command you to this day, then all these curses shall come upon you and overtake you. . . .* (Deut. XXVIII, 15–24)

From this it is clear that the positive and negative precepts are held to be efficacious and not merely expressive: observing them draws down prosperity, infringing them brings danger. We are thus entitled to treat them in the same way as we treat primitive ritual avoidances whose breach unleashes danger to men. The precepts and ceremonies alike are focussed on the idea of the holiness of God which men must create in their own lives. So this is a universe in which men prosper by conforming to holiness and perish when they deviate from it. If there were no other clues we should be able to find out the Hebrew idea of the holy by examining the precepts by which men conform to it. It is evidently not goodness in the sense of an all-embracing humane kindness. Justice and moral goodness may well illustrate holiness and form part of it, but holiness embraces other ideas as well.

Granted that its root means separateness, the next idea that emerges is of the Holy as wholeness and completeness. Much of Leviticus is taken up with stating the physical perfection that is required of things presented in the temple and of persons approaching it. The animals offered in sacrifice must be without blemish, women must be purified after childbirth, lepers should be separated and ritually cleansed before being allowed to approach it once they are cured. All bodily discharges are defiling and disqualify from approach to the temple. Priests may only come into contact with death when their own close kin die. But the high priest must never have contact with death.

. . .

He must be perfect as a man, if he is to be a priest.

This much reiterated idea of physical completeness is also worked out in the social sphere and particularly in the warriors' camp. The culture of the Israelites was brought to the pitch of greatest intensity when they prayed and when they fought. The army could not win without the blessing and to keep the blessing in the camp they had to be specially holy. So the camp was to be preserved from defilement like the Temple. Here again all bodily discharges disqualified a man from entering the camp as they would disqualify a worshipper from approaching the altar. A warrior who had had an issue of the body in the night should keep outside the camp all day and only return after sunset, having washed. Natural functions producing bodily waste were to be performed outside the camp (Deut. XXIII, 10–15). In short the idea of holiness was given an external, physical expression in the wholeness of the body seen as a perfect container.

. . .

Other precepts develop the idea of wholeness in another direction. The metaphors of the physical body and of the new undertaking relate to the perfection and completeness of the individual and his work. Other precepts extend holiness to species and categories. Hybrids and other confusions are abominated.

LEV. XVIII

23. And you shall not lie with any beast and defile yourself with it, neither shall any woman give herself to a beast to lie with it: it is perversion, . . .

The word "perversion" is a significant mistranslation of the rare Hebrew word *tebhel*, which has as its meaning mixing or confusion. The same theme is taken up in Leviticus XIX, 19.

You shall keep my statutes. You shall not let your cattle breed with a different kind; you shall not sow your field with two kinds of seed; nor shall there come upon you a garment of cloth made of two kinds of stuff.

All these injunctions are prefaced by the general command:

Be holy, for I am holy.

We can conclude that holiness is exemplified by completeness. Holiness requires that individuals shall conform to the class to which they belong. And holiness requires that different classes of things shall not be confused.

Another set of precepts refines on this last point. Holiness means keeping distinct the categories of creation. It therefore involves correct definition, discrimination and order. Under this head all the rules of sexual morality exemplify the holy. Incest and adultery (Lev. XVIII, 6–20) are against holiness, in the simple sense of right order. Morality does not conflict with holiness, but holiness is more a matter of separating that which should be separated than of protecting the rights of husbands and brothers.

Then follows in Chapter XIX another list of actions which are contrary to holiness. Developing the idea of holiness as order, not confusion, this list upholds rectitude and straight-dealing as holy, and contradiction and double-dealing as against holiness. Theft, lying, false witness, cheating in weights and measures, all kinds of dissembling such as speaking ill of the deaf (and presumably smiling to their face), hating your brother in your heart (while presumably speaking kindly to him), these are clearly contradictions between what seems and what is. This chapter also says much about generosity and love, but these are positive commands, while I am concerned with negative rules.

We have now laid a good basis for approaching the laws about clean and unclean meats. To be holy is to be whole, to be one; holiness is unity, integrity, perfection of the individual and of the kind. The dietary rules merely develop the metaphor of holiness on the same lines.

First we should start with livestock, the herds of cattle, camels, sheep and goats which were the livelihood of the Israelites. These animals were clean inasmuch as contact with them did not require purification before approaching the Temple. Livestock, like the inhabited land, received the blessing of God. Both land and livestock were fertile by the blessing, both were drawn into the divine order. The farmer's duty was to preserve the blessing. For one thing, he had to preserve the order of creation. So no hybrids, as we have seen, either in the fields or in the herds or in the clothes made from wool or flax. To some extent men covenanted with their land and cattle in the same way as God covenanted with them. Men respected the first born of their cattle, obliged them to keep the Sabbath. Cattle were literally domesticated as slaves. They had to be brought into the social order in order to enjoy the blessing. The difference between cattle and the wild beasts is that the wild beasts have no covenant to protect them. It is possible that the Israelites were like other pastoralists who do not relish wild game. The Nuer of the South Sudan, for instance, apply a sanction of disapproval of a man who lives by hunting. To be driven to eating wild meat is the sign of a poor herdsman. So it would be probably wrong to think of the Israelites as longing for forbidden meats and finding the restrictions irksome. Driver is surely right in taking the rules as an *a posteriori* generalisation of their habits. Cloven hoofed, cud chewing ungulates are the model of the proper kind of food for a pastoralist. If they must eat wild game, they can eat wild game that shares these distinctive characters and is therefore of the same general species. This is a kind of casuistry which permits scope for hunting antelope and wild goats and wild sheep. Everything would be quite straightforward were it not that the legal mind has seen fit to give ruling on some borderline cases. Some animals seem to be ruminant, such as the hare and the hyrax (or rock badger), whose constant grinding of their teeth was held to be cud-chewing. But they are definitely not cloven-hoofed and so are excluded by name. Similarly for animals which are cloven-hoofed but are not ruminant, the pig and the camel. Note that this failure to conform to the two necessary criteria for defining cattle is the only reason given in the Old Testament for avoiding the pig; nothing whatever is said about its dirty scavenging habits. As the pig does not yield milk, hide nor wool, there is no other reason for keeping it except for its flesh. And if the Israelites did not keep pig they would not be familiar with its habits. I suggest that originally the sole reason for its being counted as unclean is its failure as a wild boar to get into the antelope class, and that in this it is on the same footing as the camel and the hyrax, exactly as is stated in the book.

After these borderline cases have been dismissed, the law goes on to deal with creatures according to how they live in the three elements, the water, the air and the earth. The principles here applied are rather different from those covering the camel, the pig, the hare and the hyrax. For the latter are excepted from clean food in having one but not both of the defining characters of livestock. Birds I can say nothing about, because, as I have said, they are named and not described and the translation of the name is open to doubt. But in general the underlying principle of cleanness in animals is that they shall conform fully to their class. Those species are unclean which are imperfect members of their class, or whose class itself confounds the general scheme of the world.

To grasp this scheme we need to go back to Genesis and the creation. Here a three-fold classification unfolds, divided between the earth, the waters and the firmament. Leviticus takes up this scheme and allots to each element its proper kind of animal life. In the firmament two-legged fowls fly with wings. In the water scaly fish swim with fins. On the earth four-legged animals hop, jump or walk. Any class of creatures which is not equipped for the right kind of locomotion in its element is contrary to holiness. Contact with it disqualifies a person from approaching the Temple. Thus anything in the water which has not fins and scales is unclean (XI, 10–12). Nothing is said about predatory habits or of scavenging. The only sure test for cleanness in a fish is its scales and its propulsion by means of fins.

Four-footed creatures which fly (XI, 20–26) are unclean. Any creature which has two legs and two hands and which goes on all fours like a quadruped is unclean (XI, 27). Then follows (v. 29) a much disputed list. In some translations, it would appear to consist precisely of creatures endowed with hands instead of front feet, which perversely use their hands for walking: the weasel, the mouse, the crocodile, the shrew, various kinds of lizards, the chameleon and mole (Danby, 1933), whose forefeet are uncannily hand-like. This feature of this list is lost in the New Revised Standard Translation which used the word "paws" instead of hands.

The last kind of unclean animal is that which creeps, crawls or swarms upon the earth. This form of movement is explicitly contrary to holiness (Lev. XI, 41–44). Driver and White use "swarming" to translate the Hebrew *shěrec*, which is applied to both those which teem in the waters and those which swarm on the ground. Whether we call it teeming, trailing, creeping, crawling or swarming, it is an indeterminate form of movement. Since the main animal categories are defined by their typical movement, "swarming" which is not a mode of propulsion proper to any particular element, cuts across the basic classification. Swarming things are neither fish, flesh nor fowl. Eels and worms inhabit water, though not as fish; reptiles go on dry land, though not as quadrupeds; some insects fly, though not as birds. There is no order in them. Recall what the Prophecy of Habacuc says about this form of life:

For thou makest men like the fish of the sea, like crawling things that have no ruler. (I, v. 14)

The prototype and model of the swarming things is the worm. As fish belong in the sea so worms belong in the realm of the grave, with death and chaos.

The case of the locusts is interesting and consistent. The test of whether it is a clean and therefore edible kind is how it moves on the earth. If it crawls it is unclean. If it hops it is clean (XI, v. 21). In the Mishnah it is noted that a frog is not listed with creeping things and conveys no uncleanness (Danby, p. 722). I suggest that the frog's hop accounts for it not being listed. If penguins lived in the Near East I would expect them to be ruled unclean as wingless birds. If the list of unclean birds could be retranslated from this point of view, it might well turn out that they are anomalous because they swim and dive as well as they fly, or in some other way they are not fully bird-like.

Surely now it would be difficult to maintain that "Be ye Holy" means no more than "Be ye separate." Moses wanted the children of Israel to keep the commands of God constantly before their minds:

DEUT. XI

18. *You shall therefore lay up these words of mine in your heart and in your soul; and you shall bind them as a sign upon your hand, and they shall be as frontlets between your eyes.*

19. *And you shall teach them to your children, talking of them when you are sitting in your house, and when you are walking by the way, and when you lie down and when you rise.*

20. *And you shall write them upon the doorposts of your house and upon your gates.*

If the proposed interpretation of the forbidden animals is correct, the dietary laws would have been like signs which at every turn inspired meditation on the oneness, purity and completeness of God. By rules of avoidance holiness was given a physical expression in every encounter with the animal kingdom and at every meal. Observance of the dietary rules would thus have been a meaningful part of the great liturgical act of recognition and worship which culminated in the sacrifice in the Temple.

Edmund R. Leach

ANTHROPOLOGICAL ASPECTS OF LANGUAGE: ANIMAL CATEGORIES AND VERBAL ABUSE

Nature is, by nature, undifferentiated and unclassified. It is man who, in his social behavior and his language, distinguishes fish from fowl, man from god. In this ingenious article, Edmund Leach expands Mary Douglas's hypothesis that human classificatory systems depend not only on our matching names and things, but on avoiding or tabooing those things which fall on the boundaries between categories or names. Thus, Leach argues, we eat fish, birds, and beasts—inhabitants of water, air, and land—but avoid reptiles which live on land and sea, or insects, which move between land and air. Eating prohibitions enforce a simplified, disjunctive classification of natural things. Further, he suggests, the reason we refuse to consider dogs edible is that, in our society, dogs are too much like men. By avoiding dog meat, we enforce a cultural rule which forbids men to eat men. And, in our horror at the accusation "you're a bitch"—but not, "you're a polar bear"—we provide further evidence to the notion that ambivalent entities have a potency which may be manipulated (and worshiped) as well as feared. The argument introduces an additional complexity, however, in taking into account the fact that neither the tabooed nor the sacred is of a piece. If dogs are inedible, pigs are edible if castrated, deer edible (in season), and lions and tigers are not eaten at all: these degrees of taboo, or sacredness, correspond to the relative distance of animals from a postulated SELF. These same degrees are paralleled in the social classification of unmarriageable close kin, "kissing cousins," marriageable neighbors, and unmarriageable strangers. Sex and eating are symbolically associated in many cultures; here Leach is suggesting that, rather than simple binary oppositions, complex systems of social classification provide a model for both dietary and sexual taboos. For other expositions on the use of animals in symbolic classification, see R. Bulmer's essay, "Why is the Cassowary not a Bird?" (1967), and S. J. Tambiah, "Animals are Good to Think and Good to Prohibit" (1969).

Reprinted from *New Directions in the Study of Language* by Eric H. Lenneberg (1964), pp. 23–63 by permission of the M.I.T. Press, Cambridge, Massachusetts.

The central theme of my essay is the classical anthropological topic of "taboo." This theme, in this guise, does not form part of the conventional field of discourse of experimental psychologists; yet the argument that I shall present has its psychological equivalents. When psychologists debate about the mechanism of "forgetting" they often introduce the concept of "interference," the idea that there is a tendency to repress concepts that have some kind of semantic overlap (Postman, 1961). The thesis which I present depends upon a converse hypothesis, namely, that we can only arrive at semantically distinct verbal concepts if we repress the boundary percepts that lie between them.

To discuss the anthropological aspect of language within the confines of space allotted to me here is like writing a history of England in thirty lines. I propose to tackle a specific theme, not a general one. For the anthropologist, language is a part of culture, not a thing in itself. Most of the anthropologist's problems are concerned with human communication. Language is one means of communication, but customary acts of behavior are also a means of communication, and the anthropologist feels that he can, and should, keep both modes of communication in view at the same time.

LANGUAGE AND TABOO

This is a symposium about language but my theme is one of nonlanguage. Instead of discussing things that are said and done, I want to talk about things that are not said and done. My theme is that of taboo, expression which is inhibited.

Anthropological and psychological literature alike are crammed with descriptions and learned explanations of apparently irrational prohibitions and inhibitions. Such "taboo" may be either behavioral or linguistic, and it deserves note that the protective sanctions are very much the same in either case. If at this moment I were really anxious to get arrested by the police, I might strip naked or launch into a string of violent obscenities: either procedure would be equally effective.

Linguistic taboos and behavioral taboos are not only sanctioned in the same way, they are very much muddled up: sex behavior and sex words, for example. But this association of deed and word is not so simple as might appear. The relationship is not necessarily causal. It is not the case that certain kinds of behavior are taboo and that, therefore, the language relating to such behavior becomes taboo. Sometimes words may be taboo in themselves for linguistic (phonemic) reasons, and the causal link, if any, is then reversed; a behavioral taboo comes to reflect a prior verbal taboo. In this paper I shall only touch upon the fringe of this complex subject.

A familiar type of purely linguistic taboo is the pun. A pun occurs when we make a joke by confusing two apparently different meanings of the same phonemic pattern. The pun seems funny or shocking because it challenges a taboo which ordinarily forbids us to recognize that the sound pattern is ambiguous. In many cases such verbal taboos have social as well as linguistic aspects. In English, though not I think in American, the word *queen* has a homonym *quean*. The words are phonetically indistinguishable (KWĪN). Queen is the consort of King or even a female sovereign in her own right; quean which formerly meant a prostitute now usually denotes a homosexual male. In the nonhuman world we have queen bees and brood queen cats, both indicating a splendid fertility, but a quean is a barren cow. Although these two words pretend to be different, indeed opposites, they really denote the same idea. A queen is a female of abnormal status in a positive virtuous sense; a quean is a person of depraved character or uncertain sex, a female of abnormal status in a negative sinful sense. Yet their common abnormality turns both into "supernatural" beings; so also, in metaphysics, the contraries God and the Devil are both supernatural beings. In this case, then, the taboo which allows us to separate the two ambiguous concepts, so that we can talk of queens without thinking of queans, and vice versa, is simultaneously both linguistic *and* social.

We should note that the taboo operates so as to distinguish two identical phonemic patterns; it does not operate so as to suppress the pattern altogether. We are not inhibited from saying KWĪN. Yet the very similar phonemic pattern produced by shifting the dental N to bilabial M and shortening the medial vowel (KWĬM) is one of the most unprintable obscenities in the English language. Some American informants have assured me that this word has been so thoroughly suppressed that it has not crossed the Atlantic at all, but this does not seem entirely correct as there is dictionary evidence to the contrary.[1] It is hard to talk about the unsayable but I hope I have made my initial point. Taboo is simultaneously both behavioral and linguistic, both social and psychological. As an anthropologist, I am particularly concerned with the social aspects of taboo. Analytical psychologists of various schools are particularly concerned with the individual taboos which center in the oral, anal, and genital functions. Experimental psychologists may concern themselves with essentially the same kind of phenomenon when they examine the process of forgetting, or various kinds of muscular inhibition. But all these varieties of repression are so meshed into the web of language that discussion of any one of three frames, anthropological, psychological, or linguistic, must inevitably lead on to some consideration of the other two.

ANIMAL CATEGORIES AND VERBAL OBSCENITIES

In the rest of this paper I shall have relatively little to say about language in a direct sense, but this is because of the nature of my problem. I shall be discussing the connection between animal categories and verbal obscenities. Plainly it is much easier to talk about the animals than about the obscenities! The latter will mostly be just off stage. But

[1] The Oxford English Dictionary says nothing of the obscenity but records *Quim* as a "late Scottish variant" of the now wholly obsolete *Queme* = "pleasant." Partridge (1949) prints the word in full (whereas he balks at f*ck and c*nt). His gloss is "the female pudend" and he gives *queme* as a variant. Funk and Wagnalls, and Webster, latest editions, both ignore the term, but H. Wentworth and S. B. Flexner (1961) give: *quim* n. 1 = queen; 2 (taboo) = the vagina. That this phonemic pattern is, in fact penumbral to the more permissible *queen* is thus established.

The American dictionaries indicate that the range of meanings of *queen (quean)* are the same as in England, but the distinction of spelling is not firmly maintained.

the hearer (and the reader) should keep his wits about him. Just as queen is dangerously close to the unsayable, so also there are certain very familiar animals which are, as it were, only saved by a phoneme from sacrilege or worse. In seventeenth century English witchcraft trials it was very commonly asserted that the Devil appeared in the form of a Dog—that is, God backwards. In England we still employ this same metathesis when we refer to a clergyman's collar as a "dog collar" instead of a "God collar." So also it needs only a slight vowel shift in *fox* to produce the obscene *fux*. No doubt there is a sense in which such facts as these can be deemed linguistic accidents, but they are accidents which have a functional utility in the way we use our language. As I shall show presently, there are good sociological reasons why the English categories *dog* and *fox*, like the English category queen *(quean)*, should evoke taboo associations in their phonemic vicinity.

As an anthropologist I do not profess to understand the psychological aspects of the taboo phenomenon. I do not understand what happens when a word or a phrase or a detail of behavior is subject to repression. But I can observe what happens. In particular I can observe that when verbal taboos are broken the result is a specific social phenomenon which affects both the actor and his hearers in a specific describable way. I need not elaborate. This phenomenon is what we mean by obscenity. Broadly speaking, the language of obscenity falls into three categories: (1) dirty words—usually referring to sex and excretion; (2) blasphemy and profanity; (3) animal abuse—in which a human being is equated with an animal of another species.

These categories are not in practice sharply distinguished. Thus the word "bloody," which is now a kind of all-purpose mildly obscene adjective, is felt by some to be associated with menstrual blood and is thus a "dirty" word, but it seems to be historically derived from profanity—"By our Lady." On the other hand, the simple expletive "damn!"—now presumed to be short for "damnation!"—and thus a profanity—was formerly "goddam" (God's animal mother) an expression combining blasphemy with animal abuse. These broad categories of obscenity seem to occur in most languages.

The dirty words present no problem. Psychologists have adequate and persuasive explanations of why the central focus of the crudest obscenity should ordinarily lie in sex and excretion. The language of profanity and blasphemy also presents no problem. Any theory about the sacredness of supernatural beings is likely to imply a concept of sacrilege which in turn explains the emotions aroused by profanity and blasphemy. But animal abuse seems much less easily accounted for. Why should expressions like "you son of a bitch" or "you swine" carry the connotations that they do, when "you son of a kangaroo" or "you polar bear" have no meaning whatever?

I write as an anthropologist, and for an anthropologist this theme of animal abuse has a very basic interest. When an animal name is used in this way as an imprecation, it indicates that the name itself is credited with potency. It clearly signifies that the animal category is in some way taboo and sacred. Thus, for an anthropologist, animal abuse is part of a wide field of study which includes animal sacrifice and totemism.

RELATION OF EDIBILITY AND SOCIAL VALUATION OF ANIMALS

In his ethnographic studies the anthropologist observes that, in any particular cultural situation, some animals are the focus of ritual attitudes whereas others are not; moreover, the intensity of the ritual involvement of individual species varies greatly. It is never at all obvious why this should be so, but one fact that is commonly relevant and always needs to be taken into consideration is the edibility of the species in question.

One hypothesis which underlies the rest of this paper is that animal abuse is in some way linked with what Radcliffe-Brown called the ritual value of the animal category concerned. I further assume that this ritual value is linked in some as yet undetermined way with taboos and rules concerning the killing and eating of these and other animals. For the purposes of illustration, I shall confine my attention to categories of the English language. I postulate, however, that the principles which I adduce are very general, though not necessarily universal. In illustration of this, I discuss as an appendix to my main argument the application of my thesis to categories of the Kachin language spoken by certain highland groups in northeast Burma.

Taboo is not a genuine English word, but a category imported from Polynesia. Its meaning is not precisely defined in conventional English usage. Anthropologists commonly use it to refer to prohibitions which are explicit and which are supported by feelings of sin and supernatural sanction at a conscious level; incest regulations provide a typical example; the rules recorded in Leviticus XI, verses 4–47, which prohibited the Israelites from eating a wide variety of "unclean beasts," are another. In this paper, however, I shall use the concept of food taboo in a more general sense, so that it covers all classes of food prohibition, explicit and implicit, conscious and unconscious.

CULTURAL AND LINGUISTIC DETERMINATION OF FOOD VALUES

The physical environment of any human society contains a vast range of materials which are both edible and nourishing, but, in most cases, only a small part of this edible environment will actually be classified as potential food. Such classification is a matter of language and culture, not of nature. It is a classification that is of great practical importance, and it is felt to be so. *Our* classification is not only correct, it is morally right and a mark of our superiority. The fact that frogs' legs are a gourmet's delicacy in France but not food at all in England provokes the English to refer to Frenchmen as Frogs with implications of withering contempt.

As a consequence of such cultural discriminations, the edible part of the environment usually falls into three main categories:

1. Edible substances that are recognized as food and consumed as part of the normal diet.
2. Edible substances that are recognized as possible food, but that are prohibited or else allowed to be eaten only under special (ritual) conditions. These are substances which are *consciously tabooed*.
3. Edible substances that by culture and language are not recognized as food at all. The substances are *unconsciously tabooed*.

Now in the ordinary way when anthropologists discuss food taboos they are thinking only of my second category; they have in mind such examples as the Jewish prohibitions against pork, the Brahmin prohibition against beef, the Christian attitude to sacramental bread and wine. But my third category of edible substances that are not classed as food deserves equal attention. The nature of the taboo in the two cases is quite distinct. The Jewish prohibition against pork is a ritual matter and explicit. It says, in effect, "pork is a food, but Jews must not eat it." The Englishman's objection to eating dog is quite as strong but rests on a different premise. It depends on a categorical assumption: "dog is not food."

In actual fact, of course, dogs are perfectly edible, and in some parts of the world they are bred for eating. For that matter human beings are edible, though to an Englishman the very thought is disgusting. I think most Englishmen would find the idea of eating dog equally disgusting and in a similar way I believe that this latter disgust in largely a matter of verbal categories. There are contexts in colloquial English in which man and dog may be thought of as beings of the same kind. Man and dog are "companions"; the dog is "the friend of man." On the other hand man and food are antithetical categories. Man is not food, so dog cannot be food either.

Of course our linguistic categories are not always tidy and logical, but the marginal cases, which at first appear as exceptions to some general rule, are often especially interesting. For example, the French eat horse. In England, although horsemeat may be fed to dogs, it is officially classed as unfit for human consumption. Horsemeat may not be sold in the same shop that handles ordinary butchers' meat, and in London where, despite English prejudice, there are low foreigners who actually eat the stuff, they must buy it in a shop labeled *charcuterie* and not *butcher!* This I suggest is quite consistent with the very special attitude which Englishmen adopt toward both dogs and horses. Both are sacred supernatural creatures surrounded by feelings that are ambiguously those of awe and horror. This kind of attitude is comparable to a less familiar but much more improbable statutory rule which lays down that Swan and Sturgeon may only be eaten by members of the Royal Family, except once a year when Swan may be eaten by the members of St. John's College, Cambridge! As the Editor of *The New Yorker* is fond of telling us, "There will always be an England!"

Plainly all such rules, prejudices, and conventions are of social origin; yet the social taboos have their linguistic counterparts and, as I shall presently show, these accidents of etymological history fit together in a quite surprising way. Certainly in its linguistic aspects horse looks innocent enough, but so do dog and fox. However, in most English colloquial, horse is *'orse* or *'oss* and in this form it shares with its companion *ass* an uncomfortable approximation to the human posterior.[2]

[2]English and American taboos are different. The English spell the animal *ass* and the buttocks *arse* but, according to Partridge (1949), *arse* was considered almost unprintable between 1700 and 1930 (though it appears in the O.E.D.). Webster's Third Edition spells both words as *ass*, noting that *arse* is a more polite variant of the latter word, which also has the obscene meaning, sexual intercourse. Funk and Wagnalls (1952) distinguish *ass* (animal) and *arse* (buttocks) and do not cross reference. Wentworth and Flexner (1961) give only *ass* but give three taboo meanings, the rectum, the buttocks, and the vagina.

The problem then is this. The English treat certain animals as taboo—sacred. This sacredness is manifested in various ways, partly behavioral, as when we are forbidden to eat flesh of the animal concerned, partly linguistic, as when a phonemic pattern penumbral to that of the animal category itself is found to be a focus of obscenity, profanity, etc. Can we get any insight into why certain creatures should be treated this way?

TABOO AND THE DISTINCTIVENESS OF NAMABLE CATEGORIES

Before I proceed further, let me give you an outline of a general theory of taboo which I find particularly satisfactory in my work as an anthropologist. It is a theory which seems to me to fit in well with the psychological and linguistic facts. In the form in which I present it here, it is a "Leach theory" but it has several obvious derivations, especially Radcliffe-Brown's discussions of ritual value, Mary Douglas's thinking (still largely unpublished) on anomalous animals, and Lévi-Strauss's version of the Hegelian-Marxist dialectic in which the sacred elements of myth are shown to be factors that mediate contradictories.

I postulate that the physical and social environment of a young child is perceived as a continuum. It does not contain any intrinsically separate "things." The child, in due course, is taught to impose upon this environment a kind of discriminating grid which serves to distinguish the world as being composed of a large number of separate things, each labeled with a name. This world is a representation of our language categories, not vice versa. Because my mother tongue is English, it seems self evident that *bushes* and *trees* are different kinds of things. I would not think this unless I had been taught that it was the case.

Now if each individual has to learn to construct his own environment in this way, it is crucially important that the basic discriminations should be clear-cut and unambiguous. There must be absolutely no doubt about the difference between *me* and *it*, or between *we* and *they*. But how can such certainty of discrimination be achieved if our normal perception displays only a continuum? A diagram may help. Our uninhibited (untrained) perception recognizes a continuum (Figure 1).

We are taught that the world consists of "things" distinguished by names; therefore we have to train our perception to recognize a discontinuous environment (Figure 2).

We achieve this second kind of trained

FIGURE 1
The line is a schematic representation of continuity in nature. There are no gaps in the physical world.

FIGURE 2
Schematic representation of what is named. Many aspects of the physical world remain unnamed in natural languages.

perception by means of a simultaneous use of language and taboo. Language gives us the names to distinguish the things; taboo inhibits the recognition of those parts of the continuum which separate the things (Figure 3).

The same kind of argument may also be represented by a simplified Venn diagram employing two circles only. Let there be a circle *p* representing a particular verbal category. Let this be intersected by another circle $\sim p$ representing the "environment" of *p*, from which it is desired to distinguish *p*. If by a fiction we impose a taboo upon any consideration of the overlap area that is common to both circles, then we shall be able to persuade ourselves that *p* and $\sim p$ are wholly distinct, and the logic of binary discrimination will be satisfied (Figure 4).

FIGURE 3
The relationship of tabooed objects to the world of

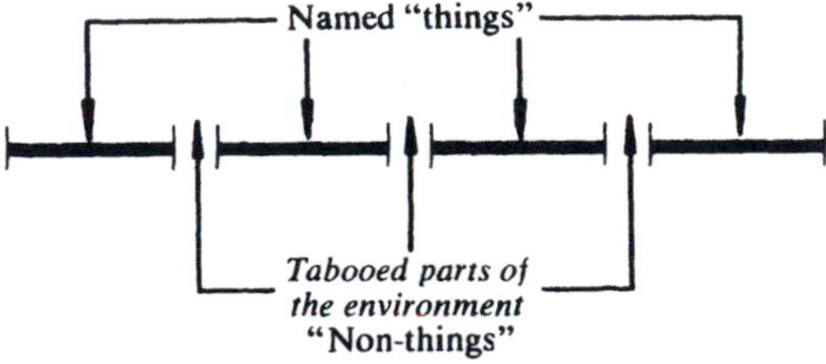

FIGURE 4
The relationship between ambiguity and taboo.

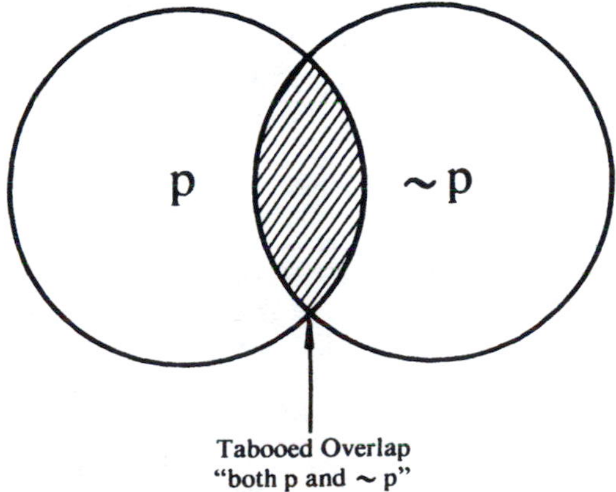

Language then does more than provide us with a classification of things; it actually molds our environment; it places each individual at the center of a social space which is ordered in a logical and reassuring way.

In this paper I shall be specially concerned with verbal category sets which discriminate areas of social space in terms of "distance from Ego (self)." For example, consider the three sets (a), (b), (c).

(a) Self · · Sister · · Cousin · · Neighbor · · Stranger
(b) Self · · House · · Farm · · Field · · Far (Remote)
(c) Self · · Pet · · Livestock · · "Game" · · Wild Animal

For each of these three sets, the words, thus arranged, indicate categories that are progressively more remote from Self, but I believe that there is more to it than that. I hope to be able to show that, if we denote these word sets as

(a) A1 B1 C1 D1 E1
(b) A2 B2 C2 D2 E2
(c) A3 B3 C3 D3 E3

then the relational statement A1:B1:C1:D1:E1 is the same as the relational statement A2:B2:C2:D2:E2 or the relational statement A3:B3:C3:D3:E3. In other words, the way we employ the words in set (c), a set of animals, allows us to make statements about the human relationships which belong to set (a).

But I am going too fast. Let us go back to my theory of taboo. If we operate in the way I have suggested, so that we are only able to perceive the environment as composed of separate things by suppressing our recognition of the nonthings which fill the interstices, then of course what is suppressed becomes especially interesting. Quite apart from the fact that all scientific enquiry is devoted to "discovering" those parts of the environment that lie on the borders of what is "already known," we have the phenomenon, which is variously described by anthropologists and psychologists, in which whatever is taboo is a focus not only of special interest but also of anxiety. Whatever is taboo is sacred, valuable, important, powerful, dangerous, untouchable, filthy, unmentionable.

I can illustrate my point by mentioning diametrically contrasted areas where this approach to taboo fits in well with the observable facts. First, the exudations of the human body are universally the objects of intense taboo—in particular, feces, urine, semen, menstrual blood, hair clippings, nail parings, body dirt, spittle, mother's milk.[3] This fits the theory. Such substances are ambiguous in the most fundamental way. The child's first and continuing problem is to determine the initial boundary. "What am I, as against the world?" "Where is the edge of me?" In this fundamental sense, feces, urine, semen, and so forth, are both me and not me. So strong is the resulting taboo that, even as an adult addressing an adult audience, I cannot refer to these substances by the monosyllabic words which I used as a child but must mention them only in Latin. But let us be clear, it is not simply that these substances are felt to be dirty—they are powerful; throughout the world it is precisely such substances that are the prime ingredients of magical "medicines."

At the opposite extreme, consider the case of the sanctity of supernatural beings. Religious belief is everywhere tied in with the discrimination between living and dead. Logically, *life* is simply the binary antithesis of *death;* the two concepts are the opposite sides of the same penny; we cannot have either without the other. But religion always tries to separate the two. To do this it creates a hypothetical "other world" which is the antithesis of "this world." In this world life and death are inseparable; in the other world they are separate. This world is inhabited by imperfect mortal men; the other world is inhabited by immortal nonmen (gods). The category god is thus constructed as the binary antithesis of man. But this is inconvenient. A remote god in another world may be logically sensible, but it is emotionally unsatisfying. To be useful, gods must be near at hand, so religion sets about reconstructing a continuum between this world and the other world. But note how it is done. The gap between the two logically distinct categories, this world/other world, is filled in with tabooed ambiguity. The gap is bridged by supernatural beings of a highly ambiguous kind—incarnate deities, virgin mothers, supernatural monsters which are half man/half beast. These marginal, ambiguous creatures are specifically credited with the power of mediating between gods and men. They are the object of the most intense taboos, more sacred than the gods themselves. In an objective sense, as distinct from theoretical theology, it is the Virgin Mary, human mother of God, who is the principal object of devotion in the Catholic church.

[3] An interesting and seemingly unique partial exception to this catalogue is "tears." Tears can acquire sacredness, in that the tears of Saints have been turned into relics and tears are proper at sacred situations, e.g., funerals, but tears are not, I think, felt to be dirty or contaminating after the manner of other exudations.

So here again it is the ambiguous categories that attract the maximum interest and the most intense feelings of taboo. The general theory is that taboo applies to categories which are anomalous with respect to clear-cut category oppositions. If A and B are two verbal categories, such that B is defined as "what A is not" and vice versa, and there is a third category C which mediates this distinction, in that C shares attributes of both A and B, then C will be taboo.

But now let us return to a consideration of English animal categories and food taboos.

ANIMAL AND FOOD NAMES IN ENGLISH

How do we speakers of English classify animals, and how is this classification related to the matters of killing and eating and verbal abuse?

The basic discrimination seems to rest in three words:

FISH: creatures that live in water. A very elastic category, it includes even crustacea—"shell fish."

BIRDS: two-legged creatures with wings which lay eggs. (They do not necessarily fly, e.g., penguins, ostriches.)

BEASTS: four-legged mammals living on land.

Consider Table 1. All creatures that are edible are fish or birds or beasts. There is a large residue of creatures, rated as either *reptiles* or *insects*, but the whole of this ambiguous residue is rated as not food. All reptiles and insects seem to be thought of as evil enemies of mankind and liable to the most ruthless extermination. Only the bee is an exception here, and significantly the bee is often credited with quite superhuman powers of intelligence and organization. The hostile taboo is applied most strongly to creatures that are most anomalous in respect of the major categories, e.g., snakes—land animals with no legs which lay eggs.

The fact that birds and beasts are warm-blooded and that they engage in sexual intercourse in a "normal" way makes them to

TABLE 1
ENGLISH LANGUAGE DISCRIMINATIONS OF LIVING CREATURES

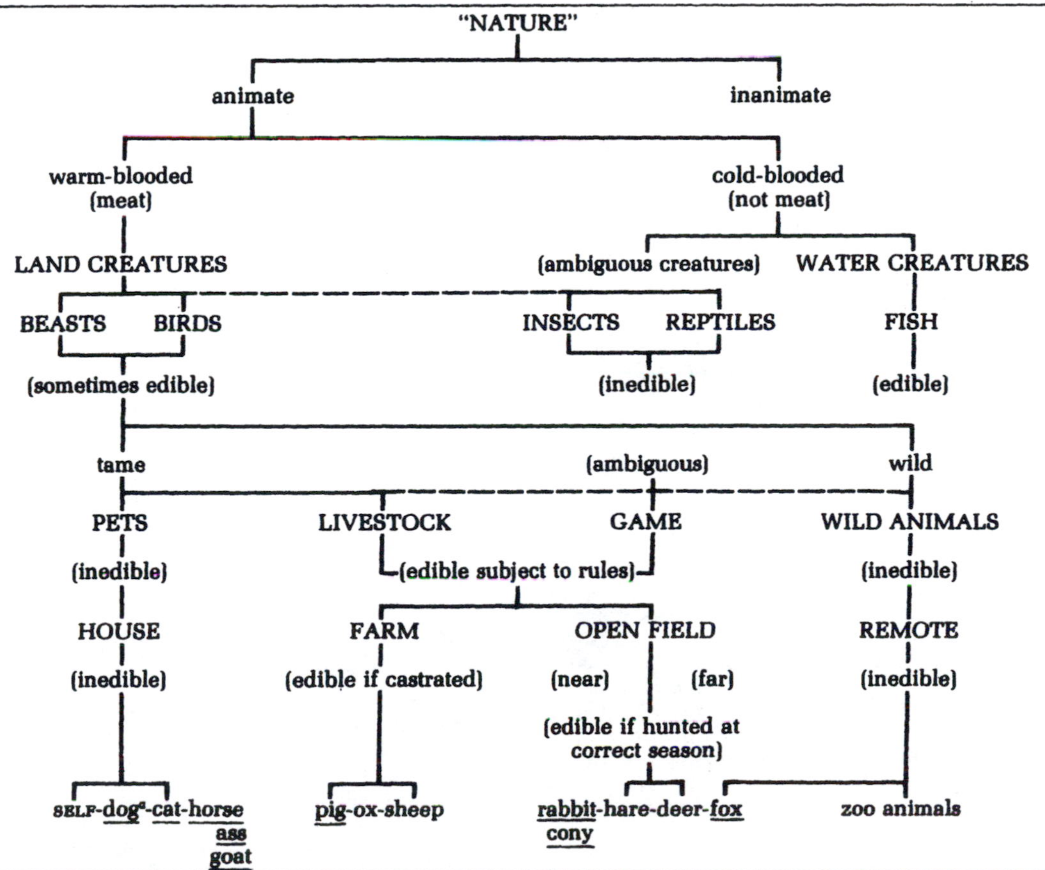

*The species underlined on the bottom line are those which appear to be specially loaded with taboo values, as indicated by their use in obscenity and abuse or by metaphysical associations or by the intrusion of euphemism.

some extent akin to man. This is shown by the fact that the concept of *cruelty* is applicable to birds and beasts but not to fish. The slaughter of farm animals for food must be carried out by "humane" methods;[4] in England we even have humane rat traps! But it is quite proper to kill a lobster by dropping it alive into boiling water. Where religious food taboos apply, they affect only the warm-blooded, near human, meat of birds and beasts; hence Catholics may eat fish on Fridays. In England the only common fish subject to killing and eating restrictions is the salmon. This is an anomalous fish in at least two respects; it is red-blooded and it is simultaneously both a sea fish and a fresh water fish. But the mammalian *beasts* are much closer to man than the egg-laying *birds*. The Society of the Prevention of Cruelty to Animals, The Anti-Vivisection Society, Our Dumb Friends League and such organizations devote most of their attention to four-footed creatures, and as time is short I shall do the same.

STRUCTURE OF FOOD AND KINSHIP TERMINOLOGIES

Anthropologists have noted again and again that there is a universal tendency to make ritual and verbal associations between eating and sexual intercourse. It is thus a plausible hypothesis that the way in which animals are categorized with regard to edibility will have some correspondence to the way in which human beings are categorized with regard to sex relations.

Upon this matter the anthropologists have assembled a vast amount of comparative data. The following generalization is certainly not a universal, but it has a very wide general validity. From the point of view of any male SELF, the young women of his social world will fall into four major classes:

1. Those who are very close—"true sisters," always a strongly incestuous category.
2. Those who are kin but not very close—"first cousins" in English society, "clan sisters" in many types of systems having unilineal descent and a segmentary lineage organization. As a rule, marriage with this category is either prohibited or strongly disapproved, but premarital sex relations may be tolerated or even expected.
3. Neighbors (friends) who are not kin, potential affines. This is the category from which SELF will ordinarily expect to obtain a wife. This category contains also potential enemies, friendship and enmity being alternating aspects of the same structural relationship.
4. Distant strangers—who are known to exist but with whom no social relations of any kind are possible.

Now the English put most of their animals into four very comparable categories:

1. Those who are very close—"pets," always strongly inedible.
2. Those who are tame but not very close—"farm animals," mostly edible but only if immature or castrated. We seldom eat a sexually intact, mature farm beast.[5]
3. Field animals, "game"—a category toward which we alternate friendship and hostility. Game animals live under human protection but they are not tame. They are edible in sexually intact form, but are killed only at set seasons of the year in accordance with set hunting rituals.
4. Remote wild animals—not subject to human control, inedible.

Thus presented, there appears to be a set of equivalents:

incest prohibition	inedible
marriage prohibition coupled with premarital sex relations	castration coupled with edibility
marriage alliance, friend/enemy ambiguity	edible in sexually intact form; alternating friendship/hostility
no sex relations with remote strangers	remote wild animals are inedible

That this correspondence between the categories of sexual accessibility and the categories of edibility is rather more than just an accident is shown by a further accident of a linguistic kind. The archaic legal expression for game was beasts of venery. The term venery had the alternative meanings, hunting and sexual indulgence.

A similar accident yields the phonemic resemblance between *venery* and *venerate* which is reminiscent of that between *quean* and *queen*. Sex and authority are both sources of taboo (respect) but in contrary senses.

A fifth major category of English animals which cuts across the others, and is significantly taboo-loaded, is vermin. The dictionary definition of this word is comprehensively ambiguous:

mammals and birds injurious to game, crops, etc.; foxes, weasels, rats, mice, moles, owls, noxious insects, fleas, bugs, lice, parasitic worms, vile persons.

[4] The word *humane* has become distinguished from *human* only since the 17th century.

[5] Two reasons are usually offered for castrating farm animals. The first, which is valid, is that the castrated animal is more amenable to handling. The second, which I am assured is scientifically invalid, is that a castrated animal produces more succulent meat in a shorter time.

Vermin may also be described as *pests* (i.e., plagues). Although vermin and pests are intrinsically inedible, rabbits and pigeons, which are pests when they attack crops, may also be classed as game and then become edible. The same two species also become edible when kept under restraint as farm animals. I shall have more to say about rabbits presently.

Before we go further, let me review the latest part of my argument in rather different form. The thesis is that we make binary distinctions and then mediate the distinction by creating an ambiguous (and taboo-loaded) intermediate category. Thus:

p	both *p* and ~*p*	~*p*
man (not animal)	"man-animal" ("pets")	not man (animal)
TAME (friendly)	GAME (friendly/hostile)	WILD (hostile)

We have already given some indication that ritual value (taboo) attaches in a marked way to the intermediate categories *pets* and *game*, and I shall have more to say about this, but we shall find that even more intense taboo attitudes are revealed when we come to consider creatures which would only fit into the interstices of the above tabulation, e.g., goats, pigs, and horses which are not quite pets, rabbits which are not quite game, and foxes which are wild but treated like game in some respects (see bottom of Table 1).

In Table 2 are listed the more familiar names of the more familiar English animals. These name sets possess certain linguistic characteristics.

Nearly all the house pets, farm, and field (game) animals have monosyllabic names: dog, cat, bull, cow, ox, and so on, whereas among the more remote wild beasts monosyllables are rare. The vocabulary is most elaborated in the farm category and most attenuated in the inedible house-pet and wild-beast categories.

Thus farm animals have separate terms for 1) an intact male, (2) an intact female, (3) a suckling, (4) an immature female, (5) a castrated male (e.g., bull, cow, calf, heifer, bullock, with local variants). This is not surprising in view of the technical requirements of farming, but it seems odd that the pet vocabulary should be so restricted. Thus dog has only: dog, bitch, pup, and of these bitch is largely taboo and seldom used; cat has only: cat, kitten.

If sex discrimination must be made among pets, one can say "bitch" and "tom cat." This implies that a dog is otherwise presumed male and a cat female. Indeed cat and dog are paired terms, and seem to serve as a paradigm for quarreling husband and wife.

Among the field animals all males are *bucks* and all females *does*. Among the wild animals, in a small number of species we distinguish the young as *cubs*. In a smaller number we distinguish the female as a variant of the male: tiger—tigress; lion—lioness; but most are sexless. Fox is a very special case, exceptional in all respects. It is a monosyllable, the male is a *dog*, the female a *vixen*, the young a *cub*. Elephants and some other "zoo animals" are distinguished as bulls, cows, and calves, a direct borrowing from the farm-animal set.

A curious usage suggests that we are ashamed of killing any animal of substantial size. When dead, bullock becomes *beef*, pig becomes *pork*, sheep becomes *mutton*, calf becomes *veal*, and deer becomes *venison*. But smaller animals stay as they are: lamb, hare, and rabbit, and all birds are the same alive or dead. Goats are "nearly pets" and correspondingly (for the English) goat meat is nearly inedible. An English housewife would be outraged if she thought that her mutton was goat!

ANIMAL ABUSE AND EATING HABITS

Most of the monosyllables denoting familiar animals may be stretched to describe the qualities of human beings. Such usage is often abusive but not always so. Bitch, cat, pig, swine, ass, goat, cur (dog) are insults; but lamb, duck, and cock are friendly, even affectionate. Close animals may also serve as near obscene euphemisms for unmentionable parts of the human anatomy. Thus cock = penis, pussy = female pubic hair, and, in America, ass = arse.

The principle that the close, familiar animals are denoted by monosyllables is so general that the few exceptions invite special attention. The use of phonetically complex terms for "close" animals seems always to be the result of a euphemistic replacement of a tabooed word. Thus *donkey* has replaced *ass*, and *rabbit* has replaced *coney*. This last term now survives only in the fur trade where it is pronounced to rhyme with Tony, but its etymological derivation is from Latin *cuniculus*, and the 18th century rabbit was a cunny, awkwardly close to *cunt*, which only became printable in English with the licensed publication of *Lady Chatterley's Lover*. It is interesting that while the adult cunny has switched to the innocuous rabbit, baby language has retained bunny. I gather

TABLE 2
ENGLISH SUBCATEGORIES OF FAMILIAR ANIMALS

	Female	*Male*	*Infant*	*Young Male*[a]	*Young Female*[a]	*Castrated Male*	*Baby Language*	*Carcass Meat*
Dog	Bitch		Puppy				Bow wow	
Hound			Whelp				Doggy	
Cat		(Tom)	Kitten				Pussy	
Goat	(Nanny)	(Billy)	Kid				?	Mutton
Pig	Sow	Boar	Piglet	Hogget[b]	Gilt	Hog[c] Porker	Piggy	Pork, bacon, ham
Ass							Ee-yaw	
Horse[d]	Mare	Stallion	Foal	Colt	Filly	Gelding	Gee-gee	
Cow (ox)[e]	Cow	Bull	Calf		Heifer	Steer Bullock	Moo-Cow	Veal; beef[f]
Sheep	Ewe	Ram	Lamb	Teg			Baa-lamb	Mutton
Fowl	Hen	Cock	Chick	Cockerel	Pullet	Capon	?	Chicken
Duck	Duck	Drake	Duckling				Quack-quack	
Goose	Goose	Gander	Gosling					
Pigeon			Squab					
Rabbit	Doe	Buck					Bunny	
Hare	Doe	Buck	Leveret					
Deer	Doe Hind	Buck Stag[g]						Venison
Swan			Cygnet					
Fox	Vixen	Dog	Cub[h]					

[a]*Other sex distinctions:*
Most birds other than duck and goose may be distinguished as cocks and hens.
The whale, walrus, elephant, moose, and certain other large animals are distinguished as bulls and cows.
Lion and tiger are presumed male since they have feminine forms lioness, tigress.
The female of certain other species is marked by prefixing the pronoun "she"; thus, she-bear.

[b]*Hogget*—a boar in its second year. The term may also apply to a young horse (colt) or to a young sheep (teg).

[c]*Hog*—may also refer to pigs in general as also swine.

[d]Note also *pony*, a small horse suitable for children.

[e]*Ox (Oxen)*—properly the term for the species in general, but now archaic and where used at all refers to a castrated male. The common species term is now *cow (cows)* or *cattle*. Cattle is in origin the same as capital = "live stock." The archaic plural of *cow* is *kine* (cf. *kin*).

[f]*Beef*—in singular = dead meat, but beeves plural refers to live animals = bullocks.

[g]*Hart*—an old stag with sur-royal antlers.

[h]*Cub (whelp)*—includes young of many wild animals: tiger, bear, otter, etc.

that in contemporary New York a Bunny Club has at least a superficial resemblance to a London eighteenth century Cunny House.[6]

Some animals seem to carry an unfair load of abuse. Admittedly the pig is a general scavenger but so, by nature, is the dog and it is hardly rational that we should label the first "filthy" while making a household pet of the second. I suspect that we feel a rather special guilt about our pigs. After all, sheep provide wool, cows provide milk, chickens provide eggs, but we rear pigs for the sole purpose of killing and eating them, and this is rather a shameful thing, a shame which quickly attaches to the pig itself. Besides which, under English rural conditions, the pig in his backyard pigsty was, until very recently, much more nearly a member of the household than any of the other edible animals. Pigs, like dogs, were fed from the leftovers of their human masters' kitchens. To kill and eat such a commensal associate is sacrilege indeed!

In striking contrast to the monosyllabic names of the close animals, we find that at the other end of the scale there is a large class of truly wild animals, most of which the ordinary individual sees only in a zoo. Such creatures are not classed as potential food at all. To distinguish these strangers as lying outside our English social system, we have given them very long semi-Latin names—elephant, hippopotamus, rhinoceros, and so forth. This is not due to any scholastic perversity; these words have been a part of the vernacular for a thousand years or so.

The intermediate category of fully sexed,

[6] In general, birds fall outside the scope of this paper, but while considering the ambiguities introduced by the accidents of linguistic homonyms we may note that all edible birds are *fowl* (i.e., foul = filthy); that *pigeon* has replaced *dove*, perhaps because of the association of the latter with the Holy Ghost; and that the word *squabble* (a noisy quarrel, particularly between married couples) is derived from *squab*, a young pigeon.

tame-wild, field animals which we may hunt for food, but only in accordance with set rules at special seasons of the year, is in England now much reduced in scope. It now comprises certain birds (e.g., grouse, pheasant, partridge), hares, and, in some places, deer. As indicated already, rabbits and pigeons are both marginal to this category. Since all these creatures are protected for part of the year in order that they may be killed in the other, the collective name *game* is most appropriate. Social anthropologists have coined the expression *joking relationship* for a somewhat analogous state of affairs which is frequently institutionalized between affinally related groups among human beings.

Just as the obscene rabbit, which is ambiguously game or vermin, occupies an intermediate status between the farm and field categories (Table 1), the fox occupies the borderline between edible field and inedible wild animals. In England the hunting and killing of foxes is a barbarous ritual surrounded by extraordinary and fantastic taboos. The intensity of feeling aroused by these performances almost baffles the imagination. All attempts to interfere with such customs on the grounds of "cruelty" have failed miserably. Some aspects of fox-hunting are linguistic and thus directly relevant to my theme. We find, for example, as commonly occurs in other societies in analogous contexts, that the sacredness of the situation is marked by language inversions, the use of special terms for familiar objects, and so on.

Thus foxes are hunted by packs of dogs and, at the conclusion of the ritual killing, the fox has its head and tail cut off, which are then preserved as trophies, but none of this may be said in plain language. It is the fox itself that can be spoken of as a *dog*, the dogs are described as *hounds*, the head of the fox is a *mask*, its tail a *brush*, and so on. It is considered highly improper to use any other words for these things.

Otters, stags, and hares are also sometimes hunted in a comparable ritual manner, and here again the hunting dogs change their identity, becoming either hounds or beagles. All of which reinforces my original hypothesis that the category *dog*, in English, is something very special indeed.

The implication of all this is that if we arrange the familiar animals in a series according to their social distance from the human SELF (Table 1, bottom) then we can see that the occurrence of taboo (ritual value), as indicated by different types and intensities of killing and eating restrictions, verbal abuse, metaphysical associations, ritual performance, the intrusion of euphemism, etc., is not just randomly distributed. The varieties of taboo are located at intervals across the chart in such a way as to break up the continuum into sections. Taboo serves to separate the SELF from the world, and then the world itself is divided into zones of social distance corrresponding here to the words farm, field, and remote.

I believe that this kind of analysis is more than just an intellectual game; it can help us to understand a wide variety of our nonrational behavior. For example, anyone familiar with the literature will readily perceive that English witchcraft beliefs depended upon a confusion of precisely the categories to which I have here drawn attention. Witches were credited with a power to assume animal form and with possessing spirit familiars. The familiar might take the form of any animal but was most likely to appear as a dog, a cat, or a toad. Some familiars had no counterpart in natural history; one was described as having "paws like a bear but in bulk not fully as big as a coney." The ambiguity of such creatures was taken as evidence of their supernatural qualities. As Hopkins, the celebrated seventeenth century witchfinder, remarked, "No mortal alone could have invented them."

But my purpose has been to pose questions rather than to offer explanations. The particular diagrams which I have presented may not be the most useful ones, but at least I have established that the English language classification of familiar animals is by no means a simple matter; it is not just a list of names, but a complex pattern of identifications subtly discriminated not only in kind but in psychological tone. Our linguistic treatment of these categories reflects taboo or ritual value, but these are simply portmanteau terms which cover a complex of feeling and attitude, a sense perhaps that aggression, as manifested either in sex or in killing, is somehow a disturbance of the natural order of things, a kind of necessary impiety.

A NON-EUROPEAN EXAMPLE

If this kind of analysis were applicable only to the categories of the English language it would amount to no more than a parlor game. Scientifically speaking, the analysis is interesting only in so far as it opens up the possibility that other languages analyzed according to similar procedures might yield comparable patterns. A demonstration on these lines is not easy: one needs to know a language very well indeed before one can play a game of this kind. Nevertheless it is worth trying.

Kachin is a Tibeto-Burman language spoken by hill tribesmen in Northeast Burma. Since it is grammatically and syntactically wholly unlike any Indo-European language it should provide a good test case. At one time I spoke the language fluently though I cannot do so now. I have a firsthand anthropological understanding of Kachin customary behaviors.

Kachin is essentially a monosyllabic language in which discrimination is achieved by varying the "prefixes" of words rather than by tonal variation, though, as in other Tibeto-Burman languages, tones play their part. It follows that homonyms are very common in this language, and the art of punning and *double entente* is a highly developed cultural feature. A special form of lovers' poetry (*nchyun ga*) depends on this fact. A single brief example will suffice as illustration:

Jan du	*gawng lawng*	*sharat a lo*
At sunset	the clapper of the cattle bell	swings back and forth.
Mai bawt	*gawng nu*	*sharat a lo*[7]
The (buffalo's)	short tail and the base of the bell	are wagged.

Nothing could be more superficially "innocent" than this romantic image of dusk and cattle bells. But the poem takes on a very different appearance once it is realized that *jan du* (the sun sets) also means "the girl comes (has an orgasm)" while *mai bawt* (the short tail) is a common euphemism for the human penis. The rest of the Freudian images can easily be worked out by the reader!

On the other hand, it cannot be said that the Kachin is at all "foulmouthed." Precisely because of his cultivated expertness at *double entente*, he can almost always appear to be scrupulously polite. But verbal obscenities do exist, including what I have called animal abuse; the latter are mainly concentrated around the dog (*gwi*).

Kachins are a primitive people living in steep mountained forest country. Their diet consists mainly of rice and vegetables, but they keep cattle, pigs, and fowls. There are very few edible creatures which they will not eat, though they draw the line at dogs and rats and human beings. The domesticated animals are killed only in the context of a sacrificial ritual. The meat of such sacrifices is eaten by members of the attendant congregation, and sacrifices are frequent. Despite this frequency, the occasion of a sacrifice is a sacred occasion (*na*) and there is a sense in which all domestic animals are sacred.

Until very recently the Kachins had an institution of slavery. It is an indication of their attitude to animals rather than of their attitude to slaves that a slave was classed as a *yam*, a category which includes all domesticated animals. It is also relevant that the word *ni* meaning near also means tame.

The linguistic correlates of all this are not simple. In general, everything that has a place in ritual occasions falls into the wide category WU (U) meaning pollution. This has sundry sub-categories:

(a) birds
(b) various species of bamboo
(c) creatures classed as *nga*—mainly fish and cattle
(d) creatures classed as *wa*—mainly human beings and pigs.

Ignoring the human beings and the bamboo, this is a category of polluted foods, i.e., foods which may properly be eaten only in the context of sacrifice. It contrasts with ordinary clean food and meat (*shat, shan*). Other creatures such as dog (*gwi*) and rat (*yu*) may sometimes be offered in sacrifice, but these would not be eaten except as part of some special magical performance. I have arranged these and other terms (Table 3) on a scale of social distance comparable to that shown for English language categories in Table 1. The parallels are very striking. Let us consider the items in this table reading from left to right, that is to say, from very close to very far.

The closest creatures are the dog and the rat. Both are inedible and heavily loaded with taboo. To call a man a dog is an obscenity; *yu* (rat) also means witchcraft. In some contexts it may also mean affinal relative on the wife's or mother's side. For a variety of structural reasons which I have described in other publications, a Kachin's feelings toward these *mayu ni* are ordinarily highly ambivalent. My wife's mother, a strongly incestuous category, is *ni*, which we have already seen also means very near, and tame.

The domesticated creatures that are edible if sacrificed have been considered already. These "farm" creatures are much more closely identified with the self than the corresponding English categories. They are as human as slaves; they all live in the same house as their owners. The term *wa* (pig) also means man, father, tooth. It is veritably a part of "me"!

[7]All Kachin linguistic usages cited here except the obscene connotation of *jan du* can be verified from O. Hanson.

In the English schema I suggested that field (game) animals have the same structural position, in terms of social distance, as the category of potential wives. In the Kachin case the category of animals comparable to English game are the forest animals hunted for meat. They live in the forest (*nam*). Now the Kachin have a prescriptive rule of marriage which requires a man to marry a girl of a certain category; this category is also *nam*. But in other respects the Kachin case is the inverse of the English situation. An Englishman has free choice in obtaining a wife, but he must go further afield than a first cousin; on the other hand he hunts his game according to precise rules. In contrast the Kachin has his category of possible wives defined in advance and, as first preference, should choose a particular first cousin (the mother's brother's daughter). But he is subject to no rules when he hunts in the forest.

The creatures of the forest which are thus obtained for meat by hunting are mainly deer of various sizes. The smaller ones are found close to the village. Like the English rabbit these are regarded as vermin as well as game, since they raid the rice fields. The larger deer are found in the deep forest. There are in all four categories of deer: *hkyi* and *tsu* are both small species living close in, *shan* and *shat* are large creatures living far out. All these words have homonym meanings: *hkyi:* feces, filth; *tsu:* a disembodied human spirit, ghost; *shan:* ordinary (clean) meat food; *shat:* ordinary (clean) food of any kind.

Thus the pattern is quite consistent. The more remote animals are the more edible, and the homonym meanings of the associated words become less taboo loaded as the social distance is increased.

However, the over-all situation is not quite so simple. Monkeys of many kinds abound. They are sometimes eaten, occasionally tamed as pets, and their blood is credited with magical aphrodisiac qualities. They seem to be thought of as wild animals rather abnormally close to man, like the little deer *tsu*. A monkey is *woi*, a term which also means grandmother. The status of squirrels is very similar. The squirrel figures prominently in Kachin mythology, since it was the death of a squirrel that led man to become mortal. Squirrels are hunted and eaten, but again the attitude is ambiguous. Squirrels are *mai* (tails), but *mai* as we have already seen means a human penis.

Moreover, as remoteness is increased, we finally reach, as in English, a category of unknown and therefore inedible creatures, and the pattern is then reversed. There are two great beasts of the forest which the ordinary Kachin knows about but seldom sees. The first is the elephant, called *magwi* but also *gwi*. Since *gwi* is a dog this may seem odd, but the usage is very similar to that by which the English call the male fox a dog. The other is the tiger (*sharaw*, *raw*) which stands as the prototype for all fabulous monsters. *Numraw*, literally woman tiger, is a creature which figures prominently in Kachin mythology; she (?) has many attributes of the Sphinx in the Oedipus story, an all-devouring horror of uncertain sex, half man, half beast.[8]

[8] This greatly simplifies a very complex mythological category. The *numraw* (also *maraw*) are "luck" deities, vaguely comparable to the furies (erinyes) of Greek mythology. The *numraw* are not always female nor always of one kind. *Baren numraw* lives in the water and seems to be thought of as some kind of alligator, *wa numraw* is presumably a wild boar, and so on.

TABLE 3
KACHIN CATEGORIES OF FAMILIAR ANIMALS
(for comparison with bottom three lines of Table 1)

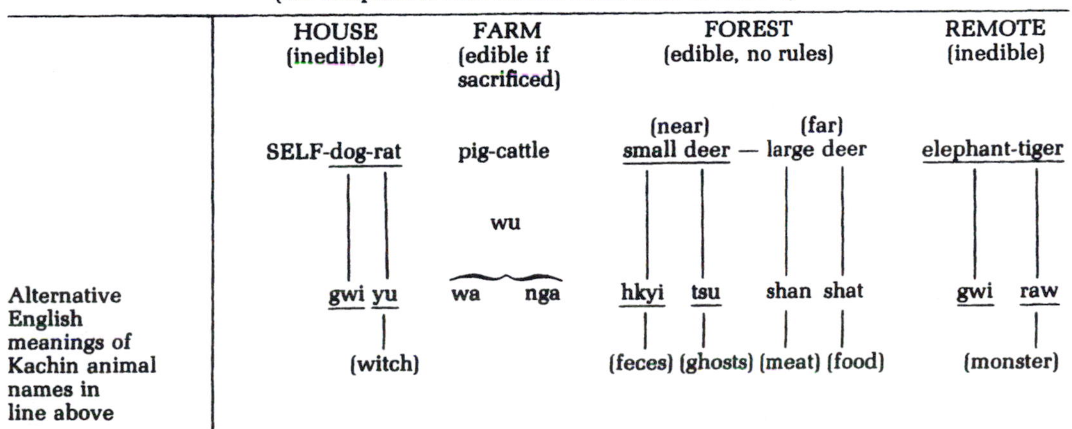

This over-all pattern, as displayed in Table 3, is certainly not identical to that found in English, but it is clearly very much the same kind of pattern, and the resemblances seem too close to be the product of either mere accident, as that phrase would ordinarily be understood, or the obsessional prejudices of myself as investigator. I suggest that the correspondences are at least sufficient to justify further comparative studies. On the other hand, I readily agree that it is easy to be over-persuaded by such evidence, especially when dealing with a language such as Kachin where the incidence of homonyms is very high.

In writing of English I suggested that there was a correspondence between the sequence of sex relationships: sister (incest); cousin (premarital relations possible, no marriage); neighbor (marriage possible); stranger (marriage impossible); and the sequence of "edibility relationships" displayed in Table 1. How far does this apply for Kachin? How does one make the comparison? The difficulty is that Kachin has a kinship system quite different from that of English. True sisters are a strongly incestuous category, but remote classificatory clan sisters are persons with whom liaisons are possible but marriage is not. Elder sister is *na* and younger sister is *nau*. The homonyms are *na*, a sacred holiday, an occasion on which a ritual sacrifice is made; *nau*, a sacred dance occurring on *na* occasions to the accompaniment of sacrifice. This of course fits very nicely with my thesis, for Table 3 can now be translated into human as opposed to animal relationships (in Table 4).

Perhaps all this is too good to be true, but I think that it deserves further investigation.

Those who wish to take my argument seriously might well consider its relevance to C. Lévi-Strauss's most remarkable book *La Pensée sauvage* (1962). Though fascinated by that work I have also felt that some dimension to the argument is missing. We need to consider not merely that things in the world can be classified as sacred and not sacred, but also as more sacred and less sacred. So also in social classifications it is not sufficient to have a discrimination me/it, we/they; we also need a graduated scale close/far, more like me/less like me. If this essay is found to have a permanent value it will be because it represents an expansion of Lévi-Strauss's thesis in the direction I have indicated.

TABLE 4
KACHIN CATEGORIES OF HUMAN RELATIONSHIPS

	Incest	*No Marriage, Illicit Relations*	*Marriage*	*Remote Nonrelative*
SELF	NI	NA/NAU	NAM	RAW[a]
	mother-in-law	'sister'	marriageable cross-cousin	
	near	sacred occasion	forest	forest fire
	(inedible)	(edible if sacrificed)	(edible)	(inedible)

[a] There are two relevant homonyms of *raw* = tiger. *Raw* as a verb means cease to be related; it applies in particular when two affinally related groups cease to recognize their relationship. *Raw* also means forest fire. It is thus the dangerous aspect of the forest, where *nam* is friendly.

FOUR
THE ANALYSIS OF MYTH

Introduction

In many respects the study of myth may be seen as a microcosm of the development of anthropology. Nearly all of the theoretical and methodological trends which have been current at one time or another in the past century in Europe and in America have had something to say about myth. Some ideas on the nature of myth belong very much to their time and have ceased to provoke much more than a smile or a sigh of wonderment. An example is the celebrated debate which raged at the turn of the twentieth century between the German philologist F. Max Müller and the Scottish anthropologist Andrew Lang. Müller contended that modern Indo-European myth was a "disease of language," a fragmentary and degenerate survival of phrases and words from an ancient Indo-European solar cult. Lang, influenced by the work of Sir James Frazer (author of *The Golden Bough*), countered this diffusionist fantasy with the evolutionary notion that primitive peoples everywhere had similar beliefs, tales, and customs, and that these survived in classic Greek and Roman myths and in modern European folklore. Lang spent decades in mustering evidence from the corners of the earth to refute Müller's naïve notions. Ironically, Lang's own assumptions about universal evolutionary stages of development from barbarism to civilization (with concomitant change in kind and function of myth) shared some of Müller's rather simplistic ideas concerning cultural process and origins. This debate, now something of a curiosity in the history of folklore studies and anthropology, is well reported in Richard Dorson's paper "The Eclipse of Solar Mythology" (1955).

Other anthropological works about myth have fared better with time and more comprehensive ethnographic data than those of the solar mythologists, diffusionists, and evolutionists. In fact, some have endured so well that their basic tenets have become a part of what we "assume" about the nature of belief systems in nonliterate societies. Such a perennial classic is Bronislaw Malinowski's *Myth in Primitive Psychology* (1926), in which he disposed once and for all of the notion that myth was a trivial cultural decoration. He suggested, on the basis of extensive field work in the Trobriand Islands, that myth was an integral part of social life, that it provided a "charter for belief," a sacred underpinning and legitimizer for all that people do and think. Although he has been rightly criticized for the static nature of his concept of "myth as charter" (Leach, 1954, and Firth, 1961), students of oral tradition in general and of myth in particular owe him a considerable debt.

Malinowski also has a respected place in the development of the anthropological tradition of field work, a way of gathering primary data which places emphasis on intensive observation of and participation in the daily lives of those whom the anthropologist is studying. With regard to myth studies, the obvious advantage of this method over the use of libraries and archives is that it enables the observer to rely on firsthand performances of narratives in their proper cultural contexts. Slightly before the time of Malinowski's major field work, Franz Boas, in America, and A. R. Radcliffe-Brown, in England, were also responsible for doing and encouraging others to do field collections and holistic interpretations of oral traditional material. All have been influential in the development of anthropological thinking about mythology. Good discussions and bibliographies on the history of anthropological treatment of myth can be found in Cohen (1969), Dundes (1963 and 1965), and Georges (1968).

Definitions of myth have been debated since primitive religion became a topic of scholarly attention. The term "myth" at best serves as a unifying concept which enables anthropologists to talk about etiological narratives and other forms which, for the society involved, make up a body of "assumed knowledge" about the universe, the natural and supernatural worlds, and man's place in the totality. At best, the term "myth" is a weak one, for it implies a uniform, sacred explanatory power for etiological narratives everywhere. The disadvantages inherent in this assumption are obvious. For example, secular narratives which are classed as *märchen* in European taxonomies frequently enter the oral traditions of societies which have experienced contact with the West as narratives which have some sacred significance. What is a secular tale for one society often becomes a sacred myth for another, and vice versa. Furthermore, most societies have their *own* taxonomies of verbal behavior. Such taxonomies often reveal that even within a single society all genres of etiological narrative do not have equal sacred value or explanatory power. The term "myth," therefore, should be used advisedly as a convenient general label for an enormous diversity of narrative styles, contents, forms and functions.

This chapter presents several anthropological approaches to myths from Western and non-Western societies. Most of the writers share the point of view that significant statements about myth should be context-conscious. That is to say that myth texts stand alone only feebly. Myths and other narratives, as well as analysis of them, must be accompanied by considerable ethnographic background if they are to become intelligible for one who does not know them as part of his own cultural experience. (See Bascom, 1953, and Dundes, 1963, for clear statements of this point of view.) But unlike Franz Boas, an important precursor of this contextual approach to myth interpretation (see his *Kwakiutl Culture as Reflected in Myth*, 1935), few anthropologists today assume a one-to-one relationship between myth on the one hand and cognitive or social reality on the other. The relationship between the two is far more subtle and elusive than this. William Lessa's paper "The Apotheosis of Marespa" shows how complex this interweaving of mythic, social, and historical factors can be.

Whereas the culture-reflector method generally treats myth as a reservoir of information about the cultural whole, the psychoanalytic methods of myth analysis—based on the work of Sigmund Freud, Géza Róheim, Carl Jung, and others—usually approach myth as an expressive phenomenon whose primary referents are the individual and his unconscious conflicts with societal constraints on the one hand and his biological, animal nature on the other. The method generally assumes certain symbolic representations of these conflicts to be universal. In an interesting paper included in this chapter, Professor Dundes explores the psychoanalytic implications of a widely encountered myth motif, that of the creation of the earth from dirt or mud brought from the bottom of the primeval waters. Bibliographies of other good studies in this vein may be found in Fischer (1963) and Kiell (1963).

The second part of this chapter is devoted to a new tradition of myth analysis, which approaches the phenomena of myth as ideal statements about social categories and their interrelationships. In other words, myths are treated not as simple culture reflectors or as universal unconscious projections of individual conflicts, but, rather, as cultural codes or logical models by means of which the human mind can order experience, especially contradictions in experience. This general orientation to myth analysis has received increasing attention recently largely because of the influence of Claude Lévi-Strauss. Among his many contributions to the study of myth have been *La Pensée sauvage* (1962) and his ambitious *Mythologiques* series on the New World (1968, 1969, 1971, 1973), the latter of which has impressed many as the major piece of myth scholarship of our time. A relatively early formulation (1955) of his method of analysis is reprinted in this chapter. Lévi-Strauss's brilliant contributions to the study of myth have been wide-ranging. Among them, he has focused our attention on the logic of myths. This perspective requires that primary attention be given to myth form (structure); myth content for him is a complementary consideration. Related to his interest in logical homologies (structure) in various texts and other expressive domains is his insistence that *all* versions of myths are "correct" versions. In focusing our attention upon "binary oppositions"—nature/culture, high/low, sky/earth, raw/cooked, and so on—and the role of myths in mediating these oppositions, and upon the ways in which myths are like a "science of the concrete"—instead of the *p* and *q* of mathematical thinking, we have jaguars and wild pigs related to each other in formal logic—Lévi-Strauss has added a dimension to the study of myths that anthropologists can ill afford to ignore in spite of the methodological pitfalls facing the analyst who chooses to work with the concepts. Perhaps most important of all has been Lévi-Strauss's rekindling of anthropological interest in myth studies. Useful summaries, applications, and critiques of his treatment of myth may be found in Hayes and Hayes (1970), Leach (1967; 1970), Rossi (1974), and Nathhorst (1969).

Although they have generally been sympathetic with Lévi-Strauss's objectives in the study of myth, British social anthropologists have provided some of the more incisive criticism of his methods and conclusions, which often seem to be intuitively derived and difficult to verify (see Cohen, 1969; Hayes and Hayes, 1970; and Leach, 1967). In this empirical tradition, R. G. Willis's paper on the Fipa of Africa represents an explicit challenge to Lévi-Strauss's methods. Willis suggests that the analysis of mythological thought need not eschew concrete ethnographic data and *can* be accommodated within the normal parameters of social anthropological investigation. (See John Middleton's collection *Myth and Cosmos*, for other examples of analysis in this tradition.)

Gary Gossen, in the final article of this chapter, challenges the adequacy of European genres of verbal behavior in analyzing non-Western oral traditions. He describes the Chamula's own taxonomy of speech "styles" and shows that Western categories such as myth, folktale, legend, folk music, and pun distort the true nature of Chamula oral tradition. Only by studying the full range of verbal behavior manifest in a culture can the true significance of any single genre be perceived. A general introduction to this type of holistic approach can be found in a book by Munro Edmunson entitled *Lore* (1971).

The methods of analysis included in this chapter may often seem to contradict one another. That, however, need not be the case. The diversity of approaches represented here illustrates that meaning in myth, like the symbols of which myth is often composed, may become clearer by analyzing it on many different levels and from many different points of view.

William A. Lessa

THE APOTHEOSIS OF MARESPA

In this article, William Lessa utilizes his field data on the Micronesian atoll of Ulithi to illuminate two problems in the study of myth. First, his analysis supports Clyde Kluckhohn's argument that neither ritual nor myth is necessarily prior to the other (see Chapter 2). Second, he skillfully documents the process by which both myth and ritual reflect as well as affect changes in cosmological beliefs.

The people of Ulithi practice ancestor worship. Each lineage possesses a number of lesser ghosts who gradually pass into oblivion as the memory of the deceased individuals fades. At the head of this amorphous pool of lineage ancestors stands a class of ancestral ghosts who, by virtue of their conceived ability to render greater service to their

---

Reprinted in abridged form from A. L. Kaeppler and H. Arlo Nimmo (eds.), *Directions in Pacific Traditional Literature* (Honolulu: Bishop Museum Press, 1976), by permission of the author and the publishers.

descendants, are remembered for as long as they continue to be effective and reliable. In addition to these lineage ghosts, on Ulithi there are two "great ghosts" named Iongolap and Marespa who possess such superior powers that they have transcended kinship boundaries and are embraced by many local lineages as their own major ghosts. In the unabridged article, Lessa documents the historical process by which one of these ghosts, Marespa, was transformed from an ancestor into a deity. According to Ulithian myths, Marespa died when he was only a few months old but returned to earth as a ghostly spirit with power to predict typhoons, reveal the fate of voyagers at sea, warn of impending epidemics, forecast an abundance of fish, describe events in distant places, and so on. Many persons were possessed by Marespa, and his renown grew to such an extent that three major shrines were devoted to him. Not only did he move beyond the confines of his own lineage, he also transcended Ulithi itself and became known on neighboring islands in the Caroline group. Through a detailed analysis of the historical and ethnographic record, Lessa attempts to establish Marespa's genealogy and estimates the date of his birth and death as 1839. The exact reasons for Marespa's apotheosis are unknown, and Lessa is careful to stay within the bounds of his data. But the question of why a child who never exerted influence as a living individual should become deified remains an intriguing one. Lessa's intimation that Marespa's lineage was that of the hereditary paramount chiefs of the area provides a possible clue. For those interested in pursuing this problem, further comparative and ethnographic material on Ulithi may be found in some of the author's own publications (see Lessa, 1956, 1961, 1962, 1966; Lessa and Spiegelman 1954).

My central purpose is to provide an instance from Micronesia of the deification of a mortal by his kinsmen. It is supported by a considerable amount of evidence, some of it written, most of it oral, and all of it having a high degree of internal consistency that should give no offense to credibility. I shall also endeavor to show that both myth and ritual arose out of this event. In doing so I, of course, do not deny that other myths and other rituals may have arisen out of fantasy or dreams, or that one may inspire the other in sequence.

But in tracing the simultaneous development of myth and ritual from a real event. I hope to bury still further those uncompromising aspects of the ritualistic theory, made popular by the Cambridge school and Lord Raglan, which allege that all myths originate in ritual and that no myths have an historical basis. I shall oppose, too, an opposite theory—just as repugnant but less polemically championed—that all rituals have their antecedents in myths. . . .

Ulithi Atoll, the locale of the apotheosis under consideration, has been the object of my field research on four separate occasions totaling a year. The bulk of the data pertinent to the present article was gathered in 1948; other probings took place during the summer of 1960, when I made an effort to amplify certain points that were not clear from the previous inquiries.

The atoll is situated in the western Carolines, not far from Yap. The natives are simple agriculturalists, dependent for subsistence chiefly on the coconut and various arums, supplementing their predominantly starchy diet with fish, pork, and chicken. There were only 421 inhabitants in the island group in 1949, but in the middle of the last century there were probably about 700. Social structure is dominated by matrilineages, with a modified form of patrilocal residence and a modified type of Crow kinship terminology. The lineages are important because the pagan religion centers essentially around a system of ancestor worship in which the ghosts of lineage mates are the object of an everyday cult. To be sure, there is also a belief in celestial gods, paralleled by some less lofty terrestrial spirits; in practice, however, the ghosts of departed relatives are most significant to the natives. Since 1937 there has been a steady and now almost complete conversion to Roman Catholicism, but at the time when the earlier field study was made, many of the older and more influential people were still pagans and most others had a keen remembrance of the old cult. There is virtually no social stratification; wealth is evenly distributed. Land is held by the lineages and portioned out to individual families for their own needs. There are various kinds of chiefs, including those with territorial jurisdiction and others with lineage authority. Political problems are the concern of the village council of elders, with chiefs functioning primarily either as lineage leaders or as liaison agents with outside islands. It should be mentioned that divorce is easy and remarriage common (prior to conversion to Christianity). . . .

THE PROCESS OF APOTHEOSIS

Apotheosis, defined as the act of raising a person who has died to the rank of a god, may be of two kinds. It is logically possible for a god to have developed from a mortal whose kinship status is not a factor. But where kinship does enter in, the situation is different and we are confronted with the problem as to where ancestor worship leaves off and apotheosis begins. It is necessary to make at least some effort to define the difference.

Where a ghost comes to be venerated beyond the confines of a kin group, where he is not one of the ancestors of the people who have come to embrace him, then he has attained the qualities of a god. Furthermore, when he has become the object of a myth-making process whereby experiences and attributes are given him beyond those of merely powerful, superior men, then again he may be said to have acquired the status of a deity. Ancestor worship already presupposes his historicity. It also entails the transference to him of specifically religious acts and attitudes, including worship and sacrifice. What it does not include is the "public" character of his cult and the leveling of supernatural sanctions against wrongdoers beyond his kinsmen. An additional but purely incidental distinction, perhaps, is that a god enjoys some measure of perdurability, whereas a worshiped ancestor suffers the fate of evanescence.

Regarding Marespa, the question of historicity has already been dealt with. So has his emergence as a supralineage spirit. What remains is to demonstrate that he had transcended the shamanistic sphere and had achieved functions beyond prognostication and familial admonishments—or at least was in the process of doing so before his posthumous career was terminated by the encroachments of Christianity and the skeptical world of alien powers.

We may begin with traditional narrative. I did not in the course of my research on Ulithi attempt to uncover the presence of Marespa tales, but in my notes I have found a simple story that partially lifts the boy out of the ancestral sphere and into the realm of the gods. The tale is short and was narrated to me by an elderly man who first heard it as a boy from some people who were making leis for a *fangelmarespa*. Rather than present it verbatim, I have thought it wise to paraphrase it and incorporate various explanatory notes that will make it more intelligible and meaningful. It goes as follows:

Marespa died. His ghost went to live inside a taro leaf. There was a spirit named Mitou whose function was to catch the souls of living people and take them up to Ialulep, the foremost god of Lang, the sky world. Mitou went to Marespa and made him his "child," and Marespa did everything that he told him. They had a net and with it they would start out in the east and make their way west as far as the Philippines, trying to catch the souls of people and make them die. They worked only at the full moon. Once when the moon was full they started out to do their work. There was a spirit named Sathawolemethau, who lived on a long log in the sea, and when they tried to catch him they could not because be broke the net and escaped. Marespa said to Sathawolemethau, "Be ready! I will come the next full moon and catch you." He replied, "You are a very wicked man. You are catching all your 'children' on these islands. You were born on earth." Marespa had not known that he was born on earth until he found this out from the spirit. He felt remorse. One full moon he and his friend came back to catch souls, but Marespa set free all those caught in the net. His friend was unaware of this. Every time Marespa and his friend went to catch souls, he would do that. One time when Marespa was in Lang, another spirit named Ilurang said to him, "You were born on this island (Ulithi)." Then Marespa entered into mediums. They made a fangelmarespa *for him and the people of the island prayed to him. After that, other islands too made* fangelmarespa. *That is why Marespa became our ghost.*

I am indebted to Inez de Beauclair for a brief reference to a Marespa story that she obtained from a middle-aged man from Ngulu whom she interviewed on Yap. She writes: "He told a strange story, in which Marespa figured as guiding a man dropped to the bottom of the sea, reaching the *falu* (men's house) of the dead, who were all sitting silently twisting coconut fibre ropes (sennit)" (de Beauclair, pers. comm., Apr. 23, 1965).

Obviously, for Marespa the myth-making process had never reached the stage achieved by that other "great ghost," Iongolap. I am convinced, however, that had Marespa enjoyed the more or less pristine cultural milieu in which Iongolap's genesis as a god had proceeded, things might have been otherwise.

Songs from various islands still preserving some paganism have served to perpetuate memories of Marespa, and of this there is no better example than that of Ifaluk.

In 1947 during the course of field work on this little atoll, Burrows and Spiro came to know him under the name of Mwarisepa or Morisepa, listing him as one of the ten "foreign supernaturals" known on the atoll. They reported that he was said to be the ghost of a boy who died at sea, and they presumed that he was from Ulithi because he was invoked in a series of songs attributed to that island group but still being sung on Ifaluk. "This spirit," they wrote, "helps mariners lost at sea" (Burrows and Spiro, 1953, p. 349).

Burrows had occasion to revisit Ifaluk in 1953 while it was still pagan and collected among others a number of religious dance songs that were published posthumously in his book, *Flower in My Ear* (1963). Of these songs, known as ur, three are concerned almost entirely with Mwarisepa (pp.389–394, 394–400, 400–403), while three others make passing reference to him (pp.141, 363–370, 379–389). Although ur in general are "not intended to express adoration directly, but rather to please the gods with entertainment" (Burrows, 1963, p. 63), those in question reveal an unmistakably supplicative attitude toward the young godling. He is ardently courted, and with good reason. In his home in the sky he takes pity on those on earth; he talks to them with kindly words. He guides mariners safely to shore and saves the people from sickness. One song tells us that the former chiefs used to be bad men, but now because of him the chiefs agree to pray for the people's welfare. The god teaches the women their *bwarux* or serenade dance songs, and he dances with them, each woman giving him a garland of flowers. The songs are like paeans—praising, thanking, exulting. The women are anxious always for him to descend from his abode in the sky and they try to coax him with blossoms, songs, and dances. He is not averse to their blandishments, although something further also draws him earthward (Burrows, 1963, p. 393).

The boy in the sky remembers, down on earth below
His mother still among the living,
Remembers when he was a babe in her arms.
He comes down to earth,
Wanting to stay there with her
Or take her to the sky with him. . . .

Deprecation of Mwarisepa is hinted at by Burrows and Spiro when they say that "people on Ifaluk seem to have no active faith in him" (Burrows and Spiro, 1953, p. 349), but it should be remembered that they were recording an impression of him formed late in time by the Ifaluk. Regardless of this, one of the songs itself, undoubtedly composed much earlier in time, contains the following passage (Burrows, 1963, p. 385):

Sometimes he speaks the truth,
Sometimes he lies, they say. . . .

But the song hastens to defend him against such calumny (Burrows, 1963, p. 385).

His talk does not swerve from the truth
Whatever backbiters may say.
He gives the people the truth!

It will be recalled, however, that all six of the ur having anything to do with Marespa originated on Ulithi; even so, he must have been held in some esteem on Ifaluk for the pagan natives to have preserved his memory for so long in the dances they danced and the songs they sang.

De Beauclair tells me that on Yap she heard of and collected parts of a women's dance song that had been inspired by Marespa. It deals with the catastrophe that met a fleet from Ulithi sailing to Fais. The canoes were punished by the chief, Sorek (Marespa's nephew, Sorekh?) by means of the most powerful Yapese magic, the red earth *eria*, put on the masts. This happened during German times (de Beauclair, pers. comm., Apr. 23, 1965). I regret that I do not know from her account how Marespa himself participated in this episode, but it is interesting to see him associated with the kind of magic power which Yap is said to use to close and open the seaways.

In turning now to the rituals that came to be built up around Marespa we shall, of course, ignore those associated purely with lineage ancestor worship and proceed to those that treated the boy as a godling. First is an annual ritual of major importance performed on Ulithi over a period of two lunar months and designed to bring an abundance of fish to the atoll. This rite would open up on Mogmog with the fish magician, commissioned to act by the paramount chief, taking a loincloth to the *fangelmarespa* on that island and leaving it with the custodian. The whole ritual was an elaborate and dangerous one, taking place for the most part during sea trips about the atoll, and in the course of events there would be prayers to many great sky and ocean deities, so that to a certain extent Marespa may be said to have been associated with the gods.

Marespa was linked with an even greater annual event, comparable in magnitude with the expeditions made by members of the intricate *kula* ring off eastern New Guinea made famous by Malinowski's writings. This annual event was the so-called tribute voyage to Yap. I have already alluded to the trips made to Yap by its satellite islands, and much has been written about them by German ethnographers, as well as myself. I shall confine myself to excerpts from an eyewitness account from the point of view of Ulithi and try to make simple what is in fact a complex matter.

The purpose of the expeditions was to bring "rent," political tribute, and religious offerings to Gagil district in Yap. I shall discuss only the offerings, called *mepel*. They were for both Iongolap and Marespa.

Of the great fleet of canoes assembled on Ulithi from all over the eastern islands, about five or more were from the atoll. Coconut oil for Marespa was put in the windward and leeward cabins of the canoe belonging to the paramount chief of Ulithi, who, of course, was a member of the Fasilus lineage. The other canoes, too, carried oil, but in this instance for their own lineage ghosts, not Marespa. The paramount chief would pray to Marespa for a safe voyage, while the navigators of each of the other canoes prayed to the great navigation god, Ialuluwe. Strict precedent determined that the lead canoe and its pilot be always from the island of Falalop.

On reaching Yap a sort of quarantine was placed on all the canoes to guard against any harm from spirits that might have followed the canoes to Yap. The passengers remained in their canoes, with the sails down but the masts up, until a certain magician for travel, who lived in Gagil district, had taken steps to lift the quarantine. He would walk up to each canoe, and as he did so, men and women would shout "Hai! Hai!" as they pounded the ground with coconuts and blew on shell trumpets to drive away the spirits. The magician would work purificatory magic over each canoe, and when he was finished the paramount chief from Ulithi would disembark with his men. They carried *mepel* for Iongolap and Marespa and these were hung in a house on a spot called Lamrui. In front of the house on the west side were about ten stone slabs used as back rests by chiefs and other important people as the prayers were being said with the offerings. These stones were not exclusively used for this one occasion, however, but also for any important meetings throughout the year concerning Iongolap and Marespa. The reason the offerings were brought to Yap was that the Yapese of Gatschapar village recognized the great power of both of the two great ghosts, Iongolap and Marespa. (We know from other accounts that the islands east and south of Ulithi were likewise required to take *mepel* to Yap.)

The return voyage from Yap to Ulithi was surrounded with further ritual and prayer. Marespa was again called upon to safeguard the travelers and their canoes.

I have not endeavored to ascertain other ways in which the Marespa cult involved ritual but am sure that Marespa was often invoked ritualistically not only in prayer but other ways as well, if the example of his companion ghost, Iongolap, is of any value. The career of the one closely follows the other and it is most likely that it followed a well-established pattern in the Carolines. Indeed, although I have not referred to them, there are ample examples in the literature of the apotheosis of local Carolinian ghosts, although I have found none that approximated the high status of the two "great ghosts."

CONCLUSION

I have, then, described an instance of the deification of a small boy on Ulithi. He died, became a lineage ghost, transcended the bounds of his lineage, and finally was well on his way to becoming a full divinity when his metamorphosis was interrupted by Westernization. This instance deals with the question as to whether or not humans are ever at all deified, and more particularly whether real persons give rise to religious rituals and myths.

This article has not purported to be a comprehensive discussion of the myth-ritual theory, but it is possible that examples such as that of Marespa will help refute the more dogmatic kind of ritual theory, which, maintaining as it does that all myth has a ritual origin, is obviously untenable. Much of what the ritualists have to say is perfectly true, but by their own criteria their position becomes invalid if even one instance can successfully be opposed to their notion that myths never have historicity but emerge only out of ritual.

Alan Dundes

EARTH-DIVER: CREATION OF THE MYTHOPOEIC MALE

In this interesting paper, Alan Dundes presents a psychoanalytic interpretation of a myth motif which has strikingly wide distribution in both the Old World and the New World. Following one of the basic assumptions of the psychoanalytic tradition—that people everywhere share unconscious biological attributes and urges which come into conflict with social constraints—he attempts to relate the widespread occurrence of the male earth-diver motif to the (theoretically) universal presence of unconscious male pregnancy envy and desire to give anal birth. In other words, since he is deprived of truly giving birth, the mythopoeic male unconsciously "asserts himself" in creating the earth itself from what is often mud or fecal material from the primeval waters. Dundes uses orthodox Freudian theory together with his own impressive control of world folk literature to build a case in favor of this interpretation of the motif. He is aware of the speculative and controversial nature of his problem and he presents his material with a scholarly moderation which has not always characterized psychological interpretations of myth. For a similar treatment of the symbolism in initiation rites, see Dundes' intriguing article, "A Psychoanalytic Theory of the Bullroarer" (1976), and more generally, his article, "Projection in Folklore: A Plea for Psychoanalytic Semiotics" (1976).

This paper and other temperate psychoanalytic writings will perhaps be of increasing interest in relation to some of the recent anthropological treatments of religious symbolism, particularly those of Victor Turner (see his *Forest of Symbols*, 1967). The differences between the theoretical and methodological approaches are considerable and perhaps irreconcilable, yet it is possible that culture-specific formulations about the nature of religious symbolism may find some common ground with universal psychological prototypes. For example, male/female-right/left-up/down discriminations, which occur widely in religious symbolism, appear to refer to something quite fundamental in human nature.

The reader may wish to consult the bibliographies listed in Dundes (1965), Kiell (1963), and Fischer (1963) for further reading on psychoanalytic studies of myth and folklore. Géza Róheim's *The Gates of the Dream* (1952) and Sigmund Freud and D. E. Oppenheim's *Dreams in Folklore* (1958) will also provide interesting (and orthodox) reading on the topics of myth, dreams, and psychoanalysis.

Reprinted from *American Anthropologist*, LXIV (1962), 1032–1051, by permission of the author and the American Anthropological Association.

Few anthropologists are satisfied with the present state of scholarship with respect to primitive mythology. While not everyone shares Lévi-Strauss's extreme pessimistic opinion that from a theoretical point of view the study of myth is "very much the same as it was fifty years ago, namely a picture of chaos" (1958: 50), still there is general agreement that much remains to be done in elucidating the processes of the formation, transmission, and functioning of myth in culture.

One possible explanation for the failure of anthropologists to make any notable advances in myth studies is the rigid adherence to two fundamental principles: a literal reading of myth and a study of myth in monocultural context. The insistence of most anthropologists upon the literal as opposed to the symbolic interpretation, in terms of cultural relativism as opposed to transcultural universalism, is in part a continuation of the reaction against 19th century thought in which universal symbolism in myth was often argued and in part a direct result of the influence of two dominant figures in the history of anthropology, Boas and Malinowski. Both these pioneers favored studying one culture at a time in depth and both contended that myth was essentially nonsymbolic. Boas often spoke of mythology reflecting culture, implying something of a one-to-one relationship. With this view, purely descriptive ethnographic data could be easily culled from the mythological material of a particular culture. Malinowski argued along similar lines: "Studied alive, myth, as we shall see, is not symbolic, but a direct expression of its subject matter" (1954:101). Certainly, there is much validity in the notion of mythology as a cultural reflector, as the well documented researches of Boas and Malinowski demonstrate. However, as in the case of most all-or-nothing approaches, it does not account for all the data. Later students in the Boas tradition, for example, noted that a comparison between the usual descriptive ethnography and the ethnographical picture obtained from mythology revealed numerous discrepancies. Ruth Benedict (1935) in her important Introduction to *Zuni Mythology* spoke of the tendency to idealize and compensate in folklore. More recently, Katherine Spencer has contrasted the correspondences and discrepancies between the ethnographical and mythological accounts. She also suggests that the occurrence of folkloristic material which contradicts the ethnographic data "may be better explained in psychological than in historical terms" (1947:130). However, anthropologists have tended to mistrust psychological terms, and consequently the pendulum has not yet begun to swing away from the literal to the symbolic reading of myth. Yet it is precisely the insights afforded by advances in human psychology which open up vast vistas for the student of myth. When anthropologists learn that to study the products of the human mind (e.g., myths) one must know something of the mechanics of the human mind, they may well push the pendulum towards not only the symbolic interpretation of myth but also towards the discovery of universals in myth.

Freud himself was very excited at the possibility of applying psychology to mythology. In a letter to D. E. Oppenheim in 1909, he said, "I have long been haunted by the idea that our studies on the content of the neurosis might be destined to solve the riddle of the formation of myths. . . ." (Freud and Oppenheim, 1958:13). However, though Freud was pleased at the work of his disciples, Karl Abraham and Otto Rank, in this area, he realized that he and his students were amateurs in mythology. In the same letter to Oppenheim he commented: "We are lacking in academic training and familiarity with the material." Unfortunately, those not lacking in these respects had little interest in psychoanalytic theory. To give just one example out of many, Lewis Spence in his preface to *An Introduction to Mythology* stated: "The theories of Freud and his followers as to religion and the origin of myth have not been considered, since, in the writer's opinion, they are scarcely to be taken seriously." What was this theory which was not to be taken seriously? Freud wrote the following: "As a matter of fact, I believe that a large portion of the mythological conception of the world which reaches far into the most modern religions, is *nothing but psychology projected to the outer world.* The dim perception (the endopsychic perception, as it were) of psychic factors and relations of the unconscious was taken as a model in the construction of a *transcendental reality,* which is destined to be changed again by science into *psychology of the unconscious*" (1938:164). It is this insight perhaps more than any other that is of value to the anthropologist interested in primitive myth.

There is, however, an important theoretical difficulty with respect to the psychoanalytic interpretation of myth. This difficulty stems from the fact that there are basically two ways in which psychoanalytic theory may be applied. A myth may be analyzed *with* a knowledge of a particular myth-maker, or a myth may be analyzed *without* such knowledge. There is some doubt as to whether the two methods are equally valid and, more specifically, whether the second is as valid as the first. The question is, to employ an analogy, can a dream be analyzed without a knowledge of the specific dreamer who dreamed it? In an anthropological context, the question is: can a myth be interpreted without a knowledge of the culture which produced it? Of course, it is obvious that any psychoanalyst would prefer to analyze the dreamer or myth-maker in order to interpret more accurately a dream or myth. Similarly, those anthropologists who are inclined to employ psychoanalysis in interpreting myths prefer to relate the manifest and latent content of myths to specific cultural contexts. However, this raises another important question. Do myths reflect the present, the past, or both? There are some anthropologists who conceive of myths almost exclusively in terms of the present. While tacitly recognizing that traditional myths are of considerable antiquity, such anthropologists, nevertheless, proceed to analyze a present-day culture in terms of its myths. Kardiner's theory of folklore, for instance, reveals this bias. Speaking of the myths of women in Marquesan folklore, Kardiner observes, "These myths are the products of the fantasy of some individual, communicated and probably changed many times before we get them. The uniformity of the stories points to some common experience of all individuals in this culture, not remembered from the remote past, but currently experienced." According to Kardiner, then, myths are responses to current realities (1939:417, 214). Róheim summarizes Kardiner's position before taking issue with it. "According to Kardiner, myths and folklore always reflect the unconscious conflicts of the present generation as they are formed by the pressure brought to bear on them by existing social conditions. In sharp contrast to Freud, Reik, and myself, a myth represents not the dim past but the present" (1940: 540).

The evidence available from folklore scholarship suggests that there is remarkable stability in oral narratives. Myths and tales re-collected from the same culture show considerable similarity in structural pattern and detail despite the fact that the myths and tales are from different informants who are perhaps separated by many generations. Excluding consideration of modern myths (for the myth-making process is an ongoing one), one can see that cosmogonic myths, to take one example, have not changed materially for hundreds of years. In view of this, it is clearly not necessarily valid to analyze a *present-day* culture in terms of that culture's traditional cosmogonic myths, which in all likelihood date from the prehistoric *past*. An example of the disregard of the time element occurs in an interesting HRAF-inspired cross-cultural attempt to relate child-training practices to folk tale content. Although the tales were gathered at various times between 1890 and 1940, it was assumed that "a folk tale represents a kind of summation of the common thought patterns of a number of individuals. . . ." (McClelland and Friedman, 1952:245). Apparently common thought patterns are supposed to be quite stable and not subject to cultural change during a 50 year period. Thus just one version of a widely diffused North American Indian tale type like the Eye Juggler is deemed sufficient to "diagnose the modal motivations" of the members of a culture. Nevertheless, Kardiner's theoretical perspective is not entirely without merit. Changes in myth do occur and a careful examination of a number of variants of a particular myth may show that these changes tend to cluster around certain points in time or space. Even if such changes are comparatively minor in contrast to the over-all structural stability of a myth, they may well serve as meaningful signals of definite cultural changes. Thus, Martha Wolfenstein's comparison of English and American versions of Jack and the Beanstalk (1955) showed a number of interesting differences in detail, although the basic plot remained the same. She suggested that the more phallic details in the American versions were in accord with other cultural differences between England and America. Whether or not one agrees with Wolfenstein's conclusions, one can appreciate the soundness of her method. The same myth or folk tale can be profitably compared using versions from two or more separate cultures, and the differences in detail may well illustrate significant differences in culture. One thinks of Nadel's (1937) adaptation of Bartlett's experiment in giving an artificial folk tale to two neighboring tribes in Africa and his discovery that the variations fell along clear-cut cultural lines, rather than along individualistic lines. However, the basic theoretical problem remains unresolved. Can the myth as a whole be analyzed meaningfully? Margaret Mead in commenting briefly on Wolfenstein's study begs the entire question. She states: "What is important here is that Jack and the Beanstalk, when it was first made up, might have had a precise and beautiful correspondence to the theme of a given culture at a given time. It then traveled and took on all sorts of forms, which you study and correlate with the contemporary cultural usage" (Tax, 1953: 282). The unfortunate truth is that rarely is the anthropologist in a position to know when and where a myth is "first made up." Consequently, the precise and beautiful correspondence is virtually unattainable or rather unreconstructible. The situation is further complicated by the fact that many, indeed, the majority of myths are found widely distributed throughout the world. The historical record, alas, only goes back so far. In other words, it is, practically speaking, impossible to ascertain the place and date of the first appearance(s) of a given myth. For this reason, anthropologists like Mead despair of finding any correspondence between over-all myth structure and culture. Unfortunately, some naïve scholars manifest a profound ignorance of the nature of folklore by their insistent attempts to analyze a specific culture by analyzing myths which are found in a great many cultures. For example, the subject of a recent doctoral dissertation was an analysis of 19th century German culture on the basis of an analyses of the content of various Grimm tales (Mann, 1958). Although the analyses of the tales were ingenious and psychologically sound, the fact that the Grimm tales are by no means limited to the confines of Germany, and furthermore are undoubtedly much older than the 19th century, completely vitiates the theoretical premise underlying the thesis. Assuming the validity of the analyses of the tales, these analyses would presumably be equally valid wherever the tales appeared in the same form. Barnouw (1955) commits exactly the same error when he analyzes Chippewa personality on the basis of a Chippewa "origin legend" which, in fact, contains many standard North American Indian tale types (Wycoco). It is clearly a fallacy to analyze an international tale or widely diffused myth *as if* it belonged to only one culture. Only if a myth is known to be unique, that is, peculiar to a given culture, is this kind of analysis warranted. It is, however, perfectly good procedure to analyze the differences which occur as a myth enters another culture. Certainly, one can gain considerable insight into the mechanics of acculturation by studying a Zuni version of a European cumulative tale or a native's retelling of the story of Beowulf. Kardiner is at his best when he shows how a cultural element is adapted to fit the basic personality structure of the borrowing culture. His account of the Comanche's alteration of the Sun Dance from a masochistic and self-destructive ritual to a demonstration of feats of strength is very convincing (1945: 93).

The question is now raised: if it is theoretically only permissible to analyze the differentiae of widely diffused myths or the entire structure of myths peculiar to a particular culture, does this mean that the entire structure of widely diffused myths (which are often the most interesting) cannot be meaningfully analyzed? This is, in essence, the question of whether a dream can be analyzed without knowledge of the dreamer. One answer may be that to the extent that there are human universals, such myths may be analyzed. From this vantage point, while it may be a fallacy to analyze a world-wide myth as if it belonged to only one culture, it is not a fallacy to analyze the myth as if it belonged to all cultures in which it appears. This does not preclude the possibility that one myth found in many cultures may have as many meanings as there are cultural contexts (Boas, 1910c: 383). Nevertheless, the hypothesis of a limited number of organic human universals suggests some sort of similar, if not identical, meaning. It should not be necessary to observe that, to the extent that anthropologists are scientists, they need not fear anathematic reductionism and the discovery of empirically observable universals. The formula $e = mc^2$ is nonetheless valid for its being reductionistic.

A prime example of an anthropologist interested in universals is Kluckhohn. In his paper "Universal Categories of Culture," Kluckhohn contends that "The inescapable fact of cutural relativism does not justify the conclusion that cultures are in all respects utterly disparate monads and hence strictly noncomparable entities" and "Valid cross-cultural comparison could best proceed from the invariant points of reference supplied by the biological, psychological, and sociosituational 'givens' of human life" (1953:520,521). Of even more interest is Kluckhohn's conviction that these "givens" are manifested in myth. In "Recurrent Themes in Myths and Mythmaking," he discusses "certain features of mythology that are apparently universal or that have such wide distribution in space and time that their generality may be presumed to result from recurrent reactions of the human psyche to situations and stimuli of the same general order" (1959:268). Kluckhohn's recurrent themes appear somewhat similar to Freud's typical dreams. Although Freud specifically warned against codifying symbolic translations of dream content, and although he did clearly state his belief that the same dream content could conceal a different meaning in the case of different persons or contexts, he did consider that there are such things as typical dreams, "dreams which almost every one has dreamed in the same manner, and of which we are accustomed to assume that they have the same significance in the case of every dreamer" (1938:292,39). While there are not many anthropologists who would support the view that recurrent myths have similar meaning irrespective of specific cultural context, that does not mean that the view is false. For those who deny universal meanings, it might be mentioned that the reasons why a particular myth has widespread distribution have yet to be given. The most ardent diffusionist, as opposed to an advocate of polygenesis or convergence, can do little more than show how a myth spreads. The how rarely includes the why. In order to show the plausibility of a symbolic and universal approach to myth, a concrete example will be analyzed in some detail.

One of the most fascinating myths in North American Indian mythology is that of the earth-diver. Anna Birgitta Rooth in her study of approximately 300 North American Indian creation myths found that, of her eight different types, earth-diver had the widest distribution. Earl W. Count who has studied the myth for a number of years considers the notion of a diver fetching material for making dry land "easily among the most widespread single concepts held by man" (1952:55). Earth-diver has recently been studied quite extensively by the folklorist Elli Kaija Köngas (1960) who has skillfully surveyed the mass of previous pertinent scholarship. The myth as summarized by Ermine Wheeler-Voegelin is:

In North American Indian myths of the origin of the world, the culture hero has a succession of animals dive into the primeval waters, or flood of waters, to secure bits of mud or sand from which the earth is to be formed. Various animals, birds, and aquatic creatures are sent down into the waters that cover the earth. One after another animal fails; the last one succeeds, however, and floats to the surface half dead, with a little sand or dirt in his claws. Sometimes it is Muskrat, sometimes Beaver, Hell-diver, Crawfish, Mink who succeeds, after various other animals have failed, in bringing up the tiny bit of mud which is then put on the surface of the water and magically expands to become the world of the present time (1949:334)

Among the interesting features of this myth is the creation from mud or dirt. It is especially curious in view of the widespread myth of the creation of man from a similar substance (Frazer, 1935:4-15). Another striking characteristic is the magical expansion of the bit of mud. Moreover, how did the idea of creating the earth from a particle of dirt small enough to be contained beneath a claw or fingernail develop, and what is there in this cosmogonic myth that has caused it to thrive so in a variety of cultures, not only in aboriginal North America but in the rest of the world as well?

Freud's suggestion that mythology is psychology projected upon the external world does not at a first glance seem applicable in the case of the earth-diver myth. The Freudian hypothesis is more obvious in other American Indian cosmogonic conceptions, such as the culture hero's Oedipal separation of Father Sky and Mother Earth (Róheim, 1921:163) or the emergence myth, which appears to be man's projection of the phenomenon of human birth. This notion of the origin of the emergence myth was clearly stated as early as 1902 by Washington Matthews with apparently no help from psychoanalysis. At that time Matthews proposed the idea that the emergence myth was basically a "myth of gestation and of birth." A more recent study of the emergence myth by Wheeler-Voegelin and Moore makes a similar suggestion en passant, but no supporting details are given 1957:73-74). Róheim, however, had previously extended Matthews' thesis by suggesting that primitive man's conception of the world originated in the prenatal perception of space in the womb (1921:163). In any event, no matter how close the emergence of man from a hole in Mother Earth might appear to be to actual human birth, it does not appear to help in determining the psychological prototype for the earth-diver myth. Is there really any "endo-psychic" perception which could have served as the model for the construction of a cosmogonic creation from mud?

The hypothesis here proposed depends upon two key assumptions. The two assumptions (and they are admittedly only assumptions) are: (1) the existence of a cloacal theory of birth; and (2) the existence of pregnancy envy on the part of males. With regard to the first assumption, it was Freud himself who included the cloacal theory as one of the common sexual theories of children. The theory, in essence, states that since the child is ignorant of the vagina and is rarely permitted to watch childbirth, he assumes that the lump in the pregnant woman's abdomen leaves her body in the only way he can imagine material leaving the body, namely via the anus. In Freud's words: "Children are all united from the outset in the belief that the birth of a child takes place by the bowel; that is to say, that the baby is produced like a piece of faeces" (1953:328). The second assumption concerns man's envy of woman's child-bearing role. Whether it is called "parturition envy" (Boehm) or "pregnancy envy" (Fromm), the basic idea is that men would like to be able to produce or create valuable material from within their bodies as women do. Incidentally, it is this second assumption which is the basis of Bruno Bettelheim's explanation of puberty initiation rites and the custom of couvade. His thesis is that puberty rites consist of a rebirth ritual of a special kind to the effect that the initiate is born anew *from males*. The denial of women's part in giving birth is evidenced by the banning of women from the ceremonies. Couvade is similarly explained as the male's desire to imitate female behavior in childbirth. A number of psychoanalysts have suggested that man's desire for mental and artistic creativity stems in part from the wish to conceive or produce on a par with women (Jones, 1957:40; Fromm, 1951:233; Huckel, 1953:44). What is even more significant from the point of view of mythology is the large number of clinical cases in which men seek to have babies in the form of feces, or cases in which men imagine themselves excreting the world. Felix Boehm makes a rather sweeping generalization when he says: "In all analyses of men we meet with phantasies of anal birth, and we know how common it is for men to treat their faeces as a child" (1930:455; see also Silberer, 1925:393). However, there is a good deal of clinical evidence supporting the existence of this phantasy. Stekel (1959:45), for example, mentions a child who called the feces "Baby." The possible relevance of this notion to the myth of the origin of man occurred to Abraham (1948:320), Jung (1916:214), and Rank (1922:54). Jung's comment is: "The first people were made from excrement, potter's earth and clay." (Cf. Schwarzbaum, 1960:48.) In fact, Jung rather ingeniously suggests that the idea of anal birth is the basis of the motif of creating by "throwing behind oneself" as in the case of Deucalion and Pyrrha. Nevertheless, neither Abraham, Jung, nor Rank emphasized the fact that anal birth is especially employed by men. It is true that little girls also have this phantasy, but presumably the need for the phantasy disappears upon the giving of birth to a child. (There may well be some connection between this phantasy and the widespread occurrence of geophagy among pregnant women [Elwin, 1949:292, n. 1].)

Both the assumptions underlying the hypothesis attempting to explain the earthdiver myth are found in Genesis. As Fromm points out (1951:234), the woman's creative role is denied. It is man who creates and, in fact, it is man who gives birth to woman. Eve is created from substance taken from the body of Adam. Moreover, if one were inclined to see the Noah story as a gestation myth, it would be noteworthy that it is the man who builds the womb-ark. It would also be interesting that the flood waters abate only after a period roughly corresponding to the length of human pregnancy. Incidentally, it is quite likely that the Noah story is a modified earth-diver myth. The male figure sends a raven once and a dove twice to brave the primordial waters seeking traces of earth. (Cf. Schwarzbaum, 1960:52), n. 15a.) In one apocryphal account, the raven disobeys instructions by stopping to feast on a dead man, and in another he is punished by having his feathers change color from white to black (Ginzberg, 1925:39, 164). Both of these incidents are found in American Indian earth-diver myths (Rooth, 1957:498). In any case, one can see that there are male myths of creation in Genesis, although Fromm does not describe them all. Just as Abraham, Jung, and Rank had anal birth without pregnancy envy, Fromm has pregnancy envy without anal birth. He neglects to mention that man was created from dust. One is tempted to speculate as to whether male creation myths might be in any way correlated with highly patriarchal social organization.

Of especial pertinence to the present thesis is the clinical data on phantasies of excreting the universe. Lombroso, for example, describes two artists, each of whom had the delusion that they were lords of the world which they had excreted from their bodies One of them painted a full-length picure of himself, naked, among women, ejecting worlds (1895:201). In this phantasy world, the artist flaunting his anal creativity depicts himself as superior to the women who surround him. Both Freud and Stekel have reported cases in which men fancied defecating upon the world, and Abraham cites a dream of a patient in which the patient dreamed he expelled the universe out of his anus (Freud, 1949:407, Stekel, 1959:44; Abraham, 1948:320). Of course, the important question for the present study is whether or not such phantasies ever occur in mythical form. Undoubtedly, the majority of anthropologists would be somewhat loath to interpret the earth-diver myth as an anal birth fantasy on the basis of a few clinical examples drawn exclusively from Western civilization. However, the dearth of mythological data results partly from the traditional prudery of some ethnographers and many folklorists. Few myths dealing with excretory processes find their way into print. Nevertheless, there are several examples, primarily of the creation of man from excrement. John G. Bourke (1891:266) cites an Australian myth of such a creation of man. In India, the elephant-headed god Ganesh is derived from the excrement of his mother (Berkeley-Hill, 1921:330). In modern India, the indefatigable Elwin has collected quite a few myths in which the earth is excreted. For instance, a Lanjhia Saora version describes how Bhimo defecates on Rama's head. The feces is thrown into the water which immediately dries up and the earth is formed (1949:44). In a Gadaba myth, Larang the great Dano devoured the world, but Mahaprabhu "caught hold of him and squeezed him so hard that he excreted the earth he had devoured

. . . . From the earth that Larang excreted, the world was formed again" (1949:37). In other versions, a worm excretes the earth, or the world is formed from the excreta of ants (1949:47; 1954:9). An example closer to continental North America is reported by Bogoras. In this Chukchee creation myth, Raven's wife tells Raven to go and try to create the earth, but Raven protests that he cannot. Raven's wife then announces that she will try to create a "spleen-companion" and goes to sleep. Raven "looks at his wife. Her abdomen has enlarged. In her sleep she creates without effort. He is frightened, and turns his face away." After Raven's wife gives birth to twins, Raven says, "There, you have created men! Now I shall go and try to create the earth." Then "Raven flies and defecates. Every piece of excrement falls upon water, grows quickly, and becomes land." In this fashion, Raven succeeds in creating the whole earth (Bogoras, 1910:152). Here there can be no doubt of the connection between pregnancy envy and anal creation. Unfortunately, there are few examples which are as clear as the Chukchee account. One of the only excremental creation myths reported in North America proper was collected by Boas. He relates (1895:159) a Kwakiutl tale of Mink making a youth from his excrement. However, the paucity of American Indian versions does not necessarily reflect the non-existence of the myth in North America. The combination of puritanical publishing standards in the United States with similar collecting standards may well explain in part the lack of data. In this connection it is noteworthy that whereas the earlier German translation of Boas' Kwakiutl version refers specifically to excrement, the later English translation speaks of a musk-bag (1910a:1959). Most probably ethnographers and editors alike share Andrew Lang's sentiments when he alludes to a myth of the Encounter Bay people, "which might have been attributed by Dean Swift to the Yahoos, so foul an origin does it allot to mankind" (1899:166). Despite the lack of a great number of actual excremental myths, the existence of any at all would appear to lend support to the hypothesis that men do think of creativity in anal terms, and further that this conception is projected into mythical cosmogonic terms.

There is, of course, another possible reason for the lack of overtly excremental creation myths and this is the process of sublimation. Ferenczi in his essay "The Ontogenesis of the Interest in Money" (1956) has given the most explicit account of this process as he traces the weaning of the child's interest from its feces through a whole graduated series of socially sanctioned substitutes ranging from moist mud, sand, clay, and stones to gold or money. Anthropologists will object that Ferenczi's ontogenetic pattern is at best only applicable to Viennese type culture. But, to the extent that any culture has toilet training (and this includes any culture in which the child is not permitted to play indiscriminately with his feces), there is some degree of sublimation. As a matter of fact, so-called anal personality characteristics have been noted among the Yurok (Posinsky), Mohave (Devereux), and Chippewa (Barnouw, Hallowell). Devereux (1951:412) specifically comments upon the use of mud as a fecal substitute among the Mohave. Moreover, it may well be that the widespread practices of smearing the body with paint or daubing it with clay in preparation for aggressive activities have some anal basis. As for the gold-feces equation, anthropologists have yet to explain the curious linguistic fact that in Nahuatl the word for gold is *teocuitlatl,* which is compound of *teotl,* "god" and *cuitlatl,* "excrement." Gold is thus "excrement of the gods" or "divine excrement" (Saville, 1920:118). This extraordinary confirmation of Freudian symbolism which was pointed out by Reik as early as 1915 has had apparently little impact upon anthropologists blindly commited to cultural relativism. (See also Róheim, 1923:387. However, for an example of money/feces symbolism in the dream of a Salteaux Indian, see Hallowell, 1938.) While the gold-feces symbolism is hardly likely in cultures where gold was unknown, there is reason for assuming that some sort of sublimation does occur in most cultures. (For American Indian instances of "jewels from excrements" see Thompson, 1929:329, n. 190a. In this connection, it might be pointed out that in Oceanic versions of the creation of earth from an object thrown on the primeval waters, as found in Lessa's recent comprehensive study (1961), the items thrown include, in addition to sand, such materials as rice chaff, betel nut husks, and ashes, which would appear to be waste products.) If this is so, then it may be seen that a portion of Ferenczi's account of the evolutionary course of anal sublimation is of no mean importance to the analysis of the earth-diver myth. Ferenczi states: "Even the interest for the specific odour of excrement does not cease at once, but is only displaced on to other odours that in any way resemble this. The children continue to show a liking for the smell of sticky materials with a characteristic odour, especially the strongly smelling degenerated produce of cast off epidermis cells which collects between the toes, nasal secretion, ear-wax, and the dirt of the nails, while many children do not content themselves with the moulding and sniffing of these substances, but also take them into the mouth" (1956:273). Anyone who is familiar with American Indian creation myths will immediately think of examples of the creation of man from the rubbings of skin . . . , birth from mucus from the nose, etc. The empirical fact is that these myths do exist! With respect to the earth-diver myth, the common detail of the successful diver's returning with a little dirt under his fingernail is entirely in accord with Ferenczi's analysis. The fecal nature of the particle is also suggested by its magical expansion. One could imagine that as one defecates one is thereby creating an ever-increasing amount of earth. (Incidentally, the notion of creating land masses through defecation has the corollary idea of creating bodies of water such as oceans through micturition. . . . For example, in the previously mentioned Chukchee myth, Raven, after producing the earth, began to pass water. A drop became a lake, while a jet formed a river.)

The present hypothesis may also serve to elucidate the reasons why Christian dualism is so frequently found in Eurasian earth-diver versions. Earl Count considers the question of the dualistic nature of earth-diver as one of the main problems connected with the study of the myth (1952:56). Count is not willing to commit himself as to whether the earth-diver is older than a possible dualistic overlay, but Köngas agrees with earlier scholars that the dualism is a later development (Count, 1952:61; Köngas, 1960:168). The dualism usually takes the form of a contest between God and the devil. As might be expected from the tradition of philosophical dualism, the devil is associated with the body, while God is concerned with the spiritual element. Thus it is the devil who dives for the literally lowly dirt and returns with some under his nails. An interesting incident in view of Ferenczi's account of anal sublimation is the devil's attempt to save a bit of earth by putting it in his mouth. However, when God expands the earth, the stolen bit also expands, forcing the devil to spit it out, where upon mountains or rocks are formed (Köngas, 1960:160–161). In this connection, another dualistic creation myth is quite informative. God is unable to stop the earth from growing and sends the bee to spy on the devil to find a way to accomplish this. When the bee buzzes, in leaving the devil to report back to God, the devil exclaims, "Let him eat your excrement, whoever sent you!" God did this and the earth stopped growing (Dragomanov, 1961:3). Since the eating of excrement prevented the further growth of the earth, one can see the fecal nature of the substance forming the earth. In still another dualistic creation myth, there is even an attempt made to explain why feces exists at all in man. In this narrative, God creates a pure body for man but has to leave it briefly in order to obtain a soul. In God's absence, the devil defiles the body. God upon returning, has no alternative but to turn his creation inside out, which is the reason why man has impurities in his intestines (Campbell, 1956:294). These few examples should be sufficient to show that the dualism is primarily a matter of separating the dross of matter from the essence of spirit. The devil is clearly identified with matter and in particular with defecation. In a phrase, it is the devil who does the dirty work. Thus Köngas is quite right in seeing a psycho-physical dualism, that is, the concept of the soul as being separable from the body, as the basis for the Christian traditional dualism. However, she errs in assuming that both creator and his "doppelgänger" are spiritual or concerned with the spiritual (1960:169). Dualism includes one material entity and, specifically in earth-diver dualism, one element deals with dirt while the other creates beauty and valuable substance from the dirt.

It should be noted that earth-diver has been previously studied from a psychoanalytic perspective. Géza Róheim, the first psychoanalytic anthropologist, made a great number of studies of the folklore and mythology of primitive peoples. In his earlier writings, Róheim tended to follow along the lines suggested by Freud, Abraham, and Rank in seeing folk tales as analogous to dreams (1922: 182), but later, after he discovered, for example, that the Aranda word *altjira* meant both dream and folk tale (1941: 267), he began to speculate as to a more genetic relationship between dream and folk tale or myth. In a posthumously published paper, "Fairy Tale and Dream" (1953a), this new theory of mythology and the folk tale is explained. "To put this theory briefly: It seems that dreams and myths are not merely similar but that a large part of mythology is actually derived from dreams. In other words, we can not only apply the standard technique of dream interpretation in analyzing a fairy tale but can actually think of tales and myths as having arisen from a dream, which a person dreamed and then told to others, who retold it again, perhaps elaborated in accord with their own dreams" (1953a: 394; for a sample of Róheim's exegesis of what he terms a dream-derived folk tale, see 1953b). The obvious criticism of this theory has been made by E. K. Schwartz in noting that "one can accept the same psychoanalytic approach and techniques for the understanding of the fairy tale and the dream, without having to accept the hypothesis that the fairy tale is nothing else but an elaboration of a dream" (1956: 747–748). Thus Schwartz, although he lists 12 characteristics of fairy tales which he also finds in dreams, including such features as condensation, displacement, symbolism, etc., does conclude that it is not necessary to assume that fairy tales are dreams. Róheim, in *The Gates of the Dream*, a brilliant if somewhat erratic full-length treatment of primitive myth and dream, had already addressed himself to this very criticism. He phrases the criticism rhetorically: "Then why assume the dream stage, since the unconscious would contain the same elements, even without dreams?" His answer is that the dream theory would explain not only the identity in content but also the striking similarity in structure and plot sequence (1951: 348). Actually, the fundamental criticism is not completely explained away. There is no reason why both dream and myth cannot be derived from the human mind without making the myth only indirectly derived via the dream.

Róheim's theory comes to the fore in his analysis of earth-diver. In fact, he even states that the earth-diver myth is "a striking illustration of the dream origin of mythology" (1951: 423). Róheim has assumed the existence of what he calls a basic dream in which the dreamer falls into something, such as a lake or a hole. According to Róheim, this dream is characterized by a "double vector" movement consisting both of a regression to the womb and the idea of the body as penis entering the vagina. In interpreting the earth-diver as an example of this basic dream, Róheim considers the diving into the primeval waters of the womb as an erection. Of considerable theoretical interest is Róheim's apparent postulation of a monogenetic origin of earth-diver: "*The core of the myth is a dream actually dreamed once upon a time by one person.* Told and retold it became a myth. . . ." (1951: 428). Actually, Róheim's over-all theory of the dream origin of myth is not at all necessarily a matter of monogenesis. In fact, he states that it is hardly likely as a general rule that an original dream was dreamed by one person in a definite locality, from which the story spread by migration. Rather, "many have dreamed such dreams, they shaped the narrative form in many centers, became traditional, then merged and influenced each other in the course of history" (1951: 348).

The validity of Róheim's interpretation of earth-diver depends a great deal on, first of all, his theory of the dream origin of myth and, secondly, the specific nature of his so-called basic dream. One could say, without going as far as to deny categorically Róheim's theoretical contentions, that neither the dream origin of myth nor the existence of the "basic dream" is necessary for an understanding of the latent content of the earth-diver myth. Curiously enough, Róheim himself anticipates in part the present hypothesis in the course of making some additional comments on earth-diver. In discussing the characteristic trait of the gradual growth of the earth, Róheim cites an Onondaga version in which he points out the parallelism between a pregnant woman and the growing earth. From the point of view of the present hypothesis, the parallelism is quite logically attributable to the male creator's desire to achieve something like female procreativity. Thus the substance produced from his body, his baby so to speak, must gradually increase in size, just as the process of female creativity entails a gradually increasing expansion. (Here again, the observation of the apparently magically expanding belly of a pregnant woman is clearly a human universal.) Róheim goes on to mention what he considers to be a parallel myth, namely that of "the egg-born earth or cloacal creation." As will be shown later, Róheim is quite correct in drawing attention to the egg myth. Then following his discussion of the Eurasian dualistic version in which the devil tries to keep a piece of swelling earth in his mouth, Róheim makes the following analysis: "If we substitute the rectum for the mouth the myth makes sense as an awakening dream conditioned by excremental pressure" (1951: 429). In other words, Róheim does recognize the excremental aspects of earth-diver and in accordance with his theory of the dream origin of myth, he considers the myth as initially a dream caused by the purely organic stimulus of the need to defecate. Róheim also follows Rank (1912, 1922: 89) in interpreting deluge myths as transformations of vesical dreams (1951: 439–465). Certainly, one could make a good case for the idea that some folk tales and myths are based upon excremental pressures, perhaps originally occurring during sleep. In European folklore, there are numerous examples, as Freud and Oppenheim have amply demonstrated, of folk tales which relate how individuals attempt to mark buried treasure only to awake to find they have defecated on themselves or on their sleeping partners. It is quite possible that there is a similar basis for the Winnebago story reported by Radin (1956: 26–27) in which Trickster, after eating a laxative bulb, begins to defecate endlessly. In order to escape the rising level of excrement, Trickster climbs a tree, but he is forced to go higher and higher until he finally falls down right into the rising tide. Another version of this Trickster adventure is found in Barnouw's account of a Chippewa cycle (1955: 82). The idea of the movement being impossible to stop once it has started is also suggested in the previously cited Eurasian account of Gods's inability to stop the earth's growth. That God must eat excrement to stop the movement is thematically similar to another Trickster version in which Trickster's own excrement, rising with flood waters, comes perilously close to his mouth and nose. However, the fact that there may be "excremental pressure myths" with or without a dream origin does not mean that excremental pressure is the sole underlying motivation of such a myth as earth-diver. To call earth-diver simply a dream-like myth resulting from a call of nature without reference to the notions of male pregnancy envy and anal birth theory is vastly to oversimplify the psychological etiology of the myth. Róheim, by the way, never does reconcile the rather phallic interpretation of his basic dream with the excremental awakening dream interpretation of earth-diver. A multi-causal hypothesis is, of course, perfectly possible, but Róheim's two interpretations seem rather to conflict. In any event, Róheim sees creation myths as prime examples of his dream-myth thesis. He says, "It seems very probably that creation myths, wherever they exist, are ultimately based on dreams" (1951: 430).

The idea of anal creation myths spurred by male pregnancy envy is not tied to the dream origin of myth theory. That is not to say that the dream theory is not entirely possible but only to affirm the independence of the two hypotheses. In order to document further the psychological explanation of earth-diver, several other creation myths will be very briefly discussed. As already mentioned, Róheim drew attention to the cosmic egg myths. There is clinical evidence suggesting that men who have pregnancy phantasies often evince a special interest in the activities of hens, particularly with regard to their laying of eggs (Eisler, 1921: 260, 285). The hens appear to defecate the eggs. Freud's famous "Little Hans" in addition to formulating a "lumf" baby theory also imagined that he laid an egg (1949: 227–228). Lombroso (1895: 182) mentions a demented pseudo-artist who painted himself as excreting eggs which symbolized worlds. Ferenczi, moreover, specifically comments upon what he calls the "symbolic identity of the egg with faeces and child." He suggests that excessive fondness for eggs "approximates much more closely to primitive coprophilia than does the more abstract love of money:" (1950: 328). Certainly the egg-creation myth is common enough throughout the world (Lukas, 1894), despite its absence in North America. It is noteworthy that there are creations of men from eggs . . . and creation of the world from a cosmic egg. . . . As in the case of feces (or mud, clay, or dirt), the cloacal creation is capable of producing either men or worlds or both.

Another anal creation myth which does occur in aboriginal North America has the spider as creator. The Spider myth, which is one of Rooth's eight creation myth types found in North America, is reported primarily in California and the Southwest. The spider as creator is also found in Asia and Africa. Empirical observation of spiders would quite easily give rise to the notion of the spider as a self-sufficient creator who appeared to excrete his own world, and a beautiful and artistic world at that. Although psychoanalysts have generally tended to interpret the spider as a mother symbol (Abraham, 1948: 326–332; cf. Spider Woman in the Southwest), Freud noted at least one instance in folklore where the thread spun by a spider was a symbol of evacuated feces. In a Prussian-Silesian tale, a peasant wishing to return to earth from heaven is turned into a spider by Peter. As a spider, the peasant spins a long thread by which he descends, but he is horrified to discover as he arrives just over his home that he could spin no more. He squeezes and squeezes to make the thread longer and then suddenly wakes up from his dream to discover that "something very human had happened to him while he slept" (Freud and Oppenheim 1958: 45). The spider as the perfect symbol of male artistic creativity is described in a poem by Whitman entitled "The Spider." In the poem, the spider is compared to the soul of the poet as it stands detached and alone in "measureless oceans of space" launching forth filament out of itself (Wilbur and Muensterberger

1951: 405). Without going into primitive Spider creation myths in great detail, it should suffice to note that, as in other types of male myths of creation, the creator is able to create without any reference to women. Whether a male creator spins material, molds clay, lays an egg, fabricates from mucus or epidermal tissue, or dives for fecal mud, the psychological motivation is much the same.

Other cosmogonic depictions of anal birth have been barely touched upon. As Ernest Jones has shown in some detail (1951: 266–357), some of the other aspects of defecation such as the sound (creation by thunder or the spoken word), or the passage of air (creation by wind or breath), are also of considerable importance in the study of mythology. With respect to the latter characteristic, there is the obvious Vedic example of Pragapati who created mankind by means of "downward breathings" from the "back part" cited by Jones (1951: 279). One account of Pragapati's creation of the earth relates the passing of air with the earth-diver story. "Pragapati first becomes a wind and stirs up the primeval ocean; he sees the earth in the depths of the ocean; he turns himself into a boar and draws the the earth up" (Dragomanov, 1961: 28). Another ancient male anal wind myth is found in the Babylonian account of Marduk. Marduk conquers Tiamat by the following means: "The evil wind which followed him, he loosed it in her face.... He drove in the evil wind so that she could not close her lips. The terrible winds filled her belly" (Guirand, 1959: 51). Marduk then pierces Tiamat's belly and kills her. The passage of wind by the male Marduk leads to the destruction of the female Tiamat. Marduk rips open the rival creator, the belly of woman, which had given birth to the world. There is also the Biblical instance of the divine (af) flatus moving on the face of the waters. Köngas (1960: 169) made a very astute intuitive observation when she suggested that there was a basic similarity between the spirit of God moving upon the primeval water and the earth-diver myth. The common denominator is the male myth of creation whereby the male creator uses various aspects of the only means available, namely the creative power of the anus.

Undoubtedly anthropologists will be sceptical of any presentation in which evidence is marshalled à la Frazer and where the only criteria for the evidence appears to be the gristworthyness for the mill. Nevertheless, what is important is the possibility of a theory of universal symbolism which can be verified by empirical observation in the field in decades to come. Kluckhohn, despite a deep-seated mistrust of pan-human symbolism, confesses that his own field work as well as that of his collaborators has forced him to the conclusion that "Freud and other psychoanalysts have depicted with astonishing correctness many central themes in motivational life which are universal. The styles of expression of these themes and much of the manifest content are culturally determined but the underlying psychological drama transcends cultural difference" (Wilbur and Muensterberger, 1951: 120). Kluckhohn bases his assumptions on the notion of a limited number of human "givens," such as human anatomy and physiology. While it is true that thoughts about the "givens" are not "given" in the same sense, it may be that their arising is inevitable. In other words, man is not born with the idea of pregnancy envy. It is acquired through experience, that is, through the mediation of culture. But if certain experiences are universal, such as the observation of female pregnancy, then there may be said to be secondary or derived "givens," using the term in an admittedly idiosyncratic sense. This is very important for the study of myth. It has already been pointed out that from a cultural relativistic perspective, the only portion of mythology which can be profitably studied is limited to those myths which are peculiar to a particular culture or those differences in the details of a widely diffused myth. Similarly, the literal approach can glean only so much ethnographic data from reflector myths. Without the assumption of symbolism and universals in myth, a vast amount of mythology remains of little use to the anthropologist. It should also be noted that there is, in theory, no conflict between accepting the idea of universals and advocating cultural relativism. It is not an "either/or" proposition. Some myths may be universal and others not. It is the all-or-nothing approach which appears to be erroneous. The same is true for the polygenesis-diffusion controversy; they also are by no means mutually exclusive. In the same way, there is no inconsistency in the statement that myths can either reflect or refract culture. (The phrase was suggested by A. K. Ramanujan.) Lévi-Strauss (1958: 51) criticizes psychoanalytic interpretations of myth because, as he puts it, if there's an evil grandmother in the myths, "it will be claimed that in such a society grandmothers are actually evil and that mythology reflects the social structure and the social relations; but should the actual data be conflicting, it would be readily claimed that the purpose of mythology is to provide an outlet for repressed feelings. Whatever the situation may be, a clever dialectic will always find a way to pretend that a meaning has been unravelled." Although Lévi-Strauss may be justified insofar as he is attacking the "Have you stopped beating your wife?" antics of some psychoanalysts, there is not necessarily any inconsistency stemming from data showing that in culture A evil grandmothers in fact are also found in myth, while in culture B conscious norms of pleasant grandmothers disguise unconscious hatred for "evil" grandmothers, a situation which may be expressed in myth. In other words, myths can and usually do contain both conscious and unconscious cultural materials. To the extent that conscious and unconscious motivation may vary or be contradictory, so likewise can myth differ from or contradict enthnographic data. There is no safe monolithic theory of myth except that of judicious eclecticism as championed by E. B. Tylor. Mythology must be studied in cultural context in order to determine which individual mythological elements reflect and which refract the culture. But, more than this, the cultural relative approach must not preclude the recognition and identification of transcultural similarities and potential universals. As Kluckhohn said, "... the anthropologist for two generations has been obsessed with the differences between peoples, neglecting the equally real similarities—upon which the 'universal culture pattern' as well as the psychological uniformities are clearly built" (Wilbur and Muensterberger, 1951: 121). The theoretical implications for practical field work of seeking psychological uniformities are implicit. Ethnographers must remove the traditional blinders and must be willing to collect *all* pertinent material even if it borders on what is obscene by the ethnographer's ethnocentric standards. The ideal ethnographer must not be afraid of diving deep and coming up with a little dirt; for, as the myth relates, such a particle may prove immensely valuable and may expand so as to form an entirely new world for the students of man.

Claude Lévi-Strauss

THE STRUCTURAL STUDY OF MYTH

The eminent French anthropologist Claude Lévi-Strauss has been providing the anthropological world with a most stimulating and provocative series of articles and books in the past decade, several of them dealing with the analysis of myths, rituals, and native categories of thought. In our judgment, his key paper on myth is "The Structural Study of Myth," which was first published in the *Journal of American Folklore* in 1955 but was revised by the author for his *Anthropologie structurale* (1958) and then translated into English for *Structural Anthropology* (1963).

In this article Lévi-Strauss makes the suggestion that our sociological and psychological interpretations of mythology have up to this point been far too facile. As he expresses it:

> *If a given mythology confers prominence to a certain character, let us say an evil grandmother, it will be claimed that in such a society grandmothers are actually evil and that mythology reflects the social structure and the social relations; but should the actual data be conflicting, it would be readily claimed that the purpose of mythology is to provide an outlet for repressed feelings. Whatever the situation may be, a clever dialectic will always find a way to pretend that a meaning has been unravelled.*

He therefore suggests that the basic function of myth is to furnish a culture with a "logical" model by means of which the human mind can

Reprinted from the *Journal of American Folklore*, LXVII (1955), 428–444, by permission of the author and The American Folklore Society, Inc.

evade unwelcome contradictions, and he proceeds to apply this theory to the Oedipus myth and to the Zuni emergence myth.

As the student who attempts to put this provocative theory to a test will soon discover, there are a number of exceedingly difficult operational problems, of which we will mention only a few. Lévi-Strauss suggests that the analysis proceed by dividing the myth into "the shortest possible sentences, and writing each sentence on an index card bearing a number corresponding to the unfolding of the story." The problem here is that if the analyst is operating in the native language (say Zuni), how does he decide on what are "the shortest possible sentences?" Lévi-Strauss then goes on to propose that the cards be arranged into columns, so that ultimately the myth reads like an orchestra score. There is a question as to whether two or more analysts, working independently, will end up with the same cards in the same columns. Finally, we may ask precisely how an analyst moves from short sentences on index cards to the quite general themes presented in, for example, the four columns devoted to the Oedipus myth.

But having presented these operational difficulties, we are left with the conviction that there is a novel, and we hope ultimately testable, theory in this notion of Lévi-Strauss about mythology. We present his article in order that new students can profit by the insights and proceed to cope with the methodological problems.

1.0. Despite some recent attempts to renew them, it would seem that during the past twenty years anthropology has more and more turned away from studies in the field of religion. At the same time, and precisely because professional anthropologists' interest has withdrawn from primitive religion, all kinds of amateurs who claim to belong to other disciplines have seized this opportunity to move in, thereby turning into their private playground what we had left as a wasteland. Thus, the prospects for the scientific study of religion have been undermined in two ways.

1.1. The explanation for that situation lies to some extent in the fact that the anthropological study of religion was started by men like Tylor, Frazer, and Durkheim who were psychologically oriented, although not in a position to keep up with the progress of psychological research and theory. Therefore, their interpretations soon became vitiated by the outmoded psychological approach which they used as their backing. Although they were undoubtedly right in giving their attention to intellectual processes, the way they handled them remained so coarse as to discredit them altogether. This is much to be regretted since, as Hocart so profoundly noticed in his introduction to a posthumous book recently published, psychological interpretations were withdrawn from the intellectual field only to be introduced again in the field of affectivity, thus adding to "the inherent defects of the psychological school . . . the mistake of deriving clear-cut ideas . . . from vague emotions." Instead of trying to enlarge the framework of our logic to include processes which, whatever their apparent differences, belong to the same kind of intellectual operations, a naïve attempt was made to reduce them to inarticulate emotional drives which resulted only in withering our studies.

1.2. Of all the chapters of religious anthropology probably none has tarried to the same extent as studies in the field of mythology. From a theoretical point of view the situation remains very much the same as it was fifty years ago, namely, a picture of chaos. Myths are still widely interpreted in conflicting ways: collective dreams, the outcome of a kind of esthetic play, the foundation of ritual. . . . Mythological figures are considered as personified abstractions, divinized heroes or decayed gods. Whatever the hypothesis, the choice amounts to reducing mythology either to an idle play or to a coarse kind of speculation.

1.3. In order to understand what a myth really is, are we compelled to choose between platitude and sophism? Some claim that human societies merely express, through their mythology, fundamental feelings common to the whole of mankind, such as love, hate, revenge; or that they try to provide some kind of explanations for phenomena which they cannot understand otherwise: astronomical, meteorological, and the like. But why should these societies do it in such elaborate and devious ways, since all of them are also acquainted with positive explanations? On the other hand, psychoanalysts and many anthropologists have shifted the problems to be explained away from the natural or cosmological towards the sociological and psychological fields. But then the interpretation becomes too easy: if a given mythology confers prominence to a certain character, let us say an evil grandmother, it will be claimed that in such a society grandmothers are actually evil and that mythology reflects the social structure and the social relations; but should the actual data be conflicting, it would be readily claimed that the purpose of mythology is to provide an outlet for repressed feelings. Whatever the situation may be, a clever dialectic will always find a way to pretend that a meaning has been unraveled.

2.0. Mythology confronts the student with a situation which at first sight could be looked upon as contradictory. On the one hand, it would seem that in the course of a myth anything is likely to happen. There is no logic, no continuity. Any characteristic can be attributed to any subject; every conceivable relation can be met. With myth, everything becomes possible. But on the other hand, this apparent arbitrariness is belied by the astounding similarity between myths collected in widely different regions. Therefore the problem: if the content of a myth is contingent, how are we going to explain that throughout the world myths do resemble one another so much?

2.1. It is precisely this awareness of a basic antinomy pertaining to the nature of myth that may lead us towards its solution. For the contradiction which we face is very similar to that which in earlier times brought considerable worry to the first philosophers concerned with linguistic problems; linguistics could only begin to evolve as a science after this contradiction had been overcome. Ancient philosophers were reasoning about language the way we are about mythology. On the one hand, they did notice that in a given language certain sequences of sounds were associated with definite meanings, and they earnestly aimed at discovering a reason for the linkage between those sounds and that meaning. Their attempt, however, was thwarted from the very beginning by the fact that the same sounds were equally present in other languages though the meaning they conveyed was entirely different. The contradiction was surmounted only by the discovery that it is the combination of sounds, not the sounds in themselves, which provides the significant data.

2.2. Now, it is easy to see that some of the more recent interpretations of mythological thought originated from the same kind of misconception under which those early linguists were laboring. Let us consider, for instance, Jung's idea that a given mythological pattern — the so-called archetype — possesses a certain signification. This is comparable to the long supported error that a sound may possess a certain affinity with a meaning: for instance, the "liquid" semivowels with water, the open vowels with things that are big, large, loud, or heavy, etc., a kind of theory which still has its supporters. Whatever emendations the original formulation may now call for, everybody will agree that the Saussurean principle of the arbitrary character of the linguistic signs was a prerequisite for the acceding of linguistics to the scientific level.

2.3. To invite the mythologist to compare his precarious situation with that of the linguist in the prescientific stage is not enough. As a matter of fact we may thus be led only from one difficulty to another. There is a very good reason why myth cannot simply be treated as language if its specific problems are to be solved; myth *is* language: to be known, myth has to be told; it is a part of human speech. In order to preserve its specificity we should thus put ourselves in a position to show that it is both the same thing as language, and also something different from it. Here, too, the past experience of linguists may help us. For language itself can be analyzed into things which are at the same time similar and different. This is precisely what is expressed in Saussure's distinction between *langue* and *parole*, one being the structural side of language, the other the statistical aspect of it, *langue* belonging to a revertible time, whereas *parole* is non-revertible. If those two levels already exist in language, then a third one can conceivably be isolated.

2.4. We have just distinguished *langue* and *parole* by the different time referents which they use. Keeping this in mind, we may notice that myth uses a third referent which combines the properties of the first two. On the one hand, a myth always refers to events alleged to have taken place in time: before the world was created, or during its first stages—anyway, long ago. But what gives the myth an operative value is that the specific pattern described is everlasting; it explains the present and the past as well as the future. This can be made clear through a comparison between myth and what appears to have largely replaced it in modern societies, namely, politics. When the historian refers to the French Revolution it is always as a sequence of past happenings, a non-revertible series of events the remote consequences of which may still be felt at present. But to the French politician, as well as to his followers, the French Revolution is both a sequence belonging to the past—as to the historian—and an everlasting pattern which can be detected in the present French social structure and which provides a clue for its interpretation, a lead from which to infer the future developments. See, for instance, Michelet who was a politically-minded historian. He describes the French Revolution thus: "This day . . . everything was possible. . . . Future became present . . . that is, no more time, a glimpse of eternity." It is that double structure, altogether historical and ahistorical, which explains that myth, while pertaining to the realm of the *parole* and calling for an explanation as such, as well as to that of the *langue* in which it is expressed, can also be an absolute object on a third level which, though it remains linguistic by nature, is nevertheless distinct from the other two.

2.5. A remark can be introduced at this point which will help to show the singularity of myth among other linguistic phenomena. Myth is the part of language where the formula *traduttore, tradittore* reaches its lowest truth-value. From that point of view it should be put in the whole gamut of linguistic expressions at the end opposite to that of poetry, in spite of all the claims which have been made to prove the contrary. Poetry is a kind of speech which cannot be translated except at the cost of serious distortions; whereas the mythical value of the myth remains preserved, even through the worst translation. Whatever our ignorance of the language and the culture of the people where it originated, a myth is still felt as a myth by any reader throughout the world. Its substance does not lie in its style, its original music, or its syntax, but in the story which it tells. It is language, functioning on an especially high level where meaning succeeds practically at "taking off" from the linguistic ground on which it keeps on rolling.

2.6. To sum up the discussion at this point, we have so far made the following claims: 1. If there is a meaning to be found in mythology, this cannot reside in the isolated elements which enter into the composition of a myth, but only in the way those elements are combined. 2. Although myth belongs to the same category as language, being, as a matter of fact, only part of it, language in myth unveils specific properties. 3. Those properties are only to be found *above* the ordinary linguistic level; that is, they exhibit more complex features beside those which are to be found in any kind of linguistic expression.

3.0. If the above three points are granted, at least as a working hypothesis, two consequences will follow: 1. Myth, like the rest of language, is made up of constituent units. 2. These constituent units presuppose the constituent units present in language when analyzed on other levels, namely, phonemes, morphemes, and semantemes, but they, nevertheless, differ from the latter in the same way as they themselves differ from morphemes, and these from phonemes; they belong to a higher order, a more complex one. For this reason, we will call them *gross constituent units*.

3.1. How shall we proceed in order to identify and isolate these gross constituent units? We know that they cannot be found among phonemes, morphemes, or semantemes, but only on a higher level; otherwise myth would become confused with any other kind of speech. Therefore, we should look for them on the sentence level. The only method we can suggest at this stage is to proceed tentatively, by trial and error, using as a check the principles which serve as a basis for any kind of structural analysis: economy of explanation; unity of solution; and ability to reconstruct the whole from a fragment, as well as further stages from previous ones.

3.2. The technique which has been applied so far by this writer consists in analyzing each myth individually, breaking down its story into the shortest possible sentences, and writing each such sentence on an index card bearing a number corresponding to the unfolding of the story.

3.3. Practically each card will thus show that a certain function is, at a given time, predicated to a given subject. Or, to put it otherwise, each gross constituent unit will consist in a relation.

3.4. However, the above definition remains highly unsatisfactory for two different reasons. In the first place, it is well known to structural linguists that constituent units on all levels are made up of relations and the true difference between our gross units and the others stays unexplained; moreover, we still find ourselves in the realm of a non-revertible time since the numbers of the cards correspond to the unfolding of the informant's speech. Thus, the specific character of mythological time, which as we have seen is both revertible and non-revertible, synchronic and diachronic, remains unaccounted for. Therefrom comes a new hypothesis which constitutes the very core of our argument: the true constituent units of a myth are not the isolated relations but *bundles of such relations* and it is only as bundles that these relations can be put to use and combined so as to produce a meaning. Relations pertaining to the same bundle may appear diachronically at remote intervals, but when we have succeeded in grouping them together, we have reorganized our myth according to a time referent of a new nature corresponding to the prerequisite of the initial hypothesis, namely, a two-dimensional time referent which is simultaneously diachronic and synchronic and which accordingly integrates the characteristics of the *langue* on one hand, and those of the *parole* on the other. To put it in even more linguistic terms, it is as though a phoneme were always made up of all its variants.

4.0. Two comparisons may help to explain what we have in mind.

4.1. Let us first suppose that archaeologists of the future coming from another planet would one day, when all human life had disappeared from the earth, excavate one of our libraries. Even if they were at first ignorant of our writing, they might succeed in deciphering it—an undertaking which would require, at some early stage, the discovery that the alphabet, as we are in the habit of printing it, should be read from left to right and from top to bottom. However, they would soon find out that a whole category of books did not fit the usual pattern: these would be the orchestra scores on the shelves of the music division. But after trying, without success, to decipher staffs one after the other, from the upper down to the lower, they would probably notice that the same patterns of notes recurred at intervals, either in full or in part, or that some patterns were strongly reminiscent of earlier ones. Hence the hypothesis: what if patterns showing affinity, instead of being considered in succession, were to be treated as one complex pattern and read globally? By getting at what we call *harmony*, they would then find out that an orchestra score, in order to become meaningful, has to be read diachronically along one axis—that is, page after page, and from left to right—and also synchronically along the other axis, all the notes which are written vertically making up one gross constituent unit, i.e. one bundle of relations.

4.2. The other comparison is somewhat different. Let us take an observer ignorant of our playing cards, sitting for a long time with a fortune-teller. He would know something of the visitors: sex, age, look, social situation, etc. in the same way as we know something of the different cultures whose myths we try to study. He would also listen to the séances and keep them recorded so as to be able to go over them and make comparisons—as we do when we listen to myth telling and record it. Mathematicians to whom I have put the problem agree that if the man is bright and if the material available to him is sufficient, he may be able to reconstruct the nature of the deck of cards being used, that is: fifty-two or thirty-two cards according to case, made up of four homologous series consisting of the same units (the individual cards) with only one varying feature, the suit.

4.3. The time has come to give a concrete example of the method we propose. We will use the Oedipus myth which has the advantage of being well-known to everybody and for which no preliminary explanation is therefore neeeded. By doing so, I am well aware that the Oedipus myth has only reached us under late forms and through literary transfigurations concerned more with esthetic and moral preoccupations than with religious or ritual ones, whatever these may have been. But as will be shown later, this apparently unsatisfactory situation will strengthen our demonstration rather than weaken it.

4.4. The myth will be treated as would be an orchestra score perversely presented as a unilinear series and where our task is to reestablish the correct disposition. As if, for instance, we were confronted with a sequence of the type: 1,2,4,7,8,2,3,4,6,8,1,4,5,7,8, 1,2,5,7,3,4,5,6,8 . . ., the assignment being to put all the 1's together, all the 2's, and 3's, etc.; the result is a chart:

1	2		4			7	8
	2	3	4		6		8
1			4	5		7	8
1	2			5		7	
		3	4	5			
					6		8

4.5. We will attempt to perform the same kind of operation on the Oedipus myth, trying out several dispositions until we find one which is in harmony with the principles enumerated under 3.1. Let us suppose, for the sake of argument, that the best arrangement is the [one shown in Chart 1] (although it might certainly be improved by the help of a specialist in Greek mythology).

4.6. Thus, we find ourselves confronted with four vertical columns each of which include several relations belonging to the same bundle. Were we to *tell* the myth, we would disregard the columns and read the rows from left to right and from top to bottom. But if we want to *understand* the myth, then we will have to disregard one half of the diachronic dimension (top to bottom) and read from left to right, column after column, each one being considered as a unit.

4.7. All the relations belonging to the same column exhibit one common feature which it is our task to unravel. For instance, all the events grouped in the first column on the left have something to do with blood relations which are over-emphasized, i.e. are subject to a more intimate treatment than they should be. Let us say, then, that the first column has as its common feature the *overrating of blood relations*. It is obvious that the second column expresses the same thing, but inverted: *underrating of blood relations*. The third column refers to monsters being slain. As to the fourth, a word of clarification is needed. The remarkable connotation of the surnames in Oedipus' father-line has often been noticed. However, linguists usually disregard it, since to them the only way to define the meaning of a term is to investigate all the contexts in which it appears, and personal names, precisely because they are used as such, are not accompanied by any context. With the method we propose to follow the objection disappears since the myth itself provides its own context. The meaningful fact is no longer to be looked for in the eventual sense of each name, but in the fact that all the names have a common feature: i.e. that they may eventually mean something and that all these hypothetical meanings (which may well remain hypothetical) exhibit a common feature, namely they refer to *difficulties to walk and to behave straight*.

4.8. What is then the relationship between the two columns on the right? Column three refers to monsters. The dragon is a chthonian being which has to be killed in order that mankind be born from the earth; the Sphinx is a monster unwilling to permit men to live. The last unit reproduces the first one which has to do with the *autochthonous origin* of mankind. Since the monsters are overcome by men, we may thus say that the common feature of the third column is *the denial of the autochthonous origin of man.*

4.9. This immediately helps us to understand the meaning of the fourth column. In mythology it is a universal character of men born from the earth that at the moment they emerge from the depth, they either cannot walk or do it clumsily. This is the case of the chthonian beings in the mythology of the Pueblo: Masauwu, who leads the emergence, and the chthonian Shumaikoli are lame ("bleeding-foot," "sore-foot"). The same happens to the Koskimo of the Kwakiutl after they have been swallowed by the chthonian monster, Tsiakish: when they returned to the surface of the earth "they limped forward or tripped sideways." Then the common feature of the fourth column is: *the persistence of the autochthonous origin of man.* It follows that column four is to column three as column one is to column two. The inability to connect two kinds of relationships is overcome (or rather replaced) by the positive statement that contradictory relationships are identical inasmuch as they are both self-contradictory in a similar way. Although this is still a provisional formulation of the structure of mythical thought, it is sufficient at this stage.

4.10. Turning back to the Oedipus myth, we may now see what it means. The myth

CHART 1

Kadmos seeks his sister Europa ravished by Zeus			
		Kadmos kills the dragon	
	The Spartoi kill each other		
			Labdacos (Laios' father) = *lame* (?)
	Oedipus kills his father Laios		
			Laios (Oedipus' father) = *left-sided* (?)
		Oedipus kills the Sphinx	
Oedipus marries his mother Jocasta			
	Eteocles kills his brother Polynices		
			Oedipus = *swollen foot* (?)
Antigone buries her brother Polynices despite prohibition			

has to do with the inability, for a culture which holds the belief that mankind is autochthonous (see, for instance, Pausanias, VIII, xxix, 4: vegetals provide a *model* for humans), to find a satisfactory transition between this theory and the knowledge that human beings are actually born from the union of man and woman. Although the problem obviously cannot be solved, the Oedipus myth provides a kind of logical tool which, to phrase it coarsely, replaces the original problem: born from one or born from two? born from different or born from same? By a correlation of this type, the overrating of blood relations is to the underrating of blood relations as the attempt to escape autochthony is to the impossibility to succeed in it. Although experience contradicts theory, social life verifies the cosmology by its similarity of structure. Hence cosmology is true.

4.11.0. Two remarks should be made at this stage.

4.11.1. In order to interpret the myth, we were able to leave aside a point which has until now worried the specialists, namely, that in the earlier (Homeric) versions of the Oedipus myth, some basic elements are lacking, such as Jocasta killing herself and Oedipus piercing his own eyes. These events do not alter the substance of the myth although they can easily be integrated, the first one as a new case of auto-destruction (column three) while the second is another case of crippledness (column four). At the same time there is something significant in these additions since the shift from foot to head is to be correlated with the shift from: autochthonous origin negated to: self-destruction.

4.11.2. Thus, our method eliminates a problem which has been so far one of the main obstacles to the progress of mythological studies, namely, the quest for the true version, or the *earlier* one. On the contrary, we define the myth as consisting of all its versions; to put it otherwise: a myth remains the same as long as it is felt as such. A striking example is offered by the fact that our interpretation may take into account, and is certainly applicable to, the Freudian use of the Oedipus myth. Although the Freudian problem has ceased to be that of autochthony versus bisexual reproduction, it is still the problem of understanding how one can be born from *two:* how is it that we do not have only one procreator, but a mother plus a father? Therefore, not only Sophocles, but Freud himself, should be included among the recorded versions of the Oedipus myth on a par with earlier or seemingly more "authentic" versions.

5.0. An important consequence follows. If a myth is made up of all its variants, structural analysis should take all of them into account. Thus, after analyzing all the known variants of the Theban version, we should treat the others in the same way: first, the tales about Labdacos' collateral line including Agavé, Pentheus, and Jocasta herself; the Theban variant about Lycos and Amphion and Zetos as the city founders; more remote variants concerning Dionysos (Oedipus' matrilateral cousin), and Athenian legends where Cecrops takes the place of Kadmos, etc. For each of them a similar chart should be drawn, and then compared and reorganized according to the findings: Cecrops killing the serpent with the parallel episode of Kadmos; abandonment of Dionysos with abandonment of Oedipus; "Swollen Foot" with Dionysos *loxias*, i.e. walking obliquely; Europa's quest with Antiope's; the foundation of Thebes by the Spartoi or by the brothers Amphion and Zetos; Zeus kidnapping Europa and Antiope and the same with Semele; the Theban Oedipus and the Argian Perseus, etc. We will then have several two-dimensional charts, each dealing with a variant, to be organized in a three-dimensional order so that three different readings become possible: left to right, top to bottom, front to back. All of these charts cannot be expected to be identical; but experience shows that any difference to be observed may be correlated with other differences, so that a logical treatment of the whole will allow simplifications, the final outcome being the structural law of the myth. [See Figure 1.]

5.1. One may object at this point that the task is impossible to perform since we can only work with known versions. Is it not possible that a new version might alter the picture? This is true enough if only one or two versions are available, but the objection becomes theoretical as soon as a reasonably large number has been recorded (a number

FIGURE 1

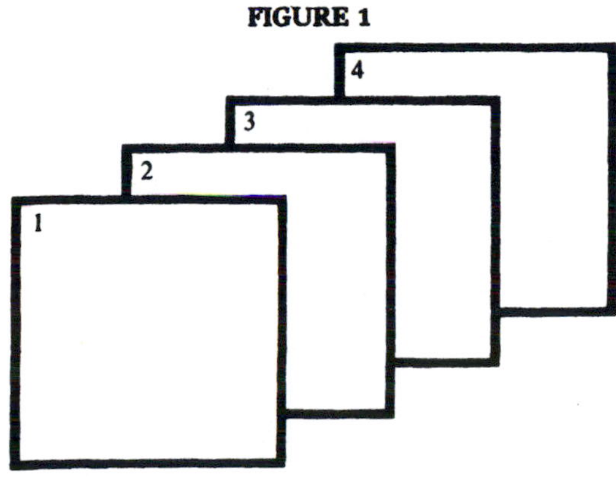

which experience will progressively tell, at least as an approximation). Let us make this point clear by a comparison. If the furniture of a room and the way it is arranged in the room were known to us only through its reflection in two mirrors placed on opposite walls, we would theoretically dispose of an almost infinite number of mirror-images which would provide us with a complete knowledge. However, should the two mirrors be obliquely set, the number of mirror-images would become very small; nevertheless, four or five such images would very likely give us, if not complete information, at least a sufficient coverage so that we would feel sure that no large piece of furniture is missing in our description.

5.2. On the other hand, it cannot be too strongly emphasized that all available variants should be taken into account. If Freudian comments on the Oedipus complex are a part of the Oedipus myth, then questions such as whether Cushing's version of the Zuni origin myth should be retained or discarded become irrelevant. There is no one true version of which all the others are but copies or distortions. Every version belongs to the myth.

5.3. Finally it can be understood why works on general mythology have given discouraging results. This comes from two reasons. First, comparative mythologists have picked up preferred versions instead of using them all. Second, we have seen that the structural analysis of *one* variant of *one* myth belonging to one tribe (in some cases, even *one* village) already requires two dimensions. When we use several variants of the same myth for the same tribe or village, the frame of reference becomes three-dimensional and as soon as we try to enlarge the comparison, the number of dimensions required increases to such an extent that it appears quite impossible to handle them intuitively. The confusions and platitudes which are the outcome of comparative mythology can be explained by the fact that multi-dimensional frames of reference cannot be ignored, or naïvely replaced by two- or three-dimensional ones. Indeed, progress in comparative mythology depends largely on the cooperation of mathematicians who would undertake to express in symbols multi-dimensional relations which cannot be handled otherwise.

6.0. In order to check this theory, an attempt was made in 1953–54 towards an exhaustive analysis of all the known versions of the Zuni origin and emergence myth: Cushing, 1883 and 1896; Stevenson, 1904; Parsons, 1923; Bunzel, 1932; Benedict, 1934. Furthermore, a preliminary attempt was made at a comparison of the results with similar myths in other Pueblo tribes, Western and Eastern. Finally, a test was undertaken with Plains mythology. In all cases, it was found that the theory was sound, and light was thrown, not only on North American

CHART 2

INCREASE			DEATH
mechanical growth of vegetals (used as ladders)	emergence led by Beloved Twins	sibling incest	gods kill children
food value of wild plants	migration led by the two Newekwe		magical contest with people of the dew (collecting wild food *versus* cultivation)
		sibling sacrificed (to gain victory)	
food value of cultivated plants		sibling adopted (in exchange for corn)	
periodical character of agricultural work			
			war against Kyanakwe (gardeners *versus* hunters)
hunting	war led by two war-gods		
			salvation of the tribe (center of the world found)
warfare		sibling sacrificed (to avoid flood)	
DEATH			PERMANENCY

mythology, but also on a previously unnoticed kind of logical operation, or one known only so far in a wholly different context. The bulk of material which needs to be handled almost at the beginning of the work makes it impossible to enter into details, and we will have to limit ourselves here to a few illustrations.

6.1. An over-simplified chart of the Zuni emergence myth would read as [shown in Chart 2].

6.2. As may be seen from a global inspection of the chart, the basic problem consists in discovering a mediation between life and death. For the Pueblo, the problem is especially difficult since they understand the origin of human life on the model of vegetal life (emergence from the earth). They share that belief with the ancient Greeks, and it is not without reason that we chose the Oedipus myth as our first example. But in the American case, the highest form of vegetal life is to be found in agriculture which is periodical in nature, i.e. which consists in an alternation between life and death. If this is disregarded, the contradiction surges at another place: agriculture provides food, therefore life; but hunting provides food and is similar to warfare which means death. Hence there are three different ways of handling the problem. In the Cushing version, the difficulty revolves around an opposition between activities yielding an immediate result (collecting wild food) and activities yielding a delayed result—death has to become integrated so that agriculture can exist. Parsons' version goes from hunting to agriculture, while Stevenson's version operates the other way around. It can be shown that all the differences between these versions can be rigorously correlated with these basic structures. [See Chart 3.]

Since fiber strings (vegetal) are always superior to sinew strings (animal) and since (to a lesser extent) the gods' alliance is preferable to their antagonism, it follows that in Cushing's version, men begin to be doubly underprivileged (hostile gods, sinew string); in Stevenson, doubly privileged (friendly gods, fiber string); while Parsons' version confronts us with an intermediary situation (friendly gods, but sinew strings since men begin by being hunters). Hence:

	CUSHING	PARSONS	STEVENSON
gods/men	-	+	+
fiber/sinew	-	-	+

6.3. Bunzel's version is from a structural point of view of the same type as Cushing's. However, it differs from both Cushing's and Stevenson's inasmuch as the latter two explain the emergence as a result of man's need to evade his pitiful condition, while Bunzel's version makes it the consequence of a call from the higher powers—hence the inverted sequences of the means resorted to for the emergence: in both Cushing and Stevenson, they go from plants to animals; in Bunzel, from mammals to insects and from insects to plants.

6.4. Among the Western Pueblo the logical approach always remains the same; the starting point and the point of arrival are the simplest ones and ambiguity is met with halfway. [See Figure 2.]

The fact that contradiction appears in the middle of the dialectical process has as its result the production of a double series of dioscuric pairs the purpose of which is to operate a mediation between conflicting terms [as shown in Chart 4], which consists in combinatory variants of the same function (hence the war attribute of the clowns which has given rise to so many queries).

6.5. Some Central and Eastern Pueblos proceed the other way around. They begin

CHART 3

	CUSHING	PARSONS	STEVENSON
Gods } Kyanakwe }	allied, use fiber strings on their bows (gardeners)	Kyanakwe alone, use fiber string	Gods } Men } allied, use fiber string
	VICTORIOUS OVER	VICTORIOUS OVER	VICTORIOUS OVER
Men	alone, use sinew (hunters) (until men shift to fiber)	Gods } Men } allied, use sinew string	Kyanakwe alone, use sinew string

CHART 4

1. 3 divine messengers	2 ceremonial clowns		2 war-gods
2. homogeneous pair: dioscurs (2 brothers)	siblings (brother and sister)	couple (husband and wife)	heterogeneous pair: grandmother/ grandchild

by stating the identity of hunting and cultivation (first corn obtained by Game-Father sowing deer-dewclaws), and they try to derive both life and death from that central notion. Then, instead of extreme terms being simple and intermediary ones duplicated as among the Western groups, the extreme terms become duplicated (i.e., the two sisters of the Eastern Pueblo) while a simple mediating term comes to the foreground (for instance, the Poshaiyanne of the Zia), but endowed with equivocal attributes. Hence the attributes of this "messiah" can be deduced from the place it occupies in the time sequence: good when at the beginning (Zuni, Cushing), equivocal in the middle (Central Pueblo), bad at the end (Zia), except in Bunzel where the sequence is reversed as has been shown.

6.6. By using systematically this kind of structural analysis it becomes possible to organize all the known variants of a myth as a series forming a kind of permutation group, the two variants placed at the far-ends being in a symmetrical, though inverted, relationship to each other.

7.0. Our method not only has the advantage of bringing some kind of order to what was previously chaos; it also enables us to perceive some basic logical processes which are at the root of mythical thought. Three main processes should be distinguished.

7.1.0. The trickster of American mythology has remained so far a problematic figure. Why is it that throughout North America his part is assigned practically everywhere to either coyote or raven? If we keep in mind that mythical thought always works from the awareness of oppositions towards their progressive mediation, the reason for those choices becomes clearer. We need only to assume that two opposite terms with no intermediary always tend to be replaced by two equivalent terms which allow a third one as a mediator; then one of the polar terms and the mediator become replaced by a new triad and so on. Thus we have:

INITIAL PAIR	FIRST TRIAD	SECOND TRIAD
Life		
	Agriculture	
		Herbivorous animals
		Carrion-eating animals (raven; coyote)
	Hunt	
		Prey animals
	War	
Death		

With the unformulated argument: carrion-eating animals are like prey animals (they eat animal food), but they are also like food-plant producers (they do not kill what they eat). Or, to put it otherwise, Pueblo style: ravens are to gardens as prey animals are to herbivorous ones. But it is also clear that herbivorous animals may be called first to act as mediators on the assumption that they are like collectors and gatherers (vegetal-food eaters) while they can be used as animal food though not themselves hunters. Thus we may have mediators on the first order, of the second order, and so on, where each term gives birth to the next by a double process of opposition and correlation.

7.1.1. This kind of process can be followed in the mythology of the Plains where we may order the data according to the sequence:

FIGURE 2

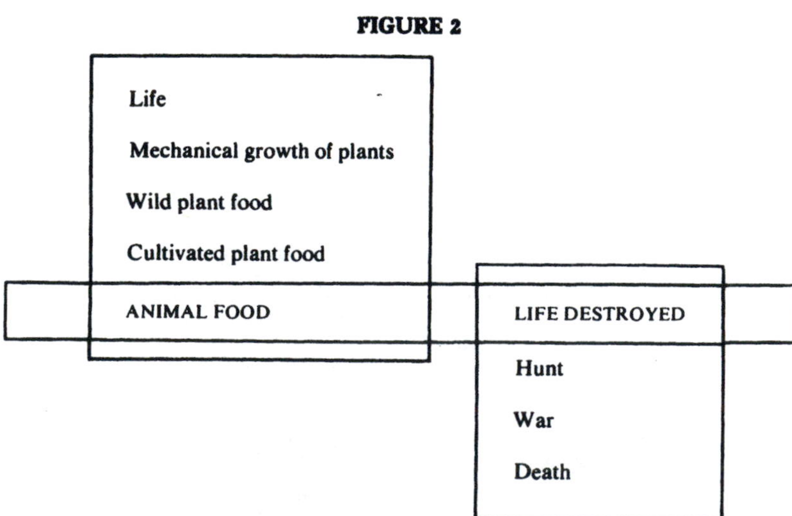

Unsuccessful mediator between earth and sky
(Star husband's wife)

Heterogeneous pair of mediators
(grandmother/grandchild)

Semi-homogeneous pair of mediators
(Lodge-Boy and Thrown-away)

While among the Pueblo we have:

Successful mediator between earth and sky
(Poshaiyanki)

Semi-homogeneous pair of mediators
(Uyuyewi and Matsailema)

Homogeneous pair of mediators
(the Ahaiyuta)

7.1.2. On the other hand, correlations may appear on a transversal axis (this is true even on the linguistic level; see the manifold connotation of the root *pose* in Tewa according to Parsons: coyote, mist, scalp, etc.). Coyote is intermediary between herbivorous and carnivorous in the same way as mist between sky and earth; scalp between war and hunt (scalp is war-crop); corn smut between wild plants and cultivated plants; garments between "nature" and "culture"; refuse between village and outside; ashes between roof and hearth (chimney). This string of mediators, if one may call them so, not only throws light on whole pieces of North American mythology—why the Dew-God may be at the same time the Game-Master and the giver of raiments and be personified as an "Ash-Boy"; or why the scalps are mist producing; or why the Game-Mother is associated with corn smut; etc.—but it also probably corresponds to a universal way of organizing daily experience. See, for instance, the French for vegetal smut, *nielle*, from Latin *nebula*; the luck-bringing power attributed to refuse (old shoe) and ashes (kissing chimneysweepers); and compare the American Ash-Boy cycle with the Indo-European Cinderella: both phallic figures (mediator between male and female); master of the dew and of the game; owners of fine raiments; and social bridges (low class marrying into high class); though impossible to interpret through recent diffusion as has been sometimes contended since Ash-Boy and Cinderella are symmetrical but inverted in every detail (while the borrowed Cinderella tale in America—Zuni Turkey-Girl—is parallel to the prototype) [as shown in Chart 5].

7.2.0. Thus, the mediating function of the trickster explains that since its position is halfway between two polar terms he must retain something of their duality, namely an ambiguous and equivocal character. But the trickster figure is not the only conceivable form of mediation; some myths seem to devote themselves to the task of exhausting all the possible solutions to the problem of bridging the gap between *two* and *one*. For instance, a comparison between all the variants of the Zuni emergence myth provides us with a series of mediating devices, each of which creates the next one by a process of opposition and correlation:

messiah > dioscurs > trickster > bisexual being >
sibling pair > married couple > grandmother-grandchild >
4 terms group > triad

In Cushing's version, this dialectic is accompanied by a change from the space dimension (mediating between sky and earth) to the time dimension (mediating between summer and winter, i.e., between birth and death). But while the shift is being made from space to time, the final solution (triad) re-introduces space, since a triad consists in a dioscur pair *plus* a messiah simultaneously present; and while the point of departure was ostensibly formulated in terms of a space referent (sky and earth) this was nevertheless implicitly conceived in terms of a time referent (first the messiah calls; *then* the dioscurs descend). Therefore the logic of myth confronts us with a double, reciprocal exchange of functions to which we shall return shortly (7.3).

7.2.1. Not only can we account for the ambiguous character of the trickster, but we may also understand another property of mythical figures the world over, namely, that the same god may be endowed with contradictory attributes; for instance, he may be

CHART 5

	EUROPE	AMERICA
Sex	female	male
Family status	double family	no family
Appearance	pretty girl	ugly boy
Sentimental status	nobody likes her	in hopeless love with girl
Transformation	luxuriously clothed with supernatural help	stripped of ugliness with supernatural help

good and bad at the same time. If we compare the variants of the Hopi myth of the origin of Shalako, we may order them so that the following structure becomes apparent:

$$(\text{Masauwu: } x) \simeq (\text{Muyingwu: Masauwu}) \simeq (\text{Shalako: Muyingwu}) \simeq (y\text{: Masauwu})$$

where *x* and *y* represent arbitrary values corresponding to the fact that in the two "extreme" variants the god Masauwu, while appearing alone instead of associated with another god, as in variant two, or being absent, as in three, still retains intrinsically a relative value. In variant one, Masauwu (alone) is depicted as helpful to mankind (though not as helpful as he could be), and in version four, harmful to mankind (though not as harmful as he could be); whereas in two, Muyingwu is relatively more helpful than Masauwu, and in three, Shalako more helpful than Muyingwu. We find an identical series when ordering the Keresan variants:

$$(\text{Poshaiyanki: } x) \simeq (\text{Lea:Poshaiyanki}) \simeq (\text{Poshaiyanki: Tiamoni}) \simeq (y\text{: Poshaiyanki})$$

7.2.2. This logical framework is particularly interesting since sociologists are already acquainted with it on two other levels: first, with the problem of the pecking order among hens; and second, it also corresponds to what this writer has called *general exchange* in the field of kinship. By recognizing it also on the level of mythical thought, we may find ourselves in a better position to appraise its basic importance in sociological studies and to give it a more inclusive theoretical interpretation.

7.3.0. Finally, when we have succeeded in organizing a whole series of variants in a kind of permutation group, we are in a position to formulate the law of that group. Although it is not possible at the present stage to come closer than an approximate formulation which will certainly need to be made more accurate in the future, it seems that every myth (considered as the collection of all its variants) corresponds to a formula of the following type:

$$^{f}x(a) : {}^{f}y(b) \simeq {}^{f}x(b) : {}^{f}a{-}I(y)$$

where, two terms being given as well as two functions of these terms, it is stated that a relation of equivalence still exists between two situations when terms and relations are inverted, under two conditions: 1. that one terms be replaced by its contrary; 2. that an inversion be made between the *function and the term* value of two elements.

7.3.1. This formula becomes highly significant when we recall that Freud considered that *two traumas* (and not one as it is so commonly said) are necessary in order to give birth to this individual myth in which a neurosis consists. By trying to apply the formula to the analysis of those traumatisms (and assuming that they correspond to conditions 1. and 2. respectively) we should not only be able to improve it, but would find ourselves in the much desired position of developing side by side the sociological and the psychological aspects of the theory; we may also take it to the laboratory and subject it to experimental verification.

8.0. At this point it seems unfortunate that, with the limited means at the disposal of French anthropological research, no further advance can be made. It should be emphasized that the task of analyzing mythological literature, which is extremely bulky, and of breaking it down into its constituent units, requires teams work and secretarial help. A variant of average length needs several hundred cards to be properly analyzed. To discover a suitable pattern of rows and columns for those cards, special devices are neeeded, consisting of vertical boards about two meters long and one and one-half meters high, where cards can be pigeon-holed and moved at will; in order to build up three-dimensional models enabling one to compare the variants, several such boards are necessary, and this in turn requires a spacious workshop, a kind of commodity particularly unavailable in Western Europe nowadays. Furthermore, as soon as the frame of reference becomes multi-dimensional (which occurs at an early stage, as has been shown in 5.3.) the board-system has to be replaced by perforated cards which in turn require I.B.M. equipment, etc. Since there is little hope that such facilities will become available in France in the near future, it is much desired that some American group, better equipped than we are here in Paris, will be induced by this paper to start a project of its own in structural mythology.

8.1.0. Three final remarks may serve as conclusion.

8.1.1. First, the question has often been raised why myths, and more generally oral literature, are so much addicted to duplication, triplication or quadruplication of the same sequence. If our hypotheses are accepted, the answer is obvious: repetition has as its function to make the structure of the myth apparent. For we have seen that the synchro-diachronical structure of the myth permits us to organize it into diachronical sequences (the rows in our tables) which should be read synchronically (the columns). Thus, a myth exhibits a "slated" structure which seeps to the surface, if one may say so, through the repetition process.

8.1.2. However, the slates are not absolutely identical to each other. And since the purpose of myth is to provide a logical model capable of overcoming a contradiction (an impossible achievement if, as it happens, the contradiction is real), a theoretically infinite number of slates will be generated, each one slightly different from the others. Thus, myth grows spiral-wise until the intellectual impulse which has originated it is exhausted. Its growth is a continuous process whereas its structure remains discontinuous. If this is the case we should consider that it closely corresponds, in the realm of the spoken word, to the kind of being a crystal is in the realm of physical matter. This analogy may help us understand better the relationship of myth on one hand to both *langue* and *parole* on the other.

8.1.3. Prevalent attempts to explain alleged differences between the so-called "primitive" mind and scientific thought have resorted to qualitative differences between the working processes of the mind in both cases while assuming that the objects to which they were applying themselves remained very much the same. If our interpretation is correct, we are led toward a completely different view, namely, that the kind of logic which is used by mythical thought is as rigorous as that of modern science, and that the difference lies not in the quality of the intellectual process, but in the nature of the things to which it is applied. This is well in agreement with the situation known to prevail in the field of technology: what makes a steel ax superior to a stone one is not that the first one is better made than the second. They are equally well made, but steel is a different thing than stone. In the same way we may be able to show that the same logical processes are put to use in myth as in science, and that man has always been thinking equally well; the improvement lies, not in an alleged progress of man's conscience, but in the discovery of new things to which it may apply its unchangeable abilities.

R. G. Willis

THE HEAD AND THE LOINS: LÉVI-STRAUSS AND BEYOND

R. G. Willis's paper, on a myth of a Bantu people of Africa, is both an excellent piece of analysis and a pertinent critique of Lévi-Strauss's methods for deriving binary discriminations in mythical thought. One of the most justifiable and frequently voiced criticisms of Lévi-Strauss's work is that the binary oppositions or discriminations which he claims to be the fundamental logical categories of mythical thought are in fact extremely difficult to verify or replicate with concrete ethnographic data. Some have suggested that this "intuitive flaw" makes his conceptual formulations extremely vulnerable to common, "grass-roots" ethnographic facts (Maybury-Lewis and others in Hayes and Hayes, 1970, and Leach, 1967a). Willis contends that binary discriminations in Fipa myth do have empirical referents in Fipa social life, and that without these concrete social facts, a Lévi-Straussian structural analysis of Fipa mythology might amount to no more than a "passionless structure of remote and mathematical beauty." Far from rejecting Lévi-Strauss's concepts, Willis uses and enriches them with ethnographic and affective data from Fipa social life. His paper may serve, therefore, as an object lesson to many who are stimulated and fascinated by the French professor's formulations, but who nevertheless remain skeptical of them. Willis has demonstrated that constructive skepticism of Lévi-Strauss and solid ethnographic data go very well together.

Reprinted from *Man*, II (1967), 519–534, by permission of the author and the Royal Anthropological Institute of Great Britain and Ireland.

This article examines, in a central African context, the relation between myth and social organization. This is a question which has been raised implicitly but acutely by the recent work of Lévi-Strauss (1964). The development of the analytical exposition of Amerindian mythology in *Le Cru et le cuit* strongly suggests that the structural solidity for the analyst of mythological thought varies inversely with its distance from ethnographical reality: the more remote its connexion with observable social facts, the more substantial it can be shown to be, and vice versa. By contrast, this article attempts to show how the analysis of mythological thought, which is intrinsically paradoxical and elusive, *can* be accommodated within the normal parameters of social anthropological investigation. The subject is a myth collected among the Fipa of south-west Tanzania.

MYTH AND MYTH-MAKERS

The Fipa are a Bantu people fairly distantly related linguistically to the Bemba. They inhabit a high, rolling and largely treeless plateau near the south end of Lake Tanganyika, which forms the western boundary of their country; another lake, Rukwa, marks the easterly limit of Fipa territory. The people live in compact village settlements and numbered 86,462 at the last census in 1957. In the middle of the Fipa plateau there is a mountain called Itweelele which is the centre of a small kingdom (or chiefdom) about four miles in diameter called Milansi; this tiny kingdom is supposed to be the oldest and original source of authority in Ufipa (the name given to the land of the Fipa). Traditionally Ufipa was further divided into two kingdoms ruled by rival but related dynasties called Twa; these two kingdoms, Nkansi and Lyangalile, are supposed to have been one in the earliest days. The origin of Twa power and its relation to the aboriginal kingdom of Milansi form the subject of the myth to be considered.

The story appears several times in early writings of the colonial period about the Fipa—an indication of its central importance as an embodiment of the Fipa sense of their own identity. I collected a number of different versions of this key myth, some of the variations in which corresponded to the differing, and sometimes opposed, political interests of focal groups in Fipa society (Willis, 1964); all versions, however, possessed the same common structure, which is typified in the following (translated) text which I collected in 1964 from an illiterate old man:

There were once three sisters who came from a far country in search of somewhere to settle. They reached Ufipa from the east and went round the western part of the country. After walking for a long time they at length reached a hillock and they said to themselves, "Let us rest here." One of the women sat down on a rock, another on the ground and a third was holding a red fruit called isuku. The one who was holding the fruit isuku became known as the Child of Isuku, the one who was sitting on the ground was called Earth-Person and the one who sat on the rock as the Child of the Stone.

Meanwhile the king of Milansi said one day to his wife: "Something is going to happen to us before long. If certain strange people come here be sure not to give them my royal stool, even if they say, 'Give it to us.' If you do they will take away our kingdom."

Soon afterwards he went into the wilderness to hunt, spending the night out there. The three women meanwhile had arrived at the place called Kanda, where even today you can see their footprints. Not long afterwards they arrived at Itweelele mountain, the home of the king of the Fipa. There they were met by the queen, his wife, and they said to her, "Give us stools so that we may sit down."

The queen took out one stool and the leader of the three women passed it on to her younger sister; she then produced another and the leader passed it on to her elder sister, saying, "I don't want that one but the king's own stool: bring it to me."

The queen refused. Then the strange woman entered the hut herself and finally overbore the queen so that she was obliged to surrender the royal stool. Taking it, the stranger said, "This country is mine: may the people live long." Then the three sisters sat down.

Meanwhile the king, where he was in the wilderness, heard a buzzing noise in his ears and knew it meant that the long-awaited strangers had arrived. Straight away he returned to the royal village, and when he reached it he met the three sisters. They greeted one another with all courtesy, then the king went inside his hut with his wife.

"O wife, what did I tell you?" he said. "Did I not warn you against giving my royal stool to the strangers? Now they have taken the kingdom from us."

Next morning the three regal sisters said to the king, "Let us go to the top of the mountain, so that you may show us the limits of your domain." Now it happened that the king had allowed his underarm hair to grow very long, and, when they reached the summit, he felt ashamed of exhibiting it to the three women. So he kept his arm low, and said, "My country ends just there."

"Why, his country extends only as far as the mountain!" the three women said, and their leader stood erect and pointed, saying, "My rule extends from Lake Tanganyika in the west to Lake Rukwa in the east; and from Unyamwanga in the south to Lyamfipa [an escarpment at the northern end of the Fipa plateau] in the north!"

So it was that the rule of the Twa began in Ufipa; and the king of Milansi remained as priest of Itweelele, the sacred mountain.

This is a moving and a tragic tale. Considered purely as a story, as entertainment (which is why Fipa like to tell and hear it) it is effective for much the same reasons that *Hamlet* and *Cinderella* are effective as stories: because its form is psychologically arresting and satisfying. In the Fipa myth an initial situation of conflict is brought to a climax (and note how artfully the tension is prolonged and heightened during the episode with the stools); the inevitable moment of triumph and tragedy occurs when the strange and majestic woman asserts her claim to sovereignty over the country of Fipa, in a way that (as we know already) must compel acceptance by the established king: she performs the symbolic act of sitting on the royal stool of Milansi.

So the Twaci (the feminine form of Twa) have conquered. What happens now? Here the story surprises us with an unexpected "twist": the king returns, sees and knows he has lost, in spite of all his efforts to avoid such a consummation—and he accepts his fate with calm and dignity, royally in fact. In his defeat, the king establishes his *moral superiority* over the aggressive intruders, a superiority which is given formal recognition later in the Twa acceptance of the permanent rule of the king and his line over Milansi and the sacred mountain of Itweelele, and his perpetual priesthood. This surprising development recreates, on another and higher plane, the initial situation of opposition and tension between Milansi and Twa.

The final episode, the ascent of the mountain and the demarcation of the two, territorially unequal, kingdoms of Milansi and the Twa, introduces a new affective element into the story—that of comedy: like us, Fipa find the incident of the under-arm hair amusing. In this episode too, the king gives further evidence of his social self-control: his sense of shame (*insoni*) over his inappropriate growth of hair leads him to sacrifice a claim he might still have made to a wider territorial sovereignty, for the story implies that Milansi's domain originally embraced the whole country. The final irony is that the king himself, by his own action, effectively cedes the land of Fipa to the strangers, at the same time as he, seemingly, makes a claim to the central core of his old kingdom—a claim which is almost contemptuously granted by the Twaci women, interested as they are in real power.

In thus summarizing and interpreting the story, we have encountered its most obvious structural characteristic, one which it shares with most, if not all, members of the genus "story": an initial situation, in which two basic elements or factors are brought into relation, unfolds, as it were in spiral form, through successive stages of crisis, partial resolution, renewed crisis, and final reformulation. The concluding resolution contains latent ambiguities (Did the king really mean to give away the country or does it still belong to him? Did the Twaci recognition of Milansi's authority over the sacred mountain mean that the Twa think of the king of Milansi as their superior? Or is Milansi really Twa territory and the king there as a political dependant? etc.) which gives the effect of continuing the dialectical "spiral" indefinitely, and accounts for the story's "timeless" quality.

Obviously too, the existence of contradictions which the narrative appears to resolve but succeeds only in transforming into new and latent contradictions, relates to the function of the story as what Malinowski (1948: 120) called a "sociological charter"—a retrospective justification and validation for an existing and rather complex social order, in which there is inherent and fundamental inner conflict.

This article is principally concerned to reveal and analyze the configuration of opposed, complementary and associated ideas and values which Fipa see as contained in the basic situation of the sovereignty myth: the relation of Milansi and Twa. Through what I call its "conceptual-affective structure," itself formed from the basic "bricks" of mythological thought—sets of binary discriminations—the myth, I shall argue, both reflects and maintains the formal similarity of two apparently disparate dimensions of Fipa society: sovereignty and descent.

To begin with, let us return to the manifest subject of the myth, the kingdoms of Milansi and the Twa. These two foci of Fipa concepts and values are linked in a relation of complementary opposition which inheres in the fact that they represent two qualitatively different and incommensurate kinds of sovereignty (ritual and political, respectively); that nevertheless they are interdependent (the Twa derive their legitimacy, their right to rule, from Milansi; Milansi in turn depends upon Twa power, on the ability of the Twa administrative-military apparatus to maintain Ufipa as a political entity); and that both terms, Milansi and Twa, have attributes implying superiority *and* inferiority vis-á-vis the other: Milansi is the ritual superior of the Twa, but its political and territorial inferior;

Milansi is the senior kingdom, but strength, in the form of organized coercive force, is all on the side of the Twa.

The more important concepts associated with the Milansi-Twa relation, and their differential value-loading, are summarized in the following diagram, in which a double-headed arrow represents a relation of complementary opposition and "plus" and "minus" signs represent relative values:

MILANSI TWA

Ritual authority(+)↔Ritual dependency(−)
Political dependency(−)↔Political supremacy(+)
Seniority(+)↔Juniority(−)
Lack of power(−)↔Possession of Power(+)

More abstractly, the opposition and combination of differentially-valued concepts in the Milansi-Twa relation could be represented as follows:

$$\begin{Bmatrix} + & \leftrightarrow & - \\ - & \leftrightarrow & + \end{Bmatrix}$$

These conceptual oppositions are entirely explicit in the minds of all Fipa who concern themselves with such matters. Thus the reigning king of Nkansi, the northern and larger of the two Twa "states," said to me of the king of Milansi, "He is our priest." At the same time he objected to my referring to the latter personage by the title "*Mweene*," implying political sovereignty, and said he should be called *i Waku Milansi*, "the one of Milansi," on the model of titles given to subordinate administrators in the Twa kingdoms. For his part, the present king of Milansi, Catakwa Mauto, told me that the whole of Ufipa was "his" country, and the Twa ultimately derived their authority from him.

DESCENT: "HEAD" AND "LOINS"

If we now turn from the Fipa conceptual scheme of sovereignty to another social dimension, that of descent, we encounter a further system of ideas. It will be argued that there is a formal similarity amounting to structural congruence between this idea-system and that associated with sovereignty.

Fipa conceptualize descent, experienced as a complex of consanguineal, marital and affinal relations, in terms of two composite symbols: "head" (*unntwe*) and "loins" (*unnsana*). At the most abstract level, "head" stands for the organizing and controlling function or aspect of the most inclusive Fipa descent group or category, the *uluko*, with its elected chief, the *umweenekasi*, and its network of reciprocal rights and duties binding members together; the symbol "head" evokes the *uluko* as a formal and continuing entity. The symbol "loins," at a similarly abstract level, evokes for Fipa the *uluko* in its regenerative and developmental capacities and functions: the descent group as a changing entity, in reciprocal relationship, through exchange of women and bridewealth, with the world outside it.

Less abstractly, "head" is associated with masculinity or maleness, patrilineality, paternity, intellect and authority and "loins" with femininity or femaleness, matrilineality, maternity, sexuality and reproduction. In terms of social categories, and consistently with these abstract associations, "head" denotes patrilateral relatives and "loins" denotes matrilateral relatives; these are ego-centred categories.

At the most concrete level, the two symbols refer, as the English terms used to translate them imply, to distinct and separate regions or parts of the human body. The literal meaning of *unntwe* is "head," in the physiological sense; but although I translate *unnsana* as "loins," this is not an exact equivalent. Physiologically *unnsana* refers to the lower abdomen and lower back in both men and women; it adjoins, though it does not include, the genital regions in both sexes. Even so the word *unnsana* has marked sexual associations for Fipa, probably because complete control of the muscles of this region is considered a prerequisite of erotic maturity; it is the object of a style of ventral dancing called *imiteete*, which is taught to pubescent girls and which boys imitate, to facilitate such control.

"Head" and "loins" then are foci for sets of ideas from markedly different areas and levels of experience within the world of Fipa descent: they are what Turner calls "dominant symbols" (1964c: 35, 50).

But not only do these two symbols separately focus and englobe clusters of ideas, but these ideas are themselves polarized in oppositional pairs analogously to the relation of complementary opposition between the "dominant" or "key" symbols, "head" and "loins." Some of these concepts have already been mentioned. They include, for example, "maleness" ("head"), which is opposed to "femaleness" ("loins"), "intellect" ("head") opposed to "sexuality" ("loins") and "authority" ("head") opposed to "reproduction" ("loins"); from the latter opposition (authority versus reproduction) is derived that between "seniority" ("head") and "juniority" ("loins"). To the first terms in all these pairs Fipa give a relatively higher value, so that this cluster of concepts can be represented in the following way:

$$(+)\left\{\begin{array}{rcl} & \text{“HEAD”} \leftrightarrow \text{“LOINS”} & \\ \text{maleness} & \leftrightarrow & \text{femaleness} \\ \text{intellect} & \leftrightarrow & \text{sexuality} \\ \text{authority} & \leftrightarrow & \text{reproduction} \\ \text{seniority} & \leftrightarrow & \text{juniority} \end{array}\right\}(-)$$

But this is far from being the whole story. In another cluster of polarized concepts associated respectively with "head" and "loins" the relative value-loading is reversed. For, as Fipa see it, "weight," "numbers," "strength" and "fellowship" are associated with *unnsana*, "loins"; and "lightness," "fewness," "weakness" and "constraint" are the corresponding attributes of *unntwe*, "head." A well known Fipa proverb says, "The loins are heavy, the head is light" (*Uk' unnsana kwanwama, uk'unntwe kwapepela*): it is the women who come into the descent group, the *unnsana* side, Fipa says, who make the *uluko* strong. Another proverb contrasts the "meat" associated with "loins" with its entire lack on the "head" side: in the huts of his mother and her siblings a man can expect food and friendship while the father and his siblings are supposed to be far less forthcoming. To the father's sister (*imaangu seenje*) is attributed a power of lethal cursing over her brother's children.

We thus have a further cluster of conceptual pairs associated with the dominant symbols "head" and "loins" and which is relatively valued in the opposite sense from the first cluster:

$$(-)\left\{\begin{array}{rcl} & \text{“HEAD”} \leftrightarrow \text{“LOINS”} & \\ \text{lightness} & \leftrightarrow & \text{heaviness} \\ \text{fewness} & \leftrightarrow & \text{numbers} \\ \text{weakness} & \leftrightarrow & \text{strength} \\ \text{constraint} & \leftrightarrow & \text{fellowship} \end{array}\right\}(+)$$

The complementary opposition of the dominant symbols "head" and "loins" is thus characterized by a contrary valuation of some of the most important pairs of subordinate and associated concepts. From our consideration of the meaning for Fipa of the descent-based symbolism of "head" and "loins" there thus emerges a picture of a conceptual-affective structure which could be most abstractly represented as follows:

$$\left\{\begin{array}{c} + \leftrightarrow - \\ - \leftrightarrow + \end{array}\right\}$$

This is the same representation as that derived from our analysis of the manifest meaning of the sovereignty myth.

EXPLICIT AND IMPLICIT PATTERNS

Empiricist critics of structural analysis in anthropology often raise the question—frequently with justice, no doubt—of how far the "pattern" elicited in any particular case reflects the thinking of the people being analyzed; coupled with this question there is usually the implication that the "structure" supposedly revealed is, to a greater or lesser extent, a creation of the analyst, who has arbitrarily imposed an order of his own on the ethnographical material. This accusation lurks behind the charge of "formalism" frequently levelled against Lévi-Strauss (cf. Yalman, 1967). In dealing with the Fipa material I have sought, on purely methodological grounds, to avoid this pitfall for the unwary structuralist: as far as the main argument is concerned, I have confined myself to sets of complementary oppositions which are perfectly explicit in Fipa thinking. Having made what I hope can be accepted as a *prima facie* case for the existence of a structural congruence between the idea-systems associated respectively with sovereignty and with descent, I feel the more justified in going on to strengthen that case with evidence from less clearly formulated areas of Fipa thought.

In dealing with this material, a regularity of another kind emerges: a conceptual opposition that is implicit in one dimension—sovereignty or descent—is always explicit in the other, as in the following examples.

1. *Male(ness)–Female(ness).* This complementary opposition is explicit in the descent context. A Fipa who is asked for his descent name "on the head side" (*uk'unntwe*) will reply with a name he inherits from his father and which is transmitted patrilineally; asked for his name "on the loins side" (*uk'unnsana*), he will mention one of another category of names which he inherits from his mother. But the same opposition is also implicit at the level of sovereignty: the dynasty of Milansi was founded by a *man*, while the Twa trace their origin to a *woman*. The intrinsic maleness of Milansi may be seen in the fact that all the rulers recorded in oral tradition and including the present incumbent have been men, whereas women, as well as men, have at various times ruled in the two Twa kingdoms of Nkansi and Lyangalile.

2. *Up–down.* This relation is explicit, as a fact of geography, in the political dimension. Milansi, the royal village of the kingdom of the same name, is and always has been—according to tradition—situated on the slopes of Itweelele, the sacred mountain. The royal

villages of the Twa, on the other hand, have always been situated at one point or another on the Fipa plateau—never on a mountain. That is to say, Milansi is recognized by Fipa as being "up" or "high," in relation to the centres of Twa power, which are "down" or "low." An analogous relation is implicit in Fipa conceptualization of the principles of descent and derives from the physiological model of the two symbolic terms, "head" and "loins": in the human body, in its normal erect posture, "head" is "up" or "high" and "loins" are "down" or "low."

3. *Fixed–moving.* Here again the oppositional relation is explicit between Milansi and the Twa. The royal village of Milansi is and always has been geographically fixed; but the location of Twa royal villages, up to the colonial period, was frequently changing—Twa rulers sometimes changed the site of their capitals several times during the course of a single reign. Again an analogous relation is implicit in the context of descent and inheres in the fact that Fipa marriage is predominantly virilocal: it is men, the "head" side in descent terms, who stay put, while women, the "loins" side, move.

MYTHS AND "MYTHICAL THINKING"

Although Lévi-Strauss has so much to tell us about myths, he does not explicitly define the concept "myth." Instead, he seems to proffer an implied "operational" definition, which would take some such form as: "myths are linguistic phenomena characterized by a multi-dimensional structure of binary oppositions; separate myths can be shown by analysis to form transformation groups in which constituent elements and oppositions in different myths are reciprocally complementary." It is also characteristic of myth and "mythical thinking," according to Lévi-Strauss, that the number of structural dimensions in any myth, and the number of myths in a transformation group, are in principle unlimited: in this way myths produced by societies widely separated in space (and presumably also, in time) can be shown to be related, and to illuminate one another.

On these terms, and without committing ourselves at this stage on the "logical status" (Yalman, 1967: 86) of Lévi-Strauss's analytical framework, the thinking of the Fipa would appear to conform well enough to the Lévi-Straussian formalization of the "mythical." The two idea-systems considered in this article, the first derived from analysis of the sovereignty myth, and the second from analysis of Fipa notions about descent, can be shown, by following standard Lévi-Straussian procedure, to form a single "transformation group."

To begin with, certain elements—oppositional pairs—in these two systems are common to both: e.g., seniority versus juniority; and up versus down. Other pairs in the two idea-systems, Milansi-Twa and "head"-"loins" appear on analysis to be analogues of one another and therefore capable of reciprocal transformation, thus:

SYSTEM 1		SYSTEM 2
Milansi		"head"
ritual authority	⇄	authority—intellect
territorial inferiority	⇄	"lightness"
weakness	⇄	"fewness"

SYSTEM 1		SYSTEM 2
Twa		"loins"
political power (=proliferation of offices	⇄	sexuality—reproduction
territorial superiority	⇄	"heaviness"
strength	⇄	"numbers"

Moreover, if we now return to our point of departure, the Fipa sovereignty myth, it can be seen to be rich in clues and references to an underlying system of binary discriminations in the best Lévi-Straussian tradition. Thus the version given here associates a fruit called *isuku* with one of the Twaci women, who is called Mwaana Kasuku (*isuku* and *Kasuku* are derived from the Fipa word for "redness," *ukasuke*). Ethnographical evidence shows that the colours red and white are symbolically significant for Fipa. The Twa rulers of the country were traditionally buried in a red ox-skin; and red, being associated with blood, was a symbol of war and violence: men painted red marks on their faces before going into battle. Red is therefore particularly appropriate as the colour of the Twaci women (in some versions of the myth they are themselves said to have been of reddish hue), the bringers of change and war to the originally simple and peaceful land of the Fipa.

The colour white, on the other hand, is symbolic of spiritual power for Fipa and hence appropriate to Milansi, the ritual capital of Ufipa. In another sense white is appropriate to Milansi as the guardian of peace, as opposed to the turbulent Twa. In the sphere of descent, spiritual authority is also attributed to the *umweenekasi*, the head of the *uluko*, whose duty it is to mediate with the ancestral spirits on behalf of his group.

Returning to the myth again, another of the

Twaci women is called Earth-Person (*Unnsi*); this association of Twa with the earth naturally suggests to anyone acquainted with the Lévi-Straussian idiom that Milansi might, by way of opposition, be associated with the sky: and sure enough, Fipa tradition says that Milansi "fell with the earth" from the sky at the beginning of time (Willis, 1964)—and the same is said of the first king of Milansi, Ntatakwa. In similar vein, the name of the third Twaci woman, "Child of the Stone," could be seen as belonging to the same oppositional group, with "stone" as metonymous for "earth."

Perhaps enough has now been said to indicate that Fipa notions about sovereignty and descent belong to a wider cosmological pattern of dualistic classification and opposition which is *the same kind of pattern* as that which Lévi-Strauss has sought to reveal elsewhere in the "primitive" world. This kind of "mythical" thinking, as Lévi-Strauss has said (1964: *passim*), has the characteristic of appearing to the analyst as "unending": always revealing new dimensions, new series of oppositions. Such thought, in this case among the Fipa, admits of no exhaustive or conclusive exposition; but this same characteristic, once recognized, points to the existence within the basic oppositional forms of Fipa thought of more abstruse cognitive potentialities than we have yet indicated. Thus I would argue that in the opposed concepts of Milansi and Twa, "head" and "loins," there are contained, partly latent and partly explicit, notions of complementary duality akin to those which have exercised the minds of philosophers and theologians through the ages: such as the ideas of "being and becoming," "transcendent and contingent" and "continuity and change." The name "Milansi," briefly translated, means "the eternal village"—an implied contrast with the transitory settlements of the Twa. A similar opposition of ideas of continuity and fixity, on the one hand, and of movement and change on the other, is associated with the opposed symbols "head" and "loins." In their most basic thought categories Fipa thus unite in complementary opposition the ideas of society as a continuing entity, and therefore in some sense unchanging, and as the subject of historical mutation.

The time has now come however to leave these rarified and irremediably hypothetical heights and consider more closely the nature of mythological thought and, within the Fipa context, the central question of its relation to more substantial aspects of the social order.

THOUGHT IN AURAL CULTURES

It seems to me that in his analysis of the structure of mythological thought Lévi-Strauss has formalized the experience of every fieldworker who has gained some intimacy with the thought-forms of a pre-literate society. In what McLuhan calls "aural" (or sometimes "oral") cultures thought is integral, it entertains contradictions (which can be resolved only by conversion into other contradictions, as in *La Geste d'Asdiwal*), it has no centre and no boundaries (Stearn, 1967: 52). The apparent "centre" of Lévi-Strauss's exposition of Amerindian mythology in *Le Cru et le cuit*—the "myth of reference"—has been arbitrarily chosen, as the author admits, for the purpose of the argument (Lévi-Strauss, 1964: 10). The subsequent arrangement of the material is in a sense no less arbitrary, based as it is on the working-out of an elaborate analogy with the structure of music. But this unexpected approach, in which a few basic themes in the repertoire of Amerindian mythology are repetitively explored and developed, is palpably in harmony with the spirit of mythological thinking: it works. The book is itself fashioned in the shape of a gigantic myth—as Lévi-Strauss says, "in spiral form" ("*en spirale*") (1964: 12).

Some part of the as-yet-unassimilated significance of this experiment in controlled *participation mystique*, I would suggest, derives from the fact that every myth is an allegory of the field experience, just as the inner life of the fieldworker is necessarily mythical. For an "observer"—the word is itself indicative of cultural bias—from a "visual" culture to immerse himself in what McLuhan calls an integral, "ear" culture is to suffer a profound disorientation. He enters a world of apparent contradictions which are resolvable, it seems, only and always in an inappropriate context, at another "level": the "resolution" is thus always provisional, always dissolving into contradictions, which are equivocally resolved in similar manner. Yet from the first the contradictions are *felt*, rather than seen, to form a pattern which is regular even, or rather especially, in its very discontinuities. This is why Lévi-Strauss has chosen music, which is structure apprehended through the ear instead of the eye, to represent the spirit of mythological thought.

It is not surprising that the edifice Lévi-Strauss has constructed in *Le Cru et le cuit* escapes the empirical constraints which he initially seeks to place upon it, emphasizing ". . . la position centrale de nos mythes, et leur adhérence aux contours essentials de l'organisation sociale et politique" (1964: 63).

But just as, for the fieldworker, a true rendering of indigenous thought involves abandoning the neat categories of social compartmentalization he had brought with him, so in mythical analysis, "chaque matrice de significations renvoie à une autre matrice, chaque mythe à d'autres mythes" (1964: 346). And the brilliant work of synthesis represented by *Le Cru et le cuit* is achieved at the cost of jettisoning sociological correlates in favour of "the human spirit" (*l'esprit*) as the ultimate point of reference: ". . . l'unique réponse que suggère ce livre est que les mythes signifient l'esprit, qui les élabore au moyen du monde dont il fait lui-même partie. Ainsi peuvent être simultanément engendrés, les mythes eux-mêmes par l'esprit qui les cause, et par les mythes, une image du monde déjà inscrite dans l'architecture de l'esprit" (1964: 346).

This is not a position which suggests possibilities of practical and theoretical advance—at least in social anthropology. It opens an enormous gulf between social thought—the collective representations of a vast culture area—and social action, the institutions to which these thought-forms must in some way correspond. The question that arises is: can mythological thought, which is endlessly dualistic, elaborate the more complex conceptual structures appropriate to systems of social relations?

One way in which this *might* be done is suggested by an earlier work of Lévi-Strauss, his *La geste d'Asdiwal* (1958), in which the myth goes through successive oppositional transformations at various levels—geographical, economic, sociological and cosmological. All these oppositions are, according to Lévi-Strauss's interpretation of the Asdiwal myth, reflections of a basic social contradiction inherent in the custom of matrilateral cross-cousin marriage among the Tsimshian Indians. This theory, which has been subjected to some criticism, is essentially speculative and unverifiable. As a solution to the problem of the relation between mythological thought and social organization it is unsatisfactory. The Fipa example, on the other hand, points to a way in which dualistic ideas can be combined so as to form, as it were, a higher order of conceptual organization which will be appropriate to the complexity of its social referents.

If we now return to the Fipa sovereignty myth, we see that its manifest meaning relates to a system of ideas and values which, though of considerable complexity, is contained within the complementary opposition of two "key" terms, "Milansi" and "Twa." We have also drawn attention to the existence of another system of ideas and values in the universe of descent, derived from and contained within the complementary opposition of the dominant symbols "head" and "loins"; and we have argued that there is a structural congruence between these two conceptual-affective systems. If this latter point is conceded, the sovereignty myth becomes not merely a "charter," in Malinowski's sense, for the relation between the kingdoms of Milansi and the Twa, but is also, at another level, an allegory of the world of descent, as Fipa experience it. The myth has meaning at different cognitive levels in two apparently unrelated dimensions of Fipa society. The first meaning (concerning the relation between ritual and political sovereignty) is overt and manifest; the second meaning, in terms of descent, is latent; both meanings, it must be presumed, contribute to the significance for Fipa of the sovereignty myth.

The interpretation of the Fipa sovereignty myth put forward in this paper does not preclude its analysis in terms of a system of binary discriminations in the standard Lévi-Straussian manner; indeed the assumption, already made explicit, is that the myth is basically structured in accordance with such a system. But the central significance of the myth for Fipa, it is argued, is its embodiment, at different cognitive levels, of what I have called "conceptual-affective" structures which directly reflect social organization. In these structures clusters of ideas, which are opposed on the model of englobing "key" oppositions, are themselves divided into opposed subclusters or sub-sets—vertically, as it were—by a contrary value-loading. Figure 1, as shown above attempts to convey some of the complexity of this conceptual-affective system. In it a single arrow (→) represents the operation of logical or empirical or logicoempirical) transformation; a double arrow (↔) represents the complementary opposition of two concepts; a plus or a minus sign indicates the relative value given to the concepts enclosed within the round brackets; square brackets enclose the two idea-systems; and the sign ≡ indicates structural congruence between them.

The actual situation is a good deal more complex than this. The diagram shows only a few of the more important, and entirely explicit, oppositional concepts associated with the two pairs of key ideas; a more comprehensive representation would have to indicate the theoretically infinite number of oppositional pairs which *could* be derived from the key oppositions and, in doing so, it would also be desirable to indicate another variable quantity—the relative explicitness or otherwise of all these ideas in Fipa thinking. The diagram may be incomplete in another way, since other idea-systems may exist, structurally congruent with those related to sovereignty and descent, in other dimensions of Fipa society: this article describes two which I have been able to isolate and analyze.

The approach to mythical analysis attempted in this article is in a sense opposite to that exemplified in Lévi-Strauss's recent work (1964). Where Lévi-Strauss *begins* "at the most concrete level . . . in the heart of a population" (1964:9) and ends amidst "the architecture of the spirit" (346), this approach begins with the myth, veiled as it is in primal music and mystery, and works towards the socially concrete, in terms of identifiable institutions and systems of relations.

Further reflection suggests that these two approaches, and others too, may all be necessary, or at least desirable: the demonstration that myth, and myths, can be understood in terms of a system of binary discriminations does not exhaust the possibilities of structural analysis, as Burridge has pointed out (1967). For if, on the one hand, the implication of the Lévi-Straussian procedure and precedent is that the full meaning of, for example, the Fipa myth can emerge only when it is examined in the course of an analysis ranging over the whole corpus of Bantu mythology, on the other hand the method results in and operates through an intractable paradox. The synoptic approach exemplified in *Le Cru et le cuit,* in which Lévi-Strauss has taken the entire mythical heritage of the Amerindians for his province, achieves astonishing coherence and complexity—but at the price of severing virtually all links with the solid ground of ethnography. In following so faithfully the spirit of mythological thought, Lévi-Strauss has been obliged, in the manner of that thought itself, to elude the straightforward categories of everyday tribal life for the elliptical linkages of *participation mystique* (Lévy-Bruhl). It has been Lévi-Strauss's achievement to discover a rigorous logical pattern, a paradoxically abstract "science of the concrete," behind these seemingly random juxtapositions.

The object of the more recent work of

FIGURE 1
Conceptual-affective systems of sovereignty and descent.

MILANSI
\+
−
Senior → High → Ritual authority → Political dependence → Territorial inferiority → Weakness
Junior → Low → Ritual dependence → Political supremacy → Territorial superiority → Strength
−
\+
TWA

≡

"HEAD"
\+
−
Senior → Male → Intellect-Control → Lightness → Few → Weakness
Junior → Female → Sexuality-Reproduction → Heaviness → Many → Strength
−
\+
"LOINS"

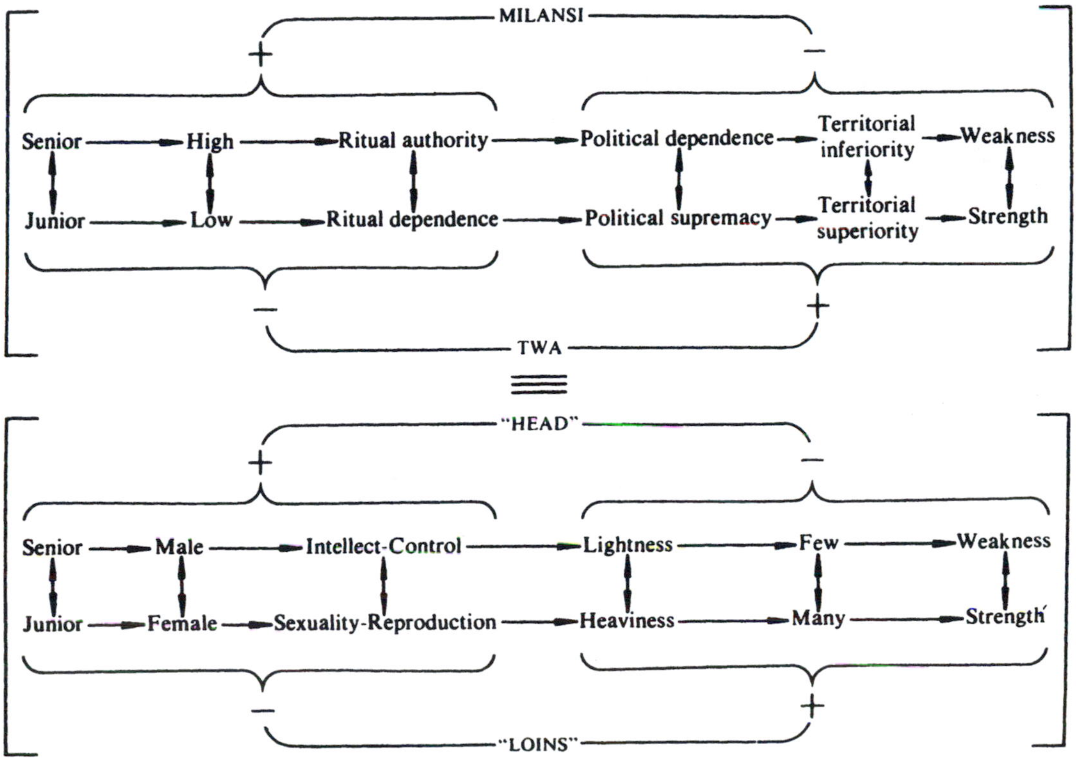

Lévi-Strauss, it seems to me, has not been to elaborate any kind of empirically verifiable "map" of mythological thought, but to demonstrate, through sympathetic and uninhibited participation in *la pensée sauvage*, the vastness and richness of the territory yet to be explored by social anthropology. Reading *Le Cru et le cuit*, in particular, is like inhabiting the mind of some super-ethnographer as he undergoes a field experience ranging through seemingly limitless expanses of time and space.

These portentous "field notes" are a notable challenge to the assumptions of particularistic and relativistic empiricism. But they will remain theoretically barren unless translated, like all such information, into the common language of social anthropology. What is needed to complement the synoptic labours of Lévi-Strauss and to begin the complex task of incorporating the immense new territory he has prospected into the body of our discipline, is not less structuralism but more—at the "grass-roots" level of ethnography. In this article I have tried to indicate, in the context of my own fieldwork, how such an approach could be made. Structuralist and obviously "Lévi-Straussian" in inspiration, it is also empirically-oriented, since it relates to "concrete" social institutions.

SUMMARY

In conclusion, the following assumptions and hypotheses seem to arise from or be suggested by, the arguments in this article.

1. Thought in pre-literate or "aural" cultures is characterized by what Lévy-Bruhl called *participation mystique*, Lévi-Strauss has described in terms of an "unending" series of conceptual oppositions, resolutions and transformations, and McLuhan has most recently called "a total field of simultaneous relations, without centre or margin" (Stearn, 1967:52).

2. "Myths" and "mythological thinking" are, *at a certain level of analysis* (which has become almost synonymous with the name of Lévi-Strauss) alike insofar as they are composed of formally similar systems of oppositions and "participations" (or "binary discriminations").

3. But, according to the evidence adduced in this article, "myths" are also *particular* in that they relate, through what I have called their conceptual-affective structure, or structures, to one or more organisational aspects of the society that produced them. This conclusion, or hypothesis, if found to be generally true by comparison with other societies, would have at least one significant consequence: it would restrict the anthropological use of the term "myth," which in the work of Lévi-Strauss seems indistinguishable from the wider category of "story," to oral forms exhibiting the necessary structural characteristics.

4. Conceptual-affective systems, or structures, in the sense the term has been used here, are aspects of social institutions and systems of relations. They are made out of the basic mythological "bricks" of oppositions and participations and their relatively greater complexity is explained by the presence of an affective, "value" component which results in cross-cutting internal oppositions of clusters of concepts within the total system. In a "myth" all the major constituent elements of such structures (value-loaded ideas) are directly or symbolically embodied.

It is precisely the affective element in mythological thought, on which Lévy-Bruhl particularly insisted (1949:167-9), that evaporates during the course of an overall analysis of *Le Cru et le cuit* dimensions, leaving a passionless structure of remote and mathematical beauty: the "music" takes on form, but loses its emotional content, which can be derived only from communication with human beings—the "field" situation.

5. Analysis of the Fipa material has suggested that a single myth can include, and relate to, more than one conceptual-affective structure—because these structures, though aspects of institutions and systems of relations which are "disparate" to conventional analysis, are in fact, like the numberless versions of the myth itself, formally congruent. The evidence presented here suggests that the central Fipa myth is a "sociological charter" of a depth and comprehensiveness which might well have surprised Malinowski, and that the language of the charter is a sort of ultra-Lévi-Straussian one.

Gary H. Gossen

CHAMULA GENRES OF VERBAL BEHAVIOR

In this cogent paper, Gary Gossen presents a taxonomy of Chamula genres of verbal behavior classified from the point of view of the Chamulas. These genres range from "ordinary speech" to highly formalized "ancient words." He then goes on to suggest that this folk oral tradition constitutes an ethical statement whose categories display attributes which also organize other aspects of Chamula expressive behavior. The structure of the oral tradition is shown to be isomorphic with the structures of other aspects of Chamula life such as religion and world view. His Chamula data demonstrate that the categories of the universe are encoded not only in "myth" but also in gossip, riddles, and proverbs. For an ethnographic description of Chamula the reader is referred to Gossen's article "Temporal and Spatial Equivalents in Chamula Ritual Symbolism" reprinted in Chapter 3, and also his more recently published book, *Chamulas in the World of the Sun: Time and Space in a Maya Oral Tradition* (1974).

Reprinted in abridged form from the *Journal of American Folklore*, 84 (331) (1971), 145–167, by permission of the author and the American Folklore Society, Inc.

The principal purpose of this paper is to present a brief taxonomy of Chamula folk genres of verbal behavior. This will contribute some substantive data to what is becoming increasingly well known: that European genre labels are often inadequate for description of non-Western oral traditions. Secondly, I will suggest that the whole domain of Chamula verbal behavior offers more opportunities for context-conscious interpretation of the meaning of oral tradition in Chamula life than single genres considered separately. This approach constitutes an application of certain "emic" methods of data collection and analysis which have been known in anthropology as ethnoscience, ethnomethodology, ethnographic semantics, and ethnography of communication. Consideration of the importance of folk genres of non-Western oral traditions has appeared only sporadically until quite recently, although folklorists and anthropologists in the past decade have been giving more and more attention to native classification of genres and related behavior settings. Thirdly, although I generally agree that native taxonomies have intrinsic descriptive value, I do not think they stand alone as ends in themselves for the purpose of analysis. I wish to go beyond this to suggest that Chamula oral tradition constitutes an ethical statement whose categories (genres) are organized according to attributes which also organize other aspects of Chamula expressive behavior and values. In this way, the structure of the whole of Chamula oral tradition may be seen to be isomorphic with the structures of other aspects of Chamula life such as religion and world view.

Finally, I hope to show that a holistic approach to Chamula verbal behavior is useful for describing and analyzing linguistic aspects of the socialization process. Formal genres that relate to ritual settings presuppose knowledge of other, more informal genres, which are learned in secular settings at an earlier age. This leads to a criticism of the tendency among many folklorists and anthropologists to deal with "standard narrative genres" (particularly myth, legend and folktale) in preference to the (apparently) less substantial "minor genres." This tendency is unfortunate, for, at least in the case of the Chamulas, the less formal narrative and nonnarrative genres are vitally important for passing on information and for regulating social relations, as well as serving as aids in recognizing, understanding, and performing the more formal genres. In fact, the Chamula data indicate that the categories of the universe are as well encoded in gossip, riddles, and proverbs as they are in myth—Claude Lévi-Strauss's statement that myth has "special meaning" notwithstanding.

. . .

THE TAXONOMY OF VERBAL BEHAVIOR

Oral tradition in this conservative community remains vitally and dynamically alive. For the vast majority of Chamulas it is a crucial source of information about the present and the only source of information about the past. Transistor radios are still luxuries possessed by only the wealthy. Even for the few who have radios, the Spanish language (in which all radio programs are broadcast) makes it difficult for them to understand. In short, far from being marginal and moribund, the oral tradition is absolutely critical for maintenance of the social order as Chamulas know it. Consequently, facility in use of ordinary and special forms of language is an ability that nearly all successful political and religious officials and shamans possess.

A bewildering number of processes, abstractions, and things can be glossed as *k'op*, which refers to nearly all forms of verbal behavior, including oral tradition. The term *k'op* can mean the following: word, language, argument, war, subject, topic, problem, dispute, court case, or traditional verbal lore. Chamulas recognize that correct use of language (that is, the Chamula dialect of Tzotzil) distinguishes them not only from nonhumans, but also from their distant ancestors and from other contemporary Indian and Spanish-speaking groups. According to Chamula narrative accounts, no one could speak in the distant past. That was one of the reasons why the sun-creator destroyed the experimental people of the First and Second Creations. The more recent people learned to speak Spanish and then everyone understood one another. Later, the nations and *municipios* were divided because they began quarreling. The sun deity changed languages so that people would learn to live together peacefully in small groups. Chamulas came out well in the long run, for their language was the best of them all (they refer to Tzotzil as *bae'i k'op* or "true language"). Language, then, came to be the distinguishing trait of social groups. It was because of the importance Chamulas attached to correct verbal behavior as a defining trait of their own indentity that I considered the range and organization of behavior included in *k'op* to be worthy of detailed attention in my research.

The taxonomy of *k'op*, which follows in Figures 1 and 2, was elicited several separate times from six male informants ranging in age from eighteen to sixty-five over the period of one year. I used both formal question frames and informal discussion to discover these categories. The two methods were complementary, in that formal question frame interviewing (for example, *hay tos* _____?_____*ˀoy šaval li Hoˀote*, "How many kinds of _____?_____ would you say there are?") produced a taxonomy and genre labels I could use to identify types of texts after I had recorded or transcribed them (for

FIGURE 1
A brief scheme of a folk taxonomy of Chamula verbal behavior.

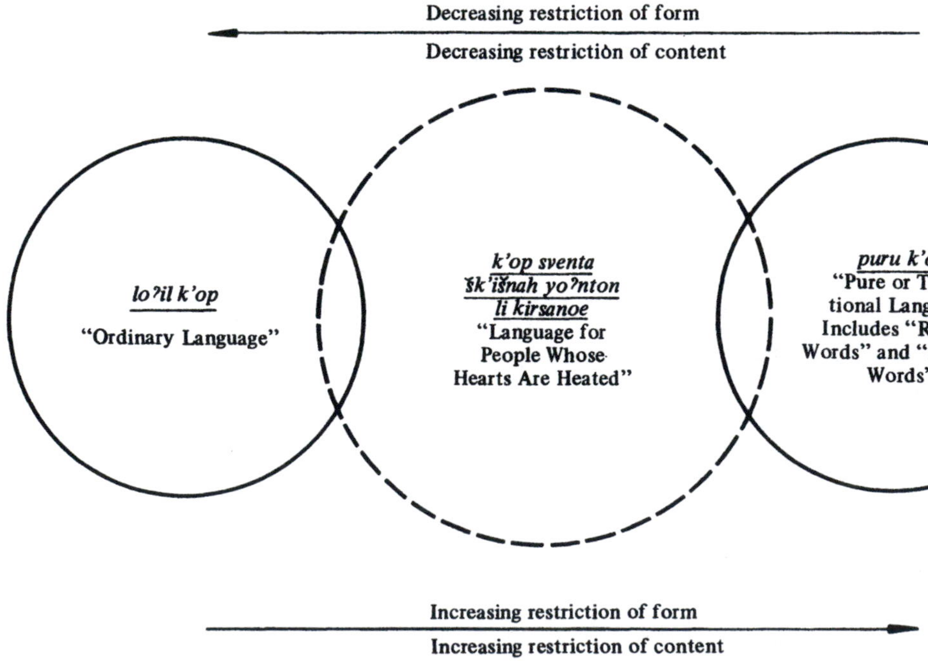

example, *mi haʔ _____ʔ_____ lie*, "Is this a _____?_____?"). In addition to its utility in providing explicit native genre labels for organizing my collection and being sure of getting comprehensive "coverage," the taxonomy also gave me some needed security and efficiency in helping me develop a specific Tzotzil vocabulary for working with a kind of information my informants took for granted. As important as the taxonomy itself were the clues it suggested for deciding on useful kinds of supporting information I might collect for all texts. Specifically, since time associations of the genres appeared as the principal attribute that distinguished the two supercategories of "Pure Words" ("Recent Words" and "Ancient Words;" see figures 1 and 2), it occurred to me early in my field work that temporal attributes of the genres might provide a key for understanding the whole of the oral tradition as it related to other aspects of Chamula life and thought. Since I also knew from my interviewing on cosmology that spatial categories originally determined temporal categories (that is, the sun's first vertical trip around the earth set up the categories of day and night, seasons and years) and that time past remained alive at the edges of the universe, I decided I would elicit explicit temporal and spatial data for all texts, in addition to basic informant and contextual data. . . . A simplified scheme (Figure 1) and a more detailed taxonomy (Figure 2) are given.

The two figures should be more or less self explanatory. The reader will probably note that I have not made an effort to describe the taxonomy as a grid of uniform or symmetrical criteria and distinctive features. Such a scheme would be a distortion of the way in which Chamulas view the taxonomy. For example: time is a relevant criterial attribute for distinguishing level 3 categories of "New Words" and "Recent Words;" for other cate-

FIGURE 2
A folk taxonomy of Chamula verbal behavior.

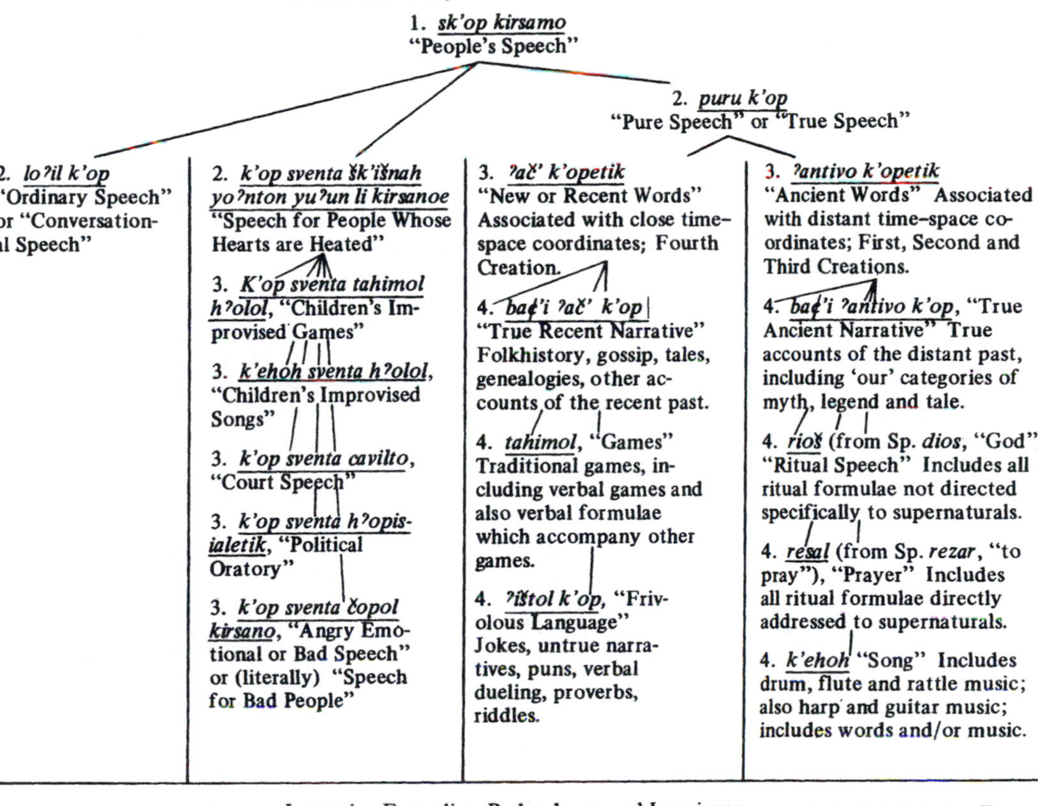

Exegesis: *ta škopoh noʔoš li kirsanoe*, "The people simply talk."

Exegesis: *ta šlok' ta yoʔnton huhune*, "It comes from the heart of each one."

Exegesis: *mu snaʔ shel sbaik*, "They do not know how to change themselves."

gories at the same level (3) of the taxonomy, place of performance is a defining feature ("Court Speech"); for still others at the same level (3), performer of the words is the relevant feature ("Children's Improvised Games"). Therefore, although I use the term "level" in referring to the scheme, I do not attach any uniform "deep structure" information to it. Levels are used only as descriptive conventions. Although I frequently recorded taxa at level 5 in the field, I have not recorded them in this abbreviated version of the classification because responses at this level were far from uniform from informant to informant. I include level 5 items in a few of the brief genre descriptions below, but only when the majority of my informants recognized them. Much more useful than any abstract explanatory grid one might impose on the taxonomy are the Chamula explanations of the super-categories. These are included in Figure 2.

"Ordinary Language" (*lo'il k'op*) is restricted in use only by the dictates of the social situation and grammaticality or intelligibility of the utterance. It is believed to be totally idiosyncratic and without noteworthiness in style, form, or content; it is everyday speech. As one moves from left to right in Figures 1 and 2, progressively more constraints of various sorts are apparent in what a person says (content) and how he says it (form). The intermediate category ("Language for People Whose Hearts Are Heated") contains kinds of verbal behavior that are neither "Ordinary Language" nor "Pure Words." They are restricted with regard to form (that is, how people will speak), but they are unpredictable as far as content is concerned. A common Chamula explanation for this kind of emotional speech emphasizes the individual, idiosyncratic qualities of the performance: "It comes from the heart of each person." The term referring to all of these intermediate forms, "Language for People Whose Hearts Are Heated," implies an elevated, excited, but not necessarily religious attitude on the part of the speaker. This state of excitement produces a style of verbal behavior in the intermediate forms that also occurs in the genres of "True Words." Yet, because content in the former depends on the individual whim of the speaker, these forms are not included by Chamulas as a part of "Pure Words." It is only with the joint presence of prescribed content and prescribed form in genres to which all people ideally have equal access that we reach "Pure Words" on the right hand side of the continuum shown in Figures 1 and 2. As Chamulas told me, " 'Pure Words' do not know how to change." In a sense, then, the heat metaphor, which implies a transition into a more stylized form of speech, continues from the intermediate category into the domain of "Pure Words," which contains the "genuine" Chamula genres of oral tradition. The implication is an obvious but, I believe, important one: Chamula oral tradition ("Pure Words") is only a part of a continuum of styles of verbal behavior occurring in other, less standardized contexts. The classes of verbal behavior that are transitional carry vital information for making sense of what is "Pure Words." Furthermore, Chamula children begin to learn some of the transitional forms (particularly improvised games and songs and emotional speech) long before they begin to experiment with "Pure Words." It therefore seems crucial to consider the whole of verbal behavior rather than just those genres having constant form and content. This will be discussed in greater detail below.

Within "Pure Words," the criterion of time association is the most important one in distinguishing the secular forms ("Recent Words," associated with the present Fourth Creation) from those having greater ritual and etiological significance ("Ancient Words," associated with the First, Second and Third Creations). Several apparent discrepancies in the scheme strike the non-Chamula observer. For example, it is highly probable that certain stylistic features of "Ancient Words" may also be found in verbal aspects of "Children's Improvised Games," which are thought to be idiosyncratic expressions of individual whims in the present. (Repetition of a single pattern of syntax four to six times, with substitution of only one new word for every repetition is a common feature of both "Children's Improvised Games" and "True Ancient Narrative.") This does not constitute an internal inconsistency in the taxonomy, but rather illustrates a simple notion that is too often ignored: children probably would not be able to recognize, understand, or learn the formal genres of "Ancient Words" if they did not experiment with the content, styles, rhythms, and syntax in their informal play behavior.

Another example of apparent inconsistency is also instructive. Gossip might seem to the American or European observer to be excluded from anyone's oral tradition, for it cannot become truly "traditional" overnight. Tradition is, however, a relative thing. In Chamula, gossip does belong to "Pure Speech" most of the time. Gossip, as the Chamulas see it, is not idiosyncratic or original in the way that intermediate types of verbal behavior are. Gossip is part of "True Recent Narrative" because it is a statement of fact, a segment of information known by several people in a single form, which ideally will be passed on as a whole. All, theoretically, have equal access to it. To illustrate: the gossip among women at a waterhole about the chief magistrate's oration to the Chamulas at a past festival is "True Recent Narrative," whereas the oration itself is not. The oration ("Political Oratory") belongs to the transitional category of "Speech for People Whose Hearts are Heated" because no one knew what he was going to say, only how he would say it. Another illustration may help to clarify the taxonomic criteria. Emotional speech ("Speech for Bad People") uses devices of cadence, repetition, syntax, and metaphor that are also found in "Pure Words." However, it is not considered "Pure Words" unless a murder or some other noteworthy event follows the quarrel in which the "Speech for Bad People" was used. In that case the murder, together with the language used, would probably be worthy of retelling as "True Recent Narrative."

BRIEF GENRE DESCRIPTIONS AND ILLUSTRATIONS

It is now time to offer brief descriptions and illustrations of the genres. After this, I shall discuss them as a unit again, for the whole tells considerably more about Chamula sòciety and thought than any one or even the sum of the parts. The whole behaves as an impressive information system which is logically tied to Chamula cosmology and world view. However, the role of each part should be briefly clarified. Parts A, B, and C below refer to the second level taxa in Figure 2.

A. "ORDINARY SPEECH"

This has been discussed above. Here let me repeat simply that this is conventional speech. No one thinks about it as a special form, except to contrast the "correct" Chamula dialect with the "incorrect" neighboring Tzotzil dialects. It has no restrictions as to form and content except that it be intelligible, grammatical and appropriate.

B. "SPEECH FOR PEOPLE WHOSE HEARTS ARE HEATED"

Generally speaking, these intermediate forms of emotional speech contain predictable stylistic devices, but do not contain predictable content. They can be said to be idiosyncratic.

1. *"Children's Improvised Games."* These games, including verbal and nonverbal components alike, tend usually to be imperfect children's imitations of adult behavior. They are distinct from "Games" which belong to "Recent Words" (below) because the latter have rules which are predictable and obligatory from one performance to the next. "Children's Improvised Games" do not behave in this way. Typical examples are small boys' imitations of their fathers' ritual behavior and everyday tasks in the corn field. Little girls between two and four also imitate their mothers' weaving and tortilla-making. Parents do not criticize these imperfect imitations, but neither do they recognize them as standard "Games." Parents frequently say, regarding these forms of play, that "they come from the heart of each one." The most typical verbal component of these games is also related to language learning. It is verbatim repetition of phrases, often three or four times. For example, as a child pretends to herd imaginary sheep he may yell:

Lok'an!	*lok'an!*	*lok'an!*
Get out!	Get out!	Get out!

This form of repetition is related not only to the other forms of "Speech for People Whose Hearts Are Heated," but also to the genres of "Pure Words," as we shall see below.

2. *"Children's Improvised Songs."* These songs, like the games above, are imperfect children's imitations of "Song," a genre that occurs in "Pure Words." The most typical content of these songs is a child's narration of what he is doing as he is playing or working. One reason adults exclude these songs from the "proper" class of "Song" is that "Song" is ideally used only for ritual contexts. This ideal is constantly abused by adults themselves, who use the religious music in numerous secular contexts. However, the crucial difference appears to be that adults know the right tunes to go with the right words; children do not. Furthermore, most children cannot play the instruments (harp and guitar) that should accompany "Song." Therefore, even though children use the "right" melody (form) with improvised words (content), adults do not accept it as legitimate "Song."

An important linguistic component of "Children's Improvised Song" is experimentation with metaphoric couplets, which are the most important stylistic building blocks of the formal genres of "Ancient Words." For example, the following song line came from a child's song of speculation about what animal soul he had. The small boy (four years old) sang it as he struck a cat with a stick:

pinto čon un bi.
Spotted animal (you are).

pinto bolom un bi.
Spotted jaguar (you are).

The melody was "correct" and even the words could conceivably occur in a true "Song," called *Bolom Čon* ("Jaguar Animal"), but the child's attitude was incorrect. He was idly looking at a domestic cat and was presumptuously speculating that he, as a mere child, might have an animal soul companion as powerful as the jaguar, who, everyone knows, is the animal soul companion only of rich and powerful adults. Furthermore, it was not sung in any semblance of a ritual context. The performance was therefore imperfect on several counts. However, the couplet which is cited above has a structure like hundreds which exist in more formal genres: same syntax in two lines, with a one-word synonym substitution in the second line.

3. *"Court Speech."* "Court Speech" refers to the language used by political officials, defendants, plaintiffs, and witnesses at court hearings that occur every day of the year except fiesta days. Verbal competence is absolutely crucial to anyone's success in court. Emotions, of course, play a vital part in all court happenings. The stylistic canons for "heated hearts" are nearly always apparent in "Court Speech." However, because each case is theoretically unique, one does not know what people will say, only how they will say it. The outstanding stylistic traits of "Court Speech" are metaphoric couplets (discussed above) and parallel syntax. The following example of parallel syntax is taken from the chief magistrate's condemnation of a woman who had been caught red-handed with stolen sheep. Note that the repeated syntax, with one word substitutions, is related to the metaphoric couplet and serves as an intensifier of the message. The magistrate's heart is very much heated.

ʔoy ša shayibuk velta šavelk'anik
Many times already you have stolen!

šavelk'an li čihe; You steal sheep;	*šavelk'an ti ʔalak'e* you steal chickens!
šavelk'an ti ʔisak'e; You steal potatoes;	*šavelk'an ti maʔile* you steal squash!
šavelk'an ti k'u ʔile; You steal clothing;	*šavelk'an ti ʔitahe* you steal cabbage!
šavelk'an ti tuluk'e; You steal turkeys;	*skotol k'usi šavelk'an* you steal anything!

ʔaʔša noʔos muyuk bu šavelk'anbe sbek'yat li kirsanoetik
The only thing you don't steal from people are their testicles;

ʔaʔnoʔoš čaloʔ
And those you only eat!

The redundant style helps to make the last line more embarrassing for the defendant, for it accuses her of oral-genital contact, which is disapproved of as animal-like; it is a metaphoric restatement of the animal-like qualities of her habitual thievery which have just been stated in parallel structures nine times. We will see below that, although this speech is idiosyncratic in content, the form of redundancy and parallelism is repeated throughout the oral tradition.

4. *"Political Oratory."* "Political Oratory" includes all public announcements made by religious and political officials outside ritual settings. Like "Court Speech," "Political Oratory" has highly predictable stylistic components; yet each performance is theoretically different, which is why it does not qualify as "Pure Speech." Since the stylistic devices that characterize it have already been discussed above—parallel syntax, metaphoric couplets, redundancy of message, verbatim repetition—no example will be given.

5. *"Speech for Bad People."* The Chamula term for this genre is somewhat misleading, for this category of speech really refers to any heated, emotional, drunken, or angry discussion. Heat is ideally desirable, for it is an aspect of sacred symbols, including the sun-creator himself. It is when heat gets out of control that Chamulas condemn it. This dual aspect of the heat metaphor is implied by the diversity of attitudes included in the class of "Speech for People Whose Hearts Are Heated." "Court Speech" can be desirable in that it defends the community's well-being. However, "Speech for Bad People" can very easily lead to machete fights and killings. Therefore, emotional and excited speech can be desirable if controlled and used in defense of the norm; it is undesirable if uncontrolled and used offensively against the norm. "Speech for Bad People" thus refers to the language of those whose hearts heat up to the point of no control.

The characteristic linguistic forms of this uncontrolled, emotional speech are as follows: multiple metaphoric restatements that may be in couplet form but also in the form of longer restatements of sentence-length, parallel syntax with one- and two-word substitutions, and simple verbatim repetition. Like other forms of the intermediate class, individual performances are unique and theoretically cannot be repeated.

C. "PURE WORDS"

"Pure Words" includes those genres having constraints of three types: Form, content, and social setting. "Pure Words" includes the stable genres of Chamula oral tradition. As a unit, "Pure Words" carries a veritable arsenal of defense for the Chamula way of life. Part of the strength of these genres seems to relate to the fact that the cyclical view of time, the very underpinning of the Chamula view of cosmic order, serves as an attribute that both unifies "Pure Words" and subdivides it into two major classes, "Recent Words" and "Ancient Words." "Recent Words" were learned or acquired in the present, Fourth Creation; "Ancient Words" were learned in, or acquired in, or refer to the First, Second, and Third Creations. Generally speaking, "Recent Words" assume the present social order in Chamula and they are preserved and taught by informal means. "Ancient Words" relate to the coming and formal maintenance of the Chamula social order. As such, "Ancient Words" provide the formulas and mythical precedents for ritual action. In order to appreciate the meaning of the temporal dimensions of this part of the taxonomy, it should be remembered that Chamulas do not subscribe to a "Golden Age" view of the past.

The First, Second, and Third Creations were chaotic and difficult times for the inhabitants of the earth. Being imperfect, they were destroyed by the sun-creator. It is only with the present Fourth Creation that the sun-creator (Christ) is pleased. And even in this Creation it is only the Chamulas who know correct behavior according to the sun's will. Other people on earth still practice some of the barbarities of the first three creations. Chamulas think that the three destructions were incomplete at the edges of the earth and that people there preserve various kinds of asocial behavior long ago surpassed by the Chamulas. It is not unlike the European view of human social evolution in the late nineteenth century: those most unlike Europe and living far away were savages; those intermediate in customs and social distance were barbarians; those most like Europeans, living at the center of the universe, enjoyed true civilization. The others might catch up someday. This is precisely the way Chamulas view their universe, but they are not so arrogant as the Europeans were. They believe that the human condition, particularly in Chamula, is very desirable but also very fragile. Every technique must be used to preserve its integrity. "Pure Words" help enormously in this endeavor.

1. *"Recent Words: True Recent Narrative."* "True Recent Narrative" includes "true" narrative accounts of Fourth Creation events that are worth repeating as a unit and to which all ideally have equal access. The historical depth of the Fourth Creation is not standard. For some it goes back only to the time of their grandfathers. For others it goes back to a nebulous time, long ago, when there were already good (that is, Chamula) people on earth. Generally speaking, the period refers to a time not radically unlike the present in terms of distribution of people, customs, and languages. In nearly all cases, "True Recent Narrative" tells of threats to the social order; famines, epidemics, natural disasters, depletion of natural resources; wars, political disputes, foreign intrusions into Chamula territory; immoral Chamulas, evil Ladinos; pranks and punishments attributed to supernaturals; gossip about corrupt officials, murders, theft, moral decay; changing lineage alliances. Nearly all carry a moral: look what happened when people behaved improperly. Only rarely is a genuinely positive event preserved as "True Recent Narrative." An example is genealogical history (seldom deeper than four generations), in which some ancestor is praised for living uprightly and leaving the present generation a lot of land. No one owns the narratives, nor is there any restriction as to where and when they may be told or who may be present. Narratives are presented as evidence and are told only as appropriate circumstances dictate or as answers to questions and inquiries. For example, accounts of misfortunes associated with droughts would be told if a drought threatened. Chamulas do not have tale-telling sessions as such. Even gossip which includes many "True Recent Narratives," is told ostensibly to inform others of recent threats to and changes in the established order. Few tell of personal good fortune, for that would invite accusations of witchcraft. In sum, "True Recent Narrative" is a kind of catalogue of the human dilemma.

Stylistic traits of "True Recent Narrative" are familiar continuities from "Speech for People Whose Hearts Are Heated." However, the joint presence of these traits with fixed content that is supposedly true qualifies these narratives as a genre of "Pure Words." Individuals may add emphasis in the telling of the event, but they should stick to the facts. There is a device, the greater or lesser density of "stacking" of metaphoric couplets, which serves speakers and listeners as a measure of what in the narrative is judged to be important and what is trivial. Greater redundancy of an idea, in the form of metaphoric couplets, parallel syntax or longer semantic restatement, underlines the importance of the idea. The example which follows illustrates typical composition and a point of emphasis in a single couplet based on parallel syntax. The following fragment, from a text entitled "The Time of the Fever," tells of the influenza epidemic of 1918, which followed the Mexican Revolution.

veno
Well, then,

K'alal ʔital ti k'ak' al čamel ti vonee
When the fever came long ago

pero veno haʔ la smul ti hkaransa
It was because of the crimes of the *carrancistas.*

ʔiliktal tahmek ta ʔolon ʔosil
It came from Hot Country.

la la ščik'ik tal ti htotike
Our Father, the Sun, brought it upon them

la la ščik'ik tal ti santoetike
The saints called it down upon them.

pere ʔora tana ʔun
But then something else happened.

2. *"Recent Words: Frivolous Language."* What "True Recent Narrative" accomplishes with prose accounts of true breaches of the social order, "Frivolous Language" accomplishes with laughter. The genre actually consists of five subgenres (which might be called fifth level taxa in the context of Figure 2). All of these express or refer to ambiguous or deviant behavior, and all elicit laughter from participants and onlookers. Laughter appears to underline the norm by placing the deviant or ambiguous item of behavior in sharp relief against the norm. Using this technique, they effect social control in informal settings and also in formal settings, when other means are not applicable. In all of the subgenres of "Frivolous Language" stylistic constraints are rigid and great emphasis is given to multiple meanings. Form, content, social setting, and range of alternative meanings are more or less constant, thus qualifying them for inclusion in "Pure Words." Very brief descriptions of the genres are given below.

a. "Lies" (hut k'op). "Lies" are prose jokes which tell of admittedly untrue events. The subgenre might be glossed as a "tall tale." Nearly always there is a superficial theme which makes the "Lie" sound like "True Recent Narrative," but there is always a second, usually sexual, theme which lies beneath the apparent surface theme. This form is popular boys' joking behavior and requires considerable linguistic competence for telling and appreciation. The second meaning usually involves some item of deviant behavior such as copulation with animals, adultery, or premarital promiscuity. The laughter which "Lies" elicit emphasizes by contrast what the norm is and should be. "Lies" share almost all stylistic traits with "True Recent Narrative." The difference lies in the verity of the events reported and in the semantic dimension.

b. "Genuine Frivolous Talk" (baʢi ʔištol loʔil). This most widely used sub-genre of "Frivolous Language" consists of hundreds of fixed sets of suggestive words and phrases that have minimal sound shifts from one to the next. Words or phrases are spoken alternately by two players as a form of verbal dueling. The player who cannot respond to a challenge loses. As in "Lies" there is a surface meaning and a second or more meanings. It is a characteristic form of boys' and men's joking behavior and frequently accompanies bantering about sexuality and sexual fantasies in this rather straight-laced society. It also accompanies some overt homosexual behavior permitted of adolescents and young men. "Genuine Frivolous Talk" requires a great deal of finesse with the language, both for performance and appreciation. As such, it serves as a training ground for aspiring politicians and religious officials. It is a form in which young boys strive to achieve excellence, for skill with language is highly prized and respected. It behaves in a way not unlike "signifying" and "ranking" in black communities in the United States.

An example follows. Note that only one phoneme shift occurs, but that the shift carries with it a powerful pun. This fragment is a part of a fixed series that can run to as many as forty exchanges.

PLAYER I: *ʔak'bun ʔaviš*
Give me your older sister.
PLAYER II: *ʔak'bo ʔaviš*
Give it to your sister.

The first line implies a request for Player II's older sister's sexual services. The complex meaning relates to the fragility of the brother-in-law relationship in Chamula. In the first place, the players are potential brothers-in-law. In the second place, the relationship is a difficult one, for although a brideprice is always given to the bride's family by the groom's family, she moves to her husband's hamlet to live. This causes bad feelings between the families. Therefore, the request for his sister's free premarital sexual services is preposterous and potentially dangerous and, hence, funny. However, Player II "one-ups" Player I by suggesting that he have sexual relations with his own older sister instead of with Player II's older sister. Incest, of course, is a greater offense than premarital promiscuity. Much that is proscribed in Chamula society is thus underlined and reinforced by the laughter generated by verbal dueling.

c. *"Obscure Words" (k'ehel k'op).* Although glossed as "proverb," this subgenre of "Frivolous Language" has a different nature and apparently more complex role than proverbs have in Western societies. Ultimately, Chamula "Obscure Words" make normative statements, but they do this by suggestion, never by actual explicit statement. In fact, they will often state the opposite of the norm. The reason for this is that their social setting demands circumlocution. There are many barriers (such as sex, affinal relationship, age, rank) which make it difficult or impossible for people to address one another freely in many social settings, public and private. Yet when some form of deviant behavior takes place, even in a public setting, the most inferior child may call down an offending elder by using "Obscure Words." Because they imply normative deviation by metaphor and try indirectly to correct it, and because the referent situation is usually obvious to offender, speaker, and others, they are remarkably funny. Both linguistic form and range of possible referent situations are more or less constant. An example follows:

ta štal li Hoʔe
It is going to rain,

pere la štakih ta ʔora.
but it will soon dry up.

The deviant addressed was (in the specific performance I witnessed) an old woman who, by pretending to squat innocently under the cover of her long skirt, was actually fouling sacred space in the Ceremonial Center by urinating there surreptitiously. A young man called her down by using this "Obscure Word." The rain referred to her improper voiding in a public place; the drying up was a suggestion that she go elsewhere. If stated directly, the criticism could have earned him a court case, fine, and jail sentence. As it was, the old woman suffered considerable embarrassment, the crowd got a laugh, and the moral order was upheld.

d. *"Riddles" (hak'om k'op).* Chamula riddles behave as jokes and nearly always involve double meanings, usually emphasizing sexual or ambivalent topics which are points of stress in Chamula society. They are generally of two types, classified by linguistic form: fixed formulas and prose. In both cases, the form and content are more or less fixed, although the ambiguous referents (that is "possible answers") may fluctuate within a given range of alternatives. An example of the formulaic form follows:

QUESTION: *hmeʔ kumagre haval*
My comadre is face-up,

kumpagre nuhul
My compadre is face-down.

k'usi ʔun
What is it?

ANSWER: *teša*
A roof tile.

Ceramic roof tiles are arranged on alternate rafters in curved-side-up, curved-side-down interlocking sequence; hence the sexual pun. The reference to the sex life of one's ritual kin (from Spanish *compadres*, "coparents") is ordinarily improper, for one should have a strict respect relationship with them. The "Riddle" actually emphasizes the importance of this respectful ritual relationship, which is a potential source of loans, labor, and general support. This fact is possibly expressed metaphorically in the image of the tile, a roof material that is expensive and better than thatching, for it affords better rain protection and lasts longer. The tile is thus analogous to the *compadrazgo* relationship, which costs something to establish but gives security in return. It should therefore be treated with respect. The humor generated by the "Riddle" emphasizes this. The prose form of "Riddles" deals with similar topics, but the question asked is stated in a longer and more involved way.

e. *"Buried Words" (mukul k'op).* This subgenre behaves as a prose riddle, but is usually used to refer to specific situations, to describe and control specific cases of normative deviation. It uses the familiar parallel structures, discussed above, but the key words are nearly always sexual or scatological puns. Like "Obscure Words," "Buried Words" frequently call attention to some error in personal appearance or behavior. In a sense they tell an offender what is "wrong" by involving him in a suggestive guessing game. The humor underlines the norm but also mitigates potential hard feelings and quarrels.

3. *"Recent Words: Games."* This genre includes verbal and nonverbal aspects of those games having definite rules and names. It is sometimes divided further into children's games, which are combined verbal and nonverbal performances, and adults' games, which are mostly verbal. The latter overlap with the subgenre of "Frivolous Lan-

guage." Space does not permit full discussion of these games, but in reference to children's games, it is important to note that they include rule-governed action of both a verbal and nonverbal nature. This implies that the verbal/nonverbal distinction is not particularly significant to Chamulas. It is rather the rule-governed aspect, the moral dimension, the predictability, which matter as criteria for inclusion of the genre in "Pure Words." Most Chamula children's games assign roles to players according to relative age. The older children have more authority and more "human" roles; the younger children have roles more appropriate to their lesser experience in the rule-governed universe. The themes of the games usually concern important social category distinctions, such as people and demons, people and animals, good people and bad people. The themes attempt to duplicate category relationships in Chamula society. Thus, rank coexists with equality and very seldom are there "winners" in any sort of free competition.

The verbal component is usually a combination of fixed lines of emotional speech and set formulas. The emotion lines accompanying the action are verbatim repetitions (usually in twos and threes) of key words and phrases. Frequently there are also set phrases, which must be said to make the game "correct." One such line comes from a kind of hide-and-go-seek game called Peter Lizard (*petul ʔokoȼ'*) in which the child playing Peter Lizard hides, while the other children try to find him, shouting:

buyot Where are you?	*buyot* Where are you?

buyot, petul ʔokóȼ
Where are you, Peter Lizard?

When they find him (he helps by giving whistle signals), they pursue him and eventually trap him by piling on top of him. Thus, both actions and speech have constraints of form and content in true Chamula "Games."

4. *"Ancient Words: True Ancient Narrative."* This narrative genre shares many stylistic traits and performance aspects with "True Recent Narrative" (see above). The important difference between the two is content, this being related to the temporal dimension. Like all genres of "Ancient Words," "True Ancient Narrative" reports or refers to events of the first three creations. As such, most of the narrations are etiological and explanatory. They tell of the origin of the earth, people, animals, customs. They include numerous anecdotes about the way life was in the first three creations; how animals, people, and inanimate objects could talk; how animals tricked one another; how all of these interacted with supernaturals. Chamulas often divide this genre into three subgenres: accounts of the First, Second, and Third Creations. Events, of course, become progressively more like modern Chamula life as one progresses from the First to the Third Creation. There are no prescribed settings for telling these tales.

Related to the role of "True Ancient Narrative" in stating the coming of the present order is a greater message redundancy than one finds in "True Recent Narrative." This greater density of metaphoric couplets and parallel structures, which I call "metaphoric stacking," appears to be related to a tendency for narrators to use greater redundancy for emphasis. Items of assumed knowledge about the nature of order appear to require more of this emphasis than the threats to order which are reported in "True Recent Narrative." An example of this pattern follows. It is a fragment from a narrative about the Second Creation relating the origin of Ladinos from the offspring of a Second Creation Ladino woman and her dog. Note the symmetry of this fragment, built of couplets.

parallel couplet	*šinulan ʔanȼ* The Ladino woman, šinulan ȼeb The Ladino girl;
interrogative couplet	k'uyepal ʔoy How many were there? čib sbi Two of them.
parallel couplet	ȼ'akal ta šanav Behind her it walked, ȼ'akal ta sbeʔ in Behind her it travelled
semantic couplet	ščʔuk sȼ'iʔ She and the dog, muyuk bu ta šanav stuk She did not walk alone.

Not all texts are as symmetrical and redundant as this one, nor is symmetry necessarily present throughout a text. The fragment, however, illustrates a general tendency for all genres of "Ancient Words" to utilize greater stylistic redundancy than "Recent Words." This relates to the kind of information carried; it is crucial, basic knowledge that must be understood by all and formally maintained.

5. *"Ancient Words: Prayer."* "Prayer" is ritual language addressed to supernaturals. It

consists wholly of formal, bound couplets. I have never heard a "Prayer" composed of smaller elements. Its use implies a ritual setting. All adult Chamulas know some "Prayers"; religious specialists know hundreds. In all cases the components remain the same: highly redundant, metaphoric couplets with prescribed content and a more or less fixed order, the content and order of the couplets being determined by the specific ritual setting.

An example follows. It is a fragment from a layman's "Prayer" of salutation to the image of San Juan (Chamula's patron saint) in the Chamula church.

parallel couplet
muk'ta san huan
Great San Juan,
muk'ta patron
Great patron,

parallel couplet
lital ta yolon ʔavok
I have come before your feet;
lital ta yolon ʔak'ob
I have come before your hands;

parallel couplet
šciʔuk hnup
With my wife,
šciʔuk hčiʔil
With my companion,

parallel couplet
šciʔuk kol
With my children,
šciʔuk hnič'on
With my offspring.

This text illustrates a pattern of "Ancient Words": that the greater the symbolic significance of a transaction, the more condensed and redundant will be the language used to conduct it.

6. *"Ancient Words: Ritual Speech."* "Ritual Speech" includes all ritual language not directed to supernaturals. Like "Prayer," all adult Chamulas must know some kinds of "Ritual Speech": religious and political specialists know the dozens of kinds required for their respective tasks. "Ritual Speech" is used by ritual officials and laymen to talk among themselves on the elevated plane of the ritual setting. It is constantly present in Chamula life, from drinking ceremonies to installation of new ritual officials to bride-petitioning rites. Since it always accompanies ritual transactions, its content is as varied as these settings. The style (with some exceptions, such as drinking toasts) is very much like that of "Prayer," and it is remarkably constant from one setting to the next. Like "Prayer," it is built almost entirely of bound formal couplets, which are theoretically irreducible components for the composition of "Ritual Speech." The relationship of redundancy of style and content to the high symbolic significance of the transaction applies to "Ritual Speech" as it does to "Prayer."

7. *"Ancient Words: Song."* "Song" may be seen as the opposite end of a continuum of formalism and redundancy beginning with "Ordinary Language" (*loʔil k'op*). "Song" has all of the formal stylistic attributes of "Prayer" and "Ritual Speech," plus musical form and instrumental accompaniment. "Song" is present at nearly all Chamula public rituals and at most private ones. No major Chamula ritual performance takes place without musicians. (Holy Week festivities are a near exception to this rule.) "Song" is a form of language addressed to supernaturals or giving them information about the progress of a ritual. As such, "Song" should not ideally be secular. But in practice it is widely used in secular settings. The ritual content in the lyrics, however, is not changed in secular settings in which I have seen and heard "Song" performed. Pieces with words (which musicians and ritual officials sing to the accompaniment of harp, guitar, and rattle) and without words (played on drum and flute and, occasionally, on horn, accordion and ocarina by specialists for certain major fiestas) are classed as "Song" (*k'ehoh*). The instruments are said to sing just as people do. "Song" is an extreme statement of redundancy, for the musical form and couplet structure make it possible to repeat them *ad infinitum* until the ritual events they accompany have concluded. An example follows. It is a fragment from a "Song" for one of the ritual officials in charge of San Juan's cult.

parallel couplet
sk'ak'alil ʔak'inale
It is the day of your fiesta!
sk'ak'alilʔapaškue
It is the day of your celebration!

parallel couplet
muk'ulil san huane
Great San Juan,
muk'ulil patrone
Great Patron.

parallel couplet
k'uyepal čihšanavotik ʔo ta hlikel bi
How soon we are to begin walking!
k'uyepal čihšanavotik ʔo ta htabel bi
How soon we will be taking you in procession!

parallel couplet	sk'ak'alil ʔaničim ba It is the day of your flowery countenance, sk'ak'alil ʔaničim sat It is the day of your flowery face.
nonsense syllables as parallel structures	la la li la lai la ʔo la la li la lai la ʔa la la li la lai la ʔa la la li la lai la ʔo

GENRES AND COSMOS

The time has come to try to pull some of the pieces back together. It has been my argument throughout that there is more that holds Chamula oral tradition together, as a reservoir of knowledge, than separates it into diverse genres. It makes more sense together, for that is the way it is learned, used, and even changed.

In this section, I should like to argue that a metalanguage of time and space binds together the normative, the credible, and the desirable in oral tradition as the same categories of time and space hold the moral universe together (as discussed above). That this might be the case should come as no surprise, for language is viewed by Chamulas as a distinctively human trait, which occurs in its perfect form in the Chamula dialect of Tzotzil (*ba¢'ik'op*, the "true language"). It should rather come as a surprise if the organization of linguistic information about the universe did not show a significant relationship to the structure of the universe itself. The taxonomy (Figure 2) suggests that time is indeed a relevant variable to consider, for "Pure Words" are themselves divided into "Ancient Words" and "Recent Words," according to their associations in the First through Fourth Creations. Even "Ordinary Speech" and "Speech for People Whose Hearts Are Heated" have a neutral temporal dimension in that they are ephemeral phenomena of the Fourth Creation; they do not have predictable form and content.

What do the present and the past mean in terms of space? Chamulas constantly insisted that behavior that had been surpassed by Chamulas after the First, Second and Third Creations still survived at the edges of their spatial universe. This suggested that time and space were aspects of the same cosmological reality, just as they were in the beginning when the sun-creator initiated the First Creation and all later temporal categories with his first spatial orbit around the universe. It therefore seemed reasonable to suppose that the order-giving and order-maintaining information in the oral tradition might demonstrate the same time-space unity. To examine this further, I compared the temporal and spatial variables of 184 texts of "True Recent Narrative" and "True Ancient Narrative." On a simple graph I plotted values of the time each narrative had taken place with the most distant placename mentioned in the same text. These specific temporal and spatial data as well as genre label were elicited for each text (discussed above). The time axis began with the present and went progressively back to the First Creation. The space axis began with Chamula and had categories of space increasingly unlike Chamula and socially distant. Results indicated that Chamula beliefs about the universe were clearly replicated in both the taxonomy and the content of their narratives. Events that took place relatively close to Chamula and merely threatened the moral universe took place in the Fourth Creation and belonged to "True Recent Narrative"; events that took place in progressively more distant spatial categories of the universe also took place, progressively, in the Third, Second, and First Creations. Extrapolated from the narrative genres to all genres, this sugggests that analogous values of time and space work together as dimensions of logic, credibility, and function in Chamula oral tradition. I also suggest that these same dimensions may regulate change in and accretions to the oral tradition. . . .

SUMMARY AND CONCLUSIONS

Chamula oral tradition is not only associated with norms but also actively involved in teaching, reinterpreting, and maintaining them. "Recent Words" and "Speech for People Whose Hearts Are Heated" teach and enforce by relatively informal means in the present the moral order that "Ancient Words" maintain by ritual means and formal explanations reaching back in time. It should not be surprising that fundamental social categories like time and space bear a relationship to the content, categories, function, and style of traditional verbal behavior. Language is, after all, a social fact *par excellence*. Oral tradition in Chamula is a crucial aspect of language. Taken separately, Chamula genres are but fragments of the totality of specialized verbal competence successful adults must master. The whole carries more information than the sum of the parts. In a nut shell, then, this paper makes a case for looking at the whole in addition to the parts. Some implications follow:

First, if our consideration of Chamula oral tradition were restricted to what we call myth, folktales, legend, folk music, or pun, we could hope for no more than a distorted view of the collective representations of the community. These Western genres are not significant, as such, in Chamula. Furthermore, even if they were significant to Chamulas, these few "standard genres" would account for no more than a fraction of the vast amount of information contained in the many classes of Chamula verbal behavior. For example, to attempt to understand Chamula religion and cosmology using "True Ancient Narrative" alone would present distortions similar to those that might come from discussing a kinship system without discussing the terms below "ego" or the terms for affines. In kinship studies, anthropologists make every effort to emphasize the culture-specific meaning of kin terms within a whole system. Why not do the same for verbal behavior? This perspective might introduce some much-needed caution into the cross-cultural "comparative method" as it is frequently found in folklore studies.

Second, my Chamula data show that no genre of "Pure Words" has any special logical primacy over any other genre for purposes of analysis. There is as much information about cosmology and social categories in a recent item of gossip in "True Recent Narrative" as there is in an item of "Ritual Speech." The form is simply different. This calls into question the inordinate amount of attention anthropologists have consistently given to myth and ritual. The "minor" genres, if noted, might supply the same information—perhaps in less cryptic form than the formal genres. They might even provide objective tests for such useful intuitive notions as "nature" and "culture." This would allow us to interpret myth as another code for information that is given explicitly elsewhere in the oral tradition. Such an intracultural comparison of genres offers exciting prospects when combined with such methods as structural analysis.

Third, a holistic approach to Chamula oral tradition permits a useful perspective for observing how children acquire adult verbal competence. The Chamula data indicate that children learn their oral tradition as stylistic and generic continuum. "Prayer," for example, is a sophisticated form that is learned as a separate form relatively late in childhood and presupposes certain religious information and ability to use parallel syntax style and redundancy. Children learn these things much earlier in their linguistic play with "Games" and "Frivolous Talk." To ignore the whole would be to ignore a very significant dimension of Chamula communication: oral tradition behaves as a system of interpenetrating styles and information.

Finally, a holistic approach helps to emphasize that patterns of ideal behavior are found throughout the cultural fabric, from court procedure to play, from games to ritual, from joking to prayer. A study of these structural patterns offers a comprehensive view of the meaning of esthetic forms, possibly providing an illustration of the old-fashioned idea that esthetics are ethics.

FIVE
THE SYMBOLIC ANALYSIS OF RITUAL

Introduction

In its broadest sense ritual may include all behavior from "How are you?" and the etiquette of daily greetings to the solemnities of the High Mass, from magical spells uttered in a Trobriand garden to the studied dignity of the Zuni Shalako ceremony. Leach, who uses the term "ritual" in its broadest sense, emphasizes that the distinction between what people say and what they do should not be confused with that between myth and ritual (see Kluckhohn, Chapter Two). Speech (prayers, spells, chants) comprises an integral part of ritual behavior, as much so as gesture and the manipulation of objects. Ritual is not the dumb, silent cousin of myth. Turner, while underlining the importance of speech in his detailed consideration of prayer and native exegesis, would restrict the term ritual to the classes of behavior which accompany social transitions and use ceremony to denote behaviors which serve to confirm a particular social status. Whether they use ritual in a wide or narrow sense, most writers would agree that ritual (in Turner's sense) shows continuities with ceremony and everyday etiquette and, for some purposes, it may be useful to call all these kinds of behavior ritual (in Leach's sense).

Religious ritual, for Durkheim and his followers (see Chapter One), is a set of practices through which the participants relate to the sacred. Sacred and profane activities are seen as antithetical, profane activities typically being economic and subsistence routines. Within the broad category of religious rites, Titiev (see Chapter Seven), for instance, would distinguish between calendrical and critical rites, depending on whether a ritual is regular or occasional in its performance. Curing and magic (see Chapters Six and Seven) are critical rites and Zinacantecan cargo ritual is calendrical. Those rituals which mark social transition, be it territorial (the treatment of the guest, the visitor), succession to office, or part of the life cycle (birth, initiation, marriage, death), comprise a general class, termed rites of passage in Arnold van Gennep's classic work on their shared characteristics. Ndembu initiation and the Crow vision quest fall into this general class which may be further subdivided into rites of separation, transition, and incorporation. Each phase of the rite of passage has its typical symbolic expressions: separation may be marked by haircutting and cutting or severing in general; incorporation is indicated by tying a knot, putting on a belt, a ring, a bracelet, or a veil. Turner directs himself to characteristic expressions of transition, or liminality, an area slighted in van Gennep's treatment.

It is worth nothing that the Freudian theory which would equate the behavior of obsessional neurotics in our culture with that of performers of religious rites in all cultures (see Kluckhohn, Chapter Two) is not relevant to the writings in this chapter. Teeth filing, for instance, might be a rite of separation for van Gennep and his followers, while, for the Freudian, it would represent symbolic castration related to Oedipal anxieties. In Freud's paper on "Obsessive Acts and Religious Practices" (1948–1950), the private rite, performed in isolation, e.g., meticulously laying one's clothes by the bedstool in a particular order, with its strictly followed compulsions and prohibitions, its impelling sense of guilt, is equated with religious rites. The primary difference between the two is that neuroses are bound to sexual drives and motives, and their repression, and religious rites derive from the suppression of egoistic, antisocial impulses. Thus sacred license, a culminating moment in a rite of passage and, for van Gennep, a rite of incorporation, would be seen by the Freudian in relation to the suppression and denial of egoistic desires associated with religious belief and practice. In part because of the cavalier equation by some students of psychoanalysis of symptomatic behavior (involuntary acts, resulting directly from inner drives and conflicts) and symbolic action (voluntary acts, which may, or may not, correspond to inner psychological dispositions and needs)—ritual tears may be wiped away by a smile and a "hello," only to be resumed again—explanation of ritual in terms of fundamental psychological needs and motives is no longer in vogue. The writings in this chapter typify the current trend in that they direct themselves less to functional problems than to problems of symbolic analysis and of explicating the internal logic of the ritual itself. The problem is not so much what the ritual does for people as what it says to them, how it is intelligible to the participants.

Edmund R. Leach

TWO ESSAYS CONCERNING THE SYMBOLIC REPRESENTATION OF TIME

It is a truism that time, especially in its calendrical aspects, has been endowed by men everywhere with sacred meaning. A look at a Roman Catholic calendar gives testimony to the persistence of the ancient connection that has been made between sacred rituals and the yearly round, based in large measure on the ever-recurring change of seasons, in animal and plant life, and in celestial phenomena, these serving as a simple kind of measurement. Social and religious life are regulated by and come to center around "natural" calendars, the moon being overwhelmingly important in the simpler societies, and traces of the lunar month can be found even today in almost all calendrical systems.

In his analysis of the symbolization of time, Leach has restated some of the standard notions of time and given them novel interpretations. His first essay, "Cronus and Chronos," opens with the suggestion that we tend to think of time both in terms of repetition and of irreversibility, especially the latter, and that much of the religion is concerned with trying to deny the reality of death by equating the second of these two concepts with the first. Some primitives, however, do not experience time in either of these two ways but perceive it as a sequence of oscillations between opposite poles. The rest of the essay is devoted toward demonstrating that this third concept involves a third entity, to wit, the thing that does the oscillating, and that an animistic concept of

Reprinted form Edmund R. Leach, *Rethinking Anthropology* (London: The Athlone Press, University of London, 1961), pp. 124–136, by permission of the author and The Athlone Press.

this sort is bound up with a belief in reincarnation, justified by a mythology, an example of which is provided from classical Greece.

In his second essay, "Time and False Noses," Leach's indebtedness to the Durkheimian school of sociology is again apparent, as it was in the first, where the influence of Lévi-Strauss was specifically acknowledged. Leach gives his solution to the question of why men throughout the world mark their calendars by festivals, at which time they indulge either in formality, masquerade, or role reversal. He sees these three involved, respectively, with three phases of sacred time: *separation*, with its rites of sacralization; a marginal state of *suspended animation*, when ordinary time stops; and *aggregation*, with its rites of desacralization. He attempts to structure the three practices of formality, masquerade, and role reversal in terms of opposites, placing the first and third in opposition to the second.

INTRODUCTORY NOTE

These two short essays originally appeared in the Toronto University publication *Explorations*. The amendments which have been made to the text of "Cronus and Chronos" are largely due to the very helpful suggestions of Mr. M. I. Finley of Jesus College, Cambridge.

I. CRONUS AND CHRONOS

My starting point in this essay is simply *time* as a word in the English language. It is a word which we use in a wide variety of contexts and it has a considerable number of synonyms, yet is oddly difficult to translate. In an English-French dictionary *time* has one of the longest entries in the book, time is *temps*, and *fois*, and *heure*, and *age*, and *siécle*, and *saison* and lots more besides, and none of these are simple equivalents; *temps* perhaps is closest to English *time*, but *beau temps* is not a "lovely time"!

Outside of Europe this sort of ambiguity is even more marked. For example, the language of the Kachin people of North Burma seems to contain no single word which corresponds at all closely to English *time;* instead there are numerous partial equivalents. For example, in the following expressions the Kachin equivalent of the word *time* would differ in every case:

The *time* by the clock is	*ahkying*
A long *time*	*na*
A short *time*	*tawng*
The present *time*	*ten*
Spring *time*	*ta*
The *time* has come	*hkra*
In the *time* of Queen Victoria	*lakhtak, aprat*
At any *time* of life	*asak*

and that certainly does not exhaust the list. I do not think a Kachin would regard these words as in any way synonyms for one another.

This sort of thing suggests an interesting problem which is quite distinct from the purely philosophical issue as to what is the *nature* of Time. This is: How do we come to have such a verbal category as *time* at all? How does it link up with our everyday experiences?

Of course in our own case, equipped as we are with clocks and radios and astronomical observatories, time is a given factor in our social situation; it is an essential part of our lives which we take for granted. But suppose we had no clocks and no scientific astronomy, how then should we think about time? What obvious attributes would time then seem to possess?

Perhaps it is impossible to answer such a very hypothetical question, and yet, clocks apart, it seems to me that our modern English notion of time embraces at least two different kinds of experience which are logically distinct and even contradictory.

Firstly, there is the notion of repetition. Whenever we think about measuring time we concern ourselves with some kind of metronome; it may be the ticking of a clock or a pulse beat or the recurrence of days or moons or annual seasons, but always there is something which repeats.

Secondly, there is the notion of nonrepetition. We are aware that all living things are born, grow old and die, and that this is an irreversible process.

I am inclined to think that all other aspects of time, duration for example or historical sequence, are fairly simple derivatives from these two basic experiences:

(a) that certain phenomena of nature repeat themselves,
(b) that life change is irreversible.

Now our modern sophisticated view tends to throw the emphasis on the second of these aspects of time. "Time," says Whitehead, "is sheer succession of epochal durations": it goes on and on. All the same we need to recognize that this irreversibility of time is psychologically very unpleasant. Indeed, throughout the world, religious dogmas are largely concerned with denying the final "truth" of this common sense experience.

Religions of course vary greatly in the manner by which they purport to repudiate the "reality" of death; one of the commonest devices is simply to assert that death and birth are the same thing—that birth follows death, just as death follows birth. This seems to amount to denying the second aspect of time by equating it with the first.

I would go further. It seems to me that if it were not for religion we should not attempt to embrace the two aspects of time under one category at all. Repetitive and nonrepetitive events are not, after all, logically the same. We treat them both as aspects of "one thing," *time*, not because it is rational to do so, but because of religious prejudice. The idea of Time, like the idea of God, is one of those categories which we find necessary because we are social animals rather than because of anything empirical in our objective experience of the world.

Or put it this way. In our conventional way of thinking, every interval of time is marked by repetition; it has a beginning and an end which are "the same thing"—the tick of a clock, sunrise, the new moon, New Year's day . . . but every interval of time is only a section of some larger interval of time which likewise begins and ends in repetition . . . so, if we think in this way, we must end by supposing that "Time itself" (whatever that is) must repeat itself. Empirically this seems to be the case. People *do* tend to think of time as something which ultimately repeats itself; this applies equally to Australian aborigines, Ancient Greeks, and modern mathematical astronomers. My view is that we think this way not because there is no other possible way of thinking, but because we have a psychological (and hence religious) repugnance to contemplating either the idea of death or the idea of the end of the universe.

I believe this argument may serve to throw some light upon the representation of time in primitive ritual and mythology. We ourselves, in thinking about time, are far too closely tied to the formulations of the astronomers; if we do not refer to time as if it were a coordinate straight line stretching from an infinite past to an infinite future, we describe it as a circle or cycle. These are purely geometrical metaphors, yet there is nothing intrinsically geometrical about time as we actually experience it. Only mathematicians are ordinarily inclined to think of repetition as an aspect of motion in a circle. In a primitive, unsophisticated community the metaphors of repetition are likely to be of a much more homely nature: vomiting, for example, or the oscillations of a weaver's shuttle, or the sequence of agricultural activities, or even the ritual exchanges of a series of interlinked marriages. When we describe such sequences as "cyclic" we innocently introduce a geometrical notation which may well be entirely absent in the thinking of the people concerned.

Indeed in some primitive societies it would seem that the process is not experienced as a "succession of epochal durations" at all; there is no sense of going on and on in the same direction, or round and round the same wheel. On the contrary, time is experienced as something discontinuous, a repetition of repeated reversal, a sequence of oscillations between polar opposites: night and day, winter and summer, drought and flood, age and youth, life and death. In such a scheme the past has no "depth" to it, all past is equally past; it is simply the opposite of now.

It is religion, not common sense, that persuades men to include such various oppositions under a single category such as *time*. Night and day, life and death are logically similar pairs only in the sense that they are both pairs of contraries. It is religion that identifies them, tricking us into thinking of death as the night time of life and so persuading us that non-repetitive events are really repetitive.

The notion that the time process is an oscillation between opposites—between day and night or between life and death—implies the existence of a third entity—the "thing" that oscillates, the "I" that is at one moment in the daylight and another in the dark, the "soul" that is at one moment in the living body and at another in the tomb. In this version of animistic thinking the body and the grave are simply alternative temporary residences for the life-essence, the soul. Plato, in the *Phaedo*, actually uses this metaphor explicitly: he refers to the human body as the *tomb of the soul* (psyche). In death the soul goes from this world to the underworld; in birth it comes back from the underworld to this world.

This is of course a very common idea both in primitive and less primitive religious thinking. The point that I want to stress is that this type of animism involves a particular conception of the nature of time and, because of this, the mythology which justifies a belief in reincarnation is also, from another angle, a mythological representation of "time" itself. In the rest of this essay I shall attempt to illustrate this argument by reference to familiar material from classical Greece.

At first sight it may appear that I am arguing in a circle. I started by asking what sort of concrete real experience lies at the back of our abstract notion of time. All I seem to have done so far is to switch from the oscillations of abstract time to the oscillations of a still more abstract concept, soul. Surely this is worse than ever. For us, perhaps, yes. We can "see" time on a clock; we cannot see people's souls; for us, souls are more abstract than time. But for the Greeks, who had no clocks, time was a total abstraction, whereas the soul was thought of as a material substance consisting of the marrow of the spine and the head, and forming a sort of concentrated essence of male semen. At death, when the body was placed in the tomb this marrow coagulated into a live snake. In Greek ancestor cults the marked emphasis on snake worship was not a residue of totemism: it was simply that the hero-ancestor in his chthonic form was thought to be an actual snake. So for the Greeks, of the pre-Socratic period anyway, the oscillation of the soul between life and death was quite materially conceived—the soul was either material bone-marrow (in the living body) or it was a material snake (in the tomb).

If then, as I have suggested, the Greeks conceived the oscillations of time by analogy with the oscillations of the soul, they were using a concrete metaphor. Basically it is the metaphor of sexual coitus, of the ebb and flow of the sexual essence between sky and earth (with the rain as semen), between this world and the underworld (with marrow-fat and vegetable seeds as semen), between man and woman. In short, it is the sexual act itself which provides the primary image of time. In the act of copulation the male imparts a bit of his life-soul to the female; in giving birth she yields it forth again. Coitus is here seen as a kind of dying for the male; giving birth as a kind of dying for the female. Odd though this symbolism may appear, it is entirely in accord with the findings of psychoanalysts who have approached the matter from quite a different point of view.

All this I suggest throws light upon one of the most puzzling characters in classical Greek mythology, that of Cronus, father of Zeus. [Aristotle] (*de Mundo* Ch. 7) declared that Cronus (Kronos) was a symbolical representation of Chronos, Eternal Time—and it is apparently this association which has provided our venerable Father Time with his scythe. Etymologically, however, there is no close connection between *kronos* and *chronos*, and it seems unlikely that [Aristotle] should have made a bad pun the basis for a major issue of theology, though this seems to be the explanation generally put forward. Whatever may have been the history of the Cronus cult—and of that we know nothing—the fact that at one period Cronus was regarded as a symbol for Time must surely imply that there was something about the mythological character of Cronus which seemed appropriate to that of a personified Time. Yet it is difficult for us to understand this. To us Cronus appears an entirely disreputable character with no obvious temporal affinities.

Let me summarize briefly the stories which relate to him:

1. Cronus, King of the Titans, was the son of Uranus (sky) and Ge (earth). As the children of Uranus were born, Uranus pushed them back again into the body of Ge. Ge to escape this prolonged pregnancy armed Cronus with a sickle with which he castrated his father. The blood from the bleeding phallus fell into the sea and from the foam was born Aphrodite (universal fecundity).

2. Cronus begat children by his sister Rhea. As they were born he swallowed them. When the youngest, Zeus, was born, Rhea deceived Cronus by giving him a (phallic) stone wrapped in a cloth instead of a new-born infant. Cronus swallowed the stone instead of the child. Zeus thus grew up. When Zeus was adult, Cronus vomited up his swallowed children, namely: Hades, Poseidon, Hestia, Hera, Demeter, and also the stone phallus, which last became a cult object at Delphi. Zeus now rebelled against King Cronus and overthrew him; according to one version he castrated him. Placed in restraint, Cronus became nevertheless the beneficent ruler of the Elysian Fields, home of the blessed dead.

3. There had been men when King Cronus ruled but no women; Pandora, the first woman, was created on Zeus's instructions. The age of Cronus was a golden age of bliss and plenty, when the fields yielded harvests without being tilled. Since there were no women, there was no strife! Our present age, the age of Zeus, will one day come to an end, and the reign of Cronus will then be resumed. In that moment men will cease to grow older: they will grow younger. Time will repeat itself in reverse: men will be born from their graves. Women will once more cease to be necessary, and strife will dissappear from the world.

4. About the rituals of Cronus we know little. In Athens the most important was the festival known as Kronia. This occurred at

harvest time in the first month of the year and seems to have been a sort of New Year celebration. It resembled in some ways the Roman saturnalia (Greek Cronus and Roman Saturn were later considered identical). Its chief features seems to have been a ritual reversal of roles—masters waiting on slaves and so on.

What is there in all this that makes Cronus an appropriate symbol for Time? The third story certainly contains a theme about time, but how does it relate to the first two stories? Clearly the time that is involved is not time as we ordinarily tend to think of it—an endless continuum from past to future. Cronus' time is an oscillation, a time that flows back and forth, that is born and swallowed and vomited up, an oscillation from father to mother, mother to father and back again.

Some aspects of the story fit well enough with the views of Frazer and Jane Harrison about Corn Spirits and Year Spirits (*eniautos daimon*). Cronus, as the divine reaper, cuts the "seed" from the "stalk" so that Mother Earth yields up her harvest. Moreover, since harvest is logically the end of a sequence of time, it is understandable enough that, given the notion of time as oscillation, the change over from year's end to year's beginning should be symbolized by a reversal of social roles—at the end point of any kind of oscillation everything goes into reverse. Even so the interpretation in terms of vegetation magic and nature symbolism does not get us very far. Frazer and Jane Harrison count their Corn Spirits and Year Spirits by the dozen and even if Cronus does belong to the general family this does not explain why Cronus rather than any of the others should have been specifically identified as a symbol of Time personified.

My own explanation is of a more structural kind. Fränkel has shown that early Greek ideas about time underwent considerable development. In Homer *chronos* refers to periods of empty time and is distinguished from periods of activity which are thought of as days (*ephmeros*). By the time of Pindar this verbal distinction had disappeared, but a tendency to think of time as an "alteration between contraries" active and inactive, good and bad, persisted. It is explicit in Archilochus (seventh century B.C.). In the classical period this idea underwent further development so that in the language of philosophy, time was an oscillation of vitality between two contrasted poles. The argument in Plato's *Phaedo* makes this particularly clear. Given this premise, it follows logically that the "beginning of time" occurred at that instant when, out of an initial unity, was created not only polar opposition but also the sexual vitality that oscillates between one and the other—not only God and the Virgin but the Holy Spirit as well.

Most commentators on the Cronus myth have noted simply that Cronus separates Sky from Earth, but in the ideology I have been discussing the creation of time involves more than that. Not only must male be distinguished from female but one must postulate a third element, mobile and vital, which oscillates between the two. It seems clear that the Greeks thought of this third element in explicit concrete form as male semen. Rain is the semen of Zeus; fire the semen of Hėphaestos; the offerings to the dead (*panspermia*) were baskets of seeds mixed up with phallic emblems; Hermes the messenger of the gods, who takes the soul to Hades and brings back souls from the dead, is himself simply a phallus and a head and nothing more.

This last symbolic element is one which is found to recur in many mythological systems. The logic of it seems clear. In crude pictorial representation, it is the presence or absence of a phallus which distinguishes male from female, so, if time is represented as a sequence of role reversals, castration stories linked up with the notion of a phallus trickster who switches from side to side of the dichotomy "make sense." If Kerenyi and Jung are to be believed there are psychological explanations for the fact that the "messenger of the gods" should be part clown, part fraud, part isolated phallus, but here I am concerned only with a question of symbolic logic. If time be thought of as alternation, then myths about sex reversals are representations of time.

Given this set of metaphors Cronus's myth *does* make him "the creator of time." He separates sky from earth but he separates off at the same time the male vital principle which, falling to the sea reverses itself and becomes the female principle of fecundity. The shocking part of the first story, which at first seems an unnecessary gloss, contains, as one might have expected, the really crucial theme. So also in the second story the swallowing and vomiting activities of Cronus serve to create three separate categories—Zeus, the polar opposites of Zeus, and a material phallus. It is no accident that Zeus's twice born siblings are the five deities named, for each is the "contrary" of Zeus in one of his recognized major aspects: the three females are the three aspects of womanhood, Hestia the maiden, Hera the wife, Demeter the mother; they are the opposites of Zeus in his roles as divine youth (*Kouros*), divine husband, divine father and divine son (Dionysus). Hades, lord of the underworld and the dead, is the opposite of Zeus, lord of the bright day and the living; Poseidon, earth shaker, god of the sea (salt water), is the opposite of Zeus, sky shaker (thunderer), god of rain and dew.

The theme of the child which is swallowed (in whole or part) by its father and thereby given second birth, crops up in other parts of Greek mythology—e.g. in the case of Athena and Dionysus. What is peculiar to the Cronus story is that it serves to establish a mythological image of interrelated contraries, a theme which recurs repeatedly in mature Greek philosophy. The following comes from Cary's translation of the *Phaedo:*

> *"We have then," said Socrates, "sufficiently determined this—that all things are thus produced, contraries from contraries?"*
> *"Certainly."*
> *"What next? Is there also something of this kind in them, for instance, between all two contraries a mutual twofold production, from one to the other, and from the other back again . . . ?"*

For men who thought in these terms, "the beginning" would be the creation of contraries, that is to say the creation of male and female not as brother and sister but as husband and wife. My thesis then is that the philosophy of the *Phaedo* is already implicit in the gory details of the myth of Cronus. The myth is a creation myth, not a story of the beginning of the world, but a story of the beginning of time, of the beginning of becoming.

Although the climate may seem unfamiliar, this theme is not without relevance for certain topics of anthropological discussion. There is for instance Radcliffe-Brown's doctrine concerning the identification of alternating generations, whereby grandfather and grandson tend to exhibit "solidarity" in opposition to the intervening father. Or there is the stress which Lévi-Strauss has placed upon marriage as a symbol of alliance between otherwise opposed groups. Such arguments when reduced to their most abstract algebraic form may be represented by a diagram such as this:

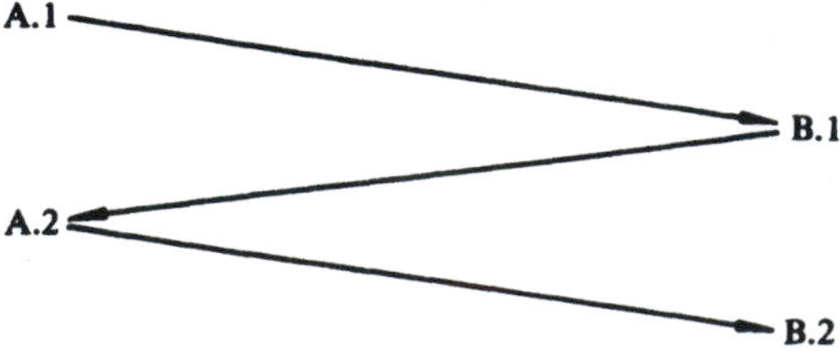

In Radcliffe-Brown's argument the As and the Bs, that are opposed yet linked, are the alternating generations of a lineage; in Lévi-Strauss's, the As and the Bs are the males of contending kin groups allied by the interchange of women.

My thesis has been that the Greeks tended to conceptualize the time process as a zig-zag of this same type. They associated Cronus with the idea of time because, in a structural sense, his myth represents a separation of A from B and a creation of the initial arrow A → B, the beginning of life which is also the beginning of death. It is also nicely relevant that Heraclitus should have defined "a generation" as a period of thirty years, this being calculated "as the interval between the procreation of a son by his father and the procreation of a son's son by the son," the interval, that is A.1 → B.1 → A.2.

I don't want to suggest that all primitive peoples necessarily think about time in this way, but certainly some do. The Kachins whom I mentioned earlier have a word *majan*, which, literally, ought to mean "woman affair." They use it in three main contexts to mean (*a*) warfare, (*b*) a love-song, and (*c*) the weft threads of a loom. This seems to us an odd concatenation yet I fancy the Greeks would have understood it very well. Penelope sits at her loom, the shuttle goes back and forth, back and forth, love and war, love and war; and what does she weave? You can guess without looking up your *Odyssey—a shroud* of course, the time of Everyman 'Tis love that makes the world go round; but women are the root of all evil. (The Greek Ares god of war was paramour of Aphrodite goddess of love.)

II. TIME AND FALSE NOSES

Briefly my puzzle is this. All over the world men mark out their calendars by means of festivals. We ourselves start each week with a Sunday and each year with a fancy dress party. Comparable divisions in other calendars are marked by comparable behaviours. The varieties of behaviour involved are rather limited yet curiously contradictory. People dress up in uniform, or in funny clothes, they eat special food, or they fast; they behave in a solemn restrained manner, or they indulge in license.

Rites de passage, which mark the individual's social development—rituals of birth, puberty, marriage, death—are often similar. Here too we find special dress (smart uniform or farcical make-believe), special food (feast or fast), special behaviour (sobriety or license). Now why?

Why should we demarcate time in this

way? Why should it seem appropriate to wear top hats at funerals, and false noses on birthdays and New Year's Eve?

Frazer explained such behaviours by treating them as survivals of primitive magic. Frazer may be right, but he is inadequate. It is not good enough to explain a world-wide phenomenon in terms of particular, localized, archaic beliefs.

The oddest thing about time is surely that we have such a concept at all. We experience time, but not with our senses. We don't see it, or touch it, or smell it, or taste it, or hear it. How then? In three ways:

Firstly we recognize repetition. Drops of water falling from the roof; they are not all the same drop, but different. Yet to recognize them as being different we must first distinguish, and hence define, time-intervals. Time-intervals, durations, always begin and end with "the same thing," a pulse beat, a clock strike, New Year's Day.

Secondly we recognize aging, entropy. All living things are born, grow old and die. Aging is the irreversible fate of us all. But aging and interval are surely two quite different kinds of experience? I think we lump these two experiences together and describe them both by one name, time, because we would like to believe that in some mystical way birth and death are really the same thing.

Our third experience of time concerns the rate at which time passes. This is tricky. There is good evidence that the biological individual ages at a pace that is ever slowing down in relation to the sequence of stellar time. The feeling that most of us have that the first ten years of childhood "lasted much longer" than the hectic decade 40–50 is no illusion. Biological processes, such as wound healing, operate much faster (in terms of stellar time) during childhood than in old age. But since our sensations are geared to our biological processes rather than to the stars, time's chariot appears to proceed at ever increasing speed. This irregular flow of biological time is not merely a phenomenon of personal intuition; it is observable in the organic world all around us. Plant growth is much faster at the beginning than at the end of the life cycle; the ripening of the grain and the sprouting of the sown grain proceed at quite different rates of development.

Such facts show us that the regularity of time is not an intrinsic part of nature; it is a man made notion which we have projected into our environment for our own particular purposes. Most primitive peoples can have no feeling that the stars in their courses provide a fixed chronometer by which to measure all the affairs of life. On the contrary it is the year's round itself, the annual sequence of economic activities, which provides the measure of time. In such a system, since biological time is erratic, the stars may appear distinctly temperamental. The logic of astrology is not one of extreme fatalism, but rather that you can never be quite sure what the stars are going to get up to next.

But if there is nothing in the principle of the thing, or in the nature of our experience, to suggest that time must necessarily flow past at constant speed, we are not required to think of time as a constant flow at all. Why shouldn't time slow down and stop occasionally, or even go into reverse?

I agree that in a strictly scientific sense it is silly to pretend that death and birth are the same thing, yet without question many religious dogmas purport to maintain precisely that. Moreover, the make-believe that birth follows death is not confined to beliefs about the hereafter, it comes out also in the pattern of religious ritual itself. It appears not only in *rites de passage* (where the symbolism is often quite obvious) but also in a high proportion of sacrificial rites of a sacramental character. The generalizations first propounded by Hubert and Mauss and van Gennep have an extraordinarily widespread validity; the rite as a whole falls into sections, a symbolic death, a period of ritual seclusion, a symbolic rebirth.

Now *rites de passage,* which are concerned with demarcating the stages in the human life cycle, must clearly be linked with some kind of representation or conceptualization of time. But the only picture of time that could make this death-birth identification logically plausible is a pendulum type concept. All sorts of pictorial metaphors have been produced for representing time. They range from Heraclitus's river to Pythagoras's harmonic spheres. You can think of time as going on and on, or you can think of it as going round and round. All I am saying is that in fact quite a lot of people think of it as going back and forth.

With a pendulum view of time, the sequence of things is discontinuous; time is a succession of alternations and full stops. Intervals are distinguished, not as the sequential markings on a tape measure, but as repeated opposites, tick-tock tick-tock. And surely our most elementary experiences of time flow are precisely of this kind: day-night day-night; hot-cold hot-cold; wet-dry wet-dry? Despite the word *pendulum,* this kind of metaphor is not sophisticated; the essence of the matter is not the pendulum but the alternation. I would maintain that the notion that time is a "discontinuity of repeated contrasts" is probably the most elementary and primitive of all ways of regarding time.

All this is orthodox Durkheimian sociology. For people who do not possess calendars of the Nautical Almanac type, the year's progress is marked by a succession of festivals. Each festival represents, for the true Durkheimian, a temporary shift from the Normal-Profane order of existence into the Abnormal-Sacred order and back again. The total flow of time then has a pattern which might be represented by such a diagram as the one shown in Figure 1.

Such a flow of time is man made. It is ordered in this way by the Societies (the "moral persons" to use Durkheimian terminology) which participate in the festal rites. The rites themselves, especially sacrificial rites, are techniques for changing the status of the moral person from profane to sacred, or from sacred to profane. Viewed in this Durkheimian way, the total sequence embraces four distinct phases or "states of the moral person."

Phase A. The rite of sacralization, or separation. The moral person is transferred from the Secular-Profane world to the Sacred world; he "dies."

Phase B. The marginal state. The moral person is in a sacred condition, a kind of suspended animation. Ordinary social time has stopped.

Phase C. The rite of desacralization, or aggregation. The moral person is brought back from the Sacred to the Profane world; he is "reborn," secular time starts anew.

Phase D. This is the phase of normal secular life, the interval between successive festivals.

So much for Durkheim, but where do the funny hats come in? Well, let me draw your attention to three features in the foregoing theoretical argument.

Firstly let me emphasize that, among the various functions which the holding of festivals may fulfil, one very important function is the ordering of time. The interval between two successive festivals of the same type is a "period," usually a named period, e.g. "week," "year." Without the festivals, such periods would not exist, and all order would go out of social life. We talk of measuring time, as if time were a concrete thing waiting to be measured; but in fact we *create time* by creating intervals in social life. Until we have done this there is no time to be measured.

Secondly, don't forget that, just as secular periods begin and end in festivals, so also the festivals themselves have their ends and their beginnings. If we are to appreciate how neatly festivity serves to order time, we must consider the system as a whole, not just individual festivals. Notice for example how the 40 days between Carnival (Shrove Tuesday) and Easter is balanced off by the 40 days between Easter and Ascension, or how New Year's Eve falls precisely midway between Christmas Eve and Twelfth Night. Historians may tell you that such balanced intervals as these are pure accidents, but is history really so ingenious?

And thirdly there is the matter of false noses, or to be more academic, role reversal. If we accept the Durkheimian analysis of the structure of ritual which I have outlined above, then it follows that the rituals of Phase A and the rituals of Phase C ought, in some sense, to be the reverse of one another. Similarly, according to the diagram, Phase B ought somehow to be the logical opposite to Phase D. But Phase D, remember, is merely ordinary secular life. In that case a logically appropriate ritual behaviour for Phase B would be to play normal life back to front.

Now if we look at the general types of behaviour that we actually encounter on

FIGURE 1

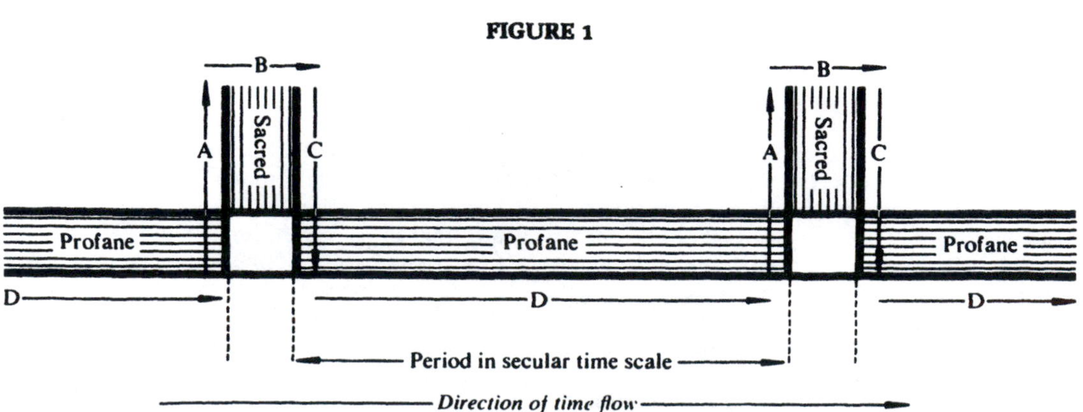

ritual occasions we may readily distinguish three seemingly contradictory species. On the one hand there are behaviours in which formality is increased; men adopt formal uniform, differences of status are precisely demarcated by dress and etiquette, moral rules are rigorously and ostentatiously obeyed. An English Sunday, the church ceremony at an English wedding, the Coronation Procession, University Degree taking ceremonials are examples of the sort of thing I mean.

In direct contrast we find celebrations of the Fancy Dress Party type, masquerades, revels. Here the individual, instead of emphasizing his social personality and his official status, seeks to disguise it. The world goes in a mask, the formal rules of orthodox life are forgotten.

And finally, in a few relatively rare instances, we find an extreme form of revelry in which the participants play-act at being precisely the opposite to what they really are; men act as women, women as men, Kings as beggars, servants as masters, acolytes as Bishops. In such situations of true orgy, normal social life is played in reverse, with all manner of sins such as incest, adultery, transvestitism, sacrilege, and *lése-majesté* treated as the natural order of the day.

Let us call these three types of ritual behaviour (1) formality, (2) masquerade, (3) role reversal. Although they are conceptually distinct as species of behaviour, they are in practice closely associated. A rite which starts with formality (e.g., a wedding) is likely to end in masquerade; a rite which starts with masquerade (e.g., New Year's Eve; Carnival) is likely to end in formality. In these puritanical days explicit role reversal is not common in our own society but it is common enough in the ethnographic literature and in accounts of Mediaeval Europe. You will find such behaviours associated with funerals, or with *rites de passage* (symbolic funerals) or with the year's end (e.g., in Europe: Saturnalia and the Feast of Fools).

My thesis is then that *formality* and *masquerade*, taken together, form a pair of contrasted opposites and correspond, in terms of my diagram to the contrast between Phase A and Phase C. *Role reversal* on the other hand corresponds to Phase B. It is symbolic of a complete transfer from the secular to the sacred; normal time has stopped, sacred time is played in reverse, death is converted into birth. This Good King Wenceslas symbolism is something which has a world wide distribution because it makes logical sense independently of any particular folklorish traditions or any particular magical beliefs.

Edmund R. Leach

RITUALIZATION IN MAN IN RELATION TO CONCEPTUAL AND SOCIAL DEVELOPMENT

Ritual is often viewed as a nonrational means (however efficacious for the actors) to achieve culturally defined ends; its symbols are characterized as condensed, containing multiple meanings, and, as action, it is elaborate, drawn out, highly repetitive human behavior. Leach suggests a novel way to view the protracted repetitiveness of ritual behavior; phrasing the problem in terms of communication theory, he asks, why the redundancy? Why does ritual seem to say the same thing—repeat the same message, in so many ways, through different channels? The information embodied in ritual action and speech pertains to the local habitat and social life of a particular culture. The often noted economy and condensation of ritual symbols are considered highly efficient means of information storage and transmission—one way in which members of a culture encode and communicate relevant cultural knowledge through the generations. In Leach's view, then, ritual in nonliterate societies has affinities, not with irrational, prelogical, or mystical thought, but with modern mathematics and the information storage of computers.

Reprinted from *Philosophical Transactions of the Royal Society of London*, 1966, Series B, No. 772, Vol. 251, pp. 403–408, by permission of the author and the Royal Society.

It has become plain that the various contributors to this Symposium use the key term *ritual* in quite different ways. The ethologists are consistent with one another; Professor Hinde's definition will serve for all: "ritualization refers to the evolutionary changes which the signal movements of lower vertebrates have undergone in adaptation to their function in communication." Such a definition has no relevance for the work of social anthropologists. Unfortunately, although *ritual* is a concept which is very prominent in anthropological discourse, there is no consensus as to its precise meaning. This is the case even for the anthropologist contributors to this Symposium; for example, I myself use the term in a different way from Professor Fortes whose paper immediately follows my own. Even so certain major differences between the positions of the ethologist and the social anthropologist need to be noted. For the ethologist, ritual is adaptive repetitive behaviour which is characteristic of a whole species; for the anthropologist, ritual is occasional behaviour by particular members of a single culture. This contrast is very radical. Professor Erikson has suggested, by implication, that we may bridge the gap by referring to "culture groups" as "pseudo-species." This kind of analogy may be convenient, in certain very special kinds of circumstance, but it is an exceedingly dangerous kind of analogy. It is in fact precisely this analogy which provides the basis for racial prejudice wherever we encounter it. It cannot be too strongly emphasized that ritual, in the anthropologist's sense, is in no way whatsoever a genetic endowment of the species.

Anthropologists are in the main concerned with forms of behaviour which are not genetically determined. Three types of such behaviour may be distinguished:

1. Behaviour which is directed towards specific ends and which, *judged by our standards of verification*, produces observable results in a strictly mechanical way . . . we can call this "rational technical" behaviour.
2. Behaviour which forms part of a signalling system and which serves to "communicate information" not because of any mechanical link between means and ends but because of the existence of a culturally defined communication code . . . we can call this "communicative" behaviour.
3. Behaviour which is potent in itself in terms of the cultural conventions of the actors but *not* potent in a rational-technical sense, as specified in (1), or alternatively behaviour which is directed towards evoking the potency of occult powers even though it is not presumed to be potent in itself . . . we can call this "magical" behaviour.

These distinctions commonly apply to aspects of individual acts rather than actions considered as wholes, but crude examples are: (1) cutting down a tree, (2) an Englishman shaking hands, (3) an Englishman swearing an oath.

The orthodox convention in anthropology, to which Professor Fortes still adheres, is to reserve the term *ritual* for behaviours of class (3) only and to call behaviours of class (2) by some other term, e.g. etiquette, ceremonial. For complex reasons which cannot be developed here I myself hold that the distinction between behaviours of class (2) and behaviours of class (3) is either illusory or trivial so that I make the term *ritual* embrace both categories.

Although swearing an oath can be a brief and simple action which all anthropologists would rate as ritual, a "typical" ritual, as conceived by most anthropologists, would be a performance of a much more prolonged and complex kind . . . e.g., the whole sequence of operations surrounding the disposal of the dead. It is characteristic of such complex ritual sequences that they have a "structure" which is in a crude sense analogous to a prose passage in that the sequence as a whole is self-segmented into elements of decreasing scale. Where, in a prose passage, we can distinguish successively paragraphs, sentences, phrases, words, syllables, phonemes, so in a complex ritual we can distinguish sub-sequences and ritual elements of different "levels." Professor Turner's paper provides some illustrations of this point. Professor Turner's paper also demonstrates the enormous complexity of the problems which face the anthropologist who seeks to interpret or decode the "messages" embodied in a ritual sequence. One feature, however is very plain and virtually universal. A ritual sequence when performed "in full" tends to be very repetitive; whatever the message may be that is supposed to be conveyed, the redundancy factor is very high.

Here it is worth reflecting on a general point of communication theory. If a sender seeks to transmit a message to a distant receiver against a background of noise, ambiguity is reduced if the same message is repeated over and over again by different channels and in different forms. For example, suppose that on a windy day I want to say something to a companion standing on a hill some distance away. If I want to make sure that my message has been understood I will not only repeat it several times over in different forms, but I will add visual signals to my verbal utterances. In so far as human rituals are "information bearing procedures" they are message systems of this redundant, interference loaded, type.

From an ethologist's point of view an example of ritualized adaptation of *Homo sapiens* is the capacity for speech, but the evolutionary developments which resulted in this capacity took place a very long time ago and the findings of contemporary anthropology have absolutely no bearing on the matter. Nevertheless, the relation between speech and ritual (in the anthropologist's sense) deserves close attention. When anthropologists talk about ritual they are usually thinking, primarily, of behaviours of a non-verbal kind, so it is worth reminding my anthropologist colleagues that (as I use the term) speech itself is a form of ritual; non-verbal ritual is simply a signal system of a different, less specialized, kind. To non-anthropologist readers I would simply say that the focus of interest in this paper is the relation between ritual as a communication system and ordinary speech as a communication system.

Professor Lorenz told us that the ethologists have two prime questions to ask about any ritual sequence. The philo-genetic question "How come?" and the functional question "What for?" The enormous complexity of the ritual sequences which anthropologists have to study make any guesses of the "How come?" type more or less absurd. Functional explanations of the "What for?" kind may look more plausible. A very general, very plausible, functional proposition is that an isolated human society must be so organized and so adapted to its environment that it can survive. For the sake of simplicity let us then confine our attention to ultra-primitive human societies as they existed in their erstwhile self-sufficient economic condition.

One common characteristic of such primitive peoples is that they are illiterate. Another is that each particular primitive society seems to be very well adapted to the environmental conditions in which it exists. Thus the Eskimos, the Australian Aborigines, and the Kalahari Bushmen all manage to live quite comfortably in conditions in which an ordinary white man would find himself incapable of sustaining life at all. This is possible because these people are somehow capable of transmitting from generation to generation an extremely elaborate body of information about the local topography, and its contents and how it may best be utilized. How is this achieved in the absence of any written documents or of any kind of formal schooling? In brief, my answer is that the performance of ritual serves to perpetuate knowledge which is essential for the survival of the performers. But this is altogether too slick. I need to explain how.

The first point to understand is an importance difference between the kind of verbal classifications which we employ and those found in primitive society.

We act as if we believed that all the things in the world belonged to "natural kinds"—I am not concerned here with the truth or falsity of this proposition but only with the fact that in our ordinary life we tend to assume that we can ask of any object whatsoever: "What is it?" and that there is a unique particular correct answer to that question. In primitive society, on the other hand, it is broadly true that only things which are in some sense useful or significant to the speaker have names. With this limitation it is still possible for the classification of the things in the world to be enormously complex, but in general the vocabulary of primitive peoples is not cluttered up with concepts which are wholly irrelevant to the user—as is invariably the case with written languages.

Put in a different way one may say that when man attaches a particular category word to a class of objects he *creates* that class of objects. If an object has no name it is not recognized as an object and in a social sense "it does not exist." Thus the world of primitive man's experience contains fewer kinds of things than the world of our experience; but the fewer things all have names and they are all of social significance.

It is characteristic of many ritual and mythical sequences in primitive society that the actors claim to be recapitulating the creation of the world and that this act of creation is mythologized as a list of names attached to persons, places, animals and things. The world is created by the process of classification and the repetition of the classification of itself perpetuates the knowledge which it incorporates.

The next point I would emphasize is that although the languages of primitive non-literate peoples contain relatively few concepts which are purely abstract, this does not mean that primitive man is incapable of apprehending abstract notions. To take a case in point which is of cardinal importance to anthropologists the words Nature and Culture are both high-level abstractions. The social anthropologist sees his task as being specifically concerned with what is cultural rather than natural. I think it goes almost without saying that concepts such as Nature and Culture do not occur in primitive languages, yet primitive people must still be aware of the distinction Nature/Culture, for a concern with the distinction between Man and non-Man must always have a central place in any system of human knowledge. But how? I only have time to provide a single illustration. Professor Lévi-Strauss has recently drawn attention to a group of South American Indian myths which constantly hark back to a contrast between raw meat and cooked meat on the one hand (that is a human—i.e. *cultural*—mode of transformation) and a contrast between fresh vegetables and putrid vegetables on the other (that is a non-human—i.e. *natural* —mode of transformation). Raw meat, cooked meat, fresh vegetables, putrid vegetables are all explicit concrete things, but placed in a pattern these few categories can serve to express the highly abstract idea of the contrast between cultural process and natural process. Furthermore, this patterning can be expressed *either in words (raw, cooked, fresh, putrid)* and displayed in a myth, *or* alternatively it can be expressed in *things* with the ritual manipulation of appropriate objects. *In such ways as this the patterning of ritual procedures can serve as a complex store of information.*

We ourselves ordinarily store our information by patterned arrangements of a small number of simple signs marked on paper or punched cards or computer tape. Primitive peoples use the objects which they employ in ritual in analogous ways—the message is not conveyed by the objects as such but by their patterned arrangement and segmental order. [Here again Professor Turner's paper provides some exemplification of what I mean.]

Non-literate peoples have every incentive to economize in their use of information storing messages. Since all knowledge must be incorporated in the stories and rituals which are familiar to the living generation, it is of immense advantage if the same verbal categories (with their corresponding objects) can be used for multiple purposes.

Broadly speaking the information which must be stored and transmitted from generation to generation is of two kinds: (1) information about Nature: that is about the topography, the climate, usable and dangerous plants, animals, inanimate things and so on; (2) information about Society: the relations of men to other men, the nature of social groups, the rules and constraints which make social life possible. These broad categories of "information about Nature" and "information about Society" belong to separate fields, and no great ambiguity is likely to be introduced if we express both kinds of information in the same kind of language. Australian totemism which has fascinated but baffled several generations of anthropologists seems to be a phenomenon of this kind. Australian aborigines classify the categories of human society by means of the same words which they use to classify the categories of Nature so that a group of human beings, a verbal concept, and a class of natural objects may all be thought of as representations of the same entity. It is only because we use words in a different way that we find this strange. For example, it makes sense in English to say: "A kangaroo is a different species of mammal from a wallaby." It also makes sense to say: "A Londoner is a different kind of man from a Parisian." But in English it does *not* make sense to economize with concepts and say: A kangaroo–Londoner is a different species-kind of mammal–man from a wallaby–Parisian." But it is only because of our linguistic conventions that this last sentence does not make sense—it is in no way ambiguous. The peculiarity of Australian totemic myths and rituals is that they constantly make condensed statements of precisely this kind. Since modern computers do the same thing I cannot really feel that our own normal mode of expression can properly be said to be the more highly developed; it merely takes up more verbal space.

A rather similar point is that in primitive society it is hardly possible to make any clearcut distinction between information which is expressed in verbal form and information which is expressed in non-verbal action.

A generation ago Jane Harrison, Malinowski and others made a clear distinction between myth on the one hand and ritual on the other, and argued that ritual was the dramatization of myth, while myth was a recapitulation of the drama, but this seems to me too simple. "Ritual" as one observes it in primitive communities is a complex of words and actions. There are doubtless some purposes for which it is useful to distinguish, within this complex, actions which are ritual, words which are spells, and words which are myth. But it is not the case that the words are one thing and the rite another. The uttering of the words is itself a ritual.

Educated peoples in our society have such

a mastery of grammatically ordered speech that they can put *all* forms of information into words—and most of us tend to imagine that this is a normal capacity. But I think that Dr. Bernstein will bear me out if I say that it is not. For ordinary non-literate people there are many kinds of information which are never verbalized but *only* expressed in action. Verbal utterance then consists of chunks of conventionalized and often wholly non-grammatical "noise behaviour." *In its proper context* the totality of the behaviour—words plus action—conveys meaning, but the meaning is conveyed because of what we know already about the context; if you record the performance on a tape and play it back, you will often find that what was said, taken by itself, was virtually gibberish.

This is true even of "ordinary conversation" among intimates but it is much more true of ritual sequences. In any ritual performance some of the actors are likely to be novices but the majority will have participated in the "same kind" of ritual many times before; indeed the stability of the form of the ritual through time is dependent on the fact that it is familiar to most of the actors. But while the familiarity of the actors makes it possible to reproduce past performances with little variation this same familiarity allows the combination of words and actions to be drastically condensed without final loss of communication value . . . precisely as happens in the conversation of intimates.

One implication of this is that attempts to interpret the "meaning" of ritual by anthropological intuition must be viewed with great scepticism. This kind of interpretation has been very common in the past and we have had some examples put forward even in this Symposium. I would assert quite categorically that no interpretation of ritual sequences in man is possible unless the interpreter has a really detailed knowledge of the cultural matrix which provides the context for the rite under discussion. The gap between Sir James Frazer and Professor Turner is very wide and it seems to me that Sir Maurice Bowra has not fully appreciated this fact.

The distinction between condensed, action-supported, ritual utterance and fully grammatical ordered utterance does not lie between primitive man and modern man but between the thought of non-literate, partially verbalized man, and that of fully literate, fully verbalized man. Both types occur in our own society. In the latter mode concepts are apprehended as *words* which exist as distinct abstract entities capable of manipulation by themselves irrespective of any particular referent; in the former mode concepts lie in the relations between things, and between persons, and between persons and things, so that words are a kind of amalgam linking up things and persons. In this mode of thought the name of a thing or of an action is not separable from that to which it refers, and things and persons which belong to the same verbal category are thereby fused together in a manner which to us seems "mystical" or "non-logical." I do not rate this as *primitive* thinking but rather as *economical* thinking. In primitive society the whole of knowledge has to be encapsulated into a memorizable set of formalized actions and associated phrases: in such circumstances the use of a separate word for every imaginable category (which is the normal objective of literate people) would be a thoroughly wasteful procedure.

These really are the main points I want to make in this brief paper:

1. In ritual, the verbal part and the behavioural part are not separable.

2. As compared with written or writable speech the "language" of ritual is enormously condensed; a great variety of alternative meanings being implicit in the same category sets. This is also an attribute of mathematics. Primitive thought is transformational in the sense that mathematics is transformational.

3. We tend to think this odd because of our own speech habits, but in fact our writable speech contains a vast amount of redundancy. This redundancy is valuable when, as is normally the case with us, we wish to convey information at a distance by means of speech alone without reference to context. In contrast the more condensed message forms which are characteristic of ritual action are generally appropriate to all forms of communication in which speaker and listener are in face to face relations and share a common body of knowledge about the context of the situation. In these restricted circumstances, which are normal in primitive society, the condensed and multi-faceted concepts to which I have been referring do not lead to ambiguity. In any event in ritual sequences the ambiguity latent in the symbolic condensation tends to be eliminated again by the device of thematic repetition and variation. This corresponds to the communication engineer's technique of overcoming noisy interference by the use of multiple redundancy.

Victor W. Turner

BETWIXT AND BETWEEN: THE LIMINAL PERIOD IN *RITES DE PASSAGE*

In his seminal essay *The Rites of Passage,* Arnold van Gennep characterized a class of rituals with three successive and distinct moments in ritual time: separation, margin, and aggregation. Working within van Gennep's framework, Turner concentrates on the properties of the hitherto neglected, and supposedly amorphous, period in rites of passage, the marginal or liminal period. Initiation rites have particularly well-marked liminal periods, where neophytes typically are removed, secluded, darkened, hidden, without rank or insignia; in terms of social structure, neophytes are invisible. In effect, the initiate is "betwixt and between," neither here nor there, no longer a child and not yet an adult. During this period of transition between states, symbolic themes characteristically concern death and decomposition, or gestation and parturition, referring to the culturally defined person the initiate has been and will become. Because of the economy of symbolic reference, the opposed states—the having been and the becoming—may be represented by a single object, act, or phrase. Turner's originality lies in uncovering the potential richness and cultural significance of what all too often is dismissed as a residual category, an interstructural phase which does not bear much study.

Reprinted from Victor W. Turner, "Betwixt and Between: The Liminal Period in *Rites de Passage*," *The Proceedings of the American Ethnological Society* (1964), Symposium on New Approaches to the Study of Religion, pp. 4–20, by permission of the author and the University of Washington Press.

In this paper, I wish to consider some of the sociocultural properties of the "liminal period" in that class of rituals which Arnold van Gennep has definitively characterized as "*rites de passage*." If our basic model of society is that of a "structure of positions," we must regard the period of margin or "liminality" as an interstructual situation. I shall consider, notably in the case of initiation rites, some of the main features of instruction among the simpler societies. I shall also take note of certain symbolic themes that concretely express indigenous concepts about the nature of "interstructural" human beings.

Rites de passage are found in all societies but tend to reach their maximal expression in small-scale, relatively stable and cyclical societies, where change is bound up with biological and meteorological rhythms and recurrences rather than with technological innovations. Such rites indicate and constitute transitions between states. By "state" I mean here "a relatively fixed or stable condition" and would include in its meaning such social constancies as legal status, profession, office or calling, rank or degree. I hold it to designate also the condition of a person as determined by his culturally recognized degree of maturation as when one speaks of "the married or single state" or the "state of infancy." The term "state" may also be applied to ecological conditions, or to the physical, mental or emotional condition in which a person or group may be found at a particular time. A man may thus be in a state of good or bad health; a society in a state of war or peace or a state of famine or of plenty. State, in short, is a more inclusive concept than status or office and refers to any type of stable or recurrent condition that is culturally recognized. One may, I suppose, also talk about "a state of transition," since J. S. Mill has, after all, written of "a state of progressive movement," but I prefer to regard transition as a process, a becoming, and in the case of *rites de passage* even a transformation—here an apt analogy would be water in process of being heated to boiling point, or a pupa changing from grub to moth. In any case, a transition has different cultural properties from those of a state, as I hope to show presently.

Van Gennep himself defined "*rites de passage*" as "rites which accompany every change of place, state, social position and age." To point up the contrast between "state" and "transition," I employ "state" to include all his other terms. Van Gennep has shown that all rites of transition are marked by three phases: separation, margin (or *limen*), and aggregation. The first phase of separation comprises symbolic behavior signifying the detachment of the individual or group either from an earlier fixed point in the social structure or a set of cultural conditions (a "state"); during the intervening liminal period, the state of the ritual subject (the "passenger") is ambiguous; he passes through a realm that has few or none of the attributes of the past or coming state; in the third phase the passage is consummated. The ritual subject, individual or corporate, is in a stable state once more and, by virtue of this, has rights and obligations of a clearly defined and "structural" type, and is expected to behave in accordance with certain customary norms and ethical standards. The most prominent type of *rites de passage* tends to accompany what Lloyd Warner (1959, 303) has called "the movement of a man through his lifetime, from a fixed placental placement within his mother's womb to his death and ultimate fixed point of his tombstone and final containment in his grave as a dead organism—punctuated by a number of critical moments of transition which all societies ritualize and publicly mark with suitable observances to impress the significance of the individual and the group on living members of the community. These are the important times of birth, puberty, marriage, and death." However, as van Gennep, Henri Junod, and others have shown, *rites de passage* are not confined to culturally defined life-crises but may accompany any change from one state to another, as when a whole tribe goes to war, or when it attests to the passage from scarcity to plenty by performing a first-fruits or a harvest festival. *Rites de passage*, too, are not restricted, sociologically speaking, to movements between ascribed statuses. They also concern entry into a new achieved status, whether this be a political office or membership of an exclusive club or secret society. They may admit persons into membership of a religious group where such a group does not include the whole society, or qualify them for the official duties of the cult, sometimes in a graded series of rites.

Since the main problem of this study is the nature and characteristics of transition in relatively stable societies, I shall focus attention on *rites de passage* that tend to have well-developed liminal periods. On the whole, initiation rites, whether into social maturity or cult membership, best exemplify transition, since they have well-marked and protracted marginal or liminal phases. I shall pay only brief heed here to rites of separation and aggregation, since these are more closely implicated in social structure than rites of liminality. Liminality during initiation is, therefore, the primary datum of this study, though I will draw on other aspects of passage ritual where the argument demands this. I may state here, partly as an aside, that, I consider the term "ritual" to be more fittingly applied to forms of religious behavior associated with social transitions, while the term "ceremony" has a closer bearing on religious behavior associated with social states, where politico-legal institutions also have greater importance. Ritual is transformative, ceremony confirmatory.

The subject of passage ritual is, in the liminal period, structurally, if not physically, "invisible." As members of society, most of us see only what we expect to see, and what we expect to see is what we are conditioned to see when we have learned the definitions and classifications of our culture. A society's secular definitions do not allow for the existence of a not-boy-not-man, which is what a novice in a male puberty rite is (if he can be said to be anything). A set of essentially religious definitions co-exist with these which do set out to define the structurally indefinable "transitional-being." The transitional-being or "liminal *persona*" is defined by a name and by a set of symbols. The same name is very frequently employed to designate those who are being initiated into very different states of life. For example, among the Ndembu of Zambia the name *mwadi* may mean various things: it may stand for "a boy novice in circumcision rites," or "a chief-designate undergoing his installation rites," or, yet again, "the first or ritual wife" who has important ritual duties in the domestic family. Our own terms "initiate" and "neophyte" have a similar breadth of reference. It would seem from this that emphasis tends to be laid on the transition itself, rather than on the particular states between which it is taking place.

The symbolism attached to and surrounding the liminal *persona* is complex and bizarre. Much of it is modeled on human biological processes, which are conceived to be what Lévi-Strauss might call "isomorphic" with structural and cultural processes. They give an outward and visible form to an inward and conceptual process. The structural "invisibility" of liminal *personae* has a twofold character. They are at once no longer classified and not yet classified. In so far as they are no longer classified, the symbols that represent them are, in many societies, drawn from the biology of death, decomposition, catabolism, and other physical processes that have a negative tinge, such as menstruation (frequently regarded as the absence or loss of a fetus). Thus, in some boys' initiations, newly circumcised boys are explicitly likened to menstruating women. In so far as a neophyte is structurally "dead," he or she may be treated, for a long or short period, as a corpse is customarily treated in his or her society. (See Stobaeus' quotation, probably from a lost work of Plutarch, "initiation and death correspond word for word and thing for thing.") The neophyte may be buried, forced to lie motionless in the posture and direction of customary burial, may be stained black, or may be forced to live for a while in the company of masked and monstrous mummers representing, *inter alia,* the dead, or worse still, the un-dead. The metaphor of dissolution is often applied to neophytes; they are allowed to go filthy and identified with the earth, the generalized matter into which every specific individual is rendered down. Particular form here becomes general matter; often their very names are taken from them and each is called solely by the generic term for "neophyte" or "initiand." (This useful neologism is employed by many modern anthropologists.)

The other aspect, that they are not yet classified, is often expressed in symbols modeled on processes of gestation and parturition. The neophytes are likened to or treated as embryos, newborn infants, or sucklings by symbolic means which vary from culture to culture. I shall return to this theme presently.

The essential feature of these symbolizations is that the neophytes are neither living nor dead from one aspect, and both living and dead from another. Their condition is one of ambiguity and paradox, a confusion of all the customary categories. Jakob Boehme, the German mystic whose obscure writings gave Hegel his celebrated dialectical "triad," liked to say that "In Yea and Nay all things consist." Liminality may perhaps be regarded as the Nay to all positive structural assertions, but as in some sense the source of them all, and, more than that, as a realm of pure possibility whence novel configurations of ideas and relations may arise. I will not pursue this point here but, after all, Plato, a speculative philosopher, if there ever was one, did acknowledge his philosophical debt to the teachings of the Eleusinian and Orphic initiations of Attica. We have no way of knowing whether primitive initiations merely conserved lore. Perhaps they also generated new thought and new custom.

Dr. Mary Douglas, of University College, London, has recently advanced (in a magnificent book *Purity and Danger* [1966]) the very interesting and illuminating view that the concept of pollution "is a reaction to protect cherished principles and categories from contradiction." She holds that, in effect, what is unclear and contradictory (from the perspective of social definition) tends to be regarded as (ritually) unclean. The unclear is the unclean: e.g., she examines the prohibitions on eating certain animals and crustaceans in Leviticus in the light of this hypothesis (these being creatures that cannot be unambiguously classified in terms of traditional criteria). From this standpoint, one would expect to find that transitional beings are particularly polluting, since they are neither one thing nor another; or may be both; or neither here nor there; or may even be nowhere (in terms of any recognized cultural topography), and are at the very least "betwixt and between" all the recognized fixed points in space-time of structural classification. In fact, in confirmation of Dr. Douglas's hypothesis, liminal *personae* nearly always and everywhere are regarded as polluting to those who have never been, so to speak, "inoculated" against them, through having been themselves initiated into the same state. I think that we may perhaps usefully discriminate here between the statics and dynamics of pollution situations. In other words, we may have to distinguish between pollution notions which concern states that have been ambiguously or contradictorily defined, and those which derive from ritualized transitions between states. In the first case, we are dealing with what has been defectively defined or ordered, in the second with what cannot be defined in static terms. We are not dealing with structural contradictions when we discuss liminality, but with the essentially unstructured (which is at once destructured and prestructured) and often the people themselves see this in terms of bringing neophytes into close connection with deity or with superhuman power, with what is, in fact, often regarded as the unbounded, the infinite, the limitless. Since neophytes are not only structurally "invisible" (though physically visible) and ritually polluting, they are very commonly secluded, partially or completely, from the realm of culturally defined and ordered states and statuses. Often the indigenous term for the liminal period is, as among Ndembu, the locative form of a noun meaning "seclusion site" (*kunkunka, kung'ula*). The neophytes are sometimes said to "be in another place." They have physical but not social "reality," hence they have to be hidden, since it is a paradox, a scandal, to see what ought not to be there! Where they are not removed to a sacred place of concealment they are often disguised, in masks or grotesque costumes or striped with white, red, or black clay, and the like.

In societies dominantly structured by kinship institutions, sex distinctions have great structural importance. Patrilineal and matrilineal moieties and clans, rules of exogamy, and the like, rest and are built up on these distinctions. It is consistent with this to find that in liminal situations (in kinship-dominated societies) neophytes are sometimes treated or symbolically represented as being neither male nor female. Alternatively, they may be symbolically assigned characteristics of both sexes, irrespective of their biological sex. (Bruno Bettelheim [1954] has collected much illustrative material on this point from initiation rites.) They are symbolically either sexless or bisexual and may be regarded as a kind of human *prima materia*—as undifferentiated raw material. It was perhaps from the rites of the Hellenic mystery religions that Plato derived his notion expressed in his *Symposium* that the first humans were androgynes. If the liminal period is seen as an interstructural phase in social dynamics, the symbolism both of androgyny and sexlessness immediately becomes intelligible in sociological terms without the need to import psychological (and especially depth-psychological) explanations. Since sex distinctions are important components of structural status, in a structureless realm they do not apply.

A further structurally negative characteristic of transitional beings is that they *have* nothing. They have no status, property, insignia, secular clothing, rank, kinship position, nothing to demarcate them structurally from their fellows. Their condition is indeed the very prototype of sacred poverty. Rights over property, goods, and services inhere in positions in the politico-jural structure. Since they do not occupy such positions, neophytes exercise no such rights. In the words of King Lear they represent "naked unaccommodated man."

I have no time to analyze other symbolic themes that express these attributes of "structural invisibility," ambiguity and neutrality. I want now to draw attention to certain positive aspects of liminality. Already we have noted how certain liminal processes are regarded as analogous to those of gestation, parturition, and suckling. Undoing, dissolution, decomposition are accompanied by processes of growth, transformation, and the reformulation of old elements in new patterns. It is interesting to note how, by the principle of the economy (or parsimony) of symbolic reference, logically antithetical processes of death and growth may be represented by the same tokens, for example, by huts and tunnels that are at once tombs and wombs, by lunar symbolism (for the same moon waxes and wanes), by snake symbolism (for the snake appears to die, but only to shed its old skin and appear in a new one), by bear symbolism (for the bear "dies" in autumn and is "reborn" in spring), by nakedness (which is at once the mark of a newborn infant and a corpse prepared for burial), and by innumerable other symbolic formations and actions. This coincidence of opposite processes and notions in a single representation characterizes the peculiar unity of the liminal: that which is neither this nor that, and yet is both.

I have spoken of the interstructural character of the liminal. However, between neophytes and their instructors (where these exist), and in connecting neophytes with one another, there exists a set of relations that compose a "social structure" of highly specific type. It is a structure of a very simple kind: between instructors and neophytes there is often complete authority and complete submission; among neophytes there is often complete equality. Between incumbents of positions in secular politico-jural systems there exist intricate and situationally shifting networks of rights and duties proportioned to their rank, status, and corporate affiliation. There are many different kinds of privileges and obligations, many degrees of superordination and subordination. In the liminal period such distinctions and gradations tend to be eliminated. Nevertheless, it must be understood that the authority of the elders over the neophytes is not based on legal sanctions; it is in a sense the personification of the self-evident authority of tradition. The authority of the elders is absolute, because it represents the absolute, the axiomatic values of society in which are expressed the "common good" and the common interest. The essence of the complete obedience of the neophytes is to submit to the elders but only in so far as they are in charge, so to speak, of the common good and represent in their persons the total community. That the authority in question is really quintessential tradition emerges clearly in societies where initiations are not collective but individual and where there are no instructors or *gurus*. For example, Omaha boys, like other North American Indians, go alone into the wilderness to fast and pray (Hocart, 1952, 160). This solitude is liminal between boyhood and manhood. If they dream that they receive a woman's burden-strap, they feel compelled to dress and live henceforth in every way as women. Such men are known as *mixuga*. The authority of such a dream in such a situation is absolute. Alice Cummingham Fletcher tells of one Omaha who had been forced in this way to live as a woman, but whose natural inclinations led him to rear a family and to go on the warpath. Here the *mixuga* was not an invert but a man bound by the authority of tribal beliefs and values. Among many Plains Indians, boys on their lonely Vision Quest inflicted ordeals and tests on themselves that amounted to tortures. These again were not basically self-tortures inflicted by a masochistic temperament but due to obedience to the authority of tradition in the liminal situation—a type of situation in which there is no room for secular compromise, evasion, manipulation, casuistry, and maneuver in the field of custom, rule, and norm. Here again a cultural explanation seems preferable to a psychological one. A normal man acts abnormally because he is obedient to tribal tradition, not out of disobedience to it. He does not evade but fulfills his duties as a citizen.

If complete obedience characterizes the relationship of neophyte to elder, complete equality usually characterizes the relationship of neophyte to neophyte, where the rites are collective. This comradeship must be distinguished from brotherhood or sibling relationship, since in the latter there is always the inequality of older and younger, which often achieves linguistic representation and may be maintained by legal sanctions. The liminal group is a community or comity of comrades and not a structure of hierarchically arrayed positions. This comradeship transcends distinctions of rank, age, kinship position, and, in some kinds of cultic group, even of sex. Much of the behavior recorded by ethnographers in seclusion situations falls under the principle: "Each for all, and all for each." Among the Ndembu of Zambia, for example, all food brought for novices in circumcision seclusion by their mothers is shared out equally among them. No special favors are bestowed on the sons of chiefs or headmen. Any food acquired by novices in the bush is taken by the elders and apportioned among the group. Deep friendships between novices are encouraged, and they sleep around lodge fires in clusters of four or five particular comrades. However, all are supposed to be linked by special ties which persist after the rites are over, even into old age. This friendship, known as *wubwambu* (from a term meaning "breast") or *wulunda*, enables a man to claim privileges of hospitality of a far-reaching kind. I have no need here to dwell on the lifelong ties that are held to bind in close friendship those initiated into the same age-set in East African Nilo-Hamitic and Bantu societies, into the same fraternity or sorority on an American campus, or into the same class in a Naval or Military Academy in Western Europe.

This comradeship, with its familiarity, ease and, I would add, mutual outspokenness, is once more the product of interstructural liminality, with its scarcity of jurally sanctioned relationships and its emphasis on axiomatic values expressive of the common weal. People can "be themselves," it is frequently said, when they are not acting institutionalized roles. Roles, too, carry responsibilities and in the liminal situation the main burden of responsibility is borne by the elders, leaving the neophytes free to develop interpersonal relationships as they will. They confront one another, as it were, integrally and not in compartmentalized fashion as actors of roles.

The passivity of neophytes to their instructors, their malleability, which is increased by submission to ordeal, their reduction to a uniform condition, are signs of the process whereby they are ground down to be fashioned anew and endowed with additional powers to cope with their new station in life. Dr. Richards, in her superb study of Bemba girls' puberty rites, *Chisungu*, has told us that Bemba speak of "growing a girl" when they mean initiating her (1956, 121). This term "to grow" well expresses how many people think of transition rites. We are inclined, as sociologists, to reify our abstractions (it is indeed a device which helps us to understand many kinds of social interconnection) and to talk about persons "moving through structural positions in a hierchical frame" and the like. Not so the Bemba and the Shilluk of the Sudan who see the status or condition embodied or incarnate, if you like, *in* the person. To "grow" a girl into a woman is to effect an ontological transformation; it is not merely to convey an unchanging substance from one position to another by a quasi-mechanical force. Howitt saw Kuringals in Australia and I have seen Ndembu in Africa drive away grown-up men before a circumcision ceremony because they had not been initiated. Among Ndembu, men were also chased off because they had only been circumcised at the Mission Hospital and had not undergone the full bush seclusion according to the orthodox Ndembu rite. These biologically mature men had not been "made men" by the proper ritual procedures. It is the ritual and the esoteric teaching which grows girls and makes men. It is the ritual, too, which among Shilluk makes a prince into a king, or, among Luvale, a cultivator into a hunter. The arcane knowledge or "*gnosis*" obtained in the liminal period is felt to change the inmost nature of the neophyte, impressing him, as a seal impresses wax, with the characteristics of his new state. It is not a mere acquisition of knowledge, but a change in being. His apparent passivity is revealed as an absorption of powers which will become active after his social status has been redefined in the aggregation rites.

The structural simplicity of the liminal situation in many initiations is offset by its cultural complexity. I can touch on only one aspect of this vast subject matter here and raise three problems in connection with it. This aspect is the vital one of the communication of the *sacra*, the heart of the liminal matter.

Jane Harrison has shown that in the Greek Eleusinian and Orphic mysteries this communication of the *sacra* has three main components (1903, 144–160). By and large, this threefold classification holds good for initiation rites all over the world. *Sacra* may be communicated as: (1) exhibitions, "what is shown"; (2) actions, "what is done"; and (3) instructions, "what is said."

"Exhibitions" would include evocatory instruments or sacred articles, such as relics of deities, heroes or ancestors, aboriginal *churingas*, sacred drums or other musical instruments, the contents of Amerindian medicine bundles, and the fan, cist and tympanum of Greek and Near Eastern mystery cults. In the Lesser Eleusinian Mysteries of Athens, *sacra* consisted of a bone, top, ball, tambourine, apples, mirror, fan, and woolly fleece. Other *sacra* include masks, images, figurines, and effigies; the pottery emblems (*mbusa*) of the Bemba would belong to this class. In some kinds of initiation, as for example the initiation into the shaman-diviner's profession among the Saora of Middle India, described by Verrier Elwin (1955), pictures and icons representing the journeys of the dead or the adventures of supernatural beings may be shown to the initiands. A striking feature of such sacred articles is often their formal simplicity. It is their interpretation which is complex, not their outward form.

Among the "instructions" received by neophytes may be reckoned such matters as the revelation of the real, but secularly secret, names of the deities or spirits believed to preside over the rites—a very frequent procedure in African cultic or secret associations (Turner, 1962a, 36). They are also taught the main outlines of the theogony, cosmogony, and mythical history of their societies or cults, usually with reference to the *sacra* exhibited. Great importance is attached to keeping secret the nature of the *sacra*, the formulas chanted and instructions given about them. These constitute the crux of liminality, for while instruction is also given in ethical and social obligations, in law and in kinship rules, and in technology to fit neophytes for the duties of future office, no interdiction is placed on knowledge thus imparted since it tends to be current among uninitiated persons also.

I want to take up three problems in considering the communication of *sacra*. The first concerns their frequent disproportion, the second their monstrousness, and the third their mystery.

When one examines the masks, costumes, figurines, and such displayed in initiation situations, one is often struck, as I have been when observing Ndembu masks in circumcision and funerary rites, by the way in which certain natural and cultural features are represented as disproportionately large or small. A head, nose, or phallus, a hoe, bow, or meal mortar are represented as huge or tiny by comparison with other features of their context which retain their normal size. (For a good example of this, see "The Man Without Arms" in *Chisungu* [Richards, 1956, 211], a figurine of a lazy man with an enormous penis but no arms.) Sometimes things retain their customary shapes but are portrayed in unusual colors. What is the point of this exaggeration amounting sometimes to caricature? It seems to me that to enlarge or diminish or discolor in this way is a primordial mode of abstraction. The outstandingly exaggerated feature is made into an object of reflection. Usually it is not a univocal symbol that is thus represented but a multivocal one, a semantic molecule with many components. One example is the Bemba pottery emblem *Coshi wa ng'oma*, "The Nursing Mother," described by Audrey Richards in *Chisungu*. This is a clay figurine, nine inches high, of an exaggeratedly pregnant mother shown carrying four babies at the same time, one at her breast and three at her back. To this figurine is attached a riddling song:

My mother deceived me!
Coshi wa ng'oma!
So you have deceived me;
I have become pregnant again.

Bemba women interpreted this to Richards as follows:

> Coshi wa ng'oma *was a midwife of legendary fame and is merely addressed in this song. The girl complains because her mother told her to wean her first child too soon so that it died; or alternatively told her that she would take the first child if her daughter had a second one. But she was tricking her and now the girl has two babies to look after. The moral stressed is the duty of refusing intercourse with the husband before the baby is weaned, i.e., at the second or third year. This is a common Bemba practice* (1956, 209–210).

In the figurine the exaggerated features are the number of children carried at once by the woman and her enormously distended belly. Coupled with the song, it encourages the novice to ponder upon two relationships vital to her, those with her mother and her husband. Unless the novice observes the Bemba weaning custom, her mother's desire for grandchildren to increase her matrilineage and her husband's desire for renewed sexual intercourse will between them actually destroy and not increase her offspring. Underlying this is the deeper moral that to abide by tribal custom and not to sin against it either by excess or defect is to live satisfactorily. Even to please those one loves may be to invite calamity, if such compliance defies the immemorial wisdom of the elders embodied in the *mbusa*. This wisdom is vouched for by the mythical and archetypal midwife *Coshi wa ng'oma*.

If the exaggeration of single features is not irrational but thought-provoking, the same may also be said about the representation of monsters. Earlier writers—such as J. A. McCulloch (1913) in his article on "Monsters" in *Hastings Encyclopedia of Religion and Ethics*—are inclined to regard bizarre and monstrous masks and figures, such as frequently appear in the liminal period of initiations, as the product of "hallucinations, night-terrors and dreams." McCulloch goes on to argue that "as man drew little distinction (in primitive society) between himself and animals, as he thought that transformation from one to the other was possible, so he easily ran human and animal together. This in part accounts for animal-headed gods or animal-gods with human heads." My own view is the opposite one: that monsters are manufactured precisely to teach neophytes to distinguish clearly between the different factors of reality, as it is conceived in their culture. Here, I think, William James's so-called "law of dissociation" may help us to clarify the problem of monsters. It may be stated as follows: when *a* and *b* occurred together as parts of the same total object, without being discriminated, the occurrence of one of these, *a*, in a new combination *ax*, favors the discrimination of *a*, *b*, and *x* from one another. As James himself put it, "What is associated now with one thing and now with another, tends to become dissociated from either, and to grow into an object of abstract contemplation by the mind. One might call this the law of dissociation by varying concomitants" (1918, 506).

From this standpoint, much of the grotesqueness and monstrosity of liminal *sacra* may be seen to be aimed not so much at terrorizing or bemusing neophytes into submission or out of their wits as at making them vividly and rapidly aware of what may be called the "factors" of their culture. I have myself seen Ndembu and Luvale masks that combine features of both sexes, have both animal and human attributes, and unite in a single representation human characteristics with those of the natural landscape. One *ikishi* mask is partly human and partly represents a grassy plain. Elements are withdrawn from their usual settings and combined with one another in a totally unique configuration, the monster or dragon. Monsters startle neophytes into thinking about objects, persons, relationships, and features of their environment they have hitherto taken for granted.

In discussing the structural aspect of liminality, I mentioned how neophytes are withdrawn from their structural positions and consequently from the values, norms, sentiments, and techniques associated with those positions. They are also divested of their previous habits of thought, feeling, and action. During the liminal period, neophytes are alternately forced and encouraged to think about their society, their cosmos, and the powers that generate and sustain them. Liminality may be partly described as a stage of reflection. In it those ideas, sentiments, and facts that had been hitherto for the neophytes bound up in configurations and accepted unthinkingly are, as it were, resolved into their constituents. These constituents are isolated and made into objects of reflection for the neophytes by such processes as componental exaggeration and dissociation by varying concomitants. The communication of *sacra* and other forms of esoteric instruction really involves three processes, though these should not be regarded as in series but as in parallel. The first is the reduction of culture into recognized components or factors; the second is their recombination in fantastic or monstrous patterns and shapes; and the third is their recombination in ways that make sense with regard to the new state and status that the neophytes will enter.

The second process, monster- or fantasy-making, focuses attention on the components of the masks and effigies, which are so radically ill-assorted that they stand out and can be thought about. The monstrosity of the configuration throws its elements into relief. Put a man's head on a lion's body and you think about the human head in the abstract. Perhaps it becomes for you, as a member of a given culture and with the appropriate guidance, an emblem of chieftainship; or it may be explained as representing the soul as against the body; or intellect as contrasted with brute force, or innumberable other things. There could be less encouragement to reflect on heads and headship if that same head were firmly ensconced on its familiar, its all too familiar, human body. The man-lion monster also encourages the observer to think about lions, their habits, qualities, metaphorical properties, religious significance, and so on. More important than these, the relation between man and lion, empirical and metaphorical, may be speculated upon, and new ideas developed on this topic. Liminality here breaks, as it were, the cake of custom and enfranchises speculation. That is why I earlier mentioned Plato's self-confessed debt to the Greek mysteries. Liminality is the realm of primitive hypothesis, where there is a certain freedom to juggle with the factors of existence. As in the works of Rabelais, there is a promiscuous intermingling and juxtaposing of the categories of event, experience, and knowledge, with a pedagogic intention.

But this liberty has fairly narrow limits. The neophytes return to secular society with more alert faculties perhaps and enhanced knowledge of how things work, but they have to become once more subject to custom and law. Like the Bemba girl I mentioned earlier, they are shown that ways of acting and thinking alternative to those laid down by the deities or ancestors are ultimately unworkable and may have disastrous consequences.

Moreover, in initiation, there are usually held to be certain axiomatic principles of construction, and certain basic building blocks that make up the cosmos and into whose nature no neophyte may inquire. Certain *sacra*, usually exhibited in the most arcane episodes of the liminal period, represent or may be interpreted in terms of these axiomatic principles and primordial constituents. Perhaps we may call these *sacerrima*, "most sacred things." Sometimes they are interpreted by a myth about the world-making activities of supernatural beings "at the beginning of things." Myths may be completely absent, however, as in the case of the Ndembu "mystery of the three rivers." . . . This mystery (*mpang'u*) is exhibited at circumcision and funerary cult association rites. Three trenches are dug in a consecrated site and filled respectively with white, red, and black water. These "rivers" are said to "flow from Nzambi," the High God. The instructors tell the neophytes, partly in riddling songs and partly in direct terms, what each river signifies. Each "river" is a multivocal symbol with a fan of referents ranging from life values, ethical ideas, and social norms, to grossly physiological processes and phenomena. They seem to be regarded as powers which, in varying combination, underlie or even constitute what Ndembu conceive to be reality. In no other context is the interpretation of whiteness, redness, and blackness so full; and nowhere else is such a close analogy drawn, even identity made, between these rivers and bodily fluids and emissions: whiteness = semen, milk; redness = menstrual blood, the blood of birth, blood shed by a weapon, etc.; blackness = feces, certain products of bodily decay, etc. This use of an aspect of human physiology as a model for social, cosmic, and religious ideas and processes is a variant of a widely distributed initiation theme: that the human body is a microcosm of the universe. The body may be pictured as androgynous, as male or female, or in terms of one or other of its developmental stages, as child, mature adult, and elder. On the other hand, as in the Ndembu case, certain of its properties may be abstracted. Whatever the mode of representation, the body is regarded as a sort of symbolic template for the communication of *gnosis*, mystical knowledge about the nature of things and how they came to be what they are. The cosmos may in some cases be regarded as a vast human body; in other belief systems, visible parts of the body may be taken to portray invisible faculties such as reason, passion, wisdom and so on; in others again, the different parts of the social order are arrayed in terms of a human anatomical paradigm.

Whatever the precise mode of explaining reality by the body's attributes, *sacra* which illustrate this are always regarded as absolutely sacrosanct, as ultimate mysteries. We are here in the realm of what Warner (1959, 3–4) would call "nonrational or nonlogical symbols" which

> *arise out of the basic individual and cultural assumptions, more often unconscious than not, from which most social action springs. They supply the solid core of mental and emotional life of each individual and group. This does not mean that they are irrational or maladaptive, or that man cannot often think in a reasonable way about them, but rather that they do not have their source in his rational processes. When they come into play, such factors as data, evidence, proof, and the facts and procedures of rational thought in action are apt to be secondary or unimportant.*

The central cluster of nonlogical *sacra* is then the symbolic template of the whole system of beliefs and values in a given culture, its archetypal paradigm and ultimate measure. Neophytes shown these are often told that they are in presence of forms established from the beginning of things. (See Cicero's comment [De Leg. II. 14] on the Eleusinian Mysteries: "They are rightly called initiations [beginnings] because we have thus learned the first principles of life.") I have used the metaphor of a seal or stamp in connection with the ontological character ascribed in many initiations to arcane knowledge. The term "archetype" denotes in Greek a master stamp or impress, and these *sacra*, presented with a numinous simplicity, stamp into the neophytes the basic assumptions of their culture. The neophytes are told also that they are being filled with mystical power by what they see and what they are told about it. According to the purpose of the initiation, this power confers on them capacities to undertake successfully the tasks of their new office, in this world or the next.

Thus, the communication of *sacra* both teaches the neophytes how to think with some degree of abstraction about their cultural milieu and gives them ultimate standards of reference. At the same time, it is believed to change their nature, transform them from one kind of human being into another. It intimately unites man and office. But for a variable while, there was an uncomitted man, an individual rather than a social *persona*, in a sacred community of individuals.

It is not only in the liminal period of initiations that the nakedness and vulnerability of the ritual subject receive symbolic stress. Let me quote from Hilda Kuper's description of the seclusion of the Swazi chief during the great *Incwala* ceremony. The *Incwala* is a national First-Fruits ritual, performed in the height of summer when the early crops ripen. The regiments of the Swazi nation assemble at the capital to celebrate its rites, "whereby the nation receives strength for the new year." The *Incwala* is at the same time "a play of kingship." The king's well-being is identified with that of the nation. Both require periodic ritual strengthening. Lunar symbolism is prominent in the rites, as we shall see, and the king, personifying the nation, during his seclusion represents the moon in transition between phases, neither waning nor waxing. Dr. Kuper, Professor Gluckman (1954), and Professor Wilson have discussed the structural aspects of the *Incwala* which are clearly present in its rites of separation and aggregation. What we are about to examine are the interstructural aspects.

During his night and day of seclusion, the king, painted black, remains, says Dr. Kuper, "painted in blackness" and "in darkness"; he is unapproachable, dangerous to himself and others. He must cohabit that night with his first ritual wife (in a kind of "mystical marriage"—this ritual wife is, as it were, consecrated for such liminal situations).

> *The entire population is temporarily in a state of taboo and seclusion. Ordinary activities and behavior are suspended; sexual intercourse is prohibited, no one may sleep late the following morning, and when they get up they are not allowed to touch each other, to wash the body, to sit on mats, to poke anything into the ground, or even to scratch their hair. The children are scolded if they play and make merry. The sound of songs that has stirred the capital for nearly a month is abruptly stilled; it is the day of* bacisa *(cause to hide). The king remains secluded; . . . all day he sits naked on a lion skin in the ritual hut of the harem or in the sacred enclosure in the royal cattle byre. Men of his inner circle see that he breaks none of the taboos . . . on this day the identification of the people with the king is very marked. The spies (who see to it that the people respect the taboos) do not say, "You are sleeping late" or "You are scratching," but "You cause the king to sleep," "You scratch him (the king)"; etc.* (Kuper, 1947, 219–220).

Other symbolic acts are performed which exemplify the "darkness" and "waxing and waning moon" themes, for example, the slaughtering of a black ox, the painting of the queen mother with a black mixture—she is compared again to a half-moon, while the king is a full moon, and both are in eclipse until the paint is washed off finally with doctored water, and the ritual subject "comes once again into lightness and normality."

In this short passage we have an embarrassment of symbolic riches. I will mention only a few themes that bear on the argument of this paper. Let us look at the king's position first. He is symbolically invisible, "black," a moon between phases. He is also under obedience to traditional rules, and "men of his inner circle" see that he keeps them. He is also "naked," divested of the trappings of his office. He remains apart from the scenes of his political action in a sanctuary or ritual hut. He is also, it would seem, identified with the earth which the people are forbidden to stab, lest the king be affected. He is "hidden." The king, in short, has been divested of all the outward attributes, the "accidents," of his kingship and is reduced to its substance, the "earth" and "darkness" from which the normal, structured order of the Swazi kingdom will be regenerated "in lightness."

In this betwixt-and-between period, in this fruitful darkness, king and people are closely identified. There is a mystical solidarity between them, which contrasts sharply with the hierarchical rank-dominated structure of ordinary Swazi life. It is only in darkness, silence, celibacy, in the absence of merriment and movement that the king and people can thus be one. For every normal action is involved in the rights and obligations of a structure that defines status and establishes social distance between men. Only in their Trappist sabbath of transition may the Swazi regenerate the social tissues torn by conflicts arising from distinctions of status and discrepant structural norms.

I end this study with an invitation to investigators of ritual to focus their attention on the phenomena and processes of mid-transition. It is these, I hold, that paradoxically expose the basic building blocks of culture just when we pass out of and before we reenter the structural realm. In *sacerrima* and their interpretations we have categories of data that may usefully be handled by the new sophisticated techniques of cross-cultural comparison.

Robin Horton

RITUAL MAN IN AFRICA

Horton begins with a critique of Gluckman, who reduces ritual to social relations, and Turner, who sees religion as a universal and nonreducible human aspiration. While granting that much of African ritual involves communion with supernatural beings, and hence is not reducible to nonreligious terms, Horton emphasizes the concern of African religions with puzzling observations in the natural and social realms. Such speculations are seen as analogous with the construction of models or theories in Western science; they are attempts to explain and influence the commonplace workings of nature and society. Scientific models, after all, are constructed by partial analogy with known and observable phenomena in the world of the scientist; the scientist's model is an attempt to explain the flux, the seeming disorder, of the natural world with reference to parsimonious underlying mechanisms. Just as it may not make sense to ask the scientist what color a proton is, so African cosmologies may remain silent as to the appearance of a deity, whether he is tall or short, thin or fat. The issue here is what should be considered an appropriate translation label for religious beliefs and practices. Horton would submit that the language of religion and science—often viewed as antithetical spheres of Western discourse—are both necessary in rendering African religious systems intelligible.

Reprinted in abridged form from *Africa*, XXXIV (1964), 85–104, by permission of the author and the International African Institute.

This paper starts with a critique of two recent essays on African religion—Professor Max Gluckman's essay "Les Rites de Passage," and Dr. V. W. Turner's *Chihamba: the White Spirit.* Though the first is a generalized interpretation of African rituals, and the second a close study of one rite in a particular culture, the two make an interesting comparison. First of all, they are inspired by strongly contrasted theoretical premises. Secondly, one represents a well-established approach to the study of ritual, while the other includes a powerful objection to this approach. Thirdly, the two essays exhibit a polarity of attitude which I suspect has a wider currency both in Social Anthropology and in Comparative Religion. In what follows, I shall argue that the polarization of thought suggested by these two essays is basically unhelpful to the study of African religions; and I shall go on and suggest an approach which seems to me a fruitful middle way into the subject.

Gluckman's essay takes as its point of departure an appraisal of van Gennep's work on *rites de passage*—i.e., those rituals which in pre-industrial societies accompany major changes of role and status. Gluckman praises van Gennep for his analysis of the mechanism of such rites, and for his exposition of the way in which they help to make role changes easier for all those involved. But, he says, van Gennep gives no adequate explanation of why *rites de passage* are so common in "tribal societies," and so rare in modern industrial states. Van Gennep simply begs the question by saying that, to the semi-civilized mind, no act is entirely free from the sacred. According to Gluckman, it would in fact have been impossible for him to have provided an explanation: for he lacked the consistent vision of social relations essential to such a task. Gluckman sets out to make up for the deficiency which he sees in his predecessor's work. He contrasts his own approach, which sees rituals primarily "in terms of social structure," with the older approach of van Gennep, Tylor, and Frazer, who are said to have treated rituals "as the fruits of mental processes and ideas." . . .

In modern industrial society, as Gluckman points out, people tend to play their various roles with different partners in different places; and these circumstances obviate the need for any additional devices designed to prevent confusion of roles. In "tribal society," on the other hand, people tend to play several different roles with the same partners in the same setting: hence there is a need for role-segregating devices of which ritual, together with other types of ceremonial, is one.

. . .

How successful is Gluckman's attempt to tackle the problems left unsolved by van Gennep? On the one hand, his characterization of the differences in role-organization between tribal and industrial societies seems definitely illuminating. So too does his thesis that a concern for harmonious social life in tribal societies must give rise to a host of role-segregating and role-defining devices which are unnecessary in industrial society. On the other hand, though ritual can be pressed into the service of role-definition and role-segregation, there is surely more to it than this. Most African ritual is directed to entities that are inaccessible to normal observation, and are in addition personal beings. To many people these properties present the central problem of Comparative Religion. Why, in tribal societies especially, should there be constant resort to entities *of this kind* in every conceivable human predicament? And why, coming back to Gluckman, should it be entities *of this kind* that are invoked on so many occasions when there is a transition or affirmation of important roles? If one grants that all human populations spend a certain amount of ingenuity on securing harmony in their social life, it follows that difficulties in maintaining harmony, which Gluckman shows to be inherent in the role-organization of "tribal societies," will evoke a multitude of counter-active responses. But there is nothing to show that the elaboration of ritual is the only effective kind of response, or indeed that the required counteractive functions could not be discharged by a whole assortment of activities and institutions other than ritual. In fact, there is nothing in the essence of ritual which makes it a particularly obvious solution to the problem of maintaining harmony in tribal societies: for sectional and individual rites abound in African communities, and they are concerned as much with disruption as with harmony. Finally, why should it be entities with the characteristic properties of "the mystical" that are invoked as a link between fluctuations of the social order and fluctuations of nature? Why should not people just assume a direct and unmediated link between the one and the other—as when a man believes that walking under a ladder is likely to be followed by misfortune? For the anthropologist who asks questions of this kind, Gluckman's essay is likely to bring no stilling of curiosity.

Some indication of why Gluckman does not attempt to answer questions of this sort comes from the introductory paragraphs of his essay. Here, as we have seen, he not only contrasts the nineteenth-century view of rituals as "the fruits of mental processes and ideas" with the modern view which sees them "in terms of social relations." He goes on to assert that modern minds are bored by the nineteenth-century approach. What this seems to mean is that while van Gennep, Tylor, Frazer, and other nineteenth-century writers treated religious beliefs as serious attempts to account for the world and its workings, those of their modern successors who follow Gluckman are unable to see such beliefs as having any serious intellectual content, and so tend to treat them as nothing more than a sort of all-purpose social glue. Again, while the nineteenth-century writers felt that the invisibility, personality, and other equally curious properties attributed to mystical beings posed fascinating problems that demanded answers, their modern successors find little of interest in any aspect of religion other than its postulated capacity to keep society running smoothly.

But why this curious change of emphasis which, in sweeping so many unsolved problems out of sight, seems more of a sideways movement than one of intellectual progress? The change cannot be simply ascribed to changes in personal religious conviction; for as far as I know all the writings involved reflect an agnostic outlook. What seems more important is that whereas the earlier writers were living in an environment dominated by religious believers, the modern agnostic is often the product of a milieu in which such believers are rather marginal beings. Hence, while the earlier writers found no difficulty in conceiving of people who really did look out on the world through religious spectacles, their successors find this a difficult feat of imagination. Again, for the earlier writers religion was a dangerous force whose every characteristic had to be charted and accounted for—even if only as an intelligence operation prior to a campaign. In the social milieu of modern agnosticism, however, religion has largely ceased to be regarded as effective. Hence attentive concern has given way to incurious apathy. But agnostic pronouncements on religion have evoked a number of recent reactions from Christian colleagues; and it is here that we move from Gluckman to Turner.

The setting of Turner's essay is the Ndembu culture of Central Africa—a culture whose population consists of shifting cultivators and hunters living in small villages organized about nuclei of matrilateral kin. The villages are unstable, being prone to conflicts and fission arising from land shortage, disputes between husbands and wives' brothers, struggles for headmanship, etc. Turner has described these communities and their cycles of conflict in his previous book *Schism and Continuity in an African Society*. . . .

When we come to *Chihamba* fresh from a reading of *Schism and Continuity*, we are in for a surprise. For this is not just a detailed study of one of the rituals presented in outline in the former book: it is a work informed by a very different theoretical approach.

. . .

In *Chihamba*, Turner is much more interested in the meaningful content of the ritual performance than in its unintended integrative functions. And this interest has led him to give us one of the most detailed and best-documented descriptions of a piece of ritual to appear in anthropological literature.

When a man or woman has been afflicted in the mode of *Chihamba*, this means that a female ancestor, in alliance with the male nature-spirit *Kavula*, is the cause of the trouble. The superficial intention of the ritual which ensues is to extricate afflicted people from their dangerous relationship with *Kavula* and the ancestress, and to establish a more beneficial bond with them.

The highlights of the *Chihamba* ritual are as follows. First, the afflicted victims are summoned to a hut where a hidden male adept, impersonating *Kavula*, asks them why they have sought him out, reviles them, and gives them special ritual names. On the next day, adepts clear a ritual enclosure in the bush, and there bury a bundle of symbolic objects. In so doing they are at once burying misfortune and installing *Kavula*. Later, they set up in the enclosure an image of *Kavula* made from a wooden framework covered by a white blanket and capped by an inverted wooden mortar.

While these preparations are going on, other adepts start to chase the candidates for submission to the ritual back and forth between the enclosure and the house of the senior victim of affliction. Songs sung at this time imply that the candidates have become slaves of *Kavula*, and to emphasize this they are made to carry heavy slave-yokes. With each chasing the candidates are brought closer and closer to the sacred enclosure until, at sundown, they are brought up one by one to make humble obeisance before the image of *Kavula*. Then, immediately afterwards, they are made to strike the image on the head with sacred rattles. The image shakes and finally keels over. *Kavula* is declared dead and all the participants return to the village.

The next day, candidates are taken out to a species of tree called *Ikamba da Chihamba*. A senior female adept bares the white taproot of this tree, which is said to represent *Kavula*. Then a senior male adept cuts off a branch of the root; and this, together with other symbolic vegetable objects, is taken back to the village. Here again, this episode is said to be a "wounding" of *Kavula*. On the way back to the village the adepts stop to draw a white clay image of *Kavula* on the ground. They cover this with a medicine basket, and make a double arch at its foot with a split sapling. The candidates are made to crawl up to the image and greet it as they greeted the forest image on the previous day. Then they too are ceremonially "killed" by having a knife passed over their shoulders.

Back in the village the final important step is the setting-up, for each of those who have submitted to the ritual, of a personal shrine to the *Chihamba* spirits. These will henceforth be a source of benefit to their former victims. The setting-up of shrines begins with that of the senior female candidate. To make the latter's shrine, a bundle of twigs cut from trees symbolic of the *Chihamba* spirits is thrust into a hole, tamped with stream mud and libated with beer. A pot is placed near the bundle, and the blood of a cock poured into it. Finally, a piece of the *Ikamba da Chihamba* root is placed near by. Later, the shrines of the other candidates are set up in a similar manner. Four weeks afterwards the participants in *Chihamba* are released from their ritual taboos, and all is finished.

Through much of this ritual sequence, events are carried forward by the performance of elaborate symbolic actions and the manipulation of innumerable symbolic objects, the latter being largely drawn from the trees and plants of the surrounding forest. Turner has some interesting things to say about the structure of this luxuriant symbolism. Its chief features are: (*a*) that elementary symbols tend to be organized and used in complexes; (*b*) that each elementary symbol tends to have a large "fan" of diverse potential meanings; and (*c*) that different selections from this fan of meanings are mobilized when a given symbol features in different complexes. Hence, though a given symbol has a restricted overt significance in any given context of use, it carries with it a vast penumbra of dimly apprehended latent meanings. It is these latent meanings, Turner suggests, which make people react with fear and awe to some of the more commonly recurring symbols, and which lead them to think of such symbols as charged with a mysterious power. Although much that Turner says on this score is sufficiently interesting to merit pages of discussion, he himself soon passes on from the structure of Ndembu symbolism to its actual content; and, in order to stick to the theme of this paper, we must follow him.

Turner admits that a good deal of the symbolism and organization of the *Chihamba* ritual reflects more general features of Ndembu social life. Thus the death and rebirth both of *Kavula* and of the candidates is one example of a common idiom for the expression of radical changes of status—used here to signify and indeed to bring about a crucial change in the relations between men and the spirits. Much the same could be said of the complementary action of the male *Kavula* and the female ancestress, and of the complementary position in the ritual of senior male adepts and senior female candidates: for this theme of male-female complementarity clearly echoes the basic principle of Ndembu social organization, which is that male authority is dependent on descent through the female line.

But, says Turner, there is much more in the *Chihamba* ritual which we cannot begin to understand if we insist that it is a mere reflection of Ndembu social structure. This is especially true of the spirit *Kavula*, of his personality, and of the symbols associated with him. If we go carefully through the attributes assigned to *Kavula*, we shall find that he sums up in his being almost all the major forces which Ndembu see operating in their world. Thus he is associated with gerontocratic authority, with the unity of the whole of Ndembuland, with the fertility of crops and people, with rainfall and the elements, and with hunting. At the same time, he is associated with disease and death, and with the destructive powers of lightning. But *Kavula* is not just the sum of all these forces: he is something beyond them and more than them. And it is to emphasize this that the *Chihamba* ritual lays such stress on paradox. Thus, by presenting *Kavula* first as one in the forest image, and then as many in the personal shrines made at the end of the ritual, Ndembu show that he transcends the opposition between the one and the many. Again, by commanding candidates to strike down *Kavula* after they have given him the obeisance due to a chief, they show that he transcends the opposition between authority and subordination. And by presenting him in renewed life after he has been killed, they not only show that he transcends the opposition between death and life, they also show by means of allegory his ultimate elusiveness from conceptual control. In fact, one might regard the whole of the *Chihamba* ritual as a lesson that *Kavula* is at once identifiable with most of the major forces in the Ndembu world, and at the same time transcends them all.

What, then, is *Kavula?* This question can only be answered, Turner feels, in terms of the traditional Thomist distinction between particular existing things and the pure existence which is the ground and support of all of them. *Kavula* is the Ndembu representation of this pure existence, or, as Turner puts it following Etienne Gilson, this "pure-act-of-being." Because it is in the nature of language to be concerned with particular existing things, a literal conceptualization of pure-act-of-being is impossible; and this is why *Kavula* can only be defined with the aid of symbol and paradox. This too is why the *Chihamba* ritual appears as a concentration of white symbols: for whiteness represents both that which is whole or total and that which is devoid of particular attributes. On this interpretation, the *Chihamba* ritual must be seen as an attempt both to say obliquely what cannot be said directly about pure-act-of-being, and to express dependence on this primal entity. These ends, says Turner, cannot be treated as the product of some specific kind of social organization. For they are not merely the ends of Ndembu worshippers: they are the ends of "ritual man" the world over.

To help convince the reader that *Chihamba* is "the local expression of a universal-human problem," Turner traces its close parallels with two better-known representations of pure-act-of-being—that found in the New Testament story of Christ's Death and Resurrection, and that found in Herman Melville's saga of the doomed quest for the great white whale Moby Dick. Although he clearly feels that the Christian representation carries with it certain unique claims to truth and value, he nevertheless sees basic similarities between the representations of *Kavula*, Christ, and the white whale. Thus in all three there is the feeling of the impossibility of direct statement, and the development of symbol and allegory to "grasp the ungraspable." There is the predominance of white symbols, aimed at representing that which is at once the ground of all things and the transcender of all things. There is the great development of paradox, and especially of the theme of the striking-down which yet does not annihilate—an allegory of that which by its very nature can never be finally pinned down by human thought.

Anthropologists in the tradition of Frazer and Durkheim, says Turner, would prefer not to recognize these constants of the religious situation. They would rather explain away religious phenomena or reduce them to non-religious terms. For, like Melville's Captain Ahab, they seek to destroy that belief in a deity which wounds and menaces their self-sufficiency. But only if they become humble in the face of religious experience, like the harpooner Queequeg, can they ever discover anything worth while about "ritual man."

Any reader of Turner's essay will be struck by a deep feeling for the importance of religious ritual in human intellectual and emotional life—a feeling notably absent from too many current analyses. Readers of my own persuasion will also be refreshed by the message that different areas of human social behaviour need to be explained in terms of different motives—a welcome change from the kind of anthropological interpretation that apparently assumes no human motives other than the quest for social harmony, the quest for power, and the quest for food. Having said this, however, I must confess uneasiness about the particular framework of interpretation that Turner favours.

First of all, it is clear from Turner's essay that the Ndembu already have in *Nzambi* a supreme being who, even though he does not feature prominently in their ritual, certainly occupies a significant place in their thought. Now if *Kavula* really is an attempt to represent pure-act-of-being, the primal entity that underlies and supports all things in man's world, why do Ndembu not identify him with *Nzambi* or at least treat him as the latter's special manifestation? The nearest Turner gets to showing that they do either of these is with an informant who says that "*Kavula* is more like *Nzambi* than an ancestor spirit." But judging from the context of this statement it seems specifically designed to emphasize the non-ancestral nature of *Kavula*, and would probably have been applicable to other non-ancestral spirits (*Chihamba*, p. 22). It is rather as if the Thomist philosophers, having worked out their theory of pure-act-of-being, were to claim that the latter's representation was to be found neither in God nor in Jesus Christ, but in the most important of the archangels. One would certainly want some explanation of what would seem to be a deliberate obscurantism on their part.

It is even a little doubtful whether *Kavula* really does sum up in his person all the major social and natural forces which Ndembu see operating in their world, and whether he transcends all the salient oppositions and contrasts in this world. We have already noted that, in the *Chihamba* ritual, *Kavula* acts as the husband of an afflicting ancestress. And there is more than a hint that this ancestress embodies a set of forces which are distinct from and complementary to those summed up in the person of *Kavula*. Thus at one point she is said to be associated with narrow and localized matrilineage loyalties, while *Kavula* is associated with the unity of all Ndembu or even of all Lunda. Again, she is said to be associated with matrilineal descent, while *Kavula* is associated with male authority over women (*Chihamba*, pp. 77–78). Instead of transcending all salient oppositions and contrasts, then, *Kavula* appears to be on one side of at least some of them.

Perhaps one could only give a conclusive verdict on Turner's interpretation if all the various connotations of *Kavula* were plotted alongside those of the various other categories of non-ancestral and ancestral spirit. Since Turner says that the present essay is merely a progress report, to be followed by a full-scale book on Ndembu religion, one hopes that he may eventually lay out his material in this way, and so enable us to make a more definite assessment.

At once more important and more controversial than Turner's application of Thomist concepts to the translation of Ndembu ideas is his advocacy of such concepts as the appropriate translation instruments for religious ideas generally. This emerges in the last chapter of *Chihamba*, where, so far as I can grasp his rich and complex analysis, he seems to be asserting the following propositions:

1. The difficulty of grasping the nature of pure existence (or pure-act-of-being in Turner's terminology) as distinct from particular existing things and their properties is "indissociable from the very structure of language and conceptualization." That is, it is a human universal. (See *Chihamba*, p. 82, para. 2.)

2. We can define "Ritual Man" as one who has a sense of dependence on pure existence or pure-act-of-being, and as one who, in all ages and places, is passionately engaged in trying to overcome the inherent difficulty of expressing this sense of dependence. (See p. 84, para. 1; and p. 87, para. 2.)

3. The concept of "Ritual Man," defined in these terms, might be made central to the comparative study of religion. This is implied by the analogy with the concept of "Economic Man" as used in economics, and with that of "The Reasonable Man" as used in law. (See p. 84, para. 1.)

Turner also appears to be asserting a less specific thesis, which is entailed by the foregoing, but could also be asserted independently. This thesis can be summarized in the following propositions:

4. All the behaviour and belief we call religious, from one end of the world to the other, is a product of the same essential human aspiration. Though some people may deny having such an aspiration because it involves a sense of dependence on a supreme being which is wounding to self-sufficiency, it is in fact universal. (P. 84, para. 1; p. 92 end of para. 1.)

5. The essential aspiration of religion cannot be explained in terms of any other human aspirations nor can it be reduced to any other such aspirations. (P. 86, para. 2.)

6. This follows from (4). For the European anthropologist, acceptance of religious insights couched in the idiom of his own culture is the key to understanding of religions generally. Rejection of such insights makes this wider understanding impossible. (P. 84, para. 1; p. 92, end of para. 1.)

Now there is nothing prima facie wrong with this set of propositions. True, they appear to be closely connected with the author's own religious beliefs; but this need not necessarily be a defect. A first step in the analysis of an alien religious system must always be the search for an area of discourse in one's own language which can appropriately serve as a translation instrument. And in so far as he is thoroughly at home in the religious discourse of his own culture, the Christian would seem to be at an advantage over the agnostic in this matter. The reasonableness of this argument receives support from the defects of most of the religious analyses carried out by agnostic anthropologists. Since their errors and their omissions are often so patently related to their personal hostility or apathy to things religious, the remedy seems straightforward enough: the Christian must make full use of his own religious discourse in translating the religious ideas of alien cultures.

Reasonable as they seem, however, the propositions which Turner appears to be asserting in the last chapter of *Chihamba* must stand or fall by their applicability to the raw data of religious belief and behaviour throughout the world. And here, of course, we shall be particularly interested in their applicability to African data.

Before confronting Turner's narrower thesis with the data, it might be as well to remind ourselves of the essentials of the Thomist position from which this thesis starts out. According to Thomist premises, everything in the world around us has certain definitive properties (its essence) and, in addition, the property of existence. Since the essences of things can be thought of apart from their existence, they are said to be contingent. Existence in itself, however, is logically prior to the other properties; hence pure being is the necessary ground and support of all the other attributes of all the particular things in the world. Not only this: pure being is identical with its own essence; and since its essence cannot be thought of apart from its existence, it is self-necessitating. It is this pure being, necessary ground of all things and sufficient reason for its own existence, that Thomists identify with the Absolute, the First Cause, the Godhead, etc. But having established the necessity of pure being, one can make no further direct statements about it: for language, by its very nature, is concerned only with the distinguishing properties of individual things (essences). Thus it is that in order to delineate pure being one is driven into the obliqueness of symbol and allegory.

Now Turner implies that this conception of pure being, of its relation to the world, and of the difficulties of making direct statements about it, is forced upon all men by the very structure of their thought and language (*Chihamba*, p. 82, para 2). But this cannot be true. For the whole complex of problems and preoccupations sketched here is indissociable from the particular meaning which Thomists attach to the word "exists." Since they treat this as a predicate which in some respects is on the same level as "is-hard," "is-green," "is-alive," and so on, it is possible for them to have meaningful discussions about an entity which has the sole attribute of existence—i.e., pure being. But there is another conceptual framework, just as widely current in modern Western culture, in which "exists" has quite a different meaning. Within this framework, to say that "X has properties Y *and* exists" is merely to say that "the statement 'X has properties Y' is true." Here, no sense can be attached to statements about pure existence; and the problems and preoccupations associated with this concept just do not arise. Although this latter conceptual framework is commonly associated with logical positivism, it is also one in which many Protestant thinkers are at home; and correspondingly, their thought about God's relation to the world tends to follow very different lines from that of the Thomists. Since by no means even all Christian thinkers acknowledge the usefulness and relevance of the Thomist conceptual framework, it would appear to be a poor candidate for the translation of religious ideas on a world-wide basis.

When we come to the study of African traditional religions, the picture seems equally unpromising. In so far as nearly all known African traditional religions feature a supreme being who is the creator and sustainer of all that is, one could perhaps say that such religions take account of something vaguely akin to the Thomist pure-act-of-being. But where we have nothing that evidently corresponds to the crucial Thomist distinctions between existence and essence, and between self-necessitating and contingent entities, the kinship would seem to be vague indeed. More important still, it would be a distortion to say that African religion was in any way centred on the struggle to adumbrate in symbols what could not be directly said about this primal entity, or that such a struggle "engaged the passionate attention of ritual man" throughout the continent. Indeed, though African thought-systems are very variable in this respect, the predominant atmosphere in many of them is one of apathy about the supreme being. Often, he is acknowledged to be the ultimate sustainer of everything in the world; but at the same time people say little about him either directly or in symbolism. Their thought and energy is focused mainly on the lesser spirits who, though they are the creation of the supreme being, are directly associated with most of the happenings in people's immediate environment. These lesser spirits are just as real to their worshippers as the supreme being; and relations with them are surely as much a part of religion as relations with this being.

What of the wider thesis implicit in the last chapter of *Chihamba*—the thesis that the same essential human aspiration is at the root of religious activity in all ages and in all places; that this aspiration is not to be explained by or reduced to any others; and that acknowledgment of this aspiration in one's own life gives one the only real key to understanding religions of other cultures very different from one's own?

. . .

Perhaps the best way to set about testing the usefulness of Turner's wider thesis is to start out with a sketch of contemporary Christian preoccupations that might be acceptable to most branches of the faith. For the sake of argument, let us adopt the following. Christians are centrally preoccupied with a supreme being whose reality transcends the space-time order. Knowledge of this being and of His perfect love and goodness gives life a depth, fullness, and richness which non-believers confined to the space-time plane can never suspect. It is as if life had one less dimension for the non-believer; and this is why he is often compared to a blind man. Much as modern Christianity has to say about the joys of living in the light of God's love and goodness, however, it shows little interest in furnishing a detailed interpretation of connections between phenomena in the space-time world. Efforts to give it such an interest, like that of Teilhard de Chardin, are not even greatly approved of by the Churches. Indeed, one could say that the Churches take the detailed working of the space-time world with no further explanatory comment than the statement that whatever happens in this realm is ultimately ordained by God.

If we take this sketch of Christian preoccupations into the field of African traditional religions, two great questions arise. First, does our sketch in any way tally with a sketch one might make of the central preoccupations of African religions? Secondly, can familiarity with Christian preoccupations and acceptance of their validity give us some special key to the understanding of African religions?

As with Turner's narrower Thomist thesis, the answers once again seem rather negative. First of all, there is the frequent apathy about the supreme being, and the concentration of intellectual and emotional energies on the figures of the lesser spirits. Again, though there is a good deal in African traditional religions which suggests the central Christian experience of intense personal communion with a loving God, such communion seems more often associated with the lesser spirits than with the supreme being. Finally and most strikingly, the primary intention of much African religious thought seems to be just that mapping of connections between space-time phenomena which modern Christian thought feels is beyond its proper domain. Though, by the standards of the more advanced contemporary sciences, these religions seldom provide valid explanations or make completely successful predictions, there is a very real sense in which they are just as concerned with explanation and prediction as the sciences are. In this respect, they are as close to the latter as they are to modern Christianity.

So far as a confrontation of modern Christianity with traditional African religions is concerned, then, it looks as though the essential aspiration of the one is often the marginal aspiration of the other, and vice versa. This being so, Christian discourse can be a translation instrument of only limited use where African religions are concerned; and familiarity with it cannot promise any general key to understanding which is not available to the agnostic.

Again, this confrontation throws doubt on the proposition that religious aspirations are not to be explained in terms of any others or reduced to them. As I have said, many African traditional religions, with their passionate interest in the explanation and prediction of space-time events, are as close to the sciences as they are to modern Christianity. Hence I venture to suggest that, over much of Africa, Ritual Man is not really a distinctive being, but is rather a sub-species of Theory-building Man.

This last suggestion leads directly to the constructive part of my argument. Professor Gluckman's programme for interpreting African ritual depends on the assumption of a dominant concern for the harmonious and smooth running of social life. Turner's reaction to this sort of programme depends on the assumption of a dominant concern with "saying the unsayable" about the ultimate ground of all particular forms of existence. I prefer to be thoroughly old-fashioned and go back to the sort of assumption that guided Tylor, Frazer, and van Gennep—that the really significant aspiration behind a great deal of African religious thought is the most obvious one; i.e. the attempt to explain and influence the working of one's everyday world by discovering the constant principles that underlie the apparent chaos and flux of sensory experience. In so far as we make this aspiration central to our analysis, we shall find ourselves searching for translation instruments not so much in the realm of Christian discourse as in that of the sciences and their theoretical concepts.

All this may sound at first like some dreadful humanist commando raid—designed to snatch Africa from the hands of the Thomists only to deliver it into the ranks of the scientists. It is, of course, nothing of the sort; for, as the reader will see, the analysis that follows takes full account of the crucial things that divide the pre-scientific thought-systems of Africa from the thought of the sciences. Nevertheless, as I shortly hope to show, an exploration of the common patterns of reasoning that underlie these crucial differences could be a valuable preliminary to the interpretation of African religious thought.

Now one very common way of trying to explain a set of observed phenomena is in terms of a scheme of underlying processes or events. To provide the basis of a satisfying explanation this scheme must be such as to display the diversity and complexity of observed phenomena as the product of an underlying unity, simplicity, and regularity. Thus an important part of modern chemical thought is the body of theory which explains the vast diversity of recorded substances as a product of the combination and recombination of a limited number of elements according to a few relatively simple rules. Given certain assumptions about regularities of events in the theoretical scheme, and certain identifications of these events with observed phenomena, it becomes possible to deduce the occurrence of the latter as necessary. And when such deduction is applied to future occurrences, we have prediction. Thus the theory of chemical elements and their combination can be used either to show the necessity of the occurrence of certain substances already observed, or to predict the future occurrence of substances not yet observed.

When they are used in the sciences, such explanatory and predictive schemes are known as "theoretical models." And the commonly approved criteria for accepting or rejecting such models are what we call "the Rules of Scientific Method." By and large, these criteria are simply an inventory of the conditions which make for maximum efficiency in fulfilling the aims of explanation and prediction. The African religious systems which contain the counterparts of these theoretical models are, as we have said, sustained by the same basic aims of explanation and prediction. They differ from the thought-systems of science most notably in the absence of any guiding body of explicit acceptance/rejection criteria that would ensure the efficiency with which they pursue their aims.

In devoting itself almost exclusively to exploring the rules for acceptance and rejection of theoretical models, modern philosophical analysis has concentrated on that aspect of Western scientific thought which most distinguishes it from the thought-systems of Africa. In more recent years, however, the philosophers have begun to turn their attention to another aspect in which the resemblances are probably more significant than the differences. Here I am thinking of the actual generation of theoretical models—the process whereby an area of puzzling observations provokes speculation as to a possible underlying mechanism, and gives birth to the tentative explanatory scheme which "scientific logic" then goes to work on.

Perhaps the only thing we know for certain about this process is that most theoretical models are drawn from phenomena already observed in the visible and tangible world. The investigator is impressed by an analogy between the puzzling observations he wants to explain and the structure of certain phenomena whose behaviour has already been well explored. Because of this analogy, he postulates a scheme of events with structure akin to that of the prototype phenomena, and equates this scheme with the reality "behind" the observations that puzzle him. Such well-known models as those involving the molecule, the planetary atom, the electric current, and the light wave all have fairly obvious prototypes in the world of everyday phenomena. Similarly, we can often see the prototypes of African religious models in the social life of the peoples who have evolved them.

What is not so well established is why a particular set of phenomena is drawn upon as the prototype of an explanatory model in a particular situation. As Stephen Toulmin has remarked, there is no possible step of inductive or deductive inference which can lead unambiguously from a given set of puzzling observations to a given theoretical model. And as for the perception of structural analogy which is the basis of the model-making process, this too would seem to permit a considerable range of choice in any given observational situation. Indeed, Toulmin's appraisal has led him to state that in the thought of science, as well as in that of prescience, model-making probably owes as much to the wider thought-patterns and fashions of the age as it does to the nature of the observations to be explained.

This brings us to the point at which we can reintroduce one of the central questions that we raised in connection with Gluckman's essay. What cultural variables are responsible for the fact that Western scientific thought tends to choose things rather than people as the basis of its explanatory models, while African thought-systems by and large tend to make the opposite choice?

Though I do not think we are yet in a position to give a fully satisfactory answer to this question, we can perhaps get a clue to some of the factors involved by going back to what the philosophers of science define as the essential feature of an explanatory model. According to them, the logic of explanation demands first and foremost that the underlying events postulated by any theoretical model should be connected in an orderly and regular fashion: for explanation *is* the demonstration of order underlying apparent chaos and of regularity underlying apparent haphazardness. Hence, to qualify as a suitable prototype for a model, a set of phenomena needs not only to be thoroughly familiar, but also to be manifestly orderly and regular in its behaviour.

Now in technologically backward communities which have a relatively simple social organization and are not in a state of rapid and self-conscious change, people's activities in society present the most markedly ordered and regular area of their experience, whereas their biological and inanimate environment is by and large less tidily predictable. Hence it is chiefly to human activities and relationships that such communities turn for the sources of their most important explanatory models. It is probably fair to say that much of traditional African society typifies this pattern.

. . .

Again, take what, for the want of a better word, one may call the "imcompleteness" of the African gods. Between different African religions, and even between different sectors of the same religion, there is a good deal of variation in the number of dimensions of human life which are incorporated into the figures of the various gods. Nearly always, however, some dimensions are missing. What these are varies from case to case. Perhaps one only notices that they are missing if one has the naivety to ask all the questions about a god that one would ask about a man. Does he beget children? How many has he? What kind of a house does he live in? Is he handsome? How tall is he? Is he kind to his wives? One has only to go a little way along this road before getting the sort of blank stare which indicates that one has been asking entirely meaningless questions. Probably one will be told curtly: "We are talking about the spirits; not about men".

That there is nothing in this situation peculiar to African gods becomes apparent if one asks the same sort of questions about the theoretical entities of the sciences. What is the temperature of a hydrogen molecule? What is the colour of a proton? However appropriate such questions would have been if asked of the prototype phenomena from which these entities were drawn, they are certainly quite out of order if asked of the entities themselves. The reason is directly connected with the explanatory function of theoretical entities. Earlier, we noted that the creation of a new theoretical model takes place when an investigator traces an analogy between the structure of certain puzzling observations and that of certain phenomena whose regularities of behaviour he is already familiar with. He draws on these phenomena as the basis of a model which he equates with the reality underlying his initial observations. But the structural analogy between the observations and the proprototype phenomena seldom involves more than a limited aspect of the latter. And it is only this limited aspect that is taken over and incorporated into the model. The rest is left behind: for, from the point of view of explanatory function, it is just so much dross. Thus the atomic physicist Rutherford, in forming his revolutionary planetary model of the atom, left behind such features as the colour and temperature of the planets as irrelevant to his explanatory task. In just the same way, when he fashions the gods from people, the African thinker leaves behind as irrelevant many features of human activity and physical appearance.

Another feature of African traditional thought which now becomes less puzzling is the often-remarked tendency towards definition of the various units of society in "mystical" or religious terms. Thus the Kalabari village is defined as that group of people which has its own *amatemeso* —the personal force that guides the thread of its history. The autonomous Ibo political unit is the largest group of communities sharing a common cult of *ala*—spirit of the earth. The Ashanti state is that unit which is guided and held together by the souls of the royal ancestors. And so on. Such definitions, again, are a logical consequence of the explanatory role of religious ideas. For theoretical models inevitably dictate the ways in which the data they explain are classified and hence described. Things apparently diverse at the level of observation may be manifestations of a single process in the model, and will be classified accordingly; while things which show superficial similarities at the level of observation may be manifestations of diverse aspects of the model, and classification, again, will proceed accordingly. Hence the sheerest description may contain implicit references to the model. A chemist, asked to give a thorough description of some substance in his laboratory, can hardly avoid mentioning such characteristics as molecular weight and formula, which refer implicitly to a massive body of chemical theory. In the same way, an African villager, who is trying to discribe what his community is, can hardly avoid implicit reference to religious concepts. In so far as one can only start to understand social relations through familiarity with the terms in which those involved think about them, it is probably true to say that he who wishes to understand many African societies must first understand their religions.

We can now reconsider some of the questions raised by Professor Gluckman. First: why is ritual, in the sense of approach to mystical powers, such a frequent accompaniment of *rites de passage* in which an individual is taken from one role to another? The answer seems clear in the light of what has been said in the last few paragraphs. These changes of role usually involve incorporation into a new group or a new set of relationships; and, as we have seen, a corporate group is apt to be defined in terms of the personal beings who are "behind" the coordinated activities of its members. It is these beings who keep the group flourishing, or weaken it in response to breaches of group norms. Because membership of the group implies having one's life partially controlled by such beings, becoming a member logically involves a process of being put under their control.

The second question which interests Gluckman is: why, in so many African rituals where the members of a corporate group approach a mystical power, do those concerned participate in a manner which lays exaggerated emphasis on the patterns of behaviour proper among each other in the wider context of social life? Here again, I think, the answer follows clearly from what has already been said about African religious ideas. In most African societies, the strength and welfare of corporate groups is seen as intimately bound up with their members' close observance of their moral norms. Consequently with this, the spirits that underpin the various corporate groups of a society nearly always support the moral norms of such groups; and their strengthening action is conditional upon observance of these norms. When a group assembles to approach its guiding spirit, it is therefore appropriate that its members, in their behaviour to one another during the ritual, should demonstrate their readiness to observe group norms.

The sketch of an approach to African traditional religions I have given in the last few paragraphs is brief, impressionistic, and highly tentative. Yet I think it indicates a line of inquiry more fruitful than that favoured by Gluckman. For it seems capable of explaining the salient morphological features of African religious beliefs *as well as* the relation of these beliefs to the social organization. Again, I hope my sketch has shown clearly enough that Turner's answer to the agnostic anthropologist is by no means the only permissible one and that one might even be able to go further in the interpretation of his Ndembu material in the terms sketched above than in his own Thomist terms. Thus one can look at the beliefs about *Kavula* and the ancestress as means of bringing intellectual order into a variety of everyday experience: more specifically, that they constitute the basis of a theoretical model which enables one to place such diverse oppositions as masculinity/femininity, pan-Lunda loyalties/matrilineage loyalties, authority/descent (and possibly others such as settlement area/forest), as instances of the operation of a single pair of underlying forces related to one another as contrasting complementaries. This would make *Kavula* very different from a representation of pure-act-of-being; but it would avoid some of the crucial difficulties of Turner's interpretation.

I am not, of course, trying to say that the approach I have suggested here is the only way towards an understanding of African religions; nor am I saying that it must exclude the sort of insight which modern Christians are equipped to provide. Indeed, as I noted earlier, there is a good deal in African traditional religions which recalls the Christian experience of communion with a loving God—even though in the African context such communion seems to be associated more with the lesser spirits than with the supreme being. Involving as it does intense personal relationships with beings beyond the human social order, the communion aspect of African religion tends to take people outside the daily round of visible and tangible experience. In this sense it moves thought in the opposite direction from the explanatory aspect, which starts in the realm of unobservable beings, and brings these to bear on visible and tangible things. Formally opposed though they are, these two aspects of religion are found intermingled in many African cultures. Nor is the tension between these two opposites always an unfruitful one: for in the shamans, prophets, and mystics of traditional religion, we see people who both pass out of the sphere of visible and tangible things in their communion, and also return from time to time with explanatory schemes which make new sense of the visible and tangible world.

This intermingling of explanation and communion seems to have been typical of Christianity down through medieval times. But after the revolution of thought in seventeenth-century Europe there was a steady differentiation, science progressively taking over the explanatory aspect, and religion becoming more and more a matter of communion. Opposites once fruitfully mingled became clearly distinguished and even set against one another. So much so that today a rare feat of imagination is required of the man who would both commit himself wholeheartedly to the ideals of Western science and at the same time remain fully committed to the Christian faith.

Hence, if it is true that the primary problem of the social anthropologist is one of finding the areas of discourse in his own language whose logic comes nearest that of the alien discourse he wishes to analyse, the would-be student of African religions is faced with a heavy task. For he must bring together in his own single mind areas of discourse which modern Western culture tends to make the preserve of different categories of people.

Roy A. Rappaport

RITUAL, SANCTITY, AND CYBERNETICS

In this highly sophisticated analysis of the functions of ritual and sanctity in human society, Roy Rappaport refines the ecological interpretation of Tsembaga ritual advanced in his well-known book, *Pigs for the Ancestors* (1968). Drawing on ethology, cybernetics, and systems theory, the author argues that ritual is primarily a mode of communication which transmits practical information about the physiological, psychological, and sociological conditions of individuals and groups of individuals. But Rappaport goes beyond this purely functional interpretation and attempts to account for the formal characteristics of the ritual mechanism used to communicate such information. Sanctity, defined as the unquestioning acceptance of unverifiable statements, is a crucial aspect of ritual performances because of the symbolic nature of human communication. Unlike animal communication in which the occurrence of any signal necessarily "means" its referent, human communication is based on an arbitrary connection between symbols and that which they symbolize. The meaning of any symbol is a matter of culturally established conventions. Human beings, then, can lie, and this presents a serious threat to the effectiveness of communication in human society. Far from being an inconsequential embellishment on the true functions of ritual, sanctity strengthens the veracity of the practical information communicated in ritual performances. Its functional significance stems from its ability to elicit from people non-random, predictable responses to ritual messages and thereby maintain a degree of orderliness in human social relations. Rappaport argues that because sanctity is a quality that adheres to things rather than being a thing in itself, religious concepts can adapt to changing ecological and social circumstances without losing their sacred potency. Finally, Rappaport suggests that the concept of sanctity originates in certain processes of child development and socialization. While this last point remains controversial, Rappaport presents us with a persuasive extension of his ecological interpretation of ritual. For another approach to the ecological analysis of religion systems, see G. Reichel-Dolmatoff, "Cosmology as Ecological Analysis: A View From the Rain Forest" (1976).

Reprinted in abridged form from *American Anthropologist*, 73 (1971), 59–76, by permission of the author and the American Anthropological Association.

I

The roles that ritual and sanctity play in communication, and in the regulation of the systems in which they participate are examined in this essay in an attempt to gain some additional understanding of the nature of religion.

This essay differs from an earlier study I made of Tsembaga ritual (Rappaport, 1967; 1968) in important ways. Whereas the earlier analysis focused upon the functions of ritual in a complex ecological system, the present attempts to elucidate those formal characteristics of Tsembaga ritual and belief—and through them, if possible, ritual and belief in general—which make them suitable to fulfill the functions the earlier analysis ascribed to them. Thus, although the arguments that I advance may have some generality, I shall have to allude to Tsembaga ethnography, and incorporate some of the earlier analysis. . . .

It will be well, before proceeding, to make clear my use of such terms as "system," "regulate," and "control." I shall then review briefly some salient features of Maring ethnology and then discuss the formal characteristics of ritual that suit them for communication and regulatory functions. The discussion of ritual will lead to suggestions concerning the nature of sanctity and its role in communication and control.

II

I do not use the term "system" to designate collections of entities which share some ontological characteristic, as might be implied by such phrases as "belief system," or "kinship terminological system." The term "system" is meant merely to designate a collection of specified variables in which a change in the value or state of any one will result in a change in the value or state of at least one of the others. The ontological characteristics of the components of the physical world from which the variables are derived are irrelevant; we may include in the compass of a single system or subsystem variables abstracted from cultural, biological, and inorganic phenomena.

I use the terms "regulate" and "control" in a systemic, indeed a cybernetic, sense. A regulating mechanism, control mechanism or homeostat is one that maintains the values of one or more of the variables included in a system within a range or ranges that defines the continued existence of the system. Such ranges of viability may often be established empirically. Population size serves as a familiar example. We may be able to demonstrate, or at least have good reason for believing, that below a certain size a particular population will be too small to reproduce or defend itself, above a particular size it will destroy its subsistence base. The viable range, i.e., the set of possible states between these limits, is sometimes called the "goal range." Regulation is the process which maintains the value of the variable within the goal range, usually through negative feed-back. A familiar example from the universe of machines is the operation of the thermostat.

The terms "regulation" and "control" refer to operations which are central to "adaptation." Adaptation here refers to the processes by which organisms or groups of organisms, through responsive changes in their own states, structures, or compositions, maintain homeostasis in and among themselves in the face of both short term environment fluctuations and long term changes in the composition or structure of their environments.

III

We may now turn to the Tsembaga, one of about twenty politically autonomous local territorial groups of Maring speaking people living on the northern fall of the Bismarck Range in the Australian Trust Territory of New Guinea. They number about 200 people and their territory encompasses about three square miles of mountainside.

The Tsembaga participate in two distinct systems. First, they are a population in the ecological sense, that is, one the components in a system of inter-species trophic (or feeding) exchanges occurring within a bounded area, Tsembaga territory. Conversely, Tsembaga territory and the biota inhabiting it (including the Tsembaga) constitute an ecosystem.

The Tsembaga participate in exchanges of women, valuables, and trade goods with other similar local groups occupying areas external to their territory. Another characteristic of relations between adjacent territorial groups is warfare, one of the processes by which land is redistributed among local groups and people redispersed over land. Thus, as the Tsembaga are participants in an ecosystem, a system of *localized inter-species* exchanges, so are they participants in a regional system, a system, of *non-localized intra-species* exchanges.

Of course events in the local system affect events in the regional system and vice versa. Therefore these two systems are not separate systems but subsystems of a larger system which they together comprise. I have argued elsewhere (1967, 1968) that rituals, arranged in protracted cycles (up to twenty years), articulate the local and regional systems, and, furthermore, regulate relations within each of the subsystems and in the larger systems as a whole. To be more specific, I have interpreted the ritual cycles of the Tsembaga and other Maring as regulating mechanisms and have argued that their operation helps to maintain an undegraded biotic environment, limits fighting to frequencies which do not endanger the survival of the regional population, adjusts man/land ratios, facilitates trade, distributes local surpluses of pig throughout the regional population in the form of pork and assures to members of the local group rations of high quality protein.

We may begin an outline of the operation of the ritual cycle with the termination of warfare. Principal antagonists invariably are local groups, such as Tsembaga. Unless it has been driven off its land, when hostilities have ceased a local group ritually plants a shrub called *rumbim* at a traditional place. This act, symbolizing the connection of the group to its tèrritory, is accompanied by a massive slaughter of pigs. Only juveniles survive; the rest are offered to the ancestors in reciprocation for their assistance in the fighting. But this sacrifice is not believed by the actors to discharge their debt to their deceased forebears, and the latter are told that when there are sufficient pigs a larger offering will be made to them. While they remain in debt to their ancestors the living cannot initiate new hostilities, for it is believed that martial success is impossible without the assistance of ancestors and that the assistance of the ancestors will not be forthcoming until they are repaid in pigs for their help in the last fight. A "truce of God" thus prevails until there are sufficient pigs to absolve the living of their debt to the dead. Thus, the number of pigs regarded as sufficient to repay the ancestors and the length of time it takes to acquire them are crucial factors in regulating the frequency of warfare.

Outside of the rituals associated with warfare and festivals, the slaughter and consumption of pigs is largely limited to the rituals associated with illness and injury. These are occasions in which it is likely that the affected organisms are experiencing physiological stress, and I have argued (Rappaport, 1965:84ff) that reserving the limited amount of domestic pork available for consumption during stressful periods is highly functional for the Maring. Be this as it may, the amount of time required to accumulate sufficient pigs is obviously related to the success and well-being of the pigs' masters, since the slaughter of the beasts is associated with human misfortune. But, rapidly or slowly, the pig population does expand and sooner or later the pigs' ration of substandard sweet potatoes incidentally obtained in the course of harvesting for humans becomes insufficient, and additional acreage needs to be put into production especially for the pigs. The increment may be substantial. When the Tsembaga herd was at maximum in 1963, 36 percent of the acreage in production was devoted to the support of 170 pigs. The burden of the increased gardening falls upon women, and their complaints of overwork become increasingly strident as the number of animals in their charge increases. At the same time, garden invasions by pigs become more frequent and often lead to serious disputes. When the complaints of the women and the garden invasions become intolerable to a sufficient number of men to dominate the consensus, there are sufficient pigs to repay the ancestors. To put this in ecological terms, there are sufficient pigs to repay the ancestors when the relationship of pigs to humans changes from one of mutualism to one of parasitism or competition. Empirical investigations indicate that this point lies below the carrying capacity of the territory for pigs. When the herd reaches such a size (170 in 1962–1963), the *rumbin* is ritually uprooted and a year-long festival is staged, during which friendly groups are entertained from time to time and during which there are massive pig sacrifices which reduce the herd to tolerable size. This pork is then distributed to former allies. At the termination of its festival, a local group has fulfilled its obligations to ancestors (and allies) and is again free to open hostilities. The initiation of warfare is thus limited to once per ritual cycle.

The ritual cycle thus operates as a homeostat in the local subsystem by keeping such variables as the size of the pig population, women's labor, lengths of fallow periods, and other variables within viable ranges; it operates as a homeostat in the regional subsystem by regulating the frequency of warfare, while periodically allowing the expansion of more ecologically competent groups at the expense of those less competent. It further operates as a transducer—a device which transmits energy or information from one subsystem into another—for it articulates the local system to the regional system.

Our argument concerning sanctity demands that we examine more closely one aspect of the year-long festival, the entertainment of visiting groups. The Tsembaga entertained visiting groups on thirteen different occasions during their festival in 1962–1963. These occasions resemble in important ways events which seem to occur among a wide range of non-human animals.

First, they include massed epigamic, or courtship, displays (Wynne-Edwards 1962: 17). Men dance in formations before the young women who are thereby acquainted with eligible males of local groups otherwise unfamiliar to them. The context also permits the young women to discriminate among this sample in terms of both endurance (signaled by how vigorously and how long a man dances) and wealth (signaled by the richness of a man's shell and feather finery).

More importantly, such massed dancing communicates information to the participants concerning the size of the groups. In many species of birds and insects such displays take place as a prelude to actions which adjust size or density (Wynne-Edwards, 1962:16). Such is also the case among the Maring. The massed dancing of the visitors at a *kaiko* entertainment communicates to the hosts, while the *rumbim* truce is still in effect, information concerning the amount of support they may expect from the visitors in the aggression that they may embark upon following the termination of the pig festival.

There are no chiefs or other political authorities capable of commanding the support of a body of followers among the Maring, and whether or not to assist another group in warfare is a decision resting with each individual male. Allies are not recruited by appealing for help to other local groups as such. When a group is in need of military assistance, each of its members appeals to his cognatic and affinal kinsmen in other local groups. These kinsmen, in turn, urge other of their co-residents and kinsmen to "help them fight." The channels through which invitations to dance are extended are precisely those through which appeals for military support are issued. Dance invitations are not extended by one group to another, but from one kinsman to another. Those invited then urge their co-residents to "help them dance." Dancing and fighting are regarded as in some sense equivalent. This equivalence is expressed in the similarity of some pre-fight and pre-dance rituals, and the Maring say that those who come to dance come to fight. The size of a visiting dancing contingent is consequently taken to indicate the number and strength of warriors whose assistance may be expected in the next round of warfare.

IV

We may now examine those aspects of rituals which suit them to function as homeostats and communication devices. I shall take up communications first, because it is the more inclusive category and the more fundamental to ritual.

Let us note first that the term "ritual" is not confined to religious practices. Freud (1907) applied the closely related or even synonymous term "ceremony" to the behavior of some neurotics as well as to religious rituals, in an attempt to elucidate their putative similarities, and the latest Webster International Dictionary widens the perspective further when it informs us that the term "ritual" in its broadest sense refers to "any practice . . . regularly repeated in a set precise manner so as to satisfy one's sense of fitness. . . ." (1965:1961).

This definition, which easily subsumes the rites of the faithful, the performances of headwaiters and the obsessional behavior of some neurotics, explicitly identifies three aspects of rituals: namely, that they are composed of conventional, even stereotyped movements or postures, that they are performed "regularly" (at times fixed by clock, calendar or specified circumstance), and that they have affective or emotional value. There is, in addition, an implication that at least some of the components of rituals, in some instances even entire rituals, are non-instrumental in the sense that they do not contribute directly to the biological or economic well-being of the performer.

A rather wide range of human behavior may thus be labeled ritual but the term has even more general application. Ethologists have also used the term ritual to refer to animal displays, some of which bear close formal resemblance to human rituals. Animal rituals are likely to involve stereotyped, apparently non-instrumental postures and movements, and, as apparently useless paraphernalia are often manipulated in human rituals, so apparently useless biological structures are often waved, vibrated, suffused with color, or expanded in animal rituals. Like human rituals, animal rituals seem to occur under specified circumstances or at fixed times, and some animal rituals, like some human rituals, occur only in special places. As the faithful of a certain persuasion congregate on Sunday mornings only in a certain church, so the starlings congregate at dusk only in certain trees.

Ethologists have generally interpreted animal rituals as communication events. In light of such an interpretation even the very quality of the grotesque characteristic of some stereotyped ritual posturing becomes understandable. For a signal to be effective it must be distinguishable from ordinary instrumental activity. The more bizarre the ritual movement of structures the more easily may they be recognized as ritual. . . . Accordingly, for our present purposes I define ritual, both animal and human, as conventional acts of display through which one or more participants transmit information concerning their physiological, psychological, or sociological states either to themselves or to one or more other participants. Such a definition is hardly radical; similar ones have been adopted by Wallace (1966:236), Leach (1954:14), and Goffman (1956).

Both the content and the occurrence of rituals are important in communication. As far as content is concerned, many writers have dealt with ways in which information concerning social arrangements are represented (communicated) in the course of public rituals, and we need not discuss the matter here. But "pattern" or "structural" information is not all that is transmitted by the contents of rituals. So is quantitative information.

We may note first that despite the stereotypic nature of rituals there is considerable room for variation in performance. Different numbers of organisms may participate, for instance, and in some displays this is the whole point of the exercise (Wynne-Edwards, 1962: 16ff, passim). Nor is quantitative variation in performance limited to numbers of participants. In the potlatches of the Northwest Coast and in the pig feasts of some Melanesians rather precise information concerning social status and political influence is communicated by variations in the number of valuables distributed. Indeed, it might be suggested that these rituals are public counting devices operating by principles similar to those employed in analogue computers. In these machines numbers are represented by directly metrical quantities, such as voltages or rotations of wheels. In epideictic displays populations are represented by samples of themselves. In the potlatch representation is also directly metrical if less intrinsic. Here political influence is represented by numbers of commodities such as blankets and copper plaques. We may note here an additional possible function of these rituals. They not only count, they translate aspects of phenomena which are not themselves directly metrical into directly metrical and therefore comparable terms. It becomes easy to compare the political influence of two Melanesian big men when they are engaged in competitive feasting. One simply counts the valuables thrown into the struggle.

If it is obvious that quantitative information can be transmitted through the content of ritual, it is perhaps less obvious that qualitative information may be transmitted by ritual occurrence. The mere occurrence of a non-calendrical ritual may be a signal. Since any ritual included in the repertoire of a people can, at a particular time, only be occurring or not occurring, ritual occurrence can be regarded as a binary mechanism or variable (a mechanism or variable having only two possible states). As such, occurrence can transmit binary information, which is qualitative information, information of a "yes-no" rather than a "more-less" sort. Of considerable interest and importance here, however, is that although the occurrence of a non-calendrical ritual may transmit a *"yes-no" signal,* it may have been triggered by the achievement or violation of a particular state or range of states of a *"more-less" variable* (i.e., one whose value can proceed through a continuous range of states), or even by the achievement or violation of a complex state or range of complex states involving the relationship among a number of such variables. Thus, the occurrence of the ritual may be a simple qualitative representation of complex quantitative information.

The importance of this aspect of ritual communication may be illustrated by reference to the ritual uprooting of the *rumbim* plant. The occurrence of this ritual, which commences the festival culminating the cycle, indicates or signals that a local ecosystem has achieved a certain complex quantitative state. The quantitative information that the qualitative or yes-no ritual statement (uprooting the *rumbin*) summarizes is not available to populations other than the one performing the ritual, and even if it were it would be subject to perhaps erroneous interpretation. Being summarized are not merely the constantly fluctuating values of a number of separate variables such as numbers of pigs, acreage in production, garden yields, settlement pattern, number of women, and clinical status of the human population, but the continually changing relationships among them. It would be difficult indeed to translate quantitative information concerning the constantly fluctuating state of the local subsystem directly into terms that would be unambiguously meaningful to other populations in the regional subsystem. This difficulty is overcome if a mechanism is available to summarize the quantitative information and translate it into a qualitative signal.

Uprooting the *rumbim* is such a mechanism, for its occurrence signals *unambiguously* that the local subsystem has achieved a certain state and that, therefore, the local population may now undertake previously proscribed actions likely to affect the regional subsystem. The absence of ambiguity from this message derives from the binary character of the ritual transduction device, which reduces a great complex mass of more-less information to a simple yes-no statement. In the ordinary course of things such a statement is free of ambiguity.

We may further note by way of clarification that the more-less information with which our illustration is concerned—information about labor, pigs, gardens, soils—is not directly meaningful in the regional system which is concerned with warfare. By "not directly meaningful" I mean that it cannot effect non-random proportional changes in the regional system. But the ritual, as transducer, summarizes and translates this quantitative information into a simple non-ambiguous and meaningful statement: "the non-belligerent is becoming a potential belligerent." Control transduction in physiological systems also seems to rely heavily upon binary mechanisms and information precisely because of the difficulties inherent in translating quantitative information directly from one subsystem to another (Goldman, 1960).

In sum, both ritual content and ritual occurrence are involved in communication. While content is particularly important in the transmission of quantitative or more-less information and is of significance mainly *within* single systems or subsystems, occurrence is particularly important in the transmission of qualitative or yes-no information, and is important in the transmission of information *across the borders* of separate and unlike systems or subsystems.

Let us now turn briefly to the regulatory functions of Maring rituals. Simple regulatory mechanisms typically perform three operations. First is the detection of changes in the state of the regulated variable. In a thermostat this operation is accomplished by a column of mercury or a bimetallic bar. Second, the value of the regulated variable is compared with a reference, or ideal, value. In the thermostat this value is fed in through a dial. Third, if there is a discrepancy between the reference and the detected value an error signal is transmitted to an effector, which initiates a corrective program. In the thermostat, the effector is a switch which turns the corrective program—heat from a furnace—on and off.

The Maring ritual cycle is more complicated than the thermostat not because more fundamental types of control operation are involved but because more variables are regulated. Whereas the thermostat regulates only temperature, the Maring ritual cycle regulates directly the frequency of warfare, the size of pig populations and population density, and through these variables yet others, such as acreage in production, women's labor, and lengths of fallow.

The picture is further complicated by a kind of economy of form. In some instances one ritual performs several control operations. For instance, the uprooting of the *rumbin*, insofar as it involves the entertainment of visiting dancers, operates as a detector with respect to military support. Insofar as it opens the way for animal sacrifices throughout the festival, it affects pig herd size; insofar as the slaughter of pigs accompanies it, this ritual incorporates a portion of the corrective program, i.e., the set of actions undertaken to correct deviations in herd size from a "reference" or "ideal" value. But the aim here is not to expand an analysis presented in detail elsewhere and sketched briefly earlier in this essay of the part that rituals play in the regulation of the ecological and regional relations of the Tsembaga. It is rather to discuss the formal characteristics of rituals which make them suitable to fulfill such functions.

Both ritual content and ritual occurrence are important in regulatory operation, and their importance rests upon the same formal characteristics that make them important in communication. This is hardly surprising since regulation is often a function of communication.

As far as contents are concerned, it is perhaps sufficient to recall that display, which may be the distinguishing characteristic of ritual, often offers opportunities for representing the states of important variables, such as population size, numbers of available marriage partners, the numbers of men who may provide military support, the political importance of different men. Thus, ritual contents are likely to be of particular importance in the operation of detection, the operation of assessing the states of critical variables. Insofar as the values of variables as detected in displays are compared during the ritual with reference or ideal values presumably derived from elsewhere (for instance, men's expectations or notions about how many men *should* be in a particular visiting dance contingent, or how many are necessary if aggression is to be undertaken), ritual contents are also important in the comparator operation.

As in the case of communication, the place of ritual occurrence in regulation is less obvious than the place of ritual contents. It may be observed first that in mechanical, electronic and physiological systems in which the states of other components may vary through a continuous range the output states of the regulator, that is, the state of its effector, is limited to two. As noted, the thermostat effector is a switch which, in response to a violation of an acceptable temperature range, goes on or off. The operation of a binary regulating device is remarkably simple. Indeed, its response to fluctuations in the state of a regulated component is the simplest conceivable: if change exceeds certain limits the regulator simply switches from one to the other of its two possible states.

Perhaps the very simplicity of the binary regulatory minimizes the likelihood of its malfunctions, but a more subtle aspect of binary operation is, I believe, of greater interest and importance. As I have argued elsewhere (1968: 234), "Binary control eliminates the possibility of error from one phase of system operation: i.e., with binary operation an inappropriate response to a system-endangering change in the value of a variable can not be selected from a set of possible responses because the set of possible responses has only one member. To put it in anthropomorphic terms, the binary regulating mechanism, once it receives a signal that a variable has transgressed its tolerable range, does not have to decide what to do. It can do only one thing or nothing at all."

This statement seems to be as applicable to Tsembaga ritual as to mechanical regulators. Despite the complexity of the system its regulatory operations are simple, for the programs undertaken to correct deviations of variables from their acceptable or "goal" ranges are fixed. All that the actors need decide is whether in fact such a deviation has occurred. The Tsembaga reach such decisions through discussions, through which a consensus eventually forms.

While Maring ritual regulation benefits from its very simplicity it must be recognized that it also suffers from simplicity's limitations. Consensus concerning deviations from acceptable conditions forms slowly, and corrective programs are both inflexible and unlikely to be proportional to deviations. While such sluggish and imprecise regulation has been sufficient to maintain the Tsembaga and other Maring in a relatively stable environment it is likely that the novel challenges presented frequently in rapidly changing environments might require more rapid and more flexible regulatory mechanisms, such as discrete human authorities occupying recognized offices. Polynesian chiefs, for instance, are more expensive to keep than ritual cycles and can make more mistakes. But they can respond to system-endangering changes in the environment with more sensitivity, speed, precision, and flexibility than ritual cycles.

V

Rituals, then, because of certain formal characteristics, are suitable for both communication and regulatory functions. But no *religious* notion inheres in our definition of ritual, nor does any religious belief seem to be vital to the functions which we have ascribed to ritual. Why, then, is it that religious beliefs should so often be associated with rituals and what indeed do we mean by religious beliefs? A comparison of religious rituals with the secular rituals of men and animals proves helpful here.

Earlier I underlined formal characteristics common to all rituals. Here I emphasize an important difference between religious and secular rituals: in the secular case the semantic content of the ritual is exhausted by the social information transmitted in the ritual. For example, when a baboon presents his rump, he transmits a statement of submission to a dominant animal. There are no meanings to be discovered in the content of this ritual other than that of submission. To put this a little differently, the semantic content of the ritual and the semantic content of the messages transmitted between those participating in the ritual are coextensive. This is also true of such human rituals as bowing and saluting.

Religious rituals seem to be different. For example, the culturally avowed purpose of rituals in which the Maring transmit messages about military support is to honor deceased ancestors. The messages transmitted in the ritual and the purposes of the ritual are thus distinct from each other. Since the ostensible purpose of the ritual is recognized in its contents, we may obviously say that the semantic content of the ritual and the semantic content of the social messages transmitted between participants in the ritual are *not* coextensive. Such lack of coextensiveness is characteristic, perhaps definitive, of religious rituals. In addition to messages concerning the physiological, psychological, and sociological states of the participants, a religious ritual *always* includes an additional term, such as a statement about or to spirits, who are usually, if not always, associated with the culturally avowed purpose of the ritual.

That there is semantic differentiation between messages and statements of purpose does not mean that the two are unrelated. They are related in an important way. Attention to the purpose of the ritual sanctifies the messages which are transmitted within it.

It may seem that this is a roundabout way to come to a shopworn definition of the religious as the sacred. But the procedure has not been an attempt merely to show that religious rituals are sacred while others are not, but to show that the sanctity of religious rituals stands in a certain relation to the communication which occurs in the rituals. Before returning to this point, I want to suggest that since the essence of ritual is communication, and since religious ritual is presumably found only among humans, there is likely to be a connection between sanctity and the special characteristics of human communication.

Linguists and ethologists, I think, generally agree that the most important distinction between human and animal signaling lies in the relationship of signals to their referents. I believe that this aspect of communication events distinguishes human from animal ritual as nicely as it does language from mere affective vocalization. This becomes clear in comparisons of formally similar rituals among men and beasts, for instance, the epigamic displays of peacocks or European ruffs on the one hand and New Guinea Highlanders on the other. In both, special feather paraphernalia adorning males is moved in stereotyped ways in the presence of females as a prelude to mating. But inasmuch as the peacock grew his fan himself, it is plausible to assume that the rustling of the fan is as much a part of his sexual arousal as his tumescence. His display, that is, is related to his arousal as a distant nimbus is to forthcoming rain. It is a perceptible aspect of an event indicating the presence of other imperceptible aspects of the same event. It is, in other words, a "sign."

Obviously, the relationship of the signal to the event in the human ritual is different. The waving of bird plumes and dancing are not intrinsic to the interest of the Maring dancer in women. They are merely arbitrary indications of that interest. As such the signal is not related to the referent as the nimbus is to rain, but as the word "rain" is to actual precipitation. In other words, it is a "symbol."

The advantages of symbolic over nonsymbolic communication are so enormous that some anthropologists have claimed that the emergence of the symbol can be compared in novelty and importance to the emergence of life. With symbolic communication an unlimited variety of messages may be transmitted through the combination of a very small number of basic units, and discourse upon past, future, distant, and imaginary events becomes possible. These advantages have been thoroughly discussed by many authors and need not be belabored here. The point I want to make is that considering the fundamental importance of symbolic communication surprisingly little attention has been paid to a problem which is a concomitant of its very virtues, a problem which is central to our present concerns.

When communication is limited to signs, that is, when the signal is intrinsic to its referent, it is impossible for the signal to occur in the absence of its referent or for it not to occur in the presence of its referent. The implication is that it is impossible for lies to be transmitted by signs. Misinterpretation, misreading of received information, is of course possible, but the willful transmission of false information is not.

Lying seems possible if and only if a signal is not intrinsic to its referent. A Maring, for instance, can indicate an interest in women when he has no such interest. If this seems trivial, note that he can also indicate a willingness to help in warfare when he has no such intention, and similarly a group can plant *rumbim* when it does not plan to leave off warfare. Lies are the natural offspring of symbols. They are transmitted by symbolic communication and symbolic communication only. Although there seems to be some very limited use of symbols by infra-human animals and some instances of possible lying among them have been observed we can assert with considerable confidence that although man is not, perhaps, the world's only liar he is surely the world's foremost liar. Certainly his reliance upon symbolic communication exceeds that of other animals to such an extent that it is probably for man alone that the transmission of false information becomes a serious problem.

His very survival may be involved. It is plausible to argue that the survival of any population depends upon social interactions characterized by some minimum degree of orderliness and that orderliness depends upon communication. But communication is effective only if the recipients of messages are willing to accept, as being in at least some minimum degree reliable, the messages which they receive. If they are unwilling or unable to give credence to received information, it is plausible to assume that their responses to particular stimuli will approach randomness. To the extent that actions are random they are unpredictable and are thus likely to elicit further apparently random responses on the parts of other actors. Randomness begets greater randomness, reducing orderliness more and more, perhaps eventually to such a degree that the population could not fulfill its biological needs. Credibility gaps are extremely dangerous, and societies which rely upon symbolic communication are faced with the problem of assuring some minimum degree of both credibility and credence in the face of the ever-present possibility of falsehood.

Concerning some messages there may be little problem. It is possible, for instance, to transmit the proposition 1 + 1 = 3, but the recipient of such a message has at his disposal a set of logical operations for verifying or falsifying such a statement. Given the meaning assigned to the terms, 1 + 1 *always* equals two; to deny it, as does the statement 1 + 1 = 3, is to be self-contradictory and therefore false. Similarly, we might have little difficulty with a statement such as the application of heat to liquid water causes it to solidify as ice. Such a statement, while not internally illogical, as is 1 + 1 = 3, could again be invalidated empirically. But much socially important information is concerned not with the laws pertaining to variables, but with their contemporary states, and their contemporary states usually can not be ascertained by extrapolation from earlier experience, even when the earlier experience can be framed in terms of empirical law (for example, to know from experience that ice melts if sufficient heat is applied to it says nothing about the temperature of a particular body of H_2O at the present time). In sum, the recipients of messages concerning the states of variables are not always in a position to perform the operations necessary to verify or falsify either empirically or logically the information upon which they must act. In some instances, indeed, there may be no known operations of verification. This is particularly true and particularly important with respect to social commitments. For example, how do the hosts at a Maring festival know that those who have come to dance will come to fight? There seems to be no procedure by which their statements of commitment can be verified. How, then, can they be depended upon?

Let us be reminded that this message is transmitted in the course of a religious ritual, a ritual that has a purpose to honor dead ancestors, distinct from its message concerning military support. It is thus plausible to assume a belief on the part of at least some of the participants in the existence of deceased ancestors; to assume otherwise would make nonsense of the proceedings. We can thus say that fundamental to Maring religious rituals are such propositions as "Deceased ancestors persist as sentient beings."

Now statements such as the ancestors are alive and well in the other world are neither logically necessary truths nor are they subject to empirical confirmation or disconfirmation. Yet they are taken to be *unquestionably* true. Indeed, to paraphrase some theologians and philosophers (Bochenski, 1965; Hick, 1963), it is this characteristic rather than substantive content that is the criterion of religious discourse; since religious discourse is sacred discourse I take this characteristic to be the criterion of sanctity as well. *Sanctity,* I am asserting, *is the quality of unquestionable truthfulness imputed by the faithful to unverifiable propositions.* Sanctity thus is not ultimately a property of physical or metaphysical objects, but of discourse about such objects. It is not, for instance, the divinity of Christ, but the assertion of his divinity, which is sacred.

Following this line I suggest that it is not its substance which distinguishes religion from other aspects of human life, but rather the sacred nature of its assertions. The term religion, in my view, refers to public discourse which includes at least one sacred statement and the conventional social actions undertaken with respect to this discourse.

While sanctity inheres ultimately in such non-material propositions as "The Godhead is a trinity," setting them above any doubt, it penetrates to (sanctifies) sentences concerning material objects and activities. Tight theological discourse may serve as the vehicle for transporting sanctity from an ultimate sacred proposition such as "The lord our God the lord is one" to sentences such as "Eating pork is evil," or "Pork may not be eaten," but the connection may be merely an association in time or space; that is, the connection may be ritualistic rather than linguistic. Messages such as "we will lend you military support," or "we have renounced warfare," when they are transmitted in a religious ritual, and are thus sanctified, are taken to be true, or at least sufficiently reliable to serve as the basis of important social action. Sanctity, although it inheres ultimately in unverifiable nonmaterial propositions, is socially important as meta-statement about assertions of a material nature, such as "we will support you in warfare" or of a partly material nature such as "giving is blessed." Statements, all of whose terms are material, may be amenable to verification, but the receivers of messages containing such statements may be in no position to verify them. However, *to sanctify statements is to certify them.*

. . .

Ritual, thus, not only invokes in the participants private religious experiences, it provides a mechanism for translating these private experiences into messages of social import; it also provides a means for certifying these messages.

The outlines of an encompassing cybernetic loop may now be suggested. Inasmuch as religious experience is an intrinsic part of the more inclusive emotional dynamics of the organism, and inasmuch as the emotional dynamics of an organism must be closely related to its material state, it is plausible to assume that religious experiences are affected by material conditions. But the latter are, particularly in primitive societies, in some degree a function of the operation of the control hierarchy which the religious experience itself supports. Thus the willingness, indeed the ability, of the members of a congregation to affirm through religious experience the ultimate sacred propositions which sanctify the control hierarchy may be in considerable measure a function of the effectiveness of the hierarchy in maintaining equilibria in and among those variables which define their material well-being in the long run, and thus adaptation. That is, if malfunctions in the control hierarchy adversely affect for protracted periods the states of social and ecological variables bearing directly upon the material well-being of the congregation, its members are likely to become, first, unable to affirm through private religious experience the ultimate sacred propositions supporting the control hierarchy and, second, perhaps later, unwilling even to participate in the rituals relating to them. Sooner or later, regulatory mechanisms themselves must be adjusted if men are not to seek new gods. It seems that ultimate sacred propositions and the control hierarchies which they support must be compatible with the affective processes of the communicants. This in itself could have corrective implications.

But if regulatory mechanisms or entire control hierarchies are sanctified, and that which is sanctified is taken to be unquestionably true, how is change possible?

Three aspects of religious discourse are significant with respect to change. The first is that the ultimate sacred sentences are propositions; the second is that they usually contain no material terms. That they are propositions prevents them from containing specific directives; if they contain no material terms they are prevented from becoming irrevocably bound to any particular social form. This means that the association of specific directives and social forms with ultimate sacred statements is not intrinsic, but is rather the product of interpretive acts. Any product of interpretation allows reinterpretation, but reinterpretation does not challenge ultimate sacred statements; it merely disputes previous interpretations.

The third characteristic of religious discourse of importance here is that it is often, if not usually, cryptic. In some cases the ultimate sacred statements are themselves cryptic; in others they may seem clear, but they are abstracted from cryptic contexts such as myths or the reports of revelations, and an apocryphal quality is often characteristic of the discourse which sanctifies sentences concerning particular social forms or containing specific directives by connecting them to ultimate sacred propositions. The importance of reducing ambiguity and vagueness in messages of social import was earlier noted. In contrast, it is perhaps necessary that considerable ambiguity and vagueness cloak the discourse from which sanctification flows. If a proposition is going to be taken to be unquestionably true, it is important that no one understand it. Lack of understanding insures frequent reinterpretation.

An important implication of such change through reinterpretation is that ultimate sacred propositions must remain non-specific with respect to particular regulatory mechanisms or processes. A possible malfunction of sanctification may be noted in this connection. It sometimes happens that sentences directly involved in regulation (thus including material terms and sometimes cast in the form of explicit directives) are taken not merely as sanctified by ultimate sacred propositions but as themselves ultimate sacred propositions. When this occurs, the control hierarchy becomes highly resistant to adjustment through reinterpretation with perhaps disastrous results. Possible modern instances of such confusion in the level of sanctity to which sentences are to be assigned are to be found in the resistance of the Vatican to the use of mechanical and chemical birth control devices, and perhaps also in its insistence upon clerical celibacy. To an outsider, it seems that both birth control devices and clerical marriage could be made acceptable through reinterpretation without challenge to dogma.

Although sanctification is subject to malfunctions, it may be asserted that sanctity contributes to the maintenance of systemic integrity even through changes in systemic structure and composition. Indeed, it may make this maintenance possible. Thus if the term "adaptation" is given the meaning earlier suggested, then the concept of the sacred is surely an important component of human adaptation.

VII

The sacred, we have argued, has played an important role in the adaptation of technologically simple communities to their social, biotic, and physical environments. But the role of the sacred changes with changing political circumstances, and these changes in turn seem in considerable degree to be a function of technological development.

It has already been noted that sentences concerning a wide variety of regulatory mechanisms may be sanctified. Among the Maring, for instance, most sentences are instructions for corrective programs, for example, sentences such as "the ancestors demand the slaughter of all adult and adolescent pigs during the festival." In other societies sanctification seems to invest sentences concerning authorities or regulatory agencies rather than specific programs, sentences such as "the chief has great mana," or "Henry is by grace of God King."

Although we, and perhaps the faithful, cast such sentences in the declarative, they imply that the directives of the regulatory agencies or authorities to which they allude should or must be obeyed. If political power is taken to be the product (in an arithmetic sense, much as force is the product of mass times acceleration) of [men] × [resources] × [organization] it would seem that as far as securing compliance with directives is concerned, sanctity operates as a functional alternative to political power among some of the world's peoples. Indeed, if authorities are taken to be loci in commumications networks from which directives emanate we may be able to discern in history and ethnography a continuum from societies, such as the Maring, that are regulated by sacred conventions in the absence or near absence of human authorities through societies in which highly sanctified authorities have little actual power (such as Polynesian chiefs), to societies in which authorities have great power but less sanctity. It would be plausible to expect this continuum to correlate roughly with technological development, for advanced technology places in the hands of authorities coercive instruments that are not only effective but also likely to be unavailable to those subject to them.

Our argument implies that the development of technology disrupts the cybernetics of adaptation. In the technologically undeveloped society, authority is maintained by sanctification, but sanctity itself is maintained by religious experience which is responsible to the effectiveness of the control hierarchy in maintaining variables defining adaptation in viable ranges. In the technologically developed society authority is freed, to the extent that technology has provided it with coercive instruments, from the constraints imposed by the need to maintain its sanctity and therefore from the corrective operations that the maintenance of sanctity implies.

This is not to say that authorities even in technologically advanced societies dispense entirely with sanctity. It is to say that the relationship between sanctity and authority changes. Previously a characteristic of the discourse associated with the regulation of the entire system, sanctity comes more and more to be concentrated in the discourse of a subsystem, "the church." When it is so confined, sacred discourse is likely to continue to ratify authority, but it tends also to become decreasingly concerned with the environment of the here and now and increasingly concerned with ethics and with the environment of the hereafter, the promise of which stirs the meek to religious experience. Religious experience, however, and the rituals in which it occurs, previously part of an encompassing corrective loop, are eventually left with little more than certain functions long recognized by students of society: they reduce anxieties produced by stressors over which the faithful have little or no control, and they contribute to the discipline of social organization. To the extent that the discourse of religion, religious ritual and religious experience contribute to the maintenance of orderliness and the reduction of anxiety without contributing to the correction of the factors producing the anxiety and disorder they are not adaptive but pathological. Indeed, their operation seems to resemble that of neuroses.

Whereas in the technologically undeveloped system authority is contingent upon sanctification, in technologically more developed societies sanctity becomes an instrument of authority. Compliance and docility are cultivated more efficiently and less expensively by religious experiences inspired by hopes of post-mortem salvation than by the coercion of police and inquisitions. Yet, although force may remain hidden, and although religious experience may be encouraged, in some systems the unquestionable status of the discourse for which sanctity is claimed rests ultimately upon force. In such societies authority is no longer contingent upon sanctity; the sacred, or discourse for which sanctity is claimed, has become contingent upon authority. . . .

But although sanctity may become degraded in the churches of technologically developed societies, "true sanctity," that uniting the organism through its affective life to processes which may correct social and ecological malfunctions, remains a continuing possibility. Throughout history revitalistic movements have emerged in streets, in universities, in fields among men sensing, and perhaps suffering from, the malfunction of control hierarchies that cannot reform themselves. In the early stages of such movements, at least, the unquestionable status of ultimate propositions rests upon affirmation through the religious experiences of the participants who believe that they are participating in corrective action. Sometimes they are mistaken. Although such movements have not infrequently been more disruptive than that to which they are a response, they may nevertheless be regarded as one of the processes through which cybernetic systems including men, and sometimes other living things as well, rid themselves of the pathology of unresponsiveness.

VIII

This discussion has assumed the existence of a full-blown concept of sanctity. Another set of questions might be asked concerning the origin of the sacred, for it does not seem to be logically entailed by symbolic communication, as does falsehood.

Waddington (1961) has argued that before a man or animal can function as a unit in a proto-cultural or cultural system he must be prepared for the role of receiver or acceptor of socially transmitted information. A recent lead provided by Erikson (1968:713ff) suggests that we examine very closely in this regard the phylogeny of rituals of ontogeny, paying particular attention to their affective component. Experimental and clinical evidence suggests that among the higher vertebrates if the infant does not learn certain things at certain times he has difficulty learning them at all and his later learning of other material is also likely to be impaired. This early learning is social in that it requires other organisms, and communication in some sense is always involved. In discussing human infants Erikson notes that this early communication takes place in "daily rituals of greeting and nurturance."

It is reasonable to refer to these interactions of mother and child as rituals, for although there is variation from one mother to the next, each handles her child in a more or less stereotyped way and vocalizes her own repetitive, stereotyped variety of baby talk at times fixed by the clock or particular circumstances. Although some of her behavior is concerned with the fulfillment of the child's bodily needs some of her actions, such as her conventional coos and caresses, are non-instrumental.

Perhaps this early interaction must be ritualized, for what the mother must communicate to the child is her dependability, and what better way to communicate dependability than through the performance of stereotyped, repetitive acts at fixed times? What the child is learning specifically in these earliest ritual experiences is that he will not be abandoned by her upon whom he depends utterly (Erikson, 1968:716); that is, the infant is learning to trust, and it is interesting to note Erikson's suggestion that the mother whom he is learning to trust is experienced as a "hallowed presence" (1968:714). It may be suggested that the trust vested in this "hallowed presence" is a necessary precondition for the acceptance of symbolic messages, first from the mother herself and then from others, as true or at least sufficiently reliable to be acted upon. It seems that failure in these early ritual contacts has severe effects upon the later development of communicative ability in humans (Erikson, 1968:714; Frank, 1966).

Erikson's lead suggests that perhaps gradually, as symbolic communication became increasingly complex, the concept of sanctity arose out of the trust which, learned earliest of all things in the mother-offspring dependency relationship, is a necessary precondition for the acceptance of messages which the recipient cannot verify. There may be opportunities here for profitable dialogue among the members of several disciplines or even for interdisciplinary research of the evolution of the socialization of the young, focusing particularly upon the rituals of ontogeny. It is likely that we shall never know whether this suggestion is more than possible. Nevertheless, we may conclude by asserting that the concept of the sacred is not only made possible by man's symbolic communication. It makes symbolic communication and the social and ecological orders depending upon symbolic communication possible.

Renato I. Rosaldo, Jr.

METAPHORS OF HIERARCHY IN A MAYAN RITUAL

Working within the framework provided by van Gennep, Hubert and Mauss, and Leach, who have characterized the formal properties of ritual action, Rosaldo examines a calendrical ritual, honoring an important local saint, performed in a highland Maya community of Chiapas, Mexico. Just as the subject of much modern poetry is poetry itself, so this ritual performed by members of the Zinacantecan civil-religious hierarchy concerns hierarchy itself. A formal analysis, something on the order of a grammar of ritual action, takes as its units the various representations of hierarchy—sitting in rows, walking in lines, serving drinks in a fixed order—which are shown to be combined in ways consistent with classic theories of ritual. While the various representations of hierarchy are continuous with obligatory and widespread acts in hamlet life denoting the recognition of a difference in age, in the ritual context they stand for differences in wealth. Though the tokens—bowing or whatever—of rank order remain the same, the contradictions between these two hierarchies (age and wealth) are problematic for the performers and may contribute to the power and sacred quality of the ritual itself.

Reprinted in abridged form from *American Anthropologist*, LXX (1968), 524–536, by permission of the author and the American Anthropological Association.

This is a study of a ritual performed by members of the religious cargo system in Zinacantan, a Tzotzil township of some 7000 in the highlands of Chiapas, Mexico. Zinacantecos are milpa farmers who live in a ceremonial center and a number of scattered hamlets. When a man decides to fulfill his religious obligations he leaves home and moves into the ceremonial center for a year. There he becomes a full-time ritual performer. "At the present time virtually all Zinacanteco adult males participate in the cargo system" (Cancian, 1965: 126).

There are four levels to the religious hierarchy; to perform as a second level official a man must perform in a first level position, to reach the fourth level he must go through the first three. It is expensive to be a religious official, so those who take another cargo position, on the next level, return to their hamlets and wait for some years, hoeing corn and saving money. Within each level of the cargo system religious officials are ranked one above the other in a single lineal hierarchy. This hierarchy is not so much a chain of command as a set of honorific positions. In their own hamlets men know one another by name; in the ceremonial center officials who perform together call one another by their titles—*martomorei* rather than Jose—and they "often do not know each other's full names" (Cancian, 1965: 34). The official rank order—seen in drinking order, processions, and seating arrangements—roughly corresponds to the cost and prestige of each cargo position (Cancian, 1965: 80–96).

My paper concerns the expressions of hierarchy in the weekly ceremonies performed by four of the cargo officials in the chapel of Our Lord of Esquipulas, one of the more important saints in the ceremonial center. The officials are ranked as follows:

1. *martomorei bankilal*
2. *martomorei ʔiȼ'inal*
3. *mexon bankilal*
4. *mexon ʔiȼ'inal*

Both *martomoreietik* spend about the

same for their cargoes—much more than the two *mexonetik*—and prestige correlates with the traditional rank order of the four officials who attend Our Lord of Esquipulas. It is the conventional way in which members of the religious hierarchy act out their own rank order that shall comprise my analysis.

In their descriptions of ritual for Esquipulas, informants narrate in painstaking detail the various kinds of obligatory behavior that indicate relative rank: cargo-holders bow to one another, walk in lines, sit in rows, drink in a fixed order, and so on. . . .

My thesis is that these Zinacantecan representations of social status, in and of themselves, comprise an articulate mode of ritual action. For the official these gestures are clear, coherent, and systematic; rules for such behavior do not require verbal rationalization—like rules of grammar, they are recognized when they are violated. Bowing and other related acts are at once expressions of hierarchical social order and of ritual order. Gestures derived from the ritual of daily affairs, they underlie and shape the cargo rite.

CARGO RITUAL

Ritual for Esquipulas is extremely scheduled. Every Sunday of the year at least two cargo officials, a martomorei and a mexon, perform the same ceremony in honor of Our Lord of Esquipulas: they uncover the medallions of the saint, *xlok' ʔual*. On alternate Saturdays they also change the flowers on the arch above the household and chapel altars, *balteʔ*. The martomorei bankilal keeps Esquipulas' medallions four weeks, then gives them to martomorei ʔiȼ'inal—his lesser counterpart, equal in all but prestige—and the medallions go back and forth throughout the year. During some major "fiestas" the officials have additional duties; they may participate in a swearing-in ceremony or a large ritual meal, but the weekend ceremony is performed as ever. At planting time and harvest time the ceremonies remain the same; they do not vary with the natural cycle. In short, it is hard to imagine a ritual more regular in its performance, one more free from unpredictable contingencies. Such rites "are always social or communal in character" (Titiev, 1960: 294). Cargo ritual is decidedly social in content as well; it repeatedly represents a hierarchical order of society.

My language may call to mind the "effervescent" collective representations of a Durkheimian societal rite (1915). But not all scheduled rituals are the same; cargo ceremony appears private and esoteric, with none of the thrill and excitement of a crowd. Durkheim's ideal type aptly characterizes a major "fiesta," taken as a whole, but not that part of it performed by the cargo-holder. Ruth Bunzel, speaking of Chichicastenango, brings out this contrast in a passage that could well have referred to Zinacantan:

> *To me, an outsider, seeing the fiesta as an expression of the social life of a great village, the unwonted concentration of people, the mounting excitement, the changing temper of the ceremonies and of the crowd, the dramatic contrasts, the abandoned drunkenness of Manuel and the austere sobriety of Juan were the significant facts, and the prayers and explanations that Juan related to me with such meticulous care, were just another long speech in the* cofradias. *In the cumulative excitement of a big fiesta the inner sacred core, what the prayers characterized as "the heart and soul" of the ceremony, gets drowned in an uproar of drum and bells and marimbas and fireworks* (1952: 252).

Cargo ritual is removed from the intense activity of the "fiesta" it sometimes accompanies, its audience is limited, at most, to two ritual advisors, three musicians, and a handful of helpers, the officials' close kinsmen and neighbors.

These rites lack dramatic quality. They appear to be elaborate, protracted, redundant communiqués about hierarchy and rank; over and over they emphasize and maximize order among men. They contrast sharply with curing ceremonies in which the shaman, a man with a calling, prays in deep resonant tones, reminiscent of medieval plain-song. The curer preserves and creates the customs; at many points in the ceremony he is consulted—should the chicken be boiled with herbs? What kind of herbs? How many of each herb? This charismatic figure directs parts of his ceremony; he does more than follow a programmed set of actions. Cargo-holders, on the other hand, perform the same ceremony every weekend of the year, just as, they say, it was performed in the past. They preserve the ancient custom.

Their song, dance, incense, high-backed sandals, all suggest that these men indeed are an incarnation of customs seen in the codices or the *Popol-Vuh*. But a cargo-holder's life-long occupation is corn farming; he takes on his role as an official when he is an adult, with no previous formal training. Formal instruction for ritual performance begins in the ceremonial center, where old men and musicians, experienced in the cargo ritual, serve as advisors, guiding the officials through their first month or so of service. But they cannot teach everything. Consider that the biweekly ceremonies are long and complex, and that over their twenty-four hour period the cargo-holder becomes drunk to the point of passing out. How does a drunken man learn, perhaps find meaningful, at least perform, such a set of actions?

Cargo ritual is not autonomous; it exists at once as a system in its own right and as part of a more general system of social action. The corn farmer immediately recognizes most of his ritual duties because he already has become familiar with them in the social and ceremonial contexts of his own hamlet. The code of such ritual is shaped primarily by other social convention, by hamlet ceremonies, and by that aspect of social behavior that symbolizes relative social status. The main subject of ritual performed by members of the religious hierarchy is hierarchy itself, expressed in the conventional code of Zinacantan.

CARGO RITUAL AND SOCIAL CONVENTION

I will illustrate some of the ways in which social conventions relate to, and make intelligible, the ritual performed for Our Lord of Esquipulas. These conventional modes of behavior are considered arbitrary cultural products, as much so as the acoustic shape of words. Clearly some acts—bowing to express respect, for instance—are widespread enough to call for a psychological explanation, but that is another story. My present purpose is to describe vocabulary and usage of Zinacanteco ritual language.

Zinacantecan rituals are not closed systems; they mutually influence and shape one another. Cargo rites, though recognizably the same from one year to the next, are flexible, and permit various degrees of innovation. It is above all in their ideology that they are static; innovation quickly becomes normative—the great transformation of twenty-three years ago is now the rule, the ancient custom. In 1944, for unknown reasons, the cargo-holders elaborated on their weekly ceremonies, and began not only to take out, but also to count, the medallions of Our Lord of Esquipulas. This change is a case of borrowing from another sector of ritual life.

The count, which shares many features of the shaman's divination, now occupies a central place in this ritual. Before beginning the count, or any action he calls "work," the official loosens the kerchief on his head, as does the shaman. The martomorei counts the medallions—Mexican and Guatemalan coins from one to thirty pesos in value—while the mexon records the count with grains of corn, one per peso. The outcome is uncertain; the number of grains more than the value of the coins indicates the fortune of the official—the more the better. Similarly, in divination "the number of floating grains indicates the number of lost parts of the *ch'ulel*" (Vogt, 1965a: 45). The official, for an important part of his ceremony, adopts the sacred conventions of the shaman and makes them his own.

At the same time, this ritual reflects and reinforces patterns of hamlet life; much of the ritual action is a condensed elaborate version of daily social intercourse in Zinacantan, in particular of the various ways in which individuals signal their recognition of difference in age. In drinking, the eldest male is served first, then the next oldest, and so on; in cargo ritual it is the highest ranking official who drinks first. When two men meet on the path and stop to talk, the younger bows to the older. The cargo-holder elaborates on this action and, at many points in the ceremony, bows repeatedly to a higher ranking man, while speaking to him formally, in couplets.

Cargo-holders, in one salient case, invert the expression of rank order seen in daily conduct. On the narrow paths of Zinacantan the eldest male walks ahead; the rest follow in order of relative age. In cargo processions it is the low ranking man who walks first. It seems reasonable to interpret this action in relation to the etiquette of daily affairs: when there is a "formal greeting situation"—when, for example, a man comes to ask a woman's hand in marriage—the youngest male leads the procession to the door of the house. Here, the Zinacanteco puts his worst foot forward. In their processions officials do not simply walk from one place to another; they stop to pray a number of times: at the cross by the door of the house, before crosses on the path—often "considered as a doorway to the abode of the gods" (Early, 1965: 63). As in daily life, they invert their order to say they are greeting, presenting themselves to, the gods.

In any particular year few people witness cargo rites, yet most would find the elements or ritual acts of these ceremonies familiar. I found I could read prayers, which vary in content from one cargo-holder to another, to several young men, who had neither held cargoes, nor seen the ritual for Esquipulas, and they would recognize the speakers and situation. These rites, private in their performance, are written in a public language.

THE RITUAL

Now I shall describe a part of the ceremony held in honor of Our Lord of Esquipulas, with a view to showing how the language of social conventions is used in ritual. A complete narrative of these rites is impossible in my limited space (for other material on this ritual see Cancian [1965: 52–55] and Early [1965: 110–113; 1966: 337–354]). What follows, then, is an account of the first two or three hours of the bi-weekly ritual: the flower-change ceremony (balteʔ) at the house of the martomorei.

Women are present in the household, but do not enter into this description; they do not participate in ranking, except when the officials enter and leave the house and speak with the eldest woman. As the cargo-holder faces the sacred altar, on the east side of the house, the women are seated on the floor to his left, in no particular order. They pass food from left to right, from the hearth to the men who sit on chairs, arranged and ranked on the right-hand side. A woman with a named role keeps the supply of sugar cane liquor and gives it to the boys who in turn serve it to the men. As Hertz (1960) would expect, women sit on the ground, on the left, in disorder; they comprise the counterpart of masculine metaphors of hierarchy.

The martomorei (*Mr*), seated before his household altar, turns to his mexon (*M*) and says in formal couplet speech:

Let us speak together
Let us speak to the musicians.
We shall change the flowers
we shall change the leaves
of the sacred seat
of the sacred place
of the flowery face
of the flowery countenance
of Lord Esquipulas my father
of Lord Esquipulas my owner.
We are here on sacred Saturday
we are here on sacred Sunday.
We have united
we have come together
to spend
to pass
the sacred Saturday
the sacred Sunday
of Lord Esquipulas my father
of Lord Esquipulas my owner.

While speaking—as if to rehearse the lines they will say to the musicians and to the saint—they repeatedly perform the conventional everyday greeting gesture of bowing and releasing. *M*, lower in rank, bows to *Mr*, who touches him on the forehead with the back of his hand.

Then *M* gets up, followed *Mr*, and goes to speak with the musicians, first the violinist (Mu_1), then the harpist (Mu_2), finally the guitarist (Mu_3), as diagramed in Figure 1. Cargo-holder and musician speak almost simultaneously, saying the same thing: they are going to change the flowers and leaves for Our Lord of Esquipulas. They too bow and release repeatedly, the younger man this time bowing to the older.

FIGURE 1
Cargo-holders greeting the musicians and praying before the household altar at the beginning of the flower-change ceremony in the house of *Mr*.

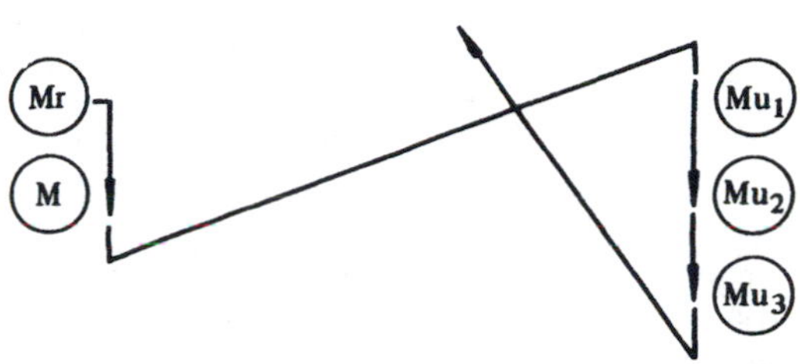

Now the cargo-holders go before the household altar and kneel to pray. They touch the altar with the back of their right hand and bow to touch it with their foreheads, while they pray to God, Jesus Christ, My Lord Esquipulas; they shall change his flowers and leaves.

Each group of men begins its task; musicians sing and play, cargo-holders change the flowers. *Mr* and *M* take off their woolen cloaks, loosen the kerchiefs tied around their heads, then proceed to remove the ferns, geraniums, and pine boughs from the flowered arch of the household altar. As the cargo-holders finish, the musicians sing a verse which all recognize as a signal to drink. Two little boys, one for *Mr*, the other for *M*, take their liter bottles and shot glasses and begin to serve all present in this order: *Mr*, *M*, Mu_1, Mu_2, Mu_3, helpers (by sex, men first, and age, oldest first). After drinking, the officials continue their work and put new flowers on the arch above the household altar. When the new flowers are in place, everybody drinks again, and in the same order.

The old dry flowers and boughs, lying on a reed mat before the altar, still have to be thrown out. *Mr* and *M* slip two one-fifth liter bottles of liquor beneath the dried flowers, and take the reed mat with its trash into the cornfield. When they throw out the dead leaves, one of the men discovers a bottle and suggests they drink it. But if the liquor has been bewitched, it means instant death to he who drinks, they say. Not wanting to die alone, they drink a little and set aside the rest for the musicians. They return to the house, *M* again preceding *Mr*, and approach the musicians to speak and drink with them.

M asks Mu_1 to drink a little with him: he says he found a bottle in the trash. The bottle may, or may not, be good, who knows? But since the officials drank from it, the musicians should as well. The musicians are not certain they should trust what the cargo-holders say, they reply. It would be best if M drank first before their eyes. This joke is as much a part of the biweekly ceremony as changing the flowers itself.

The flower change at the house of the martomorei ends in the opposite way that it began. Everyone drinks from shot glasses, in the same order as before. Then the cargo-holders light candles and incense, and kneel before the altar to pray: God, Jesus Christ, Our Lord Esquipulas; they have changed his flowers and leaves. They rise and, M before Mr, go speak to the musicians (order: Mu_1 Mu_2, Mu_3), saying, as they bow and release again and again, that they have changed the flowers and leaves of Our Lord of Esquipulas. They have finished and begin to dance before going to change the flowers in the chapel.

After changing the flowers in the chapel they dance once again. Cargo-holders and musicians then return to the house of the martomorei where they eat and rest for a short while. The first ceremony has ended, the flowers and leaves have been changed. About two A.M. on Sunday the officials rise to take out the medallions of Our Lord of Esquipulas; this initiates the second ceremony, called *xlok' ʔual*. While in the house of the martomorei, they count the medallions, dance, and eat. Then they move on to the chapel to place the medallions on the saint, dance, eat, and dance again, until mid-afternoon when they return for the last time to the house of the martomorei. This completes the weekend ritual for Esquipulas.

A FORMAL ANALYSIS

Even my descriptive account does not include all the facts about the ceremony; the analysis that follows is more selective, yet comprehensive. It isolates certain observable and salient features of this ritual, that is, the extreme and repetitious way in which cargo officials order and rank themselves, then subsumes every instance of a wide range of seemingly diverse phenomena—all defined as "ranking"—under a simple model. Ranking includes the following kinds of action: a cargo-holder bows to some people and, by touching their foreheads, releases those who bow to him; he sits, with his fellow officials, in neat single file rows; they all march in a straight line; drinks are served in a fixed order, one man first, another second, and so on. Every instance of programmed ranking by participants in the rite may be represented by a concise formal notation. Here I derive relative rank from seating and procession orders, I encode only those acts where exchange, verbal or material, takes place. This notation refers to a series of overt ritual acts which informants consistently emphasize in their descriptions of the ceremonies.

I shall consider the order in which people are served drinks an expression of, or metaphor for, hierarchy. When people drink from the shot glasses, the liquor is served first to the highest in rank, then on down to the lowest. Let an arrow, running from left to right, denote this rank order as follows: →. "Prayer" is more difficult to represent because it may occur in either of two ways: (1) in the chapel there is free variation in rank orientation, the high man kneels on either side of the altar, and (2) in his home the martomorei ranks highest and kneels on the north side of his altar. These two metaphors for hierarchy occur in different places; they are in complementary distribution and may be seen as variants of the same message about ranking. My notation corresponds to what takes place in the chapel; but an arrow running in two directions—with heads on either end—represents both cases of "prayer": ↔.

I encode the elaborate bowing and releasing between cargo-holders and musicians as shown in Figure 2. The upper arrow, running from right to left, denotes that the officials invert their rank order prior to, and while speaking with the musicians; the lower arrow indicates that the musicians are spoken to in rank order, highest to lowest (Mu_1, Mu_2, Mu_3). The two arrows are the same in length and represent a sequence of gestures rather than relative number of actors; in the chapel four, not two, cargo-holders invert their order to speak with the musicians, yet the notation remains the same.

FIGURE 2
Descriptive and formal notation for bowing and releasing between cargo-holders and musicians.

Descriptive Diagram
East
(household altar)

Formal Notation

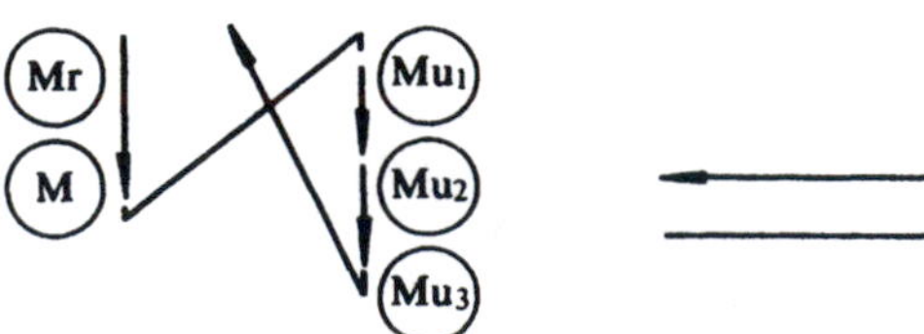

The same notation (⇆) also refers to the drinking and joking between cargo-holders and musicians after the old flowers are thrown out; here the men drink from bottles, not shot glasses, in this order: *M*, *Mr*, Mu_1, Mu_2, Mu_3. Again officials invert their order; musicians do not. On this level of analysis, the basic structural units or elements are messages or metaphors of rank order and hierarchy rather than concrete actions. It is not these elements themselves, but the relations among them which shall comprise my analysis.

I

A formal account of the flower change at the house of the martomorei eliminates the drama, but it reveals a high degree of structure in the ritual, something not apparent in a conventional description. Figure 3—like the method Lévi-Strauss (1963a) proposes for diagraming the structural study of myth—reads, from left to right and top to bottom, as the temporal sequence of metaphors in the ceremony, and vertically, as repetitions of the same metaphor. This represents the following sequence: cargo-holders invert their order and speak with the musicians (⇆), then they pray (↔). Everyone, from highest to lowest is served a shot of liquor (→); they drink again (→). The officials have just thrown out the dry flowers and come drink and joke with the musicians (⇆). All present drink for the third time (→); officials then pray (↔), and speak with the musicians (⇆). This pattern recurs over and over during the ritual for Our Lord of Esquipulas.

The same diagram describes, for example, the flower change at the chapel. The equivalence of these two portions of the ritual is not obvious from observation: in the chapel the two cargo-holders join the other martomorei and mexon to redecorate five, rather than one, flowered arches; this flower change takes longer to perform than the first, but the number and sequence of messages about rank remain constant. Two ceremonies, then, appear to be distinct, but formally—seen as a sequence of metaphors for hierarchy—they are the same.

After the flower changes in the house and chapel, the officials dance and sing with the musicians, who are seated playing their instruments. Ritual dancing differs from the flower change only in that it omits one of the messages about rank, "prayer" (↔) [see Figure 4]. Zinacantecos call the flower change "work" (*abtel*); dancing is relaxation—the cargo-holders "rest the heart of the gods" (*ta hkux yoʔ on kahvaltik*). While the two portions of the ritual formally resemble one another, it is appropriate that the flower change contain more messages about rank. Formal elaboration and something like "sacredness" go together.

FIGURE 3
A formal description of the flower change at the house of the martomorei.

Flower Change

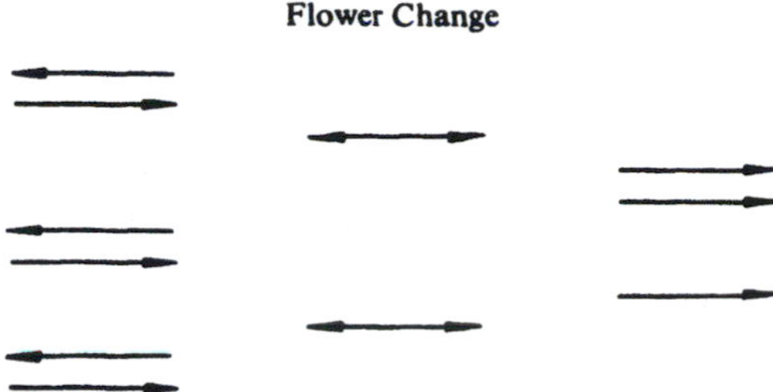

FIGURE 4
A formal description of dancing at the house of the martomorei and in the chapel.

Dancing

TABLE 1
SUMMARY DESCRIPTION OF THE COMPLETE BALTEʔ

balteʔ	
at house *Mr*	eat (coffee and bread) change flowers dance
at chapel	change flowers dance
at house *Mr*	eat (meal)

Flower change and dance, in the house and chapel, plus two periods of eating constitute the entire six hour (Saturday, usually 6–12 P.M.) flower change ceremony, the balteʔ (Table 1). Like what has preceded, the two segments glossed as "eat" share certain formal properties (Vogt, 1965b: 345–349); in the first case people eat coffee and bread, served on the ground, and in the second instances they have beef with broth and "tortillas," wash their mouths, then eat coffee and bread. Whether they are served on the ground or at the table varies, depending on what the musicians want. The relationship between the two "eats" is homologous with that between "change flowers" and "dance"; in both cases, structurally similar units differ in that an element of one is lacking in the other.

TABLE 2
SUMMARY DESCRIPTION OF THE FIRST SEVEN SEGMENTS OF THE XLOK' ʔUAL

	xlok' ʔual
at house *Mr*	eat (coffee and bread)
	count medallions
	dance
at chapel	eat (meal)
	place medallions on saint
	dance
	eat (egg, coffee, bread)

Ritual time in the balteʔ, then, is an ordered alternation between greater and lesser units of the same order. "Cyclical," "repetitive," or other familiar Western terms do not describe this alternation as aptly as do the Tzotzil relational concepts bankilal and ʔic'inal, which appear in Zinacantan "as a way of classifying phenomena in almost any domain in the universe" (Vogt, 1965b: 351). These concepts, represented in the kin terminology, are confined in most Zinacantecan hamlets to male siblings (J. F. Collier, personal communication): *hbankil* refers to a man's older brother; *ki¢'in* refers to a younger. Cargo-holders go one step further and use these as terms of address. The two martomoreietik call the mexonetik—men who spend much less on their cargoes than they—mexon and are addressed in turn as *htot* martomorei, following the rule for terms of address across generations (male or female speaker); but the martomoreietik, who share title and cost of cargo, call one another hbankil and ki¢'in, "More and less, two of a kind": the relation of bankilal and ʔi¢'inal obtains between the martomoreietik, brothers, and, I suggest, segments of the ritual for Esquipulas. The same principle structures ritual time and social space during the cargo performance. It is order among men—metaphors of hierarchy—that shapes each segment of the balteʔ, and it seems reasonable that the relations of these segments and certain human relations structurally coincide.

The same alternations obtain in taking out the medallions of the saint, xlok' ʔual, the ceremony that follows the balteʔ after a break for sleep. The first seven segments of the xlok' ʔual—lasting from about 2 A.M. to 10 A.M. on Sunday—formally resemble the balteʔ; as shown in Table 2. "Count medallions" and "place medallions on saint" occupy the same structural position as "flower change" in the balteʔ. Yet xlok' ʔual differs with its additional "eat"; here, the second "eat" is a meal that must be served on a table; the third takes place outside the chapel. That xlok' ʔual is the same as, and more than, the balteʔ is consistent with other indications of its relative importance. This ceremony is the defining feature of ritual for Esquipulas; as opposed to the semiweekly flower change, it is performed whenever the cargo-holders participate in a "fiesta" and every Sunday of the year.

After the third "eat," from about ten to two on Sunday, the crystalline structure of the ritual becomes less and less apparent. During certain segments of the rite, people drink twice instead of three times. Informants, even in ideal simulations, note that such performance is at once odd and occurs every week—the *mayol*, they explain, wants to go home, and acts drunk, puts on his hat, refuses to dance. Or the musicians get hungry. Furthermore, dance follows dance, and each segment is protracted, with fewer metaphors of hierarchy per unit time, by the clock. It is no accident that this ritual becomes less structured, more continuous; this is the way with other Zinacanteco ritual practices. An otherwise different rite, curing, begins at the patient's house with a similar degree of structure, with much bowing, releasing, and passing of the shot glass. As the ceremony proceeds and the shaman and his party walk and pray before crosses on various sacred mountains, these messages about rank are more widely spaced. The long curing trek has affinities with the repetitious two-step, the rhythm of the cargo-holders' drawn out ritual dance late on Sunday morning.

II

My thesis has been that the alternation of segments—alike in kind, greater and lesser in degree—marks the flow of time in the weekend ritual. The principle that underlies the sequence of segments is bankilal and ʔi¢'inal; when the ritual begins, this pattern is compact and salient, becoming less clearly marked as the ceremony proceeds. This rhythm, I think, is analogous to the way a Zinacanteco conceives of the relation between an older and younger brother, or two religious officials with the same title, or, for that matter, a number of other aspects of his world. What matters is that ritual time is cut up into pieces that are basically the same, yet a little different. I would not insist on the interpretation that these alternations somehow grow out of, or mirror, the social relations of males, same generation, with close ties (either family or title), but I suspect that this is the case, and all these relations are formally equivalent.

While the rite as a whole is seen as a rhythmic alternation, the nature and structure of metaphors for hierarchy within each segment remain to be seen. I shall now consider the rules by which messages about rank are combined in "flower change," "count the medallions," "take out the medallions," "dance," and other phases of the ritual. Two principles govern the occurrence of metaphors in all segments: (1) entrance and exit of each phase are marked by metaphors that are counterparts, either the same or the opposite, and (2) intervening ritual action is marked by three repetitions of drink from the shot glass (→). I add a rule: each segment of the ritual tends toward symmetry, except for messages that vary from segment to segment and are contingent on the ritual action itself.

To illustrate the operation of these principles, in Figure 5 I show the flower change and the count of medallions in the house of the martomorei. The notation remains the same.

The count has a novel metaphor (+→), which represents the fact that all present come forward (order: musicians, male helpers, female helpers, officials) to pray before the medallions. I bracket the second occurence of this metaphor because it was performed in 1964, but not in 1965 and 1966.

Two of the above metaphors are motivated by aspects of the ritual action: (1) ⇆ occurs in the middle of the flower change because the officials have thrown away the dried flowers and must greet the musicians on reentering the house, and (2) +→ occurs because people must pray when the saint's medallions are taken out of their chest. These messages, contingent or motivated, are not predictable in a schema valid across segments; they are high in information, pointing up the distinction of one segment from another. The presence of an elaborate metaphor (+→) seems to correlate with variation in "sacredness" across two segments that occupy the same structural position in the ritual. In both "flower change" and "count" the cargo-holder loosens his kerchief, as does the shaman; but during the count the official seems to imitate the sacred divination—the count tells his fortune. Consistent with a heightening of "sacred" behavior is the appearance of a novel and complex metaphor: all participants pray (+→).

Aside from such motivated messages, the middle section of each segment is marked by three repetitions of drink (→); this seems to be a particularly rich metaphor. When drink is served people are in various positions, corresponding to their social or ritual status; women to the north and men to the south; musicians seated along the south wall, in a row; martomorei on the north side of the altar (its right hand), mexon on the south, and so on. But, as the young boy pours drinks, he includes everybody in a single hierarchy—all present are served, one before the other. While rank is absolute, groups are united. At the same time that drink ranks men, it signifies complete equality; each person receives the same kind and amount of liquor. The participants are joined in an inclusive hierarchy, with equal portions for all. The unifying message of drink differs radically from the discontinuous metonymy Lévi-Strauss (1963b) and Leach (1964) discuss, where one category of men might receive fruit wine and another sugar cane liquor. In cargo ritual, as with many religious ceremonies, the differences among men appear to have been overcome (Lienhardt, 1964: 148). Drink, the central and critical portion of every segment, is another expression of the oft-repeated words of formal couplet speech: "We have united; we have all come together."

FIGURE 5
A formal description of flower change and count in the house of the martomorei.

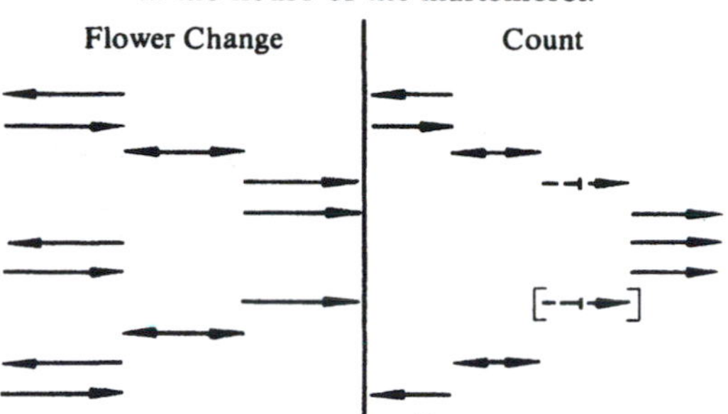

All segments have "drink" as their center; they also have well-characterized limits. In considering entrance and exit I include all acts of bowing and releasing, accompanied by speech in couplet form. Three kinds of behavior mark entrance and exit: (1) couplet speech with the musicians, (2) prayers that immediately follow, and echo, speech to the musicians: the officials kneel, bow, release—they greet the gods as men—and repeat the phrases they have just spoken, and (3) on occasion, just following the prayer, speech with elderly women, in the same manner. Couplet speech is easily recognized: the two lines are identical, differing only in their terminal words. In general, the second terminal word is phonetically longer than the first, and often, the less common, more elegant, or archaic. Thus in

c'ul senior ʔeskipula htot
c'ul senior ʔeskipula kahval

htot has one syllable and *kahval* two, and kahval means "my lord," and is elegant, while htot is simply "my father." It is significant that when the officials reenter the house after throwing out the dried flowers they bow, release, and joke with the musicians, but they do not speak in couplets. The point here is that coming into the house, even with bowing and releasing, does not equal entrance to a "sacred" phase of the ritual: "sacred" phases have clearly marked boundaries.

Leach, in an attempt to refine classic theories of ritual, predicts that entrance and exit of "sacred" segments—like "flower change" and "count" will be "contrasted opposites" (1961:136), i.e., entrance ⇆ ↔ and exit ↔ ⇆. He fails, however, to predict the many other phases of the ritual that end as they begin, such as the dancing. To account for my data I must return to the more general and accurate formulations of Hubert and Mauss (1964: 46,48) and van Gennep (1960:24): rites of entrance and exit are "counterparts," either the same or the reverse. My material, though, does make some refinement possible; I can specify the difference between the segments that end and begin in the same way and those that are opposites. By now it should be no surprise that inversion occurs only in the phases termed "work," where the official loosens his kerchief as a shaman. The cargo-holder seems to signal his creation of a "sacred phase" by finishing in the opposite way that he began.

CARGO-HOLDERS, MUSICIANS, AND HELPERS

A description of cargo ceremonies in terms of rank creates something on the order of a grammar of ritual action. Formal relations are both intelligible and prescribed; this is not a trivial grammar, for three reasons: (1) structure is revealed in the ritual, (2) rank is ever-present and obligatory in Zinacantecan social life, and (3) elaboration of metaphors for hierarchy corresponds to increased "sacredness" in ritual action.

I will now relate the principles of ranking to patterned modes of behavior in the ritual for Esquipulas. My purpose is to discover some reasons for the institutionalized joking between cargo-holders and musicians, and for the more spontaneous disputes that often arise among the officials themselves. What follows suggests that hierarchy is a matter of deep concern for the participants, and that it poses a moral dilemma, which is part of the ritual's meaning and its power.

The three categories of individuals who participate in the weekend ritual are defined over and over in messages about rank. I list them in Table 3. The principles of ranking differ for each of the groups as does the way in which they are recruited for service.

The helpers are friends and relatives of the official who selects them, and they are ranked, as in daily life, by age. For the cargo-holders "a universalistic criterion, economic resources, determines eligibility" (Cancian, 1964:342), and it is their titled office that determines position in the hierarchy. Musicians, on the other hand, are chosen for their ability to play an instrument and through personal acquaintance and recommendation. In ranking, officials speak to musicians in accord with the instrument they play, first violin, then harp, last guitar, but the younger of the two men bows. The musician's status is mixed, at once acquired and ascribed.

Musicians and officials cooperate to perform a ritual, but their relationship is ambiguous. Musicians instruct the newly initiated cargo-holder in his duties. As one informant explained, they are like shamans: public servants possessing special ritual knowledge, they are paid for their services in food and drink. Cancian describes the relation between the two kinds of groups in this manner:

In Zinacantan today, quite different kinds of prestige accrue to individuals who provide the two kinds of service, that of the cargo-holder and that of the ritual specialist. The ritual specialists are respected for their knowledge and their services to the saints and the community, but in the last analysis it is the people who supply the money, the cargo-holders, who receive the lion's share of

TABLE 3
CARGO-HOLDERS, MUSICIANS, AND HELPERS WHO PARTICIPATE IN THE RITUAL FOR ESQUIPULAS

I Cargo-Holders *hpas ʔabtelik*	II Musicians *hvabahobetik*	III Helpers *hcomiletik*
1. *martomorei bankilal*	1. *hvob violin*	1. eldest male
2. *martomorei ʔi¢'inal*	2. *hvob ʔarpa*	2. ...
3. *mexon bankilal*	3. *hvob kitara*	3. youngest male
4. *mexon ʔi¢'inal*		

> *the prestige. The prestige given the cargo-holders is rather finely graded according to how much they have spent* [1964:341].

In effect, musicians are food-drink receivers, the cargo-holders food-drink givers; they depend on one another. The structural relation between musicians and officials has the "conjuctive and disjunctive components" that Radcliffe-Brown associates with the joking relation [1952:95].

It is appropriate that joking between these two groups occurs, for the most part, when officials are giving—a drink from their bottles or a ritual meal. Giving during the meal is mediated by young men who serve; here, joking centers around sex and other themes. But, when the officials give most overtly, when they hand the musicians a bottle of liquor, jokes focus explicitly on status relations. During the flower change there is the programmed joke about trust and mistrust between the two groups of men. At other times, as the official offers the bottle, the musician grasps hand and bottle, saying the cargo-holder does not really want to give. Or the musician releases his opposite with his left hand instead of right. In one sequence the cargo-holder speaks to the musician as if he were asking his future father-in-law for his daughter's hand. The joking relation between the two categories of men is structurally analogous to that between affines in other areas of the world; they laugh about what divides and unites them.

Joking here is programmed and defined by a conflict in roles—a formal opposition with a formal solution. Another set of conflicts—more spontaneous and overt—obtains among the cargo-holders themselves. Their arbitrary ranking may subordinate older to younger, and peer to peer. In 1966 martomorei ʔiȼ'inal was older than bankilal, and sensitive to this difference. He changed the normal seating arrangement for ritual meals as shown in Figure 6. In past years older officials have taken the positions assigned by their titles; other Zinacantecos find it hard to believe that a man would not take his given place. Rank order is not a matter of indifference.

Disputes related to ritual performance cannot be predicted; these most explicit statements of conflict often become public court cases. In 1965, for instance, martomorei bankilal was very drunk when it came time to count the saint's medallions; he came out 110 short. ʔiȼ'inal, who usually wound up 30 to 50 ahead, wondered aloud, "How can a man count so badly?" He was promptly hit by the son of bankilal. This incident was discussed before members of the civil hierarchy, with

FIGURE 6
Normal and changed seating arrangements for officials at the ritual meal.

1964-1965 (normal) East		1966 (changed) East	
Mr$_1$	Mu$_1$	Mr$_1$	(Mr$_2$)
(Mr$_2$)	Mu$_2$	M$_1$	Mu$_1$
M$_1$	Mu$_3$	M$_2$	Mu$_2$
M$_2$			Mu$_3$

emphasis on the embarrassing count. In the end, amends were made, as might be expected, with a number of rounds of drink. Such squabbles arise for a number of reasons—personalities of the actors, difficulties in getting along with strangers, and so on—but their primary reference is inherent in ranking itself.

The rank order among officials for Esquipulas roughly corresponds to a hierarchy based on relative wealth and prestige in the community. A man does not ordinarily have the opportunity to display and flaunt his wealth; witchcraft threatens the show-off. In cargo ritual the bowing and releasing behavior—in daily life, a metaphor expressing respect for age—is, in effect, a recognition of economic superiority. A metaphor for ascribed status (age) is translated into one for acquired status (wealth). Not only does the cargo system reflect and confer prestige within the community, but also, in its ritual, it gives men a culturally appropriate way to act out a social order based on acquired status, an order forbidden in hamlet life.

Metaphors of hierarchy in cargo ritual are those of daily life; Leach correctly says that ritual denotes "*aspects* of almost any kind of action" (1964:13). It also is true, as has been seen, that ritual and daily life may be two different kinds of action. Leach fails to see that these two sectors of social life may be at once continuous and discontinuous (1954:10–14); here it makes more sense to speak of "both-and" than "either-or." "Both-and" because helpers are ranked, as in daily life, by age, and cargo-holders by wealth. Messages about rank in Zinacantan are not like inkblots that each person, or category of person, reads in his own way; the meaning of a bow is never questioned. A single message, in ritual and in daily life, unambiguously denotes two principles of ranking, acquired status and ascribed.

If the ways Zinacantecos denote relative social status are the "model schema of the social structure in which they live" (Leach,

1961b:299), there remains a profound difference between everyday affairs and ritual action. This is the difference between a rank order where anyone, by simply growing older, reaches the top, and a hierarchy closed at the top to the man who lacks the economic means to ascend. The former is one hypothetical model of a just society, with equal distribution of commodities (portions of drink) and equal opportunity to rise; the latter is more open to question. Adult males live in both worlds, they must acknowledge the existence of both hierarchies. To the extent that this dilemma is felt by the participants, the contradictions between these two systems must give the relation among the cargo-holders its problematic, and its "sacred," quality.

Evon Z. Vogt and Catherine C. Vogt

LÉVI-STRAUSS AMONG THE MAYA

In this joint article by Professor and Mrs. Vogt the concepts of Claude Lévi-Strauss are applied to the "Great Vision" ceremony, the longest and most complex curing ritual performed in the contemporary Maya Indian community of Zinacantan which Evon Vogt and his colleagues have been studying for the past twenty years. The Vogts indicate that while a traditional functional interpretation addressed to the question "what function does this ritual serve?" can show how the curing ceremony maintains social harmony and relieves the anxieties of the individuals concerned, it fails to explain most of the specific episodes and symbols in the ritual. For an interpretation of the symbolic details of the ceremony it is necessary to turn to a structural analysis utilizing the binary opposition of "nature" versus "culture". More recently, Evon Vogt has published a monograph, *Tortillas for the Gods: A Symbolic Analysis of Zinacanteco Rituals* (1976), in which he reports on still further interpretative discoveries of the rich symbolism of Zinacanteco curing ceremonies, especially on the manner in which the "inner souls" of the ritual plants encode crucial messages for the patient.

Reprinted with abridgments from *Man*, Vol. 5, No. 3 (1970), 379–392 with permission of the authors and the Royal Anthropological Institute of Great Britain and Ireland.

> *Lévi-Strauss, following the clues left by many thinkers before him, has found his way into an immense area of human experience which remains uncharted, full of traps and all kinds of theoretical monsters. It will never be possible again to treat mental life—myth, ritual—of the people we have been concerned with as a mere epiphenomenon of the "concrete" facts of economics, politics, and kinship. . . . The study of the structure and functions of customary thought still lies in the future. On this terrain, though Lévi-Strauss is certainly not the first adventurer, he may turn out to be the first successful cartographer* (Yalman 1967: 88–89).

Whether or not one agrees with all the theoretical premises and methodological assumptions involved (which we do not!), the interpretation of myths and rituals has certainly been vastly stimulated by the recent work of Professor Claude Lévi-Strauss. In focusing our attention upon "binary oppositions"—nature/culture; high/low; sky/earth; black/white and so on—and the role of myths and rituals in mediating these oppositions, Lévi-Strauss has added a dimension to the study of culture that anthropologists can ill afford to ignore in spite of the methodological pitfalls facing the analyst who chooses to work with these concepts.

In this article we propose to utilise field data gathered over the past thirteen years of research among the highland Maya Indians of Zinacantan, Mexico, to explore the symbolic meanings of certain ritual features of one of their curing ceremonies. The data to be examined concern the Zinacanteco concepts of the human soul and its animal spirit companion that shares this soul, and the ritual episodes that occur in the largest, most expensive Zinacanteco curing ceremony, the so-called *muk'ta ʔilel* (the "Great Vision"). A preliminary description and interpretation of these ritual features has already been published (Vogt, 1970), but both new field data from Zinacantan and new interpretative discoveries have prompted this further article.

After describing the concepts of the soul and the ritual episodes observed in the "Great Vision" ceremony, we shall suggest interpretations of the symbolic meanings involved using (1) the more traditional functional approach to the interpretation of the data; (2) an interpretation in terms of conceptual replication (see Vogt 1965a); and, finally; (3) a structural interpretation that relates the ritual data to a binary opposition in Zinacanteco culture, specifically that between "nature" and "culture." In exploring this nature/culture opposition we shall attempt to delineate as clearly as possible which aspects of the symbolism are parts of the accepted body of explicit customs of the Zinacantecos, and which are parts of a model constructed by ethnographers to help us order the data from Zinacantan.

THE MUNICIPIO OF ZINACANTAN

Zinacantan is a Tzotzil-speaking municipio in the Highland Maya area of Chiapas, Mexico, where we have been engaged in fieldwork each season since 1957. The municipio, with an elevation of 6,000 to 8,000 feet, and a population of approximately 8,000 Indians, is located just to the west of San Cristóbal Las Casas. Subsistence is based primarily upon maize grown with a system of swidden agriculture. The settlement pattern is typically Mayan, with ceremonial centre and outlying hamlets. About 400 Zinacantecos live in the centre; the other 7,600 live in the fifteen outlying hamlets. The ceremonial centre contains the Catholic churches, the *cabildo* (town hall), and an open-air market which functions during important fiestas. A series of sacred mountains and waterholes which figure prominently in religious life are located in and around this ceremonial focus. The most important feature of the social structure in the centre is a religious hierarchy with sixty-one positions in four levels. These positions are filled on an annual basis with the 'office-holders' moving with their families into the ceremonial centre to live during their terms of office, then returning to their hamlets to farm maize during the interim rest periods.

The social structure of the hamlets is based upon patrilocal extended families living in house compounds, localised lineages and waterhole groups composed of two or more localised patrilineages. While the office-holders perform ceremonies in the centre, ritual life in the hamlets is in the hands of *h?iloletik* (shamans). There are now about 160 *h?iloletik* among the Zinacantecos. Most of them are men, but some are women, and some are as young as fifteen years of age. To become *h?ilol*, one dreams three times that one's "inner soul" (see below) has been called before the council of the ancestral deities inside the most important sacred mountain and taught how to perform ceremonies. The ceremonies performed include curing ceremonies, semi-annual ceremonies (in May and October) for waterhole and lineage groups in the hamlets, new house ceremonies, agricultural ceremonies, rainmaking ceremonies, and three annual ceremonies for the New Year, the Middle of the Year, and the End of the Year. Zinacantecos believe that a shaman has the power to "see" the deities inside the mountains, hence the designation as *h?ilol* which means literally "seer."

ZINACANTECO SOULS

The Zinacanteco belief system conceives of "souls" of two types: *ch'ulel* and *chanul.* The term "soul" is used advisedly and in quotes to indicate that the familiar European concepts of "souls" and "spirits" are inadequate for precise ethnographic description of these concepts. In a very general way, of course, these Zinacanteco "souls" signify that the people are "animistic" in the terms described by Sir Edward B. Tylor. They also indicate the local manifestation of widespread Middle American beliefs about animal spirits (see Foster, 1944) but leave much unsaid about the complex and subtle meanings implied by the words *ch'ulel* and *chanul* for the Zinacanteco. To him, the *ch'ulel* is an inner, personal "soul" placed in the heart of each unborn embryo by the ancestral deities who live in the sacred mountains. By being placed in the heart, this soul is also to be found in the bloodstream and is composed of thirteen parts, one or more of which may be lost in a variety of ways, causing sickness for an individual. To recover the lost parts of the soul requires the services of an *h?ilol* and a curing ceremony.

Although temporarily divisible into parts when various kinds of "soul-loss" occur, the *ch'ulel* is considered to be eternal and indestructible. At death, the *ch'ulel* leaves the body but remains associated with the grave of the deceased for the period of time that the person lived on earth. It then rejoins the "pool" of souls kept by the ancestral deities, who later utilise it for another unborn embryo.

The *ch'ulel* (as an entity) can leave the living body of a person during sleep to visit the souls of other Zinacantecos or the deities.

It can also "drop out" of the body temporarily in times of fright or intense excitement. Informants tell of the *shi?el* ("soul loss") experienced by many persons when the first aircraft swooped low over Zinacantan twenty-five years ago as an example of fright, and they cite an orgasm during sexual intercourse as an example of intense excitement.

The *ch'ulel* tends to leave the body of a small child easily, since it is not yet firmly "fixed" in its new receptacle. Parents, therefore, are expected to treat a baby or small child with the utmost care and affection lest its *ch'ulel* leave—from fright or ill-treatment suffered by the child. The baptismal ceremony is believed to "fix" the *ch'ulel* more firmly in the child's body; but even after baptism a mother may still sweep the ground where she has been sitting for some time with her young child, in order to gather up all the parts of his *ch'ulel* that otherwise might remain at that spot.

At a deeper level of causation in Zinacanteco thought, *shi?el* is believed to be due either to punishment by the ancestral deities (whose power may cause a person to encounter serious accident or can send a frightening lightning bolt to knock out one or more parts of the *ch'ulel*), or to witchcraft performed by an evil person (a cave ritual in which the evil one "sells" one or more parts of the victim's *ch'ulel* to *Yalval Balamil* ("Earth Lord"), who uses the victim as a servant in his underworld house). With the loss of one or more parts of his *ch'ulel* from the deities' punishment or an enemy's witchcraft, the victim becomes sick, and an *h?ilol* must be fetched to diagnose and cure his illness.

The diagnostic procedure entails *pik ch'ich* ("touch blood")—the "pulsing" of the patient by the shaman. As he feels the pulse at both wrists and both elbows, it is believed that the blood "talks," providing the shaman with information as to whether *shi?el* has occurred; and revealing, if it has, its cause and the ceremony required to recover the lost parts of the soul and to restore them to the patient.

Human beings are not unique in possessing a *ch'ulel*, however. Everything important and valuable to Zinacanteco life is also believed by them to possess a *ch'ulel*. Thus, domesticated plants, such as maize, beans and squash, and farming tools have them; salt has a very strong *ch'ulel*; houses, their interior cooking fires, wooden crosses wherever erected (on mountains, inside caves, beside waterholes, in house patios), the saints' statues in chapels and churches, and even the musical instruments used in ceremonies, as well as the various deities in the Zinacanteco pantheon, all possess a *ch'ulel*. It soon becomes evident to an ethnographer in Zinacantan that the most important interaction in the universe is not between persons, nor between persons and objects, as we would perceive them; it is, instead, between the *ch'uleletik* possessed by these persons and objects.

The second type of "soul" which Zinacantecos believe themselves to possess is the *chanul*, which is a kind of "animal spirit companion" or "spiritual *alter ego*." Within a majestic volcano called *bankilal muk'ta vits* ("senior large mountain") that lies to the east of Zinacantan centre and dominates the ridges surrounding the centre in its valley, the Zinacantecos believe that there are several supernatural corrals in which the ancestral deities watch over and care for 8,000 *chanuletik*, one for each Zinacanteco. One corral contains jaguars, the "animal spirit companions" of the most important Zinacantecos (the shamans, the competent cargoholders, the ambitious political leaders). A second one contains ocelots—"animal spirit companions" of less important persons; and a third and fourth corral hold coyotes and

FIGURE 1
Human and animal "souls" in Zinacantan.

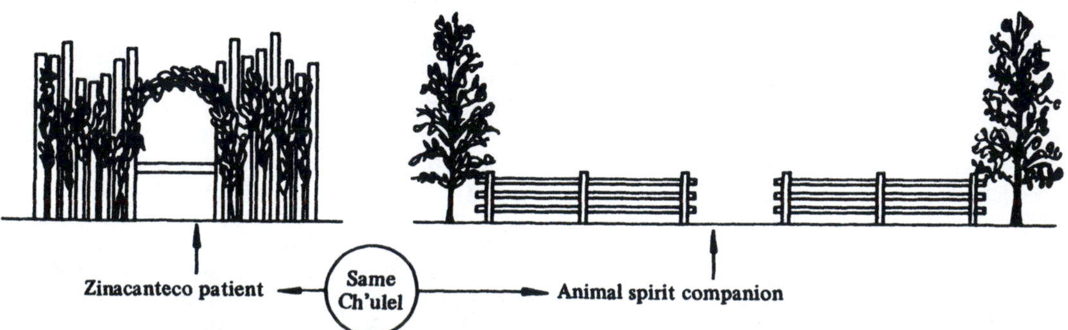

smaller animals (e.g. opossums) respectively—the "animal spirit companions" of Zinacantecos who for economic or other reasons do not have ritual power or political prestige.

The ancestral deities who care for the *chanuletik* do so under the supervision of the supernatural *muk'ta ʔalkalte* ("Senior Alcalde")—the ancestral gods' equal to the highest ranking member of the Zinacantecos religious hierarchy. This supernatural Senior Alcalde has his house inside the mountain near the corrals; and, although this province cannot be seen except in dreams or by the ritual "seers," the household cross of the Senior Alcalde is a visible shrine on the crest of the volcano and is visited by Zinacantecos during ceremonies.

The moment that a Zinacanteco baby is born, a corresponding animal is born. They share for life the *ch'ulel* given them jointly by the ancestral deities (see Figure 1). Whatever happens of note, good or bad, to the Zinacanteco also happens to his *chanul* and vice versa. If a Zinacanteco engages in wrong-doing or behaviour that angers the ancestral deities, they retaliate by letting his animal spirit companion out of its corral. It then becomes visible to men as it wanders on the mountain slopes and is prey to any hunter or larger animal. The person whose animal companion is released is then in mortal danger, because anything that happens to his animal spirit companion—from being caught in thickets, to being attacked by larger animals, or, worst of all, being shot by man—also happens simultaneously to him.

The knowledge of the kind of animal spirit companion a Zinacanteco has is ordinarily revealed to him in a dream during childhood. His *ch'ulel* visits its animal *alter ego* in the dream, allowing the dreamer to "see" the animal. The child may or may not discuss this important dream with his parents the following morning. The parents, however, may already be aware of the kind of animal with which the child *should* share his *ch'ulel*, since Zinacantecos believe that name and soul are transmitted together, as a package, down the patrilineage. They do not necessarily pass from father to son, nor from father's sister to mother's daughter, since it will be recalled that a *ch'ulel* stays with the grave of the deceased for as long as he lived on earth. When a young child dies, the patrilineage can use the name and the ancestral deities can use the *ch'ulel* and its associated *chanul* quite soon again. Quite the reverse occurs with the death of an old man or woman, for many years must pass before an old person's name (and soul) may be used again by a new member of the patrilineage. When it does occur, the new member (baby) becomes a *k'esholil* ("replacement" or "substitute") for the deceased within the lineage. And if the ancestor had distinguished himself in any way to be well remembered, it would be expected that the child would, perforce, later dream that his *chanul* was a jaguar.

THE "GREAT VISION" CEREMONY

At the most fundamental etiological level, social disorder and illness are interwoven with these concepts of "souls." Disruptive social behaviour (fighting and quarrelling with kinsmen, failing to accept community service when one has the necessary resources to expand, or failing to make contributions when the officials arrive to collect for ceremonies) leads the ancestral deities to mete out punishment.

To appease the enraged deities, or to remove the witchcraft of an enemy—which will eradicate the misfortune or illness suffered by the victim—a shaman's services are essential. Diagnoses are varied but, for any case of "lost *chanul*," the "Great Vision" must be held to round up the wandering animal spirit companion. This is the longest and most complex curing ritual performed by a Zinacanteco shaman for an individual, and illustrates a case in point for a perceptive comment by Lévi-Strauss:

> *Examined superficially and from the outside, the refinements of ritual can appear pointless. They are explicable by a concern for what one might call "micro-adjustment"—the concern to assign every single creature, object or feature to a place within a class* (1966: 10).

The "Great Vision" ceremony involves the patient, the shaman, the patient's family, relatives and friends in a ritual period of up to thirty-six hours. It includes a pilgrimage to the shrines of at least five sacred mountains, ritual meals and a ceremonialised placing of the patient in a decorated bed where he must remain for many days following the lengthy ritual. A brief description of the ceremony follows.

The ceremony commences with the shaman's arrival at the house of the patient to pray over the assembled offerings of candles, incense, and rum liquor. The patient and two black chickens (the same sex as the patient) are bathed in water from seven sacred waterholes to which has been added a special assortment of wild plants. The patient is then dressed in freshly washed and incensed clothes and made to drink a cupful of blood drained from the neck vein of the chicken destined to be left at the mountain shrine as an offering to the ancestral deities. The shaman daubs some of the blood on the patient's forehead, sews up the dead chicken's neck wound, and places the fowl on a pine-needle-covered plate.

A ritual meal of chicken, tortillas and liquor is served to the shaman, the patient, and several assistants. They leave on the pilgrimage after reciting prayers and shouldering the requisite supplies and ritual offerings. Visiting the five sacred mountains to renew the pine bough and flower decorations on the crosses there, pausing each time to set and light candles, burn incense, pray, and drink liquor at specified intervals, the curing party proceeds with the lengthy circuit—including a difficult ascent to the summit of Senior Large Mountain to pray at the household shrine of the supernatural Senior Alcalde. The black chicken on the pine-needle-covered plate is left here and said to be a *k'esholil* ("replacement")—the hope being that the ancestral deities will accept the offering as a substitute for the life of the patient.

After visiting the last of the five sacred mountains, the curing party returns to the patient's house. The patient is escorted under a flower-decorated arch and placed in a platform bed that is surrounded by thirteen bundles of pine boughs, flowers, and other leafy tree branches. The second black chicken is killed and placed on the bed beside the patient. A final meal served to the shaman and the assistants marks the end of the formal curing ceremony.

During the following days (the number varies) when the patient must remain in his decorated bed—except to relieve himself, and even then he must be accompanied—the second chicken is stewed and served to the patient *only*. The patient must save the feathers and the bones of the chicken for further ritual. At the end of the patient's taboo period, the shaman returns to remove the boughs from around the bed, and uses the boughs to rub the patient's body before placing them in a sack that two assistants take to the crest of a sacred mountain called *Kalvaryo*, where the ancestral deities are believed to convene. The assistants hang the sack there in the branches of a sacred tree and return to help the shaman bury the bones and feathers of the second chicken in a deep hole behind the household cross in the patio outside the patient's house. With this ritual episode completed, the patient hopefully recovers. But what deeper meanings are there to be found in these field data?

SOME ALTERNATIVE INTERPRETATIONS

Part of the answer can be elicited from Zinacantecos by simply asking them what they *think* they are doing during the curing ritual. Interviewing in this manner provides data on what Victor Turner appropriately calls "native exegesis" or the explanation of a native informant (Turner 1967; 1968). Thus any Zinacanteco can tell you that the patient is ill because the ancestral deities are angry with him; that they have allowed his *chanul* to wander outside its safe corral; and that the members of the curing party are praying to the ancestral deities who live inside the mountains as they make the lengthy circuit; that the ancestral deities must be placated with prayers, candles (which to the deities are "tortillas" and "meat"), the drinking of liquor (shared by the deities from that which is purposefully poured on the ground for them), and the gift of the black chicken as a substitute for the patient's life, and so forth.

Further hints can be derived from questions about the "operational meaning" of a ritual, as Victor Turner phrases an ethnographer's observance of the *behaviour* of persons with respect to, or in presence of, a sacred symbol (Turner, 1967: 51). Thus, our observing the placing of thirteen bundles of tree boughs around the patient's bed elicited the information that they did, indeed, have a relation to the thirteen parts of the patient's "soul."

Turner refers to a third level of inquiry in the analysis of ritual as the seeking out of the "positional meaning" of a symbol—i.e. its relationship to other symbols in a totality whose elements acquire their significance from the system as a whole (Turner, 1967: 51). Thus, we can speculate that a pine bough in itself is not a sacred symbol but that in its associative use during the curing ceremony it takes on sacred significance. In addition, we can speculate that placing the patient in the tree-bough- and flower-decorated bed soothes the patient with the special treatment tendered, the floral beauty to be seen and its aroma to be savoured. It also brings to mind the desired "spiritual" goal of the ritual—that of replacing the patient's animal spirit companion in its corral. The relation of the ritual act to the desired supernatural end seems evident when we learn that the word for the decorated arch is "doorway" or "gateway" and the decorated bed is called a "corral" during the ceremony. Immediately we think of the animal spirit companion being led back through the "doorway" of the mountain or "gateway" of the supernatural corral (see Figure 1).

Having elicited some possible symbolic meanings of the ritual, we now present three approaches to the interpretation of the ritual and its symbols. The first is a familiar *functional interpretation* that derives from the theories of Radcliffe-Brown and Malinowski, answering the question "what function does this ritual serve?" (e.g. Radcliffe-Brown, 1952; Malinowski, 1948). A Zinacanteco engages in disruptive behaviour—he fights with his kinsmen, gets drunk repeatedly and beats his wife, or he refused to take a religious cargo position, and, instead, accumulates money or spends it ostentatiously. Tensions build up in his relations with his family and neighbours; and, eventually, he falls ill. The shaman who is called prescribes the Great Vision ceremony, which functions to draw kinsmen together to co-operate in the patient's cure, to appease the deities with prayers and offerings, to relieve his guilty feelings in respect of his poor behaviour, and to remove some of his surplus wealth—thereby restoring his favour with gods and men. Thus the curing ceremony functions to maintain or preserve social harmony (à la Radcliffe-Brown) as well as to relieve the anxieties of the individual (à la Malinowski); but most of the *specific* episodes and symbols of the ritual are left unexplained by this approach.

The interpretation in terms of *conceptual replication* (Vogt, 1965a) poses the question, "what themes are repeated in rituals that are to be found elsewhere in the culture?" and can be applied to the Great Vision ceremony in the following way:

The word stem-*pet* in Tzotzil means "to embrace." The concept of "embracing" has the broad association in Tzotzil of watching over, guarding, caring for, instructing, being responsible for, and occurs in Zinacantan in the following contexts: the socialisation process in the family, the baptismal ceremony, the wedding ceremony and the curing ceremony—as well as in the concept regarding the role and activities of the ancestral deities.

The father (*tot*) and mother (*meʔ*) of a Zinacanteco child are expected to "embrace" their baby, i.e. to guard against loss of its tenuously-attached *ch'ulel*, to protect and care for it as it grows, to instruct it regarding the correct behaviour patterns.

In baptism, a child's godfather and godmother become "embracers" of the child during the ceremony, literally holding the child during the ceremony as they ritually promise to assume guardianship of the child throughout his life or as long as they themselves live.

In a wedding (the native ceremony performed at home after the church service), a ritual specialist called *hpetom* ("embracer") assumes a major role. He leads the bride and groom together into the groom's father's house where they are to live, and helps them to remove their outer wedding finery. He advises them how to create a good marriage that will last and asks the groom's mother to be patient and understanding with her new daughter-in-law. He leads the bride's family into the house and introduces them to the groom's parents, smoothing any friction that might arise. He is the wise, loving and concerned "guarantor" that the new marriage will be a fine and lasting one. And, in fact, if troubles do arise later, he will be called upon to help resolve the difficulties.

In curing ceremonies, the patient calls the shaman *tot* ("father"), and is guarded, cared for, advised ("embraced") by the shaman in the procedure of recovering his lost soul.

The ancestral deities are called the *totilmeʔiletik*, a word derived from "fathers" and "mothers," and as we have seen, are expected to "embrace" (guard and care for) the animal spirit companion. In short, all guardian or parental-like figures in Zinacanteco culture are spoken of and conceived of as being "embracers." The pattern is replicated in the supernatural and terrestrial worlds, and we see and hear the theme repeated in rituals ad infinitum.

Other conceptual replications have been found in our data from Zinacantan, but even they do not solve the symbolic mysteries remaining in the curing ceremony, e.g., why must the chickens be black, why does the patient drink the blood, why is one chicken left as an offering to the deities and the other cooked and served only to the patient, and why are the bones and feathers of the patient's chicken carefully saved and later buried deep in the ground near the household shrine? For some possible answers to these questions we turn to Lévi-Strauss's binary opposition of nature versus culture.

NATURE VERSUS CULTURE IN ZINACANTAN

We begin by asking what linguistic evidence there is that Zinacantecos explicitly recognise an opposition between nature and culture. At this most general level of contrast, there are no Tzotzil words, and there is literally "no way of talking about" what we mean by nature and culture. It would not even help if we interviewed the few bilingual Zinacantecos in their second language of Spanish to pose questions about *naturaleza* and *cultura*, since they are essentially meaningless concepts to them (see Vogt, 1970).

But these facts should not surprise us, as it is precisely one of Lévi-Strauss's major points about "savage thought" that we should not expect to discover oppositions at this general level of contrast. Rather, "savage thought" follows the rules of the "science of the concrete," and the more general categories are expressed in more concrete contrasts such as "raw/cooked," "wet/dry," "male/female," etc. At this more concrete level of contrast we discover that Zinacantecos do make a basic distinction between *naetik* (literally "houses," but connoting the space on the earth that is filled by houses occupied by Zinacantecos in their everyday life) and *te'tik* (literally "trees" or "forest" but connoting the space that is unused by people for living, although exploited by them from time to time as in wood cutting and plant gathering). These are polar opposites to the Zinacantecos, who add an intermediate category of *chobtik* to describe the cultivated fields which by the process of swidden agriculture temporarily transforms patches of *te'tik* into the fields of maize, beans, and squash.

The conversion of the domain of nature into culture, in these terms, is observed in two fundamental ways in Zinacantan. There is first a utilitarian, space-filling extension of culture into nature as the construction of houses and fields changes *te'tik* into *naetik* and the intermediate category of *chobtik*. There is, secondly, a ritual, sacred extension as Zinacantecos label and interact with parts or the whole domain of *te'tik* in their ceremonial life; or, in other words, as they develop and maintain beliefs about aspects of their natural habitat, that "wilder" area lying outside and beyond their houses and fields. It is most important for the ethnographer (and for our argument) to know that the Zinacantecos believe the mountains and hills (both called *vits*) to be the home and domain of the ancestral deities, and that the subsurfaces, both around and below the settlements, are the home and domain of the earth gods. The ancestral deities are pictured as elderly Indian ancestors. Communication with them is achieved through prayers, particularly those said in front of the shrines at the foot of and on top of the sacred mountains. Those on top of mountains are the ancestral deities' household shrines (symbolically equivalent to the household shrines in Zinacanteco patios); those at the foot of the mountains are the outer gateways of the deities' house compounds (equivalent to Zinacanteco property gateways where a caller will pause first to shout his arrival before entering the patio).

The earth gods are called *Yahval Balamiletik* (literally "Earth Lords") and are pictured as fat, greedy ladinos, eager to capture the inner "souls" of the Indians. Communication with them is achieved via any opening in the surface of the earth, such as waterholes, limestone sinks, or caves (all of which are called *ch'en*).

It is highly significant that extensions (or encroachments) made by Zinacantecos into the domain of nature are done so accompanied by ritual. The building of a new house entails the new use of a piece of land taken from nature, the taking of wood for posts and rafters, of mud for the wattle-and-daub walls, and of grass for the thatched roofs. For the land and materials used, the earth gods must be compensated by a house dedication ceremony, including prayers asking their pardon and offerings of candles, incense, and liquor. The carving out of a new maize field in the domain of nature likewise involves taking and using land belonging to the earth gods; and, again, they must be compensated for, by agricultural ceremonies performed with prayers and offerings.

Similarly, the pilgrimages to the mountain shrines to communicate with the ancestral gods or those to waterholes, limestone sinks, and caves to pray to the earth gods are highly ritualised, for, besides showing proper respect to the deities and gods, the Zinacanteco is venturing into the domain of nature (an area fraught with the unexpected and the dangerous) from the domain of culture (an area of familiarity and predictability).

In commonly held Zinacanteco attitudes about the domain of *naetik* as compared with the domain of *te'tik* there is also some evidence for the contrast between culture and nature. This evidence is not as solid, for unlike the linguistic distinction between *naetik* and *te'tik* that is universally made in Zinacantan, attitudes about these domains vary from individual to individual both in content and in intensity. But our data do show strong tendencies among Zinacantecos to view the domain of *naetik* as familiar and safe, and to view the domain of *te'tik* as unfamiliar and dangerous. The domain of *te'tik* is dangerous because of the hazards one may encounter there in the form of *pukuhetik* or *h'ik'aletik*. The *pukuhetik* are various "demons" such as the *poslom* which travels as a ball of fire and hits people, causing a bad swelling. The *h?ik'aletik* are small, black-skinned, curly-haired men with winged feet who soar out of their caves at dusk, like bats, searching for food and sex. They suck the blood of men, and rape women with their two-meter long penises. So potent is their sexuality that their progeny appear three days after conception (Laughlin, 1963: 190–191; Blaffer, 1969).

More convincing evidence in the belief system for an opposition between nature and culture is found in the Zinacanteco concepts of "souls" described earlier. The relationships between the categories of *nature/culture, naetik/te?tik,* and *man/chanul* are summarised in Figure 2.

FIGURE 2
Nature/culture relationship.

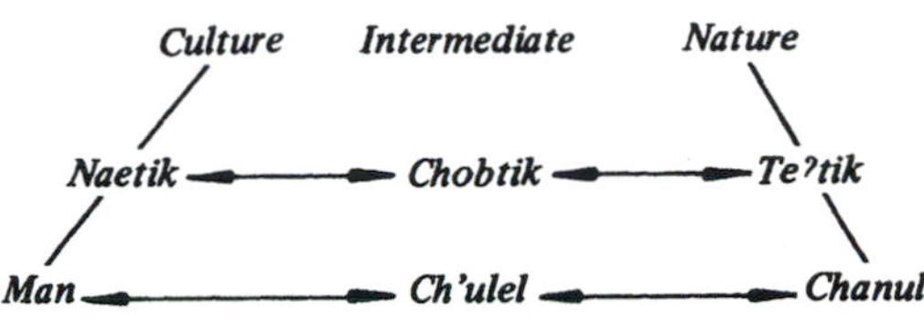

THE CONCEPTUAL BALANCE OF NATURE AND CULTURE

Edmund Leach begins a recent review of two works of Lévi-Strauss with these words:

> *The problem is: Just where do we fit in? Are we better or worse or indeed in any way different from our prehistoric ancestors or our primitive contemporaries? We are animals and, therefore, a part of Nature, but we are also self-conscious human beings who can somehow or other conceive of ourselves as outside observers, looking on* (Leach, 1967a: 6).

Later in the same review, he questions:

> *How is it and why is it that men, who are part of Nature, manage to see themselves as "other than" Nature even though, in order to subsist, they must constantly maintain 'relations with' Nature?* (Leach, 1967a: 8).

The "how" and the "why" of man's seeing himself as "other than" nature may remain unanswered, but we have presented evidence that the Zinacanteco does distinguish the domains of nature and culture. We would propose that the concept of the Zinacanteco sharing his inner "soul" with an animal spirit companion involves two complementary processes—the culturalisation of nature and the naturalisation of culture. The result is a symbolic structure expressing the balance or homeostasis between these two opposite processes. We further suggest that these balanced nature/culture relationships also provide a symbolic language for denoting structural relations in Zinacantan society.

A Zinacanteco is *naturalised* (i.e. conceived as being part of nature) by sharing his inner "soul" with a wild animal spirit companion. This "soul's" well-being maintains the life and health of the Zinacanteco and is the means by which he communicates at the basically most important level with other men, with valued cultural objects (houses, fire, cross-shrines, maize), and with the deities. Throughout his life, he is consciously aware that he shares this essential "soul" of his with a wild animal within the domain of Nature.

But nature, in turn, is *culturalised* in this instance, in the corraling of a wild animal spiritual companion. The Zinacanteco recognises the relationship between man and animal (culture and nature) and has conceptualised his belief in his "other than" qualities in this way. The ancestral deities' role in the "corraling" and "embracing" of his wild animal spirit companion symbolically *culturalises* nature, and is comparable to the "embracing" of a child by his parents and to the controlling of an individual's unruly behaviour by the social rules in Zinacanteco society.

The balance between nature and culture is thereby set and maintained so long as a Zinacanteco behaves within the socially approved norms. His good behaviour guarantees that his animal spirit companion will be "embraced" by the deities within the corral—and by extension, that he will enjoy good health. Imbalance occurs when a Zinacanteco transgresses the social norms and the deities set loose his animal spirit companion—and by extension, put his life in danger. The curing ceremony then serves as a symbolic way of restoring the balance between nature and culture in the following way:

Man (culture) enacts an animal (nature) role in allowing himself to be led into, and cared for in, a corral (bed). This compensatory act for his animal spirit companion (which is hopelessly lost in the woods) demonstrates to the deities that the man is repentant and is cognisant of the joint danger he shares with his animal spirit companion. Since it was the man who initiated all the trouble by his transgression of social norms as he acted wildly and impulsively and caused his animal spirit to be turned out of the supernatural corral, it is his obligation to be penned, guarded over, and cared for (in effect, re-socialised to normal behaviour) until such time as his animal counterpart is once again returned to the corral, and the balance between Nature and Culture is restored to its normal state.

But, what about the black chickens? What symbolic role do they play? Chickens are anomalous—they exemplify an over-domesticated or over-culturalised nature figure. They have wings, yet cannot fly. They can walk about, yet are "corraled" by depending on people to feed them grain; they stay near houses even when not penned and roost in the trees in the house patio at night. Thus, the chicken is an appropriate symbolic mediator between culture and nature.

Note that both chickens (the same sex as the patient) are bathed in the same water that is used to bathe the patient. Note also that blood from the sacrificial chicken is daubed on the patient, and then the patient proceeds to drink the rest of the blood drained from the chicken's neck—thereby absorbing and ingesting part of the inner "soul" of the chicken and establishing a spiritual link with the chicken before it is taken to be "fed" to the ancestral deities in the mountains so that the deities will reciprocate by caring for the patient's animal spirit companion.

The second chicken that is killed and placed in the patient's bed may also be construed as helping to restore a balance between nature and culture—an offering left out in nature is balanced by the offering left to culture in the patient's bed-corral and later eaten by the patient. We would further argue that since this second chicken is to remain in the domain of culture, the feathers and bones *must* be carefully saved and deeply buried (beyond a depth to which any animals—nature—could dig them up and eat them) in the house patio which is an essential part of *naetik* as opposed to *te?tik*. Finally, the plants used to surround the patient's platform bed are taken from nature and are returned to nature where they belong, in the branches of a tree since they are all tree plants: laurel leaves, pine boughs, bromileads, etc.

But, then, why *must* the chickens be black? We know that black and red are important ceremonial colours in Zinacantan as evidenced by the black ceremonial robes and bright red head turbans worn by the high-ranking office-holders during their rituals. In this ceremonial regalia, the office-holders *look very similar* to the chickens whose black feathers and red combs combine these colours in the same proportions. Furthermore, the Tzotzil words for office-holders and sacrificial chickens are significantly the same: *k'esholiletik* ("substitutes" or "replacements"). The office-holders are "replacements" because they succeed each other in office on an annual basis. The sacrificial chicken is serving as a "substitute" for the life of the patient when it is offered to the gods in the mountains. We surmise that the message in this symbolic complex is that black chickens are like office-holders because they are in good communication with the deities and because they are both sacrifices—the office-holder sacrificing his time, resources and energy for the benefit of the community, the chicken sacrificing his life for the benefit of the patient. The identification is even closer in some of the office-holder's prayers, as for example, when the Senior Alcalde administers the oath of office to an incoming Alférez with these words (Vogt, 1969: 490).

. . . He came to receive,
He came to take,
The holy, divine oath,
Here under your feet,
Here under your hands,
Your servant,
Your rooster.

So office-holders and roosters are both sacrificial offerings clothed in black and red.

We have now obviously reached the limits of legitimate speculation and must leave the decoding of further questions for more insightful fieldworkers collecting more data on future trips to Zinacantan.

. . .

In contrasting games and rituals Lévi-Strauss has written:

Games thus appear to have a disjunctive effect; they end in the establishment of a difference between individual players or teams where originally there was no indication of inequality. And at the end of the game they are distinguished into winners and losers. Ritual, on the other hand, is the exact reverse; it conjoins, for it brings about a union (one might even say communion in this context) or in any case an organic relation between two initially separate groups. In the case of games the symmetry is therefore preordained. . . . Asymmetry is engendered. . . . The reverse is true of ritual. There is an asymmetry which is postulated in advance between profane and sacred, faithful and officiating, dead and living, initiated and uninitiated, etc. and the "game" consists in making all the participants pass to the winning side by means of events, the nature and ordering of which is genuinely structural (Lévi-Strauss, 1966: 32).

In this Zinacanteco curing ritual, the asymmetry postulated in advance is between nature and culture—in the sense that both the patient and his animal spirit have become over-naturalised (i.e. out of control). The patient has broken social rules and as a consequence his animal spirit has been let out of its corral by the ancestral gods. The ritual moves to restore a balance, to conjoin, or bring about a union again between the two domains as the animal spirit is safely returned to its supernatural corral and the patient is controlled in behaviour and restored to good grace with his fellow men and the ancestral gods.

In conclusion, we should like to raise a methodological point about which aspects of this interpretation are parts of the accepted customs explicitly recognised by the Zinacantecos and which aspects are parts of a model constructed to order the data from Zinacanteco ritual behaviour.

In attempting to establish the distinctions between *naetik* and *te'tik* all the lines of evidence cited are explicitly discussed by the Zinacantecos.

The ethnographic model-building begins on p. 283 where we begin to develop a language which is quite obviously not utilised in ordinary discourse by Zinacantecos. A crucial part of the model has been discussed with Zinacanteco informants: the conceptual similarity between the corral of the *chanul* and the decorated platform bed into which the patient places himself at the end of the ceremony. At the onset of the fieldwork, data were collected on the beliefs about the *ch'ulel* and the *chanul*. Later we elicited the data that the decorated bed is called a "corral." We then asked Zinacanteco informants about this conceptual similarity, and the response was "I've never thought about that before, but getting the *chanul* back in his corral and having the sick person climb into a bed that is called a 'corral' do seem to be the same." It was, in short, an illuminating suggestion to them. Beyond this, we have not gone; nor are we very hopeful of going much further. Certainly when the statements reached the level of a meta-language in which the assertion is made that ". . . the Zinacanteco sharing of his inner 'soul' with an animal spirit companion involves two complementary processes—the culturalisation of nature and the naturalisation of culture" we have gone beyond explicit Zinacanteco comprehension. Any tests for the validity of our interpretation, at this level of analysis, must depend upon an examination of the logical steps taken in moving from the "science of the concrete" to the model we have attempted to construct to order the data.

Robert H. Lowie

THE VISION QUEST AMONG THE NORTH AMERICAN INDIANS

The vision quest among the Indians and Eskimo of North America was a ritualistic means of acquiring supernatural power through personal contact with the supernatural. But there have been many misunderstandings regarding the quest. As Ruth Fulton Benedict has demonstrated in her authoritative monograph, "The Concept of the Guardian Spirit in North America" (1923), the vision experience was not at all always associated with acquiring a guardian spirit. It was used in California by shamans wishing to effect a cure; among the Montagnais and Mistassini to promote success in a hunt; among the Plains Indians for mourning, warpaths, revenge, curing disease, calling the bison, naming a child, acquiring a design, entering a secret society, and so on; power or commands were received directly rather than by acquiring a guardian spirit. Nor was the vision quest, as Hutton Webster supposed, synonymous with the puberty rite; it was not a rite of passage except in certain areas. True, the two often went together, but frequently the vision cycle led only to supernatural power and the puberty rite qualified only for membership in the tribe. The two concepts were remarkably distinct in California. Another mistake is to regard the vision quest as something sought by all young men of the tribe. Some Indians reserved the quest

only for shamans seeking a tutelary spirit to be used to punish trespassers on family hunting grounds and to fight with rival shamans in supernatural contests. Often the attempt to induce a vision failed and the individual might resort to acquiring a share in someone else's vision through purchase. It should be remembered, too, that visions were not always sought; west of the Rockies they ordinarily came involuntarily. Benedict has reminded us that guardian spirits could be acquired by means other than a vision. She insists that the vision and not the guardian spirit was the unifying religious fact of North America.

The hallucinatory side of the vision quest is of interest because it supports the hypothesis that religious ritual often affords an opportunity for self-transcendence, either through consciousness-changing drugs, purgatives, self-torture, or fasting. It leads to what is usually referred to as the "religious thrill," which many theorists regard as the source of religion. But while the experience is an individual and solitary one, it is culturally patterned both in the methods for inducing the vision and in the contents which are revealed. It is a socially created ritual, and not one whose genesis is to be sought in the unique experience of the individual.

The account of the vision quest that follows comes from Lowie's considerable field experience with American Indians, especially the Crow. For an illustration of the power of such visions to affect an Indian's life, see John G. Neihardt's moving book, *Black Elk Speaks* (1961). The reader wishing to go beyond the descriptive type of account should consult the article by Benedict mentioned earlier.

Reprinted from Robert H. Lowie, *Indians of the Plains* (New York: McGraw-Hill Book Co. and the American Museum of Natural History, 1954), pp. 157–161, by permission of the American Museum of Natural History.

Most North American Indians attached great importance to visions, and in the Plains these took precedence in the religious life. However, the spirits did not always appear to their prospective protégé, but might merely become audible to him, issuing instructions and promising definite benefits. In Siberia and parts of western North America supernatural visitants were not sought; in fact, often the spirit compelled a native to accept his guardianship much against the future protégé's wishes. By way of contrast, Woodland and Plains Indians deliberately went out to a lonely spot in order to obtain a revelation. Some Crow individuals received favors unsought when in a predicament. Occasionally it even happened that a spirit came under ordinary circumstances from a pure desire to befriend the mortal. However, the normal procedure was to go into solitude, fast and thirst for four days, and supplicate the spirits to take pity on the sufferer. A Crow usually cut off a finger joint of his left hand or in some other way mortified his flesh by way of arousing supernatural pity.

Certain tribal differences are noteworthy with respect to the vision quest. In the Woodlands, Ojibwa and Winnebago parents regularly instructed boys, possibly not over seven years of age, to fast in order to obtain the blessing of a spirit, and on the Plains the Hidatsa elders likewise prompted their children to seek a revelation at an early age. But no such admonition was customary among the Crow. There a lad grew up, constantly hearing that all success in life was derived from visions; hence, being eager for horses and for social recognition, an adolescent would go out to fast, praying for rich booty, for a chance to strike a coup, or for some other benefit. A mature man or woman would seek a vision whenever a special cause arose—if his children were sick, if he had lost his property, if he longed to revenge the killing of a close relative, and so on. Again, the Arapaho seem to have sought a vision only as adults.

We naturally wonder what really happened on such quests. There is no doubt that the vast majority of informants firmly believed in the reality of the experiences they described. In order to explain this phenomenon psychologically, several factors have to be considered. First of all, the god seeker was usually under a strong emotional impulse—either yearning to shine before his fellows or desiring relief from want or disease or the grief over an unavenged kinsman. By seclusion in a lonely spot, by his fast, by self-mutilation, he naturally intensified his emotional state. What is more, the myths told by his people and the accounts of the supernatural experiences of contemporary tribesmen had left an imprint on his mind and helped to shape the sense impressions that came to him. His longings at the time blended with the visionary pattern of his tribe and with the sounds or sights actually experienced under highly abnormal conditions so as to inspire an interpretation of things seen and heard. Individual peculiarities likewise entered: an Indian of a predominantly auditory type might imagine a whole series of distinguishable sounds—the call of a bird, the rustling of leaves, the neighing of a horse, the speech of an alien tribe, and what not. If his was a decidedly visual type, he would see specific details, as when a would-be raider caught sight of a mount he was to steal—say, a bay horse with docked tail, heavy mane, and a zigzag line painted down its legs. A man who subsequently arranged his sensations for his own enlightenment or to give a clear statement to an audience was in the position of ourselves when trying to give a coherent account of a dream. Without trying to deceive or to invent, he would unconsciously bridge over obscure points, filling in the gaps, adapting his memories of the experience to one of the tribal vision patterns familiar to him from listening to earlier accounts.

A good example of such a pattern is the following. Several Crow informants independently tell how on their lonely vigil they saw a spirit or several spirits riding along, how the rocks and trees in the neighborhood turned into enemies who attacked the horsemen, but were unable to inflict any harm. The symbolical meaning of these apparitions is that the spirits are making the visionary invulnerable. This is, of course, a generally prized blessing, but several persons could not independently conceive the identical image of spiritual riders shot at by transformed bits of the landscape, especially when the very same motif appears also in traditional stories apart from the narration of the teller's personal experiences. Evidently the image, however it may have originated, became part of tribal folklore and was readily worked into the report of their revelations by persons who particularly craved invulnerability. Again, it was certainly a part of the tribal pattern that most Crow Indians obtained their spiritual blessings on the fourth night of their seclusion, four being the mystic number within the area.

The supernatural beings who befriend man vary enormously in character. Animals were very frequent visitants of Plains Indians; buffalo, elk, bears, eagles (sometimes conceived as birds producing thunder by flapping their wings), and sparrow hawks constantly figure in the narratives, but also quite lowly beasts such as dogs or rabbits. A Pawnee legend even describes the invocation of mosquitoes, and according to Cree tradition a mosquito gave one tribesman the gift of chieftaincy. Curious contradictions do not seem to have been recognized as such by the Indians. In a Crow story a rabbit pursued by a hawk promises to give supernatural power to an Indian if he will shield him from the bird of prey. Correspondingly, a Pawnee boy gets supernatural aid from mice who are unable to extricate themselves from a relatively simple difficulty. That is, though animals are possessed of supernatural powers, they may be dependent on mortals for specific services, for which they reward them. Celestial patrons are also frequent, stars figuring prominently among the Pawnee. Fanciful creatures of more or less human shape likewise appear in visions, e.g., a dwarf with a very powerful musculature. Sometimes the patron comes in human guise but in disappearing assumes his true shape or otherwise gives a clue to his identity.

The Crow interpreted the relationship between patron and protégé as that of a father and his child, and accounts of visions often explicitly quote the spirit as pronouncing the formula of adoption: "I will have you for my child." In any case the spirit normally taught the Crow a sacred song, instructed him just how he must dress in battle or if a man was to become a doctor what medicines or curing devices he must use, and frequently imposed certain taboos as to diet or behavior. Any infraction of the rules was liable to precipitate a loss of the guardian's protection or even a dire calamity. Often the visionary not only wore some token of his vision or painted it on, say, his shield cover, but also on the strength of successive visions assembled the ingredients to build up a "medicine bundle," i.e., a wrapper containing a set of sacred objects indicated by the spirit. A Pawnee bundle contained as a minimum one pipe, tobacco, paints, certain birds, and corn—all assembled in a container of buffalo hide that was hung from the wall of the lodge. The opening of a bundle and the treatment of its contents were accompanied by definite rites. As already stated, it is often difficult to tell whether the native consistently considered such objects sacred in their own right, in other words, made them fetishes wholly independent of any personal spirit, or whether they become sacred only as gifts of the spirit; very likely the attitude of a person varied at different times.

If because of visions, one individual worshiped above all a supernatural buffalo, another an eagle, and a third the morning star, the question arises how these several beings ranked in relation to one another. With the Comanche and the Crow this problem arose only when there was a clash of interests between tribesmen, each man falling back on the protection of his own guardian and the issue showing whose patron was the stronger. In the absence of a coherent system of the universe, the religious consciousness assigned priority to individual visitants. Thus, an Indian once told the author that a feather he cherished as memento of his vision of a bird was the greatest thing in the world. At the opposite extreme stood the Pawnee, who had brought their beliefs into a logical system, venerating a Supreme Being named Tirawa, a sky-dwelling creator who rules the universe, his commands being executed by lesser deities. Utterances by Dakota medicine men suggest a similar fondness for metaphysical speculation and integration. A question that remains unanswered is whether the average Pawnee or Dakota individual in his daily life was actually guided by priestly generalizations or whether in practice, without overtly rejecting them, he followed the Crow pattern.

Though all persons coveted a revelation, not all were able to obtain one. Those who did not succeed naturally did not wish to be thereby doomed to failure throughout life. The Crow and some other tribes resolved the dilemma by permitting a successful visionary to sell part of his power to less fortunate tribesmen, adopting them as his supernatural patron had adopted *him*, making for each of his disciples a replica of his sacred paraphernalia, teaching him the sacred songs, and warning against breach of any taboo associated with his medicine.

Edmund Wilson

THE ZUNI SHALAKO CEREMONY

One of the most important Southwestern Indian ceremonials is the Zuni Shalako, which is the high point in the annual Zuni ceremonial calendar. Since the ceremony takes place in late November or early December in Zuni Pueblo, located in an isolated region of western New Mexico, relatively few Americans have seen this colorful and dramatic affair. When one of our foremost writers and literary critics, Edmund Wilson, visited Zuni and attended the Shalako in the autumn of 1947, we were provided with this absorbing and perceptive account, which first appeared as an article in the *New Yorker* and was later published in his book, *Red, Black, Blond and Olive* (1956).

The account is an accurate ethnographic description of the main features of the Shalako, but more important, it provides in its interpretations an understanding of the meaning and significance of a rite of intensification for an American Indian culture. As Wilson expresses it, "It seems as if the dancer by his pounding were really generating energy for the Zunis; by his discipline, strengthening their fortitude; by his endurance, guaranteeing their permanence." Watching the dance, the people receive strength and revitalization. The dance is the climactic event of the year and sets the moral standard. As Wilson observes, the whole social structure of the Zuni revolves around the ceremony, and by keeping the dances up throughout the night "they know that their honor and stamina, their favor with the gods, are unimpaired."

An interesting treatment of the Shalako by a French scholar, Jean Cazeneuve, *Les Dieux dansant à Cibola* (1957), is the first full-scale account of the ceremony.

Reprinted in abridged form from Edmund Wilson *Red, Black, Blond and Olive* (London: W. H. Allen & Co. Ltd., 1956), pp. 3–4, 9–12, 23–31, and 33–42, by permission of the publisher.

Ever since reading, some years ago, a book called *Dancing Gods*, by Miss Erna Fergusson, which describers the ceremonials of the Pueblo Indians in New Mexico and Arizona, I had had an ambition to attend what seemed from her account the most spectacular of them: the Zuni festival called Shalako. But this takes place under what are, for an Easterner, rather inconvenient conditions: in midwinter, at a date which varies and which may be set only a few days in advance; and at a place, in northwestern New Mexico, which is off the tourist route and not very easily accessible. When I did finally get a chance to visit the Shalako festival, I discovered certain other difficulties.

The little pueblo of Zuni is one of the Indian communities that have survived, since the arrival of the whites, most successfully as a social organism. Its strength and cohesion it seems mainly to owe to the extraordinary tribal religion: a complicated system of priesthoods, fraternities, and clans which not only performs the usual functions of religions but also supplies it with a medical service, a judiciary machinery, and yearlong entertainment. This cult includes the whole community, distributing and rotating offices, and organizing it so tightly that it is completely self-contained, in a way that perhaps no white community is, and equipped to resist the pressures that have disintegrated other Indian groups. The ceremonies are partly in the nature of the enactment of a national myth, and they present a sort of sacred drama whose cycle runs through the entire year. The legends show a good deal of imagination and the impersonations a good deal of art, and the cast is so enormous that a very considerable proportion of the little town of twenty-six hundred has, at one time or another, a chance to play some role. With this, the Zuni religion imposes an effective discipline, involving periods of continence and fasting, and insisting on truthfulness—"speaking with one tongue"—and on civility and gentleness in personal relations. The Zunis as a group are extremely self-controlled, industrious, and self-reliant.

. . .

Coming down into the village proper—among one-story adobe houses and the beehive-shaped outdoor ovens that are both the same purplish pink as the bare grassless earth they are made of—is a descent into a foreign country. The air is full of piñon smoke that has a smell as rich and fragrant as roast chestnuts. The dogs come out everywhere to bark at you—half-wild and rather horrid mongrels: some look like degenerate huskies, others as if they were crossed with coyotes. I saw one family of half-grown pups in which every one was different. I was reminded for a moment by the earth and the smell, the women wearing gay shawls and carrying baskets or jars on their heads, of the towns in southern Europe. But this is something remote from Europe, at once newer and older: a piece of prehistoric America that has absorbed some of the customs of the United States.

There are great preparations in evidence: everywhere men chopping wood and women baking loaves in the ovens; outside the houses hang sheepskins, fresh from the dozens of sheep that will be barbecued or stewed for the feasts. Against the monotonous background, the blankets are bright green or red. The people have an Eskimo Mongoloid look: stout, compact, and not very tall, with round black eyes that shine. Some of the men have frank friendly faces, but all look as if they had been cut out of some very hard substance, and they are in general reserved and solemn, talking little among themselves and not even glancing at visitors. The women have bulky swathed bodies on feet and legs made enormous by a kind of wound puttees, and their wrapped and wadded bodies go along on legs that seem spindling. There are many small primitive corrals, mere rows of rough stakes, with sheep, burros, cattle, and horses. Here and there is a domesticated wild turkey or an eagle in a wooden cage, both kept to furnish feathers for costumes. Beyond rises Corn Mountain, which belongs to the Zunis and to which they belong, now transformed by the setting sun: the upper part of the mesa is for a moment vividly reddened, and its markings and outlines become distinct, then suddenly it is all left in shadow. On the other side of the sky, the clouds are a dull brickish red that corresponds with the color of the mesa and harmonizes with that of the soil. The little Zuni River shines palely as twilight falls.

The town is no longer the anthill (the Zunis themselves called it the Middle Anthill of the World) that the travelers of the eighteen-eighties found and that the Taos pueblo still is—with the houses piled up in terraces and scaled by outside ladders. There is a nucleus of these old buildings left that encloses the little plaza, but the Zunis have prospered so much that they have built themselves capacious houses, which now cover a relatively large area. They seem to put them wherever they like, at various distances from and angles to one another, and there is scarcely in the whole pueblo anything that can be called a street. The typical Zuni house has only a single story and not more than three or four rooms. These rooms are hung with shawls and blankets, and one of the more pretentious houses is decorated with maps. I saw none that showed any signs of squalor—though the Zunis' ideas about bedding are not so nice as ours—and none that did not smell clean. In spite of the generally high standard of living, there are different degrees of wealth, and the families I visited were pretty well off. Yet, even with their chairs and beds, these houses, to a non-Indian, seem rather bare, because they are still the dwellings of people who have for millennia been used to sitting and sleeping on the ground and have not yet had the time to acquire the sense of furniture. The pieces are set around without system, often at great distances from one another, just as the conversations that take place when a white visitor calls are full of immense silences that are the product not of embarrassment but of the natural taciturnity of the Indian. There are two or three houses with a second floor, but this is merely "conspicuous waste," as the owners do not live in the upper part but use it, if at all, to store corn. Lately, the Zunis have shifted from round to square beams, because the women have found that the latter are easier to dust—a motivation of a kind which, as a visiting anthropologist says, could hardly be guessed in the ruins of the past by a student of archaeology.

Some of these houses have curious features that are the result of their having been built to receive the Shalako gods, or Shalakos. There are six of these gods, and tradition demands that each of them be received in a house especially built for the purpose. There have also in the past been two houses to entertain other groups of divinities. Now, the building of these eight houses and the banquets, on a medieval scale, with which the gods are welcomed have in some cases ruined for the whole of the year the families that have undertaken them. So the Zunis sometimes cheat on the expense and merely replaster old houses or build on a new room or two or entertain two Shalakos in one house. Even so, this means that every year there are several new houses, equipped for the requirements of the Shalako dance. They must have each a long room, which sometimes runs to sixty feet, and a ceiling at least twelve feet high to accommodate the enormous masks. Each must also have a row of windows that opens on the Shalako room from another large chamber next to it and from which certain special groups have the privilege of watching the performance, as if from theater boxes. These windows, which have regular sashes and panes, with little paper stickers on them to advertise the company that makes them, are one of the queerest examples of the mixture in Zuni of the old and the new. When the celebration is over, and a family comes to live in the house, the windows become a nuisance and are usually walled up.

. . .

I started for the first night of the Shalako festival (December 16 this year), with a small party of other visitors, at about four in the afternoon. All cars going down the hill were stopped by the police and searched for liquor. This, I was later told, failed almost completely in its purpose, since the Zunis by way of their grapevine would send the word back to Gallup for their bootleggers to come in around the hills.

We arrived at the pueblo just in time for the advent of the Council of the Gods, a group in which the Shalakos are not included. A fording place of mud and stones had been built across the Zuni River, and the gods, coming down from a stone formation known as the White Rocks, made their entrance over it into the town. The young Fire God comes first—a boy in his early teens, his nude body painted black and spotted with red, yellow, white and blue, wearing a black spotted mask, like a helmet that covers the whole of his head, and carrying a smoldering brand. We missed his arrival, however, and did not see him till later. The main procession, which was now approaching, produced an uncanny impression. First comes the high god of the festival, Sayatasha, the Rain God of the North; and behind him his deputy, Hututu, the Rain God of the South. Sayatasha, in his mask, has what looks from a distance like a blank black-and-white pierrot face, between a black-banged wig and a black-and-white striped ruff, and he is dressed in a white gown. He stalks pompously in a long slow stride, accompanied by a short sharp rattle, made by shaking a cluster of deer scapulae every time he puts down his foot. It is the rhythm of authority and dignity which is reserved for him alone and—like the music for Wotan in the *Ring*—accompanies him all through the ceremonies. As he comes closer, we make out his accoutrements. A long flat horn, in place of an ear, sticks out from the right side of his mask, like an upcurved turquoise pennon; it has a heavy black fringe on its underside and a white feather dangling at the end. This horn presages long life for the Zuni people; and the left eye, a long black streak prolonged through an outstanding wooden ear, also heavily fringed, invokes a special long life for the "people of one heart." The right eye, not extended beyond the face, is intended to threaten short life to those who practice witchcraft. Sayatasha has a bow and arrows, and "prayer plumes"—that is, sticks with feathers attached that are supposed to give wings to the prayers. His follower Hututu is much the same, except that he has two ears and no horn, and that his eyes are set in a single black stripe which stretches across his mask, and from the tip of one ear to that of the other. Each is followed by a Yamuhakto, or Wood Carrier, who comes to pray for the trees, so that the people may have firewood and beams for their houses. The masks of the Yamuhakto are turquoise and bell-glass-shaped, with expressionless holes for the eyes and mouth, and each of these masks is surmounted with an untrimmed black wig, a tuft of yellow macaw feathers, and a kind of long green wand, from which hang down toward the shoulders long tassels of many-colored yarns. The Yamuhakto are wearing white buckskin skirts, and the naked upper parts of their bodies are painted a kind of purple and festooned with great garlands of beads. They carry deer antlers and bunches of feathers. All four of these principal divinities are wearing enormous round collars—shaped like life preservers and striped black-on-white like peppermints—that extend far beyond their faces and conceal the joint made by the mask. The two whippers, the Salimopiya, come last, carrying yucca switches. Both have bell-glass-shaped masks, noses like long pipes, eyeholes that are connected like spectacles, yellow topknots of feathers that stick out behind like weather vanes, and huge ruffs of black raven feathers. Both are nude except for a loincloth and wear spruce wreaths on wrists and ankles; but they are decorated in different ways: one, the Warrior of the Zenith, has a mask that is checkered in bright squares of color, with much yellow and red, which represents a spectrum of the midday sun, and red sunbursts where the ears would be. The other, the Warrior of the Nadir, is wearing a black mask with blue eyes and a blue snout.

All these figures proceed at a rhythm that is set by Sayatasha's rattle, but involves at least three different gaits. Hututu paces at a shorter stride than Sayatasha, and the Salinopiyas move with a quicker, a running step. All the time one hears a soft lively whistling that resembles the calling of birds. One cannot tell which of the figures is making these sounds, because one cannot see their faces; and, arising from no visible human source, scanning no human chant, yet filling the quiet air, the song seems the genuine voice of deities that are part of Nature. So they pass, while the people wait in silence, across the little dwindled river, where a dead dog lies on the bank and old tin cans and paper boxes have been caught here and there on the mud flats; they march up between the rude corrals, in one of which a big sow is grunting.

The Council now blesses the village, proceeding to six different points, where small holes have been dug in the ground. The people come out of the houses and sprinkle the divinities with sacred meal, and the Council, at every excavation, plants prayer plumes and sprinkles meal and performs some solemn maneuvers. Sayatasha and Hututu, each with his Yamuhakto, make two units that parade back and forth, while the Salimopiya mark time, never slackening their running pace but turning around in one spot. The climax of the ceremony comes when Sayatasha and Hututu walk up to one another and stop. Sayatasha cries, "Hu-u-u," and his vis-à-vis answers "Hu-tu-tu. Hu-tu-tu." The livelier calls, one decides, must be made by the Salinopiya, since they seem to match the brisker tempo. It is evident that all these calls have been imitated directly from bird-cries—one remembers the expertness at this of Fenimore Cooper's Indians—bird-cries, perhaps, heard at dusk or at night and attributed to elemental beings. Though owls, with the Indians, have a bad reputation, being usually connected with witchcraft, Hututu is obviously an owl. I assumed at first that the voices were whistles in the snouts of the Salimopiyas, but learned that they were produced by the throat and lips. I was told of a conversation in English in which one Zuni had said to another, "Gee, you make that noise good!" At one year's Shalako, Miss Bunzel says, the Salimopiyas were severely criticized for not being sufficiently handsome, for not showing sufficient animation, and for not giving loud enough calls. Yet the whistling is never shrill, it is always under perfect control; and the confrontation of Sayatasha and Hututu is performed with an unearthly impressiveness. At last, with much ceremonial, they enter the house prepared for them—it has a cozy, brand-new, suburban look. Though we whites have been behaving with discretion, the Indians are afraid we may go too close and warn us to keep our distance.

In the meantime, the six Shalakos, the guests of honor, have been sitting out in front of a cabin, in which the actors put on their costumes, in a field back of one of the trading posts. These creatures are gigantic birds, the messengers of the rain gods, which, erect, stand ten or twelve feet tall. They have cylindrical turquoise faces with protruding eyes that roll up and down, long wooden beaks that snap, and upcurving tapering turquoise horns on either side of their heads. They wear big ruffs of raven feathers, black-banged wigs and towering fan-shaped crests of black-and-white eagle tail-feathers. But their entrance into the village is arranged to take place just at the moment when twilight is falling, and one can now see them only dimly as, proceeding in single file and escorted by men in black blankets, they make their way to the river and, with a rhythmic jingle of bells fastened around their ankles, come slowly across the ford. The dark is blotting them out at the moment they arrive on the hither side; they squat in a row of six on the road by which the Council came. Now, with night, it grows very cold. The visitors hang around for a time—there is a group of young men and women, anthropological students from the University of New Mexico—afraid to ask the Zunis what is going to happen next or when it is going to happen. We lean on the egg-shaped ovens, and one of the girls gets a present of a loaf of white Zuni bread, made from sour dough, which she breaks up and offers around: it is still warm and tastes delicious. But the last orange-yellow light has faded out of the sky to our left, and still the birds do not move. The Zunis have gone indoors, and the whites drift away, too. Only the Indian Agent and I remain.

An hour and a half pass. We walk up and down to unfreeze our feet. The Shalakos utter from time to time a single reiterated bird-note, which sounds as if it came, not from close at hand, but from the other side of the river; and at intervals they clack their beaks—which we can hear with remarkable distinctness—not at random, but one at a time, like counting-off in the Army. At one point, while they are making this sound, the bell in one of the churches, with a strange irrelevance, begins to ring. The men, wrapped in black blankets, go back and forth silently with flashlights, which are never allowed to play on the birds. They are only revealed now and then for a second by the swerve of an occasional Zuni car. An airplane passes above us, winking green and red. The Indians begin to emerge and line up along the road; we assume that the show is starting, but we still have a long time to wait. At last, with other blanket-swathed figures, a group of twelve men arrives, jingling bells on their ankles; surprisingly, they seem costumed like characters in a production of *Romeo and Juliet*. These are the Shalako impersonators. (The birds, during the interval of waiting, have apparently been worked by "managers," who accompany and supervise them.) For each bird there are two dancers, who will alternate through the night. These twelve dancers, appointed a year ago, have been in training for their work ever since. Their roles, which bring much prestige, are exacting and responsible ones. Besides learning the difficult dances and memorizing endless speeches, they have had to build the Shalako houses. Though they begin by impersonating the gods, these latter, the night of the festival, will actually enter into them, and the men, with their masks, become sacred objects. If anyone touches a Shalako, or if the Shalako stumbles or falls—as it seems one of them did last year—the dancer is supposed to be struck dead by the god. A mistake on the part of the impersonator means either that someone has seen his mask while it was still in the dressing room and has not been whipped for impiety or that he himself has been making love to somebody else's wife and is unworthy to play the role. When a disaster of this kind occurs, the crowd must at once go away: the Salimopiya drive them off with whips. The dancer, of course, does not actually die, but his family go into mourning and behave as if he had. And though the Shalako actor must pull the cords that control the beak and the eyes, he is never—on pain of instant death—allowed to look up toward the top of the mask to watch the mystery in operation. Nobody except the manager may understand the Shalako's mechanics. These, then, were the dancers whom we now heard returning from six different points of the pueblo. We counted the jingling groups till the sixth had disappeared in the shadow where the birds were sitting.

Then suddenly, at some signal, a chorus of voices was raised. The Shalakos were on their feet. They came up from the road to the river and filed past us with their escort and choir; and the effect of this was thrilling and lovely in a way that it would be hard to imagine. The great birds, not rigidly erect but bent forward with the dignity of their kingly crests and their beardlike feathery ruffs, as if they were intent on their errand and knew each its destination, did not, in the frosty night, the pale moonlight, and the window lamplight, appear in the least comic, as they had in the pictures that one had seen; they hardly seemed even grotesque. And the welcoming hymns that accompanied them, in a harmony one did not understand but with the voices intertangled and singing against one another, had a beauty one could not have expected—not wild but both solemn and joyful—not entirely unlike our own anthems. Each of the Shalako birds is brought to the house prepared for it, and when it has come, it kneels down in front of the door, while prayer meal is sprinkled before it. The warm yellow light from inside gives comfort and life in the winter dark. The chants of reception are sung, and the bird, curt and proud in acceptance, snaps its beak in response to the welcome. Then the Shalako goes into the house and takes its seat before a turquoise altar. The impersonator comes out from inside, while a blanket is held up to screen him, and he and his alternate make offerings of seeds. Then they take seats beside the host, who hands them a cigarette, which he and they pass back and forth as they smoke it. The host addresses as "Father!" that one of the impersonators who is supposed to speak for the Shalako, and the latter replies, "Son!" They exchange other terms of relationship; then the host asks it, "How have you prayed for us? If you will tell us that, we shall be very glad to know it."

"I have come," says the Shalako, "from the sacred lake, and I have come by all the springs." He enumerates all the springs that the Zunis in their wanderings passed, when they were looking for a site for their town. "I have come to see my people. For many years I have heard of my people living here at Itiwana (the Middle), and for long I have wanted to come. I want them to be happy, and I have been praying for them; and especially I want the women to be fortunate with their babies. I bring my people all kinds of seeds, all the different kinds of corn, and all the different kinds of fruit and wild green things. I have been praying for my people to have long life; and whoever has an evil heart should stand up in the daylight. I have been praying that my people may have all different kinds of seeds and that their rooms may be full of corn of all colors and beans of all colors and pumpkins and water gourds, and that they may have plenty of fresh water, so that they may look well and be healthy because of the pumpkins and the beans and the corn. I want to see them healthy.... Yes, I have worked hard and prayed for all my people. I do not want any of the roots to rot. I do not want anyone to sicken and die, but I want everyone to stand firmly on his feet all year. This is how I have prayed for you."

. . .

The dances do not begin till midnight, for the ceremonies connected with the reception of the gods are affairs of tremendous length. The speech made by Sayatasha alone—which the actor has had to learn by heart—takes him six hours to deliver. I did not try to visit the house where this god was being entertained. The old lady from California who was suspected of sinister designs, had walked in and sat down in front, and immediately been asked to leave. The Agent himself with his wife had been moved on from there by an officious visiting Navaho. The whole atmosphere was quietly hostile. Elsewhere a discourteous visitor was invited "kindly" to remove his hat; and another, who was standing at the door, was ordered not to come in by a boy of about twelve, who fixed him with a hateful eye. When the visitor tried to explain that his intention had been merely to look on from there, the boy grimly told him, "Don't look!" I did not, therefore, go into the house, but simply peered through the misted windows—where some of the Indians had also gathered—casually walking away and then walking up again. One cannot in the least blame the Zunis for wanting to keep strangers out of these ceremonies, for they are services of the most solemn kind, comparable in dignity and devotion to any that I have ever seen.

Besides the six houses prepared for the reception and the dances of the Shalakos, there are supposed to be one for the Council of the Gods and one for another group, called the Koyemshi, or Old Dance Men; but just as two pairs of Shalakos had doubled up this year, so the Koyemshi and the Council have combined. As I gazed in through the panes at these latter, the Council were beyond my vision, but I got a good view of the Koyemshi. These are a group of ten clown-priests, familiarly known as the Mudheads, who play roles of the first importance, being threaded in and out of ceremonies which continue through the whole year. When the Zunis, according to their legend, were wandering in search of a home, they sent out a brother and sister on a prospecting expedition. But the boy raped the girl in her sleep, and she gave birth to a brood of nine idiots. These are the Mudheads, who stand as a warning of the danger of incestuous unions.

Largely naked and painted pink, they wear masks that are pink and bald and knobbed with enormous warts, and have imbecile round pop-eyes, gaping mouths like tadpoles or frogs, and fleshy topknots or catfish antennae. Each of these masks differs slightly from the others, and the roles of the Mudheads differ. One tries to repeat sacred rituals and always breaks down into gibberish; one is a coward, who hides under ladders and hangs back behind the rest; another is called the Bat and is supposed to be blind, so that he is always stumbling about and bumping into things; another believes himself invisible and hides his head like an ostrich; another can only laugh; another is glum, etc. When they are in character and wearing their masks, they pass in and out of the houses, performing all sorts of antics or—in infantile simpleton voices that seem to whimper and wheedle, to bubble and ooze from their masks—entertaining the spectators with ribald jokes that often probe into their private affairs. When the festival was announced by them eight days before, it was in such terms as these: "In eight days my people come. You must look around for nice girls and stay with them. . . . I come to tell you that in eight days everyone will be happy and have a good time. Men should trade wives." But they, too, are sacred beings, venerated as well as loved. During the year of their impersonation, the actors in the mythical dramas partly lose their own identities and become for the people of the pueblo the personages they represent. In the case of Sayatasha, the actor even loses his own name and is known by the name of the god. The affection and reverence felt for the mythical role that a man is playing is said sometimes to contrast sharply with the opinion his neighbors have had of him.

It is strange now to see these ten men (the incestuous Father makes the tenth), their masks pushed up on the tops of their heads, here dedicating themselves with prayer, after days of retreat and fasting, to the impish and ridiculous parts it is their duty to resume at midnight. Some of them are rather old, and have arms of skin-and-bone and aquiline Dantesque profiles. The audience sits on one side of the room, with a space between it and the celebrants. The Koyemshi, by themselves in a row, sit against the opposite wall; the man of the house sits facing them, flanked with five men of his own clan, the Dogwood, and four men of the Frog clan, his wife's, each drawn up so close to his vis-à-vis that their knees are almost touching. Long cigarettes made of reeds have been lighted from burning coals and are being passed back and forth between the Mudhead and the man who is receiving him, each taking six whiffs and waving the cigarette in the direction of the six Zuni points of the compass—North, South, East, West, Up, and Down. The Father recites a long speech like that of Sayatasha, while the others answer, "*Athlu*" (Amen). Says the Father of the Koyemshi to his hosts, "I leave my children with you for five days. They will dance in your houses; they will then go to the home of the gods in the East. . . . Give us food that we may eat, and next year we will bring you all kinds of seeds." They have little packets of seeds concealed under their black neckclothes, and the knobs on their heads are filled with seeds.

The young people came and went, looking in for a time through the windows or lingering on the porch. This part of the evening's ceremonies did not interest them much. A boy who had been in the war greeted two other boys with a "*Come sta, signori?*" and they showed off with Italian conversation. A boy and a girl had a moment of necking as they sat on the rail of the porch. He enveloped her plump round figure, dressed in poinsettia red, with a wing of his black blanket-cloak, and for a moment they rubbed their cheeks. Then he carried her off as she softly laughed, still with his cloak about her.

The monotonous chanting of the ritual went on without pause for hours: an unvarying repetition of six beats that ended in a kind of short wail.

The first Shalako house I visited, when, later, the dancing began, made upon me a tremendous impression. The rooms where the dances are held are dazzling with electric light and blazing with decorations. The walls are completely covered with brilliant blankets and shawls, pale buckskins, and queer blue or green hangings, made by the Navahos, on which square-headed elongated figures represent the Navaho gods. At one end of the room is a turquoise altar, ornamented with eagle feathers. A group of fetishistic animals, carved from stone, is set out in a row before it. In the audience, most of the men, having discarded their modern clothes, are wrapped in their best black blankets, and the women wear over their heads their best green or red or flowered shawls, and sometimes a kind of black apron, made of silk with fancy designs.

Against this background and before this audience, a Shalako and his alternate are dancing, balancing one another in a bizarre moving composition that seems to fill and charge the whole room. The unmasked dancer here is putting on such an extraordinary performance that he distracts attention from the bird. His costume has a suggestion of the Renaissance that may have been derived from the Spaniards. He wears a tight-fitting white buckskin cap with a curtain that hangs down behind, like the headwear of Giotto's Dante, and a fillet of red ribbon with silver bells. His black shirt is trimmed at the shoulders and sleeves with ribbons of many colors; his black kilts are embroidered in blue and circled with embroidered sashes. His knees are painted red, and the lower part of his legs is yellow, and he has tassels of blue yarn tied below the knees. With his brown bare feet he treads up and down—at a rate, as one observer has calculated, of about four times as many steps a minute as a marathon runner takes—in a quick, sharp, unflagging rhythm. This rhythm is also marked with a pointed yucca wand held before him in the right hand at an unwavering phallic angle. His eyelids are dropped, his eyes seem closed; the firm line of his mouth is drawn down—as if, in dedicating himself to his role, he has achieved a solemn sublimation and is shut off from the rest of the world. His whole demeanor is perfectly disciplined as he slowly moves thus back and forth from one end of the room to the other. And the Shalako, towering above him, actually seems lighter than he and dancing to an easier rhythm, as it turns in place or marks time or—astonishing in its swiftness and grace—swoops the length of the floor in a birdlike flight, never butting into the wall or ceiling and never so much as brushing the spectators, who sit close on either side.

These spectators rarely move, they are receptive, quiet, and calm; and the white visitor, too, becomes rapt. He, too, feels the thrill and the awe at the elemental power summoned. It seems as if the dancer by his pounding were really generating energy for the Zunis; by his discipline, strengthening their fortitude; by his endurance, guaranteeing their permanence. These people who sit here in silence, without ever applauding or commenting, are sustained and invigorated by watching this. It makes the high point of their year, at which the moral standard is set. If the Zunis can still perform the Shalako dances, keeping it up all night, with one or other of the performers always dancing and sometimes both dancing at once, they know that their honor and their stamina, their favor with the gods, are unimpaired. The whole complicated society of Zuni in some sense depends on this dance. Our ideas of energy and power have tended to become, in the modern world, identified with the natural forces—electricity, combustion, etc.—which we manipulate mechanically for our benefit, and it is startling to see human energy invoked and adored as a force that is at once conceived as a loan from the nonhuman natural forces and as a rival pitted against them; or rather, to put it in terms that are closer to the Zuni point of view, to see all the life of the animal world and the power of the natural elements made continuous with human vitality and endowed with semihuman form.

Here, too, one finds theater and worship before they have become dissociated, and the spectacle suggests comparisons in the fields of both religion and art. In the theatrical connection, it seems curious at first to be reminded of the Russian Ballet, but the reason soon becomes quite plain. It must have been true that Dyaghilev brought into the conventional ballet, with its formal routines and patterns, something that was genuinely primitive. He had really opened the way for an infusion of old Russia—by giving new life to the music of Rimsky and Borodin, who had already returned to folk material; through the Mongolian wildness of Nizhinsky; through the barbaric splendors of Bakst; through the atavistic stridencies and iterative beat of the Stravinsky of *Le Sacre du Printemps*. The kind of thing one sees in the Shalako dance must be something like the kind of thing that was revived by the Russian Ballet—not brought to the point of refinenent to which Dyaghilev was able to carry it, but, in its color and variety and style, in the thoroughness of the training involved and the scrupulous care for detail, a great deal more accomplished and calculated than one could easily conceive without seeing it. In the other, the religious, connection, one comes quite to understand the student of comparative religions quoted by Erna Fergusson, who said that it was "no wonder missionaries have had no luck in converting these people to Christianity. It will never be done. The essential mental rhythm of the two races is too far apart. You could imagine reducing that Shalako figure two feet or even four; you could not possibly turn it into Christ on the Cross." The difficulty, one sees, would be to induce the flourishing Zunis—who have maintained their community for centuries, as sound and as tough as a nut, by a religion that is also a festive art—to interest themselves in a religion that has its origin in poverty and anguish. The Zunis, moreover, have no sense of sin; they do not feel that they need to be pardoned. What the Shalako bird brings is not pardon, but good cheer and fecundity. It is formidable; the children hide from it the day it comes into town, and if anybody falls asleep, it leans over and wakes him by snapping its beak. But the great bird loves the people, and the people love the bird. They build a house for it and spread it a feast, and it dances before them all night to show them its satisfaction.

In each of the other two Shalako houses, two Shalakos were dancing together, occasionally assisted by Mudheads. At one place, where I looked through a window, I saw people holding a blanket while the Shalako sat down in a corner; and the alternate changed places with the weary man who had just been performing his role. In the house of Sayatasha, the Council of the Gods, with their masks off, were performing stately evolutions, accompanied by the adolescent Fire God, who—slim and handsome in his speckled nudity—danced with the dropped eyelids and resolute lips of the Shalako impersonator. But the great success of the evening was a Shalako who danced alone. It was marvelous what this dancer could do, as he balanced his huge bird-body. He would slowly pavane across the floor; he would pirouette and teeter; he would glide in one flight the whole length of the room as smoothly as a bird alighting. The masks are constructed like crinolines; there are hoops sewn inside a long cylinder that diminishes toward the top; and the whole thing hangs from a slender pole attached to the dancer's belt. So the movements are never stiff. The Shalakos, ungainly though they may seem at first when one watches them from afar by daylight, are created in the dance as live beings; and this one was animated from top to toe, vibrating as if with excitement—gleaming with its turquoise face, flashing its white embroidered skirt, while its foxskins flapped like wings at the shoulders. The dance conveyed both delicacy and ecstasy, and the music—produced by a small group of men who sat, as if in a huddle, facing one another, as they chanted, beat a drum and shook rattles—exercised a peculiar enchantment. There are many different songs for the dances, and they vary in mood and pace; but each consists of a single theme repeated over and over, with a rest after so many bars and occasional changes in tempo, which momentarily relieve the dancer. In this case, the recurrent lapses—during which the Shalako, poised for flight, marked time and snapped his beak at the end of his room-long runway—would be followed by brisk pickings-up, when the bird would skim across the floor; and this reprise always had about it an element of the miraculous, of the miracle of the inexhaustible energy, leaping up after every subsidence with the same self-assertive joy. Carried along by the rhythm yourself, alternately let down and lulled, then awakened and stimulated, in a sequence that never faltered, you were held by a kind of spell. The great blue-and-white creature irresistibly took on for you, too, an extra-human personality, became a thing you could not help watching, a principle of bounding and soaring life that you could not help venerating. A white woman who had once seen the dance told me that it had given her a shudder and thrill, in her chair at the end of the room, to feel the eaglelike bird swooping down on her. And I found that it was only with effort that I, too, could withstand its hypnotic effect. I had finally to take myself in hand in order to turn my attention and to direct myself out of the house. For something in me began to fight the Shalako, to reject and repulse its influence just at the moment when it was most compelling. One did not want to rejoin the Zunis in their primitive Nature cult; and it was hardly worth while for a Protestant to have stripped off the mummeries of Rome in order to fall a victim to an agile young man in a ten-foot mask.

Yet the effect of it lingered and haunted me even after I was back in my guest-house. Kept wakeful as I was with coffee, the monotonously repetitive music, and indefatigable glowing bird that had dominated the crowded room, drawn toward it all upward-turned eyes, suspended in a trance all wills, stayed with me and continued to trouble me. I was glad to find a letter in my room which recalled me to my own urban world and which annoyed me, when I read it, so much that I was distracted from the vision of the Shalako.

J. S. Slotkin
THE PEYOTE WAY

Peyote (a name derived from the Nahuatl word *peyotl*) was used in the ceremonies of Indians in central and northern Mexico in pre-Columbian times. The Huichol Indians living in the Sierra Madre mountains of western Mexico still make long pilgrimages on foot to collect peyote for their ceremonies each year (see Myerhoff, Chapter Three). From Mexico the custom of taking peyote spread to the United States Indians and by 1890 it had become an important form of religion among the Plains tribes. Today, as Slotkin points out, Peyote religion is the most widespread contemporary religion among the Indians of the United States. It is organized as the Native American Church and has become a kind of Indian version of Christianity, having adopted white Christian theology, ethics, and eschatology and modified these features to make them more compatible with traditional Indian culture.

The following selection provides a brief but illuminating description of "the Peyote Way," written by an anthropologist who was a member and officer of the Native American Church. In addition to the other technical reports published by Slotkin and mentioned in the selection, there is also a monograph by Weston LaBarre, *The Peyote Cult* (1938), and a popular book by Aldous Huxley, *Doors to Perception* (1954), which describes Huxley's experiences in taking mescaline, the same drug that is found in peyote. An excellent monograph of the contemporary American Indian Peyote Cult is David Aberle's *The Peyote Religion Among the Navaho* (1965), and a more recent study of an ancient peyote religion can be found in Barbara Myerhoff's book, *The Peyote Hunt: The Sacred Journey of the Huichol Indians* (1974).

Reprinted from *Tomorrow*, IV, No. 3 (1955–1956), 64–70, by permission of Garrett Publications.

Peyote (*Lophophora williamsi*) is a spineless cactus which grows in the northern half of Mexico and for a short distance north of the Texas border. It has attracted attention because it is used as a sacrament in religious rites conducted by Indians in the United States and Canada belonging to the Native American Church. The Peyote Religion or Peyote Way, as it is called by members, is the most widespread contemporary religion among the Indians, and is continually spreading to additional tribes.

From the viewpoint of almost all Peyotists, the religion is an Indian version of Christianity. White Christian theology, ethics, and eschatology have been adopted with modifications which make them more compatible with traditional Indian culture. The religion probably originated among the Kiowa and Comanche in Oklahoma about 1885.

The Peyote rite is an all-night ceremony, lasting approximately from sunset to sunrise, characteristically held in a Plains type tipi. Essentially the rite has four major elements; prayer, singing, eating the sacramental Peyote, and contemplation. The ritual is well defined, being divided into four periods; from sunset to midnight, from midnight to three o'clock, from three o'clock to dawn, and from dawn to morning. Four fixed songs sung by the rite leader, analogous to the fixed songs in the Catholic Mass, mark most of these divisions.

The rite within the tipi begins with the Starting Song; the midnight period is marked by the Midnight Water Song; there is no special song at three o'clock; at dawn there is the Morning Water Song, and the rite ends with the Quitting Song. At midnight sacred water is drunk again and a communion meal eaten.

Usually five people officiate at the rite. Four are men: the leader, often referred to as the Roadman because he leads the group along the Peyote Road (that is, the Peyotist way of life) to salvation; the drum chief who accompanies the leader when he sings; the cedar chief who is in charge of the cedar incense; and the fire chief who maintains a ritual fire and acts as sergeant-at-arms. A close female relative of the leader, usually his wife, brings in, and prays over, the morning water.

In clockwise rotation, starting with the leader, each male participant sings a set of four solo songs; he is accompanied on a water drum by the man to his right. The singing continues from the time of the Starting Song to that of the Morning Water Song; the number of rounds of singing therefore depends upon the number of men present. On most occasions there are four rounds, so that each man sings a total of sixteen songs.

During the rite Peyote is taken in one of the following forms: the fresh whole plant except for roots (green Peyote), the dried top of the plant (Peyote button), or an infusion of the Peyote button in water (Peyote tea). Some people have no difficulty taking Peyote. But many find it bitter, inducing indigestion or nausea. A common complaint is, "It's hard to take Peyote."

The amount taken depends upon the individual, and the solemnity of the ritual occasion. There is great tribal variability in amount used, and accurate figures are virtually impossible to obtain. But in general one might say that under ordinary circumstances the bulk of the people take less than a dozen Peyotes. On the most serious occasions, such as rites held for someone mortally sick, those present take as much Peyote as they can; the capacity of most people seems to range from about four to forty Peyote buttons.

Peyotists have been organized into the Native American Church since 1918. These church groups run the gamut of comprehensiveness from the single local group on the one extreme, to the intertribal and international federation known as the Native American Church of North America, on the other extreme.

In a series of other publications I have discussed the early history of Peyotism ("Peyotism, 1521–1891," *American Anthropologist*, LVII [1955], pp. 202–230), presented an historical and generalized account of the religion (in a book to be published in 1956[1]), and given a detailed description of the Peyote Religion in a single tribe ("Menomini Peyotism," *Transactions of the American Philosophical Society*, XLII [1952], Part 4)—all from the viewpoint of a relatively detached anthropologist. The present essay is different. Here I concentrate on the contemporary uses of, and attitudes toward, sacramental Peyote, and write as a member and officer of the Native American Church of North America. Of course the presentation is mine, but I think susbstantially it represents the consensus of our membership.

Long ago God took pity on the Indian. (Opinions vary as to when this happened: when plants were created at the origin of the world, when Jesus lived, or after the white man had successfully invaded this continent.) So God created Peyote and put some of his power into it for the use of Indians. Therefore the Peyotist takes the sacramental Peyote to absorb God's power contained in it, in the same way that the white Christian takes the sacramental bread and wine.

Power is the English term used by Indians for the supernatural force called *mana* by anthropologists; it is equivalent to the New Testament *pneuma*, translated as Holy Spirit or Holy Ghost. Power is needed to live. As a Crow Indian once remarked to me as we were strolling near a highway, man is like an auto; if the car loses its power it cannot go. Physically, power makes a person healthy, and safe when confronted by danger. Spiritually, power gives a person knowledge of how to behave successfully in everyday life, and what to make of one's life as a whole. The Peyotist obtains power from the sacramental Peyote.

Physically, Peyote is used as a divine healer and amulet.

For sick people Peyote is used in various ways. In a mild illness Peyote is taken as a home remedy. Thus when a man has a cold, he drinks hot Peyote tea and goes to bed. In more serious illnesses Peyote is taken during the Peyote rite. Such an illness is due not only to lack of sufficient power, but also to a foreign object within the body. Therefore a seriously sick person who takes Peyote usually vomits, thus expelling the foreign object which is the precipitating cause of the illness; then more Peyote is taken in order to obtain the amount of power needed for health.

In cases of severe illness, the rite itself is held for the purpose of healing the patient; it is often referred to as a doctoring meeting. In addition to having the sick person take Peyote, as in less desperate cases, everyone else present prays to God to give the patient extra power so he or she will recover.

Members may keep a Peyote button at home, or on their person, to protect them from danger. The latter is particularly true of men in the armed forces. The power within the Peyote wards off harm from anything in the area of its influence. In cases of great danger, as when a young man is about to leave for military service, a prayer meeting is held at which everyone present beseeches God to give the man extra power to avoid harm.

Spiritually, Peyote is used to obtain knowledge. This is known as learning from Peyote. Used properly, Peyote is an inexhaustible teacher. A stock statement is, "You can use Peyote all your life, but you'll never get to the end of what there is to be known from Peyote. Peyote is always teaching you something new." Many Peyotists say that the educated white man obtains his knowledge from books—particularly the Bible; while the uneducated Indian has to obtain his knowledge from Peyote. But the Indian's means of achieving knowledge is superior to that of the white man. The latter learns from books

[1] Ed. note: *The Peyote Religion: A Study in Indian-White Relations* (Glencoe, Ill.: The Free Press, 1956).

merely what other people have to say; the former learns from Peyote by direct experience.

A Comanche once said, "The white man talks *about* Jesus; we talk *to* Jesus." Thus the individual has a vividly direct experience of what he learns, qualitatively different from inference or hearsay. Therefore the Peyotist, epistemologically speaking, is an individualist and empiricist; he believes only what he himself has experienced.

A Peyotist maxim is, "The only way to find out about Peyote is to take it and learn from Peyote yourself." It may be interesting to know what others have to say; but all that really matters is what one has directly experienced—what he has learned himself from Peyote. This conception of salvation by knowledge, to be achieved by revelation (in this case, through Peyote) rather than through verbal or written learning, is a doctrine similar to that of early Middle Eastern Gnosticism.

The mere act of eating Peyote does not itself bring knowledge. The proper ritual behavior has to be observed before one is granted knowledge through Peyote. Physically, one must be clean, having bathed and put on clean clothes. Spiritually, one must put away all evil thought. Psychologically, one must be conscious of his personal inadequacy, humble, sincere in wanting to obtain the benefits of Peyote, and concentrate on it.

Peyote teaches in a variety of ways.

One common way in which Peyote teaches is by heightening the sensibility of the Peyotist, either in reference to himself or to others.

Heightened sensibility to oneself manifests itself as increased powers of introspection. One aspect of introspection is very important in Peyotism. During the rite a good deal of time is spent in self-evaluation. Finally the individual engages in silent or vocal prayer to God, confessing his sins, repenting, and promising to follow the Peyote Road (that is, the Peyotist ethic) more carefully in the future. If he has spiritual evil within him, Peyote makes him vomit, thus purging him of sin.

Heightened sensibility to others manifests itself as what might be called mental telepathy. One either feels that he knows what others are thinking, or feels that he either influences, or is influenced by, the thoughts of others. In this connection a frequent phenomenon is speaking in tongues, which results from the fact that people from different tribes participate in a rite together, each using his own language; Peyote teaches one the meaning of otherwise unknown languages.

For example, during the rite each male participant in succession sings solo four songs at a time. Recently a Winnebago sitting next to me sang a song with what I heard as a Fox text (Fox is an Algonquian language closely related to Menomini, the language I use in the rite), sung so clearly and distinctly I understood every word.

When he was through, I leaned over and asked, "How come you sang that song in Fox rather than Winnebago (a Siouan language unintelligible to me)?"

"I did sing it in Winnebago," he replied. The afternoon following the rite he sat down next to me and asked me to listen while he repeated the song; this time it was completely unintelligible to me because the effects of Peyote had worn off.

A second common way in which Peyote teaches is by means of revelation, called a vision. The vision is obtained because one has eaten enough Peyote under the proper ritual conditions to obtain the power needed to commune with the spirit world. The vision provides a direct experience (visual, auditory, or a combination of both) of God or some intermediary spirit, such as Jesus, Peyote Spirit (the personification of Peyote), or Waterbird.

The nature of the vision depends upon the personality and problems of the individual. The following are typical: He may be comforted by seeing or hearing some previously unexperienced item of Peyotist belief, or departed loved ones now in a happy existence. He may be guided on the one hand by being shown the way to solve some problem in daily life; on the other hand, he may be reproved for evil thoughts or deeds, and warned to repent.

A third way in which Peyote teaches is by means of mystical experience. This is relatively uncommon. It is limited to Peyotists of a certain personality type among the more knowledgeable members of the church; roughly speaking, they have what white people would call a mystical temperament. These Peyotists, in turn, rarely have visions, and tend to look upon them as distractions. The mystical experience may be said to consist in the harmony of all immediate experience with whatever the individual conceives to be the highest good.

Peyote has the remarkable property of helping one to have a mystical experience for an indefinite period of time, as opposed to most forms of mystical discipline under which the mystical experience commonly lasts for a matter of minutes. Actually I have no idea of how long I could maintain such an experience with Peyote, for after about an hour or so it is invariably interrupted by some ritual detail I am required to perform.

What happens to the Peyotist phenomenologically that makes possible the extraordinary results I have described? It seems to depend on both the physiological and psychological effects of Peyote.

Physiologically, Peyote seems to have curative properties. Many times, after a variety of illnesses brought about by fieldwork conditions, I have left a Peyote meeting permanently well again.

Another physiological effect of Peyote is that it reduces the fatigue to an astonishing extent. For instance, I am not robust, but after taking Peyote I can participate in the rite with virtually no fatigue—a rite which requires me to sit on the ground, crosslegged, with no back rest, and without moving, for 10 to 14 hours at a stretch; all this in the absence of food and water.

Psychologically, Peyote increases one's sensitivity to relevant stimuli. This applies to both external and internal stimuli. Externally, for example, the ritual fire has more intense colors when I am under the influence of Peyote. Internally, I find it easier to introspect upon otherwise vague immediate experiences.

At the same time, Peyote decreases one's sensitivity to irrelevant external and internal stimuli. Very little concentration is needed for me to ignore distracting noises inside or outside the tipi. Similarly, extraneous internal sensations or ideas are easily ignored.

Thus, on one occasion I wrote in my field diary, "I could notice no internal sensations. If I paid very close attention, I could observe a vague and faint feeling that suggested that without Peyote my back would be sore from sitting up in one position all night; the same was true of my crossed legs. Also my mouth might be dry, but I couldn't be sure."

The combination of such effects as absence of fatigue, heightened sensitivity to relevant stimuli, and lowered sensitivity to irrelevant stimuli, should make it easier to understand how the individual is disposed to learn from Peyote under especially created ritual conditions. To any reader who becomes intrigued by Peyote, two warnings should be given. First, I have discussed the effects of Peyote on those who used it as a sacrament under ritual conditions. The described responses of white people to Peyote under experimental conditions are quite different; in fact, they tend to be psychologically traumatic. Second, Peyote is a sacrament in the Native American Church, which refuses to permit the presence of curiosity seekers at its rites, and vigorously opposes the sale or use of Peyote for nonsacramental purposes.

SIX
THE PURPOSES OF SHAMANISM

Introduction

In the comparative analysis of religious organization one of the useful analytical distinctions has been the contrast between the "shaman" and the "priest." These two polar types of ceremonial practitioners are found in all parts of the world, and the difference between their religious roles provides a significant index of contrasts between different types of religious systems.

A "shaman" is a ceremonial practitioner whose powers come from direct contact with the supernatural, by divine stroke, rather than from inheritance or memorized ritual; a "priest" is a ceremonial practitioner who often inherits his position and who learns a body of codified and standardized ritual knowledge from older priests and later transmits it to successors. Shamanism is more usually found in the loosely structured food-gathering cultures, where the more common ceremonial is a curing rite performed for one or more patients within the context of an extended family group. The ceremonial takes place on a noncalendrical basis, usually when a person falls ill and needs the ritual. The priest, and especially the organization of priests into elaborate sets of priesthoods, is characteristically found in tightly structured and relatively elaborate food-producing—usually agricultural—societies, where the more common ceremonial is a public rite performed for the benefit of a whole village or community. The ceremony typically takes place on a calendrical basis at the proper time within the annual ceremonial calendar. Many societies, of course, have both shamans and priests, as, for example, in Navaho society where the hand-tremblers who diagnose illness are technically shamans, in the sense that they derive their power directly from a supernatural source, while the singers who perform the curing ceremonies are technically priests, in the sense that they have learned standardized ritual by apprenticing themselves to an older singer. But our evidence suggests that the presence of these singers has been a relatively recent development in Navaho history, a pattern which the Navahos borrowed from contact with the Southwestern Pueblos. Earlier in their history all Navaho ceremonial practitioners were probably of the shamanistic type. Among the neighboring Apache tribes the practitioners are still more shamanistic in type, as indicated in the Opler article in Chapter Eight.

Another way of looking at the difference between shamans and priests is in terms of communication between supernaturals and men. Shamans are essentially mediums, for they are the mouthpieces of spirit beings. Priests are intermediaries between people and the spirits to whom they wish to address themselves. This is what Evans-Pritchard has in mind when, writing about the priests and prophets (shamans) of the Nuer of the Sudan, he says: "Whereas in the priest man speaks to God, in the prophet . . . God speaks to man."

The outstanding area for the study of shamanism has been Siberia—in fact, the very word comes from the Tungus word "shaman"—and northern and western North America. The selections from Bogoras and Rasmussen provide excellent descriptive accounts of shamanistic performances among the Chukchee and Eskimo. But the phenomenon is by no means restricted to this area, as will be apparent in the other articles in this chapter.

In this fourth edition of the *Reader* we have chosen to focus upon the "shaman" rather than the "priest" as a ceremonial practitioner. The behavior of priests and the organization of priesthoods are touched upon in many selections, especially in the pieces by Edmund Wilson, Ruth Bunzel, Renato Rosaldo, and others. But it appears to us that there are perhaps more intriguing problems still unsolved in the questions of recruitment, roles, performances, and defining characteristics of the shamans of the world. Our selections begin with the classic descriptions of shamanistic performances provided by Bogoras and Rasmussen. We then offer a provocative theoretical article by Rodney Needham on the possible relationship between percussion and transition in shamanistic and other types of rituals in the world. The selection from Lévi-Strauss is a fine example of how a shamanistic cure among the Cuna Indians of Panama closely parallels the procedures used in contemporary psychoanalysis. The final selection by Richard A. Shweder is a pioneering attempt to utilize experimental procedures to show how the cognitive capacities of shamans are definitively different from those of nonshamans in the Maya Indian society of Zinacantan in Southern Mexico. Students interested in pursuing this subject further might consult I. M. Lewis's book, *Ecstatic Religion: An Anthropological Study of Spirit Possession and Shamanism* (1971).

Waldemar Bogoras

SHAMANISTIC PERFORMANCE IN THE INNER ROOM

The anthropological literature reveals few phenomena more interesting, and none more dramatic, than the shamanistic performance. In the following selection Bogoras calls upon his intimate knowledge of the nomadic, reindeer-herding Chukchee of Siberia to provide a description of the shaman in action. He reveals the consummate artistry of the shaman without becoming so enamored of the shaman's skill as to be unable to view his performance objectively. The Chukchee shaman employs superb verbal and manual skills—ventriloquism, singing, beating the omnipresent drum, sleight of hand—to capture his audience in a semi-trance state.

Although Bogoras discusses the procedural techniques of the shaman and at times tends to portray him as a ventriloquist and conjurer, it must be remembered that the Chukchee do not visit a shaman with a critical analysis of his technique in mind. They cannot suspect him of fraud or wither him with ruthless logic, for if he is a fraud then so are they, and if he is open to logical criticism then so are they, since they both share the same logical premises. It should be clear then that the Chukchee cannot afford the luxury of skepticism, for they need the shaman and his wonderful powers. When the shaman becomes hysterical in his

Reprinted from Waldemar Bogoras, *The Chukchee*, Vol. VII of Franz Boas (ed.), *The Jesup North Pacific Expedition* ("Memoirs of the American Museum of Natural History," Vol. XI, Parts 2 and 3 [Leiden: E. J. Brill, 1904–1909]), pp. 433–441, by permission of the American Museum of Natural History.

spirit possession, the audience knows this as a sign that they will soon hear the voices of powerful spirits able to divine their vital problems. When the shaman transports himself to the spirit world to divine or cure, the audience does not look for tricks; they anxiously and respectfully await answers.

The typical shamanistic performance is carried out in the following manner. After the evening meal is finished and the kettles and trays are removed to the outer tent, all the people who wish to be present at the séance enter the inner room, which is carefully closed for the night. Among the Reindeer Chukchee, the inner room is especially small, and its narrow space causes much inconvenience to the audience, which is packed together in a tight and most uncomfortable manner. The Maritime Chukchee have more room, and may listen to the voices of the spirits with more ease and freedom. The shaman sits on the "master's place," near the back wall; and even in the most limited sleeping-room, some free space must be left around him. The drum is carefully looked over, its head tightened, and, if it is much shrunken, it is moistened with urine and hung up for a short time over the lamp to dry. The shaman sometimes occupies more than an hour in this process, before he is satisfied with the drum. To have more freedom in his movements, the shaman usually takes off his fur shirt, and remains quite naked down to the waist. He often removes also his shoes and stockings, which of course gives free play to his feet and toes.

In olden times, shamans used no stimulants; but at present they often smoke a pipeful of strong tobacco without admixture of wood, which certainly works like a strong narcotic. This habit is copied from the Tungus shamans, who make great use of unmixed tobacco as a powerful stimulant.

At last the light is put out and the shaman begins to operate. He beats the drum and sings his introductory tunes, at first in a low voice; then gradually his voice increases in volume, and soon it fills the small closed-up room with its violent clamor. The narrow walls resound in all directions.

Moreover, the shaman uses his drum for modifying his voice, now placing it directly before his mouth, now turning it at an oblique angle, and all the time beating it violently. After a few minutes, all this noise begins to work strangely on the listeners, who are crouching down, squeezed together in a most uncomfortable position. They begin to lose the power to locate the source of the sounds; and, almost without any effort of imagination, the song and the drum seem to shift from corner to corner, or even to move about without having any definite place at all.

The shaman's songs have no words. Their music is mostly simple, and consists of one short phrase repeated again and again. After repeating it many times, the shaman breaks off, and utters a series of long-drawn, hysterical sighs, which sound something like "Ah, ya, ka, ya, ka, ya, ka!" After that, he comes back to his songs. For this he draws his breath as deep as possible in order to have more air in his lungs, and to make the first note the longest.

Some of the tunes, however, are more varied, and are not devoid of a certain grace. Not a few are improvised by the shaman on the spot; others are repeated from séance to séance. Each shaman has several songs of his own, which are well known to the people; so that if anybody uses one of them, for instance at a ceremonial, the listeners recognize it immediately, and say that such and such a man is using the particular song of such and such a shaman.

There is no definite order for the succession of the songs, and the shaman changes them at will, sometimes even returning to the first one after a considerable interval has elapsed. This introductory singing lasts from a quarter of an hour to half an hour or more, after which the ke'let make their first appearance.

The shaman sings all alone, and the auditors take no part in the performance. From time to time, however, some one of the listeners will cry out, "Hık, hık!" or Hıč, hıč!" (interjection of wonder) or "Qai'vo" ("of course") or Emño'lık" ("certainly")—all of which are meant to express the full approbation by those present of the doings of the shaman. The Chukchee have a special word for these exclamations, "o'cıtkΘk" ("to give answering calls"). Without an očitkΘ'lin (participle), a Chukchee shaman considers himself unable to perform his calling in a proper way; therefore novices, while trying to learn the shamanistic practices, usually induce a brother or a sister to respond, thus encouraging the zeal of the performer. Some shamans also require those people who claim their advice or treatment to give them answering calls during the particular part of the performance which refers to their affairs. The storytellers of the Chukchee also usually claim the assistance of their listeners, who must call out the same exclamations.

Among the Asiatic Eskimo, the wife and other members of the family form a kind of chorus, which from time to time catches up the tune and sings with the shaman. Among the Russianized Yukaghir of the lower Kolyma the wife is also the assistant of her shaman husband, and during the performance she gives him encouraging answers, and he addresses her as his "supporting staff."

In most cases the ke'let begin by entering the body of the shaman. This is marked with some change in his manner of beating the drum, which becomes faster and more violent; but the chief mark is a series of new sounds, supposed to be peculiar to the ke'let. The shaman shakes his head violently, producing with his lips a peculiar chattering noise, not unlike a man who is shivering with cold. He shouts hysterically, and in a changed voice utters strange, prolonged shrieks, such at "O to, to, to, to," or "I pi, pi, pi, pi"—all of which are supposed to characterize the voice of the ke'let. He often imitates the cries of various animals and birds which are supposed to be his particular assistants. If the shaman is only a "single-bodied" one—that is, has no ventriloquistic power—the ke'let will proceed to sing and beat the drum by means of his body. The only difference will be in the timbre of the voice, which will sound harsh and unnatural, as becomes supernatural beings.

With other shamans the ke'let appear all at once as the "separate voices." They manifest themselves with sounds and shrieks of the same harsh and unnatural character, and these are located outside the body of the shaman. After that a varied exhibition begins, in which the performance of the shaman far transcends anything attainable by a person of ordinary powers.

The Chukchee ventriloquists display great skill, and could with credit to themselves carry on a contest with the best artists of the kind of civilized countries. The "separate voices" of their calling come from all sides of the room, changing their place to the complete illusion of their listeners. Some voices are at first faint, as if coming from afar; as they gradually approach, they increase in volume, and at last they rush into the room, pass through it and out, decreasing, and dying away in the remote distance. Other voices come from above, pass through the room and seem to go underground, where they are heard as if from the depths of the earth. Tricks of this kind are played also with the voices of animals and birds, and even with the howling of the tempest, producing a most weird effect.

I heard a voice which professed to be an echo. It repeated faithfully all sounds and cries which we chose to produce in its presence, including phrases in English or Russian. The foreign words were, of course, slightly mispronounced, still the reproduction proved the "spirit" to be possessed of a fine ear, catching quickly the sounds of an unknown language. The only way in which the "spirit" could imitate the clapping of our hands (another test to which we put him) was by clacking his tongue, which caused much mirth even among the native listeners. I heard also the "spirits" of a grasshopper, horsefly, and mosquito, who imitated exceedingly well the sounds produced by the real insects.

In proof of his accuracy as to the location of the sounds, the shaman Qora'wge, previously spoken of, made one of his "spirits" shout, talk, and whisper directly into my ear, and the illusion was so perfect that involuntarily I put my hand to my ear to catch the "spirit." After that he made the "spirit" enter the ground under me and talk right in between my legs, etc. All the time that he is conversing with the "separate voices," the shaman beats his drum without interruption in order to prove that his force and attention are otherwise occupied.

I tried to make a phonographic record of the "separate voices" of the "spirits." For this purpose I induced the shaman Scratching-Woman to give a séance in my own house, overcoming his reluctance with a few extra presents. The performance, of course, had to be carried out in utter darkness: and I arranged my machine so as to be able to work it without any light. Scratching-Woman sat in the farthest corner of the spacious room, at a distance of twenty feet from me. When the light was put out, the "spirits," after some "bashful" hesitation, entered, in compliance with the demand of the shaman, and even began to talk into the funnel of the graphophone. The records show a very marked difference between the voice of the shaman himself, which sounds from afar, and the voices of the "spirits," who seemed to be talking directly into the funnel.

All the while, Scratching-Woman was beating the drum incessantly to show that he was in his usual place, and occupied with his usual function, that of beating the drum without interruption. He brought some of the entering "spirits" to my special notice. One was a fawn of a wild reindeer, found by him in the wilderness beside the carcass of its mother, which had been killed by a wolf. The fawn, when he found it, was trying to suck the carcass. The strange sight had evidently struck Scratching-Woman, and he took the fawn for one of his assisting ke'let. The "spirit" manifested his presence by characteristic short snorts, peculiar to the fawn when calling for its mother. Another "spirit" entered with a dismal howl. This was the wolf who killed the reindeer dam.

Scratching-Woman explained that when he desired to wreak his vengeance on some one of his foes, he transformed himself into this wolf, taking care beforehand to turn the other party into a reindeer. Then, of course, he was quite certain of victory. The idea that shamans, in case of need, not only may send their "spirits" to a destined place, but also may turn themselves into any of their "spirits," and carry out their intentions, appears in many tales.

For instance, in the tale of the Shaman with Warts (Kuku'lpin), this shaman, during a shamanistic contest, asks his adversary, "Which ke'lE are you going to employ?" The other answers, "The small black hawk." — "And you?"—"The great diver." Then they turn into these birds, and the contest begins.

Those episodes of the tales in which men in distress have recourse to their animal amulets—either reviving them and bidding them fight their enemies, or transforming themselves into their living likenesses—are evidently quite analogous.

Still another of the ke'let introduced by Scratching-Woman was a raven who cawed lustily. The shaman used him when working with magic medicine, because the raven could devour all germs of sickness and disease. Still another was a little mouse, who could travel very fast underground, and was employed on errands requiring haste.

There followed the leather bucket, which forms a part of a "bonebreaking set," and is used as a receptacle for pounded bones. Once when Scratching-Woman was hunting wild reindeer, he succeeded in wounding a strong buck in the right foreleg, but still he could not overtake it. Then he called for the Skin Bucket, bade it overtake the buck and entrap its head. After that the reindeer was easily caught.

After having entered the room and produced a few sounds, by way of making his presence known, the "spirit" usually offers to "try his breath," that is, he beats the drum for a while, singing a tune in the special harsh voice peculiar to the "spirits." This, however, lasts only a short time, after which the "spirit" declares that his breath is ebbing away. Then he either begins to talk, or straightaway takes his departure with characteristic quivering sounds somewhat similar to the buzzing of a fly. These sounds are called by the Chukchee "gibbering" (moomga'tırgın), and are always associated with the "spirits." The same name is applied to the chattering alluded to before.

Often the shaman declares to the "spirit" first entering, that the sound of his drum is bad, or even that the cover of it is broken, and this is corroborated by a few dull strokes. The "spirit" must then mend the drum by breathing upon it, which he does accordingly. This treatment is resorted to especially in cases of magic medicine. After the drum is mended, the shaman explains to the patient that it is a good sign. He says also, that if the "spirit" were not able to mend the drum, it would forebode a bad turn in the disease.

I must again repeat that the animal "spirits" produce their own characteristic sounds. The walrus and the bear roar, the reindeer snorts, the wolf howls, the fox bays, the raven caws. The last three, however, are able to talk but use a particular timbre of voice, and intersperse among their words, from time to time, their peculiar cries.

In most cases the ventriloquistic performance soon takes on a dramatic character. A number of "spirits" appear in succession. They talk to the shaman and to one another, pick quarrels, abuse and denounce one another. It is superfluous to add that only one voice may talk at a time, so that even the most lively dialogue consists of a series of interpolations following each other in succession. The talk of the "spirits" is often carried on in strange, quite unintelligible words, such as "papire kuri muri," etc. To make it understood, the shaman has to call for an interpreter, who from that time on takes part in all conversations, and also explains to the auditors the words of the other "spirits." Thus the shaman is supposed to be unable to understand the language of the "separate spirits."

The same idea obtains among other neighboring tribes. The most curious case of all is that of the shamans of the Russians and the Russianized natives of the Kolyma and the Anadyr, who know no other language than the Russian. The "spirits," however, even when speaking through the mouth of the shaman, employ only the usual unintelligible gibberish mixed with some distorted and mispronounced phrases in the Koryak, Yakut, and Yukaghir languages. After a while the shaman calls for an interpreter, and at last, after some controversy, the spirits send for one who can speak Russian and who translates the orders of the "spirits."

The Chukchee shamans have no special language of their own, with the exception of a few words and expressions. Thus the drum is called "a'ᵋtwet" ("canoe"), which is an additional proof of the preponderance of maritime pursuits in the former life of the people. The idea of shamanistic ecstasy is expressed by the word "an·ña'arkın" ("he sinks"), which refers to the belief that the shaman, during the period of ecstasy, is able to visit other worlds, and especially that underground.

Among the northwestern branch of the Koryak, the "spirits" are said to use a special mode of pronunciation, similar to that used by the southeastern Koryak and the Chukchee. A few words are also said to be peculiar to them. Among the Asiatic Eskimo the "spirits" are said to have a special language. Many words of it were given to me by the shamans, and most of them are analogous to the "spirit" language known to various Eskimo tribes of America, both in Alaska and on the Atlantic side.

Tricks of various kinds break up the monotony of the performance, which may last for several hours. The "spirits" will scratch from the outside at the walls of the sleeping-room, running around it in all directions, so that the clattering of their feet is quite audible. In contrast to this, the motion of the ke'let inside of the room produces but slight noise. The rustling of their flight is similar to the buzzing of a mosquito, and the rattling of their tiny feet as they run over the surface of the drum is hardly perceptible.

Often, however, a mischievous "spirit" suddenly tugs at the skin spread in the center of the room with such force that things lying on it fly about in all directions. Therefore the housemates of the shaman usually take the precaution to remove kettles and dishes from the room. Sometimes an invisible hand seizes the whole sleeping-room by its top, and shakes it with wonderful strength, or even lifts it up high, letting in for a moment the twilight from the outer tent. This, of course, is possible only with the movable tent of the Reindeer people, where the sleeping-room is fastened none too firmly. Other invisible hands toss about lumps of snow, spill cold water and urine, and even throw blocks of wood, or stones, at the imminent risk of hurting some of the listeners.

All these things happened several times in my presence. The "spirits" would ask me, through the shamans, whether I really felt afraid; and, when I did not give a satisfactory answer, the "spirits" would try to increase my respect for them by such material manifestations. I must mention that the audience is strictly forbidden to make any attempts whatever to touch the "spirits." These latter highly resent any intrusion of this kind, and retaliate either on the shaman, whom they may kill on the spot, or on the trespassing listener, who runs the risk of having his head broken, or even a knife thrust through his ribs in the dark. I received warnings of this kind at almost every shamanistic performance. In some cases the shaman would lay a bare knife within his own reach as an additional warning against any infringement.

The size of the sleeping room is so small that it is really wonderful how a shaman can keep up the illusion even under cover of the dark and with the protection of his resentful "spirits." Many times I sat so near the performer that I could almost touch him with my outstretched hand, and the warning against too great inquisitiveness on my part was of course quite necessary.

All these tricks strangely resemble the doing of modern spiritualists, and without doubt they cannot be carried out without the help of human assistants.

The second part of the shamanistic performance is of a magical character. To give a clearer idea of it, I will describe a few instances.

The shaman Tilu'wgi, of whom I shall speak again, after some preliminary intercourse with the "spirits," called a peculiar ke'lE of his, who said she was an old maid, living alone in her house, and she expressed apprehension lest we should laugh at her talk with the peculiar feminine pronunciation. After that, however, she proceeded to give the magic instructions and explanations.

She told one of those present Enmu'wgi by name, who had recently been vanquished in a wrestling-match, that his defeat was caused by the use of malignant incantations by his adversary, and she advised him to take the matter into his own hands.

This female "spirit" reproached one of my fellow travelers, a great hunter, with ill-treating those "walking afoot," which is the usual periphrasis for the bears. When he tried to defend himself, the female "spirit" reminded him of a hunting expedition, in

which he took part about two months before, which was directed against a bear sleeping in its den. From the old Chukchee point of view, this certainly was a rather dangerous pursuit. In the end the "spirit" said that the man in question, because of his offenses against those "walking afoot," was in danger of losing his powers of endurance in walking. To his question as to the means of warding off the danger, the female "spirit" said that he must procure for himself the skin of the nose of a newly killed bear, and perform a thanksgiving ceremonial over it. That, probably, would appease those "walking afoot."

Afterward she told another listener that she saw that in the last autumn he had killed a wild reindeer buck. Though this happened far away from his herd, he should have made a sacrifice to the buck, which he omitted to do; therefore the following winter he was visited by bad luck, in that the wolves attacked his herd, and killed nine fat bucks. To check the recurrence of such a misfortune, it is necessary to take a small crotch of willow cut on the place of the attack by wolves, and perform over it the required ceremonial.

Galmu′urgin, the soothsaying shaman already spoken of, who gave a prescription at the very beginning of the séance predicted in my presence to the master of the tent that the next fall many reindeer would come to his house. "One buck will stop on the right side of the entrance, and pluck at the grass, attracted by a certain doe of dark-gray hair. This attraction must be strengthened with a special incantation. The reindeer buck, while standing there, must be killed with a bow, and the arrow to be used must have a flat rhomboid point, This will secure the successful killing of all the other wild reindeer."

After that the shaman recollected himself for a while, and addressed the brother of the master, who, with one companion, lived in a separate camp. This companion was married to one of his relatives. The shaman said that, before the fall, they would part company, nor would they look at each other with clear eyes; and, by the way, his prediction was fulfilled much earlier than the time designated.

To still another of the listeners he said that he feared lest the "bad things" might conceive a desire to approach his house. By this he meant the "spirits of disease." In order to thwart their intentions, the man was told to go through some special preventive ceremonies during the celebration of the ceremonial of the antlers, which was then at hand. The ceremonies consisted in drawing several lines across the snow near the tent, and putting some small stones before the entrance. These were supposed to transform themselves into a large river, and high, inaccessible cliffs, on the route of the "bad beings."

In this way the usual shamanistic performance is carried on in the inner room, and with the light put out.

In other cases the shaman actually "sinks"; that is, after some most violent singing, and beating of the drum, he falls into a kind of trance, during which his body lies on the ground unconscious, while his soul visits "spirits" in their own world, and asks them for advice. Chukchee folklore is full of episodes referring to such shamanistic trances; but in real life they happen very rarely, especially in modern times, when shamans are so much less skillful than of old. Even the word "an·ña′arkın" ("to sink"), from the explanation of modern shamans, has reference simply to the immersion of the performer into the depths of shamanistic ecstasy without its literal fulfillment.

In folk stories the shamans sink into the other worlds chiefly for the purpose of finding one of the missing souls of a patient who claims their power for his treatment. In important cases, even at the present day, the shamans, when treating a well-to-do patient, will at least pretend to have sunk into the required unconsciousness. On one or two occasions I had an opportunity of witnessing such a state, but the whole performance was of a rather poor kind.

It began, as usual, in the dark; but when the shaman suddenly broke off beating the drum, the lamp was again lighted and the face of the shaman immediately covered with a piece of cloth. The mistress of the house, who was the wife of the shaman, took up the drum and began to beat it with light, slow strokes. This lasted the entire time that the shaman lay under the cloth, or about a quarter of an hour. Then he suddenly awoke, and, removing the cloth from his face, sat up in his place, took the drum from his wife, beat it for a while, and sang a few tunes as in the beginning. After that he began to give the patient magical advice regarding his illness, which, however, was nothing else than an elaborate incantation in dramatized form.

Knud Rasmussen

A SHAMAN'S JOURNEY TO THE SEA SPIRIT

Shamans ordinarily deal with spirits by acting as their mouthpieces while in a state of possession; this article illustrates a less usual procedure in which the shaman's soul dissociates itself from his body and travels to the spirit world.

In this moving account, Knud Rasmussen, one of the great authorities on the Eskimo, describes one of the principal rituals of an Eskimo shaman—to make a journey to the bottom of the sea to propitiate the Spirit of the Sea (often called "Sedna" or "Sea Goddess" in other monographs on the Eskimo). The Eskimos believe that this goddess controls the sea mammals, whence come the most important food, fuel, and skins for clothing, and sends nearly all the worst misfortunes to the Eskimo people. These misfortunes are due to misdeeds and offenses committed by men and they gather in dirt and impurity over the body of the goddess. It is necessary for the shaman to go through a dangerous ordeal to reach the sea goddess at the bottom of the sea. He must then stroke her hair and report the difficulties of his people. The goddess replies that breaches of taboos have caused her to send the misfortunes, whereupon the shaman returns for the mass confession from all the people who have committed misdeeds. Presumably when all sins are confessed, the sea goddess releases the game, returns lost souls, cures illnesses, and generally makes the world right with the Eskimos again.

Reprinted in abridged form from Knud Rasmussen, *Report of the Fifth Thule Expedition, 1921–1924*, Vol. VII, No. 1, *Intellectual Culture of the Iglulik Eskimos* (Copenhagen: Gyldendalske Boghandel, Nordisk Forlag, 1929), pp. 123–129, by permission of Rudolf Sand.

The girl who was thrown into the sea by her own father and had her finger joints so cruelly cut off as she clung in terror to the side of the boat has in a strange fashion made herself the stern goddess of fate among the Eskimos. From her comes all the most indispensable of human food, the flesh of sea beasts; from her comes the blubber that warms the cold snow huts and gives light in the lamps when the long arctic night broods over the land. From her come also the skins of the great seal which are likewise indispensable for clothes and boot soles, if the hunters are to be able to move over the frozen sea all seasons of the year. But while Takánakapsâluk gives mankind all these good things, created out of her own finger joints, it is she also who sends nearly all the misfortunes which are regarded by the dwellers on earth as the worst and direst. In her anger at men's failing to live as they should, she calls up storms that prevent the men from hunting, or she keeps the animals they seek hidden away in a pool she has at the bottom of the sea, or she will steal away the souls of human beings and send sickness among the people. It is not strange, therefore, that it is regarded as one of a shaman's greatest feats to visit her where she lives at the bottom of the sea, and so tame and conciliate her that human beings can live once more untroubled on earth.

When a shaman wishes to visit Takánakapsâluk, he sits on the inner part of the sleeping place behind a curtain, and must wear nothing but his kamiks and mittens. A shaman about to make this journey is said to be ɴak·a·ʒɔq: one who drops down to the bottom of the sea. This remarkable expression is due perhaps in some degree to the fact that no one can rightly explain how the journey is made. Some assert that it is only his soul or his spirit which makes the journey; others declare that it is the shaman himself who actually, in the flesh, drops down into the underworld.

The journey may be undertaken at the instance of a single individual, who pays the shaman for his trouble, either because there is sickness in his household which appears incurable, or because he has been particularly unsuccessful in his hunting. But it may also be made on behalf of a whole village threatened by famine and death owing to

scarcity of game. As soon as such occasion arises, all the adult members of the community assemble in the house from which the shaman is to start, and when he has taken up his position—if it is winter, and in a snow hut, on the bare snow; if in summer, on the bare ground—the men and women present must loosen all tight fastenings in their clothes, the lacings of their footgear, the waistbands of their breeches, and then sit down and remain still with closed eyes, all lamps being put out, or allowed to burn only with so faint a flame that is is practically dark inside the house.

The shaman sits for a while in silence, breathing deeply, and then, after some time has elapsed, he begins to call upon his helping spirits, repeating over and over again: "The way is made ready for me; the way opens before me!"

Whereat all present must answer in chorus: "Let it be so!"

And when the helping spirits have arrived, the earth opens under the shaman, but often only to close up again; he has to struggle for a long time with hidden forces, ere he can cry at last:

"Now the way is open."

And then all present must answer: "Let the way be open before him; let there be way for him."

And now one hears at first under the sleeping place: "Halala—he—he—he, halala—he—he—he!" and afterwards under the passage, below the ground, the same cry: "Halele—he!" And the sound can be distinctly heard to recede farther and farther until it is lost altogether. Then all know that he is on his way to the ruler of the sea beasts.

Meanwhile, the members of the household pass the time by singing songs in chorus, and here it may happen that the clothes which the shaman has discarded come alive and fly about round the house, above the heads of the singers, who are sitting with closed eyes. And one may hear deep sighs and the breathing of persons long since dead; these are the souls of the shaman's namesakes, who have come to help. But as soon as one calls them by name, the sighs cease, and all is silent in the house until another dead person begins to sigh.

In the darkened house one hears only sighing and groaning from the dead who lived many generations earlier. This sighing and puffing sounds as if the spirits were down under water, in the sea, as marine animals, and in between all the noises one hears the blowing and splashing of creatures coming up to breathe. There is one song especially which must be constantly repeated; it is only to be sung by the oldest members of the tribe, and is as follows:

We reach out our hands
to help you up;
We are without food,
we are without game.
From the hollow by the entrance
you shall open,
you shall bore your way up.
We are without food,
and we lay ourselves down
holding out hands
to help you up!

An ordinary shaman will, even though skillful, encounter many dangers in his flight down to the bottom of the sea; the most dreaded are three large rolling stones which he meets as soon as he has reached the sea floor. There is no way round; he has to pass between them, and take great care not to be crushed by these stones, which churn about, hardly leaving room for a human being to pass. Once he has passed beyond them, he comes to a broad, trodden path, the shaman's path; he follows a coastline resembling that which he knows from on earth, and entering a bay finds himself on a great plain, and here lies the house of Takánakapsâluk, built of stone, with a short passageway, just like the houses of the tunit. Outside the house one can hear the animals puffing and blowing, but he does not see them; in the passage leading to the house lies Takánakapsâluk's dog stretched across the passage taking up all the room; it lies there gnawing at a bone and snarling. It is dangerous to all who fear it, and only the courageous shaman can pass by it stepping straight over it as it lies; the dog then knows that the bold visitor is a great shaman, and does him no harm.

These difficulties and dangers attend the journey of an ordinary shaman. But for the very greatest, a way opens right from the house whence they invoke their helping spirits; a road down through the earth, if they are in a tent on shore, or down through the sea, if it is in a snow hut on the sea ice, and by this route the shaman is led down without encountering any obstacle. He almost glides as if falling through a tube so fitted to his body that he can check his progress by pressing against the sides, and need not actually fall down with a rush. This tube is kept open for him by all the souls of his namesakes, until he returns on his way back to earth.

Should a great shelter wall be built outside the house of Takánakapsâluk, it means that she is very angry and implacable in her feelings towards mankind, but the shaman must fling himself upon the wall, kick it down and level it to the ground. There are some who declare that her house has no roof, and is open at the top, so that she can better watch, from her place by the lamp, the doings of mankind. All the different kinds of game: seal, bearded seal, walrus, and whale are collected in a great pool on the right of her lamp, and there they lie puffing and blowing. When the shaman enters the house, he at once sees Takánakapsâluk, who, as a sign of anger, is sitting with her back to the lamp and with her back to all the animals in the pool. Her hair hangs down loose all over one side of her face, a tangled, untidy mass hiding her eyes, so that she cannot see. It is the misdeeds and offenses committed by men which gather in dirt and impurity over her body. All the foul emanations from the sins of mankind nearly suffocate her. As the shaman moves towards her, Isarrataitsoq, her father, tries to grasp hold of him. He thinks it is a dead person come to expiate offenses before passing on to the Land of The Dead, but the shaman must then at once cry out: "I am flesh and blood" and then he will not be hurt. And he must grasp Takánakapsâluk by one shoulder and turn her face towards the lamp and towards the animals, and stroke her hair, the hair she has been unable to comb out herself, because she has no fingers; and he must smooth it and comb it, and as soon as she is calmer, he must say:

"Those up above can no longer help the seals up by grasping their foreflippers."

Then Takánakapsâluk answers in the spirit language: "The secret miscarriages of the women and breaches of taboo in eating boiled meat bar the way for the animals."

The shaman must now use all his efforts to appease her anger, and at last, when she is in a kindlier mood, she takes the animals one by one and drops them on the floor, and then it is as if a whirlpool arose in the passage, the animals disappear in the sea. This means rich hunting and abundance for mankind.

It is then time for the shaman to return to his fellows up above, who are waiting for him. They can hear him coming a long way off; the rush of his passage through the tube kept open for him by the spirits comes nearer and nearer, and with a mighty "Plu—a—he—he" he shoots up into his place behind the curtain: "Plu-plu," like some creature of the sea, shooting up from the deep to take breath under the pressure of mighty lungs.

Then there is silence for a moment. No one may break this silence until the shaman says: "I have something to say."

Then all present answer: "Let us hear, let us hear."

And the shaman goes on, in the solemn spirit language: "Words will arise."

And then all in the house must confess any breaches of taboo they have committed.

"It is my fault, perhaps," they cry, all at once, women and men together, in fear of famine and starvation, and all begin telling of the wrong things they have done. All the names of those in the house are mentioned, and all must confess, and thus much comes to light which no one had ever dreamed of; everyone learns his neighbor's secrets. But despite all the sin confessed, the shaman may go on talking as one who is unhappy at having made a mistake, and again and again break out into such expressions as this:

"I seek my grounds in things which have not happened; I speak as one who knows nothing."

There are still secrets barring the way for full solution of the trouble, and so the women in the house begin to go through all the names, one after another; nearly all women's names; for it was always their breaches of taboo which were most dangerous. Now and again when a name is mentioned, the shaman exclaims in relief:

"Taina, taina!"

It may happen that the woman in question is not present, and in such a case, she is sent for. Often it would be quite young girls or young wives, and when they came in crying and miserable, it was always a sign that they were good women, good penitent women. And as soon as they showed themselves, shamefaced and weeping, the shaman would break out again into his cries of self-reproach:

"I seek, and I strike where nothing is to be found! I seek, and I strike where nothing is to be found! If there is anything, you must say so!"

And the woman who has been led in, and whom the shaman has marked out as one who has broken her taboo, now confesses:

"I had a miscarriage, but I said nothing, because I was afraid, and because it took place in a house where there were many."

She thus admits that she has had a miscarriage, but did not venture to say so at the time because of the consequences involved, affecting her numerous housemates; for the rules provide that as soon as a woman has had a miscarriage in a house, all those living in the same house, men and women alike, must throw away all the house contains of qituptɔq: soft things, i.e., all the skins on the sleeping place, all the clothes, in a word all soft skins, thus including also ilupᴇrɔq: the sealskin covering used to line the whole interior of a snow hut as used among the Iglulingmiut. This was so serious a matter for the household that women sometimes dared not report a miscarriage; moreover, in the case of quite young girls who had not yet given birth to any child, a miscarriage might accompany their menstruation without their knowing, and only when the shaman in such a case as this, pointed out the girl as the origin of the trouble and the cause of Takánakapsâluk's anger, would she call to mind that there had once been, in her menstruation skin (the piece of thick-haired caribou skin which women place in their under-breeches during menstruation) something that looked like "thick blood." She had not thought at the time that it was anything particular, and had therefore said nothing about it, but now that she is pointed out by the shaman, it recurs to her mind. Thus at last the cause of Takánakapsâluk's anger is explained, and all are filled with joy at having escaped disaster. They are now assured that there will be abundance of game on the following day. And in the end, there may be almost a feeling of thankfulness towards the delinquent. This then was what took place when shamans went down and propitiated the great Spirit of the Sea.

Rodney Needham

PERCUSSION AND TRANSITION

Although the hypothesis advanced by Needham—that there is a connection in human life between percussion and transition—has broader implications than the more specialized study of the phenomenon of shamanism, the postulated relationship occurs very frequently and was first noted by Needham in shamanistic performances. Hence, we have included his article in this chapter to call attention to his novel hypothesis and to stimulate further research into this phenomenon that occurs not only in shamanistic rituals but in many other types of transition rituals in both tribal and modern societies. We suggest that percussive sound not be labeled as "noise" since in terms of communications theory, "noise" consists of sounds that interfere with the meaningful messages being transmitted, or are "nonmessages." And, clearly, if Needham is correct, the percussive sounds are transmitting meaningful messages about a transition in social life. Apart from this small matter of terminology, we find the article both cogent and stimulating and the hypothesis very promising for further exploration. We suggest for further exploration the reading of William C. Sturtevant's comment entitled "Categories, Percussion and Physiology" (1968), which especially calls attention to Andrew Neher's paper "A Physiological Explanation of Unusual Behavior in Ceremonies Involving Drums" (1962) and discusses the psychological states produced by rhythmical drumming.

Reprinted from *Man*, II (1967), 606–614, by permission of the author and the Royal Anthropological Institute of Great Britain and Ireland.

La faculté de sentir est la première faculté de l'âme.

—Laromiguière (1826, 1, 86)

This article indicates a problem which seems to relate to matters of fundamental importance in social anthropology. The present observations are tentative, and I am not in a position to construct a formal argument. Moreover, I have deliberately cited as few authorities as possible, partly for the reason that the relevant literature is so immense that I can neither list it all nor pretend to know what is best in it, and partly because the intended force of this article is that I think everybody will recognize at once what phenomena and institutions it is about and will not need any direction to pertinent facts.

What I hope for especially in publishing these uncertain remarks is that colleagues will help to frame the appropriate conceptual terms for coming to grips with the large and universal matters that are at issue. Alternatively, perhaps it can be shown that there is no problem after all, or that there is a problem but that is has been badly defined. It may even be that this has all been worked out before, but I suspect that in such a case I am not the only one to be ignorant of the fact.

The problem initially presented itself in this form: why is noise that is produced by striking or shaking so widely used in order to communicate with the other world?

This formulation changed as my reflections on the question shaped themselves, and the scope of the enquiry became far wider, but let me begin with the particular puzzle which first caught my attention and which others may also find as intriguing. The starting point is the common report, encountered again and again in the ethnographical literature, that a shaman beats a drum in order to establish contact with the spirits. It is so well described, and has been so thoroughly recognized as a characteristic feature of a shaman's activities, that the question seems not to have been asked (so far, at least, as I can discover) just why he beats a drum, and why this banging noise is essential if he is to communicate with spiritual powers.

My own first recourse was to turn to Wilken's famous study of shamanism in Indonesia, and to see whether he had anything to say about the matter. He does not, it turns out, isolate this specific problem, but he does help to place the question in a wider context. He points out, namely, that a drum is beaten, not only at a shamanic séance, but also on other occasions in order to call the spirits (Wilken, 1887: 479n. 156), i.e., that drumbeating, though indeed characteristic of the shaman, is not peculiar to his office but is a widely recognized means of making contact with the spiritual world. The obvious comment, however, is that a shaman does not always beat a drum, and that neither do other people always do so when they want to communicate with the other world. But as Eliade says in discussing shamanic ritual, "there is always some instrument that, in one way or another, is able to establish contact with the 'world of the spirits' " (1964: 179), and this in itself is surely a very curious fact.

What are these instruments? Here is a list: drum, gong, bell, cymbal, tambourine, xylophone, metallophone, rattle, rasp, stamping tube, sticks (struck against each other), sticks on stretched mats, resounding rocks, clashing anklets. No doubt this catalogue is very incomplete, but it is already impressively extensive and varied. I am not saying, of course, that these instruments are used only in order to contact the spirits, or that no other instruments are used for this purpose; but they are all, to even a casual recollection, employed in order to communicate with the other world—and they are all *percussive*. With this defining term, yet other means can be isolated, which strictly speaking are non-instrumental, of doing the same thing, for example, clapping, striking the palm against various surfaces of the body, or simply stamping the feet or drumming with the heels. All over the world it is found that percussion, by any means whatever that will produce it, permits or accompanies communication with the other world.

But is "percussion" really the defining feature? It is not the most general, for the first characteristic of these instruments and procedures is simply that they generate noise. This is an interesting fact, for it is certainly not necessary that noise of any kind shall attract or greet spirits; smoke, gestures, dances, or objects such as masks or images can all do as much, and they are of course actually employed together with noise. This definition will not serve, however, for there are innumerable methods of producing noise in addition to those which we are considering. The second most general feature is that the methods in question make rhythmic noise; rhythm has already attracted sociological attention (Bücher, 1899), and it is certainly a cultural phenomenon of great importance, but it is clearly not specific enough to answer to our purpose. Melody, on the other hand, is far too specific and is obviously inappropriate as a criterion; some of our noise-makers produce distinct notes and are capable of elaborating melodies or of generating other tonal effects, but others (e.g., rattles, sticks, clapping) cannot do so. This brief survey of types of noise-production is very elementary, and a long way from being exhaustive, but it is enough to confirm the first indication that the defining feature is indeed percussion.

How, next, is one to make sense of this association between percussion and the spiritual world? This is a difficult question to approach in the first place because this range of noise-makers does not (so far as I know) correspond to a standard musicological category; percussion instruments are of course commonly distinguished, but not the total range of percussive devices and procedures under consideration, since not all of these are instruments. In the second place, even familiar percussion instruments may not be grouped together in description or analysis, but they may be divided up according to material of manufacture, construction, quality of sound, origin, and so forth. For example, to take an old but eminently useful authority, the *Encyclopaedia of Religion and Ethics* devotes one article to "Drums and Cymbals" (Crawley, 1912), another to "Gongs and Bells" (Wheeler, 1913), and appends to the latter a semi-independent article on "American Bells" (Chamberlain, 1913). These are in fact most interesting and valuable surveys, well worth recommending today, but together they cover only four of the fourteen types of noise-maker in my provisional classification, and the fragmentary treatment of them introduces a gratuitous source of difficulty in grappling with the problem. The real difficulty, however, is presented by the problem itself, in that if the relationship in question has not been isolated before (or even if it is not commonly recognized) one then lacks the support and the stimulation, in the form of analytical terms and ideas, which the discipline otherwise normally provides. I readily admit that I do not know (although I have tried hard enough to find out) what previous work may have been done in this connection, but I feel fairly sure that the relationship between percussion and communication with the other world is not an everyday preoccupation among social anthropologists.

There is, however, one work which is of special interest, namely the paper "The origin of bell and drum" by Maria Dworakowska (1938). It touches on part of my present problem, and it is methodologically instructive too. Dworakowska begins with the blunt declaration: "The bell is usually considered to be exclusively a musical or signalling instrument although this is quite erroneous" (1938: 1). (This sentence has a promising ring which reminds one that it is really Hocart or the late Lord Raglan who might best have dealt with the present problem.) She states that the bell plays a role similar to that of the drum among many peoples, and contends that there is a "genetic union" between the two instruments. To this assimilation she adds the gong, "a form which is as closely allied to the bell as to the drum." Her first intention is to construct an evolutionary series, the first member of which would be the drum and the last the bell of western Europe. This is a conventional kind of ethnological aim, and intrinsically a most interesting one; but where Dworakowska engages the special attention of the social anthropologist is in her explicit rejection of museum criteria in favour of a sociological concentration on "a striking similarity between the bell and the drum as regards the role which they play in everyday life, in magic and in religion" (1938: 9). I need not recapitulate the details in her exposition of the facts, nor her consideration of other approaches to the instruments, but will take up directly the hypothesis which she advances. Her argument is that the drum is a "continuation of the coffin-log" (22–23), which may or may not be historically sound, but what is more immediately relevant is that Dworakowska argues centrally that "there is a close connection between the drum and the dead" (20–22), so that the genetic series of drum, gong, bell and cognate instruments are all characteristically part of the cult of the dead.

I have outlined this argument not only because it may not be well known, but also because of the value in Dworakowska's procedure. She deliberately ignores the materials, methods of manufacture, forms and mechanisms of the instruments in order to concentrate on their social meaning; she examines these particular instruments because of their recognized prominence in cultures all around the world; and she makes a connexion, even if not a wholly satisfactory one, between certain types of percussion instruments and the dead. Her argument is also negatively instructive, in that it does not deal with, and cannot explain, the use of so many other means of producing percussive sound; it neglects, by its essentially developmental cast, the constant factors which may be operative throughout any historical changes; and it is framed in terms which are unduly circumstantial (a certain original instrument, a certain initial religious institution) and are insufficiently general or abstract.

Dworakowska's paper, then, is an encouraging and useful example, but it is not fundamental enough. A far more promising approach, in this respect, is that of Crawley, who writes: "The music of the drum is more closely connected with the foundations of aurally generated emotion than that of any other instrument. It is complete enough in itself to cover the whole range of human feeling" (1912: 91). This is the right approach, I think, because it is psychological. Now it has been well enough shown, of course, that "en aucun cas la sociologie ne saurait emprunter purement et simplement à la psychologie telle ou telle de ses propositions, pour l'appliquer telle quelle aux faits sociaux" (Durkheim [1901] 1967: XIX), but the more nearly a cultural phenomenon approaches the universal the more necessary it becomes to seek the grounds of it in the general psychic characters of mankind. In the present case, the remarkably wide distribution of percussive noise-makers, employed in communication with the other world, indicates that an historical or sociological interpretation would be quite inappropriate. It is this circumstance that makes the problem especially difficult for the social anthropologist, for whereas the discipline provides notions and techniques which serve relatively well in explaining social institutions or the structure of collective representations, it provides as yet no way of understanding the elementary forms of experience. Psychology, on the other hand, has on the whole turned away from such concerns, and for obvious scientific reasons has concentrated increasingly on more limited and manipulable phenomena. Psycho-analytical work is likely in principle to be more enlightening, and that of Jung in particular is highly suggestive, but studies in this field have so far not expanded their compass to match the worldwide evidence which the anthropologist takes for granted and which must be addressed if an integral understanding of humanity is ever to be achieved.

But if Crawley's psychological (and even neurological) orientation is right, his specific proposition about the drum is not so satisfactory. We all know something of the effects of the drum because we have felt them, but is it possible, to begin with, to put the proposition to empirical test? There is no readily apparent means, at any rate, of doing so with the proposition as it stands, and to a rigidly positivistic view this would rob it of any decisive value. It might then be maintained that Crawley's assertions, whatever their immediate appeal, are merely subjective and metaphorical. This criticism raises a general issue of epistemological or heuristic principle; it calls into question not only Crawley's proposition but also others of the kind which might be equally plausible and seem on other grounds to be appropriate to the type of problem. My own response to this form of objection would be that by rigidly confining oneself to empirically testable propositions one will never get very far in understanding man and his works. There are methodological justifications of this position, not to speak of other considerations of a philosophical kind, but since the issue is basically one of intellectual temper rather than resoluble argument there is little point in offering a defence here. For the present, it will suffice to concede that the position is defensible, and that Crawley's (and similar) views need not be rejected simply because it may not be possible to test them objectively.

A related criticism is that the very terms of the proposition are difficult to define: closeness of connexion, in this regard, is an extremely obscure idea; "aurally generated emotion" is not a precise description; and it is not at all clear how the music of the drum might be "complete," and in such a way that it might cover "the whole range," whatever this may comprise, of human feeling. But as Kant himself writes, "If we could not undertake anything with a concept until we had defined it, all philosophizing would be in a bad way" (1787: 759 n). Let me emphasize again, also, that the issue is not the suitability of the particular words that Crawley chooses to employ, nor the degree of his expository skill, nor the exactness of his observation. The difficulties of expression and interpretation encountered in his proposition about the drum are typical, it seems to me, of the generality of attempts to describe elemental feelings, and one cannot expect to begin with clear definitions of the problem. It is not so much the particular terms that cause the trouble, but the inherent difficulty in translating the phenomena into any terms at all.

But how, in this case, is one to make sense of the bangs, thumps, taps, rattles, and other reverberations which indisputably have such a wide social importance, and the individual effects of which are known. One expedient is to adopt the premise that everybody knows the subject, and that there is therefore no need to strive for a precise formulation—just as one does not bother, after all, to demonstrate the importance of sex, or to define erotic sensations. This, of course, is a position which should be adopted only when others are obviously unnecessary or have appeared unfeasible, which cannot yet be claimed in this case; but there seem nevertheless to be some grounds for adopting it. One might even suggest, indeed, that it is an unavoidable position, at some stage of the enquiry, and one that is peculiarly appropriate to the phenomena themselves. In the matter of dealing with the universal psychic appeal of a certain kind of noise, presumably the question of exact discrimination by the distinctive categories of any single culture should not be decisive. This is not the sphere of rational discourse and inference, even, but that of feeling. Admittedly, society itself defines and organizes feelings, and conditions its members to respond to certain sounds rather than to others—in one society the effect will be produced by the drum, in another by the gong, and in another by clapping—but practically everywhere it is found that percussion is resorted to in order to communicate with the other world, and it is the non-cultural affective appeal of percussion which I have to try to relate to the concept of spiritual existence.

Essentially, Crawley seems to be right: drums do have the kind of effect which he attempts impressionistically to describe, and so do other percussion instruments. Gongs also have such an effect, especially perhaps the deeper ones, and similarly with bells. The effect in question is not so patent in the case of some other items in the list above, such as rattles and sticks, but all these noisemakers tend to produce a comparable affective impact. This impact is produced, let me repeat, not simply by rhythm or melody or a certain note or period of resonance, but by percussion. There is no need to go intensively into the literature on the neurological grounds of this kind of effect: apart from the common experience of percussive musical instruments, the internal quaking produced by thunder, and the similar effects of gunfire or other explosive noises which vibrate the environment are well-known. (The word "percussion" comes from the Latin *quatere*, to strike, shake.) There is no doubt that sound-waves have neural and organic effects on human beings, irrespective of the cultural formation of the latter. The reverberations produced by musical instruments thus have not only aesthetic but also bodily effects. These effects may be more or less consciously undergone, but they are in any case unavoidable. The sounds mark off points on a scale of intensity the effects of which range from an agonizing disruption of the organism down to subliminal thrills or other bodily responses which contribute to the conscious affective appreciation of the sounds. Prominent among such sounds are those produced by percussion, which may well be said to involve "the foundations of aurally generated emotion."

From the point of view of culture history, also, it may be important that percussive sounds are the easiest to make, and the most obviously possible: they do not depend upon special materials, techniques, or ideas, but can readily be made with the human body alone or by its abrupt contact with any hard or resonant part of the environment. In two senses, therefore, it may be concluded that percussion is a primary and elemental phenomenon.

So far, then, I have generalized one term ("noise produced by striking or shaking") in the matter under investigation, and I have placed the shaman's drum in a far wider context of percussive phenomena and their physiological effects. But this leaves a corresponding term ("communication with the other world") which then seems much too explicit and ideational to account for so general a relation.

How am I to generalize this second term? Wilken (1887) has pointed out that drums are used not only to establish contact with spirits, but also to repel them, but this is still a form of communication with the other world. What other situations and institutionalized forms of behaviour are marked by percussion? Once the question is put in this way, it is seen that percussive devices are used in very large number of situations other than that of contacting spirits. Dworakowska has indeed indicated the importance of bells and drums in the normal course of social life, in healing, prophylaxis, hunting, warfare, funerals, etc. (1938: 9–12); and one has only to review ethnographical literature to appreciate that percussion is typical of a remarkably wide range of other situations such as birth, initiation, marriage, accession to office, sacrifice, lunar rites, calendrical feasts. declaration of war, the return of head-hunters, the reception of strangers, the inauguration of a house or a communal building, market days, sowing, harvest, fishing expeditions, epidemics, eclipses, and so on. Often the instruments are identified with the events, and are themselves the material symbols of them; their players may be not just normal participants but indispensable officiants at the rites and ceremonies which are distinguished by the sounds.

What is it that these events have in common? Obviously that they are *rites de passage*. In other words, the class of noisemakers is associated with the formal passage from one status or condition to another. Once again, though, I am not saying that such rites cannot be accomplished without percussive noisemakers, or that only such devices are used to mark them, but simply that there is a constant and immediately recognizable association between the type of sound and the type of rite. What I am proposing, namely, is that there is a significant connexion between percussion and transition.

This, I suggest, is the definitive relation, and the nature of the connexion is the real problem. There is certainly no intrinsic relationship between the phenomena, yet the association is too firm for the answer to be sought in the contingent particulars of cultural tradition. An obvious and conventional resort is to look at other usual means of marking the transition from one category to another. One such expedient is the use of a special vocabulary (van Gennep, 1909: 241; [1960: 169]; cf. 1908), which might even be thought formally comparable, to some slight extent, in that it involves the production of distinctive sounds. Another means is the assumption of special clothes, ornaments, or masks—or alternatively the divestiture of all such external distinctions; and yet another is to change location, so that the passage from one social or mystical status to another is symbolized, as van Gennep shows, by a territorial passage. But these comparisons are not helpful, for a number of reasons; firstly, these institutions are individually less general and more variable than the feature of percussion; secondly, they themselves are severally and typically accompanied by percussive sounds; and, thirdly, they are simply alternative means of marking transition, so that they merely pose the same fundamental problem but in more complex forms. Moreover, they actually lead away from the specific question, in that they demand an analysis of transition rites as such. But the necessary feature of transition will equally inescapably be marked in some way or other (i.e., not only by a tripartite ritual), and the question posed here is why precisely percussion should be so prominently and so very widely employed as a specially suitable kind of marker. The answer is not going to be arrived at, I suspect, by this kind of comparison, for the things compared in this case belong to different orders. On the one hand the institutions (beating of drums, etc.) have been defined reductionally by physical criteria (sound-waves, neural responses) which have no social content, whereas on the other hand institutions (sacrifice, etc.) which are equally social have merely been classed together sociologically in a way which retains their social and contingent nature. These considerations give all the more reason to revert to "transition" as the second term in the relation.

This offers a formally satisfactory definition of the problem, but in the end it only shows all the more clearly how profound and seemingly intractable a problem it is. What I am dealing with is the conjunction of two primal, elementary, and fundamental features: (1) the affective impact of percussion, (2) the logical structure of category-change. According to common notions, these components pertain to two quite disparate modes of apprehension: emotion and reason. Yet empirically there seems to be a significant connexion between them. This connexion cannot be derived exclusively from one or the other mode, i.e., either affectively or else logically, since by definition neither contains or implies the distinctive and irreducible features of the other. Nor is there, it would appear, anything in the social context of transition which might account externally for the connexion between these conventionally disjoined features. It would be easy enough to say that we should ignore common notions, or even a philosophically established opposition between feeling and thought, and instead consider directly the association that is postulated; but to do so would still leave an evident contrast between percussion and transition, and it is the ineluctable disparity, however defined, which frames the problem.

It seems, therefore, that one is committed to an anthropological kind of "depth analysis," in a synoptic attempt to transcend conventional academic distinctions and to account for human phenomena, psychic and social, in their integrity. Turner (1966) and more especially Beidelman (1964; 1966a; 1966b) have provided valuable exploratory examples of this sort of investigation, and much of my own work on classification (e.g., Needham, 1967) has been directed by the same concern. So far, I think it will be agreed, this kind of research has served, at a theoretical level (as distinct from ethnographical interpretation) only to delineate the problems involved, not to solve them. This at least is the position in which I find myself at this point in the face of this new problem. But I do not find such a conclusion especially dismaying for whereas social anthropology (like philosophy) has had considerable success in discerning and formulating problems, it is very much a matter of opinion whether it can be said ever to have solved any of them. In the present instance I shall be gratified if it is only thought that these problematical comments have contributed in any way to a clearer conception of the primary factors of human experience, and particularly of the basic importance of feeling in coming to terms with phenomenal reality.

Whether or not it is agreed that there is a real problem here, or that my own rather baffled observations are at all cogent, at least there is a methodological precept which it may prove useful for the ethnographer and the theoretical social anthropologist to keep in mind, namely to pay special attention to percussion. For the rest, I conclude simply and mnemonically by restating the the problem in the form of the unduly forthright and apparently unlikely hypothesis:

There is a connexion between percussion and transition.

NOTE: This paper was originally given, in its present form, as lecture at the University of Oxford in April, 1967. Certain further facts have since come to my notice and should be noted here.

1. The question why a shaman beats a drum has in fact been adverted to by van der Leeuw. Without posing this specific question, or considering the issue in any detail, he very briefly states that drumming and dancing induce a state of ecstasy in the shaman (1933, ch. 26. 2).

This possibility has been gone into more fully by Francis Huxley, in a fascinating paper which was published while the present article was in press. Writing about voodoo in Haiti, he reports that: "It is the drummers who largely provoke dissociation; they are skillful in reading the signs, and by quickening, altering, or breaking their rhythm they can usually force the crisis on those [dancers] who are ready for it" (1967: 286). Sometimes the dancer collapses before he has been possessed by the commanding presence of the god; he is put on his feet by the audience, who send him out on to the dance floor again "till the buffets of sound have their full effect" (286).

The effect in question is said to be produced through disturbances of the inner ear, an organ which modulates postural attitude, muscle tonus, breathing rhythms, heartbeat, blood pressure, feelings of nausea and certain eye reflexes. Huxley convincingly proposes that "the apparatus of drumming, dancing, and singing" can not only affect the inner ear, but is actually "aimed at it in an effort to dissociate the waking consciousness from its organization in the body" (287).

From what I have shown above, however, it is unfortunately plain that even a radical explanation of this kind, though very apt (as Crawley would have agreed) in the case of certain instruments, does not answer to the range of phenomena and related considerations to which the shaman's drum is merely an introduction. (It may be remarked, incidentally, that the vocational mark of a voodoo priest or priestess is a rattle [294].)

2. Professor Maurice Freedman has independently furnished a splendid complement to the argument of the present article, both supporting the hypothesis and extending the range of relevant phenomena, in his observations on Chinese marriage ritual.

When the bride leaves her home and is separated from her family she is in "a phase of transition" from which she will emerge only in her bridal chamber at the end of her journey. During this phase she may be "possessed," according to one authority (Johann Frick), by the God of Happiness (Freedman, 1967: 16). "The special character of the transition is marked by another feature: as the procession moves off, as it arrives, and sporadically along the route, firecrackers are let off" (17).

Freedman comments upon the little intellectual curiosity which has been excited by firecrackers, and he then proposes his own provisional interpretation. Crackers are part of a series of noise-producers which stretches from salt in the fire at one end to the cannon at the other. "Noise is used as a marker. It punctuates approaches to and separations from spirits and certain formal approaches to and separations from humans" (17). In these contexts neither the fear of evil spirits nor the expression of joy—which are motives expressed by Chinese themselves—need be relevant: "The marker [i.e., noise] is . . . neutral."

Freedman goes on to consider further connexions of noise with symbols such as fire, light, and colour, and to suggest certain ideological components of setting off firecrackers; but it is his relational discernment of a connexion between *explosions* and transition which makes such a remarkable contribution to the line of enquiry taken up here. I did indeed make a reference above to the effects of gunfire "and other explosive noises," but I had missed the fact that such sounds (percussive in the extreme) are also symbolically relevant. Yet in our own culture, after all, solemn entrances and exists are most prominently marked by explosions: a head of state is greeted with a twenty-one gun salute, and rifle volleys are fired at the graveside of a dead soldier. Marriage rites are relevant, too, for at a European wedding there is a traditional parallel to the Chinese firecrackers: pans—more recently replaced by tin cans—are tied behind the wedding carriage, where they bang, resound and clash like mad.

Now this last is a crucial fact which shows a more fundamental correspondence with firecrackers, and with cordite salutations, namely that in these cases there is no rhythm. The jangling cacophony of the pans is quite random, and the furious rattle of Chinese fireworks (numbers of which are set off at once, moreover, so that they produce bursts of overlapping reports) is equally non-rhythmical. The same is true of European transition-marking by means of firearms, for in both of the ceremonies instanced the interval between the shots is too long to compose any rhythm. What counts, therefore (and I am grateful to Freedman for having led me to see this new proof), is not rhythm, and certainly not melody, but nothing other than percussion.

The arresting convergence and mutual implications of the papers by Crawley, Dworakowska, Huxley and Freedman (on topics as initially disparate as drums and cymbals, bell and drum, voodoo, and Chinese marriage rites), together with my own tentative conspectus, seem to show at least that there really is something in the hypothesis. But this in turn only shows again that there is a real problem.

Claude Lévi-Strauss

THE EFFECTIVENESS OF SYMBOLS

Illness and disease are not merely physiological phenomena. Indeed, anthropologists have long noted the widespread use of curative symbols and their effect on patients. Such symbols, and the cultural context in which they are embedded, organize the ways in which the underlying physiological reality of illness is perceived, experienced, and dealt with. Beginning with this premise, Claude Lévi-Strauss analyzes a song used by Cuna Indian shamans to facilitate difficult childbirth. He suggests that the effectiveness of the song lies in its power to psychologically manipulate the patient's generative organs. The shaman's song provides a mythic language in which the patient can express the inexpressible incoherence of pain and disorder. By attaining this psychological release, the shaman also effects a physiological cure. In explaining the effectiveness of such symbolic operations, Lévi-Strauss draws a parallel between shamanistic and psychoanalytic curing, asserting that both attempt a cure by creating a myth which the patient then must relive; in the case of shamanism it is a collective myth, in psychoanalysis the patient's own personal myth. But Lévi-Strauss goes even further and asserts that shamanistic and psychoanalytic curing are one and the same because both parallel a universal, unconscious symbolic function of the human mind which structures the preconscious and conscious in all individuals, regardless of their cultural conditioning or idiosyncratic history. While many have criticized this last point as well as the vagueness with which Lévi-Strauss links the psychological aspects of shamanistic curing to the physiological ones [see Jerome Neu's article, "Lévi-Strauss on Shamanism" (1975) for a psychologist's critique of Lévi-Strauss's position], few would question his insights into the psychological power and efficacy of therapeutic symbols. A more general anthropological statement on the relationship of healing to its wider socio-cultural context can be found in Arthur Kleinman's essay, "Medicine's Symbolic Reality" (1974).

Reprinted form Claude Lévi-Strauss, *Structural Anthropology*, Chapter 10, translated from the French by Claire Jacobson and Brook Grundfest Scheepf (New York: Basic Books, Inc., 1963; London: Allen Lane, The Penquin Press, 1968), by permission of the author and the publishers.

The first important South American magico-religious text to be known, published by Wassén and Holmer,[1] throws new light on certain aspects of shamanistic curing and raises problems of theoretical interpretation by no means exhaustively treated in the editors' excellent commentary. We will re-examine this text for its more general implications, rather than from the linguistic or Americanist perspective primarily employed by the authors.

The text is a long incantation, covering eighteen pages in the native version, divided into 535 sections. It was obtained by the Cuna Indian Guillermo Haya from an elderly informant of his tribe. The Cuna, who live within the Panama Republic, received special attention from the late Erland Nordenskiöld, who even succeeded in training collaborators among the natives. After Nordenskiöld's death, Haya forwarded the text to Nordenskiöld's successor, Dr. Wassén. The text was taken down in the original language and accompanied by a Spanish translation, which Holmer revised with great care.

The purpose of the song is to facilitate difficult childbirth. Its use is somewhat exceptional, since native women of Central and South America have easier deliveries than women of Western societies. The intervention of the shaman is thus rare and occurs in case of failure, at the request of the midwife. The song begins with a picture of the midwife's confusion and describes her visit to the shaman, the latter's departure for the hut of the woman in labor, his arrival, and his preparations—consisting of fumigations of burnt cocoa-nibs, invocations, and the

[1] Nils M. Holmer and Henry Wassén, *Mu-Igala or the Way of Muu, a Medicine Song from the Cunas of Panama* (Göteborg: 1947).

making of sacred figures, or *nuchu*. These images, carved from prescribed kinds of wood which lend them their effectiveness, represent tutelary spirits whom the shaman makes his assistants and whom he leads to the abode of Muu, the power responsible for the formation of the fetus. A difficult childbirth results when Muu has exceeded her functions and captured the *purba*, or "soul," of the mother-to-be. Thus the song expresses a quest: the quest for the lost *purba*, which will be restored after many vicissitudes, such as the overcoming of obstacles, a victory over wild beasts, and, finally, a great contest waged by the shaman and his tutelary spirits against Muu and her daughters, with the help of magical hats whose weight the latter are not able to bear. Muu, once she has been defeated, allows the *purba* of the ailing woman to be discovered and freed. The delivery takes place, and the song ends with a statement of the precautions taken so that Muu will not escape and pursue her visitors. The fight is not waged against Muu herself, who is indispensable to procreation, but only against her abuses of power. Once these have been corrected, relations become friendly, and Muu's parting words to the shaman almost correspond to an invitation: "Friend *nele*, when do you think to visit me again?"

Thus far we have rendered the term *nele* as shaman, which might seem incorrect, since the cure does not appear to require the officiant to experience ecstasy or a transition to another psychic state. Yet the smoke of the cocoa beans aims primarily at "strengthening his garments" and "strengthening" the *nele* himself, "making him brave in front of Muu." And above all, the Cuna classification, which distinguishes between several types of medicine men, shows that the power of the *nele* has supernatural sources. The native medicine men are divided into *nele, inatuledi, and absogedi*. The functions of the *inatuledi and absogedi* are based on knowledge of songs and cures, acquired through study and validated by examinations, while the talent of the *nele*, considered innate, consists of supernatural sight, which instantly discovers the cause of the illness—that is, the whereabouts of the vital forces, whether particular or generalized, that have been carried off by evil spirits. For the *nele* can recruit these spirits, making them his protectors or assistants.[2] There is no doubt, therefore, that he is actually a shaman, even if his intervention in childbirth does not present all the traits which ordinarily accompany this function. And the *nuchu*, protective spirits who at the shaman's bidding become embodied in the figurines he has carved, receive from him—along with invisibility and clairvoyance—*niga*. *Niga* is "vitality" and "resistance," which make these spirits *nelegan* (plural of *nele*) "in the service of men" or in the "likeness of human beings," although endowed with exceptional powers.

From our brief synopsis, the song appears to be rather commonplace. The sick woman suffers because she has lost her spiritual double or, more correctly, one of the specific doubles which together constitute her vital strength. (We shall return to this point.) The shaman, assisted by his tutelary spirits, undertakes a journey to the supernatural world in order to snatch the double from the malevolent spirit who has captured it; by restoring it to its owner, he achieves the cure. The exceptional interest of this text does not lie in this formal framework, but, rather, in the discovery—stemming no doubt from a reading of the text, but for which Holmer and Wassén deserve, nonetheless, full credit—that *Mu-Igala*, that is, "Muu's way," and the abode of Muu are not, to the native mind, simply a mythical itinerary and dwelling-place. They represent, literally, the vagina and uterus of the pregnant woman, which are explored by the shaman and *nuchu* and in whose depths they wage their victorious combat.

This interpretation is based first of all on an analysis of the concept of *purba*. The *purba* is a different spiritual principle from the *niga*, which we defined above. Unlike the *purba* the *niga* cannot be stolen from its possessor, and only human beings and animals own one. A plant or a stone has a *purba* but not a *niga*. The same is true of a corpse; and in a child, the *niga* only develops with age. It seems, therefore that one could, without too much inaccuracy, interpret *niga* as "vital strength," and *purba* as "double" or "soul," with the understanding that these words do not imply a distinction between animate and inanimate (since everything is animate for the Cuna) but correspond rather to the Platonic notion of "idea" or "archetype" of which every being or object is the material expression.

The sick woman of the song has lost more than her *purba;* the native text attributes fever to her—"the hot garments of the disease"—and the loss or impairment of her sight—"straying . . . asleep on Muu Puklip's path." Above all, as she declares to the sha-

[2] E. Nordenskiöld, *An Historical and Ethnological Survey of the Cuna Indians*, Henry Wassén (ed.), Vol. X of *Comparative Ethnographical Studies* (Göteborg: 1938), pp. 80 ff.

man who questions her, "It is Muu Puklip who has come to me. She wants to take my *niga purbalele* for good." Holmer proposes translating *niga* as physical strength and *purba (lele)* as soul or essence, whence "the soul of her life." It would perhaps be bold to suggest that the *niga*, an attribute of the living being, results from the existence of not one but several *purba*, which are functionally interrelated. Yet each part of the body has its own *purba*, and the *niga* seems to constitute, on the spiritual level, the equivalent of the concept of organism. Just as life results from the cooperation of the organs, so "vital strength" would be none other than the harmonious concurrence of all the *purba*, each of which governs the functions of a specific organ.

As a matter of fact, not only does the shaman retrieve the *niga purbalele;* his discovery is followed immediately by the recapture of other *purba*, those of the heart, bones, teeth, hair, nails, and feet. The omission here of the *purba* governing the most affected organs—the generative organs—might come as a surprise. As the editors of the text emphasize, this is because the *purba* of the uterus is not considered as a victim but as responsible for the pathological disorder. Muu and her daughters, the *muugan*, are, as Nordenskiöld pointed out, the forces that preside over the development of the fetus and that give it its *kurgin*, or natural capacities. The text does not refer to these positive attributes. In it Muu appears as an instigator of disorder, a special "soul" that has captured and paralyzed the other special "souls," thus destroying the cooperation which insures the integrity of the "chief body" from which it draws its *niga*. But at the same time, Muu must stay put, for the expedition undertaken to liberate the *purba* might provoke Muu's escape by the road which temporarily remains open; hence the precautions whose details fill the last part of the song. The shaman mobilizes the Lords of the wild animals to guard the way, the road is entangled, golden and silver nets are fastened, and, for four days, the *nelegan* stand watch and beat their sticks. Muu, therefore, is not a fundamentally evil force: she is a force gone awry. In a difficult delivery the "soul" of the uterus has led astray all the "souls" belonging to other parts of the body. Once these souls are liberated, the soul of the uterus can and must resume its cooperation. Let us emphasize right here the clarity with which the native ideology delineates the emotional content of the physiological disturbance, as it might appear, in an implicit way, to the mind of the sick woman.

To reach Muu, the shaman and his assistants must follow a road, "Muu's way," which may be identified from the many allusions in the text. When the shaman, crouching beneath the sick woman's hammock, has finished carving the *nuchu*, the latter rise up "at the extremity of the road" and the shaman exhorts them in these terms:

> *The (sick) woman lies in the hammock in front of you.*
> *Her white tissue lies in her lap, her white tissues move softly.*
> *The (sick) woman's body lies weak.*
> *When they light up (along) Muu's way, it runs over with exudations and like blood.*
> *Her exudations drip down below the hammock all like blood, all red.*
> *The inner white tissue extends to the bosom of the earth.*
> *Into the middle of the woman's white tissue a human being descends.*

The translators are doubtful as to the meaning of the last two sentences, yet they refer to another native text, published by Nordenskiöld, which leaves no doubt as to the identification of the "white inner tissue" with the vulva. . . .

"Muu's way," darkened and completely covered with blood owing to the difficult labor, and which the *nuchu* have to find by the white sheen of their clothes and magical hats, is thus unquestionably the vagina of the sick woman. And "Muu's abode," the "dark whirlpool" where she dwells, corresponds to the uterus, since the native informant comments on the name of this abode . . . in terms of . . . "woman's turbid menstruation," also called "the dark deep whirlpool" and "the dark inner place."

The original character of this text gives it a special place among the shamanistic cures ordinarily described. These cures are of three types, which are not, however, mutually exclusive. The sick organ or member may be physically involved, through a manipulation or suction which aims at extracting the cause of the illness—usually a thorn, crystal, or feather made to appear at the opportune moment, as in tropical America, Australia, and Alaska. Curing may also revolve, as among the Araucanians, around a sham battle, waged in the hut and then outdoors, against harmful spirits. Or, as among the Navaho, the officiant may recite incantations and prescribe actions (such as placing the sick person on different parts of a painting traced on the ground with colored sands and pollens) which bear no direct relationship to the specific disturbance to be cured. In all these cases, the therapeutic method (which as we know is often effective) is difficult to interpret. When it deals directly with the unhealthy organ, it is too grossly concrete (generally, pure deceit) to be granted intrinsic value. And when it consists in the repetition of often highly abstract ritual, it is difficult for us to understand its direct bearing on the illness. It would be convenient to dismiss these difficulties by declaring that we are dealing with psychological cures. But this term will remain meaningless unless we can explain how specific psychological representations are invoked to combat equally specific physiological disturbances. The text that we have analyzed offers a striking contribution to the solution of this problem. The song constitutes a purely psychological treatment, for the shaman does not touch the body of the sick woman and administers no remedy. Nevertheless it involves, directly and explicitly, the pathological condition and its locus. In our view, the song constitutes a *psychological manipulation* of the sick organ, and it is precisely from this manipulation that a cure is expected.

To begin, let us demonstrate the existence and the characteristics of this manipulation. Then we shall ask what its purpose and its effectiveness are. First, we are surprised to find that the song, whose subject is a dramatic struggle between helpful and malevolent spirits for the reconquest of a "soul," devotes very little attention to action proper. In eighteen pages of text the contest occupies less than one page and the meeting with Muu Puklip scarcely two pages. The preliminaries, on the other hand, are highly developed and the preparations, the outfitting of the *nuchu*, the itinerary, and the sites are described with a great wealth of detail. Such is the case, at the beginning, for the midwife's visit to the shaman. The conversation between the sick woman and the midwife, followed by that between the midwife and the shaman, recurs twice, for each speaker repeats exactly the utterance of the other before answering him:

> The (sick) woman speaks to the midwife: "I am indeed being dressed in the hot garment of the disease."
> The midwife answers her (sick woman): "You are indeed being dressed in the hot garment of the disease, I also hear you say."

It might be argued that this stylistic device is common among the Cuna and stems from the necessity, among peoples bound to oral tradition, of memorizing exactly what has been said. And yet here this device is applied not only to speech but to actions:

> The midwife turns about in the hut.
> The midwife looks for some beads.
> The midwife turns about (in order to leave).
> The midwife puts one foot in front of the other.
> The midwife touches the ground with her foot.
> The midwife puts her other foot forward.
> The midwife pushes open the door of her hut; the door of her hut creaks.
> The midwife goes out . . .

This minute description of her departure is repeated when she arrives at the shaman's, when she returns to the sick woman, when the shaman departs, and when he arrives. Sometimes the same description is repeated twice in the same terms. The cure thus begins with a historical account of the events that preceded it, and some elements which might appear secondary ("arrivals" and "departures") are treated with luxuriant detail as if they were, so to speak, filmed in slow-motion. We encounter this technique throughout the text, but it is nowhere applied as systematically as at the beginning and to describe incidents of retrospective interest.

Everything occurs as though the shaman were trying to induce the sick woman—whose contact with reality is no doubt impaired and whose sensitivity is exacerbated—to relive the initial situation through pain, in a very precise and intense way, and to become psychologically aware of its smallest details. Actually this situation sets off a series of events of which the body and internal organs of the sick woman will be the assumed setting. A transition will thus be made from the most prosaic reality to myth, from the physical universe to the physiological universe, from the external world to the internal body. And the myth being enacted in the internal body must retain throughout the vividness and the character of lived experience prescribed by the shaman in the light of the pathological state and through an appropriate obsessing technique.

The next ten pages offer, in breathless rhythm, a more and more rapid oscillation between mythical and physiological themes, as if to abolish in the mind of the sick woman the distinction which separates them, and to make it impossible to differentiate their respective attributes. First there is a description of the woman lying in her hammock or in the native obstetrical position, facing eastward, knees parted, groaning, losing her blood, the vulva dilated and moving. Then the shaman calls by name the spirits of intoxicating drinks; of the winds, waters, and woods; and even—precious testimony to the plasticity of the myth—the spirit of the "silver steamer of the white man." The themes converge: like the sick woman, the *nuchu* are dripping with blood; and the pains of the sick woman assume cosmic proportions: "The inner white tissue extends to the bosom of the earth. . . . Into the bosom of the earth her exudations gather into a pool, all like blood, all red." At the same time, each spirit, when it appears, is carefully described, and the magical equipment which he receives from the shaman is enumerated at great length: black beads, flame-colored beads, dark beads, ring-shaped beads, tiger bones, rounded bones, throat bones, and many other bones, silver necklaces, armadillo bones, bones of the bird *kerkettoli*, woodpecker bones, bones for flutes, silver beads. Then general recruitment begins anew, as if these guarantees were still inadequate and all forces, known or unknown to the sick woman, were to be rallied for the invasion. Yet we are released to such a small extent into the realm of myth that the penetration of the vagina, mythical though it be, is proposed to the sick woman in concrete and familiar terms. On two occasions, moreover, "muu" designates the uterus directly, and not the spiritual principle which governs its activity. Here the *nelegan*, in order to enter Muu's way, take on the appearance and the motions of the erect penis:

> The *nelegan's* hats are shining white, the *nelegan's* hats are whitish.
> The *nelegan* are becoming flat and low (?), all like bits, all straight.
> The *nelegan* are beginning to become terrifying (?), the *nelegan* are becoming all terrifying (?), for the sake of the (sick) woman's *niga purbalele*.

And further, below:

> The *nelegan* go balancing up on top of the hammock, they go moving upward like *nusupane*.

The technique of the narrative thus aims at recreating a real experience in which the myth merely shifts the protagonists. The *nelegan* enter the natural orifice, and we can imagine that after all this psychological preparation the sick woman actually feels them entering. Not only does she feel them, but they "light up" the route they are preparing to follow—for their own sake, no doubt, and to find the way, but also to make the center of inexpressible and painful sensations "clear" for her and accessible to her consciousness. "The *nelegan* put good sight into the sick woman, the *nelegan* light good eyes in the (sick) woman. . . ."

And this "illuminating sight," to paraphrase an expression in the text, enables them to relate in detail a complicated itinerary that is a true mythical anatomy, corresponding less to the real structure of the genital organs than to a kind of emotional geography, identifying each point of resistance and each thrust:

> The *nelegan* set out, the *nelegan* march in a single file along Muu's road, as far as the Low Mountain,
> The *nelegan* set out, etc., as far as the Short Mountain,
> The *nelegan*, etc., as far as the Long Mountain,
> The *nelegan*, etc., (to) Yala Pokuna Yala, (not translated)
> The *nelegan*, etc., (to Yala Akkwatallekun Yala, (not translated)
> The *nelegan*, etc., (to) Yala Ilamalisuikun Yala, (not translated)
> The *nelegan*, etc., into the center of the Flat Mountain.
> The *nelegan* set out, the *nelegan* march in a single file along Muu's road.

The picture of the uterine world, peopled with fantastic monsters and dangerous animals, is amenable to the same interpretation—which is, moreover, confirmed by the native informant: "It is the animals," he says, "who increase the diseases of the laboring woman"; that is, the pains themselves are personified. And here again, the song seems to have as its principal aim the description of these pains to the sick woman and the naming of them, that is, their presentation to her in a form accessible to conscious or unconscious thought: Uncle Alligator, who moves about with his bulging eyes, his striped and variegated body, crouching and wriggling his tail; Uncle Alligator Tiikwalele, with glistening body, who moves his glistening flippers, whose flippers conquer the place, push everything aside, drag everything; Nele Ki(k)kirpanalele, the Octopus, whose sticky tentacles are alternately opening and closing; and many others besides: He-who-has-a-hat-that-is-soft, He-who-has-a-red-colored-hat, He-who-has-a-variegated-hat, etc., and the guardian animals: the black tiger, the red animal, the two-colored animal, the dust-colored animal; each is tied with an iron chain, the tongue hanging down, the tongue hanging out, saliva dripping, saliva foaming, with flourishing tail, the claws coming out and tearing things "all like blood, all red."

To enter into this hell à la Hieronymus Bosch and reach its owner, the *nelegan* have to overcome other obstacles, this time material: fibers, loose threads, fastened threads, successive curtains—rainbow-colored, golden, silvery, red, black, maroon, blue, white, wormlike, "like neckties," yellow, twisted, thick and for this purpose, the shaman calls reinforcements: Lords of the wood-boring insects, who are to "cut, gather, wind and reduce" the threads, which Holmer and Wassén identify as the internal tissues of the uterus.

The *nelegan's* invasion follows the downfall of these last obstacles, and here the tournament of the hats takes place. A discussion of this would lead us too far from the immediate purpose of this study. After the liberation of the *niga purbalele* comes the descent, which is just as dangerous as the ascent, since the purpose of the whole undertaking is to induce childbirth—precisely, a difficult descent. The shaman counts his helpers and encourages his troops; still he must summon other reinforcements: the "clearers of the way," Lords-of-the-burrowing animals, such as the armadillo. The *niga* is exhorted to make its way toward the orifice:

> *Your body lies in front of you in the hammock,*
> *(Her) white tissue lies in her lap,*
> *The white inner tissue moves softly,*
> *Your (sick) woman lies in your midst . . .*
> *. . . thinking she cannot see.*
> *Into her body they put again (her)* niga purbalele . . .

The episode that follows is obscure. It would seem that the sick woman is not yet cured. The shaman leaves for the mountains with people of the village to gather medicinal plants, and he returns to the attack in a different way. This time it is he who, by imitating the penis, penetrates the "opening of muu" and moves in it "like *nusupane* . . . completely drying the inner place." Yet the use of astringents suggests that the delivery has taken place. Finally, before the account of the precautions taken to impede Muu's escape, which we have already described, we find the shaman calling for help from a people of Bowmen. Since their task consists in raising a cloud of dust "to obscure . . . Muu's way," and to defend all of Muu's crossroads and byroads, their intervention probably also pertains to the conclusion.

The previous episode perhaps refers to a second curing technique, with organ manipulation and the administration of remedies. Or it may perhaps match, in equally metaphorical terms, the first journey, which is more highly elaborated in the text. Two lines of attack would thus have been developed for the assistance to the sick woman, one of which is supported by a psychophysiological mythology and the other by a psychosocial mythology—indicated by the shaman's call on the inhabitants of the village—which, however, remains undeveloped. At any rate, it should be observed that the song ends after the delivery, just as it had begun before the cure. Both antecedent and subsequent events are carefully related. But it is not only against Muu's elusive stray impulses that the cure must, through careful procedures, be effected; the efficacy of the cure would be jeopardized if, even before any results were to be expected, it failed to offer the sick woman a resolution, that is, a situation wherein all the protagonists have resumed their places and returned to an order which is no longer threatened.

The cure would consist, therefore, in making explicit a situation originally existing on the emotional level and in rendering acceptable to the mind pains which the body refuses to tolerate. That the mythology of the shaman does not correspond to an objective reality does not matter. The sick woman believes in the myth and belongs to a society which believes in it. The tutelary spirits and malevolent spirits, the supernatural monsters and magical animals, are all part of a coherent system on which the native conception of the universe is founded. The sick woman accepts these mythical beings or, more accurately, she has never questioned their existence. What she does not accept are the incoherent and arbitrary pains, which are an alien element in her system but which the shaman, calling upon myth, will re-integrate within a whole where everything is meaningful.

Once the sick woman understands, however, she does more than resign herself; she gets well. But no such thing happens to our sick when the causes of their diseases have been explained to them in terms of secretions, germs, or viruses. We shall perhaps be accused of paradox if we answer that the reason lies in the fact that microbes exist and monsters do not. And yet, the relationship between germ and disease is external to the mind of the patient, for it is a cause-and-effect relationship; whereas the relationship between monster and disease is internal to his mind, whether conscious or unconscious: It is a relationship between symbol and thing symbolized, or, to use the terminology of linguists, between sign and meaning. The shaman provides the sick woman with a *language*, by means of which unexpressed, and otherwise inexpressible, psychic states can be immediately expressed. And it is the transition to this verbal expression—at the same time making it possible to undergo in an ordered and intelligible form a real experience that would otherwise be chaotic and inexpressible—which induces the release of the physiological process, that is, the reorganization, in a favorable direction, of the process to which the sick woman is subjected.

In this respect, the shamanistic cure lies on the borderline between our contemporary physical medicine and such psychological therapies as psychoanalysis. Its originality stems from the application to an organic condition of a method related to psychotherapy. How is this possible? A closer comparison between shamanism and psychoanalysis—which in our view implies no slight to psychoanalysis—will enable us to clarify this point.

In both cases the purpose is to bring to a conscious level conflicts and resistances which have remained unconscious, owing either to their repression by other psychological forces or—in the case of childbirth—to their own specific nature, which is not psychic but organic or even simply mechanical. In both cases also, the conflicts and resistances are resolved, not because of the knowledge, real or alleged, which the sick woman progressively acquires of them, but because this knowledge makes possible a specific experience, in the course of which conflicts materialize in an order and on a level permitting their free development and leading to their resolution. This vital experience is called *abreaction* in psychoanalysis. We know that its precondition is the unprovoked intervention of the analyst, who appears in the conflicts of the patient through a double transference mechanism, as a flesh-and-blood protagonist and in relation to whom the patient can restore and clarify an initial situation which has remained unexpressed or unformulated.

All these characteristics can be found in the shamanistic cure. Here, too, it is a matter of provoking an experience; as this experience becomes structured, regulatory mechanisms beyond the subject's control are spontaneously set in motion and lead to an orderly functioning. The shaman plays the same dual role as the psychoanalyst. A prerequisite role—that of listener for the psychoanalyst and of orator for the shaman—establishes a direct relationship with the patient's conscious and an indirect relationship with his unconscious. This is the function of the incantation proper. But the shaman does more than utter the incantation; he is its hero, for it is he who, at the head of a supernatural battalion of spirits, penetrates the endangered organs and frees the captive soul. In this way he, like the psychoanalyst, becomes the object of transference and, through the representations induced in the patient's mind, the real protagonist of the conflict which the latter experiences on the border between the physical world and the psychic world. The patient suffering from neurosis eliminates an individual myth by facing a "real" psychoanalyst; the native woman in childbed overcomes a true organic disorder by identifying with a "mythically transmuted" shaman.

This parallelism does not exclude certain differences, which are not surprising if we note the character—psychological in the one case and organic in the other—of the ailment to be cured. Actually the shamanistic cure seems to be the exact counterpart to the psychoanalytic cure, but with an inversion of all the elements. Both cures aim at inducing an experience, and both succeed by recreating a myth which the patient has to live or relive. But in one case, the patient constructs an individual myth with elements drawn from his past; in the other case, the patient receives from the outside a social myth which does not correspond to a former personal state. To prepare for the abreaction, which then becomes an "adreaction," the psychoanalyst listens, whereas the shaman speaks. Better still: When a transference is established, the patient puts words into the mouth of the psychoanalyst by attributing to him alleged feelings and intentions; in the incantation, on the contrary, the shaman speaks for his patient. He questions her and puts into her mouth answers that correspond to the interpretation of her condition, with which she must become imbued:

My eyesight is straying, it is asleep on Muu Puklip's path.
It is Muu Puklip who has come to me. She wants to take my niga purbalele *for good.*
Muu Nauryaiti has come to me. She wants to possess my niga purbalele *for good.*
etc.

Furthermore, the resemblance becomes even more striking when we compare the shaman's method with certain recent therapeutic techniques of psychoanalysis. R. Desoille, in his research on daydreaming, emphasized that psychopathological disturbances are accessible only through the language of symbols. Thus he speaks to his patients by means of symbols, which remain, nonetheless, verbal metaphors. In a more recent work, with which we were not acquainted when we began this study, M. A. Sechehaye goes much further. It seems to us that the results which she obtained while treating a case of schizophrenia considered incurable fully confirm our preceding views on the similarities between psychoanalysis and shamanism. For Sechehaye became aware that speech, no matter how symbolic it might be, still could not penetrate beyond the conscious and that she could reach deeply buried complexes only through acts. Thus to resolve a weaning complex, the analyst must assume a maternal role, carried out not by a literal reproduction of the appropriate behavior but by means of actions which are, as it were, discontinuous, each symbolizing a fundamental element of the situation—for instance, putting the cheek of the patient in contact with the breast of the analyst. The symbolic load of such acts qualifies them as a language. Actually, the therapist holds a dialogue with the patient, not through the spoken word, but by concrete actions, that is, genuine rites which penetrate the screen of consciousness to carry their message directly to the unconscious.

Here we again encounter the concept of manipulation, which appeared so essential to an understanding of the shamanistic cure but whose traditional definition we must broaden considerably. For it may at one time involve a manipulation of ideas and, at another time, a manipulation of organs. But the basic condition remains that the manipulation must be carried out through symbols, that is, through meaningful equivalents of things meant which belong to another order of reality. The *gestures* of Sechehaye reverberate in the unconscious *mind* of the schizophrenic just as the *representations* evoked by the shaman bring about a modification in the organic *functions* of the woman in childbirth. Labor is impeded at the beginning of the song, the delivery takes place at the end, and the progress of childbirth is reflected in successive stages of the myth. The first penetration of the vagina by the *nelegan* is carried out in Indian file and, since it is an ascent, with the help of magical hats which clear and light up the way. The return corresponds to the second phase of the myth, but to the first phase of the physiological process, since the child must be made to come down. Attention turns toward the *nelegan*'s feet. We are told that they have shoes. When they invade Muu's abode, they no longer march in single file but in "rows of four;" and, to come out again in the open air, they go "in a row." No doubt the purpose of such an alteration in the details of the myth is to elicit the corresponding organic reaction, but the sick woman could not integrate it as experience if it were not associated with a true increase in dilatation. It is the effectiveness of symbols which guarantees the harmonious parallel development of myth and action. And myth and action form a pair always associated with the duality of patient and healer. In the schizophrenic cure the healer performs the actions and the patient produces his myth; in the shamanistic cure the healer supplies the myth and the patient performs the actions.

The analogy between these two methods would be even more complete if we could admit, as Freud seems to have suggested on two different occasions, that the description in psychological terms of the structure of psychoses and neuroses must one day be replaced by physiological, or even biochemical, concepts. This possibility may be at hand, since recent Swedish research has demonstrated chemical differences resulting from the amounts of polynucleids in the nerve cells of the normal individual and those of the psychotic. Given this hypothesis or any other of the same type, the shamanistic cure and the psychoanalytic cure would become strictly parallel. It would be a matter, either way, of stimulating an organic transformation which would consist essentially in a structural reorganization, by inducing the patient intensively to live out a myth—either received or created by him—whose structure would be, at the unconscious level, analogous to the structure whose genesis is sought on the organic level. The effectiveness of symbols would consist precisely in this "inductive property," by which formally homologous structures, built out of different materials at different levels of life—organic processes, unconscious mind, rational thought—are related to one another. Poetic metaphor provides a familiar example of this inductive process, but as a rule it does not transcend the unconscious level. Thus we note the significance of Rimbaud's intuition that metaphor can change the world.

The comparison with psychoanalysis has allowed us to shed light on some aspects of shamanistic curing. Conversely, it is not improbable that the study of shamanism may one day serve to elucidate obscure points of Freudian theory. We are thinking specifically of the concepts of myth and the unconscious.

We saw that the only difference between the two methods that would outlive the discovery of a physiological substratum of neurosis concerns the origin of the myth, which in the one case is recovered as an individual possession and in the other case is received from collective tradition. Actually, many psychoanalysts would refuse to admit that the psychic constellations which reappear in the patient's conscious could constitute a myth. These represent, they say, real events which it is sometimes possible to date and whose authenticity can be verified by checking with relatives or servants. We do not question these facts. But we should ask ourselves whether the therapeutic value of the cure depends on the actual character of remembered situations, or whether the traumatizing power of those situations stems from the fact that at the moment when they appear, the subject experiences them immediately as living myth. By this we mean that the traumatizing power of any situation cannot result from its intrinsic features but must, rather, result from the capacity of certain events, appearing within an appropriate psychological, historical, and social context, to induce an emotional crystallization which is molded by a pre-existing structure. In relation to the event or anecdote, these structures—or, more accurately, these structural laws—are truly atemporal. For the neurotic, all psychic life and all subsequent experiences are organized in terms of an exclusive or predominant structure, under the catalytic action of the initial myth. But this structure, as well as other structures which the neurotic relegates to a subordinate position, are to be found also in the normal human being, whether primitive or civilized. These structures as an aggregate form what we call the unconscious. The last difference between the theory of shamanism and psychoanalytic theory would, then, vanish. The unconscious ceases to be the ultimate haven of individual peculiarities—the repository of a unique history which makes each of us an irreplaceable being. It is reducible to a function—the symbolic function, which no doubt is specifically human, and which is carried out according to the same laws among all men, and actually corresponds to the aggregate of these laws.

If this view is correct, it will probably be necessary to re-establish a more marked distinction between the unconscious and the preconscious than has been customary in psychology. For the preconscious, as a reservoir of recollections and images amassed in the course of a lifetime, is merely an aspect of memory. While perennial in character, the preconscious also has limitations, since the term refers to the fact that even though memories are preserved they are not always available to the individual. The unconscious, on the other hand, is always empty—or, more accurately, it is as alien to mental images as is the stomach to the foods which pass through it. As the organ of a specific function, the unconscious merely imposes structural laws upon inarticulated elements which originate elsewhere—impulses, emotions, representations, and memories. We might say, therefore, that the preconscious is the individual lexicon where each of us accumulates the vocabulary of his personal history, but that this vocabulary becomes significant, for us and for others, only to the extent that the unconscious structures it according to its laws and thus transforms it into language. Since these laws are the same for all individuals and in all instances where the unconscious pursues its activity, the problem which arose in the preceding paragraph can easily be resolved. The vocabulary matters less than the structure. Whether the myth is re-created by the individual or borrowed from tradition, it derives from its sources—individual or collective (between which interpenetrations and exchanges constantly occur)—only the stock of representations with which it operates. But the structure remains the same, and through it the symbolic function is fulfilled.

If we add that these structures are not only the same for everyone and for all areas to which the function applies, but that they are few in number, we shall understand why the world of symbolism is infinitely varied in content, but always limited in its laws. There are many languages, but very few structural laws which are valid for all languages. A compilation of known tales and myths would fill an imposing number of volumes. But they can be reduced to a small number of simple types if we abstract, from among the diversity of characters, a few elementary functions. As for the complexes—those individual myths—they also correspond to a few simple types, which mold the fluid multiplicity of cases.

Since the shaman does not psychoanalyze his patient, we may conclude that remembrance of things past, considered by some the key to psychoanalytic therapy, is only one expression (whose value and results are hardly negligible) of a more fundamental method, which must be defined without considering the individual or collective genesis of the myth. For the myth *form* takes precedence over the *content* of the narrative. This is, at any rate, what the analysis of a native text seems to have taught us. But also, from another perspective, we know that any myth represents a quest for the remembrance of things past. The modern version of shamanistic technique called psychoanalysis thus derives its specific characteristics from the fact that in industrial civilization there is no longer any room for mythical time, except within man himself. From this observation, psychoanalysis can draw confirmation of its validity, as well as hope of strengthening its theoretical foundations and understanding better the reasons for its effectiveness, by comparing its methods and goals with those of its precursors, the shamans and sorcerers.

Richard A. Shweder

ASPECTS OF COGNITION IN ZINACANTECO SHAMANS: EXPERIMENTAL RESULTS

Ever since the time that ethnographers began to observe the behavior of shamans in the various tribal cultures of the world there have been comments and speculations about the extent to which the shamans are somehow different from the nonshamans in these societies. The shamans have always been observed to occupy special roles in their social systems and to perform special rituals. But are they also psychologically different or distinct in some definable ways? The early ethnographers like Bogoras (1904–1909), Paul Radin (1937), and others suggested that the behavior of shamans displayed "neurotic," or even "psychotic," symptoms. But a more common observation, as more data were collected, was to the effect that while *some* shamans might be "half crazy," more of them in any given society displayed no such symptoms. This brief but pioneering article by Shweder opens up a whole new area for exploration as he reports on his experimental results to the effect that the Zinacanteco shamans possess certain cognitive capacities that clearly distinguish them from nonshamans in this society. The extent to which these findings may be true in other societies remains to be investigated, but we suggest that Shweder has pointed up a new way in which we may come to understand the distinctive characteristics of shamans. The paper was prepared especially for this volume.

THE COGNITIVE ROLE OF SHAMANS IN ZINACANTAN

Among the Zinacanteco Indians of Chiapas, Mexico, the shaman's role is interpretive and constructive. The *h'ilol* (meaning "one who sees" or "seer") is a part-time specialist who diagnoses illness by means of divine revelation and by means of pulsing the blood of the infirmed, and who administers remedies, performs new-house ceremonies, lineage and year renewal ceremonies, rain-making ceremonies, and agricultural rituals, and tries to ritually avert epidemics (Silver, 1966: 42, 268; Vogt, 1969: 416–420). But it is as curer that his repertoire of cognitive skills is most apparent.[1]

The healthy Zinacanteco shares his imminent soul (*c'ulel*) with a wild animal (*canul*). Under normal circumstances the animal counterpart is held in custody in a mythical corral by the ancestral gods and the supernatural equivalent of the native police force (Silver, 1966:19). A man's vulnerability is increased, and the conditions which are sufficient for the genesis of illness, distress, anxiety, and fear are created when the canul is free of its bondage. Freedom is the result of escape or abandonment by displeased gods. The freedom is a negative one. In its natural state of wildness the canul is endangered by all the contingencies of untamed and undomesticated nature. Illness results from such uncontrolled and uncontrollable encounters.

The native belief conceives of the supernatural, and especially the ancestral gods, as a sort of "superego," a control which imposes order upon the disordered and chaotic wild. The sick individual is like a man with high

[1] The research was conducted in the summer of 1967 under the auspices of Professor Evon Z. Vogt's Harvard Chiapas Project. I thank him warmly for his patience and invaluable assistance. I wish to thank George Collier, Robert Hahn, José (Cep) Hernández, Klaus Koch, and Evon Z. Vogt for helpful suggestions on an earlier report of this data, and Candy, my wife, for reordering the data. The research was supported by a grant from NIMH-02100.

dependency needs alone in the jungle, forced to fend for himself, yet incapable of adaptation to his surroundings, and wishing only to understand why he is condemned to such jeopardy and what he must do to escape from his unsought and unwanted freedom.

The curer's role in this situation is to bring the canul back to the corral (Silver, 1966: 43) and convince the ancestral gods to tend to the canul properly, feed him, and contain him. There are other themes in the native belief, but from my perspective the shaman emerges as an agent of ancestral control and order who tames the wild by placing it into a cultural framework, the corral, where ancestral authority supports customary behavior, and the integrity of the individual person is unmaligned and protected.

From the native point of view the shaman has extraordinary cognitive capacities.[2] The shaman is recruited when he realizes his innate calling in a dream or vision and is thereby selected by the ancestral gods as one capable of "seeing" into the supernatural.

Diagnosis is not related to biological information, but to information concerning divine, supernatural intent. Diagnosis can be variable from patient to patient even when they have similar objective symptoms, and the shaman is free to creatively determine the appropriate explanation of the illness in the light of what he knows of the individual, the family, and the circumstances surrounding the illness. The shaman, of course, may take none of this information into consideration.

The cure is a propitiation, a show of respect to the gods, an attempt to convince them to place things back in order, to not leave anyone abandoned in the wilds. The shaman is indispensable because only he is capable of supernatural revelation into the significance and cure of the illness. The shaman is the individual who in the face of those contingencies of the environment which threaten the Zinacanteco with ill health, anxiety, distress, and fear interprets the uninterpretable and leads the way to security and health.

THE SAMPLE

In the summer of 1967 I designed an experiment the aim of which was to distinguish the cognitive style of Zinacanteco shamans from non-shamans. There are approximately 8,000 Zinacantecos, of whom 118 were male shamans in 1966 (Silver, 1966: 24). Thirty-three of these 118 male shamans were selected for testing. They were matched with thirty-three non-shaman males on the basis of three criteria: age, socioeconomic status, and degree of acculturation.

Since Zinacantecos do not convey to the anthropologist much confidence in their knowledge of their exact age, I considered it wise to age-match on the basis of three age categories: ages 22–30, 31–49, and 50 years and over. This division of the age continuum corresponds roughly to the triadic distinction made in Zinacantan between a man who has reached the appropriate age for marriage (*vinik xa*), a man who has reached the halfway point en route to becoming a respected elder (*oʔlolvinik*), literally "half man," and old man (*baz'i mol xa*) (Fred Whelan: personal communication, summer 1967).

Socioeconomic status matching was based on subjective ratings and reduced to three categories: rich, middle, poor. In some cases up to three native informants who knew a particular subject were asked to rate him in terms of wealth as rich, middle, or poor. If two of the three concurred, the rating was accepted. In no case did all three informants produce different ratings. A pool of five informants made it possible to always have available three informants who knew all of my 66 subjects. A similar subjective rating was compiled in 1967 by Frank Cancian for household heads in the village of ʔApas. Cancian had two informants rate subjects on three quantitative scales: 1–10, 1–8, 1–3. Wherever possible I used this data as a further confirmation of, or arbitrator between, the judgments of two informants.

Finally, subjects were matched by the degree of their acculturation. Since Zinacantecos speak a preconquest Mayan tongue called Tzotzil, the handiest (perhaps best) indicator of acculturation was the ability to speak Spanish.

EXPERIMENTAL DESIGN

Subjects were presented with and forced to confront concrete examples of chaos, i.e., diffuse, unstructured stimuli. The experimental design consisted of six *series* of photographs of objects familiar to Zinacantecos. Each series developed through twelve stages from a complete blur to perfectly defined focus. The six series (twelve photos each) were as follows: Evon Z. Vogt with a horse, a market scene, a close-up shot of a foot in a ritual sandal, San Lorenzo, a close-up shot of an ear, and a turkey. The seventy-two photos were arranged into twelve rounds. Each round presented all six scenes in the first degree of focus (a full blur). With each sub-

[2] I use cognitive to include perceptual processes.

sequent round there was a gradual development from blur to focus. The last round presented all six scenes in full focus.

Subjects were given the following instructions: "Look carefully and for as long as you like at each photograph I show you. With each photograph if you are sure you know what the photograph is of, tell me. If you are not sure, say 'I don't know.' "

For three of the six series three alternative responses were presented to the subject. For example, with the turkey series the following additional instructions were given: "With this photograph there are three possibilities as to what the photograph is of. It is either a man with a ball, flowers, or a turkey. If you are sure you know what it is tell me. If you are not sure say 'I don't know.' "

All instructions were administered in the native tongue by means of a tape recorder; the design presented to the subject by a Tzotzil informant.

The main independent variable was the difference between shamans and non-shamans matched for age, socioeconomic status, and degree of acculturation. The main dependent variables were the subject's willingness to say "I don't know" to stimuli which were undefinable, and below the threshold of recognition, and the formal patterns to be found in the responses given throughout the experiment.

The point in each series at which the object of the series was recognizable was determined by independent experiments with native informants. These norms of objective recognition set the cutoff point in the photograph design before which a refusal to say "I don't know" was taken to indicate an imposition of form by the subject on diffuse and unorganized stimuli.

RESULTS [3]

Shamans are significantly different from non-shamans in three aspects of cognitive style. The significance of the differences is determined by the application to the data of Student's T test between matched groups. First, shamans avoid bafflement more than non-shamans. They are imposers of form on diffuse sense data. Second, shamans are more productive in their responses; they are more generative of different responses. Third, shamans seem to have available to themselves their own constructive categories and remain relatively insensitive to the alternative categories provided by the experimenter. Below I list the experimental evidence for each of these three distinctive cognitive capacities of shamans, and the statistical level of significance of the evidence.

1. HIGH AVOIDANCE OF BAFFLEMENT—IMPOSERS OF FORM ON UNSTRUCTURED SENSE DATA

In response to the photographic series where no alternative responses were given to the subject, shamans say "I don't know" less than non-shamans (.006) and classify the photos in the series at an earlier point in the sequence (.04). The dramatic nature of the shaman's refusal to say "I don't know" is revealed by comparing the number of shamans and non-shamans who say "I don't know" five or less times over the entire design. If the norms on objective visual recognition are used as a standard, a subject ought to say "I don't know" fifty-nine times during the experiment. In fifty-nine of the seventy-two photos in the whole design it is simply impossible to determine the true nature of the series.

Twenty-three of thirty-three shamans respond with "I don't know" less than five times. Only eight of the thirty-three non-shamans follow the same pattern.

There is a larger increase in the number of "I don't know" responses given by non-shamans when confronting a series where no alternatives are supplied as opposed to a series where alternative responses are provided (.03). Non-shamans also delay the point in the sequence at which they are willing to classify the stimuli (.04).

These results indicate the shaman's capacity to be an *imposer* of form. He refuses to be baffled by stimuli which are diffuse and lacking in significance. It is crucial to note that the difference between the two groups in the number of "I don't know" responses is directional but *not* significant (.10) for the series where alternative responses were presented by the experimenter. In other words, when alternatives and choices of meaning are apparent there is a reduced need to utilize the special array of cognitive capacities possessed by the shaman. In response to a series with readily available alternative responses non-shamans behave in a very "shaman-like" manner. They also stop saying "I don't know." They have a form (the alternatives) with which to order the chaos set before their eyes. They, so to speak, do not need a shaman. It is in situations where significance is not clear, and alternative responses lacking that the shaman's abilities are at a premium.

The same function of the shaman as im-

[3] These results have been cited by Vogt (1969:476).

poser of form in situations where alternative responses are not forthcoming is revealed by the point of earliest classification in the two groups. When moving from a series with provided alternatives to a series with no alternatives provided the shamans continue to impose form early in the sequence, while non-shamans switch to an "I don't know" response mode and remain baffled.

2. HIGH GENERATIVE CAPACITY—MORE PRODUCTIVE

The number of *different* categories suggested by shamans to classify photos over a fixed number of identifications per series is higher both for series with, and without, alternatives provided by the experimenter (.005 and .001). The shaman either has a richer repertoire of categories with which to classify incoming stimuli or uses his available repertoire more creatively.

3. AVAILABILITY OF OWN CONSTRUCTIVE CATEGORIES—"INNER-DIRECTEDNESS" OF RESPONSES

In those series where alternative responses were provided by the experimenter, shamans more often gave responses which were *not* included in the presented choices (.03). If we add to this consideration the fact that shamans are generally unwilling to say "I don't know" when confronted with chaotic stimulation the shaman appears to be cognitively "inner-directed," utilizing his internal classificatory powers to dominate external disorder.

It is my belief that these aspects of the cognitive style of the shaman, the avoidance of bafflement and the imposition of form, the productivity of response patterns, and the self-centeredness of classification are functions of personality and somewhat enduring across situations. The test situation was not a role context. The shamans were not recruited to perform rituals. In the case of avoidance of bafflement, it seems justified to call it a "need" to avoid bafflement. The instructions demanded "I don't know" responses. Unless the shaman, standing as he was before a diffuse and unidentifiable stimulus, found these instructions frustrating his need for certainty he could easily have said "I don't know," as so many non-shamans chose to do.

In closing this section on test results I should note that with only one exception there were no differences between the two groups in the final degree of accuracy of responses. The close-up shot of an ear was the exception. For some reason shamans had considerable difficulty in making a correct identification of the ear, even in full focus!

ROLE EXPERIENCE AND PREEXISTING PERSONALITY

Once it has been ascertained that shamans have some distinctive cognitive capacities it might be asked whether these capacities have developed with experience in performing the role, or whether they are part of the array of personality features which exist before a man becomes a shaman, and which help filter him into the role. Considerable data of a more refined and extensive nature than I have been able to collect would be needed to resolve this issue with any rigor. I can only suggest a way to formulate the problem so as to be able to test it, and exhibit the results of the test on my more crude data.

If role experience is sufficient to account for such distinctive cognitive capacities of shamans as the need to impose form, productivity of response pattern, and "inner-directedness" of classification, then we should expect an increase in the magnitude of these variables in the responses of shamans as their experience in the role increases. If we could rank all thirty-three shamans in terms of some measure of role experience, and then rank them again in terms of the magnitude of the three distinctive cognitive variables in their response patterns, we should expect a significant correlation between the two rankings.

A number of measures of role experience suggest themselves: the number of years a man has been a shaman, the number of ceremonies he has performed, the frequency with which he performs ceremonies.

But difficulties arise when considering the ranking of shamans by their scores on variables distinctive of their cognitive style. Ideally we would like *one* measure which would indicate the extent to which a given shaman reflects in his test scores the cognition distinctive of shamans. However, we have three distinctive capacities. We do not know how to weigh and combine each of these three features into one measure. I treated all three features as equal in weight and simply added them together. This is bound to be wrong and is one reason this discussion is only suggestive.

The thirty-three shamans were ranked on all three distinctive cognitive capacities. Each ranking of thirty-three scores was divided into eight ranks. Each shaman was given a mean rank over the three rankings and partitioned again into one of eight ranks.

This final rank was an ordering based on the equal weighting of the three distinctive capacities.

The final ranking was correlated with a ranking of the shamans into eight ranks or divisions on the basis of a number of measures of role experience. The number of years as shaman lent the strongest support to the role experience hypothesis but fell short of statistical significance (.14; Kendall's Rank Order Correlation Coefficient was used). The result, however, is certainly directional.

The hypothesis that cognitive capacities such as avoidance of bafflement and imposition of form on unstructured stimuli, productivity of response, and "inner-directedness", of classification are aspects of the personality which existed before the role of shaman was assumed suggests a different, although not exclusive, test of the data. Of those *non-shamans* whose cognitive styles are quantitatively the same as those of a prototypical shaman, a significant number should be in the younger half of the non-shaman sample.

The median age for non-shamans in my sample is forty years. It happens that after this age a man becoming a shaman is somewhat suspected of insincerity (Silver, 1966:46). I noted the age of every non-shaman with "shaman-like" responses. If preexisting personality is a factor in selection for the role, we can assume that "shaman-like" personalities will have been selected for the role by the age of forty, decreasing the "shaman-like" personalities in the non-shaman sample who are over forty. The preexisting personality hypothesis also proved nonsignificant but directional (X^2 = 1.88, .18 significance level).

This second suggestion is even more tentative than the first. It can easily be argued that to have a "shaman-like" cognitive style is not necessarily to become a shaman. But both the role experience and the preexisting personality hypotheses test out in the right direction, and the data is limited. Perhaps a predisposing personality interacts with experience in the role, as a proper combination of sufficient data might indicate.[4]

CONCLUSION

Zinacanteco Indians believe that their shamans have distinctive cognitive capacities. An experiment indicated that indeed they do. Their special qualities include a need to avoid bafflement and impose form on unstructured stimuli, a highly productive and generative response pattern, and an "inner-directed" or self-centered style of classification.

[4] It is also possible that my evidence provides indirect support for the view that the process of becoming a shaman involves a sudden and radical reorganization "of values, attitudes and beliefs which 'make sense' of a hitherto confusing and anxiety-provoking world" (Wallace, 1961:192). In such a case we do not expect statistical support for either the role-experience or preexisting personality hypotheses. The shaman's cognitive style would not have existed previous to the conversion experience, and would be a "fait accompli" soon after it.

SEVEN
INTERPRETATIONS OF MAGIC, WITCHCRAFT, AND DIVINATION

Introduction

The three concepts of magic, witchcraft, and divination are more than heuristic labels; they are real in that they represent actual classes of actions and beliefs intimately related to the human problem of control in known cultures. All men strive to control their social and physical environments and to determine, or at least to have prior knowledge of, their own lives. Through manipulation, explanation, and prediction the operations of magic, witchcraft, and divination work toward this vital human end.

While magic is overwhelmingly private and individual in nature, there are many instances of magic being conducted publicly as an attempt to benefit a whole society. Private magic may be either malevolent (black) or well-intentioned (white); it may be designed to destroy a rival or to cure an ailing child. Public magic is always directed toward the welfare of the group which performs it, but it may be calculated to bring evil to other groups or tribes. The term "sorcerer" refers to a practitioner of black magic, while "medicine man" usually refers to a man who performs primarily white magic and cures through natural means, dealing only secondarily in black magic. The "law of sympathy," so basic to magic, will be thoroughly discussed by Sir James Frazer in his article of this section.

The magical formula usually consists of a spoken and acted ritual, often called a "spell," and of material objects, often called "medicine." A "fetish" is an object or a bundle of objects, such as the famous Plains Indian medicine bundle, which has magical properties. While a fetish is sometimes thought to contain a spirit, it is used magically and is not, as is frequently claimed, worshiped. Neither should the term be used in the psychiatric sense of an inanimate object compulsively used in attaining sexual gratification.

Although magic often has an emotional origin, the performance of magic is routine, and while the ritual may appear to be dramatic, it is almost always nonemotional. This is especially so if, as often happens, a client takes his complaint to a magical specialist who has no emotional involvement with the problem.

Magic gives the individual confidence in the face of fear and provides an outlet for hostility. Magic explains misfortune and failure and reveals the cause of illness. Magic assigns a human cause to terrifying events, and in so doing converts these events into a human rather than an extrahuman context. Socially, magic may act to drain off tensions which might otherwise result in physical combat and death. Unfortunately, magic creates problems as well. People die from fear of sorcery or fall ill from putatively magical attacks, and whole societies may live in constant fear of black magic. Whatever the reasons for magic in human society, purely functional explanations of its utility in regulating social relations are clearly inadequate.

Witchcraft is the exercise of evil through an immanent power. Witchcraft, unlike sorcery, is derived from within, and cannot be learned. A witch's power to do evil may lie dormant and not be used or it may be increased by practice, but it is nearly always inherited. Whereas magic may be either malevolent or beneficent, witchcraft is invariably evil. A witch frequently has an animal form such as a cat, a werewolf, or a bat. Witches can project evil over great distances without moving, or they may transport themselves at great speeds in order to do some needed mischief. The evil eye and evil tongue are variants of witchcraft; some people can cause terrible harm simply by looking or speaking, often without evil intent. Witchcraft, like magic and divination, is undoubtedly worldwide, and its antiquity is great.

Witchcraft is far more than a grisly aberration of the human spirit; despite its macabre elements, it has positive functional value. All societies have the problem of providing an outlet for aggressions engendered by the conflicts, antagonisms, and frustrations of social living. Witches exist as convenient scapegoats for such aggressions. All societies also spawn individuals who in some degree do not find satisfactions within their culture, and a person of this sort may find an acceptable self-identity by considering himself to be a witch. Witchcraft may serve to regulate sex antagonism or to provide a means of demanding cultural conformity by furnishing a criminal act or state of which deviants may be accused. Like magic, witchcraft may also explain unhappiness, disease, and bad luck. Similarly, witchcraft has its dysfunctional aspects. Witches do real harm, cause real fears, and promote dangerous conflicts. As with magic, it is difficult to construct a balance sheet which can indicate the relative value of these practices within any sociocultural system.

For further information on these and other points, the reader should consult Evans-Pritchard, *Witchcraft, Oracles, and Magic Among the Azande* (1937); Clyde Kluckhohn, *Navaho Witchcraft* (1944); John Middleton and Edward Winter (eds.), *Witchcraft and Sorcery in East Africa* (1963); John Middleton (ed.), *Magic, Witchcraft, and Curing* (1967); Lucy Mair's book, *Witchcraft* (1969), also provides a useful summary. Other relevant volumes include *Witchcraft Confessions and Accusations* (1970) edited by Mary Douglas, Keith Thomas's book, *Religion and the Decline of Magic* (1971), a history of magic in sixteenth- and seventeenth-century England, and John Connor's article, "The Social and Psychological Reality of European Witchcraft Beliefs" (1975).

Divination, the art or practice of foreseeing future events or discovering hidden knowledge through supernatural means, is a cultural universal. From the Kaingang of South America, who seek answers in the volume of their belching, to the Hollywood movie star who daily consults a horoscope, divination assumes infinite forms and intensities. There are two general types of divination, inspirational and noninspirational. In the former, answers are revealed through a change in the psychology or emotional state of the individual. Shamanism, crystal gazing, and shell hearing are some inspirational forms of divination. Noninspirational divination may be either fortuitous, such as finding meanings in black cats, hairpins, sneezing, and countless other omens, or deliberate, by means of astrology, scapulimancy, chiromancy, ordeals, and the like. For a penetrating study of divination in a tribal context the reader is referred to Victor W. Turner, *Ndembu Divination: Its Symbolism and Techniques* (1961).

All men, as we know them, eagerly seek to know the unknowable and to control the uncontrollable. Divination allows man to control chance and to know the future. Divination permits the man who is immobilized by a difficult decision to make a choice, and to make it with confidence. Or have you never flipped a coin? Man is an animal doubly cursed; he knows that there is a future, and he fears that he cannot control it. That divination lessens these curses is attested to by the flourishing vigor of many forms of divinatory art in modern Western European culture, despite all the efforts of religion and science to brand such practices as sinful or ignorant.

The articles in this chapter fall roughly into three categories. The first, represented by Titiev's article, addresses the definitional problem of the difference between magic and religion. The second group, represented by Frazer, Tambiah, and Evans-Pritchard, concerns itself with the logical structure of "magical" thought. Frazer maintains that the magician's logic is a misapplication of the association of ideas; it is a logic based on false premises. Tambiah, in his turn, attempts to show that magic and science, while both based on the logical use of analogy, employ *different kinds* of analogy such that the two systems of thought are incommensurable. Unlike Frazer, Tambiah chooses not to judge magic in terms of strict canons of Western notions of induction and verification. Finally, the implications of Evans-Pritchard's essay raise the problem of self-contained, "closed" systems of thought such as Azande notions of witchcraft which, while providing explanations of unfortunate events, are unverifiable in terms of Western concepts of inductive proof. It would appear that such "beliefs" can stand only as long as their veracity goes unquestioned. How is the rationality of such systems of thought to be evaluated? The questions raised by this second group of articles address issues of crucial concern to anthropology as well as philosophy. If thought may be said to be a crucial element of what it means to be human, a true understanding of any culture must sooner or later address this question of thought and rationality and the problems of cross-cultural comparison it raises. Students interested in pursuing these issues might consult Brian Wilson (ed.) *Rationality* (1970), and a volume edited by Robin Horton and Ruth Finnegan entitled *Modes of Thought* (1973). While this question of rationality seems to lead us well beyond the bounds of magic, witchcraft, and divination, it lies at the heart of both the conceived efficacy of such practices and the manner in which we as anthropologists are to interpret them. Finally, the third section of this chapter includes the articles by Cannon, Turner, and Moore which seek to illustrate the various functions of witchcraft and divination in human society.

Mischa Titiev

A FRESH APPROACH TO THE PROBLEM OF MAGIC AND RELIGION

There has recently been an intensified interest in defining religion, particularly as it relates to magic. The following article, by Mischa Titiev, is a modest effort to clear the atmosphere without departing from what is essentially a Frazerian position. It may be contrasted with two articles by Murray and Rosalie Wax, "The Magical World View" (1962) and "The Notion of Magic" (1963), which severely attack any effort to sustain the more traditional views of magic as expressed by not only Frazer himself but also Tylor, Durkheim, and others. The Waxes' articles provide a useful review of the controversy in its historical and intellectual aspects. Less polemic efforts at grappling with the definitional problems on a broad basis have been made by Horton (1960) and Goody (1961).

Titiev's proposal to distinguish between calendrical and critical rituals has a familiar ring, although his use of the distinction is novel. Chapple and Coon, in their *Principles of Anthropology*, had earlier made a distinction between rites of intensification and rites of passage, the first usually being cyclical and recurrent, the latter nonrecurrent, but their aim was to explore these rituals in terms of the restoration of disturbed equilibrium. What Titiev has done is to show that many of the traits adhering to calendrical rituals are those we usually regard as religious, whereas many of those associated with critical rites are customarily considered to be magical. Yet he does not press the use of these criteria beyond reason, recognizing, as do indeed even those who favor the Frazerian type of dichotomy, that there simply is no hard and fast rule.

Reprinted with omission of a figure from the *Southwestern Journal of Anthropology*, XVI:3 (1960), 292–298, by permission of the author and the *Southwestern Journal of Anthropology*.

About seventy years ago the great scholar of primitive religion, Sir James G. Frazer, found it advisable to divide all phenomena involving the supernatural into the two categories of magic and religion. Almost at once large numbers of social scientists found Frazer's dichotomy useful and began to emphasize the criteria which, in their opinion, separated the one category from the other. In the course of time it became customary to stress four factors, although others were sometimes invoked. The four attributes that came to be most often cited run somewhat as follows.

1. Magic *compels* the world of the supernatural to do its bidding. It fails to get results only if errors of procedure or text have been made, or if stronger counter-magic has been brought to bear. Religion, on the other hand, say the supporters of Frazer's dichotomy, never guarantees results. Its use is limited to *supplication*, and its practitioners never resort to manipulation or coercion.

2. Magic, according to Durkheim and his followers, has no "church." That is to say, magical rites may be public or private but, unlike those that are religious, they do not have to have a large body of celebrants; they do not need to be held in public before a congregation of worshippers; and they may have no social or communal aspects whatsoever.

3. Magical utterances have a tendency to degenerate into spells or formulas, some of which have little or no meaning even to those who say them. It is implied that religious pronouncements are usually meaningful in terms of a society's customary language.

4. Practitioners of magic, even in primitive societies, are often set apart in one fashion or another from socially recognized priests. With occasional exceptions it is only acknowledged priests who go through a period of formal training and who then qualify to perform communal or publicly sanctioned religious exercises, leaving shamans and others to deal in magic.

Although most writers on the subject have continued to accept Frazer's distinction, somewhat apathetically, it must be confessed, others have held the criteria to be unsatisfactory because they cannot be precisely determined and because they so frequently overlap. Indeed, some contemporary anthropologists have found the customary divisions between magic and religion to be so vague and indeterminate that they have refused to recognize the traditional dichotomy and now prefer to treat both sets of practices as one. Indicative of this attitude is Dr. Hsu's statement, written only a few years ago, that "whichever criterion we employ, we are led to the conclusion that magic and religion, instead of being treated as mutually exclusive entities, must be grouped together as magico-religion or magico-religious phenomena. This is a position increasingly endorsed by anthropologists." Nevertheless, even if we grant that modern critics have many points in their favor, there are a number of anthropologists who still believe that a distinction needs to be made between what they feel are two essentially different kinds of human behavior, each of which makes an appeal to the supernatural world for help, guidance, or comfort.

As a fresh start toward a workable dichotomy, it may be well to distinguish two kinds of activities on a new basis, one that rests on a criterion that is precise, but has not been traditionally utilized by former analysts. In all primitive societies one set of practices involving the supernatural always takes place recurrently, and may, accordingly, be termed CALENDRICAL; while the other set, which is celebrated only intermittently, and then only when an emergency or crisis seems to have arisen, may be called CRITICAL.

Because of their very nature calendrical rituals can always be scheduled and announced long in advance of their occurrence. This gives the people of a community ample time to develop a shared sense of anticipation, and an opportunity to get ready for a big event. On the other hand, it must be realized that if a celebration is to be performed at a definite time of season in the future, it cannot possibly take into account the immediate desires for supernatural assistance or comfort of the whole society or of any of its parts. To cite one instance, the gigantic figure of Shalako appears in Zuni each December, regardless of the frame of mind of any particular inhabitants of the village.

One can find calendrical rites even in Christianity. Christmas is an example. Throughout the Western world it is celebrated annually on the twenty-fifth day of December, regardless of the wants or needs, on that particular day, of individual Christians or of any congregation of Christians.

As a rule, calendrical performances are entrusted to officially-sanctioned priests, rather than to other persons who may deal with the supernatural; and since ceremonies based on a calendar cannot possibly be geared to anyone's immediate desires, they can be interpreted only as having value for an entire society. In this sense, especially, calendrical observances may be said always to have a "church," and to correspond, on the whole, more nearly to established concepts of religion than to those of magic.

Moreover, since they are always social or communal in character, calendrical rites invariably tend to disappear when a society loses its distinctiveness or radically alters its old ways of life. Thus, when the Hopi Indians of Oraibi began to show greater interest in White than in native culture, the pueblo's calendrical observances were among the first cultural items to suffer disintegration.

In a similar vein, long before the establishment of Israel, the Jews were of particular interest to social scientists partly because they managed to give the impression of being a single society, even though it was patently obvious that they were not, inasmuch as they were scattered among many, many nations. What, then, gave observers the impression that the Jews constituted *a society*? Above all else, it was the fact that regardless of their places of residence the Jewish people steadfastly continued to observe such traditional calendrical (social) ceremonies as Passover and Yom Kippur. It is noteworthy in this context that whenever Jews become assimilated into any originally alien society, they stop observing their ancient calendrical rituals.

Quite different in nearly every respect are those practices, also based on a belief in the supernatural, that we have termed critical. They are, let us recall, customarily designed to meet the pressing needs of a given moment. For this reason they can never be held only because a particular time has arrived, nor can they be announced, scheduled, or prepared for far in advance. In some cases critical ceremonies may be performed by priests, but in a large number of instances they are conducted by other personages.

Unlike calendrical observances which are *invariably* communal or broadly social, critical rituals may be designed to benefit either a whole society, a relatively small group, or even a single individual. It should be obvious that every now and then a critical rite may be held to counteract a public emergency, as when a prolonged drought affects all the farmers in a given community, or when an entire nation prays for peace. However, crises on this scale are comparatively rare. For the most part critical ceremonies are staged only when a private or personal emergency has arisen, as might be the case if something important has been stolen or mislaid, or if a child has fallen gravely ill, or in the event that an individual has entered on a new social position that disturbs his former dealings with the members of his society. In such cases critical rituals are designed to benefit only those who have asked, and sometimes paid, for them. A reexamination of the rich material from Africa, as well as from other regions, pertaining to the services rendered by seers, diviners, fortune-tellers, medicine-men, and so forth, shows that their approach to the supernatural is far more often on behalf of persons who have a problem than it is for the sake of whole societies or communities. These instances show that critical observances do not inevitably need to have a "church." Since, at the same time, they do not necessarily have to be performed by socially sanctioned priests, they tend in a number of ways to correspond quite closely to traditional concepts of magic.

It should be noted further that whereas calendrical rites ordinarily disappear when a society diminishes in power or loses its identity, critical rites may persist long after an entire society has collapsed, and in a new social setting may form the basis for a large number of the carry-overs that students of religion generally call superstitions.

Since the distinction here made cannot be maintained without the existence of some form of a calendar, it is essential to show that even the most primitive and non-literate of people may have a simple way of keeping track of the year's progress. In the northern hemisphere, whose varied religions are far better known to anthropologists than are those of the people who live south of the equator, the easiest method involves no more than noting, from exactly the same spot each day, where the sun seems to rise. When this is done regularly the sun apparently travels from north to south between June 21 and December 21, and from south to north during the remaining six months. Whenever the eastern horizon happens to be irregular it appears as if the sun comes up now from a mountain peak, now from a bit of forest, now from an open stretch, and so on. In this way the coincidence of a sunrise with a particular landmark may serve as a seasonal checkpoint, and as an indication of the time when a given calendrical rite ought to be announced or performed. The terminal or turning points in the sun's annual course mark the solstices. In many communities of the northern hemisphere, even if the June solstice is unnoticed, it is customary to hold important calendrical rituals on or about December 21.

The main reason for this difference of attitude and behavior seems to stem from the fact that whenever it reaches either of its solstice points the sun at first makes so little daily progress in the opposite direction that it appears to rise in the same spot or, in a manner of speaking, to hesitate or to stand still for three or four days. When this "hesitation" takes place on June 21, there is little to fear, for vegetation is usually plentiful, crops are growing, and the weather is balmy. But it is quite another matter when the sun pauses at its southern terminal and appears reluctant to move northward, in the direction of spring and summer. Such a threatened stoppage would, indeed, be a calamity. It might result in perpetual winter, no fodder for animals, and no crops for man. That is why strenuous efforts are sometimes made to get the sun to turn from its southern to its northern path; and that is also why winter solstice observances so commonly take the form of new-fire rites, or else include a number of symbols expressive of man's desire for increased light and heat.

Never should it be thought that calendrical ceremonies, because they may disregard the needs of the moment, are only of secondary importance. Far from it! Analysis of their intent reveals that they are designed primarily to strengthen the bonds of cohesion that hold together all of a society's members or else to aid the individuals who form a social unit to adjust to one another and to their external environment.

Our dichotomy should not be interpreted as a device for classifying every conceivable aspect of primitive religion. For instance, it does not apply smoothly to all the manifestations of the famed rites of passage. It is true that three of van Gennep's stages—birth, marriage, and death—are critical, because they are concerned primarily with individuals and cannot be precisely determined in advance; whereas the fourth—puberty or tribal initiation—is often calendrically observed. Yet, all of the rites of passage drastically change a person's social relationships, and therefore, all of them may be classed, as they usually are, as critical.

For many anthropologists in the United States, especially, the old distinction between magic and religion has lost much of its pristine vitality and freshness. Unless we are prepared to lump all supernatural phenomena into a single category, we need a fresh basis for classification and analysis. That is what the proposed difference between calendrical and critical rites is meant to provide. The likelihood is strong that every social unit's system of supernatural practices contains both calendrical and critical elements. In partnership, these may be seen to function as vital parts of every primitive society's nonempirical method for trying to gain desired ends.

James G. Frazer
SYMPATHETIC MAGIC

Although Sir James G. Frazer was not an outstanding theorist, he was adept at compiling and classifying fact, had some feeling for problem, and stimulated a whole generation of ethnologists to take an interest in the theoretical questions involved in the subject of magic. His classic work, *The Golden Bough*, is one of the best known of all ethnological publications. Many a layman who has never heard of or read other anthropological books has at least perused this one, usually in its abridged, one-volume form.

The portion of this vast work that is reprinted here presents Frazer's well-known distinction between "imitative" and "contagious" magic. This classification, while it assuredly does not encompass the whole range of magical phenomena, does cover the greatest portion. Frazer shows that the common factor in these two kinds of magic is the sympathetic principle: things act on each other at a distance through a "secret sympathy." As long as Frazer restricted himself to classificatory interests of this sort, he remained unchallenged. But when he turned to either historical or analytic problems, he enjoyed less immunity. For example, his argument that magic is older than religion because it is

Reprinted in abridged form from James George Frazer, *The Golden Bough: A Study in Magic and Religion* (12 vols.; 3d ed., rev. and enl.; London: Macmillan & Co., Ltd., 1911–1915), I, 52–219, by permission of Trinity College, Cambridge and Macmillan & Co., Ltd.

psychologically simpler than the concept of spirit agents and because it is more uniform than religious cults does not stand up against criticism. As Marett and Goldenweiser have demonstrated, Frazer's separation of magic from religion has some merit, but it goes too far, because it overlooks the vast areas in which the alleged differences actually overlap and because it tends to obscure the common supernatural basis for each. Frazer's view that magic is comparable to science because both involve mental operations that are alike breaks down because, as Malinowski has insisted, the magical practitioner himself makes a distinction between things that lie in the empirical realm and those that lie in the supernatural.

The following article contains a great many illustrative examples of the nature of magic. The functions of magic are not explicitly considered, but many of them may be recognized in Frazer's descriptions of diverse magical practices. It is cautioned that the author's closing dictum that magic has been "... the mother of freedom and truth," can be true only in a most allegorical sense.

1. THE PRINCIPLES OF MAGIC

If we analyze the principles of thought on which magic is based, they will probably be found to resolve themselves into two: first, that like produces like, or that an effect resembles its cause; and, second, that things which have once been in contact with each other continue to act on each other at a distance after the physical contact has been severed. The former principle may be called the "Law of Similarity," the latter the "Law of Contact or Contagion." From the first of these principles, namely the Law of Similarity, the magician infers that he can produce any effect he desires merely by imitating it: from the second he infers that whatever he does to a material object will affect equally the person with whom the object was once in contact, whether it formed part of his body or not. Charms based on the Law of Similarity may be called "Homeopathic or Imitative Magic." Charms based on the Law of Contact or Contagion may be called "Contagious Magic." To denote the first of these branches of magic the term Homeopathic is perhaps preferable, for the alternative term Imitative or Mimetic suggests, if it does not imply, a conscious agent who imitates, thereby limiting the scope of magic too narrowly. For the same principles which the magician applies in the practice of his art are implicitly believed by him to regulate the operations of inanimate nature; in other words, he tacitly assumes that the Laws of Similarity and Contact are of universal application and are not limited to human actions. In short, magic is a spurious system of natural law as well as a fallacious guide of conduct; it is a false science as well as an abortive art. Regarded as a system of natural law, that is, as a statement of the rules which determine the sequence of events throughout the world, it may be called "Theoretical Magic"; regarded as a set of precepts which human beings observe in order to compass their ends, it may be called "Practical Magic." At the same time it is to be borne in mind that the primitive magician knows magic only on its practical side; he never analyzes the mental processes on which his practice is based, never reflects on the abstract principles involved in his actions. With him, as with the vast majority of men, logic is implicit, not explicit; he reasons, just as he digests his food, in complete ignorance of the intellectual and physiological processes which are essential to the one operation and to the other. In short, to him magic is always an art, never a science; the very idea of science is lacking in his undeveloped mind. It is for the philosophic student to trace the train of thought which underlies the magician's practice; to draw out the few simple threads of which the tangled skein is composed; to disengage the abstract principles from their concrete applications; in short, to discern the spurious science behind the bastard art.

If my analysis of the magician's logic is correct, its two great principles turn out to be merely two different misapplications of the association of ideas. Homeopathic magic is founded on the association of ideas by similarity: contagious magic is founded on the association of ideas by contiguity. Homeopathic magic commits the mistake of assuming that things which resemble each other are the same: contagious magic commits the mistake of assuming that things which have once been in contact with each other are always in contact. But in practice the two branches are often combined; or, to be more exact, while homeopathic or imitative magic may be practiced by itself, contagious magic will generally be found to involve an application of the homeopathic or imitative principle. Thus generally stated the two things may be a little difficult to grasp, but they will readily become intelligible when they are illustrated by particular examples. Both trains of thought are in fact extremely simple and elementary. It could hardly be otherwise, since they are familiar in the concrete, though certainly not in the abstract, to the crude intelligence not only of the savage, but of ignorant and dullwitted people everywhere. Both branches of magic, the homeopathic and the contagious, may conveniently be comprehended under the general name of "Sympathetic Magic," since both assume that things act on each other at a distance through a secret sympathy, the impulse being transmitted from one to the other by means of what we may conceive as a kind of invisible ether, not unlike that which is postulated by modern science for a precisely similar purpose, namely, to explain how things can physically affect each other through a space which appears to be empty.

It may be convenient to tabulate as follows the branches of magic according to the laws of thought which underlie them:

Sympathetic Magic
(Law of Sympathy)

Homeopathic Magic
(Law of Similarity)

Contagious Magic
(Law of Contact)

I will now illustrate these two great branches of sympathetic magic by examples, beginning with homeopathic magic.

2. HOMEOPATHIC OR IMITATIVE MAGIC

Perhaps the most familiar application of the principle that like produces like is the attempt which has been made by many peoples in many ages to injure or destroy an enemy by injuring or destroying an image of him, in the belief that just as the image suffers, so does the man, and that when it perishes he must die. A few instances out of many may be given to prove at once the wide diffusion of the practice over the world and its remarkable persistence through the ages. For thousands of years ago it was known to the sorcerers of ancient India, Babylon, and Egypt, as well as of Greece and Rome, and at this day it is still resorted to by cunning and malignant savages in Australia, Africa, and Scotland. Thus the North American Indians, we are told, believe that by drawing the figure of a person in sand, ashes, or clay, or by considering any object as his body, and then pricking it with a sharp stick or doing it any other injury, they inflict a corresponding injury on the person represented. So when a Cora Indian of Mexico wishes to kill a man, he makes a figure of him out of burnt clay, strips of cloth, and so forth, and then, muttering incantations, runs thorns through the head or stomach of the figure to make his victim suffer correspondingly.

If homeopathic or imitative magic, working by means of images, has commonly been practiced for the spiteful purpose of putting obnoxious people out of the world, it has also, though far more rarely, been employed with the benevolent intention of helping others into it. In other words, it has been used to facilitate childbirth and to procure offspring for barren women. Thus among the Eskimos of Bering Strait a barren woman desirous of having a son will consult a shaman, who commonly makes, or causes her husband to make, a small doll-like image over which he performs certain secret rites, and the woman is directed to sleep with it under her pillow. In Anno, a district of West Africa, women may often be seen carrying wooden dolls strapped, like babies, on their backs as a cure for sterility. In the seventh month of a woman's pregnancy common people in Java observe a ceremony which is plainly designed to facilitate the real birth by mimicking it. Husband and wife repair to a well or to the bank of a neighboring river. The upper part of the woman's body is bare, but young banana leaves are fastened under her arms, a small opening, or rather fold, being left in the leaves in front. Through this opening or fold in the leaves on his wife's body the husband lets fall from above a weaver's shuttle. An old woman receives the shuttle as it falls, takes it up in her arms and dandles it as if it were a baby, saying, "Oh, what a dear little child! Oh, what a beautiful little child!" Then the husband lets an egg slip through the fold, and when it lies on the ground as an emblem of the afterbirth, he takes his sword and cuts through the banana leaf at the place of the fold, obviously as if he were severing the navel-string.

The same principle of make-believe, so dear to children, has led other peoples to employ a simulation of birth as a form of adoption, and even as a mode of restoring a supposed dead person to life. If you pretend to give birth to a boy, or even to a great bearded man who has not a drop of your blood in his veins, then, in the eyes of primitive law and philosophy, that boy or man is really your son to all intents and purposes. Thus Diodorus tells us that when Zeus persuaded his jealous wife Hera to adopt Hercules, the goddess got into bed, and clasping the burly hero to her bosom, pushed him through her robes and let him fall to the ground in imitation of a real birth; and the historian adds that in his own day the same mode of adopting children was practiced by the barbarians. At the present time it is said to be still in use in Bulgaria and among the Bosnian Turks. A woman will take a boy whom she intends to adopt and push or pull him through her clothes; ever afterwards he is regarded as her very son, and inherits the whole property of his adoptive parents. In ancient Greece any man who had been supposed erroneously to be dead, and for whom in his absence funeral rites had been performed, was treated as dead to society till he had gone through the form of being born again. He was passed through a woman's lap, then washed, dressed in swaddling clothes, and put out to nurse. Not until this ceremony had been punctually performed might he mix freely with living folk.

Another beneficent use of homeopathic magic is to heal or prevent sickness. In ancient Greece, when a man died of dropsy, his children were made to sit with their feet in water until the body was burned. This was supposed to prevent the disease from attacking them. In Germany yellow turnips, gold coins, gold rings, saffron, and other yellow things are still esteemed remedies for jaundice, just as a stick of red sealing wax carried on the person cures the red eruption popularly known as St. Anthony's fire, or the bloodstone with its red spots allays bleeding. Another cure prescribed in Germany for St. Anthony's fire is to rub the patient with ashes from a house that has been burned down; for it is easy to see that as the fire died out in that house, so St. Anthony's fire will die out in that man.

One of the great merits of homeopathic magic is that it enables the cure to be performed on the person of the doctor instead of on that of his victim, who is thus relieved of all trouble and inconvenience, while he sees his medical man writhe in anguish before him. For example, the peasants of Perche, in France, labor under the impression that a prolonged fit of vomiting is brought about by the patient's stomach becoming unhooked, as they call it, and so falling down. Accordingly, a practitioner is called in to restore the organ to its proper place. After hearing the symptoms he at once throws himself into the most horrible contortions, for the purpose of unhooking his own stomach. Having succeeded in the effort, he next hooks it up again in another series of contortions and grimaces, while the patient experiences a corresponding relief. Fee five cents. In like manner a Dyak medicine man, who has been fetched in a case of illness, will lie down and pretend to be dead. He is accordingly treated like a corpse, is bound up in mats, taken out of the house, and deposited on the ground. After about an hour the other medicine men loose the pretended dead man and bring him to life; and as he recovers, the sick person is supposed to recover too.

Further, homeopathic and in general sympathetic magic plays a great part in the measures taken by the rude hunter or fisherman to secure an abundant supply of food. On the principle that like produces like, many things are done by him and his friends in deliberate imitation of the result which he seeks to attain; and, on the other hand, many things are scrupulously avoided because they bear some more or less fanciful resemblance to others which would really be disastrous.

Nowhere is the theory of sympathetic magic more systematically carried into practice for the maintenance of the food supply than in the barren region of Central Australia. Here the tribes are divided into a number of totem clans, each of which is charged with the duty of propagating and multiplying their totem for the good of the community by means of magical ceremonies and incantations. The great majority of the totems are edible animals and plants, and the general result supposed to be accomplished by these ceremonies or *intichiuma*, as the Arunta call them, is that of supplying the tribe with food and other necessaries. Often the rites consist of an imitation of the effect which the people desire to produce; in other words, their magic is of the homeopathic or imitative sort. Thus among the Arunta the men of the witchettygrub totem perform a series of elaborate ceremonies for multiplying the grub which the other members of the tribe use as food. One of the ceremonies is a pantomime representing the fully developed insect in the act of emerging from the chrysalis.

The Indians of British Columbia live largely upon the fish which abound in their seas and rivers. If the fish do not come in due season, and the Indians are hungry, a Nootka wizard will make an image of a swimming fish and put it into the water in the direction from which the fish usually appear. This ceremony, accompanied by a prayer to the fish to come, will cause them to arrive at once. The islanders of Torres Straits use models of dugong and turtles to charm dugong and turtles to their destruction. The Toradjas of Central Celebes believe that things of the same sort attract each other by means of their indwelling spirits or vital ether. Hence they hang up the jawbones of deer and wild pigs in their houses, in order that the spirits which animate these bones may draw the living creatures of the same kind into the path of the hunter. In the island of Nias, when a wild pig has fallen into the pit prepared for it, the animal is taken out and its back is rubbed with nine fallen leaves, in the belief that this will make nine more wild pigs fall into the pit, just as the nine leaves fell from the tree.

The western tribes of British New Guinea employ a charm to aid the hunter in spearing dugong or turtle. A small beetle, which haunts coconut trees, is placed in the hole of the spear haft into which the spearhead fits. This is supposed to make the spearhead stick fast in the dugong or turtle, just as the beetle sticks fast to a man's skin when it bites him. When a Cambodian hunter has set his nets and taken nothing, he strips himself naked, goes some way off, then strolls up to the net as if he did not see it, lets himself be caught in it, and cries, "Hello! what's this? I'm afraid I'm caught." After that the net is sure to catch game. A Malay who has baited a trap for crocodiles, and is awaiting results, is careful in eating his curry always to begin by swallowing three lumps of rice successively; for this helps the bait to slide more easily down the crocodile's throat. He is equally scrupulous not to take any bones out of his curry; for, if he did, it seems clear that the sharp-pointed stick on which the bait is skewered would similarly work itself loose, and the crocodile would get off with the bait. Hence in these circumstances it is prudent for the hunter, before he begins his meal, to get somebody else to take the bones out of his curry, otherwise he may at any moment have to choose between swallowing a bone and losing the crocodile.

This last rule is an instance of the things which the hunter abstains from doing lest, on the principle that like produces like, they should spoil his luck. For it is to be observed that the system of sympathetic magic is not merely composed of positive precepts; it comprises a very large number of negative precepts, that is, prohibitions. It tells you not merely what to do, but also what to leave undone. The positive precepts are charms: the negative precepts are taboos. In fact the whole doctrine of taboos, or at all events a large part of it, would seem to be only a special application of sympathetic magic, with its two great laws of similarity and contact. Though these laws are certainly not formulated in so many words nor even conceived in the abstract by the savage, they are nevertheless implicitly believed by him to regulate the course of nature quite independently of human will. He thinks that if he acts in a certain way, certain consequences will inevitably follow in virtue of one or the other of these laws; and if the consequences of a particular act appear to him likely to prove disagreeable or dangerous, he is naturally careful not to act in that way lest he should incur them. In other words, he abstains from doing that which, in accordance with his mistaken notions of cause and effect, he falsely believes would injure him; in short, he subjects himself to a taboo. Thus taboo is so far a negative application of practical magic. Positive magic or sorcery says, "Do this in order that so and so may happen." Negative magic or taboo says, "Do not do this, lest so and so should happen." The aim of positive magic or sorcery is to produce a desired event; the aim of negative magic or taboo is to avoid an undesirable one. But both consequences, the desirable and the undesirable, are supposed to be brought about in accordance with the laws of similarity and contact. And just as the desired consequence is not really affected by the observance of a magical ceremony, so the dreaded consequence does not really result from the violation of a taboo. If the supposed evil necessarily followed a breach of taboo, the taboo would not be a taboo but a precept of morality or common sense. It is not a taboo to say, "Do not put your hand in the Fire"; it is a rule of common sense, because the forbidden action entails a real, not an imaginary, evil. In short, those negative precepts which we call taboo are just as vain and futile as those positive precepts which we call sorcery. The two things are merely opposite sides or poles of one great disastrous fallacy, a mistaken conception of the association of ideas. Of that fallacy, sorcery is the positive and taboo the negative pole. If we give the general name of magic to the whole erroneous system, both theoretical and practical, then taboo may be defined as the negative side of practical magic. To put this in tabular form:

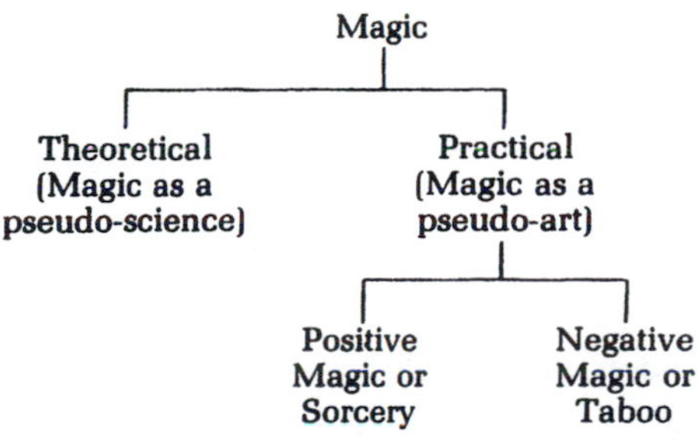

I have made these remarks on taboo and its relations to magic because I am about to give some instances of taboos observed by hunters, fishermen, and others, and I wished to show that they fall under the head of Sympathetic Magic, being only particular applications of that general theory. Among the Eskimos of Baffin Land boys are forbidden to play cat's cradle, because if they did so their fingers might in later life become entangled in the harpoon-line. Here the taboo is obviously an application of the law of similarity, which is the basis of homeopathic magic; as the child's fingers are entangled by the string in playing cat's cradle, so they will be entangled by the harpoon-line when he is a man and hunts whales. Again, among the Huzuls of the Carpathian Mountains, the wife of a hunter may not spin while her husband is eating, or the game will turn and wind like the spindle, and the hunter will be unable to hit it. Here again the taboo is clearly derived from the law of similarity. So, too, in most parts of ancient Italy women were forbidden by law to spin on the highroads as they walked, or even to carry their spindles openly, because any such action was believed to injure the crops. Probably the notion was that the twirling of the spindle would twirl the cornstalks and prevent them from growing straight. So, too, among the Ainos of Saghalien a pregnant woman may not spin nor twist ropes for two months before her delivery, because they think that if she did so the child's guts might be entangled like the thread. For a like reason in Bilaspore, a district of India, when the chief men of a village meet in council no one present should twirl a spindle; for they think that if such a thing were to happen, the discussion, like the spindle, would move in a circle and never be wound up. In the East Indian Islands of Saparoea, Haroekoe, and Noessalaut, any one who comes to the house of a hunter must walk straight in; he may not loiter at the door, for were he to do so, the game would in like manner stop in front of the hunter's snares and then turn back, instead of being caught in the trap. For a similar reason it is a rule with the Toradjas of Central Celebes that no one may stand or loiter on the ladder of a house where there is a pregnant woman, for such delay would retard the birth of the child; and in various parts of Sumatra the woman herself in these circumstances is forbidden to stand at the door or on the top rung of the house-ladder under pain of suffering hard labor for her imprudence in neglecting so elementary a precaution.

Among the taboos observed by savages none perhaps are more numerous or important than the prohibitions to eat certain foods, and of such prohibitions many are demonstrably derived from the law of similarity and are accordingly examples of negative magic. Just as the savage eats many animals or plants in order to acquire certain desirable qualities with which he believes them to be endowed, so he avoids eating many other animals and plants lest he should acquire certain undesirable qualities with which he believes them to be infected. In eating the former he practices positive magic; in abstaining from the latter he practices negative magic.

The reader may have observed that in some of the foregoing examples of taboos the magical influence is supposed to operate at considerable distances; thus among the Blackfeet Indians the wives and children of an eagle hunter are forbidden to use an awl during his absence, lest the eagles should scratch the distant husband and father; and again no male animal may be killed in the house of a Malagasy soldier while he is away at the wars, lest the killing of the animal should entail the killing of the man. This belief in the sympathic influence exerted on each other by persons or things at a distance is of the essence of magic. Whatever doubts science may entertain as to the possibility of action at a distance, magic has none; faith in telepathy is one of its first principles. A modern advocate of the influence of mind upon mind at a distance would have no difficulty in convincing a savage; the savage believed in it long ago, and what is more, he acted on his belief with a logical consistency such as his civilized brother in the faith has not yet, so far as I am aware, exhibited in his conduct. For the savage is convinced not only that magical ceremonies affect persons and things afar off, but that the simplest acts of daily life may do so too. Hence on important occasions the behavior of friends and relations at a distance is often regulated by a more or less elaborate code of rules, the neglect of which by the one set of persons would, it is supposed, entail misfortune or even death on the absent ones. In particular when a party of men are out hunting or fighting, their kinsfolk at home are often expected to do certain things or to abstain from doing certain others, for the sake of ensuring the safety and success of the distant hunters or warriors. I will now give some instances of this magical telepathy both in its positive and in its negative aspect.

In Laos when an elephant hunter is starting for the chase, he warns his wife not to cut her hair or oil her body in his absence; for if she cut her hair the elephant would burst the toils, if she oiled herself it would slip through them. When a Dyak village has turned out to hunt wild pigs in the jungle, the people who stay at home may not touch oil or water with their hands during the absence of their friends; for if they did so, the hunters would all be "butter-fingered" and the prey would slip through their hands. While a Gilyak hunter is pursuing the game in the forest, his children at home are forbidden to make drawings on wood or on sand; for they fear that if the children did so, the paths in the forest would become as perplexed as the lines in the drawings, so that the hunter might lose his way and never return. A Russian political prisoner once taught some Gilyak children to read and write; but their parents forbade them to write when any of their fathers was away from home; for it seemed to them that writing was a peculiarly complicated form of drawing, and they stood aghast at the idea of the danger to which such a drawing would expose the hunters out in the wild woods.

Many of the indigenous tribes of Sarawak are firmly persuaded that were the wives to commit adultery while their husbands are searching for camphor in the jungle, the camphor obtained by the men would evaporate. Husbands can discover, by certain knots in the tree, when their wives are unfaithful; and it is said that in former days many women were killed by jealous husbands on no better evidence than that of these knots. Further, the wives dare not touch a comb while their husbands are away collecting the camphor; for if they did so, the interstices between the fibers of the tree, instead of being filled with the precious crystals, would be empty like the spaces between the teeth of a comb. In the Kei Islands, to the southwest of New Guinea, as soon as a vessel that is about to sail for a distant port has been launched, the part of the beach on which it lay is covered as speedily as possible with palm branches, and becomes sacred. No one may thenceforth cross that spot till the ship comes home. To cross it sooner would cause the vessel to perish. Moreover, all the time that the voyage lasts three or four young girls, specially chosen for the duty, are supposed to remain in sympathetic connection with the mariners and to contribute by their behavior to the safety of and success of the voyage.

Where beliefs like these prevail as to the sympathetic connection between friends at a distance, we need not wonder that above everything else, war, with its stern yet stirring appeal to some of the deepest and tenderest of human emotions, should quicken in the anxious relations left behind a desire to turn the sympathetic bond to the utmost account for the benefit of the dear ones who may at any moment be fighting and dying far away. Hence, to secure an end so natural and laudable, friends at home are apt to resort to devices which will strike us as pathetic or ludicrous, according as we consider their object or the means adopted to effect it. Thus in some districts of Borneo, when a Dyak is out headhunting, his wife or, if he is unmarried, his sister must wear a sword day and night in order that he may always be thinking of his weapons; and she may not sleep during the day nor go to bed before two in the morning, lest her husband or brother should thereby be surprised in his sleep by an enemy. Among the Sea Dyaks of Banting in Sarawak the women strictly observe an elaborate code of rules while the men are away fighting. Some of the rules are negative and some are positive, but all alike are based on the principles of magical homeopathy and telepathy. Amongst them are the following. The women must wake very early in the morning and open the windows as soon as it is light; otherwise their absent husbands will oversleep themselves. The women may not oil their hair, or the men will slip. The women may neither sleep nor doze by day, or the men will be drowsy on the march. The women must cook and scatter popcorn on the veranda every morning; so will the men be agile in their movements. The rooms must be kept very tidy, all boxes being placed near the walls; for if any one were to stumble over them, the absent husbands would fall and be at the mercy of the foe. At every meal a little rice must be left in the pot and put aside; so will the men far away always have something to eat and need never go hungry. On no account may the women sit at the loom till their legs grow cramped, otherwise their husbands will likewise be stiff in their joints and unable to rise up quickly or to run away from the foe. So in order to keep their husbands' joints supple the women often vary their labors at the loom by walking up and down the veranda. Further, they may not cover up their faces, or the men would not be able to find their way through the tall grass or jungle. Again, the women may not sew with a needle, or the men will tread on the sharp spikes set by the enemy in the path. Should a wife prove unfaithful while her husband is away, he will lose his life in the enemy's country.

Among the Thompson Indians of British

Columbia, when the men were on the warpath, the women performed dances at frequent intervals. These dances were believed to ensure the success of the expedition. The dancers flourished their knives, threw long, sharp-pointed sticks forward, or drew sticks with hooked ends repeatedly backward and forward. Throwing the sticks forward was symbolic of piercing or warding off the enemy, and drawing them back was symbolic of drawing their own men from danger. The hook at the end of the stick was particularly well adapted to serve the purpose of a life-saving apparatus. The women always pointed their weapons towards the enemy's country. They painted their faces red and sang as they danced, and they prayed to the weapons to preserve their husbands and help them to kill many foes. Some had eagledown stuck on the points of their sticks. When the dance was over, these weapons were hidden. If a woman whose husband was at the war thought she saw hair or a piece of scalp on the weapon when she took it out, she knew that her husband had killed an enemy. But if she saw a stain of blood on it, she knew he was wounded or dead. When the men of the Yuki tribe of Indians in California were away fighting, the women at home did not sleep; they danced continually in a circle, chanting and waving leafy wands. For they said that if they danced all the time, their husbands would not grow tired. When a band of Carib Indians of the Orinoco had gone on the warpath, their friends left in the village used to calculate as nearly as they could the exact moment when the absent warriors would be advancing to attack the enemy. Then they took two lads, laid them down on a bench, and inflicted a most severe scouring on their bare backs. This the youths submitted to without a murmur, supported in their sufferings by the firm conviction, in which they had been bred from childhood, that on the constancy and fortitude with which they bore the cruel ordeal depended the valor and success of their comrades in the battle.

Among the many beneficent uses to which a mistaken ingenuity has applied the principle of homeopathic or imitative magic, is that of causing trees and plants to bear fruit in due season. In Thüringen the man who sows flax carries the seed in a long bag which reaches from shoulders to his knees, and he walks with long strides, so that the bag sways to and fro on his back. It is believed that this will cause the flax to wave in the wind. In the interior of Sumatra rice is sown by women who, in sowing, let their hair hang loose down their back, in order that the rice may grow luxuriantly and have long stalks. Similarly, in ancient Mexico a festival was held in honor of the goddess of maize, or "the long-haired mother," as she was called. It began at the time "when the plant had attained its full growth, and fibers shooting forth from the top of the green ear indicated that the grain was fully formed. During this festival the women wore their long hair unbound, shaking and tossing it in the dances which were the chief features in the ceremonial, in order that the tassel of the maize might grow in like profusion, that the grain might be correspondingly large and flat, and that the people might have abundance."

The notion that a person can influence a plant homeopathically by his act or condition comes out clearly in a remark made by a Malay woman. Being asked why she stripped the upper part of her body naked in reaping the rice, she explained that she did it to make the rice-husks thinner, as she was tired of pounding thick-husked rice. Clearly, she thought that the less clothing she wore the less husk there would be on the rice. The magic virtue of a pregnant woman to communicate fertility is known to Bavarian and Austrian peasants, who think that if you give the first fruit of a tree to a woman with child to eat, the trees will bring forth abundantly next year. On the other hand, the Baganda believe that a barren wife infects her husband's garden with her own sterility and prevents the trees from bearing fruit; hence a childless woman is generally divorced.

Thus on the theory of homeopathic magic a person can influence vegetation either for good or for evil according to the good or the bad character of his acts or states: for example, a fruitful woman makes plants fruitful, a barren woman makes them barren. Hence this belief in the noxious and infectious nature of certain personal qualities or accidents has given rise to a number of prohibitions or rules of avoidance: people abstain from doing certain things lest they should homeopathically infect the fruits of the earth with their own undesirable state or condition. All such customs of abstention or rules of avoidance are examples of negative magic or taboo.

In the foregoing cases a person is supposed to influence vegetation homeopathically. He infects trees or plants with qualities or accidents, good or bad, resembling and derived from his own. But on the principle of homeopathic magic the influence is mutual: the plant can infect the man just as much as the man can infect the plant. In magic, as I believe in physics, action and reaction are equal and opposite. The Cherokee Indians are adept in practical botany of the homeopathic sort. Thus wiry roots of the catgut plant or devil's shoestring (*Tephrosia*) are so tough that they can almost stop a plowshare in the furrow. Hence Cherokee women wash their hands with a decoction of the roots to make the hair strong, and Cherokee ballplayers wash themselves with it to toughen their muscles. It is a Galelareese belief that if you eat a fruit which has fallen to the ground, you will yourself contract a disposition to stumble and fall; and that if you partake of something which has been forgotten (such as a sweet potato left in the pot or a banana in the fire), you will become forgetful. The Galelareese are also of the opinion that if a woman were to consume two bananas growing from a single head she would give birth to twins. The Guarani Indians of South America thought that a woman would become a mother of twins if she ate a double grain of millet. Near Charlotte Waters, in Central Australia, there is a tree which sprang up to mark the spot where a blind man died. It is called the Blind Tree by the natives, who think that if it were cut down all the people of the neighborhood would become blind. A man who wishes to deprive his enemy of sight need only go to the tree by himself and rub it, muttering his wish and exhorting the magic virtue to go forth and do its baleful work. In this last example the infectious quality, though it emanates directly from a tree, is derived originally from a man—namely, the blind man—who was buried at the place where the tree grew. Similarly, the Central Australians believe that a certain group of stones at Undiara are the petrified boils of an old man who long ago plucked them from his body and left them there; hence any man who wishes to infect his enemy with boils will go to these stones and throw miniature spears at them, taking care that the points of the spears strike the stones. Then the spears are picked up, and thrown one by one in the direction of the person whom it is intended to injure. The spears carry with them the magic virtue from the stones, and the result is an eruption of painful boils on the body of the victim. Sometimes a whole group of people can be afflicted in this way by a skillful magician.

These examples introduce us to a fruitful branch of homeopathic magic, namely to that department of it which works by means of the dead; for just as the dead can neither see nor hear nor speak, so you may on homeopathic principles render people blind, deaf, and dumb by the use of dead men's bones or anything else that is tainted by the infection of death. Thus among the Galelareese, when a young man goes a-wooing at night, he takes a little earth from a grave and strews it on the roof of his sweetheart's house just above the place where her parents sleep. This, he fancies, will prevent them from waking while he converses with his beloved, since the earth from the grave will make them sleep as sound as the dead. Burglars in all ages and many lands have been patrons of this species of magic, which is very useful to them in the exercise of their profession. Thus a South Slavonian housebreaker sometimes begins operations by throwing a dead man's bone over the house, saying, with pungent sarcasm, "As this bone may waken, so may these people waken"; after that not a soul in the house can keep his or her eyes open. Similarly, in Java the burglar takes earth from a grave and sprinkles it round the house which he intends to rob; this throws the inmates into a deep sleep. In Europe similar properties were ascribed to the Hand of Glory, which was the dried and pickled hand of a man who had been hanged. If a candle made of the fat of a malefactor who had also died on the gallows was lighted and placed in the Hand of Glory as in a candlestick, it rendered motionless all persons to whom it was presented; they could not stir a finger any more than if they were dead. An ancient Greek robber or burglar thought he could silence and put to flight the fiercest watchdogs by carrying with him a brand plucked from a funeral pyre. Again, Servian and Bulgarian women who chafe at the restraints of domestic life will take the copper coins from the eyes of a corpse, wash them in wine or water, and give the liquid to their husband to drink. After swallowing it, the husbands will be as blind to his wife's peccadilloes as the dead man was on whose eyes the coins were laid.

Again, animals are often conceived to possess qualities or properties which might be useful to man, and homeopathic or imitative magic seeks to communicate these properties to human beings in various ways. Thus some Bechuanas wear a ferret as a charm, because, being very tenacious of life, it will make them difficult to kill. Others wear a certain insect, mutilated, but living, for a similar purpose. Yet other Bechuana warriors wear the hair of a hornless ox among their own hair, and the skin of a frog on their mantle, because a frog is slippery, and the ox, having no horns, is hard to catch; so the man who is provided with these charms believes that he will be as hard to hold as the ox and the frog. One of the ancient books of India prescribes that when a sacrifice is offered for victory, the earth out of which the altar is to be made should be taken from a place where a boar has been wallowing, since the strength of the boar will be in that earth. When you are playing the one-stringed lute, and your fingers are stiff, the thing to do it to catch some long-legged field spiders and roast them, and then rub your fingers with the ashes; that will make your fingers as lithe and nimble as the spiders' legs—at least so think the Galelareese. Among the western tribes of British New Guinea, a man who has killed a snake will burn it and smear his legs with the ashes when he goes into the forest; for no snake will bite him for some days afterwards. If a South Slavonian has a mind to pilfer and steal at market, he has nothing to do but to burn a blind cat, and then throw a pinch of its ashes over the person with whom he is haggling; after that he can take what he likes from the booth, and the owner will not be a bit the wiser, having become as blind as the deceased cat with whose ashes he has been sprinkled. The thief may even ask boldly "Did I pay for it?" and the deluded huckster will reply, "Why certainly."

On the principle of homeopathic magic, inanimate things, as well as plants and animals, may diffuse blessing or bane around them, according to their own intrinsic nature and the skill of the wizard to tap or dam, as the case may be, the stream of weal or woe. In Samarkand women give a baby sugar candy to suck and put glue in the palm of its hand, in order that when the child grows up his words may be sweet and precious things may stick to his hands as if they were glued. The Greeks thought that a garment made from a fleece of a sheep that had been torn by a wolf would hurt the wearer, setting up an itch or irritation in his skin. They were also of the opinion that if a stone which had been bitten by a dog were dropped in wine, it would make all who drank of that wine to fall out among themselves. Among the Arabs of Moab a childless woman often borrows the robe of a woman who has had many children, hoping with the robe to acquire the fruitfulness of its owner. The Caffres of Sofala, in East Africa, had a great dread of being struck with anything hollow, such as a reed or a straw, and greatly preferred being thrashed with a good thick cudgel or an iron bar, even though it hurt very much. For they thought that if a man were beaten with anything hollow, his inside would waste away till he died.

In Madagascar a mode of counteracting the levity of fortune is to bury a stone at the foot of the heavy house-post. The common custom of swearing upon a stone may be based partly on a belief that the strength and stability of the stone lend confirmation to an oath. Thus the old Danish historian Saxo Grammaticus tells us that "the ancients, when they were to choose a king, were wont to stand on stones planted in the ground, and to proclaim their votes, in order to foreshadow from the steadfastness of the stones that the deed would be lasting." But while a general magical efficacy may be supposed to reside in all stones by reason of their common properties of weight and solidity, special magical virtues are attributed to particular stones, or kinds of stone, in accordance with their individual or specific qualities of shape and color. The Indians of Peru employed certain stones for the increase of maize, others for the increase of potatoes, and others again for the increase of cattle. The stones used to make maize grow were fashioned in the likeness of cobs of maize, and the stones destined to multiply cattle had the shape of sheep. The ancients set great store on the magical qualities of precious stones; indeed it has been maintained, with great show of reason, that such stones were used as amulets long before they were worn as mere ornaments. Thus the Greeks gave the name of tree-agate to a stone which exhibits treelike markings, and they thought that if two of these gems were tied to the horns or neck of oxen at the plow, the crop would be sure to be plentiful. Again, they recognized a milkstone which produced an abundant supply of milk in women if only they drank it dissolved in honey-mead. Milkstones are used for the same purpose by Greek women in Crete and Melos at the present day; in Albania nursing mothers wear the stones in order to ensure an abundant flow of milk. Again, the Greeks believed in a stone which cured snake bites, and hence was named the snakestone; to test its efficacy you had only to grind the stone to powder and sprinkle the powder on the wound. The wine-colored amethyst received its name, which means "not drunken" because it was supposed to keep the wearer of it sober; and two brothers who desired to live in unity were advised to carry magnets about with them, which, by drawing the twain together, would clearly prevent them from falling out.

Dwellers by the sea cannot fail to be impressed by the sight of its ceaseless ebb and flow, and are apt, on the principles of that rude philosophy of sympathy and resemblance which here engages our attention, to trace a subtle relation, a secret harmony, between its tides and the life of man, of animals, and of plants. In the flowing tide they see not merely a symbol but a cause of exuberance, of prosperity, and of life, while in the ebbing tide they discern a real agent as well as a melancholy emblem of failure, of weakness, and of death. The Breton peasant fancies that clover sown when the tide is coming in will grow well, but that if the plant be sown at low water or when the tide is going out, it will never reach maturity, and that the cows which feed on it will burst. His wife believes that the best butter is made when the tide has just turned and is beginning to flow, that milk which foams in the churn will go on foaming till the hour of high water is past, and that water drawn from the well or milk extracted from the cow while the tide is rising will boil up in the pot or saucepan and overflow into the fire. According to some of the ancients, the skins of seals, even after they had been parted from their bodies, remained in secret sympathy with the sea, and were observed to ruffle when the tide was on the ebb. Another ancient belief, attributed to Aristotle, was that no creature can die except at ebb tide. In Portugal, all along the coast of Wales, and on some parts of the coast of Brittany, a belief is said to prevail that people are born when the tide comes in, and die when it goes out. Dickens attests the existence of the same superstition in England. "People can't die along the coast," said Mr. Peggotty, "except when the tide's pretty nigh out. They can't be born, unless it's pretty nigh in—not properly born till flood."

Another application of the maxim that like produces like is seen in the Chinese belief that the fortunes of a town are deeply affected by its shape, and that they must vary according to the character of the thing which that shape most nearly resembles. Thus it is related that long ago the town of Tsuen-cheu-fu, the outlines of which are like those of a carp, frequently fell a prey to the depredations of the neighboring city of Yung-chun, which is shaped like a fishing net, until the inhabitants of the former town conceived the plan of erecting two tall pagodas in their midst. These pagodas, which still tower above the city of Tsuen-cheu-fu, have ever since exercised the happiest influence over its destiny by intercepting the imaginary net before it could descend and entangle in its meshes the imaginary carp.

Sometimes homeopathic or imitative magic is called in to annul an evil omen by accomplishing it in mimicry. The effect is to circumvent destiny by substituting a mock calamity for a real one. In Madagascar this mode of cheating the fates is reduced to a regular system. Here every man's fortune is determined by the day or hour of his birth, and if that happens to be an unlucky one his fate is sealed, unless the mischief can be extracted, as the phrase goes, by means of a substitute. The ways of extracting the mischief are various. For example, if a man is born on the first day of the second month (February), his house will be burnt down when he comes of age. To take time by the forelock and avoid this catastrophe, the friends of the infant will set up a shed in a field or in a cattle fold and burn it. If the ceremony is to be really effective, the child and his mother should be placed in the shed and only plucked, like brands, from the burning hut before it is too late. Once more, if fortune has frowned on the man at his birth and penury has marked him for her own, he can easily erase the mark in question by purchasing a couple of cheap pearls, price three halfpence, and burying them. For who but the rich of this world can thus afford to fling pearls away?

3. CONTAGIOUS MAGIC

Thus far we have been considering chiefly that branch of sympathetic magic which may be called homeopathic or imitative. Its leading principle, as we have seen, is that like produces like, or, in other words, that an effect resembles its cause. The other branch of sympathetic magic, which I have called Contagious Magic, proceeds upon the notion that things which have once been conjoined must remain ever afterwards, even when quite dissevered from each other, in such a sympathetic relation that whatever is done to the one must similarly affect the other. Thus the logical basis of Contagious Magic, like that of Homeopathic Magic, is a mistaken association of ideas; its physical basis, if we may speak of such a thing, like the physical basis of Homeopathic Magic, is a material medium of some sort which, like the ether of modern physics, is assumed to unite distant objects and to convey impressions from one to the other. The most familiar example of Contagious Magic is the magical sympathy which is supposed to exist between a man and any severed portion of his person, as his hair or nails; so that whoever gets possession of human hair or nails may work his will, at any distance, upon the person from whom they were cut. This superstition is worldwide; instances of it in regard to hair and nails may be noticed later on in this work. I will now illustrate the principles of Contagious Magic by examples, beginning with its application to various parts of the human body.

The Basutos are careful to conceal their extracted teeth, lest these should fall into the hands of certain mythical beings called *baloi,* who haunt graves, and who could harm the owner of the tooth by working magic on it. In Sussex some fifty years ago a maidservant remonstrated strongly against the throwing away of children's cast teeth, affirming that should they be found and gnawed by any animal, the child's new tooth would be, for all the world, like the teeth of the animal that had bitten the old one. In proof of this she named old Master Simmons, who had a very large pig's tooth in his upper jaw, a personal defect that he always averred was caused by his mother, who threw away one of his cast teeth by accident into the hog's trough. A similar belief had led to practices intended, on the principles of homeopathic magic, to replace old teeth by new and better ones. Thus in many parts of the world it is customary to put extracted teeth in some place where they will be found by a mouse or a rat, in the hope that, through the sympathy which continues to subsist between them and their former owner his other teeth may acquire the same firmness and excellence as the teeth of these rodents.

Other parts which are commonly believed to remain in a sympathetic union with the body, after the physical connection has been severed, are the navel-string and the afterbirth, including the placenta. So intimate, indeed, is the union conceived to be, that the fortunes of the individual for good or evil throughout life are often supposed to be bound up with one or other of these portions of his person, so that if his navel-string or afterbirth is preserved and properly treated, he will be prosperous; whereas if it be injured or lost, he will suffer accordingly. Certain tribes of Western Australia believe that a man swims well or ill, according as his mother at his birth threw the navel-string into water or not. In Ponape, one of the Caroline Islands, the navel-string is placed in a shell and then disposed of in such a way as shall best adapt the child for the career which the parents have chosen for him. Thus if they wish to make him a good climber, they will hang the navel-string on a tree. Among the Cherokees the navel-string of a girl is buried under a corn mortar, in order that the girl may grow up to be a good baker; but the navel-string of a boy is hung up on a tree in the woods, in order that he may be a hunter.

Even in Europe many people still believe that a person's destiny is more or less bound up with that of his navel-string or afterbirth. Thus in Rhenish Bavaria the navel-string is kept for a while wrapt up in a piece of old linen, and then cut or pricked to pieces according as the child is a boy or a girl, in order that he or she may grow up to be a skillful workman or a good seamstress. In Berlin the midwife commonly delivers the dried navel-string to the father with a strict injunction to preserve it carefully, for as long as it is kept the child will live and thrive and be free from sickness. In Beauce and Perche the people are careful to throw the navel-string neither into water nor into fire, believing that if that were done the child would be drowned or burned.

A curious application of the doctrine of contagious magic is the relation commonly believed to exist between a wounded man and the agent of the wound, so that whatever is subsequently done by or to the agent must correspondingly affect the patient either for good or evil. Thus Pliny tells us that if you have wounded a man and are sorry for it, you have only to spit on the hand that gave the wound, and the pain of the sufferer will be instantly alleviated. In Melanesia, if a man's friends get possession of the arrow which wounded him, they keep it in a damp place or in cool leaves, for then the inflammation will be trifling and will soon subside. Meantime the enemy who shot the arrow is hard at work to aggravate the wound by all means in his power. For this purpose he and his friends drink hot and burning juices and chew irritating leaves, for this will clearly inflame and irritate the wound. Further, they keep the bow near the fire to make the wound which it has inflicted hot; and for the same reason they put the arrowhead, if it has been recovered, into the fire. Moreover, they are careful to keep the bowstring taut and to twang it occasionally, for this will cause the wounded man to suffer from tension of the nerves and spasms of tetanus. Similarly when a Kwakiutl Indian of British Columbia had bitten a piece out of an enemy's arm he used to drink hot water afterwards for the purpose of thereby inflaming the wound in his foe's body. If a horse wounds its foot by treading on a nail, a Suffolk groom will invariably preserve the nail, clean it, and grease it every day, to prevent the foot from festering. A few years ago a veterinary surgeon was sent for to attend a horse which had ripped its side open on the hinge of a farm gatepost. On arriving at the farm he found that nothing had been done to the wounded horse, but that a man was busy trying to pry the hinge out of the gatepost in order that it might be greased and put away, which, in the opinion of the Cambridge wiseacres, would conduce to the recovery of the animal. Similarly, Essex rustics opine that, if a man has been stabbed with a knife, it is essential to his recovery that the knife should be greased and laid across the bed on which the sufferer is lying. So in Bavaria you are directed to anoint a linen rag with grease and tie it on the edge of the axe that cut you, taking care to keep the sharp edge upwards. As the grease on the axe dries, your wound heals.

The sympathetic connection supposed to exist between a man and the weapon which wounded him is probably founded on the notion that the blood on the weapon continues to feel with the blood in his body. For a like reason the Papuans of Tumleo, an island off German New Guinea, are careful to throw into the sea the bloody bandages with which their wounds have been dressed, for they fear that if these rags fell into the hands of an enemy he might injure them magically thereby. Once when a man with a wound in his mouth, which bled constantly, came to the missionaries to be treated, his faithful wife took great pains to collect all the blood and cast it into the sea. Strained and unnatural as this idea may seem to us, it is perhaps less so than the belief that magic sympathy is maintained between a person and his clothes, so that whatever is done to the clothes will be felt by the man himself even though he may be far away at the time. In Tanna, one of the New Hebrides, a man who had a grudge at another and desired his death would try to get possession of a cloth which had touched the sweat of his enemy's body. If he succeeded, he rubbed the cloth carefully over with the leaves and twigs of a certain tree, rolled and bound cloth, twigs and leaves into a long sausage-shaped bundle, and burned it slowly in the fire. As the bundle was consumed, the victim fell ill, and when it was reduced to ashes, he died. In this last form of enchantment, however, the magical sympathy may be supposed to exist not so much between the man and the cloth as between the man and the sweat which issued from his body. But in other cases of the same sort it seems that the garment by itself is enough to give the sorcerer a hold upon his victim. In Prussia they say that if you cannot catch a thief, the next best thing you can do is to get hold of a garment which he may have shed in his flight; for if you beat it soundly, the thief will fall sick. This belief is firmly rooted in the popular mind. Some eighty or ninety years ago, in the neighborhood of Berend, a man was detected trying to steal honey, and fled, leaving his coat behind him. When he heard that the enraged owner of the honey was mauling his lost coat, he was so alarmed that he took to his bed and died.

Again magic may be wrought on a man sympathetically, not only through his clothes and severed parts of himself, but also through the impressions left by his body in sand or earth. In particular, it is a worldwide superstition that by injuring footprints you can injure the feet that made them. Thus the natives of southeastern Australia think that they can lame a man by placing sharp pieces of quartz, glass, bone, or charcoal in his footprints. In North Africa the magic of footprints is sometimes used for more amiable purposes. A woman who wishes to attach her husband or lover to herself will take earth from the print of his right foot, tie it up with some of his hairs in a packet, and wear the packet next to her skin.

Similar practices prevail in various parts of Europe. Thus in Mecklenburg it is thought that if you drive a nail into a man's footprint he will fall lame; sometimes it is required that the nail should be taken from a coffin. A like mode of injuring an enemy is resorted to in some parts of France. It is said that there was an old woman who used to frequent Stow in Suffolk, and she was a witch. If, while she walked, anyone went after her and stuck a nail or a knife into her footprint in the dust, the dame could not stir a step until it was withdrawn. An old Danish mode of concluding a treaty was based on the same idea of the sympathetic connection between a man and his footprints; the covenanting parties sprinkled each other's footprints with their own blood, thus giving a pledge of fidelity. In ancient Greece superstitions of the same sort seem to have been current, for it was thought that if a horse stepped on the track of a wolf he was seized with numbness; and a maxim ascribed to Pythagoras forbade people to pierce a man's footprints with a nail or a knife.

The same superstition is turned to account by hunters in many parts of the world for the purpose of running down the game. Thus a German huntsman will stick a nail taken from a coffin into the fresh spoor of the quarry, believing that this will hinder the animal from escaping. The aborigines of Victoria put hot embers in the tracks of the animals they were pursuing. Hottentot hunters throw into the air a handful of sand taken from the footprints of the game, believing that this will bring the animal down. Thompson Indians used to lay charms on the tracks of wounded deer; after that they deemed it superfluous to pursue the animal any further that day, for being thus charmed it could not travel far and would soon die.

But though the footprint is the most obvious it is not the only impression made by the body through which magic may be wrought on a man. The aborigines of southeastern Australia believe that a man may be injured by burying sharp fragments of quartz, glass, and so forth in the mark made by his reclining body; the magical virtue of these sharp things enters his body and causes those acute pains which the ignorant European puts down as rheumatism. We can now understand why it was a maxim with the Pythagoreans that in rising from bed you should smooth away the impression left by your body on the bedclothes. The rule was simply an old precaution against magic, forming part of a whole code of superstitious maxims which antiquity fathered on Pythagoras, though doubtless they were familiar to the barbarous forefathers of the Greeks long before the time of that philosopher.

4. THE MAGICIAN'S PROGRESS

We have now concluded our examination of the general principles of sympathetic magic. The examples by which I have illustrated them have been drawn for the most part from what may be called private magic, that is, from magical rites and incantations practiced for the benefit or the injury of individuals. But in savage society there is commonly to be found in addition what we may call public magic, that is, sorcery practiced for the benefit of the whole community. Wherever ceremonies of this sort are observed for the common good, it is obvious that the magician ceases to be merely a private practitioner and becomes to some extent a public functionary. The development of such a class of functionaries is of great importance for the political as well as the religious evolution of society. For when the welfare of the tribe is supposed to depend on the performance of these magical rites, the magician rises into a position of much influence and repute, and may readily acquire the rank and authority of a chief or king. The profession accordingly draws into its ranks some of the ablest and most ambitious men of the tribe, because it holds out to them a prospect of honor, wealth, and power such as hardly any other career could offer. The acuter minds perceive how easy it is to dupe their weaker brother and to play on his superstition for their own advantage. Not that the sorcerer is always a knave and imposter; he is often sincerely convinced that he really possesses those wonderful powers which the credulity of his fellows ascribes to him. But the more sagacious he is, the more likely he is to see through the fallacies which impose on duller wits. Thus the ablest members of the profession must tend to be more or less conscious deceivers; and it is just these men who in virtue of their superior ability will generally come to the top and win for themselves positions of the highest dignity and the most commanding authority. The pitfalls which beset the path of the professional sorcerer are many, and as a rule only the man of coolest head and sharpest wit will be able to steer his way through them safely. For it must always be remembered that every single profession and claim put forward by the magician as such is false; not one of them can be maintained without deception, conscious or unconscious. Accordingly the sorcerer who sincerely believes in his own extravagant pretensions is in far greater peril and is much more likely to be cut short in his career than the deliberate impostor. The honest wizard always expects that his charms and incantations will produce their supposed effect; and when they fail, not only really, as they always do, but conspicuously and disastrously, as they often do, he is taken aback: he is not, like his knavish colleague, ready with a plausible excuse to account for the failure, and before he can find one he may be knocked on the head by his disappointed and angry employers.

The general result is that at this stage of social evolution the supreme power tends to fall into the hands of men of the keenest intelligence and the most unscrupulous character. If we could balance the harm they do by their knavery against the benefits they confer by their superior sagacity, it might well be found that the good greatly outweighed the evil. For more mischief has probably been wrought in the world by honest fools in high places than by intelligent rascals. Once your shrewd rogue has attained the height of his ambition, and has no longer any selfish end to further, he may, and often does, turn his talent, his experience, his resources, to the service of the public. Many men who have been least scrupulous in the acquisition of power have been most beneficent in the use of it, whether the power they aimed at and won was that of wealth, political authority, or what not. In the field of politics the wily intriguer, the ruthless victor, may end by being a wise and magnanimous ruler, blessed in his lifetime, lamented at his death, admired and applauded by posterity. Such men, to take two of the most conspicuous instances, were Julius Caesar and Augustus. But once a fool always a fool, and the greater the power in his hand the more disastrous is likely to be the use he makes of it. The heaviest calamity in English history, the breach with America, might never have occurred if George the Third had not been an honest dullard.

Thus, so far as the public profession of magic affected the constitution of savage society, it tended to place the control of affairs in the hands of the ablest man: it shifted the balance of power from the many to the one: it substituted a monarchy for a democracy, or rather for an oligarchy of old men; for in general the savage community is ruled not by the whole body of adult males, but by a council of elders. The change, by whatever causes produced, and whatever the character of the early rulers, was on the whole very beneficial. For the rise of monarchy appears to be an essential condition of the emergence of mankind from savagery. No human being is so hidebound by custom and tradition as your democratic savage; in no state of society consequently is progress so slow and difficult. The old notion that the savage is the freest of mankind is the reverse of the truth. He is a slave, not indeed to a visible master, but to the past, to the spirits of his dead forefathers, who haunt his steps from birth to death, and rule him with a rod of iron. What they did is the pattern of right, the unwritten law to which he yields a blind, unquestioning obedience. The least possible scope is thus afforded to superior talent to change old customs for the better. The ablest man is dragged down by the weakest and dullest, who necessarily sets the standard, since he cannot rise, while the other can fall. The surface of such a society presents a uniform dead level, so far as it is humanly possible to reduce the natural inequalities, the immeasurable real differences of inborn capacity and temper, to a false superficial appearance of equality. From this low and stagnant condition of affairs, which demagogues and dreamers in later times have lauded as the ideal state, the Golden Age, of humanity, everything that helps to raise society by opening a career to talent and proportioning the degrees of authority to men's natural abilities, deserves to be welcomed by all who have the real good of their fellows at heart. Once these elevating influences have begun to operate—and they cannot be forever suppressed—the progress of civilization becomes comparatively rapid. The rise of one man to supreme power enables him to carry through changes in a single lifetime which previously many generations might not have sufficed to effect; and if, as will often happen, he is a man of intellect and energy above the common, he will readily avail himself of the opportunity. Even the whims and caprices of a tyrant may be of service in breaking the chain of custom which lies so heavy on the savage. And as soon as the tribe ceases to be swayed by the timid and divided counsels of the elders, and yields to the direction of a single strong and resolute mind, it becomes formidable to its neighbors and enters on a career of aggrandizement, which at an early stage of history is often highly favorable to social, industrial, and intellectual progress. For extending its sway, partly by force of arms, partly by the voluntary submission of weaker tribes, the community soon acquires wealth and slaves, both of which, by relieving some classes from the perpetual struggle for a bare subsistence, afford them an opportunity of devoting themselves to that disinterested pursuit of knowledge which is the noblest and most powerful instrument to ameliorate the lot of man.

Intellectual progress, which reveals itself in the growth of art and science and the spread of more liberal views, cannot be dissociated from industrial or economic progress, and that in its turn receives an immense impulse from conquest and empire. It is no mere accident that the most vehement outbursts of activity of the human mind have followed close on the heels of victory, and that the great conquering races of the world have commonly done most to advance and spread civilization, thus healing in peace the wounds they inflicted in war. The Babylonians, the Greeks, the Romans, the Arabs are our witnesses in the past: we may yet live to see a similar outburst in Japan. Nor, to remount the stream of history to its sources, is it an accident that all the first great strides towards civilization have been made under despotic and theocratic governments, like those of Egypt, Babylon, and Peru, where the supreme ruler claimed and received the servile allegiance of his subjects in the double character of a king and a god. It is hardly too much to say that at this early epoch despotism is the best friend of humanity and, paradoxical as it may sound, of liberty. For after all there is more liberty in the best sense—liberty to think our own thoughts and to fashion our own destinies—under the most absolute despotism, the most grinding tyranny, than under the apparent freedom of savage life, where the individual's lot is cast from the cradle to the grave in the iron mold of hereditary custom.

So far, therefore, as the public profession of magic has been one of the roads by which the ablest men have passed to supreme power, it has contributed to emancipate mankind from the thralldom of tradition and to elevate them into a larger, freer life, with a broader outlook on the world. This is no small service rendered to humanity. And when we remember further that in another direction magic has paved the way for science, we are forced to admit that if the black art has done much evil, it has also been the source of much good; that if it is the child of error, it has yet been the mother of freedom and truth.

S. J. Tambiah

THE FORM AND MEANING OF MAGICAL ACTS: A POINT OF VIEW

By drawing on the concrete ethnographic data provided in Evans-Pritchard's famous book, *Witchcraft, Oracles, and Magic Among the Azande* (1937), S. J. Tambiah presents an insightful explication of the logic embedded in magical behavior. His concern is not so much with the specific content of magical spells or rituals as it is with the mode of thought which underlies them. The essay addresses three major points. First, Tambiah emphasizes the similar use of *analogy* in both scientific and magical thinking but then goes on to make a radical distinction between different ways of using analogy. The scientific use of analogy depends on the causal relationship between objects and their qualities such that predictions can be made from *known* sets of causal relationships to similar, but *unknown* sets. In this manner, empirically verifiable hypotheses and comparisons can be generated. Analogy employed in magic, however, depends on a persuasive or evocative transference of the value or meaning implied in one set of relationships to a second set of relationships, although a relation of similarity or causality does not necessarily obtain between these two sets. Magic, Tambiah maintains, is neither simply a science that has failed (as Frazer asserts in his essay in this chapter) nor an incipient "rational" science (as Horton suggests in Chapter Five). Rather, the empirical mode of science and the persuasive, "performative" mode of ritual magic represent two types of thought; the criteria of one cannot—and should not—be applied to the other. Nor is one mode of thought necessarily superior to the other, as Tambiah points out in the second part of his essay. There, he analyzes the "performative" nature of ritual acts and speech, and certain aspects of ordinary language. He borrows Austin's concept of the "performative utterance" to show that *thinking* and *action* are intimately connected not only in ritual or magical behavior but in everyday behavior as well. Making a promise or issuing a command resembles a magical spell in that both rely on the fact that neither merely *describes* an action. Their very utterance is itself an action which effects a change in the world. It is on these criteria of persuasion, transference, and expansion of meaning that magical acts must be evaluated and analyzed, for it is upon them that the conceived efficacy of such acts rests. For further discussion of the issues raised here, see "The Magical Power of Words" (1968) by S. J. Tambiah, and "It's All Uphill: The Creative Metaphors of Ilongot Magical Spells" (1975) by Michelle Z. Rosaldo.

Reprinted in abridged form from R. Horton and R. Finnegan (eds.), *Modes of Thought* (London: Faber and Faber Ltd., 1973), 199–229, by permission of the author and the publisher.

Finally, Tambiah concludes his essay by addressing the wider implications of his argument. He questions the preconceptions embedded in such categories as "magic," "science," and "religion" which imply that all social and cultural development must necessarily follow that taken to be true for Western Europe: that there is a universal development from magic to religion or from religious mysticism to secular rationality. Tambiah rightly points out that the danger of such facile universalization of our own particular civilization's historical experience lies in its power to distort our perceptions and understanding of other cultures.

INTRODUCTION

Like one of the proverbial blind men who probed different parts of the elephant's body, I shall investigate merely a fragmentary portion of the gigantic question: is there a basic difference in the modes of thought of "traditional pre-scientific" and "modern science-oriented" societies? This was implicitly the theme of Evans-Pritchard's justly famous "dialogue" with Lévy-Bruhl. I shall attempt here only a mini-dialogue with Evans-Pritchard concerning the theoretical implications of his Zande data on magic.

My general thesis will be as follows. The *analogical* mode of thought has always been exploited by man generally. While both "magic" and "science" are characterized by analogical thought and action, they comprise differentiated varieties whose validity it would be inappropriate to measure and verify by the same standards. Magical acts, usually compounded of verbal utterance and object manipulation, constitute "performative" acts by which a property is imperatively transferred to a recipient object or person on an analogical basis. Magical acts are ritual acts, and ritual acts are in turn performative acts whose positive and creative meaning is missed and whose persuasive validity is misjudged if they are subjected to that kind of empirical verification associated with scientific activity. Neither magic nor ritual constitutes applied science in the narrow sense.

In contrast, the exploitation of analogical thought in science consists in making the known or apprehended instance serve as a model for the incompletely known in the phenomenon to be explained. The model serves to generate a prediction concerning the *explicandum,* which is then subject to observation and verification tests to ascertain the prediction's truth value.

Now "performative" acts of a persuasive kind are by no means confined to the primitive: modern industrial societies also have their rites and ceremonies which achieve their effects by virtue of conventional normative understandings. However, science (strictly defined) is an achievement perhaps only of certain complex and literate civilizations: in the West at least where it has attained its fullest development, science probably developed and differentiated out of certain forms of traditional and magical thought and activity, but this should not automatically serve as a universal linear scheme, nor should there be a retrospective and backward thrust by which the "rationality" of magic is pitted against the "rationality" of science, to the former's inevitable and foregone detriment. Indeed it is precisely because many Western anthropologists have approached the ritual performances of other societies from the perspective of their own historical experience and intellectual categories that they have misunderstood the semantic basis of magical acts. . . .

. . . [Although Evans-Pritchard subjected Zande magic and witchcraft to the westerner's criteria of scientific induction and verification,] fresh insights break through here and there in [his book *Witchcraft, Oracles and Magic Among the Azande* (1937).] One such is contained in the passing phrase "imitative symbolism," and another in the idea of "homoeopathy," once again discussed briefly in two pages (pp. 449–450). Here we find the seeds of an approach to Zande magic (and indeed other magical systems) which I shall call "analogical action."

Apparently the Azande themselves recognized the analogical and metaphorical basis for the use of material substances in their rites. . . . Evans-Pritchard writes:

> *They (the Azande) say, "We use such-and-such a plant because it is like such-and-such a thing," naming the object towards which the rite is directed. Likewise they say, "We do so-and-so in order that so-and-so may happen," naming the action which they wish to follow. Often the similarity between medicine and desired happening is indicated in the spell.*[1]

Evans-Pritchard proceeds to give the example (which he also gave in 1929) of the tall *bingba* grass, which is profuse in growth and has featherlike branches, being used by ver-

[1] Evans-Pritchard, *Witchcraft, Oracles and Magic Among the Azande,* p. 449.

bal direction and by direct action to make the oil-bearing melon *(kpagu)* flourish.

There are many examples of analogical action in word and deed scattered throughout the book. A systematic assembling and examination of these examples may provide an alternative interpretation to the one proposed by Evans-Pritchard.

Scrutinize these preliminary examples with this objective in view:

1. When the Azande prick the stalks of bananas with crocodiles' teeth they say "Teeth of crocodile are you, I prick bananas with them, may bananas be prolific like crocodiles' teeth."
2. Azande tie *gbaga* (the fruit of a palm tree) to their girdles as a medicine of masculinity and to secure sexual potency. When tying they say: "You are *gbaga*. May I be very potent sexually. May I not become sexually weak. . . ."
3. Here is an expressive example that could equally well come from Ceylon or Thailand: If a man is a victim of *menzere* (sorcery) medicine, he goes to a much-frequented cross-roads, kneels there and verbally disperses it: ". . . If it is *menzere* may it follow all paths and not return."
4. Finally, there is the celebrated case of the stone placed in the fork of a tree to retard the sun: "You stone, may the sun not be quick to fall today. You stone, retard the sun on high so that I can arrive first at that homestead to which I journey, then the sun may set."

Note here that the Azande refer to the stone used as *ngua uru* which Evans-Pritchard translates as "sun-medicine."

It is my submission that, had Evans-Pritchard followed leads of this sort, he could have thrown more light on why within the range of plant life and arboreal substances (which form the major category of "medicines") used by the Azande, certain woods or roots or leaves rather than others were chosen to represent specialized ideas. Furthermore, the utterances and spells are in fact, as we have seen in these examples, critical for telling us which feature of an object-symbol is the focus of attention on an analogical basis. A shift of theoretical interest from "inherent potency" of medicines to "analogical transfer of their qualities" might have made the botanical enumeration of Zande medicines not so tedious and unnecessary as Evans-Pritchard feared.

Here is a critical passage which we may take as the text for our discussion in that it encapsulates the "closed" system of Zande thought, a central theme of the book (and grist for the Popperian mill):

I do not know whether more than a verbal analogy is implied in the Zande name for mumps (the affected parts are massaged with an unguent): imawirianzoro, *sickness of the little* (wiri) anzoro *birds (finches) which have lumps on their necks. But it may well be so, for we know that in primitive patterns of thought objects which have a superficial resemblance are often linked up by nomenclature and ritual and are connected in mystical patterns of thought. In Zande therapeutics this mystical connexion is found in notions about cause and cure. Ringworm resembles in appearance fowls' excrement, and fowls' excrement is at the same time both cause and cure of ringworm. Blepharoptosis resembles a hen's egg, and a hen's egg is its cure. Generally the logic of therapeutic treatment consists in the selection of the most prominent external symptoms, the naming of the disease after some object in nature which it resembles, and the utilization of the object as the principal ingredient in the drug administered to cure the disease. The circle may even be completed by belief that the symptoms not only yield to treatment by the object which resembles them but are caused by it as well.*

A number of words appear in this commentary that are worthy of "practical criticism": "superficial resemblance" can get its meaning only by unstated comparison with the notion of deeper identity from a scientific causal viewpoint; "mystical connection" can only mean unobservable and unknown connection by comparison with empirically observable connection. The backdrop then is the standards of verification of science. . . .

. . . [Let] us examine carefully the kinds of analogies that exist and their uses. First of all what do we mean by analogy? Basically analogy depends on the recognition of similarities between the instances compared, and, as many philosophers have recognized, analogy stands as a prototype of reasoning from experience. J. S. Mill's paradigm serves well as a definition: "two things resemble each other in one or more respects; a certain proposition is true of the one; therefore it is true of the other." Lloyd elucidating Keynes's thinking on the subject (in *A treatise on probability*) remarks that "both Bacon's own inductive method, based on the use of 'exclusions and rejections,' and Mill's Methods of Agreement and Difference, aim at the determination of the resemblances and differences between particular instances, at the determination of what Keynes called the Positive and Negative Analogies." [2]

Hesse in an instructive essay,[3] on which I draw, lists four kinds of analogies. For my purposes, I shall modify her examples, and elaborate in new directions fundamentally two types of analogy—the *scientific predic-*

[2] Lloyd, *Polarity and Analogy: Two Types of Argumentation in Greek Thought*, University Press, Cambridge, 1966, p. 173.

[3] M. B. Hesse, *Models and analogies in science*, Newman History and Philosophy and Science series, 14, Sheed and Ward, London, 1963.

Figure 1

CAUSAL RELATIONS	SIMILARITY RELATIONS	
	Properties of sound	*Properties of light*
	echoes loudness pitch etc.	reflection brightness colour

tive and the *conventional persuasive*. First, let us bear in mind that "positive analogy" relates to properties shared or points of similarity between the things compared, "negative" analogy to their points of difference or properties they do not share, and "neutral analogy" to properties of the things compared of which we do not yet know whether they are of positive or negative character.

Of the two fundamentally different types of analogies that can be distinguished, one serves as a model in science generating hypotheses and comparisons which are then subject to verification inductively. In this use, the known or apprehended instance serves as the "model" and the unknown or incompletely known is the *explicandum*, the phenomenon to be explained by means of a theory.

Let us take some examples of analogies that might be used in science [see Figure 1]. In this analogy, following Hesse, I indicate two kinds of dyadic relations that should be recognized, the *horizontal* and *vertical* relations. If it is to serve as a material analogy in science, the pairs of horizontal terms (echoes: reflection, etc.) should be either identical or *similar*, and the vertical relations (between the properties of sound such as echoes, loudness, etc.) should be "*causal*," which term given a wide interpretation should mean at least a tendency to *co-occurrence*, in that certain properties are necessary or sufficient conditions for the occurrence of other properties.

In the second "looser" example given [in Figure 2] the horizontal relation may show similarities of *structure* or of *function*, and the vertical relation that of whole to its parts depending on some theory of inter-relation of parts, evolutionary or adaptive.

Now it is essential to note that analogies can usefully serve as theoretical models only if the horizontal dyadic relations are relations of similarity (i.e. judged by identities and differences), if the vertical relations of the model are *causal* in some scientifically acceptable sense and if those of the *explicandum* also promise relations of the same kind, and if the essential properties and causal relations of the model have not been shown to be part of the negative analogy between model and *explicandum*. If these conditions are satisfied then predictions can legitimately be made from any set of known, say three, terms to an unknown fourth. For example, in the case of the sound and light analogies stated before, if we have established the similarity of "echoes" to "reflection," then from the known property of "loudness" in sound we may expect to find the "similar" property of "brightness" in light. Or in the bird and fish analogy, one can predict from the known parts of the bird skeleton to a "missing" part of the fish skeleton. To put it differently, the fun lies in extrapolating from the domain of positive analogy into the domain of neutral analogy as these were defined above. Ultimately of course these predictions should be capable of verification or falsification in terms of observation statements.

Figure 2

CO-OCCURRENCE	SIMILARITIES	
	Bird	*Fish*
	wing lungs feathers	fin gill scales

There is another kind of traditional analogy used widely in human discourse that does not owe its genesis and use to the pursuit of "scientific" knowledge. It would therefore be ridiculous to weigh and measure its adequacy in terms of inductive verification. Consider the following analogy that may occur in political rhetoric: the employer is to his workers as a father is to his children.

$$\frac{\text{father}}{\text{children}} : \frac{\text{employer}}{\text{workers}}$$

Let us say that the purpose of this analogy is propagandist, that it is disseminated by employers in order to "evoke" attitudes in workers rather than to "predict" them.

Now, it should be noted that in this example the vertical relations are not specifically causal; nor is it necessary that if three terms occur, the fourth also must. Even more importantly, there is not in this example any horizontal relation of similarity between the terms, except in virtue of the fact that the two pairs are up to a point *related by the same vertical relation.* (There may be other persuasive analogies in which, in spite of horizontal similarities between terms, the critical relation is still the vertical one.)

How must this analogy work if it is to succeed as political rhetoric? The relation of father to children bears some relation of employer to workers (positive analogy) in the sense let us say that just as the father provides for the material needs of his children so does the employer provide work and wages for his workers. Let us next say that the relation of children to father (and vice versa) is much more than this dependence; children should love their father, obey and respect him and so on. These meanings are not necessarily implied in the employer-worker relation (negative analogy). It is precisely this expansion of meaning or the transfer of these additional values to the employer–worker relations that is sought by invoking the father–children analogy. Since in this case the ultimate aim is to make the workers believe that they are like "children," there is a sense in which we can say that the operation consists in "transferring" (rather than "predicting") from the postulated three terms, the value of "children" to the fourth term, the "workers." It is for this reason that this analogy and its variants are labelled "persuasive," "rationalizing" or "evocative."

It is my thesis that in ritual operations by word and object manipulation, the analogical action conforms to the "persuasive" rather than the "scientific" model. I shall later illustrate the argument that in Zande rites (as well as those of many other societies) the operation rests on the explicit recognition of *both similarity* (positive analogy) *and difference* (negative analogy) *between the vertical relations of the paired terms.* And the rite consists in persuasively transferring the properties of the desired and desirable vertical relation to the other which is in an undesirable condition, or in attempting to convert a potential not-yet-achieved state into an actualized one. The manipulation is made operationally realistic by directing the transfer not only by word but, as in the Zande case, by bringing a material piece of the object in the desirable–desired analogy into contact with the object in need of the transfer. There are nuances in this basic manipulation which are best illustrated when dealing with the concrete cases.

Thus a vital difference exists between the use of "analogy" in science and ritual. Barring a few instances, in most Zande magical rites (especially those considered important by the people concerned), the analogical relation or comparison and the wished-for effect is stated *verbally* simultaneously with or before the carrying out of the so-called "homoeopathic" act (of influencing certain objects by manipulating other objects which resemble them). Why must the analogy of attraction be stated in word and deed for it to be effective? No classical philosopher or historian of science appears to have asked this when propounding that the principle of "like attracts like" activated primitive thought and action. In a laboratory of today, the only time a scientist may be found to foretell and verbally explain his actions while simultaneously doing his experiment would be, for example, when he is teaching a class the procedure involved in conducting that experiment. (And of course he does not expect that his words will automatically make the experiment come out right, as we know from the failed experiments in science classes we have attended in school.) Outside some such situation, his sanity would be suspect if he gave instructions aloud to his apparatus to do his bidding.

Note also how extraordinary the magical operation must look in terms of the traditional explanation (of like attracts like) when placed in relation to the use of analogy made by a scientist. Supposing a scientist constructs an electronic brain-model to "simulate" in some ways a human biochemically structured brain. The former is useful as a predictive model only in those areas where the material make-up of the analogue is not essential to the model (i.e. constitutes the innocuous negative analogy) but where the pattern of mutual relation of the parts and the behavioural relations expressed by it are the essential features. If, say, a man is weak in arithmetic the scientist does not bring a brain-model that can add and place it in contact with the head of the former so that his additions may be thus "caused" to be correct. But this is precisely what we are told the primitive magician might attempt to do! (On the other hand the scientist may demonstrate the working of an adding machine to our hypothetical subject, and it is possible that after sufficient demonstration of its workings his abilities might increase. This is a technique of "persuasion" through contact. Could it be that this is the logic of the magical operations as well . . . ?)

SOME ZANDE ANALOGIES

We have already noted that for the first time, well towards the end of the Azande book, Evans-Pritchard broached the question of the analogical basis of magical rites as seen by the actors. It is however a pity that he did not compile a more thorough indigenous exegesis on why certain "medicines" were used, and what properties or features of the substance used were singled out as "similar" to those of the recipient of the rite. Hence in the examples he cryptically cites, the logic of their use is open to an alternative interpretation that is as plausible as Evans-Pritchard's own implicitly theory-dictated view that the medicines and drugs, chosen on the basis of superficial resemblances and to which is given mystical significance, are empirically ineffective and scientifically false, although used as if they had automatic effects. Let us look at some Zande cases:

1. At a certain time of their growth the stems of the creeper *araka* lose their leaves. These are replaced by a double row of bands, joined to the stalks, which little by little dry, split, and fall in small pieces just as the extremities of the hands and feet disappear in "*la lépre mutilante*." This creeper is highly thought of as furnishing treatment for this kind of leprosy.

I suggest that the analogical reasoning in this example [see Figure 3] is more complex than is implied by a simplistic "like attracts like" in that it brings to view both similarities and differences, positive and negative analogies, in the *vertical relations* of the terms. In the case of the creeper, the falling of its extremities is a *phase of its growth cycle*, whereas in the case of human beings the decay of limbs through leprosy is a *disease that leads to degeneration and death*. Thus this comparison proceeds to use the *araka* creeper in the rite as a vehicle or agent of life, the message being: may the leprosy disappear and health appear, just as the shedding process in the creeper stimulates growth. The rite expresses the wish that one "vertical" relation that is undesired be replaced by another desired one; it itself represents symbolic not causal action.

2. Let us next take the celebrated example already cited of a man indulging "in the action of placing a stone in the tree and relating by a few words this action to a desired end [see Figure 4]." We should bear in mind that the man is on a journey and wishes to arrive home before sunset.

We can plausibly say that here the initial

Figure 3

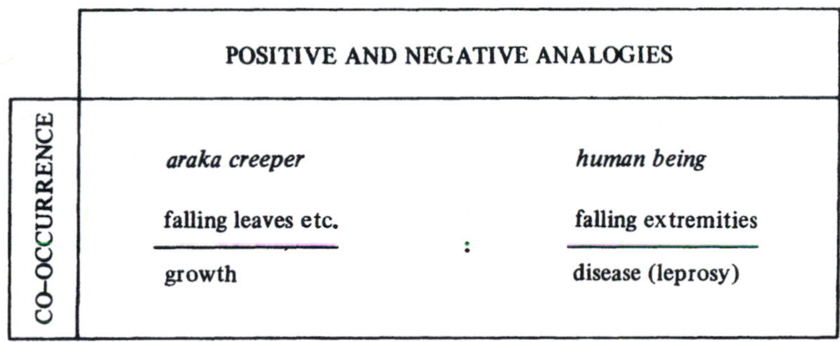

Figure 4

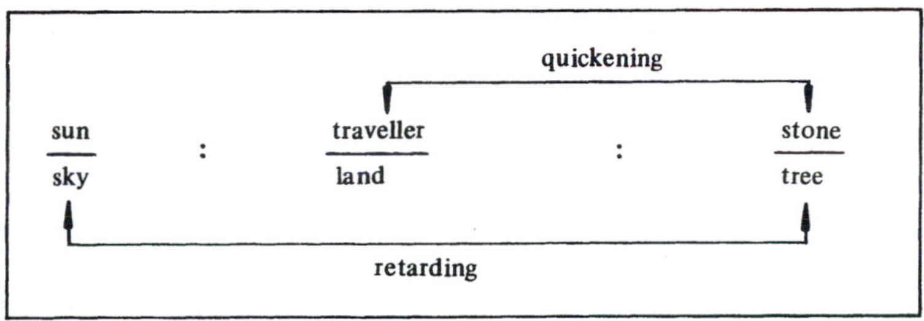

comparison is between the sun "travelling" towards sunset (in the sky) and a man travelling (on land) to his homestead. The sun and the man are therefore similar in their situations but their interests are not identical (the difference that constitutes the negative analogy). The man wishes to travel faster than the sun. It is in this context that we must view the operation of putting a stone in the fork of a tree and thus wedging it. It represents the desired positive effect of retarding the sun and the implicit counter effect (or negative analogy) of quickening his footsteps home, which in fact the traveller actually does by performing this rite.

3. To examine now a case of "homeopathic" treatment of a disease [Figure 5]. Ringworm in children is called *imanduruakondo* (*ima* = sickness, nduruakondo = fowl house).

It is so called because the scabby patches of the disease resemble fowls' excrement: hence they appear to consider the disease due to the afflicted child having eaten food grown on a dung heap in the vicinity of a fowl house: hence also they consider the remedy to consist in fowls' excrement dried and reduced to ashes and mixed into a paste with a little palm-oil and applied to the ringworm.

While the "like attracts like" argument would say that the fowls' excrement is (falsely) used to attract the scabs on the skin which it (falsely) resembles, I am tempted to say that the analogy is interesting and is capable of being acted upon creatively because, once again, of the positive and negative features it exhibits. The relation of fowl to excrement is one of *elimination* of (unwanted) waste product, while that of scabby skin on child is one of (unwanted) *adherence* to body. Hence it is that the fowl's excrement can convey the desired idea of eliminating the scabs when applied to the body, because while in one sense similar to it, it is also essentially different. . . .

Enough Zande examples have been given to suggest how the analogical thought and action of the persuasive types are exploited. A well-known example such as the cure of elephantiasis by the use of ashes from a piece of burnt elephant's leg looks much less bizarre when subjected to similar analysis. Nor is this underlying logic peculiar to the Azande. Numerous cases were documented by Malinowski: one example that neatly illustrates analogical action, is that in which the Trobrianders, having postulated an analogy (or homology) between the yam house with yams stored in it and the human belly with food inside it, act upon the former in order to influence the latter. "The Trobriand logic is that the rite is really a metaphorical analogy urging the human belly to restrain its hunger and greed for food." The application of "similarity and difference" analogically also serves to unravel the logic of some Trobriand food taboos. . . .

HOW TO UNDERSTAND RITUAL (WHICH INCLUDES "MAGIC")?

I have perhaps so far only indicated negatively how "magic" should not be viewed and not positively how it might be viewed in terms of a new perspective. I have argued that to view magic as an attempt at science that failed (or more crudely a "bastard science" in the manner of Frazer, or more sophisticatedly as a "closed" system of thought that allows for no verification and falsification of its principles *à la* Popper) is to assert that in their magic and ritual the primitives tried to achieve results through "causal" reasoning and failed. I have also argued that while it is the case that much primitive magic is based on analogical thought and action as is Western science, the difference between them is that whereas in science the use of an analogy is closely linked to prediction and verification, and its adequacy judged in terms of inductive support, or of meeting standards of probability criteria, or standing up to tests of falsifiability

Figure 5

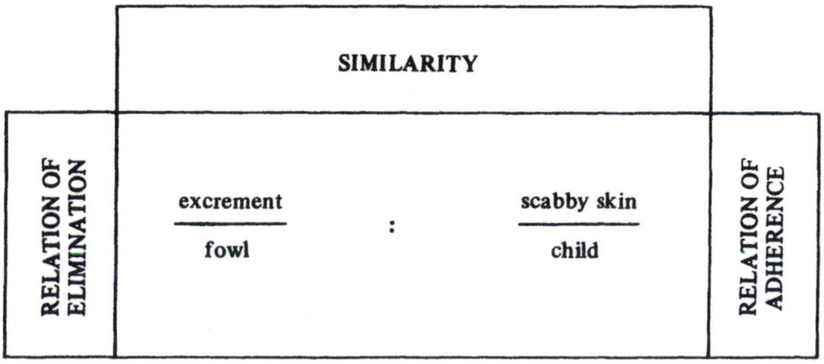

SIMILARITY

RELATION OF ELIMINATION

$\dfrac{\text{excrement}}{\text{fowl}} : \dfrac{\text{scabby skin}}{\text{child}}$

RELATION OF ADHERENCE

and the like, the semantics of a magical rite are not necessarily to be judged in terms of such "true/false" criteria of science but on different standards and objectives. The corresponding objectives in (magical) ritual are "persuasion," "conceptualization," "expansion of meaning" and the like, and the criteria of adequacy are better conveyed by notions such as "validity," "correctness," "legitimacy," and "felicity" of the ceremony performed.

It is this latter assertion that I wish to elucidate now. In my essay on "The Magical Power of Words"[4] I took some steps towards understanding the form and meaning of ritual in terms of its inner semantic frame and outer pragmatic frame. My starting point with regard to the former was that most "magical rites" (as indeed most rituals) combine word and deed and that the rite is devoted to an "imperative transfer" of effects, which some might phrase as the "telic" and others as the "illocutionary" or "performative" nature of the rite. The semantics of the transfer itself, the logic of construction of the transfer, in the Trobriand case depends on (1) metaphorical and analogical transfers by word mediated by realistic contact transfer through objects used as "transformers," and (2) on imperative verbal transfer of energy to a "whole" through the metonymical naming of the parts. One of the points I made was that the same laws of association that apply to ordinary language apply to magical language. . . .

In Austin's *How to Do Things with Words* the chief topic of elaboration is what he calls the "performative" or "illocutionary" act, in which the uttering of the sentence cannot merely be described as saying something, but is, or is a part of, the *doing of an action*. When in a marriage ceremony the man says "I do take this woman to be my lawful wedded wife" (or some such formula), or the man says in a will "I give and bequeath . . . ," to utter these sentences in the appropriate circumstances "is not to *describe* my doing of what I should be said in so uttering to be doing or to state I am doing it: it is to do it."

What ultimately I think Austin arrives at towards the end of his exercise is a classification of speech acts, "the issuing of utterances in a speech situation," which makes any stating "performing an act."

. . . How many senses may there be in which to say something is to do something, or in saying something we do something, or even by saying something we do something?

[4] *Man*, N.S., 3, 1968.

The following classification of speech acts may help to answer the question:

1. to perform a *locutionary* act: to utter a sentence with a certain sense and reference (an assertion, a descriptive statement of fact) which is *true or false in a referential sense*.
2. to perform an *illocutionary* act: this relates to an utterance which has a *certain conventional force*, a performative act *which does something* (as implied in promising, ordering, apologizing, warning etc.). Usually the explicit illocutionary utterance is reducible or analysable into a form with a verb in the first person singular present indicative active (i.e. the "I," the "active" and the "present" seem appropriate). These statements cannot be subject *to the true–false test*, but are *normatively judged* as "happy"/"unhappy," valid/invalid, correct/ defective etc.
3. to perform a *perlocutionary* act: this refers to what we bring about or achieve *by saying something* (as connoted by convincing, persuading, misleading etc.). It refers to both the intended and unintended *consequence* upon the hearer of words uttered by the speaker. (By saying it I convinced him . . .)

These three are analytically separate but in reality not exclusive categories: both locutionary and illocutionary acts can have consequences listed as perlocutionary; and an illocutionary act can have referring and predicating elements together with the performative. We could perhaps say that an imperative illocutionary act attempts to get the world to conform to words, whereas "true" when ascribed to illocutions attributes success in getting words to conform to the world.

Now adapting these ideas for our purposes, we can say that ritual acts and magical rites are of the "illocutionary" or "performative" sort, which simply by virtue of being enacted (under the appropriate conditions) achieve a change of state, or do something effective (e.g. an installation ceremony undergone by the candidate makes him a "chief"). This performative aspect of the rite should be distinguished from its locutionary (referential, information-carrying) and perlocutionary (consequences for the participants) features.

It was quite evident to Austin that, while he focuses on the role of speech in illocutionary acts, the utterance was not the sole thing necessary if the illocutionary act was to be deemed to have been performed, and also that *actions other than speech* whether physical or mental were entailed for the full realization of the performance. Indeed it is even possible at the other extreme to enact a performative act without uttering words at all—a hypothetical example would be the establishing of blood brotherhood by the physical exchange of blood (without an exchange of words).

The vast majority of ritual and magical acts combine word and deed. Hence it is appropriate to say that they use words in a performative or illocutionary manner, just as the action (the manipulation of objects and persons) is correspondingly performative.

I shall attempt to formalize in a few words the essentials of what I see as the form and meaning of magical ritual acts. The rite usually consists of a close interweaving of *speech* (in the form of utterances and spells) and *action* (consisting of the manipulation of objects). The *utterance* can be analysed with respect to its "predicative" and "illocutionary" frames. In terms of predication and reference the words exploit analogical associations, comparisions and transfers (through simile, metaphor, metonym etc.) The illocutionary force and power by which the deed is directed and enacted is achieved through use of words commanding, ordering, persuading and the like: "Whistle, whistle, I send you after a thief . . . ," so commands an Azande spell. . . .

The action can be similarly analysed. The objects manipulated are chosen analogically on the basis of similarity and difference to convey meaning. From the performative perspective, the action consists of an operation done on an object-symbol to make an imperative and realistic transfer of its properties to the recipient. Or to put it differently, two objects are seen as having resemblances and differences, and an attempt is made to transfer the desirable quality of one to the other which is in a defective state.

Now it is clear that the words and action closely combine to form an amalgam which is the magical or ritual *act*. The interrelation between the two media—speech and object manipulation—can take different forms. What I want to emphasize here is that this way of looking at "magical art" breaks through the Saussurean *langue/parole* distinction. On the one hand, the magical act bears predicative and referential *langue*-type meanings and on the other it is a performative act. Both frames are co-existent, and it is as a *performative* or "illocutionary" act directed by analogical reasoning that magic gets its distinctiveness.

Now it is *inappropriate* to subject these performative rites to verification, to test whether they are true or false in a referential or assertive sense or whether the act has effected a result in terms of the logic of "causation" as this is understood in science. Let me illustrate the point by considering the Thai rite of blessing a new house by Buddhist monks (so that evil spirits may be driven out and prosperity result) through the recitation of sacred verses and the performance of certain acts. Several conditions have to be satisfied if a performance of this rite is not, to use Austin's word, to become an "infelicity": that there exists a conventional procedure properly enacted only by authorized persons, e.g. monks, householders etc.; that, in this particular instance, the monks who took part were entitled to conduct the ceremony, and that the actual ceremony was executed both correctly and completely.

Quite another set of conditions relates to the *bona fides* of the actors. For example, the rite is intended for beneficiaries who expect to conduct themselves in certain ways and who have the right intentions. In fulfilment of this, it is necessary that the participants, in the actual rite performed, satisfy these expectations and actually so conduct themselves subsequently.

Now suppose that after the performance of the rite it is found that one or more of these conditions were not fulfilled—the monks may have been bogus, the ceremony incorrectly performed, or the householder never intended to live in the house with his family but planned to use it for an illicit purpose—we cannot in these circumstances say that the rite itself was false or empirically ineffective in a causal sense. The ceremony *itself* cannot ever be said to have been proved to be false or untrue or ineffective; however, any particular enactment of it may be said to be void, unworthy or defective. A bigamist who on false pretences has gone through a second marriage ceremony, does not on that account make the institution of marriage false, wrong or ineffective; what can be said is that he has undergone the ceremony in bad faith and that he has not properly "married" a second time.

The conclusions therefore are that (1) while to particular instances of ritual enactments of the illocutionary or performative type *normative* judgements of efficacy (legitimacy, defectiveness, propriety, etc.) may be applied, it is inappropriate to judge their efficacy in terms of *vertification statements* and inductive rules, and (2) while ritual in general as an institution cannot be declared to be defective, particular instances of it may be so declared, if the proper conditions of performance were not met. It is at this point that I wish to join issue with Evans-Pritchard first and then Robin Horton afterwards.

Evans-Pritchard in his classic study of Zande witchcraft, oracles and magic, having elucidated the coherence and close linkage of these systems of belief, felt it necessary to ask how they fitted into the observer-imposed ritual/empirical categories and how they related to Zande "practical" day-to-day activity. More pointedly, Evans-Pritchard, naturally interested in a "European" intellectual problem, asked how magic, which was oriented to achieving effects, compared with Western empiricism based on canons of proof and experimentation. Evans-Pritchard gave various reasons why the Azande did not disbelieve in magic even when the expected or wished-for magical effect did not materialize. His answer was that although Azande may be sceptical about the skills and knowledge of particular witch doctors or their poor medicines or the correct performance of particular performances, and the like, their belief in the efficacy of the system itself was not thereby assailed. Now, whereas Evans-Pritchard gave this as evidence of why Zande magic cannot be empirically proven wrong, he did not perhaps fully appreciate that the answers he received were appropriate to all conventional performative and illocutionary acts—particular performances may for various reasons be "unhappy" or "incorrect" and therefore inefficacious while the convention itself is unassailable.

Robin Horton compounds the "error" in his challenging essays, suggestively entitled "African Traditional Thought and Western Science."[5] On the one hand Horton argues that African traditional thought (with its supernatural entities couched in a personal idiom) and Western science (with its concepts couched in an impersonal idiom) are similar in that reference to theoretical entities is used to link events in the visible, tangible world (natural effects) to their antecedents in the same world (natural causes). On the other hand, however—and here is the sting—this same African thought-system whose aim is explanatory and predictive (just like science) refuses to subject itself (like good science) to falsifiability and other verification tests. Indeed African traditional thought (just as Evans-Pritchard elucidated it) is a "closed system"; the believer cannot get outside the web of his thought, he cannot be agnostic, there is no vision of alternatives; furthermore it portrays unreflective thinking, i.e. traditional thought lacks logic and philosophy and reflection upon the rules of explanation. Evans-Pritchard's demonstration is driven home in traditional thought by a process of *secondary elaboration;* other current beliefs are utilized in such a way as to "excuse" each failure as it occurs and thus the major theoretical assumptions are protected even in the face of negative evidence. By comparison the collective memory of the European scientific community is littered with the wreckage of discarded theories . . . true, but Horton's enthusiasm for Popper's idealizations may benefit from some of Kuhn's scepticism.

I think it is possible to differ from Horton on the basic assumptions of the comparisons between traditional and scientific thought. One does not deny that traditional societies reflect the patterns he enumerates. But I think it is fundamentally mistaken to say that African religion and ritual are concerned with the same intellectual tasks that science in Western society is concerned with: this is a case of analogy abused. The net result of such comparative pursuit is to land oneself where Frazer found himself—magical rituals are like science with the difference that they are mistaken and false.

My counter-argument is that to view most ritual and magical acts as if they were directed to the purposes of scientific activity—to discover natural causes, predict empirical consequences in terms of a theory of causation—is inappropriate and not productive of maximum understanding. Analogical thought of Western science and of primitive ritual have different implications. Like "illocutionary" and "performative" acts ritual acts have consequences, effect changes, structure situations not in the idiom of "Western science" and "rationality" but in terms of convention and normative judgement, and as solutions of existential problems and intellectual puzzles. These orders of thought and action after all are to be found in Western societies as well—they co-exist with science and thrive outside its field of action or relevance. (It would be interesting to know what Horton thinks is the relation between science and religion in Western society.)

But returning to the problem of magic itself: have I merely evaded answering what magic is by embedding it in ritual and seeing it as an analogical *cum* performative act? By and large I think this is a correct representation of it. But I must also go on to say that in so far as magical rites try to effect a transfer they are often geared to achieving practical results—such as cure of disease or production of a fine harvest, etc.—as much as they are geared to effecting social results. Although we should not judge their *raison d'être* in terms of applied science, we should however recognize that many (but not all)

[5] *Africa*, 37, 1967.

magical rites are elaborated and utilized precisely in those circumstances where non-Western man has not achieved that special kind of "advanced" scientific knowledge which can control and act upon reality to an extent that reaches beyond the realm of his own practical knowledge. Let us not forget what Evans-Pritchard's conclusion was. Zande rites were most "mystical" where the diseases they dealt with were the most acute and chronic. These rites then are on a different wave length from scientific technology; or at least in primitive societies it is better to assimilate witchcraft and magic to "ritual" rather than to "applied science."

Let us also not forget one of Evans-Pritchard's most pregnant observations, that the Zande belief in witchcraft does not exclude "empirical knowledge of cause and effect" but that it provides a social and cultural method of acting upon the world: "In every case witchcraft is the socially relevant cause, since it is the only one which *allows intervention* and determines social behaviour.[6] Thus through ritual man imposes meaning on the world, anticipates the future, retrospectively "rationalizes" the past and effects results.

It is perhaps because magic and applied science are so to say on different wave lengths, yet may (partially) overlap over the ground they cover, that the results of the spread of modern science and technology in so-called "traditional" societies are complex, inconsistent and non-linear. An effective pesticide may over time render a "magical rite" for killing pests redundant and unnecessary. But a sacrifice which creates the cosmos persists because it "creates" the world in a sense that is different from that known in the laboratory. How does one understand the Hindu theory of sacrifice which asserts claims vaster than the causal act itself? And

[6] Evans-Pritchard, *Witchcraft, Oracles and Magic*. . . , p. 73 (my italics, S.J.T.).

in the new urban communities of developing societies, "drugs" may replace traditional "medicines," but scientific "scepticism" and "prediction" do not replace astrology, or consulting of oracles or of diviners, for the guidance of human actions and for providing meaning in perplexing situations.

But what may be true of non-Western societies may not he true of Western civilization in its recent past. . . .

We should heed this warning in our comparative studies. By simply naming rituals of non-Western societies as "magic," and the substances they use as "medicines" and "drugs," we cannot thereby attribute to the phenomena so named, by virtue of that naming, characteristics that may be peculiar to one's own contemporary civilization. It is only a short step from here to go on to measure these same ritual practices and ideas as equivalent to, but of course misguided and falling short of, empirical science. It is not that such a perspective is wrong but that it may hide from view the positive, persuasive and creative, though "non-scientific," features of analogical thought and action expressed in magical rites. The dangers of excessive historical universalization should be kept in view. The rise of industry, capitalism and experimental science in Europe in recent centuries found its counterpart in sociological theorizing in Weber's doctrine of growing "rationality" and "rationalization" in Western civilization—an inevitable historical process towards efficiency of social forms like bureaucracy, towards pragmatic orientation whereby means were closely linked to ends, and towards the generation of context-free, neutral and universal constructs and principles. I am merely indicating that this is a particular historical experience which need not and should not be universalized if it entails automatic projections of how things traditional inevitably become things rational.

E. E. Evans-Pritchard

WITCHCRAFT EXPLAINS UNFORTUNATE EVENTS

In few societies of the world does witchcraft assume a more focal interest than among the Azande, a large and complex group situated

Reprinted in excerpted form from E. E. Evans-Pritchard, "The Notion of Witchcraft Explains Unfortunate Events," *Witchcraft, Oracles and Magic Among the Azande* (Oxford: Clarendon Press, 1937), Part I Chap. 4, by permission of the Oxford University Press.

both north and south of the Sudan–Zaire border. The Azande recognize witchcraft to be a psychic act, and they clearly differentiate it from sorcery, which concerns itself with spells and medicines. They believe that a person is a witch because of an inherited organ or substance called *mangu*. Mangu is oval, is located somewhere between the breastbone and the intestines, and is variously described as reddish, blackish, or hairy. A male can inherit mangu only from a male, a female only from a female. An autopsy may be performed to determine the presence or absence of mangu. Since an accusation of witchcraft may result in a stigma or a fine, or both, autopsies are sometimes carried out to clear a family name.

Witchcraft explains unfortunate events, but only if these events are unusual and inexplicable. An event which is clearly due to carelessness, sorcery, or a taboo violation would not be explained as being due to witchcraft. It is the uncommon event, the event which cannot be understood through normal causal interpretation, which is "obviously" due to witchcraft. The logic used in positing witchcraft as the cause of such strange events is impeccable. It is the basic premise, not the logic, which is at fault.

There are many plausible functions of Zande witchcraft. A man who is too successful, for example, one who finds three honeycombs in one day, is accused of witchcraft. Such accusations militate against any strong striving for success. The economic efficiency of the *kpolo* (extended family) is maintained by directing all conflicts outside the kpolo through accusations of witchcraft. A member of one's own extended family cannot be accused of witchcraft. The fact that the Azande have not engaged in feuds or raids may indicate the ability of accusations and angers against witches to absorb latent hostilities.

Most important, however, is the usefulness of witchcraft in explaining why an event occurred. Science cannot tell us what happened, beyond mentioning the laws of probability. The Azande find both comfort and an opportunity to retaliate in their explanation of why an unfortunate and unusual event took place.

It is an inevitable conclusion from Zande descriptions of witchcraft that it is not an objective reality. The physiological condition which is said to be the seat of witchcraft, and which I believe to be nothing more than food passing through the small intestine, is an objective condition, but the qualities they attribute to it and the rest of their beliefs about it are mystical. Witches, as Azande conceive them, cannot exist.

The concept of witchcraft nevertheless provides them with a natural philosophy by which the relations between men and unfortunate events are explained and with a ready and stereotyped means of reacting to such events. Witchcraft beliefs also embrace a system of values which regulate human conduct.

Witchcraft is ubiquitous. It plays its part in every activity of Zande life; in agricultural, fishing, and hunting pursuits; in domestic life of homesteads as well as in communal life of district and court; it is an important theme of mental life in which it forms the background of a vast panorama of oracles and magic; its influence is plainly stamped on law and morals, etiquette and religion; it is prominent in technology and language; there is no niche or corner of Zande culture into which it does not twist itself. If blight seizes the groundnut crop it is witchcraft; if the bush is vainly scoured for game it is witchcraft; if women laboriously bail water out of a pool and are rewarded by but a few small fish it is witchcraft; if termites do not rise when their swarming is due and a cold useless night is spent in waiting for their flight it is witchcraft; if a wife is sulky and unresponsive to her husband it is witchcraft; if a prince is cold and distant with his subject it is witchcraft; if a magical rite fails to achieve its purpose it is witchcraft; if, in fact, any failure or misfortune falls upon any one at any time and in relation to any of the manifold activities of his life it may be due to witchcraft. Those acquainted either at firsthand or through reading with the life of an African people will realize that there is no end to possible misfortunes, in routine tasks and leisure hours alike, arising not only from miscalculation, incompetence, and laziness, but also from causes over which the African, with his meager scientific knowledge, has no control. The Zande attributes all these misfortunes to witchcraft unless there is strong evidence, and subsequent oracular confirmation, that sorcery or one of those evil agents which I mentioned in the preceding section has been at work, or unless they are clearly to be attributed to incompetence, breach of a taboo, or failure to observe a moral rule.

When a Zande speaks of witchcraft he does not speak of it as we speak of the weird witchcraft of our own history. Witchcraft is to him a commonplace happening and he seldom passes a day without mentioning it. Where we talk about the crops, hunting, and our neighbors' ailments the Zande introduces into these topics of conversation the subject of witchcraft. To say that witchcraft has blighted the groundnut crop, that witchcraft has scared away game, and that witchcraft has made so-and-so ill is equivalent to saying in terms of our own culture that the groundnut crop has failed owing to blight, that game is scarce this season, and that so-and-so has caught influenza. Witchcraft participates in all misfortunes and is the idiom in which Azande speak about them and in which they explain them. Witchcraft is a classification of misfortunes which while differing from each other in other respects have this single common character, their harmfulness to man.

Unless the reader appreciates that witchcraft is quite a normal factor in the life of Azande, one to which almost any and every happening may be referred, he will entirely misunderstand their behavior towards it. To us witchcraft is something which haunted and disgusted our credulous forefathers. But the Zande expects to come across witchcraft at any time of the day or night. He would be just as surprised if he were not brought into daily contact with it as we would be if confronted by its appearance. To him there is nothing miraculous about it. It is expected that a man's hunting will be injured by witches, and he has at his disposal means of dealing with them. When misfortunes occur he does not become awe-struck at the play of supernatural forces. He is not terrified at the presence of an occult enemy. He is, on the other hand, extremely annoyed. Some one, out of spite, has ruined his groundnuts or spoiled his hunting or given his wife a chill, and surely this is cause for anger! He has done no one harm, so what right has anyone to interfere in his affairs? It is an impertinence, an insult, a dirty, offensive trick! It is the aggressiveness and not the eerieness of these actions wich Azande emphasize when speaking of them, and it is anger and not awe which we observe in their response to them.

Witchcraft is not less anticipated than adultery. It is so intertwined with everyday happenings that it is part of a Zande's ordinary world. There is nothing remarkable about a witch—you may be one yourself, and certainly many of your closest neighbors are witches. Nor is there anything awe-inspiring about witchcraft. We do not become psychologically transformed when we hear that someone is ill—we expect people to be ill—and it is the same with Azande. They expect people to be ill, i.e., to be bewitched, and it is not a matter for surprise or wonderment.

But is not Zande belief in witchcraft a belief in mystical causation of phenomena and events to the complete exclusion of all natural causes? The relations of mystical to commonsense thought are very complicated and raise problems that confront us on every page of this book. Here I wish to state the problem in a preliminary manner and in terms of actual situations.

I found it strange at first to live among Azande and listen to naïve explanations of misfortunes which, to our minds, have apparent causes, but after a while I learned the idiom of their thought and applied notions of witchcraft as spontaneously as themselves in situations where the concept was relevant. A boy knocked his foot against a small stump of wood in the center of a bush path, a frequent happening in Africa, and suffered pain and inconvenience in consequence. Owing to its position on his toe it was impossible to keep the cut free from dirt and it began to fester. He declared that witchcraft had made him knock his foot against the stump. I always argued with Azande and criticized their statements, and I did so on this occasion. I told the boy that he had knocked his foot against the stump of wood because he had been careless, and that witchcraft had not placed it in the path, for it had grown there naturally. He agreed that witchcraft had nothing to do with the stump of wood being in his path but added that he had kept his eyes open for stumps, as indeed every Zande does most carefully, and that if he had not been bewitched he would have seen the stump. As a conclusive argument for his view he remarked that all cuts do not take days to heal but, on the contrary, close quickly, for that is the nature of cuts. Why, then, had his sore festered and remained open if there were no witchcraft behind it? This, as I discovered before long, was to be regarded as the Zande explanation of sickness. Thus, to give a further example, I had been feeling unfit for several days, and I consulted Zande friends whether my consumption of bananas could have had anything to do with my indisposition and I was at once informed that bananas do not cause sickness, however many are eaten, unless one is bewitched. I have described at length Zande notions of disease in Part IV, so I shall record here a few examples of witchcraft being offered as an explanation for happenings other than illness.

Shortly after my arrival in Zandeland we were passing through a government settlement and noticed that a hut had been burnt to the ground on the previous night. Its owner was overcome with grief as it had contained the beer he was preparing for a mortuary feast. He told us that he had gone the previous night to examine his beer. He had lit a handful of straw and raised it above his head so that light would be cast on the pots, and in so doing he had ignited the thatch. He, and my companions also, were convinced that the disaster was caused by witchcraft.

One of my chief informants, Kisanga, was a skilled wood carver, one of the finest carvers in the whole kingdom of Gbudwe. Occasionally the bowls and stools which he carved split during the work, as one may well imagine in such a climate. Though the hardest woods be selected they sometimes split in process of carving or on completion of the utensil even if the craftsman is careful and well acquainted with the technical rules of his craft. When this happened to the bowls and stools of this particular craftsman he attributed the misfortune to witchcraft and used to harangue me about the spite and jealousy of his neighbors. When I used to reply that I thought he was mistaken and that people were well disposed towards him he used to hold the split bowl or stool toward me as concrete evidence of his assertions. If people were not bewitching his work, how would I account for that? Likewise a potter will attribute the cracking of his pots during firing to witchcraft. An experienced potter need have no fear that his pots will crack as a result of error. He selects the proper clay, kneads it thoroughly till he has extracted all grit and pebbles, and builds it up slowly and carefully. On the night before digging out his clay he abstains from sexual intercourse. So he should have nothing to fear. Yet pots sometimes break, even when they are the handiwork of expert potters, and this can only be accounted for by witchcraft. "It is broken—there is witchcraft," says the potter simply. Many similar situations in which witchcraft is cited as an agent are instanced throughout this and following chapters.

In speaking to Azande about witchcraft and in observing their reactions to situations of misfortune it was obvious that they did not attempt to account for the existence of phenomena, or even the action of phenomena, by mystical causation alone. What they explained by witchcraft were the particular conditions in a chain of causation which related an individual to natural happenings in such a way that he sustained injury. The boy who knocked his foot against a stump of wood did not account for the stump by reference to witchcraft, nor did he suggest that whenever anybody knocks his foot against a stump it is necessarily due to witchcraft, nor yet again did he account for the cut by saying that it was caused by witchcraft, for he knew quite well that it was caused by the stump of wood. What he attributed to witchcraft was that on this particular occasion, when exercising his usual care, he struck his foot against a stump of wood, whereas on a hundred other occasions he did not do so, and that on this particular occasion the cut, which he expected to result from the knock, festered whereas he had had dozens of cuts which had not festered. Surely these peculiar conditions demand an explanation. Again, if one eats a number of bananas this does not in itself cause sickness. Why should it do so? Plenty of people eat bananas but are not sick in consequence, and I myself had often done so in the past. Therefore my indisposition could not possibly be attributed to bananas alone. If bananas alone had caused my sickness, then it was necessary to account for the fact that they had caused me sickness on this single occasion and not on dozens of previous occasions, and that they had made only me ill and not other people who were eating them. Again, every year hundreds of Azande go and inspect their beer by night and they always take with them a handful of straw in order to illuminate the hut in which it is fermenting. Why then should this particular man on this single occasion have ignited the thatch of his hut? I present the Zande's explicit line of reasoning—not my own. Again, my friend the wood carver had made scores of bowls and stools without mishap and he knew all there was to know about the selection of wood, use of tools, and conditions of carving. His bowls and stools did not split like the products of craftsmen who were unskilled in their work, so why on rare occasions should his bowls and stools split when they did not split usually and when he had exercised all his usual knowledge and care? He knew the answer well enough and so, in his opinion, did his envious, backbiting neighbors. In the same way, a potter wants to know why his pots should break on an occasion when he uses the same material and technique as on other occasions; or rather he already knows, for the reason is known in advance, as it were. If the pots break it is due to witchcraft.

We must understand, therefore, that we shall give a false account of Zande philosophy if we say that they believe witchcraft to be the sole cause of phenomena. This proposition is not contained in Zande patterns of thought, which only assert that witchcraft brings a man into relation with events in such a way that he sustains injury.

My old friend Ongosi was many years ago injured by an elephant while out hunting, and his prince, Basongoda, consulted the oracles to discover who had bewitched him. We must distinguish here between the elephant and its prowess, on the one hand, and the fact that a particular elephant injured a particular man, on the other hand. The Supreme Being, not witchcraft, created elephants and gave them tusks and a trunk and huge legs so that they are able to pierce men and fling them sky high and reduce them to pulp by kneeling on them. But whenever men and elephants come across one another in the bush these dreadful things do not happen. They are rare events. Why, then, should this particular man on this one occasion in a life crowded with similar situations in which he and his friends emerged scatheless have been gored by this particular beast? Why he and not someone else? Why on this occasion and not on other occasions? Why by this elephant and not by other elephants? It is the particular and variable conditions of an event and not the general and universal conditions that witchcraft explains. Fire is hot, but it is not hot owing to witchcraft, for that is its nature. It is a universal quality of fire to burn, but it is not a universal quality of fire to burn you. This may never happen; or once in a lifetime, and then only if you have been bewitched.

In Zandeland sometimes an old granary collapses. There is nothing remarkable in this. Every Zande knows that termites eat the supports in course of time and that even the hardest woods decay after years of service. Now a granary is the summerhouse of a Zande homestead and people sit beneath it in the heat of the day and chat or play the African hole game or work at some craft. Consequently it may happen that there are people sitting beneath the granary when it collapses and they are injured, for it is a heavy structure made of beams and clay and may be stored with eleusine as well. Now why should these particular people have been sitting under this particular granary at the particular moment when it collapsed? That it should collapse is easily intelligible, but why should it have collapsed at the particular moment when these particular people were sitting beneath it? Through years it might have collapsed, so why should it fall just when certain people sought its kindly shelter? We say that the granary collapsed because its supports were eaten away by termites. That is the cause that explains the collapse of the granary. We also say that people were sitting under it at the time because it was in the heat of the day and they thought that it would be a comfortable place to talk and work. This is the cause of people being under the granary at the time it collapsed. To our minds the only relationship between these two independently caused facts is their coincidence in time and space. We have no explanation of why the two chains of causation intersected at a certain time and in a certain place, for there is no interdependence between them.

Zande philosophy can supply the missing link. The Zande knows that the supports were undermined by termites and that people were sitting beneath the granary in order to escape the heat and glare of the sun. But he knows besides why these two events occurred at a precisely similar moment in time and space. It was due to the action of witchcraft. If there had been no witchcraft people would have been sitting under the granary and it would not have fallen on them, or it would have collapsed but the people would not have been sheltering under it at the time. Witchcraft explains the coincidence of these two happenings.

Walter B. Cannon
"VOODOO" DEATH

The phenomenon of death caused by witchcraft and sorcery or due to taboo violation is common and widespread. Such deaths are frequent in aboriginal Australia, Polynesia, South America, and Africa. Similar phenomena are occasionally reported from almost every corner of the world.

Both early observers and modern investigators have accepted such deaths as being due to fear; that is, there is ample evidence that no poison or physical agent is necessary to bring about the demise of the victim. Where belief in sorcery, witchcraft, or supernatural sanctions is firmly held, fear alone can kill. While competent investigators had not doubted the actuality of "voodoo" death, it remained for Cannon to establish the physiological mechanisms by which fear, such as can be engendered by sorcery, can kill a human being. For this purpose, Cannon was able to draw upon his classic studies of the physiological changes due to hunger, rage, fear, and pain (see his classic *The Wisdom of the Body*, 1932).

In this article the author demonstrates that through fear the body is stimulated to meet an emergency. Through the sympathetic nervous system, muscles are prepared for action by the production of large amounts of adrenalin and sugar and by the contraction of certain blood vessels. When the emergency is not met by action, or is prolonged, a state of shock may result. The blood pressure is reduced, the heart deteriorates, and blood plasma escapes into the tissues. Lack of food and water compound this deleterious physiological state. A continuation of this condition may lead to death within a very few days. In more recent work on the problem of "voodoo" death, David Lester (1972) supplements Cannon's physiological hypothesis by proposing a psychological theory akin to the despair of the "giving up–given up" complex often found in terminally ill patients, and Barbara Lex (1974) supports Cannon's interpretations of "voodoo" death with further physiological data on the sensitization of the autonomic nervous system.

Although this article deals with witchcraft, fear, and death in primitive societies, its implications are far-reaching. The psychogenic ailments of modern "civilized" man defy understanding, but we know that fear through suggestion and autosuggestion afflicts the modern hypochondriac and ulcer patient much as it does the Australian who is bewitched or "sung."

Reprinted in abridged form from *American Anthropologist*, XLIV (1942), 169–181, by permission of the American Anthropological Association.

In records of anthropologists and others who have lived with primitive people in widely scattered parts of the world is the testimony that when subjected to spells or sorcery or the use of "black magic" men may be brought to death. Among the natives of South America and Africa, Australia, New Zealand, and the islands of the Pacific, as well as among the Negroes of nearby Haiti, "voodoo" death has been reported by apparently competent observers. The phenomenon is so extraordinary and so foreign to the experience of civilized people that it seems incredible; certainly if it is authentic it deserves careful consideration.

A question which naturally arises is whether those who have testified to the reality of voodoo death have exercised good critical judgment. Although the sorcerer or medicine man or chief may tacitly possess or may assume the ability to kill by bone-pointing or by another form of black magic, may he not preserve his reputation for supernatural power by the use of poison? Especially when death has been reported to have occurred after the taking of food may not the fatal result be due to action of poisonous substances not commonly known except to priests and wizards? Obviously, the possible use of poisons must be excluded before voodoo death can be accepted as an actual consequence of sorcery or witchcraft. Also it is essential to rule out instances of bold claims of supernatural power when in fact death resulted from natural causes; this precaution is particularly important because of the common belief among aborigines that illness is due to malevolence. I have endeavored to learn definitely whether poisoning and spurious claims can quite certainly be excluded from instances of death, attributed to magic power, by addressing inquiries to medically trained observers.

Dr. S. M. Lambert of the Western Pacific Service of the Rockefeller Foundation wrote to me concerning the experience of Dr. P. S. Clarke with Kanakas working on the sugar plantations of North Queensland. One day a Kanaka came to his hospital and told him he would die in a few days because a spell had been put upon him and nothing could be done to counteract it. The man had been known by Dr. Clarke for some time. He was given a very thorough examination, including an examination of the stool and the urine. All was found normal, but as he lay in bed he gradually grew weaker. Dr. Clarke called upon the foreman of the Kanakas to come to the hospital to give the man assurance, but on reaching the foot of the bed, the foreman leaned over, looked at the patient, and then turned to Dr. Clarke saying, "Yes, doctor, close up him he die" (i.e., he is nearly dead). The next day, at 11 o'clock in the morning, he ceased to live. A post-mortem examination revealed nothing that could in any way account for the fatal outcome.

Another observer with medical training, Dr. W. E. Roth, who served for three years as government surgeon among the primitive people of north central Queensland, has also given pertinent testimony. "So rooted sometimes is this belief on the part of the patient," Roth wrote, "that some enemy has 'pointed' the bone at him, that he will actually lie down to die, and succeed in the attempt, even at the expense of refusing food and succor within his reach: I have myself witnessed three or four such cases."

Dr. J. B. Cleland, Professor of Pathology at the University of Adelaide, has written to me that he has no doubt that from time to time the natives of the Australian bush do die as a result of a bone being pointed at them, and that such death may not be associated with any of the ordinary lethal injuries. In an article which included a section on death from malignant psychic influences, Dr. Cleland mentions a fine, robust tribesman in Central Australia who was injured in the fleshy part of the thigh by a spear that had been enchanted. The man slowly pined away and died, without any surgical complication which could be detected. Dr. Cleland cites a number of physicians who have referred to the fatal effects of bone-pointing and other terrifying acts. In his letter to me he wrote, "Poisoning is, I think, entirely ruled out in such cases among our Australian natives. There are very few poisonous plants available and I doubt whether it has ever entered the mind of the central Australian natives that such might be used on human beings."

Dr. Herbert Basedow, in his book, *The Australian Aboriginal*, has presented a vivid picture of the first horrifying effect of bone-pointing on the ignorant, superstitious, and credulous natives, and the later more calm acceptance of their mortal fate:

The man who discovers that he is being boned by any enemy is, indeed, a pitiable sight. He stands aghast, with his eyes staring at the treacherous pointer, and with his hands lifted as though to ward off the lethal medium, which he imagines is pouring into his body. His cheeks blanch and his eyes become glassy and the expression of his face becomes horribly distorted.... He attempts to shriek but usually the sound chokes in his throat, and all that one might see is froth at his mouth. His body begins to tremble and the muscles twist involuntarily. He sways backwards and falls to the ground, and after a short time appears to be in a swoon; but soon after he writhes as if in mortal agony, and, covering his face with his hands, begins to moan. After a while he becomes very composed and crawls to his wurley. From this time onwards he sickens and frets, refusing to eat and keeping aloof from the daily affairs of the tribe. Unless help is forthcoming in the shape of a countercharm administered by the hands of the Nangarri, or medicine man, his death is only a matter of comparatively short time. If the coming of the medicine man is opportune he might be saved.

The Nangarri, when persuaded to exercise his powers, goes through an elaborate ceremony and finally steps toward the awe-stricken relatives, holding in his fingers a small article—a stick, a bone, a pebble, or a talon—which, he avows, he has taken from the "boned" man and which was the cause of the affliction. And now, since it is removed, the victim has nothing to fear. The effect, Dr. Basedow declares, is astounding. The victim, until that moment far on the road to death, raises his head and gazes in wonderment at the object held by the medicine man. He even lifts himself into a sitting position and calls for water to drink. The crisis is passed, and the recovery is speedy and complete. Without the Nangarri's intervention the boned fellow, according to Dr. Basedow, would certainly have fretted himself to death. The implicit faith which a native cherishes in the magical powers of his tribal magician is said to result in cures which exceed anything recorded by the faith-healing disciples of more cultured communities.

Perhaps the most complete account of the influence of the tribal taboo on the fate of a person subjected to its terrific potency has come from W. L. Warner, who worked among primitive aborigines in the Northern Territory of Australia. There are two definite movements of the social group, he declares, in the process by which black magic becomes effective on the victim of sorcery. In the first movement the community contracts; all people who stand in kinship relation with him withdraw their sustaining support. This means that all his fellows—everyone he knows—completely change their attitudes toward him and place him in a new category. He is now viewed as one who is more nearly in the realm of the sacred and taboo than in the world of the ordinary where the community finds itself. The organization of his social life has collapsed, and, no longer a member of a group, he is alone and isolated. The doomed man is in a situation from which the only escape is by death. During the death-illness which ensues, the group acts with all the outreachings and complexities of its organization and with countless stimuli to suggest death positively to the victim, who is in a highly suggestible state. In addition to the social pressure upon him the victim himself, as a rule, not only makes no effort to live and to stay a part of his group but actually, through the multiple suggestions which he receives, co-operates in the withdrawal from it. He becomes what the attitude of his fellow tribesmen wills him to be. Thus he assists in committing a kind of suicide.

Before death takes place, the second movement of the community occurs, which is a return to the victim in order to subject him to the fateful ritual of mourning. The purpose of the community now, as a social unit with its ceremonial leader, who is a person of very near kin to the victim, is at last to cut him off entirely from the ordinary world and ultimately to place him in his proper position in the sacred totemic world of the dead. The victim, on his part, reciprocates this feeling. The effect of the double movement in the society, first away from the victim and then back, with all the compulsive force of one of its most powerful rituals, is obviously drastic.

The social environment as a support to morale is probably much more important and impressive among primitive people, because of their profound ignorance and insecurity in a haunted world, than among educated people living in civilized and well-protected communities. Dr. S. D. Porteus, physician and psychologist, has studied savage life extensively in the Pacific islands and in Africa; he writes:

Music and dance are primitive man's chief defenses against loneliness. By these he reminds himself that in his wilderness there are other minds seconding his own . . . in the dance he sees himself multiplied in his fellows, his action mirrored in theirs. There are in his life very few other occasions in which he can take part in concerted action and find partners. . . . The native aboriginal is above all fear-ridden. Devils haunt to seize the unwary; their malevolent magic shadows his waking moments, he believes that medicine men know how to make themselves invisible so that they may cut out his kidney fat, then sew him up and rub his tongue with a magic stone to induce forgetfulness, and thereafter he is a living corpse, devoted to death. . . . So desperate is this fear that if a man imagines that he has been subjected to the bone-pointing magic of the enemy he will straight away lie down and die.

Testimony similar to the foregoing, from Brazil, Africa, New Zealand, and Australia, was found in reports from the Hawaiian Islands, British Guiana, and Haiti. What attitude is justified in the presence of this accumulation of evidence? In a letter from Professor Lévy-Bruhl, the French ethnologist long interested in aboriginal tribes and their customs, he remarked that answers which he had received from inquiries could be summed up as follows. The ethnologists, basing their judgment on a large number of reports, quite independent of one another and gathered from groups in all parts of the world, admit that there are instances indicating that the belief that one has been subjected to sorcery, and in consequence is inevitably condemned to death, does actually result in death in the course of time. On the contrary, physiologists and physicians—men who have had no acquaintance with ethnological conditions—are inclined to consider the phenomenon as impossible and raise doubts regarding clear and definite testimony.

Before denying that voodoo death is within the realm of possibility, let us consider the general features of the specimen reports mentioned in foregoing paragraphs. First, there is the elemental fact that the phenomenon is characteristically noted among aborigines—among human beings so primitive, so superstitious, so ignorant that they are bewildered strangers in a hostile world. Instead of knowledge they have a fertile and unrestricted imagination which fills their environment with all manner of evil spirits capable of affecting their lives disastrously. As Dr. Porteus pointed out, only by engaging in communal activities are they able to develop sufficient *esprit de corps* to render themselves resistant to the mysterious and malicious influences which can vitiate their lives. Associated with these circumstances is the fixed assurance that because of certain conditions, such as being subject to bone-pointing or other magic, or failing to observe sacred tribal regulations, death is sure to supervene. This is a belief so firmly held by all members of the tribe that the individual not only has that conviction himself but is obsessed by the knowledge that all his fellows likewise hold it. Thereby he becomes a pariah, wholly deprived of the confidence and social support of the tribe. In his isolation the malicious spirits which he believes are all about him and capable of irresistibly and calamitously maltreating him, exert supremely their evil power. Amid this mysterious mark of grim and ominous fatality what has been called "the gravest known extremity of fear," that of an immediate threat of death, fills the terrified victim with powerless misery.

In his terror he refuses both food and drink, a fact which many observers have noted and which, as we shall see later, is highly significant for a possible understanding of the slow onset of weakness. The victim "pines away"; his strength runs out like water, to paraphrase words already quoted from one graphic account; and in the course of a day or two he succumbs.

The question which now arises is whether an ominous and persistent state of fear can end the life of a man. Fear, as is well known, is one of the most deeply rooted and dominant of the emotions. Often, only with difficulty can it be eradicated. Associated with it are profound physiological disturbances, widespread throughout the organism. There is evidence that some of these disturbances, if they are lasting, can work harmfully. In order to elucidate that evidence I must first indicate that great fear and great rage have similar effects in the body. Each of these powerful emotions is associated with ingrained instincts—the instinct to attack, if rage is present; the instinct to run away or escape, if fear is present. Throughout the long history of human beings and lower animals these two emotions and their related instincts have served effectively in the struggle for existence. When they are roused they bring into action an elemental division of the nervous system, the so-called "sympathetic" or sympathico-adrenal division, which exercises a control over internal organs, and also over the blood vessels. As a rule the sympathetic division acts to maintain a relatively constant state in the flowing blood and lymph, i.e., the "internal environment" of our living parts. It acts thus in strenuous muscular effort; for example, liberating sugar from the liver, accelerating the heart, contracting certain blood vessels, discharging adrenaline, and dilating the bronchioles. All these changes render the animal more efficient in physical struggle, for they supply essential conditions for continuous action of laboring muscles. Since they occur in association with the strong emotions, rage and fear, they can reasonably be interpreted as preparatory for the intense struggle which the instincts to attack or to escape may involve. If these powerful emotions prevail, and the bodily forces are fully mobilized for action, and if this state of extreme perturbation continues in uncontrolled possession of the organism for a considerable period, without the occurrence of action, dire results may ensue.

When, under brief ether anesthesia, the cerebral cortex of a cat is quickly destroyed so that the animal no longer has the benefit of the organs of intelligence, there is a remarkable display of the activities of lower, primary centers of behavior, those of emotional expression. This decorticate condition is similar to that produced in man when consciousness is abolished by the use of nitrous oxide; he is then decorticated by chemical means. Commonly the emotional expression of joy is released (nitrous oxide is usually known as "laughing gas"), but it may be that of sorrow (it might as well be called "weeping gas"). Similarly, ether anesthesia, if light, may release the expression of rage. In the sham rage of the decorticate cat there is a supreme exhibition of intense emotional activity. The hairs stand on end, sweat exudes from the toe pads, the heart rate may rise from about 150 beats per minute to twice that number, the blood pressure is greatly elevated, and the concentration of sugar in the blood soars to five times the normal. This excessive activity of the sympathico-adrenal system rarely lasts, however, more than three or four hours. By that time, without any loss of blood or any other events to explain the outcome, the decorticate remnant of the animal, in which this acme of emotional display has prevailed, ceases to exist.

What is the cause of the demise? It is clear that the rapidly fatal result is due to a persistent excessive activity of the sympathico-adrenal system. One of my associates, Philip Bard, noted that when the signs of emotional excitement failed to appear, the decorticate preparation might continue to survive for long periods; indeed, its existence might have to be ended by the experimenter. Further evidence was obtained by another of my associates, Norman E. Freeman, who produced sham rage in animals from which the sympathetic nerves had been removed. In these circumstances the behavior was similar in all respects to the behavior described above, excepting the manifestations dependent upon sympathetic innervation. The remarkable fact appeared that animals deprived of their sympathetic nerves and exhibiting sham rage, so far as was possible, continued to exist for many hours without any sign of breakdown. Here were experiments highly pertinent to the present inquiry.

What effect on the organism is produced by a lasting and intense action of the sympathico-adrenal system? In observations Bard found that a prominent and significant change which became manifest in animals displaying sham rage was a gradual fall of blood pressure toward the end of the display, from the high levels of the early stages to the low level seen in fatal wound shock. Freeman's research produced evidence that this fall of pressure was due to a reduction of the volume of circulating blood. This is the condition which during World War I was found to be the reason for the low blood pressure observed in badly wounded men—the blood volume is reduced until it becomes insufficient for the maintenance of an adequate circulation. Thereupon deterioration occurs in the heart, and also in the nerve centers which hold the blood vessels in moderate contraction. A vicious circle is then established; the low blood pressure damages the very organs which are necessary for the maintenance of an adequate circulation, and as they are damaged they are less and less able to keep the blood circulating to an effective degree. In sham rage, as in wound shock, death can be explained as due to a failure of essential organs to receive a sufficient supply of blood or, specifically, a sufficient supply of oxygen, to maintain their functions.

The gradual reduction of blood volume in sham rage can be explained by the action of the sympathico-adrenal system in causing a persistent constriction of the small arterioles in certain parts of the body. If adrenaline, which constricts the blood vessels precisely as nerve impulses constrict them, is continuously injected at a rate which produces the vasoconstriction of strong emotional states, the blood volume is reduced to the degree seen in sham rage. Freeman, Freedman, and Miller performed that experiment. They employed in some instances no more adrenaline than is secreted in response to reflex stimulation of the adrenal gland, and they found not only marked reduction of the blood plasma but also a concentration of blood corpuscles as shown by the percentage increase of hemoglobin. It should be remembered, however, that in addition to this circulating vasoconstrictor agent there are in the normal functioning of the sympathico-adrenal system the constrictor effects on blood vessels of nerve impulses and the co-operation of another circulating chemical substance besides adrenaline, viz., sympathin. These three agents, working together in times of great emotional stress, might well produce the results which Freeman and his collaborators observed when they injected adrenaline alone. In the presence of the usual blood pressure, organs of primary importance, e.g., the heart and the brain, are not subjected to constriction of their vessels, and therefore they are continuously supplied with blood. But this advantage is secured at the deprivation of peripheral structures and especially the abdominal viscera. In these less essential parts, where constriction of the arterioles occurs, the capillaries are ill-supplied with oxygen. The very thin walls of the capillaries are sensitive to oxygen-want and when they do not receive an adequate supply they become more and more permeable to the fluid part of the blood. Thereupon the plasma escapes into the perivascular spaces. A similar condition occurs in the wound shock of human beings. The escape of the plasma from the blood vessels leaves the red corpuscles more concentrated. During World War I we found that the concentration of corpuscles in skin areas might be increased as much as fifty percent.

A condition well known as likely to be harmful to the wounded was a prolonged lack of food or water. Freeman, Morison, and Sawyer found that loss of fluid from the body, resulting in a state of dehydration, excited the sympathico-adrenal system; thus again a vicious circle may be started, the low blood volume of the dehydrated condition being intensified by further loss through capillaries which have been made increasingly permeable.

The foregoing paragraphs have revealed how a persistent and profound emotional state may induce a disastrous fall of blood pressure, ending in death. Lack of food and drink would collaborate with the damaging emotional effects to induce the fatal outcome. These are the conditions which, as we have seen, are prevalent in persons who have been reported as dying as a consequence of sorcery. They go without food or water as they, in their isolation, wait in fear for their impending death. In these circumstances they might well die from a true state of shock, in the surgical sense—a shock induced by prolonged and tense emotion.

It is pertinent to mention here that Wallace, a surgeon of large experience in World War I, testified to having seen cases of shock in which neither trauma nor any of the known accentuating facts of shock could account for the disastrous condition. Sometimes the wounds were so trivial that they could not reasonably be regarded as the cause of the shock state; sometimes the visible injuries were negligible. He cites two illustrative instances. One was a man who was buried by the explosion of a shell in a cellar; the other was blown up by a buried shell over which he had lighted a fire. In both the circumstances were favorable for terrifying experience. In both all the classic symptoms of shock were present. The condition lasted more than 48 hours, and treatment was of no avail. A post-mortem examination did not reveal any gross injury. Another remarkable case which may be cited was studied by Freeman at the Massachusetts General Hospital. A woman of 43 years underwent a complete hysterectomy because of uterine bleeding. Although her emotional instability was recognized, she appeared to stand the operation well. Special precautions were taken, however, to avoid loss of blood, and in addition she was given fluid intravenously when the operation was completed. That night she was sweating, and refused to speak. The next morning her blood pressure had fallen to near the shock level, her heart rate was 150 beats per minute, her skin was cold and clammy, and the measured blood flow through the vessels of her hand was very slight. There was no bleeding to account for her desperate condition, which was diagnosed as shock brought on by fear. When one understands the utter strangeness, to an inexperienced layman, of a hospital and its elaborate surgical ritual, and the distressing invasion of the body with knives and metal retractors, the wonder is that not more patients exhibit signs of deep anxiety. In this instance a calm and reassuring attitude on the part of the surgeon resulted in a change of attitude in the patient, with recovery of a normal state. That the attitude of the patient is of significant importance for a favorable outcome of an operation is firmly believed by the well-known American surgeon, Dr. J. M. T. Finney, for many years Professor of Surgery at the Johns Hopkins Medical School. He has publicly testified, on the basis of serious experiences, that if any person came to him for a major operation, and expressed fear of the result, he invariably refused to operate. Some other surgeon must assume the risk!

Further evidence of the possibility of fatal outcome from profound emotional strain was reported by Mira in recounting his experiences as a psychiatrist in the Spanish war of 1936–1939. In patients who suffered from what he called "malignant anxiety" he observed signs of anguish and perplexity, accompanied by a permanently rapid pulse (more than 120 beats per minute), and a very rapid respiration (about three times the normal resting rate). These conditions indicated a perturbed state deeply involving the sympathico-adrenal complex. As predisposing conditions Mira mentioned "a previous lability of the sympathetic system" and "a severe mental shock experienced in conditions of physical exhaustion due to lack of food, fatigue, sleeplessness, etc." The lack of food appears to have attended lack of water, for the urine was concentrated and extremely acid. Toward the end the anguish still remained, but inactivity changed to restlessness. No focal symptoms were observed. In fatal cases death occurred in three or four days. Post-mortem examination revealed brain hemorrhages in some cases, but, excepting an increased pressure, the cerebrospinal fluid showed a normal state. The combination of lack of food and water, anxiety, very rapid pulse and respiration, associated with a shocking experience having persistent effects, would fit well with fatal conditions reported from primitive tribes.

The suggestion which I offer, therefore, is that voodoo death may be real, and that it may be explained as due to shocking emotional stress—to obvious or repressed terror. A satisfactory hypothesis is one which allows observations to be made which may determine whether or not it is correct. Fortunately, tests of a relatively simple type can be used to learn whether the suggestion as to the nature of voodoo death is justifiable. The pulse toward the end would be rapid and "thready." The skin would be cool and moist.

A count of the red blood corpuscles, or even simpler, a determination by means of a hematocrit of the ratio of corpuscles to plasma in a small sample of blood from skin vessels would help to tell whether shock is present; for the "red count" would be high and the hematocrit also would reveal "hemoconcentration." The blood pressure would be low. The blood sugar would be increased, but the measure of it might be too difficult in the field. If in the future, however, any observer has opportunity to see an instance of voodoo death, it is to be hoped that he will conduct the simpler tests before the victim's last gasp.

Victor W. Turner

DIVINATION AS A PHASE IN A SOCIAL PROCESS

The following excerpt from *The Drums of Affliction* is an especially cogent example of Victor Turner's seminal thinking about the relationship of divination to social process. Divination is seen not just as a means of diagnosing the cause of an affliction and prescribing a cure. Rather, for a society without centralized political institutions, divination is shown to be a mechanism for social redress. The Ndembu diviners have learned by experience to reduce their social system to a few basic principles, and to manipulate these until they arrive at a decision that accords with the views of the majority of their clients. Thus the diviner must take into account both the specific structure of the society and a set of moral values, and these are represented in the symbolism of divination. The symbols are mnemonics which are purposely vague and flexible so as to leave the diviner free to make a detailed interpretation of the configuration of symbols that corresponds to the diagnosis he is making of the state of relationships between his clients.

Reprinted with slight abridgments from Victor W. Turner, *The Drums of Affliction* (Oxford: Oxford University Press, 1968) by permission of the author and the International African Institute.

Divination is a phase in a social process which begins with a person's death or illness, or with reproductive trouble, or with misfortune at hunting. Informal or formal discussion in the kinship or local group of the victim leads to the decision to consult a diviner. The actual consultation or seance, attended by the victim's kin and/or neighbours, is the central episode in the process. It is followed by remedial action according to the diviner's verdict, action which may consist of the destruction or expulsion of a sorcerer/witch, or of the performance of ritual by cult specialists to propitiate or exorcise particular manifestations of shades, or of the application of medicines according to the diviner's prescription by a leech or medicine man.

Death, disease and misfortune are usually ascribed to tensions in the local kin group, expressed as personal grudges charged with the mystical power of sorcery or witchcraft, or as beliefs in the punitive action of ancestor spirits. Diviners try to elicit from their clients responses which give them clues to the current tensions in their groups of origin. Divination, therefore, becomes a form of social analysis, in the course of which hidden conflicts are revealed so that they may be dealt with by traditional and institutionalized procedures. It is in the light of this function of divination as a mechanism of social redress that we must consider its symbolism, the social composition of its consultative sessions, and its procedures of interrogation.

We must always remember that the standards against which social harmony and disharmony are assessed are those of Ndembu culture and not of Western social science. They are those of a society which, possessing only a rudimentary technology and limited empirical skills and knowledge, consequently has a low degree of control over its material environment. It is a society highly vulnerable to natural disasters, such as disease, infant mortality, and intermittent food shortages. Furthermore, its ethical yardsticks are those of a community composed of small residential groups of close kin. Since kinship guides co-residence and confers rights to succeed to office and inherit property, the major problems of Ndembu society bear on the maintenance of good relations between kin, and on the reduction of competition and rivalry between them. Furthermore, since persons of incompatible temperaments and characters are frequently forced into daily propinquity by kinship norms which enjoin respect and co-operation among them, interpersonal hostilities tend to develop that are forbidden direct expression. Hidden grudges (*yitela*) rankle and grow, as Ndembu are well aware. In the idiom of Ndembu culture these grudges are associated with the mystical power of sorcery/witchcraft.

Ndembu themselves list jealousy, envy, greed, pride, anger, lust, and the desire to steal as causes of discord in group life, and these vices are by no means unfamiliar to us. Nevertheless, these symptoms of a disordered human nature spring from a specific social structure. In their attempts to diminish the disastrous consequences of these "deadly sins" in social life, Ndembu bring into operation institutionalized mechanisms of redress that are ordered towards the maintenance of that social structure. Divination, as we have seen, is one of those mechanisms, and in it we can observe many idiosyncratic features.

In the first place, the diviner clearly knows that he is investigating within a social context of a particular type. He first establishes the location of the Senior Chief's area, then that of the Sub-chief's, then the vicinage, and finally the village of the victim. Each of these political units has its own social characteristics—its fractional divisions, its inter-village rivalries, its dominant personalities, its nucleated and dispersed groups of kindred—each possessing a history of settlement or migration. An experienced diviner will be familiar with the contemporary state of these political systems from previous consultations and from the voluminous gossip of wayfarers. Next he finds out the relationship between the victim and those who have come to consult him. He is assisted in this task by his knowledge of the categories of persons who typically make up the personnel of a village: the victim's matrilineal kin, his patrilateral kin, his affines, and unrelated persons. He finds out the victim's relationship to the headman, and he then focuses his attention on the headman's matrilineage, and discovers into how many sub-lineages it may be segmented.

By the time he has finished his interrogation, he has a complete picture of the current structure of the village, and of the position occupied in it by the victim and by those who came to consult him. Since it is common for representatives of each of its important segments, as well as affines of members of its matrilineal nucleus, to visit a diviner in the event of an important man's death, and since these representatives may not make the same responses to key questions, the diviner does not have to look far for indications of structural cleavages in the village. Diviners are also aware that there is a general association between the kind of misfortune about which he is consulted, the sex of the victim, the composition of the group of clients, and the size and structure of the political or residential unit from which they come. Thus only a few close kin or affines will normally consult a diviner about a woman's barrenness or a hunter's bad luck. But a large party, representative of all segments of a Sub-chiefdom, will come to him when a Sub-chief dies. This association does not always hold true, however, for the death or even illness of a child may sometimes be taken as the occasion to bring into the open the dominant cleavage in a large village if the time is felt to be ripe. But diviners have learnt by experience—their own and their society's, incorporated in divinatory procedure and symbolism—to reduce their social system to a few basic principles and factors, and to juggle with these until they arrive at a decision that accords with the view of the majority of their clients at any given consultation.

They are guided, however, not by an objective analysis of the social structure, but rather by an intuition into what is just and fitting in terms both of Ndembu moral values and an ethical code which would be recognized as valid by all human groups. Just as Africans have been shown to operate in their judicial processes with the universally recognized concept of the "reasonable man," or "man of sense," so do they operate in their divinatory processes with the universally recognized concept of the "good man" or "moral man," *muntu wamuwahi*. This is the man who bears no grudges, who is without jealousy, envy, pride, anger, covetousness, lust, greed, etc., and who honours his kinship obligations. Such a man is open, he has "a white liver," he has nothing to conceal from anyone, he does not curse his fellows, he respects and remembers his ancestors. The diviner looks for sorcerers and witches among those who do not measure up to this standard of morality. Indeed, he looks for them among the positive transgressors, among those whom his clients admit to be wrongdoers or "slippery customers." In the cases of illness, infertility, and bad luck at hunting, he applies the same measure of the "moral man" to individuals, although he also applies the yardstick of the "moral group," which lives in mutual amity and collectively reveres its ancestors and respects its political authorities. But here it would seem he is on the look out not so much for "mortal sins" as for "venial sins," for grudges that have not grown murderous, for offences that may yet be forgiven, for quarrels that have not yet split up a group.

A sinner (*mukwanshidi*) is defined by Ndembu as "one who has ill feeling for other people (*mukwanshidi watiyang'a kutama nawakwawa antu*)." *Kutama*, "to be bad, evil, unpleasant, ugly," is linked with symbolism of blackness, darkness, death, sterility, and night in Ndembu ritual. It is the opposite of *ku-waha*, "to be good, morally upright, pleasant, beautiful." It is also linked with witchcraft/sorcery, theft, adulterous lust, and murder. *Ku-tana* is associated with "secret things" (*yiswamu*), with the concealment of thoughts or possessions from others. What is "good," for Ndembu, is the open, the public, the unconcealed, the sincere. A man is said to be "good" when he performs his duties from "the liver," not from calculated policy with a show of outward politeness under which malice is concealed. A man is bad when there is a marked inconsistency, or disparity, between his public behaviour and his private thoughts and feelings. The former is outwardly correct, but it conceals malice and envy. Thus the hypocrite is the real sinner. We find in the diviner's basket a representation of the weeping hypocrite (*Katwambimbi*), and several references to the duplicity of "bad" people, i.e. of the witches and sorcerers.

Thus the diviner has to take into account both the specific structure of Ndembu society and a set of moral values and norms. Both these referents are represented in the symbolism of divination. The symbols are mnemonics, reminders of certain general rubrics of Ndembu culture, within which the diviner can classify the specific instance of behaviour that he is considering. Moreover, they have to be of such a nature as to lend themselves to configurational analysis. It is the *constellation* of symbols rather than the individual symbol which forms the typical unit of interpretation. A symbol may appear as a substantive, and in this role it may possess, say, half a dozen basic senses. By noting the reactions of the clients and attenders, the diviner can make a guess, or "formulate a hypothesis," which will enable him to establish the particular sense of the substantival symbol: he can then allocate senses to the modifiers. Here the vagueness and flexibility of the series of referents of each symbol leave him free to make a detailed interpretation of the configuration of symbols corresponding to the diagnosis he is making of the state of relationships between his clients and the deceased, and between the living kin concerned in the matter. And once he has established a *chidimbu*, a definite point of divination, and obtained agreement on its veracity or likelihood, he has a point of departure for further enquiry, something firm to go on. He may then deduce logical consequences from the *chidimbu*, regarded as a set of premises. Furthermore, he has established a certain psychological ascendancy over his audience, so that they tend to become less guarded in their replies, for with growing credulity in his divinatory powers they become more eager to give him the hard data he requires. I believe that this is one of the reasons why a basket-diviner tries to find the name of the deceased quite early in the seance. Diviners, as we have seen, have learnt that the vast majority of Ndembu names can be classified under relatively few main heads—"water," "hoofed animals," "chieftainship," etc., and after the manner of the English party game, "Twenty Questions," they can quickly proceed from the general to the particular. In a society not specially remarkable for its power of abstract thinking, the diviner's ability to do this must appear little short of miraculous. When the diviner names the deceased, therefore, he has won the credulity of his audience to such an extent that he can elicit key information without much difficulty. In other words, the logician is felt to be a magician.

It may be said in conclusion that the diviner occupies a central position with reference to several fields of social and cultural relationships. He acts as a mechanism of redress and social adjustment in the field of local descent groups, since he locates areas and points of tension in their contemporary structures. Furthermore, he exonerates or accuses individuals in those groups in terms of a system of moral norms. Since he operates in emotionally charged situations, such norms are restated in a striking and memorable fashion. Thus he may be said to play a vital role in upholding tribal morality. Moral law is most vividly made known through its breach. Finally, the diviner's role is pivotal to the system of rituals of affliction and anti-witchcraft/sorcery rituals, since he decides what kind of ritual should be performed in a given instance, when it should be performed, and sometimes who should perform it. Since diviners are consulted on many occasions, it is clear that their role as upholders of tribal morality and rectifiers of disturbed social relationships—both structural and contingent—is a vital one in a society without centralized political institutions.

Omar Khayyam Moore

DIVINATION—A NEW PERSPECTIVE

While divination is usually regarded as a means of overcoming ambiguity and of legitimizing a course of action, Moore's ingenious theory is that divination, by supplying a chance mechanism, directs some human activities toward randomness and may thereby serve a useful role in avoiding regularity where such regularity may be disadvantageous. He suggests in this article that scapulimancy may send Naskapi hunters off in random directions and thereby *increase* their chances of encountering the caribou herds they seek. His hypothesis needs further exploration, but it is certainly novel and merits investigation.

Reprinted from *American Anthropologist* LIX (1957), 69–74, by permission of the author and the American Anthropological Association.

The purpose of this paper is to suggest a new interpretation of certain kinds of magical practices, especially divination. First, however, I should perhaps explain briefly the motivation for undertaking this analysis. The initial impetus came from experimental investigations of the problem-solving activities of groups. These experiments quite naturally involved the study and classification of ineffective problem-solving techniques, and it appeared that fresh insight into this whole matter might be gained through examining some "classic" cases of ineffective solutions to problems. Magic is, by definition and reputation, a notoriously ineffective method for attaining the specific ends its practitioners hope to achieve through its use. On the surface, at least, it would seem then that magical rituals are classic cases of poor solutions to problems, and for this reason should be of theoretical interest from the standpoint of research on human problem solving.

Most, if not all, scientific analyses of magic presuppose that these rituals as a matter of fact do not lead to the desired results. If the carrying out of a magical rite is followed by the hoped for state of affairs, then this is to be explained on other grounds. Scientific observers, of course, employ the criteria furnished by modern science to judge the probable efficacy of magical activities as methods for producing the ends-in-view of magicians. One of the puzzles most theories of magic seek to resolve is why human beings cling so tenaciously to magic if it does not work. Many contemporary explanations of this puzzle make use of the concept "positive latent function," that is, that even though magic fails to achieve its "manifest" ends, except by accident or coincidence, it serves its practitioners and/or their society in other critically important ways. The position developed here is compatible with the viewpoint that magical rituals may be sustained by numerous latent functions. However, it conceivably could serve as a prophylaxis against the overelaboration of these functions; in any case, it could serve as a supplementary explanation of the phenomena.

Put baldly, the thesis to be advanced here is that some practices which have been classified as magic may well be directly efficacious as techniques for attaining the ends envisaged by their practitioners. Perhaps the best way to render plausible this somewhat counter-intuitive proposition is to consider in some detail an actual magical rite as it has been described by a highly competent anthropologist.

The Montagnais-Naskapi, most northerly of eastern Indian tribes, live in the forests and barren ground of the interior plateau of the Labradorian Peninsula. Speck (1935) has conducted field studies of the Naskapi and in the account that follows, primary reliance is placed upon his reports. According to Speck, "The practices of divination embody the very innermost spirit of the religion of the Labrador bands. Theirs is almost wholly a religion of divination" (p. 127). It is of interest to learn exactly how divination is carried out and what ends the Naskapi expect to achieve through it.

Animal bones and various other objects are used in divination. The shoulder blade of the caribou is held by them to be especially "truthful." When it is to be employed for this purpose the meat is pared away, and the bone is boiled and wiped clean; it is hung up to dry, and finally a small piece of wood is split and attached to the bone to form a handle. In the divinatory ritual the shoulder blade, thus prepared, is held over hot coals for a short time. The heat causes cracks and burnt spots to form, and these are then "read." The Naskapi have a system for interpreting the cracks and spots, and in this way they find answers to important questions. One class of questions for which shoulder-blade augury provides answers is: What direction should hunters take in locating game? This is a critical matter, for the failure of a hunt may bring privation or even death.

When a shoulder blade is used to locate game, it is held in a predetermined position with reference to the local topography, i.e., it is directionally oriented. It may be regarded as "a blank chart of the hunting territory . . ." (Speck, p. 151). Speck states (p. 151) ". . . as the burnt spots and cracks appear these indicate the directions to be followed and sought." If there is a shortage of food, the shoulder-blade oracle may be consulted as often as every three or four days and, of course, the directions that the hunts take are determined thereby.

There are certain other relevant aspects of divination that must be mentioned before turning to an analysis of the ritual. Speck explains (p. 150):

> *In divining with the burnt shoulder blade the procedure is first to dream. This, as we shall see, is induced by a sweat bath and by drumming or shaking a rattle. Then, when a dream of seeing or securing game comes to the hunter, the next thing to do is to find where to go and what circumstances will be encountered. And since the dream is vague, and especially since it is not localized, the hunter-dreamer cannot tell where his route is to lie or what landmarks he will find. So he employs the shoulder blade. As one informant put it, the divination rite cleared up the dream. "We generally use the caribou shoulder blade for caribou hunting divination, the shoulder blade or hip bone of beaver for beaver divination, fish-jaw augury for fishing, and so on." Drumming, singing, and dreaming, next divination by scapula, then, combine as the modus operandi of the life-supporting hunt.*

It is well to pause at this point to take note of certain features of these rites.

The Naskapi do not control the exact patterning of cracks and spots in the shoulder blade and, furthermore, it would not be in accord with their beliefs about divination to attempt such control; rather, they are interested in observing whatever cracks and spots appear. This means that the final decision about where to hunt, for instance, does not represent a purely personal choice. Decisions are based on the outcome of a process extrinsic to their volition—and this outcome is dependent upon the interaction of a number of relatively uncontrolled variables such as bone structure, temperature of fire, length of time bone is exposed to heat, etc.

It may be clarifying to perform a "mental experiment" in order to analyze some of the possible consequences of basing a decision on the outcome of an impersonal and relatively uncontrolled process. Imagine that the Naskapi carried out their divinatory rites as described with this exception; they did not base their decisions on the occurrence of cracks and spots in the burnt blade. They dreamed, sang, drummed, burned a shoulder blade, but ignored the cracks and spots. Under these hypothetical circumstances, decisions still would have to be made about where to hunt the game.

One question which this "mental experiment" raises is: Would the Naskapi be likely to enjoy more success in hunting if they did not permit decisions to rest upon the occurrence of cracks and spots? Would it not be sounder practice for them simply to decide where, in their best judgment, game may be found and hunt there? Of course, when the Naskapi do have information about the location of game, they tend to act upon it. Ordinarily, it is when they are uncertain and food supplies get low that they turn to their oracle for guidance.

It can be seen that divination based on the reading of cracks and spots, serves to break (or weaken) the causal nexus between final decisions about where to hunt and individual and group preferences in this matter. Without the intervention of this impersonal mechanism it seems reasonable to suppose that the outcome of past hunts would play a more important role in determining present strategy; it seems likely their selections of hunting routes would be patterned in a way related to recent successes and failures. If it may be assumed that there is some interplay between the animals they seek and the hunts they undertake, such that the hunted and the hunters act and react to the other's actions and potential actions, then there may be a marked advantage in avoiding a fixed pattern in hunting. Unwitting regularities in behavior provide a basis for anticipatory responses. For instance, animals that are "overhunted" are likely to become sensitized to human beings and hence quick to take evasive action. Because the occurrence of cracks and spots in the shoulder blade and the distribution of game are in all likelihood independent events, i.e., the former is unrelated to the outcome of past hunts, it would seem that a certain amount of irregularity would be introduced into the Naskapi hunting pattern by this mechanism.

We can indicate the point of the foregoing discussion in the following way. In the first place, the Naskapi live a precarious life; their continued existence depends on the success of their day-to-day hunting. And it is prima facie unlikely that grossly defective approaches to hunting would have survival value. Like all people, they can be victimized by their own habits; in particular, habitual success in hunting certain areas may lead to depletion of the game supply—it may lead, that is, to a success-induced failure. Under these circumstances, a device which would break up habit patterns in a more or less random fashion might be of value. The question is: To what degree, if any, does shoulder-blade augury do this?

It should be remembered that it is difficult for human beings to avoid patterning their behavior in a regular way. Without the aid of a table of random numbers or some other randomizing instrument, it is very unlikely that a human being or group would be able to make random choices even if an attempt were made to do so. The essential soundness of the last statement is recognized in scientific practice. Whenever, in the course of a scientific investigation, it is essential to avoid bias in making selections, every effort is made to eliminate the factor of personal choice. As Yule and Kendall have succinctly stated, "Experience has, in fact, shown that the human being is an extremely poor instrument for the conduct of a random selection."

Of course, it is not maintained here that the burnt shoulder blade is an unbiased randomizing device. It is likely that the bones would crack and form spots in certain ways more often than others. Regularity stemming from this source may to some degree be lessened because the Naskapi change campsites, yet in the rituals they maintain the same spatial orientation of the bones (for, as previously mentioned, the bones are oriented map-like with reference to the topography). Hence, a crack or spot appearing in the same place in the bone on a new occasion of divination at another campsite, would send them on a different route. An impersonal device of the kind used by the Naskapi might be characterized as a crude "chance-like" instrument. It seems that the use of such a device would make it more difficult to anticipate their behavior than would otherwise be the case.

It is not possible on the basis of the available evidence to determine even approximately whether shoulder-blade divination as practiced by the Naskapi actually serves to increase their hunting success, although a plausible argument has been advanced indicating that this might be the case.

If the Naskapi were the only people who engaged in scapulimancy, the question of its efficacy would perhaps not be of general theoretical interest. However, scapulimancy was widely practiced in North America and has been reported from Asia, India, and Europe. There are other divinatory rituals that also involve the use of impersonal chance-like devices in arriving at decisions, for example, the ancient Chinese divination by cracks in burnt tortoise shells. One-hundred and twenty-five different figures formed by these cracks were distinguished for oracular purposes. All manner of objects and events have been used in divination. Some arrangements are perhaps not obviously chance-like, but prove to be so when analyzed, as for instance Azande divination. The basic divinatory equipment associated with the Azande "poison oracle" consists of poison, probably strychnine, and fowls. The Azande have little control over the potency of the poison they administer to the fowls since they do not make their own poison, and not all fowls have the same tolerance for this poison. The Azande ask questions of the poison oracle and base decisions on whether the fowls live or die. They have no way of knowing in advance what the outcome will be.

The heuristic analysis given here is potentially relevant to all situations in which human beings base their decisions on the outcome of chance mechanisms. It is obvious, however, that light would be shed on the actual workability of these procedures only in terms of a thorough-going investigation of the problems men face within the societal context in which these problems occur. Certainly the apparent irrelevance of such techniques is no guarantee of their inutility. On the contrary, if shoulder-blade augury, for example, has any worth as a viable part of the life-supporting hunt, then it is because it is in essence a very crude way of randomizing human behavior under conditions where avoiding fixed patterns of activity may be an advantage. The difficulty of providing an empirical test for this hypothesis points to the fact that it is an open question.

Years ago Tylor noted that "the art of divination and games of chance are so similar in principle that the very same instrument passes from one use to the other." Tylor's observation is acute. However, it would appear that the relationship in "principle" is not between divination and games of chance, but between divination and games of strategy. It is only very recently that the distinction between games of chance and games of strategy has been drawn clearly. We are indebted to von Neumann and Morgenstern for clarifying this. It is beyond the scope of this paper to discuss the theory of games of strategy, but it is worth pointing out that this theory makes evident how some classes of interactional problems can be solved optimally by means of a "mixed" or "statistical" strategy. In order to employ a statistical strategy it is necessary to have, adapt, or invent a suitable chance mechanism. Its being "suitable" is critical, for unless the chance device will generate appropriate odds for the problem at hand, then its potential advantage may be lost. It should go without saying that no one assumes that preliterate magicians are in any position to get the most out of their crude chance-like devices. Nevertheless, it is possible that through a long process of creative trial and error some societies have arrived at some approximate solutions for recurring problems.

SUMMARY

It is the object of this paper to suggest a new interpretation of some aspects of divination. It should be emphasized that this interpretation is offered as a supplement to existing theories of magic and not as a replacement. An examination of many magical practices suggests that the utility of some of these techniques needs to be reassessed. It seems safe to assume that human beings require a functional equivalent to a table of random numbers if they are to avoid unwitting regularities in their behavior which can be utilized by adversaries. Only an extremely thorough study of the detailed structure of problems will enable scientists to determine to what degree some very ancient devices are effective.

EIGHT
THE MEANING OF GHOSTS AND ANCESTOR WORSHIP

Introduction

Universal problems faced by all human societies are created by what Malinowski has called "the supreme and final crisis of life"—death. These problems, many-faceted to be sure, may be considered on two levels: those that face the individual and those that force adjustments on the society as a whole.

For all sane individuals eventual extinction of the organism, in the corporeal sense at least, forms an ever-present part of life expectancy; no normal human considers his own potential span to be eternal. Further, the death of a spouse or close relative disturbs an individual's social relations, often necessitating deliberate changes in family relations, economic activities, emotional exchange, and many other areas where the life pattern of the deceased formerly impinged on the lives of the survivors. Moving to a higher level of abstraction—the societal rather than the individual—the death of any member of the interacting group is likely to create points of stress which will pervade the entire social structure, particularly in small societies living in face-to-face relationships. Depending on the social importance of the deceased, the amount of disturbance felt within the system will vary. When the middle-aged but still vigorous male family head dies he leaves a vastly greater number of roles and functions unfulfilled than does, let us say, a female infant from a socially unimportant family. Yet the loss of any member from the group will have repercussions in a much wider circle than that composed of kin alone. For examples of how funerals and other mortuary institutions meet the social problems arising from human mortality, see Robert Hertz's classic essay on death reprinted in his book *Death and the Right Hand* (1960), and a more recent article by William Carter entitled "Secular Reinforcement in Aymara Death Ritual" (1968).

All cultures have techniques and methods which serve, if not to eliminate, at least to reduce problems arising out of the fact of human mortality. This they do both by reducing the individual's anxiety stemming from the contemplation of his own demise and by facilitating the orderly resumption of interpersonal relations following the death of a member of the group.

It could hardly be said that members of

any culture anticipate with relish the prospect of passing from the delights of earthly existence, regardless of how few these may be; it is probably a fair generalization to say that most humans, given the option, would choose to remain among the living a while longer when the final moment of departure arrives. Myth and fiction sometimes permit an alternative but life itself never does. But though it is not possible to postulate eternal corporeal existence for members of a culture—the corpse is difficult to overlook—it is possible to extend culture-like conditions, bridging out from the known to the unknown, for the departed spirit to enjoy. Without attempting to suggest causality or primacy to either the spirit concept or that of life after death, it may be said that virtually all cultures provide both the concept of some nonmaterial aspect of life which will survive death and some beliefs regarding where and how this spirit would exist.

It might be suggested, though it is at present a better research hypothesis than a cultural law, that the individual's attitude toward death is strongly conditioned by the cultural belief regarding what becomes of that part of consciousness which survives the death crisis. Implicit belief in, and anticipation of, the survival of the cognitive being beyond the grave might do much to alleviate individual anxieties regarding termination of the material self—it merely continues to exist in another, and possibly more pleasant, form. The willingness of members of religious groups to die for causes justified by religious beliefs stands in evidence for this point. Attitudes of early Christians sacrificed for their faith, the willingness of Moslems to engage in "holy wars," and the apparent acceptance of their fates by many Aztec sacrificial victims, all attest to the overcoming of individual fears of death when promised recompense in an afterworld. This same point could be made for the Masai, the Plains Indian, and the Eskimo; death loses its sting when it is not conceived of as the complete end of the self. This cultural potential, the possibility of partially alleviating individual fears regarding death through the implicit belief in an afterlife, stands as another virtually universal feature of human existence. Referring to the belief in the survival of the human spirit after death, Frazer wrote with some petulance that "it seems probable that the great majority of our species will continue to acquiesce in a belief so flattering to human vanity and so comforting to human sorrow." A recent study of death and concepts of death can be found in Arien Mack (ed.), *Death in American Experience* (1973).

But what of the living, those who are not immediately contemplating an exit? Belief in an afterworld may assuage an individual's fears but, at the same time, it places him in more or less intimate contact with a host of nonmortal beings, either the departed members of his own group, as is the case with many simple cultures, or with the spirits of all departed human beings, as is the case with Christianity. Does the knowledge that the spirits of the dead were formerly relatives, countrymen, or fellow humans result in the enthusiastic participation of the living with the nonliving? Apparently not, except in a few cases. As Frazer has so convincingly demonstrated in a three-volume study of the subject (*The Fear of the Dead in Primitive Religion*, 1933–1936), most cultures have developed attitudes of fear and dread regarding the spirits of the deceased. Sometimes these fears are mild and noninstitutionalized, as among the Hopi. At other times they are expressed through elaborate mechanisms which serve to pacify the ghosts or to mislead them by guile, as when the Bambwa sacrifice a goat near a shrine close to the ghost's alleged abode, or certain Australian tribes impose years of silence on widows so that the spirits of their jealous husbands will not be able to detect them. Anthropological literature is filled with fantastic examples of the efforts to which the living will go to ensure against the return of ghosts, even to the extent of supplying the dead with money for their expenses of the journey to the other world—a custom not only of the Khasis of Assam, the Burmese, the Lolos, and the Mosquito Indians, but of the ancient Greeks as well, who inserted a coin in the mouth of the corpse so that the deceased could pay Charon for ferrying him across the river Styx.

Apparently basic to the institutionalized fear of ghosts is the belief that after death, though the spirit of the individual continues to exist in the afterworld, the basic "personality" structure of the spirit undergoes a striking change—it becomes malevolent. Regardless of what the person may have been like in life, his spirit is potentially dangerous to the living. As the following articles reveal, however, this conception of spirits of the dead is not always the case. In many groups, ghosts may be only partially evil or dangerous, and in still others, they may be conceived of as ever-present members of the social group who have increased powers to influence the lives of the living, either favorably or unfavorably. When the ghosts are thought to be most concerned with members of their own kin groups, and the members of the kin groups feel that the ghosts require propitiation in order to aid their living kinsmen, ancestor worship prevails. The spirits of the dead are revered, though that reverence is possibly never free from some feelings of fear and awe. Sometimes repressive and harsh, at other times benign and beneficial, the ghosts or ancestral spirits coexist with the living, influencing and even determining the fortunes of the tribal members. A useful collection for the comparative study of ancestor worship in Africa and East Asia is *Ancestors* (1976) edited by William H. Newell.

The articles in this chapter are intended to indicate something of the range of attitudes and beliefs that exist regarding death, ghosts, and ancestors, to indicate the ways in which these attitudes and practices are interrelated with other aspects of culture, and to offer some analyses of the various phenomena.

Morris E. Opler

AN INTERPRETATION OF AMBIVALENCE OF TWO AMERICAN INDIAN TRIBES

This article, prefaced by a Freudian proposition regarding ambivalence, contains excellent ethnographic documentation of attitudes and behaviors associated with death in Chiricahua and Mescalero Apache cultures. The ambivalent feeling that living members of the groups manifest toward the dead—mourning and grief expressed on the one hand, and dread and possibly hatred expressed on the other—is explained in purely cultural terms. Rejecting the Freudian position regarding "primordial parricides" and a consequent guilt feeling arising from this hypothetical event, Opler suggests that the apparent ambivalences may be explained through an analysis of interpersonal relations, the nature of power, and the ecological circumstances of the cultures. Fear of the dead is seen as a function of kinship and local group systems, of patterns of authority, of fear of sorcery and witchcraft, plus the basic need for interpersonal cooperation as a requisite for survival in the hostile environment.

As is true of most conclusions drawn from bodies of data partially inferred from individual psychological processes, other interpretations could be made than that presented here by Opler. Nonetheless, Opler's work stands as a well-documented, closely reasoned analysis of what is possibly a panhuman phenomenon—ambivalent feelings on the part of the living toward the deceased.

Opler has provided further data to substantiate his thesis in an article, "Further Comparative Anthropological Data Bearing on the Solution of a Psychological Problem," published in 1938. There Opler shows how the typical Apache mourning behavior displayed toward adults who die in the prime of life is *not* displayed at the death of the very old nor at the death of infants. The reasons are evident: the extremely old are less likely to be feared because they have lived so long and experienced so much that there is no reason for them to suspect their surviving kinsmen of death wishes or sorcery and to take revenge for these. Conversely, in the case of the extremely young, the social personality has not yet been formed, and the clash of wills and desires that characterizes adult life has not occurred with these infants.

Reprinted in abridged form from the *Journal of Social Psychology*, VII (February, 1936), 82–115, by permission of the author and The Journal Press.

Some time ago, in a review of *Totem and Taboo*, A. L. Kroeber referred to a number of Freud's suggestions as contributions "which every ethnologist must sooner or later take into consideration." Kroeber singled out Freud's discussion of ambivalence as particularly provocative and, in part, said of it: "Again the strange combination of mourning for the dead with the fear of them and taboos against them is certainly illumined if not explained by this theory of ambivalence."

Whether or not the ethnologist has taken this phase of Freud's writings into consideration, it remains true that few students of preliterate peoples have conducted inquiries designed to test or modify the psychoanalytic theory and conclusions upon the point.

At one time during my stay on the [Mescalero Apache] reservation, a very able and intelligent informant who wished to give me the fullest possible understanding of the culture undertook to explain native customs and beliefs for me. This Apache offered a number of native rationalizations pertaining to various rites and practices, and then bravely started to explain the peculiar belief that an Apache who possesses supernatural power and successfully practices the rite connected with it for any length of time, finally will be forced to sacrifice a close relative or permit himself to die. My informant floundered in a web of ambiguities for a few minutes and then had to confess that the whole matter was not clear to him. He could see, he said, why the power of some outsider, one who wished you ill perhaps, was to be feared; but why the power of a relative, one who could refuse you nothing in everyday life, should be a source of terror, he was unable to explain. This Apache was manifestly bewildered by the glaring inconsistency in the attitude toward kin upon which he had stumbled. On one hand he had been urged throughout his life to assist, and, in turn, to depend upon his relatives in all matters, to support them, whatever the consequences to himself, and even to avenge all wrongs inflicted upon them. Yet it was also within the traditional pattern to believe that these same people become, par excellence, a source of morbid fear for him. This contradiction or conflict in emotion and attitude towards the same person or group of people which this native sensed, we readily recognize as an expression of ambivalence.

The example cited is one of the most striking cases of contradictory attitude in respect to the same person which Apache culture affords and is the one which would, perhaps, be most noticeable to the native. But this instance by no means stands alone. The cultural forms are marked, at many points, by unmistakable evidence of such contrary emotions, and whole complexes are liberally tinged with such mixed feelings. A conspicuous affirmation of the last statement is the entire complex which has to do with death and the disposal of the dead. It will repay us to turn to this set of practices and beliefs.

One of the most impressive elements of Apache burial is the dispatch with which it must be conducted. Whenever possible burial takes place the same day on which death occurred. If this is impossible because the deceased has died in the evening, the burial always takes place the following day. The time during which the living and the dead are in contact is reduced to a minimum, a logical procedure in view of the dread sickness it is believed can be contracted from the dead, from the sight of the corpse, or from the possessions of the deceased.

As the last statement may suggest, no time is lost in disposing of the personal possessions of the dead. A certain number of his belongings are taken along by the burial party and interred with him; the rest are burned or broken into pieces at the spot where death took place. It is incumbent upon a dead Apache's relatives to dispose, in this way, of everything which had been used by him or had been in close personal contact with him. Even articles owned jointly with other members of the family, if they had been used to any extent by the deceased, had to be sacrificed. To retain any of these objects would bring back the ghost; the dead would return to claim his possessions. In any case the retention of some personal possession of a dead man would be sure to act as a reminder of him, and to think of the dead is one way of inviting the presence of the ghost and of subsequently succumbing to the serious "ghost" or "darkness sickness." In keeping with this fear of the return of the ghost to claim objects recognized by him, it is considered dangerous even to cherish presents given one by the deceased before his death.

Not only are the possessions of the dead relative destroyed or buried, but the very dwelling in which death took place is razed as well. The framework is usually burned, but even if it is not reduced to ashes, one may be sure that no Apache will enter a deserted house or use wood from it unless he is very certain that no death has occurred there. Nor does the destruction of the dwelling pave the way for a new, uncontaminated home on the old site. The family moves immediately to a new locality, one that will not be conducive to memories centering about the departed.

The effort to efface the memory of the dead relative goes much further. Those who assume the unwelcome task of dressing the corpse and burying it, burn, upon their return, all the clothes they wore while performing these duties. They also bathe their bodies in the smoke of a sage called "ghost medicine" which is thought unpleasant to ghosts and efficacious in keeping them at a distance. In fact, all members of the bereaved family are likely to "fumigate" themselves in this manner and to resort for some days to various devices which are considered useful in avoiding dreams of the dead or in warding off the visits of ghosts. Such practices consist in crossing the forehead or bed with ashes, or hanging some crossed pieces of "ghost medicine" above the head before retiring.

At the grave, just before their return, the members of the burial party take a final precautionary measure. They brush off their own bodies with green grass which they then lay at the grave in the form of a cross. The conception is that when this is done, any danger of falling victim to "ghost sickness" will be brushed away and left at the grave of the dead.

No more people than are strictly necessary to carry the possessions and prepare the grave participate in the burial. The site of the grave is not discussed thereafter; ordinarily no one would ask about the location of the grave, and no one would volunteer such information.

After the foregoing it is almost unnecessary to add that the grave is never revisited and that anyone found lingering around a grave site is suspect of witchcraft. As among so many other peoples, graves and the bones and possessions of the dead play a prominent role in ideas concerning sorcery.

To this point we have been primarily concerned with the measures taken to erase from the scene any material reminders of a dead relative and to avoid illness which may derive from actual contact with or sight of the corpse. But there are quite as many steps taken to obliterate less tangible reminders of the loss the family has suffered, and it may be instructive to turn to some of these now.

There is, first of all, a strong taboo against mentioning the name of the deceased. If it becomes necessary, for any reason, to mention his name, a phrase meaning "who used to be called" must be added.

As a result of this taboo it proved extremely difficult for me to obtain reliable genealogical material. It was considerably easier to persuade Apaches to discuss and reveal rites and ceremonies than it was to bring them to the point of talking freely of the kinship ties which had existed between them and those now dead.

The unwillingness to utter the name of the recent dead is a characteristic true of all members of these two tribes, whether they are relatives of the deceased or not. With the passage of time the taboo becomes less binding upon nonrelatives. Not so in respect to the relatives, however. For them there is no diminution of the strength of the taboo, and others, no matter what they may do elsewhere, must strictly refrain from any mention of the dead in the presence of these relatives. In fact, nothing is more insulting, provocative, and certain to precipitate conflict than to call out the name of a dead man in the presence of his relative. A surprising number of feuds between families have had such an origin or include such an episode in their histories.

Just as the calling of a dead man's name within the hearing of his relative is accounted the gravest of insults and acts of hostility, so it is considered a graceful compliment to the family of the deceased and to the memory of the dead to take elaborate precautions that the name be not called. In cases of the death of prominent men who have been named after some object or animal, that animal or object is given an alternative name or another name. Thus when a Mescalero leader named Beso (from the Spanish *peso*) died, everyone was obliged to say *dinero* instead of *peso*, especially when within earshot of members of the dead man's family.

There is another practice which utilizes similiar reasoning. If an Apache called two relatives by the same kinship term, and one of these relatives dies, for a long time afterward he will refrain from using this term to the survivor. To use the term formerly addressed to the one who has died will awaken memories of him and deepest grief, it is felt.

It is interesting to note that the very existence of death cannot be allowed terminological sanction. The verb that connotes the coming of death is used only in connection with animals. Of a person the most that can be said in everyday speech is, "He is gone."

The insistence that nothing be left as it was before a death, lest it act as a reminder of the bereavement, finds expression in all departments of native life. There is the practice, for example, of never leaving the bedding as it was when in use, when camp is to be broken. If death should occur and the individual should not return to that place, the sight of his bed as last used by him would only bring sorrow to his relatives.

These attitudes are reflected in the ceremonial complex, moreover. Ceremonies usually continue through four days or nights. If a death occurs in any nearby camp after the rite has begun, when the news is brought to the officiating shaman, he terminates his work at once. The ceremonial gifts which had to be given him before he could enter upon his duties he returns to the donors. Now all is as it was before, and after the passage from one to four days the whole ceremony is repeated from the beginning.

Despite the brevity and condensation of this description of Apache customs concerning death rites, it should be reasonably clear that there is a whole set of important practices designed to suppress and obliterate all mention and memory of the dead relative. In introducing this material I have termed it an indicator of ambivalent attitudes. In the Freudian sense this would suggest that the struggle to remove the possessions, the name, even the memory of the deceased from consciousness, is nothing else than an elaborate attempt to guard against the fear of the dead which results from the unconscious hate and resentment felt for this person during his life.

It may be asked why such an interpretation, so farfetched at first thought, need be accepted. The Apaches themselves say that there is no deep-seated mystery concerning the genesis of these acts and rites. They will tell you that an Apache loves his kin—a great deal more than the white man cares for his relatives, they may add significantly. To dwell on the memory of the dead would be to emphasize the loss and deepen the grief. Therefore they engage in the practices which arouse our curiosity.

The reasoning sounds honest and logical and might be acceptable if it were not for another congeries of attitudes and practices of an altogether different flavor which exists at the time of death, side by side with those we have already noted. These last are direct and vehement expressions of grief and evidences of mourning which are in no way subdued, curbed, or repressed. When an Apache learns of a close relative's death, he tears the clothes from his back. The women wail, the men cry openly and unashamed. Close relatives cut their hair, an act which alone will mark their bereavement for at least a year. For some time they wear only such clothing as is absolutely necessary for minimum warmth, and for a generous span of time they shun the dances and festivities. Often relatives mourn thus for a long time. An old woman, whose husband has been dead many years, still can be heard bewailing her loss occasionally.

Without laboring the point or extending the discussion, enough has been said, perhaps, to indicate that contradictory practices mark the Apache rites of death; there is the tendency to publicly signify grief and attest to the loss, and an elaborately socialized machinery for banishing that grief and the objects and words which might awake it.

But to state the Freudian conception, namely, that these two sets of practices result from ambivalent emotional attitudes toward the dead; that one set derives from the affection and regard which normal human relations sponsor, and the other from unconscious dislike and fear that are no less poignant and real; to state this, merely, is not to prove it.

Indeed, it could be most reasonably argued that it is gratuitous elaboration and special pleading to conjure up fear and unconscious hate as the stimulus for the practices which serve to eradicate mention and memory of the dead. It might be insisted with as much cogency that both sets of practices can be reasonably traced to one source, the affection and regard for the dead relative. It takes no great imaginative powers to suppose that genuine love for the dead relative could expend itself through more than one channel, and that the actualizations of these emotional flows could even appear contradictory. It is intelligible that under the impact of a deeply felt loss there would be the impulse to cry out and testify to grief, and no less the realization that the future must be faced alone, that the living must somehow carry on, that memories which weaken without aiding must be laid aside.

With these two interpretations possible from the data, the inquiry is reduced bluntly to this question: Is there any concrete and conclusive evidence in Apache culture of avowed fear of the dead, and especially of dead relatives, which might give body and validity to the hypothesis that the avoidance of the dead, of their graves, their names, their possessions, and their memories is attributable to fear rather than to regard?

Fortunately the study of Apache culture affords an unequivocal answer. Fear of the dead, and fear of the dead relatives particularly, does not have to be inferred. Instead its existence is asserted and emphasized by the natives. This fear is not merely an amorphous dread which seizes individuals in varying ways and must be relieved according to personal requirements. It has become formalized into a body of beliefs and concepts, and these have been woven into the fabric of the ceremonial life.

Now Apache ceremonial life, while it has other functions, is principally concerned with the healing of the sick. The gravest illnesses are contracted, it is believed, from contact with certain animals, such as bear, snake, and the like, or from being frightened or endangered by certain natural forces, such as lightning. Each of these sicknesses has its own characteristics and symptoms, and such diseases can be cured by shamans who have supernatural power from, and therefore considerable influence over, the animal or agency which has caused the illness. But there are also some people of malevolent disposition who have likewise had supernatural experiences with these potent animals or forces of nature and who have gained a ceremony and considerable power thereby. These are the witches, who manipulate their power for evil often, and are the ultimate source of much sickness and death. The witch who "knows" Bear may cause his enemy to suffer from "bear disease." His victim's sole hope is to command the services of another who "knows" Bear, who uses such power for beneficent purposes only, and whose power is stronger than that of the witch. It is likewise possible for a person to use his ceremony for the benefit of some, yet seek to harm others. He may be a shaman at one point of his career and a witch at another. He may be both at the same time.

With this hint of background we may proceed to the expression of the fear of the dead in Apache society. The fear, in obedience to the native pattern, is expressed in terms of sickness, and the sickness, eloquently enough for our argument, is expressed in terms of fear.

The particular illness attributable to persecution by the ghosts of the dead is known by three names, "ghost sickness," "owl sickness," and "darkness sickness." Ordinarily the Apache will not dare to use the words "ghost" or "owl" and will therefore give the last name only. The term "ghost sickness" is self-explanatory. The disease is also called "owl sickness" because the ghost is said to come back in the shape of an owl; owls are the ghosts of the departed. The blackest omen of which an Apache can think is the hoot of an owl around camp. The proximity of the bird, especially shortly after the death of a relative, evokes the greatest terror, and is often sufficient grounds for the requisite "ghost" or "owl ceremony." I could fill many more pages with native accounts of the dread and despair inspired by the appearance of the owl around camp or by its call. Ghosts are said to trouble people most often at night when it is dark, and most shamans who cure "ghost sickness" will not conduct their ceremony except at night. For these reasons, and also because a person afflicted with the malady is especially nervous and easily frightened at night, the name "darkness sickness" is the approved euphemism for the disease.

It is of special interest to note that the disease always strikes "from the head to the heart." All its symptoms are those of fright and include irregular beating of the heart, a choking sensation, and faintness at first seizure. As long as the illness lasts the patient suffers from excessive timidity, much trembling, weeping, and headache.

Although ghosts of nonrelatives may and do cause fear and sickness, it is far more common that the disease be the result of an encounter with the ghost of a deceased relative.

In the first place it is noteworthy that the most elaborate precautions are entered upon by the close relatives immediately after an Apache's death. Since these relatives have most contact with the corpse and the possessions of the dead, this is quite to be expected. Nevertheless, the end result and the general feeling are that the relative has more to fear from the ghost than anyone else.

Again, it is a matter of interest that most ghost ceremonies are held soon after a death in a family, and that the patient or patients are usually relatives of the deceased.

There is another impressive indication of the close nexus between relationship and fear of ghosts and owls. The hooting of the owl is accepted as speech in the Apache language which can be understood if one listens closely. The owl, according to my informants, has many unpleasant remarks to make to its uneasy hearers. It has been known to make the hair-raising statement, "I'm going to drink your blood." But more often the words of the owl have to do with its relationship to the one it is addressing. "I am your dead relative"—this is the most common sentence discerned by the tortured imagination of the Apache when the owl hoots nearby.

The owl is also prone to give ominous warnings concerning relatives. The bird is not infrequently heard reporting such melancholy news as, "All your people (relatives) are going to die." One woman, after the departure of a war party, heard this message repeated over and over by an owl, "I used to be one of your relatives." The next day the men returned without her son; he had been killed.

The owl, according to one Apache, "represents the spirit of a person" which "works by entering the body of an owl and exercises evil influence in this way." "That man is already dead and comes back. He turned to owl." "It's a ghost. It comes out of the grave, and it goes back." These are representative dicta of the natives concerning the owl.

From this equation of ghost with owl flows the belief that the ghost can appear as an owl and then transform itself at will into the semblance of the figure it bore in life. And it is possible for a shade of the dead to appear and, upon being accosted, to change into an owl and disappear.

Now to see or hear an owl is unlucky and harrowing enough, but to see the form of a ghost as you knew him in life, or, worse still, to be able to distinguish his features, is well-nigh fatal. It is the general consensus of opinion, backed by the authority of many cases, that the person who can discern the features of the ghost before him has not long to live.

Even though the evidence which has been offered is but a fraction of what could be presented, I hope that enough has been said to establish the connection between the taboos directed against the dead and fear of the dead. It should be abundantly clear, too, that the burden of both the taboos and the fear falls primarily and with unremitting force on the relatives of the deceased. But if the Apache must guard against the ill will of the dead, he must guard himself just as sedulously against the machinations of the living. Something has been said above of the duality of supernatural power as conceived of by the Apache, and of the possibility of wielding such power in the spirit of malice and revenge as well as for purposes good and holy. Granting the existence and duality of supernatural power, there is nothing obscure about the basis of fear of witches. A case will illustrate this. I was once talking to a man about charges of witchcraft which had been directed against X. The man with whom I was talking then admitted to me, "Well, I'm a little afraid of X myself." He told me how he and X had opposed each other in a dispute which nearly ended in blows. Knowing X's reputation for possessing much supernatural power, and believing him to be thoroughly unscrupulous, he wondered whether X's resentment might not spill over into supernatural channels and work some immense disaster to him. In this case there was a cause for revenge and a subsequent outgrowth of fear. In all cases of ordinary witchcraft, some reason for the murderous supernatural attack is advanced, if it is only that the witch was jealous of the sick one's good looks or envious of his promising career. When a shaman sings over a patient and determines that his client is witched, he very often describes what led the witch to such extremes. "Do you remember when you attended that dance two years ago?" he might ask. "You gave something to drink to everyone there but one woman. You did not know it, but you forgot her and she was very angry. She determined to get even for this insult. She has waited till now so no suspicion will fall upon her." The conception is that always, if one can but put a finger on it, there is some injury or insult which will account for recourse to witchcraft.

But the Apache is not only beset by fear of the supernatural power of those who have reason to hate and harm him; he must also face the possibility that the supernatural power of those who are closest and dearest to him, the supernatural power of his own relatives, may be utilized to effect his very death. The reader will remember that we began our paper with this very paradox. At that time it seemed an insoluble contradiction which puzzled my willing Apache informant as much as it puzzled us. Now we are in a position to see the concept as one more mark of the underlying fear directed toward relatives. We have already dealt with the fear of the ghosts of the dead felt by living relatives. Now we have to consider the Apache's fear of the supernatural power of his living relatives.

The fear is based on the peculiar belief which already has been introduced. It is asserted that if one who has a ceremony from a certain power, heals and prospers by means of it for many years, the time will come when his power will remind him of the benefits bestowed, of the long life that has been permitted him, of the guidance and security that have been granted. Then the power will ask payment in return for all this help, and, coming to the point, will announce that the payment must be the sacrifice of a child or close relative of the shaman. To refuse is to sign one's own death warrant; if the relative does not die, the shaman must die in his stead. Thus there is the saying, "He sacrifices his relative to prolong his own life."

I was once working in his tent with an Apache well above middle age, when I happened to glance out of the doorway and saw his father, a very old man, approaching on horseback. I innocently said, "Here comes your father. Shall I call him over?" I was not a little disturbed to hear an emphatic, "No!" uttered in a hoarse, strained whisper. Instead, I was directed in that same tense tone of voice, to stand at the door and describe the old man's movements. "Where is he now? What's he doing? Is he going away?" These were the questions thrown at me, and I answered in some bewilderment. As it happened the old man was just passing through his son's field on the way to another camp. I reported his departure and turned to demand an explanation of such unusual conduct. My friend was perspiring freely and breathing heavily. He talked readily enough about the matter. "I don't mind admitting I'm afraid of the old man," he said. "He's got all kinds of power. They say he has done a lot of good with it. Well, maybe he has done good years ago. But I haven't seen any good that he's done in the last ten years. I don't like to have him monkeying around this camp."

It is decidedly easier to establish the existence of ambivalence in Apache society, and to advance material concerning the fear of the ghosts of dead relatives and the power of living ones, than it is to account for and explain all this. One explanation has already been offered us. It is Freud's suggestion "that ambivalence, originally foreign to our emotional life, was acquired by mankind from the father complex. . . ."

There are a number of objections to such a view. In characteristic Freudian manner it would derive ambivalence from the omnipotent Oedipus complex, that hypothetical source from which so much is made to flow. Freud would have us believe that Apache ambivalence exists, not because there is anything in present Apache culture to warrant it, but because some of the younger men of a protohuman horde slew their father countless years ago. A "psyche of mass" which no psychologists have been able to understand, explain, or substantiate is supposed to have carried on and preserved the memory of the parricide for the unconscious of our Apaches. Just how this parricide can account for the fear of dead female relatives and the fear of the power of living female relatives it is difficult to imagine, and how this hypothesis can illuminate the equally strong fear of relatives other than parents has yet to be demonstrated. Divorce from reality in the interests of a threadbare theory and insistence upon tying excellent clinical data to the coattails of the unconvincing Oedipus story have done not a little to delay the benefits which should result from Freud's contributions.

I have found it more convincing, realistic, and illuminating to interpret Apache ambivalence in terms of forces and elements which actually operate in the society and whose effects are open to observation and evaluation. It will be profitable, therefore, to outline one or two aspects of Apache culture which I feel have a direct bearing upon our problem.

The Mescalero and Chiricahua Apaches were hunting and food-gathering nomads ranging over the semiarid territory which now includes northwestern Texas, southern New Mexico, southeastern Arizona, and the adjoining section of northern Old Mexico. They lived on the wild game and plant life of the region and so were constantly on the move as the fruits ripened in one locality or game seemed more abundant in another. As one would expect from this simple economy and roving life, their artifacts were few and crude. The life was arduous, and productivity was achieved only as a result of earnest effort to which all individuals had to contribute. It was the obligation of the Apache to fit himself for any situation, and, if possible, to excel his fellows in all important pursuits. From his earliest years the Apache boy was taught to develop his strength and talents and to compete with others in tests of endurance and fortitude. Most of the games played by the children were designed to prepare them for the strenuous life of the future. At the time of puberty the boy was subjected to a prolonged ordeal of hardening and training. With this successfully passed there remained a series of four warpath expeditions which he had to attend, not as a warrior, but as an apprentice, and on these trips he was again under the severe scrutiny of the older men who looked for any signs of weakness or incompetence in the youth. Often a relative would arrange to have a distinguished hunter or warrior with much supernatural power perform a ceremony for the young man, so that he would become outstanding in those activities.

The girl, too, was urged quite as much to perfect herself in the women's tasks. In short, the Apache had infinite pride in his strength, his hunting ability, his warpath prowess, and in all the traits and aptitudes which marked him as an exceptional individual.

In the light of the meager technological advancement of the Apaches, this attitude is what might be expected. Each warrior had to know how to make his bow and arrows and to use them effectively. Everyone had to be trained and encouraged to take his place in the economy and to help win a livelihood from the barren country which constituted a large part of the Apache range. The point I wish to emphasize is the appreciation of himself as an individual of capacity and ability which every normal Apache was likely to develop. This personal independence was manifest throughout life and pervaded all types of activity.

But while it is true that each Apache had to be trained to cope with the dangers and trials which a nomadic life of hunting, raiding, and warfare imposed, it is certainly not true that he was an arrant individualist, owing obedience, cooperation, and discipline to no group. I should like, very briefly, to outline the composition of a strong unit to which the individual owed deepest loyalty, to touch upon the probable reasons for its strength, and to indicate the part it normally played in the affairs of each Apache.

It is apparent that the economy which the Apache practiced would not support a large population. From the time of earliest records to the present, the two tribes we are considering were few in numbers and there is no reason to think that their population was on the increase at the time of first white contact. Yet these two small tribes traversed and controlled a vast territory, necessary to a hunting and gathering people in a locality where soil and climate combine to limit the food supply. It was imperative, moreover, that the people be well distributed over the range; too great a number trying to subsist in a limited area would have soon exhausted the available plant and animal life. Yet some concentration of population was required, if only for defense. As far back as my informants could remember, they had always had invaders to repel. For the Mescaleros, first it was the Tonkawas, then the Comanches, later the Mexicans and the Americans. Again, a good many of the tasks which had to be discharged required the assistance of a number of men or women. A raid to obtain valuable horses is a case in point. Enough men had to participate to secure and drive away the animals quickly, and the raid was most likely to succeed when lookouts could be posted before and behind the line of march. When the women were roasting the mescal in underground ovens and preparing this important food for winter use, enough of them had to assist to perform the necessary labor.

It occasions no surprise, then, to learn that the Apaches were distributed over their range in groups whose size and composition reflected the need for a small, close-knit body of people, sufficient for the execution of the necessary tasks dictated by the simple technology, possessing means of defense and the requisite mobility.

The group which offered these valuable characteristics and which became the central unit of Apache social organization was the extended domestic family. Residence after marriage among the Apaches was matrilocal, and so the extended domestic family ordinarily included an older married couple, their married and unmarried daughters, their sons-in-law, their married daughters' children, and their unmarried sons. The individual dwellings of the several families comprising this group were scattered a short distance from one another; altogether these camps composed a cluster of related families who shared the varied fortunes of battle, feast, work, and ceremony.

It was not uncommon for two or more extended domestic families which were united by marriage to camp near one another. This larger social division I have called the local group, for its members were generally known by a name descriptive of some mountain or natural landmark near which they roamed. This local group represented the greatest concentration of population realized by these Apaches except during brief periods of feast or ceremony. The Apache's life, therefore, was spent largely in company with his relatives by blood and affinity.

Apache social organization is characterized by other social divisions but they are of minor importance. There are the band and the tribe. Each is demarcated from the other by a definite range and slight differences of dialect and customs. While their existence was recognized by the native, he was considerably less interested in them than is the anthropologist. The Apache was sensible of the greater uniformity of speech and culture within what we call a tribe, but the Apache tribe was so remotely concerned with the problems and activities of the individual that neither of the two peoples under discussion possessed native tribal names. For all practical purposes, the allegiance and fundamental interest of the Apache were limited to the group of relatives represented by the extended domestic family, or at least by the local group.

It would be difficult to overestimate the unity of the extended domestic family. The women, the mother and daughters, were inseparable. They acted together in the accomplishment of all tasks, whether it were food gathering, food preparation, or the cooking.

The mother's home was the center of all domestic activity. All game shot by the father, unmarried sons, or sons-in-law was brought to this domestic hub. Here the daughters aided their mother with the cooking, and then each married daughter carried some of the prepared food to her own dwelling and ate with her husband and children, since the son-in-law must never see his wife's mother.

There is powerful opposition to the disruption of this nucleus of relatives. The son-in-law, as has been mentioned, is bound to his wife's family by ties of avoidance, by special forms of speech and conduct, and these carry with them obligations of continuous economic assistance and absolute respect. He must live near his parents-in-law and work for them. He is always at their command. If the young man should wish to marry a second wife (for polygamy was practiced) it would have to be a younger sister or cousin of his first wife, a member of the same relationship cluster. If his wife died, her relatives could force the widower to take a sister or female cousin of the deceased to wife. In case of domestic discord, the husband could not take easy offense and leave the camp of his parents-in-law without sufficient provocation. To do so would be to excite the enmity of a large and powerful group, and to be a marked man in its territory thereafter. So much for the structural safeguards which maintain the extended domestic family.

It will be appreciated that an organization of such strength and rigidity must exercise tremendous influence over the children which are reared in its charge. Something of the domination of this body of relatives over the affairs of the growing child has already been indicated when we were discussing that part played by relatives in the marriage choice. In all other matters of import the child is quite as dependent. If he needs a ceremony performed, it usually rests upon the bounty of his relatives to defray expenses. His instruction and training are supplied by relatives, or if outsiders are involved, the relatives pay for such services. Even as a mature person the individual can accomplish little without the aid of his relatives.

It may be wondered, perhaps, why so much space has been devoted to a discussion of Apache social groupings in a paper supposedly concerned with psychological problems. I think it is sufficient justification to point out that since the ambivalences we are attempting to comprehend are directed primarily against the members of the extended domestic family and the local group, it is plainly necessary (if we take the position that the ambivalences are stimulated by present, determinable factors) to study the common interests and also the probable causes of antagonism which these social units engender.

I am going to suggest the hypothesis that the ambivalences marked by the Apache practice of mourning for the dead and yet barring from sight or hearing anything that may arouse memories of the dead and consequent distress marked by fear, and the equally contradictory convention of avowing affection for kin and yet living in perpetual fear of their power—that these are the result of repressed and unconscious resentment and dislike of relatives which have their roots in the actual circumstances and events of Apache life.

The reader may smile at this. He may think, "Well, it is probably less fantastic to derive ambivalence from unconscious resentment against meddling relatives than it is to seek its meaning in fear of the vengeance of the sire of a primal horde, but, unfortunately, this hypothesis seems as impossible to prove as the other."

The situation may not be quite so desperate, however. After all, it should be possible to determine whether there are tangible causes of antagonism between relatives in Apache culture and whether these points of friction are substantial enough to cause noticeable disruption, and thus find a way into the field notes of the ethnologist. An affirmative answer of these two inquiries would afford much more conviction to my hypothesis. Therefore I am going to subject my hypothesis to four germane questions: (1) Is there any reason, inherent in Apache society, to expect conflict of desires between an Apache and his relative or body of relatives? (2) Do such conflicts occur openly enough and frequently enough to call themselves to the attention of an observer of the culture? (3) Can such open and public conflicts as do occur be definitely correlated with the existence or strength of ambivalence? (4) Agreeing that clashes between relatives may occur because of marked divergences in personalities and aims, how shall we account for the socialization of such oppositions, and their appearances as ambivalences, taboos, and customs to which all, including those who seemingly get along well with their kin, are subject?

In answer to the first question it may be said that while the strength and unity of the extended domestic family were prime necessities for the functioning of Apache culture at its technological level, and while innumerable benefits and kindnesses flowed to the individual Apache from such an arrangement, it also had its suppressive and irritating side. Merely to view the matter theoretically and apart from actual cases, it would seem inevitable that to train the youth to self-reliance and pride in personal achievement and yet leave him so completely under the control of a body of kin, would be to invite dissatisfaction and discord.

Let us now turn to our second inquiry and determine whether the undercurrent of revolt and dissatisfaction that seems theoretically possible really existed. I have abundant reason to believe that the absolutism of control over the individual by older kin or kin in a greater position of authority is compensated for by a definite tenseness in these relations which not infrequently flares up into acrimonious disputes.

The matter is not one into which it is easy to delve. The important material bearing on the point is not obtained through general questions which aim at understanding the formal outlines of the culture. Only considerable contact with the natives over a respectable length of time, and the establishment of close and friendly contacts can furnish the requisite data. An actual incident of field work will illustrate the point. During the early stages of my Mescalero research I hired an elderly informant and had no reason to complain of his services. As many others did after him, he gave me the ideal picture of Apache society. He emphasized, as will any reliable informant, the great respect and obedience which the Apache husband owes to his wife's relatives, and he enumerated the avoidances, polite forms, and usages which mark such observances. No one would have gathered from his sober and consistent discourse, that any Apache would dare slight these obligations or could live among his people if he had done so. About a year later I learned that this same informant, when a young man, had not only violated the proprieties to the extent of seeing his mother-in-law, but had come within an ace of scalping the poor lady. He had led an armed, one-man revolt against his wife's family, bottled them up together in a dwelling, and was only subdued by force in a successful attack from the rear.

Once the surface of things was scratched, it was not difficult to find comparable material which told a tale of resistance of individuals against domination by relatives of blood and affinity. Stories were obtained describing how girls fled from home rather than submit to marriage with repugnant men chosen by their relatives. A number of such unfortunates are said to have been killed by bears. I have the case of a young woman forced into a "shotgun" marriage by her father. She was so incensed that she refused to see her father any more, and she lived, in contrast to the usual Apache rule, with her husband's relatives.

One elderly informant, after I had absorbed considerable Apache decorum, rather shocked me by asserting that his mother-in-law was "no good." Upon investigation it turned out that the mother-in-law, after some family difficulties, had insulted him outrageously. Angered at something he had done, and in spite of the strict rule of avoidance, she faced him in the company of some others and freely aired her opinion of him. Another bitter antagonism between son-in-law and mother-in-law was masked behind avoidance and polite forms for some years. Then it culminated in a hand-to-hand scuffle in which the man emerged victorious but with considerable damage to his reputation. Still another mother-in-law, after scrupulous attention to all the forms for a long time, is reported to have assisted her daughter in driving her son-in-law out of camp under a barrage of rocks.

If we are satisfied that differences between Apache kin can arise and often terminate somewhat violently, we can pass to the next question and ask whether there is any discernible correlation between the expressions of ambivalence and conflicts such as we have been describing above. To answer briefly, I believe that evidence for such a correlation exists. It is certain that when conflict between relatives occurs, the fear of the power of the relative becomes stronger and avowed. The reader will remember the informant who was thrown into such a panic at the approach of his father. It will perhaps clarify the incident to remark that at the time of this scene, these two were opposing each other upon an issue which meant much to them. The father was about to instruct the son's bitterest political foe in his personal power.

We may say that when fear of the ghosts of relatives or fear of the power of living relatives is admitted and avowed, there is a definite correlation between this fear and tangible factors which led these people to oppose and dislike each other. We also note that exceptionally tranquil and satisfactory relations between individuals who are kin diminish the likelihood of the development of such fears, at least in overt form. If these be accepted as valid generalizations a long stride has been taken toward the validation of my hypothesis, for the connection between ambivalence and experience has been made in these instances.

But, while we have accounted for such manifestations of ambivalence in terms of conflict between the respect which the Apache is taught to tender all relatives and the antagonism and dislike which he cannot help feeling towards some of them, the general problem of ambivalence in Apache society is not yet entirely clarified.

After all, most Apache youths do not attempt to scalp their mothers-in-law, and most Apache mothers-in-law do not stone their sons-in-law.... While I have listed a number of the more spectacular deviations from Apache canons of good conduct, the truth of the matter is that the ordinary Apache obeyed the mores of his society and behaved himself so as to precipitate little scandal. And yet every Apache, though most were not involved in any open and discernible conflicts with relatives, practiced all the taboos of the death rite and believed in the possibility of their sacrifice by relatives—elements which we have said are indicative of fear and resentment felt toward kin.

I believe we will understand the matter better if we regard the cases of admitted and overt hostility toward relatives as symptoms of a far more general psychic disorder. These are the exceptional cases where friction has been so continuous and galling that the trouble could not subside and be dismissed.

While the occasional explosions furnish valuable clues to the nature of disagreements in the society, such incidents were not the general rule. Nevertheless, I have little doubt that most Apaches at some stage of their careers found the control of their affairs by relatives somewhat at variance with their own plans and desires. There is ample evidence to show that individual marriage choices were overruled and personal inclinations rejected any time they interfered with the best interests of the larger group. But, though the individual often felt circumscribed, limited, and curbed by the decisions of his relatives, he generally subordinated his personal inclinations to their rulings. To do otherwise, to invite an open rupture, would be to cut himself off from future economic and moral assistance. No man stood more isolated and alone than one who could not depend on his kin to furnish him a haven. It goes without saying that only extreme provocation would induce an Apache to break with his relatives. What resentment he felt when his wishes were thwarted, he swallowed.... He bowed to the inevitable and was guided by tradition and his own best interests. He suppressed the memory of the whole incident, banished it from consciousness, and followed whither the cultural forms led.

But the repression of conscious wishes does not make them less real for unconscious mental life. The longings, which had to be denied that the extended domestic family might flourish, lodged their protest in the unconscious. The resentment, which could not normally be expressed in everyday life if the solidarity and unity essential to the health of the society were to be maintained, emerged in the guise of a mysterious terror of the dead relatives and a puzzling dread of the power of living relatives. The disguise is ingenious. Everything is arranged to mask from consciousness the reality of the ill feeling against the relative. The ghost of the dead becomes an owl, and one can revile the owl, shoot at it, drive it away from camp with good conscience. The fact that it is your relative whom you treat in this manner is obscured by the feeling that you are thus harassing an evil bird. You fear the supernatural power of your relative, but again the grim truth is glossed over. For some unexplained reason his power forces him to act against you. In conscious thought the power is represented as malevolent and blameworthy, and the relative escapes the greater part of the censure. But these sops to the traditions and amenities which guide conscious thought are rather transparent, and, as we have seen, they yield readily to analysis when a total picture is presented.

In conclusion I would say that the material and interpretation offered are an attempt to explain aspects of Apache psychology, conscious and unconscious, from the circumstances under which actual people lived in a society that really existed. Such an approach stands in direct contrast to the general trend of "depth psychology" wherein it has been the fashion to derive psychological phenomena, and even social phenomena, from such remote events and concepts as "primal parricides" and "primordial images." If what has been written here proves suggestive and worthy of consideration, it is hoped that other and more penetrating studies of mental life from this angle will be accomplished, and that the important relationship between culture and psychology will be richly exploited.

James L. Brain

ANCESTORS AS ELDERS IN AFRICA—FURTHER THOUGHTS

Ancestors play an important part in African religion. They are vested with mystical power and retain a jural role in the world of the living, particularly in the lives of their descendants. Indeed, African kin-groups are often described as communities of both the living and dead. Ancestors are regarded as ambivalent, at best capricious. While their benevolence is generally insured through propitiation and sacrifice, it is believed that ancestors readily punish their descendants for any neglect of such ritual obligations. Ancestor cults differ from cults of the dead in that not all the dead are propitiated. Only certain dead occupying particular genealogical positions are recognized as proper ancestors, and the behavior of the ancestors reflects a particular status in the political jural domain rather than their individual personalities. The living relate to their ancestors through the exclusive status of the elders of the kin-group, and this ritual and political authority of living elders is in turn derived from their close genealogical links to the ancestors. In this selection, James Brain takes issue with an assertion made by Igor Kopytoff that because there is no word for "ancestor" in many African languages, there is no distinction between living and dead elders. While agreeing with Kopytoff that the term "worship" is inappropriate to describe the practices involved in ancestor cults, Brain challenges the validity of the semantic analysis on which Kopytoff bases his argument through a detailed exegesis of the Swahili word *mzimu*. He shows that while there is no specific term for "ancestor," there *is* a term for "ancestral spirit" which belongs to a noun class not normally used for living persons. Utilizing his data on the social structure of the Luguru of Tanzania, Brain then goes on to show that while elders in Africa are accorded a high degree of respect and authority, this does not necessarily equate them with the ancestors. Ancestors, as deceased elders, possess a qualitatively different kind of authority and power which their living descendants cannot exercise. For another interesting view on this topic, see Victor Uchendu, "Ancestorcide! Are African Ancestors Dead?" (1976). For further descriptions and interpretations of ancestor cults in Africa, see Colson 1954; Middleton 1960; Goody 1962; Fortes 1959, 1961, 1965, and Shelton 1972.

Reprinted in slightly abridged form from *Africa*, 43 (1973), 122–133 by permission of the author and the International African Institute.

In the essay which follows an attempt will be made to answer and elaborate on some of the points raised by Kopytoff in his article "Ancestors as Elders in Africa" (*Africa*, xli, 2 April 1971, pp. 129–142), an article which will, no doubt, stimulate much argument and discussion. To do this I shall utilize both published sources and material collected in Uluguru in Eastern Tanzania.

Like him, I have long rejected the term "ancestor worship" as being quite inappropriate to describe the phenomenon found in many African societies, whatever the case may be in other parts of the world. However, I cannot accept his rejection of the terms "cult" and "sacrifice" as being inappropriate, and I do not find acceptable his dictum that:

> *Insistence on the conceptual primacy of this division between the living and the dead is . . . an ethnocentric distortion of the African world view, a distortion that prevents our understanding of what we have persisted in calling "ancestor cults" and "ancestor worship"* (op. cit. 136).

His separation of cults of the dead and cults of the ancestors following Fortes (1965) and Gluckman (1937), and indeed, Durkheim (1915), is well taken. Fortes brings the point out clearly by noting that while Catholics and Jews have, in effect, what might be called a cult of the dead, they certainly do not have an ancestral cult, but that this point has less than universal acceptance among anthropologists is soon made clear by reading of the literature. For instance, Middleton, in his work on Lugbara religion notes that it: "comprises several cults, that of the dead being the most important. Most sacrifices are made to the dead." (1960: 23) Yet his excellent description is quite plainly that of an ancestral cult. One also meets semantic problems in the descriptions of the beings involved. Most writers refer to "spirits," but Middleton and Beattie (1967) use "ghosts," and Monica Wilson prefers "shades," (1959).

Leaving these points aside, I wish to turn to one of the major points of dispute with Kopytoff—his assertion that "ethnographies often discuss 'ancestral cults' and the position of elders without giving native terms for one or the other and especially for both at the same time" (op. cit. 134). He takes us through a fascinating and valuable list of root terms in Bantu languages signifying "elder," "old," "great," and so on, it being his contention, indeed the very core of his argument, that there is no difference between dead ancestors and living elders, and that because Africans have no specific term for ancestors other than that applied to "fathers," "grandfathers," or "elders," therefore they perceive no real difference between the two categories, and that it is only we in our ethnocentric obtuseness who have tried to foist on to the evidence the category of "ancestral spirit" as having some different kind of power from that possessed by living elders. To an extent I find that I am in agreement with him, but certain points seem to me to be quite wrong and having discussed them with an anthropologically trained African and found that he confirmed my ideas as correct, I feel that they must be raised.

It is quite true, as Kopytoff notes, that most Bantu languages do not have a specific word for "ancestors" and that one finds the same terms used as those for "our elders" or "our grandfathers," but to this one might reply that the same is true of English, since although we do have "ancestors" we often talk of "forefathers" or "forbears." However, far more important is the disregard for the fact that though Bantu languages may have no word for "ancestor," they *do* have a word for "ancestral spirit." In Swahili the term is *mzimu*, plural *mizimu*, variants of which occur in many Bantu languages, and it is of interest that it is in a noun class usually associated with natural phenomena like trees, growing things, rivers, the moon, and so on, rather than that associated with persons, a point which Beattie observes when writing of the Nyoro, where, he tells us:

> *A ghost* (muzimu, *plural* mizimu) *is the disembodied spirit of someone who has died. When a man is alive this vital principle is called* mwoyo (*plural* myoyo) *which may be rather loosely translated as "soul," and is believed to dwell in the breast or diaphragm. But a ghost is not just a person who has died; it is a being of quite a different order from the living. . . . Ghosts are left by people, but they are not people* (Beattie, 1967: 255).

Mary Tew writes of the Maravi of the Malawi area that their religion "was a form of ancestor cult, the spirit of the dead being called *Mzimu*," (1950:46) and similarly, Elizabeth Colson notes that the ancestral spirits of the Plateau Tonga are called *mizimu*, singular *muzimu*, (1960:373) as does Abrahams of the Nyamwezi, (1967), Prins of the Digo, (1961) and Willis of the Fipa, Nyamwanga and Iwa (1966). Their neighbours the Pimbwe refer to *kizimu*, plural *vizimu*, the same root word, though the *ki- vi-* prefix rather than the *m(u) mi-* may be a diminutive as in Swahili or an amplicative as in Ha/Rundi, in either case the point is still that this is a different noun class from that in which living persons are put.

Some writers *have* used the normal "person" type prefixes when describing spirits, for instance d'Hertefelt tells us that: "The major concern of the Rwanda was with the *abazimu* (spirits of the dead . . .)" (1966: 431), and Maquet also refers to the *bazimu* (1961: 88). They may be perfectly correct, but it is known that the neighbouring Rundi and Ha quite definitely use *muzimu*, plural *mizimu*, and it is an easily made mistake if one is rather ethnocentrically transferring our categories, using "he" or "she" rather than "it" when referring to a spirit. That this can occur is demonstrable from the work of Beidelman, who in his survey of the matrilineal peoples of Eastern Tanzania in 1967 refers to the ancestral spirits among the Luguru as *waximu* when more correctly it should be *mitsimu* (p. 33), among the Kaguru was *wasimu* instead of *misimu*, and gives the *wazimu* as the plural for the Ngulu, Zaramo, and Zigula (pp. 49, 59, 19, 71), when in each case it should be *mizimu*, though he does refer to the Zaramo spirits as both *wazimu* and *mizimu*. That he has now accepted that this is erroneous is evident from his recent monograph on the Kaguru in which he refers to "the ghosts (*misimu*)" (1971: 33). All this may seem unnecessarily pedantic, but I submit that it is extremely important since the assignment of words to particular noun classes in Bantu languages is not at all fortuitous and is a definite reflection of the feelings of the speakers about particular objects. It is noteworthy that in Swahili the only other words referring to beings and assigned to this class are *mungu* plural *miungu*—god or God, and *mtume* plural *mitume*—apostle or prophet, in both cases representing superhuman beings. If people do, as Kopytoff tells us, really regard ancestors as not being qualitatively different from elders, why then assign the name for them to a non-person noun class?

. . .

The term *mzimu* is not universal among the Bantu-speaking peoples. The Ambo of Zambia called their "shades" *mipashi*, (Stefaniszyn, 1964) and the Lungu of the same area refer to *imipasi* (Willis, op. cit.). The Yao use *masoka* (Tew, op. cit.) and a similar term *mahoka* occurs among the "Bena of the Rivers" (Culwick, 1935), while "The Sonjo believe in the existence of spirits or ghosts of the dead and call them *virioka*" (Gray, 1963: 123). The term *mahoka* does occur, though rarely, in Swahili. Perhaps most interesting of all is the usage of the Ndebele of Rhodesia. We are told that "All castes of the Ndebele nation have the common belief of the Bantu peoples in some form of survival after death and in the power of the ancestor-spirits (*amadhlozi*, sing. *idhlozi*) to affect the welfare of the living" (Kuper, 1954: 103). The great interest of this term is the root of the word, *loz-*, which is one variant of *loj-*, *loy-* and *log-* found in many Bantu languages with the meaning of witchcraft. In Ndebele witchcraft is called *ukuloya*, but this does not invalidate the idea, one can find two or more variants in any language, for instance in Swahili *kuloga* means "to bewitch" and the word *kiroja*, *kiloga*, or *kioja* means "something terrifying or amazing." Probably the Ndebele would deny a connection between ancestors and witches, yet the word they use for "ancestral spirit" clearly makes the association. It may well be that the *viroka* of the Sonjo is also from the same root as the *log-* of other languages. To press this point further, some of the Luhya of western Kenya believe that an *mzimu* is not an ancestral spirit but rather the power that can be used *by* the spirits to punish their descendants. In Swahili, as in Luguru, the term can mean not only "ancestral spirit" but also "burial place" and "place of sacrifice," and also it describes the power vested in ancestors, and also, it would seem, in elders. Thus we have both a denial of and a reinforcement of Kopytoff's points. On the one hand there is no doubt that the Luguru have a word for "ancestral spirit"—*mtsimu* (though to describe "ancestors" they use *wakulu*—great ones, elders), on the other hand it seems that the same power lies at the disposal of any elder who has authority.

The key word here is authority. One who has authority is in contact with power, whatever the power may be. Kopytoff tells us that "I must have driven my informants to distraction by insisting on pursuing the question of the 'why' and the 'where from' of the powers of the living elders. It took a kind of methodological (and cultural) leap of faith to accept as a terminal ethnographic datum that if the dead can appropriately do supernatural things, why not also the living?" (op. cit. footnote to p. 137). No doubt others of us must have had similar experiences with informants, perhaps conditioned by our western background of dividing powers of good as coming from God and evil as coming from Satan. Yet in most African cosmologies, while there is a recognition of good and evil among the living and that there are evil forces in some kind of spirit world, the dead ancestor is not separated by virtue of his goodness or wickedness. As Kopytoff quotes Fortes on the subject of the Tallensi: "What matters in ancestors is their jural status . . . the personality and character, the virtues or vices, success or failures, popularity or unpopularity, of a person during his lifetime make no difference to his attainment of ancestorhood." (Fortes, 1965: 133). Returning to the name given to ancestral spirits by the Ndebele, *amadhlozi*, with its implication of witchcraft, I would suggest that in peoples' minds the powers of witches, ancestors, and elders all derive from the same source, analogous with that which elsewhere is believed to confer *mana*. To make a simplistic parallel, a thief who enters a bank and makes a hold-up using a gun is utilizing precisely the same power as the policeman who follows him and shoots him, but whereas the policeman has the legitimate authority to do what he does, the thief, manipulating the same power, has not. That this concept is certainly true of some Bantu societies is evident from the work of Monica Wilson on the Nyakyusa, where, she notes:

> *many of our informants were agreed that the power of witchcraft and the power to see and fight witches were one and the same. The essential distinction lies in the use to which the power is put; wrongly used it is "witchcraft"* (ubulosi); *rightly used to defend the village or to punish evil-doers it is "the breath of men"* (imbepo sya bandu) *and how any particular case is labelled*

depends upon the viewpoint of the speaker (Wilson, 1959: 66).

While this might be taken to support Kopytoff's case that ancestors and elders are much the same, we must also examine what an African, W. E. Abraham, has to say. He notes that:

In what is called ancestor worship, ancestors are invoked to give succour to their family descendants. A great deal of respect is shown to them on such occasions. The basis of the respect is twofold, first that the ancestors are our predecessors, our elders, and for this reason alone command our respect; and second that in their spiritual state they note more than we can, being in unhindered touch with the essence of things (*my emphasis*) . . . *the rites of ancestor worship are not rites of worship* but methods of *communication* (Abraham, 1966: 63).

It is evident that although in one sense Abraham sees the ancestors as elders, in another he sees them as having an edge over the living elders in that they can observe not only people's actions but be aware of their inner thoughts.

In support of Kopytoff's position both Uchendu (1965: 11–12) and Kenyatta (1938: 255) speak of the "constant interaction" or "communion" with the ancestors, but it is my interpretation that there is always a perception of qualitative difference between ancestors and elders. Kenyatta indeed writes that an elder is respected for his "seniority and wisdom, and he, in turn, respects the seniority of the ancestral spirits" (ibid.). Nevertheless, the graduation of elder to ancestor is directly contingent upon his position of authority in life. As Middleton puts it, "all ghosts are ancestors, but not all ancestors are ghosts" (1960:34), using "ghosts" to denote those who have died and become important because when recounting genealogies they "are given as the apical ancestors of segments and lines of descent and ones so seen as having been 'big' men" (ibid).

Perhaps we might accept that there are actually three themes in many African religions. Describing the discussions which led to the production of *African Systems of Thought,* Fortes tells us that Bradbury "emphasised the recognition of the collective dead, side by side with named individual ancestors and lines of ancestors among the Edo" (op. cit. 17) so that we can see that there is a totality of rites and beliefs surrounding: (*a*) the recently dead; (*b*) the collective dead; and (*c*) the ancestors as named figures of authority in a genealogical schema. Kopytoff would have us believe that: "If there be a cult here, it is a cult of *bambuta,* of elders living and dead" (op. cit. 133). If we take Durkheim's definition of cult as: "a system of diverse rites, festivals and ceremonies which *all have this characteristic, that they reappear periodically*" (op. cit. 63), then surely we can accept that there is a cult of ancestors in Africa? As Durkheim so cogently observed, we talk of marriage rites and rites of birth, "because the events on the occasion of which these rites take place imply no periodicity" (ibid.). There may certainly be rites connected with elderhood, but to describe these as a cult would be giving a different definition of "cult" from that generally accepted. On the other hand I am entirely in agreement with Kopytoff that "worship" is an inappropriate word to describe the cults directed towards ancestors, and agree with him that the powers of ancestors to affect the living are not necessarily different from those of living elders. I would, however, reaffirm that ancestors have the edge over living elders in that they are aware of what may be hidden from the latter. I hope that it has been adequately demonstrated that his claim that Bantu languages have no word for ancestral spirit is patently absurd (even though there may be no word for "ancestor"), and I repeat that it is significant that the words used are placed in noun classes not normally utilized for living persons, so that our ascription of ancestors to a different category from that of living elders is not semantically inaccurate.

Let us now turn to consideration of ethnographic evidence which, it is hoped, will substantiate my support for and opposition to Kopytoff's position. To do this I shall try to describe some of the beliefs of the Luguru people of eastern Tanzania, one of the cluster of matrilineal peoples listed by Beidelman in the Ethnographic Survey series (1967) as: Zaramo, Kwere, Luguru, Kutu, Kaguru, Sagara, Vidunda, Ngulu, and Zigula, names largely descriptive of their habitat. In the case of the Luguru the name clearly means hills or mountains and is appropriate in that they live in a large mountain mass running approximately north and south, having a central spine with peaks rising to as much as 8,000 feet. There is no plateau, the land is broken up into ridges and valleys which are extremely inaccessible except on foot. The slopes are mostly steep and the agricultural practices of the Luguru, while they do not cause as much erosion as was at one time thought, have been the despair of successive generations of agronomists. The whole area is densely populated but Luguru have been, until recently, extremely reluctant to move into the ample fertile plains available at the foot of the mountains, and even today there is only a trickle of emigration. The reasons for this are partly climatic and partly cultural. The climate in the mountains is healthy and bracing, malaria is rare, and there are good supplies of clean water coming from the forest reserve on the central ridge, water which can be led in small channels to irrigate gardens all the year round, so that though cash incomes are very low, there is never any shortage of food. Probably more important than the climate is attachment to descent groups which are sub-divisions of about fifty named clans, many of which occur throughout the culture area. These local descent groups have usually been described as matrilineages, (see Beidelman, 1967; Christensen, 1963; Fosbrooke & Young, 1960), but sub-clan seems a more appropriate term in that while the leader of the unit can recount his descent for anything up to twelve generations or more, "commoner" members of the group can rarely go back more than two or three generations, while acknowledging common descent with all other members of the group, and indeed with all members of the total clan, which is the exogamous unit.

Each sub-clan lays claim to a specific area of land which often has on it a grove of trees in which the ancestral graves are to be found. Sometimes these are remains of the original dense forest, at others they are trees which have grown up around the graves and been preserved. In one case there is a large piece of original forest left at least ten acres in extent beside a modern highway. All these groves stand out sharply in an otherwise denuded landscape, since all trees have been cleared except for isolated very large *mng'ong'o* trees which themselves are associated with ancestral spirits. At some time in the past segmentation must have taken place, and in some cases we have oral traditions of this having occurred, but there has been no further segmentation for many generations, and today it is possible to find lowland areas in which the immigrants from the hills outnumber the land-owning group, but yet who still see their orientation to the graves in the hills, and do not form a new autonomous lineage. Fosbrooke remarks that it would be easy for a new group to form since the insignia involved are not elaborate and could easily be made (1960:53), but in fact this does not occur, and many plains-dwellers return to the hills for ancestral rites. The localized sub-clan is led by an elder known as *mwenye issi* (Lug.) or *mwenye ardhi* (Swah.), the basic meaning being the same, approximately "the holder of the land," the term "warden" is perhaps appropriate. He is also known as *mwenye shoka*—the holder of the axe, and also as *mwenye mtsimu*, this latter term being of particular interest for this essay, meaning as it does "owner/guardian/holder/warden of the *mtsimu*," the term to which reference has already been made and to which we shall return. The warden is said in the literature to "rule the name," a curious example of misunderstanding which today has even come to be accepted by Africans of the area. It always seemed odd to me that a word referring to a Luguru custom should use an essentially Arabic/Swahili term, and I guessed that it should be *kutwala*, found in Swahili as *kutwaa*—to take. Inquiries have shown that the correct Luguru term is *kuhala tawa*—to take the name, and it seems probable that earlier researchers using Swahili heard a Luguru-ized version of the Swahili *kutwaa* used to translate *kuhala* and thought it was *kutawala*—to rule (cf. Mitchell, 1956:114). The warden is selected from among the sisters' sons of the previous office-holder, sometimes before his death, sometimes after. In many cases it seems that the selection is confirmed by the public acclaim of the women of the sub-clan. His authority is ritual rather than political but his influence on all activities, even today under conditions of party rule, is very strong. Uluguru is very densely populated, land is very short, and in consequence the power of the wardens has been and remains strong, since land allocation is in their hands, and even today they have, in the main, effectively prevented the introduction of profitable cash crops to the area, perceiving their primary duty to be to safeguard the land for the sub-clan for food production. It seems somewhat odd that whereas in Tanzania the effective powers of chiefs were removed by legislation shortly after independence a decade ago, yet in Uluguru the power of the wardens remains unimpaired since the present political authorities, like their colonial predecessors, have yet to recognize that they constitute any kind of political force, the official "chief," a colonial creation of "indirect rule" in an acephalous society, having been removed long ago. Certain of the wardens achieved great prominence as rainmakers and continue to have great ritual importance.

Although in the areas nearest to Morogoro, the area and regional headquarters, inheritance is usually from father to son, elsewhere both inheritance and succession are in the female line, and the authority of the maternal uncle over his sisters' children remains very strong. That the inheritance pattern is changing did not seem to be of great significance to some informants, among them a warden, the reason being a most interesting one. The Luguru kinship terminology is in most respects an Iroquois or bifurcate merging type, but it has one feature of a Crow type which is relevant to this attitude. During a man's lifetime his children refer to and address his sister's son as *mtani*—cross cousin/joking partner, but after his death this man becomes *tata* (Lug.) or *baba* (Swah.)—father, since he has succeeded to the position, and may even inherit his maternal uncle's wife if she is of suitable age. Thus, it was claimed, even if a man's child inherited his property instead of a nephew, he would be bound to share things with his "father." Although, or perhaps because, there is great emphasis on line, evidenced by the Crow-type terminology, the father's descent group is of great importance, and the name of the father's clan is used as an appellation for any child, e.g. a child (or adult) whose clan is Bena, but whose father was Chiru, will be called Mchiru (or if a girl Mlamchiru). An illegitimate child will have a *lukolo* but no *mtala*, whereas children of slave women captured in war have an *mtala* but no *lukolo* and are termed *wanawana*—children of children. It should be mentioned that the warden's "name" is not that of the clan but is a specific one relating to his sub-clan, and it is said "the name does not die, only the person."

The Luguru say that a person gets blood from both sides, not solely from the mother. In marriage both father and maternal uncle have to give permission, but it is said that whereas today the father's consent is often more important, in the past the reverse was true. Observations showed that in fact the authority of the maternal uncle is still very strong, though the "ideal" for many Luguru today is to emphasize the father's authority, perhaps because all are nominal Catholics or Muslims. Marriage, as I have shown elsewhere (Brain, 1969), is said to be matrilocal, but in fact tends to be so until the first child is born and weaned, when the "delayed right of bride removal" is exercised, and the man takes his wife to his own sub-clan land to live close to his maternal uncle, who did the same thing in a previous generation. It is now common for a man's mother to leave her husband and to join her son and brother on clan land. There is a difference of opinion as to whether the most preferred match is to the mother's brother's daughter or to the father's sister's daughter. In some cases this may be one and the same person. If marriage to the mother's brother's daughter does take place then there is no need for later removal, since by making this marriage the man has moved to clan land. Unusually, both men and women have rights in land; both from the mother's and the father's sub-clans, so that any married couple may have land in at least four places, and possibly more by the payment of *ngoto* tribute to the warden of another sub-clan.

One of the most important institutions of the culture area is a joking relationship between clans. Opinions differ as to whether the relationship is only with the members of a particular sub-clan or with all members of the whole clan wherever they may be. The latter seems more likely since a similar arrangement exists between total groups of peoples. I hope to discuss this elsewhere, but some mention of it must be made here because the presence of joking partners is essential to all rites connected with the ancestors. The relationship is known as *ugongo* (Lug.) or *utani* (Swah.), and as I have pointed out (Brain, 1971), one is confronted with a hen/egg situtation. Since a cross-cousin is called *mtani* in Luguru, one wonders whether they are called this because one jokes with them, or is the relationship called *utani* in Swahili because one behaves as one does towards cross-cousins? Although there are themes of hostility—a subject well covered by Beidelman, 1966—inherent in the relationship, this is not an aspect that is at all evident to Luguru, who reject any such idea as absurd. As one informant put it, "You can say these things to them because they are your best friends."

There is a mild joking relationship with grandfathers, but not with grandmothers. The reasons are clear. The father's mother will be concerned lest her son should favour his son over her daughter's children. The mother's mother is definitely an authority figure within her descent group. While this is in no sense a matriarchal society, women are accorded considerably more respect than in many African societies, evidenced by: (*a*) their important role in choosing a new sub-clan head, and (*b*) by their having rights in land. Relations with grandmothers were described thus: "My father's mother? I have to fear her, she bore my father, I cannot joke with her, I cannot work magic on her, I must care for her. My mother's mother? She is fierce and gentle, she teaches me everything, do thus, do thus, hold a hoe . . . but one isn't too much afraid of either of them, they are like my wives, they teach you everything."

The authority figures in any person's life then are:

(a) The head of the sub-clan and his sister's sons, who together form something like an aristocracy within the sub-clan.
(b) The maternal uncle and, if still alive, his maternal uncle and mother.
(c) The father and his sister (*sangazi* = female father), their mother and maternal uncle. It must be remembered that land comes from both sides.
(d) The elder brother. He is known as *sekuru*, the same term as is applied to grandfather and meaning precisely that, "great father." The Swahili term for elder brother, *kaka*, is also used and sometimes applied to the grandfather. As Kopytoff points out, this term has the root-*ka* meaning older, greater etc. When asked why the same term is used to both relatives the answer is always in terms of "they are both my elders." This might be seen as an example of "the merging of alternate generations." The elder brother has great authority over his younger siblings, and will, of course, on the death of the maternal uncle, assume his role.

Let us now turn to what is said about ancestral spirits and the term *mtsimu*, plural *mitsimu* (or *mzimu, mizimu* Swah.). The following is the substance of a conversation with a warden who has the reputation of being an acknowledged expert on Luguru tradition:

> *Mitsimu* are the spirits of our grandfathers who died, of our grandmothers, some people say these are *mitsimu*, they bring sickness to a person for his faults. Also, as I say, when your maternal uncle (*mkolo* Lug. ref., *mtumba* Lug. address, *mjomba* Swah.) departs and bequeaths you his name there must be a supernatural event (*lazima utokee na maujiza*, Swah.), then they say the name is seeking a person, his maternal uncle's name, then they say that is *mtsimu*. Or suppose you want to go to Dar es Salaam and you ask permission from your maternal uncle and he says "You can't go!" and you say "I'm going!" and then he says, "All right, you'll see for yourself!" Then where you are going there is sure to turn out some danger. From the *mitsimu*.

The Luguru say that the earth was created by God—*mulungu*, but that he is not normally concerned with human affairs. He is not prayed to or sacrificed to, sacrifices are made to the *mitsimu*. Nor is it believed that the *mitsimu* are in any way mediators between man and God. There is bound to be some confusion here since all Luguru today claim to be Muslim or Christian and manifestly both religions pray to God. However, this certainly does not prevent members of either group from carrying out sacrifices (*tambiko* Lug. and Swah.) to the *mitsimu*, which is still done regularly in all parts. Today, with the departure of almost all the Europeans from the area it is far easier to get people to talk about such sacrifices than it was ten years ago. Sacrifices are made when misfortune strikes, after consultation with a diviner/doctor, usually said to be someone from a distance who will bring no personal bias to the case. For all sacrifices the presence of joking partners is essential.

Ancestors are remembered at specific periodic intervals, before cultivation, at the time of the first fruits, and although, as one informant put it, "they are remembered at the time of misfortune, even at the time of joy too they are remembered; for instance if my child reaches puberty and I want to organize a dance for her, I cannot do it until I have sacrificed to the elders to give them their portion." The same informant, a Catholic, also remarked, "We sacrifice to our elders, to all those who died, not one person." Sacrifices usually take place at grave sites which are cleared beforehand by the joking partners, but may sometimes take place at a cross-roads, or at the foot of a large tree.

On the other hand, as one might expect, those ancestors turned to in the event of misfortune, are those to whom one looks for authority, to a dead maternal uncle, his mother, a dead father or his maternal uncle or mother. Moreover, when one's own ancestors prove ineffective then a delegation will go to one of the rainmakers, most often the one known as Kingalu, who will consult his local oracles and give advice and medicine which is taken back to the home area, when further sacrifices are made there, sometimes involving ritual mock fights between neighbouring joking partner sub-clans on their boundaries. For really serious affairs Kingalu makes a journey to his *mtsimu* located some eighty miles away in Ungulu, where he sacrifices to the spirit of the original Kingalu and communes with it, something only possible to him alone, though he approaches the shrine accompanied by his sister's son and the warden of the sub-clan with which he has *ugongo*.

One final point before examining these facts in the light of Kopytoff's hypothesis is that it is generally believed that any older person who thinks that a youth is behaving in an unsuitable manner may warn him, and in extreme cases may visit, and be seen to visit, the ancestral graves, when the offender will be punished by sickness. One cannot but be struck by the similarity to "ghost invocation" among the Lugbara, as described by Middleton, and there can be no doubt that this is a highly effective sanction on behaviour.

To summarize then, I agree that the term "ancestor worship," but not "ancestor cult" is "semantically inappropriate." The latter term in my view and in the view of two anthropologically trained African colleagues is valid. It is misleading to state that there is no word for "ancestors" while ignoring the wide occurrence of a word for "ancestral spirits." Although it is true that Africans generally treat their elders with more respect and reverence than is customary in western society, this does not necessarily place them on a par with the ancestors, who are believed to be aware not only of the actions but also of the thoughts of their living descendants. Gifts made to elders are not the equivalent of sacrifices made to ancestors, who clearly are the subject of a cult, in the generally accepted meaning of the term. At the same time it is accepted that elders in a position of authority do possess, in some undefined way powers either in their own right, or by appeal to the ancestors, these powers being very similar if not the same as those manipulated by witches for illicit ends. It is emphasized that the term used for ancestral spirit in both Swahili and Luguru can mean: the spirit of an important deceased elder; the power possessed by elders and/or ancestors; a burial place and by extention a place of sacrifice, or a place of awe and mystery, e.g. a lake, an underground river, a high place; finally, it is said by the Luguru that a lone baboon appearing on the edge of crop land is an *mtsimu* come to inspect the work and is not harmed, and the appearance of any unusual animal such as a lion or elephant is taken to be a warning from the *mtsimu* that people are not behaving correctly. While all the dead are remembered as a collectivity, it is only the important figures who are named in rituals, first the men and then the women. Where is *kutsimu (kuzimu* Swah.), the place inhabited by the spirits? As well ask a modern Christian where heaven and hell are situated. Some say "down below," some say "up above." At a really serious sacrifice the rite is held high up on an awe-inspiring mountain top. Why? "If it is high the cry will be heard above and below, to right and to left." And the senior elder will say:

> *Mkagone vigonile fungo munhu mkulu kagona*
> *Kakunza kalamsigwa na wegenda maze*
> *Mkagone Mndo, mkagoneni Kingalu . . . (names other famous names)*
> *Mkagone mwake, Mwanambena, mkagone Mwanasinembo . . . (names others)*
>
> *May you all sleep curled up like a civet cat, the great one*
> *was waked by the fetchers of water*
> *Sleep Mndo, sleep Kingalu . . .*
> *Sleep you women, sleep Mwanambena, sleep Mwanasinembo . . . (etc.).*

He then pours out beer on the stone marking the graves and says:

> *Mbwali ntambika utulekere tu wana totambika*
> *Iwana wakumbuka kumtambikieni yamkile wose mkagone*
>
> *I sacrifice with beer which you left to us, we your children sacrifice, the children remember you all, to sacrifice to you all who went before, may you all sleep* (Text of prayers for one sub-clan)

Maurice Freedman

RITUAL ASPECTS OF CHINESE KINSHIP

In this excerpt from a longer article, Maurice Freedman presents a concise and illuminating description of the various aspects of Chinese ancestor worship—the domestic cult, the lineage cult, and geomantic practices. The domestic cult focuses on memorialism—remembering, tending, and consoling deceased members of the household, and the subjugation of the living to their authority. While the domestic cult encompasses *personal* relationships between the living and the dead, the lineage cult represents the *collectively* held links between a solidary group of male agnates and their patrilineal forebears. Twice-yearly ceremonies conducted in the lineage hall affirm the identity of the kin-group through praise and sacrifice to a body of ancestors that it holds in

Reprinted in abridged form from Maurice Freedman, "Ritual Aspects of Chinese Kinship and Marriage," in M. Freedman (ed.), *Family and Kinship in Chinese Society* (Stanford: Stanford University Press, 1970), 164–179, by permission of the publisher.

distinction from other similar kin-groups. Finally, the third aspect of Chinese ancestor worship involves geomancy—"the mystical determination of fortune by the acts of men on their environment." In contrast to that aspect of the soul which is venerated at the domestic or lineage hall altar, the ancestral soul in the grave can be manipulated expressly for individual gain. A man seeks to orient his ancestor's grave in such a manner that the mystical benefits derived from it will accrue to him alone. Geomancy, then, not only reverses the relationship between the living and their ancestors found in domestic and lineage cults, but it also encourages competition between kinsmen.

Several authors have differed with Freedman's description of Chinese ancestor worship, and interested readers should consult Emily Ahern, *The Cult of the Dead in a Chinese Village* (1973) for an in-depth description and analysis of ancestor worship in Taiwan. Interesting comparative material also can be found in Robert Smith, *Ancestor Worship in Contemporary Japan* (1974) and Maurice Freedman's excellent comparison of Chinese and African ancestors in *Chinese Lineage and Society: Fukien and Kwangtung* (1966:144–154). Finally, mention must be made of a volume edited by Arthur Wolf entitled *Religion and Ritual in Chinese Society* (1974) which includes Wolf's insightful essay, "Gods, Ghosts, and Ancestors," an extensive analysis of the place of ancestor worship in rural Taiwanese society.

ANCESTOR WORSHIP

Little was achieved in the study of Chinese ancestor worship until it was made clear that there are two distinct kinds of worshiped ancestors: domestic and extra-domestic. The universality of ancestor worship among the Chinese is the universality of the domestic cult, which, even when it dispenses with wooden tablets, always entails the representation of dead forebears and their ritual service. As we shall presently see, household ancestor worship is not the Chinese domestic religion par excellence, but from several points of view it is the more important half of the total cult of the ancestors. The part of the cult centering on lineage ancestors (the dramatic and awe-inspiring parade of ritualized piety) cannot be universal, for lineages are not everywhere found in China. Where they exist, and consequently both parts of the cult are present, the two parts differ in the ancestors they serve, the attitudes maintained toward them by the worshipers, the role ascribed to the ancestors, and the rites performed. The halves of the cult each belong to different phases of group life and have different implications for our understanding of Chinese social organization. The first formulation of the two classes of ancestors will, however, need to be modified a little later on, when we come to consider the possibility that ancestors are worshiped who are neither domestic (although they are in domestic shrines) nor the apical members of clearly structured lineages and their segments.

The domestic religion of the Chinese has many facets, but there is a sense in which the supreme domestic cult is that of the so-called Kitchen God, Tsao Chün, for in his worship each household (i.e., each unit defined in relation to its separate cooking place) stands out as a distinct religious entity.

> *In the village, the god, besides the ancestor spirits, who receives sacrifices most frequently is the kitchen god—his wife being sometimes included. The kitchen god . . . is the supernatural inspector of the household, sent by the emperor of heaven. His duty is to watch the daily life of the house and to report to his superior at the end of each year . . . . Based on the report, the fortunes of the household will be decided* (Fei, 1939: 99f.).

It is a picture familiar to anyone who knows Chinese home life. We can see that each Kitchen God shrine (which, however, need not be more than a place where incense sticks are put up) is the defining focus for a household in respect of its commensality. A separate household usually has a separate kitchen, and its Tsao Chün shrine is physically distant from those of related households; but two or more households may in some circumstances share a kitchen, and then the cooking place with its own shrine becomes the locus of differentiation. (It is clear that Stove God would be a better English name for Tsao Chün.) By the worship of this deity the domestic unit is linked into the hierarchy of groups with gods that gives Chinese bureaucracy its religious aspect.

This clear ritual segmentation of households does not coincide with the segmentation of units based on ancestor worship.

Every house has an altar in its main hall (or at least in its main room when it cannot rise to the luxury of a hall); in it are set both the images of the gods that the household chooses to worship and its ancestor tablets (or substitutes). The household may be both wider and narrower than an ancestor-worshiping group. Not every member of a household is necessarily the descendant, or the wife of a descendant, of a dead forebear represented on the altar. The unit defined by a collection of ancestor tablets may include people distributed over several households. Imagine a house in which, by family partition, the immediate families of different brothers severally occupy distinct living quarters and yet maintain the hall of the house and its altar in common—by no means a rare pattern. Each household will keep a Tsao Chün shrine, for each eats separately; but the brothers, their wives, and their children will as a group collectively worship the ancestors on the altar.

Just as the household is tied into one religious hierarchy through Tsao Chün, so the family, whatever its precise constitution, is linked at least in principle to a ritual hierarchy of nearer and more distant ancestors. When each socially mature man or woman dies, a tablet is made for him and placed on the domestic altar. The qualification for being so treated is the attainment of parenthood, whether actual or merely potential, as when a man posthumously acquires an heir through an adoption; parenthood may also be only nominal in the sense that members of a junior generation accept the responsibility for caring for the tablet. A boy or girl of marriageable age dying single may be posthumously married—even perhaps to another dead mate—in order to establish a place on the altar. What the system rigidly excludes is the immediate entry of the tablets of dead children, for they are not considered potential ancestors and have committed an unfilial act by the mere fact of dying young. (Yet it may be possible after the lapse of a generation or more for the restless spirit of such an unfortunate and wicked child to be appeased by his being married off in a ghostly union so that he may join the ranks of the honored dead on the altar.) The tablet of a dead man rests (if for the moment we exclude the possibility of uxorilocal residence) on the altar that houses his father's, unless of course his family has by now moved from the place where that altar is kept. A married woman's tablet is installed in the altar belonging to her husband's family. A spinster is not supposed to die in her paternal house; if she is to stay unmarried even after death, then a non-domestic shrine must be found to accommodate her tablet, if indeed she is to have one.

As the generations unfold, new tablets are added automatically to the domestic stock, but old ones are being removed, for only some three or four generations are characteristically represented. A superannuated tablet is burnt or buried near the grave of the person for whom it stands. In principle, then, domestic ancestor worship works on a cycle in which the youngest living generation worships before an altar that houses the tablets of ancestors, some four generations above it—a religious correlate of the Chinese abstraction that the core of agnatic kinship is formed by those related within the patrilineal *wu fu*, the five mourning grades. But for several reasons a particular domestic altar may not present so orderly and self-limiting a set of tablets.

In the first place, the agnatic thread linking any set may be broken. If a man enters into that form of marriage in which he lives uxorilocally and fathers children to his wife's surname, both he and his wife come to rest as tablets on an altar that will now contain parents-in-law and son-in-law and parents and daughter. Moreover, it is possible for a set to include the tablet of a non-agnatic relative or even a non-relative when that person has been a member of the house and has nobody outside it ritually to serve him. This apparent anomaly raises a crucial question (that we shall examine later) about the nature of the ritual tie between living and dead.

Second, tablets cannot build up in a regular pattern when one or more of a group of brothers move out of the house. In a new house a fresh stock may begin when the most senior member dies off; his descendants there may worship him yet still go to the old house to take part in worship, within a wider group, of more senior generations. On the other hand, especially when a new house is set up at a distance from the old, the new stock may begin with a "general" tablet on which are recorded the details extracted from the individual tablets left behind; thus worship in the new house may be addressed to the same collection of ancestors as is worshiped in the old house.

Finally, by an extension of the principle that families resulting from a recent division may come together at the altar maintained by one of them, one such altar may continue over many generations—well beyond the "standard" four—to house tablets serving as the focus for a large group of agnates scattered over numerous houses. Such an altar is physically domestic, and it is ritually domestic for the people in whose house it stands; but, acting as a ritual center for a long line of agnates, it has become akin to the altar constructed in an ancestral hall.

Before we turn to the matter of ancestral halls, however, we ought to consider an aspect of the character of ancestor tablets and the manner of their keeping. An individual tablet is usually "dotted": it has a red dot (ink or blood) imposed on it to establish a *hun* (soul) of the dead person in it, or at least to provide the *hun* with a place to settle. That ritual act sets up one instrument and distinguishes it from all others that may come to be made for the same person. As far as domestic worship is concerned, the "dotted" tablet should act as the focus when all those who are the descendants of the person for whom it stands wish to serve it jointly. In theory, a stock of tablets passes down the generations by primogeniture, and it is in connection with his right-duty to maintain the stock that the oldest son may claim and get an extra share of property when a patrimony is divided up among brothers. It follows (again in theory) that when a domestic shrine serves as the ritual center for a large nondomestic group of agnates, that shrine will have been transmitted from oldest son to oldest son, younger sons having established their own domestic altars. In reality, however, the primogenitory rule may have been broken, and the chief altar may have passed down a line that excludes some oldest sons.

We may now make the transition to ancestral halls. When a domestic tablet is destroyed or buried, having served its tour of duty, that event may mark the end of the ritual memory of the person for whom the tablet was made. And indeed, most Chinese pass into oblivion in this fashion, a similar process or erosion taking place in the treatment of tombs, as we shall see. Appearances to the contrary, the Chinese have never overburdened themselves with ancestors. But another tablet may be made for the same person and installed in an ancestral hall; once in such an altar, the tablet will remain as long as the hall stands. Often, in the cities when a tablet is similarly deposited in a club building or temple for safe and ritual keeping, it escapes the annihilation to which a normal domestic life, so to speak, would have condemned it. But it cannot play the role in an agnatic community played by a tablet in an ancestral hall, except possibly where it has been placed in a shrine belonging to a clan association.

Ancestral halls must be clearly distinguished from temples and from domestic shrines. Temples are devoted to gods, even though some urban temples may accommodate ancestor tablets. An ancestral hall is a building put up and maintained by a patrilineal group to house their ancestor tablets and serve as the center of their ritual and secular activities. Though it may display one or more deities in side-shrines, it is dominated by the symbols of ancestors. It is physically quite distinct from any normal living accommodation. The commonest form of ancestral hall is that which belongs to a lineage, but any such lineage that is finely segmented may contain a hierarchy of halls, each of them the ritual center of a segment. A hall requires for its building and its maintenance and for the upkeep of its rites that it be endowed; hence, a hall is a mark of riches, and a segment that enjoys the ownership of a hall is a rich unit within a community of units.

The segments that form within a Chinese lineage are based on some sort of income-producing property, most commonly land. Some segments are not rich enough to build a hall, and so find their ritual foci in the tombs (they may in reality be cenotaphs) of the apical ancestors from whom they trace their origin or in the shrines incorporated in domestic altars. The segments lowest down in the hierarchy (that is to say, of the shallowest genealogical depth) are almost certain to own no ritual center other than such a tomb or shrine. It becomes clear, then, that whereas from the point of view of traditional Chinese, domestic ancestor worship is a necessity, ancestor worship in halls is a luxury, expressing and reinforcing the honor of a segment but not resting on an absolute religious obligation.

The segmentary order of a Chinese lineage, as we now know, is typically asymmetrical. Segments well enough endowed to own halls stand out against both coordinate segments that cannot afford halls and groups of agnates that lack the means even to be organized into segments. Social differentiation is given one of its ritual faces. The factors that will explain why deep lineages appear in some parts of China and not in others will also explain why hall worship is found unevenly in the country. What accounts for differing degrees of genealogical elaboration will help us understand why nondomestic ancestor worship is differently elaborated.

The ancestral hall contains in the place of honor the tablet of the founding ancestor.

Logically, if the segments tracing their origin to the sons of the founder also have their several halls, we should expect to find no other tablets in the main hall. But that situation we do not in fact find. The only lineage halls with a single tablet would appear to be those belonging to Hakka (or at any rate those in the southeastern part of the country) in which the solitary tablet is not that of the first ancestor but a general tablet for agnatic ancestors as a group—the hall equivalent of the general tablets we sometimes find in domestic shrines. It would seem that families will install a tablet for one of their dead members not only in the lowest segment hall to which they belong, but perhaps also in every higher segment hall of which they are members and in the lineage hall. In this way, one tablet becomes many. (The installation does not, however, have necessarily to wait upon a man's death; living men sometimes have their own tablets put on an altar where they will stand, for the time being, shrouded auspiciously in red, eventually to merge into the general company of the dead.) Indeed, if we reflect for a moment on the significance of hall tablets, we see that the duplication makes good sense. The installation of a tablet is the assertion of the prestige of those descended from the person represented or of the person himself if he installs his own. That prestige, though desirable enough in the lowest-level hall, is yet more desirable in the halls to which larger groups of agnates have recourse. Of course, in the old days when tablets could be entered in the lineage or some other high-level hall only when the descendants were titled scholars or were for some other reason thought worthy of the privilege (perhaps hard cash being paid for it), many tablets found in the lower halls were not duplicated in the halls at or near the summit of the system.

I think it is useful at this point in the argument to examine the best ethnography we have to date on the distribution of tablets in ancestral halls. The new information was collected in the early 1960's in one of the great lineages of Hsin-an county, Kwangtung—since 1899 living under British rule in the Hong Kong New Territories. The village of Sheung Shui (the Cantonese form of its name) is traditionally the settlement of a single lineage bearing the surname Liao. Numerous "trusts" or estates held jointly have evolved at various generation levels, but only three ancestral halls now result from them: the lineage hall, a hall in the fourth generation, and one in the seventh. (see Baker, 1968). The main ancestral hall—the lineage hall—houses three groups of tablets, of which the most important (and centrally placed) consists of the tablets of certain ancestors senior to the lineage founder, of the founder and his wife, of his only son and that man's wives and three sons, and, in addition, six tablets of the fourth generation, four tablets of the fifth, and one of the fifteenth (this last something of a puzzle, unless the fact that it belongs to a man who was a "Battalion Second Captain" has something to do with his inclusion in the main group of ancestors). The next most important group is formed by the tablets of ancestors "of particularly high academic success": two tablets for *chü-jen*, provinicial graduates. The final group is of 156 tablets belonging to men who subscribed money at various times to restore the hall; there are tablets for members of each generation from the sixth to the eighteenth, the latter generation flourishing about the beginning of the present century. It is interesting to note that when in 1932 the hall was last restored and partly converted into a school, an entirely different method of rewarding donors was resorted to: their framed photographs were put up, but not to be worshipped or tended—apart from anything else, it would be awkward to treat them ritually, for the photographs include two of men who are not members of the lineage.

The lineage has three primary segments, stemming from the three members of the third generation (the founder, we recall, had only one son). None of these segments, however, has a hall. The second hall in Sheung Shui defines the segment springing from a fourth-generation ancestor: the older of the sons of the founder of the second primary segment. In this hall there are again three groups of tablets. The central group (of 139) consists of a "composite" tablet for the first three generations of the lineage and individual tablets for the apical ancestor of the segment and his wife, the remainder being tablets each of which stands for a man and his wife or wives. These last include men from the fifth to seventeenth generations, several tablets being duplicated in the lineage hall; it is not at all clear why these tablets appear on the central altar. The second group is made up of three tablets of men of high honor. The final group is of 115 tablets for men who donated money for the building and the restoration of the hall; the men are drawn from the thirteenth to the nineteenth generations.

The third hall has as its apical ancestor a man of the seventh generation, a descendant of the brother of the apical ancestor of the second hall. Here there is only one group of tablets, 70 in all, some of them duplicated in the lineage hall. The group consists of individual tablets for the apical ancestor of the segment, his wife, and their sons and wives; for the ten men of the next generation, the ninth; and for various men of the tenth to fifteenth generations, some sort of merit having apparently decided their entry. All these tablets seem to have been installed when the hall was built in the early nineteenth century. Well endowed, the segment to which this hall belongs apparently has not needed to solicit donations against the privilege of setting up tablets.

Few of these facts are in conflict with my earlier general statements; we see . . . the duplication of tablets in halls and their roles as points of reference and markers of prestige. But Baker stresses in relation to my earliest treatment of the subject that there is in his material on Sheung Shui no support whatever for the view that ancestors in their tablets can be promoted from domestic to hall shrines, "the only way of securing a place there being to be alive (and sufficiently wealthy) at the time the hall is restored" (Baker 1968: 62). As a matter of fact, this last statement can apply only to the groups of tablets that represent donors in the lineage and fourth-generation halls; the evidence shows that the tablets of the earliest generations in the main altars of all three halls must have been installed after death, and it seems to me that this may well have been the case with more recent tablets in the central altars of the lineage and fourth-generation halls. As for the domestic cult, Baker says that ancestors are worshiped "for a much longer period" than is provided for in my model, "many homes having paper 'tablets' representing 'all the ancestors of the Liao surname,' while others have paper 'tablets' recording the names of individual ancestors of ten generations or more (wooden tablets have disappeared from the home)."

Now, men installing their own hall tablets (and leaving them auspiciously shrouded while they live) certainly will not have prevented their tablets being put up in the houses where they die; thus for some generations at any rate such men will be worshiped both in the hall and in a domestic shrine. But nobody lasts indefinitely in a domestic shrine (except in the vague sense that he is embraced in a "general" tablet of the kind Baker describes: "all the ancestors of the Liao surname"), and a man's only chance of a posthumous installation in a hall lies in his descendants procuring his admission, on some ground of eminence, to one or more of the central altars of the halls. Such an installation is no longer possible; but that may be because for the last generation at least the system has declined; certainly no new ancestral hall will now or in the future come into existence to make it possible for people to establish their ancestors in a permanent shrine belonging to a segment.

In Sheung Shui, as we have seen, individual tablets (in reality just sheets of red paper) may be kept in domestic altars for "ten generations or more." Two questions arise. First, has this lengthy retention something to do with the fact that eminent ancestors can no longer be put into hall shrines? Second, and more important, are some of the remoter ancestors kept in domestic shrines because they are in fact the foci of large and nondomestic groups of agnates? In connection with this second question I refer to other present-day evidence, drawn from a village study made in Taiwan. In Hsin Hsing there is a multiplicity of agnatic groups, none of which is very large. It would appear that only one of them has collective property and none an ancestral hall. Yet the *tsu* (as they call themselves, using the term we normally translate as "lineage") participate in the common worship of ancestors on their death-dates, as do lesser groups within the *tsu*, the loci for such worship being domestic shrines. The relation between domestic worship proper and worship at a domestic shrine by some nondomestic group is indicated in Gallin's statement (1966: 248): "Generally, a single ancestor is worshipped for about two or three generations, or as long as someone remembers him in his lifetime. When no one remains who remembers him alive, he, together with other more or less forgotten ancestors . . . is worshipped only on one designated day of the year, and then perhaps by the *tsu*." In cases such as this we are witnessing the bringing together, within the context of a domestic shrine, of ritual attitudes and practices that are clearly segregated when hall and house worship are independently developed.

Ancestor worship in China is not confined to shrines, the tablet being only one of two localizations of an ancestor. The other is the grave. Lineages and segments that maintain halls may, by means of their economic resources, keep up grand tombs for apical ancestors and may conduct periodic communal worship at them. Lacking ancestral halls, lineages and segments may fall back on tombs as the only places for their joint worship. Just as a distinction is to be made between worship at domestic shrines and worship in halls, so it can be made in the worship at graves: families cherish the tombs of their more recent forebears, gradually abandoning them as they recede in time; the graves of remoter ancestors are tended only when they serve as points of reference for lineages and their segments. As Baker puts it for Sheung Shui (1968: 62):

> The most distant ancestor's grave known by me to be worshipped was that of a great-grandfather of the youngest agnatic descendant present. . . . Beyond this limit in generation depth graves are not worshipped by individual families, but grave-worshipped ancestors may be "promoted" to communal grave-worship and thus saved from extinction of memory, in much the same way as are the tablet-worshipped ancestors of Freedman's account.

Up to this point we have mapped out what might be called the general structural arrangements of Chinese ancestor worship. Now we must explore the nature of the ritual activity associated with those arrangements, beginning again with domestic worship. On any domestic altar there may be two kinds of tablet: individual and collective, the latter designating "all the ancestors." This possible combination helps us to see that domestic worship has two sides: on the one hand a family addresses itself on the major annual festivals to its ancestors and reports to them as a collectivity; on the other hand, individual ancestors are tended on their death-dates, perhaps with their favorite food being set before them and the family as a whole paying its respects. The distinction between the two classes of devotion does not, however, depend on there being two different kinds of tablet. Ancestors as a collectivity can be worshiped in the absence of any tablet that represents them as such, and individual ancestors do not require individual tablets to insure that they are worshiped on their death-dates. (Some families keep sheets of paper or boards on which important death-dates are recorded as a guide.) Yet, although these two aspects are present, it is the worship of individual ancestors that is the more distinctive of domestic worship. Indeed, it is the highly individualizing and personal character of ancestor worship in the house that marks it off sharply from worship conducted by nondomestic groups.

Although the head of a family should formally put himself in charge of the rites conducted before the ancestors, whether at the festivals or on the death-dates of particular ancestors, the routine tendance—the daily offering of incense and the special offerings made on the first and fifteenth days of every lunar month—is carried out by women. Everywhere in China, at least outside the families of the small Confucian elite, the routine care of ancestors falls essentially to women—as indeed does nearly every part of domestic religion. On their shoulders rests the responsibility for remembering the death-dates of the ancestors for whom the family is concerned; it is they who are likely to pray to the ancestors for well-being and peace; and, as I have argued elsewhere, to the limited extent that ancestors can intervene detrimentally in the lives of their descendants, it is women who are probably the agents for the unfavorable interpretation of ancestral behavior. There are enough hints in the literature that in many places in China the most conspicuous role of men in domestic religion is in the conduct of the main rites for the Kitchen God. It may seem highly paradoxical that in the ritual sphere men should emerge as leaders of the household and women generally appear as prime agents in the rites of the family, but we might suggest that on the one side men are appropriately associated with the kind of domestic discipline for which Tsao Chün stands, and that on the other side they cannot be in too intimate a relationship with domestic ancestors because of the latter's potential power to inflict harm.

From the point of view of men, ancestors are essentially benign, their kindliness perhaps springing from the gradualness with which a son takes over responsibility from his father (for him the key domestic ancestor). Despite the ritual primacy of the oldest son (which we have already seen to be expressed in his custodianship of the family's stock of tablets and his right to an extra share of inheritance), there is, in real life, equality between brothers and no transfer from father to son of a power to control the other mature sons. The head of a family does not draw from his ancestors the capacity to punish by nonhuman means; he does not stand before the other members of the family with an array of disciplinary ancestors behind him. The ancestors represent protectiveness and solicitude. And yet they have rights—chiefly, to be served on their death-dates and provided with agnatic descendants—which, if they are denied, may lead them to cause sickness or some other discomfort to the living. The punitive element in ancestral behavior is a minor one, but (we may argue) it is of sufficient importance to make it difficult for men to deal closely with their dead forebears, that role being assumed by women. On marriage women are estranged from their own ancestors and placed under their husbands', to whom they now have special access and from whom they hope for protection and blessings even as they fear possible retribution.

The interpretation may well be wrong, but the evidence for the crucial place of women in domestic ancestor worship is accumulating. I was struck by the prominence of this womanly role in Singapore; Gallin records it; and a Chinese writer has recently done the same in respect of another village in Taiwan, although he appears to treat what he has seen as a sign that men have abdicated their role in favor of women in recent times. He writes of the village of Chin Chiang Ts'o that he and his colleagues did not see a single case in which a male *chia-chang* (family head) led his sons and grandson in domestic ancestor worship. Men (he goes on) have become indifferent, have neglected their responsibilities, and are now represented by women. I prefer to accept the observations and not draw any moral about modern social change.

We have seen that a collection of tablets in a domestic shrine may include a tablet of a non-ancestor, and the presence of such an outsider, who will automatically share in the general offerings made at the altar, forces us to examine the implication of statements that Chinese worship their ancestors. Some Chinese writing about peasants deny that "worship" is the right word, and it hardly needs to be said that Confucian agnosticism has made it possible for the educated elite to look upon (or at least to present) their reverential treatment of their ancestors as a form of decorous ceremony. I think that Yang (1948: 90) is unjustified in asserting that Chinese "do not worship their ancestors in the way the gods are worshiped," for it can be shown for the mass of Chinese that first, the same ritual elements enter into the approach to ancestors as in that to the gods (offerings, libations, incense, and so on), and second, both gods and ancestors fall into the category of *shen*, "spirit." (It does not follow, of course, that ancestors and gods are treated exactly alike. In an important paper entitled "Gods, Ghosts, and Ancestors," as yet unpublished, Arthur Wolf discusses the differences in ritual treatment on the basis of his Taiwan field data.) But a difficulty seems to arise from the fact that Chinese also speak of their actions for the dead as commemoration. In Singapore I found that Hokkien Chinese most commonly used the term *ki-liam* (Mandarin: *chi-nien*), "to commemorate," in the context of domestic ancestor worship, and it is clear that the desire to keep a person's memory green is a crucial element in the total system of ideas. The ancestral portraits of former times and the photographs of today are by themselves evidence of that notion: they are in no sense worshiped (except when photographs have been inserted into tablets or placed on altars as substitutes for them). As a Chinese, a person feels under an obligation to perpetuate the memory of somebody with whom he has lived. At the same time, the further obligation is incurred to prevent him from going unfed, whence his share in the offerings made in general at the altar. That is to say, the presence of outsiders on an altar highlights the fact that domestic ancestor worship is compounded of memorialism, devotion to the needs of the dead, and subjection to their vague authority.

Shifting our attention to the rites conducted in ancestral halls we see at once that we are dealing with a different kind of ancestor. There is a sense in which there are now no individual ancestors but rather a sort of ancestral collectivity, the common spiritual property of a corporate group. True, the names of key ancestors are picked out in the grand rites and people may decorate (and even perhaps pay private attention to) the tablet of some ancestor for whom they are specially concerned; but the atmosphere in the hall is overwhelmingly one in which a group of male agnates (or at least their elders and elite on their behalf) dramatize their existence by praising and sacrificing to a body of ancestors that they hold in distinction from other groups of like order. The twice-yearly rites and festivities are a manifestation, to both the worshipers and those from whom they are differentiated by those acts, of a claim to a special standing and distinction bound up with the reciprocal relationship of honor between living and dead. Men glorify their ancestors and parade them as the source of their being. For their part the ancestors bask in the glow of the solidarity and achievements of their descendants.

This is a world of men. Their wives enter the hall only as tablets—a dumb and wooden fate. And even then, they are rarely admitted in the same numbers as men, for as we have seen in the case of the Sheung Shui halls, the wives of the most senior ancestors are likely to be represented, but not those of the men who have been installed on account of their special honor or generosity. The ancestral hall is not merely the site of agnation; it is the locus of the political life of the agnatic community, and in that life women can have no public place. The contrast with domestic worship is sharp: that sphere belongs above all to women; the ancestors are capable of some immediate intervention in the lives of their descendants; it is a realm of personal relationships between living and dead. In the halls the ancestors are raised by men to a plane from which notions of punitive behavior are excluded, whence only pride and generalized benignity flow.

The very same systematic difference is to be seen between the rites performed at the graves of recent forebears and those at structurally significant tombs of remoter ancestors. When family parties go out to the graves (ideally sited in the hills) to care for and make offerings at them—which they do at least at Ch'ing Ming—they enter into the same kind of relationship with individual forebears as we find in domestic worship. The women are prominent; personal appeals to the dead may be made; the delicacies offered are likely to be adjusted to the tastes of the departed. But the rites at the great tombs of distant ancestors are all pomp and splendor, a kind of alfresco version of what (if a group has a hall) will have taken place indoors, perhaps with chants of praise and bursts of music.

Yet as soon as we begin to consider the role of tombs in ancestor worship, we are forced to recognize that the term "ancestor worship" cannot embrace all that the Chinese do ritually to make their ancestors significant in their lives. When they worship at the graves they address themselves to entities that are identical with, or at least of the same order as, those tended in domestic shrines. (The distinction depends on the analysis one makes of the *hun* elements of the nonphysical personality.) But in this context the buried ancestor is presenting only one of two sides of his nature, for he is not merely a disembodied soul but also a mystified set of bones. As the former he is attached to a tablet and hovers above his grave; as the latter he is permanently in the earth, where his relationship to his "physical" surroundings has a direct bearing on the fate of his descendants. We are now in the realm of *feng-shui*, "geomancy," the mystical determination of fortune by the acts of men on their environment.

In the *feng-shui* of graves (that is, of *yin* habitations)—as distinct from that of buildings (*yang* habitations)—men seek to site their tombs where the "winds and waters" are most favorable; they look to this siting as a means of establishing or maintaining good fortune—riches, rank, and progeny—and they expect the ancestral bones to respond to the treatment to which they subject them. The worship of ancestors, which hinges on the moral duty of *hsiao* ("filial piety"), is counterbalanced by the "disrespect" of ancestors implied in the *feng-shui* of graves.

We have seen that tombs may be used as foci of lineages and their segments, either supplementing or replacing halls; and in the context of ancestor worship these graves are symbols of agnatic solidarity. But in geomancy the tombs mean something different, introducing fine points of differentiation among agnates. A man seeks to site a grave in such a way that the benefit it is designed to produce will flow to him alone or to him in the company of close patrilineal kinsmen. The benefit resulting from good siting ramifies along the lines of agnatic descent from the man or woman buried in the grave (a woman's agnatic descendants being her own children and the patrilineal issue of her sons); the remoter the buried ancestor, the wider will be the spread of beneficiaries, so that it becomes part of the strategy of choice in *feng-shui* to fasten onto a near ancestor in order to restrict the range of the people with whom one will be forced to share the benefits procured. The great tombs of apical ancestors yield geomantic profits of too general a character; agnates differentiate themselves by exploiting the *feng-shui* of their proximate forebears.

The point that in geomancy competition between agnates is of the essence is brought home most dramatically by the behavior of brothers, among whom in the Chinese system there is a built-in tendency to be rivalrous when they are adult. All brothers must of course benefit from the geomantically sited tomb of a common parent, but in fact the rules of *feng-shui* presuppose that they will not profit equally, for it is laid down that it is virtually impossible so to site and orient a tomb that all children will enjoy a like happiness. The evidence is abundant that brotherly squabbling attends the attempt to get agreement on precisely where, in which direction, and at what time to bury a parent. By *feng-shui* men seek to individualize their fate, pressing individualism to the point where each can strive to climb above his fellows, and at their expense, for one man's gain is seen as another's loss.

Ancestors in their tablets and as they receive offerings at their graves are *shen* and their affinities are with Heaven (*t'ien*). Men cannot expect them to pour out their blessings without reciprocity; the ancestors are moral beings. Ancestors as bones, on the contrary, partake of the nature of Earth (*ti*);

they are morally neutral, and the benefits of which they are the vehicle are amoral. Men use their buried forebears for their selfish ends, manipulating in the context of *feng-shui* the ancestors whom they revere in the realm of worship. It is a remarkable feature of Chinese religion that the ancestors can be shown, in segregated spheres, to be symbols of authority and honor on the one hand and symbols of the satisfaction of greed on the other. That latter aspect of the treatment and conception of ancestors is poorly reflected in the literature. Is it because the *feng-shui* of graves is a kind of negative ancestor worship about which Chinese writers themselves are uncomfortable and which the foreign observers of China have been unable to see, partly perhaps by their being overpersuaded by the Confucian models set before them?

The brief excursion into geomancy in turn suggests the possibility that there remain much wider fields within which to inquire into the symbolic roles of Chinese ancestors. In this connection I may cite the pioneering work done in the last few years by Aijmer. In a recently published paper (1968) he has sketched out a set of ideas that explore the *yin* aspects (other than that revealed in *feng-shui*) of the ancestors, particularly in regard to their agricultural role in the underground, and has looked at the various key festivals of the Chinese year as forming a system of alternating visits between the living and their ancestors in both their *yin* and *yang* guises. He writes (1968: 96):

> During these festivals, *Qingming*, *Duanwu*, and *Zhongyang* [Ch'ing Ming, Tuan Wu, and Ch'ung Yang], there appears to be no particular concern about the ancestor tablets. New Year seems to be the big event for them. Thus *Qingming* implies a visit to the *yin* ancestors and *Duanwu* a return visit from the latter. *Zhongyang* implies a visit to the *yang* ancestors and New Year a return visit from them.

I leave the subject at this juncture. As with every other topic in the study of Chinese society, when we begin to systematize our understanding of it, the investigation branches off into directions—perhaps unforeseen at first—that lead to numerous points in the total system of Chinese social behavior and the total system of Chinese ideas. About these systems we have at the moment only general notions.

Ruth Bunzel

THE NATURE OF KATCINAS

One of the most common souvenirs bought by travelers in the American Southwest is the small, brightly painted wooden doll called the "katcina." Often erroneously called an Indian "god" or "fetish," the dolls, in fact, serve as visual aids in educating Pueblo Indian children in the intricacies of the Katcina Cult found among these Indians. The katcina spirits, in part thought to be tribal ancestral spirits and in part the spirits of departed tribal members, are of many forms and fill many roles: Pautiwa is the chief of katcina village; Chakwena Woman aids in rabbit hunts; the Koyemshi are clowns. Katcina spirits are participants in, rather than the objects of, Pueblo ceremonials. Enacted by men in the masks and body decorations appropriate to particular spirits or types of spirits, katcinas take part in fertility ceremonies, rain dances, and many of the ceremonies involved in the yearly round. They mingle in the streets with the people, discipline unruly children in their homes, chide deviants publicly, and, in front of all the people during ceremonials in the plazas, they often dramatize the values and beliefs basic to Pueblo Indian culture.

Recalling that katcinas are thought to be, in part, the spirits of the dead, Zuni attitudes toward these "ghosts" stand in contrast to those of the Apaches cited in a previous article.

Extracted with editorial modifications from "Zuni Katcinas," *47th Annual Report of the Bureau of American Ethnology*, pp. 837–1086 (Washington, D.C.: Smithsonian Institution Press, 1932), by permission of the author and the publisher.

The Katcina Cult is one of the six major cults of Zuni, and might indeed be called the dominant Zuni cult. It includes many of the most beautiful and spectacular ceremonies, and the ceremonies which attract the most popular attention. Furthermore, it is the one cult which personally reaches all people, since all males belong to it and are required to participate in its ceremonies. Moreover, at the present time it is an ascendant cult. At a time when the societies are declining in membership, and the priesthoods experience difficulties in filling their ranks, when ceremonies lapse because no one competent to perform them survives, the Katcina Society is extending its activities. More katcina dances are held each year than in Mrs. Stevenson's time, and the dances last longer. It is true that some of the older dances are no longer performed, but on the other hand for each dance that lapses two new ones are introduced. It is the most vital, the most spectacular, and the most pervasive of Zuni cults; whatever foreign elements it may at one time or another have incorporated, its ideology and form are aboriginal and characteristic, and for the average Zuni it is the focal point of religious, social, and aesthetic experience.

The Katcina Cult is built upon the worship, principally through impersonation, of a group of supernaturals called in Zuni terminology *koko*. The koko live in a lake, *Hatin kaiakwi* (whispering spring), west of Zuni, near St. Johns, Arizona. In the bottom of this lake they have a village (*Koluwalawa*, katcina village) reached by ladders through the lake. Here they spend their time singing and dancing, and occasionally they come to Zuni to dance for their "daylight" fathers. They live on the spiritual essence of food sacrificed to them in the river, and clothe themselves with the feathers of prayer sticks. They turn into ducks when traveling back and forth to Zuni.

The first katcinas were the children of humans lost through contact with contamination, unwilling sacrifices to atone for sin. By origin and later association they are identified with the dead. Mortals on death join the katcinas at katcina village and become like them.

In addition to being identified with the dead the katcinas are especially associated with clouds and rain. When they come to dance they come in rain. They are equivalent to the Shiwana of Keresan pueblos.

In ancient times, the katcina used to come to Zuni to dance for their people in order that they might be gay. But always when they left someone "went with them," that is, died, and so they decided not to come any more. But they authorized masked dances and promised "to come and stand before them." So now when a katcina dance is held the katcinas come merely as rain, and no one dies. So the institution of masked dancing, originated according to legend to assuage the loneliness of parents for their lost children, has become a rain-making ceremony.

The power of katcina ceremonies resides in the masks which, whether ancient tribal property or individually owned modern masks, are believed to contain divine substance, by means of which the katcina whose representation is worn "makes himself into a person." Masks are treated with the utmost reverence. The awe which Zunis feel for all sacred and powerful objects is intensified in this case by the fact that masks are representations of the dead, and, indeed, the very substance of death. Therefore the use of masks is surrounded by special taboos. One must never try on a mask when not participating in a ceremony, else one will die. One must never use human hair or the hair of a live horse on a mask, else that person or horse will surely die. If one is incontinent during a katcina ceremony the mask will choke him or stick to his face during the dance.

The katcinas are very intimate and affectionate supernaturals. They like pretty clothes and feathers; they like to sing and dance, and to visit. Above all they like to come to Zuni to dance.

The folk tales about individual katcinas describe them at home in their kitchens, scrambling for their feathers at the solstices, quarreling amiably among themselves, meddling in one another's affairs. They have a village organization similar to that of Zuni. Pautiwa is "the boss," as Zunis say. His pekwin, who delivers his messages, is Kaklo. His principal administrative duties seem to be to keep his people quiet long enough to give a courteous welcome to visitors, to receive messages from Zuni, and to decide when to dance there and who shall go. Pautiwa "makes the New Year" at Zuni. His representative brings in the Ca'lako crook and crooks for other special ceremonies, such as the initiation and the dance of the Kanakwe, thus determining the calendar of katcina ceremonies for the year. Whenever the people at Zuni decide they want one of the regular katcina dances they send prayer sticks to katcina village (kiva chiefs plant prayer sticks four days before a dance) and Pautiwa decides whom to send.

Hamokatsik, the mother of the katcinas, looks after their clothing when they prepare for dances.

In addition to the official visits of the katcinas when invited with prayer sticks, they sometimes pay unexpected visits on missions of good will. They come to plant and harvest for deserted children, to affirm the supernatural power of the pious and despised. Pautiwa visits in disguise poor and despised maidens, and leaves wealth and blessing behind him. Katcinas in disguise bring proud girls to their senses by the amiable disciplinary methods so characteristically Zunian.

In reading these folk tales we cannot but be struck by their resemblance in feeling and tone to medieval tales of saints and angels—such tales as that of the amiable angel who turned off the wine tap left open by the monk who was so pious that he didn't even stop to turn off the tap when summoned for prayer. The particular situations in which katcinas prove helpful and their special techniques differ, of course, from those of saints and angels. Medieval saints do not ordinarily humble proud maids by contriving in spite of impossible tests to sleep with them and so instruct them in the delights of normal human association and the advantages of humility. But in spite of these differences the popular attitudes and feeling for the role of supernaturals in commonplace human affairs are curiously similar. Undoubtedly this modern folklore concerning katcinas has been strongly colored by Catholic influences.

But for all their generally amiable and benign character, there is a certain sinister undertone to all katcina ceremonies. It is said more often of the katcinas than of other supernaturals that they are "dangerous." The katcinas inflict the most direct and dramatic punishments for violation of their sanctity. If a priest fails in his duties, he does not get rain during his retreat, he may suffer from general bad luck, he may become sick and may even die if he does nothing to "save his life." But the katcina impersonator who fails in his trust may be choked to death by his mask during the ceremony. There is always a certain feeling of danger in wearing a mask. In putting on a mask the wearer always addresses it in prayer: "Do not cause me any serious trouble." A man wearing a mask or, in katcina dances without mask, one wearing katcina body paint, is untouchable. He is dangerous to others until his paint has been washed off. Zunis watching katcinas dance shrink from them as they pass through narrow passages, in order not to touch their bodies.

The first katcinas were children sacrificed to the water to atone for sin; afterwards when they came to dance, bringing their blessing of rain and fertility, "they took someone with them"; that is, they exacted a human life from the village. It was only when masks were substituted for the actual presence of the katcinas that this heavy toll was lightened.

There are hints in ritual that ideas of human sacrifice may lie but a little way beneath the surface in the concept of masked impersonation. The great ceremony of the Ca'lako opens with the appointment of a group of impersonators of the gods. For a year they are set apart. They do no work of their own. In the case of the Saiyataca party they even assume the names of the gods whom they are to impersonate. At the end of their term of office they have elaborate ceremonies in which they appear in mask; that is, in the regalia of death. After all-night ceremonies they depart for the home of the dead. "Everyone cries when they go," as a Zuni informant says. "It is very sad to see them go, because we always think that we shall never see them again." The final ceremony of the departure of the Ca'lako is especially suggestive of this interpretation. When out of sight of the village the Ca'lako are pursued by young men. When caught they are thrown down and killed, and the mask is treated like the body of a fallen deer—"for good luck in hunting." On returning the impersonators are met outside the village by their aunts and taken at once to their houses to be bathed before they are safe from human contact.

Identification with the god, and the killing of the god, for fecundity, as found in ancient Mexico, seem to be ideas in keeping with Zuni concepts. But Zuni temperament would repudiate the bloody sacrifice. It may well be that the particular technique of impersonation, with its atmosphere of the sinister and dangerous, is the symbolic representation of the extirpated fact. Tales of the former existence of human sacrifice in the pueblos continually crop up.

Frazer, quoting Bourke, gives an account of the sacrifice of a youth at the fire festival (tribal initiation) of the Hopi. Mrs. Stevenson refers to the report of human sacrifice at Zia. There are cases of human sacrifices for fertility among the Pawnee and the Sioux. The prevalence of all forms of human sacrifice among the Aztecs is too well known to require comment. Among the Aztecs, however, are found two striking features: The dancing of priests in the flayed skin of the sacrificial victim, and the identification of the sacrificial victim with god, as for example, in the sacrifice of Tezcatlipoca. In the battle with the katcinas at Acoma the katcinas are ritualistically slain so that their blood may fertilize the earth. In the prayers of the scalp dance there are frequent allusions to blood as a fertilizing medium, so possibly the whole complex of human sacrifice is not so remote historically or conceptually as might at first appear.

The persistent rumors of an early prevalence of human sacrifice in the pueblos may be without foundation, but the reworking of a cult that once included human sacrifice is quite in accord with pueblo tendency to absorb ritual from all sides and mitigate all its more violent features.

NINE
DYNAMICS IN RELIGION

Introduction

"Men have become like gods," Sir Edmund Leach asserts in his B.B.C. Reith Lectures for 1967. "Isn't it about time that we understood our divinity? Science offers us total mastery over our environment and over our destiny, yet instead of rejoicing we feel deeply afraid. Why should this be? How might these fears be resolved?" (Leach, 1967:1) Encompassed within this half-statement, half-question are the two broad themes running through many anthropological and sociological approaches to religious change. The first concerns explanations of the process of secularization: the de-anthropomorphization and "disenchantment" of a world formerly inhabited by Olympian gods, myriad ancestral spirits, or nature deities; the development of self-concious and explicitly coherent rationalized religious doctrines; the perennial war between Religion and Science. The second theme addresses the problem of why, in the face of such growing secularization, does religion persist, and as some of the articles in this chapter indicate, do new ones arise? Precisely why *do* we continue to fear, as Leach puts it, our own "divinity"? The following selections are intended to show how anthropologists have dealt with aspects of these two broad questions of religious change.

The dynamic aspects of religion are doubly intractable to anthropological analysis. First, the process of religious change is frequently a latent one, carried on beneath apparently changeless sacred symbols. The salient expressions of religious concepts can remain the same while their content and meaning change, either gradually or dramatically. Second, the very manner in which religious concepts are held and expressed leaves them inherently ambiguous and somewhat ambivalent. As Geertz suggests (see Chapter Two), religion experienced in the midst of ritual may differ markedly from religion remembered in the midst of everyday life; the worshipper absorbed in his experience, like a dreamer in his dream, may take it as profoundly real but be unable later to recall or report the precise nature of that felt reality.

Further, the symbols used to express religious concepts themselves require a degree of skepticism—an "as if" attitude—from the ritual performers or participants. The efficacy of any symbol, especially a sacred one, lies precisely in its ability not to be merely what it seems. A cross in a church is something more than a cross; a Zuni Katcina's painted visage something more than a mask. This simultaneous perception of both the symbol's *representational intention* (e.g., a mask as a god's face) and the *concrete means* by which this effect is created (perceiving the mask as a mask) necessitates a certain degree of psychical distancing; pretending, if you will, but utterly serious pretending. The experience becomes doubly ambiguous; things become what they objectively are not, or do they? Clearly, religious change is not simply a matter of "belief" or "disbelief" or a "shift in beliefs," but rather, it is a complex interplay of balance and proportion between conviction and skepticism, and seriousness and mere diversion. These two factors—the latent quality of religious change, and the frequent ambiguity with which religious concepts are held and expressed—make the dynamic aspects of religion difficult to locate, and still more, difficult to measure.

Early anthropological studies of religious change were encompassed by a wider concern with acculturation—the way in which cultures change through contact with one another. While anthropologists were often quick to rectify the misconception that "primitive" religions did not undergo modifications, the lack of historical data left these assertions largely unsubstantiated, both on the ideological level of religious dogma and creed as well as on the sociological level of political, economic, and social structural causality. But the increasing impact of the West on non-Western cultures soon provoked a rash of "nativistic," "revivalistic" or "revitalization" movements—religiously inspired responses to the stresses of colonization, acculturation, and domination. Anthropological explanations of this kind of religious change were couched in terms of the social and economic inequities of the contact situation and produced what has come to be called *deprivation theory:* the assumption that religious change grows out of psychological, social, economic, or political deprivation.

Two classic examples of deprivation theory are included in this chapter. Ralph Linton's essay is an early attempt to define the essence of the phenomenon and to provide a workable typology of the movements. In a more recent paper, Anthony Wallace defines the concept of "revitalization" and outlines certain uniform processes found in such religious movements.

But deprivation theory, while logically and intuitively powerful, provides little insight into any particular movement, the form it takes, or its history. Hill's short essay on the Ghost Dance, one of the most famous religious movements of the North American Indians, and Cochrane's piece on Melanesian "cargo" cults in the South Pacific, both rely on deprivation theory but point out its inadequacies. Hill does this by showing that the Navaho did not accept the Ghost Dance of 1890 because of their culturally conditioned ambivalence toward the dead. Cochrane in turn asserts that a true understanding of cargo cults can only be attained by grasping the significance of Melanesian concepts of status and power. Clearly, an adequate explanation of such movements must go beyond an analysis of the kind of deprivation involved to elucidate the social and cultural context out of which they grow. The proper study of such self-evident examples of religious dynamism thus can provide insights both into subtler aspects of religious change and also into the more general processes of culture change.

But the dynamic aspects of religion are not limited to ghost dances or cargo cults. Religion is intimately bound to wider social and cultural processes, and as these change, so does religion. But explicating precisely how and why religion affects—and is affected by—these other phenomena is a complex and seemingly intractable task. Although the selection in this chapter by Eric Hobsbawm does not directly address this relationship between religion and society, it does draw a cogent parallel between religiously motivated millenarian movements and modern political revolutions. In both cases, a movement can be maintained only through the unquestioning conviction of its followers that its goal, be it a political utopia or an earthly paradise, can and must be achieved. The final selection by Clifford Geertz deals with the more specific problem of religious change on the Indonesian island of Bali. He clearly shows that religion can play a stabilizing role during periods of rapid change while simultaneously providing a symbolic language through which these changes can be carried out. The rationalization or secularization of religion need not automatically vitiate its potency as a meaningful force in social action.

For an interesting treatment of the source and dynamics of ritual practices and religious concepts, see Adolf Jensen's book, *Myth and Cult Among Primitive Peoples* (1963), especially chapters 1–3. An extensive survey of new religions in the United States can be found in a volume edited by I. I. Zaretsky and Mark P. Leone entitled *Religious Movements in Contemporary America* (1974); and a specific case study is Francine Daner's *The American Children of Krsna: A Study of the Hare Krsna Movement* (1976). Readers also might want to consult a book on the psychological aspects of contemporary religious movements entitled *Case Studies in Spirit Possession* (1977), edited by Vincent Crapanzano and Vivian Garrison. For a further theoretical statement on deprivation theory, see David Aberle, "A Note on Relative Deprivation Theory as Applied to Millenarian and Other Cult Movements" (1962).

Ralph Linton

NATIVISTIC MOVEMENTS

The impact of European culture upon the small, primitive societies of the world during the past four centuries has frequently led to the appearance of what have come to be known as "nativistic movements," wherein the primitive societies have reacted, sometimes violently, against domination by the Europeans and engaged in organized attempts to revive or perpetuate certain aspects of their native cultures in the face of this pressure to change. Since the religious systems of the primitive societies typically embodied the central values of their cultures, these nativistic movements almost always involved some type of religious or magical procedures as their essential elements and hence have provided us with crucial data on dynamics in religion.

This general paper of Ralph Linton's is an attempt to define and classify the types of nativistic movements that have occurred in culture-contact situations and to identify the conditions under which these various types of movements arise. Linton makes it clear that nativism can appear in the dominant group as well as in the subordinate group in a culture-contact situation, although the more dramatic manifestations tend to occur in the subordinate society.

Reprinted from *American Anthropologist*, XLV (1943), 230–240, by permission of the American Anthropological Association.

At the time that the centennial meeting of the American Ethnological Society was planned, the writer was invited to contribute a paper on nativistic movements in North America. When he attempted to prepare this it soon became evident that there was a need for a systematic analysis of nativistic phenomena in general. Although the Social Science Research Council's Committee on Acculturation had made some progress in this direction much remained to be done. The present paper is an attempt to provide such a systematic analysis and is presented in the hope that its formulations may be modified and expanded by further research.

The first difficulty encountered in the study of nativistic movements was that of delimiting the field. The term "nativistic" has been loosely applied to a rather wide range of phenomena, resembling in this respect many other terms employed by the social sciences. For the writer to determine arbitrarily which of several established usages is to be considered correct and which incorrect is not only presumptuous but also one of the surest ways to promote misunderstanding of the theoretical contributions he hopes to make. The only satisfactory definition under such circumstances is one based upon the common denominators of the meanings which have come to be attached to the term through usage. With this as a guide, we may define a nativistic movement as "Any conscious, organized attempt on the part of a society's members to revive or perpetuate selected aspects of its culture."

Like all definitions, the above requires amplification to make its implications clear. Its crux lies in the phrase "conscious, organized effort." All societies seek to perpetuate their own cultures, but they usually do this unconsciously and as a part of the normal processes of individual training and socialization. Conscious, organized efforts to perpetuate a culture can arise only when a society becomes conscious that there are cultures other than its own and that the existence of its own culture is threatened. Such consciousness, in turn, is a by-product of close and continuous contact with other societies; an acculturation phenomenon under the definition developed by the above-mentioned committee.

The phrase "selected aspects of its culture" also requires elaboration. Nativistic movements concern themselves with particular elements of culture, never with cultures as wholes. This generalization holds true whether we regard cultures as continuums of long duration or follow the usual ethnographic practice of applying the term "a culture" to the content of such a continuum at a particular point in time. The avowed purpose of a nativistic movement may be either to revive the past culture or to perpetuate the current one, but it never really attempts to do either. Any attempt to revive a past phase of culture in its entirety is immediately blocked by the recognition that this phase was, in certain respects, inferior to the present one and by the incompatibility of certain past culture patterns with current conditions. Even the current phase of a culture is never satisfactory at all points and also includes a multitude of elements which seem too trivial to deserve deliberate perpetuation. What really happens in all nativistic movements is that certain current or remembered elements of culture are selected for emphasis and given symbolic value. The more distinctive such elements are with respect to other cultures with which the society is in contact, the greater their potential value as symbols of the society's unique character.

The main considerations involved in this selective process seem to be those of distinctiveness and of the practicability of reviving or perpetuating the element under current conditions. Thus the Ghost Dance laid great stress on the revival of such distinctive elements of Indian culture as games and ceremonial observances, elements which could be revived under agency conditions. At the same time it allowed its adherents to continue the use of cloth, guns, kettles, and other objects of European manufacture which were obviously superior to their aboriginal equivalents. In fact, in many cases the converts were assured that when the dead returned and the whites were swept away, the houses, cattle and other valuable property of the whites would remain for the Indians to inherit.

All the phenomena to which the term "nativistic" has been applied have in common these factors of selection of culture elements and deliberate, conscious effort to perpetuate such elements. However, they differ so widely in other respects that they cannot be understood without further analysis. At the outset it is necessary to distinguish between those forms of nativism which involve an attempt to revive extinct or at least moribund elements of culture and those which merely seek to perpetuate current ones. For convenience we will refer to the first of these forms as *revivalistic nativism*, to the second as *perpetuative nativism*. These two forms are not completely exclusive. Thus a revivalistic nativistic movement will be almost certain to include in its selection of elements some of those which are current in the culture although derived from its past. Conversely a perpetuative nativistic movement may include elements which had been consciously revived at an earlier date. However, the emphases of these two forms are distinct. The revivalistic type of nativism can be illustrated by such movements as the Celtic revival in Ireland, with its emphasis on the medieval Irish tradition in literature and its attempt to revive a moribund national language. The perpetuative type of nativism can be illustrated by the conditions existing in some of the Rio Grande Pueblos or in various Indian groups in Guatemala. Such groups are only vaguely conscious of their past culture and make no attempts to revive it, but they have developed elaborate and conscious techniques for the perpetuation of selected aspects of their current culture and are unalterably opposed to assimilation into the alien society which surrounds them.

There is a further necessity for distinguishing between what we may call *magical nativism* and *rational nativism*. It may well be questioned whether any sort of nativistic movement can be regarded as genuinely rational, since all such movements are, to some extent, unrealistic, but at least the movements of the latter order appear rational by contrast with those of the former.

Magical nativistic movements are often spectacular and always troublesome to administrators, facts which explain why they have received so much attention from anthropologists. Such movements are comparable in many respects to the messianic movements which have arisen in many societies in time of stress. They usually originate with some individual who assumes the role of prophet and is accepted by the people because they wish to believe. They always lean heavily on the supernatural and usually embody apocalyptic and millennial aspects. In such movements moribund elements of culture are not revived for their own sake or in anticipation of practical advantages from the elements themselves. Their revival is part of a magical formula designed to modify the society's environment in ways which will be favorable to it. The selection of elements from the past culture as tools for magical manipulation is easily explainable on the basis of their psychological associations. The society's members feel that by behaving as the ancestors did they will, in some usually undefined way, help to recreate the total situation in which the ancestors lived. Perhaps it would be more accurate to say that they are attempting to recreate those aspects of the ancestral situation which appear desirable in retrospect.

Such magical nativistic movements seem to differ from ordinary messianic and millennial movements in only two respects. In the nativistic movements the anticipated millennium is modeled directly on the past, usually with certain additions and modifications, and the symbols which are magically manipulated to bring it about are more or less familiar elements of culture to which new meanings have been attached. In non-nativistic messianic movements, the millennial condition is represented as something new and unique and the symbols manipulated to bring it about tend to be new and unfamiliar. Even in these respects the differences are none too clear. New elements of culture often emerge in connection with magical nativistic movements, as in the case of the distinctive Ghost Dance art. Conversely, messianic movements may lean heavily upon the familiar symbolism of the culture, as in the case of most Christian cults of this type. The basic feature of both messianic cults and magical nativistic movements is that they represent frankly irrational flights from reality. Their differences relate only to the ways in which such flights are implemented and are, from the point of view of their functions, matters of minor importance.

What we have chosen to call rational nativistic movements are a phenomenon of a quite different sort. While such movements resemble the magical ones in their conscious effort to revive or perpetuate selected elements of culture, they have different motivations. What these are can be understood more readily if we reintroduce at this point the distinction previously made between revivalistic and perpetuative nativistic movements. Rational revivalistic nativistic movements are, almost without exception, associated with frustrating situations and are primarily attempts to compensate for the frustrations of the society's members. The elements revived become symbols of a period when the society was free or, in retrospect, happy or great. Their usage is not magical but psychological. By keeping the past in mind, such elements help to re-establish and maintain the self-respect of the group's members in the face of adverse conditions. Rational perpetuative nativistic movements, on the other hand, find their main function in the maintenance of social solidarity. The elements selected for perpetuation become symbols of the society's existence as a unique entity. They provide the society's members with a fund of common knowledge and experience which is exclusively their own and which sets them off from the members of other societies. In both types of rational nativistic movement the culture elements selected for symbolic use are chosen realistically and with regard to the possibility of perpetuating them under current conditions.

It must be emphasized that the four forms of nativistic movement just discussed are not absolutes. Purely revivalistic or perpetuative, magical or rational movements form a very small minority of the observed cases. However, these forms represent the polar positions of series within which all or nearly all given nativistic movements can be placed. Moreover, it will usually be found that a given nativistic movement lies much closer to one end of such a scale than to the other if it is analyzed in terms of the criteria used to establish the polar positions. If we combine the polar positions in the two series, the result is a fourfold typology of nativistic movements, as follows:

1. Revivalistic-magical
2. Revivalistic-rational
3. Perpetuative-magical
4. Perpetuative-rational

Forms 1, 2, and 4 in this typology recur with great frequency, while form 3 is so rare that the writer has been unable to find any clearly recognizable example of it. The reason for this probably lies in the conditions which are usually responsible for magical nativistic movements. The inception of such movements can be traced almost without exception to conditions of extreme hardship or at least extreme dissatisfaction with the *status quo*. Since the current culture is associated with such conditions and has failed to ameliorate them, magical efficacy in modifying these conditions can scarcely be ascribed to any of its elements. Nevertheless, a perpetuative-magical movement might very well arise in the case of a society which currently occupies an advantageous position but sees itself threatened with an imminent loss of that position. It is highly probable that if we could canvass the whole range of nativistic movements examples of this type could be found.

An understanding of the various contact situations in which nativistic movements may arise is quite as necessary for the study of these phenomena as is a typology of such movements. There have been many cases of contact in which they have not arisen at all. The reasons for this seem to be so variable and in many cases so obscure that nothing like a satisfactory analysis is possible. The most that we can say is that nativistic movements are unlikely to arise in situations where both societies are satisfied with their current relationship, or where societies which find themselves at a disadvantage can see that their condition is improving. However, such movements may always be initiated by particular individuals or groups who stand to gain by them and, if the prestige of such initiators is high enough, may achieve considerable followings even when there has been little previous dissatisfaction.

Although the immediate causes of nativistic movements are highly variable, most of them have as a common denominator a situation of inequality between the societies in contact. Such inequalities may derive either from the attitudes of the societies involved or from actual situations of dominance and submission. In order to understand the motives for nativistic movements the distinction between these two sources of inequality must be kept clearly in mind. Inequality based on attitudes of superiority and inferiority may exist in the absence of real dominance, although situations of dominance seem to be uniformly accompanied by the development of such attitudes. As regards attitudes of superiority and inferiority, two situations may exist. Each of the groups involved in the contact may consider itself superior or one group may consider itself superior with the other acquiescing in its own inferiority. There seem to be no cases in which each of the groups involved in a contact considers itself inferior. The nearest approach to such a condition is the recognition of mixed inferiority and superiority, i.e., the members of each group regard their own culture as superior in certain respects and inferior in others. Such a condition is especially favorable to the processes of culture exchange and ultimate assimilation of the two groups. It rarely if ever results in the development of nativistic movements.

The type of situation in which each society considers itself superior is well illustrated by the relations between Mexicans and Indians in our own Southwest. In this case factors of practical dominance are ruled out by the presence of a third group, the Anglo-American, which dominates Indian and Mexican alike. Although the two subject groups are in close contact, each of them feels that any assimilation would involve a loss of prestige. The transfer of individuals from one social-cultural continuum to the other is met by equal resistance on both sides and the processes of assimilation never have a chance to get under way. Under such circumstances the life of each of the societies is conscious of its own culture and consciously seeks to perpetuate its distinctive elements. At the same time this consciousness of difference is devoid of envy or frustration and produces no friction. The members of each group pursue their own goals with the aid of their own techniques and, although the situation does not preclude economic rivalries—witness the constant quarrels over water rights—it does preclude social rivalries. It seems that the establishment of such attitudes of mutual social exclusiveness, without hatred or dominance, provides the soundest basis for organizing symbiotic relationships between societies and should be encouraged in all cases where the attitudes of one or both of the groups in contact preclude assimilation.

Contact situations comparable to that just discussed are not infrequent, but they seem to be less common than those in which both groups agree on the superiority of one of the parties. It must be repeated that such attitudes are not necessarily linked with conditions of actual dominance. Thus the Japanese during the early period of European contact acquiesced in the European's estimate of his own superiority and borrowed European culture elements eagerly and indiscriminately although maintaining national independence. Again, the disunited German states of the eighteenth century acknowledged the superiority of French culture and were eager for French approval even when no political factors were involved.

When two groups stand in such a mutually recognized relationship of superiority and inferiority, but with no factors of actual dominance involved, the contact will rarely if ever give rise to nativistic movements of the magical type. The relationship cannot produce the extreme stresses which drive the members of a society into such flights from reality. On the other hand, the contact may well give rise to rational nativistic movements, but these will rarely if ever appear during the early contact period. At first the superior group is usually so sure of its position that it feels no reluctance toward borrowing convenient elements from the culture of the inferior one. Conversely, the inferior group borrows eagerly from the superior one and looks forward to full equality with it as soon as the cultural differences have been obliterated. During this period impecunious members of the superior group are likely to turn their prestige to practical advantage by marrying rich members of the inferior one and, for a time, genuine assimilation appears to be under way. In such a situation the nativistic trends will normally appear first in the superior group, which is naturally jealous of its prestige. The movements inaugurated will generally be of the perpetuative-rational type, designed to maintain the *status quo*, and will include increasing reluctance to borrow elements of culture from the inferior group and the increase of social discrimination against its members and those of the superior group who consort with them.

When such a nativistic movement gets well under way in the superior group, there will usually be a nativistic response from the inferior one. Finding themselves frustrated in their desire for equality, with or without actual assimilation, the inferiors will develop their own nativistic movements, acting on the well-known sour-grapes principle. However, these movements will be of the revivalistic-rational rather than the perpetuative-rational type. The culture elements selected for emphasis will tend to be drawn from the past rather than the present, since the attitudes of the superior group toward the current culture will have done much to devaluate it. In general, symbolic values will be attached, by preference, to culture elements which were already on the wane at the time of the first contact with the superior group, thus embodying in the movement a denial that the culture of the other group ever was considered superior.

We have already said that attitudes of superiority and inferiority seem to be present in all cases of contact involving actual dominance. Combining these two sets of factors we get the following possible situations for contact groups:

1. Dominant-superior
2. Dominant-inferior
3. Dominated-superior
4. Dominated-inferior

These situations assume agreement on the part of the groups involved not only with respect to dominance, readily demonstrable, but also with respect to attitudes. The frequent lack of such agreement makes it necessary to add a fifth situation, that in which the dominant and dominated group each considers itself superior. The other possible combinations, those involving attitudes of inferiority on the part of both dominant and dominated and those involving attitudes of mixed inferiority and superiority on both sides, may be ruled out from the present discussion. The first of these possible combinations simply does not occur. The second occurs rather frequently, but as in the cases where it occurs without domination, normally results in assimilation rather than the production of nativistic movements.

The idea that nativistic movements may arise in dominant as well as dominated groups appears strange to us, since most of our experience of such movements comes from the contact of Europeans with native peoples. However, we must not forget that Europeans have occupied a singularly favored position in such contacts. Even where the European settles permanently among a native population, he remains a mere outlier of white society and, thanks to modern means of transportation and communication, can keep close touch with the parent body. This parent body is shielded from contact and assimilation and is thus able to send out to its colonial ruling groups constant increments of individuals who are culturally unmixed. Moreover, the technological superiority of European culture has, until recently, rendered the dominance of colonial groups secure. The nativism of Europeans has, therefore, been largely unconscious and entirely of the perpetuative-rational type. It has manifested itself in such things as the practice of sending children back to Europe to be educated or the Englishman's insistence on dressing for dinner even when alone in a remote outpost of empire. Most dominant groups have been less fortunate. They have found themselves threatened, from the moment of their accession to power, not only by foreign invasion or domestic revolt but also by the insidious processes of assimilation which might, in the long run, destroy their distinctive powers and privileges. This threat was especially menacing when, as in most of the pre-machine age empires, the dominant and dominated groups differed little if at all in physical type. Among such rulers the frustrations which motivate nativistic movements in inferior or dominated groups were replaced by anxieties which produced very much the same results.

Returning to the contact situations previously tabulated, we find that dominant-superior groups tend to initiate perpetuative-rational forms of nativism as soon as they achieve power and to adhere to them with varying intensity as long as they remain in power. Thus the various groups of nomad invaders who conquered China all attempted to maintain much of their distinctive culture and at the height of their power they issued repressive measures directed not only against the Chinese but also against those of their own group who had begun to adopt Chinese culture. It seems probable that revivalist-rational forms of nativism will not arise in a dominant-superior group, at least as regards elements of culture which were moribund at the time of their accession to power, although this form of nativism might develop with respect to culture elements which had fallen into neglect during the period of power. It seems possible also that, under conditions of extreme threat, some form of brief revivalist-magical nativism might arise in such a group, but information that might verify these conjectures is lacking.

The situation in which a dominant group acknowledges its cultural inferiority to the dominated is one which must arise very infrequently. However, examples of it are provided by such cases as that of the Goths at the time of their conquest of Italy. Such a group immediately finds itself caught on the horns of a dilemma. It can remove its feelings of inferiority only by undergoing cultural if not society assimilation with the conquered society, while such assimilation is almost certain to cost it its dominant position. It seems probable that such a society might develop nativistic movements either when its desire for cultural assimilation with the conquered was frustrated or when it found its dominant position seriously threatened, but again information is lacking.

There is abundant information on nativistic movements among dominated groups and in discussing these we stand on firm ground. A dominated group which considers itself superior will normally develop patterns of rational nativism from the moment that it is brought under domination. These patterns may be either revivalist or perpetuative but are most likely to be a combination of both. One of the commonest rationalizations for loss of a dominant position is that it is due to a society's failure to adhere closely enough to its distinctive culture patterns. Very often such nativism will acquire a semi-magical quality founded on the belief that if the group will only stand firm and maintain its individuality it will once again become dominant. Fully developed magical-revivalist nativism is also very likely to appear in groups of this sort since to the actual deprivations entailed by subjection there are added the frustrations involved by loss of dominance. These frustrations are somewhat mitigated in the cases where the dominant group recognizes the superiority of the dominated group's culture. Such attitudes strengthen the rational nativistic tendencies of the dominated group and diminish the probabilities for magical-revivalist nativism of the more extreme type. Lastly, in cases where the dominant group concurs with the dominated in considering certain aspects of the latter's culture superior but will not grant the superiority of the culture as a whole, this attitude will stimulate the dominated group to focus attention upon such aspects of its culture and endow them with added symbolic value.

A dominated group which considers itself inferior, a condition common among societies of low culture which have recently been brought under European domination, is extremely unlikely to develop any sort of rational nativism during the early period of its subjection. It may, however, develop nativism of the revivalist-magical type if it is subjected to sufficient hardships. The threshold of suffering at which such movements may develop will vary greatly from group to group and will be influenced not only by the degree of hardship but also by the society's patterns of reliance upon the supernatural. A devout society will turn to nativism of this sort long before a skeptical one will. If the hardships arising from subjection are not extreme, the inferior group will usually show great eagerness to assume the culture of the dominant society, this eagerness being accompanied by a devaluation of everything pertaining to its own. Nativistic movements tend to arise only when the members of the subject society find that their assumption of the culture of the dominant group is being effectively opposed by it, or that it is not improving their social position. The movements which originate under these circumstances are practically always rational with a combination of revivalist and perpetuative elements. In this respect they resemble the nativistic movements which originate in inferior groups which are not subject to domination and there can be little doubt that the primary causes are the same in both cases. These movements are a response to frustration rather than hardship and would not arise if the higher group were willing to assimilate the lower one.

Rational nativistic movements can readily be converted into mechanisms for aggression. Since the dominated society has been frustrated in its earlier desires to become acculturated and to achieve social equality, it can frustrate the dominant society in turn by refusing to accept even those elements of culture which the dominant group is eager to share with it. Dominated societies which have acquired these attitudes and developed conscious techniques for preventing further acculturation present one of the most difficult problems for administrators. Passive resistance requires much less energy than any of the techniques needed to break it down, especially if the culture patterns of the dominant group preclude the use of forcible methods.

One final aspect of nativistic movements remains to be considered. The generalizations so far developed have been based upon the hypothesis that societies are homogeneous and react as wholes to contact situations. Very frequently this is not the case, especially in societies which have a well-developed class organization. In such societies nativistic tendencies will be strongest in those classes or individuals who occupy a favored position and who feel this position threatened by culture change. This factor may produce a split in the society, the favored individuals or groups indulging in a rational nativism, either revivalistic or perpetuative, while those in less favored positions are eager for assimilation. This condition can be observed in many immigrant groups in America where individuals who enjoyed high status in the old European society attempt to perpetuate the patterns of that society while those who were of low status do their best to become Americanized.

In a rapidly shrinking world the study of nativistic movements, as of acculturation in general, has ceased to be a matter of purely academic interest. As contacts between societies become more frequent and more general, the need for an understanding of the potentialities of such contact situations becomes more urgent. The troubles which they usually involve can be traced, with few exceptions, to two factors: exploitation and frustration. The first of these is the easier to deal with and may well disappear with the spread of modern science and techniques to all parts of the world. The second is more difficult to deal with, since its removal entails fundamental changes in attitudes of superiority and inferiority. Without these there would be no bar to the assimilation of societies in contact situations or to the final creation of a world society. However, this seems to be one of those millennial visions mentioned elsewhere in this report. Failing assimilation, the happiest situation which can arise out of the contact of two societies seems to be that in which each society is firmly convinced of its own superiority. Rational revivalistic or perpetuative nativistic movements are the best mechanism which has so far been developed for establishing these attitudes in groups whose members suffer from feelings of inferiority. It would appear, therefore, that they should be encouraged rather than discouraged.

Anthony F. C. Wallace
REVITALIZATION MOVEMENTS

The publication of this paper by Anthony F. C. Wallace represents another landmark in anthropological attempts to formulate the general characteristics of major cultural-system innovations that typically involve religious patterns. Wallace suggests that these major innovations, variously called "nativistic movements," "cargo cults," "messianic movements," "revolutions," etc., are characterized by a uniform process which he calls "revitalization." He outlines the structure of the process in terms of five somewhat overlapping stages: Steady State; Period of Individual Stress; Period of Cultural Distortion; Period of Revitalization; and finally a New Steady State again. In his sophisticated use of culture-pattern and psychological theory, Wallace has added important theoretical dimensions to our understandings of "revitalization move-

Reprinted in abridged form from *American Anthropologist*, LVIII (1956), 264–281, by permission of the author and the American Anthropological Association

ments" and has suggested that the historical origin of a great proportion of religious phenomena has been in such movements. Interested readers will find a full application of his ideas in his recently published book *The Death and Rebirth of the Seneca* (1970).

INTRODUCTION

Behavioral scientists have described many instances of attempted and sometimes successful innovation of whole cultural systems, or at least substantial portions of such systems. Various rubrics are employed, the rubric depending on the discipline and the theoretical orientation of the researcher, and on salient local characteristics of the cases he has chosen for study. "Nativistic movement," "reform movement," "cargo cult," "religious revival," "messianic movement," "utopian community," "sect formation," "mass movement," "social movement," "revolution," "charismatic movement," are some of the commonly used labels. This paper suggests that all these phenomena of major cultural-system innovation are characterized by a uniform process, for which I propose the term "revitalization." The body of the paper is devoted to two ends: (1) an introductory statement of the concept of revitalization, and (2) an outline of certain uniformly-found processual dimensions of revitalization movements.

THE CONCEPT OF REVITALIZATION

A revitalization movement is defined as a deliberate, organized, conscious effort by members of a society to construct a more satisfying culture. Revitalization is thus, from a cultural standpoint, a special kind of culture change phenomenon: the persons involved in the process of revitalization must perceive their culture, or some major areas of it, as a system (whether accurately or not); they must feel that this cultural system is unsatisfactory; and they must innovate not merely discrete items, but a new cultural system, specifying new relationships as well as, in some cases, new traits. The classic processes of culture change (evolution, drift, diffusion, historical change, acculturation) all produce changes in cultures as systems; however, they do not depend on deliberate intent by members of a society, but rather on a gradual chain-reaction effect: introducing A induces change in B; changing B affects C; when C shifts, A is modified; this involves D . . . and so on *ad infinitum*. This process continues for years, generations, centuries, millennia, and its pervasiveness has led many cultural theorists to regard culture change as essentially a slow, chain-like, self-contained procession of super-organic inevitabilities. In revitalization movements, however, A, B, C, D, E . . . N are shifted into a new *Gestalt* abruptly and simultaneously in intent; and frequently within a few years the new plan is put into effect by the participants in the movement.

. . .

The term "revitalization" implies an organismic analogy. This analogy is, in fact, an integral part of the concept of revitalization. A human society is here regarded as a definite kind of organism, and its culture is conceived as those patterns of learned behavior which certain "parts" of the social organism or system (individual persons and groups of persons) characteristically display. A corollary of the organismic analogy is the principle of homeostasis: that a society will work, by means of coordinated actions (including "cultural" actions) by all or some of its parts, to preserve its own integrity by maintaining a minimally fluctuating, life-supporting matrix for its individual members, and will, under stress, take emergency measures to preserve the constancy of this matrix. Stress is defined as a condition in which some part, or the whole, of the social organism is threatened with more or less serious damage. The perception of stress, particularly of increasing stress, can be viewed as the common denominator of the panel of "drives" or "instincts" in every psychological theory.

As I am using the organismic analogy, the total system which constitutes a society includes as significant parts not only persons and groups with their respective patterns of behavior, but also literally the cells and organs of which the persons are composed. Indeed, one can argue that the system includes nonhuman as well as human subsystems. Stress on one level is stress on all levels. For example, lowering of sugar level (hunger) in the fluid matrix of the body cells of one group of persons in a society is a stress in the society as a whole. This holistic view of society as organism integrated from cell to nation depends on the assumption that society, as an organization of living matter, is definable as a network of intercommunication. Events on one subsystem level must affect other subsystems (cellular vis-à-vis institutional, personal vis-à-vis societal) at least as information; in this view, social organization exists to the degree that events in one subsystem are information to other subsystems.

There is one crucial difference between the principles of social organization and that of the individual person: a society's parts are very widely interchangeable, a person's only slightly so. The central nervous system cells, for example, perform many functions of coordinating information and executing adaptive action which other cells cannot do. A society, on the other hand, has a multiple-replacement capacity, such that many persons can perform the analogous information-coordination and executive functions on behalf of society-as-organism. Furthermore, that regularity of patterned behavior which we call culture depends relatively more on the ability of constituent units autonomously to perceive the system of which they are a part, to receive and transmit information, and to act in accordance with the necessities of the system, than on any all-embracing central administration which stimulates specialized parts to perform their function.

It is therefore functionally necessary for every person in society to maintain a mental image of the society and its culture, as well as of his own body and its behavioral regularities, in order to act in ways which reduce stress at all levels of the system. The person does, in fact, maintain such an image. This mental image I have called "the mazeway," since as a model of the cell-body-personality-nature-culture-society system or field, organized by the individual's own experience, it includes perceptions of both the maze of physical objects of the environment (internal and external, human and nonhuman) and also of the ways in which this maze can be manipulated by the self and others in order to minimize stress. The mazeway is nature, society, culture, personality, and body image, as seen by one person. . . .

We may now see more clearly what "revitalization movements" revitalize. Whenever an individual who is under chronic, physiologically measurable stress, receives repeated information which indicates that his mazeway does not lead to action which reduces the level of stress, he must choose between maintaining his present mazeway and tolerating the stress, or changing the mazeway in an attempt to reduce the stress. Changing the mazeway involves changing the total *Gestalt* of his image of self, society, and culture, of nature and body, and of ways of action. It may also be necessary to make changes in the "real" system in order to bring mazeway and "reality" into congruence. The effort to work a change in mazeway and "real" system together so as to permit more effective stress reduction is the effort at revitalization; and the collaboration of a number of persons in such an effort is called a revitalization movement.

The term revitalization movement thus denotes a very large class of phenomena. Other terms are employed in the existing literature to denote what I would call subclasses, distinguished by a miscellany of criteria. "Nativistic movements," for example, are revitalization movements characterized by strong emphasis on the elimination of alien persons, customs, values, and/or material from the mazeway (Linton, 1943). "Revivalistic" movements emphasize the institution of customs, values, and even aspects of nature which are thought to have been in the mazeway of previous generations but are not now present (Mooney, 1892–1893). "Cargo cults" emphasize the importation of alien values, customs, and material into the mazeway, these things being expected to arrive as a ship's cargo as for example in the Vailala Madness (Williams, 1923, 1934). "Vitalistic movements" emphasize the importation of alien elements into the mazeway but do not necessarily invoke ship and cargo as the mechanism. "Millenarian movements" emphasize mazeway transformation in an apocalyptic world transformation engineered by the supernatural. "Messianic movements" emphasize the participation of a divine savior in human flesh in the mazeway transformation (Wallis, 1918, 1943). These and parallel terms do not denote mutually exclusive categories, for a given revitalization movement may be nativistic, millenarian, messianic, and revivalistic all at once; and it may (in fact, usually does) display ambivalence with respect to nativistic, revivalistic, and importation themes.

Revitalization movements are evidently not unusual phenomena, but are recurrent features in human history. Probably few men have lived who have not been involved in an instance of the revitalization process. They are, furthermore, of profound historical importance. Both Christianity and Mohammedanism, and possibly Buddhism as well, originated in revitalization movements. Most denominational and sectarian groups and orders budded or split off after failure to revitalize a traditional institution. One can ask whether a large proportion of religious phenomena have not originated in personality transformation dreams or visions characteristic of the revitalization process. Myths, legends, and rituals may be relics, either of the manifest content of vision-dreams or of the doctrines and history of revival and import cults, the circumstances of whose origin have been distorted and forgotten, and whose connection with dream states is now ignored. Myths in particular have long been noted to possess a dream-like quality, and have been more or less speculatively-interpreted according to the principles of symptomatic dream interpretation. It is tempting to suggest that myths and, often, even legends, read like dreams because they *were* dreams when they were first told. It is tempting to argue further that culture heroes represent a condensation of the figures of the prophet and of the supernatural being of whom he dreamed.

In fact, it can be argued that all organized religions are relics of old revitalization movements, surviving in routinized form in stabilized cultures, and that religious phenomena per se originated (if it is permissible still in this day and age to talk about the "origins" of major elements of culture) in the revitalization process—i.e., in visions of a new way of life by individuals under extreme stress.

THE PROCESSUAL STRUCTURE

A basic methodological principle employed in this study is that of event-analysis (Wallace, 1953). This approach employs a method of controlled comparison for the study of processes involving longer or shorter diachronic sequences (vide Eggan, 1954, and Steward, 1953). It is postulated that events or happenings of various types have genotypical structures independent of local cultural differences; for example, that the sequence of happenings following a severe physical disaster in cities in Japan, the United States, and Germany will display a uniform pattern, colored but not obscured by local differences in culture. These types of events may be called behavioral units. Their uniformity is based on generic human attributes, both physical and psychological, but it requires extensive analytical and comparative study to elucidate the structure of any one. Revitalization movements constitute such a behavioral unit, and so also, on a lower level of abstraction, do various subtypes within the larger class, such as cargo and revival cults. We are therefore concerned with describing the generic structure of revitalization movements considered as a behavioral unit, and also of variation along the dimensions characteristic of the type.

The structure of the revitalization process, in cases where the full course is run, consists of five somewhat overlapping stages: (I) Steady State; (II) Period of Individual Stress; (III) Period of Cultural Distortion; (IV) Period of Revitalization (in which occur the functions of mazeway reformulation, communication, organization, adaptation, cultural transformation, and routinization), and finally, (V) New Steady State. These stages ar described briefly in the following sections.

I. *Steady State.* For the vast majority o the population, culturally recognized techniques for satisfying needs operate with such efficiency that chronic stress within the system varies within tolerable limits. Some severe but *still* tolerable stress may remain general in the population, and a fairly constant incidence of persons under, for them, intolerable stress may employ "deviant" techniques (e.g., psychotics). Gradual modification or even rapid substitution of techniques for satisfying some needs may occur without disturbing the steady state, as long as (1) the techniques for satisfying other needs are not seriously interfered with, and (2) abandonment of a given technique for reducing one need in favor of a more efficient technique does not leave other needs, which the first technique was also instrumental in satisfying, without any prospect of satisfaction.

II. *The Period of Increased Individual Stress.* Over a number of years, individual members of a population (which may be "primitive" or "civilized," either a whole society or a class, caste, religious, occupational, acculturational, or other definable social group) experience increasingly severe stress as a result of the decreasing efficiency of certain stress-reduction techniques. The culture may remain essentially unchanged or it may undergo considerable changes, but in either case there is continuous diminution in its efficiency in satisfying needs. The agencies responsible for interference with the efficiency of a cultural system are various: climatic, floral and faunal change; military defeat; political subordination; extreme pressure toward acculturation resulting in internal cultural conflict; economic distress; epidemics; and so on. The situation is often, but not necessarily, one of acculturation, and the acculturating agents may or may not be representatives of Western European cultures. While the individual can tolerate a moderate degree of increased stress and still maintain the habitual way of behavior, a point is reached at which some alternative way must be considered. Initial consideration of a substitute way is likely, however, to increase stress because it arouses anxiety over the possibility that the substitute way will be even less effective than the original, and that it may also actively interfere with the execution of other ways. In other words, it poses the threat of mazeway disintegration. Furthermore, admission that a major technique is worthless is extremely threatening because it implies that the whole mazeway system may be inadequate.

III. *The Period of Cultural Distortion.* The prolonged experience of stress, produced by failure of need satisfaction techniques and by anxiety over the prospect of changing behavior patterns, is responded to differently by different people. Rigid persons apparently prefer to tolerate high levels of chronic stress rather than make systematic adaptive changes in the mazeway. More flexible persons try out various limited mazeway changes in their personal lives, attempting to reduce stress by addition or substitution of mazeway elements with more or less concern for the *Gestalt* of the system. Some persons turn to psychodynamically regressive innovations; the regressive response empirically exhibits itself in increasing incidences of such things as alcoholism, extreme passivity and indolence, the development of highly ambivalent dependency relationships, intragroup violence, disregard of kinship and sexual mores, irresponsibility in public officials, states of depression and self-reproach, and probably a variety of psychosomatic and neurotic disorders. Some of these regressive action systems become, in effect, new cultural patterns.

In this phase, the culture is internally distorted; the elements are not harmoniously related but are mutually inconsistent and interfering. For this reason alone, stress continues to rise. "Regressive" behavior, as defined by the society, will arouse considerable guilt and hence increase stress level or at least maintain it at a high point; and the general process of piecemeal cultural substitution will multiply situations of mutual conflict and misunderstanding, which in turn increase stress-level again.

Finally, as the inadequacy of existing ways of acting to reduce stress becomes more and more evident, and as the internal incongruities of the mazeway are perceived, symptoms of anxiety over the loss of a meaningful way of life also become evident: disillusionment with the mazeway, and apathy toward problems of adaptation, set in.

IV. *The Period of Revitalization.* This process of deterioration can, if not checked, lead to the death of the society. Population may fall even to the point of extinction as a result of increasing death rates and decreasing birth rates; the society may be defeated in war, invaded, its population dispersed and its customs suppressed; factional disputes may nibble away areas and segments of the population. But these dire events are not infrequently forestalled, or at least postponed, by a revitalization movement. Many such movements are religious in character, and such religious revitalization movements must perform at least six major tasks.

1. *Mazeway Reformulation.* Whether the movement is religious or secular, the reformulation of the mazeway generally seems to depend on a restructuring of elements and subsystems which have already attained currency in the society and may even be in use, and which are known to the person who is to become the prophet or leader. The occasion of their combination in a form which constitutes an internally consistent structure, and of their acceptance by the prophet as a guide to action, is abrupt and dramatic, usually occurring as a moment of insight, a brief period of realization of relationships and opportunities. These moments are often called inspiration or revelation. The reformulation also seems normally to occur in its initial form in the mind of a single person rather than to grow directly out of group deliberations.

With a few exceptions, every religious revitalization movement with which I am acquainted has been originally conceived in one or several hallucinatory visions by a single individual. A supernatural being appears to the prophet-to-be, explains his own and his society's troubles as being entirely or partly a result of the violation of certain rules, and promises individual and social revitalization if the injunctions are followed and the rituals practiced, but personal and social catastrophe if they are not. These dreams express: (1) the dreamer's wish for a satisfying parental figure (the supernatural, guardian-spirit content), (2) world-destruction fantasies (the apocalyptic, millennial content), (3) feelings of guilt and anxiety (the moral content), and (4) longings for the establishment of an ideal state of stable and satisfying human and supernatural relations (the restitution fantasy or Utopian content). In a sense, such a dream also functions almost as a funeral ritual: the "dead" way of life is recognized as dead; interest shifts to a god, the community, and a new way. A new mazeway *Gestalt* is presented, with more or less innovation in details of content. The prophet feels a need to tell others of his experience, and may have definite feelings of missionary or messianic obligation. Generally he shows evidence of a radical inner change in personality soon after the vision experience: a remission of old and chronic physical complaints, a more active and purposeful way of life, greater confidence in interpersonal relations, the dropping of deep-seated habits like alcoholism. Hence we may call these visions "personality transformation dreams."

. . .

2. *Communication.* The dreamer undertakes to preach his revelations to people, in an evangelistic or messianic spirit; he becomes a prophet. The doctrinal and behavioral injunctions which he preaches carry two fundamental motifs; that the convert will come under the care and protection of certain supernatural beings; and that both he and his society will benefit materially from an identification with some definable new cultural system (whether a revived culture or a cargo culture, or a syncretism of both, as is usually the case). The preaching may take many forms (e.g., mass exhortation vs. quiet individual persuasion) and may be directed at various sorts of audiences (e.g., the elite vs. the down-trodden). As he gathers disciples, these assume much of the responsibility for communicating the "good word," and communication remains one of the primary activities of the movement during later phases of organization.

3. *Organization.* Converts are made by the prophet. Some undergo hysterical seizures induced by suggestion in a crowd situation; some experience an ecstatic vision in private circumstances; some are convinced by more or less rational arguments, some by considerations of expediency and opportunity. A small clique of special disciples (often including a few already influential men) clusters about the prophet and an embryonic campaign organization develops with three orders of personnel: the prophet; the disciples; and the followers. Frequently the action program from here on is effectively administered in large part by a political rather than a religious leadership. Like the prophet, many of the converts undergo a revitalizing personality transformation.

Max Weber's concept of "charismatic leadership" well describes the type of leader-follower relationship characteristic of revitalization movement organizations (1947). The fundamental element of the vision, as I have indicated above, is the entrance of the visionary into an intense relationship with a supernatural being. This relationship, furthermore, is one in which the prophet accepts the leadership, succor, and dominance of the supernatural. Many followers of a prophet, especially the disciples, also have ecstatic revelatory experiences; but they and all sincere followers who have not had a personal revelation also enter into a parallel relationship to the prophet: as God is to the prophet, so (almost) is the prophet to his followers. The relationship of the follower to the prophet is in all probability determined by the displacement of transference dependency wishes onto his image; he is regarded as an uncanny person, of unquestionable authority in one or more spheres of leadership, sanctioned by the supernatural. Max Weber denotes this quality of uncanny authority and moral ascendency in a leader as charisma. Followers defer to the charismatic leader not because of his status in an existing authority structure but because of a fascinating personal "power," often ascribed to supernatural sources and validated in successful performance, akin to the "mana" or "orenda" of ethnological literature. The charismatic leader thus is not merely permitted but expected to phrase his call for adherents as a demand to perform a duty to a power higher than human. Weber correctly points out that the "routinization" of charisma is a critical issue in movement organization, since unless this "power" is distributed to other personnel in a stable institutional structure, the movement itself is liable to die with the death or failure of individual prophet, king, or war lord.

. . .

4. *Adaptation.* The movement is a revolutionary organization and almost inevitably will encounter some resistance. Resistance may in some cases be slight and fleeting but more commonly is determined and resourceful, and is held either by a powerful faction within the society or by agents of a dominant foreign society. The movement may therefore have to use various strategies of adaptation: doctrinal modification; political and diplomatic maneuver; and force. These strategies are not mutually exclusive nor, once chosen, are they necessarily maintained through the life of the movement. In most instances the original doctrine is continuously modifed by the prophet, who responds to various criticisms and affirmations by adding to, emphasizing, playing down, and eliminating selected elements of the original visions. This reworking makes the new doctrine

more acceptable to special interest groups, may give it a better "fit" to the population's cultural and personality patterns, and may take account of the changes occurring in the general milieu. In instances where organized hostility to the movement develops, a crystallization of counter-hostility against unbelievers frequently occurs, and emphasis shifts from cultivation of the ideal to combat against the unbeliever.

5. *Cultural Transformation.* As the whole or a controlling portion of the population comes to accept the new religion with its various injunctions, a noticeable social revitalization occurs, signalized by the reduction of the personal deterioration symptoms of individuals, by extensive cultural changes, and by an enthusiastic embarkation on some organized program of group action. This group program may, however, be more or less realistic and more or less adaptive: some programs are literally suicidal; others represent well conceived and successful projects of further social, political, or economic reform; some fail, not through any deficiency in conception and execution, but because circumstances made defeat inevitable.

6. *Routinization.* If the group action program in nonritual spheres is effective in reducing stress-generating situations, it becomes established as normal in various economic, social, and political institutions and customs. Rarely does the movement organization assert or maintain a totalitarian control over all aspects of the transformed culture; more usually, once the desired transformation has occurred, the organization contracts and maintains responsibility only for the preservation of doctrine and the performance of ritual (i.e., it becomes a church)....

V. *The New Steady State.* Once cultural transformation has been accomplished and the new cultural system has proved itself viable, and once the movement organization has solved its problems of routinization, a new steady state may be said to exist. The culture of this state will probably be different in pattern, organization or *Gestalt*, as well as in traits, from the earlier steady state; it will be different from that of the period of cultural distortion.

VARIETIES AND DIMENSIONS OF VARIATION

I will discuss four of the many possible variations: the choice of identification; the choice of secular and religious means; nativism; and the success-failure continuum.

1. *Choice of Identification.* Three varieties have been distinguished already on the basis of differences in choice of identification: movements which profess to *revive* a traditional culture now fallen into desuetude; movements which profess to *import* a foreign cultural system; and movements which profess neither revival nor importation, but conceive that the desired cultural endstate, which has never been enjoyed by ancestors or foreigners, will be realized for the first time in a future *Utopia.* The Ghost Dance, the Xosa Revival, and the Boxer Rebellion are examples of professedly revivalistic movements; the Vailala Madness (and other cargo cults) and the Taiping Rebellion are examples of professedly importation movements. Some formulations like Ikhnaton's monotheistic cult in old Egypt and many Utopian programs, deny any substantial debt to the past or to the foreigner, but conceive their ideology to be something new under the sun, and its culture to belong to the future.

. . .

Culture areas seem to have characteristic ways of handling the identification problem. The cargo fantasy, although it can be found outside the Melanesian area, seems to be particularly at home there; South American Indian prophets frequently preached of a migration to a heaven-on-earth free of Spaniards and other evils, but the promised-land fantasy is known elsewhere; North American Indian prophets most commonly emphasized the revival of the old culture by ritual and moral purification, but pure revival ideas exist in other regions too. Structural "necessity" or situational factors associated with culture area may be responsible. The contrast between native-white relationships in North America (a "revival" area) and Melanesia (an "importation" area) may be associated with the fact that American Indians north of Mexico were never enslaved on a large scale, forced to work on plantations, or levied for labor in lieu of taxes, whereas Melanesians were often subjected to more direct coercion by foreign police power. The Melanesian response has been an identification with the aggressor (vide Bettelheim, 1947). On the other hand, the American Indians have been less dominated as individuals by whites, even under defeat and injustice. Their response to this different situation has by and large been an identification with a happier past. This would suggest that an important variable in choice of identification is the degree of domination exerted by a foreign society, and that import-oriented revitalization movements will not develop until an extremely high degree of domination is reached.

2. *The Choice of Secular and Religious Means.* There are two variables involved here: the amount of secular action which takes place in a movement, and the amount of religious action. Secular action is here defined as the manipulation of human relationships; religious action as the manipulation of relationships between human and supernatural beings. No revitalization movement can, by definition, be truly nonsecular, but some can be relatively less religious than others, and movements can change in emphasis depending on changing circumstances. There is a tendency, which is implicit in the earlier discussion of stages, for movements to become more political in emphasis, and to act through secular rather than religious institutions, as problems of organization, adaptation, and routinization become more pressing. The Taiping Rebellion, for instance, began as religiously-preoccupied movements; opposition by the Manchu dynasty and by foreign powers forced it to become more and more political and military in orientation.

A few "purely" political movements like the Hebertist faction during the French Revolution, and the Russian communist movement and its derivatives, have been officially atheistic, but the quality of doctrine and of leader-follower relationships is so similar, at least on superficial inspection, to religious doctrine and human-supernatural relations, that one wonders whether it is not a distinction without a difference. Communist movements are commonly asserted to have the quality of religious movements, despite their failure to appeal to a supernatural community, and such things as the development of a Marxist gospel with elaborate exegesis, the embalming of Lenin, and the concern with conversion, confession, and moral purity (as defined by the movement) have the earmarks of religion. The Communist Revolution of 1917 in Russia was almost typical in structure of religious revitalization movements: there was a very sick society, prophets appealed to a revered authority (Marx), apocalyptic and Utopian fantasies were preached, and missionary fervor animated the leaders. Furthermore, many social and political reform movements, while not atheistic, act through secular rather than religious media and invoke religious sanction only in a perfunctory way. I do not wish to elaborate the discussion at this time, however, beyond the point of suggesting again that the obvious distinctions between religious and secular movements may conceal fundamental similarities of sociocultural process and of psychodynamics, and that while all secular prophets have not had personality transformation visions, some probably have, and others have had a similar experience in ideological conversion.

Human affairs around the world seem more and more commonly to be decided without reference to supernatural powers. It is an interesting question whether mankind can profitably dispense with the essential element of the religious revitalization process before reaching a Utopia without stress or strain. While religious movements may involve crude and powerful emotions and irrational fantasies of interaction with nonexistent beings, and can occasionally lead to unfortunate practical consequences in human relations, the same fantasies and emotions could lead to even more unfortunate practical consequences for world peace and human welfare when directed toward people improperly perceived and toward organs of political action and cultural ideologies. The answer would seem to be that as fewer and fewer men make use of the religious displacement process, there will have to be a corresponding reduction of the incidence and severity of transference neuroses, or human relationships will be increasingly contaminated by character disorders, neurotic acting out, and paranoid deification of political leaders and ideologies.

3. *Nativism.* Because a major part of the program of many revitalization movements has been to expel the persons or customs of foreign invaders or overlords, they have been widely called "nativistic movements." However, the amount of nativistic activity in movements is variable. Some movements—the cargo cults, for instance—are antinativistic from a cultural standpoint but nativistic from a personnel standpoint. Handsome Lake was only mildly nativistic; he sought for an accommodation of cultures and personalities rather than expulsion, and favored entry of certain types of white persons and culture-content. Still, many of the classic revivalistic movements have been vigorously nativistic, in the ambivalent way discussed earlier. Thus nativism is a dimension of variation rather than an elemental property of revitalization movements.

A further complication is introduced by the fact that the nativistic component of a revitalization movement not uncommonly is very low at the time of conception, but increases sharply after the movement enters the adaptation stage. Initial doctrinal formulations emphasize love, co-operation, understanding, and the prophet and his disciples expect the powers-that-be to be reasonable and accepting. When these powers interfere with the movement, the response is apt to take the form of an increased nativistic component in the doctrine. Here again, situational factors are important for an understanding of the course and character of the movement.

4. *Success and Failure.* The outline of stages as given earlier is properly applicable to a revitalization movement which is completely successful. Many movements are abortive; their progress is arrested at some intermediate point. This raises a taxonomic question: how many stages should the movement achieve in order to qualify for inclusion in the category? Logically, as long as the original conception is a doctrine of revitalization by culture change, there should be no requisite number of stages. Practically, we have selected only movements which passed the first three stages (conception, communication, and organization) and entered the fourth (adaptation). This means that the bulk of our information on success and failure will deal with circumstances of relatively late adaptation, rather than with such matters as initial blockage of communication and interference with organization.

Two major but not unrelated variables seem to be very important in determining the fate of any given movement: the relative "realism" of the doctrine; and the amount of force exerted against the organization by its opponents. "Realism" is a difficult concept to define without invoking the concept of success or failure, and unless it can be so defined, is of no use as a variable explanatory of success or failure. Nor can one use the criterion of conventionality of perception, since revitalization movements are by definition unconventional. While a great deal of doctrine in every movement (and, indeed, in every person's mazeway) is extremely unrealistic in that predictions of events made on the basis of its assumptions will prove to be more or less in error, there is only one sphere of behavior in which such error is fatal to the success of a revitalization movement: prediction of the outcome of conflict situations. If the organization cannot predict successfully the consequences of its own moves and of its opponents' moves in a power struggle, its demise is very likely. If, on the other hand, it is canny about conflict, or if the amount of resistance is low, it can be extremely "unrealistic" and extremely unconventional in other matters without running much risk of early collapse. In other words, probability of failure would seem to be negatively correlated with degree of realism in conflict situations, and directly correlated with amount of resistance. Where conflict-realism is high and resistance is low, the movement is bound to achieve the phase of routinization. Whether its culture will be viable for long beyond this point, however, will depend on whether its mazeway formulations lead to actions which maintain a low level of stress.

SUMMARY

This programmatic paper outlines the concepts, assumptions, and initial findings of a comparative study of religious revitalization movements. Revitalization movements are defined as deliberate, conscious, organized efforts by members of a society to create a more satisfying culture. The revitalization movement as a general type of event occurs under two conditions: high stress for individual members of the society, and disillusionment with a distorted cultural *Gestalt*. The movement follows a series of functional stages: mazeway reformulation, communication, organization, adaptation, cultural transformation, and routinization. Movements vary along several dimensions, of which choice of identification, relative degree of religious and secular emphasis, nativism, and success or failure are discussed here. The movement is usually conceived in a prophet's revelatory visions, which provide for him a satisfying relationship to the supernatural and outline a new way of life under divine sanction. Followers achieve similar satisfaction of dependency needs in the charismatic relationship. It is suggested that the historical origin of a great proportion of religious phenomena has been in revitalization movements.

W. W. Hill

THE NAVAHO INDIANS AND THE GHOST DANCE OF 1890

Among the many nativistic movements that have been developed in the wake of the impact of white American culture upon the native Indian cultures of the United States, two are of special interest: the Ghost Dance and the Peyote Cult. The Ghost Dance was a classic example of Linton's magical-revivalistic type of movement and appeared in two waves, both originating among the Northern Paiute Indians in Nevada. The first Ghost Dance started in 1870 and spread mainly to Northern California; the second started in 1890 and spread mainly eastward to the Plains tribes. It was believed that through the intervention of the Great Spirit or his emissary, the earth would be transformed into a paradise for both the living and the resurrected dead. In anticipation of this golden age, believers had to return to the aboriginal form of life. The millennium was to be established through divine agency; believers needed only watch and pray. The Peyote Cult, on the other hand, represented a more passive movement and incorporated many Christian elements and symbols (see Slotkin, Chapter Five).

In an article entitled "Acculturation and Messianic Movements" (1941) Bernard Barber suggested that the differential spread of the 1870 and 1890 Ghost Dance movements could be accounted for by the relative amounts of deprivation in the two areas. He then described the Peyote Cult as an alternative response to deprivation which, because it was essentially nonviolent and nonthreatening to white American culture, could spread and survive in areas where the Ghost Dance was forcibly exterminated. When the Ghost Dance did not produce the hoped-for results, or was forcibly stamped out by Indian agents and soldiers, the same tribes began to accept the Peyote Cult, which crystallized around passive acceptance and resignation in the face of continuing deprivation. In response to Barber's thesis, W. W. Hill shows convincingly in the following paper that although Barber's general hypothesis may be sound, special cultural patterns in a particular tribe can be crucial in leading a people to reject a movement that is embraced by neighboring tribes. Using the Navaho as a case in point, Hill demonstrates that fear of the dead and ghosts, which is an underlying and pervasive pattern in Navaho culture, was the critical factor in their rejection of the Ghost Dance. As Hill expresses it, "The Navaho were frightened out of their wits for fear the tenets of the movement were true"—that is, that the ghosts would come back. This article clearly shows that deprivation theory by itself cannot explain the occurrence of such movements.

The outstanding account of the Ghost Dance is found in James Mooney's "The Ghost-Dance Religion" (1896). Students might also want to consult W. LaBarre, *The Ghost Dance: The Origins of Religion* (1970).

Reprinted from *American Anthropologist*, 46 (1944), 523–527 by permission of the American Anthropological Association.

For years it has been the custom for most anthropologists to revert to economic determinism for an explanation of messianic phenomena. Recently, however, Bernard Barber in his paper "Acculturation and Messianic Movements" called our attention to approaches other than economic, i.e., social, and during the past year Ralph Linton in his article "Nativistic Movements" has outlined a whole new field for researches in the dynamics associated with revivalistic and perpetuative aspects of cultures. Stimulated by these two works I examined my field material on the Ghost Dance of 1890 among the Navaho and, because the data therein varied so from accounts of other tribes, decided to present it for publication.

To those acquainted with Navaho Indians

any mention of their association with the Ghost Dance of 1890 must seem anomalous. While strictly speaking no direct participation did occur, this messianic development reached the Navaho and the impact registered profoundly on the minds of the individuals of the period. According to Mooney, news of the movement was conveyed to the Navaho via the Paiute. This was confirmed by some Navaho. However, others assigned it to the Southern Ute, while still others were unable to give any provenience. Most, however, agreed that while it was known throughout the reservation, the focal point for the dissemination of the concepts was in the Shiprock, Nava [Newcomb] Tohatchi region, i.e., northwest New Mexico, a factor which lends weight to their probable diffusion from the Southern Ute.

Most of the familiar traits of the Ghost Dance complex, the resurrection of the dead, the removal of the whites, the reestablishment of the old order of life, and survival through compulsory belief and participation in the movement, were known to the Navaho. The most widespread and significant element was the reported return of the dead. This was variously expressed. Some informants simply state that the dead or ghosts were said to be returning. Elaboration on this theme included the statements that those who had died during the incarceration at Fort Sumner, and those who had been killed by enemies, were coming back, and that the headmen were leading the ghosts back to the reservation.

Other phases of the doctrine were also subject to individual elaboration. The vehicle for white elimination varied in its practical methods, some holding that they were to be exterminated, others that they would leave the Navaho area and return to their former habitat. It was thought that the arrival of the millennium would bring with it the return of the old order, social and religious, plentiful game, ample rainfall, and corn immune from disease. Those who believed in and participated in the movement were to live; those who were skeptical were to die.

It is clear that the Navaho were thoroughly cognizant of all the essential elements of the Ghost Dance of 1890. It has also been established that the movement failed to flourish or find acceptance. We have the testimony of informants alive during this period, the statement of Washington Matthews to Mooney, and Barber's conclusions to this effect. The reasons for this rejection pose some interesting problems in dynamics and configuration.

The question of why the Navaho failed to embrace a doctrine found palatable by so many Indian peoples of North America represents a situation probably unique in the history of messianic movements. Barber has suggested that the rejection was due to a lack of social and spiritual "deprivation." This corresponds to an idea expressed many years ago by Wissler, in connection with the spread of the Ghost Dance in the Plains, and termed by him the occurrence of a cultural vacuum. I should like to present, however, an alternative possibility for the rejection of the 1890 Ghost Dance by the Navaho other than Barber's "life was integrated around a stable culture pattern."

It appears that the lack of acceptance resulted from the functioning of phases of Navaho culture falling into categories described by Kluckhohn as belonging to a covert pattern or configuration. The appended accounts show Navaho attitudes toward the Ghost Dance to have been ones of extreme ambivalence. It is apparent that the acceptance or rejection, per se, on the basis of the benefits which the movement promised was absent from the minds of informants. The question of "life integrated around a stable culture pattern" (if such existed in 1890, it certainly did not in 1870 when according to informants a similar opportunity was rejected) was not a consideration in the decisions. In fact, the idea of rejection or acceptance was of minimum importance; the Navaho interest in the movement was a manifestation of anxiety as to whether or not the reports which reached them were true.

An underlying fear appears even in accounts of the most skeptical informants. It is expressed, according to Navaho pattern, in references to abnormal weather conditions which prevailed during the period, suspicion of witchcraft in connection with the purveyors of the movement, and post-factum rationalizations of dire consequences both to individuals and property. All these were secondary expressions. The real anxiety concern was with the one element which was the core of the movement, i.e., the return of the dead.

Had the "economic" or "social integration" factors been compulsive, a selective element could have been expected to operate; the Navaho might gladly have embraced parts of the complex—the restoration of the old life and the disappearance of the whites—while rejecting the tidings that the dead were to return. However, the compelling element for them was clearly their fear of the dead; so much so that all other tenets were infected by it, hence suspect and to be rejected.

For the Navaho with his almost psychotic

fear of death, the dead, and all connected with them, no greater cataclysm than the return of the departed or ghosts could be envisaged. In short, the Navaho were frightened out of their wits for fear the tenets of the movement were true. Thus, a covert pattern or configuration, deep-seated in the unconscious psychology of that people, acted as a barrier to the diffusion of a complex embraced by most of the tribes in western United States.

APPENDIX

The late Fat One's Son, Tohatchi, N.M.: "The ignorant Navaho like myself were saying at this time, 'Look over toward Nava. [Nava (Newcomb) is north of Tohatchi. The ghosts are thought to reside in the north.] They [ghosts] are there already at Nava and will soon appear on the high ridges between Nava and Cornfields.' Then they would mention the names of the different headmen who had died and who were leading the ghosts back. Among them they mentioned my own father. The majority of the people believed in this. Those who did not believe, would ask, 'What is the purpose of these ghosts coming back?' The believers would say, 'They are just coming back to live with us and to tell us of the things in the other world.' Some of the people were singing to prevent the ghosts from coming back; they were afraid of them. This lasted one whole summer but gradually died out because no ghosts appeared and because the unbelievers ridiculed the believers. They tried to find the source of this rumor but they could not find where it started. They decided that some woman must have started it." The informant said that he does not know how far the Ghost Dance spread but believes that it was known throughout the reservation. The ghosts were to bring with them much rain; there were to be quantities of game in the country again; they were to bring corn which was immune from all diseases; all the old customs were to be reinstated; everything was to be as it was in the beginning because these ghosts knew conditions on both sides [i.e., in life and death] and they were to combine things from both sides and make things perfect. Some of the men even told people that they should be thankful that their relatives were returning. "Old Manuelito, of Fort Sumner time, was the chief unbeliever. He said, 'It is our belief that if ghosts appear it is bad luck. If they do appear we will have to get rid of them.' I was living close to Manuelito so I did not believe in their return, but everyone was talking so strongly about it it was hard not to believe. A woman dreamed that in the future the ghosts would return to the land of the living. That seems to have been the start of it. Manuelito told all the leading men to try and discourage this ghost business. He said, 'We know that ghosts are bad.' He tried to get the people to think of beneficial things, like agriculture and sheep raising. He said, 'Why ask the ghosts to come back; some day you will get a chance to go there.' This ghost dance never caused any harm but this witch business did. Right after [the captivity at] Fort Sumner the Navaho were very poor."

Grey Hair, White Cone, Ariz.: "The people who were saying this were a kind of prophet people. After they had said this thing a number of girls and boys around eighteen years of age died." The informant says that he has heard this prediction of the return of the dead three times during his life. "The first time was when I was about twelve years old [1870]. I heard it again when I was about thirty years old [1890]. The last time I heard it was about fifteen years ago [about 1918]. These prophet men were thinking bad. They must have been thinking that all the Navaho were going to die. A few years after the first time I heard this [1870] there was an epidemic of measles and a great many people died. A few years after the second time [1890] an epidemic of mumps killed a great number of people. Nothing has happened as yet since the last prophecy but I am waiting to see what will."

Slim Curley, Crystal, Ariz.: "I was living at Lukachukai. I was a young man at the time. The days were just hazy and the sun was reddish. Everything looked peculiar. People began to say that the Utes and Paiutes were talking about the ghosts coming. Many of the people in the country did not believe this. You could tell because they ridiculed the idea. However, there were a number who did believe it. I remember at a gathering for gambling one night there was a man who did not believe it. This man asked another for some money, saying, 'I hear that the ghosts are coming back to this country. No doubt my mother is in the crowd and you can have intercourse with her when she returns.' Those who believed said, 'The Utes are sending word ahead that the ghosts are coming.' In the last month Chi Dodge was giving a group of medicine men a talking to. In the course of the talk he said, 'You must not start all these rumors.' He said, 'Look what happened after Fort Sumner [days]; someone started this rumor that all the white men were to be exterminated and then later this business about the ghosts coming back was started.' One old man wanted to take a party to the west to visit Changing Woman and find out what this return of the ghosts meant."

Mr. Headman, Head Springs, Ariz.: "There were Holy Men among the Navaho who told the old men and women that the dead were coming back. However, the old men and women did not believe it. They said, 'No one is going to come back once they are dead. If they come back it will mean that they will bring back all kinds of sickness. Also, if they come back there will be no rains and no corn.' They told the prophets that they should not say that the dead were coming back. The prophets said, 'When the ghosts come back all the whites . . .' —it hurts an old man like me to say these kind of words [i.e., to talk about ghosts]."

Albert G. Sandoval, Lukachukai, Ariz.: "It was known all over the reservation but most of the people did not believe it. They never danced. The Gods have left the country and have visited the people for the last time. The dead do not come back. In 1920 a preacher on the San Juan predicted a flood. The people were frightened and the majority of them left for the mountains. There was a hell of a mess. Most of the Indians took all their possessions with them. The knowledge [of the Ghost Dance] does not seem to have come from any particular source. Everyone knew of it but it just seems to have been passed along."

Pete Price, Fort Defiance, Ariz.: "The wind and the weather were very unusual at that time. Then word came that the dead were coming back to the earth. However, the majority of the people did not take this very seriously. They used to joke about it."

Mr. Left-Handed, Crown Point, N.M.: "I heard that all the Navaho who had died at Fort Sumner and all those who had been killed by enemies were coming back to life. The Navaho were all to go back where they had been living before and all the whites would have to go back to their own country. This came from around Tohatchi. There was no dance connected with the coming of the ghosts. As a rule it was not believed by the majority. Most of the people thought that this was started by the witches."

The Late Little Smith's Son, Crown Point, N.M.: "When we first heard of it I was living along Tohatchi flat. We heard that the ghosts were moving in close to where we were. Some of the young scouts told me that my father was coming back and that I had better go over and meet him. They said that all those who did not believe that the ghosts were coming back were going to die; the rest of the people would live on. This ghost business started up near Shiprock. A man there started it."

Glynn Cochrane

BIG MEN AND CARGO CULTS

In the following selection, Glynn Cochrane presents a sophisticated application of deprivation theory to "cargo cults"—nativistic movements found in the Melanesian islands of the South Pacific. Despite a wide geographical and temporal distribution throughout the area, these movements manifest many similarities. "Prophets" play a fundamental role in the inception and crystallization of the cults. Through dreams or revelations they establish contact with the supernatural—sometimes powers of the traditional religion, or Christianity, or a combination of the two—foretelling the return of the ancestors and the coming of "cargo" in the form of European goods. In anticipation of cargo, daily activities may cease, valuable pigs be slaughtered, fields and gardens left to ruin. A new code of morals often may be preached, ostensibly to strengthen community life so that the spirits will find the people worthy of cargo. When cargo fails to appear, the people blame the Europeans who are withholding it, or more frequently, their own inadequacy in doubting the prophet's word. Cochrane bases his analysis on three cults.

Reprinted in slightly abridged form from Glynn Cochrane, *Big Men and Cargo Cults*, Chapter 10

The 1919 movement refers to the "Vailala Madness" which occurred in southern New Guinea on the Gulf of Papua coast. Both the 1944 "Marching Rule" movement and the 1963 "Doliasi 'Custom' " movement occurred in the Solomon Islands, east of New Guinea. While the 1963 movement did not involve a specific cargo belief, it is of interest because it originated in the "deprived" bush tribes of Malaita, one of the six major islands of the Solomons, and was directed against the more Europeanized coastal people rather than the Europeans themselves.

Cochrane's analysis focuses on two key Melanesian concepts, those of "big man" and "rubbish man." "Big men" are the traditional leaders of Melanesian society. Their power stems from their own personal renown as feast-givers, their prowess in warfare, and their special ritual knowledge rather than from an institutionalized or inherited political authority. A "big man" is at once the leader, protector, and provider of his faction, and he maintains his exceptional social status only as long as he continues adequately to fulfill these functions. At the other end of the social scale is the "rubbish man"—lazy, indolent individuals who possess no magical, ritual, economic, or political power. A sense of shame—of no longer belonging to the community—often accompanies the downward slide to the status of "rubbish man." Cochrane hypothesizes that the somewhat abrupt appearance of Europeans in Melanesia resulted in the degradation of indigenous measures of status and prestige. Europeans possessed extraordinary organizational, economic, political, and ritual powers and were exceptional warriors as well. In short, they fulfilled all the qualifications of "big men" in the eyes of the Melanesians, yet they refused to acknowledge the responsibilities which that power traditionally had implied. They did not treat the Melanesians as men; they did not eat with them, enter into reciprocal relationships, or observe traditional customs. To be Melanesian suddenly meant to be a "rubbish man," an intolerable situation in which all the routes to success—warfare, ritual knowledge, and sorcery—were preempted by Europeans. Cargo movements, then, are spontaneous reactions against status deprivation, and cargo, rather than expressing the Melanesian's grasping materialism, is a unitary symbol of status and power; it represents a symbolic means of persuading the Europeans to recognize Melanesian concepts of manhood and worth. Interested readers should consult Cochrane's book, *Big Men and Cargo Cults* (1970), for substantiation of the author's theory. For other explanations of cargo cults, see I. C. Jarvie, "Theories of Cargo Cults: A Critical Analysis" (1963), and Peter Worsley's book, *The Trumpet Shall Sound* (1968). For an in-depth study of one cargo cult, see *Road Belong Cargo* (1964) by Peter Lawrence.

Some of the explanations that have been given for "cargo cults" have been broadly based:

It seems to me fairly obvious to assume that cargo cults tend to arise as a resultant of several factors in operation together; a markedly uneven relation between a system of wants and the means of their satisfaction; a very limited technical knowledge of how to improve conditions; specific blocks or barriers to that improvement by poverty of natural resources or opposed political interests. What constitutes a cult is a systematized series of operations to secure the means of satisfaction by non-technical methods. Yet the implications of technical methods may, as I have shown, approach cult behaviour if they are used more to give immaterial satisfaction.[1]

This kind of theory does not really tell us very much about "cargo cults." It does not indicate that there is anything distinctive about "cargo cults" or the societies in which these movements have arisen which could serve to distinguish them from political and economic-based movements which have arisen in underdeveloped territories in other parts of the world.

[1] R. Firth 1967:158.

The attempt here must simply be to provide an explanation which can satisfy curiosity. An explanation which can attempt to show that the "cargo" movements have been distinctive because Melanesian and Papuan cultural and belief systems have been unique. This explanation should be involved with two things: a factual explanation of the various movements which can be arrived at deductively, and a theoretical explanation which can contain the facts. A factual account should, considered in its entirety, suggest the theory. The theory should be no more than a minimum intellectual framework which contains, but does not "explain," the facts.

FACTUAL EXPLANATION

The origins of the movements examined go back to the time when the Melanesians and Papuans saw their first white men. Europeans posed a problem—who were they, were they spirits or men? As time went by the natives learnt that the Europeans were men. Within terms of their existing experience the Europeans were categorized by the natives as "big men," because of the attributes they possessed, and the ways in which they acted.

These European "big men" seem to have differed in two respects from the traditional "big men." Their actions and attributes gave them much more power and status than the traditional "big men," but they refused to assume the traditional responsibilities that a "big man" had towards his people. Europeans did not treat the natives as men: they did not eat with them or enter into reciprocal relationships, they did not uphold all the traditional customs, and they made far greater demands on the time of the people than the traditional "big men" had done. In every field of activity where the natives and the white men met the Europeans were superior. Natives were unable to establish their manhood in relationships with Europeans.

European contact completely destroyed the power and status of the traditional "big man." "Big men" had been symbols of their society's cultural integrity. They had guarded and sustained the indigenous culture and had, so to speak, carried it on their shoulders. When they went there was little left. Ordinary men lost the ability to establish their manhood in the organizational framework that the "big men" had provided. The natives were unable to establish their manhood in the organizational framework provided by the Europeans. They were also unable to escape the Europeans' influence.

These factors seem to have been responsible for the origin of the movements, but what factors were responsible for actually "triggering off" the movements? In 1919 the administration's agricultural experiments in the Gulf of Papua had increased European intervention in the lives of the Elema. In 1944 European administrative pressure on Malaita people increased as a result of the war. These movements appear to have been precipitated by a sudden increase in European contact.

The origin of the 1963 movement had its roots in the actions of the Solomon Islanders. The effect of the coastal people's attitude to the bush people was the same as the effect that Europeans had had in 1919 and 1944. In 1963 the movement was the result of a long process of maturation.

Areas which were affected by the movements had experienced a greater degree of European contact than other areas where the movements did not break out. For example, movements did not break out in Santa Cruz or on Bougainville, where there had been little contact between the Melanesians and the Europeans. Movements also did not affect areas which had been exposed to a very great deal of European contact. There was no cargo movement on Gela or in the Russell Islands in the Solomons.

It appears that European contact has only been germane to the problem of explaining why the movements broke out "here" instead of "there," when contact was with island societies with a particular structure and belief system. Where the indigenous authoritarian and organizational system had not had "big men," then the Europeans may not have been categorized in this way.

Where this happened the Europeans did not appear to be more powerful versions of the traditional leaders. This meant that there was no conflict between the actions and attributes of the Europeans and the actions and attributes of the traditional leaders. In turn the indigenous concepts of manhood continued to have validity since the standards and methods for achieving manhood remained traditional. In this sense movements did not break out in the towns because native urban social structure and values were Europeanized—they did not conflict with traditional values and ideas on social organization.

However, in some areas there was also no conflict because the European/"big men" treated the natives as if they were men. In this instance the European was able to discharge all the obligations of a traditional "big man." The "Vailala Madness" probably had no appeal in Orokolo village because the L.M.S. missionaries had assumed the responsibilities of a "big man." But why should some areas in Papua and Melanesia which have experienced movements be different from other areas which have not? There is a possible explanation.

The societies where the movements broke out had, in the period before the white men came, distinctive environmental and structural features which distinguished them from other areas where movements have not broken out. These features were a function of the number of people in the societies, the location and topography of the areas where they lived, and the existence of an almost continuous state of warfare.

Historically, in any independent village the number of people who lived in the village and considered themselves as an independent entity was very small, seldom more than 200. Continuous warfare, which was a feature of their lives, meant that the natives seldom combined to form larger political associations. The formation of larger political associations would have required a cessation of hostilities and would inevitably have resulted in the creation of an institutionalized political system. Two factors may have counted against this development.

The peculiar nature of these societies demanded that warfare had to continue because the activities associated with warfare were responsible for validating indigenous concepts of status and power. Warfare proved manhood. And, like gardening, warfare was thought to be a good and necessary activity. Secondly, topography of the country lent itself to the formation of small independent units. Each group lived in an easily fortified area. They were economically self-sufficient, and infanticide was practised to ensure that the population of the group did not outrun resources.

In turn these circumstances were responsible for the flexible nature of leadership. Due to the continuous state of warfare, mortality rates among the leaders were high. Since replacements had to be found quickly, this may have led to the institutionalization of the attributes of leadership. Attributes and qualities were institutionalized because men with the necessary attributes and qualities had to be chosen quickly to replace those who had fallen in battle or died as a result of illness. Continual warfare militated against the creation of hereditary systems of leadership.

The white man's peace was the first peace that these islands had known. It was this peace, and the actions of Europeans, which forced the formation of larger political units. These units were made by the white men, they were Districts and island groupings. These political associations, which were made by the white man, have continued. It is a striking thing that there has never been any attempt, in any of the areas affected by the 1944 movement, to alter the political boundaries. There has been no quarrel with the arbitrary political boundaries of the white men.

Political boundaries always seem to have followed the limits of the "big man's" power. There are now no "big men" who hold sway over island groups. Perhaps that is why larger units have not been formed by the indigenes since the white men came. This development was helped because the white man's political system was like the indigenous political system—or it appeared to be like it. The white man's system was not hereditary—District Officers came and went in much the same profusion as traditional "big men," who were killed in war activities. And the attributes possessed by the white men conformed to the traditional institutionalized attributes of a "big man." In this way the peculiar ideas and values surrounding traditional social organization in these areas may have been perpetuated.

In the areas where the movements broke out there was no institutionalized political system. Everything depended on the impermanent authority of the "big man." The peculiar nature of this traditional social organization and the peculiar nature of British Colonial administration were bedfellows—European contact maintained the "big man" system and its values. . . . The maintenance of social order was dependent on status, the status of the "big man." And the "big man's" status was dependent on his ability to achieve results.

The movements were spontaneous reactions against status deprivation. They were attempts to force Europeans (and Melanesians in the 1963 movement) to recognize indigenous concepts of status. In traditional society the Elema and the Solomon Islanders had recognized two kinds of status, the status of ordinary men and the status of "big men." The movements appear to have concentrated on forcing the Europeans to recognize these two kinds of status. Additional objectives of the movements appear to have been concerned with the kinds of European that the natives had distinguished. Europeans who were thought to be semi-friendly were to be forced to co-operate. Those who were thought to be unfriendly or hostile were to be boycotted or driven away by force of arms.

Concepts of power and status had remained static—even though the presence of Europeans had forced critical examination of traditional ideas and values—and in conformity with traditional institutionalized values. There were no new aims or objectives, only new ways of achieving traditional objectives. Political objectives were also static. The spheres of influence of the movements' leaders corresponded to the political boundaries which had been created by the white men.

Certain individuals from time to time may have made revolutionary statements but these cannot be considered as evidential. Consideration of the overall pattern of the movements, which involves appreciating the relationship between ritual and belief, does seem to show that the affected societies were only concerned with taking action which was designed to achieve recognition of indigenous concepts of status.

The "extraordinary" features of the movements represented a carryover of pre-existing styles of ritual and organizational behaviour combined with deductions which had been made about the nature of European power and status. Both in Papua and the Solomons traditional epistemological assumptions about ritual and organization remained static. This traditional knowledge, added to the deductions made about Europeans, accounted for the morphology of the movements.

Physical characteristics of the 1919 movement were also a carryover from pre-existing styles of ceremonial behaviour. In 1944 and 1963 there was no sign of any special physiological features; this is attributable to the disappearance of the traditional religious system. The physical effort which was put into cult activities was designed to show that the members could act like men—they felt that they had to try very hard.

In 1919 traditional ideas and religious beliefs were combined with ideas gained from experience of European behaviour to secure maximum effect. Epistemological assumptions about the nature of power and status remained unchanged. Ritual, or the method of demonstrating power and status, showed a blend of old and new. There were no new theories or ideas, only new rituals and activities which were designed to achieve traditional results.

In the 1944 movement traditional organizational ideas were combined with ideas gained through experience of European behaviour to secure maximum effect. Epistemological assumptions about the nature of power and status remained unchanged but organizational activities, or the method of gaining status and demonstrating power, showed a blend of old and new. There were no new ideas about the nature of power or status, only new activities which were designed to achieve traditional results.

The 1963 movement modified traditional techniques in the light of experience gained from Europeans and Melanesian behaviour. But epistemological assumptions about the nature of power and status were still traditional. Organizational activities, or the method of gaining status and demonstrating power, showed a blend of old and new. As in 1919 and 1944, there were no new ideas or theories, only new activities which were designed to achieve traditional results.

In the Gulf Division of Papua movements continued to break out until a few years ago. The later Elema movements have shown the same pattern as those of the Solomons. They still had the same organizational and structural features as the 1919 movement, but they were more pragmatic, with fewer "extraordinary" features; the "cargo" belief disappeared. In the Solomons, the only movement which has broken out since the decline of the 1944 movement, affecting the islands which have been examined, has been the 1963 movement.

Indigenous concepts of status were recognized by the Europeans in the Solomons in 1953. Movements have not reappeared in areas where indigenous status was recognized. In the Gulf Division indigenous concepts of status were not recognized by the Europeans in 1919 and the movements continued. The status of the bush people in north-east Malaita was not recognized by the coastal Melanesians in 1963 and activity continues.

Periodicity cannot be linked with political or economic issues. Economic objectives were not achieved in 1944 though they were achieved in 1963. In the Solomons and in Papua there has been a continuing indigenous syndrome of economic and political deprivation. Nor can it be said that the geographical patterning of the movements has corresponded with the most economically and politically depressed areas. Periodicity does seem to have been related to the kind of European contact experienced by the natives. Where European contact has been continuous and direct, this may have emphasized the indigenous sense of inferiority and hastened the outbreak of cult activity.

A factor which may also have influenced periodicity is the existence of leadership. In the early days of European contact, when indigenous notions about Europeans were unsophisticated, it was relatively easy for new leaders to convince their followers that they were familiar with European technological processes. A higher standard of education and technical competence is now required from the leaders. This may have had a limiting effect in some areas where other conditions are ripe for a movement.

The leaders were chosen because they appeared to have the attributes which were considered necessary to solve the problems which had been created by contact with the Europeans. In traditional society the "big man" had presented a synthesized cultural image of the society he lived in; the new leaders presented a synthesized cultural image of their contemporary society which had absorbed European ideas and techniques.

In all the movements the new "big men" gained their status in conformity with traditional epistemological assumptions about the nature of a "big man's" status and the ways in which he used his power. The theory behind the use of power was traditional. But it was overlaid with experience which had been gained as a result of European contact. The new "big men" expressed social concepts and ambitions, they expressed the cultural integrity of their societies. But they did all these things in a traditional manner and their status did not rest on an ability to reveal divine knowledge. "Big men" *were* society, not "prophets."

New problems in traditional Elema society had called for ritual solutions, new problems in traditional Solomon Island society had called for organizational solutions. The only person in native experience who was capable of implementing these solutions was the "big man." And "big men" could only be recognized when they appeared to possess the traditional institutionalized power and status attributes.

The new leaders were only able to evoke a response from their followers in so far as they were able to pattern their performance on that of the traditional "big man." Their successes and failures were evaluated in the same manner. New leaders gained their power in a traditional manner—they also lost power in a traditional manner when it was evident that they were no longer able to achieve results. The most striking feature about the new "big men" was the intensity of their operations. This feature was the result of a desire to put up a much better performance than that of the Europeans. If this was done, then the Europeans would be forced to recognize the validity of their operations, and the morality of their claims to status.

Why did the movements end? In the 1919 movement (a) the cargo did not come, (b) leaders were imprisoned and repressive action was taken by the Government, and (c) the Europeans continued to treat the Elema as "rubbish men." In 1944, (a) the cargo did not come; (b) leaders were imprisoned and repressive action was taken by the Government; and (c) Europeans recognized indigenous concepts of status. In 1963, (a) there was no cargo but all the declared objects of the movement were achieved, which in effect was the same as if cargo had arrived; (b) the leader was not imprisoned, and no repressive measures were taken by the Government; and (c) the Melanesians continued to treat the bush people as "rubbish men." In the areas affected by the 1919 and 1963 movements activity continued.

This comparison shows that the only factor which has determined the decline of the movements has been whether or not indigenous concepts of status have been recognized. Indigenous concepts of status were recognized in 1944 and the movement came to a dramatic halt. But in 1919 and 1963 it was gradually realized that the movements were not a success. Activity declined awaiting the emergence of another "big man" who could find the right ritual or organizational solution to the problems posed by the Europeans.

Disappearance of distinctive morphological features may profitably be distinguished from the phasing-out of the enabling conditions. Imprisonment of the leaders or failure of their policies in areas where indigenous concepts of status have not been recognized has merely resulted in the disappearance of distinctive morphological features associated with a particular individual's attempt at a ritual or organizational solution. This has meant that the ideological basis for the movement has remained temporarily out of sight. "Temporarily," because in these instances activity has continued as soon as a new leader comes forward who appeared to possess the necessary attributes for success.

Government action may only have been responsible, in the main, for assisting the natives to evaluate the claims of a new "big man" quickly or over a long period of time. This process would seem to depend on the nature and intensity of the Government's repressive measures.

The inference that can be drawn from the

development of these movements over a period of time is that success, and disappearance of the ideological basis of the movements, or failure of a particular organizational or ritual solution and the continuing existence of the movements' ideological basis, is linked with the recognition or nonrecognition of indigenous concepts of status by those at whom the movements were directed.

THEORY

Two kinds of social change can be distinguished. These are cultural change and structural change. The process of cultural change has been real and continuous. Analysis of structural change is really involved with explanations for non-change.

Cultural change took place mainly on the grounds of convenience, in some cases because of European pressure. Steel tools and cooking utensils of the Europeans were more robust and utilitarian than their indigenous equivalents. European clothing was more comfortable, European weapons were more efficient in hunting, and so on. These kinds of cultural change were dictated by convenience. Their adoption did not collide with the indigenous system of values or with traditional social organization. This kind of change was continuous and it took place throughout the period which has been examined. causing no resistance or resentment. As a result the natives were given a new set of preferences, but these were still determined by traditional values.

When the natives were presented with a choice between European utilitarian goods and indigenous status-giving goods they chose status rather than comfort. In this way men bought pigs instead of calico or radios. They preferred to give feasts rather than buy kerosene to light the long dark evenings. The natives were pressed to become Christians. This did not result in a great deal of conflict because Christianity was interpreted in terms of indigenous values and beliefs. The Government insisted on new methods of hygiene and housebuilding, and new criminal offences were created. This development did not result in conflict because it did not collide with traditional notions of status and power.

The multi-purpose organizational structure which was intimately linked with institutionalized notions about status and power remained relatively unaffected by European contact. Traditionally the multi-purpose organizational framework was the only relationship that affected all the members of society. There was virtually no structural change because the Europeans simply replaced the "big men" who had had control of the framework. Europeans took over the control of the multi-purpose organizational framework.

This in turn meant that indigenous attempts to establish manhood would continue to be phrased in a traditional manner, because the organizational structure and institutionalized values had survived. Attempts to establish manhood in the traditional manner failed—this system could have no validity while the Europeans continued to ignore indigenous concepts of status.

In the towns built by the Europeans there was no multi-purpose organizational framework because European executive functions were specialized. The natives in the towns adopted European values and the peculiar needs and ambitions of urban Solomon Island society were phrased in European terms.

In traditional society the structure can be described as integrated, social, stressed, and articulate. Integrated because the functioning of the multi-purpose organizational framework gave existence, impact, and credibility to a set of known rules for the determination of individual status; social, because within the complex of organizational relationships it was morally possible for an individual to increase his status; stressed because the fissiparous centrifugal tendencies given by kinship and other segmentary groupings were counteracted by the centripetal integrative force supplied through existence of a "big man;" articulate, because notions about the society's cultural integrity could be expressed through the "big man" who was in himself a synthesized cultural image.

It seems that in traditional society ordinary men relied, for the determination of their individual status, on the existence of two polar status concepts, the "big man" and the "rubbish man." By looking at either of these individuals a man could determine where he stood. He could see that his performance was better than that of a "rubbish man" but not as good as the performance of a "big man." The existence of these two kinds of polar status concept gave ordinary men a form of individual status calibration. This system had validity because concepts of status and power had become static through institutionalization.

When the Europeans had control of the multi-purpose organizational framework the system no longer worked, though its structural integrity was preserved. Ordinary men could no longer calibrate their own individual status against that of the "big man." The only standard they could evaluate their performance against was the standard of the "rubbish men." Indigenous society then became disintegrated, unsocial, unstressed, and inarticulate. Disintegrated because traditional methods of achieving status no longer had any validity; unsocial because no matter how hard they tried individuals were unable to gain status; unstressed because centrifugal tendencies given by the kinship and other segmentary groupings were not balanced by any centripetal force since there was no traditional "big man;" inarticulate, because notions about the society's cultural integrity could not be expressed through the medium of the European/"big man."

In this way all the actions and events connected with the movements that have been examined were evaluated within the natives' existing horizon of experience. The process of change exhibited by these movements has been continuous, carrying forward the past and yet in some ways breaking with it to form something new.

Eric J. Hobsbawm
MILLENARIANISM

In this excerpt from his book, *Primitive Rebels* (1959), Eric J. Hobsbawm, a noted historian, compares the qualities of "old fashioned" millenarian movements with those of modern revolutionary movements. While both kinds of movements reject the present evil or unjust world and strive to bring about a better one, they differ in that millenarian movements are essentially chiliastic. The notion of chiliasm is derived from the Christian doctrine revealed in Revelations which foretells Christ's return and his rule on earth for a thousand years; it refers generally to a period of great happiness, perfect government, or freedom from imperfections in human existence which is to be brought about by divine revelation or by a miracle. Conversely, revolutionary movements strive to realize their vision of a perfect world through an explicit political ideology, organization, strategy, tactics, and social program. While these two types of social movements differ radically in their modes of implementation, Hobsbawm insightfully points out that a similar spirit of utopianism or "impossibilism" motivates the members of both millenarian and revolutionary movements. A faith that the new and better—if not perfect—world can be achieved, and the present realization of the utopia among the members of the movement themselves makes anything seem possible, if only for the moment. Obviously, the power of convictions and faith in human experience are not limited to religion, mysticism, or noninstrumental behavior, and this Hobsbawm clearly shows. For an anthropologist's view on millenarianism, see Kenelm Burridge, *New Heaven, New Earth: A Study of Millenarian Activities* (1969). Readers should also consult Lucy Mair, "Independent Religious Movements in Three Continents" (1959), for a broader comparative perspective.

Reprinted in abridged form from Eric J. Hobsbawm, *Primitive Rebels*, Chap. 4 (New York: W. W. Norton & Company, Inc., 1959; Manchester, Eng.: Manchester University Press, 1959), by permission of the author and the publishers.

Of all the primitive social movements discussed in this book, millenarianism is the one least handicapped by its primitiveness. For the only thing really primitive about it is external. The essence of millenarianism, the hope of a complete and radical change in the world which will be reflected in the millennium, a world shorn of all its present deficiencies, is not confined to primitivism. It is present, almost by definition in all revolutionary movements of whatever kind, and "millenarian" elements may therefore be discovered by the student in any of them, insofar as they have ideals. This does not mean that therefore *all* revolutionary movements are millennial in the narrower sense of the word, let alone that they are primitive. . . . Indeed, it is impossible to make much sense of modern revolutionary history unless one appreciates the differences between primitive and modern revolutionary movements, in spite of the ideal which they have in common, that of a totally new world.

The typical old-fashioned millenarian movement in Europe has three main characteristics. First, a profound and total rejection of the present, evil world, and a passionate longing for another and better one; in a word, revolutionism. Second, a fairly standardized "ideology" of the chiliastic type. . . . The most important ideology of this sort before the rise of modern secular revolutionism, and perhaps the only one, is Judeo-Christian messianism. At all events it seems that classical millenarian movements occur only, or practically only, in countries affected by Judeo-Christian propaganda. This is only natural, for it is difficult to construct a millenarian ideology within a religious tradition which sees the world as a constant flux, or series of cyclical movements, or as a permanently stable thing. What makes millenarians is the idea that the world as it is may—and indeed will—come to an end one day, to be utterly re-made thereafter, a conception which is alien to such religions as Hinduism and Buddhism. It does not follow that the actual beliefs of any millenarian movement will be chiliastic in the strictly Jewish or Christian sense. Third, millenarian movements share a fundamental vagueness about the actual way in which the new society will be brought about.

It is difficult to put this last point more precisely, for such movements range from the purely passive at one extreme, to those which skirt modern revolutionary methods at the other—indeed, as we shall see, to those which merge naturally into modern revolutionary movements. However, it may perhaps be clarified as follows. Modern revolutionary movements have—implicitly or explicitly—certain fairly definite ideas on how the old society is to be replaced by the new, the most crucial of which concerns what we may call the "transfer of power." The old rulers must be toppled from their positions. The "people" (or the revolutionary class or group) must "take over" and then carry out certain measures—the redistribution of land, the nationalization of the means of production, or whatever it may be. In all this the organized effort of the revolutionaries is decisive, and doctrines of organization, strategy and tactics, etc., sometimes very elaborate, are evolved to aid them in their task. The sort of things revolutionaries do is, let us say, to organize a mass demonstration, throw up barricades, march on the town hall, run up the tricolour, proclaim the Republic one and indivisible, appoint a provisional government, and issue a call for a Constituent Assembly. (This, roughly, is the "drill" which so many of them learned from the French Revolution. It is not, of course, the only possible procedure.) But the "pure" millenarian movement operates quite differently, whether because of the inexperience of its members or the narrowness of their horizons, or because of the effect of millenarian ideologies and preconceptions. Its followers are not makers of revolution. They expect it to make itself, by divine revelation, by an announcement from on high, by a miracle—they expect it to happen somehow. The part of the people before the change is to gather together, to prepare itself, to watch the signs of the coming doom, to listen to the prophets who predict the coming of the great day, and perhaps to undertake certain ritual measures against the moment of decision and change, or to purify themselves, shedding the dross of the bad world of the present so as to be able to enter the new world in shining purity. Between the two extremes of the "pure" millenarian and the "pure" political revolutionary all manner of intermediate positions are possible. . . .

When a millenarian movement turns into, or is absorbed by, a modern revolutionary movement, it therefore retains the first of its characteristics. It normally abandons the second at least to some extent, substituting a modern, that is in general a secular, theory of history and revolution: nationalist, socialist, communist, anarchist or of some other type. Lastly it adds a superstructure of modern revolutionary politics to its basic revolutionary spirit: a programme, a doctrine concerning the transfer of power, and above all a system of organization. This is not always easy, but millenarian movements differ from some of the others discussed in this book in opposing no fundamental *structural* obstacles to modernization. At any rate, as we shall see, such movements have been successfully integrated into modern revolutionary ones; just possibly also into modern reformist ones. . . .

It is not always easy to recognize the rational political core within millenarian movements, for their very lack of sophistication and of an effective revolutionary strategy and tactics makes them push the logic of the revolutionary position to the point of absurdity or paradox. They are impractical and utopian. Since they flourish best in periods of extraordinary social ferment and tend to speak the language of apocalyptic religion, the behaviour of their members is often rather odd by normal standards. They are therefore as easily misinterpreted as William Blake, who until quite recently was commonly regarded not as a revolutionary, but simply as an eccentric other-worldly mystic and visionary. When they wish to express their fundamental critique of the existing world, they may, like the millenarian anarchist strikers in Spain, refuse to marry until the new world has been instituted; when they wish to express their rejection of mere palliatives and lesser reforms, they may (again like the Andalusian strikers of the early 20th century) refuse to formulate demands for higher wages or anything else, even when urged to do so by the authorities. When they wish to express their belief that the new world ought to be fundamentally different from the old, they may, like the Sicilian peasants, believe that somehow even the climate can be changed. Their behaviour may be ecstatic to the point where observers describe it in terms of mass hysteria. On the other hand their actual programme may be vague to the point where observers doubt whether they have one. Those who cannot understand what it is that moves them—and even some who do—may be tempted to interpret their behaviour as wholly irrational or pathological or at best as an instinctive reaction to intolerable conditions.

Without wishing to make it appear more sensible and less extraordinary than it often is, it is advisable for the historian to appreciate the logic, and even the realism—if the word can be used in this context—which moves them, for revolutionary movements are difficult to understand otherwise. It is their peculiarity that those who cannot see what all the bother is about are disabled from saying anything of great value about them, whereas those who do (especially when among primitive social movements) cannot often speak in terms intelligible to the rest. It is especially difficult, but necessary, to understand that utopianism, or "impossibilism" which the most primitive revolutionaries share with all but the most sophisticated, and which makes even very modern ones feel a sense of almost physical pain at the realization that the coming of Socialism will not eliminate *all* grief and sadness, unhappy love-affairs or mourning, and will not solve or make soluble *all* problems; a feeling reflected in the ample literature of revolutionary disillusionment.

First, utopianism is probably a necessary social device for generating the superhuman efforts without which no major revolution is achieved. From the historian's point of view the transformations brought about by the French and Russian Revolutions are astonishing enough, but would the Jacobins have undertaken their task simply to exchange the France of the Abbé Prévost for the France of Balzac, the Bolsheviks to exchange the Russia of Tchehov for that of Mr. Khrushchev? Probably not. It was essential for them to believe that "the ultimate in human prosperity and liberty will appear after their victories." Obviously they will not, though the result of the revolution may nevertheless be very worth while.

Second, utopianism can become such a social device *because revolutionary movements and revolutions appear to prove that almost no change is beyond their reach.* If the revolutionaries needed proof that "human nature can be changed"—i.e. that no special problem is insoluble—the demonstration of its changes in such movements and at such moments would be quite sufficient:

> This other man had I dreamed
> A drunken vainglorious lout . . .
> Yet I number him in the song;
> He, too, has resigned his part
> In the casual comedy;
> He, too, has been changed in his turn,
> Transformed utterly:
> A terrible beauty is born.

It is this consciousness of *utter* change, not as an aspiration but as a fact—at least a temporary fact—which informs Yeats' poem on the Easter Rising, and tolls, like a bell, at the end of his stanzas: All changed, changed utterly. A terrible beauty is born. Liberty, equality, and above all fraternity may become real for the moment in those stages of the great social revolutions which revolutionaries who live through them describe in the terms normally reserved for romantic love: "bliss was it in that dawn to be alive, but to be young was very Heaven." Revolutionaries not only set themselves a standard of morality higher than that of any except saints, but at such moments actually carry it into practice, even when it involves considerable technical difficulty, as in the relation between the sexes. Theirs is at such times a miniature version of the ideal society, in which all men are brothers and sacrifice all for the common good without abandoning their individuality. If this is possible within their movement, why not everywhere?

As for the masses of those who do not belong to the revolutionary élite, the mere fact of becoming revolutionary and of recognizing the "power of the people" seems so miraculous that anything else seems equally possible. An observer of the Sicilian Fasci has correctly noted this logic: if a sudden vast mass movement could be stamped out of the ground, if thousands could be shaken out of the lethargy and defeatism of centuries by a single speech, how could men doubt that great and world-overturning events would soon come to pass? Men *had* been utterly changed and were being visibly transformed. Noble men who in their lives followed the dictates of the good society—poverty, brotherliness, saintliness, or whatever else they were—could be observed working among them even by the unregenerate, and provided further proof of the reality of the ideal. We shall see the political importance of these local revolutionary apostles among the Andalusian village anarchists, but every observer of modern revolutionary movements is aware of it in almost all of them, and of the pressure upon the revolutionary élite to live up to the role of moral exemplars: not to earn more or live better, to work harder, to be "pure," to sacrifice their private happiness (as happiness is interpreted in the old society) in full public view. When normal modes of behaviour creep in again—for instance, after the triumph of a new revolutionary régime—men will not conclude that the changes for which they long are impracticable for long periods or outside exclusive groups of abnormally devoted men and women, but that there has been "backsliding" or "betrayal." For the possibility, the reality, of the ideal relationship between human beings has been proved in practice, and what can be more conclusive than that?

The problems facing millenarian movements are or look simple in the intoxicating periods of their growth and advance. They are correspondingly difficult in those which follow revolutions or risings.

Since none of the movements discussed in this book have so far been on the winning side, the question what happens when they discover that their victory does not in fact solve *all* human problems does not greatly concern us. Their defeat does, for it faces them with the problem of maintaining revolutionism as a permanent force. The only millenarian movements which avoid this are the completely suicidal ones, for the death of all their members makes it academic. Normally defeat soon produces a body of doctrine to explain why the millennium has not come and the old world can therefore expect to go on for a while. The signs of imminent doom were not read right or some other mistake has been made. (The Jehovah's Witnesses have quite a large exegetical literature to explain why the failure of the world to end on the date originally predicted does not invalidate the prediction.) To recognize that the old world will continue is to recognize that one must live in it. But how?

Some millenarians, like some revolutionaries, do indeed tacitly drop their revolutionism and turn into *de facto* acceptors of the *status quo*, which is all the easier if the *status quo* becomes more tolerable for the people. Some may even turn into reformist ones, or perhaps discover, now that the ecstasy of the revolutionary period is over, and they are no longer swept away by it, that what they wanted really does not require quite so fundamental a transformation as they had imagined. Or, what is more likely, they may withdraw into a passionate inner life of "the movement," or "the sect," leaving the rest of the world to its own devices except for some token assertions of millennial hopes, and perhaps of the millennial programme: for instance pacifism and the refusal to take oaths. Others, however, do not. They may merely retire to wait for the next revolutionary crisis (to use a non-millenarian term) which must surely bring with it the total destruction of the old world and the institution of the new. This is naturally easiest where the economic and social conditions of revolution are endemic, as in Southern Italy, where every political change in the 19th century, irrespective from what quarter it came, automatically produced its ceremonial marches of peasants with drums and banners to occupy the land, or in Andalusia where ... millenarian revolutionary waves occurred at roughly ten-year intervals for some sixty or seventy years. Others ... retain enough of the old fire to attach themselves to, or to turn into, revolutionary movements of a non-millennial type even after long periods of apparent quiescence.

There, precisely, lies their adaptability. Primitive reformist movements are easily lost in a modern society, if only because the task of securing an equitable regulation of social relations within the existing framework, the creation of tolerable or comfortable conditions here and now, is technically specialized and complicated, and much better done by organizations and movements built to the specifications of modern societies: co-operative marketing organizations are better at the job of giving peasants a fair deal than Robin Hoods. But the fundamental object of social-revolutionary movements remains much more unchanged, though the concrete conditions of the fight for it vary, as may be seen by comparing the passages in which the great utopian or revolutionary writers make their critique of existing societies with those in which they propose specific remedies or reforms. Millenarians can . . . readily exchange the primitive costume in which they dress their aspirations for the modern costume of Socialist and Communist politics. Conversely as we have seen even the least millenarian modern revolutionaries have in them a streak of "impossibilism" which makes them cousins to the Taborites and Anabaptists, a kinship which they have never denied. The junction between the two is therefore readily made, and once made, the primitive movement can be transformed into a modern one.

Clifford Geertz

"INTERNAL CONVERSION" IN CONTEMPORARY BALI

Drawing on Max Weber's distinction between the ideal types of "traditional" and "rational" religions, Clifford Geertz examines the complexities of religious change in Bali. Rather than describing the rise of new religions or religiously inspired social movements, Geertz focuses his analysis on the dynamics within a single religious system, its traditional bases and the uncertainties of its future. He demonstrates the concrete symbolism and action-centered aspects of traditional Balinese religion and then goes on to show its movement toward rationalization, both on the level of personal experience and on the level of dogma and creed. Encompassed within his ethnographic description of Balinese Hinduism are two fundamental points of relevance for both the comparative study of religion as well as the analysis of social and cultural change in general. First, he stresses Weber's notion that while the movement from "traditional" to "rational" religion can take on various guises, it is the form, not the content, of such movements away from the "magical realism" of traditional religion that defines them as "rationalized." It is the displacement of the divine from this world into the other, supernatural one, and the subsequent efforts to bridge this metaphysical gulf which produce the two main types of self-conscious, explicitly coherent religious rationalization: the formulation of a formal, legal-moral code derived from divine revelation, or an institutionalized communion with the divine through individual mystical experience. Second, Geertz shows that there is nothing inherently conservative about religious symbols. They may, and often do, serve as templates for present customs as well as vehicles for revolutionary—or revolutionizing—programs. Indeed, while religion is deeply affected by other social, economic, and political changes, it cannot simply be reduced to them. Readers may be interested to note that in 1962, "Balinese Religion" was officially recognized as a "Great Religion" in Indonesia, and the process of religious rationalization there has grown apace. Geertz describes these and other more recent developments in his essay, "Religious Change and Social Order in Soeharto's Indonesia" (1972). Other articles which deal with similar issues are Clifford Geertz, "Ritual and Social Change: A Javanese Example" (1957), and Alice Dewey, "Ritual as a

Reprinted from J. Bastin and R. Roolvink (eds.), *Malayan and Indonesian Studies Presented to Sir Richard Winstedt* (Oxford: Oxford University Press, 1964) pp. 282–302, by permission of the author and the publisher.

Mechanism for Urban Adaptation" (1970). For a more detailed statement on his approach to the comparative study of religion, see Clifford Geertz, *Islam Observed: Religious Development in Morocco and Indonesia* (1968), and a collection of essays by Geertz entitled *The Interpretation of Cultures* (1973).

Every race has its lumber-room of magical beliefs and practices, and many such survivals are gracious and beautiful and maintain the continuity of a civilization. It is to be hoped that modern materialist ideas will not obliterate them entirely and leave Malay culture jejune.

—Richard Winstedt: *The Malay Magician*

We hear much these days about political and economic modernization in the new states of Asia and Africa, but little about religious modernization. When not ignored entirely, religion tends to be viewed either as a rigidly archaic obstacle to needed progress or a beleaguered conservator of precious cultural values threatened by the corrosive powers of rapid change. Little attention is paid to religious development in and of itself, to regularities of transformation which occur in the ritual and belief systems of societies undergoing comprehensive social revolutions. At best, we get studies of the role that established religious commitments and identifications play in political or economic processes. But our view of Asian and African religions as such is oddly static. We expect them to prosper or decline; we do not expect them to change.

With respect to Bali, perhaps the most richly stocked lumber-room of gracious and beautiful magical beliefs and practices in Southeast Asia, such an approach is virtually universal, and the dilemma of choosing between a quixotic cultural antiquarianism and a barren cultural materialism seems, therefore, to be an especially cruel one. In this essay, I want to suggest that this dilemma is, in all likelihood, a false one, that the continuity of Balinese civilization can be maintained though the fundamental nature of its religious life be totally transformed. And further, I want to point to a few faint, uncertain signs that such a transformation is in fact already under way.

THE CONCEPT OF RELIGIOUS RATIONALIZATION

In his great work on comparative religion, the German sociologist Max Weber set forth a distinction between two idealized polar types of religions in world history, the "traditional" and the "rationalized," which, if it is overgeneralized and incompletely formulated, is yet a useful starting point for a discussion of the process of genuinely religious change.

The axis of this contrast turns upon a difference in the relationship between religious concepts and social forms. Traditional religious concepts (Weber also calls them magical) rigidly stereotype established social practices. Inextricably bound up with secular custom in an almost point-for-point manner, they draw "all branches of human activity . . . into the circle of symbolic magic" and so insure that the stream of everyday existence continues to flow steadily within a fixed and firmly outlined course. Rationalized concepts, however, are not so thoroughly intertwined with the concrete details of ordinary life. They are "apart," "above," or "outside" of them, and the relations of the systems of ritual and belief in which they are embodied to secular society are not intimate and unexamined but distant and problematic. A rationalized religion is, to the degree that it is rationalized, self-conscious and worldly-wise. Its attitude to secular life may be various, from the resigned acceptance of genteel Confucianism to the active mastery of ascetic Protestantism; but it is never naive.

With this difference in relationship between the religious realm and the secular goes a difference also in the structure of the religious realm itself. Traditional religions consist of a multitude of very concretely defined and only loosely ordered sacred entities, an untidy collection of fussy ritual acts and vivid animistic images which are able to involve themselves in an independent, segmental, and immediate manner with almost any sort of actual event. Such systems (for, despite their lack of formal regularity, they are systems) meet the perennial concerns of religion, what Weber called the "problems of meaning"—evil, suffering, frustration, bafflement, and so on—piecemeal. They attack them opportunistically as they arise in each particular instance—each death, each crop failure, each untoward natural or social occurrence—employing one or another weapon chosen, on grounds of symbolic appropriateness, from their cluttered arsenal of myth and magic. (With respect to the less defensive activities of religion—the celebration of human continuity, prosperity, and solidarity—the same strategy is employed.) As the approach to fundamental spiritual issues which traditional religions take is discrete and irregular, so also is their characteristic form.

Rationalized religions, on the other hand, are more abstract, more logically coherent, and more generally phrased. The problems of meaning, which in traditional systems are expressed only implicitly and fragmentarily, here get inclusive formulations and evoke comprehensive attitudes. They become conceptualized as universal and inherent qualities of human *existence* as such, rather than being seen as inseparable aspects of this or that specific event. The question is no longer put merely in such terms as, to use a classic example from the British anthropologist Evans-Pritchard, "Why has the granary fallen on my brother and not on someone else's brother?" but rather, "Why do the good die young and the evil flourish as the green bay tree?" Or, to escape from the conventions of Christian theodicy, not, "By what means can I discover who practiced witchcraft against my brother, thereby causing the granary to fall on him?" but, "How can one know the truth?" Not, "What specific actions must I perform in order to wreak vengeance upon the witch?" but, "What are the bases upon which punishment of evildoers can be justified?" The narrower, concrete questions, of course, remain; but they are subsumed under the broader ones, whose more radically disquieting suggestions they therefore bring forward. And with this raising of the broader ones in a stark and general form arises also the need to answer them in an equally sweeping, universal, and conclusive manner.

The so-called world religions developed, Weber argued, as responses to the appearance in an acute form of just this sort of need. Judaism, Confucianism, Philosophical Brahmanism, and, though on the surface it might not seem to be a religion at all, Greek Rationalism, each emerged out of a myriad of parochial cults, folk mythologies, and ad hoc by-beliefs whose power had begun to fail for certain crucial groups in the societies concerned. This sense, on the part, largely, of religious intellectuals, that the traditional conglomerate of rituals and beliefs was no longer adequate, and the rise to consciousness of the problems of meaning in an explicit form, seems to have been part, in each case, of a much wider dislocation in the pattern of traditional life. The details of such dislocations (or of those amidst which later world religions, descended from these first four, appeared) need not detain us. What is important is that the process of religious rationalization seems everywhere to have been provoked by a thorough shaking of the foundations of social order.

Provoked, but not determined. For, aside from the fact that profound social crisis has not always produced profound religious creativity (or any creativity at all), the lines along which such creativity has moved when it has appeared have been most varied. Weber's whole grand comparison of the religions of China, India, Israel, and the West rested on the notion that they represented variant directions of rationalization, contrastive choices among a finite set of possible developments away from magical realism. What these diverse systems had in common was not the specific content of their message, which deepened in its particularity as it expanded in its scope, but the formal pattern, the generic mode, in which it was cast. In all of them, the sense of sacredness was gathered up, like so many scattered rays of light brought to focus in a lens, from the countless tree spirits and garden spells through which it was vaguely diffused, and was concentrated in a nucleate (though not necessarily monotheistic) concept of the divine. The world was, in Weber's famous phrase, disenchanted: the locus of sacredness was removed from the rooftrees, graveyards, and road-crossings of everyday life and put, in some sense, into another realm where dwelt Jahweh, Logos, Tao, or Brahman.

With this tremendous increase in "distance," so to speak, between man and the sacred goes the necessity of sustaining the ties between them in a much more deliberate and critical manner. As the divine can no longer be apprehended *en passant* through numberless concrete, almost reflexive ritual gestures strategically interspersed throughout the general round of life, the establishment of a more general and comprehensive relationship to it becomes, unless one is to abandon concern with it altogether, imperative. Weber saw two main ways in which this can be brought about. One is through the construction of a consciously systematized, formal, legal-moral code consisting of ethical commands conceived to have been given to man by the divine, through prophets, holy writings, miraculous indications, and so on. The other is through direct, individual experiential contact with the divine via mysticism, insight, aesthetic intuition, etc., often with the assistance of various sorts of highly organized spiritual and intellectual disciplines, such as yoga. The first approach is, of course, typically, though not exclusively, mid-Eastern; the second typically, though also not exclusively, East Asian. But whether, as seems unlikely, these are the only two possibilities, or not, they both do bridge the enormously widened gap, or attempt to bridge it, between the profane and the sacred in a self-conscious, methodical, explicitly coherent manner. They maintain, for those who are committed to them, a sense of a meaningful tie between man and the removed divine.

As with all Weber's polar contrasts, however, that between traditional and rational (the opposite of which is not irrational, but unrationalized) is as thoroughly blurred in fact as it is sharply drawn in theory. In particular, it must not be assumed that the religions of nonliterate peoples are wholly lacking in rationalized elements and those of literate ones rationalized through and through. Not only do many so-called primitive religions show the results of significant amounts of self-conscious criticism, but a popular religiosity of a traditional sort persists with great strength in societies where religious thought has attained its highest reaches of philosophical sophistication. Yet, in relative terms, it is hardly to be doubted that the world religions show greater conceptual generalization, tighter formal integration, and a more explicit sense of doctrine than do the "little" ones of clan, tribe, village, or folk. Religious rationalization is not an all-or-none, an irreversible, or an inevitable process. But, empirically, it is a real one.

TRADITIONAL BALINESE RELIGION

As the Balinese are, in a broad sense, Hindus, one might expect that a significant part, at least, of their religious life would be relatively well rationalized, that over and above the usual torrent of popular religiosity there would exist a developed system of either ethical or mystical theology. Yet this is not the case. A number of overintellectualized descriptions of it to the contrary notwithstanding, Balinese religion, even among the priests, is concrete, action-centered, thoroughly interwoven with the details of everyday life, and touched with little, if any, of the philosophical sophistication or generalized concern of classical Brahmanism or its Buddhist offshoot. Its approach to the problems of meaning remains implicit, circumscribed and segmental. The world is still enchanted and (some recent stirrings aside for the moment) the tangled net of magical realism is almost completely intact, broken only here and there by individual qualms and reflections.

How far this absence of a developed body of doctrine is a result of the persistence of the indigenous (that is, pre-Hindu) element, of the relative isolation of Bali from the outside world after the fifteenth century or so and the consequent parochialization of its culture, or of the rather unusual degree to which Balinese social structure has been able to maintain a solidly traditional form, is a moot question. In Java, where the pressure of external influences has been relentless, and where traditional social structure has lost much of its resilience, not just one but several relatively well-rationalized systems of belief and worship have developed, giving a conscious sense of religious diversity, conflict, and perplexity still quite foreign to Bali. Thus, if one comes, as I did, to Bali after having worked in Java, it is the near total absence of either doubt or dogmatism, the metaphysical nonchalance, that almost immediately strikes one. That, and the astounding proliferation of ceremonial activity. The Balinese, perpetually weaving intricate palm-leaf offerings, preparing elaborate ritual meals, decorating all sorts of temples, marching in massive processions, and falling into sudden trances, seem much too busy practicing their religion to think (or worry) very much about it.

Yet, again, to say that Balinese religion is not methodically ordered is not to say that it is not ordered at all. Not only is it pervaded with a consistent, highly distinctive tone (a kind of sedulous threatricalism which only extended description could evoke), but the elements which comprise it cluster into a number of relatively well-defined ritual complexes which exhibit, in turn, a definite approach to properly religious issues no less reasonable for being implicit. Of these, three are of perhaps greatest importance: (1) the temple system; (2) the sanctification of social inequality; and (3) the cult of death and witches.

1. *The temple system* is a type example of the wholesale fashion in which the diverse strands of a traditional religion twine themselves through the social structure within which they are set. Though all the temples, of which there are literally thousands, are built on a generally similar open-court plan, each is entirely focused on one or another of a number of quite specifically defined concerns: death, neighborhood patriotism, kin-group solidarity, agricultural fertility, caste pride, political loyalty, and so on. Every Balinese belongs to from two or three to a dozen such temples; and, as the congregation of each is composed of those

families who happen to use the same graveyard, live in the same neighborhood, farm the same fields, or have other links, such memberships and the heavy ritual obligations they involve buttress rather directly the sort of social relationships out of which Balinese daily life is built.

The religious forms associated with the various temples, like the architecture broadly similar from temple to temple, are almost wholly ceremonial in nature. Beyond a minimal level, there is almost no interest in doctrine, or generalized interpretation of what is going on, at all. The stress is on orthopraxy, not orthodoxy—what is crucial is that each ritual detail should be correct and in place. If one is not, a member of the congregation will fall, involuntarily, into a trance, becoming thereby the chosen messenger of the gods, and will refuse to revive until the error, announced in his ravings, has been corrected. But the conceptual side is of much less moment: the worshippers usually don't even know who the gods in the temples are, are uninterested in the meaning of the rich symbolism, and are indifferent to what others may or may not believe. You can believe virtually anything you want to actually, including that the whole thing is rather a bore, and even say so. But if you do not perform the ritual duties for which you are responsible you will be totally ostracized, not just from the temple congregation, but from the community as a whole.

Even the execution of ceremonies has an oddly externalized air about it. The main such ceremony occurs on each temple's "birthday," every 210 days, at which time the gods descend from their homes atop the great volcano in the center of the island, enter iconic figurines placed on an altar in the temple, remain three days, and then return. On the day of their arrival the congregation forms a gay parade, advancing to meet them at the edge of the village, welcoming them with music and dance, and escorting them to the temple where they are further entertained; on the day of their departure they are sent off with a similar, though sadder, more restrained procession. But most of the ritual between the first and the last day is performed by the temple priest alone, the congregation's main obligation being to construct tremendously complex offerings and bring them to the temple. There is, on the first day, an important collective ritual at which holy water is sprinkled on members of the congregation as, palms to forehead, they make the classic Hindu obeisance gesture to the gods. But even in this seemingly sacramental ceremony only one member of the household need participate, and it is usually a woman or an adolescent who is so delegated, the men being generally unconcerned so long as a few drops of the charmed water falls protectively upon some representative of their family.

2. *The sanctification of social inequality* centers on the one hand around the Brahmana priesthood and on the other around the enormous ceremonies which the dozens of kings, princes, and lordlings of Bali give to express and reinforce their ascendency. In Bali, the symbolization of social inequality, of rank, has always been the linchpin of supravillage political organization. From the very earliest stages, the primary moving forces in the process of state formation have been more stratificatory than political, have been concerned more with status than with statecraft. It was not a drive toward higher levels of administrative, fiscal, or even military efficiency that acted as the fundamental dynamic element in the shaping of the Balinese polity, but rather an intense emphasis on the ceremonial expression of delicately graduated distinctions in social standing. Governmental authority was made to rest, secondarily and quite precariously, on more highly valued prestige differences between social strata; and the actual mechanisms of political control through which an authoritarian oligarchy exercises its power were much less elaborately developed than were those through which a traditional cultural elite demonstrates its spiritual superiority—that is, state ritual, court art, and patrician etiquette.

Thus, where the temples are primarily associated with egalitarian village groups—perhaps the fundamental structural principle around which they are organized is that within the temple context all differences in social rank between members of the congregation are irrelevant—the priesthood and the spectacular ceremonies of the upper caste tie gentry and peasantry together into relationships that are frankly asymmetrical.

While any male member of the Brahmana caste is eligible to become a priest, only a minority undertake the extended period of training and purification that is prerequisite to actual practice in the role. Though it has no organization as such, each priest operating independently, the priesthood as a whole is very closely identified with the nobility. The ruler and the priest are said to stand side by side as "full brothers." Each without the other would fall, the first for lack of charismatic potency, the second for lack of armed protection. Even today, each noble house has a symbiotic tie with a particular priestly house which is considered to be its spiritual counterpart, and in the precolonial period not only were the royal courts largely manned by priests, but no priest could be consecrated without permission of the local ruler and no ruler legitimately installed except by a priest.

On the commoner or lower-caste side each priest "owns" a number of followers, allotted to his house at one point or another by this or that noble house and subsequently inherited from generation to generation. These followers are scattered, if not altogether randomly, at least very widely—say three in one village, four in the next, several more in a third, and so on—the reason for this practice evidently being a wish on the part of the nobility to keep the priesthood politically weak. Thus, in any one village a man and his neighbor will ordinarily be dependent upon different priests for their religious needs, the most important of which is the obtaining of holy water, an element essential not just for temple ceremonies but for virtually all important rituals. Only a Brahmana priest can address the gods directly in order to sanctify water, as only he has, as the result of his ascetic regimen and his caste purity, the spiritual strength to traffic safely with the tremendous magical power involved. The priests are thus more professional magicians than true priests: they do not serve the divine nor elucidate it, but, through the agency of ill-understood sanskritic chants and beautifully stylized sacred gestures, they utilize it.

A priest's followers refer to him as their *siwa*, after the god by whom he is possessed during the entranced portions of his rite, and he refers to them as his *sisija*, roughly "clients"; and in such a way the hierarchical social differentiation into upper and lower castes is symbolically assimilated to the spiritual contrast between priests and ordinary men. The other means through which rank is given religious expression and support, the prodigious ceremonies of the nobility, employs an institution of political rather than ritual clientage—*corvée* to underscore the legitimacy of radical social inequality. Here, it is not the content of the ceremonial activity which is important, but the fact that one is in a position to mobilize the human resources to produce such an extravaganza at all.

Usually focused around life-cycle events (tooth-filing, cremation), these ceremonies involve the collective efforts of great masses of subjects, dependents, etc., over a considerable stretch of time, and form, therefore, not just the symbol but the very substance of political loyalty and integration. In precolonial times the preparation and performance of such grand spectacles seem to have consumed more time and energy than all other state activities, including warfare, put together, and so, in a sense, the political system can be said to have existed to support the ritual system, rather than the other way round. And, despite colonialism, occupation, war, and independence, the pattern in great part persists—the gentry is still, in Cora Du Bois's fine phrase, "the symbolic expression of the peasantry's greatness," and the peasantry, still the lifeblood of the gentry's pretensions.

3. *The cult of death and witches* is the "dark" side of Balinese religion, and, though it penetrates into virtually every corner of daily life, adding an anxious note to the otherwise equable tenor of existence, it finds its most direct and vivid expression in the ecstatic ritual combat of those two strange mythological figures: Rangda and Barong. In Rangda, monstrous queen of the witches, ancient widow, used-up prostitute, child-murdering incarnation of the goddess of death, and, if Margaret Mead is correct, symbolic projection of the rejecting mother, the Balinese have fashioned a powerful image of unqualified evil. In Barong, a vaguely benign and slightly ludicrous deity, who looks and acts like a cross between a clumsy bear, a foolish puppy, and a strutting Chinese dragon, they have constructed an almost parodic representation of human strength and weakness. That in their headlong encounters these two demons, each saturated with that mana-like power the Balinese call *sakti*, arrive inevitably at an exact stand-off is therefore not without a certain ultimate significance for all its magical concreteness.

The actual enactments of the battle between Rangda and Barong usually, though not inevitably, take place during a death temple's "birthday" ceremony. One villager (a man) dances Rangda, donning the fierce mask and repulsive costume; two others, arranged fore and aft as in a vaudeville horse, dance the elegant Barong. Both entranced, the hag and dragon advance warily from opposite sides of the temple yard amid curses, threats, and growing tension. At first Barong fights alone, but soon members of the audience begin falling involuntarily into trance, seizing krisses, and rushing to his aid. Rangda advances toward Barong and his helpers, waving her magical cloth. She is hideous and terrifying, and, although they hate her with a terrible rage and want to destroy her, they fall back. When she, held at bay by Barong's *sakti*, then turns away, she suddenly becomes irresistibly attractive (at least so my informants reported) and they advance on her eagerly from the rear, sometimes even trying to mount her from behind; but, with a turn of her head and a touch of her cloth, they fall helpless into a coma. Finally she withdraws from the scene, undefeated, but at least checked, and Barong's desperately frustrated assistants burst into wild self-destructive rages, turning their krisses (ineffectively, because they are in trance) against their chests, desperately hurling themselves about, devouring live chicks, and so on. From the long moment of tremulous expectancy which precedes the initial appearance of Rangda to this final dissolution into an orgy of futile violence and degradation, the whole performance has a most uncomfortable air of being about to descend at any moment into sheer panic and wild destruction. Evidently it never does, but the alarming sense of touch-and-go, with the diminishing band of the entranced desperately attempting to keep the situation minimally in hand, is altogether overwhelming, even for a mere observer. The razor-thin dimensions of the line dividing reason from unreason, eros from thanatos, or the divine from the demonic, could hardly be more effectively dramatized.

THE RATIONALIZATION OF BALINESE RELIGION

Except for a few odd sports of limited consequence such as Bahai or Mormonism (and leaving aside, as equivocal cases, the so-called political religions such as Communism and Fascism), no new rationalized world religions have arisen since Mohammed. Consequently, almost all of the tribal and peasant peoples of the world who have shed, to whatever degree, the husk of their traditional faiths since that time, have done so through conversion to one or another of the great missionary religions—Christianity, Islam, or Buddhism. For Bali, however, such a course seems precluded. Christian missionaries have never made much progress on the island and, connected as they are with the discredited colonial regime, their chances would now seem poorer than ever. Nor are the Balinese likely to become Muslims in large numbers, despite the general Islamism of Indonesia. They are, as a people, intensely conscious and painfully proud of being a Hindu island in a Muslim sea, and their attitude toward Islam is that of the duchess to the bug. To become either Christian or Muslim would be tantamount, in their eyes, to ceasing to be Balinese, and, indeed, an occasional individual who is converted is still considered, even by the most tolerant and sophisticated, to have abandoned not just Balinese religion but Bali, and perhaps reason, itself. Both Christianity and Islam may influence further religious developments on the island; but they have virtually no chance of controlling them.

Yet, that a comprehensive shaking of the foundations of the Balinese social order is, if not already begun, in the very immediate offing, is apparent on all sides. The emergence of the unitary Republic and the enclosure of Bali as a component within it has brought modern education, modern governmental forms, and modern political consciousness to the island. Radically improved communications have brought increased awareness of, and contact with, the outside world, and provided novel criteria against which to measure the worth both of their own culture and that of others. And inexorable internal changes—increased urbanization, growing population pressure, and so on—have made maintenance of traditional systems of social organization in unchanged form progressively more difficult. What happened in Greece or China after the fifth century B.C.—the disenchantment of the world—seems about to happen, in an altogether different historical context and with an altogether different historical meaning, in mid-twentieth century Bali.

Unless, as is of course a real possibility, events move too fast for them to maintain their cultural heritage at all, the Balinese seem likely to rationalize their religious system through a process of "internal conversion." Following, generally and not uncritically, the guidelines of the Indian religions to which they have been so long nominally affiliated, but from whose doctrinal spirit they have been almost wholly cut off, they seem on the verge of producing a self-conscious "Bali-ism" which, in its philosophical dimensions, will approach the world religions both in the generality of the questions it asks and in the comprehensiveness of the answers it gives.

The questions, at least, are already being asked; particularly by the youth. Among the educated or semieducated young men of eighteen to thirty who formed the ideological vanguard of the Revolution, there have appeared scattered but distinct signs of a conscious interest in spiritual issues of a sort which still seem largely meaningless to their elders or their less *engagés* contemporaries.

For example, one night, at a funeral in the

village where I was living, a full-scale philosophical discussion of such issues broke out among eight or ten young men squatted around the courtyard "guarding" the corpse. As the other aspects of traditional Balinese religion which I have described, funeral ceremonies consist largely of a host of detailed little busy-work routines, and whatever concern with first and last things death may stimulate is well submerged in a bustling ritualism. But these young men, who involved themselves but minimally in all this, the necessary observances being mostly performed by their elders, fell spontaneously into a searching discussion of the nature of religion as such.

At first they addressed themselves to a problem which has haunted the religious and the students of religion alike: how can you tell where secular custom leaves off and religion, the truly sacred, begins? Are all the items in the detailed funeral rite really necessary homage to the gods, genuinely sacred matters? Or are many simply human customs performed out of blind habit and tradition? And, if so, how can you differentiate the one from the other?

One man offered the notion that practices which were clearly connected with grouping people together, strengthening their bonds with one another—for example, the communal construction of the corpse litter by the village as a whole, or the kin-group's preparation of the body—were custom, and so not sacred, while those connected directly with the gods—the family obeisance to the spirit of the deceased, the purification of the body with holy water, and so on—were properly religious. Another argued that those elements which appeared generally in ritual observances, which you find virtually everywhere, from birth to death, in the temples and at the Rangda plays (again, holy water is a good example), were religious, but those which occurred only here and there, or were limited to one or two rites, were not.

Then the discussion veered, as such discussions will, to the grounds of validity for religion as such. One man, somewhat Marxist-influenced, propounded social relativism: when in Rome do as the Romans do, a phrase he quoted in its Indonesian form. Religion is a human product. Man thought up God and then named him. Religion is useful and valuable, but it has no supernatural validity. One man's faith is another man's superstition. At bottom, everything comes down to mere custom.

This was greeted with universal disagreement, disapproval, and dismay. In response, the son of the village head offered a simple, nonrational belief position. Intellectual arguments are totally irrelevant. He knows in his heart that the gods exist. Faith is first, thought secondary. The truly religious person, such as himself, just knows that the gods truly come into the temples—he can feel their presence. Another man, more intellectually inclined, erected, more or less on the spot, a complex allegorical symbology to solve the problem. Tooth-filing symbolizes man becoming more like the gods and less like the animals, who have fangs. This rite means this, that that; this color stands for justice, that for courage, etc. What seems meaningless is full of hidden meaning, if only you have the key. A Balinese cabalist. Yet another man, more agnostic, though not a disbeliever, produced the golden mean for us. You can't really think about these things because they don't lie within human comprehension. We just don't know. The best policy is a conservative one—believe just about half of everything you hear. That way you won't go overboard.

And so it went through a good part of the night. Clearly these young men, all of whom (save the village chief's son who was a government clerk in a nearby town) were peasants and smiths, were better Weberians than they knew. They were concerned on the one hand with segregating religion from social life in general, and on the other with trying to close the gap between this world and the other, between secular and sacred, which was thus opened up, by means of some sort of deliberately systematic attitude, some general commitment. Here is the crisis of faith, the breaking of the myths, the shaking of the foundations in a pretty unvarnished form.

The same sort of new seriousness is beginning to appear, here and there, in liturgical contexts as well. In a number of the temple ceremonies—particularly those at which, as is increasingly the case, a Brahmana priest officiates directly rather than, as has been customary, merely providing holy water for the use of the low-caste temple priest—there is appearing an almost pietistic fervor on the part of some of the young male (and a few of the young female) members of the congregation. Rather than permitting but one member of their family to participate for all in the genuflexion to the gods, they all join in, crowding toward the priest so as to have more holy water sprinkled on them. Rather than the context of screaming children and idly chatting adults within which this sacrament usually takes place, they demand, and get, a hushed and reverent atmosphere. They talk, afterward, about the holy water not in magical but emotionalist terms, saying that their inward unease and uncertainty is "cooled" by the water as it falls upon them, and they too speak of feeling the gods' presence directly and immediately. Of all this, the older and the more traditional can make little; they look on it, as they themselves say, like a cow looking at a gamelan orchestra—with an uncomprehending, bemused (but in no way hostile) astonishment.

Such rationalizing developments on the more personal level demand, however, a comparable sort of rationalization at the level of dogma and creed if they are to be sustained. And this is in fact occurring, to a limited extent, through the agency of several recently established publishing firms which are attempting to put scholarly order into the classical palm-leaf literature upon which the Brahmana priesthoods' claim to learning rests, to translate it into modern Balinese or Indonesian, to interpret it in moral-symbolic terms, and to issue it in cheap editions for the increasingly literate masses. These firms are also publishing translations of Indian works, both Hindu and Buddhist, are importing theosophical books from Java, and have even issued several original works by Balinese writers on the history and significance of their religion.

It is, again, the young educated men who for the most part buy these books, but they often read them aloud at home to their families. The interest in them, especially in the old Balinese manuscripts, is very great, even on the part of quite traditional people. When I bought some books of this sort and left them around our house in the village, our front porch became a literary center where groups of villagers would come and sit for hours on end and read them to one another, commenting now and then on their meaning, and almost invariably remarking that it was only since the Revolution that they had been permitted to see such writings, that in the colonial period the upper castes prevented their dissemination altogether. This whole process represents, thus, a spreading of religious literacy beyond the traditional priestly castes—for whom the writings were in any case more magical esoterica than canonical scriptures—to the masses, a vulgarization, in the root sense, of religious knowledge and theory. For the first time, at least a few ordinary Balinese are coming to feel that they can get some understanding of what their religion is all about; and more important, that they have a need for and a right to such understanding.

Against such a background, it might seem paradoxical that the main force behind this religious literacy and philosophical-moral interpretation movement is the nobility, or part of it, that it is certain, again generally younger, members of the aristocracy who are collating and translating the manuscripts and founding the firms to publish and distribute them.

But the paradox is only an apparent one. As I have noted, much of the nobility's traditional status rested on ceremonial grounds; a great part of the traditional ceremonial activity was designed so as to produce an almost reflexive acceptance of their eminence and right to rule. But today this simple assumption of eminence is becoming increasingly difficult. It is being undermined by the economic and political changes of Republican Indonesia and by the radically populist ideology which has accompanied these changes. Though a good deal of large-scale ceremonialism still persists on Bali, and though the ruling class continues to express its claim to superiority, in terms of ritual extravagance, the day of the colossal cremation and titanic tooth-filing seems to be drawing to a close.

To the more perceptive of the aristocracy the handwriting on the wall is thus quite clear: if they persist in basing their right to rule on wholly traditional grounds they will soon lose it. Authority now demands more than court ceremonialism to justify it; it demands "reasons"—that is, doctrine. And it is doctrine that they are attempting to provide through reinterpreting classical Balinese literature and re-establishing intellectual contact with India. What used to rest on ritual habit is now to rest on rationalized dogmatic belief. The main concerns upon which the content of the "new" literature focuses—the reconciliation of polytheism and monotheism, the weighing of the relative importance of "Hindu" and "Balinese" elements in "Hindu-Balinese" religion, the relation of outward form to inward content in worship, the tracing of the historico-mythological origins of caste rankings, and so on—all serve to set the traditional hierarchical social system in an explicitly intellectual context. The aristocracy (or part of it) have cast themselves in the role of the leaders of the new Bali-ism so as to maintain their more general position of social dominance.

To see in all this a mere Machiavellianism, however, would be to give the young nobles both too much credit and too little. Not only are they at best partially conscious of what they are doing, but, like my village theologians, they too are at least in part religiously rather than politically motivated. The transformations which the "new Indonesia" has brought have hit the old elite as hard as any other group in Balinese society by questioning the foundations of their belief in their own vocation and thus their view of the very nature of reality in which they conceive that vocation to be rooted. Their threatened displacement from power appears to them as not just a social but a spiritual issue. Their sudden concern with dogma is, therefore, in part a concern to justify themselves morally and metaphysically, not only in the eyes of the mass of the population but in their own, and to maintain at least the essentials of the established Balinese world view and value system in a radically changed social setting. Like so many other religious innovators, they are simultaneously reformists and restorationists.

Aside from the intensification of religious concern and the systematization of doctrine, there is a third side to this process of rationalization—the social-organizational. If a new "Bali-ism" is to flourish, it needs not only a popular change of heart and an explicit codification, but a more formally organized institutional structure in which it can be socially embodied. This need, essentially an ecclesiastical one, is coming to revolve around the problem of the relation of Balinese religion to the national state, in particular around its place—or lack thereof—in the Republican Ministry of Religion.

The Ministry, which is headed by a full cabinet member, is centered in Djakarta, but has offices scattered over much of the country. It is entirely dominated by Muslims, and its main activities are building mosques, publishing Indonesian translations of the Koran and commentaries, appointing Muslim marriage-closers, supporting Koranic schools, disseminating information about Islam, and so on. It has an elaborate bureaucracy, in which there are special sections for Protestants and Catholics (who largely boycott it anyway on separatist grounds) as distinct religions. But Balinese religion is thrown into the general residual category perhaps best translated as "wild"—that is, pagan, heathen, primitive, etc.—the members of which have no genuine rights in, or aid from, the Ministry. These "wild" religions are considered, in the classical Muslim distinction between "peoples of the Book" and "religions of ignorance," as threats to true piety and fair game for conversion.

The Balinese naturally take a dim view of this and have constantly petitioned Djakarta for equal recognition with Protestantism, Catholicism, and Islam as a fourth major religion. President Sukarno, himself half-Balinese, and many other national leaders sympathize, but they cannot, as yet, afford to alienate the politically powerful orthodox Muslims and so have vacillated, giving little effective support. The Muslims say that the adherents of Balinese Hinduism are all in one place, unlike the Christians who are scattered all over Indonesia; the Balinese point out that there are Balinese communities in Djakarta and elsewhere in Java, as well as in south Sumatra (transmigrants), and instance the recent erection of Balinese temples in east Java. The Muslims say, you have no Book, how can you be a world religion? The Balinese reply, we have manuscripts and inscriptions dating from before Mohammed. The Muslims say, you believe in many gods and worship stones; the Balinese say, God is One but has many names and the "stone" is the vehicle of God, not God himself. A few of the more sophisticated Balinese even claim that the real reason why the Muslims are unwilling to admit them to the Ministry is the fear that if "Bali-ism" were to become an officially recognized religion, many Javanese, who are Islamic in name only and still very Hindu-Buddhist in spirit, would convert, and "Bali-ism" would grow rapidly at the expense of Islam.

In any case, there is an impasse. And, as a result, the Balinese have set up their own independent, locally financed "Ministry of Religion," and are attempting through it to reorganize some of their most central religious institutions. The main effort, so far, has been concentrated (with largely indifferent results) upon regularizing the qualifications for Brahmana priests. Instead of resting the priestly role mainly on its hereditary aspect, which in itself they, of course, do not question, or on the ritual virtuosity involved, the "Ministry" wishes to rest it on religious knowledge and wisdom. It wants to insure that the priests know what the scriptures mean and can relate them to contemporary life, are of good moral character, have attained at least some degree of genuine scholarship, and so on. Our young men will no longer follow a man just because he is a Brahmana, the officials say; we must make him a figure of moral and intellectual respect, a true spiritual guide. And to this end they are attempting to exercise some control over ordination, even to the point of setting qualifying examinations, and to make the priesthood a more corporate body by holding meetings of all the priests in an area. The representatives of the "Ministry" also tour the villages giving educational speeches on the moral significance of Balinese religion, on the virtues of monotheism and the dangers of idol worship, and so on. They are even attempting to put some order into the temple system, to establish a systematic classification of temples, and perhaps eventually to elevate one kind, most likely the village origin-temple to pre-eminence in a universalistic pattern comparable to that of a mosque or a church.

All this is, however, still largely in the paper-planning stage, and it cannot be claimed that very much actual reorganization of the institutional structure of Balinese religion has in fact taken place. But there is an office of the "Ministry" in each Balinese regency now, headed by a salaried Brahmana priest (a regularly paid "official" priesthood being in itself something of a revolution), assisted by three or four clerks, most of them also members of the Brahmana caste. A religious school, independent of the "Ministry" but encouraged by it, has been established, and even a small religious political party centered around a ranking noble and dedicated to forwarding these changes has been founded, so that at least the faint beginnings of religious bureaucratization are manifest.

What will come of all this—the intensified religious questioning, the spread of religious literacy, and the attempt to reorganize religious institutions—remains simply to be seen. In many ways, the whole drift of the modern world would seem to be against the sort of movement toward religious rationalization which these developments portend, and perhaps Balinese culture will, in the end, be swamped and left jejune by just the sort of "modern materialist ideas" which Sir Richard Winstedt fears. But not only do such overall drifts—when they do not turn out to be mirages altogether—often pass over deeply rooted cultural configurations with rather less effect upon them than we would have thought possible, but, for all its present weakness, the regenerative potential of a triangular alliance of troubled youth, threatened aristocrats, and aroused priests should not be underestimated. Today in Bali some of the same social and intellectual processes which gave rise to the fundamental religious transformations of world history seem to be at least well begun, and whatever their vicissitudes or eventual outcome, their career can hardly help but be an instructive one. By looking closely at what happens on this peculiar little island over the next several decades we may gain insights into the dynamics of religious change of a specificity and an immediacy that history, having already happened, can never give us.

BIOGRAPHIES OF AUTHORS

JANE MONNIG ATKINSON (1949–) was born in Missouri and did her undergraduate studies at Bryn Mawr College. She is currently a Ph.D. candidate at Stanford University, writing her dissertation on curing and shamanism among the To Wana of Indonesia. In addition to her work in Indonesia, she has had field training among the Ilongots of Northern Luzon in the Philippines.

WALDEMAR BOGORAS (VLADIMIR GERMANOVICH BOGORAZ) (1865–1936) was a Russian who was exiled in his youth to Siberia. At the invitation of his friend Waldemar Jochelson he joined the Jesup North Pacific Expedition, working with the Chukchee, Koryak, Yukaghir, and Lamut. For a while he lived in the United States and then returned to Russia, where he was associated with the Academy of Sciences Museum of Anthropology and Ethnography in Leningrad. He wrote novels under the pseudonym "Tan." Among his numerous monographs are *The Chukchee* (1904–1909), *Chukchee Mythology* (1910), and *Koryak Texts* (1917).

JAMES LEWTON BRAIN (1923–) was born in England. He received his Postgraduate Diploma from the University of London and his doctorate from Syracuse University in 1968. He is currently Professor of Anthropology at the State University of New York, New Paltz. He served as Community Development Officer for Tanzania and Uganda (1951–1963), and has done field work among the Buha in Western Tanzania and the Uluguru in Eastern Tanzania. He is the author of "Sex, Incest, and Death: Initiation Rites Reconsidered," *(Current Anthropology*, Vol. 18, No. 2, 1977).

RUTH LEAH BUNZEL (1898–) was born in New York City and received her doctorate from Columbia in 1929, where she was trained under Franz Boas and where she is presently a Research Associate. During the war she was an analyst for the Office of War Information. Her main field research has been done in connection with Zuni ceremonialism, but she has had additional research experience in Middle America and is the author of "Introduction to Zuni Ceremonialism," "Zuni Origin Myths," "Zuni Katcinas," and "Zuni Ritual Poetry," all of which appeared in the *47th Report Bureau of American Ethnology, 1929–1930* (1932), as well as *Chichicastenango: A Guatemalan Village* (1952). She has also investigated American and Chinese national character.

WALTER BRADFORD CANNON (1871–1945) took his A.B. (1896), A.M. (1897), and M.D. (1900) at Harvard University and was the holder of numerous honorary degrees from universities throughout the world. He was George Higginson Professor of Physiology at Harvard from 1906 until his retirement in 1942. He was responsible for solving the acute World War I problem of traumatic shock, and he discovered the adrenalin-like hormone "sympathin." Many of his studies dealt with homeostasis, a term which he introduced to the literature. His publications include *Bodily Changes in Pain, Hunger, Fear and Rage* (1915; revised 1929), *Traumatic Shock* (1923), and *The Wisdom of the Body* (1932).

D. GLYNN COCHRANE (1940–) was born in Northern Ireland. He received his M.A. from Dublin University and his doctorate from Oxford University. He is presently department chairman and Professor of Anthropology and Public Administration at the Maxwell Graduate School, Syracuse University. His field work was done in the Southwest Pacific. He is the author of *Big Men and Cargo Cults* (1970).

MARY DOUGLAS (1921–) was born in Italy and received her doctorate from Oxford in 1951. She is presently a Professor of Anthropology at the University College, London. Her field work was done in the Kasai district of the former Belgian Congo. She is the author of *Purity and Danger* (1966), *Natural Symbols* (1970), *Implicit Meanings: Essays in Anthropology* (1975), and editor of *Rules and Meanings: The Anthropology of Everyday Knowledge* (1973).

ALAN DUNDES (1934–) is Professor of Anthropology and Folklore at the University of California, Berkeley. Born in New York City, he received both his bachelor's and master's degrees from Yale, obtaining his doctorate from Indiana University in 1962. He has served as a member of the executive board of the American Folklore Society. He is the author, with Alessandro Falassi, of *La Terra in Piazza: An Interpretation of the Palio of Siena* (1975), and editor of *The Study of Folklore* (1965). He has done field research in Siena, Italy, and among the Florida Seminole and the Potawatomi in Kansas.

ÉMILE DURKHEIM (1858–1917), a Frenchman by birth, was descended from a long line of rabbis and at an early age prepared for the rabbinate, but soon decided to become a teacher. He attended the École Normale Supérieure, where he was much influenced by Fustel de Coulanges and Émile Boutroux. For a few years he taught philosophy at various lycées and then turned to sociology. To prepare himself for improving his doctoral dissertation, he spent a year in Paris and Germany. At the University of Bordeaux in 1887 he gave the first course in social science ever offered in France. Six years later he defended his two doctoral theses, one of them being his *De la division du travail social* (1893). He founded the *Année Sociologique* in 1898. He taught sociology for thirty years at Bordeaux and the University of Paris. He was a prolific writer and, in turn, has been the object of scores of expository and critical books and articles.

EDWARD EVAN EVANS-PRITCHARD (1902–1973) was Professor of Social Anthropology at Oxford. He received his master's degree at Oxford and his doctorate at the University of London. He taught and did research at the Egyptian University at Cairo, the University of London, and Cambridge, and was knighted in 1971. He carried on field work in the Sudan, the Belgian Congo, Ethiopia, and Kenya. Among his books are *Witchcraft, Oracles and Magic Among the Azande* (1937), *Nuer Religion* (1956), and *Theories of Primitive Religion* (1965).

JAMES GEORGE FRAZER (1854–1941) was born in Glasgow and educated at Glasgow University and Trinity College, Cambridge. He was called to the bar in 1879, and in 1907 became Professor of Social Anthropology at the University of Liverpool. He was knighted in 1914. Frazer had a strong interest in comparative religion, and it was in this field that he made his chief contributions to anthropological theory. Among his numerous writings the most famous is *The Golden Bough* (1st ed., 1890; 3d ed., 12 vols., 1911–1915). He also wrote *The Belief in Immortality and the Worship of the Dead* (1913–1924), *Folk-Lore in the Old Testament* (1918), *Myths of the Origin of Fire* (1930), and *The Fear of the Dead in Primitive Religion* (1933–1936).

MAURICE FREEDMAN (1920–1975) was born in England and educated at the London School of Economics where he taught from 1951 to 1970. He was Professor of Social Anthropology at Oxford at the time of his death. His publications include *Family and Kinship in Chinese Society* (ed.) (1970), *Chinese Lineage and Society* (1966), *Lineage Organization in Southeastern China* (1958), and *Chinese Family and Marriage in Singapore* (1957).

CLIFFORD GEERTZ (1926–) is Professor of the Social Sciences at the Institute for Advanced Study, Princeton, New Jersey. He was born in San Francisco. After attending Antioch College he went to Harvard and there received his doctorate in social anthropology in 1956. He has carried on field research in Java, Bali, and Morocco. Among his publications are *The Religion of Java* (1960), *Agricultural Involution: The Processes of Ecological Change in Indonesia* (1963), *Peddlers and Princes: Social Development and Economic Change in Two Indonesian Towns* (1963), *Islam Observed* (1968), and *The Interpretation of Cultures* (1973).

GARY HAMILTON GOSSEN (1942–) received his doctorate from Harvard University in 1970. He is presently Associate Professor of Anthropology and chairperson of the Committee on Latin American Studies at the University of California, Santa Cruz. He has done field work in Mexico, Costa

Rica, Spain, and on the Potawatomi Indian Reservation (Kansas) and is currently conducting a project on oral history and symbolism among the Maya Indians of Rincón Chamula (Chiapas, Mexico). He is the author of *Chamulas in the World of the Sun: Time and Space in a Maya Oral Tradition* (1974).

C. R. HALLPIKE (1938–) was born in London. He was educated at Oxford University, receiving his D.Phil. in 1968. He has served as a post-doctoral research fellow at Dalhousie University (1968–1969), a research associate at Dalhousie (1972–1973), and is presently an independent researcher. He has done field research among the Konso of Ethiopia and the Tauade in Papua. He is the author of *The Konso of Ethiopia: A Study of the Values of a Cushitic People* (1972), *Bloodshed and Vengeance in the Papuan Mountains: The Generation of Conflict in Tauade Society* (1977), and is currently completing a book, *The Foundations of Primitive Thought* (n.d.).

WILLARD WILLIAMS HILL (1902–1974) was chairman of the Department of Anthropology at the University of New Mexico from 1948 to 1964. He received his doctorate from Yale. Most of his field research was done among the Navaho, on whom he was one of the outstanding authorities, but he also worked with the Pueblo, Ute, and Pomo Indians. He is the author of *Navaho Warfare* (1936), *The Agricultural and Hunting Methods of the Navaho Indians* (1938), and *Navaho Material Culture* (with Clyde Kluckhohn and Lucy Wales Kluckhohn; 1971).

ERIC JOHN HOBSBAWM (1917–) was born in Alexandria. He was educated at Cambridge University, receiving his Ph.D. in 1951. Currently he is Professor of Social and Economic History at the Birkbeck College of the University of London. He is a Fellow of the British Academy, and an honorary foreign member of the American Academy of Arts and Sciences. Professor Hobsbawm has done field work in the Mediterranean, Latin America, and the United Kingdom. He is the author of *Primitive Rebels* (1959) and *Bandits* (1969).

GEORGE CASPAR HOMANS (1910–) is a sociologist who was trained at Harvard, where he has taught since 1939 except for a period of military service. He is now Professor of Sociology at Harvard. He has served as president of the American Sociological Association (1963–1964). He is the author of *The Human Group* (1950), *Social Behavior* (1961), *Sentiments and Activities* (1962), and *The Nature of Social Science* (1967).

ROBIN HORTON (1932–) is a Senior Research Fellow in the Institute of African Studies, University of Ibadan, Nigeria. His special interests are in the ethnography of the Ibo-speaking peoples of the Niger delta and in more general problems relating to the sociology of ideas. He is the author of *Kalabari Sculpture* (1966).

CLYDE KLUCKHOHN (1905–1960) was born in Iowa and did graduate work at the universities of Vienna, Oxford, and Harvard, where he received his doctorate and taught until his death. He served as chairman of the Department of Anthropology at Harvard and was one of the organizers of the Department of Social Relations at that institution, where he also served from 1947 to 1954 as director of the Russian Research Center. He was one of the outstanding authorities on the Navaho Indians, with whom he did extensive field work for a quarter of a century. He was active in the reorganization of the American Anthropological Association, being elected president of that body in 1947; but his dedication to his profession ranged beyond this and he was frequently called upon to serve in various administrative and advisory capacities. Of his numerous publications, those bearing on Navaho religion include *Navaho Classification of Their Song Ceremonials* (1938), *An Introduction to Navaho Chant Practice* (1940), both of which were written with Leland C. Wyman, and *Navaho Witchcraft* (1944).

ALFRED LOUIS KROEBER (1876–1960) was born in Hoboken, New Jersey, and trained in anthropology at Columbia by Boas, receiving his doctorate in 1901. From that year until his retirement in 1946 he taught at the University of California at Berkeley and was for many years curator of its museum of anthropology. He was not only one of the most prolific writers in his discipline (over 500 publications) but one of the most active in its various societies, having served as president of the American Folklore Society (1906), the American Anthropological Association (1917–1919), and the Linguistic Society of America (1940). He was also the recipient of several honorary degrees and awards. Most of his field research was done with the Indians of California. Of his publications, some of the most noteworthy were the *Handbook of the Indians of California* (1925), *Configurations of Culture Growth* (1944), and, especially, *Anthropology* (1923; revised 1948), which as a textbook exerted an important influence on generations of students.

EDMUND RONALD LEACH (1910–) was born in England and educated at Cambridge and the London School of Economics. His fieldwork has been extensive, having been conducted in China, Formosa, Iraq, Burma, Borneo, and Sri Lanka. He is presently

Professor of Social Anthropology and the Provost of King's College at Cambridge University. He is a Fellow of the British Academy, a trustee of the British Museum, and was knighted in 1975. His books include *Political Systems of Highland Burma* (1954), *Pul Eliya: A Village in Ceylon* (1961), *Rethinking Anthropology* (1961), *Claude Lévi-Strauss* (1970), and *Culture and Communication* (1976); he is editor of *The Structural Study of Myth and Totemism* (1967) and *Dialectic in Practical Religion* (1968).

WILLIAM ARMAND LESSA (1908–) is Professor Emeritus of Anthropology at the University of California, Los Angeles, and an Honorary Fellow of the Association for Social Anthropology in Oceania. Born in Newark, he began his work in Anthropology with Hooton as an undergraduate at Harvard and later received the doctorate in social anthropology from the University of Chicago. He served as first vice-president of the American Folklore Society (1960) and as secretary of the American Anthropological Association (1952–1954). He has done field work in Hawaii, China, Ulithi Atoll, and Samoa. Among his books and monographs, the one most relevant to the field of religion is his *Tales from Ulithi Atoll: a Comparative Study of Oceanic Folklore* (1961). He is also the author of *Chinese Body Divination* (1968).

CLAUDE LÉVI-STRAUSS (1908–) is Directeur d'Études at the École Pratique des Hautes Études in Paris and has held this post since 1950. He has also been Professeur au Collège de France in Paris since 1959. He was born in Brussels and educated at the University of Paris, where he obtained his Agrégé de Philosophie in 1931 and his Docteur ès Lettres in 1949. Early in his career he taught at the University of São Paulo and the New School for Social Research, New York. Later he served as cultural attaché to the French embassy in the United States. His field work was done in South and Central Mato Grosso, Brazil (1935–1936), and North and West Mato Grosso and South Amazonas (1938–1939). He has gained world recognition in anthropology for his pursuit of what has been called the "structural method." Among his writings are *Tristes tropiques* (1955; trans. 1961), *Le Totémisme aujourd'hui* (1962; trans. 1963), *La Pensée sauvage* (1962; trans. 1966), *Structural Anthropology* (1963), *Mythologiques I: Le Cru et le cuit* (1964; trans. 1969), *Mythologiques II: Du Miel aux cendres* (1966), *Mythologiques III: L'Origine des maniéres de table* (1968), and *L'Homme Nu* (1971).

RALPH LINTON (1893–1953) studied anthropology for brief periods at Pennsylvania and Columbia but received his doctorate from Harvard. After serving as assistant curator of the Chicago Natural History Museum, he taught at Wisconsin and Columbia, and was Sterling Professor of Anthropology at Yale at the time of his death. From 1939 to 1945 he was editor of the *American Anthropologist*, and in 1946 was president of the American Anthropological Association. His field researches took him to various parts of the world, including the Marquesas, Madagascar, South Africa, Peru, and Brazil. He is the author of *The Study of Man* (1936), *The Cultural Background of Personality* (1945), and *The Tree of Culture* (1955, posthumous), as well as numerous monographs and articles.

ROBERT HARRY LOWIE (1883–1957) at the time of his death was Professor Emeritus of Anthropology at the University of California, Berkeley. He was born in Vienna and educated in the United States, receiving the doctorate in 1908 from Columbia, where he studied under Boas. From 1907 to 1921 he was associated with the American Museum of Natural History and after that he went to Berkeley. He was editor of the *American Anthropologist* from 1924 to 1933, and president of the American Folklore Society, the American Ethnological Society, and the American Anthropological Association. He wrote numerous books, among them *Primitive Society* (1920), *Primitive Religion* (1924; revised, 1948), and *The History of Ethnological Theory* (1937).

BRONISLAW MALINOWSKI (1884–1942) was born and educated in Poland, where he took his Ph.D. in physics and mathematics. When ill health forced him to leave the University of Cracow in order to recuperate, he accidentally came across a copy of Frazer's *The Golden Bough*, which awakened his interest in the study of culture. He went to England in 1910 and studied under C. G. Seligman at the London School of Economics. Beginning in 1914 he spent two-and-a-half years doing research in the Pacific islands, chiefly in the Trobriands, which were made famous by his many books, including *Argonauts of the Western Pacific* (1928) and *Coral Gardens and Their Magic* (1935). In 1927 he was appointed to the first Chair in Anthropology at the University of London, where his weekly seminars became famous. At the time of his death he was a Visiting Professor at Yale University. An article written by S. F. Nadel, "Malinowski on Magic and Religion," appears in *Man and Culture—An Evaluation of the Work of Bronislaw Malinowski*, edited by Raymond Firth (1957).

OMAR KHAYYAM MOORE (1920–) was

born in Utah and received his doctorate from Washington University in 1949. He is currently Professor of Sociology at the University of Pittsburgh, where he is also director of the Clarifying Environments Program. He is president and chairman of the board of the Responsive Environments Foundation, Inc. His publications include "The Formal Analysis of Normative Concepts" (*American Sociological Review*, 1957) and "Problem Solving and the Perception of Persons" (Tagiuri and Petrullo, 1958).

BARBARA GAY MYERHOFF (1935–) was born in Cleveland, Ohio, and educated at the University of Chicago and the University of California at Los Angeles, where she received her doctorate in 1968. She is presently Professor of Anthropology and chairperson of the department at the University of Southern California. In addition, she is currently a research associate at the Andrus Gerontology Center, University of Southern California. She has done field work in South Central Mexico and in various parts of California. She is the author of *Peyote Hunt: The Sacred Journey of the Huichol Indians* (1974) and *The Divided Cloak* (In press). She is coeditor, with Sally Falk Moore, of *Secular Ritual: Forms and Meanings* (1977).

RODNEY NEEDHAM (1923–) was born in England and received his doctorate from Washington University in 1949. He is presently Professor of Social Anthropology at Oxford. He has written a number of articles, some of which are "The Left Hand of the Mugwe" (1960), "Blood, Thunder and Mockery of Animals" (1964), and "Right and Left in Nyoro Symbolic Classification" (1967). He is also the author of *Structure and Sentiment* (1962), *Belief, Language, and Experience* (1972), and the editor of *Right and Left: Essays on Dual Symbolic Classification* (1973).

MORRIS EDWARD OPLER (1907–) is Professor Emeritus of Anthropology at Cornell University and also at the University of Oklahoma. Born in Buffalo, New York, he received his Ph.D. from the University of Chicago in 1933. He served as a vice-president (1962) and then president (1963) of the American Anthropological Association. His field work was done in the American Southwest and in northern India. Among his works are *Myths and Tales of the Jicarilla Apache Indians* (1938), *Myths and Legends of the Lipan Apache Indians* (1940), *An Apache Life-Way* (1941), *Myths and Tales of the Chiricahua Apache Indians* (1942), *The Character and Derivation of the Jicarilla Holiness Rite* (1943), and *Apache Odyssey* (1969).

SHERRY B. ORTNER (1941–) is Associate Professor of Anthropology at the University of Michigan in Ann Arbor. Born in Brooklyn, she received her A.B. from Bryn Mawr College and her doctorate from the University of Chicago in 1970. She has done field research among the Sherpas of Nepal, and is the author of *Sherpas Through Their Rituals* (1977).

TALCOTT PARSONS (1902–) was born in Colorado. After attending the London School of Economics, where he studied with Ginsberg and Malinowski, he went to the University of Heidelberg and there received the doctorate in sociology and economics. He began teaching at Harvard in 1927, at first in economics and later in sociology, and is now Professor of Sociology. He was the first chairman of the Department of Social Relations at that institution (1946–1957), being one of its founders. From 1967 to 1971, he served as president of the American Academy of Arts and Sciences. He has translated and edited some of the works of Max Weber. Among his own writings are *The Structure of Social Action* (1937), *The Social System* (1951), and *Structure and Process in Modern Societies* (1960).

ALFRED REGINALD RADCLIFFE-BROWN (1881–1955) was born and educated in England, where he trained in anthropology under Haddon and Rivers at Cambridge University. His first field trip took him to the Andaman Islands from 1906 to 1908, and his fellowship thesis for Trinity College was a conventional reconstruction of Andaman culture history. But while teaching at the London School of Economics and at Cambridge he became aware of the French sociologists, especially Durkheim and Mauss, and eventually completely rewrote his Andamanese materials in terms of the meaning and function of their rites, myths, and institutions. From 1910 to 1912 he did field research in Australia. He spent a considerable part of his life abroad, being affiliated with the Pretoria Museum, the University of Cape Town, the University of Sydney, the University of Chicago, Yenching University, the University of São Paulo, Farouk I University, and Grahamstown. He was called to the newly created Chair of Social Anthropology at Oxford in 1937. Radcliffe-Brown is author of *The Andaman Islanders* (1922). Three collections of his essays, addresses, and seminar lectures have been published: *Structure and Function in Primitive Society* (1952), *A Natural Science of Society* (1957), and *Method in Social Anthropology* (1958).

ROY A. RAPPAPORT (1926–) is Professor of Anthropology and department chairman at the University of Michigan. He is currently a member of the Executive Board of the Central States Anthropological Society. His undergraduate work was done at Cornell University and he received his Ph.D. from Columbia University in 1966. He has undertaken field research in the Society Islands, New Guinea, and is the author of *Pigs for the Ancestors: Ritual in the Ecology of a New Guinea People* (1968).

KNUD RASMUSSEN (1879–1933) was born in Greenland, of partially Eskimo parentage. He learned to speak an Eskimo dialect before he was competent in Danish. He had as playmates during his childhood Eskimos who were entirely Christianized, and as a boy he dreamed of exploring and living in the unknown northland. He made the first of nearly a dozen major expeditions to the polar regions from 1902 to 1904, and this trip resulted in the publication of *The People of the Polar North* (1905), which established him as an authority on the Eskimos. Although particularly interested in folklore, he contributed greatly to knowledge about Greenland and the polar regions. He wrote on geography, natural history, language, general ethnology, and many other subjects, and in recognition of his research and writings he was awarded a Ph.D. from the University of Copenhagen. He was editor or author of several multivolume works on the Eskimo, of which *Report of the Fifth Thule Expedition, 1921–24* was one.

MICHELLE ZIMBALIST ROSALDO (1944–) was born in New York City. She studied as an undergraduate at Radcliffe and received her Ph.D. from Harvard in 1972. She is presently Assistant Professor of Anthropology at Stanford University, and has served as a member of the Institute for Advanced Study, Princeton (1975–1976). She has done field work in Andalucia, Spain; Chiapas, Mexico; and the Philippines. She is co-editor (with Louise Lamphere) of *Woman, Culture and Society* (1974).

RENATO IGNACIO ROSALDO, JR. (1941–) was born in Champaign, Illinois, and did both his undergraduate and graduate studies at Harvard, receiving his doctorate in 1970. He is presently Associate Professor of Anthropology at Stanford University, and has served as a member of the Institute for Advanced Study, Princeton (1975–1976). He has done field research in Ecuador, Peru, Chiapas, Mexico, and among the Ilongot of Northern Luzon, Philippines.

RICHARD ALLAN SHWEDER (1945–) was born in New York City, and received his Ph.D. in Anthropology from Harvard in 1972. He is currently Assistant Professor of Human Development at the University of Chicago where he serves on the Committee on Human Development. He is also a member of the Social Science Research Council's Committee on Social and Affective Development During Childhood. Professor Shweder has done field work in Chiapas, Mexico; Orissa, India; and in Kenya.

JAMES SYDNEY SLOTKIN (1913–1958) at the time of his death was Associate Professor in the Department of Social Sciences of the University of Chicago, at which institution he received his training in anthropology. His field research was conducted among the Menomini Indians. Among his pertinent publications are *The Peyote Religion* (1956) and *The Menomini Powwow Religion* (1957).

STANLEY JAYARAJA TAMBIAH (1929–) was born in Sri Lanka and received his doctorate from Cornell University in 1955. Formerly a Lecturer in Anthropology and Fellow of King's College at Cambridge University and Professor of Anthropology at the University of Chicago, he is now Professor of Anthropology at Harvard University. His field research has been conducted in Sri Lanka and Thailand. He has been awarded the Curl Bequest Prize and the Rivers Memorial Medal by the Royal Anthropological Institute. He is the author of *Buddhism and the Spirit Cults in Northeast Thailand* (1970), and *World Conqueror and World Renouncer: A Study of Buddhism and Polity in Thailand Against a Historical Background* (1976).

MISCHA TITIEV (1901–) is Professor Emeritus of Anthropology at the University of Michigan. He was born in Russia and educated at Harvard, where he received the doctorate in 1935. He is an authority on the Hopi Indians, having written *Notes on Hopi Witchcraft* (1942) and *Old Oraibi: A Study of the Hopi Indians of Third Mesa* (1944). In 1948 he did field research with the Araucanian Indians of Chile, and in 1951 with rural Japanese. He is the author of *The Science of Man* (1954; rev. 1963), *Introduction to Cultural Anthropology* (1959), and other works.

VICTOR WITTER TURNER (1920–) was born in Scotland and obtained his doctorate from the University of Manchester in 1955. He was chairman of the African Studies Committee at Cornell from 1964 to 1968; chairman of the Committee on Social Thought at the University of Chicago in 1976 and 1977; and has been chairman of the Advisory Council to the Anthropology Department of Princeton since 1973. He is presently the William R. Kenan, Jr. Professor of Anthropology in the Center for Advanced

Studies at the University of Virginia. He has done field work in Zambia, Uganda, Mexico, Ireland, Italy, and France. He is the author of *Ndembu Divination* (1961), *Chihamba, The White Spirit* (1962), *The Forest of Symbols* (1967), *The Drums of Affliction* (1968), *The Ritual Process* (1969), *Dramas, Fields, and Metaphors* (1974) and *Image and Pilgrimage in Christian Culture* (1977).

EDWARD BURNETT TYLOR (1832–1917) was the foremost anthropologist of his time. Although not a university graduate, having been privately educated, he became Keeper of the University Museum at Oxford and a reader there from 1884 until 1896, when he was given a professorship. He had an unusually wide range of interests. He went to Mexico in 1856 in the company of a prehistorian, and visited some Pueblo villages in 1884, but he was not a fieldworker. However, his critical appraisals and analyses of secondary materials were significant contributions to the nascent fund of anthropological knowledge. He was not strictly an evolutionist, for he insisted on the important part played in the development of culture by diffusion. His best-known works are *Researches in the Early History of Mankind and the Development of Civilization* (1865), *Primitive Culture: Researches into the Development of Mythology, Philosophy, Religion, Language, Art, and Custom* (1871), and *Anthropology: An Introduction to the Study of Man and Civilization* (1881).

CATHERINE CHRISTINE HILLER VOGT (1921–   ) was born in Salina, Kansas and educated at the University of Chicago. She currently serves as a research assistant in anthropology and as co-master of Kirkland House at Harvard University. She has accompanied her husband throughout his extensive field research in the Southwest and in Mexico and has worked in the Harvard Chiapas Project archives, indexing and compiling data.

EVON ZARTMAN VOGT, JR. (1918–   ) was born in Gallup, New Mexico, and educated at the University of Chicago, where he received his doctorate in 1948. Since then he has been teaching at Harvard where he is now Professor of Social Anthropology, Curator of Middle American Ethnology, and Master of Kirkland House. He has done extensive field work among the Navaho Indians of New Mexico and the Tzotzil Indians of Chiapas, Mexico. His publications include *Navaho Veterans* (1951), *Modern Homesteaders* (1955), *Water Witching U.S.A.* (with Ray Hyman; 1959), *Desarrollo Cultural de los Mayas* (with Alberto Ruz; 1964), *Zinacantan: A Maya Community in the Highlands of Chiapas* (1969), *The Zinacantecos of Mexico: A Modern Way of Life* (1970), and *Tortillas for the Gods: A Symbolic Analysis of Zinacanteco Rituals* (1976).

ANTHONY F. C. WALLACE (1923–   ) was born in Toronto. He did both his undergraduate work and graduate work at the University of Pennsylvania, receiving his doctorate there in 1950. He is now Professor of Anthropology at the University of Pennsylvania and Medical Research Scientist at the Eastern Pennsylvania Psychiatric Institute. He is a past president of the American Anthropological Association (1971–1972). He has done work among the Iroquois Indians in New York and Ontario and is the author of *Religion: An Anthropological View* (1966), and *The Death and Rebirth of the Seneca* (1970).

JOHN MAMORU WATANABE (1952–   ) was born in California and did his undergraduate work at the University of California, Santa Cruz. He is currently a Ph.D. candidate in social anthropology at Harvard University. His field work will be conducted in the Cuchumatan Highlands of western Guatemala.

ROY GEOFFREY WILLIS (1927–   ) was born in England and studied at Oxford where he received his doctorate in 1966. He was a Visiting Associate Professor at the Department of Anthropology of the University of Virginia in 1975–1976, and is presently Reader in Social Anthropology at the University of Edinburgh, Scotland. He has done field research among the Fipa of southwest Tanzania, and is the author of *Man and Beast* (1974).

EDMUND WILSON (1895–1972) was a literary critic and writer with an interest in problems of comparative religion. After his graduation from Princeton in 1916 he served as managing editor of *Vanity Fair* from 1920 to 1921, as associate editor of the *New Republic* from 1926 to 1931, and as book review editor of the *New Yorker* from 1944 to 1948. He published almost a score of books, including *The Scrolls from the Dead Sea* (1955), in connection with which he visited the Dead Sea site where the scrolls were found.

ERIC R. WOLF (1923–   ) is Distinguished Professor of Anthropology at Herbert H. Lehman College, City University of New York. Born in Vienna, Professor Wolf studied at Queens College and received his doctorate from Columbia in 1951. He has done field work in Puerto Rico, Mexico, and the Italian Alps. He is the author of *Sons of the Shaking Earth* (1959), and *Peasants* (1966).

SELECTED MONOGRAPHS ON NON-WESTERN RELIGIOUS SYSTEMS

AHERN, EMILY. *The Cult of the Dead in a Chinese Village*. Stanford, Calif.: Stanford University Press, 1973.

In this detailed study of ancestor worship in a Taiwan village, the author analyzes the complex interrelationships between Chinese kinship, lineage organization, and religion. The conclusion is drawn that the form and degree of elaboration of ancestor cults can only be understood in the wider context of community social organization, corporateness, and wealth.

BARTH, FREDRIK. *Ritual and Knowledge Among the Baktaman of New Guinea*. New Haven, Conn.: Yale University Press, 1975.

The author analyzes the Baktaman ritual system as an embodiment and transmission of traditional knowledge. The study focuses on the complex, multi-leveled initiation ceremony and on the changing significance of religious symbols for novices at various levels of initiation. Based on these data, the author proposes that the meaning of Baktaman religious symbols does not derive from the interconnectedness of a logically structured system but rather from the fan of connotations and associations derived for each separate symbol through ritual manipulation.

BARTON, R. F. *The Religion of the Ifugaos*. ("Memoirs of the American Anthropological Association," No. 65.) Menasha, Wis., 1946.

This account of "the most extensive and pervasive religion that has yet been reported . . . outside of India" introduces the gods and describes their uses and some occasions on which they are invoked. Interesting features of the work are an attempt at quantification—for example, counting the times a particular benefit is sought in a sample of rites—and an examination of the historical development of the religion based on comparative data from related groups.

BATESON, GREGORY. *Naven: A Survey of the Problems Suggested by a Composite Picture of the Culture of a New Guinea Tribe Drawn from Three Points of View*. Stanford, Calif.: Stanford University Press, 1958.

The *naven* ceremony of the Iatmul of New Guinea is a celebration of important achievements, especially when accomplished for the first time. The ceremony is performed for a person by a classificatory mother's brother and marked by sex role reversals by the participants. Bateson attempts to explain the ceremony by placing it in its full cultural context, in which he distinguishes structure and function, and relating it to the ethos or emotional tone of the society.

BELLAH, ROBERT N. *Tokugawa Religion: The Values of Pre-Industrial Japan*. New York: The Free Press, 1957.

The author uses Max Weber's sociological frame of reference to demonstrate the influence of certain religious and political value orientations found in the feudal Tokugawa period which, he proposes, formed the matrix for the prodigious and vigorous later economic and political development of Japan into an industrial nation.

BOGORAS, WALDEMAR. *The Chukchee*, Vol. VII of Franz Boas (ed.), *The Jesup North Pacific Expedition*. ("Memoirs of the American Museum of Natural History," Vol. XI, Parts 2 and 3.) Leiden: E. J. Brill, 1904–1909.

Based on extensive field work among the reindeer-breeding peoples of Siberia, this monograph presents a wealth of detail on Chukchee cosmology and on the ritual means for securing the benefits of good spirits and warding off the effects of evil ones. (The sketches of these spirits by Chukchee are illuminating.) Seasonal sacrifices are associated with the life cycle of the reindeer, while other ritual centers around the hearth, each household having its own sacred objects and signs.

BOWERS, ALFRED W. *Mandan Social and Ceremonial Organization*. Chicago: The University of Chicago Press, 1950.

Although this book is concerned with ritual, describing a variety of ceremonies each built around a specific need (buffalo, eagles, rain), it is valuable also as mythology, since all the rites are dramatizations of myths. Each centers about a bundle of objects which represent the characters and incidents of the myth.

BRICKER, VICTORIA REIFLER. *Ritual Humor in Highland Chiapas*. Austin: University of Texas Press, 1973.

This volume contains an insightful description and comparative analysis of ritual humor in three Tzotzil-speaking communities—Zinacantan, Chamula, and Chenalho. With first-hand data based on intensive field work in the three communities, Professor Bricker shows that patterns of ritual humor are related to the basic moral values of these Highland Maya cultures.

BUNZEL, RUTH. "Introduction to Zuni Ceremonialism," *47th Annual Report of the Bureau of American Ethnology*, pp. 467–545. Washington, D.C., 1932.

In this summary of the rich and varied ceremonialism of Zuni, the author points out that the apparent complexity is one of organization rather than content. She demonstrates this by abstracting a pattern of ritual elements common to all rites and by listing the major cults and their internal organization and interactions. Special emphasis is placed on the aesthetic functions of the ritual in Zuni life.

BUNZEL, RUTH. *Chichicastenango: A Guatemalan Village*. ("Publications of the American Ethnological Society," Vol. XXII.) Locust Valley, N.Y.: J. J. Augustin, 1952.

This study of a Guatemalan community contains a great deal of detail on the organizational aspects of the local religion—the selection and functioning of the rotating officials of the church—and on the *fiesta* round. In addition, consideration is given to the role of the ancestors as supplements to the Catholic saints, the use of the ancient calendar, divination by seeds, and the ideas of sin and penance.

CASO, ALFONSO. *The Aztecs: People of the Sun*. Norman: University of Oklahoma Press, 1960.

Caso sees the worship of the gods (especially the sun) and their maintenance by sacrifices as the central motivating force behind the Aztec nation. He examines the gods—their powers and their demands—and suggests that the requirements of the religion had a profound formative influence on the society. Illustrations in color from the codices contribute to the exposition and make this an attractive book.

EVANS, I. H. N. *The Religion of the Tempasuk Dusuns of North Borneo*. New York: Cambridge University Press, 1953.

The author gives a detailed account of Dusun religion and custom set in a background of daily life, pointing out the similarities to beliefs and practices found not only in other parts of Borneo but also in the Philippines, Indonesia, and Malaya. Among such similarities he cites the idea of multiple souls, soul wandering and capture, the importance of priestesses or mediums, as well as striking resemblances in ceremonial practice.

EVANS-PRITCHARD, E. E. *Witchcraft, Oracles and Magic Among the Azande*. Oxford: Clarendon Press, 1937.

Throughout this skillful account the author explores the dynamics of Zande belief—the balance between faith and skepticism and between empirical and mystical causes. To the Azande, witchcraft is the socially relevant cause of an illness and death; it is a purely psychical act, imputed to others (usually social deviants) and denied in oneself.

EVANS-PRITCHARD, E. E. *Nuer Religion*. Oxford: Clarendon Press, 1956.

In this study Evans-Pritchard describes a religion which is distinctive in its markedly monotheistic tendency, its strong sense of dependence on God, and the idea of punishment for sin and the consequent guilt, confession, and expiatory sacrifice. He suggests that Nuer religious thought, in which one spirit has many manifestations, is a reflection of the segmentary structure of the society.

FIRTH, RAYMOND. *The Work of the Gods in Tikopia*. ("London School of Economics and Political Science Monographs on Social Anthropology," Nos. 1 and 2.) London: Percy Lund, Humphries & Co., 1940.

Firth gives a step-by-step, eye-witness account, enriched by his closeness to the people and the vernacular, of the ritual cycle in this small Pacific society. He stresses the unity, perceived by the people themselves, of the series of rites—consecration of canoes and temples, harvest and planting, sacred dances, moral exhortation, and taboos on noise and amusement. Attention is given throughout to the sources of variation, by conscious innovation or error, in the tradition—the dynamics of ritual.

FLETCHER, ALICE, and LA FLESCHE, FRANCIS. "The Omaha Tribe," *27th Annual Report of the Bureau of American Ethnology*, pp. 15–672. Washington, D.C., 1911.

This study emphasizes ritual, both that of the secret societies and that performed by the clans for the tribe. The camp circle has two ritual divisions—the northern, the clans of which are responsible for rites concerned with creation and the cosmos, and the southern, whose clans perform the rites of war, maize, buffalo, and the sacred pole which "holds the tribe together."

FORTUNE, R. F. *Sorcerers of Dobu*. New York: E. P. Dutton & Co., Inc., 1932.

The author sees jealousy of possession as a keynote to this culture and traces it in the attitudes toward, and uses of, the incantations which are the means of control over the supernatural. Both garden magic and spells for inflicting disease are privately owned and secret and are employed largely to protect one's property from others. Divination by watergazing is a technique for locating the sorcerer who has caused a particular illness.

FORTUNE, R. F. *Manus Religion*. ("Memoirs, American Philosophical Society," Vol. III.) Philadelphia, 1935.

Dr. Fortune presents an exhaustive account of every facet of Manus religion with a wealth of illustrative case material, native opinions, and so on. Due to his intimacy with the villagers, he describes their personalities and emotional reactions as accurately as the average individual could describe those of his European neighbor.

FOSTER, GEORGE M. *Empire's Children: The People of Tzintzuntzan*. ("Smithsonian Institution, Institute of Social Anthropology, Publications," No. 6.) Washington, D.C., 1948.

In this community, considered by the author as one of the least rural in all rural Mexico, Catholicism of a Mexican variety has replaced the old religion in its entirety. The Church, with its rotating offices, its associations, and its ceremonial calendar, is a social and spiritual focus for the community.

GEERTZ, CLIFFORD. *The Religion of Java*. New York: The Free Press, 1960.

Javanese religion is seen as having a Great and a Little tradition, each of which blends an animistic and a Hindu heritage. Their world view and social behavior are contrasted with a third element, *santri*, the more nearly orthodox Islamic tradition. The author links each with residence and occupation, but even more importantly with religious orientation and political alignments. The study emerges as an analysis of the Javanese value system.

GOODY, JACK. *Death, Property and the Ancestors: A Study of the Mortuary Customs of the Lodagaa of West Africa*. Stanford, Calif.: Stanford University Press, 1962.

The author describes the funeral rituals through which a deceased member of a lineage becomes an ancestor. A comparison of two neighboring tribes reveals a correlation between patterns of inheritance and patterns of sacrifices to specific ancestors. Goody interprets this as an example of the ritualization of social organization, in this case the principle of unilineal descent, in which supernatural sanctions are used to reinforce the system of authority within the social group.

GOSSEN, GARY H. *Chamulas in the World of the Sun: Time and Space in a Maya Oral Tradition*. Cambridge, Mass.: Harvard University Press, 1974.

Gossen offers an analysis of the cosmology, symbolism, and verbal behavior of the Tzotzil-speaking Chamulas who live in the highlands of Chiapas in southeastern Mexico. The interpretations are based upon a systematic collection of oral traditions within the framework of their own folk classification. The author shows how the underlying structure of Chamula categories of time and space provides a key to the understanding of the style, structure, and performance of their folklore.

GRINNELL, GEORGE B. *The Cheyenne Indians*. 2 vols. New Haven, Conn.: Yale University Press, 1923.

In an account reflecting several decades of acquaintance with the Cheyenne, the author describes in detail two of the four major ceremonies, pointing up the importance of the personal ordeal, private or public, in securing success and averting evil. Healing, also rich in ceremony, receives lengthy consideration.

GUSINDE, MARTIN. *Die Feuerland Indianer*. Band 2. *Die Yamana*. Mödling bei Wien: Verlag der Internationalen Zeitschrift "Anthropos," 1937.

This work contains an account of the religious concepts and practices of the primitive

Yahgan of Tierra del Fuego. The author gives particular attention to the myths, which are concerned with the creation of the world and the invention (by a legendary family) of important parts of the social life.

HERSKOVITS, MELVILLE J. *Dahomey*. 2 vols. Locust Valley, N.Y.: J. J. Augustin, 1938.

The political complexity of this West African monarchy is here shown to be paralleled by an elaborate theology and a set of specialized religious institutions. In addition to ancestor worship carried on by extended families, there are rites for royal ancestors (at one time including human sacrifice), divination, and rituals performed by the highly trained priests of five separate cults.

HUNT, EVA. *The Transformation of the Hummingbird: Cultural Roots of a Zinacantecan Mythical Poem.* Ithaca, N.Y.: Cornell University Press, 1977.

This monograph is a masterful structural-symbolic analysis of a mythical poem from Zinacantan which uses a historical approach to relate the poem to its original antecedents in pre-Hispanic Mesoamerican mythology and then to relate the symbols to the natural, cosmic, and cultural orders. The author shows that the historical and cultural roots of the poem are still alive in contemporary Zinacantecan life as a part of "... a sacred armature that organizes, blends, and gives ultimate meaning to the puzzle pieces in the present."

JUNOD, HENRI A. *The Life of a South African Tribe*. 2d ed., revised and enlarged. London: Macmillan & Co., Ltd., 1927.

This missionary's work on the Thonga deals rather sympathetically with religious observances and gives explanations for them in native terms. The worship of ancestors is central, and divination with dice is used to determine the occasions for sacrifice; a great variety of the latter are employed for rain making and growth, purification after death, punishment and reconciliation of enemies, and, combined with magic, medicine.

LANTIS, MARGARET. *Alaskan Eskimo Ceremonialism*. ("Publications of the American Ethnological Society," Vol. XI.) Locust Valley, N.Y.: J. J. Augustin, 1947.

This survey draws together material on ceremonials from the various Eskimo groups of Alaska, pointing out the distribution and variation of ceremonies at life crises, memorial feasts for the dead, secret societies which impersonate devils to frighten the uninitiated, and hunting ritual (the latter most highly developed). The author attempts a reconstruction of historical relationships on the basis of the distributional data.

LEÓN-PORTILLA, MIGUEL. *Time and Reality in the Thought of the Maya.* Boston: Beacon Press, 1973 (Translation of Tiempo y realidad en el pensamiento Maya: ensayo de acercamiento, Mexico: Universidad Nacional Autonoma de México, 1968).

In this analysis of ancient Maya cosmology and religious symbolism, León-Portilla uses ethno-historic documents, chronicles, and linguistic and archaeological data to support his basic hypothesis that religious belief and many aspects of cognitive reality for the ancient Maya were a part of an obsessive and all-encompassing vision of temporal cycles. The solar cycles were particularly important in this cosmological system and served to delimit not only temporal, but also spatial, categories. He demonstrates that many of the Mayas' artistic, literary, and intellectual achievements developed as expressions of their concern with the reckoning of time. Professor Alfonso Villa Rojas' appendix to this volume will orient the reader to temporal and spatial aspects of the cosmologies of contemporary Indian groups of Mexico and Guatemala who are descendants of the ancient Maya.

LIENHARDT, GODFREY. *Divinity and Experience: The Religion of the Dinka.* Oxford: Oxford University Press, 1961.

This analysis of the religion of the Dinka, a pastoral people of East Africa, is concerned principally with cosmology rather than ritual. The author discusses the Dinka concept of "Divinity" (connoting formlessness or event rather than the more substantive term "God"), the political and religious ascendance of the clans of spear-masters, and the part played by cattle sacrifices in the ceremonials, which he interprets as being social-symbolic dramas paralleling events, not altering them. Cattle are offered as foils for disaster and as substitutes for men who would otherwise be the victims.

LOWIE, ROBERT H. *The Crow Indians.* New York: Farrar & Rinehart, 1935.

Lowie's insight into Crow culture and his wide knowledge of others give both depth and perspective to this work. He sees the vision quest or guardian-spirit complex as the dominant pattern in Crow relations with the supernatural, and traces this and the idea of "medicine" in a variety of communal ceremonies.

McILWRAITH, T. F. *The Bella Coola.* 2 vols. Toronto: University of Toronto Press, 1948.

This monograph on a vanishing Northwest Coast society presents a view of the world in which all the forces and beings in nature are conceived as persons. Religious belief and practice are consequently multifaceted and ubiquitous. Inheritance of myths and dances through sibs, shamanism, and a series of origin stories involving the ingenious Raven are features of considerable interest.

MALINOWSKI, BRONISLAW. *Coral Gardens and Their Magic.* 2 vols. London: George Allen & Unwin, Ltd., 1935.

Focusing on agriculture in the Trobriands, Malinowski here enlarges upon his ideas about magic with a coherent and colorful illustration of its nature, its role, and its relationship to technology and practical work. Although there are references to myths which underpin land tenure and the cultivation of gardens, this is primarily a book about practice and not about a system of beliefs.

MEAD, MARGARET. *The Mountain Arapesh,* Vol. II, *Supernaturalism.* ("Anthropological Papers of the American Museum of Natural History," Vol. XXXVII, Part 3, pp. 317–451.) New York, 1940.

In this monograph Mead describes the Arapesh world view, pointing out the absence of cosmology and the recurrence of the basic contrast between the physiological nature of men and women in ideas about human beings, spirits associated with the kin groups, life, and death. She traces this contrast in selected myths and rituals, primarily in rites of passage and harvest ceremonies.

MIDDLETON, JOHN. *Lugbara Religion: Ritual and Authority Among an East African People.* London: Oxford University Press, published for the International African Institute, 1960.

This book is more a sociological analysis of the place of ritual and belief in Lugbara social life than an exposition of their theology. It emphasizes the cult of the dead and its role in the maintenance of lineage authority. Competition for power within the lineage and household is shown to involve manipulation of this cult and, through it, the power of the ancestors.

MORLEY, SYLVANUS G. *The Ancient Maya.* 3d ed., revised by George W. Brainerd. Stanford, Calif.: Stanford University Press, 1956.

Morley draws on a lifetime of work in Maya archaeology and ethnology for this description of the Maya gods and the calendrical ritual directed to them. He traces the development of pantheon, priesthood, and ritual as this can be seen in the archaeological record.

MURPHY, ROBERT F. *Mundurucú Religion,* ("University of California Publications in American Archaeology and Ethnology," Vol. XLIX, No. 1.) Berkeley, 1958.

Murphy examines the transformations which the religion of the Mundurucú, an Indian tribe in Brazil, is undergoing today due to profound changes in their culture and social organization. Until very recently the core of their religious beliefs was the relationship between humans and game animals, now declining due to a different economic orientation. He also emphasizes the continued persistence and importance of sorcery.

NADEL, S. F. *Nupe Religion.* London: Routledge & Kegan Paul, Ltd., 1954.

Nadel's description and discussion of the theology, divination and other rituals, medicine, and witchcraft of this tribe of the Sudan reflects both anthropological sophistication and exhaustive field research. Consideration is given to the borrowing of elements of religion from other tribes and to conversion to Islam, both of which provide insight into the indigenous system.

NASH, JUNE. *In the Eyes of the Ancestors: Belief and Behavior in a Maya Community.* New Haven, Conn.: Yale University Press, 1970.

While focusing on the roles of belief and ritual in social change, the author offers an in-depth description of the religious beliefs and practices of a highland Maya community in southern Mexico. By placing religion in a wider social and economic context, she clearly illustrates how social change occurs in the "dissonance between the way things are done and social goals."

NIMUENDAJÚ, CURT. *The Eastern Timbira.* Translated by Robert H. Lowie. ("University of California Publications in American Archaeology and Ethnology," Vol. XLI.) Berkeley, 1946.

The chief emphasis in this study of a Brazilian tribe is on ceremonial and its organization. The annual dry-season rites are the initiation of age classes or dances performed by hereditary men's societies. In the rainy season these societies and ceremonial moieties participate in planting, growth, and harvest ritual.

OPLER, MORRIS E. *An Apache Life-Way.* Chicago: The University of Chicago Press, 1941.

Seeking to convey the Apache's view of life in, as nearly as possible, the Apache's own terms, Opler arranges his material on religious beliefs and practices in the order of their introduction in the individual life cycle. To the same end, he makes extensive use of verbatim reports of his informants on ritual (girls' puberty ceremony, shamanistic ceremonies for curing, love, hunting, and war) and cosmology.

ORTIZ, ALFONSO. *The Tewa World: Space, Time, Being, and Becoming in a Pueblo Soci-*

ety. Chicago: The University of Chicago Press, 1969.

The author, who was born a member of the pueblo studied, describes Tewa mythology, world view, and ritual in relation to the moiety system which divides society, for ceremonial purposes, into "Summer people" and "Winter people." Besides tracing the wide ramifications of the dual mode of classification at both the social and symbolic levels, he determines the mechanisms by which unity is maintained in the face of these divisions.

RADCLIFFE-BROWN, A. R. *The Andaman Islanders*. Cambridge: Cambridge University Press, 1922.

After describing the customs and beliefs of the Andamanese, Radcliffe-Brown proceeds to interpret the ceremonies and some of the myths from the point of view of social anthropology. He suggests that both of these serve to maintain and transmit the sentiments on which the social system depends, and shows how certain features of the marriage, funeral, and puberty rites contribute to this end.

RADIN, PAUL. "The Winnebago Tribe," *37th Annual Report of the Bureau of American Ethnology*, pp. 35–550. Washington, D.C., 1923.

Radin discusses Winnebago religious concepts and describes the four major kinds of ceremony: the clan feast; the rites of four societies of individuals blessed by the same spirit; the Medicine dance, whose membership is voluntary; and the dance following success in war. He provides perspective by a consideration of the introduction of a modern cult, Peyote.

RASMUSSEN, KNUD. *Report of the Fifth Thule Expedition, 1921–24*, Vol. VII, No. 1, *Intellectual Culture of the Iglulik Eskimos*. Copenhagen: Glydendalske Boghandel, Nordisk Forlag, 1929.

Rasmussen prefaces his work with a group of Eskimo autobiographies which bring out the difficulties of life in the far north. He proceeds, with the aid of myths and first-person statements from articulate informants, to show how the Eskimo views this life. Shamanism, amulets, and magic words as means of reducing the uncertainties of existence are described.

REDFIELD, ROBERT. *Tepoztlan: A Mexican Village*. Chicago: The University of Chicago Press, 1930.

With characteristic and appealing simplicity Redfield describes the fusion of Spanish and Aztec elements which constitutes the religion of these Mexican peasants. He follows the yearly round of *fiestas* and discusses the concepts of *santo* (saint) and *veterano* (military hero) as foci of the sentiments of the community.

REDFIELD, ROBERT, and VILLA ROJAS, ALFONSO. *Chan Kom: A Maya Village*. ("Carnegie Institution of Washington Publications," No. 448.) Washington, D.C., 1934.

In this Maya village the authors find two separate complexes of sacred ritual, each with its own practitioners and general sphere of operations. One uses prayers from the Catholic liturgy recited by professional *cantores*; this complex is usually chosen for baptism, marriage, and death. The other uses Maya priests and prayers to the spirits of the milpa, the village, and the rain, and is used for agriculture and illness.

REICHEL-DOLMATOFF, GERARDO. *Amazonian Cosmos; The Sexual and Religious Symbolism of the Tukano Indians*. Chicago: The University of Chicago Press, 1971.

Based upon sustained work with one informant who had left his tribe and was living in Bogotá, this recent volume provides an astonishingly intricate view of the cosmology and ceremonies of the Tukano Indians who live in Northwest Amazonia. The work contains data on the tribal creation myth, the cosmological beliefs, and the ceremonies which focus upon sexual symbolism and the intimate interrelationships between men and the natural world.

REINA, RUBEN E. *The Law of the Saints: A Pokomam Pueblo and Its Community Culture*. Indianapolis and New York: The Bobbs-Merrill Co., Inc., 1966.

Reina presents a thorough ethnography of Chinautla—a colorful Guatemalan community of modern Maya Indians, Spanish-speaking Ladinos and Mengalas, those of Spanish descent who have assumed the Indian life style. He integrates his description with the abstract concept of the "Law of the Saints," which is a kind of ideal model for the customary, the good, and the desirable. Formally responsible for maintaining the community's adherence to ideal behavior are the members of the religious *cofradías*, the organizations in charge of the pueblo's fiestas and religious celebrations.

RIVERS, W. H. R. *The Todas*. London: Macmillan & Co., Ltd., 1906.

The core of the religious life of this people of India's Nilgiri hills is the care of the sacred water buffaloes. This work is done in village dairies, graded by degree of sanctity, by an ordained priesthood; the elaborateness of ritual and the personal requirements of the priests vary accordingly. Religious practices of the common people include rites of passage and the observance of taboos on periodic sacred days.

ROSCOE, JOHN. *The Bakitara.* Cambridge: Cambridge University Press, 1923.

A major focus of this monograph from East Africa is the ritual surrounding the king, described as both "the great high priest of the nation" and "almost a deity himself." Supplementing the king were rain makers, diviners of many kinds, and priests devoted to each of the nineteen gods concerned with cattle raising.

SCHÄRER, HANS. *Ngaju Religion: The Conception of God Among a South Borneo People.* The Hague: Martinus Nijhoff, 1963.

The Ngaju cosmology is seen as expressing unity, at all levels, as the union of opposites, the divisions of the world created by a pervasive dualistic principle of classification. God, an ambivalent and bisexual deity, combines in himself the Hornbill and Watersnake (lesser deities), upperworld and underworld, man and woman, sun and moon, good and evil, life and death, hornbill and watersnake ceremonial moieties, etc. The basic social norms, *hadat,* are rooted in this divine order; thus transgressions of custom invite natural disaster.

SELIGMAN, C. G., and SELIGMAN, BRENDA Z. *The Veddas.* Cambridge: Cambridge University Press, 1911.

The Seligmans present a detailed account of the culture and religions of the Veddas of Ceylon, who for many years served as a sort of stockpile of a "primitive people." Their religion centers around the ancestral spirits, who enter into the bodies of shamans or other persons in order to communicate with their descendants. Strikingly, belief in magic and sorcery appear to be lacking here.

SHIROKOGOROFF, S. M. *The Psychomental Complex of the Tungus.* London: Kegan Paul, 1935.

This monograph gives systematic treatment to the beliefs of a Siberian people in spirits residing in nature and in the dead and to the methods (most of them individual) of managing these spirits. Particular attention is given to shamanism—the rituals and paraphernalia, the psychological aspects of both performance and belief, the social position of the shaman, and the possible sources of the complex.

SMITH, ROBERT J. *Ancestor Worship in Contemporary Japan.* Stanford, Calif.: Stanford University Press, 1974.

This is the first comprehensive English-language monograph on Japanese ancestor worship. The author outlines the historical development of ancestor worship in Japan, current practices concerning ancestors, and the significance of ancestors in contemporary Japanese society. The place of ancestors in Japanese cosmology and their putative role in human affairs are described. The relationship between ancestor worship and larger political and administrative processes as well as its possible future in a modernizing and highly mobile population are also considered.

SPECK, FRANK G. *Naskapi.* Norman: University of Oklahoma Press, 1935.

This work on the religion of the hunting bands of Labrador stresses the individual nature of religious observance and links it with dispersed nomadic settlement; aside from feasts in celebration of hunting success, no religious assembly is known. The author discusses the spiritual guide and the ritual of hunting in which this spirit is invoked by sweat baths, songs, drumming, and divination.

SPENCER, BALDWIN, and GILLEN, F. J. *The Arunta.* 2 vols. London: Macmillan & Co., Ltd., 1927.

A major part of this monograph is concerned with totemism—the relationship between the individual and his totem and the associated *churinga* (sacred object); the traditions, in which totemic ancestors and local topography are linked; and the various rituals whereby the totem animal or plant is increased and the young are initiated into the secrets of the sacred.

STANNER, W. E. H. *On Aboriginal Religion.* ("Oceania Monographs," No. 11.) Sydney, 1963.

This is a masterful and unique effort to examine Australian religion, with the author endeavoring to study it in itself and not as a mirror of something else.

TAMBIAH, S. J. *Buddhism and The Spirit Cults in North-East Thailand.* Cambridge: Cambridge University Press, 1970.

The author describes the four dominant ritual complexes in the religion of a Thai village. After presenting these ritual complexes as a synchronic, ordered scheme of collective representations, he examines their relationships both to the wider field of social institutions as well as to the grand Buddhist literary and historical traditions. By examining the continuities and transformations in this religious tradition, the author demonstrates the linkages between his synchronic structural description of this religious system and the rich historical roots out of which it grew.

TITIEV, MISCHA. *Old Oraibi.* ("Papers of the Peabody Museum of American Archaeology and Ethnology," Vol. XXI, No. 1.) Cambridge, Mass., 1944.

Titiev describes Hopi ceremonialism in all its complexity and interprets the various rituals in terms of the basic concepts of continuity of life after death and the duality of the year. The colorful Katcina Cult, centering around the impersonation of the dead, displays these concepts as fundamentals, while other rituals, performed by secret societies, share them to some extent.

TOBING, PHILLIP ODER LUMBAN. *The Structure of the Toba-Batak Belief in the High God*. Amsterdam: Jacob van Campen, 1956.

The author, himself a Toba-Batak, presents the total cosmology of the Toba-Batak as a manifestation of their high god whose primary embodiment is the tree of life, a giant banyan tree whose branches form the upperworld, whose trunk is the middleworld of everyday life, and whose roots are the underworld where the yearly circling of a *naga* (dragon) around the cardinal points expresses the unity of time and space. This basic conception pervades Toba-Batak life, being symbolized in microcosm in the village, house, ritual space, and even the groups in the marriage exchange.

TSCHOPIK, HARRY, JR. *The Aymara of Chucuito, Peru. I. Magic* ("Anthropological Papers of the American Museum of Natural History," Vol. XLIV, Part 2, pp. 137–308.) New York, 1951.

The aim of this monograph is to suggest a relationship between a highly specialized system of magic (described in detail) and certain salient features of Aymara personality. The author suggests that the specialization of practitioners (six kinds, distinguished by the problems each handles), the proliferation of specific rites, and the private nature of most magic are compatible with the characteristic ways of expressing anxiety and hostility.

TURNER, VICTOR W. *Chihamba, the White Spirit: A Ritual Drama of the Ndembu*. Manchester: Manchester University Press, for the Rhodes-Livingstone Institute, 1962.

In this monograph Turner describes in detail the Chihamba ritual of the Ndembu of Zambia, which is designed to overcome attacks by an ancestress and a nature spirit, and he includes the native explanation of each step. This is followed by a discussion of symbolism in general and a comparative analysis of "white" color symbolism around the world.

TURNER, VICTOR W. *The Forest of Symbols: Aspects of Ndembu Ritual*. Ithaca, N.Y.: Cornell University Press, 1967.

This book is a collection of essays, both theoretical and descriptive, on the ritual system of the Ndembu of Zambia. The author analyzes the rites as systems of symbols whose meanings are revealed through native exegesis, their use in the ceremonies, and their relations within the ritual setting. Certain basic themes, such as the rivalry between male and female and the importance of red, white, and black as life forces, are revealed even in dissimilar rites.

TURNER, VICTOR W. *The Drums of Affliction: A Study of Religious Processes Among the Ndembu of Zambia*. Oxford: Oxford University Press, 1968.

This more recent volume of Victor Turner's is not only important theoretically, but also contains additional detailed ethnographic descriptions and analyses of the meaning of symbolism in the rituals of affliction of the Ndembu. The volume includes a discussion of divination and of the rituals as social dramas in full cultural context.

UNDERHILL, RUTH. *Papago Indian Religion*. New York: Columbia University Press, 1946.

The author approaches the description of Papago ceremonies from the point of view of the contrast between two coexistent methods of contact with the supernatural—the communal and the individual. Whether of rainmaking ceremony or guardian-spirit quest, the descriptions are well written and enhanced by the inclusion of poetic songs and texts.

VAILLANT, GEORGE C. *Aztecs of Mexico*. Garden City, N.Y.: Doubleday & Co., 1941.

On the basis of Conquest documents, Vaillant constructs a brief but vivid and discerning picture of Aztec religion. He describes some of the hierarchy of gods who gave their names to the days of the ritual year, and demonstrates with clarity how this ritual calendar set the times for ceremonies—often human sacrifices—performed by the priesthood, itself a hierarchy.

VOGT, EVON Z. *Zinacantan: A Maya Community in the Highlands of Chiapas*. Cambridge, Mass.: Harvard University Press, 1969.

This ethnography on a contemporary Tzotzil-speaking tribe in southern Mexico provides data on the economic system and social structure followed by a full-length description of the religious system, including chapters on myths, ritual symbols, cosmological beliefs, shamanism, and the complex ceremonies of the cargo system attached to the cult of the saints. Not only is the syncretism between Maya and Catholic elements examined, but the monograph also suggests how contemporary Maya data may illuminate the social structure and religion of the ancient Maya as well as provide some general insights as to how the tribal society copes with the modern world that is just now reaching into the remote highlands of Chiapas.

VOGT, EVON Z. *Tortillas for the Gods: A Symbolic Analysis of Zinacanteco Rituals*. Cambridge, Mass.: Harvard University Press, 1976.

Following a theoretical introduction on concepts and methods for decoding the symbolic meaning of rituals, this monograph provides a structural analysis of the principal rites performed in Zinacantan—the ceremonies designed to bless a new home, to firmly "fix" the innate soul in an infant, to cure illness, to honor the saints, and "renew" the year. The interpretations include the myths of the holy mountains, the roles of the animal companions and supernatural ancestors, the symbolism of plants and colors, and the messages encoded in maize divinations and in the rites of the shamans and cargoholders.

WARNER, W. LLOYD. *A Black Civilization: A Social Study of an Australian Tribe*. Rev. ed. New York: Harper & Row, Publishers, Inc., 1958.

Totemism among the Murngin of Australia and its elaborate, myth-dramatizing ritual are carefully described and sociologically interpreted in this work. In addition, the role of magicians ("black" ones to cause illness and "white" ones to cure it) is examined, with special reference to arrangements in a northern subgroup which lacks this means of dealing with disease.

REFERENCES CITED

ABERLE, DAVID. "A Note on Relative Deprivation Theory as Applied to Millenarian and Other Cult Movements," in Sylvia L. Thrupp (ed.), *Millennial Dreams in Action*. ("Comparative Studies in Society and History," Supplement 2.) The Hague, 1962.

ABERLE, DAVID. *The Peyote Religion Among the Navaho*. Chicago: Aldine, 1965.

ABRAHAM, KARL. "Selected Papers on Psychoanalysis." *The International Psycho-Analytical Library*, No. 13. London: Hogarth Press, 1948.

ABRAHAM, W. E. *The Mind of Africa*. Chicago: University of Chicago Press, 1966.

ABRAHAMS, R. G. *The Peoples of Greater Unyamwezi, Ethnographic Survey of Africa*. London: International African Institute, 1967.

AHERN, EMILY. *The Cult of the Dead in a Chinese Village*. Stanford, Calif.: Stanford University Press, 1973.

AIJMER, GORAN. "A Structural Approach to Chinese Ancestor Worship," *Bijdragen tot de taal-, land-, en volkenkunde*, pt. 124, 1968.

BAKER, HUGH D. *A Chinese Lineage Village: Sheung Shui*. Stanford, Calif.: Stanford University Press, 1968.

BANTON, MICHAEL (ed.). *Anthropological Approaches to the Study of Religion*. ("Association of Social Anthropologists Monographs," No. 3.) London: Tavistock Publications, 1965; New York: Praeger, 1966.

BARBER, BERNARD. "Acculturation and Messianic Movements," *American Sociological Review*, VI (1941), 663–669.

BARNOUW, VICTOR. "A Psychological Interpretation of a Chippewa Origin Legend," *Journal of American Folklore*, LXVIII (1955), 73–85, 211–223, 341–355.

BARTH, FREDRIK. *Ritual and Knowledge Among the Baktaman of New Guinea*. New Haven, Conn.: Yale University Press, 1975.

BASCOM, WILLIAM R. "The Sanctions of Ifa Divination," *Journal of the Royal Anthropological Institute*, LXXI (1941), 43–54.

BASCOM, WILLIAM R. "Folklore and Anthropology," *Journal of American Folklore*, LXVI (1953), 283–290.

BASCOM, WILLIAM R. "The Myth-Ritual Theory," *Journal of American Folklore*, LXX (1957), 103–114.

BEALS, RALPH C. "The Comparative Ethnology of Northern Mexico Before 1750," *Ibero-Americana:* 2. Berkeley: University of California Press, 1932.

BEALS, RALPH C. "Problems of Mexican Indian Folklore," *Journal of American Folklore*, 56 (1943), 8–16.

BEATTIE, J. "The Ghost Cult in Bunyoro," in John Middleton (ed.), *Gods and Rituals*. New York: Natural History Press, 1967.

BEIDELMAN, T. O. "Pig (Guluwe): An Essay on Ngulu Sexual Symbolism and Ceremony," *Southwestern Journal of Anthropology*, XX (1964), 359–392.

BEIDELMAN, T. O. "Swazi Royal Ritual," *Africa*, XXXVI (1966), 373–405.

BEIDELMAN, T. O. "Utani: Some Kaguru Notions of Death, Sexuality and Affinity," *Southwestern Journal of Anthropology*, XXII (1966), 354–380.

BEIDELMAN, T. O. *The Matrilineal Peoples of Eastern Tanzania*. London: International African Institute, 1967.

BEIDELMAN, T. O. *The Kaguru*. New York: Holt, Rinehart and Winston, 1971.

BENEDICT, RUTH. *The Concept of the Guardian Spirit in North America*. "Memoirs of the American Anthropological Association, No. 29." Menasha, Wisconsin: American Anthropological Association, 1923.

BENEDICT, RUTH. *Patterns of Culture*. Boston: Houghton Mifflin, 1934.

BENEDICT, RUTH. *Zuni Mythology*. ("Columbia University Contributions to Anthropology," No. 21.) 1935.

BENEDICT, RUTH. *The Chrysanthemum and the Sword*. Cleveland: World Publishers, 1967.

BENITEZ, FERNANDO. *En la tierra magica del peyote*. Mexico: Ediciones Era, 1968.

BERG, CHARLES. *The Unconscious Significance of Hair*. London: George Allen & Unwin, 1951.

BERKELEY-HILL, OWEN. "The Anal-Erotic Factor in the Religion, Philosophy, and Character of the Hindus," *International Journal of Psycho-analysis*, II (1921), 306-338.

BETTELHEIM, BRUNO. "Individual and Mass Behavior in Extreme Situations," in T. M. Newcomb et al. (eds.), *Readings in Social Psychology*. New York: Holt, Rinehart and Winston, 1947.

BETTELHEIM, BRUNO. *Symbolic Wounds, Puberty Rites and the Envious Male*. New York: The Free Press, 1954.

BLAFFER, SARAH. *The Blackman of Zinacantan*. A. B. Thesis. Radcliffe College, 1969.

BOAS, FRANZ. *Indianische Sagen von der nordpacifischen Küste Amerikas*. Berlin: A. Asher, 1895.

BOAS, FRANZ. *Kwakiutl Tales*. ("Columbia University Contributions to Anthropology," No. 2.) New York, 1910.

BOAS, FRANZ. "The Origin of Totemism," *Journal of American Folklore*, XXIII (1910), 392-393.

BOAS, FRANZ. "Psychological Problems in Anthropology," *American Journal of Psychology*, XXI (1910), 371-384.

BOAS, FRANZ. "Kwakiutl Culture as Reflected in Mythology," *Memoirs of the American Folklore Society*, No. 28. 1935.

BOCHENSKI, J. M. *The Logic of Religion*. New York: New York University Press, 1965.

BOEHM, FELIX. "The Femininity-Complex in Men," *International Journal of Psycho-analysis*, XI (1930), 444-469.

BOGORAS, WALDEMAR. *The Chukchee*, Vol. VII of Franz Boas (ed.), *The Jesup North Pacific Expedition*. ("Memoirs of the American Museum of Natural History," Vol. XI, Parts 2 and 3.) Leiden: E. J. Brill, 1904-1909.

BOGORAS, WALDEMAR. *Chuckchee Mythology*. ("Jesup North Pacific Expedition," Publication 8.) "Memoirs of the American Museum of Natural History," Vol. XII. Leiden, 1910.

BOURKE, JOHN G. *Scatalogic Rites of All Nations*. Washington, D.C.: W. H. Lowerdermilk, 1891.

BRAIN, JAMES L. "Matrilineal Descent and Marital Stability: A Tanzanian Case," *Journal of Asian and African Studies*, 4:2 (1969), 122-131.

BRAIN, JAMES L. "Kingalu: A Myth of Origin from Eastern Tanzania," *Anthropos*, LXVI (1971).

BRAIN, JAMES L. "Ancestors as Elders in Africa—Further Thoughts," *Africa*, 43 (1973), 122-133.

BRICKER, VICTORIA REIFLER. *Ritual Humor in Highland Chiapas*. Austin: University of Texas Press, 1973.

BÜCHER, A. *Arbeit und Rhythmus*. 2d Ed. Leipzig, 1899.

BULMER, R. "Why Is the Cassowary Not a Bird? A Problem of Zoological Taxonomy Among the Karam of the New Guinea Highlands," *Man*, n.s., 2 (1967). 5-25.

BUNZEL, RUTH L. "Introduction to Zuni Ceremonialism," *47th Annual Report of the Bureau of American Ethnology*, pp. 467-545. Washington, D.C., 1932.

BUNZEL, RUTH L. "Zuni Katcinas," *47th Annual Report of the Bureau of American Ethnology*, pp. 837-1086. Washington, D.C., 1932.

BUNZEL, RUTH L. *Chichicastenango: A Guatemalan Village*. ("Publications of the American Ethnological Society," Vol. XXII.) Locust Valley, N.Y.: J. J. Augustin, 1952.

BURRIDGE, K. O. L. "Lévi-Strauss and Myth," in E. R. Leach (ed.), *The Structural Study of Myth and Totemism*. ("Association of Social Anthropologists Monographs," No. 5.) London: Tavistock Publications, 1967.

BURRIDGE, K. O. L. *New Heaven, New Earth: A Study of Millenarian Activities*. Oxford: Basil Blackwell, 1969.

BURROWS, EDWIN G. *Flower in My Ear*. Seattle: University of Washington Press, 1963.

BURROWS, EDWIN G., and MELFORD E. SPIRO. *An Atoll Culture: Ethnography of Ifaluk in the Central Carolines*. New Haven, Conn.: Human Relations Area Files, 1953.

CAMPBELL, JOSEPH. *The Hero with a Thousand Faces*. New York: Meridian, 1956.

CANCIAN, FRANK. "Some Aspects of the Social and Religious Organization of a Maya Society," *XXXV Congreso Internacional de Americanistas, Actas y Memorias*, I (1962), 336-343.

CANCIAN, FRANK. *Economics and Prestige in a Maya Community: The Religious Cargo System in Zinacantan*. Stanford, Calif.: Stanford University Press, 1965.

CANNON, WALTER B. *The Wisdom of the Body*. (1932). Paperback edition, New York: W. W. Norton, 1963.

CANNON, WALTER B. " 'Voodoo' Death," *American Anthropologist*, XVIV (1942), 169-181.

CARROLL, JOHN B. (ed.). *Language, Thought, and Reality: Selected Writings of Benjamin Lee Whorf*. Cambridge, Mass.: The M.I.T. Press; and New York: Wiley, 1956.

CARTER, WILLIAM. "Secular Reinforcement in Aymara Death Ritual," *American Anthropologist*, 70 (1968), 238-263.

CAWTE, J. E. "Further Comment on the Australian Subincision Ceremony" (letter to the editor), *American Anthropologist*, 70 (1968), 961-964.

CAZENEUVE, JEAN. *Les Dieux dansant á Cibola*. Paris: Gallimard Publishers, 1957.

CHAMBERLAIN, ALEXANDER F. "American Bells," *Encyclopedia of Religious Ethics*, VI (1913), 316-318.

CHAPPLE, E. D., and C. S. COON. *Principles of Anthropology*. New York: H. Holt and Co., 1942.

COCHRANE, GLYNN. *Big Men and Cargo Cults*. New York: Oxford University Press, 1970.

COFER, CHARLES N. (ed.). *Verbal Learning and Verbal Behavior*. New York: McGraw-Hill, 1961.

COHEN, PERCY. "Theories of Myth," *Man*, IV (1969), No. 3, 337-353.

COLSON, ELIZABETH. "Ancestral Spirits and Social Structure Among the Plateau Tonga," *International Archives of Ethnography*, XLVII, Part 1 (1954), 21-68.

COMTE, AUGUSTE. *Cours de philosophie positive*. Paris: Borrani et Droz, 1835-1852.

CONNOR, JOHN W. "The Social and Psychological Reality of European Witchcraft Beliefs," Psychi-

atry, 38:4 (1975), 366–380.

COUNT, EARL W. "The Earth-Diver and the Rival Twins: A Clue to Time Correlation in North-Eurasiatic and North American Mythology," in Sol Tax (ed.), *Indian Tribes of Aboriginal America*. Selected Papers of the 19th International Congress of Americanists. Chicago: The University of Chicago Press, 1952.

CRAPANZANO, VINCENT, and VIVIAN GARRISON (eds.). *Case Studies in Spirit Possession*. New York: John Wiley and Sons, 1977.

CRAWLEY, A. E. "Drums and Cymbals," *Encyclopedia of Religious Ethics*, V (1912), 89–94.

CRAWLEY, A. E. *Dress, Drinks and Drums: Further Studies of Savages and Sex*. Edited by T. Besterman. London: Methuen, 1931.

CULWICK, A. T., and G. M. CULWICK. *Ubena of the Rivers*. London: Allen and Unwin Co., 1935.

DANER, FRANCINE. *The American Children of Krsna: A Study of the Hare Krsna Movement*. New York: Holt, Rinehart and Winston, 1976.

DE BEAUVOIR, SIMONE. *The Second Sex*. New York: Knopf, 1952.

DEVEREUX, GEORGE. "Cultural and Characterological Traits of the Mohave Related to the Anal Stage of Psychosexual Development," *Psychoanalytic Quarterly*, XX (1951), 398–422.

DE WAAL MALEFIJT, ANNEMARIE. *Religion and Culture: An Introduction to Anthropology of Religion*. New York: Macmillan, 1968.

DEWEY, ALICE. "Ritual as a Mechanism for Urban Adaptation," *Man*, n.s., 5 (1970), 438–449.

D'HERTEFELT, MARCEL. "The Rwanda of Rwanda," in J. L. Gibbs (ed.), *The Peoples of Africa*, New York: Holt, Rinehart and Winston, 1966.

DORSON, RICHARD. "The Eclipse of Solar Mythology," *Journal of American Folklore*, LXVIII (1955), 393–416. Reprinted in Alan Dundes (ed.), *The Study of Folklore*. Englewood Cliffs, N.J.: Prentice-Hall, 1965.

DOUGLAS, MARY. *Purity and Danger*. London: Routledge & Kegan Paul, 1966.

DOUGLAS, MARY. "The Meaning of Myth," in E. R. Leach (ed.), *The Structural Study of Myth and Totemism*. ("Association of Social Anthropologists Monographs," No. 5.) London: Tavistock Publications, 1967.

DOUGLAS, MARY. "Pollution," *Encyclopedia of the Social Sciences*, XII (1968), 336–341.

DOUGLAS, MARY. *Natural Symbols*. New York: Random House, 1970.

DOUGLAS, MARY (ed.). *Witchcraft Confessions and Accusations*. London: Tavistock Publications, 1970.

DOUGLAS, MARY (ed.). *Rules and Meanings: The Anthropology of Everyday Life*. Baltimore: Penguin Books, 1973.

DOUGLAS, MARY. *Implicit Meanings*. London: Routledge & Kegan Paul, 1975.

DRAGOMANOV, MIXAILO PETROVIC. "Notes on the Slavic Religio-Ethical Legends: The Dualistic Creation of the World," *Russian and East European Series*, XXIII (1961). Bloomington: Indiana University Publications.

DUNDES, ALAN. "Earth-Diver: Creation of the Mythopoeic Male," *American Anthropologist*, LXIV (1962), 1032–1051.

DUNDES, ALAN. "From Etic to Emic Units in the Structural Study of Folktales," *Journal of American Folklore*, LXXV (1963), 95–105.

DUNDES, ALAN (ed.). *The Study of Folklore*. Englewood Cliffs, N.J.: Prentice-Hall, 1965.

DUNDES, ALAN. "A Psychoanalytic Theory of the Bullroarer," *Man*, n.s., 11 (1976), 220–238.

DUNDES, ALAN. "Projection in Folklore: A Plea for Psychoanalytic Semiotics," *Modern Language Notes*, 91 (1976), 1500–1533.

DURKHEIM, ÉMILE. *Le Suicide*. Paris, 1897. Translated from the French by John A. Spaulding and George Simpson. Paperback edition, New York: The Free Press, 1951.

DURKHEIM, ÉMILE. *Année Sociologique*. Vol. IV, Paris, 1899.

DURKHEIM, ÉMILE. *The Elementary Forms of the Religious Life*. Translated from the French by Joseph Ward Swain. London: George Allen & Unwin, 1915. Paperback edition, New York: The Free Press, 1954.

DURKHEIM, ÉMILE, and MARCEL MAUSS. *Primitive Classification*. Translated by Rodney Needham. London: Cohen & West; Chicago: University of Chicago Press, 1963.

DWORAKOWSKA, M. "The Origin of Bell and Drum," *Pr. Etnol. Warsaw 5*. Warsaw: Nakladem Towarzystwa Nankowego Warszawskiego, 1938.

EARLY, JOHN D. *The Sons of San Lorenzo in Zinacantan*. Ph.D. dissertation, Harvard University, 1965.

EARLY, JOHN D. "El ritual Zinacanteco en honor del Señor Esquipulas," in Evon Z. Vogt (ed.), *Los Zinacantecos: Un Pueblo de los Altos de Chiapas*. Mexico, D. F.: Instituto Nacional Indigenista, 1966, pp. 337–354.

EDMONSON, MUNRO. *Lore: An Introduction to the Science of Folklore and Literature*. New York: Holt, Rinehart and Winston, 1971.

EGGAN, FRED. "Social Anthropology and the Method of Controlled Comparison," *American Anthropologist*, 56 (1954), 743–763.

EISERLAN, F. C., et al. (eds.). *Abingdon Bible Commentary*. London: Epworth Press, 1929.

EISLER, M. J. "A Man's Unconscious Phantasy of Pregnancy in the Guise of Traumatic Hysteria: A Clinical Contribution to Anal Erotism," *International Journal of Psychoanalysis*, II (1921), 255–286.

EL GUINDI, FADWA. *Religion in Culture*. Dubuque, Iowa: William C. Brown, 1977.

ELIADE, MIRCEA. *The Sacred and the Profane: The Nature of Religion*. New York: Harcourt Brace Jovanovich, 1959. [German edition, 1957.] Paperback edition, New York: Harper & Row, 1961.

ELIADE, MIRCEA. "The Yearning for Paradise in Primitive Tradition," in H. A. Murray (ed.), *Myth and Mythmaking*. New York: Brazillier, 1960, pp. 61–75.

ELIADE, MIRCEA. *Shamanism: Archaic Techniques of Ecstasy*. Rev. ed. Translated by W. T. Trask (Bollingen Series 76.). New York: Pantheon, 1964.

ELIADE, MIRCEA. *Australian Religions: An Introduction*. Ithaca, N.Y.: Cornell University Press, 1973.

ELWIN, VERRIER. *Myths of Middle India*. Madras: Oxford University Press, 1949.

ELWIN, VERRIER. *Tribal Myths of Orissa*. Bombay: Oxford University Press, 1954.

ELWIN, VERRIER. *The Religion of an Indian Tribe*.

London: Geoffrey Cumberlege, 1955.

ENDICOTT, KIRK M. *An Analysis of Malay Magic.* New York: Oxford University Press, 1970.

ERIKSON, ERIC H. "The Development of Ritualization," in Donald Cutler (ed.), *The Religious Situation.* Boston: Beacon Press, 1968, pp. 711–733.

EVANS-PRITCHARD, E. E. *Witchcraft, Oracles and Magic Among the Azande.* New York: Oxford University Press, 1937.

EVANS-PRITCHARD, E. E. *Nuer Religion.* New York: Oxford University Press, 1956.

EVANS-PRITCHARD, E. E. "Religion," in E. E. Evans-Pritchard et al., *The Institutions of Primitive Society.* Oxford: Basil Blackwell, 1956.

EVANS-PRITCHARD, E. E. *Social Anthropology and Other Essays.* New York: Free Press, 1962.

EVANS-PRITCHARD, E. E. *Theories of Primitive Religions.* New York: Oxford University Press, 1965.

FAIRCHILD, HOXIE N. (ed.). *Religious Perspectives in College Teaching.* New York: Ronald Press, 1952.

FEI HSIAO-TUNG. *Peasant Life in China: A Field Study of Country Life in the Yangtze Valley.* New York: E. P. Dutton, 1939.

FERENCZI, SANDOR. "Further Contributions to the Theory and Technique of Psycho-analysis," *The International Psycho-analytical Library,* No. 11. London: Hogarth Press, 1950.

FERENCZI, SANDOR. *Sex in Psycho-analysis.* New York: Dover, 1956.

FERNANDEZ, JAMES. "The Mission of Metaphor in Expressive Culture," *Current Anthropology,* 15:2 (1974), 119–145.

FIRTH, RAYMOND. *History and Traditions of Tikopia.* ("The Polynesian Society," Memoir No. 33.) Wellington, New Zealand, 1971.

FIRTH, RAYMOND. *Tikopia Ritual and Belief.* Boston: Beacon Press, 1967.

FIRTH, RAYMOND. *Symbols: Public and Private.* Ithaca, N.Y.: Cornell University Press, 1973.

FISCHER, J. L. "The Sociopsychological Analysis of Folktales," *Current Anthropology,* IV (1963), 235–295.

FORTES, MEYER. *Oedipus and Job in West African Religion.* London: Cambridge University Press, 1959.

FORTES, MEYER. "Pietas and Ancestor Worship," *Journal of the Royal Anthropological Institute,* 91 (1961), 166–191.

FORTES, MEYER. "Introduction," in M. Fortes and G. Dieterlen (eds.), *African Systems of Thought.* New York: Oxford University Press, 1965a.

FORTES, MEYER. "Some Reflections on Ancestor Worship in Africa," in M. Fortes and G. Dieterlen (eds.), *African Systems of Thought.* London: Oxford University Press, 1965b.

FORTES, MEYER. "Totem and Taboo," in *Proceedings of the Royal Anthropological Institute,* (1966), 5–22.

FOSBROOK, H., and R. A. YOUNG. *Land and Politics Among the Luguru of Tanzania.* London: Routledge and Kegan Paul, 1960.

FOSTER, GEORGE M. "Nagualism in Mexico and Guatemala," *Acta Americana,* 2 (1944), 85–103.

FOX, JAMES J. "Sister's Child as Plant: Metaphors in an Idiom of Consanguinity," in R. Needham (ed.), *Rethinking Kinship and Marriage.* London: Tavistock Publications, 1972.

FRANK, LAWRENCE K. "Tactile Communication," in Alfred G. Smith (ed.), *Communication and Culture.* New York: Holt, Rinehart and Winston, 1966.

FRAZER, JAMES G. *Psyche's Task: A Discourse Concerning the Influence of Superstition on the Growth of Institutions.* London: Macmillan, 1909.

FRAZER, JAMES G. *The Golden Bough: A Study in Magic and Religion.* 12 vols. 3d ed., revised and enlarged. London: Macmillan, 1911–1915. Abridged edition, 1922; reprinted New York: St. Martins Press, 1955.

FRAZER, JAMES G. *Sir Roger de Coverley, and Other Literary Pieces.* London: Macmillan, 1920.

FRAZER, JAMES G. *Folklore in the Old Testament.* Abridged edition. London: Macmillan, 1923.

FRAZER, JAMES G. *The Fear of the Dead in Primitive Religion.* 3 vols. London: Macmillan, 1933–1936.

FRAZER, JAMES G. *Creation and Evolution in Primitive Cosmogonies.* London: Macmillan, 1935.

FREEDMAN, MAURICE. *Chinese Lineage and Society: Fukien and Kwangtung.* London: Athalone Press, 1966.

FREEDMAN, MAURICE. *Rites and Duties, or: Chinese Marriage.* London: G. Bell & Sons, 1967.

FREEDMAN, MAURICE. "Ritual Aspects of Chinese Kinship and Marriage," in M. Freedman (ed.), *Family and Kinship in Chinese Society.* Stanford: Stanford University Press, 1970, 164–179.

FREUD, SIGMUND. *Totem and Taboo: Resemblances Between the Psychic Life of Savages and Neurotics.* Authorized English translation, with Introduction, by A. A. Brill. New York: Moffat Yard & Co., 1918. Paperback edition, New York: Vintage Books, 1952.

FREUD, SIGMUND. *The Basic Writings of Sigmund Freud.* New York: Modern Library, 1938.

FREUD, SIGMUND. *Moses and Monotheism.* Translated by Katherine Jones. New York: Alfred A. Knopf, Inc., 1939.

FREUD, SIGMUND. *Collected Papers, Vol. III.* London: Hogarth, 1949.

FREUD, SIGMUND. "Obsessive Acts and Religious Practices," *Collected Papers,* Vol. II. Translated by Joan Rivière. 5 vols. London: Hogarth Press and the Institute of Psycho-Analysis, 1948–1950.

FREUD, SIGMUND. *A General Introduction to Psycho-Analysis.* New York: Permabooks, 1953.

FREUD, SIGMUND and OPPENHEIM, D. E. *Dreams in Folklore.* New York: International Universities Press, 1958.

FROMM, ERICH. *The Forgotten Language.* New York: Grove Press, 1951.

FUNG, YU-LAN. *A History of Chinese Philosophy.* Translated by Derk Bodde. Peiping: H. Vetch, 1937.

FURST, PETER T. "West Mexican Tomb Sculpture as Evidence for Shamanism in Pre-Hispanic Mesoamerica," *Anthropologica,* 15 (1965), 29–60.

FURST, PETER T. "Huichol Conceptions of the Soul," *Folklore Americas,* 27:2 (1967), 39–106.

FURST, PETER T. "The Parching of the Maize: An Essay on the Survival of Huichol Ritual," *Acta Ethnologica et Linguistica,* 14 (1968), Vienna.

FURST, PETER T., and BARBARA G. MYERHOFF. "Myth as History: The Jimson Weed Cycle of the Huichols of Mexico," *Anthropologica,* 17 (1966), 3–39.

FUSTEL DE COULANGES, N. D. *La Cité antique.* Paris: Durand, 1864. [Also published in English translation as *The Ancient City*, various editions, including paperback by Doubleday, 1963.]

GALLIN, BERNARD. *Hsin Hsing, Taiwan: A Chinese Village in Change*. Berkeley: University of California Press, 1966.

GEERTZ, CLIFFORD. "Ritual and Social Change: A Javanese Example," *American Anthropologist*, 59 (1957), 32–54.

GEERTZ, CLIFFORD. "Ethos, World-view and the Analysis of Sacred Symbols," *Antioch Review* (Winter, 1958), 421–437.

GEERTZ, CLIFFORD. *The Religion of Java*. New York: The Free Press, 1960.

GEERTZ, CLIFFORD. "Ideology as a Cultural System," in D. Apter (ed.), *Ideology of Discontent*. New York: The Free Press, 1964.

GEERTZ, CLIFFORD. " 'Internal Conversion' in Contemporary Bali," in J. Bastin and R. Roolvink (eds.), *Malayan and Indonesian Studies Presented to Sir Richard Winstedt*. New York: Oxford University Press, 1964.

GEERTZ, CLIFFORD. "Religion as a Cultural System," in Michael Banton (ed.), *Anthropological Approaches to the Study of Religion*. ("Association of Social Anthropologists Monographs," No. 3.) London: Tavistock Publications, 1965; New York: Praeger, 1966.

GEERTZ, CLIFFORD. *Islam Observed: Religious Development in Morocco and Indonesia*. Chicago: University of Chicago Press, 1968.

GEERTZ, CLIFFORD. "Religious Change and Social Order in Soeharto's Indonesia," *Asia*, 27 (1972), 62–84.

GEERTZ, CLIFFORD. *The Interpretation of Cultures*. New York: Basic Books, 1973.

GENNEP, ARNOLD L. VAN. "Essai d'une théorie des langues spéciales," *Rev. Etud. Ethnogr. Social.*, I (1908), 276–277.

GENNEP, ARNOLD L. VAN. *The Rites of Passage*. London: Routledge and Kegan Paul, Ltd.; Chicago: The University of Chicago Press, 1960. [French edition, *Les Rites de Passage*. Paris: E. Nourry, 1909.]

GEORGES, ROBERT (ed.). *Studies on Mythology*. Homewood, Ill.: The Dorsey Press, 1968.

GIBBON, E. *The Decline and Fall of the Roman Empire* (abridgment by D. M. Low). London: Chatto and Windus, 1960.

GINZBERG, LOUIS. *The Legends of the Jews*, I. Philadelphia: Jewish Publication Society of America, 1925.

GLUCKMAN, MAX. "Mortuary Customs and the Belief in Survival after Death among the South-eastern Bantu," *Bantu Studies*, 10 (1937).

GLUCKMAN, MAX. *Rituals of Rebellion in South-east Africa*. Manchester: Manchester University Press, 1954.

GLUCKMAN, MAX. *Essays on the Ritual of Social Relations*. Manchester: Manchester University Press, 1962.

GLUCKMAN, MAX (ed.). *Closed Systems and Open Minds: The Limits of Naivety in Social Science*. Edinburgh: Oliver and Boyd, 1964.

GLUCKMAN, MAX (ed.). *Custom and Conflict in Africa*. New York: Barnes and Noble, 1964.

GLUCKMAN, MAX. "The Frailty of Authority," in Max Gluckman (ed.), *Custom and Conflict in Africa*. New York: Barnes and Noble, 1964, 27–53.

GOFFMAN, ERVING. "The Nature of Deference and Demeanor," *American Anthropologist*, 58, (1956), 473–503.

GOLDENWEISER, ALEXANDER A. "Religion and Society: A Critique of Émile Durkheim's Theory of the Origin and Nature of Religion," *The Journal of Philosophy, Psychology, and Scientific Methods*, XIV (1931), 113–124.

GOLDMAN, STANFORD. "Further Consideration of Cybernetic Aspects of Homeostasis," in M. C. Yevits and Scott Cameron (eds.), *Self-Organizing Systems*. New York: Pergamon Press, 1960.

GOODE, WILLIAM J. *Religion Among the Primitives*. New York: The Free Press, 1951.

GOODY, JACK. "Religion and Ritual: The Definitional Problem," *British Journal of Sociology*, XII (1961), 142–164.

GOODY, JACK. *Death, Property, and the Ancestors: A Study of the Mortuary Customs of the Lodagaa of West Africa*. Stanford: Stanford University Press, 1962.

GOSSEN, GARY H. *Time and Space in Chamula Oral Tradition*. Ph.D. dissertation, Department of Anthropology, Harvard University, 1970.

GOSSEN, GARY H. "Chamula Genres of Verbal Behavior," *Journal of American Folklore*, 84 (1971), 145–167.

GOSSEN, GARY H. *Chamulas in the World of the Sun: Time and Space in a Maya Oral Tradition*. Cambridge, Mass.: Harvard University Press, 1974.

GRAY, ROBERT F. *The Sonjo of Tanganyika*. New York: Oxford University Press, 1963.

GREY, GEORGE. *Polynesian Mythology and Ancient Traditional History of the New Zealand Race*. London: John Murray, 1855.

GUIRAND, FELIX. "Assyro-Babylonian Mythology," in *Larousse Encyclopedia of Mythology*. New York: Prometheus Press, 1959.

HADDON, A. C., and W. H. R. RIVERS. *Reports of the Cambridge Anthropological Expedition to Torres Straits* (6 vols.). Cambridge: Cambridge University Press, 1935.

HALLOWELL, A. IRVING. "Freudian Symbolism in the Dream of a Salteaux Indian," *Man*, XXXVIII (1938), 47–48.

HALLOWELL, A. IRVING. "Myth, Culture and Personality," *American Anthropologist*, XLIX (1947), 544–556.

HALLPIKE, C. R. "Social Hair," *Man*, n.s., 4 (1969), 256–264.

HALLPIKE, C. R. "Is There a Primitive Mentality?" *Man*, n.s., 11 (1976), 253–270.

HARRISON, JANE. *Prolegomena to the Study of Greek Religion*. London: Cambridge University Press, 1903.

HARRISON, JANE. *Themis: A Study of the Social Origins of Greek Religion*. Cambridge: Cambridge University Press, 1912.

HASTINGS, J. *A Dictionary of the Bible*, Vol. 4. Edinburgh: T. and T. Clark, 1902.

HAYES, E. NELSON, and TANYA HAYES (eds.). *Claude Lévi-Strauss: The Anthropologist as Hero*. Cambridge, Mass., and London: The M.I.T. Press, 1970.

HERTZ, R. *Death and the Right Hand*. Translated by Rodney and Claudia Needham. London: Cohen & West; New York: The Free Press, 1960. (First published in 1909.)

HICK, JOHN. *Philosophy of Religion*. Englewood Cliffs, N.J.: Prentice Hall Co., 1963.

HILL, W. W. "The Navaho Indians and the Ghost Dance of 1890." *American Anthropologist*, XLVI (1944), 523–527.

HOAGLAND, HUDSON. "Some Comments on Science and Faith," in "Conference on Science, Philosophy, and Religion." New York, 1941. (Mimeographed.)

HOBSBAWM, ERIC J. *Primitive Rebels*. New York: W. W. Norton, 1959.

HOCART, A. M. *Kings and Councillors*. Cairo: Egyptian University, Faculty of Arts, 1936.

HOCART, A. M. *The Life-Giving Myth*. London: Methuen, 1952.

HOCART, A. M. *Social Origins*. London: Methuen, 1954.

HOLMER, NILS M., and HENRY WASSEN. *Mu-Igala or the Way of Muu, A Medicine Song from the Cunas of Panama*. Göteborg: Etnografiska Museet, 1947.

HOMANS, GEORGE C. "Anxiety and Ritual: The Theories of Malinowski and Radcliffe-Brown," *American Anthropologist* XLIII (1941), 164–172.

HORTON, ROBIN. "A Definition of Religion, and Its Uses," *Journal of the Royal Anthropological Institute*, XC (1960), 201–226.

HORTON, ROBIN. "The Kalabari World View: An Outline and Interpretation," *Africa*, XXXII (1962), No. 3, 197–220.

HORTON, ROBIN. "Ritual Man in Africa," *Africa*, XXXIV (1964), No. 2, 85–104.

HORTON, ROBIN, and RUTH FINNEGAN (eds.). *Modes of Thought*. London: Faber and Faber Ltd., 1973.

HOWARD, W. F. "First and Second Corinthians," in F. C. Eiserlan et al. (eds.), *Abingdon Bible Commentary*. London: Epworth Press, 1929.

HOWELLS, W. W. *The Heathens: Primitive Man and His Religions*. Garden City, N.Y.: Doubleday, 1948. Paperback edition, New York: Natural History Press.

HUBERT, HENRI, and MARCEL MAUSS. *Sacrifice: Its Nature and Function*. Translated by W. D. Halls. Chicago: University of Chicago Press, 1964.

HUCKEL, HELEN. "Vicarious Creativity," *Psychoanalysis* II (1953), 44–50.

HUME, DAVID. *Four Dissertations. I, The Natural History of Religion*. . . . London: A. Millar, 1757.

HUNT, EVA. *The Transformation of the Hummingbird: Cultural Roots of a Zinacantecan Mythic Poem*. Ithaca, N.Y.: Cornell University Press, 1977.

HUXLEY, ALDOUS. *Doors to Perception*. New York: Harper & Row, 1954.

HUXLEY, FRANCIS. "Anthropology and ESP," in J. R. Smythies (ed.), *Science and ESP*. London: Routledge & Kegan Paul, 1967.

HYMAN, STANLEY EDGAR. "The Ritual View of Myth and the Mythic," *Journal of American Folklore*, LXVIII (1955), 462–472.

JAKOBSON, ROMAN, and MORRIS HALLE. *Fundamentals of Language*. The Hague: Mouton, 1956.

JAMES, WILLIAM. *Principles of Psychology*. Vol. I. New York: Holt, Rinehart and Winston, 1918.

JARVIE, I. C. "Theories of Cargo Cults: A Critical Analysis," *Oceania*, 34 (1963), 1–31, 108–136.

JENSEN, ADOLF. *Myth and Cult Among Primitive Peoples* Translated by M. T. Choldin and W. Weissleder. Chicago: University of Chicago Press, 1963.

JOHNSON, F. *A Standard Swahili Dictionary*. London: Oxford University Press, 1939.

JONES, ERNEST. "Essays in Applied Psycho-analysis, II." *The International Psycho-analytical Library*, No. 41. London: Hogarth Press, 1951.

JONES, ERNEST. "How to Tell Your Friends from Geniuses," *Saturday Review*, XL (August 10, 1957), 9–10, 39–40.

JUNG, CARL GUSTAV. *Psychology of the Unconscious*. New York: Moffat Yard, 1916.

KAEPPLER, A. L., and H. ARLO NIMMO (eds.). *Directions in Pacific Traditional Literature*. Honolulu: Bishop Museum Press, 1976.

KANT, IMMANUEL. *Kritik der reunen Vernunft*. 2d ed. Riga, 1787.

KARDINER, ABRAM. *The Individual and His Society*. New York: Columbia University Press, 1939.

KARDINER, ABRAM. *The Psychological Frontiers of Society*. New York: Columbia University Press, 1945.

KENYATTA, JOMO. *Facing Mount Kenya: The Tribal Life of the Gikuyu*. London: Secker and Warburg, 1938.

KIELL, NORMAN (ed.). *Psychoanalysis, Psychology and Literature*. Madison: University of Wisconsin Press, 1963.

KITAGAWA, JOSEPH M. "The Nature and Program of the History of Religions Field," *Divinity School News* (November, 1957), 13–25.

KLEINMAN, ARTHUR. "Medicine's Symbolic Reality: On a Central Problem in the Philosophy of Medicine," *Inquiry*, 16 (1974), 206–213.

KLUCKHOHN, CLYDE. "Myths and Rituals: A General Theory," *Harvard Theological Review*, XXXV (January, 1942), 45–79.

KLUCKHOHN, CLYDE. *Navaho Witchcraft*. ("Peabody Museum Papers," No. 22.) Cambridge, Mass., 1944.

KLUCKHOHN, CLYDE. "Universal Categories of Culture," in *Anthropology Today: An Encyclopedic Inventory*, prepared under the chairmanship of A. L. Kroeber. Chicago: The University of Chicago Press, 1953.

KLUCKHOHN, CLYDE. "Recurrent Themes in Myths and Mythmaking." *Proceedings of the American Academy of Arts and Sciences*, LXXXVIII (1959), 268–279.

KÖNGAS, ELLI KAIJA. "The Earth-Diver," *Ethnohistory* VII (1960), 151–180.

KOPYTOFF, IGOR. "Ancestors as Elders in Africa," *Africa*, XLI: 2 (1971), 129–42.

KROEBER, ALFRED L. "Totem and Taboo: An Ethnologic Psychoanalysis," *American Anthropologist*, XXII (1920), 48–55.

KROEBER, ALFRED L. "Totem and Taboo in Retrospect," *American Journal of Sociology*, XLV (1939), 446–451.

KROEBER, ALFRED L. *Anthropology*. New ed., revised. New York: Harcourt Brace Jovanovich, 1948.

KROEBER, ALFRED L. *The Nature of Culture*. Chicago: The University of Chicago Press, 1952.

KUPER, HILDA. *An African Aristocracy*. New York: Oxford University Press, for the International African Institute, 1947.

KUPER, HILDA, and A. J. B. HUGHES. *The Shona and Ndebele of Southern Rhodesia, Ethnographic Survey of Africa*. London: International African Institute, 1954.

LA BARRE, WESTON. *The Peyote Cult.* ("Yale University Publications in Anthropology," No. 13.) New Haven, Conn., 1938.

LA BARRE, WESTON. *The Ghost Dance: The Origins of Religion.* New York: Doubleday, 1970.

LA FONTAINE, J. S. (ed.). *The Interpretation of Ritual.* London: Tavistock Publications, 1972.

LAMPHERE, LOUISE, and MICHELLE ROSALDO (eds.). *Woman, Culture and Society.* Stanford, Calif.: Stanford University Press, 1974.

LANG, ANDREW. *The Making of Religion.* London: Longmans, Green & Co., 1898.

LANG, ANDREW. *Myth, Ritual and Religion.* Vol. I. London: Longmans, Green, 1899.

LANGER, SUZANNE K. *Feeling and Form: A Theory of Art.* New York: Scribner, 1953.

LANGER, SUZANNE K. *Philosophy in a New Key.* 4th ed. Cambridge, Mass.: Harvard University Press, 1960.

LAROMIGUIERE, P. *Leçons de philosophie sur les principes de l'intelligence, ou sur les causes et sur les origines des idées.* 4th ed. 3 vols. Paris: Brunot-Labbe, 1826.

LAUGHLIN, ROBERT M. *Through the Looking-Glass: Reflections on Zinacantan Courtship and Marriage.* Ph.D. dissertation, Harvard University, 1963.

LAWRENCE, PETER. *Road Belong Cargo: A Study of the Cargo Movement in the Southern Madang District, New Guinea.* Manchester: Manchester University Press, 1964.

LEACH, E. R. *Political Systems of Highland Burma.* London: G. Bell & Sons, 1954. Reprinted, Boston: Beacon Press, 1964.

LEACH, E. R. "Magical Hair," *Journal of the Royal Anthropological Institute (Man),* LXXXVIII (1958), 147–164.

LEACH, E. R. "Lévi-Strauss in the Garden of Eden: An Examination of Some Recent Developments in the Analysis of Myth," *Transactions of the New York Academy of Sciences,* Ser. II, XXIII (1961), 386–396.

LEACH, E. R. *Pul Eliya: A Village in Ceylon.* Cambridge, Mass.: Cambridge University Press, 1961.

LEACH, E. R. "Two Essays on the Symbolic Representation of Time," in *Rethinking Anthropology.* London: Athlone Press, University of London, 1961.

LEACH, E. R. "Genesis as Myth," *Discovery,* XXIII (1962), 30–35.

LEACH, E. R. "Pulleyar and the Lord Buddha: An Aspect of Religious Syncretism in Ceylon," *Psychoanalysis and the Psychoanalytic Review,* XLIX (1962), No. 2, 80–102.

LEACH, E. R. "Anthropological Aspects of Language: Animal Categories and Verbal Abuse," in Eric H. Lenneberg, *New Directions in the Study of Language.* Cambridge, Mass.: The M.I.T. Press, 1964, pp. 23–63.

LEACH, E. R. "Ritualization in Man in Relation to Conceptual and Social Development," *Philosophical Transactions of the Royal Society of London.* CCLI (1966), Ser. B, No. 772, 403–408.

LEACH, E. R. "Brain Twister," *New York Review of Books,* (Oct. 12, 1967) 6–10.

LEACH, E. R. *A Runaway World?* New York: Oxford University Press, 1967.

LEACH, E. R. (ed.). *The Structural Study of Myth and Totemism.* ("Association of Social Anthropologists," Monograph 5.) London: Tavistock Publications, 1967.

LEACH, E. R. (ed.). *Dialectic in Practical Religion.* New York: Cambridge University Press, 1968.

LEACH, E. R. *Claude Lévi-Strauss.* New York: Viking, 1970.

LEACH, E. R. *Culture and Communication.* New York: Cambridge University Press, 1976.

LEEUW, G. VAN DER. *Phänomenologie der Religion.* 2d ed. Tübingen: J. C. B. Mohr (Paul Siebeck), 1933.

LEIGHTON, ALEXANDER H., and DOROTHEA C. LEIGHTON. "Elements of Psychotherapy in Navaho Religion," *Psychiatry,* IV (1941), 515–524.

LEIGHTON, ALEXANDER H., and DOROTHEA C. LEIGHTON. "Some Types of Uneasiness and Fear in a Navaho Indian Community," *American Anthropologist,* XLIV (1942), 194–209.

LENNEBERG, ERIC H. *New Directions in the Study of Language.* Cambridge, Mass.: The M.I.T. Press, 1964.

LEON-PORTILLA, MIGUEL. *Time and Reality in the Thought of the Maya.* Boston: Beacon Press, 1973. [Spanish edition, *Tiempo y realidad en el pensamiento Maya.* Mexico: Universidad Nacional Autonoma de México, 1968.]

LESLIE, CHARLES (ed.). *Anthropology of Folk Religion.* New York: Random House, 1960.

LESSA, WILLIAM A. "Oedipus-Type Tales in Oceania," *Journal of American Folklore,* LXIX (1956), 63–73.

LESSA, WILLIAM A. "Sorcery on Ifaluk," *American Anthropologist,* LXIII (1961), 817–820.

LESSA, WILLIAM A. *Tales from Ulithi Atoll: A Comparative Study in Oceanic Folklore.* ("University of California Publications: Folklore Studies," No. 13). Berkeley and Los Angeles, 1961.

LESSA, WILLIAM A. "The Decreasing Power of Myth on Ulithi," *Journal of American Folklore,* LXXV (1962), 153–159.

LESSA, WILLIAM A. "Discoverer-of-the-Sun," *Journal of American Folklore,* LXXIX (1966), 3–51.

LESSA, WILLIAM A. "The Apotheosis of Marespa," in A. L. Kaeppler and H. Arlo Nimmo (eds.), *Directions in Pacific Traditional Literature.* Honolulu: Bishop Museum Press, 1976.

LESSA, WILLIAM, and MARVIN SPIEGELMAN. "Ulithian Personality As Seen Through Ethnographic Materials and Thematic Test Analysis." ("University of California Publications in Culture and Society," Vol. II, No. 2.) Berkeley, 1954.

LESTER, DAVID. "Voodoo Death: Some New Thoughts on an Old Phenomenon," *American Anthropologist,* 74 (1972), 386–390.

LÉVI-STRAUSS, CLAUDE. "La Geste d'Asdiwal," *École pratique des hautes études, section des sciences religieuses.* Extr. Annuaire, 1958–1959, pp. 3–43.

LÉVI-STRAUSS, CLAUDE. "The Bear and the Barber," *Journal of the Royal Anthropological Institute,* XCIII (1963), 1–11.

LÉVI-STRAUSS, CLAUDE. *Structural Anthropology.* New York: Basic Books, 1963.

LÉVI-STRAUSS, CLAUDE. *Totemism,* Boston: Beacon Press, 1963. [French edition, *Le Totémisme aujourd'hui.* Paris: Presses Universitaires de France, 1962.]

LÉVI-STRAUSS, CLAUDE. *The Savage Mind.* London:

Weidenfeld and Nicolson, 1966. [French edition, *La Pensée sauvage*. Paris: Libraire Plon, 1962.]

LÉVI-STRAUSS, CLAUDE. *Mythologiques III: L'Origine des manières de table*. Paris: Libraire Plon, 1968.

LÉVI-STRAUSS, CLAUDE. *The Elementary Structures of Kinship*. Boston: Beacon Press, 1969. [French edition, *Les Structures élémentaires de la parenté*. Paris: Les Presses Universitaires, 1949.]

LÉVI-STRAUSS, CLAUDE. *The Raw and the Cooked*. New York: Harper & Row, 1969. [French edition, *Mythologiques I: Le Cru et le cuit*. Paris: Plon, 1964.]

LÉVI-STRAUSS, CLAUDE. *Tristes tropiques*. New York: Atheneum, 1970. [French edition, *Tristes tropiques*. Paris: Plon, 1955.]

LÉVI-STRAUSS, CLAUDE. *Mythologiques IV: l'homme nu*. Paris: Plon, 1971.

LÉVI-STRAUSS, CLAUDE. *From Honey to Ashes*. New York: Harper & Row, 1973. [French edition, *Mythologiques II: du miel au cendre*. Paris: Plon, 1964.]

LÉVI-STRAUSS, CLAUDE. *Structural Anthropology II*. New York: Basic Books, 1976.

LÉVY-BRUHL, LUCIEN. *How Natives Think*. London: George Allen & Unwin, 1926. [French edition, *Les Fonctions mentales dans les sociétés primitives*. Paris: F. Alcan, 1910.] Paperback edition, New York: Washington Square Press, 1966.

LÉVY-BRUHL, LUCIEN. *Primitive Mentality*. London: Macmillan, 1923. [French edition, 1922.]

LÉVY-BRUHL, LUCIEN. *Les Carnets de Lucien Lévy-Bruhl*. Paris: Libraire Plon, 1949.

LEWIS, I. M. *Ecstatic Religion: An Anthropological Study of Spirit Possession and Shamanism*. Baltimore: Penguin Books, 1971.

LEWIS, OSCAR. "Comparisons in Cultural Anthropology," in William L. Thomas, Jr. (ed.), *Yearbook of Anthropology, 1955*. New York: Wenner-Gren Foundation for Anthropological Research, 1955.

LEX, BARBARA. "Voodoo Death: New Thoughts on an Old Explanation," *American Anthropologist*, 76 (1974), 818–823.

LIENHARDT, GODFREY. *Divinity and Experience: The Religion of the Dinka*. New York: Oxford University Press, 1961.

LIENHARDT, GODFREY. *Social Anthropology*. New York: Oxford University Press, 1964.

LINTON, RALPH. "Nativistic Movements," *American Anthropologist*, XLV (1943), 230–240.

LLOYD, G. *Polarity and Analogy: Two Types of Argumentation in Greek Thought*. Cambridge: Cambridge University Press, 1966.

LOMBROSO, CESARE. *The Man of Genius*. London: Walter Scott, 1895.

LOWIE, ROBERT H. *Primitive Society*. New York: Liveright, 1920.

LOWIE, ROBERT H. *The Crow Indians*. New York: Holt, Rinehart and Winston, 1935.

LOWIE, ROBERT H. *Primitive Religion*. Enl. ed. New York: Liveright, 1948.

LOWIE, ROBERT H. *Indians of the Plains*. ("American Museum of Natural History, Anthropological Handbooks." No. 1.) New York: McGraw-Hill, 1954.

LOWIE, ROBERT H. "Religion in Human Life," *American Anthropologist*, LXV (1963), 532–542.

LUKAS, FRANZ. "Das Ei als kosmogonische Vorsellung," *Zeitschrift des Vereins für Volkskunde*, IV (1894), 227–243.

LUMHOLTZ, CARL. *Symbolism of the Huichol Indians*, Memoirs, 2, vol. 1. New York: American Museum of Natural History, 1900.

LUMHOLTZ, CARL. *Unknown Mexico*, Vols. 1 and 2. New York: Scribner, 1902.

LUMHOLTZ, CARL. *Decorative Art of the Huichol Indians*, Memoirs, 3, vol. 3. New York: American Museum of Natural History, 1904.

MACK, ARIEN (ed.). *Death in American Experience*. New York: Schocken Books, 1973.

MAIR, LUCY. *An African People in the Twentieth Century*. London: Routledge and Kegan Paul, 1934.

MAIR, LUCY. "Independent Religious Movements in Three Continents," *Comparative Studies in Sociology and History*, 1 (1959), 113–136.

MAIR, LUCY. *Witchcraft*. New York: McGraw-Hill, 1969.

MALINOWSKI, BRONISLAW. *Myth in Primitive Psychology*. New York: W. W. Norton, 1926.

MALINOWSKI, BRONISLAW. *Sex and Repression in Savage Society*. London: Routledge & Kegan Paul, 1927.

MALINOWSKI, BRONISLAW. "Culture," in *Encyclopaedia of the Social Sciences*, IV (1931), 621–646.

MALINOWSKI, BRONISLAW. *Coral Gardens and Their Magic*. 2 vols. London: George Allen & Unwin, 1935.

MALINOWSKI, BRONISLAW. *Magic, Science and Religion, and Other Essays*. Boston: Beacon Press, 1948; and New York: The Free Press, 1948. Paperback edition. Garden City, N.Y.: Doubleday (Anchor Books), 1954.

MANN, JOHN. *The Folktale as a Reflector of Individual and Social Structure*. Ph.D. dissertation, Columbia University, 1958.

MAQUET, JACQUES. *The Premise of Inequality*. New York: Oxford University Press, 1961.

MARETT, ROBERT RANULPH. *The Threshold of Religion*. London: Methuen, 1909.

MATTHEWS, WASHINGTON. *The Night Chant: A Navaho Ceremony*. ("Memoirs of the American Museum of Natural History," No. 6.) New York, 1902.

MATTHEWS, WASHINGTON. "Myths of Gestation and Parturition," *American Anthropologist*, IV (1902), 737–742.

MC CLELLAND, DAVID C., and G. A. FRIEDMAN. "A Cross-Cultural Study of the Relationship Between Child-Training Practices and Achievement Motivation Appearing in Folk Tales," in G. E. Swanson, T. M. Newcomb, and E. L. Hartley (eds.), *Readings in Social Psychology*. New York: Holt, Rinehart and Winston, 1952.

MC CULLOCH, J. A. "Monsters," in *Hastings Encyclopaedia of Religion and Ethics*. Edinburgh: T. & T. Clark, 1913.

MIDDLETON, JOHN. "The Cult of the Dead: Ancestors of Ghosts," in *Lugbara Religion: Ritual and Authority Among an East African People*. New York: Oxford University Press, 1960a.

MIDDLETON, JOHN. *Lugbara Religion*. London: Oxford University Press, 1960b.

MIDDLETON, JOHN (ed.). *Gods and Rituals*. ("American Museum of Natural History Sourcebooks in Anthropology.") New York: The Natural History Press, 1967a.

MIDDLETON, JOHN (ed.). *Magic, Witchcraft, and Curing.* ("American Museum of Natural History Sourcebooks in Anthropology.") New York: The Natural History Press, 1967b.

MIDDLETON, JOHN (ed.). *Myth and Cosmos.* ("American Museum of Natural History Sourcebooks in Anthropology.") New York: The Natural History Press, 1967c.

MIDDLETON, JOHN, and EDWARD WINTER (eds.). *Witchcraft and Sorcery in East Africa.* London: Routledge & Kegan Paul, 1963; New York: Praeger, 1963.

MILLER, GEORGE A. "Language and Psychology," in E. H. Lenneberg (ed.), *New Directions in the Study of Language.* Cambridge, Mass.: M.I.T. Press, 1964.

MITCHELL, J. CLYDE. *The Yao Village.* Manchester: Manchester University Press, 1956.

MONEY-KYRLE, R. *The Meaning of Sacrifice.* ("The International Psycho-Analytic Library," No. 16.) London: Hogarth Press, 1930.

MOONEY, JAMES. "The Ghost-Dance Religion and the Sioux Outbreak of 1890," *14th Annual Report of the Bureau of American Ethnology, 1892–93,* Part 2. Washington, D.C.: 1896.

MOORE, OMAR K. "Divination—A New Perspective," *American Anthropologist,* LIX (1957), 69–74.

MOREAU, R. E. "Joking Relationships in Tanganyika," *Africa,* XIV (1944), 386–400.

MORGAN, WILLIAM. "Navaho Dreams," *American Anthropologist,* XXXIV (1932), 390–405.

MORGAN, WILLIAM. *Human Wolves Among the Navaho.* ("Yale University Publications in Anthropology," No. 11.) New Haven, Conn., 1936.

MÜLLER, F. MAX (trans.). *Rig-Veda-Sanhita: The Sacred Hymns of the Brahmans.* London: Trübner, 1869.

MUNN, NANCY. *Walbiri Iconography.* Ithaca, N.Y.: Cornell University Press, 1973.

MURCHISON, C. *Handbook of Social Psychology.* New York: Oxford University Press, 1931.

MURDOCK, GEORGE P. *Social Structure.* New York: Macmillan, 1949.

MURRAY, H. A. (ed.). *Myth and Mythmaking.* New York: Brazillier, 1960.

MYERHOFF, BARBARA. "The Deer-Maize-Peyote Symbol Complex Among the Huichol Indians of Mexico," *Anthropological Quarterly,* 43 (1970), 64–68.

MYERHOFF, BARBARA. *The Peyote Hunt: The Sacred Journey of the Huichol Indians.* Ithaca, N.Y.: Cornell University Press, 1974.

NADEL, S. F. "A Field Experiment in Racial Psychology," *British Journal of Psychology,* XXVIII (1937), 195–211.

NADEL, S. F. "A Study of Shamanism in the Nuba Mountains," *Journal of the Royal Anthropological Institute,* LXXVI (1946), 25–37.

NADEL, S. F. *Nupe Religion.* London: Routledge & Kegan Paul, 1954.

NASH, JUNE. *In the Eyes of the Ancestors: Belief and Behavior in a Maya Community.* New Haven, Conn.: Yale University Press, 1970.

NATHHORST, BERTEL. *Formal or Structural Studies of Traditional Tales.* (Stockholm Studies in Comparative Religion, No. 9, ACTA Universitatis Stockhomiensis.) Stockholm: Kungl Boktryckeriet P. A. Norstedt and Soner, 1969.

NEEDHAM, JAMES (ed.). *Science, Religion and Reality.* New York: Macmillan, 1925.

NEEDHAM, RODNEY. "A Structural Analysis of Purum Society," *American Anthropologist,* LX (1958), 75–101.

NEEDHAM, RODNEY. "The Left Hand of the Mugwe: An Analytical Note on the Structure of Meru Symbolism," *Africa,* XXXI (1961), 28–33.

NEEDHAM, RODNEY. "Blood, Thunder, and Mockery of Animals." *Sociologus,* 14 (1964), 136–149.

NEEDHAM, RODNEY. "Percussion and Transition," *Journal of the Royal Anthropological Institute (Man),* II (1967), No. 4, 606–614.

NEEDHAM, RODNEY. "Right and Left in Nyoro Symbolic Classification," *Africa,* XXXVII, (1967), No. 4, 425–452.

NEEDHAM, RODNEY. *Rethinking Kinship and Marriage.* London: Tavistock Publications, 1972.

NEEDHAM, RODNEY (ed.). *Right and Left.* Chicago: University of Chicago Press, 1973.

NEHER, ANDREW. "A Physiological Explanation of Unusual Behavior in Ceremonies Involving Drums," *Human Biology,* XXXIV: 2 (1962), 151–160.

NEIHARDT, JOHN G. *Black Elk Speaks.* Lincoln: University of Nebraska Press, 1961.

NEU, JEROME "Lévi-Strauss on Shamanism," *Man,* n.s., 10:2 (1975), 285–292.

NEWCOMB, T. M., et al. (eds.). *Readings in Social Psychology.* New York: Holt, Rinehart and Winston, 1947.

NEWELL, WILLIAM H. (ed.). *Ancestors.* The Hague: Mouton, 1976.

NORBECK, EDWARD. *Religion in Primitive Society.* New York: Harper & Row, 1961.

NORDENSKIOLD, E. "An Historical and Ethnological Survey of the Cuna Indians," in H. Wassen (ed.), *Comparative Ethnographical Studies,* Vol. X. Goteberg: Etnögrafiska Avendelningen, 1938.

OGDEN, C. K., and I. A. RICHARDS. *The Meaning of Meaning.* New York: Harcourt Brace Jovanovich, 1927 (Second Edition).

OPLER, MORRIS E. "An Interpretation of Ambivalence of Two American Indian Tribes," *Journal of Social Psychology,* VIII, No. 1, (February, 1936), 82–115.

OPLER, MORRIS E. "Further Comparative Anthropological Data Bearing on the Solution of a Psychological Problem," *Journal of Social Psychology,* IX (1938), 477–483.

OPLER, MORRIS E. *An Apache Life-Way.* Chicago: The University of Chicago Press, 1941.

ORTNER, SHERRY B. *Tibetan Circles.* M. A. Thesis, University of Chicago, 1966.

ORTNER, SHERRY B. "On Key Symbols," *American Anthropologist,* 75 (1973), 1338–1346.

ORTNER, SHERRY B. "Sherpa Purity," *American Anthropologist,* 75 (1973) 49–63.

ORTNER, SHERRY B. "Gods' Bodies, Gods' Food: A Symbolic Analysis of Sherpa Ritual," in Roy Willis (ed.), *The Interpretation of Symbolism.* New York: Wiley, 1975.

PARSONS, TALCOTT. *Essays in Sociological Theory: Pure and Applied.* New York: The Free Press, 1949.

PARSONS, TALCOTT. *The Social System.* New York: The Free Press, 1951.

PARSONS, TALCOTT. "Religious Perspectives in Sociology and Social Psychology," in Hoxie N. Fairchild (ed.), *Religious Perspectives in College Teaching.* New York: Ronald Press, 1952.

PARSONS, TALCOTT, R. F. BALES, and E. S. SHILS. *Working Papers in the Theory of Action*. New York: The Free Press, 1953.

PAUL, ROBERT A. "The Sherpa Temple as a Model of the Psyche," *American Ethnologist*, 3 (1976), 131–146.

PEPPER, STEPHEN. *World Hypotheses*. Berkeley: University of California Press, 1942.

PERRY, RALPH BARTON. *General Theory of Value: Its Meaning and Basic Principles Construed in Terms of Interest*. New York: Longman, Green, 1926.

POSTMAN, L. "The Present Status of Inference Theory," in Charles N. Cofer (ed.), *Verbal Learning and Verbal Behavior*. New York: McGraw-Hill, 1961, pp. 152–196.

POUILLON, JEAN, and PIERRE MARANDA. *Échanges et communications*. Mélanges Offert à Claude Lévi-Strauss. The Hague: Mouton, 1970.

POZAS, RICARDO. *Chamula: Un pueblo Indio de los altos de Chiapas*. ("Memorias del Instituto Nacional Indigenista," VII.) Mexico, 1959.

POZAS, RICARDO. *Juan the Chamula: An Ethnological Re-creation of the Life of a Mexican Indian*. Translated from the Spanish by Lysander Kemp. Berkeley and Los Angeles: University of California Press, 1962.

PRINS, A. H. J. *The Swahilli-Speaking Peoples of Zanzibar and the East African Coast*. London: International African Institute, 1961.

RADCLIFFE-BROWN, A. R. *The Andaman Islanders*. New York: Cambridge: University Press, 1922.

RADCLIFFE-BROWN, A. R. "The Sociological Theory of Totemism," *Proceedings of the Fourth Pacific Science Congress* (Java, 1929). Batavia, 1930.

RADCLIFFE-BROWN, A. R. *Taboo*. ("The Frazer Lecture," 1939.) New York: Cambridge: University Press, 1939.

RADCLIFFE-BROWN, A. R. "Religion and Society," *Journal of the Royal Anthropological Institute*, LXXV (1945), 33–43.

RADCLIFFE-BROWN, A. R. "The Comparative Method in Social Anthropology." Huxley Memorial Lecture for 1951. *Journal of the Royal Anthropological Institute*, LXXXI (1951), 15–22. [Republished in *Method in Social Anthropology*, edited by M. N. Srinivas. Chicago: The University of Chicago Press, 1958.]

RADCLIFFE-BROWN, A. R. *Structure and Function in Primitive Society*. New York: The Free Press, 1952.

RADIN, PAUL. *Primitive Religion: Its Nature and Origin*. New York: Viking, 1937.

RADIN, PAUL. *The Trickster*. New York: Philosophical Library, 1956.

RAGLAN, FITZ ROY RICHARD SOMERSET (LORD). *The Hero: A Study in Tradition, Myth, and Drama*. London: Methuen, 1936.

RANK, OTTO. "Die Symbolschichtung im Wecktraum und ihre Wiederkehr im mythischen Denken," *Jahrbuch für psychoanalytische Forschungen*, IV (1912), 51–115.

RANK, OTTO. *Psychoanalytische Beiträge zur Mythenforschung*. 2d ed. Leipzig: Internationaler Psychoanalytischer Verlag, 1922.

RAPPAPORT, ROY. "Ritual Regulation of Environmental Relations Among a New Guinea People," *Ethnology*, 6 (1967), 17–30.

RAPPAPORT, ROY. *Pigs for the Ancestors: Ritual in the Ecology of a New Guinea People*. New Haven, Conn.: Yale University Press, 1968.

RAPPAPORT, ROY. "Ritual, Sanctity, and Cybernetics," *American Anthropologist*, 73 (1971), 59–76.

RASMUSSEN, KNUD. *Report of the Fifth Thule Expedition, 1921–24*, Vol. VII, No. 1, *Intellectual Culture of the Igulik Eskimos*. Copenhagen: Gyldendalske Boghandel, Nordisk Forlag, 1929.

REICHEL-DOLMATOFF, GERARDO. "Cosmology as Ecological Analysis: A View from the Rain Forest," *Man*, n.s., 11 (1976), 307–318.

REIK, THEODOR. "Gold und Kot," *International Zeitschrift für Psychoanalyse*, III (1951), 183.

REINACH, SALOMON. *Orpheus: A History of Religions*. Translated by Florence Simmonds. Enl. New York: Liveright, 1930.

RICHARDS, A. *Chisungu*. London: Faber & Faber, 1956.

RÓHEIM, GÉZA. "Primitive Man and Environment," *International Journal of Psycho-Analysis*, II (1921), 157–178.

RÓHEIM, GÉZA. "Psycho-analysis and the Folk-Tale," *International Journal of Psycho-Analysis*, III (1922), 180–186.

RÓHEIM, GÉZA. "Heiliges Geld in Melanesien," *Internationale Zeitschrift für Psychoanalyse*, IX (1923), 384–401.

RÓHEIM, GÉZA."Psycho-analysis of Primitive Culture Types," *International Journal of Psycho-Analysis*, XIII (1932), 1–221. (Róheim Australasian Research number.)

RÓHEIM, GÉZA. "Society and the Individual," *Psychoanalytic Quarterly*, IX (1940), 526–545.

RÓHEIM, GÉZA. "Myth and Folk-Tale," *American Imago*, II (1941), 266–279.

RÓHEIM, GÉZA. The Gates of the Dream. New York: International Universities Press, 1951

RÓHEIM, GÉZA. "Fairy Tale and Dream," *The Psychoanalytic Study of the Child*, VIII (1953), 394–403.

RÓHEIM, GÉZA. "Dame Holle: Dream and Folk Tale (Grimm No. 24)," in Robert Lindner (ed.), *Explorations in Psychoanalysis*. New York: Julian Press, 1953.

ROOTH, ANNA BIRGITTA. "The Creation Myths of the North American Indians," *Anthropos*, LII (1957), 497–508.

ROSALDO, MICHELLE Z. *Context and Metaphor in Ilongot Oral Tradition*. Unpublished Ph.D. dissertation, Harvard University, 1971.

ROSALDO, MICHELLE Z. "Metaphor and Folk Classifications," *Southwestern Journal of Anthropology*, 28:1 (1972), 83–99.

ROSALDO, MICHELLE Z. "Women, Culture, and Society: A Theoretical Overview," In M. Rosaldo and L. Lamphere (eds.), *Woman, Culture and Society*. Stanford, Calif.: Stanford University Press, 1974.

ROSALDO, MICHELLE Z. "It's All Uphill: The Creative Metaphors of Ilongot Magical Spells," in M. Sanches and B. Blount (eds.), *Ritual, Reality and Creativity in Language*. New York: Seminar Press, 1975, pp. 117–204.

ROSALDO, MICHELLE Z., and JANE MONNIG ATKINSON. "Man the Hunter and Woman: Metaphors for the Sexes in Ilongot Magical Spells," in Roy Willis (ed.), *The Interpretation of Symbolism*. London: J. M. Dent; New York: Wiley, 1975, pp. 43–75.

ROSALDO, RENATO I., JR. "Metaphors of Hierarchy in a Mayan Ritual," *American Anthropologist*, 67 (1968), 524-536.

ROSALDO, RENATO I., JR. "Ilongot Kin Terms: A Bilateral System of Northern Luzon, Philippines," in *Proceedings of VIIIth International Congress of Anthropological and Ethnological Sciences.* Tokyo: Science Council of Japan, 1970 pp. 81-84.

ROSALDO, RENATO I., JR. *Ilongot Society: The Social Organization of a Non-Christian Group in Northern Luzon, Philippines.* Ph.D. Dissertation, Harvard University, 1970.

ROSSI, INO (ed.). *The Unconscious in Culture.* New York: E. P. Dutton, 1974.

SACLEUX, C. S. Dictionnaire Francais-Swahilli (second edition). Paris: Institut d'Ethnologie, 1959.

SAHAGÚN, BERNARDINO DE. *The Florentine Codex: General History of the Things of New Spain, Book II, The Ceremonies.* Translated by A. J. O. Anderson and C. E. Dibble. ("Monographs of the School of American Research," No. 14, Part 3.) Sante Fe: Museum of New Mexico. 1951.

SANTAYANA, GEORGE. *Reason in Religion,* New York: Collier Books, 1906.

SAPIR, EDWARD. "Conceptual Categories in Primitive Languages," *Science*, LXXIV (1931), 578.

SAVILLE, MARSHALL H. "The Goldsmith's Art in Ancient Mexico." ("Indian Notes and Monographs.") New York: Heye Foundation, 1920.

SCHMIDT, WILHELM. *The Origin and Growth of Religion: Facts and Theories.* Translated by H. J. Rose. New York: Lincoln MacVeagh, 1931.

SCHNEIDER, DAVID M. *American Kinship.* Englewood Cliffs, N.J.: Prentice-Hall. 1968.

SCHUTZ, A. *The Problem of Social Reality. Collected Papers*, Vol. I. The Hague: Martinus Nijhoff, 1962.

SCHWARTZ, EMANUEL K. "A Psychoanalytic Study of the Fairy Tale," *American Journal of Psychotherapy*, X (1956), 740-762.

SCHWARZBAUM, HAIM. "Jewish and Moslem Sources of a Falasha Creation Myth," in Raphael Patai, Francis Lee Utley, and Dov Noy (eds.), *Studies in Biblical and Jewish Folklore.* ("American Folklore Society," Memoir 51.) Bloomington: Indiana University Press, 1960.

SELIGMAN, E., and J. JOHNSON (eds.). *Encyclopedia of the Social Sciences.* New York: Macmillan, 1931.

SELIGMAN, C. G., and BRENDA Z. SELIGMAN. *The Veddas.* New York: Cambridge University Press. 1911.

SHELTON, AUSTIN J. "The Aged and Eldership Among the Igbo," in Cowgill and Holmes (eds.), *Aging and Modernization.* Englewood Cliffs, N. J.: Prentice-Hall, 1972.

SILBERER, HERBERT. "A Pregnancy Phantasy in a Man," *Psychoanalytic Review*, XII (1925), 377-396.

SILVER, DANIEL. *Zinacanteco Shamanism.* Unpublished Ph.D. dissertation, Department of Social Relations, Harvard University, 1966.

SINGER, MILTON. "The Cultural Pattern of Indian Civilization," *Far Eastern Quarterly*, XV (1955), 23-36.

SINGER, MILTON. "The Great Tradition in a Metropolitan Center: Madras," in M. Singer (ed.) *Traditional India: Structure and Change.* Philadelphia: American Folklore Society, 1958.

SINGER, PHILIP, and DANIEL E. DESOLE. "The Australian Subincision Ceremony Reconsidered: Vaginal Envy or Kangaroo Bifid Penis Envy," *American Anthropologist*, LXIX (1967), 355-358.

SLOTKIN, J. S. "Menomini Peyotism," *Transactions of the American Philosophical Society*, XLII, Part 4 (1952).

SLOTKIN, J. S. "Peyotism, 1521-1891," *American Anthropologist*, LVII (1955), 202-230.

SLOTKIN, J. S. "The Peyote Way," Tomorrow, IV, No. 3 (1955-1956), 64-70.

SLOTKIN, J. S. *The Peyote Religion: A Study in Indian-White Relations.* New York: The Free Press, 1956.

SLOTKIN, J. S. *The Menomini Powwow Religion.* Milwaukee, Wis.: Milwaukee Public Museum, 1957.

SMITH, ROBERT J. *Ancestor Worship in Contemporary Japan.* Stanford, Calif.: Stanford University Press, 1974.

SMITH, W. ROBERTSON. *Lectures on the Religion of the Semites:* New York: D. Appleton, 1889. Paperback edition, New York: Meridian Books, 1957.

SPECK, FRANK G. *Naskapi.* Norman: University of Oklahoma Press, 1935.

SPENCE, LEWIS. *An Introduction to Mythology.* New York: Holt, Rinehart and Winston, 1921.

SPENCER, BALDWIN, and F. J. GILLEN. *The Arunta.* 2 vols. London: Macmillan, 1927.

SPENCER, KATHERINE. "Reflection of Social Life in the Navaho Origin Myth." ("University of New Mexico Publications in Anthropology," No. 3.) 1947.

SPERBER, DAN. *Rethinking Symbolism,* Translated by Alice Morton. New York: Cambridge University Press. 1975.

STEARN, G. E. "Conversations with McLuhan," *Encounter*, XXVIII: 1967, 50-58.

STEFANISZYN, B. *Social and Ritual Life of the Ambo of Northern Rhodesia.* London: Oxford University Press, 1964.

STEKEL, WILHELM. *Patterns of Psychosexual Infantilism.* New York: Grove Press, 1959.

STEWARD, JULIAN N. "Evolution and Process," in A. L. Kroeber (ed.), *Anthropology Today.* Chicago: The University of Chicago Press, 1953.

STRATHERN, ANDREW, and MARILYN STRATHERN. "Marsupials and Magic: A Study of Spell Symbolism Among the Mbowamb," in E. Leach (ed.), *Dialectic in Practical Religion.* New York: Cambridge University Press. 1968.

STURTEVANT, WILLIAM C. "Categories, Percussion and Physiology," *Journal of the Royal Anthropological Institute (Man)*, 3:1 (1968) 133-134.

TAMBIAH, S. J. "Animals Are Good to Think and Good to Prohibit," *Ethnology*, 8 (1968), 423-459.

TAMBIAH, S. J. "The Magical Power of Words," *Man*, 3:2 (1968) 175-208.

TAMBIAH, S. J. *Buddhism and the Spirit Cults in Northeast Thailand.* New York: Cambridge University Press, 1970.

TAX, SOL, et al. (eds.). *An Appraisal of Anthropology Today.* Chicago: University of Chicago Press, 1953.

TEW, MARY. *Peoples of the Lake Nyasa Region* (Ethnographic Survey of Africa). London: International African Institute, 1950.

THOMAS, ELIZABETH MARSHALL. *The Harmless People*. New York: Knopf, 1959.

THOMAS, KEITH. *Religion and the Decline of Magic*. New York: Scribner, 1971.

THOMAS, W. I., and F. ZNANIECKI. *The Polish Peasant in Europe and America*. Chicago: University of Chicago Press, 1918.

THOMPSON, J. ERIC S. *Maya History and Religion*. Norman: University of Oklahoma Press, 1970.

THOMPSON, STITH. *Tales of the North American Indians*. Cambridge, Mass.: Harvard University Press, 1929.

THOMPSON, STITH. *Motif-Index of Folk-Literature*. Bloomington: Indiana University Press, 1955.

TITIEV, MISCHA. "A Fresh Approach to the Problem of Magic and Religion," *Southwestern Journal of Anthropology*, XVI (1960), 292–298.

TURNER, VICTOR. *Ndembu Divination: Its Symbolism and Techniques*. ("Rhodes-Livingstone Papers," No. 31.) Manchester, 1961.

TURNER, VICTOR. *Chihamba, The White Spirit*. ("Rhodes-Livingstone Papers," No. 33.) Manchester, 1962.

TURNER, VICTOR. "Three Symbols of Passage in Ndembu Circumcision Ritual," in M. Gluckman (ed.), *Essays in the Ritual of Social Relations*, Manchester: Manchester University Press, 1962, pp. 124–173.

TURNER, VICTOR. "Betwixt and Between: The Liminal Period in *Rites de Passage*," in the *Proceedings of the American Ethnological Society*, Symposium on New Approaches to the Study of Religion, 1964, pp. 4–20.

TURNER, VICTOR. *Lunda Medicine and the Treatment of Disease* ("Rhodes-Livingstone Papers," No. 15.) Manchester, 1964.

TURNER, VICTOR. "Symbols in Ndembu Ritual," in M. Gluckman (ed.), *Closed Systems and Open Minds: The Limits of Naivety in Social Anthropology*. London: Manchester University Press, 1964.

TURNER, VICTOR. "Colour Classification in Ndembu Ritual: A Problem in Primitive Classification," in *Anthropological Approaches to the Study of Religion*. ("Association of Social Anthropologists," Monograph 3.) London: Tavistock Publications, 1966.

TURNER, VICTOR. *The Forest of Symbols*. Ithaca and London: Cornell University Press, 1967.

TURNER, VICTOR. *The Drums of Affliction*. New York: Oxford University Press, 1968.

TURNER, VICTOR. *The Ritual Process*. Chicago: Aldine, 1969.

TURNER, VICTOR. *Dramas, Fields and Metaphors*. Ithaca, N.Y.: Cornell University Press, 1974.

TURNER, VICTOR. "Symbolic Studies," *Annual Review of Anthropology*, 4 (1975).

TYLOR, EDWARD B. *Primitive Culture: Researches into the Development of Mythology, Philosophy, Religion, Language, Art, and Custom*. 2d ed. 2 vols. London: John Murray, 1873.

UCHENDU, VICTOR. *The Igbo of Southeast Nigeria*. New York: Holt, Rinehart and Winston, 1965.

UCHENDU, VICTOR. "Ancestorcide! Are African Ancestors Dead?" in William Newell (ed.), *Ancestors*. The Hague: Mouton, 1976, pp. 283–296.

VOGT, EVON Z. "Ceremonial Organization in Zinacantan," *Ethnology*, 4 (1965a) 39–52.

VOGT, EVON Z. "Structural and Conceptual Replication in Zinacantan Culture," *American Anthropologist*, 67 (1965b), 342–353.

VOGT, EVON Z. "Zinacanteco 'Souls,'" *Man*, 65 (1965c), 33–35.

VOGT, EVON Z. *Zinacantan: A Maya Community in the Highlands of Chiapas*. Cambridge, Mass.: Harvard University Press (Belknap Press), 1969.

VOGT, EVON Z. "Human Souls and Animal Spirits in Zinacantan," in J. Pouillon and P. Maranda (eds.), *Échanges et Communications*. The Hague: Mouton, 1970, pp. 1148–1157.

VOGT, EVON Z. *Tortillas for the Gods: A Symbolic Analysis of Zinacanteco Ritual*. Cambridge, Mass.: Harvard University Press, 1976.

VOGT, EVON Z., and CATHERINE C. VOGT. "Lévi-Strauss Among the Maya," *Man*, 5 (1970) 379–392

WADDINGTON, C. H. *The Ethical Animal*. New York: Atheneum, 1961.

WALLACE, ANTHONY F. C. "A Science of Human Behavior," *Explorations*, No. 3. Toronto: University of Toronto, 1953.

WALLACE, ANTHONY F. C. "Revitalization Movements," *American Anthropologist*, LVIII (1956), 264–281.

WALLACE, ANTHONY F. C. *Culture and Personality*. New York: Random House, 1961.

WALLACE, ANTHONY F. C. *Religion: An Anthropological View*. New York: Random House, 1966.

WALLACE, ANTHONY F. C. *The Death and Rebirth of the Seneca*. New York: Knopf, 1970.

WALLIS, WILSON D. *Messiahs—Christian and Pagan*. Boston: R. G. Badger, 1918.

WALLIS, WILSON D. *Messiahs: Their Role in Civilization*. Washington, D.C.: American Council of Public Affairs, 1943.

WARNER, W. LLOYD. *A Black Civilization: A Social Study of an Australian Tribe*. New York: Harper & Row, 1937.

WARNER, W. LLOYD. *American Life: Dream and Reality*. Chicago: The University of Chicago Press, 1953.

WARNER, W. LLOYD. *The Living and the Dead: A Study of the Symbolic Life of Americans*. New Haven, Conn.: Yale University Press, 1959.

WARNER, W. LLOYD. *The Family of God*. New Haven, Conn.: Yale University Press, 1961.

WASSERSTROM, ROBERT. *Our Lady of the Salt*. A.B. honors thesis, Harvard College, 1970.

WAX, MURRAY, and ROSALIE WAX. "The Notion of Magic," *Current Anthropology*, IV (1963), 495–518.

WAX, ROSALIE, and MURRAY WAX. "The Magical World View," *Journal for the Scientific Study of Religion.*, I (1962), 179–188.

WEBER, MAX. *The Theory of Social and Economic Organization*. New York: The Free Press, 1947.

WHEELER, ADDISON J. "Gongs and Bells," *Encyclopedia of Religious Ethics*, VI (1913), 313–316.

WHEELER-VOEGELIN, ERMINIE. "Earth Diver," In Maria Leach (ed.), *Standard Dictionary of Folklore, Mythology and Legend*. Vol. 1. New York: Funk and Wagnalls, 1949.

WHEELER-VOEGELIN, ERMINIE, and REMEDIOS W. MOORE. "The Emergence Myth in Native North America," in W. Edson Richmond (ed.), *Studies in Folklore*. Bloomington: Indiana University Press, 1957.

WHITEHEAD, ALFRED N. *Symbolism*. New York: Putnam, 1927.

WHITING, JOHN W. M. "The Cross-Cultural Method,"

in Gardner Lindzey (ed.), *Handbook of Social Psychology*. Vol. I, pp. 523–531. Cambridge: Addison-Wesley, 1954.

WILBUR, GEORGE B., and WARNER MUENSTERBERGER (eds.). *Psychoanalysis and Culture*. New York: International Universities Press, 1951.

WILKEN, G. A. "Het shamanisme bij de volken van den Indischen Archipel," *Bijdragen tot de Taal-, Land- en Volkenkunde*, XXXVI (1887), 427–497.

WILLIAMS, F. E. *The Vailala Madness and the Destruction of Native Ceremonies in the Gulf Division*. ("Anthropology Report," No. 4.) Port Moresby: Territory of Papua, 1923.

WILLIAMS, F. E. "The Vailala Madness in Retrospect," in *Essays Presented to C. G. Seligman*, edited by E. E. Evans-Pritchard, et al. London: Kegan, Paul, Trench, Trubner, 1934.

WILLIS, R. G. "Traditional History and Social Structure in Ufipa," *Africa*, XXXIV (1964), 340–352.

WILLIS, R. G. *The Fipa and Related Peoples of South-West Tanzania and North-East Zambia*. London: International African Institute, 1966.

WILLIS, R. G. "The Head and the Loins: Lévi-Strauss and Beyond," *Journal of the Royal Anthropological Institute (Man)*, II (1967), No. 4, 519–534.

WILLIS, ROY (ed.). *The Interpretation of Symbolism*. New York: Wiley, 1975.

WILLOUGHBY, R. R. "Magic and Cognate Phenomena: An Hypothesis," in C. Murchison (ed.), *Handbook of Social Psychology*. Worcester, Mass: Clark University Press, 1935, pp. 461–519.

WILSON, BRIAN (ed.). *Rationality*. New York: Harper & Row, 1970.

WILSON, EDMUND. *Red, Black, Blond and Olive*. New York: Oxford University Press, 1956.

WILSON, MONICA. *Communal Rituals of the Nyakyusa*. New York: Oxford University Press, 1959.

WOLF, ARTHUR P. (ed.). *Religion and Ritual in Chinese Society*. Stanford, Calif.: Stanford University Press, 1974.

WOLF, ERIC. "The Virgin of Guadalupe: A Mexican National Symbol," *Journal of American Folklore*, LXXI (1958), 34–39.

WOLFENSTEIN, MARTHA. " 'Jack and the Beanstalk': An American Version," in Margaret Mead and Martha Wolfenstein (eds.), *Childhood in Contemporary Cultures*. Chicago: The University of Chicago Press, 1955.

WORSLEY, PETER. *The Trumpet Shall Sound: A Study of "Cargo Cults" in Melanesia*. 2d. aug. ed. New York: Schocken Books, 1968.

WYNNE-EDWARDS, V. C. *Animal Dispersion in Relation to Social Behavior*. Edinburgh and London: Oliver and Boyd, 1962.

YALMAN, NUR. "The Raw: the Cooked:: Nature: Culture," in E. R. Leach (ed.), *The Structural Study of Myth and Totemism*. ("Association of Social Anthropologists," Monograph No. 5). London: Tavistock Publications, 1967.

YANG, MARTIN C. *A Chinese Village: Taitou, Shangtung Province*. New York: Columbia University Press 1948.

YINGER, J. MILTON. *Religion, Society and the Individual*. New York: Macmillan, 1957.

YINGER, J. MILTON. *The Scientific Study of Religion*. New York: Macmillan, 1970.

ZARETSKY, I. I., and M. P. LEONE (eds.). *Religious Movements in Contemporary America*. Princeton, N.J.: Princeton University Press, 1974.

ZINGG, ROBERT M. *The Huichols: Primitive Artists*. New York: G. E. Stechert, 1938.

INDEX OF AUTHORS AND TITLES

04 05 06 10 9 8 7 6 5 4 3 2